KU-438-770

THE EUROPA
BIOGRAPHICAL DICTIONARY OF
British Women

OVER 1000 NOTABLE WOMEN FROM
BRITAIN'S PAST

EDITED BY

Anne Crawford, Tony Hayter, Ann Hughes
Frank Prochaska, Pauline Stafford
Elizabeth Vallance

EUROPA PUBLICATIONS LIMITED

Europa Publications Limited
18 Bedford Square, London WC1B 3JN
© Europa Publications Limited, 1983

British Library Cataloguing in Publication Data
The Europa biographical dictionary of British women
1. Women–Great Britain–Biography
I. Crawford, Anne
920.72'0941   CT3320
ISBN 0-905118-77-4

Printed and bound in England by
STAPLES PRINTERS ROCHESTER LIMITED
at The Stanhope Press

Introduction

Achievement or public recognition in some form must be the main qualification for inclusion in any biographical dictionary. A biographical dictionary of women from early times poses certain problems of selection, if only because wide public recognition was something few women have enjoyed. In compiling this book, the editors have tried to follow certain guidelines. First among the entries chosen are women whose place in history is recognized and who are therefore to some extent household names. For the rest, the bias has been towards women whose work has had some sort of public impact and who have therefore helped to widen women's horizons beyond the traditional confines of the home. These women, broadly speaking, fall into four categories:

1. Those who sought to expand women's involvement in public affairs–for example, the suffrage campaigners and suffragettes, the first women to enter the hitherto male world of the professions, and the 'feminist' writers of the late seventeenth and eighteenth centuries.

2. Those who played a part in shaping history by virtue of their participation in a movement which allowed women greater scope than was usual at the time. Examples here include women who were prominent in the religious life of the early Middle Ages; women who devoted their lives to social reform, particularly in the nineteenth century; and women who played a part in the Civil War and other periods of social upheaval, thus gaining opportunities for self-expression which they would not have had in quieter times.

3. Those who influenced the course of events in a more informal way: women who were close to government, such as the wives of kings and politicians, mistresses, ladies-in-waiting and society hostesses. Also among this group are some of the philanthropists who believed that, while a woman's place was in the home, it was her duty to use her moral influence for the betterment of society at large.

4. Those who pursued traditional female occupations: actresses, singers, entertainers and writers and artists.

This book is not meant to be a history of the role of women in society in biographical form, but the lives assembled here tend to exemplify certain trends and also mirror women's preoccupations at various times in relation to the social conditions in which they lived. The high proportion of nuns and noblewomen among the entries for the Middle Ages, for instance, is partly due to the nature of the surviving records, but it also reflects the influence that an able and independent woman could exert in the Church of the time as well as the scope of female involvement in a society where land ownership bestowed power to influence public affairs. In the eighteenth century women were expected to see the home as their principal domain. Yet at this time writing became an important outlet as well as a bridge between women's private and public worlds. Literary forms were changing: the emergence of the novel as a popular art form allowed women more varied means of self-expression.

The occupations for which women gained recognition in the Victorian age tended to be those of the leisured middle class, particularly writing and philanthropy. A real turning point came in the mid-nineteenth century when conscious and concerted efforts were made to improve the status of women before the law, in education and in the professions. Needless to say, the entries for the twentieth century are the most varied of all, including as they do women from practically all walks of life and from a wide range of professions, from medicine to landscape gardening.

The Europa Biographical Dictionary of British Women has been compiled by a team of six editors and eighty contributors. Pauline Stafford was the editor for the Anglo-Saxon period, Anne Crawford for the Middle Ages, Ann Hughes for the sixteenth and seventeenth centuries, Tony Hayter for the eighteenth century, Frank Prochaska for the nineteenth century, and Elizabeth Vallance for the twentieth century. Alexandra Pringle was consultant editor for nineteenth-century literary women, and Jane Havell for literary women of the twentieth century.

The use of capital letters in personal names in the text of entries indicates that an entry is included in the appropriate alphabetical sequence elsewhere in the book.

London, October 1983

List of Contributors

M.A.	Margaret Adolphus, MA, MLitt, freelance writer
C.B.	Claire Barwell, MA, freelance writer and journalist
G.B.	Gail Barron, MA, freelance writer
G.Q.B.	Gerald Bowler, BA, PhD, Lecturer in History, University of Regina, Canada
L.B.	Lettice Buxton, BA, writer
M.G.B.	Mary G Bott, BMus, freelance writer
P.B.	Paul Berry, writer and lecturer, author of *Daughters of Cain* and a biography of Mary Ann Clarke, *By Royal Appointment*
R.B.	Ruth Bowden, Professor of Anatomy, Royal Free Hospital School of Medicine, London
S.B.	Sheila Barwell, CMT, freelance writer
A.C.	Anne Crawford, BA, MPhil, archivist at the Bristol Record Office
A.V.C.	Anne Charvet, BA, Senior Editor, Granada Publishing
B.H.C.	Brenda Clarke, BA, Dip Ed, writer and editor
C.C.	Catherine Crawford, BA, MSc, research student, Linacre College, Oxford
D.C.	Deborah Cherry, MA, PhD, Lecturer in Art History, University of Manchester
J.C.	Jane Carpenter, BA, research student, Department of History, King's College, London
K.C.	Karen Clarke, freelance writer
P.C.	Patricia Crawford, BA, MA, PhD, Senior Lecturer in History, University of Western Australia
A.D.	Ardèle Dejey, freelance writer and editor
K.R.D.	Keith R Dockray, BA, Senior Lecturer in History, Huddersfield Polytechnic
M.D.	Maria Dowling, BA, PhD, Lecturer in Further Education, London
J.E.	Judith Evans, BA, MSc, Lecturer in Politics, Queen Mary College, London
F.F.	F Flower, Senior Assistant, Department of Printed Books, RAF Museum
C.H.G.G.	Claire Gobbi, BA, MA, Research Associate, University of Liverpool Archives Department, on secondment to the European Commission, Brussels
M.G-E.	M Glyn-Evans, freelance writer, sister of Grace Williams (q.v.)
R.G.	Ruth Gipps, MBE, DMus, FRCM, Hon RAM, FRSA, ARCM, composer and conductor
S.G.	Sally Grover, MA, ALA, Archivist, Royal Society, London
S.M.G.	Sue Goldie, MA, freelance writer
A.H.	Ann Hughes, BA, PhD, Lecturer in History, University of Manchester
B.H.	Barbara Halpern, author, daughter of Ray Strachey (q.v.)
C.H.	Clair Hughes, BA, MA, Art Historian, Council for National Academic Awards
D.H.	Derek Hyde, BA, BMus, PhD, ARCM, Principal Lecturer in Music, Nonington College, Nr Dover
D.D.H.	David Hebb, BA, MA, researcher working on 17th century piracy
G.H.	Geoffrey Hindley, MA, historical writer, author of *England in the Age of Caxton*
G.E.H.H.	George Hughes, BA, PhD, British Council Lecturer in English Literature, Hiroshima, Japan
J.H.	Jane Hayball, MA, researcher on Victorian literature and welfare rights worker
J.E.E.H.	Jane Havell, MA, freelance writer and editor

N.H.	Nathaniel Harris, BA, writer on history and the arts
P.M.H.	Patricia Higgins, BA, MA, Assistant Keeper of Manuscripts, British Library
T.H.	Tony Hayter, BA, PhD, Lecturer in History, University of Buckingham
A.L.	April London, DPhil, Assistant Professor in English, University of Ottawa, Canada
J.L.	Jeremy Lawrence, BA, MA, writer and freelance editor
J.E.L.	Jean E Lewis, BA, MA, PhD, Lecturer in Social Science and Administration, London School of Economics
J.R.L.	Jill Liddington, BA, Lecturer in Adult Education, University of Leeds
J.V.L.	Janice V Lee, BA, library clerk, House of Commons Library
P.L.	Patricia Ledward, freelance writer and author
P.G.L.	Peter Lake, BA, PhD, Lecturer in History, Bedford College, University of London
J.M.	Judith Mackrell, BA, Half-time Lecturer in English Literature, Oxford Polytechnic
L.M.	Lucy Middleton, BA, former MP, author of *Women in the Labour Movement*
L.M.M.	Linda Murray, FSA, art historian
T.M.	Tessa Murdoch, BA, PhD, Assistant Keeper, Tudor and Stuart Department, Museum of London
T.J.M.	Teri Moores, BA, Executive Officer, Department of History and Philosophy of Science, University College, London
U.S.M.	Ursula Stuart Mason, MIPR, MAWPR, MJI, author of *The Wrens*, head of Public Relations Department, National Maritime Museum
A.M.N.	Margaret Nicol, BA, PGCE, Assistant History Teacher at St. Leonards Mayfield School, Sussex
M.N	Maire Nic Suibne, freelance writer
H.O.	Hugh Olliff, BA, MA, social historian
T.O'M.	Tom O'Malley, BA, postgraduate student working on the Quakers and the Press
W.R.O.	W R Owens, BA, Research Assistant in Literature, The Open University
A.P.	Alexandra Pringle, BA, editor, Virago Press
A.K.P.	Ann Parry, BA, Archivist, Women's Royal Voluntary Service
D.R.M.P.	Major Dione Parker (Retd), Curator, Women's Royal Army Corps Museum
F.K.P.	Frank Prochaska, BA, MA, PhD, historian, author of *Women and Philanthropy in Nineteenth-Century England*
G.P.	Glen Petrie, freelance writer
J.R.	Judith Rowbotham, PhD, part-time Tutor, School of Oriental and African Studies, University of London
J.S.R.	Janice Robertson, MA, writer and freelance editor
J.S.	Joy Shakespeare, BA, postgraduate student working on mid-16th century Protestantism
J.G.S.	Julie Stark, MA, economic historian
J.H.S.	Jonathan H Sawday, freelance writer
K.S.	Keith Sutton, BA, journalist
M.S.	Mary Stott, former editor of the women's page of *The Guardian*
M.J.S.	Martin J Smith, BA, PhD, History Master, The Royal Grammar School, High Wycombe
P.A.S.	Pauline Stafford, MA, DPhil, Lecturer in History, Huddersfield Polytechnic
B.V.	Betty Vernon, BA, freelance writer, author of *Ellen Wilkinson*
E.M.V.	Elizabeth Vallance, MA, MSc, PhD, Senior Lecturer in Government and Political Science, Queen Mary College, University of London
A.W.	Alison Wall, MA, Senior Lecturer in History, University of Sydney
D.W.	Dorothy Watkins, BA, sociologist

K.W.   Keith Walker, MA, freelance writer and historian
L.W.   Linda Walker, BA, MA, Teacher and Researcher of History and Women's
       Studies in Manchester
M.Z.   Meta Zimmeck, BA, MA, MA, Researcher, Social Science Research Council

A

Aberdeen, Ishbel Maria Gordon, Lady (1857–1939), campaigner for women's rights. The youngest daughter of Lord Tweedmouth, she married John Gordon, Earl of Aberdeen and later Marquess of Aberdeen and Temair, in 1877. Her childhood brought her into contact with many great political and religious leaders including Gladstone, but her mother was the strongest influence on her, giving her a strong sense of social responsibility and deep religious convictions.

Her husband shared her interest in philanthropy and it was a very happy marriage; they had five children. They co-operated in a number of schemes, such as the Haddo House Association (the Onward and Upward Association), an educational and recreational project which started on their Aberdeenshire estates and spread throughout the Empire.

Lord Aberdeen's diplomatic activities enabled his wife to utilize her talents on a considerable scale, developing her interest in advancing the social and educational position of women. During his Governor-Generalship of Canada (1893–98) she founded the Victoria Order of Nurses (1898). While in Canada, she also became interested in the National Council of Women, and from 1893, when she became President of the International Council of Women, she was the acknowledged leader of the society, which worked to improve the social and economic lot of women and to promote peace. After the First World War, Lady Aberdeen persuaded the League of Nations to open all posts on its secretariat to women on equal terms. In Ireland, during her husband's term as Lord Lieutenant (1906–15), she made a great impact, founding the Women's National Health Association and campaigning for better conditions for Irish women. She was one of the first women to become a JP. Nonetheless she constantly emphasized the necessity for women not to neglect their domestic role, and herself took a major part in her children's upbringing and closely supervised her household. She and her husband wrote *We Twa'* (1925).

See also M. A. Sinclair, *A Bonnie Fechter*, 1952. J.R.

Abington, Frances (1737–1815), actress, reputed one of the finest contemporary performers in comedy.

Fanny Abington's career lasted half a century. She had a lowly and unsuccessful start on the London stage when it was dominated by Mrs PRITCHARD and Mrs CLIVE. She married her music-master, James Abington, and left London for the Dublin stage, where she was more successful. After several scandals, she separated from her husband.

Invited by Garrick to Drury Lane, she returned to London, where she lived under the protection of a minor landed gentleman. Mrs Clive had retired and Mrs Pritchard was dead, so Mrs Abington's success was assured. Garrick disliked her tantrums ('the worst of bad women') but admired her acting, and she remained at Drury Lane until after his retirement and death. From 1776 to 1782 she was with the Sheridan management at Covent Garden, where she was very highly paid. In 1790 she retired to nurse her dying protector. She returned briefly to Covent Garden, but she was now too stout to play the young comedy parts she had made her own, and retired finally in 1797.

Fanny Abington was known chiefly for her comic talent in coquette roles such as Miss Prue, Beatrice, and Lady Teazle (of which she was the first exponent); but she also played Shakespearian roles such as Portia, Desdemona, and Ophelia. She was a clever and ambitious woman who achieved a secure social position and became famous for her fine taste in clothes. She was painted by Zoffany, Cosway, Reynolds, and many others.

See also P. H. Highfill, K. A. Burnim, E. A. Langhans, *A Biographical Dictionary of Actors, Actresses, Musicians, Dancers, Managers and other Stage Personnel in London, 1660–1800*, vol. 1, 1973; *Theatrical Biography; or Memoirs of the Principal Performers of the Three Theatres Royal*, 1772. C.H.

Achurch, Janet (1864–1916), actress. She came from a theatrical family, her grandparents having managed the Theatre Royal, Manchester, and she first appeared in 1883 at the Olympic Theatre in the farce *Betsy Baker*. After playing in pantomime and touring in various plays, she joined F. R. Benson's company, where she had particular success as Desdemona, the Queen in *Hamlet*, Lady Macbeth, and other Shakespearean parts. She also appeared with Beerbohm Tree's company and was at the Adelphi in *Harbour Lights.* In 1895 she played in America.

In 1896 Janet Achurch produced Ibsen's *Little Eyolf* at the Avenue Theatre with herself as Rita and Mrs Patrick CAMPBELL as the Ratwife. Indeed, it is as one of the first actresses in England to play Ibsen that she is best remembered. In 1889 she took over management of the Novelty Theatre, appearing as Nora Helmer in the first English production of *A Doll's House.* She was also seen in Bernard Shaw's plays, including *Candida* and (as Lady Cecily Wayneflete) *Captain Brassbound's Conversion,* both at the Strand (1900). Shaw called her 'the only tragic actress of genius we now possess' and described her acting in his dramatic criticism (collected as *Our Theatres in the Nineties*). She toured widely with her husband Charles Charrington and was the first English actress to appear in the Khedivial Theatre, Cairo. Heavy drinking affected her health and performing ability, and she retired in 1913.   B.H.C.

Acton, Eliza (1799–1859), poet and cookery writer. Eliza Acton was born in Battle, Sussex, the daughter of a brewer. She grew up in Suffolk but was taken abroad for her health. In Paris she became engaged to an officer in the French army, though she never married; her early verse, published in Ipswich by private subscription in 1826, hints at disappointment in love and the desire for revenge against an unfaithful lover. Further poems appeared in local publications, and in 1837 she presented verses to Queen Adelaide. Her last published poetry was *The Voice of the North* (1842) in honour of Queen Victoria.

Eliza Acton's subsequent poems were rejected by the publishers Messrs Longman, who suggested that a cookery book would be more commercial. She responded with *Modern Cookery for Private Families* (1845), which has remained one of the best cookery books in the English language. Dedicated to 'the Young Housekeepers of England', it is remarkable for its clarity, style, and attention to vital detail, and was innovatory in appending a summary of ingredients and giving 'the precise time to dress the whole'. Eliza Acton's literary talent is evident, and the work is informed with a sense of the quality of life; she is intolerant of people who serve 'trash' and of 'indifferent cooks who pride themselves on never doing anything by rule'. Living at Bordyke House, Tonbridge, where she kept house for her mother, she tested all the recipes herself; many of them were her own, and she was justly upset at 'the unscrupulous manner in which large portions of my volume have been appropriated by contemporary authors', notably Mrs BEETON. *Modern Cookery* was reprinted several times within two years of its first appearance and, after complete revision in 1855 in the light of Baron Liebig's theories about the chemistry of food, continued to sell well for fifty years.

Moving to Hampstead in the 1850s, Miss Acton contributed 'Household Hints and Receipts' to Mrs Loudon's *Ladies' Companion* and in 1857 published *The English Bread-Book*, an inspiring treatise on good bread. She refers to another work in progress but never published it. Pioneering in its advocacy of higher standards in English cooking, her work has inspired many later writers.

See also E. Ray (ed.), *The Best of Eliza Acton*, 1968.   C.B.

Adams, Sarah Flower (1805–48), poet and hymnologist. She was born at Harlow, Essex, the younger daughter of the radical journalist Benjamin Flower and his wife Eliza GOULD. Her health broke down on her father's death in 1829, and she went to the Isle of Wight to recuperate. Among the verses she wrote at this time were 'The Little Church of Yaverland' and 'The Royal Progress'. Between 1833 and 1836 she contributed various stories, poems and essays to *The Monthly Repository*, edited by W. J. Fox, under the pseudonym 'S.Y.'; she also contributed to the *Westminster Review*. Specimens of her unpublished poems written for the Anti-Corn Law League are to be found in Fox's *Lectures Addressed Chiefly to the Working Classes* (1846–49).

After her marriage in 1834 to William Bridges Adams, a noted railway engineer, Sarah Flower Adams began a career on the stage, making her first appearance at Richmond in 1837 as Lady Macbeth. But ill-health frustrated her ambitions, and she returned to writing. In November 1840 she wrote the hymn 'Nearer, My God, to Thee', which was set to music by her sister, Eliza FLOWER. It was published the following year in Fox's *Hymns and Anthems*, along with several other hymns by Sarah Flower Adams, all characterized by an intense devotional feeling, and was used in the services at the South Place Unitarian Chapel, Finsbury. Only after her death did this hymn become a classic. In 1841 her 'Vivia Perpetua: A Dramatic Poem', on the subject of early Christian martyrdom, appeared; and in 1845 she published a religious catechism for children, *The Flock at the Fountain*. She did not recover from her sister's death in 1846; she died of consumption and was buried in the family vault in Foster Street Baptist cemetery, Harlow.

See also H. W. Stephenson, *The Author of Nearer, My God, to Thee*, 1922, and *Unitarian Hymn-Writers*, 1931.   M.J.S.

Adela of Blois (1062?–1138), mother of King Stephen of England and later a Cluniac nun. She was a younger daughter of William the Conqueror by MATILDA OF FLANDERS. In about 1081 she married Earl Stephen of Meaux and Brie, who some ten years later succeeded his father as Count of Blois and Chartres. Adela proved the dominant partner in the relationship and, as her friend Bishop Hildebert of Mans observed, possessed 'all that is needed to guide the helm of the state'. Thus when her easy-going husband joined the First Crusade in 1096, she became his regent at home; and, on his ignominious return from the Holy Land, it was she who urged him to go back. In 1101 he did so, only to meet a violent death the following year.

Adela's great force of character and determination could now be given free rein, and she devoted herself single-mindedly to the advancement of her children. Her three daughters were appropriately married off, and so was her eldest son William, who Adela apparently regarded as unfit to succeed his father. She ruled her husband's provinces until her second son, Theobald, was sufficiently schooled to take over in 1107. Stephen, her third son, was despatched to the English Court of her brother Henry I in 1113, and he subsequently secured his uncle's throne in 1135. Henry, her fourth son, became a Cluniac monk and ultimately a distinguished bishop of Winchester.

As she grew older and her sons reached maturity, Adela became progressively less interested in politics and more committed to religion. Her friends included such eminent churchmen as St Anselm (whom she chose, according to his biographer Eadmer, 'as after God the director and guardian of her life'), the canon lawyer Bishop Ivo of Chartres, and Peter the Venerable, Abbot of Cluny. She entertained Pope Paschal II at Chartres in 1107, and probably played a part in ending the dispute between the Papacy and her brother Henry I. In 1119 she gave shelter to the exiled Archbishop Thurstan of York; and it was probably under his influence that she determined to take the veil. Around 1122 she was received into the Cluniac priory of Marcigny-sur-Loire, where she remained until her death in March 1138.

Adela was clearly a remarkable woman, and also a formidable one, as is evident from the writings of Abbot Baudri of Bourgueil. Like the chronicler Hugh of Fleury (who dedicated his *Historia Ecclesiastica* to her) Baudri was one of Adela's protégés, and he was impressed not only by her intelligence and generosity as a patron but also by her courage (which, he declared, was equal to that of the Conqueror himself). A proud, self-willed woman who probably inspired fear rather than love, she pursued her ends—whether political or religious—with a ruthlessness which earned her the deep respect of her contemporaries.

See also R.H.C. Davis, *King Stephen*, 1967.   K.R.D.

Adelaide (1792–1849), William IV's queen. She was born at Meiningen, the eldest child of George, Duke of Saxe-Meiningen, and Princess Louise of Hohenlohe-Langenburg. In 1818 she married William, Duke of Clarence, the third son of George III. Although the match was arranged, and Clarence was twice Princess Adelaide's age, the marriage proved to be a happy one, though it failed to achieve its intended purpose of producing an heir to the throne; Adelaide's pregnancies ended with miscarriages or babies who died within a few months at most.

On 26 June 1830 Princess Adelaide's husband became king on the death of his brother George IV. The new queen's support for the Tories, and her opposition to parliamentary reform, made her unpopular during the Reform Bill crisis, and although she exerted less political influence than was generally believed, her attitude was one factor in William IV's conversion from being a supporter to an opponent of the Bill. The King's abrupt dismissal of Lord Melbourne's administration in November 1834 was also (incorrectly) attributed to her: *The Times* of 15 November declared, 'The Queen has done it all.'

On William IV's death in 1837, Adelaide became Queen Dowager. She spent her remaining years travelling extensively in England and Europe in the interests of her health, and contributed some £20,000 a year to various charitable enterprises. In particular, she financed the building of the Collegiate Church of St Paul in Valletta, Malta. Her popularity long restored, she died at Bentley Priory, Stanmore, and was buried in St George's Chapel, Windsor.

Queen Adelaide was never completely anglicized and possessed neither great beauty nor great intelligence. Nevertheless her kind and modest personality succeeded in domesticating William IV and, so far as the presence of his numerous illegitimate children allowed, restored the image of a virtuous, ordered monarchical family. In maintaining a decorous court, and in setting an example of dedicated public service, she was the first 'Victorian' queen.

See also M. Sandars, *The Life and Times of Queen Adelaide*, 1915; M. Hopkirk, *Queen Adelaide*, 1946; G. Wakeford, *Three Consort Queens*, 1971.
M.J.S.

Adeliza (?–1151?), second queen of Henry I of England. She was the daughter of Duke Godfrey of Lower Lotharingia, and married Henry in 1121. She failed to provide him with the male heir he craved, and took no part in politics or war beyond receiving the newly-arrived Empress MATILDA at her castle of Arundel in 1139. But she did gain a considerable reputation as a literary patron.
K.R.D.

Ady, Mrs Henry. See CARTWRIGHT, JULIA.

Æbbe (*fl.* 664–81), abbess. Æbbe was the half-sister of Kings Oswald and Oswiu of Northumbria, the issue of a former or subsequent liaison of their mother, Acha. Little is known of her early life save that she married and, upon being widowed, entered the Church. A tradition exists that she founded a monastery by the River Derwent, on the site of a Roman fort given to her by King Oswiu; but more reliable evidence simply states that Æbbe founded a monastery at Coldingham, of which she subsequently became the abbess. Although she was honoured for her piety and her noble birth, and attracted novices like King Ecgfrith's first wife, ÆTHELTHRYTH, she seems to have failed utterly to maintain discipline in her foundation. Instead of praying and reading, the monks and nuns feasted, drank and gossiped; the nuns also spent their leisure hours making elaborate garments. All this led St Cuthbert, who came to visit the community some time between 661 and 664, to declare that monks and nuns should be excluded from each other's company.

It is not clear when Æbbe died. According to a vision experienced by one member of the community, Coldingham was to be destroyed after Æbbe's death as a punishment for all the sins committed there. A fire is recorded as having occurred at Coldingham in 679. However, Æbbe was still alive in 681, when she is said to have cured Ecgfrith's second wife, IURMINBURG, of an illness during a visit that the royal couple made to Coldingham, by persuading Ecgfrith to release Bishop Wilfrid of York from prison. After her death Æbbe's body was translated twice: once after the Viking invasions, and again in the eleventh century, when it was brought to Durham.

See also B. Colgrave and R. A. B. Mynors (eds), *Bede's Ecclesiastical History of the English People*, 1969; B. Colgrave (ed. and trans.), *Vita Cuthberti*, 1940; B. Colgrave (ed. and trans.), Eddius, *Vita Wilfridi*, 1927.
J.C.

Ælfflaed (654–714), abbess. Ælfflaed was the daughter of King Oswiu of Northumbria and his second wife, EANFLAED. A year after her birth, Oswiu placed her in a monastery at Hartlepool that was run by HILD, a distant cousin of her mother. In 657 the community was transferred to the new foundation Hild had built at Whitby. There Ælfflaed was at first taught the traditions of the Celtic Church, for Hild was a protégée of the Irish bishop Aidan; later, after her father's famous decision at Whitby (664) in favour of the Roman and against the Celtic Church, she was educated accordingly. In 680 Hild died and Ælfflaed succeeded her, for a time sharing the responsibility of running the abbey with her mother, who probably joined the community after Oswiu's death in 670.

During her career as abbess, Ælfflaed gained a reputation for being 'the best comforter and counsellor in the land'. Her qualities were revealed by her invitation to Bishop Trumwine of Abercorn to come to Whitby after the Picts had expelled him from his see in 685; by the way she overcame her hostility to Bishop Wilfrid of York in order to persuade her family to end their feud with him in 706; and by her helping a fellow-ecclesiastic on her travels abroad (she commended her to the abbess of Pfazel). She was a friend of St Cuthbert, whom she met twice (in 684 and 685), and encouraged the arts to flourish at Whitby; the earliest surviving *Life* of Pope Gregory the Great was composed there during the last ten years of Ælfflaed's life. She was buried, with her mother, alongside the bodies of her father and maternal grandfather, which she and Eanflaed had brought to Whitby. Translated in the twelfth century, Ælfflaed is commemorated on 8 February and 11 April.

See also B. Colgrave and R. A. B. Mynors (eds), *Bede's Ecclesiastical History of the English People*, 1969; B. Colgrave (ed. and trans.) *Vita Cuthberti*, 1940; B. Colgrave (ed. and trans.), Eddius, *Vita Wilfridi*, 1927.   J.C.

Ælfflaed (*fl.* mid–9th century), princess and Queen of Mercia. Ælfflaed was the daughter of Ceolwulf, King of Mercia. The death of her uncle King Coenwulf ushered in a period of great uncertainty over the Mercian succession. Among the contenders for the throne was the family of King Wiglaf, who made good his claim in about 830. Wiglaf married his son Wigmund to Ælfflaed. Their son Wigstan's succession was opposed by another pretender, Beorhtfrith, who sought to strengthen his own claim by seeking marriage with the widowed Ælfflaed. The match was not made, Wigstan was murdered, and Ælfflaed disappears from history. Her obscure story illustrates how many royal women were wooed both as princesses and widows for the strength which their blood and connections could bring to claimants to the throne.

See also 'Life and Miracles of St Wistan', in W. D. Macray (ed.), *Chronicon Abbatiae de Evesham*, Rolls Series, 1863.   P.A.S.

Ælfflaed (*fl.* early 10th century), Anglo-Saxon queen. Soon after his father's death, King Edward the Elder took Ælfflaed as his first legitimate wife; his earlier concubine Ecgwyna disappeared. Ælfflaed was daughter of an ealdorman, Æthelm, probably the same man as an ealdorman of Wiltshire known to have died in 897. Edward had had a cousin Æthelm with strong claims to the throne. If the two Æthelms are identical, Edward was marrying his cousin's daughter, a shrewd move to strengthen his hand against Æthelm's brother, who was

in rebellion in 900. Ælfflaed bore two sons, Ælfweard and Edwin, and six daughters. There is considerable doubt concerning her fate; she was probably repudiated by Edward in about 918 and sent to the nunnery of Wilton, where two of her daughters had taken the veil.

See also P. Stafford, 'Changes in the status of the king's wife in Wessex', in *Past and Present*, 1982.   P.A.S.

Ælfflaed (before 939–*c*.1002), noblewoman and monastic benefactress. Ælfflaed was the younger daughter of the sonless Ælfgar, Ealdorman of Essex. She married Brihtnoth, the man who succeeded her father in his ealdormanry; the marriage constituted part of Brihtnoth's strategy to secure his position in eastern England. As her father's heiress, and as residuary legatee of her older sister Queen Æthelflaed, Ælfflaed disposed of enormous properties in eastern England. Her will lists nearly forty manors, though in many cases she was confirming earlier bequests of her family. Following her father and sister, she endowed the family monastery and mausoleum at Stoke-by-Nayland, and her husband's favoured abbey and burial place, Ely, also received land. The capacity of women like Ælfflaed to inherit and dispose of land was the foundation of female influence in Anglo-Saxon England; its use for religious endowment is typical.

See also D. Whitelock, *Anglo-Saxon Wills*, 1930.   P.A.S.

Ælfgifu (*fl.* 956–58), Anglo-Saxon queen. The daughter of a great south-western noble line directly descended from the West Saxon royal family, Ælfgifu married King Eadwig in 956. The King was attempting to strengthen his position and to reverse the policies of his uncle and predecessor. He and Ælfgifu therefore incurred the enmity of Eadwig's grandmother, Queen Eadgifu, and of Abbot Dunstan, leaders of the rival faction; Ælfgifu is alleged to have played a part in Dunstan's exile. Hence the unflattering picture of her and her mother as wantons, found in the partisan *Life of Dunstan*. The triumph of the King and his wife was brief. As support ebbed from Eadwig, Dunstan's party was able forcibly to separate the King and his wife on the grounds of consanguinity. Ælfgifu was well provided for; her will survives, recording her great wealth and her return of large estates in Wessex to the royal family.

See also D. Whitelock (ed.), *Anglo-Saxon Wills*, 1930.   P.A.S.

Ælfgifu of Northampton (*fl.* 1014–37), noblewoman and king's wife. Ælfgifu was the daughter of Ælfhelm, Ealdorman of York and member of a powerful north Mercian noble family. The family fell from royal favour in 1006, when Ælfhelm and his sons, suspected of treachery, were murdered and/or blinded. The resulting disaffection of the family made them obvious allies for enemies of King Æthelred, and in 1014 or 1016 the invading Danish leader Cnut (Canute) sought their friendship and married Ælfgifu, though he did not make her his queen. Ælfgifu bore him two sons, Swegn and Harold Harefoot. Stories of Harold's doubtful paternity, and even of his being smuggled into Ælfgifu's bedchamber in a bedpan, reveal less of the truth than of the fierce propaganda surrounding the dispute over the throne between 1035 and 1037 and its later elaboration at the hands of post-Conquest writers.

In 1017 Cnut took a second wife, EMMA, but Ælfgifu was not cast aside completely. In 1029 she and her son Swegn were sent as Cnut's regents to Norway, where they found little support; by 1033 their position was untenable and in 1035 they were forced to flee to Denmark. Memories of her rule were not sweet, and evil times in Norway were long synonymous with 'Ælfgifu's days'; but this may simply derive from Norwegian dislike of Danish rule. Ælfgifu had returned to England by 1037 to aid her son Harold in his attempt to gain the English throne; some of his known support in the Midlands probably came from her family. Her fate after his death in 1040 is unknown.

See also M. W. Campbell, 'Queen Emma and Ælfgifu of Northampton, Canute the Great's women', in *Medieval Scandinavia* (Odense University), vol. 4, 1971.   P.A.S.

Ælfthryth (before 950–*c.*1002), Queen of England. Ælfthryth was the daughter of Ordgar, a substantial landowner in south-west England. Her first marriage was to Æthelwold, Ealdorman of East Anglia and son of Athelstan Half-King. Æthelwold died in about 962, and by 965 she had contracted a second marriage to King Edgar. Later legends describe her seduction of the King and Edgar's complicity in the murder of her first husband; their details bear the impress of twelfth-century romance, but gossip surrounding the marriage may have been current in the tenth century. Ælfthryth's later power, and especially her involvement in the bitter succession dispute which followed Edgar's death, attracted other accusations of witchcraft and adultery. Both gossip and accusations smack of political propaganda cast in the common anti-feminist mould.

Despite the gossip, Ælfthryth's marriage was clearly a political union. Her father was made ealdorman of south-west England about the time of the wedding, and her family helped extend Edgar's control of the area. She was the King's third wife, a fact which dominated her career. She dispossessed the family of Edgar's second wife of their abbey at Barking, but her main problem was posed by the existence of Edward, a young son by Edgar's first marriage. By 966 Ælfthryth had produced a son of her own, Edmund, and while he was still an infant she and her allies at court advanced his claims to the throne against those of his older half-brother. After Edmund's death in 971, at the age of five, the Queen's efforts were directed towards securing the throne for her younger son, Æthelred.

Ælfthryth became Edgar's queen in 965; at this date, the title emphasized the full legitimacy of her marriage and the formal position she enjoyed at court. She was the first tenth-century queen known to have been important during her husband's lifetime. In the monastic revival of Edgar's reign she was given responsibility for the English nunneries and played a part in ecclesiastical patronage at a date when the Church exercised great political influence. Her intercession was sought by those seeking royal favour and she seems to have struck up a close alliance with Æthelwold, Bishop of Winchester. Æthelwold appears to have aided her in the foundation of her nunnery at Wherwell, and he may have been instrumental in securing her formal consecration as queen in 973. Ælfthryth is only the second English queen known to have been anointed, the earlier instance being the anointing of Judith on the continent.

Ælfthryth's anointing enhanced her status and may have been intended to strengthen her son's claim to the throne. Edgar's death in 975 precipitated a succession struggle in which Ælfthryth led the party supporting Æthelred.

The prince was little more than five years old, and the Queen's enemies cannot have relished the prospect of her regency. This and other factors swung the balance in favour of Edward, but his success was short-lived. In March 979 Edward was murdered while visiting his step-mother and half-brother at Corfe in Dorset; the deed was probably done at Ælfthryth's instigation. Æthelred became king, and from 979 to 985 Ælfthryth and Æthelwold of Winchester were dominant at court. Æthelred's coming of age, combined with his marriage in about 985, brought about her temporary eclipse, but she was restored to power in 993, perhaps when Æthelred's father-in-law was disgraced and his first marriage ended. Ælfthryth now secured control of her grandsons' upbringing, a role of crucial importance; her influence at court is suggested by the way in which petitioners habitually invoked her intercession. In her final years she may have retired to her nunnery at Wherwell.

See also P. Stafford, 'Sons and Mothers, family politics in the early middle ages', in D. Baker (ed.), *Medieval Women*, 1978.

P.A.S.

Ælfwyn (*fl.* 918), princess and ruler of Mercia, the only daughter of Æthelred and ÆTHEL-FLAED, Lord and Lady of the Mercians. Ælfwyn was chosen by a section of the Mercian nobility to rule the kingdom after her mother's death in 918. The choice of a woman to rule in her own right, not as the widow of a royal husband or regent for a young son, is virtually unique in early medieval Europe. It is a testimony to the greatness of her mother Æthelflaed, to the tradition of powerful queenship in Mercia, and to the Mercians' desire to remain independent of Wessex. Ælfwyn's authority was short-lived: in December 918 her uncle, the West Saxon king Edward the Elder, marched into Mercia, deprived Ælfwyn of her authority, and carried her back to Wessex and into obscurity. P.A.S.

Æthelbertha. See BERTHA.

Æthelburh, also known as Tate (*fl.* 614–33), Queen of Northumbria, the only daughter of King Æthelberht of Kent. Æthelburh was born in, or before, 614. Her mother, according to late sources, was Æthelberht's first wife, the Frankish princess BERTHA. After a Christian upbringing, presumably at the recently converted Kentish court, she was solicited in marriage by King Edwin of Northumbria, sometime between 616, after Æthelberht's death, and 625. Her brother, King Eadbald, initially rejected the proposal on the grounds that Edwin was still a pagan. But the political advantages of the match were such that Eadbald changed his mind when he learned that Edwin would tolerate Æthelburh's beliefs and was even considering embracing Christianity himself. Eadbald doubtless hoped that it would not be long before Æthelburh, aided by her spiritual adviser Paulinus (who had earlier helped to evangelize Kent), secured Edwin's conversion. Edwin's failure to accept baptism until 627 was thus seen as a gross dereliction of conjugal duty on Æthelburh's part, and she was duly chastised by the Pope. In fact, the delay had little to do with her. As his willingness to have his daughter christened in 626 demonstrates, Edwin was perfectly prepared to accept Christianity, but simply dared not make public his beliefs too early, for fear of alienating his subjects. In 633 Edwin was killed and his enemies forced Æthelburh and her two surviving children to seek refuge in Kent. There, according to local tradition, her brother supplied her with an estate at Lyminge where she founded a monastery in which she spent the remainder of her days.

See also B. Colgrave and R.A.B. Mynors (eds), *Bede's Ecclesiastical History of the English People*, 1969. J.C.

Æthelflaed (*c.* 870–918), Lady of the Mercians. Æthelflaed was the eldest child of King Alfred and his Mercian wife EALHSWITH. Her father gave her in marriage to Æthelred, Lord of the Mercians, probably in the early 880s. Æthelred was by this date effectively ruler of Mercia, sometimes referred to as 'king'; Æthelflaed became Lady of the Mercians and her title, *Hlaefdige*, was a frequent Anglo-Saxon translation of 'queen'. She was heiress to a tradition of able Mercian queens dating back to the late eighth century. Her marriage sealed an alliance between Wessex and Mercia that was essential to Alfred's success in his struggle against the Vikings.

Æthelflaed took an active part in Mercian politics even before the long illness of her husband, and ruled Mercia from his death in 911 until 918. She and Æthelred made joint grants of land to Worcester Cathedral and translated thither the bones of St Oswald. According to Irish sources it was Æthelflaed,

7

not Æthelred, who granted land to the Irish Viking Ingimund in the Wirral in 902, and she who in 907 fortified Chester against the growing threat of Viking attack from Ireland. Between 910 and 915 she built a series of fortresses around Wirral and Mersey, on the Welsh border, and in north-west Mercia, paralleling the fortress building of her brother Edward the Elder in the south-east Midlands and Essex. Brother and sister were intent on combating further Viking invasion of England and on the conquest of those areas controlled by the Viking armies. In this joint enterprise Æthelflaed was responsible for the conquest of Derby and Leicester, two Viking bases, in 917 and 918. The co-ordinated plans of Edward and Æthelflaed to advance on Nottingham and Lincoln in 918 were upset by her death on 12 June.

Co-operation with her brother the king of Wessex had been part of Æthelflaed's wider commitment to the defence of Mercia against its traditional enemies, the Welsh kings, and against the Viking threat. If Æthelflaed planned to use Viking settlers in the Wirral against the Welsh, their growing numbers thwarted her hopes. In 916 she sent a punitive expedition into North Wales and took a Welsh queen hostage, but her increasing concern was with the threat posed by the Dublin Vikings to north-west Mercia. To deal with this, Æthelflaed became one of the architects and leaders of an alliance of the northern British rulers, extending to the Scottish kings and including the Danes at York, who submitted to her. In 918 this alliance brought about the defeat of the Norse Viking, Ragnald, at Corbridge.

Æthelflaed behaved as Queen of Mercia rather than a West Saxon princess; her extraordinary power as an independent female ruler was firmly based on Mercian traditions. However, her concern for Mercian defence did not conflict with the West Saxon alliance. Her brother Edward made no attempt to oust her, and may have helped her in the crucial period after Æthelred's death. Edward recognized local Mercian loyalties and sent his eldest and illegitimate son Athelstan to be fostered by Æthelflaed, perhaps as a potential heir since she had no sons. Irish sources speak of Æthelflaed's great fame, and the Anglo-Saxon poem *Judith*, celebrating the Biblical warrior queen, may have been written for her. If English sources preserve little of her memory, it is because they emanate largely from Wessex,

whose kings became rulers of all England and hardly wished to celebrate Mercian achievements.

See also F. T. Wainwright, 'Æthelflaed, Lady of the Mercians', in *Scandinavian England* (Odense University), 1975.   P.A.S.

Æthelflaed of Damerham (before 934–after 975), Queen of England and monastic benefactress. Æthelflaed's marriage to King Edmund as his second wife (c. 945) was closely associated with the appointment of her father, Ælfgar, as Ealdorman of Essex, which it was designed to secure. At court she had a strong rival for power in the person of the queen-mother, EADGIFU; and Edmund's death soon after the marriage, and apparently before the birth of children, ended any prospect of Æthelflaed becoming of political importance; a royal widow without sons had little influence. She went on to marry an ealdorman, Athelstan, whom she also outlived. As joint heir of her father's estate and owner of dower land from two marriages, Æthelflaed was an extensive property-owner in her own right. She bequeathed some twenty-five estates to the religious houses of eastern England, principally to Ely and Stoke-by-Nayland. Such munificence from childless heiresses brought much land to the Church in the early Middle Ages.

See also D. Whitelock (ed.), *Anglo-Saxon Wills*, 1930.   P.A.S.

Æthelthryth (?–679), Queen of Northumbria and religious enthusiast, daughter of King Anna of East Anglia. Æthelthryth was born near Exning in Suffolk, probably no later than 640. In her youth she received many proposals of marriage but rejected them all, her only desire being to enter the Church. In 652, however, her parents forced her to marry an East Anglian sub-king, Tondberht, prince of the South Girvii. The match was short lived, for Tondberht died in 655, and Æthelthryth, who had allegedly succeeded in retaining her virginity, retired to the Isle of Ely, which Tondberht had given her as a morning-gift, intending to devote the rest of her life to God.

In 660, however, her family persuaded her to accept another marriage proposal, this time from King Oswiu of Northumbria's fifteen-year-old son Ecgfrith. Despite the ties of matrimony, Æthelthryth tried to live as religious a life as possible in Northumbria, endeavouring, above all, to keep her virginity intact. Ecgfrith, whose need for an heir grew ever greater as time passed, eventually sought the help of Æthelthryth's protégé, Bishop Wilfrid of York, to whom the queen had once granted an estate at Hexham. Wilfrid promised to try and persuade Æthelthryth to consummate the marriage, but in fact advised the Queen to become a nun. After much cajoling on Æthelthryth's part, Ecgfrith reluctantly agreed to allow her to receive the veil from Wilfrid and to enter his aunt ÆBBE's foundation at Coldingham in 672.

This history of non-consummation may be true; or it may represent no more than an excuse used by Ecgfrith to justify a divorce. He is said to have changed his mind a year later, so that Æthelthryth was forced to flee from the monastery. A miraculous flood prevented Ecgfrith from following her, and she made her way, with two companions, to East Anglia, disguised as a pilgrim; they stopped at Alftham, where she built a church, and at a place that became known as *Ætheldredestowe* after her staff took root there. She eventually reached Ely (673), where she built an abbey for her followers. As abbess, Æthelthryth led a life of great sanctity: wearing woollen garments, never linen; only taking baths before great festivals, after all the other nuns; and rarely eating more than once a day, except again on the days of great festivals or on occasions of extreme urgency. Her sister SEXBURGA joined the community sometime after 675, and in 679 they were visited by her old friend Wilfrid on his way to Rome. According to later traditions, Æthelthryth used this opportunity to ask the Bishop to secure privileges of recognition and immunity for her foundation from the Pope. If so, she did not live to see the results of her request. Not long after Wilfrid's departure she became ill with a tumour under her jaw and died. On her orders she was buried in a wooden coffin in the nuns' cemetery. Sixteen years later, however, Sexburga, who had succeeded her as abbess, translated her corpse, amid many miracles, to a new stone coffin. Her body was translated a second time in 1106.

See also B. Colgrave and R. A. B. Mynors (eds.), *Bede's Ecclesiastical History of the English People*, 1969; E. O. Blake (ed.), *Liber Eliensis*, Camden Series 3, vol. 92, 1962.

J.C.

Aguilar, Grace (1816–47), writer. She was born in Hackney, London, into a family of Spanish-Jewish origin and, owing to her frail health, was educated at home. She travelled over much of England with her family when young, but lived mainly in Devonshire. She began writing early, much of her work concerning the history and religion of the Jewish people. These books include *The Jewish Faith* (1845), *The Women of Israel* (1845), and especially *The Spirit of Judaism* (1842), which emphasized the spirituality of the Old Testament while criticizing contemporary Judaism for excessive formalism. For although devout, Grace Aguilar was liberal in her thinking and advocated the adoption of a less rigorous orthodoxy. However, she became best known for her many novels of domestic life, only one of which, *Home Influence* 1847, was published in her lifetime. Her deteriorating health rendered her a semi-invalid, and she died while visiting her brother in Frankfurt and was buried in the Jewish cemetery there. Her life was outwardly uneventful and her books are domestic, sentimental, and pious, although not without charm, particularly two historical narratives, the Scottish *Days of Bruce* (1852) and *The Vale of Cedars* (1853), about Jews in Spain at the time of Ferdinand and Isabella. A branch of the New York Library is named after her.

B.H.C.

Aikin, Lucy (1781–1864), writer. Born in Warrington, she was the daughter of John Aikin, physician, scholar, and man of letters. She spent her early childhood in Yarmouth and then lived with her family in London from 1792 to 1797. They subsequently moved to Stoke Newington, where she lived until her father's death in 1822. Apart from a short period spent in Wimbledon, Lucy Aikin spent the rest of her life in Hampstead, where she was buried next to her great friend, the writer Joanna BAILLIE.

Lucy Aikin's literary career began when she was seventeen, but her first important publication was the verse *Epistles on Women*, which appeared in 1810. This was followed in 1814 by her only work of fiction, *Lorimer, A Tale*. But it was with her historical works that she gained a literary reputation: *Memoirs of the Court of Queen Elizabeth*, 1818; *Memoirs of the Court of James I*, 1822; *Memoirs of the Court of Charles I*, 1833; and *The Life of Addison*, 1843. She also wrote a life of her

Albani, Emma

father and of her aunt, the writer Anna BARBAULD.

See also P. H. Le Breton (ed.), *Memoirs, Miscellanies and Letters of the Late Lucy Aikin*, 1864.   L.B.

Albani, (Marie Louise) Emma (Cecile) (1852–1930), singer. She was born at Chambly, near Montreal, the daughter of Joseph Lajeunesse, a musician, and was educated at the Convent of the Sacred Heart, Montreal, until the age of fourteen. She then went to Albany, New York, for musical training. Eventually, with the help of the Bishop and the local community, she was sent to Milan to study under Lamperti. He chose her stage-name, Albani, to honour the people of Albany who had helped her musical career.

Albani's first stage appearance was in *La Sonnambula* at Messina in 1870, and this was followed by many engagements abroad. She was singer to the German Court, and also toured Australia, America, Russia, India, and other countries. In 1873 she came to London, eventually (1878) marrying Ernest Gye, lessor of Covent Garden. After singing all the principal soprano parts in Italian opera, she enjoyed a supreme, final professional triumph when she sang Isolde in German.

After she retired from the stage, she did much to popularize little-known music, an activity for which she was created a DBE in 1925. She wrote an autobiography, *Forty Years of Song* (1911).   A.D.

Aldrich-Blake, Louisa (Brandreth) (1865–1925), surgeon. Born in Chingford, Essex, the daughter of a minister, she moved with her family to Welsh Bicknor, Herefordshire, while still young. She was educated at Cheltenham Ladies' College, and at the age of 17 determined to become a doctor. In 1887 she entered the London (Royal Free Hospital) School of Medicine for Women, embarking on a brilliant academic career.

She obtained an MB with First Class Honours in Medicine and Obstetrics in 1892, BS in 1893 (winning the University Gold Medal), took her MD in 1895, and one year later became the first woman to be awarded the Master in Surgery. However, she always wished her achievements to be judged by the same standards as a man's would be; her principal aim was to do good work, and not to advance the cause of female emancipation.

10

She continued to specialize in surgery; from 1895 to 1925 she held successively the posts of assistant, full, and senior surgeon at the Elizabeth Garrett Anderson Hospital, as well as that of anaesthetist (1895–1906) and consulting surgeon (1919–22) at the Royal Free Hospital. (She was the first woman appointed surgical registrar and anaesthetist in any teaching hospital.)

Louisa Aldrich-Blake was appointed Dean of the London School of Medicine for Women in 1914, and during her spell in office (1914–25) she more than doubled the size of the school, increased the bed space of the Royal Free Hospital, and, by introducing a new midwifery unit, drew attention to a neglected area of medical concern. As Dean, she was an exceptionally able administrator who strove constantly to increase the technical efficiency of her students.

She was 'very exacting, but good to work for'. Her surgical judgement and skill were outstanding, based on scientific premises and clinical experience. She was the ideal ambassador for women in medicine; a surgeon of great skill, a thorough administrator whose ability and conduct helped to lift the barriers of opposition to women throughout the medical profession.

Louisa Aldrich-Blake never married but devoted her life entirely to her work. In January 1925 she was appointed DBE, the second woman in the medical profession to receive this distinction.

See also G. A. Riddell, *Dame Louisa Aldrich-Blake*, 1926.   R.B.

Alexander, Cecil Frances (1818–95), hymn writer. She was born Cecil Frances Humphreys in County Wicklow, Ireland, and married William Alexander, clergyman and poet, in 1850. In 1846 she published *Verses for Holy Seasons* and two years later *Hymns for Little Children*, which included the still-popular hymns 'All Things Bright and Beautiful', 'Once in Royal David's City', and 'There is a Green Hill Far Away'. Altogether she wrote nearly four hundred hymns, among them 'Jesus Calls Us O'er the Tumult'. Her sacred poem 'The Burial of Moses' was admired by Tennyson, and notable also are her Irish national songs, such as 'The Siege of Derry' and 'The Irish Mother's Lament', as well as tracts for the Anglo-Catholic Oxford Movement. Her husband became Archbishop of Armagh and it was at the bishop's palace in Londonderry that she died.   B.H.C.

Alexandra (1844–1925), Edward VII's queen, the daughter of the King and Queen of Denmark. In the late 1850s VICTORIA and Albert had been looking for a suitable wife, beautiful, good-natured and tolerant, for their somewhat wayward eldest son, and came to favour Alexandra. The couple became engaged in 1862 and were married in 1863 at Windsor, quietly, since Victoria was still in mourning for Albert. Lovely, but without vanity, dignified without being withdrawn, Alexandra was immediately popular. She bore the Prince of Wales three sons and three daughters, and stood by him through the frustrating years during which he waited to become king. She began to go deaf rather early in life, and although the condition may have been hereditary (her mother too became deaf) it is possible that she often preferred not to hear of Edward's love affairs, which continued from early in their marriage. She was a deeply religious woman, and this, combined with her great desire to help people, led her to help establish the military nursing service which bears her name.

With the death of Victoria in 1901 she became queen. Due to the King's ill-health (he almost died of appendicitis), the Coronation was delayed until 1903 when, although she was fifty-nine, Alexandra's beauty was still apparent. Her great tolerance and magnanimity remained evident when she sent for Edward's current mistress to visit him when he was dying. She outlived him by thirteen years, dying suddenly of a heart attack, and was buried by his side at Windsor.

See also N. Lofts, *Queens of Britain*, 1977; G. and H. Fisher, *Bertie and Alex*, 1974.
                                              E.M.V.

Allen, Mary (Sophia) (1878–1964), co-founder and head of the Women Police Service. She was born in Cheltenham, the daughter of the manager of the Great Western Railway, and was educated at Princess Helena College, Ealing. Inspired by Annie KENNEY, she became a suffragette and was imprisoned three times, once for throwing a brick through a Home Office window.

In September 1914 the Women Police Volunteers was created by Margaret Damer DAWSON with the help of Mary Allen, who became Sub-Commandant (1914-19) and Comman-

dant (1919–38). It was re-formed and re-named the Women Police Service in February 1915. The force was not part of the Metropolitan Police although it had the Commissioner's approval.

Mary Allen's first duties were in Grantham and Hull, where army camps were causing public concern over drunkenness and prostitution. She spent the war years rescuing young girls from white slavery while also attempting to formulate the duties of a policewoman with little guidance from the police themselves. In 1917 she was awarded the OBE; in February 1920, however, the Metropolitan Police issued summonses against Mary Allen and four other members of the WPS, complaining that they were 'impersonating police officers' because of the similarity of their uniforms to those of the official force. The uniform was subsequently modified and the title of the WPS changed to the Women's Auxiliary Service. Their past work was universally praised.

In 1922 Mary Allen was sent to Cologne to work with the Military Police and to train German women in police work. She had great sympathy for the Germans; in 1934 she met Hitler, who impressed her as an 'idealist', and held serious discussions with Göring. It was perhaps significant that she was never out of uniform, wearing her jack-boots even at official dinners in her honour. With the approach of war, Mary Allen's fascist sympathies led to the ending of the association between the WAS and Civil Defence.

She published three books: *The Pioneer Policewoman*, 1925; *Woman at the Crossroads*, 1934; and *Lady in Blue* 1936.

See also J. Lock, *The British Policewoman: her Story.* 1979.   A.D.

Allgood, Sara (1883–1950), actress, born in Dublin and educated at Marlborough Street Training College. In 1903 she joined the Fays' Irish National Dramatic Society. Her first big success came in December 1904, when she played Mrs Fallon in *Spreading the News* on the opening night of the Abbey Theatre. Later, after playing in Liverpool 'rep', she joined the Abbey Theatre's founder, Annie HORNIMAN, in Manchester. In 1916 she married her leading man, Gerald Henson, in Australia. He died in the influenza epidemic of 1918.

After several London seasons, Sara Allgood returned to the Abbey, 'making it stronger than it had ever been' and playing the great role of Juno in Sean O'Casey's *Juno and the Paycock*.

She went to New York in 1940 for her last stage appearance, and then turned to films. Although acclaimed for her 'Celtic humour and pathos', she was given only Irish character parts and died in Hollywood, alone and in near-poverty. A.D.

Allingham, Margery (Louise) (1904–66), crime novelist. She was born in London, the daughter of a journalist, and was educated at Perse High School, Cambridge.

From the age of seven, Margery Allingham's father trained her as a writer, giving her the plot of a simple story to work on. At fifteen she left school and began writing for a living. After a period during which she wrote pulp fiction for magazines, *The Daily Express* serialized her first crime novel, *The Crime at Black Dudley* (1929), which introduced her detective hero Albert Campion. *Mystery Mile* (1930) brought her popular success, but not until after the Second World War, with the Charlie Luke stories, did she develop the psychological depth that made her one of the leaders of the new generation of crime novelists. She brought a fine literary style to her work and raised the standard of crime writing. *Tiger in the Smoke* (1952), hailed by critics as a thriller of the highest quality, is widely regarded as her best book. Others include *Death of a Ghost*, 1934, *Flowers for the Judge*, 1936, *Hide My Eyes*, 1958, and *The China Governess*, 1962.

See also J. Mann, *Deadlier than the Male* 1981. P.L.

ALOE. See TUCKER, CHARLOTTE MARIA.

Anados. See COLERIDGE, MARY (ELIZABETH).

Anderson, Adelaide (Mary) (1863–1936), civil servant. Adelaide Anderson was the daughter of a Scottish shipowner. She was educated by a governess and then in schools in France and Germany. After attending classes at Queen's College, Harley Street, she went up to Girton College, Cambridge, where she had a distinguished career. After coming down she coached young women for examinations, sat on the Educational Council of the Co-operative Union, and gave lectures to the Women's Co-operative Guild. In 1892 she joined the clerical staff of the Royal Commission on Labour.

In 1894 she became one of the first four women to be appointed by the Home Office as a factory inspector, serving from 1897 to 1921 as principal lady inspector of factories in charge of the Women's Branch of the Factory Department. Women inspectors were initially assigned to specific investigations in various parts of the country as the need arose, and not attached to the men's organization, a system which, combined with persistent understaffing, made the work particularly rigorous and inefficient. Adelaide Anderson sought a way of rationalizing it while at the same time preserving the independence of the Women's Branch; she did so by stages, forming a special residential district in West London (1898) and later (1908) decentralizing the branch into regions, each with a residential women's inspectorate, linked tentatively to the male inspectorate but firmly controlled by the principal lady inspector in London.

Adelaide Anderson demanded a very high standard from her staff and always sought to expand their duties and upgrade their qualifications. During the First World War she attempted to take over as much work as possible from the Men's Branch. For her wartime work she was awarded the CBE in 1918. The great strides made by the women's inspectorate were formally recognised in 1921 in the reorganization of the Factory Department, which involved the amalgamation of the Men's and Women's Branches. Ironically, this meant the loss of independence and (for a time) of many high posts by women. Her heart was not in these changes for, although a strong feminist, she believed that it was in the interests of women inspectors to have a separate organization, and she retired in 1921, having been awarded the DBE. She published *Women in the Factory: an Administrative Adventure, 1893–1921* in 1922.

After her retirement Adelaide Anderson travelled extensively and brought her great expertise to the study of labour conditions in foreign countries. She was a member of the Commission on Child Labour in Shanghai (1923–24) and published an account of her experiences in *Humanity and Labour in China: an Industrial Visit and its Sequel, 1923–1926* (1928). She was also a member of the Foreign Office's Advisory Committee on the China (Boxer Indemnity) Fund (1925) and of a mission sent out by the International Labour Office to Nanking in 1930–31. In 1930 she made a study of child labour for the Egyptian Government.

See also H. Martindale, *Women Servants of the State: a History of Women in the Civil Service, 1870–1938*, 1938, and *Some Victorian Portraits and Others*, 1948.   M.Z.

Anderson, Elizabeth Garrett (1836–1917), physician. Born in Whitechapel, the second of ten children, she moved with her family in 1841 to Aldeburgh in Suffolk, where her father became a wealthy merchant. She was educated in London but on her return home became increasingly dissatisfied with the conventional life of a Victorian lady. This, together with her association with such women as Emily DAVIES and Elizabeth BLACKWELL, interested her in the women's cause and particularly in medicine as a profession for women.

At this time no medical school nor examining body in Britain would accept a female candidate. Undeterred, she started unofficial training at the Middlesex Hospital in 1860 but was forced to withdraw under hostile student pressure. The following year the Society of Apothecaries was obliged to register her as a student, and after then being refused university training, she continued with private tuition from some of the country's leading doctors, financially supported by her father. After four years of study she became the first woman to qualify as a medical practitioner in Britain, settling in London as a consultant to women and children. In 1870 she graduated MD from the Sorbonne.

By now opinion, even within the medical profession, was more favourable towards her, if not towards other aspiring women doctors, and in 1871 she became one of the first women elected to the London School Board. In the following year she opened the New Hospital for Women, now named after its founder, and in 1877 she was elected to the British Medical Association, which then closed its ranks to women. Despite her initial disapproval she proceeded to take a prominent role in the London Medical School for Women, founded by Sophia JEX-BLAKE. During her time as Senior Lecturer and Dean for 23 and 20 years respectively, the School forged teaching links with the Royal Free Hospital and in 1902 became a college of London University, thus securing the future of women in medicine.

Neither her marriage in 1871 to James Skelton Anderson of the Orient Shipping Line nor the birth of their three children were allowed to halt her career, and this combination of a normal family life with an exacting profession strengthened her arguments on behalf of women. So too did her personal qualities—calmness, determination, and a heightened sense of professional courtesy. Throughout her life she supported the women's movement, deviating only in her support of the Contagious Diseases Acts. Apart from a brief flirtation with the militant Suffragette organization, the WSPU, between 1908 and 1911, she was in favour of constitutional suffrage as voiced by her sister Millicent FAWCETT. Most of her later years were spent in Aldeburgh, where she followed her father and husband as mayor, being the first woman in Britain to hold that office. Her writings include *An Enquiry into the Character of The Contagious Diseases Acts of 1866–69* (1870).

See also L. G. Anderson, *Elizabeth Garrett Anderson*, 1939; J. G. Manton, *Elizabeth Garrett Anderson*, 1965.   J.G.S.

Anderson, Dame Kitty (1903–79), distinguished head mistress, the daughter of a Middlesbrough accountant. She was educated at the High School for Girls, Saltburn-by-the-Sea, and at Royal Holloway College, London, where she read history. After teaching for six years at Burlington School in London, she was Head Mistress of Kings Norton Grammar School in Birmingham from 1939 to 1944. In 1944 she was appointed Head Mistress of the prestigious North London Collegiate School for Girls, where she exercised a beneficent influence in personal as well as administrative terms; it is said that she never forgot the name of any girl in the school. On her retirement in 1965 she became Chairman, and later (1976) Vice-President, of the Girls' Public Day School Trust. She also served on the Robbins Committee on Higher Education (1960–64) and many similar bodies.   N.H.

Andrews, Ellen. See PATEY, JANET MONACH.

Anna Matilda. See COWLEY, HANNAH.

Anne, Queen (1665–1714), Queen of Great Britain and Ireland, the daughter of James II (then Duke of York) and his first, Protestant wife, Anne HYDE. She was brought up by Lady Frances Villiers, whose death in 1677 disturbed her deeply. So did her father's conversion to Catholicism and his second marriage in 1679 to his co-religionist MARY OF MODENA. In 1681 a stay in Scotland made her realise its security value to England and presaged the Act of Union in her reign. After her marriage in 1683 to Prince George of Denmark (a colourless character twelve years her senior, to whom she remained devoted), her existence was punctuated by eighteen pregnancies. These unsuccessful attempts to produce an heir affected her physically and mentally, yet did not prevent her pursuing such interests as hunting, gardening, and music.

The enforced abdication of her father in 1688 and the Protestant succession of William and her sister MARY were reluctantly accepted by Anne (she was a dutiful daughter but also a devout Anglican), who relinquished her hereditary right in favour of the new monarchs' children. Meanwhile, by special Act of Parliament, a grant was fixed on her. In 1691 she granted to Sarah CHURCHILL, now a close friend on whom she depended greatly, a pension of £1,000 per annum; and the two women began to call each other 'Mrs Morley' and 'Mrs Freeman' as part of a curious make-believe informal relationship.

Anne's unexpected succession to the throne in 1702 revealed her to be quite a strong-minded woman. Despite being a virtual invalid she carried out all her duties; and she made a large number of appointments without advice. However, the political situation forced her to rely heavily on the Whigs and in particular on John Churchill, whom she created Duke of Marlborough for his conduct of the war against France. But, increasingly, his wife Sarah's deteriorating relationship with Anne made the Queen turn against the Whigs. Marlborough's influence with Anne was further weakened by the efforts of the Tory politician Robert Harley and his relative, Abigail Hill (Mrs MASHAM), who gradually replaced Sarah Churchill in Anne's affections. The death of Prince George in 1708 marked the nadir of Anne's life, but her determination to rule enabled her in the following year to take the lead in pressing for peace, to refuse Marlborough's demand for the captain-generalship for life, and to break with Sarah Churchill. The downfall of the Marlboroughs and the Whigs was hastened by the 'great changes' of 1710, including the acquittal of Henry Sacheverell and the Tory electoral victory.

The last years of Anne's life were dominated by her pursuit of peace in Europe and a tranquil Protestant succession: both concerns exhausted her emotionally. But the force of her personality and her popularity did much to prevent the onset of civil war which might have resulted from Jacobite discontent and the rivalry of the Tory leaders Harley and Bolingbroke. On her deathbed her refusal to appoint either of them as chief minister ensured the Hanoverian succession and the supremacy of the Whigs during the next two reigns.

See also E. Gregg, *Queen Anne*, 1980; G. M. Trevelyan, *England in the Reign of Queen Anne* 1935.   C.H.G.G.

Anne of Bohemia (1366–94), Richard II's queen, daughter of the Holy Roman Emperor, Charles IV. Anne was highly educated before her marriage in 1382 to the young King Richard II. Although there were no identifiable artists or craftsmen in her German entourage, she is generally regarded as having introduced Rhenish and Bohemian art to England. Her marriage to Richard was deeply happy, but they had no children. Anne exercised a restraining influence over the King until her death, apparently of the plague. In his grief, Richard ordered the destruction of the palace of Sheen where she had died.

See also A. Steel, *Richard II*, 1941.

A.C.

Anne of Cleves (1515–57), fourth queen of Henry VIII, the daughter of John the Pacific, Duke of Cleves and Juliers. She was betrothed to the Duke of Lorraine until 1535. Her match with Henry came about because the king was looking for allies among the German Lutheran states. Holbein painted Anne's portrait, which Henry found to his taste, and a marriage treaty was signed on 24 September 1539. Anne reached England on 27 December; Henry surprised her at Rochester on 1 January 1540, but was greatly dismayed by her appearance, which evidently failed to live up to the Holbein. The marriage was nonetheless celebrated on 6 January 1540, but on 17 April Thomas Cromwell—its architect—was arrested, signalling a change of royal policy. Henry's desire for reconciliation with the Holy Roman Emperor, and his infatuation with Katherine Howard, made him resolve to abandon Anne and the Lutheran alliance. She sensibly accepted the title 'King's sister' and a settlement of £4000, and Convocation declared her marriage void on 9 July. Though both English and German Protestants hoped the King would take her back on Katherine Howard's fall. Anne lived on privately in England, her last public appearance being at Queen Mary's coronation in 1553, when she rode and banqueted with Princess Elizabeth. She was buried in Westminster Abbey.

See also J. S. Brewer, *Letters and Papers, Foreign and Domestic, of the reign of Henry VIII . . .*, 1920; M. A. S. Hume, *The Wives of Henry VIII*, 1929.   M.D.

Anne of Denmark (1574–1619), Queen Consort of Scotland (1589–1619) and England (1603–19). Anne was the daughter of Frederick II of Denmark and Norway and Sophia of Mecklenburg. Her father died in 1588 and her marriage to James VI of Scotland (James I of England from 1603) was arranged by her mother. Anne and James were married in Norway in November 1589 and arrived in Scotland the following May. The fifteen-year-old Queen set herself to learn Scots, evidence perhaps of determination and some intellectual capacity. In general, though, she behaved as a kindly but frivolous and undistinguished woman. Her physical and mental health were impaired by childbirth: she bore her first child, Henry, in 1594; ELIZABETH, later Queen of Bohemia, in 1596; and the future Charles I in 1600. Four other children died in infancy and she suffered at least three miscarriages. Opinion on the happiness of the early years of her marriage is divided, but by 1607 she was living virtually apart from the homosexual James.

Despite her Lutheran parentage and her Calvinist intellectual husband, Anne flirted with Catholicism, refusing the communion of the Church of England at her coronation in 1603. Her suspect religion, James's homosexual preferences, and her own incapacity limited her political influence, but she is of significance as a patron of the arts. The great architect and designer Inigo Jones began work on the Queen's House, Greenwich, for Anne, and was also associated with the staging of theatrical masques, which were Anne's principal passion. The Queen's entry into London in 1603 was delayed so that Thomas Dekker could devise a suitable pageant, and amongst the masques at court in which Anne herself performed were Ben Jonson's *Masque of Blacknesse* (1605) and *Masque of Queens* (1609) and Samuel Daniel's

Tethys' Festival (1610). The Queen's patronage extended to the provinces: in 1615 a Bristol company of actors was licensed at her request. Anne was criticized for the extravagance of her artistic tastes: the *Masque of Queens* cost £3000 to stage, and one court jeweller alone provided her with £48,000 worth of jewels between 1603 and 1613. If Anne's patronage was unpopular in its day it now seems the most interesting aspect of a life in many ways unremarkable and even pathetic.

See also E. C. Williams, *Anne of Denmark*, 1970.   P.M.H.

Anning, Mary (1800–47), geologist, born at Lyme Regis, Dorset. She was the daughter of a carpenter, an enthusiastic collector of fossils and other 'curiosities' who encouraged her to develop an early interest in geology. After his death, she supported her mother and brother by selling the specimens she found to visitors and local scholars.

When still very young, Mary Anning discovered the remains of a complete animal, known in Lyme as 'the crocodile', this was in fact an ichthyosaurus. Its high standard of preservation attracted much interest, and it was eventually sold to the British Museum. In 1828 she unearthed the skeleton of a previously unknown creature, the pterodactyl; and her discovery of the plesiosaur followed a few years later.

Although she had no scientific education, Mary Anning's work made a significant contribution to the furthering of geological studies. Her extensive knowledge of local conditions enabled her to predict with great accuracy the possible locations of remains. She also developed considerable skill in the delicate operation of extracting fossils undamaged from the lias in which they lay.

Although enjoying some celebrity during her lifetime, Mary Anning's achievements are largely forgotten today, and she is unmentioned in most standard works on the history of geology. There is a commemorative window to her in Lyme Regis church, erected by members of the Geological Society of London.
                                        J.V.L.

Anspach, Margravine of. See BERKELEY, ELIZABETH.

Arber, Agnes (1879–1960), botanist and philosopher of science, born in London, the elder daughter of H. R. Robertson. She was educated

Archdale, Helen

at the North London Collegiate School for Girls and University College, London, and then went on to Newnham College, Cambridge, where she took Firsts in both parts of the Natural Sciences Tripos. After research work and a lectureship at University College, London, she married the distinguished Cambridge palaeobotanist E. A. N. Arber in 1909. Thereafter she pursued her researches at the Balfour Laboratory in Cambridge and in her private laboratory at home. In 1920 she published *Water-Plants: a Study of Aquatic Angiosperms*, which was followed by other morphological studies. From the lay point of view her most interesting publications were historical or philosophical. *Herbals, their Origin and Evolution* (1912) is a fascinating account of the works about plants printed between 1470 and 1670. The philosophical works are *The Natural Philosophy of Plant Form* (1950) and *The Mind and the Eye* (1954), which considers the nature of biological research and the bases of biological thinking in the wider context of an inquiry into the aims and validity of science as a whole. Her personal philosophy is set out in *The Manifold and the One* (1957).   N.H.

Archdale, Helen (Alexander) (1876–1949), journalist and worker for women's rights. Helen Archdale's father, Alexander Russel, was a distinguished journalist who became editor of *The Scotsman*. She went to school and university at St Andrews, and married Lieutenant-Colonel Theodore Archdale. She was a militant suffragette, twice imprisoned, and worked on *Britannia*, the organ of the Women's Social and Political Union. From 1921 to 1926 she was the first editor of the weekly review *Time and Tide*, which under her direction had a radical and feminist outlook that later disappeared when Lady RHONDDA took over. Until her death, Helen Archdale was a member of the Liaison Committee of Women's International Organizations.   N.H.

Arden, Alice (d. 1551), murderess. The wife of a prosperous Kentish landowner, Alice Arden fell in love with a man named Mosbie and resolved to murder her husband. After an attempt to poison Thomas Arden had failed, she and Mosbie enlisted the aid of several servants and two professional ruffians, 'Black Will' and 'Shakebag'. They too were thwarted

in their murderous designs on a number of occasions, and for a time Mosbie lost his nerve; he agreed to go on only when Alice begged him on her knees to go through with the deed. On the evening of 15 February 1551, Arden was attacked in his home and strangled, stabbed, and bludgeoned to death by Alice and her gang, who dumped his body in a nearby field. When suspicion fell on her, Alice soon confessed, and she and her accomplices were convicted and executed.

The crime captured the public imagination in Tudor England, and was retold in chronicles, pamphlets, and plays such as *Arden of Feversham*, sometimes attributed to Shakespeare, and *Murderous Michael*, which was performed before Queen Elizabeth. This fascination is explained by the quasi-religious horror which the age attached to murder of a husband, the punishment for which was to be burned alive. This point is further illustrated by a passage in a contemporary political tract which claimed that 'the wicked woman of Feversham in Kent, that not long since killed her husband' was, seemingly as part of her punishment, left to be sexually assaulted by any man who cared to do so.

See also R. Holinshed, *Chronicles*, 1577; J. Ponet, *Shorte Treatise of Politicke Power*, 1556; J. H. Marshburn, *Murder and Witchcraft in England*, 1971.   G.Q.B.

Argyle, Duchess of. See LOUISE (CAROLINE ALBERTA), PRINCESS.

Arnaud, Yvonne (Germaine) (1892–1958), actress, born at Bordeaux. After winning first prize for the piano at the Paris Conservatoire when aged only twelve, she toured Europe and America as a child prodigy. Her first stage appearance, in *The Quaker Girl* (1911), occurred during a break in concert tours, but thereafter she devoted herself to acting. She was famous for her French accent and her wit, elegance, and obsession for perfection; many bad plays enjoyed undeserved success thanks to her stagecraft and personality. She loved comedy but wrote, 'I hate farce. They want me to be a clown, and I loathe being a clown.'

Yvonne Arnaud's greatest triumph was in Macrae's *Traveller's Joy* (1940); her other successes include *Tons of Money, Tomorrow We Live*, and *Love for Love*. She was in British films and early broadcasts. The repertory theatre at Guildford is named after her.

A.D.

Arnim, Elizabeth Mary, Countess von (1866–1941), novelist. Born Elizabeth Beauchamp in Sydney, she was the cousin of Katherine MANSFIELD and married in 1891 the Prussian Count von Arnim. His great estate in Pomerania was the scene of her best-loved book *Elizabeth and her German Garden* (1898), in which she relates her horticultural adventures and her experiences with five babies, servants, guests, and her husband, 'The Man of Wrath'. After she had performed all her many daily duties, she formed the habit of shutting herself away and writing stories, which led to a series of light novels signed 'Elizabeth', the first being *The Benefactress* (1902).

The Count died in 1910 and in 1916 she married the second Earl Russell, brother of Bertrand Russell, but they separated in 1919. She remarked that perhaps husbands never altogether agreed with her! Her novels became more serious; *Vera* (1921), for example, reflected the misery she felt at the failure of her second marriage. However, *Enchanted April* (1923), based on her experiences on the French Riviera, almost recaptured the insouciance of her early work and was a best-seller in America. Two more novels, *The Jasmine Tree* (1934) and *Mr Skeffington* (1940), were American Book-of-the-Month Club choices. From 1939 onwards she lived in America and died at Charleston, South Carolina. Other works include *The Pastor's Wife* (1914) and *Love* (1925).

See also her autobiography, *All the Dogs of my Life*, 1936; L. de Charms, *Elizabeth of the German Garden*, 1958.　　　　　　　　P.L.

Ashby, Dame Margery Corbett (1882–1981), oustanding figure in the international movement for women's rights. She was born into a progressive-minded family in Sussex, and educated at home before going on to Newnham College, Cambridge. After coming down from Cambridge she revealed her gifts as a speaker when her father, C. H. Corbett, contested East Grinstead for the Liberals; she herself was to be a Liberal candidate on many occasions, became a lecturer for the party on educational and land questions, and was twice President of the Women's Liberal Federation.

However, her greatest contribution to public affairs was as a speaker and organizer for the women's movement; and here her mastery of French and German was an important factor in giving her international stature. She joined the International Alliance of Women when it was founded at Berlin in 1904; in 1920 she became its secretary, and in 1946 its president. She was also an effective editor of the monthly *International Women's News* and other publications. In Britain, she became Secretary to the National Union of Women's Suffrage Societies (1906–07) and later served on its executive.

These and other concerns took her into many parts of the world, and she became particularly involved with the problems of women in the developing countries. Her ability was officially recognized by occasional *ad hoc* appointments. She helped to organize a women's police service in Germany after the First World War; served as alternate delegate for the United Kingdom to the Disarmament Conference at Geneva in 1932–34; and was sent to Sweden on a propaganda mission during the Second World War. Despite all these activities, she was a successful wife (to the barrister A. B. Ashby, from 1910) and mother.　　　　　　　　N.H.

Ashford, Daisy, pseudonym of Mrs Margaret Devlin (1881–1972), whose famous 'novel' *The Young Visiters* is said to have been composed when she was nine years old; her literary efforts ceased when she was sent away to school. Years later she rediscovered the manuscript of *The Young Visiters* and lent it to a friend; the friend showed it to Chatto & Windus; and as a result it was published in 1919 with a preface by J. M. Barrie. It made a fashionable success and has remained popular ever since, being at various times dramatized and turned into a musical comedy.

The entertainment value of the *The Young Visiters* lies in its child's-eye view of high society, expressed through unintentionally comic juxtapositions, misapprehensions and misspellings. These are regular and pointed enough to raise doubts about its authenticity as a child's work, although Barrie declared himself satisfied. It begins 'Mr Salteena was an elderly man of 42' and goes on to tell how Mr S., although 'not quite a gentleman but you would hardly notice it', achieves social success by taking a special course for upstarts at 'the Crystal Pallace', but meanwhile loses Ethel Monticue to a younger rival who is 'inclined to be rich'.

17

Ashley, Katherine

Two early stories by Daisy Ashford appear in *Love and Marriage* (1965).   N.H.

Ashley, Katherine (*fl.* 1510–70), governess to the Princess (later Queen) ELIZABETH. Katherin Ashley, or Astley, was the daughter of Sir Philip Champernowne of Devonshire. Sometime in the 1530s she married John Ashley, a cousin of Anne Boleyn, and became governess to Anne's daughter, the Princess Elizabeth, who called her Kat. After the death of Henry VIII, Elizabeth and Katherine lived in the household of Thomas Seymour and his wife Katherine PARR, and there Katherine Ashley seems to have encouraged a flirtation between Seymour and Elizabeth. After Katherine Parr's death in 1548 this led to secret marriage plans, and the subsequent imprisonment of Katherine. Seymour was executed in 1549 but nothing was proved against Elizabeth, who remained loyal to her imprisoned servants, demanding of Protector Somerset that they should be returned to her. In 1555 Katherine was again imprisoned because of Elizabeth's suspected involvement in the Dudley conspiracy against the Catholic Queen MARY; various Protestant works had also been found in Katherine's possession. She remained in prison for about three months.

In 1558, on Elizabeth's accession, John Ashley returned from. exile abroad and was appointed master of the jewel house; Katherine became chief gentlewoman of the privy chamber. She seems to have encouraged the relationship between Elizabeth and Robert Dudley; her husband was in trouble in 1561 for being too outspoken on the question of the queen's marriage. Katherine died around 1570.

Elizabeth was always very fond of Katherine Ashley, and it seems that Katherine proved a good governess, since in about 1548 Roger Ascham, later Elizabeth's tutor, congratulated her on Elizabeth's academic progress and proffered advice on the Princess's education.

See also B. W. Beckingsale, *Elizabeth I*, 1963; F. A. Mumby, *The Girlhood of Queen Elizabeth*, 1909.   J.S.

Ashton, Winifred. See DANE, CLEMENCE.

Ashwell, Lena (1872–1957), actress. She was the daughter of Commander Charles Ashwell Pocock, RN, and was born on board a training ship in the Tyne. The family emigrated to Toronto when Lena was eight. She went to Lausanne in 1888 for singing lessons, and then to London, where in 1891 Ellen TERRY advised her to act. She was hampered at first by her Canadian accent, but by 1900 had become established as one of England's leading actresses with her performance as Mrs Dane in *Mrs Dane's Defence*, which she later took to Australia.

In 1907 Lena Ashwell started in management with *Irene Wycherley*, leasing the Kingsway Theatre until 1915, and meanwhile playing in Barrie's *Twelve Pound Look* (1910). During the agitation for women's suffrage she worked for the Actresses' Franchise League and later formed the Three Arts Club for women. During the First World War she organized the Lena Ashwell Concerts at the Front (1914–20), raising £100,000 in funds and receiving the OBE in 1916.

Her public spirit was equally in evidence after the war. In 1920, with the help of Clement Attlee, then Mayor of Stepney, she started a repertory company, the Once-A-Week-Players, to bring good cheap entertainment to the public; and the Lena Ashwell Players (1924–29) continued this work.

Lena Ashwell published an autobiography, *Myself a Player* (1936).   A.D.

Askewe, Anne (1521?–1546), Protestant martyr under Henry VIII. The second daughter of a Yorkshire knight, she married Thomas Kyme, with whom she 'demeaned herself like a Christian wife' and had two children; but her growing adherence to the Protestant faith brought their married life to an effective end. Whether her husband expelled her at the insistence of outraged Catholic clergy, or whether she left in the belief that it was improper to cohabit with an infidel spouse, Anne Askewe found herself in London Protestant circles in 1545.

Arrested in that year and imprisoned, she was questioned by the Lord Mayor and Bishop Bonner of London concerning the sacrament. Her replies were evasive and she was released by Bonner after signing an ambiguous declaration on transubstantiation. Bonner attributed Askewe's release to her connections and 'worshipful stock'. After she was re-arrested in 1546 and questioned by the Council at Greenwich, her replies to the bishops were bolder and she refused to sign another statement on the Mass. Eventually she was committed to the Tower. In an attempt to determine the extent of her influential connections, she was racked and asked what support she had received from women such as the Duchess of Suffolk and the Countesses of Sussex and Hertford. So severely was she injured that she had to be carried to Smithfield, the place of her execution, in a chair. The sermon at the burning was delivered by Nicholas Shaxton, and Anne Askewe commented aloud throughout it, confirming his references when correct and, when they were incorrect, saying, 'There he misseth, and speaketh without the book.' Burned for heresy with her were three others including a gentleman, John Lascells, sometimes call Anne Askewe's 'instructor'.

Anne Askewe's learning and steadfastness made her an exemplary martyr in the eyes of sixteenth-century Protestant England, and her story, based on her own account of her examinations and torture, was powerfully retold, first by John Bale and later by the Elizabethan martyrologist John Foxe.

See also J. Bale, *Select Works*, 1849; J. Foxe, *Acts and Monuments*, 1563.   G.Q.B.

Asquith, Margot (1864–1945), socialite and hostess. Born Emma Alice Margaret Tennant, she was the daughter of Sir Charles Tennant, whose family had made a fortune in chemicals. She was brought up in Peeblesshire. Given almost no formal education and allowed virtually to run wild, she yet developed an unusual combination of talents, musical, literary, and artistic, and grew up with almost no self-consciousness. It was later both her strength and her weakness that she seemed quite untouched by what others thought of her.

In 1881 she 'came out' in London together with her sister Laura, and in spite of her unprepossessing appearance—as she herself put it 'I have no face, only two profiles clapped together'—she was soon an enormous success. The keynotes of her dinner-parties were the brilliant, witty conversations she led, and her insistence that political animosities be forgotten for their duration. A group of talented young people gathered around the Tennant girls; they included Curzon, Arthur Balfour, and Alfred Lyttelton (who was to marry Laura), and were dubbed 'The Souls'.

In 1894 Margot Tennant married as his second wife Herbert Henry Asquith, the Liberal politician, despite the fact that she considered him irredeemably bourgeois and lacking in style. However, when he became

Prime Minister, she was proud of his position. She took no part in the war effort after 1914 and made little attempt to hide her own extravagant life-style, which scarcely helped Asquith, who was already being criticized as an unsatisfactory war leader (he was ousted in 1916). In 1920 and 1922 Margot's famous indiscreet memoirs appeared. Asquith died in 1927 but she survived until 1945, a lonely old woman living at the Savoy who, for all her brittle insensitivity, had influenced the social and political mores of a generation.

See also M. Bonham Carter (ed.), *The Autobiography of Margot Asquith*, 1962.

                                                   E.M.V.

Asquith of Yarnbury, Lady. See BONHAM CARTER, (HELEN) VIOLET, LADY ASQUITH OF YARNBURY.

Astell, Mary (1666–1731), author and feminist, was born at Newcastle into a gentry family of Royalist inclinations and was reportedly educated by a clergyman uncle. Her father died when she was twelve and a few years after the death of her mother in 1684 she moved to London; by 1695 she was established in Chelsea, where she lived for the rest of her life, first as an independent householder and then as a member of the household of Lady Katherine Jones, a daughter of the Countess of Ranelagh.

A profound scholar, a fearsome polemicist, and devout supporter of the conservative establishment and the Anglican faith, Mary Astell owed the philosophical inspiration for her feminist vision largely to Descartes and his neo-Platonist commentators, from whom she derived a firm belief in the authority of the thinking self and the equal spiritual and intellectual capacities of the two sexes, capacities which she felt that women should be encouraged to develop. In 1694, as a self-styled 'Lover of her Sex', she published anonymously the first part of her most important and revolutionary work, *A Serious Proposal to the Ladies for the Advancement of their True and Greatest Interest*, which was followed by a second part in 1697. In this she advocated the establishment of an institution of higher education for women, dubbed a 'Monastery, or Place of Religious Retirement' without vows, an academy where women who could afford the tuition might temporarily retire from the world to devote themselves to intellectual, religious, and charitable pursuits and the cultivation of friendship, and where they might receive the benefits of 'an ingenuous and liberal education'. The academy could also serve as a refuge for unmarried women seeking to escape a mercenary marriage or a derisory and dependent spinsterhood. In such a place, women might develop their intellectual and spiritual resources and afterwards go forth to realize their full potential in their traditional spheres as wives, mothers, teachers, and inculcators of Christian virtues.

In 1700, in her tract *Some Reflections upon Marriage,* while accepting the assumption of a male-dominated society, Mary Astell promoted the ideal of a rational and companionate marriage based on mutual kindness and esteem, and above all on friendship; more than most other reformers she emphasized the need to educate women so that they might arrange their marriages more prudently and give a better account of themselves in the married state. She argued that intellectual discipline and a serious education would produce more virtuous, sensible, effective, and happier wives, mothers, and teachers, to whom would be reserved 'the Glory of Reforming this Prophane and Profligate Age'.

She herself never married, allegedly disappointed by the failure of marriage negotiations with an eminent clergyman. Her circle of friends and associates consisted mainly of Anglican divines and clever young female disciples, including Lady Elizabeth Hastings and her four half sisters, Lady Anne Coventry, Catherine Atterbury, Elizabeth ELSTOB, and Lady Mary Wortley MONTAGU. She entered vigorously into discussions of the political, religious, and social issues of her day, and was regarded as a woman of formidable intellect by even her fiercest detractors.

See also J. K. Kinnaird, 'Mary Astell and the Conservative Contribution to English Feminism', *Journal of British Studies,* 1979; F. Smith, *Mary Astell,* 1916.   T.J.M.

Astley, Katherine. See ASHLEY, KATHERINE.

Astor, Nancy (Witcher), Viscountess Astor (1879–1964), public figure, the first woman Member of Parliament. Nancy Witcher Langhorne was born into an old Virginian family and lived the life of a Southern belle until 1897, when she married Robert Shaw, by whom she had one son; they were divorced in 1903. Soon afterwards she came to Europe,

and in 1906 she married Waldorf Astor; they had five children.

Nancy Astor's political career began in a more conventional fashion than is generally realized. In 1919 she took over her husband's seat (as Conservative Member for Plymouth, Sutton) when he inherited his father's viscountcy and went to the Lords. This was probably arranged in the expectation that Lord Astor would reclaim the seat when his planned Bill to allow peers to sit in the Lower House became law. It never did, and Nancy Astor was to survive as a politician in her own right for twenty-five years.

In Parliament, she devoted herself to the causes of women and children, temperance, education, and nursery schools, all suitably 'female' subjects, although she often presented her case with a verve, originality, and tenacity which her opponents considered scarcely feminine. She was remarkable for her ability to take the strain of being the single woman in a largely hostile House, a gentleman's club with no facilities for women. She could easily have lost her identity, but with characteristic self-confidence she refused the male definitions of what was politically important and went her own way.

She was a notoriously bad party woman and never held office, which was probably no bad thing: her genius was not for administration but for publicizing the causes which she took to heart. Her idiosyncratic feminism alienated not only her male colleagues but often her own sex, as for example, when she summoned the women of the 1929 Parliament to lunch to instruct them in setting up a 'female phalanx', a women's party, free from what were considered idiotic male priorities: she had a firm belief in the superiority of women.

Nancy Astor's strength came in part from her deep religious faith (she was a Christian Scientist) and also from a real love of political performance. She had a marvellous ability to deal with uncomfortable situations; she revelled in repartee; she was a painfully accurate mimic, a great 'turn'. She had no conception of this as graceless and strident or unfeminine, and so she was not vulnerable, as so many women are, to male criticism of 'unsuitable' female behaviour.

During the Second World War, while still an MP, Nancy Astor became Lady Mayoress of Plymouth and in 1959 she was made a Freeman of the City. She did not stand for re-election to Parliament in 1945, and although she had been made a CH in 1937, she never had the final honour she coveted—that of being the first woman in the Upper House as she had been in the Lower. It would have been a fitting recognition of the unique and difficult part she had played in establishing women in politics.

See also M. Collis, *Nancy Astor*, 1960; C. Sykes, *Nancy, the Life of Lady Astor*, 1972.

E.M.V.

Atholl, Duchess of; Katherine Marjory Stewart-Murray (1874–1960). Conservative MP and first Conservative woman minister. The daughter of Sir James Ramsay, a well-known historian, Kitty Ramsay was brought up in an aristocratic Scottish family who had been Lairds of Banff since 1232. She was educated at Wimbledon High School and the Royal College of Music where she took her ARCM. In 1899 she married the future Duke of Atholl. They had no children. Her public service began before the First World War, when from 1909 she was President of the Perthshire Red Cross Society. In 1912 she sat on the committee investigating the medical services in the Highlands and Islands, and in 1917 she was a member of the Committee of Enquiry on Scottish Tinkers. During the war, she turned the family seat, Blair Castle, into an auxiliary hospital which she ran herself.

With this background, and her acquaintance with many of the best-known politicians of the day, it is perhaps not surprising that she was pressed to stand for parliament. Although her husband had held the seat of Kinross and West Perthshire until 1917, it had not been contested since, and so the Duchess did well to win it when she stood in 1923, so becoming the first woman MP for Scotland.

An honest and diligent MP, who refused to compromise on matters of principle, she was consequently sometimes unpopular and often misunderstood, but worked hard for the causes to which she was most committed, those of women and children and the educational services. In 1924 she was appointed Under-Secretary of State to the Board of Education, the first Conservative woman to hold ministerial office. She was not, however, a supporter of women's suffrage and strongly opposed Mrs Pankhurst's scheme for a Woman's Party in parliament. Yet she was prepared to raise her voice in support of women where she saw

exploitation or oppression. She courageously spoke against the enforced circumcision of Kikuyu girls, a subject which was not, at the time, easy for a woman to discuss publicly. She was above all an opponent of totalitarianism, and as it became clear that European war was inevitable, she took a strong line against appeasement. In 1938 she resigned her seat and fought a by-election which became a straight fight between the official Conservative candidate supporting Chamberlain and the Duchess supporting Churchill and re-armament. Many influential people gave her their support, but she lost the by-election and was never to return to parliament.

For the rest of her life she continued in public service, taking evacuee children into Blair Castle during the Second World War, organizing Civil Defence in Perthshire, and after the war supporting the Poles, Czechs, and Hungarians in opposition to Soviet Russia. It was appropriate, therefore, that with the honorary doctorates awarded to her from Oxford, Glasgow, Manchester, Durham, Columbia, Leeds, and McGill, she should also have received the Order of Polonia Restituta shortly before her death at the age of eighty-six.

She published several books, including *Women and Politics* (1931) and *Working Partnership* (1958). E.M.V.

Attaway, Mrs (*fl.* 1642–47), preacher. Mrs Attaway was among the most notorious women preachers in London in the 1640s, attracting much outraged comment from sober Presbyterians like Robert Baillie and Thomas Edwards. According to these hostile accounts, she was a lace-seller living in Bell Alley, Coleman Street. She preached weekly with two other women in Bell Alley, attracting a large audience. She attacked infant baptism and argued for the right of women to preach publicly, and was associated with prominent antinomians like John Goodwin and John Saltmarsh. The activities of Mrs Attaway and other women preachers were felt to be highly threatening by the London authorities, and in 1646 several Aldermen and Common Councillors informed Parliament 'of private meetings of women preachers of new and strange doctrines and blasphemies'; as a result of this complaint Mrs Attaway was questioned by the Commons' Committee of Examinations. She was probably the target of an anonymous tract,

Tub Preachers Overturned (1647), which denounced a woman 'tubber' who sold lace in Cheapside and

> Did take a text and boldly did descant
> The lawfulness to preach of a she-saint,
> Inform'd her auditory that there was
> More need to edify 'em than sell lace.

Mrs Attaway left her husband and ran away with a fellow radical, William Jenney, a married man. She justified her action with arguments drawn from the poet Milton's *Doctrine and Discipline of Divorce:* she and her husband were incompatible and therefore the marriage was void. She had, she claimed, 'an unsanctified husband, that did not walk in the way of Sion, nor speak the language of Canaan'. Mrs Attaway thus illustrates the potentially liberating effect of religious radicalism on women's lives during the Civil War period, in both the public and, more precariously, the personal sphere.

See also Christopher Hill, *The World Turned Upside Down*, 1972.   P.M.H.

Attwell, Mabel Lucie (1879–1964), illustrator, born in Mile End, London, the daughter of a butcher. She was educated at the Coopers' Company School and later attended classes at various art schools. In 1908 she married the painter and illustrator Harold Earnshaw; they had three children.

Her strength lay in her feeling for imaginary subjects, particularly the inhabitants of fairyland. Her career began with magazine work, and this led to commissions from book publishers, notably a Raphael Tuck series of gift books that included *Alice in Wonderland* (1910) and *The Water Babies* (1915).

After her husband lost his right arm in the First World War, she became a main support of the family, and the ubiquity of her drawings made her a household name. Mabel Lucie Attwell children appeared everywhere, on calendars, postcards, nursery equipment, painting books, and annuals, and as dolls made from her own plasticine models. Despite her rather sentimental interpretation of childhood, she had a distinctive personal style, and many parents saw their offspring through her eyes, copying the clothes and hair styles of the children in her illustrations.   P.L.

Aust, Sarah (1744–1811) topographical writer. She wrote under the name 'Hon. Mrs Murray' and is chiefly known for her *Companion and*

Useful Guide to the Beauties of Scotland, to the Lakes of Westmoreland, Cumberland and Lancashire; and to the Curiosities in the District of Craven, in the West Riding of Yorkshire (1799). A second edition, with more material on the Scottish islands, appeared in 1803. The book has some interest for its information on the social conditions of the labouring classes, as well as the more customary detail of topography.   T.H.

Austen, Jane (1775–1817), novelist. The daughter of George and Cassandra Austen, she was born at Steventon, Hampshire, where her father was the rector. She was the seventh of eight children, of whom her only sister Cassandra became her lifelong companion. The two girls were sent to school at Oxford, Southampton, and Reading for short periods. Jane Austen's formal education ended when she was nine. Thereafter she was taught at home, learning French and Italian and reading widely.

Jane Austen began to write as a child, producing many short comedies and tales. In 1793 or 1794 she wrote *Lady Susan*, a short epistolary novel, and shortly afterwards began a first and unpreserved version of *Sense and Sensibility* entitled *Eleanor and Marianne*, also in letter form. In 1796–97 she wrote *First Impressions*, an early version of *Pride and Prejudice*, but when her father offered it for publication it was rejected. *Sense and Sensibility* was written in 1797–99 and *Northanger Abbey* in 1798. The latter was completed for publication in 1803 and sold for ten pounds under the title of *Susan*. In 1809 Jane Austen re-purchased it, unpublished, and it eventually appeared posthumously with *Persuasion* in 1818.

From 1801 to 1806 the Austen family lived at Bath. On a visit to the seaside in 1801 or 1802 Jane Austen met the only one of her four known suitors to make a strong impression on her. He planned to visit the family: instead they received the news of his death. This experience and that of her sister, whose fiancé died, are often suggested as sources of the deep understanding of love in Jane's novels.

In 1805 George Austen died and from 1806 to 1809 his widow and two daughters lived at Southampton. After 1803 there was a long pause in Jane's literary activity, which has been variously attributed to discouragement, unhappiness, and her dislike of her surroundings. In 1809 the three women settled in a cottage at Chawton, on the property of Jane's brother, Edward Knight. (He had changed his name on inheriting a cousin's property.) She began writing again and from 1811 worked steadily until her final illness. In 1809 she prepared *Sense and Sensibility* for the press, and on its publication in 1811 it was an immediate success. *Pride and Prejudice* (1813) and *Mansfield Park* (1814) were her next publications. *Emma* (1816) was dedicated to the Prince Regent, who greatly admired her work. *Persuasion* was written in 1815–16.

Jane Austen lived at Chawton for the rest of her life, doing most of her writing in the family sitting-room. Her world was the small country society of family and friends, and she was a devoted aunt to her many nephews and nieces. Despite the popular recognition which she received in later years, she never moved in wider literary circles. In 1816 her health worsened and in 1817 she and Cassandra took lodgings at Winchester in order to be near Jane's doctor. She died in July 1817 and was buried in Winchester Cathedral.

Jane Austen's earlier work shows her satirical reaction to the sentimental novels then current: *Sense and Sensibility* criticizes extreme romantic 'sensibility', while *Northanger Abbey* parodies the Gothic novels of the day. Her best-known work, *Pride and Prejudice*, tells of the Bennett family and the growth of love between Elizabeth and Darcy despite her initial antipathy. It also contains the characters Mr Collins, Elizabeths's rejected suitor, and the haughty, patronising Lady Catherine de Bourgh who are portrayed with merciless satire. Jane Austen's later work shows increasing gravity and control. Her account of the development of Fanny Price's character in *Mansfield Park* is her most extended portrayal of a character's growth, while *Emma* is a rich and comic study of self-deception, centred on a heroine whom Jane mistakenly thought nobody but herself would like. *Persuasion* is a quiet and beautifully controlled analysis of love and social pressures. Her other works include *The Watsons* and *Sanditon*.

Jane Austen is one of the best English novelists: her brilliant irony, intense moral concern, wit, and vitality are universally admired. She was a careful writer, revising her work thoroughly, and a marvellous delineator of human relationships. Her novels are humorous and incisive but always delicate and finely controlled. While they are set in the small world in which she herself always lived, they closely analyse that society, especially the economic problems facing young women, and the revelation of moral implications in everyday social behaviour in her work remains of universal meaning and interest.

See also Lord David Cecil, *A Portrait of Jane Austen*, 1978; R. W. Chapman, *Jane Austen: Facts and Problems*, 1948; R. W. Chapman (ed.), *Jane Austen's Letters to her sister Cassandra and others*, 1952; M. Lascelles, *Jane Austen and Her Art*, 1963; B. Roth and J. Weinsheimer, *An Annotated Bibliography of Jane Austen Studies 1952–72*, 1973.   J.H.

Austral, Florence, stage-name of Florence Fawaz or Wilson (1894–1968), singer, born at Melbourne. Her real name was Wilson, but until she adopted her professional name 'Austral' as a gesture of pride, she went under her stepfather's name, Fawaz. In 1914 she won a scholarship to Melbourne Conservatory, then continued her studies in New York. She joined the British National Opera Company and was first heard in 1922 at Covent Garden as Brünnhilde. The strength, consistent beauty, and evenness of tone of her voice made her a natural Wagnerian heroine. She appeared in the complete 'Ring' cycle, becoming the leading soprano at the Berlin State Opera (1930) after many foreign tours with her flautist husband John Amadio, including appearances at Covent Garden. She also sang in oratorio. Many excellent HMV recordings by her still exist. On her retirement she taught at the Newcastle Conservatory in Australia.

                                                    A.D.

Avery, Elizabeth (*fl.* 1647–53), religious and social radical, a member of the Fifth Monarchist sect that flourished briefly during the Civil War and Commonwealth periods. Elizabeth Avery was probably the daughter of a Puritan minister, Robert Parker, and the sister of Thomas Parker, a minister in Newbury, Berkshire, who had moved to New England by 1649. She published her Fifth Monarchist views in *Scripture Prophecies Opened* (1647). Founding her opinions on the books of Daniel and Revelation, she believed that Christ's Second Coming on earth was imminent and that existing earthly powers would be overturned. For Avery, England, and especially its

Parliament, was 'Babylon' because of the repression of religious radicals: 'the violence done unto the Saints'. Like other women preachers and prophets, for example Mrs ATTAWAY, Mary CARY, Lady Eleanor DAVIES, she aroused alarm and opposition. In 1649 *A Copy of a Letter Written by Thomas Parker to his Sister* was published; in it Parker attacked the 'heretical opinions' in her 1647 pamphlet and was particularly critical of her failure to join with her husband in religious observances, an act of defiance which challenged the fundamental patriarchal assumptions of seventeenth-century society. By 1653 Elizabeth Avery had found a spiritual home in the Dublin Fifth Monarchist church led by John Rogers, a minister who aroused controversy by his encouragement of women's full participation in his congregation.

See also Keith Thomas, 'Women and the Civil War Sects' in T. Aston (ed.), *Crisis in Europe*, 1965.   P.M.H.

Aylward, Gladys (1902–70), missionary. Born and brought up in the London suburb of Edmonton, Gladys Aylward worked first in a shop and then as a parlour-maid. Her family were Nonconformists and she was religious even as a child. She became more and more convinced that God had called her to missionary work, not just anywhere, but specifically in China. Her subsequent three-week journey to Tientsin via the Trans-Siberian railway was in itself extraordinary for a woman who had never been further from London than Swansea. Although China's ruler, Chiang Kai-Shek, was a Christian convert, the authorities (especially the regional mandarins) often disliked foreign missionaries. Hence the mission where Gladys Aylward served was disguised as an inn, The Inn of the Sixth Happiness—the name later taken for the film of her life. She worked for years in Shansi province and finally applied for naturalization—an act of great courage as it removed her from British protection, which by 1937–38, with China under attack by Japan, she might well have needed.

In 1940 she began the adventure for which she became famous, leading over a hundred children from the dangerous Shansi province to the comparative safety of Sian. She remained in China throughout the War and Civil War years, only returning to London in 1949. In 1957 she went back to the East, to Taiwan, where she started an orphanage. On her death she was buried near Taipei.

See also A. Burgess, *The Small Woman*, 1957.   E.M.V

Ayres, Ruby M(ildred) (1883–1955), popular novelist. She was born at Watford, Hertfordshire, the daughter of an architect. In 1909 she married a London insurance broker, Reginald William Pocock, and they lived at Harrow until his death in a train accident, after which she spent the last six years of her life at her sister's home in Weybridge. She had no children.

Ruby M. Ayres's, novels, of which there are over 150, are light escapist romances that mostly originated as serials for newspapers and magazines, initially for *The Daily Chronicle* and *The Daily Mirror*, then for a wide variety of other publications. She was a fast but meticulous writer who met her deadlines and never mixed up her characters even though she might be engaged on as many as six serials at a time. Her publishers once commissioned twelve books from her in a single contract. About her undoubted craftsmanship she was down-to-earth: she once said, 'First I fix the price. Then I fix the title. Then I write the book'—and, she might have added, concoct the plot.

Her novels were ephemeral; during her lifetime, and especially between the two World Wars, hers was a household name, but the vogue for her books did not last. Her novels include *Richard Chatterton VC*, 1916; *The Remembered Kiss*, 1918; *Life Steps In*, 1928; *The Man in her Life*, 1935; *Living Apart*, 1938; *Sunrise for Georgie*, 1941; and *Steering by a Star*, 1949. She also wrote for films in England and America; and had one play produced, *Silver Wedding*, 1932.   J.L.

B

Bacon, Ann (1528–1610), scholar. The second daughter of Sir Anthony Cooke of Gidea Park, Essex, she benefited greatly from the humanist education her father provided for all his five daughters. She is said to have been able to read Greek, Latin, French, and Italian as well as she could read English, and indeed her correspondence is liberally spiced with Greek and Latin quotations. Roger Ascham described Ann Cooke and Jane GREY as the two most learned women in England. Ann is traditionally held to have assisted her father in his capacity as tutor to Edward VI; but this seems unlikely, since current humanist theory held that boys should be educated by men and kept from the company of women. It is known, however, that she translated into English some sermons by the Italian Protestant Bernardino Ochino, published in 1560. She also translated Bishop Jewel's *Apology of the Church of England* from Latin with the assistance of Archbishop Parker; this was published with the author's permission in 1564.

Besides their learning, Anthony Cooke's daughters are interesting for the political alliances formed through their marriages. Mildred Cooke married William Cecil in 1545, and Ann married Nicholas Bacon, a Cambridge friend of Cecil and Parker, in 1557. It was possibly through Cecil's influence that Bacon was made Lord Keeper of the Great Seal in December 1558. Ann was seldom at court, but the Bacons often entertained Queen Elizabeth at their house of Gorhambury.

Ann Bacon was widowed in 1597. She had two sons: Anthony, born in 1558, and the famous Francis, later Lord Chancellor and Viscount St Albans, born in January 1560. She died in 1610, having lost her reason towards the end of her life.

It seems unlikely that Ann Bacon exercised much political influence, even during her husband's lifetime. But she is interesting, firstly because of her extraordinary learning, and secondly because of the strong personality which emerges from her correspondence. A Protestant of strong views, she wrote to Cecil urging the fair treatment of Puritans, and numerous letters to her sons warned them against frivolity and ungodliness. She was a great devotee of sermons, often travelling long distances to hear a noted preacher. Theodore Beza, informed of her piety and learning by her son Anthony, dedicated his *Meditations* to her.

See also C. D. Bowen, *Francis Bacon*, 1963; J. Spedding, *Life and Times of Francis Bacon*, 1878, for Ann Bacon's correspondence.

M.D.

Bacon, Gertrude (1874–1949), aeronautical pioneer. Born at Cambridge, the daughter of a scientist, she spent her childhood at Coldash in Berkshire and was educated entirely by her father, who provided a huge library for the use of his children.

In her autobiography, *Memories of Land and Sky* (1928), Gertrude Bacon writes that 'through force of circumstances I have hung on the skirts of great movements'. Because her father was a pioneer of scientific ballooning, she was the first woman in England to make a proper ascent (1898). And because he studied astronomy, she accompanied expeditions of the British Astronomical Association to view total solar eclipses in Lapland, India, and North Carolina.

She was also the first woman to fly as passenger (in the second Farman biplane ever built), and the first woman to be a passenger when the loop was being looped. Through her writings and lectures she played an important part in making favourable propaganda for aeronautics. She predicted a great future for women in commercial and popular flying. Her other publications include *The Record of an Aeronaut* (1907).

P.L.

Baddeley, Angela (Madeline Clinton-) (1904–76), actress. She was born in London and educated privately. She was the sister of another well-known actress, Hermione Baddeley, and her second husband was the actor-director Glen Byam Shaw.

Angela Baddeley's first stage appearance was at the Old Vic in *Richard III* in 1913, her last as Madame Armfeldt in *A Little Night Music* which she took over from Hermione Gingold in September 1975. In 1926 she toured Australia in the name part in *Mary Rose*, then returned to the London stage. There, her parts included Olivia Grayne in *Night Must Fall* (1935) and Cecily Cardew in *The Importance of Being Earnest* (1939), in which she played

25

Baddeley, Sophia

Lady Bracknell in 1964. She worked at the Old Vic (1949–50), touring Russia with the company in 1958–59. Her television work included *Martin Chuzzlewit* (1965) and the series *Upstairs, Downstairs* (1973–75), in which she played the cook.   A.D.

Baddeley, Sophia (1745–86), actress and singer. Sophia Baddeley began her career as a popular vocalist at the Ranelagh and Vauxhall pleasure-gardens. Her husband, the comic actor Robert Baddeley, introduced her to the stage, and her exceptional beauty helped her to make a rapid success. Her performance as Fanny Stirling in *The Clandestine Marriage* led George III to commission a portrait of her from Zoffany. She specialized in genteel comedy parts, but also played Ophelia and sang at the Shakespeare Jubilee of 1768.

Her extravagance and dissipation estranged her from her husband, though they continued to play together. She fled from her creditors to Edinburgh, where she played from 1783 to 1785. She was the subject of a scandalous biography intended to extort money from men of rank implicated in her life. Laudanum and ill-health ruined her later years, and she died in squalor.

See also P. H. Highfill, K. A. Burnim, E. A. Langhans, *A Biographical Dictionary of Actors, Actresses, Musicians, Dancers, Managers and Other Stage Personnel in London, 1660–1800*, vol. 1, 1973.   C.H.

Baden-Powell, Olave St Clair, Lady Baden-Powell (1889–1977), World Chief Guide. Her father inherited a brewery which he soon sold, making enough money to live comfortably without working. There was no tradition of public service in the family, but as a young woman she became increasingly dissatisfied with the social round, and in 1912 she met Lieutenant -General Sir Robert Baden-Powell, the hero of Mafeking and founder of the Boy Scout Movement. At the time she was twenty-three and he was already fifty-five. They married, and began the partnership which was to continue until his death and result in the extension of the scouting movement and the establishment world-wide of the Girl Guides. They had three children.

When Baden-Powell began the Scout movement with the publication of *Scouting for Boys* in 1908, some girls were keen to form a similar organization for themselves. Thus

began the Girl Guides, originally run by Baden-Powell's sister Agnes and a committee of worthy if unadventurous Edwardian ladies. The First World War made a great difference to the position of women and girls in society, and the movement became clearly in need of direction and modernization. Lady Baden-Powell, still only twenty-seven, and with no experience of Guiding, set about organizing the movement in Sussex, where she lived. She was Chief Commissioner in 1916, and in 1918 she became Chief Guide. Bit by bit she took greater responsibility for the movement, bringing it firmly into the twentieth century and giving it an appeal for the young which the original organization had lacked. Within a few years the Guides became international and the Chief Guide spent the rest of her life serving the movement in Britain and all over the world.

See also O. Baden-Powell (as told to Mary Drewery), *Window on my Heart*, 1973.

E.M.V.

Bagnold, Enid (1889–1981), novelist and dramatist. She spent most of her childhood in Jamaica, where her father was Commander, Royal Engineers. She went to school in Surrey and later in Switzerland, running away to Paris and Marburg. At nineteen she began to attend Walter Sickert's school of drawing and painting, where she developed a talent for etching and met the sculptor Gaudier-Brzeska and the writers Katherine MANSFIELD and Ralph Hodgson.

In 1914 Edith Bagnold became a VAD at the Royal Herbert Hospital, Woolwich. While there she wrote her first novel, *A Diary with Dates* (1918), about her experiences, and was consequently expelled for a breach of military discipline. *The Happy Foreigner* (1920) records her subsequent war career as a driver for the FANY in France.

Edith Bagnold married Sir Roderick Jones, who was chairman of Reuter's News Agency, in 1920. They had four children, one of whom, Laurian, was later to illustrate two of her mother's novels, *Alice and Thomas and Jane* (1930) and her most famous work, *National Velvet* (1935), which was subsequently adapted for television and for an extremely popular film. Edith Bagnold's unflagging energy as a professional writer resulted in a prodigious output of novels, plays, and poems, many of which were very well received in both England and America. Her best-known works are *Serena Blandish: or the Difficulties of Getting Married* (by a 'Lady of Quality', 1924), which was dramatised by S. N. Behrman and became a Broadway hit in 1925; *The Squire* (in America *The Door of Life*), 1937; and *The Loved and the Envied*, 1951. She published her autobiography in 1969.

See also H. S. Ede, *Savage Messiah*, 1931; K. Mansfield, *Novels and Novelists*, 1930.

J.M.

Bailey, (Lady) Mary (1890–1960), aviatrix, the daughter of Lord Rossmore of Monaghan. She married the South African millionaire Sir Abe Bailey in 1911 and already had five children when she took up flying.

She qualified as a pilot in 1926, and in the same year became the first woman to pilot herself across the Irish Sea. In 1927 she set a new altitude record when, with a passenger, she took a Gipsy Moth to 17,283 feet (5,268 metres).

In 1928 Mary Bailey flew off alone from Croydon to see her husband in South Africa: her successful flight was regarded at the time as one of the finest feats ever accomplished by a woman. Against advice she then flew back to England, choosing the western route, which had never before been flown south–north. Her successes were enthusiastically acclaimed; with characteristic modesty she remarked that she had merely set forth to join her husband and had just sat and listened to the engine. The Royal Aero Club awarded her the Britannia Trophy in 1930, and she was created a DBE the same year. In later life she continued flying, studied navigation, and was the first woman to receive a certificate for 'blind flying'.

See also W. Boase *The Sky's the Limit*, 1979.   P.L.

Baillie, Joanna (1762–1851), poet and playwright, the daughter of a clergyman, born at Bothwell, Lanark. In 1776 her father was appointed Professor of Divinity at Glasgow, but on his death in 1778 the family returned to the countryside, where Joanna Baillie began to write. In 1783 her brother, a doctor, inherited the London house of his uncle, anatomist William Hunter, and was joined there by his mother and sisters. In 1790 Joanna Baillie published anonymously her first book of poems, *Fugitive Verses*, and in 1798 the first

volume of a series of 'Plays on the Passions'; the second and third volumes followed in 1802 and 1812. The Baillie women then took a house in Hampstead whose air and society, she said, influenced her writing. Her plays went through five editions, though the good reception of *De Montfort* at Drury Lane was chiefly due to the excellent staging and acting of John Kemble and Sarah Siddons. In 1804 and 1805 more of her plays appeared in print.

Sir Walter Scott admired Joanna Baillie's work, and in 1808 their friendship was cemented when she and her sister Agnes were his guests on a tour of Scotland. The Scott family later visited them in Hampstead, where Joanna Baillie was a popular society hostess. From 1812 to 1817 she travelled in Britain and on the Continent, writing several more plays and poetry and editing a collection of poems. During the 1820s she concentrated on editing, and wrote only two short plays, *The Martyr* and *The Bride*; but in 1836 a new series appeared. These aroused even greater interest than her earlier volumes, although she specialized in portraying personifications of emotions and passions rather than living characters.

Religion had always been an important factor in her life, and old age emphasized this; yet she vigorously questioned all aspects of doctrine. Her moral beliefs led her to portray women as almost wholly virtuous, the victims of evil men. In spite of the dramatic and technical weaknesses of her plays, Joanna Baillie was considered the leading Scottish dramatist of the age. Her poetry too was praised, notably by Wordsworth. In her 'Introductory Discourse' to the plays in 1798 she enunciated clearly a theory of poetry akin to that of the Lake poets, prizing unsophisticated expression of truthful thoughts and feelings.

See also M. S. Carhart, *The Life and Work of Joanna Baillie*, 1923.   C.H.G.G.

Baldwin, Anne (*fl.* 1690–1713), publisher and bookseller; properly Abigail Baldwin, but always known as Anne. She was the wife of Richard Baldwin, a Buckinghamshire man who became a freeman of the London Stationers' Company in 1675, and was among the most important Whig publishers of the 1690s. Anne Baldwin played an important part in her husband's business, and after his death in 1698 she ran the concern alone, besides dealing with the problems caused by her husband's debts and caring for at least one small child. Working from a shop in Warwick Lane, Anne Baldwin published some 240 works between 1698 and 1713. Her publications were mainly concerned with contemporary political, religious, and foreign policy issues and show that she shared her husband's radical republican convictions. She published a new edition of Henry Nevile's republican tract *Plato Redivivus* in 1698, and Daniel Defoe was another of her authors. For a brief period in 1709–10 Anne Baldwin controlled *The Ladies Tatler*, a gossipy scandal sheet for women, edited, until the two women quarrelled, by Mary MANLEY. She published nothing after 1713: she may have died, or else retired, possibly hit, like many publishers, by the stamp duty imposed on newspapers.

Anne Baldwin played an important role in the political and literary culture of late Stuart England. Her career also exemplifies the experience of many women from the middle ranks of English society who capably carried on family businesses after their husbands' deaths.

See also E. Ludlow, *A Voyce from the Watch Tower*, (Camden Society Fourth Series, 21), 1978; E. Rostenberg, *Literary, Political, Scientific and Legal Publishing in England 1551–1700*, vol. 2, 1965. A.H.

Balfour, Clara (Lucas) (1808–78), writer and temperance lecturer. She was an only child, her father dying young. She was brought up in London by her mother, who educated her in the religious principles which were to guide her adult life. In 1827 she married James Balfour of the Ways and Means Office, and moved to Chelsea. The marriage was apparently a happy one, though there were no children.

1837 was the turning point of Clara Balfour's life. In October of that year she became convinced of the religious and social importance of the temperance movement, though the actual events that brought about this conviction remain obscure. Clara Balfour took the pledge at a nearby Bible Christians' Chapel, and thereafter considered the battle against alcohol as the chief business of her life. In 1841 she began her career as a temperance lecturer at the Greenwich Literary Institution. She continued lecturing there for thirty years on the evils of alcoholism at all social levels, but particularly among the working classes. A

popular speaker, she soon began to branch out, giving lectures on other subjects such as the influence of women on society.

The success of her first tract in 1837 encouraged Clara Balfour to turn to authorship in order to reach a wider audience. The list of her publications is vast; most are concerned with temperance but all have an underlying theological and philanthropic basis. Her works were widely read and *A Whisper to a Newly Married from a Widowed Wife* (1850) reached twenty–three editions. Many shorter writings appeared in periodicals such as *The British Workman* and *The Family Visitor*. Her work was mainly done in conjunction with the British Temperance League, and her last public appearance, in 1877, was at her election as President of the British Women's Temperance League. Her other writings include *Working Women of the Last Half Century* (1856) and *Morning Dewdrops* (1853).

See also Rev. D. Burns, *Memorial Discourse*, 1878. J.R.

Balfour, Lady Frances (1858–1931), suffragette, writer, and churchwoman, the fifth daughter of the Duke of Argyll. Her childhood was spent largely at the family homes in Scotland, where she was privately educated. As the daughter of a well-known Liberal peer she was early brought into contact with politics and politicians. In 1879 she married Eustace Balfour, an architect and youngest brother of the politician A. J. Balfour. They had five children. It was not a particularly happy marriage; Eustace turned to drink and died a hopeless alcoholic in 1911.

Despite her close contact with her brother-in-law Arthur Balfour, Lady Frances failed to exercise the political influence she craved, and her increasing irritation at her subsidiary role in society caused her to develop an interest in the cause of women's suffrage and in wider social work among women. She became closely associated with Dame Millicent FAWCETT in the National Union of Women's Suffrage Societies, and was well known as an active and effective speaker at rallies and meetings. However, while quite prepared to use strong language for the sake of the cause, and to urge it upon her male political contacts, she had little sympathy with more militant activists such as the Pankhursts. Lady Frances also became a member, and later President, of the Travellers Aid Society for Girls and Women.

She maintained a lifelong concern for women's social and working conditions. Another of her great interests was the Church of Scotland, and she took a personal pride in its reunion in 1929, having worked for that end for many years. Her energies also found an outlet through writing; she composed a number of biographies, including *The Life of George, 4th Earl of Aberdeen* (1923) and *Dr Elsie Inglis* (1918). In 1930 she published two volumes of autobiographical reminiscences, *Ne Obliviscaris*.

Lady Frances Balfour was an important figure in the movement for women's suffrage and in the struggle to improve women's conditions. This was due to her privileged position in society and her intimacy with leading politicians, but above all to her abilities as a speaker, her crusading spirit, and her personal charm.

See also Travellers Aid Society, *In Memoriam*, 1931.   J.R.

Ball, Frances (1794–1861), founder of the Irish Branch of the Institute of the Blessed Virgin Mary (Loreto Institute). Born in Dublin, she was the youngest child of a wealthy silk manufacturer. Brought up in a devout and charitable Catholic family, she was from childhood a deeply religious girl. She was educated at St Mary's Convent, IBVM, Micklegate Bar, York, and entered the order in 1814, taking the name 'Sister Mary Teresa'. Making her vows in 1816, she returned to Dublin in 1821 to found the Irish Branch of the Institute. She named her first Dublin convent 'Loreto House', and each Convent founded thereafter took the name 'Loreto', hence the name 'Loreto Institute'. During the next twenty years she founded other convents and schools in Ireland. In 1841, the Bishop of Calcutta invited her to establish a House in India, and subsequently the Institute spread all round the world, convents and schools being established in Mauritius (1845), Gibraltar (1845), Canada (1847), England (Manchester 1851). After her death the institute spread to Australia (1875), South Africa (1878), Spain (1889), East Africa (1926) and Peru (1981).

The Institute was an educational order, providing day and boarding schools for girls and free schools for poor children. The aim of the Institute was twofold: 'to lead the pupils to a knowledge and love of their Creator, and to provide them with a sound general education in all branches requisite for a girl's education'. Special emphasis was laid on character training and general culture, with much attention being paid to music, drama and art.

Towards the end of the 18th century, the penal laws under which Roman Catholics had suffered since the Reformation were relaxed and then in 1829 the Catholic Emancipation Act was passed. Catholic education began to revive in Ireland and England, and Mother Teresa Ball's schools played an important role in that revival. The Institute not infrequently met with opposition due to religious prejudice which the Sisters often helped to break down.

See also W. D. Hutch, *Mrs Ball: Foundress of the Institution of the Blessed Virgin Mary in Ireland and the British Colonies ... a biography*, 1879; E. MacDonald, *Joyful Mother of Children: Mother Frances Mary Teresa Ball*, 1961.   D.E.W.

Bancroft, Lady Marie (Effie) (1839–1921), actress and theatrical manager. The daughter of provincial actors, she was a performer from early childhood, travelling constantly and receiving no formal education. But her courage, determination, and unerring judgement made her a significant and beneficial influence on the English theatre.

She soon attracted attention in boy parts, and in 1856 obtained a London engagement at the Lyceum. From then on her talent for burlesque brought her wide acclaim; Charles Dickens described her as 'the cleverest girl I have ever seen on the stage'.

In 1865 she borrowed £1000 to take over the disreputable Queen's Theatre in Tottenham Street, known as 'The Dust Hole'. This bold decision proved justified and began a great change in the fortunes of the London stage. Prettily redecorated and launched with one or two burlesques, the new Queen's was an immediate success. In 1867 she married Squire Bancroft, a founder-member of her company, who became joint manager. Against all advice she staged the unknown author Tom Robertson's *Society*, a new and (by contemporary standards) realistic type of comedy. It was successful, and Robertson's plays became the permanent mainstay of the Bancrofts' repertoire, inaugurating a new era in stage production, with carefully designed and convincing sets for high-quality drama. The leading actors were chosen carefully and highly paid (£60–£100 weekly as against the usual £5–£10). The price of seats went up accordingly. All this raised the status of the acting profession, and society, which had abandoned the theatre during the era of burlesques and melodramas, was now lured back.

In 1880 the Bancrofts moved to the Haymarket and rebuilt it, abolishing the pit and surviving the first-night riot which this caused. They retired in 1885 after five successful years, and then collaborated in the writing of three plays, a novel and an autobiography, *Mr and Mrs Bancroft on and off the Stage* (1888), revised and published as *The Bancrofts: Recollections of Sixty Years* (1909). In 1897 a knighthood was conferred on Squire Bancroft in recognition of the services of husband and wife to the theatre.   A.D.

Barbauld, Anna (Laetitia) (1743–1825), writer and educationist. She was the daughter of the Reverend John Aikin, at whose school at Kibworth, Leicestershire, and afterwards at Warrington Academy, she received an unusually broad education in French, Italian, Latin, and Greek. In 1773, encouraged by her brother John, she published her first volume of poems, and then together they brought out a collection of essays, *Miscellaneous Pieces in Prose*.

This was followed in 1775 by Anna's *Devotional Pieces*, containing passages from the Psalms and the Book of Job. In 1789, she began writing political pamphlets, including an *Address to the Opposers of the Repeal of the Test and Corporations Acts*, and in 1791 *An Epistle to William Wilberforce on the Rejection of the Bill abolishing the Slave Trade*. Then she turned to literary criticism, attaching essays to Mark Akenside's *Pleasures of the Imagination* (1794) and to an edition of poems by William Collins (1797). After her husband died in 1808, she also edited a series in fifty volumes of the best British novelists.

In 1774 she married the Reverend Rochemont Barbauld, and from 1774 to 1785 she taught with some success at his school for boys at Palgrave in Suffolk; but her married happiness was marred by his increasingly frequent fits of insanity. She wrote two letters *On Female Studies* in 1774; like many of her contemporaries, she emphasized the need to prepare girls as wives and mothers, holding that literature, French, Italian, and other subjects, though desirable, were not essential. In an essay *On Education* she concentrated on the importance of environment in boys' upbringing, while her essay *On Prejudice* warned against lack of guidance and the too literal implementation of the fashionable maxim, 'Give your child no prejudices'. After adopting her brother's son Charles, she wrote *Lessons for Children of Two to Three Years Old* (1775) and *Hymns in-Prose for Children* (1781), which, translated into French, Italian, and German, became her most famous book. Finally, in 1811, she published a selection of pieces for girls entitled *The Female Speaker*.

See also G. Ellis, *A Memoir of Mrs Anna Laetitia Barbauld with Many of her Letters*, 1874; J. Murch, *Mrs Barbauld and her Contemporaries*, 1877.   A.M.N.

Barber, Mary (1690–1757), poet and friend of Jonathan Swift. She was born in Ireland, married a Dublin businessman, and for some years wrote poetry for family consumption. She belongs to quite a large group of eighteenth-century women who flourished under male protection. Swift rescued her from literary obscurity in 1724 and took her into his circle under the fanciful name of Sapphira. When she visited England (1730), he contrived that she should be so well received in literary society that she soon afterwards settled there permanently. Her *Poems on Several Occasions* were first published in 1734. The book's reception was not entirely favourable; perhaps too much had been expected of a protégée of Swift. Misfortunes came upon her at this time; she and her printer were involved in a legal action, and she sank under an illness described as 'gout'. Swift intervened to save her from destitution by allowing her to sell part of his literary property (*A Complete Collection of Genteel and Ingenious Conversation*), and her circumstances improved. She lived to see her poetry reappear in 1755 as part of *Poems by Eminent Ladies*, in company with Aphra BEHN and Lady Mary Wortley MONTAGU.

See also R. W. Jacobson, *Swift and his Circle*, 1945; A. W. Ward and A. R. Waller (eds.) *Cambridge History of English Literature*, vol. 9, 1932.   T.H.

Barclay-Smith, (Ida) Phyllis (?–1980), ornithologist. She was educated at Church House School, Worthing, Blackheath High School, and King's College, London. Her entire professional life was devoted to ornithology, with the exception of the Second World War period, when she worked at the Foreign Office and later as a welfare officer attached to the Ministry of Labour. She was Assistant Secretary of the Royal Society for the Protection of Birds (1924–35) and then Assistant Secretary (1935–46), Secretary (1946–78) and finally Vice-President of the International Council for Bird Preservation. She was also Honorary Secretary (1945–51) and Vice-President (1957–60) of the British Ornithologists' Union, and worked for many similar organizations, including those concerned with the hazard of oil pollution of the sea. She edited *The Avicultural Magazine* from 1939 to 1973, and published *British Birds on Lake, River, and Stream*, 1939; *British and American Game Birds* (with Hugh Pollard), 1939; *Garden Birds*, 1945; *A Book of Ducks*, 1951; and several translations from French and German.   N.H.

Barker, Jane (*fl.* 1688–1723), author, was born into a Royalist family around 1660, and brought up in Wilsthorp, near Stamford in Lincolnshire. Her earliest literary works were published in a collection of *Poetical Recreations* in 1688. Shortly afterwards, following the flight of King James II into exile, she went to France as a Jacobite sympathiser. She returned to Lincolnshire during Queen Anne's reign, but in 1715 was included in a list of disaffected Catholics. By 1718 she had moved to London, where she corresponded clandestinely with the exiled Jacobite peer, the Duke of Ormond.

In 1715 Jane Barker published a long prose romance, *Exilius; or, The Banish'd Roman*. In the dedication to the Countess of Exeter she defended her choice of this old-fashioned literary form and argued for its moral, social, and educational advantages. Her second work in this mode was *Love's Intrigues: or, The History of the Amours of Bosvil and Galesia* (1719). In 1723 she published an anthology of short tales and verse as *A Patch-Work Screen for the Ladies*, followed by her final work, *The Lining for the Patch-Work Screen* (1726). Collections of *The Entertaining Novels of Mrs Jane Barker* were published in 1719, 1736, and 1743.

Little more is known of Jane Barker's life, though some of the incidents in her writings may be autobiographical. From these it appears that she was taught medicine by her brother, and treated people who came to her in London. She never married, having, she says, 'a secret disgust against matrimony'. Her romances have little literary merit, but their fictional action, whether semi-autobiographical or not, sometimes undercuts their moral didacticism and implies that female self-fulfillment may demand more than the conventional dependence on men.

See also W. H. McBurney, 'Edmund Curll, Mrs Jane Barker, and the English Novel', *Philological Quarterly*, XXXVII, 1958; P. M. Spacks, *Imagining a Self*, 1876.   W.R.O.

Barker, Dame Lilian (Charlotte) (1874–1955), prison official and reformer. She was the daughter of a London tobacconist and received an elementary school education before teacher-training at Whitelands College, Chelsea. Her subsequent career displayed her ability to combine sympathetic understanding with good discipline, and by 1914 she had become Principal of the London County Council Women's Institute in Cosway Street, Marylebone.

For Lilian Barker, as for so many other women, the First World War brought opportunties for wider activity. Initially she organized the training of cooks for the army. Then, in 1915, she was appointed Lady Superintendent at Woolwich Arsenal, where she became responsible for the welfare of the thirty thousand women who had replaced the male workforce; conditions were greatly improved under her régime, and such amenities as canteens, rest rooms, cloakrooms, and first aid centres were installed.

After the war she became involved in training and retraining schemes for women; but when in 1923 she was offered the governorship of Aylesbury Borstal Institution for Girls, she accepted, despite the sacrifice of salary entailed. This was the role for which she was to be best remembered. Her policy at Aylesbury was a liberal one: the prison-like atmosphere of the Borstal was modified by the provision of pleasanter clothes, food, and furnishings; organized games were introduced, a swimming pool was put in, and Lilian Barker herself gave nightly talks that reinforced her strong influence over the girls. She remained as Governor until 1935, when she became the first woman Assistant Commissioner for Prisons, responsible for all women's prisons in England and Wales. She retired in 1943.

N.H.

Barnard, Lady Ann. See LINDSAY, LADY ANNE.

Barnes, Julyan. See BERNERS, JULIANA.

Barnett, Dame Henrietta Octavia (Weston) (1851–1936), social reformer. She was the daughter of Alexander Rowland, a wealthy businessman, and was born in Clapham, where she soon developed a love of country pursuits. She was, however, aware of the squalor and deprivation that existed in London, and went to work with Octavia HILL among the poor in Marylebone. There she met and married a curate, Samuel Barnett, whose quiet nature complemented her own assertive personality. From 1873 to 1906 they lived and worked in Whitechapel, where Henrietta Barnett helped her husband to found Toynbee Hall, a university settlement. Her independent activities were many. She was nominated the first woman Guardian (an official responsible for poor law relief) for the area, and in 1877 became manager of Forest Gate district school. The establishment of a holiday fund for deprived children was her idea, and she sat on the committee to enquire into Poor Law Schools; the report of this committee led to the formation of the State Children's Association in 1896. She was also closely associated with the founding of Whitechapel Art Gallery, which opened in 1901.

The contrast between the East End and the Barnetts' house on Hampstead Heath supplied the idea for building a model suburb there 'to provide a bridge between poverty and privilege—a dwelling place amidst pleasant surroundings'. Henrietta Barnett's energy and drive provided the impetus for the scheme, but she chose architects and financial advisers of proven ability to help her realize it. Hampstead Garden Suburb, which was started in 1907, catered for all sections of the community; it had special housing for the aged and infirm, good secondary schools and adult institutes, and ample recreational facilities. Despite the Anglicanism of its founder, churches of other denominations were included in the plans. It did suffer, however, from inadequate public transport and shopping facilities.

Henrietta Barnett wrote several books, alone and with her husband. These included *Practicable Socialism* (1885), which sets out their Christian Socialist beliefs, and *Matters that Matter* (1930). For her work as a social reformer she was awarded the CBE in 1917 and the DBE in 1924.

See also H. O. Barnett, *Canon Barnett, His Life, Work and Friends*, 1918; and B. Grafton Green, *Hampstead Garden Suburb*, 1977.

C.H.G.G.

Barnett, Lady Isobel (Morag) (1918–80), radio personality. She was the daughter of a doctor, and was educated at York before studying medicine at Glasgow University. In 1941 she married a solicitor, Captain Geoffrey Barnett (knighted in 1953), by whom she had one son. Soon afterwards she went into general medical practice. In the 1950s and 1960s Lady Barnett became one of the best-known of all radio and television personalities, above all in the panel game *What's My Line?*; her combination of breeding, intelligence, and quiet elegance were well suited to the still 'Reithian' tone of BBC broadcasting. Among other programmes in which she appeared were *Many a Slip*, *Petticoat Line*, and *Any Questions?* She saw her fame as fortuitous, as she made clear in her autobiography, *My Life Line* (1956).

A.D.

Barrett, Elizabeth. See BROWNING, ELIZABETH BARRETT.

Barry, Anne (1734–1801), actress, also known as Ann Dancer and Anne Crawford. She was born in Bath, but an early broken romance took her to York, where she took up acting, and an actor, William Dancer. They married in 1754, but he died young five years later. Her first recorded performance was in 1758 in Dublin, where she played Cordelia to Spranger Barry's Lear. Her early career, though at first unsuccessful, made some progress in Dublin.

She followed Barry to London in 1767 and they were married by February 1768. For the next seven years they both played at Drury Lane with increasing success. The Barrys then moved to Covent Garden, where they briefly constituted the only serious threat to Garrick's supremacy at Drury Lane; the existence of rival productions of *Romeo and Juliet* at the two theatres was a notable event. Mrs Cibber's death in 1766 left Anne Barry unchallenged in grand tragedy, in which she played Andromache, Desdemona, Belvidera, and Jane Shore.

After Spranger Barry's death in 1777 her career took a downward turn, especially after her marriage to a younger actor, Thomas Crawford, in 1778. However, she continued to perform until 1798 in London and Dublin.

See also P. H. Highfill, K. A. Burnim, E. A. Langhans, *A Biographical Dictionary of Actors, Actresses, Musicians, Dancers, Managers and Other Stage Personnel in London, 1660–1800*, Vol. 1, 1973.   C.H.

Barry, Elizabeth (1658–1713), actress, reportedly the daughter of Colonel Robert Barry, a barrister, but raised by Lady Davenant, the wife of the theatrical manager, Sir William. Her first stage appearance in 1674 was a failure, and it appears that she owed her subsequent success to the brilliant and mercurial Earl of Rochester, who was probably already smitten with her, and who recognized her talent. After intensive theatrical training from Rochester (probably in the autumn and winter of 1675–76) Elizabeth Barry went on to become the greatest actress on the Restoration stage. In December 1677 she gave birth to a daughter by Rochester but returned to acting in 1678.

By 1682 the virtual retirement of Mrs BETTERTON and Elizabeth Barry's clear superiority over other actresses made her the undisputed leading lady of the United Company, recently formed from the King's and Duke's Companies. Her majestic presence, her rich and powerful voice, and her extraordinary capacity to evoke passion and sympathy especially suited her to tragedy, but she was also highly proficient in comedy, and during her 35-year career performed both in classical roles and in plays by Otway, Crowne, Dryden, Congreve, and other contemporary dramatists.

In 1695 Elizabeth Barry was one of the leaders of a group of actors who presented a petition to the Lord Chamberlain listing their grievances concerning pay and working conditions, with the result that they were given a licence for a new company in Lincoln's Inn Fields. Barry continued in leading roles which required a mature woman until 1708, when the union of the two companies seems to have contributed to her decision to retire to her home at Acton.

Most men found Elizabeth Barry irresistibly attractive and her lovers were numerous. Contemporaries described her as wanton, mercenary, and callous. Professionally, however, she was acclaimed as the most accomplished actress of her day, and as such made a significant contribution to the development of Restoration drama; she inspired playwrights, attracted audiences, and elevated the status of women in a profession that had only recently been opened to them.

See also J. H. Wilson, *All the King's Ladies: Actresses of the Restoration*, 1958.   T.M.

Barry, Florence (1885–1965). Catholic suffragist and internationalist. The child of a Persian immigrant and an Austrian Catholic, Florence Barry was educated at a convent boarding school, a Belgian finishing school, and the School of Social Science connected with Liverpool University. Her family background gave international connections and interests; her parents' piety and her mother's work for the poor were also important influences. In 1912 Florence Barry became Honorary Secretary of St Joan's Alliance, a Catholic suffrage group, holding the post for fifty years. She began the dialogue with women in Catholic nations that led to the formation of St Joan's International Alliance, whose Secretary she also became. And in liaison with missionaries of various churches, she began the movement for the emancipation of women in the developing world. In 1951 Pope Pius XII awarded her the medal *Pro Ecclesia et Pontifice*, the highest papal honour a woman can receive. She remained unmarried.   J.E.

Barton, Elizabeth (1506?–1534), religious impostor, 'the Holy Maid of Kent'. In 1525 Barton, a young serving girl, fell ill and in a series of trances began to inveigh against the seven deadly sins and to prophesy. These utterances attracted the attention of the Archbishop of Canterbury, Warham, who sent a commission of clergymen to examine her. Their favourable report, and her miraculous healing before a crowd of thousands, enhanced her growing reputation. In 1526 Elizabeth Barton entered a Canterbury nunnery where, under the direction of Dr Edward Bocking, her prophesying took on political overtones. By boldly speaking out against Henry VIII's plans for divorce she became a centre of national attention, gaining the respectful hearing of Warham, Cardinal Wolsey, Bishop Fisher, and the papal ambassadors. She went so far as to warn the King personally that he was wrong, and prophesied that if he married Anne BOLEYN he would soon cease to be king and would die a villain's death.

With the death of Warham, Elizabeth Barton lost a valuable ally. His successor, Cranmer, moved against her in July 1533 and extracted a confession that her visions had been feigned. Her accomplices—Bocking, Edward Thwaytes (the author of *The Nun's Book*, which described her life and prophecies), and several monks—were arrested and sent to the Tower. Barton, Bocking, and five others were found guilty of treason, and at her execution in April 1534 she repeated her confession and blamed those around her who had profited from her impostures.

Elizabeth Barton was the willing instrument of a group who sought to use her possibly epileptic trances to defend CATHERINE OF ARAGON and certain traditional Catholic practices during the religious and political crisis caused by Henry VIII's wish to divorce and re-marry. It has also recently been suggested that her prophecies were the inspiration of a plot to depose Henry and replace him with Henry Courtenay, Marquis of Exeter.

See also A. Denton Cheney, 'The Holy Maid of Kent', *Transactions of the Royal Historical Society*, 1904; A. Neame, *The Holy Maid of Kent*, 1971; L. E. Whatmore, 'The Sermon against the Holy Maid of Kent', *English Historical Review*, 1943.   G.Q.B.

Bateman, Hester (1709–90), silversmith. Her husband died in 1760 and Hester became head of the family firm, helped by her children John, Peter and Jonathan. She first registered her mark in 1774. The firm concentrated on producing good sound silverware for household use; its Neo-classical style was influenced by Adam, but it was not outstandingly well designed. Hester Bateman pieces—mainly spoons, teaspoons, tea-caddies, cream jugs, and salvers—are often seen in the salerooms, indicating the large output of the firm, and they fetch good prices. The Bateman family continued to produce pieces well into the nineteenth century.

See also D. S. Shure, *Hester Bateman*, 1959; E. J. G. Smith, 'Woman Silversmiths; Hester Bateman', in *Collectors' Guide*, 1969.

T.H.

Bateson, Mary (1865–1906), historian. She was born near Whitby, the daughter of the master of St John's College, Cambridge. Privately educated, she later studied at Newnham College, Cambridge, which her parents had been among the first to promote and where she later taught. She was an advocate of female suffrage, but became persuaded that her first concern was to be a scholar and 'write true history'. Known chiefly as a medievalist, she could be versatile, as her contribution to the Cambridge Modern History on 'The French in America' shows. To this work she contributed over a hundred articles between 1893 and 1900. Her interest in municipal and monastic history is evident in her articles on the topography and antiquities of the borough and abbey of Peterborough for the *Victoria County History of Northamptonshire* (1906). She was appointed one of three editors of the projected Cambridge Medieval History, but died the same year.   B.H.C.

Bathe, Lillie de. See LANGTRY, LILLIE.

Battersea, Lady. See FLOWER, CONSTANCE, BARONESS BATTERSEA.

Baylis, Lilian (Mary) (1874–1937), theatrical manager, founder of the Old Vic and Sadler's Wells companies. Born in London of musical parents, Lilian Baylis received early training as a violinist. At seven she appeared in an entertainment arranged by her aunt Emma CONS, who was to influence her entire future.

In 1890 the Baylis family emigrated to South Africa and toured, giving musical performances. Lilian Baylis settled in Johannesburg, training a ladies' orchestra, until recalled by Emma Cons in 1898 to help with the management of the Royal Victoria Coffee Music Hall, which she had formed at the Old Vic in 1880 to provide a source of entertainment for the working classes at which alcohol was not served. On her aunt's death in 1912, Lilian Baylis became sole manager and began her life's work, providing drama, opera, and ballet for a wide audience at low cost. She was deeply religious, believing that she was divinely inspired to accomplish her work. Harcourt Williams said, 'the secret of her power is that . . . she cares passionately for her cause . . . and for people'. Asked how a meeting of the Board of Governors had gone, she replied, 'Splendidly. I had the Almighty in my pocket.'

Although not fond of Shakespeare, she thought it her duty to present all his plays at the Old Vic (1914–23). Her unerring choice of collaborators, including Matheson Lang, Ben Greet, Russell Thorndike, Robert Atkins, and Tyrone Guthrie, soon established the Old Vic as a permanent repertory theatre 'of the people' and a superb acting school where actors worked for far less than they would elsewhere.

Drama left no room at the Old Vic for the musical performing arts, so in 1931 Lilian Baylis took over Sadler's Wells Theatre for opera and ballet productions. Under Ninette de Valois ballet soon became as popular as opera.

By the time she died, Lilian Baylis had truly created a national theatre; and the Old Vic eventually became the first home of Sir Laurence Olivier's National Theatre Company. Lilian Baylis was made a CH in 1929 and was the second woman outside Oxford to be given an Honorary MA by the University in 1924.

See also P. Roberts, *The Old Vic Story*, 1976; S. and R. Thorndike, *Lilian Baylis*, 1938.

A.D.

Bayly, Ellen Ada (1857–1903), novelist and feminist. Born in Brighton, the daughter of a barrister, she was educated there in private schools. She wrote her novels under the pseudonym 'Edna Lyall', an anagram formed from nine letters of her real name. Her first book was *Won By Waiting* (1879), the story of a girl's life. *Donovan* (1882) was a three-volume work which included among its admirers Mr Gladstone, although it was the sequel *We Two* (1884) which established her reputation. She was an energetic supporter of women's emancipation, and ardently championed all liberal movements in politics. Among the causes she espoused was that of the freethinking MP Charles Bradlaugh, whose refusal to take an oath on the Bible in the House of Commons created a long-running crisis. However, she was herself of a deeply religious temperament. The earnest sense of political purpose which pervaded her writing was combined with a clear style, able constructive technique, and skilful characterization, especially of young girls. In *Doreen* (1894) she championed Irish Home Rule, and in her last novel, *The Hinderers* (1902), she opposed the Boer War.

B.H.C.

Beaconsfield, Mary Anne Disraeli, Viscountess. See DISRAELI, MARY ANNE, VISCOUNTESS BEACONSFIELD.

Beale, Dorothea (1831–1906), pioneer of women's education, the daughter of a surgeon. Her education was varied until 1847, when she went to Mrs Bray's school for girls in Paris. She returned home when that closed as a result of the 1848 revolution, and became one of the first to attend classes at the newly-opened Queen's College in London. She completed her formal education there, though she continued to teach herself new subjects, such as Hebrew, to the end of her life.

Dorothea Beale remained unmarried, though she was briefly engaged to a clergyman in 1856–57. Instead she devoted her energies to her work in female education, her enthusiasm in the cause giving rise to the rhyme 'Miss Buss and Miss Beale/Cupid's darts do not feel/How unlike us/Miss Beale and Miss Buss'. In 1849 she became mathematics tutor in the school attached to Queen's College, becoming its head in 1854. Dissatisfied with the school's administration, she resigned in 1856 and accepted the headship of the Clergy Daughters' School at Casterton. There followed an unhappy period ending with her dismissal in December 1857. In 1858 she became principal of Cheltenham Ladies' College, which was to be her chief concern for the rest of her career. She introduced a more rigorous curriculum which, though unpopular at first, attracted more pupils and so guaranteed the school's survival. As a result of her success at Cheltenham, she was invited to give evidence before the Schools Commission Enquiry in 1864, and then to edit the Commission's report on girls' education, which appeared in 1869 with a provocative preface.

Dorothea Beale was convinced of the need for adequate training for women teachers, and was involved in the setting up of St Hilda's training college for secondary teachers which was opened at Cheltenham in 1885. An Oxford extension, opened in 1893, became St Hilda's College in 1901. She made great efforts to enhance the status of women teachers, encouraging her staff to join the Teachers' Guild and becoming president of the Association of Head Mistresses (1895–97). In 1894 she gave evidence again before the Bryce Commission on Secondary Education, and in 1898 she published her views on girls' education in *Work and Play in Girls' Schools*. She was an ardent churchwoman, and religion shaped most of her life and attitudes, including her opposition to competition. She became a supporter of the movement for women's suffrage, though she was never prominent in it. She was an important pioneer in the educational field, though her overall effectiveness was limited by her concentration on Cheltenham, where she had a deep influence on her pupils. Her personal dignity made her a persuasive ambassador for female education.

See also J. Kamm, *How Different From Us*, 1958; E. Shillitoe, *Dorothea Beale*, 1920.

J.R.

Beale, Mary (1633–99), painter. She was the daughter of John Craddock, a Suffolk Puritan clergyman, and himself an amateur painter, from whom she received a good education. In 1652 Mary married Charles Beale, a member of a leading Buckinghamshire Puritan family who possessed a keen interest in the fine arts. In the later 1650s he inherited his father's post as Deputy Clerk of the Patent Office, and at about this time the couple moved from Covent Garden, where Mary was already established as an amateur painter of some repute, to a larger official lodging in Fleet Street, where Mary set up a proper 'paynting roome' and Charles displayed his valuable art collection. Mary Beale, who by 1658 was sufficiently well known to be included in Sir William Sanderson's *The Excellent Art of Painting*, may have received training from Robert Walker and was almost certainly instructed in miniature painting by the Beales' close friend Thomas Flatman, gentleman poet and painter, who referred to Mary as his 'Scholar' and subsequently taught her son Charles.

From about 1670 the Beales lived in the fashionable new area of Pall Mall, where Mary, now the breadwinner of the family since her husband's dismissal from his government post, set up in earnest as a professional painter to the nobility, gentry, and clergy, charging £5 for a standard head and shoulders and £10 for a three-quarter length portrait. She was assisted by her sons Bartholomew, later a physician, and Charles, a talented painter; her husband became an expert in artists' colours and primed the canvases. While his 'Dearest and most indefatigable Heart' frequently painted from dawn to dusk, Charles Beale attended to the housekeeping, supervised the running of the studio, kept the accounts, and conscientiously recorded the painting activities of his wife in his notebooks. Among the Beales' many friends in the scientific and artistic community was Sir Peter Lely, the leading painter of the day, who became a kindly critic of Mary's work. Mary's output was prodigious,

and although the 1670s were probably the peak years of her commercial success, she took advantage of the leaner years of the 1680s to do some experimental paintings for 'study and improvement'. Some of her finest works were painted after the Revolution of 1688.

She was highly regarded in the eighteenth century, and the later eclipse of her reputation seems to have been caused chiefly by the attribution of her best works to male contemporaries, particularly Lely. Renewed appreciation of her as an artist of considerable talent and a woman of great resource came, appropriately, in 1975 (International Women's Year) through an exhibition of her paintings at the Geffrye Museum which afforded her public recognition as England's first professional woman painter.

See also E. Walsh and R. Jeffree, 'The Excellent Mrs Mary Beale', catalogue of the Geffrye Museum exhibition, 1975.　　T.M.

Beauclerk, Lady Diana (1734–1808), amateur artist, the elder daugher of Charles Spencer, second Duke of Marlborough; she spent her childhood at Blenheim Palace. In 1757 she married the second Lord Bolingbroke but was divorced from him by an Act of Parliament in 1768. She then resigned from the post of Lady in Waiting to Queen Charlotte which she had occupied since 1761 and two days after the divorce married Topham Beauclerk, now remembered mainly as a friend of Dr Johnson. She was expert in 'soot-water' designs of cupids, painted rococo studies of children, completed works in a rustic genre, illustrated her friend Horace Walpole's 'Gothick' romance *The Mysterious Mother*, and became involved in interior design. The rooms of her houses in Twickenham (destroyed 1785–86) and Richmond were decorated with characteristic festoons of flowers.

After the death of Topham Beauclerk in 1780, Lady Beauclerk sold her houses in Great Russell Street and Little Marble Hill, Twickenham, and settled at Devonshire Cottage, Richmond. Her most important works were executed in the later part of her life. They inlcuded illustrations for Bürger's *Leonora* (1796) and Dryden's *Fables* (1797) and, after 1785, a series of commissioned designs for Josiah Wedgwood.

See also B. Erskine, *Lady Diana Beauclerk, Her Life and Work*, 1903.　　A.L.

Beaufort, Joan (*c.* 1405–1445), Queen of Scotland. She was the daughter of John, Earl of Somerset, and the grand-daughter of John of Gaunt and Katherine SWYNFORD. During his long but honourable captivity in England, James I of Scotland saw Joan and fell in love with her, describing the event in his poem 'The King's Quair'. Luckily policy marched with passion, and the Beauforts, anxious for a royal match, hastened the arrangements for his ransom and release. James and Joan were married in February 1424 and had arrived in Scotland by April. The marriage was happy, and produced one surviving son and six daughters.

In 1437 James was murdered at Perth while with the Queen and her ladies; Joan was wounded in an attempt to aid him. Within six weeks her determination to be avenged had led to the capture, torture, and execution of the murderers. The young King James II and his sisters were entrusted to the custody of their mother, with a council to assist her, but she was not made regent. Real power seemed likely to be taken by either Crichton or Livingstone, but in a bid to gain a protector and achieve power for herself, Joan married Sir James Stewart, the Black Knight of Lorne. However, she and her husband were surprised at Stirling by Livingstone and held captive. Under pressure, Joan was forced to surrender the young king's person, her dower for his upkeep, and her castle of Stirling for his residence. She and her husband were released but Joan never recovered her authority. She lived for six more years and bore Stewart three sons. Her second marriage was dictated by policy, albeit misjudged, and she chose to be buried by her beloved James I at Perth.

See also C. Bingham, *The Stewart Kingdom of Scotland, 1371–1603*, 1974.　　　A.C.

Beaufort, Margaret, Countess of Richmond and Derby (1443–1509), mother of Henry VII. She was the daughter and sole heiress of John Beaufort, Duke of Somerset. She was married four times. Her first 'marriage', arranged when she was still a young girl, was a dubious, clandestine match with John de la Pole, son of the Duke of Suffolk, her rapacious guardian. Her second, to Edmund Tudor, Earl of Richmond, lasted but a year, although three months after his death she gave birth—at barely fourteen years of age—to the future Henry VII. Her third husband, Henry Stafford, second son

of Humphrey, Duke of Buckingham, died in 1471. Only her fourth marriage, to Thomas, Lord Stanley, lasted for any length of time, and years before Stanley's death in 1504 she had separated from him in order to follow a life of austere piety.

During the last strife-ridden years of Henry VI's reign and the first decade of Edward IV's rule, Margaret Beaufort and her young son Henry spent much time in the safety of her brother-in-law's castle of Pembroke. The triumph of the Lancastrians and Henry VI's recovery of the throne in 1470/1 saw her take up residence at the royal court, but the Yorkist Edward IV's speedy return sent her back into retirement—now without her son who, given his (admittedly tenuous) claim to represent the house of Lancaster, had prudently become an exile in Brittany. Following the usurpation of Richard III in 1483, the Lancastrian Margaret Beaufort entered into an unholy alliance with the Yorkist Edward IV's widow, Elizabeth Woodville, aimed at securing both the marriage of her son Henry to the Queen's eldest daughter, Elizabeth of York, and Richard's removal from the throne. Margaret Beaufort's hopes were shattered by the failure of Buckingham's rebellion in October 1483, and she only escaped attainder thanks to the King's unwillingness to alienate her husband. Even so, Stanley was given her lands, and Margaret was ordered to be kept 'in some secret place at home, without any servants or company, so that she might not communicate with her son'. Henry VII, did of course, secure the throne for himself in 1485, with the backing of both Margaret and her husband, and his mother was then lavishly provided for. However, apart from assuming the role of trusted adviser to the King on matters of court protocol and etiquette, she preferred to live largely in retirement.

In her later years Margaret fell increasingly under the influence of her confessor, John Fisher, and adopted with enthusiasm the pious, chaste life to which she had always been temperamentally inclined. On Fisher's advice she instituted divinity professorships at both Oxford and Cambridge. In 1505 she refounded God's House at Cambridge as Christ's College, and in 1508 she began the transformation of the corrupt hospital of St John the Evangelist into St John's College, Cambridge. In a funeral oration following her death, Fisher declared that 'all England ... had cause for weeping' at the loss of this pious, merciful and generous woman.

See also J. R. Lander, *Government and Community: England 1450–1509*, 1980.

K.R.D.

Becher, Lady Eliza. See O'NEILL, ELIZA.

Becker, Lydia (Ernestine) (1827–90), campaigner for women's suffrage. She was born in Manchester, the daughter of a manufacturer. Except for a short stay at a boarding school in Everton, Liverpool, she was educated at home. As a young woman she developed an interest in botany, gave lectures in girls' schools, corresponded with Charles Darwin, and in 1864 published *Botany for Novices*. The following year she began a short-lived Ladies' Literary Society in Manchester to enable women to study scientific subjects.

In October 1865 a paper delivered by Barbara BODICHON to the Social Science Association on 'Reasons for the Enfranchisement of Women' inspired Lydia Becker's subsequent lifelong devotion to that cause. She wrote an article, 'Female Suffrage', that appeared in *The Contemporary Review* of March 1867, and became Secretary of the Manchester Women's Suffrage Committee, formed with her assistance in January 1867. At the 1868 British Association Congress in Norwich she read a paper on 'Some Supposed Differences in the Minds of Men and Women in Regard to Educational Necessities' which was widely discussed. She became an excellent public speaker, clear and logical, at a time when women rarely appeared on public platforms. In 1869 she undertook the first of many lecture tours, visiting several Northern towns. From her Manchester base she edited *The Women's Suffrage Journal* (1870–90), and in 1880 organized a women-only demonstration in support of female suffrage in the Free Trade Hall. The same year she became Secretary of the London Central Committee for Women's Suffrage and eventually its parliamentary agent, showing a formidable knowledge of parliamentary procedure.

Lydia Becker's other main interest was education. Having worked for the inclusion of a clause in the Elementary Education Act of 1870 which allowed women to serve as members of school boards, she was elected to the Manchester School Board in 1870 and served consecutive terms until her death. An able and effective Board member, she worked particu-

larly for the provision of educational facilities for girls and for the improvement of the position of women teachers. She was also Treasurer of the Married Women's Property Committee and of the Vigilance Association for the Defence of Personal Rights. She showed independence of character and great courage in the face of initial ridicule, ultimately earning respect and recognition as the leader of the early women's suffrage movement.

See also M. Holmes, *Lydia Becker*, 1913; Helen Blackburn (ed.), *Words of a Leader* (extracts from Lydia Becker's writings), 1897.

L.W.

Bedford, Countesses of. See COUCY, ISABELLA DE, COUNTESS OF BEDFORD; RUSSELL, LUCY, COUNTESS OF BEDFORD.

Bedford, Duchess of. See RUSSELL, MARY, DUCHESS OF BEDFORD.

Beeton, Isabella (1836–65), editor and journalist, famous as 'Mrs Beeton'. Isabella Mayson was born in London. Her father, who ran a linen business, died in 1840, and three years later her mother married the clerk of the course at Epsom. Isabella, now the eldest of a large family, was brought up in Epsom and educated at private schools in Islington and Heidelberg; a proficient pianist, she took lessons with Julius Benedict. In 1856, after a year's engagement, she married Samuel Orchart Beeton, journalist and publisher, and they set up house in Pinner. Isabella Beeton embarked on a professional partnership with her husband when she published her first articles in his magazine, *The Englishwoman's Domestic Magazine*, in April 1857. From contributing three articles monthly she went on to become the magazine's fashion correspondent and editor in 1860. When the Beetons launched *The Queen* in 1861 she edited the women's features, and in 1864 she advised on *The Young Englishwoman*.

When her first child died in July 1857, Isabella Beeton began planning a household encyclopedia that was to take her 'four years of incessant labour'. Conceived and published by Sam Beeton, the work was hers, though she called herself editress rather than author, since it was a compilation of ideas from many sources. *Mrs Beeton's Book of Household Management* was issued in parts from 1859, appearing as a book in 1861. Over 1000 pages long, it was the most comprehensive work on domestic affairs ever attempted. Her concern was to avert 'family discontent' as a result of mismanagement, and she offered guidelines on all household matters from polishes to picnics, the nursery to legal problems. She outlined the duties of domestic servants and likened the mistress of the house to the commander of an army. Although only twenty-five and inexperienced, she produced a manual of conduct and economy which became a landmark in nineteenth-century social history, her epigrammatic style supplying catch-phrases for the middle classes. 60,000 copies were sold in the first year, and new editions have been regularly devised. Though little remains of her original, Mrs Beeton's achievement, and her name, survive.

Despite commitments to journalism and charity, children and moving house, Isabella Beeton also produced two condensed versions of her book: *The Englishwoman's Cookery Book* (1863) and *Mrs Beeton's Dictionary of Every-Day Cookery* (1865). She died at the height of her career from puerperal fever, contracted during the birth of her fourth son.

See also S. Freeman, *Isabella and Sam: the Story of Mrs Beeton*, 1977.   C.B.

Behn, Aphra (1640–89), novelist, playwright, and poet. She was probably born at Harble-down, near Canterbury, and was the daughter of a yeoman. Practically nothing is known of the first twenty years of her life. Around 1663 she sailed with her family to Surinam in the West Indies, where she stayed for about six months. Her experience there formed the basis for her novel *Oronooko* (1688), which provides some brief biographical details. Shortly after returning to England in 1664 she married. Her husband may have been a Dutch merchant, but he apparently died in the great plague the following year.

Throughout her life Aphra Behn was an ardent Royalist, and it seems that she had some connections at court. The first unquestioned facts about her life concern her activities as a government spy in Holland in 1666–67. She was sent there by Lord Arlington, to whom she passed on useful information. However, the payments she received did not cover her expenses and she had to borrow her fare back to England. Towards the end of 1668 she was imprisoned briefly for debt. In order to survive alone she needed some means of financial support, and in 1670 she entered the fiercely competitive world of the theatre, becoming the first woman to earn her living as a professional writer.

Between 1670 and 1687 fifteen of Aphra Behn's plays were produced and published, many to great acclaim. She wrote one tragedy and a few tragi-comedies, but her forte was comedy. Her greatest triumph and best play was *The Rover* (1677), an elaborately plotted, witty sex-intrigue comedy in which she attacked forced and mercenary marriages. The character of the hero, Wilmore, perhaps contains elements drawn from John Hoyle, a rak-ish republican lawyer with whom she had had a brief, passionate love affair the previous year. The success of *The Rover* brought Aphra Behn the patronage of James II. Some of her later plays were open political satires on the Whigs, and in 1682 she was arrested for a biting attack on Monmouth in an epilogue written for an anonymous play.

She produced no more plays until 1686, turning instead to prose fiction and poetry. In 1684 she produced a long epistolary romance and a major collection of her poems. Thereafter she had to struggle increasingly against debt, and she became seriously ill with arthritis. Her last two plays were produced in 1686 and 1687, but they seem not to have brought her much money; she was forced to publish translations and occasional poems on public events in order to survive. During the last two years of her life, in a surge of creative energy, she produced several novels. The most famous, *Oronooko, or The History of the Royal Slave* (1688), contains the first attack on slavery in English literature; Oronooko is highly educated and civilized, and a powerful contrast is drawn between his nobility and the brutality of the English colonists who enslave him.

Despite the fame of *Oronooko*, Behn's best works were her plays. Many of her contemporaries were reluctant to admit her gifts, and her writing was frequently criticized as immodest. She defended herself vigorously in bold and witty prefaces, pointing out that her plays were no more bawdy than those by men, and declaring that women, as she herself had proved, were capable of writing good plays despite their lack of educational opportunities. A pioneer in her own time, she remains the most famous woman writer in England before the nineteenth century.

See also M. Duffy, *The Passionate Shepherdess*, 1977; A. Goreau, *Reconstructing*

Bell, Currer, Ellis and Acton

Aphra, 1980; F. M. Link, *Aphra Behn*, 1968; M. Summers (ed.), *The Works of Aphra Behn*, 6 vols, 1915. W.R.O.

Bell, Currer, Ellis and Acton. See BRONTË, CHARLOTTE, EMILY and ANNE.

Bell, Gertrude (Margaret Lowthian) (1868–1926), traveller, archaeologist, and government official, the daughter of Sir Hugh Bell of Washington Hall, County Durham. Gertrude Bell was educated at Queen's College, Harley Street, and at Lady Margaret Hall, Oxford, where in 1887 she took a First in History. She travelled extensively, and in 1899 visited childhood friends in Jerusalem, where she learned Arabic and in March 1900 made her first desert journey. Over the years such expeditions became ever more far-flung and hazardous until in 1913, with a *rafiq* (local guide) and her usual train of camels and tents, she made a journey round the great An Nafud desert to Hail. She made valuable contributions to the maps and archaeological records of the Middle East, and when war broke out her unique knowledge of Mesopotamian tribes proved of considerable value. She was attached to Military Intelligence in Cairo, and then in 1917 became Assistant Political Officer in Baghdad; she was four times mentioned in dispatches. After the war, when the ex-Turkish dominions were being distributed among the victors, she was Oriental Secretary to the High Commissioner in Baghdad, and as such worked to make the leader of the Arab Revolt, Faisal, King of Iraq. She became a CBE and FRGS, was President of the Salam Library, and as Honorary Director of Antiquities founded the Iraq Museum.

Gertrude Bell recorded her travels in such works as *The Desert and the Sown*, 1907, *Amurath to Amurath*, 1911, and *Palace and Mosque at Ukhaider*, 1919. Her *Letters*, 1927, provide a vivid, spontaneous self-portrait.

See also H. V. F. Winstone, *Gertrude Bell*, 1978. J.S.R.

Bell, Vanessa (1879–1961), painter. She was the daughter of Sir Leslie Stephen, a man of letters famous for his part in creating *The Dictionary of National Biography*; and she was the older sister of Virginia WOOLF and the great-niece of Julia Margaret CAMERON.

Vanessa Bell studied at the Royal Academy Schools, and also under Sargent, and about 1904 she settled with her sister Virginia and her two brothers in a house in Gordon Square, London, which became the chief meeting-place of the Bloomsbury Group. In 1907 she married the art historian and writer on aesthetics Clive Bell, and between 1913 and 1919 she worked with Roger Fry in the Omega Workshops which Fry had founded. The main purpose of the Workshops was to improve contemporary design by creating useful objects of furniture, pottery, etc. in a bold 'modern' style. Fry had become famous (or rather notorious) as the organizer of the first exhibition of Post-Impressionist painting in London (1910–11), and Vanessa Bell's style reflected the influence of such masters as Cézanne, and later of such 'Fauves' as Matisse, Derain, and Vlaminck, and also of Picasso in his early 'Blue Period'. In later years there was a general simplification of form and colour in her style (although she painted only a few entirely abstract pictures), possibly as a result of her design work and through her fifty-year-long association with the painter Duncan Grant. There are works by Vanessa Bell at the Tate Gallery in London, and the Courtauld Institute Galleries contain not only paintings but also a notable collection of the products of the Omega Workshops.

See also R. N. Shone, *Bloomsbury Portraits: Vanessa Bell, Duncan Grant, and their Circle*, 1976. L.M.M.

Bellamy, George-Anne (1731?–1788), actress, the illegitimate daughter of Lord Tyrawley; her forename was the result of a mis-hearing of 'Georgiana' at her christening. Preferring the stage to life with her father's relatives, she first appeared at Covent Garden in 1744 as Miss Prue.

After making a success in Dublin, where she first played with Garrick, she joined his company at Drury Lane in 1750. She played most of the leading tragic and romantic roles opposite him, notably Juliet. She also played Cleopatra, Volumnia, and Monimia. Though her unreliability and short temper tried Garrick sorely, her beauty and intelligence assured engagements. But as her looks faded, so did her popularity. The scandal attaching to her name through two husbands and countless lovers lost her public esteem, and during her last years she was much harassed by creditors.

George-Anne Bellamy's cheerfully scandalous autobiography is invaluable as theatrical and costume history, although somewhat unreliable as an apology for her life and loves. A contemporary review describes her acting as 'a soft wildness which commands pity'.

See also P. H. Highfill, K. A. Burnim, E. A. Langhans, *A Biographical Dictionary of Actors, Actresses, Musicians, Dancers, Managers and Other Stage Personnel in London, 1660-1800*, vol. 2, 1973; C. Hughes, *Enchanting Bellamy*, 1956.   C.H.

Benger, Elizabeth Ogilvy (1778-1827), writer. Her family background, chiefly commercial, proved no handicap to her literary ambitions; indeed her father placed her in a boys' school at the age of twelve to further her classical education. On settling in London in 1800 she thrust her way with determination into the literary company she hungered for, even employing curious stratagems to do so; she achieved access to Mrs Inchbald, for example, by impersonating a servant. In due course she became successfully established among a circle which included Dr Aikin and his daughters and Charles and Mary LAMB. After publishing (anonymously) some poetry in *The Monthly Magazine* she produced an ambitious poem *On the Slave Trade* (1809), an expensive but apparently successful work illustrated by Smirke. Two novels, *Marian* and *The Heart and the Fury*, followed; they were well received at the time but are now forgotten. Between 1818 and 1825 she wrote five historical memoirs, also ventured into travel literature, and made translations from German. In spite of her considerable output she died almost destitute after several years marred by ill health.   T.H.

Benson, Stella (1892-1933), novelist. She was born in Much Wenlock, Shropshire, the daughter of a country gentleman, and was educated privately at home and abroad. Her interest in women's suffrage shortly before the First World War led her to investigate social conditions in London's East End, where she opened a small general shop. There she wrote her first novel, *I Pose* (1915), and sent it to the publishing house of Macmillan, asking for a decision in a week. They accepted it.

In 1917 she worked on the land, and in 1918 went to America, where she supported herself by various menial jobs. She lived alone in a very small room where she finished her third novel, *Living Alone* (1919). She then returned to England, working her way via the Far East.

In China she met her future husband, John O'Gorman Anderson of the Chinese customs service. They married in England (1921), then returned to live in China. In Hong Kong she was active in the organization of a successful campaign aginst the system of licensed prostitution.

Stella Benson's first popular novel, *Tobit Transplanted* (1931), won the Femina Vie Heureuse prize and the A. C. Benson silver medal of the Royal Society of Literature. Critics hailed her as a highly original writer who combined wit and tragedy, fantasy and realism. Three years later she died in northern French Indo-China. Her other works include *Worlds Within Worlds* (1928); *Collected Short Stories* was published in 1933.

See also R. Ellis Roberts, *Portrait of Stella Benson*, 1939.   P.L.

Bentham, Ethel (?-1931), physician, pioneer of child health, and political activist. She was born in England but brought up in Dublin, where her father was a JP. She attended Alexandra School and College, Dublin, and the London School of Medicine for Women, and trained at hospitals in Brussels and Paris.

Ethel Bentham practised medicine at Newcastle-upon-Tyne and Gateshead until 1909, when she moved to London, establishing a practice in North Kensington and living with Marion PHILLIPS. Her work as principal supporter and organizer of the Margaret O. MacDonald Memorial Clinic for Children under School Age in North Kensington helped by example the development of public health provision for mothers and pre-school children. (See, for example, *The Needs of Little Children*, a paper by Margaret McMILLAN and Ethel Bentham, 1912). She was a member of the Metropolitan Asylums Board, and after the First World War a JP and member of the Children's Court.

Ethel Bentham took an active role in the women's suffrage campaign, becoming a member of the Executive of the National Union of Women's Suffrage Societies. She joined the Fabian Society in 1907 while still in Newcastle, and the Fabian Women's Group in 1908, lecturing at their summer schools. A member of the Independent Labour Party and the Women's Labour League, she was elected to Kensington Borough Council in 1912, retaining her seat for thirteen years. She was elected to the Labour Party Executive in 1917, served on the Standing Joint Committee of Industrial Women's Organizations which formulated policy for Labour Women's Conferences, and stood as Labour Party candidate at East Islington in the 1922 general election and each subsequent election until successful in 1929. In the same year she was elected to the Executive of the Labour Party. She remained a keen feminist: her last work in the Commons was to introduce the Nationality of Married Women Bill.

See also *Fabian News* (February 1931).

L.W.

Bentley, Phyllis (1894–1977), novelist, born in Halifax, the daughter of a cloth manufacturer. She was educated at Halifax High School, Cheltenham Ladies' College, and London University. During the First World War, Phyllis Bentley taught in a local Grammar School, then went to London as a secretary in the Ministry of Munitions and wrote her first novel, *Environment*, published in 1922. Later she worked at cataloguing various libraries in Yorkshire, thus enriching herself with the detailed knowledge of Yorkshire life and history that was to figure in her books. She was a regional novelist *par excellence*. Her special interest was the rise and fall of industry in her county; for example, *Inheritance* (1932) observes the advent of the industrial revolution, while *A Modern Tragedy* (1934) concerns the effects of the slump.

Leeds University honoured her with a D.Litt. (1949), she became a Fellow of the Royal Society of Literature (1958), and she was awarded the OBE (1970). Her other works include *The Rise of Henry Morcar* (1946), and an autobiography, *O Dreams, O Destinations* (1962).

See also M. Crosland, *Beyond the Lighthouse—English Women Novelists in the Twentieth Century*, 1981.

P.L.

Berengaria of Navarre (c. 1172–after 1230), Richard I's queen. She was the daughter of Sancho VI, 'the Wise', of Navarre. Berengaria's marriage to Richard I was arranged in 1191, before his departure on the Third Crusade. She was escorted to Cyprus for her wedding by Richard's mother, ELEANOR OF AQUITAINE. Richard and Berengaria were necessarily apart for much of the time in the Holy Land, and on her return the Queen settled in Maine. She is the only medieval queen of England never

to have set foot on English soil. Contemporary writers found little in Berengaria worthy of note and Richard's attitude to her was cool and offhand. There were no children of the marriage, a factor which was to have profound consequences following Richard's early death in 1199.

See also J. Gillingham, *Richard the Lionheart*, 1978.

A.C.

Berkeley, Elizabeth (1750–1820), writer, later Margravine of Anspach. The daughter of the Earl of Berkeley, Elizabeth Berkeley married the son of the Earl of Craven. They separated in 1783, and Lady Craven left England and six children for a prolonged European tour. In 1789 she published *A Journey through the Crimea to Constantinople*, and subsequently on a visit to Anspach she took up residence with the Margrave.

In Anspach she translated and wrote little plays in French for the court theatre. Lord Craven died in 1791 and the following month she married the Margrave. The Margrave then sold his lands and title; the couple moved to England and bought a house in Hammersmith, where he died in 1806.

Elizabeth Berkeley also wrote for the English theatre—notably *The Silver Tankard* (1781) and *The Princess of Georgia* (1799) —and her plays were printed by Horace Walpole at Strawberry Hill. There were comedies, and pantomimes for which she herself sometimes composed the music. Walpole wrote of her, 'She has, I fear, been infinitamente indiscreet, but what is that to you or me? She is very pretty, has parts, and is good natured to the greatest degree.'

See also *Memories of Margravine of Anspach* 1826; *Letters of Horace Walpole*, 1839; J. Genest, *Some Account of the English Stage*, 1832.

C.H.

Berry, Mary (1763–1852), writer and friend of Horace Walpole. Mary and her sister Agnes (b. 1764) were brought up in somewhat straitened circumstances. These later improved a little upon the death of a rich relation, but were never ample, and the education of the sisters was consequently sketchy. In 1783 they began a two-year sojourn in France and Italy with their father, Mary using the experience to begin her journals and correspondence.

The Berrys' association with the elderly

Horace Walpole, which was to be so momentous for both of them, began in late 1787 or early 1788. In his younger days Walpole seems to have been somewhat uneasy with women, at least in a sexual context, but he had a great capacity for friendship and he became entirely captivated by the sisters. According to one anecdote in the *Edinburgh Review* (October 1865) he was prepared to offer marriage to either of them to secure their continued society. Certainly he became very dependent on Mary in particular, although the relationship was non-physical. 'I do pique myself', he said, 'on not being ridiculous at this very late period of my life.'

Upon Walpole's death in 1797, the sisters were left legacies, and also Little Strawberry Hill, which had been their home for some years. Furthermore, they found themselves co-executors with their father, Robert Berry, of Walpole's literary property. Within a year Mary had produced a five-volume edition of his works. It is a comment on notions of modesty and the public self-effacement of women in that age that she advertised the work as edited by Robert Berry, who had played no part in it. Mary Berry's next literary production was a five-act comedy called *Fashionable Friends*; again she disclaimed authorship, this time ascribing her work to Walpole, now several years dead. It was not a success and only survived three nights at Drury Lane (1802). She was more highly praised for her edition of Walpole's correspondence with Madame du Deffand (1810). In 1819 she edited the letters of Lady Rachel Russell (a seventeenth-century collection not first published until 1773), adding an account of her subject's life. Her last work, *A Comparative View of the Social Life of England and France from the Restoration of Charles the Second to the French Revolution*, appeared in two parts (1828 and 1831). There must be few but researchers who consult it nowadays, but it was well received at the time.

There must have been numerous women in history who have been noticed by posterity merely for their association with the famous. Mary Berry belongs to that much smaller band of women who used such an association as a means to personal achievement.

See also R. W. Ketton-Cremer, *Horace Walpole*, 1946; T. Lewis (ed.), *Extracts of the Journals and Correspondence of Miss Berry 1783-1852*, 1865.   T.H.

Bertha (*fl.* 567–601), or Æthelbertha, Queen of Kent. The only surviving child of King Charibert of Paris, Bertha was born between 532 and Charibert's death in 567. She remained in Frankia, where she probably received a form of education, until sometime before 596, when King Æthelberht of Kent requested her hand in marriage. Although the match promised to confirm existing links between the two kingdoms, Æthelberht and his subjects were still pagans, unlike the recently converted Franks. Consequently, his proposal was only accepted on the understanding that Bertha might practise Christianity in Kent. As a result of this arrangement, Bertha often worshipped at the Roman church of St Martin at Canterbury. However, Bertha and her spiritual adviser, the Frankish bishop Luidhard, were apparently reluctant to evangelize Kent, and it was Augustine, sent from Rome in 596, who persuaded Æthelberht and his people to accept Christianity. A papal letter, dated June 601, chastised Bertha for failing to take the initiative, but she was also praised for the way she helped Augustine in the early years of his mission. Indeed, without the support she was able to afford him as Queen, the history of the English conversion might have been very different. Bertha died sometime before 616, leaving her husband with two children, and was buried, not in St Martin's but in a new foundation, dedicated to Saints Peter and Paul.

See also B. Colgrave and R. A. B. Mynors (eds), *Bede's Ecclesiastical History of the English People*; P. Ewald and L. Hartmann (ed.), Pope Gregory I's Letters in *Monumenta Germaniae Historica*.   J.C.

Bertie, Catherine (1520–80), Protestant exile and popular heroine. Catherine Bertie was the daughter and heiress of Lord Willoughby and Maria de SALINAS. When her father died in 1526 she became the ward of Charles Brandon, Duke of Suffolk, and his wife Mary, sister to Henry VIII. Mary died in 1533 and Catherine married the Duke. His death in 1545 was followed in 1551 by the deaths of their two sons, for whom Thomas Wilson, once their tutor, composed an epitaph, printed in his *Arte of Rhetorique* (1553). In 1552 Catherine married Richard Bertie, a scholar of humble birth. Since the death of her first husband, Catherine had been a partisan of the Protestant cause, and had become a close friend of the famous reformer Hugh Latimer. Her religion, and her sharp tongue, made her enemies, among whom was Stephen Gardiner, Bishop of Winchester; and on the accession of the Catholic Queen Mary, Richard Bertie was summoned by Gardiner to account for his wife's beliefs. Bertie received permission to travel abroad, and in January 1555 Catherine joined him with their daughter Suzan. Their son Peregrine was born at Wesel. The family spent some time at Weinheim, where John Brett, an envoy of the Queen sent to recall them, was manhandled by their household. They eventually settled in Poland, where they were granted lands in Samogitia at the request of the Polish reformer John a Lasco, who had known Catherine in England.

In 1559, after the accession of Queen Elizabeth, they returned to England, where Catherine urged Elizabeth's chief minister, William Cecil—an old friend—to push forward Church reform. Elizabeth did not always view Catherine kindly, and refused to ennoble Richard Bertie. The Willoughby title passed to Peregrine, their son, on his mother's death.

Catherine was a staunch Protestant, and in 1562 and 1578 Augustine Bernher dedicated his collection of Latimer's sermons to her, praising her zeal for the faith. Her life story, particularly her flight from England and adventures abroad, was celebrated in ballads, and in a play by Thomas Drewe. As Dowager Duchess of Suffolk, Catherine was able to wield considerable influence, which she used in supporting Protestant ministers, both English and foreign, while her adventurous life and reputation for incisive wit made her a popular heroine of the Reformation.

See also Lady C. Goff, *A Woman of the Tudor Age*, 1930; E. Read, *Catherine, Duchess of Suffolk*, 1962. J.S.

Berwick, Miss Mary. See PROCTER, ADELAIDE ANNE.

Besant, Annie (1847–1933), social reformer, theosophist, and political leader, the only daughter of a London businessman who died just after her fifth birthday. She grew up in conditions of genteel poverty with her Irish mother and elder brother. Her education, which began under a liberal tutor, was completed at a strict Evangelical school in Dorset. In 1867 she entered into a disastrous marriage with the Reverend Frank Besant, whom she later left. By 1874 she had formed a close

friendship with the free-thinker Charles Bradlaugh, and for twelve years she wrote and lectured with him, becoming co-editor of *The National Reformer* and Vice-President of the National Secular Society. Bernard Shaw called her 'the greatest orator in England', but her opinions aroused intense hostility. Annie Besant and Bradlaugh were convicted of obscenity for republishing a controversial birth control pamphlet (though the verdict was later quashed); and in 1879 she lost custody of her daughter in a high court case.

After taking a science degree at London University, she taught at the National Secular Society's Hall of Science. A romantic attachment to Edward Aveling, a fellow worker, ended in 1883 when he transferred his affections to Eleanor MARX. Annie Besant was converted to socialism and joined the Fabian Society in 1885 under the influence of Bernard Shaw, with whom a new friendship developed. Subsequently she helped to organize strikes, including that of the match-girls at Bryant and May Ltd, and publicized trade union issues in *Link*, a magazine which she founded with W. T. Stead. She was elected to the School Board for Tower Hamlets in 1889 on a programme of free secular education and free meals for poor children.

At this very time she stunned her colleagues by joining the Theosophical Society, later emigrating to India, where she preached theosophy and championed Home Rule. In 1917 she was interned for three months; and from 1917 to 1919 she was President of the Indian National Congress, losing her position in 1920 when she opposed Gandhi's plan of non-co-operation with the British.

Annie Besant was not an original thinker, but she presented issues and ideas clearly to mass audiences, and possessed organizational skills and great energy. Even her espousal of theosophy, which never gained a mass following, earned her a platform in Indian politics from which to embarrass an imperialist government. Her writings include *An Autobiography*, 1893, *Why I do not believe in God*, 1887, *Wake Up India*, 1913, and *Why I became a Theosophist*, 1889.

See also A. H. Nethercot, *The First Five Lives of Annie Besant*, 1961, and *The Last Four Lives of Annie Besant*, 1963. K.S.

Bess of Hardwick. See TALBOT, ELIZABETH, COUNTESS OF SHREWSBURY.

Best, Edna (1900–74), actress. She was born at Hove and trained at the Guildhall School of Music. After appearing in *Charley's Aunt* (1917), she toured in American farce, then played Peter Pan in 1920. She was the original Tessa in *The Constant Nymph* (1926). Her many London appearances included a co-starring role with Tallulah Bankhead in Noël Coward's *Fallen Angels* (1925). Her first film part was in *A Couple of Down and Outs* (1923); one of her most famous appearances was in *South Riding*, with Ralph Richardson (1938).

Soft-spoken, she played with a sort of contemptuous restraint. In 1939 she emigrated to the United States, where many of her best parts were in popular British plays such as Rattigan's *The Browning Version*.   A.D.

Betham, Mary Matilda (1776–1852), writer and miniaturist. The eldest daughter of the Reverend William Betham, rector of Stoke Lacey, schoolmaster and author, she had little formal education but enjoyed free access to her father's comprehensive library and occasional instruction from him. She never married, and early attempted to turn her talents to practical account. She taught herself miniature painting, and her work was characterized by a delicate touch and the sweet expressions of her faces; but her lack of technique limited her achievement. She exhibited her portraits at the Royal Academy, but her greatest fame came from her literary talent, which brought her into contact with the leading writers of the day. Coleridge, Southey, and the Lambs were all admirers of her poetry. In 1804 she published *A Biographical Dictionary of the Celebrated Women of Every Age and Country*, based on her early reading. Her most successful work was *The Lay of Marie* (1816).   J.R.

Betham-Edwards, Matilda Barbara (1836–1919), writer. She was born in Suffolk, where her father farmed, and attended school for only a short time. Her education was furthered by reading and by travel in rural France. She began writing at twenty-one and maintained a prodigious output for over sixty years. Her work comprises novels, based mostly on recollections of life in Suffolk, and interpretations of France and the French. Notable among the novels are *The White House by the Sea* (1857), *Dr Jacob* (1864), *Kitty* (1869), and *Lord of the Harvest* (1899). Among the books on France are *French Men, Women and Books* (1910) and *Twentieth Century France* (1917). *Reminiscences* appeared in 1898 and *Mid-Victorian Memories* in 1919. Amelia Blandford EDWARDS was her cousin.   B.H.C.

Betterton, Mary (*c.* 1637–1712), the first regular actress on the English stage; one of the first women, shortly after the Restoration of 1660 ended the prohibition of the drama under Cromwell, to join the Duke's Company managed by Sir William Davenant, in whose house she apparently boarded. She made her first recorded appearance on stage in June 1661 in Davenant's *The Siege of Rhodes* as Ianthe, the name by which Samuel Pepys always referred to her because of her memorable performance in that role. In December 1662, as Mary Saunderson 'of St Giles, Cripplegate, spinster, about twenty-five', she married, with the consent of her widowed mother, the great actor, playwright, and future manager Thomas Betterton.

An exceedingly attractive and talented actress, especially suited to romantic roles, Mary Betterton was also known as a kind and generous woman of unblemished character and sober life; appropriately, she was usually cast as a 'good' woman. She created many new roles in plays by contemporary dramatists and received universal acclaim for her performances in Shakespeare, particularly for her Lady Macbeth, which Colley Cibber thought in many ways superior to that of her great successor, Elizabeth BARRY. From 1682, having lost much of her physical appeal, she created only a few new roles and performed her old romantic roles less frequently, turning increasingly to maternal parts until her retirement in 1695. On her husband's death in 1710 it was said that she 'ran distracted, though she appeared rather a prudent and constant than a passionate wife'. Reportedly given a pension by Queen Anne, she survived Thomas Betterton by only two years and was buried beside him in Westminster Abbey. A childless couple, the Bettertons were noted for their kindness to aspiring young actors, particularly to Anne BRACEGIRDLE. Mary herself was greatly esteemed both as an excellent actress and as an admirable woman who led a virtuous life.

See also J. H. Wilson, *All the King's Ladies: Actresses of the Restoration*, 1958.

T.J.M.

Biddle, Esther (*fl.* 1629–96), Quaker writer and activist. She was born at Oxford and married Thomas Biddle, a cordwainer, of the Old Change, London. She was converted to Quakerism by Francis Howgill and in 1656–57 travelled as a missionary to Barbados and Newfoundland. She returned to England and in 1657 is said to have prophesied the return of Charles II. (The Quaker leader George Fox warned her not to publicize it at the time for fear of reprisals.) She seems to have helped Dorothy WHITE get a book published in 1661, and was imprisoned in November 1662 for herself writing a book, possibly *The Trumpet of the Lord Sounded Forth unto these Three Nations, as a Warning from the Spirit of Truth* (1662). She was in prison again in 1664. During the London plague of 1665 she remained in the city and in the November of that year was arrested for preaching in the street; during the arrest she was struck across the face by a halberd. She was a member of the Quaker Women's Meeting in London. In 1694 Queen Mary granted her a pass to go to France, where she had an audience with Louis XIV and begged for peace. In her old age she became poor and had to be supported by other Quakers. Like others attracted by the Quakers' advanced views on the role of women, Esther Biddle, an active minister and writer, did much to promote and sustain the movement. Her writings include *Wo to thee, City of Oxford, thy wickednesse surmounteth the wickednesse of Sodome* (1655), and *A Warning from the Lord God of Life and Power unto thee O City of London* (1660).

See also M. R. Brailsford, *Quaker Women 1650–1690*, 1915, and the unpublished *Dictionary of Quaker Biography* in Friends' House, London. **T.O'M.**

Biffin, Sarah (1784–1850), miniaturist. Of humble parentage, she was born without arms or legs in East Quantoxhead, Somerset, and she did not grow more than three feet in height. With great perseverance she taught herself to manipulate pencil, pen, painting-brush, even needle and scissors, with her mouth.

She worked for sixteen years with a drawing master who carried her about the country, exhibiting her to audiences for whom she drew landscapes and painted miniatures on ivory. Later the Earl of Morton financed further instruction for her by a well-known portrait painter. Royal patronage ensured her recognition and enabled her to become self-supporting. The Society of Artists awarded her a medal in 1821.

On her retirement to Liverpool, Sarah Biffin's skill declined, and she might have perished from age and poverty had not a friend organized a benefit subscription for her.

P.A.S.

Billington, Elizabeth (1765?–1818), singer, actress and composer. Although German by parentage, Elizabeth Weichsel was born in Soho. Her father was an oboist, her mother a singer and a pupil of J. C. Bach. Elizabeth and her brother Carl, a violinist, studied and performed together from an early age. She showed a precocious talent for the harpsichord and composition, as well as singing.

In defiance of her family she married her voice teacher, James Billington, in 1783. Later that year they were in Dublin, where Elizabeth began a series of liaisons. Billington broke with her, repudiating her debts. However, they were soon re-united and successfully performing at Smock Alley. Elizabeth Billington sang Polly in the *The Beggar's Opera*, Eurydice in *Orpheus*, and Mandane in *Artaxerxes*. In 1784 she gave birth to a daughter, who died shortly afterwards. After an affair with the notorious theatre manager Daly and a serious illness, Elizabeth left for London in 1786 with her husband.

In London, while continuing to study under famous teachers, she was a huge success and commanded large fees. During the early 1790s she sang in London, Edinburgh, and Dublin in oratorios and ballad operas and in pleasure gardens. As a result of the publication of her scandalous *Memoirs* she left for the Continent in 1794.

In Italy the Billingtons performed before the King of Naples at Sir William Hamilton's house. James Billington died suddenly and Elizabeth remained in Naples, singing in operas composed for her. In 1796 she and her brother mounted an operatic tour of Italy. She married a Frenchman in 1799 and settled near Venice, but as a result of his brutality she was back in England in 1801.

Her exotic European adventures made her even more attractive to London audiences and she characteristically signed on with both Covent Garden and Drury Lane, resolving the confusion by performing alternately at each.

Between 1802 and 1806 she was the acknowledged London *prima donna*. At her last performance in 1806 she sang Vitelli in *La Clemenza di Tito*. In 1817 her French husband re-appeared and took her back to Venice, where she died a year later, possibly as a result of ill-treatment, and leaving, it was said, two illegitimate children.

The brilliance of Elizabeth Billington's voice, her charm, kindness, and beauty were univerally acknowledged, although critics did not always appreciate her vocal embellishments. She also remained an accomplished pianist. She was the subject of many portraits by artists such as Romney, Cosway, Rowlandson, and Stothard. Sir Joshua Reynolds, apologizing for a portrait that did not do her justice, said 'How could I help it? I could not paint her voice.'

See also P. H. Highfill, K. A. Burnim, E. A. Langhans, *A Biographical Dictionary of Actors, Actresses, Musicians, Dancers, Managers and Other Stage Personnel in London, 1660-1800*, vol 2, 1973; S. Sadie (ed.), *The New Grove Dictionary of Music and Musicians*, 1981.   C.H.

Billington-Greig, Teresa (1877–1964), suffragette. Born Teresa Billington in Lancashire, the daughter of a shipping clerk, she was educated at a convent school and through Manchester University extension classes. She became a teacher, in 1904 helping to start the equal pay movement, and joined the Women's Social and Political Union in 1903. One of the first militants, she was also among the first suffragettes sent to Holloway Prison (1906). She became known as 'the woman with the dog whip', for when interrupting meetings to state her views, she whirled the whip around her to make sure she could not be ejected. Disagreeing with the Pankhursts' policies, she helped to form the Women's Freedom League in 1907 but soon felt that its aims fell short of her concept of women's freedom. She undertook a programme of writing and speaking (1911–14) and published *The Militant Suffrage Movement* (1911), criticizing the methods used in militancy, *The Consumer in Revolt* (1912), and *Towards Women's Liberty*. Her husband, Frederick Greig, supported her in all her activities.   B.H.C.

Bishop, Anna (1810–84), singer, born in London, was one of the thirteen children of Daniel Riviere, a drawing master of Huguenot descent. Initially taught by her mother, she entered the Royal Academy of Music in 1824, studying singing, piano, and composition. She left in 1828 and made her professional debut in 1831. She married her former professor, the composer Henry Rowley Bishop, in July 1831 and toured the provinces with him and the harpist Nicholas Bochsa, singing sacred music. After a busy London season she gave her first benefit concert in 1836. A tour with Bochsa in 1839 culminated in a concert at Her Majesty's Opera House, where she sang Tancredi to great acclaim. Five days later she eloped with Bochsa to Hamburg.

Widely condemned for leaving her husband and children for a convicted forger and reputed bigamist, Anna Bishop did not return to Britain until 1846. From 1839 to 1846 she toured Europe, spending a year in Russia and a record twenty-seven months as *prima donna assoluta* at San Carlo, Naples, where she gave 327 performances in twenty operas. Soon after her return to London she left for New York, touring Mexico, Cuba, and California (1847–50). In 1852 she produced and sang Flotow's *Martha* at Niblo's Garden, New York, and in 1854 she sailed for Sydney, where Bochsa died in 1856. For the next two years she toured South America; in 1858, having returned to New York, she married Martin Schultz, a diamond merchant. In London the following year, singing to an audience of 6000 at Surrey Gardens, she was praised for her 'energy, soul, and powerful and tragic expression'. She sang with the Philharmonic Society in New York in 1860 and then toured America, Canada, and Mexico. In February 1866 she sailed from California for Hong Kong but, shipwrecked on a coral reef for forty days, lost all her music, clothes, and jewellery, and did not reach Hong Kong until October. Undefeated, she continued her tour of India, Ceylon, Singapore, and Australia, returning to New York via England. She made a last world tour in 1874–76 and after three years in London retired to New York, where she made her final public appearance on 22 April 1883.

Internationally successful, Anna Bishop had a brilliant soprano voice and impressive technique, but reputedly lacked expressive power and so never achieved the renown of Jenny Lind.

See also G. Foster, *Biography of Mme Anna Bishop*, 1855; R. Northcott, *The Life of Sir*

Bishop, Isabella Bird

Henry Rowley Bishop, 1920; S. Sadie (ed.), *The New Grove Dictionary of Music and Musicians*, 1981.   C.B.

Bishop, Isabella Bird (1831–1904), traveller and writer, born Isabella Lucy Bird at Boroughbridge Hall in Yorkshire. She was the eldest daughter of a clergyman. Her family lived a somewhat nomadic life before settling in Wyton in Huntingdonshire when she was seventeen. She was a delicate, sickly child who suffered from spinal weakness, and it was on her doctor's recommendation that in 1854 she made her first trip to America. She was a keen observer and, having made extensive notes about her travels, settled down on her return to write *The Englishwoman in America*, which became an immediate success.

Isabella Bird's restless spirit and continued ill-health in Britain compelled her to undertake numerous journeys: she returned to America and also explored the hinterlands of Japan, Persia, and China, as well as the islands of the South Pacific. She travelled throughout her life, often in uncharted territory and on many occasions suffering greatly through ill-health. Nor was age a deterrent: in her sixtieth year she journeyed 2500 miles through Persia and Kurdistan, and her last journey, to Morocco, was undertaken when she was seventy. After each trip she would write in detail of her adventures, and her books were favourably received by geographers and literary critics alike.

In Britain her time was occupied by scientific and philanthropic work. After her first trip to America she helped to promote emigration there from north-west Scotland, an area she knew and loved. In 1881 she married her sister's physician, and until his death five years later, his health was her chief concern. Under his influence she became increasingly interested in medical missions and established several small hospitals in China and India; towards the end of her life she gave herself wholeheartedly to the missionary cause, her travels taking on an added significance.

In 1892 Isabella Bird Bishop was made a Fellow of the Royal Geographical Society, the first woman to be so honoured. She thoroughly deserved such an honour for her extraordinary courage in exploring dangerous lands and accomplishing feats that no one expected of a woman, and for the meticulous way in which she recorded her journeys. Her writings include *The Hawaian Archipelago*, 1875, *Unbeaten Tracks in Japan*, 1880, *Journeys in Persia and Kurdistan*, 1891, and *Korea and her Neighbours*, 1898.

See also C. Williams, *The Adventures of a Lady Traveller: The Story of Isabella Bird Bishop*, 1909; P. M. Barr, *A Curious Life for a Lady*, 1970.   J.G.S.

'Black Agnes'. See DUNBAR, AGNES.

Black, Clementina (1855?–1923), reformer of social and industrial conditions for women and writer. The daughter of a solicitor, she was brought up in Brighton, the eldest of eight children. She taught French and German to her sisters, one of whom was Constance GARNETT, and began writing stories and contributing to magazines at an early age. Her first published book was *A Sussex Idyll* (1877).

In the early 1880s Clementina Black moved to London with her sisters, living in Fitzroy Square, pursuing her studies in the British Museum, and associating with socialists and Fabians. After a period of ill-health she lived abroad with her friend the writer Amy Levy. On her return to London she spent her time in the East End working to improve industrial conditions for women and girls through militant unionism. She became Secretary of the Women's Provident and Protective League for a brief period; she left in 1889 after a disagreement over whether the League should actively support the match-girls' strike. Believing that they should, she formed the Women's Trade Union Association, whose main aim was to help women workers form trade unions along the lines of the new mass unionism that had developed in the 1880s. At the same time she founded a Women's Labour Bureau with Frances Hicks. With the reorganization of the Women's Provident and Protective League into the Women's Trade Union League, and its adoption of a more militant industrial stance, the Women's Trade Union Association was disbanded and Clementina Black directed her energies into forming the Women's Industrial Council (1894). For a time she edited its journal, *The Women's Industrial News*, and directed the work of the investigation sub-committee into conditions for women workers. She was an Executive Committee member of the Anti-Sweating League formed in 1906, and argued the need for trade boards to regulate wages in the worst-paid trades; her views are expressed in *Sweated Industry and the*

Minimum Wage (1907). She spoke at numerous meetings and conferences and in January 1907 contributed to a course of lectures on 'The Relation of the State to Women's Work', arranged jointly by the Women's Industrial Council and King's College, London. Still vigorous in her sixties, she wrote *Married Women's Work* (1915) and contributed an article, 'Report on Industry and Motherhood Inquiry', to *The Women's Industrial News* of January 1918.

Clementina Black's other activities included membership of the Christian Social Union and of the Executive Committee of the London Society for Women's Suffrage; and around 1913 she served as acting editor of *The Common Cause*. A prolific writer on the causes she advocated, she also published novels, biographies, plays for children, and several translations. Her works include *Orlando* (1880), *An Agitator* (1894), and with Stephen N. Fox *The Truck Acts* (1894). L.W.

Blackburn, Helen (1842–1903), campaigner for women's rights. She was born in Knightstown, Valencia Island, Ireland, the daughter of a civil engineer and inventor. She moved to London in 1859. Her early involvement with the women's movement was through the suffrage campaign. She served as Secretary of the London Central Committee for Women's Suffrage from 1874 to 1895, of the Bristol and West of England Society from 1880 to 1895 and of the London Central Association from 1887 to 1895. She believed that the vote was the foundation for women's emancipation and devoted considerable energy to suffrage publications including *The Women's Suffrage Calendar* (1896, 1897) and *Women's Suffrage: a record of the women's suffrage movement in the British Isles* (1902). As editor of *The Englishwoman's Review* from 1881 to 1890 she became a close associate of Jessie BOUCHERETT, the *Review's* proprietor, who was keenly interested in women's employment. Their common conservative political outlook and belief in self-help inspired their opposition to factory legislation for women workers, and in 1899 they established the Freedom of Labour Defence League. They published *The Condition of Working Women and the Factory Acts* in 1896. Helen Blackburn was a delegate to the Trades Union Congress in 1881 for the Bristol National Union

of Working Women. In 1895 she gave up most public work to look after her ailing father.

Recognized as a prodigious worker for the suffrage and for women's employment, Helen Blackburn was less admired by some for her staunch adherence to the concept of self-determination, which meant that the promoters of every fresh measure to extend the Factory Acts to women had to calculate on her opposition. Her writings include *A Handbook for Women Engaged in Social and Political Work* (1881) and, with Nora Vynne, *Women under the Factory Act* (1903). L.W.

Blackwell, Elizabeth (*fl.* 1737), botanical illustrator, born in Scotland. She eloped with Alexander Blackwell to London, where she extricated him from financial difficulties by painting, engraving and colouring *A Curious Herbal*, which appeared in two volumes in 1737 with no less than five hundred illustrations.

She then disappears from notice until 1747, the year of her husband's execution in Sweden for plotting against the Crown, when pamphlets record that she had then been on the point of joining him. C.H.

Blackwell, Elizabeth (1821–1910), the first woman physician. She was the daughter of a dissenting sugar refiner who emigrated in 1832 from Bristol to America. When their father died in debt in 1838, Elizabeth Blackwell and her two sisters opened a school for girls in Cincinnati. Her interest in women's education took a new direction when a friend who was dying of cancer remarked that her suffering would have been greatly eased had she been treated by a woman doctor. Elizabeth Blackwell applied for admission to American medical colleges, which repeatedly turned her down before she was unexpectedly accepted by Geneva College, New York, where the male medical undergraduates had, half in jest, voted for her admission. She graduated with an MD in 1849 and immediately returned to England, where she became a celebrity in medical circles. While pursuing her studies in London and Paris hospitals she contracted a disease from a patient which resulted in the loss of an eye and an end to her ambitions to become a surgeon.

In 1850 Elizabeth Blackwell returned to America and opened a dispensary among the 'fever nests' of New York's rotting tenements.

Blair, Emily

This grew until it became the New York Infirmary and College for Women. Over the next fifteen years Elizabeth Blackwell opened the American medical profession to women, helped by public admiration for the role played by women nurses in the Civil War. After a lecture tour of England in 1858, she stayed on to campaign against the conservatism of the British medical establishment. In 1871 she was one of the founders of the National Health Society (motto: 'Prevention is better than cure') and in 1875 accepted the chair of gynaecology at the new London School of Medicine for Women.

Elizabeth Blackwell wrote at length on women, health and morality, for example in *Christianity in Medicine*, 1891, *The Influence of Women in the Profession of Medicine*, 1889, and *The Human Element in Sex*, 1884. She fought against social ostracism and medical prejudice in a sometimes lonely career of struggle which paved the way for women in medicine all over the world.

See also R. Baker, *The First Woman Doctor*, 1946; D. C. Wilson, *Lone Woman*, 1970.

K.S.

Blair, Emily (Mathieson) (1890–1963), nurse, born at Lenzie near Glasgow, the daughter of a muslin manufacturer. Emily Blair was educated at Lenzie Academy and trained at the Western Infirmary in Glasgow. She served during the First World War with Queen Alexandra's Royal Naval Nursing Service Reserve before being appointed, in 1918, to Princess Mary's Royal Air Force (RAF) Nursing Service. In . 1938 she became RAF Matron-in-Chief and she was mentioned in dispatches.

In 1943 Emily Blair became Matron-in-Chief of the British Red Cross Society, responsible for the staffing and running of some 250 auxiliary hospitals and convalescent homes in the United Kingdom, and also for the training and supervision of VADs and Red Cross nurses serving overseas. She retired from this post in 1953 but was a member of the Council of the British Red Cross until her death. She was also a member of the Executive Committee and Chairman of the Nursing Advisory Board.

Emily Blair was created DBE in 1943 and awarded the Florence Nightingale Medal in 1947.

J.S.R.

Blamire, Susanna (1747–94), dialect poet, 'the muse of Cumberland', born near Carlisle. Her father was a yeoman farmer and her only formal education was at the village school at Raughton Head. However, her family was evidently sufficiently well off for her to winter in Carlisle, where she enjoyed a certain amount of social life and for a time lodged and collaborated with a fellow poet, Catherine Gilpin. Some of her poems appeared, unsigned, in magazines, and her life was passed so quietly among friends and relatives that her existence might well have been forgotten but for the efforts of two later enthusiasts for her Scots dialect poems; they recovered her surviving manuscripts and issued a collected edition of her works in 1842, almost fifty years after her death. Although she wrote some entertainingly direct story-poems in Cumbrian dialect, Susanna Blamire is now mainly remembered for Scottish songs such as 'And ye shall walk in silk attire' and 'The Traveller's Return'.

N.H.

Blaugdone, Barbara (1609–1704), Quaker minister. She was a well-educated and moderately wealthy teacher in Bristol when she was converted to Quakerism by John Audland and John Camm during their mission to the city. After her conversion all her pupils were withdrawn from her school because her new beliefs were considered dangerous. She became a travelling minister and, unusually among Quaker ministers, was able to meet her expenses out of her own pocket. In 1655 she helped to obtain the release of some Quakers imprisoned at Basingstoke. Between 1655 and 1657 she undertook missionary journeys to Ireland, pleading the Quakers' case with Ireland's ruler, Henry Cromwell. She returned to England in 1657 and worked in the West Country. She was imprisoned at Marlborough, where she went on a brief hunger strike, and later in 1657 was jailed at Exeter for disturbing a minister. At Exeter she went on hunger strike again and was whipped in her cell.

After the Restoration of 1660 Barbara Blaugdone continued her work as a minister and in 1681 was imprisoned at Bristol for attending a Quaker meeting. In 1683 she was fined £60 for non-attendance at the local Anglican church. In 1689 she wrote two pieces for publication, one of which was directed at the new King William III; they were rejected by the censorship committee of the Society of Friends because of the sensitive political climate. In 1691 she published *An Account of* the Travels, Sufferings, and Persecutions of Barbara Blaugdone, which was intended to encourage Quakers by demonstrating how a great many trials might be endured successfully. She was an important early Quaker minister who reveals the attraction of the movement for active and independent women.

See also M. R. Brailsford, *Quaker Women 1650–1690*, 1915, and the unpublished *Dictionary of Quaker Biography* in Friends' House Library, London. 　　　　T.O'M.

Blessington, Countess of. See GARDINER, MARGUERITE, COUNTESS OF BLESSINGTON.

Blind, Mathilde (1841–96), poet and biographer. Born in Mannheim, Germany, she was the daughter of a banker named Cohen but changed her name to that of her stepfather Karl Blind, a political writer and revolutionary. After leading the Baden revolt in 1848–49, Karl Blind and his family were forced to seek asylum in London, where their house was frequented by foreign exiles, in particular the great Italian revolutionary Mazzini, who exerted considerable influence over Mathilde Blind.

She was twenty-six when her first volume, *Poems*, was published under the pseudonym 'Claude Lake'. In her own time she was most famous for her biographies of George Eliot (1883) and Madame Roland (1886), written while she was living in Manchester, where she had moved to be near her close friends, the painter Ford Madox Brown and his wife. However, her chief works are now considered to be three long poems, *The Prophecy of St Oran* (1881), *The Heather on Fire* (1886), and *The Ascent of Man* (1889), an epic on Darwin's theory of evolution. Mathilde Blind travelled widely throughout her life and her visits to Italy and Egypt are reflected in her *Dramas in Miniature* (1891), *Songs and Sonnets* (1893), and *Birds of Passage* (1895). She was also a translator, notably of Strauss's *The Old Faith and the New* (1873) and *The Journal of Marie Bashkirtseff* (1890). On her death Mathilde Blind left her property to Newnham College, Cambridge.

See also *The Poetical Works of Mathilde Blind* with a memoir of her by Richard Garnett, 1891. 　　　　A.P.

Blyton, Enid (Mary) (1897–1968), writer of children's books. Born in London, Enid Blyton was educated at St Christopher's School for Girls, Beckenham; she spent some years as a teacher at Bickley Park School, Kent, and as a nursery governess in Surbiton, before her marriage in 1924 to Hugh Pollock. (Some of her books were published under the name 'Mary Pollock'.) She had two daughters, was divorced in 1942, and in the following year married Kenneth Darrell Waters.

The standards of middle-class suburbia portrayed in her books faithfully reflect her own background, although in adolescence hers was not the 'happy family' that recurs as a motif in many of her books: she disliked her mother, and her father walked out on his wife and children when Enid was fifteen. In 1923 she started writing a column for *The Teacher's World;* in 1924 appeared her first volume for children, *The Enid Blyton Book of Fairies;* and from 1926 until 1952 she edited *Sunny Stories* magazine. Her output was prodigious: she wrote over six hundred books. Her enormous popularity dates from the later 1930s (*The Adventures of the Wishing Chair*, 1937; *The Enchanted Wood*, 1939) and the 1940s. She wrote for the nursery and the younger child: she claimed that she heeded no critic over the age of eleven.

Little Noddy in Toyland (1949) established her best-known character, his fame boosted by commercial exploitation. For an older age-group she wrote mystery and adventure stories concerned with, among others, the 'Famous Five' and the 'Secret Seven'. Her characters tend, indeed, to hunt in packs ('The Adventurous Four', 'The Six Bad Boys'). Then there are her school stories, whose titles, for example *The Naughtiest Girl in the School* (1940), are reminiscent of the works of Angela BRAZIL, although free from Brazil's fey whimsicality.

Enid Blyton's vocabulary and style are limited (the tones of the nursery governess can be clearly heard) and her delineation of character is sketchy. That her books are undemanding and so easily readable has been seen both as a virtue (they get the young child reading) and as a vice (they may spoil the reader for more demanding fare).

Enid Blyton's autobiography, *The Story of my Life*, was published in 1952. 　　　　J.L.

Boadicea. See BOUDICCA.

Bocher, Joan (?–1550), Anabaptist martyr. Her origins are unknown, though she is sometimes called Joan of Kent or Joan Knel. She first appears about 1540, supplying court ladies with copies of Tyndale's Protestant vernacular New Testament. Before 1543 she was charged with heresy, but Strype (see Bibliography) claims that Henry VIII himself intervened in her favour.

Joan Bocher's brand of Anabaptism involved the assertion that Christ's nature was wholly divine, and that consequently he had no human body born of the Virgin, but merely a phantom one. She was examined by Cranmer, Latimer and others in 1548, excommunicated in April 1549, and handed over to the Privy Council for punishment. She was imprisoned for a year, and though visited by such divines as Latimer, Whitehead, Ridley and Cranmer, she remained obdurate, On 2 May 1550 she was burned at Smithfield. The legend that Cranmer's single-minded vindictiveness caused her death is unacceptable, since she was tried and condemned by due process of law. However, her death demonstrates that religious toleration for all Protestants did not exist during the Protestant reign of Edward VI.

See also A. G. Dickens, *The English Reformation*, 1967; J. Foxe, *Acts and Monuments*, 1563; J. Strype, *Memorials of Cranmer*, 1848.   M.D.

Bodichon, Barbara (1827–91), campaigner for women's rights. She was the eldest daughter of Benjamin Leigh Smith, MP for Norwich, who gave his sons and daughters an equal education. He assured her financial independence by providing her with an income of £300 a year when she came of age, and he also influenced the direction of her philanthropic interests: the deeds of the Westminster School for Infants (which he administered and financed) were transferred to her, prompting her to establish the Portman Hall School, a non-denominational co-educational school for children.

Barbara Bodichon was an ardent campaigner for women's rights and a dynamic participant in the early feminist movement, bringing to it tireless energy and a considerable fortune. In 1854 she wrote *A Brief Summary in Plain Language of the Most Important Laws Concerning Women*, and during the next two years she petitioned for changes in the Married Women's Property Acts, which at that time gave married women virtually no control over their own money. *Women and Work* (1857), her most important publication,

argued the necessity of paid work for women. Female idleness, she stated, caused illness, whereas work gave women health, dignity, and independence. Her advocacy of work for women led to her involvement in the Society for the Promotion of the Employment of Women. She also helped to set up *The Englishwoman's Journal*, contributing articles to this and other magazines.

In the following decade Barbara Bodichon supported the campaign for the enfranchisement of women, and she was among the founders of the Women's Suffrage Committee of 1866. She believed that women were not only entitled to the vote but also to higher education. With Emily DAVIES she founded Girton College, Cambridge, of which she proved a generous benefactor.

A woman of many interests, she was also a talented and skilful artist. She exhibited in London and the provinces, and was a regular contributor to the Society of Female Artists. She painted watercolour landscapes of the English countryside and views of Algeria, where she spent part of each year after her marriage to Dr Eugène Bodichon in 1857. By the age of fifty her health had deteriorated. She retired from active campaigning, but continued to paint and to exhibit her work until the early 1880s. Her paintings may be seen at Girton College, and at Hastings Art Gallery.

See also H. Burton, *Barbara Bodichon, 1827–91*, 1949; J. W. Reed (ed.), *Barbara Leigh Smith Bodichon: An American Diary, 1857–58*, 1972.   D.C.

Boleyn, Anne (1507?–1536), second Queen of Henry VIII. Anne was the daughter of Sir Thomas Boleyn, courtier and diplomatist, by Elizabeth Howard, daughter of the second Duke of Norfolk. Little is known of her early life, and she is often confused with her sister Mary. Almost certainly, however, she went to France, possibly in Mary Tudor's retinue in 1514; and she may also have served Claude of France and Marguerite de Valois. She had returned to England by 1523.

It is not known when she first attracted Henry VIII, but when divorce proceedings opened in May 1527 she was undoubtedly queen-in-waiting. Besides ousting KATHERINE OF ARAGON, Anne aimed to replace Wolsey as the King's chief adviser. In 1529, having failed to procure the divorce, Wolsey fell from power, and Anne's influence with Henry was undisputed. She persuaded him to separate from Katherine in 1531, and accompanied him on a visit to the French King in October 1532. It was probably at about this time that she became Henry's mistress, since she was pregnant by January 1533; he married her secretly, to ensure the child's legitimacy. In May Cranmer pronounced Katherine's marriage invalid, in June Anne was crowned, and in September she gave birth to Princess (later Queen) ELIZABETH. The child's sex was a blow to Henry, but the Act of Succession of 1534 disinherited Katherine of Aragon's daughter, Princess MARY, and settled the crown on his children by Anne.

Both before and after her marriage Anne was a patron of 'the reformed religion'. She brought works by Tyndale and Fish to the King's notice, protected transgressors against the religious laws, and promoted radical churchmen; her more eminent clients included Hugh Latimer, Nicholas Shaxton, William Barlow, John Skip and Matthew Parker. Her radical policy, together with her arrogance and the widespread loyalty felt towards Queen Katherine and Princess Mary, made Anne unpopular and her position precarious. Moreover, she failed to provide the King with the desired male heir. When she miscarried of a son in January 1536 her fate was sealed, for Henry had become infatuated with Jane SEYMOUR, and Katherine of Aragon, whose existence made a new marriage impossible for him, had just died.

On 1 May Anne was arrested, together with four gentlemen of Henry's Privy Chamber (including her brother George) who were allegedly her partners in adultery. In fact they were her political supporters in the King's household, and the attack on Anne was a palace revolution organized by an uneasy alliance between the rising politician Thomas Cromwell and Princess Mary's supporters. Anne was tried by her peers, found guilty, and beheaded at the Tower on 19 May. A court under Cranmer declared Anne's marriage invalid; Elizabeth was consequently illegitimate, and therefore ineligible for the succession.

Anne Boleyn is important as the direct cause of the ecclesiastical breach with Rome, as the mother of Queen Elizabeth, and as a patron of reformed religion.

See also M. L. Bruce, *Anne Boleyn*, 1972.

M.D.

Bonaventure, Thomasine (?–1510?), Cornish benefactress. Born of humble parents at Week St Mary, Thomasine Bonaventure grew rich through successive marriages to London merchants. Her last husband, whom she married in 1498, was Sir John Percyvall, then Lord Mayor of London. On his death in 1504 she returned home to Cornwall. There her benefactions included relief of the poor and prisoners, bridge building, the founding of a chantry and free school, and the provision of dowries for local girls.

G.H.

Bondfield, Margaret (Grace) (1873–1953), Labour MP and first woman Cabinet minister. She was the second youngest of the eleven children of a Somerset lace-maker, and, finishing her own education at thirteen, she became a teaching assistant to infants in the local school and then a shop assistant in Brighton. For more than ten years, she worked in shops in London and elsewhere and acquired first-hand experience of shop conditions, of pay and hours and the pernicious 'living-in' system. She became convinced that the only hope of improvement lay in trade unionism, and in 1894 joined the Shop Assistants Union. From 1896 to 1908 she was its Assistant Secretary and got to know many of the influential unionists of the time. In particular, her friendship with Mary MACARTHUR of the National Federation of Women Workers, was dramatically to influence her life and thinking. She said afterwards that 'the inside knowledge I obtained of the appalling conditions ... of women wage earners turned me into an ardent socialist'.

She therefore became involved with the newly-formed Independent Labour Party and served on its Executive. With the death of Margaret MACDONALD she became organising secretary of the Women's Labour League, and during the First World War she served on various committees in her capacity as an expert on women's employment.

After the war, she travelled to Russia and America attending conferences of trade unionists and League of Nations conventions. When Mary Macarthur died in 1921, Margaret Bondfield took over from her the chairmanship of the Standing Joint Committee of Industrial Women's Organisations. In 1923 she was made Chairman of the General Council of the TUC, being the first woman ever to hold that office.

Thus, when she entered Parliament in 1923 (as Labour Member for Northampton), Margaret Bondfield had a very full and distinguished experience of unionism and public service behind her. It is not surprising then, that early in 1924 she was appointed Parliamentary Secretary to the Ministry of Labour, becoming the first woman to hold ministerial office in Britain. She lost her seat in the 1924 election, but returned to Parliament in 1926 as member for Wallsend. In the second Labour adminstration she became Minister of Labour, the first ever woman Cabinet Minister and Privy Councillor. Her time as minister was not, however, an easy one. She was forced to finance the Unemployment Insurance Fund by increasing its borrowing powers, and had to defend this and other decisions in a hostile House. She lost her seat in the 1931 election and was never to return to Parliament, although she was prospective Labour candidate for Reading when war broke out. She did valuable war work lecturing in the United States, and her years of public service were recognized by her creation as a CH in 1948. She wrote an autobiography, *A Life's Work* (1950). E.M.V.

Bonham Carter, (Helen) Violet, Lady Asquith of Yarnbury (1887–1969), public figure. Violet Asquith was the fourth of the five children of Herbert Henry Asquith and his first wife, Helen Melland, who died when she was four. During her childhood her father was establishing himself as a leading Liberal. In 1894 he married Margot Tennant and in 1908, when Violet was twenty-one, he became Prime Minister. In 1915 she married Maurice Bonham Carter, then her father's principal private secretary. They had four children, their daughter, Laura, marrying Jo Grimond, who was to become leader of the Liberal Party.

Violet Bonham Carter became her father's most loyal political ally, using her oratorical gifts to support him at meetings all over the country. During the difficult period of his feud with Lloyd George and his rejection by the electorate, she stood by him, as she herself said, often 'in an agony of solicitude'. After Asquith's death in 1927, she remained in the forefront of Liberal politics, supporting the National Government in 1931 and Free Trade against Protectionism in 1932. By 1933–34 she was in the vanguard of the attack on the personnel and policies of the Third Reich and a staunch supporter of the League of Nations Union Crusade. During the later 1930s, she took part in the agitation for the creation of a Ministry of Supply, and supported Churchill, advocating his inclusion in the Chamberlain administration.

Violet Bonham Carter was a passionate libertarian and supporter of all institutions and concerns which she believed would enhance or protect freedom, whether personal or national. She fought alongside Eleanor RATHBONE for family allowances, and called for electoral reform and a United States of Europe, bringing to all these causes her characteristic passionate conviction and brilliance of advocacy. In view of her enormous political ability, it is perhaps strange that she never sat in the House of Commons, although she stood for Parliament in 1945 and 1951. She was created DBE in 1953 and became a Life Peer in 1964. Among her publications was *Winston Churchill As I Knew Him* (1965). E.M.V.

Bonny, Anne (1700–?), pirate, came to fame on 28 November 1721 in Jamaica, where she was convicted of acts of piracy by the Vice-Admiralty Court. The record of this trial was printed but most of our knowledge of Bonny's life derives from the account by Captain Charles Johnson (possibly a pseudonym for Daniel Defoe) in *A General History . . . of the Most Notorious Pyrates* (1724). According to Johnson and later writers, Anne was born on 8 March 1700 near Cork, the illegitimate daughter of a prosperous lawyer and a serving maid. Because of the adultery, the family was obliged to emigrate to Charlestown, South Carolina, where Anne was raised in comfortable circumstances. She is described as a high-spirited girl who found the genteel conventions of plantation society inhibiting and rebelled against her father's wishes by marrying a poor seaman, James Bonny. Cut off from home and fortune, the couple shipped out to Providence Island, a haven for pirates. There Anne encountered 'Calico' Jack Rackam, who enticed her to abandon her husband and come aboard his ship dressed as a man. It is said that during this cruise she became pregnant by Rackam and was put ashore on Cuba to have the child, after which she returned to Rackam and a life of piracy, in which activity 'no Body was more forward or courageous than she'. In her last engagement she is reported to have stayed on deck fighting while all but one of the male crew cowered in the hold. She mockingly told Rackam as he went to his death that 'if he had fought like a man, he need not have been hang'd like a Dog'. Nothing is known of her life after the trial.

From the first, Bonny has been an attractive subject for writers, who have used her to dramatize political or social ideals from Lockean liberalism to lesbian liberation. But there is little in the historical record to suggest the heroic deeds or romantic character often ascribed to her career. The piracies with which she was charged were petty incidents, and her role was not a leading one. Although convicted, she pleaded pregnancy and was released (unlike most of her male shipmates, who were hanged).   D.D.H.

Booth, Catherine (1829–90), evangelist and joint founder of the Salvation Army. Born in Ashbourne, Derbyshire, she was the daughter of John Mumford, a coachbuilder and Wesleyan lay preacher. Her upbringing was uncompromisingly religious and also rather secluded, in that ill health prevented her from attending school for any length of time. In 1844 the family moved to Brixton, where Catherine experienced 'the assurance of eternal salvation'. She joined the Wesleyan Church but four years later was excommunicated for taking part in the 'Reform Movement'. She then held a class at the reformers' chapel, where in 1851 she met William Booth, the newly appointed pastor. In June 1855 they were married.

Initially William Booth was assigned to the work of itinerant missions, and on one of these in Halifax the first of their eight children was born. In 1858 they moved to Gateshead, and there Catherine, having written a powerful pamphlet defending the rights of woman in the Church, first entered her husband's pulpit. Thereafter she preached regularly. Her fame spread and she and her husband conducted numerous revival missions throughout the country until they settled in London in 1865. There they founded the Christian Revival Association which, with the purchasing of Whitechapel Market in 1870, developed into the People's Mission. Evangelical work was undertaken among all classes of society, Catherine Booth's ministry being particularly acceptable to the rich; in this way she was able to collect funds to support both her family and

her husband's work among the poor of London's East End. By 1877 the mission had developed into the Salvation Army, an idea which suited Catherine's rigorous and emotional response to religion. The Army's ranks were open to women preachers and officers, and this owed much to her influence, as did their rescue work among prostitutes.

By this time she was suffering greatly from illness and spent much of her time writing for *The War Cry*, the official magazine of the Army, and watching the triumphs of her children in the larger family she had helped to create. She participated in the social purity agitation of 1885, which culminated in the passing of the Criminal Law Amendment Act, and also gave her wholehearted support to female suffrage. In the following two years she held numerous revival meetings throughout the country. Knowing the gravity of her illness, she gave her last, highly emotional public address at the City Temple in June 1888, after which she retired to Clacton.

Catherine Booth managed to combine a busy family life with a demanding public one, and her work for the Salvation Army, her fame as a preacher, and her defence of the rights of women to participate as equals in the Christian Church were a manifestation of Christianity's role in extending women's traditional sphere. Her writings include *Papers on Practical Religion* (1879), and *Popular Christianity* (1887).

See also C. Bramwell-Booth, *Catherine Booth; the Story of Her Loves*, 1970; W. T. Stead, *Mrs Booth of the Salvation Army*, 1900.
                                J.G.S.

Booth, Evangeline (Cory) (1865–1950), salvationist; her first name was originally Eveline, but with a characteristic sense of dramatic effect she changed it to Evangeline. She was born on Christmas day in Hackney, a district in London's impoverished East End where her parents were carrying out their evangelical mission; they were William Booth, founder of the Salvation Army, and his wife Catherine BOOTH.

Thus Evangeline Booth was born into the Army, and by the time she had reached the age of fifteen had been promoted to the rank of sergeant. She soon proved herself a brilliant orator and an able, tough-minded organizer with a flair for attracting publicity. She directed the training college in London, then

(1896) organized the Army in Canada. In 1904 she was appointed National Commander for the United States, and over the next thirty years succeeded in expanding both the Army and its activities. In 1934 she was elected General of the entire Salvation Army—the fourth person and first woman to hold the post. She retired in 1939, spending her last years in the United States.

Evangeline Booth was a woman of energy and resource. In 1896 her brother, Ballington Booth, broke with the Salvation Army and tried to bring over the American membership to his own organization, the Volunteers of America, and for this purpose called a meeting of Salvation Army officers behind locked doors. Evangeline Booth is said to have climbed a fire escape and crawled through a window to enter the building; then she made an unexpected appearance on the platform of the meeting, and spoke to such effect that the assembled officers decided to remain within the movement.

She also wrote a number of popular hymns (*Songs of the Evangel*, 1927) and published her sermons (*Towards a Better World*, 1928).

See also P. W. Wilson, *The General: the story of Evangeline Booth*, 1935.　　N.H.

Bottome, Phyllis (1884–1963), novelist and short story writer, born at Rochester in Kent. She was the daughter of an American clergyman and a Yorkshirewoman. When she was nine her father was appointed to a living on Long Island, where she spent the next few years; later she travelled widely in Europe. She was educated privately; for a time she aspired to be an actress, but her ambitions were frustrated by an attack of tuberculosis which necessitated a cure at Davos in Switzerland. During the First World War she undertook relief work in Belgium and wrote propaganda articles. In 1917 she married A. E. Forbes Dennis, whom she accompanied to post-war Vienna, which provides the setting for much of her work. She wrote the first of her novels when she was seventeen (and had it published), but now only *Private Worlds* (1934) and *The Mortal Storm* (1937) find many readers; they reflect her absorption in the psychology of Alfred Adler, whose biography she wrote (1939), and her opposition to Nazism. She is most likely to be remembered for her highly professional short stories (*The Best Stories of Phyllis Bottome*, 1963). Her

memories and reflections are recorded in *Search for a Soul*, 1948, *The Challenge*, 1953, and *The Goal*, 1961.　　N.H.

Boucherett, Jessie (Emilia) (1825–1905), campaigner for women's rights. She was born at Willingham, near Market Rasen, Lincolnshire, and educated at the Miss Byerleys' ladies' school at Avonbank, Stratford-on-Avon. Her father was the local lord of the manor and High Sheriff of Lincolnshire in 1820, and her elder sister, Louisa (1821–95) was a pioneer in the movement for boarding out pauper children.

Jessie Boucherett's interest in feminism was kindled by reading Harriet MARTINEAU's article 'The Industrial Position of Women in England' in the *The Edinburgh Review* (April 1859) and by a copy of *The English Woman's Journal*, a feminist periodical, purchased at a railway bookstall. Moving to London in 1859, she met women with similar views to hers at the *Journal* office in Langham Place, Upper Regent Street, which became the centre for women's rights activities over the next few years. From then onwards, supported by her private income, she devoted her life to women's emancipation. In 1859, with Barbara BODICHON and Adelaide Anne PROCTER, she began the Society for the Promotion of Employment for Women, which ran a school to train young women as book-keepers, clerks, and cashiers. She financed *The English-woman's Review* (1866–1910), a periodical devoted to women's emancipation, and was its first editor (1866–70) and a regular contributor. An active suffragist, she helped to organize the first suffrage petition sent to Parliament in 1866 and campaigned for the right of married women to hold property. Politically conservative, she and Helen BLACKBURN founded in 1899 the Freedom of Labour Defence League, whose object was to oppose protective legislation for women workers. Her primary interest was the employment issue, because she thought that of all women's grievances the most widely felt and least difficult to remedy was their exclusion from the means of earning a livelihood. She addressed herself to this issue in several publications: 'How to Provide for Superfluous Women' in Josephine Butler (ed.), *Woman's Work and Woman's Culture* (1869), 'The Industrial Movement' in Theodore Stanton (ed.), *The Woman Question in Europe* (1884), and in *The Condition of Working*

Women and the Factory Acts (1896), written with Helen Blackburn. She also contributed to *The Edinburgh Review* and *The Contemporary Review*, wrote on manorial history, and advocated a return to the land. Possibly her most important contribution to the women's movement was the support she gave to *The Englishwoman's Review*, whose pages charted the course of liberal feminism from its mid-Victorian origins to its Edwardian heyday.

See also J. Kamm, *Rapiers and Battleaxes*, 1966.   L.W.

Boudicca (?–AD 62), Celtic warrior queen; 'Boadicea' used to be the preferred spelling of her name. Women warriors were acceptable in Celtic society and it is thought the general status of women was comparatively high. The calamity that befell Boudicca on the death of her husband, Prasutagus, King of the Iceni in eastern Britain, came from outside: the Roman overlords of Britain flogged her, raped her daughters, and seized her lands. Her revenge was terrible. Choosing a time when the governor, Suetonius Paulinus, was campaigning against the Druids in Anglesey, she led an army to devastate Colchester, London and Verulamium, massacring the inhabitants.

Before the final battle against Suetonius, who had hastened back from Wales, Boudicca drove in her chariot among her warriors, urging them to remember the Roman atrocities they had all suffered. A contemporary, Dio Cassius, wrote 'She was huge of frame, terrifying of aspect, and with a harsh voice. A great mass of bright red hair fell to her knees.'

Although her name derives from a Celtic word meaning 'victorious', her defeat was total and she poisoned herself on the battlefield. The effect of her rebellion was to lessen the severity of Roman rule.

See also N. K. Chadwick, *The Celts*, 1971; R. G. Collingwood and J. N. L. Myres, *Roman Britain and the English Settlements*, 2nd edn, 1937.   P.L.

Bowdler, Jane (1743–84), writer. Born at Ashley near Bath, she was the sister of Harriet and Thomas Bowdler, the editors of the notoriously 'bowdlerized' *Family Shakespeare*. She suffered an early attack of smallpox and was thereafter inclined to be silent and studious. After an attack of measles in 1777 her health was permanently undermined and she suffered continuously until her death. Her work was published for the benefit of the General Hospital at Bath, as *Poems and Essays by a Lady, Lately Deceased* (1786). The volume ran through many editions and is said to have been read three times by Queen CHARLOTTE, who somewhat surprisingly found it a great comfort.

See also T. Bowdler, *Memoir of the Late John Bowdler*, 1825; N. Perrin, *Dr Bowdler's Legacy*, 1970.   G.E.H.H.

Bowen, Elizabeth (Dorothea Cole) (1899–1973), novelist and short story writer, born in Dublin of Anglo-Irish descent. She lived first at Bowen's Court, Cork, her ancestral home, then in Hythe, Kent. She was educated at Downe House School, Kent.

Elizabeth Bowen began writing short stories in 1919: these were all rejected but were later published in book form as *Encounters* (1923). She married Alan Charles Cameron in 1923 and lived in Oxford. She published her first novel, *The Hotel*, in 1927, and thereafter produced work of consistently high quality every two or three years, including *The Last September*, 1929, *To The North*, 1933, and *The House in Paris*, 1936. She became one of the most distinguished novelists of her generation.

She defined the novel as 'a non-poetic statement of a poetic truth'. Her early novels are studies of youthful disillusion and betrayal. She has said of her writing at that time, 'I was beating myself against human unknowableness; in fact I made it my theme.'

During the Second World War, Elizabeth Bowen worked for the Ministry of Information by day and as an air-raid warden by night. She continued to write constantly, being especially concerned with 'the divorce between public belief and behaviour and private intuition'. From these preoccupations came *The Heat of the Day* (1949) and wide popular acclaim. She also published essays, criticism and biography. Her novel *Eva Trout* (1969) won the James Tait Black prize. *Collected Short Stories* appeared posthumously in 1980.

Trinity College, Dublin, honoured her with a D.Litt. (1948); Oxford did likewise (1956). She received the CBE in 1948.

See also V. Glendinning, *Elizabeth Bowen: Portrait of a Writer*, 1977; H. Lee, *Elizabeth Bowen*, 1981.   P.L.

Bowen, Marjorie (1886–1952), was the best-known pseudonym of the novelist Margaret Gabrielle Long; she also published under several other names, notably 'Joseph Shearing' and 'George Preedy'. She was born on Hayling Island, where her family were living in poverty, but managed to study at the Slade School of Art and spend a year in Paris; however, the need to support her family was already an important spur to achievement. Her first novel was published when she was sixteen, and thereafter her output was prodigious; she is reckoned to have written at least 150 books. A contemporary description of her as 'the best serious writer of high romance now publishing' indicates the nature and limitations of her fiction. The majority of her works were swashbuckling historical novels such as *The Viper of Milan* (1906), but she also wrote a number based on famous criminal cases, and she was a prolific biographer (of William Cobbett, Hogarth, Mary Wollstonecraft Godwin and others). She was married twice. Her autobiography, *The Debate Continues* (1939), was published under her maiden name, Margaret Campbell.   N.H.

Bowes, Elizabeth (?1502–1568), Protestant zealot. The daughter of a Yorkshire knight, she married Richard Bowes, the captain of Norham Castle, and had fifteen children by him. Living at Berwick during the reign of Edward VI, she became deeply involved with the Scottish minister John Knox, whose counsel and preaching - strengthened her Protestant convictions. When Knox wished to marry her fifth daughter Marjory (?1534–1560), Elizabeth supported his proposal despite the opposition of her husband and his family, and Knox and Marjory were betrothed in January 1553. The accession of Mary I brought danger to Protestant preachers and in early 1554 Knox was forced to flee to the Continent, where he wrote his *Exposition of the Sixth Psalm* for Elizabeth, urging her to remain constant in the faith.

It was, Knox claimed, chiefly at the request of Elizabeth Bowes that in 1555 he returned to Scotland. Here Marjory married Knox, and in 1556, when the preacher returned to the Continent, she and Elizabeth went into exile at Geneva with him. Elizabeth Bowes' abandonment of husband and country was a brave step and attests to the power of sixteenth-century religious beliefs. Shortly after the return of Elizabeth and the Knox family from exile in 1559, Marjory died. Elizabeth, now a widow, stayed with her son-in-law to help raise her grandchildren but it is uncertain whether she continued in Knox's household after his remarriage in 1564. The date of her death is usually given as 1568.

Elizabeth Bowes was a woman of strong religious convictions and even stronger doubts. Her correspondence with Knox, which also reveals much about the Reformer, shows a woman obsessed with her own sinfulness. Knox said that she cried and complained to God more often than anyone he had known and that her constant need of counsel and reassurance was often burdensome to him. Despite this, her adherence to Protestantism in the face of family pressure (both she and Marjory went unmentioned in her husband's will), and her choice of exile, demonstrate how much of the strength of the English Reformation lay in its women disciples.

See also W. S. Reid, *Trumpeter of God*, 1974; J. Ridley, *John Knox*, 1968.   G.Q.B.

Boyle, Nina (1866–1943), suffragette, one of the more vivid personalities among those who campaigned for women's suffrage. She never resorted to the more violent methods employed in the cause, although she delighted in annoying the authorities and was imprisoned more than once. For many years she was associated with the Save the Children Fund, an activity which included relief work in Macedonia during the First World War and afterwards in Russia. She was a member of the Women's Freedom League and organized the first voluntary women police in the earliest days of the First World War. An excellent raconteuse and public speaker, she also wrote novels.

                                B.H.C.

Bracegirdle, Anne (1663?–1748), actress, the daughter of Richard Bracegirdle of Wolverhampton, who entrusted her to the care of the actors Thomas and Mary BETTERTON. This upbringing must have helped Anne's theatrical career, which started in earnest in January 1688, when she is first listed as a member of the United Company. Her first recorded performance as the young Antelina in Mountfort's *The Injured Lovers* (about March 1688) was followed by a number of *ingénue* roles which enhanced her popularity and reputation. Successful in Shakespearian parts, particularly

Desdemona and Ophelia, she also inspired and created many new roles in plays by leading contemporary dramatists. She generally played the part of the romantic *ingénue*, virtuous and chaste, and her infectious charm and vivacity made her outstanding in high comedy. Her reputation as a leading lady was firmly established by her performance as Araminta, the lovely heroine of William Congreve's first play, *The Old Bachelor* (1693). Her association with Congreve continued, and she took the heroine's part in all his plays, achieving her greatest triumphs in them.

In 1695 Anne Bracegirdle joined Thomas Betterton and Elizabeth BARRY in leading a group of actors who broke away from the United Company and set up their own company. Her premature retirement from the stage in 1707 seems to have been connected with her rivalry with a younger actress, Mrs OLDFIELD, who played with the other company, and with the pending union of the two companies.

Anne Bracegirdle never married, although she was romantically linked with Congreve and with the Earl of Scarsdale. Her discretion in her private life gave her a unique reputation as the 'Romantick Virgin', an image which she cultivated and which enhanced her popularity. Anne Bracegirdle made an important contribution to the development of Restoration drama and, as an early professional actress, to the interpretation of female roles, inspiring many new ones.

See also J. H. Wilson, *All the King's Ladies: Actresses of the Restoration*, 1958.

T.J.M.

Braddock, Bessie (1899–1970), politician. Born Elizabeth Margaret Bamber in Liverpool, she grew up in a strong radical political tradition. Her father, Hugh Bamber, was a well-paid skilled bookbinder and her mother Mary came from a well-to-do Edinburgh legal family which had lost its money, making her aware of inequality and injustice. Mary Bamber, who became National Organizer of the National Union of Distributive and Allied Workers, was a potent influence on her daughter. She was a dedicated socialist whom Sylvia Pankhurst called 'the finest fighting platform speaker in the country', and Bessie Bamber grew up in an atmosphere of dedication to the war against social deprivation. Important too in her political education were the Liverpool streets of

the early years of the century, full of hungry children and men without work, for in spite of its prosperity as a port, Liverpool had the highest rates of pauperism and infant mortality in the country. She worked for the Co-operative movement and joined the ILP. In 1922 she married Jack Braddock, who shared her political interests. They had no children, but their marriage, which lasted until Jack's death in 1963, was extremely close and 'The Braddocks' became legendary in Merseyside politics. He never went to Westminster but became Leader of the Liverpool City Council, while she stood in 1945 for the Exchange division of the city, which she represented until 1970. However, she remained deeply involved in local government as a member of the Liverpool City Council from 1930 until 1961 and as an Alderman from 1955 to 1961. In the House she was known as a defiant champion of working people, in particular of better housing conditions, better educational opportunities, and workers' organizations. She earned the reputation of being very direct, sometimes less than polite, in her speech, often displaying utter contempt for her political opponents. She was not a good party woman, for although she was fiercely partisan, she stood for certain values and gave her support to those suffering deprivation or injustice without regard to any party line. Perhaps unsurprisingly, then, she never held office but fought from the back benches for the working people to whom she had dedicated her life.

See also J. and B. Braddock, *The Braddocks*, 1963; M. Toole, *Mrs Bessie Braddock, MP*, 1957.

E.M.V.

Braddon, Mary (Elizabeth) (1837–1915), novelist, the daughter of a Cornish solicitor. She was born in London and educated privately. When she was four her mother left her father, taking the children with her. This meant that there was always a shortage of money, and in 1857 Mary became an actress to help support her mother and herself. In 1860 she left the stage to write when a Yorkshire printer offered her £10 for a story 'combining Dickens and Marryat'. In 1861 she met John Maxwell, the publisher of *Robin Goodfellow* and other magazines. He ran Mary Braddon's most famous novel, *Lady Audley's Secret* (1862), as a serial in *The Sixpenny Magazine*. A melodramatic tale of a golden-haired murderess, this story of crime in high society appeared in book form the following year and became an enormous popular success, selling nearly a million copies and making its author and publisher rich for life.

Mary Braddon's expertise as a sensational novelist is unquestionable. Although *Lady Audley's Secret* remained her most famous book, *Aurora Floyd* and *John Marchmont's Legacy* (both 1863) maintained a reputation which was to be sustained through the publication of over seventy novels. It was not for nothing that her publishers called her 'the queen of the circulating libraries'.

Mary Braddon lived with John Maxwell until his wife's death in an Irish mental hospital in 1874, when they married. Two of her sons, W. B. Maxwell and Gerald Maxwell, themselves became well-known novelists. As well as writing novels, she wrote poems and plays, edited magazines including *Temple Bar* and *Belgravia*, and contributed to *Punch* and *The World*. Although her work was attacked for its 'sensationalism' and 'immorality', it was admired by Thackeray and Stevenson. Her first novel is still the book she is remembered for, although *Ishmael* (1884) is probably the best, relying more on character than sensation. Her work is now being reappraised, for in much of her writing she shows an aptitude for social satire (particularly of codes of feminine weakness and romance) and for the creation of atmosphere.   A.P.

Bradstreet, Anne (*c.* 1612–1672), first English woman poet in America. She was the daughter of Thomas Dudley, steward to the Earl of Lincoln, and in 1628 married Simon Bradstreet, who had been brought up in the Earl's family and was then steward to the Countess of Warwick. In 1630 Anne and Simon Bradstreet and her parents sailed to New England, settling first at Charlestown, later (1634) at Ipswich, Massachusetts, and finally (1638) at nearby Merrimac; Anne had the first of her eight children in 1640. She had already written a number of poems which circulated in manuscript and brought her a considerable reputation, aided perhaps by the distinction of her family and connections (her father had already served as governor of the Massachusetts Bay colony). In 1650 her work was published in London as *The Tenth Muse, Lately Sprung up in America;* an American edition of her poems did not appear until 1678. Aspects of her life (her husband's trip to England as secretary to the colony, the deaths of grandchildren) are glanced at in some of the later verse. Much of her work is imitative of Sir Philip Sidney, the once influential Du Bartas, and similar models; and a didactic Puritanism restricts her sensibility. But she could write effectively and affectingly in shorter pieces, and sometimes spiritedly, as when she considers the subversive greatness of Queen Elizabeth:

> Now, say, have women worth? Or have they none?
> Or had they some, but with our Queen is't gone?
> Nay, Masculines, you have thus taxed us long,
> But she, though dead, will vindicate our wrong.
> Let such as say our sex is void of reason
> Know 'tis a slander now, but once was treason.   N.H.

Brahms, Caryl (1901–82), novelist and playwright notable for her skilful blending of wit with wild farce. She was born in Surrey and educated privately and at the Royal Academy of Music. She had a long career in London as a reviewer of plays and ballets, and a fascination with the theatre and its personalities is evident in much of her work.

Although she wrote *The Rest of the Evening's My Own*, 1964, and other works by herself, Caryl Brahms was most comfortable and effective when writing in collaboration. From 1937 S. J. Simon was her literary partner. They published *A Bullet in the Ballet* (1937), and two sequels (all three collected as *Stroganoff in the Ballet* (1975). They also wrote *Don't Mr Disraeli* (1940), *No Bed for Bacon* (1941), and other novels that treated historical clichés and stereotypes in a spirit of farcical exaggeration (Francis Bacon is constantly thwarted in his efforts to acquire one of the many beds in which Queen Elizabeth has slept) that was then quite unusual. Later, Caryl Brahms began a prolific collaboration with Ned Sherrin which included novels, short stories, television productions and musicals such as *Cindy-Ella*, 1962, *Sing a Rude Song*, 1970, and *The Mitford Girls*, 1981.   N.H.

Braithwaite, Dame (Florence) Lilian (1873–1948), actress. Born in Ramsgate, the daughter of a clergyman, she was educated at Hampstead and Croydon High Schools and spent a year studying the piano in Dresden. She acted with amateur companies in London before marrying the actor-manager Gerald Lawrence in 1897 and accompanying his Shakespearian company to South Africa. In 1900 she made her first London appearance in *As You Like It*, played in more Shakespeare with Sir Frank Benson in 1901, and consolidated her reputation in productions by the leading actors of the day, including Tree, Alexander and Du Maurier.

In 1912 Lilian Braithwaite played the Madonna in Reinhardt's production of *The Miracle*, but her talent for comedy proved her greatest asset; it was put to skilful use in a long succession of drawing-room dramas and light comedies, culminating in the long-running *Arsenic and Old Lace* (1942–46). She also created with great success the neurotic Florence Lancaster in Coward's *The Vortex* (1924).

An intelligent and stylish actress, notable for her wit both on and off the stage, Lilian Braithwaite served during the Second World War as chairman and chief organiser of the hospital division of ENSA. She was created DBE in 1943.   K.W.

Brassey, Lady Anna, also known as Annie (1839–87), writer and traveller. Her maiden name was Allnutt, and in 1860 she became the wife of Thomas Brassey, a prominent Liberal MP and authority on naval affairs. His wife proved an able and helpful assistant in his political career. She also joined him on the annual voyages they made in the yacht 'The Sunbeam'. The notes she made on these journeys were later assembled into books written for private circulation among her friends, and they proved so popular that she was encouraged to publish them. They were received with great interest, particularly *The Voyage in the Sunbeam: Our Home on the Ocean for Eleven Months* (1878), which described the Brasseys' world tour of 1876–77. While on her travels, Lady Anna was able to collect various interesting and curious objects, natural and ethnographical, which formed the basis of a museum at her home. It was on one of her voyages, taken for her health, that she died at sea near Brisbane, Australia, at the age of forty-seven. The previous year she had become Baroness Brassey. Her works cover the extensive travels which she undertook around the world. They include *Sunshine and Storm in the East: or Cruises to Cyprus and Constan-*

tinople, 1880, *In the Trades, the Tropics and the Roaring Forties*, 1885, and *The Last Voyage*, which was edited by M. A. Broome and published posthumously in 1889.   B.H.C.

Brazil, Angela (1868–1947), writer of school stories for girls. Born at Preston, Lancashire, she was the daughter of a cotton-mill manager; she was educated at Manchester Preparatory High School and at Ellerslie College, of which she became head girl. Her first full-length book, *A Terrible Tomboy* (1904), contains a romanticized self-portrait in 'Peggy'. This was not in fact a school story; but with *A Fourth Form Friendship* (1911) the genre that she was to make famous over the next three decades had emerged: jolly, extroverted tales characterized by adventurous 'scrapes', warm but innocent schoolgirl attachments, the gentle inculcation of knowledge on history, literature, botany and numerous other subjects, and an extravagant slang that is dated but diverting. By the time she published her last book of the sort, *The School on the Loch* (1946), the formula had become stereotyped. As well as over fifty full-length stories Angela Brazil wrote short stories that appeared in schoolgirl annuals. She never married. Her books include *The Nicest Girl in the School*, 1909, *A Patriotic Schoolgirl*, 1918, *Ruth of St Ronan's*, 1927, and the autobiographical *My Own Schooldays*, 1925.

See also M. Cadogan and P. Craig, *You're a Brick, Angela!* 1976; G. Freeman, *The Schoolgirl Ethic: the Life and Work of Angela Brazil*, 1976.   J.L.

Bride, St. See BRIGIT, ST.

Bridge, Ann, pseudonym of Mary Dolling Sanders (1891–1974), popular novelist. She was born at Bridgend in Surrey, of an English father and an American mother. She spent part of her childhood in Italy, was educated at home, and went on to study at the London School of Economics. In 1913 she married Sir Owen St Clair O'Malley, whose diplomatic career took the couple to China, Yugoslavia and other countries that were to become the settings for Ann Bridge's fiction. She carefully maintained her pseudonym for years in order to protect her husband's career; she herself said that she was before all else a wife and mother, which may have limited her achievement. Her first novel, *Peking Picnic* (1932), was an immediate success, winning the Atlantic Monthly Prize. It established the pattern of her work, in which an essentially romantic story takes place against a closely observed exotic background; examples include *Illyrian Spring*, 1935, *Enchanter's Nightshade*, 1937, *The Dark Moment*, 1952, and *Episode at Toledo*, 1966. *Permission to Resign: goings-on in the Corridors of Power*, 1971, tells how she succeeded in vindicating her husband after he had been asked to leave the Foreign Office for allegedly speculating in French currency.

N.H.

Bridgeman, Caroline Beatrix, Viscountess Bridgeman (1872–1961), politician. Of upper-class parentage, in 1895 she married the Conservative politician Viscount Bridgeman, who subsequently became Home Secretary and First Lord of the Admiralty. Her involvement with Conservative politics dated from the early years of the century, when she was associated with the Tariff Reform League Women's Association, formed to support the protectionist policies of Joseph Chamberlain.

With the rapid growth of party membership among women following the establishment of their own organization in 1918, she pressed successfully for a greater voice for women in policy-making and became the first woman chairman of the National Union of Conservative and Unionist Organizations. She remained for many years a leading figure in women's Conservatism.

Outside politics, Viscountess Bridgeman was closely involved in many aspects of public affairs, serving as a governor of the BBC (1935–39), a member of the House of Laity of the Church Assembly from 1930 and later its vice-chairman (1942–47), and as a member of the Royal Commission on London Squares. She was created DBE in 1924.

K.W.

Bridges, Dame Daisy Caroline (1894–1972), nurse. She was educated at Heathfield School, Ascot, and the Ladies' College, Cheltenham. During the First World War she worked for the British Red Cross and was mentioned in dispatches. After training at the Nightingale School of St Thomas's Hospital, she joined the staff of St Thomas's in 1925, remaining there until 1936. A Rockefeller fellowship took her to the United States and Canada in 1937–38. During the Second World War she worked in France, Egypt, and India. Having retired with the rank of Principal Matron, she served on the working party on the recruitment and training of nurses (1946–47) before her appointment as General Secretary (1948–61) of the International Council of Nurses. She published *A History of the International Council of Nurses* (1967).

N.H.

Bright, Mary (Chavelita) (1860–1945), novelist and dramatist who used the pseudonym 'George Egerton'. She was born in Melbourne, Australia, the daughter of a captain, and was educated privately.

Mary Bright was married three times. Her first husband, H. H. W. Melville, died in 1889, the year after their marriage. Two years later she married Egerton Clairmonte, a novelist who died after ten years of marriage. Her third marriage, in 1901, was to the journalist and authors' agent Reginald Golding Bright.

Mary Bright wanted to be an artist before she turned to writing. Her first novel, *Keynotes* (1893), was an exploration of married life. It was followed by *Discords*, 1894, *Symphonies*, 1897, *Fantasies*, 1898, and *Flies in Amber*, 1905. She also adapted Henry Bernstein's play *La Rafale* (as *The Whirlwind*), 1911, and translated Knut Hamsun's novel *Hunger* (1926). She was an original founder of the Irish Genealogical Research Society and lived in London, travelling in Europe and America. Her other works include: *Young Olef's Ditties*, 1895, *The Wheel of God*, 1898, *Rosa Amorosa*, 1901, and two plays, *His Wife's Family* 1908, and *The Backsliders*, 1910.

A.P.

Brightwen, Eliza (1830–1906), naturalist. She was born Eliza Elder at Banff in Scotland, but spent her childhood near London in the care of her uncle, Alexander Elder, who was a founder of the publishing company Smith, Elder, & Company. She had no regular formal education, but read a great many books on what was to be a lifelong passion, natural history. At the age of twenty-five she married a banker, George Brightwen. Their home at Stanmore in Middlesex, called 'The Grove', was surrounded by a large wooded estate, complete with shrubberies, a lake, and a large garden. Here she was able to spend her time in philanthropic work and, above all, in following up her interest in natural history by observing the animals and plants of her own garden. She had no children and her husband died in 1883.

It was not until her sixtieth year that Eliza

Brightwen began to write, but such was the impact of her books that she became one of the most popular naturalists of her time. *Wild Nature Won by Kindness* appeared in 1890, *More about Wild Nature* in 1892, *Inmates of My House and Garden* in 1895, *Glimpses into Plant Life* in 1898, *Rambles with Nature Students* in 1899 and *Quiet Hours with Nature* in 1903. *Last Hours with Nature* was published posthumously in 1908. Her books were composed from the storehouses of her own personal notes. She used nothing from othe writers and accepted no authority other than her own observation. The undoubted affinity that she had with wild creatures was described as a sort of 'natural magic'. She died at Stanmore, aged 76.

See also W. H. Chesson (ed.), *Eliza Brightwen: the Life and Thoughts of a Naturalist*, 1909. B.H.C.

Brigit, St (453–523), nun, born at Faugher near Dundalk, the daughter of the nobleman Dubhthach and his concubine Brotsech. Dubhthach allegedly tried to sell Brigit to the King of Leinster but the latter freed her. She refused to submit to her father's pressure to marry, and took the veil. Many legends accreted round her name: that, as an infant, she was surrounded by miraculous fire; that she produced prodigious supplies of dairy produce; and that she and her nuns attended a perpetual fire at Kildare which burned without ash and was unseen by male eyes. The nature of these tales suggests that her cult was confounded with that of an earlier fertility and fire goddess at Kildare. Her foundation of a double monastery there is one certain fact of her career; Brigit appointed Condlaed as monastic bishop of the house of monks and nuns. She died at Kildare on 1 February 523 and was buried there. P.A.S.

Briouse, Matilda (?–1210), the wife of William de Briouse (or Braose), lord of Brecon and for many years an intimate, lavishly rewarded friend of King John. But William's immense power, and an indiscreet reference by Matilda to the murder of Arthur of Brittany (of which the King was suspected), eventually provoked John's bitter wrath against the Briouse family. Matilda's husband fled, but she and her eldest son William were imprisoned in Windsor castle and starved to death by royal command, to the disgust of an increasingly disgruntled English baronage.

See also S. Painter, *The Reign of King John*, 1949. K.R.D.

Brittain, Vera (Mary) (1893–1970), writer, journalist, and lecturer. Her public life was devoted to peace and the liberation of women, and her deeply felt and forcibly expressed convictions excited considerable controversy. She was born in Newcastle, Staffordshire, and educated at St Monica's, Kingswood, and Somerville College, Oxford, where she was an Exhibitioner in 1914. During the First World War, she served as a VAD nurse (1915–19) in London, Malta, and France.

Vera Brittain achieved international recognition in 1933 with *Testament of Youth*, a passionately outspoken autobiographical record of the First World War in which her fiancé and only brother were killed. This caught the high tide of disillusionment with the war, and was acclaimed as 'the real war book of the women of England'. Its marked undertones of feminism and pacifism made a profound impact on contemporary thought, and became features of all her writing. *Testament of Friendship* (1940) told the story of her great friend, the novelist Winifred HOLTBY.

In 1937 Vera Brittain became a sponsor of the Peace Pledge Union, contributing regularly to numerous pacifist publications. Her pamphlet *Seed of Chaos* (1944) caused a furore in America, with headlines proclaiming 'British Woman Pacifist rouses US fury'. *Testament of Experience* (1957) continued her autobiography from 1925 to 1950, and is a significant historical record and pacifist odyssey. She chaired the *Peace News* board from 1958 to 1964 during the period of its radical commitment to non-violent direct action, and actively supported the Campaign for Nuclear Disarmament, the Anglican Pacifist Fellowship, Christian Action, the Women's International League for Peace and Freedom, and the Fellowship of Reconciliation. She travelled widely, lecturing throughout Great Britain, undertaking seven lecture tours in Canada and the USA between 1934 and 1959, and also lecturing in Holland (1936), Scandinavia (1945), Germany (1947), India and Pakistan (1949–50), and India (1963); in 1960 she addressed the University of Natal Jubilee Conference.

Brontë, Anne

Vera Brittain's twenty-nine books include novels, biography, history, travel, and a selection of letters. Among them are *Account Rendered*, 1945, *Born 1925, A Novel of Youth*, 1949, *In the Steps of John Bunyan*, 1950, *Search after Sunrise*, 1951, and *Lady into Woman: A History of Women from Victoria to Elizabeth II*, 1953. She was a dedicated Anglican, worshipping at St Martin-in-the-Fields, for which she wrote a pamphlet, *The Story of St Martin's* (1951). In 1925 she married Professor (later Sir) George E. G. Catlin, political philosopher, writer and professor at McGill University, Canada, by whom she had a son and a daughter, the politician Shirley Williams. She bridged successfully the conflicting claims of her domestic and professional life, and was warmly supportive to her family and friends.

See also P. Berry, *Testament of Faith: the Story of Vera Brittain* (in preparation); A. Bishop (ed.), *Chronicle of Youth: War Diary 1913–17*, 1981.   P.B.

Brontë, Anne (1820–49), novelist and poet, the youngest and least known of the Brontë sisters. The only formal education she received was at Miss Wooler's school at Roe Head, where she stayed for a few months in 1837. At the age of nineteen she left home, going to Blake Hall, where she was governess to the Inghams, an extremely difficult family with whom she stayed for only nine months. Her next post, with the Robinsons of Thorp Green, was more rewarding. She remained with them between 1841 and 1845, resigning only when her brother Branwell, who was tutor to the family, was dismissed after the discovery of his infatuation with Mrs Robinson. Anne too suffered from an unrequited, if more controlled, love, the object of which was her father's curate, William Weightman.

Anne Brontë's first novel, *Agnes Grey*, was written in 1845, while Emily was writing *Wuthering Heights* and Charlotte was engaged on *The Professor*. The following year all three sisters produced *Poems by Currer, Ellis, and Acton Bell*, which was not a success. *Agnes Grey* and *Wuthering Heights* were published together in 1847. After the appearance of Anne's second novel, *The Tenant of Wildfell Hall* (1848), Anne and Charlotte went to London to convince their publishers, Smith and Elder, that they (writing as Acton and Currer Bell) were two separate people.

Although some found it shocking, *The Tenant of Wildfell Hall* did very well, and a new edition was put out in the year of publication. Anne wrote a preface to this new edition in defence of herself, remarking that 'I am at a loss to conceive how a man should permit himself to write anything that would be really disgraceful to a woman, or why a woman should be censured for writing anything that would be proper and becoming for a man.' While *Agnes Grey* was largely autobiographical, *The Tenant of Wildfell Hall* was an altogether more melodramatic work, the story of a marriage ruined by the dissipation of the husband; the erring spouse may have been modelled on Branwell Brontë. However, Anne's novels give an accurate picture of middle-class country life in early nineteenth-century England, and George Moore considered *The Tenant of Wildfell Hall* to have been seriously underrated.

It is likely that Anne Brontë was strongly influenced by her sisters and that without them she would not have been inspired to write. She was a shy and retiring person, spending more of her life at her father's parsonage than either of her sisters. Soon after Emily's death in 1848 she developed tuberculosis. The following year she died at Scarborough, where she had gone for the sea air.

See also W. T. Hale, *Anne Brontë: her life and writings*, 1929; A. M. Harrison, *Anne Brontë: Her Life and Work*, 1959; Clement Shorter (ed.), *The Complete Poems of Anne Brontë*, 1921; W. H. Stevenson, *Emily and Anne Brontë*, 1968.   A.P.

Brontë, Charlotte (1816–55), novelist, born at Thornton, the daughter of the Reverend Patrick Brontë, an Irishman, and his wife Maria Branwell. In 1820 the family moved to Haworth, where Brontë became curate, and in 1821 Mrs Brontë died, leaving five daughters and one son, Branwell.

They were precocious children and in 1823 the four eldest daughters were sent to a school for clergymen's daughters at Cowan Bridge (later described, under the name Lowood, in *Jane Eyre*). Miserable conditions caused the deaths of the two eldest girls, and Emily and Anne were withdrawn to be educated at home. It was at this time that Charlotte and Branwell began to write about the imaginary island of Angria, an alternative world which was to preoccupy their imaginations for years.

From 1831 to 1832 Charlotte attended Miss Wooler's school at Roe Head. Then, after three years at home teaching her younger sisters and reading avidly, she returned to Roe Head in 1835 as a teacher. Despite some unhappiness she stayed there until Christmas 1837, when the ill health of Anne alarmed her and they went home. Charlotte returned in 1838 for a short period and also worked in 1839 and 1841 as a governess.

Charlotte continued to write, despite a discouraging response from the poet Southey, who told her that a woman should not make literature her career. Dependent for their home at the parsonage on their father's increasingly precarious health, the sisters needed employment. To further a plan to start their own school, Emily and Charlotte went in 1842 to the Hégers' finishing school in Brussels. After their initial period of six months they were engaged as pupil-teachers, but late that year the death of their aunt (the parsonage housekeeper) recalled them to Haworth. In January 1843 Charlotte returned to Brussels alone, where she developed a passion for Monsieur Héger. She returned home in January 1844, unhappy and lonely, her despondency increasing as Héger's letters became less frequent. The school plan also failed: the sisters advertised for pupils, but none came.

In 1846 *Poems by Currer, Ellis, and Acton Bell* (that is, Charlotte, Emily, and Anne Brontë) was published but received little attention. Charlotte's first novel, *The Professor*, was repeatedly rejected by publishers (it appeared posthumously). But in 1847 *Jane Eyre* was published and was a sensational success. Drawing on her own experience, and showing some influence from the Gothic novel, Charlotte's story of the passionate heroine who refuses to compromise her moral integrity or independence remains her most popular work.

The writing of *Shirley* (1849), set against a background of industrial depression and machine-breaking in the Yorkshire of 1807–12, was interrupted by the deaths of Branwell, Emily, and Anne (1848–49). *Villette* (1853), was well received, although considered somewhat 'coarse' in its portrayal of a woman passionately in love.

Now alone at home with her infirm father, Charlotte was simultaneously becoming famous. She made frequent visits to London, moving in literary circles and seeing friends, including Mrs GASKELL, whom she met in 1850 and who was to write a famous biography of Charlotte Brontë. In 1852 Charlotte rejected her fourth marriage proposal, this time from her father's curate, A. B. Nicholls. He left Haworth in May 1853 but gradually won Charlotte's love and her father's consent. They were married in June 1854 but the following March, after a long illness and at the approach of childbirth, Charlotte died and was buried at Haworth.

Charlotte Brontë was the only one of the three novelist sisters for whom writing became a career, and her work draws heavily on her own experiences. Her novels show a deep concern with the position of women and are remarkable for their portrayal of women as independent and questioning beings. The originality and almost magical quality of her writing marked her out amongst contemporary writers and she continues to be considered a major nineteenth-century novelist.

See also W. Gérin, *Charlotte Brontë: The Evolution of Genius*, 1967; R. B. Martin, *The Accents of Persuasion: Charlotte Brontë's Novels*, 1966; T. J. Wise and J. A. Symington (eds), *The Poems of Charlotte Brontë and Patrick Branwell Brontë*, 1934, and *The Brontës: Their Lives, Friendships and Correspondence*, 1932.   J.H.

Brontë, Emily (Jane) (1818–48), poet and novelist. Emily was born at Thornton, the fourth daughter of Patrick and Maria Brontë and sister to Charlotte and Anne BRONTË. From November 1824 to June 1825 Emily attended the school at Cowan Bridge which caused the deaths of her two eldest sisters. She was then taught at home but her education was unmethodical and she spent much time roaming the wild moors around Haworth, where the family lived from 1820. Her passion for this landscape was to last for life and to be a major influence on her writing. The children passed some of their time in composing minutely-written romantic stories of faraway kingdoms, Emily creating the Gondal Chronicles, to which Anne also contributed. Emily worked on these chronicles as late as 1845, incorporating her poems in them.

In 1835 Emily went as a pupil to Roe Head, where Charlotte was teaching, but the regulation and methods of instruction at the school seemed totally alien after the freedom and independence to which she had become accustomed. Ill from homesickness and general

65

unhappiness, she left after less than three months, to be replaced by Anne. In 1837 Emily taught for six months in Halifax but again felt confined and unhappy. She soon returned home, but this period away had an effect that was to appear recurrently in her work.

It now became accepted among the family that Emily was to stay at home. And so, while Charlotte and Anne were often away, Emily spent more time with Branwell, whose increasing instability and addictions were a source of great anxiety and distress. However, in 1842 Emily accompanied Charlotte to the Hégers' school at Brussels, where they spent nine months, returning to Haworth on their aunt's death. Emily spent the rest of her life at the parsonage in close contact with her father, who increasingly depended on her to read to him as his eyesight deteriorated.

Emily continued to write privately, and in the autumn of 1845 Charlotte accidentally discovered Emily's poems. Emily was furious at their disclosure, and although she agreed to a joint publication of her and her sisters' poetry, she was never happy about the enterprise. The collection appeared in 1846 as *Poems by Currer, Ellis, and Acton Bell*. Another rare outbreak of fury by Emily occurred when Charlotte accidentally made known the identity of 'Ellis Bell'.

During 1846 Emily was writing *Wuthering Heights*, her passionate story of the love of Catherine Earnshaw and Heathcliff, and reading completed sections aloud to her sisters. She was becoming increasingly involved with Branwell and his excesses, and in *Wuthering Heights* both Heathcliff and Hindley Earnshaw contain aspects of Branwell's character. The novel was published in 1847. Then in 1848 Branwell died and Emily was distraught. She refused to take medicine or proper rest for a cold caught at his funeral and died in December 1848, within three months of Branwell's death. She was buried at Haworth.

Despite her short life and small output, Emily is a major figure in English literature, since *Wuthering Heights* is generally ranked among the best novels in the language. The intensity of feeling in her work, and her almost mystical desire for union with nature, reveal her deep longing for freedom. The sheer passion and imaginative greatness of her writing triumph over its occasional technical defects.

See also W. Gérin, *Emily Brontë*, 1978; Phillip Henderson (ed.), *The Complete Poems*

66

of Emily Brontë, 1951; M. Visick, *The Genesis of Wuthering Heights*, 1958.   J.H.

Brooke, Frances (1724–89), the first Canadian novelist, the daughter of a clergyman. In 1736 Frances Moore married the Reverend John Brooke, rector of Colney in Norfolk. Her first work, published under the pseudonym Mary Singleton, was for the periodical *The Old Maid*, which ran from November 1755 to July 1756. She published a tragedy, *Virginia* (1756), followed by translations of Mme Riccoboni, the best known being *Letters from Lady Juliet Catesby* (1763); these provided practical experience of narrative style and structure, and the influence of Riccoboni persisted throughout her career.

Frances Brooke's first successful novel, *Lady Julia Mandeville*, was published anonymously in 1763, and by 1792 had gone through ten editions. It establishes an interesting parallel between the love interest and a socio-political ideal based on hierarchy, although the ending reverts to conventional romantic tragedy. In *Emily Montague* (1796), Frances Brooke retains this affinity between individual affection and social structure, thus anticipating the narrative strategy employed by the radical novelists INCHBALD, Holcroft, and Godwin. In literary and historical terms the significance of *Emily Montague* lies in its being the first novel written in Canada: Frances Brooke accompanied her husband to Quebec, where he had been appointed chaplain in 1763, and the first half of the novel contains many passages describing the colony.

Frances Brooke met with mixed success as a playwright. She mounted a vitriolic attack on Garrick in her novel *The Excursion* (1777) after he refused to produce two plays she had offered him. Her friendship with the actress Mrs Yates probably brought her contacts in the Opera House, Covent Garden, and a number of her subsequent works were produced there: a tragedy, *The Siege of Sinope* (1781), the very successful musical *Rosina* (1782), and the drama *Marion* (1788).

In old age she retired to her son's house in Sleaford, Lincolnshire, where she died shortly after her husband.   A.L.

Broughton, Rhoda (1840–1920), novelist. She was born near Denbigh in Wales, but was brought up in an Elizabethan manor house at Broughton, Staffordshire, an old family home which she later used as a setting in her novels. She was the youngest of four children and was educated by her clergyman father; her mother died while Rhoda was still a child. At twenty-two she began to write her first novel, *Not Wisely But Too Well*, which was turned down by the first publisher she sent it to and did not appear until 1867, after the publication of *Cometh Up as a Flower* (1867) established her as a daring sensational novelist.

After the death of her father when she was twenty-three, Rhoda Broughton went to live with her sister in North Wales and then in Oxford. She remained unmarried (it is thought she had an unhappy love affair as a young woman), and after her sister's death she lived with a cousin at Headington Hill, near Oxford.

Rhoda Broughton's earliest novels were her most sensational. Geraldine JEWSBURY tried to stop Bentley publishing them, and Mrs OLIPHANT said in a review 'it is a shame to women so to write'. But Rhoda Broughton continued to write, at the rate of about one novel every two years. Mary BRADDON, who had a reputation for disliking her disciples, considered Rhoda Broughton a competitor worthy of her notice, and they eventually became close friends. However, Rhoda Broughton's work became steadily less *risqué*. She found her own reputation amusing, once saying of herself, 'I began my life as Zola, I finish it as Miss YONGE.'

Her novels include *Red as a Rose is She*, 1870, *Goodbye, Sweetheart*, 1872, *Nancy*, 1873, *Joan*, 1876, *Belinda*, 1883, *Doctor Cupid*, 1886, *Foes-in-Law*, 1900, *A Waif's Progress*, 1905 and *The Devil and the Deep Sea*, 1910.   A.P.

Browning, Elizabeth Barrett (1806–61), poet. Born at Coxhoe Hall in Northumberland, Elizabeth Barrett was the eldest of eleven children. At the age of three she and her family moved south to Hope End, a large estate near Ledbury in Herefordshire. Both her father, a wealthy plantation owner, and her mother encouraged her in her early attempts at writing poetry. She proved to be a precocious child: at the age of eight she was translating Homer and composing her own verses. At the age of fourteen she wrote an epic in four books, *The Battle of Marathon*, which was privately printed and issued by her father in 1820.

In 1832, following the death of his wife, and in serious financial difficulties, Elizabeth Bar-

rett's father sold Hope End and the family moved first to Sidmouth and then to London. Though her health was very delicate, Elizabeth, encouraged by her friend John Kenyon, was introduced to many of the literary figures of the day, including Wordsworth and Walter Savage Landor. It was Kenyon, too, who encouraged her to publish a collection of her poetry, which appeared in 1838 under the title *The Seraphim and Other Poems*. In the hope of restoring her health, she moved to Torquay, but by 1841 she had returned to London following the drowning of a brother to whom she had been devoted.

Elizabeth Barrett's return to London signalled the beginning of a period of almost complete isolation from the outside world. She lived in her father's house and received no visitors. In 1844 her *Poems* were published in two volumes, and in the following year she was persuaded to meet Robert Browning, an admirer of her verse. Aided perhaps by Browning's visits, her health began to improve, but she was advised that to remain in England during the winter might prove fatal. However, her father refused to allow her to travel abroad, so she secretly married Browning in September 1846, and the couple left England a week after their wedding. Her father refused to see her again, dying still unreconciled to his daughter in 1857.

For the rest of her life Elizabeth Barrett Browning lived abroad, mainly in Florence. In 1849, after a number of miscarriages, her son Penini was born. *Sonnets From the Portuguese*, perhaps her finest work, was published in 1850, to be followed by *Casa Guidi Windows* (1851), a poem which reflects her lifelong attachment to the cause of Italian national unification. Robert Browning had always valued his wife's work more highly than his own, an estimation which many of his contemporaries seem to have shared: it was proposed that she should be offered the position of Poet Laureate on the death of Wordsworth, although it was ultimately Tennyson who was chosen. *Aurora Leigh*, which Elizabeth Barrett Browning regarded as her most important work, was published in 1857; despite almost universally hostile reviews, the poem was enthusiastically received by the public and by progressive thinkers, including the Rossettis, Swinburne, and Ruskin.

Elizabeth Barrett Browning's other works include *Prometheus Bound*, 1833, *The Cry*

Bryant, Sophie

of The Children, 1854, and *Poems Before Congress*, 1860. She died in Florence.

See also F. G. Kenyon (ed.), *Letters of Elizabeth Barrett Browning*, 1897; R. Mander, *Mrs Browning*, 1980; V. Radley, *Elizabeth Barrett Browning*, 1972.   J.H.S.

Bryant, Sophie (1850–1922), educationist and worker for women's rights. She was born in Ireland and grew up in County Cork and County Fermanagh; her teachers were her father, a parson and mathematician, and occasional governesses. In 1863 the family moved to England and three years later she won an Arnott scholarship to Bedford College. In 1869 she married Dr Bryant, a physician who died the following year. Sophie Bryant then began teaching in Highgate, and in 1875 Frances BUSS offered her a post at the North London Collegiate School to teach mathematics and German. While teaching and looking after her mother and nieces she worked for her degree, taking a BA in Mental and Moral Science and Mathematics in 1881 and becoming the first woman D.Sc. in Physiology, Logic, and Ethics in 1884.

Recommended by Miss Buss as having 'vital force', Sophie Bryant became the North London Collegiate School's second headmistress from 1895 to her retirement in 1918. An inspiration and a mentor, she challenged staff and pupils to excel and to think for themselves. Working for secondary education, opportunities for women, and the training of teachers, she served on committees of the London County Council, the University of London, and national associations. She was one of the three women on the Bryce Commission on Secondary Education in 1894, worked for twenty years on the Board of Studies in Pedagogy, and was President of the Association of Headmistresses from 1903 to 1905.

'Freedom is a condition of all development' was a belief she expressed in her efforts on behalf of Irish Home Rule and women's suffrage. She worked through the Women's Liberal Federation, founded the English Home Rule Propagandist Organisation, and lectured in England and Ireland. In 1908, as president of the Hampstead Suffrage Society, she was one of the four leaders of the march of the National Union of Suffrage Societies with Emily DAVIES, Millicent FAWCETT, and Frances BALFOUR.

Sophie Bryant contributed articles on education and philosophy to many journals, and between 1887 and 1922 published ten books on moral and religious education and Ireland, in recognition of which Dublin University awarded her an Honorary D.Litt. in 1904. Her works include *Short Studies in Character*, 1894, *The Genius of the Gael: a Study in Celtic Psychology and its Manifestations*, 1913, *Moral and Religious Education*, 1920 and *Liberty, Order, and Law under Native Irish Rule*, 1923.

An energetic climber, she disappeared in Chamonix on 12 August 1922 and was found dead a fortnight later on the slopes of Mont Blanc.

See also R. M. Scrimgeour (ed.), *The North London Collegiate School 1850–1950*, 1950.
C.B.

Buchan, Countess of. See MACDUFF, ISABEL.

Buchan, Elspeth (1738–91), religious mystic, founder of the Buchanite sect. Her parents kept an inn near Portsoy in Scotland. After the failure of her marriage to Robert Buchan she came under the influence of the Presbyterian preacher Hugh White of Irvine. White soon took the view that Elspeth Buchan was a saint and the woman mentioned in the Revelation of St John, and together they formed the sect known as the Buchanites. In 1784, having already been ejected from his ministry, White was exiled from Irvine, along with Elspeth and the sect, by the outraged authorities. The sect then migrated to a farm in Dumfriesshire and lived as a religious commune for some years, revering Elspeth Buchan as their 'spiritual mother', with the gift of prophecy and the ability to confer the Holy Ghost by breathing. Robert Burns, who for a time was in love with a girl member of the sect, described the Buchanites as 'carrying on a great farce by pretended devotion', and stigmatized their idleness and indecency. The faith of the members does not seem to have long survived the death of their leader.

See also J. F. C. Harrison, *The Second Coming: Popular Millenarianism 1780–1850*, 1979.
T.H.

Burdett-Coutts, Angela Georgina, Baroness (1814–1906), philanthropist. Born in London, she was the youngest child of the radical politician Sir Francis Burdett and his wife Sophia, a daughter of the wealthy banker Thomas Coutts. Her childhood was a privileged one of luxury and foreign travel, made all the more interesting because of her father's extensive connections, which gave her a wide and enlightened social circle. She was educated by tutors, drawing masters, and language coaches. Her governess, Hannah Meredith, became a much-loved companion whose influence strengthened Angela Burdett's Evangelical fervour.

In 1837, at the age of twenty-three, Angela Burdett became a celebrity when her step-grandmother (Thomas Coutts' widow) left her the whole of her fortune, making her the richest woman in England. Proposals of marriage poured in, though Angela Burdett-Coutts, as she now became, recognized the source of her sudden appeal and was little tempted. She did unconventionally propose marriage to her friend the Duke of Wellington in 1847, but the seventy-eight-year-old Duke diplomatically declined.

Angela Burdett-Coutts' friendships were many, and included the politicians Peel, Disraeli and Gladstone, and various writers, most notably Dickens, who for many years gave encouragement and a radical flavour to her philanthropic schemes. It was Dickens who prepared the ground for her generous contributions to the Ragged School Union and to Urania Cottage in Shepherd's Bush, a refuge for prostitutes opened in 1847. Discriminating in her charity, she was anxious that her wealth be turned to genuinely useful purposes. It was rumoured in the 1880s that by that time she had given away as much as three or four million pounds.

Angela Burdett-Coutts' charitable interests extended over a great variety of causes, from the relief of personal distress to urban redevelopment. As a lifelong pillar of the Church of England, she spent vast sums on church building in London and endowed colonial bishoprics in Cape Town, Adelaide, and elsewhere. In memory of her father, whose public spiritedness she inherited, she spent £90,000 on St Stephen's Church and its associated schools in his former constituency of Westminster. She was a patron of the London Society for the Prevention of Cruelty to Children. In Bethnal Green she built Columbia Square Market, in an unsuccessful attempt to keep food prices down in the poor districts of the East End; this venture was associated with her Columbia Square housing project for the poor. She also established Holly Village, a middle-class housing estate in Highgate. She assisted African exploration, provided nurses for the Zulu War, and gave a gunboat and a model farm to her friend Rajah Brooke of Sarawak.

In 1871 she was the first woman to be raised to the peerage in her own right. Ten years later, at the age of sixty-seven, she married the twenty-seven-year-old William Ashmead Bartlett, a match not without a touch of the ridiculous. She was a complex woman, vulnerable and headstrong and somewhat isolated by her wealth. Her charity at its best combined social responsibility with practical benefit. She was one of the many Victorian women (and admittedly the one operating on the grandest scale) who effectively turned philanthropy into a profession for women. She edited the book *Woman's Mission* (1893). Angela Burdett-Coutts is buried in Westminster Abbey.

See also E. Healey, *Lady Unknown: The Life of Angela Burdett-Coutts* 1978; D. Orton, *Made of Gold: A Biography of Angela Burdett-Coutts*, 1980; D. Owen, *English Philanthropy, 1660–1960*, 1964.   F.K.P.

Burgundy, Duchess of. See MARGARET OF YORK.

Burnett, Frances Hodgson (1849–1924), novelist and playwright, was born in Manchester, the daughter of a middle-class businessman. She was educated at local day-schools until she was fifteen, when her family emigrated to Tennessee. To contribute to the family income, she sent stories to magazines, her first being published in 1868. Her first novel, *That Lass o'Lowrie's*, was very well received in 1877. *Through One Administration* (1883), based on political life in Washington, earned her the reputation of being a 'realist' with modern views on marriage and the role of women.

Her famous children's story, *Little Lord Fauntleroy* (1886), is about a small American boy who unexpectedly inherits an earldom, travels to England, and wins the heart of his irascible elderly grandfather. The book was an immediate best-seller, and transformed Frances Hodgson Burnett's life. Together with her other most enduring children's story, *The Secret Garden* (1911), it identified her lastingly in the public mind with romantic escapism and sentimentality, and her previous reputation as a serious novelist has been largely forgotten.

Frances Hodgson Burnett married twice and had two sons. In 1888 she fought a successful law-suit against the author of a dramatization of *Little Lord Fauntleroy*, an action that helped to secure the eventual passing of the 1911 British Copyright Act. She wrote an autobiography, *The One I Know the Best of All* (1893).

See also V. Burnett, *The Romantick Lady*, 1927; A. Thwaite, *Waiting for the Party: the Life of Frances Hodgson Burnett*, 1974.

J.E.E.H.

Burney, Fanny (1752–1840), novelist. Fanny, originally Frances, Burney was born at King's Lynn, where her father Charles Burney had recently secured the post of organist at St Margaret's Church. In 1760 the family moved to London, where Dr Burney worked as a music-master, and after the death of his wife in 1762 assumed responsibility for the upbringing of his six surviving children. Fanny Burney was largely self-educated and read extensively from her father's library, especially 'improving literature': contemporary sermons, histories and conduct-books. The influence of these works and of her mother's death appear in the didactic tone, wise male monitors, and motherless heroines of her own novels, and in the scrupulous attention to propriety found in her journals.

In 1767 Dr Burney married a widow, Mrs Allan, but until 1770 she retained her own house in King's Lynn. In that year she moved to London, and the presence of a stepmother, towards whom the children of the first marriage felt great antagonism, restricted Fanny Burney's accustomed independence. As her father began to suffer increasingly from rheumatism after 1772, she served as his amanuensis in the composition of his great *History of Music*. Her own novel, *Evelina*, which she had begun in the late 1760s, was completed in 1777 and published anonymously in 1778. Initially only her sisters knew the author's identity, but after her father's glowing commendation of the work, she let him into the secret, which soon got out and made her a literary celebrity. Encouraged by her father's support, and by new acquaintances among the Streatham circle (Dr Johnson, the Thrales, Edmund Burke, Joshua Reynolds, Elizabeth MONTAGU), Fanny Burney began but failed to complete a farce, *The Witlings*, and in 1782 published her second novel, *Cecilia*.

In 1786 Fanny Burney was invited by Queen CHARLOTTE to become Second Keeper of the Robes, and took up residence at Windsor. In addition to keeping a Windsor journal, she composed a number of blank-verse tragedies during this period. Exhausted, ill, and unhappy in an uncongenial role at court, she petitioned to be released from her post and was allowed to resign in 1791. She was rewarded for her work by an annual pension of £100.

In 1792 Fanny Burney met the emigré General D'Arblay, whom she married the following year. Marriage to a man who was both French and Catholic, even though of moderate political opinions, was at a time of considerable anti-French and anti-Catholic feeling an act of considerable courage and independence. In an attempt to ease their subsequent financial difficulties she began writing her third novel, *Camilla*, published in 1796. The work sold well but received mixed reviews which greatly pained Fanny Burney. Then in 1802, during the brief peace between England and the Bonapartist régime which had replaced the Revolutionary government, Fanny Burney and her husband went to France in an unsuccessful attempt to recover his property and military rank. The outbreak of war made her return to England impossible until she was able to leave in 1812. In 1814 she published *The Wanderer*, an uninspired but commercially successful novel. In 1815 she returned to Europe during the Waterloo Campaign, in which her husband was seriously wounded. Her own formal journal was written after his death in 1818. Fanny Burney's final years were darkened by the harsh criticisms directed at her *Memoirs of Doctor Burney* (1832), and by the deaths of her only child, Alexander, and her two sisters.

See also C. Barrett (ed.), *The Diary and Letters of Madame d'Arblay*, 1904; A. R. Ellis (ed.), *The Early Diaries of Frances Burney*, 1907; J. Hemlow, *The History of Fanny Burney*, 1958; J. Hemlow et al. (eds), *The Journals and Letters of Fanny Burney (Madame D'Arblay), 1791–1840*, 1972.

A.L.

Burney, Sarah Harriet (1772–1844), novelist, the only daughter of the music historian Dr Charles Burney by his second marriage; she has been overshadowed by her half-sister Fanny BURNEY. She showed precocious literary promise and had mastered French and Italian by the age of twelve, but her novels are not remarkable for their originality. The first, *Clarentine*, appeared in 1796. Her later novels, *Geraldine Fauconberg* (1808) and *Traits of Nature* (1812), were popular enough at the time to go into second editions. After living in Florence for some years she returned to write her *Romance of Private Life* (1839).

See also J. Hemlow (ed.), *The Journals and Letters of Fanny Burney*, 1972, *passim*.

T.H.

Burton, Lady Isabel (1831–96), traveller and author. She was born in London into the old Catholic Arundell family, and was educated in English and French convents.

In 1851 she first met the explorer Richard Burton and immediately determined to marry him. Despite her family's disapproval they married ten years later. She travelled with him to Africa, South America, India and the Middle East, acting as his secretary and riding, swimming, and fencing with him. She wrote *The Inner Life of Syria* (1875) and *Arabia, Egypt, India* (1879).

After Burton's death in 1890 she took a cottage near his tomb at Mortlake, wrote his biography (certainly not a complete picture of the man), and prepared memorial editions of his work, refusing all help and advice. Contemporaries felt that she had a beneficial influence on her headstrong, unconventional husband, but later generations have found it hard to forgive her destruction of his private diaries and erotic translations from the Arabic.

She was buried by Burton's side in a replica of an Arab tent which she had had built in Mortlake cemetery as a memorial to him.

See also W. H. Williams (ed.), *The Romance of Isabel, Lady Burton*, 1897. P.S.

Bury, Elizabeth (1644–1720), diarist. Elizabeth Lawrence's father died when she was four and her mother married an East Anglian minister who was ejected in 1662, during the campaign against the Dissenters. She thus had a Nonconformist background. Her first marriage, in 1667, was to Griffith Lloyd, a Huntingdonshire gentleman who died in 1682. Thereafter she was reluctant to give up the independence which widowhood gave her, and refused several offers before her marriage in 1697 to Samuel Bury, an eminent Nonconformist minister from Bury St. Edmunds.

From an early age Elizabeth Bury kept a diary, written partly in shorthand to ensure privacy, and this formed the basis of a life of her written by her husband after her death.

From this emerges a picture of a learned, pious, and active woman who was probably typical apart from her activity as a diarist. Possibly her childlessness gave her a leisure for introspection that was not available to many similar women. Her studies included music, mathematics, philosophy, philology, history, and languages, especially Hebrew, which was important for her 'constant favourite' activity, reading the Scriptures. She was active in charitable work, distributing Bibles and material aid to the poor. Her own poor health and the 'desire of being useful among her neighbours' led her to the study of medicine. Her medical knowledge suprised many learned doctors 'by her stating the most nice and difficult cases, in such proper terms which could have been expected only from men of their own profession; and [they] have often owned that she understood a human carcass and the materia medica, much better than most of her sex' (Samuel Bury, in his *Account of the Life and Death of Mrs. Elizabeth Bury*, 1920).

P.M.H.

Buss, Frances (Mary) (1827–94), pioneer of women's education, the daughter of an artist. She was educated at schools in London until she was eighteen, when she and her mother opened their own school in Kentish Town. Her mother was an important influence, imbuing her with a strong sense of duty towards whatever project she took up, and particularly towards girls' education. Fired by this sense of duty, Frances Buss concentrated her energies on her work and her family, never marrying; she and another pioneer, DOROTHEA BEALE, were characterized in a jingle as 'Miss Buss and Miss Beale/Cupid's darts do not feel/How unlike us/Miss Beale and Miss Buss'.

Conscious of her deficient education, Frances Buss began to attend evening classes at the newly-opened Queen's College in 1848, continuing her daytime teaching. On finishing her formal education at Queen's she decided to begin a new venture, and in April 1850 opened the North London Collegiate School for Ladies (later Girls). By the end of the first year numbers had increased from 35 to 115. She offered girls a good education at moderate fees and without consideration of social position or religion.

Frances Buss was determined to raise the status of women's education and was therefore a great believer in competitive examinations.

She insisted that her staff attend the Home and Colonial School Society for training, and was instrumental in forming the Schoolmistresses' Association, of which she was President from 1867. In 1874 she helped form the Association of Head Mistresses, becoming President of that also. The Teachers' Guild (1888) was yet another product of her initiative. She was an early supporter of Girton College, Cambridge, with whose aims she was in full sympathy. In 1864 she was asked to give evidence before the Schools Enquiry Commission, an indication of the success her work was enjoying. Unlike Dorothea Beale, Frances Buss extended her attention to middle-class education generally, and also took a great interest in Board schools. In 1871 she opened the Camden Lower School. Intensely practical, she founded the School's Dorcas Society (to make clothing for the poor), starting the tradition of social service with which the North London Collegiate School became associated. Towards the end of her life her health failed, but she continued her efforts in education and philanthropy until her death. Frances Buss's democratic principles, and her wide interests in all aspects of education, made her an important figure in nineteenth-century education. Above all, she made a great contribution towards establishing the status of women's education and of women teachers.

See also M. Holmes, *Frances Mary Buss*, 1913; J. Kamm, *How Different From Us*, 1958; A. E. Ridley, *Frances M. Buss and Her Work for Education*, 1895.　　　　J.R.

Butler, Lady Eleanor (1745?–1829), Irish recluse, sister of the 17th Earl of Ormonde. At some time in the 1790s she and her cousin Sarah Ponsonby (1745?–1831) resolved to retire from society and live in seclusion. For about half a century they lived in a house named Plas Newydd in the vale of Llangollen (which gave rise to their soubriquet 'the Ladies of Llangollen'), never venturing out for even a night. This and other eccentricities together with their devotion to each other, made them known in their time throughout Europe.

See also E. Mavor, *Ladies of Llangollen*, 1973.　　　　T.H.

Butler, Lady Elizabeth (1846–1933), painter. Born Elizabeth Thompson, she was the daughter of a man of private fortune who devoted

himself to the education of his two children. She and her sister Alice (later Alice MEYNELL) spent much of their early life travelling in Europe. As a child she had a passion for drawing horses and soldiers, and when she decided to pursue art professionally she made military painting her speciality. She trained at the South Kensington Schools of Art (1866–68) and completed her studies in Italy (1868–70). In 1877 she married a distinguished soldier, Sir William Butler.

In 1874 Elizabeth Butler exhibited *Calling the Roll after an Engagement, Crimea* at the Royal Academy. This picture, which became known as *The Roll Call*, was a sensational success. It was applauded by artists and critics, protected from admiring crowds by a policeman, and sent by royal command to the Queen, who purchased it. The artist was precipitated from a life of quiet retirement into the public gaze. She became a national heroine and one of the most famous living artists. Within a few weeks a quarter of a million portrait photographs of her were sold. The public was impressed by the fact that a woman had painted this picture, which, with restrained emotion and sombre realism (by the standards of the time), portrayed exhausted, wounded, and dying Grenadier Guards lining up in the winter snows of the Crimea. The following year John Ruskin felt compelled to recant his opinion that women could not paint great pictures.

Whereas her predecessors and contemporaries in art glorified war and military commanders, Elizabeth Butler's pictures showed the horrors, pain, and senseless suffering of war, and gave a prominent place to the lower ranks. Her achievement brought her not only public acclaim but also financial reward; but she did not sustain her early success. After her marriage, the demands of her family life and her role as a military hostess inhibited her output. In search of fresh inspiration she turned from the Crimea and the Waterloo campaign to more recent military events, but these pictures failed to capture public approval and her popularity declined. She never lost her conviction that her art should express her pacifist belief.

Elizabeth Butler's paintings may be seen at Leeds City Art Gallery, Manchester City Art Gallery, and the Ferens Art Gallery, Hull. In 1922 she published *An Autobiography*.

　　　　D.C.

Butler, Josephine (Elizabeth) (1828–1906), philanthropist and social reformer. She was born into a distinguished Northumbrian family, the youngest and favourite child of John Grey of Dilston, chief Whig agent in the north. From infancy she was brought up to be well-informed in political controversy. From her mother she acquired her simple and unaffected Christian convictions, which were to be a lifelong inspiration in the work for which she believed herself divinely chosen.

In 1852 she married George Butler, teacher and later Canon of Winchester. It was an ideal partnership, in which George succeeded in providing his wife with the emotional stability she required during her stormy career. In 1857, at Oxford, Josephine Butler attempted without success to rescue a prostitute, and in the same year she befriended a young woman who had been imprisoned for killing the illegitimate baby fathered on her by a Balliol don. These two incidents inspired in her a desire not only to help the poorer class of prostitute but to explore the social and economic causes of prostitution. In the climate of the time, it was a brave decision: she was to be accused of being 'a Maenad, a shrieking sister, worse than the women she seeks to befriend'.

Josephine Butler's *Women's Work and Women's Culture* (1869) brought her to the attention of the small band of radicals who were opposing the extension of the Contagious Diseases Acts. Passed in 1864, 1866 and 1869, these Acts had imposed in eighteen garrison and naval dockyard towns the Prussian system of a morals police enforcing the compulsory registration, licensing, and medical examination of prostitutes. Not only did they represent a double standard of morality, they placed all working-class women at risk, since innocent women suspected of being prostitutes henceforth lost their reputation. As secretary of the Ladies' National Association for the Repeal of the Contagious Diseases Acts (1869–85), Josephine Butler dedicated herself single-mindedly to the cause of repeal. She succeeded by virtue of her considerable charm and courage, her shameless importuning of those political contacts she had inherited from her family, and above all through the political acumen she had learnt from her father. She mobilized provincial middle-class suspicion of central government and allied it with the puritan element within the Liberal Party, which was easily convinced of the sexual dissoluteness of the upper classes. The Acts were repealed in 1886.

Josephine Butler's leadership of the movement against the Contagious Diseases Acts was her greatest achievement, but she was also active in other campaigns. From 1867 to 1870 she was President of the North of England Council for Promoting the Higher Education of Women. In 1874 she undertook the first of several visits to the Continent to organize international opposition to prostitution and the 'white slave traffic'. Her intervention in support of W. T. Stead during the 'Maiden Tribute' campaign against child prostitution in 1885, though heroic, was clumsy and ill-conceived. She supported votes for women, but it was not a major preoccupation. In later life, fatigue, and the death of a husband upon whose judgement she had relied, made her impatient and less discriminating in her choice of targets.

Josephine Butler's integrity has been recognized by her inclusion in the Anglican Kalendar. Dr Jowett said she was 'touched with genius'. Few others demonstrated with equal skill how lobbying could be used to achieve results within the late nineteenth-century parliamentary system. Among her writings were *Personal Reminiscences of a Great Crusade* (1896) and a *Life of St Catherine of Siena* (1898).

See also A. S. G. Butler, *Portrait of Josephine Butler*, 1954; G. W. and L. A. Johnson, *Josephine E. Butler, an Autobiographical Memoir*, 1909; P. McHugh, *Prostitution and Victorian Social Reform*, 1980; G. Petrie, *A Singular Iniquity: the Campaigns of Josephine Butler*, 1971.   G.P.

Butt, Clara (1873–1936), singer. Clara Butt was the legendary contralto of whom it is said that, when she was rehearsing with massed brass bands in the Royal Albert Hall, the conductor shouted to his musicians, 'Play up, gentlemen! I can't hear you!' The story is told in various versions; the name of the conductor varies; but the singer in the tale is always Clara Butt. She learnt singing with Daniel Rootham at Bristol until she was sixteen, when she made her début at the Royal Albert Hall as Ursula in Sullivan's *Golden Legend*; three days later she sang the title role in Gluck's *Orfeo* at the Lyceum Theatre. Her success was based largely on ballad concerts, which she gave all over the British Empire, but she was also in demand for other occasions, particularly in the English musical festivals. Her voice was famous for its beauty as well as its legendary strength, though this phenomenal power was clearly demonstrated in the heavy orchestration of Elgar's *Sea Pictures* (full orchestra and organ), written especially for her and given a highly successful first performance at the Norwich Festival of 1899. She married the baritone Kennerley Rumford in 1900. In 1920 she was created DBE for her services during the war, and in that year she made a brief reappearance in opera, singing Gluck's *Orfeo* at Covent Garden. R.G.

C

Cable, (Alice) Mildred (1878–1952), missionary. Born in Guildford, Mildred Cable was the daughter of a master draper. Inspired by a meeting with a missionary in 1893, when she was old enough she applied to work with the China Inland Mission. Following the Boxer rising in 1900, she left England to work in Hwochow, where she and Evangeline and Francesca French ran a girls' school for twenty-one years. In 1926 they became itinerant missionaries, and for the next fifteen years they followed the trade routes across the uncharted Gobi desert to spread the gospel in Chinese and Turki. They travelled by cart, by camel, and on foot, wearing Chinese dress.

As missionaries and explorers, Mildred Cable and the Frenches were popular lecturers at universities and societies in England. Together they published several books including *The Gobi Desert* (1942), for which Mildred Cable was awarded the Lawrence Memorial Medal in 1942 by the Royal Central Asian Society, *Something Happened* (1933), and *Through Jade Gate and Central Asia* (1927). In 1943 they were jointly awarded the Livingstone Medal by the Royal Scottish Geographical Society. From 1941 Mildred Cable helped with the publicity and fund-raising for the British and Foreign Bible Society.

M.G.B.

Calvert, Elizabeth (?–1675), bookseller. She was the wife of the radical London bookseller Giles Calvert, by whom she had two children, Nathaniel and Giles. She inherited one third of her husband's estate on his death in 1664 and thereafter ran her own booksellers' business in the City, often falling foul of the authorities for her radical views. In 1661 she was arrested for selling the seditious book *Several Prodigies*, being released on a bond of £500 in December of that year. She was also imprisoned on similar charges in 1663. In the following year she was held from February until April and questioned about the production of another seditious book, *Mene Tekel*, and in 1665 she was again in trouble for producing illegal material. In 1667 she sent fifty books about the Fire of London to Susanna Moore, a bookseller in Bristol, which were considered 'likely to seduce persons' against the government. The following April she was

in prison again, this time for keeping a private press and selling 'unlicensed and scandalous books and pamphlets'. In 1670 three hundred seditious books 'of old date' were seized from her. During her career she published books by William Dyer, John Owen, Peter Fullwood, Samuel Petto, Benjamin Agus, and Richard Steele. When she died in 1675 she left her property to her son Giles and asked to be buried among the Baptists.

See also *Calendar of State Papers Domestic;* P. Morrison, *Index of Printers, Publishers and Booksellers in Donald Wing's Short-Title Catalogue,* 1955; H. Plomer, *A Dictionary of Printers and Booksellers in England 1641-67,* 1907.

T.O'M.

Cam, Helen Maud (1885–1968), medieval historian, last of the great British school of constitutional, administrative, and legal historians stemming from Stubbs and Maitland. She was born at Abingdon in Oxfordshire, where her father was a grammar school headmaster; later, on his appointment as rector, the family moved to Birchanger in Essex. Helen Cam received a very thorough education at home, and went as a scholar to Royal Holloway College, London, taking a First in History and being awarded an MA for work on Anglo-Saxon and Frankish studies that was partly accomplished during a year in the United States as a Fellow at Bryn Mawr College, Pennsylvania. She was assistant history mistress at the Ladies' College, Cheltenham, from 1909 to 1912, then lectured at Royal Holloway College down to 1921, when her long association with Cambridge began. At Girton College she was successively Pfeiffer Research Fellow, lecturer, director of studies in history and law, and Vice-Mistress. From 1948 to 1954 she was the first Zemurray Radcliffe Professor of History at Harvard. She continued to write and lecture after her retirement, and was still hard at work at the time of her death.

Helen Cam belonged to the breed of historian concerned with minute particulars —the painstaking investigation of 'dusty documents' that is indispensable to an understanding of the past although generally unspectacular in its outcome. Her own most distinctive contribution was in connection with the Hundred Rolls, the records of English

75

self-government as it was exercised through local courts: *Studies in the Hundred Rolls* (1921) and *The Hundred and the Hundred Rolls* (1930). Much of her best work consisted of papers, collected in *Liberties and Communities in Medieval England* (1944), and *Law-Finders and Law-Makers in Medieval England* (1962).   N.H.

Cambridge, Ada (1844–1926), novelist, born in Wiggenhall St Germains, Norfolk. She was educated at home, living in Norfolk, Cambridgeshire, and Staffordshire until 1870, when she married the Reverend George Frederick Cross and emigrated to Australia. They lived in bush districts in Victoria, then in Williamstown, a port of Melbourne, between 1893 and 1912. They had one son and one daughter.

In Australia, Ada Cambridge was able to enjoy more varied experiences than her contemporaries in England, and her novels contained some interesting and unusual material which disguised from contemporaries their fundamentally conventional nature. The first of her novels, *My Guardian*, was published in 1878. She also wrote *In Two Years' Time*, 1879, *A Mere Chance*, 1882, *The Three Miss Kings*, 1891, *A Marriage Ceremony*, 1894, *Materfamilias*, 1898, *Sisters*, 1904, and other works. *Thirty Years in Australia*, 1903, is her autobiography.   A.P.

Cameron, Julia Margaret (1815–79), photographer. The daughter of James Pattle, a Scotsman in the Bengal Civil Service, she was born in Calcutta. Orphaned at an early age, she was sent back to Europe, where she attended schools in England and France. In 1834 she returned to India, where she met Charles Cameron, a jurist working on the reform of the Indian legal system, and the couple were married in 1838.

Julia Margaret Cameron was a lively, witty woman with great resources of energy; in 1846 she raised over £10,000 for Irish famine victims. However, after the Camerons returned to England in 1848, raising a large family occupied her until middle age. As her children left home, she became increasingly depressed and lonely. Then her daughter presented her with a camera to alleviate her boredom, and Mrs Cameron was immediately captivated. She had no previous knowledge of photography, and for a year worked ceaselessly to acquire fundamental skills. Her first success

was a likeness of Annie, a local child. From 1864 onwards, domestic considerations were totally subordinated to the demands of photography. Servants and guests alike were pressed to pose. Mrs Cameron would scan the streets for likely sitters, personally persuading them to her home. She was particularly fascinated by portraiture. Abandoning the contemporary full-figure image complete with classical backdrop, she concentrated on close-ups, attempting to convey the essence of the sitter's character in a single frame. Having assiduously cultivated literary and artistic friendships, she was able to obtain introductions to many other prominent people. Her collected portraits comprise a cross-section of mid-nineteenth-century eminence, including such figures as Tennyson, Trollope, Browning, Carlyle, and Darwin.

Mrs Cameron also produced tableaux depicting scenes from the Bible and contemporary literature. In 1874 Tennyson suggested that she illustrate his *Idylls of the King*, and a series of photographs were taken. Mrs Cameron was most disappointed when these were printed in a reduced form and rendered in woodcut. She privately printed the collection in full, a venture sufficiently successful to be repeated with further scenes in 1875. In the same year the Camerons left England for Ceylon, where they owned land. Mrs Cameron died there after a short illness.

In her lifetime, Julia Margaret Cameron's work provoked mixed reactions. She had little success in competitive exhibitions, and the London Photographic Society criticized her slapdash technique and lack of professional polish. However, she persevered, encouraged by her husband's enthusiasm and sustained by her own belief in the quality of her work. Her distinctive talent is best displayed in her portraits, which have an immediacy of effect and sharpness of perception rarely found in more formal Victorian photography.

See also H. Gernsheim, *Julia Margaret Cameron*, 1948; National Portrait Gallery, *The Cameron Collection*, 1975.   J.V.L.

Campbell, Beatrice Stella. See CAMPBELL, MRS PATRICK.

Campbell, Janet Mary (1877–1954), medical reformer. She was the daughter of a banker, and was educated at Brighton High School, Neuwied Moravian School, and the London (Royal Free Hospital) School of Medicine for

Women. She graduated MB, BS in 1901. After junior hospital appointments at the Royal Free, the Belgrave Hospital for Children, and the Naylands Sanatorium, she obtained the London degrees MD (1904) and MS (1905) and also took a post-graduate course in obstetrics at Vienna.

Mary Campbell was Assistant Schools Medical Inspector to the LCC from 1905 to 1907. From 1907 to 1919 she was the first full-time woman Medical Officer to the Board of Education. In 1919 she became Chief Woman Medical Adviser to the Board, having achieved suitable status and pay for women in that post. The Ministry of Health was established in 1919 and Mary Campbell combined the advisory work to the Board of Education with that of Senior Medical Officer in charge of maternal and child welfare until 1934, when her resignation was enforced by her marriage to Michael Heseltine, Registrar of the British Medical Register. A founder-member of the Medical Women's Federation in 1917, she was successively its Honorary Secretary, Vice-President, and President (1944–46).

Breadth of outlook, an incisive and statesmanlike mind, patience, charm, and capacity for looking, listening, and wisely delegating responsibility enabled Mary Campbell to initiate constructive reforms. She was instrumental in establishing nursery schools, education in infant welfare in schools, schools for mothercraft, schooling for children in hospital, and proper supervision of physical education and of the health of women in industry. Her reports included 'The Physical Welfare of Mothers and Children' for the Carnegie United Kingdom Trust (1917) and 'A Comprehensive Report on Maternity Services' (1945).

Mary Campbell was a member of many committees, the most important of which were the War Cabinet Committee on Women in Industry and the Health Committee of the League of Nations. She was created DBE in 1924.   R.B.

Campbell, Margaret. See BOWEN, MARJORIE.

Campbell, Mrs Patrick (1865–1940), actress, born Beatrice Stella Tanner in Kensington, London. She had an unsettled childhood and unhappy schooling. At seventeen she gave up a piano scholarship and eloped with Patrick Campbell, whose name she retained throughout her professional career. They had two children in as many years, and, ailing and out

of work, he left for the colonies hoping to make money; he returned only once, without any, and in 1900 was killed in the Boer War. Some experience with an amateur group in Dulwich led Mrs Campbell to find work in the theatre. At twenty-three she made her professional début in Liverpool, and after some poorly paid tours she joined Ben Greet's open-air Shakespeare company performing in stately homes. For two years she played in melodramas at the Adelphi before *The Second Mrs Tanqueray* made her an overnight success in 1893. Praised and reviled, her playing of a contemporary 'woman with a past' was hailed as a new theatrical phenomenon, and was possibly her greatest creation.

In the next twenty years her career was erratic, but she gave strong performances in *The Notorious Mrs Ebbsmith* (1895) and *Beyond Human Power* (1901). She managed the Royalty from 1900 to 1901, producing new plays by European playwrights, and in 1904 she revived *Pelléas and Mélisande* with Sarah Bernhardt. Magda and Hedda Gabler were amongst her best roles, and in 1914 she created Eliza Doolittle, the heroine of *Pygmalion*, specially written for her by Bernard Shaw, with whom she had a notable correspondence. Five days before the opening night of *Pygmalion* she married George Cornwallis-West, ex-husband of Lady Jennie CHURCHILL, but the marriage did not last. She worked only spasmodically thereafter, although sometimes with memorable power, and she led a restless, lonely, nomadic existence that took her to Hollywood, New York, and Paris with only a cosseted dog as her companion. She died, virtually forgotten, at Pau in France.

Mrs Patrick Campbell's career has been called 'a record of talent thrown away, wasted time, lost opportunities'. She never developed the stamina, commitment, or technique to be a consistently successful professional actress. A celebrity, beautiful, wilful, and magnetic, she became a legend in her own lifetime, famous for her malicious wit and practical jokes. She could ruin a production through boredom or ill health, and cultivated a reputation (not wholly unjustified) for being unmanageable, though 'in the acting of women with brains and with natures complex, strange or highly strung, she had not her equal on the English stage'. She wrote an autobiography, *My Life and Some Letters* (1922).

See also A. Dent (ed.), *Bernard Shaw and*

Cappe, Catharine

Mrs Patrick Campbell: their Correspondence, 1952; A. Dent, *Mrs Patrick Campbell*, 1961.

C.B.

Cappe, Catharine (1744–1821), philanthropist, the daughter of Jeremiah Harrison, vicar of Craven in Yorkshire. Initially instructed by a family friend, she later went to school in York. In later life she regarded her education as deficient, attributing this to her father's distaste for intellectual women. As a young woman, influenced by a friend's example, she became a Unitarian.

While living in York, Catharine Harrison was struck by the ignorance and degradation of girls working on the manufacture of hemp. Together with other ladies, in 1784 she established a School for the Spinning of Worsted where girls also received a practical and moral education. A knitting school was opened to cater for younger girls.

The success of these institutions attracted the attention of the governors of York's Grey-Coat School for Girls, the reputation of which had long been in decline. Invited to suggest a plan for revitalizing the school, Catharine Harrison made many criticisms, and in particular she objected to the system of female apprenticeship, by which girls from the school were bound for years to any individual willing to accept them, thus making possible unchecked cruelty. Her careful arguments and circumspect approach impressed the governors, who in 1786 transferred control of the School to her Ladies' committee.

Her marriage in 1778 to the ailing Unitarian divine Newcome Cappe did not divert her from establishing a model Female Friendly Society at York in the same year. A distinctive and much imitated feature of this society was the honorary membership conferred on wealthy subscribers, who were thus persuaded to secure the Society's financial position. Approached for advice by the prestigious London Ladies' Committee for Promoting the Education and Employment of the Female Poor, Catharine Cappe produced an account of her guiding principles in her *Observations on Charity Schools and Female Friendly Societies*, published in 1804. In later years she was involved in the successful campaign for the appointment of female visitors to the women's wards of local hospitals and institutions.

Catharine Cappe did not question women's exclusion from political life. Instead, she stressed the importance of their indirect influence in effecting the moral regeneration of society, and devoted her life and abilities to establishing organizations which would first improve the women themselves. Her works include *An Account of Two Charity Schools . . . and of a Female Friendly Society* (1800) and *Memoirs of the Life of the late Mrs Catharine Cappe* written by herself (1822).

J.V.L.

Carlile (or Carlisle), Joan (1606?–79), painter, was the daughter of William Palmer, an official in the Royal Parks. In 1626 she married the poet and dramatist Lodowick Carlile, Gentleman of the Bows to Charles I and one of the Keepers of Richmond Park. One of Joan Carlile's most important works, *A Stag Hunt*, exhibited at the Tate Gallery in 1972, shows Lodowick, a keen huntsman, with her and their children, James and Penelope, and their good friend Justinian Isham. It has been described by Oliver Millar as 'one of the most charming premonitions painted in England in the Stuart period of the conversation piece in a landscape', a genre developed in the eighteenth century by Hogarth, Zoffany, and others.

An amateur painter of some distinction, with influential patrons before, during, and after the Civil War, Joan Carlile was employed chiefly in copying the works of Italian masters and reproducing them in miniature. She also painted portraits in which the influence of the court painter Van Dyck, whom she probably knew personally, can be discerned. It is said that Charles I so admired her work that he presented to her and to her mentor, Van Dyck, ultramarine valued at £500. In 1658 Sir William Sanderson paid tribute to her ability in his survey of the contemporary artistic scene, *Graphice, The Excellent Art of Painting*, in which he noted that 'in Oyal Colours we have a vertuous example in that worthy Artist, Mrs Carlisle'. A subsequently neglected artist (the *Dictionary of National Biography* mistakenly calls her Anne), of considerable stature in a field traditionally dominated by men, Joan Carlile was among the earliest, if not the earliest, English female portrait painters on record.

See also O. Millar, *The Age of Charles I: Paintings in England 1620–1649*, 1927; M. Toynbee and Sir G. Isham, 'Joan Carlisle

(1606?–1679)—An Identification', *Burlington Magazine*, 1954.   T.J.M.

Carlisle, Countesses of. See HAY, LUCY, COUNTESS OF CARLISLE; HOWARD, ROSALIND FRANCES, COUNTESS OF CARLISLE.

Carlyle, Jane (Baillie) Welsh (1801–66), writer and wife of Thomas Carlyle. Jane Welsh was the daughter of a surgeon and was an only child. A bright, self-willed, and precocious girl, she received a thorough education at her own insistence. She was sent to learn Latin at Haddington school, where she met Edward Irving, who was a master there and lived in her father's house. The only person with any real influence over her was her father, and when he died of typhus fever in 1819 she went into a decline and her health remained poor for years. She continued living with her mother, becoming a celebrated beauty renowned for her ferocious wit. She had an abundance of suitors but rejected them all because she was in love with her tutor, Edward Irving. He, however, went to live in Kirkcaldy, where he became engaged to another woman. But he continued to visit Jane Welsh at Haddington, and finally asked his fiancée to release him from his engagement; but she refused, and they were married in 1823.

Two years earlier Irving had brought the writer Thomas Carlyle to Haddington. Carlyle was immediately interested in Jane, and began a correspondence with her. She was not at first interested in him as a suitor, but after five years of courtship they were married and went to live at Comely Bank in Edinburgh. Jane Welsh Carlyle was to have a difficult marriage, beset with financial problems and doomed to solitude. In 1827 the Carlyles moved to Craigenputtock, a cottage outside Edinburgh. Four years later they moved to London, living in Gray's Inn Road until 1833, when they returned to Edinburgh. It was at this time that Jane Welsh Carlyle's life became particularly bleak. Her husband was completely immersed in his work, and she had no other company. She had to practise rigid economy, and her health began to suffer. But her life improved when they moved back to London in 1834 and settled in a house in Cheyne Row, Chelsea. For the first time she was able to look outside her marriage for companionship, forming a circle of friends of her own which included Geraldine JEWSBURY, who met her in 1841. As

Thomas's literary reputation grew, the Carlyles' financial problems became less severe, and Jane was able to have a maid in 1860. But in 1863 she was knocked down by a cab, an accident from which she never properly recovered. Three years later she went for a drive, stopped to pick up a stray dog, and was later found dead with the dog in her lap.

Despite her vivacity and evident literary talent, Jane Welsh Carlyle produced very little. She began writing poetry at the age of fourteen and continued for many years; but due largely to the circumstances of her life, her output was mainly in the form of lively, entertaining letters, which have been published in numerous collections and selections.

See also E. Adler, *Jane Welsh Carlyle*, 1907; O. H. Burdett, *The Two Carlyles*, 1930; E. Drew, *Jane Welsh and Jane Carlyle*, 1928.

A.P.

Caroline (1768–1821), George IV's queen. She was born at Wolfenbüttel, the second daughter of Charles, Duke of Brunswick, and Princess Augusta of England. On 8 April 1795 she married her first cousin, George, then Prince of Wales. The marriage was a disaster, for the Prince was repelled by her; in spite of the birth on 7 January 1796 of their daughter, Princess Charlotte (who died in 1817), the couple separated a few months later.

Rumours concerning Princess Caroline's moral conduct subsequent to the separation led to the 'Delicate Investigation' of 1806, which exonerated her of adultery, although the Commissioners censured her unconventional behaviour on several occasions. In spite of the Princess's popularity, her husband's installation as Regent in February 1811 weakened her position; excluded from court, and restricted in her access to her daughter, she left England for the Continent in August 1814. Escorted by the courtier Bartolomeo Pergami, she travelled extensively in Europe, the Mediterranean, and the Levant: in July 1816 she entered Jerusalem seated on an ass. She was constantly surrounded by spies, and her behaviour with Pergami was so indiscreet that the Prince Regent secretly established the Milan Commission to investigate her conduct and collect evidence for a divorce.

In 1820 Caroline became Queen on the death of George III, and determined to return to England to claim her rights. She dismissed the government's offer of a £50,000 annuity if she relinquished her title and remained in exile, and landed at Dover in June 1820. Her name was expunged from the liturgy, and in July the government introduced a Bill of Pains and Penalties in the House of Lords, to deprive her of the title of Queen and divorce her from the King. The Whigs championed her cause, hoping to benefit from her popularity. Thanks to Henry Brougham's brilliant defence of the Queen, and despite the convincing proofs of her misconduct, the Bill encountered such opposition that it was withdrawn in November. It is in fact possible that the Queen's relationship with Pergami was never physically consummated, for he seems to have been impotent (although this evidence was not disclosed during the proceedings). In spite of her acquittal, she was forcibly excluded from the King's coronation at Westminster Abbey in July 1821. Queen Caroline died a few weeks later at Brandenburg House, Hammersmith, and was buried in the royal vault at Brunswick.

Vulgar, eccentric, and impetuous, her conduct may well have been caused by mental imbalance. Queen Caroline was manipulated for partisan purposes by the opponents of George IV and his ministers, and both she and her husband did much to discredit the British monarchy

See also T. Holme, *Caroline*, 1979.

M.J.S.

Caroline Matilda (1751–75), Queen of Denmark and Norway, the youngest daughter of Frederick, Prince of Wales, and grand daughter of George II. In 1765 she married Prince Christian, who became King of Denmark in 1766. The marriage between the wayward Caroline Matilda and the weak-minded Christian VII was unhappy, and provided an opportunity for the ambitious and somewhat unscrupulous adventurer Johann Struensee to gain power. Struensee's knowledge of medicine, and his partial success in treating the maladies of the King, enabled him to become the chief confidant of the family. He seems to have become the Queen's lover towards the end of 1769. By the middle of 1771 he and his accomplice Brandt effectively controlled Denmark, but their tactless behaviour soon brought their fall. The Queen was placed under restraint and divorced from the King, while Struensee and Brandt were both executed. The disgraced Queen was given asylum in Hanover by her brother George III, but he declined to help her regain her position in Denmark. She died at Celle in 1775.

See also W. F. Reddaway, 'Struensee and the Fall of Bernstorff', in *English Historical Review*, XXVII, 1912.

T.H.

Caroline of Anspach (1683–1737), Princess of Brandenburg-Anspach and wife of George II. The daughter of John Frederick, Margrave of Brandenburg-Anspach, Caroline was brought up mainly in Saxony. After being orphaned at thirteen, she was cared for by the Elector Frederick of Brandenburg and his wife, Sophia Charlotte. From the Electress, Caroline acquired a taste for such subjects as history, literature, theology, and metaphysics.

In 1705, after refusing the Archduke Charles, heir to the Holy Roman Empire, Caroline married George Augustus, son of the Elector George of Hanover, and came to England in 1714, when her father-in-law came to the throne of Great Britain as George I. In 1715 George Augustus became Guardian of the Realm while his father attended to Hanoverian affairs, and for the first time he and Caroline enjoyed a certain amount of power; Caroline, sociable by nature and ambitious for herself and George Augustus, was active in receiving representatives of different political parties and interviewing ministers. At Hampton Court, and from 1718 at Richmond Lodge and Leicester House, London, she entertained on a grand scale, holding balls, galas, hunting parties, and horse races. With her husband she also patronized opera and river-fêtes and the music of Handel, attracting many wits and men of fashion to the Prince's court.

From 1727, when her husband succeeded to the throne as George II, Caroline exercised increasing political influence. At the beginning of the reign she persuaded the King to overcome his prejudice against Sir Robert Walpole and re-appoint him as his minister. After this, Walpole and the Queen developed into a formidable working partnership, eliminating rivals and influencing the King in important matters, although George II was never a matrimonial puppet. Caroline's support for Walpole remained unwavering, even in difficult times such as the excise crisis of 1733. In 1729, 1732, 1735, and 1736–37, she became regent during her husband's absence in Hanover, refusing to allow any active role to Frederick Louis, the Prince of Wales, whom she loathed. She took an active part in political affairs, especially during the Porteous Riots. In 1733–34, influenced by Walpole and her favourite, Hervey, she sought to persuade her huband to favour peace in the Polish Succession question. Caroline took advice from Walpole in private matters also; in 1735, for example, confident that she had greater influence over her husband than any mistress, she advised him to bring his current favourite, Madame de Walmoden, to England.

Caroline of Anspach died in 1737, having exercised more authority than any Queen Consort before her; and George II was heartbroken at her death. Among his subsequent mistresses she had no worthy successor, either personally or politically. Charming and beautiful, she was served well by her ministers and widely respected for her wit, vivacity, and real ability. She was a generous patron of writers, musicians, and churchmen.

See also P. Quennell, *Caroline of England: An Augustan Portrait*, 1939.   A.M.N.

Carpenter, Margaret (1793–1872), portrait painter. She was born in Salisbury, the daughter of Captain Geddes of Edinburgh. After studying art from Lord Radnor's collection at Longford Castle, she won the gold medal of the Society of Arts. In 1814 she went to London and began to exhibit at the Royal Academy and the British Institution. In 1817 she married William Carpenter, Keeper of Prints and Drawings at the British Museum; they had three children. During the next fifty years Margaret Carpenter exhibited over two hundred paintings in several places, and when her husband died in 1866 Queen Victoria gave her a pension of £100 per annum. She painted after the style of Thomas Lawrence, but often with greater sentimentality, as in *The Sisters*, which is a portrait of her two daughters. Her work includes miniatures in oil, water-colour and crayons. Examples can be seen in London at the National Portrait Gallery and the Victoria and Albert Museum, and in the Eton College Collection.

See also W. Shaw-Sparrow, *Women Painters of the World*, 1905; C. Wood, *Dictionary of Victorian Artists*, 1978.
          C.H.G.G.

Carpenter, Mary (1807–77), educationist and penologist. She was born in Exeter, the daughter of a Unitarian minister and considerable educationist; her mother supervised Unitarian schools for girls. Mary Carpenter was given an unusually liberal education, including classics, mathematics, and natural sciences, and her parents encouraged her to take up teaching in the schools under their care. At the age of 10 her family moved to Bristol, which became her home for most of the rest of her life. In her twenties she met Harriet MARTINEAU (her father's sometime private pupil), the princeling Rammohun Roy, who inspired in her an intense interest in India, and Joseph Tuckerman, a philanthropist from Massachusetts; all were to be formative influences on her.

Her own serious philanthropic work started in 1835 when, influenced by Tuckerman's work in Boston, she founded a Working and Visiting Society in Bristol, serving as its secretary and principal organizer for twenty years. In 1846 she opened Bristol's first 'Ragged School' in the Lewin's Mead section. She became increasingly interested in investigating the causes of juvenile crime, and in 1851 she published the first of the two books which were to secure her reputation, *Reformatory Schools for the Children of the Perishing and Dangerous Classes, and for Juvenile Offenders*. In it she drew the classic Victorian distinction between the deserving and undeserving poor, but with the warning that if the children of the deserving were not assisted by society, they would be recruited into the ranks of the undeserving.

Mary Carpenter put her theories into practice by devoting her personal fortune to setting up a reformatory school in Bristol in 1852. In the following year she published another influential work, *Juvenile Delinquents, their Condition and Treatment*, in which she insisted that juvenile offenders should be treated differently from adults. Her findings provided the basis for the provisions of the Juvenile Offenders Act (1854). She was subsequently consulted by the British Parliament in matters relating to education and the treatment of juvenile offenders; she also advised in Prussia and the United States. Her last years were largely devoted to the struggle to admit women to university degrees, and to medical degrees in particular.

Only in India, to which she made several visits between 1866 and 1875, did Mary Carpenter's pioneering work meet with relative failure. Her attempt to set up a Normal School for the training of women teachers was unsuccessful because the western-based curriculum was unsuitable; and the girls' schools she founded became the educational property of a class already endowed with more than its fair share of privileges.

In her own country Mary Carpenter's work was distinguished by realism and a refusal to view the poor with sentimentality. The rich, she once wrote, must recognize that, in asking the poor to be honest, they are asking them to deprive themselves of the hope of occasional luxury, in return for a wage insufficient to provide them with any share in the comforts of life.

See also J. E. Carpenter, *The Life and Work of Mary Carpenter*, 1879; J. Manton, *Mary Carpenter and the Children of the Streets*, 1976; J. J. Tobias, *Crime and Industrial Society in the Nineteenth Century*, 1967.

G.P.

Carr, Frances. See HOWARD, FRANCES, COUNTESS OF ESSEX AND SOMERSET.

Carrington, Dora (1893–1932), painter. She was the daughter of conventional middle-class parents, but was allowed to study art at the Slade (1910–13), where her teachers included Tonks and Wilson Steer and among her friends were Augustus John and Henry Lamb. She was influenced by C. R. Nevinson, in whose family circle she encountered new ideas on the emancipation of women. Her close association with Mark Gertler began about 1912, but she steadfastly refused to marry him, through fear of losing her artistic independence and because of an aversion to the sexual act.

Dora Carrington got to know the famous biographer Lytton Strachey about 1915, through Leonard and Virginia WOOLF and Lady Ottoline MORRELL, and began her close involvement with the Bloomsbury coterie, though she continued a loose attachment to Gertler. In 1917 she began a curious association with Strachey as his housekeeper at Tidmarsh Mill, near Pangbourne, and there she began a dedicated course of self-education. She continued to paint, though with extreme diffidence about her abilities and a consistent refusal to exhibit. In the Strachey circle Dora Carrington met mostly literary people: Keynes, Forster, David Garnett, Desmond McCarthy, and Leonard and Virginia WOOLF; the only artists were Duncan Grant and Vanessa BELL. Her own admirations in art stopped at Cézanne, the Post-Impressionists,

and Matisse: she loathed the works of Picasso and Braque. In 1919 she went on a walking tour of Spain with her brother Noel and his friend Ralph Partridge, and in 1921 married Partridge. In 1924 the Strachey ménage moved to Ham Spray in Sussex, and there she worked mostly on crafts. Her output declined in the late 1920s due to the strain on her imposed by Strachey's homosexuality, while Partridge had formed other attachments in London. In 1931 Strachey was found to be suffering from cancer; Dora Carrington tried to kill herself when he was dying, and after his death committed suicide. There are few of her works in public collections: a nude in the Slade School, and a portrait of Lady Strachey in the National Portrait Gallery of Scotland.

See also N. Carrington, *Carrington: Paintings, Drawings and Decorations*, 1978; D. Garnett (ed.), *Carrington: Letters and Extracts from her Diaries*, 1970.　　L.M.M.

Carter, Elizabeth (1717–1806), translator, poet, and letter writer; eldest daughter of Dr Nicholas Carter, perpetual curate of Deal Chapel. She was a proficient linguist who was educated by her father in French, Latin, Greek and Hebrew, and taught herself Italian, Spanish, German, Portuguese and Arabic. From 1734 she wrote verses for *The Gentleman's Magazine*, and her first volume of poems was published anonymously in 1738. She completed a number of translations and in 1749 began work on a translation of Epictetus, published in 1758. A friend of Dr Johnson, she wrote numbers 44 and 100 of his *Rambler*, and contributed with Lady Mary Wortley MONTAGU to the *Poems by Eminent Ladies* (1755). Her reputation rests largely on her posthumously published letters, written to such friends as Samuel Richardson, Bishop Butler, and Lord Bath. Fanny BURNEY, often a harsh critic of her own sex, described Elizabeth Carter in 1780 as 'really a noble-looking woman; I never saw age so graceful in the female sex yet; her whole face seems to beam with goodness, piety and philanthropy.'

See also Charlotte Barrett (ed.), *The Diary and Letters of Madame d'Arblay*, 1904; A. A. Hufstader, *Sisters of the Quill*, 1978.

A.L.

Carter, Lady Violet Bonham. See BONHAM CARTER, (HELEN) VIOLET, LADY ASQUITH OF YARNBURY.

Cartwright, Julia, known as Mrs Henry Ady (1851–1924), writer. She was born at Edgecote, Northamptonshire, and educated at home. In 1880 she became the wife of the Reverend W. H. Ady, who was rector of Ockham. She was the author of many books, including works on the Renaissance and on painters and painting, for example *The Pilgrim's Way*, 1892, *The Life and Work of Sir Edward Burne-Jones*, 1894, *Raphael in Rome*, 1895, *J.-F. Millet: his Life and Letters*, 1896, *The Life and Work of G. F. Watts*, 1896, *Sandro Botticelli*, 1904, *Raphael*, 1905, and *Baldassare Castiglione, The Perfect Courtier: His Life and Letters, 1478–1529*, 1908.   B.H.C.

Carus-Wilson, E(leanor) M(ay) (1897–1977), economic historian, the outstanding authority of her time on the English textile industry and England's foreign trade during the late Middle Ages. She was born at Montreal, where her father was Professor of Engineering at McGill University, and educated at St Paul's Girls' School and Westfield College, London; she was a schoolteacher for a few years before returning to the college for her MA, and later became a part-time lecturer there. Her researches were interrupted by war service (she was head of a branch of the Ministry of Food, 1940–45), after which she became a lecturer at the London School of Economics. She was Reader in Economic History at the University of London, then Professor from 1953 until her retirement in 1965.

Eileen POWER was E. M. Carus-Wilson's mentor. Most of her works consisted of pamphlets, or of essays that appeared in specialist journals; but a volume of collected studies, *Medieval Merchant Venturers* (1954), is widely used and encapsulates her main concerns. Taken together, the essays indicate the dimensions of the 'industrial revolution' that changed medieval England from an underdeveloped producer of raw wool—'the Australia of the Middle Ages'—into an exporter of manufactured textiles. The resultant expansion of Bristol as a port is the subject of the longest essay. Her other publications include *The Expansion of Exeter at the Close of the Middle Ages*, 1963, (with Olive Coleman) *England's Export Trade 1275–1547*, 1963, and (as editor) three volumes of *Essays in Economic History*, 1954.   N.H.

Cary, Elizabeth, Viscountess Falkland (1585–1639), playwright, the only child of a wealthy Oxford lawyer. An extraordinarily precocious child, she read constantly and taught herself French, Spanish, Italian, Latin, Hebrew, and even, apparently, 'Transylvanian'. She made translations from Latin and French and at the age of twelve discovered, to her father's consternation, 'many contradictions' in Calvin's *Institutes*. In 1602, being a young heiress, she was married to Sir Henry Cary, although they did not live together until about 1606. Their first child was born in 1609, and was followed by at least ten more over the next fifteen years.

Probably in the interval between marriage and living with her husband, Elizabeth Cary wrote the first published play in English known to have been the work of a woman: *The Tragedy of Mariam, the Fair Queen of Jewry* (published in 1613). Based on an account in Josephus' *Antiquities, Mariam* is a tragedy in the formal, Senecan mode, written mainly in rhymed quatrains. The chief dramatic interest is the contrast between the active Salome, who, scheming to get rid of her husband and marry her lover, meditates on inequitable divorce laws which deny women rights afforded to men, and the passive Mariam, who articulates the duties of a wife to her husband, and laments that she has been unfaithful in her mind.

In 1620 Henry Cary became Viscount Falkland, and he was sent to Ireland as Lord Deputy in 1622. To enable him to take up his post, his wife turned over to him a jointure settled on her by her father and was disinherited as a result. While in Ireland she set up schemes for teaching trades to Irish children, but these ran into difficulties due in part to her financial mismanagement.

She returned to England in 1625, and the following year became estranged from her husband when she openly announced her conversion to Roman Catholicism. This was a severe blow to Cary's career, and he abandoned her, taking the children and leaving her almost destitute. She was, however, assisted by Queen Henrietta Maria and others, and the King eventually ordered her husband to provide for her. Until her death in 1639 she lived in relative poverty, but she managed to send six of her children to France, where they were brought up as Catholics.

She became well known as a Catholic polemicist; her translation of Cardinal Perron's reply to King James's attack on his works was published in France in 1630, but copies reaching England were ordered to be burnt. In 1627 she wrote a biography of Edward II (not published until 1680, when it was wrongly ascribed to her husband). Other compositions in verse which she is reported to have written have not survived, but the publication of *Mariam* has secured her place in literary history.

See also K. B. Murdock, *The Sun at Noon*, 1939; N. C. Pearse, 'Elizabeth Cary, Renaissance Playwright', in *Texas Studies in Literature and Language*, 1977; R. Simpson (ed.), *The Lady Falkland: Her Life*, 1861.

W.R.O.

Cary, Mary (b. *c*.1621–*fl*.1653), prophetess, a member of the Fifth Monarchist millenarian sect; her ideas took shape at the age of fifteen, when she began to study the prophetic books of the Bible. Though she styled herself a 'minister' there is no evidence that she ever had a congregation. After 1651 she changed her name to Rande, presumably as a result of marrying.

Mary Cary's first publication was a theological tract, *The Glorious Excellencie of the Spirit of Adoption* (1645), but she is best known for the five books and pamphlets which she issued in the 1650s. These expounded the Fifth Monarchist belief that the millennial reign of Christ on earth was imminent, and that the saints might expedite it. Unlike other prophets, Cary disclaimed supernatural inspiration, and based her predictions on her interpretation of Scriptural texts. She related the arcane Scriptural symbols of Daniel and Revelation to contemporary events: the little horn was Charles I; the resurrection of the witnesses was the emergence of the New Model Army; the conversion of the Jews would happen in 1656; and Christ would return in person in 1701. Her account of *The Little Horn's Doom and Downfall* (1654) was issued with commendatory notes by the famous army preacher, Hugh Peters, and the leading Fifth Monarchists Henry Jessey and Christopher Feake.

Cary described the millennium as a period of material and spiritual blessings: 'the riches of the world . . . shall in a very short time be abundantly given to the Saints of the Most High'; 'Not only men, but women shall prophecy . . . not only those who have University-learning, but those who have it not; even servants and hand maides'. In anticipation of that happy time she directed the attention of the Barebones Parliament in 1653 to a series of detailed proposals for ecclesiastical, legal, and social reform. Her works are an important expression of Fifth Monarchist thought.

See also B. S. Capp, *The Fifth Monarchy Men*, 1972; A. Cohen, 'Mary Cary's *The Glorious Excellencie* Discovered', in *The British Studies Monitor*, 1980; C. Hill, *The World Turned Upside Down*, 1972.

W.R.O.

Castlemaine, Countess of. See VILLIERS, BARBARA, COUNTESS OF CASTLEMAINE AND DUCHESS OF CLEVELAND.

Catchpole, Margaret (1762–1819), heroine and/or criminal of exceptional force and resolution. Margaret Catchpole was the daughter of a Suffolk labourer. At thirteen she rode bareback to Ipswich to fetch a doctor in an emergency; later, as a domestic servant in the town, she saved one of her master's children from drowning; later still, in 1797, she disguised herself as a sailor, stole John Cobbold's (her master's) horse, and rode to London in eight and a half hours to join her seaman lover. For this last exploit she was sentenced to death, but the sentence was commuted to seven years' transportation. She nonetheless boldly broke out of Ipswich gaol to join her lover, was recaptured, sentenced to death again, and finally (1801) transported for life to Australia. There she worked first as a cook, and later as an overseer on the Rouse family property at Richmond. In spite of the circumstances of her departure from the Cobbolds, she carried on a correspondence with the family from her exile in Australia. She did not marry. After her pardon in 1814, she kept a small store in Richmond, and acted as a midwife and nurse, eventually dying from influenza which she caught while nursing a shepherd.

John Cobbold's son Richard wrote *The History of Margaret Catchpole* (1845), using many of Margaret's letters to his family as base material. He freely adapted these, however, and this has led to considerable subsequent confusion about the true facts of Margaret Catchpole's life.

See also N. Donkin, *Margaret Catchpole*, in the series 'Australians in History', 1974.

N.H.

Catherine of Braganza (1638–1705), Charles II's queen, the only daughter of King João of

Portugal. She was brought up as a devout Catholic and in strict seclusion by her mother, who planned from when her daughter was seven to marry her to a future king of England. In England the marriage was considered politically desirable and the Infanta's appearance satisfactory, but the determining factor was her dowry, which brought Charles II £360,000 plus Tangiers and Bombay. Although the negotiations were concluded in May 1661, it was a year before Catherine arrived in England, during which she was belatedly given worldly advice by her mother and rudimentary instruction in English.

Although she had instilled in her the virtues of obedience and submission, Catherine was no fool and had something of her mother's strong will, which proved of little avail when confronted with her first marital crisis, caused by the King's continued passion for his mistress, Barbara VILLIERS, the Countess of Castlemaine, and his determination to make her a lady of the Bedchamber. Catherine, who loved her husband deeply, responded initially with hysteria and remained obstinate in her refusal to grant this request until Charles's deliberate neglect, the hostility of the Court, and the dismissal of her Portuguese servants finally wore her down. However, within a year of their marriage they had settled into an amicable relationship which endured until the King's death, largely thanks to Catherine's tolerance of her husband's mistresses and his love for his illegitimate children, which added to her grief at her own childlessness. This incapacity, and the conversion to Catholicism of the Duke of York, Charles' brother and heir, made Catherine the victim of recurring plots to divorce her from the King in the hope that he would marry again and produce a Protestant heir. To his credit, Charles staunchly resisted all such schemes. Catherine's essential goodness, her refusal to meddle in political or religious affairs, and the King's determination to stand by her, also preserved her during the Popish Plot crisis, when anti-Catholic sentiment was at its peak.

Grief-stricken by the King's death in 1685, Catherine retired to Somerset House and finally returned to Portugal in 1692. She proved an able adviser to her brother, King Pedro, whose poor health led to her subsequent appointment as Queen Regent. As such, she concluded a treaty with England in 1703 and conducted a highly successful military campaign against Spain, dying at the height of her popularity and success.

See also J. Mackay, *Catherine of Braganza*, 1937.

T.J.M.

Catherine of Valois (1401–37), Henry V's queen. She was the youngest daughter of Charles VI of France; her eldest sister, ISABELLA, had been Richard II's queen. Negotiations for Catherine's marriage to Henry V dragged on for years while their countries were at war. By the treaty of Troyes in 1420 Henry won her, together with the kingdom of France on her father's death. Their son, Henry VI, was born a few months before Henry's own death in 1422, and he remained in his mother's care until he was seven. Catherine played no part in the political events of the minority, but fear of the influence that any future step-father might have on the young king led to a statute forbidding the remarriage of a queen-dowager without the king's permission. Catherine was not prepared to wait until her son was old enough to give it and in about 1428 she secretly married an obscure Welsh squire named Owen Tudor, by whom she had four children. The second son, Edmund Tudor, later Earl of Richmond, was the father of Henry VII.

See also R. A. Griffiths, *The Reign of Henry VI*, 1981.
A.C.

Catley, Anne (1745–89), actress, singer and dancer, born in London. Anne Catley was singing in taverns by the age of ten, and by the age of fourteen was the mistress of many members of the Tower of London garrison. Contemporary memoirs indicate that she became one of London's most sought-after high-class courtesans.

She made her first professional stage appearance at Vauxhall in 1762, followed by a part in *Comus* at Covent Garden. She made her name in 1763 singing the leading role in *Thomas and Sally*. The following year she was involved in complicated litigation featuring her father, her 'agent', and an aristocratic degenerate who planned to set her up as a prostitute; the outcome was obscure. Appearing in London and Dublin during the late 1760s, Anne Catley became successful and fashionable (her hair-style was particularly admired and imitated), in spite of scandalous amours and the births of two children. In

Cavell, Edith

1770–71 she appeared successfully in ballad operas at Covent Garden: *Love in a Village*, *The Padlock, Lionel and Clarissa*. In 1771 she married Colonel Francis Lascelles, but insisted that her children inherit her fortune, and her marriage remained secret until her retirement. She continued to perform throughout the 1770s, and despite constant attacks on her coarseness she commanded huge salaries and was acknowledged as an exquisite singer and attractive personality.

By 1780 she was deteriorating physically and played older parts such as Clara in Sheridan's *The Duenna*. At 37, too ill to go on, she retired to a large house in Ealing where she took to philanthropy. She died of consumption leaving a fortune to her eight children by various fathers.

See also P. H. Highfill, K. A. Burnim and E.A. Langhans, *A Biographical Dictionary of Actors, Actresses, Musicians, Dancers, Managers and Other Stage Personnel in London, 1660–1800*, vol. 3, 1975.   C.H.

Cavell, Edith (Louisa) (1865–1915), nurse. Born in Swardeston by Norwich, she was one of four children. A serious child, she was educated at first by her father, a minister, and later attended a school for modern languages; thereafter she undertook work as a governess, living for some years in Brussels. In 1895, after caring for her father, who was seriously ill, she decided that nursing was her appointed role in life and in the following year was accepted as a probationer at the London Hospital. Thereafter she worked steadily, if not outstandingly, at her chosen career, and in 1907 was invited to assist in setting up a Belgian school of nursing, modelled on the British system. She became matron of the Berkendael Institute in Brussels and in 1910 assumed similar control in the hospital of St Gilles. She was a strict disciplinarian, demanding total dedication from her nurses, but considering the difficult task in front of her, her 'cold, aloof' attitude is more easily understood. The Institute was an outstanding success and funds were raised to enlarge the school.

When war broke out Edith Cavell remained in Brussels, and it is the help which she gave to Allied fugitives, and her subsequent execution, for which she is best remembered. Initially she arranged for the escape of two British soldiers to Holland, but in little less than a year, as part of an underground network, she aided over a hundred British soldiers and another hundred Frenchmen and Belgians of military age. She did not consider the possible implications of her actions, believing it was her Christian duty to take in those who needed help. As time passed the German authorities grew suspicious of her, and in August 1915 she was arrested and detained in St Gilles prison, where she made a full confession of her activities. She was tried along with thirty-four others on 6 October 1915, and five days later she and four associates were sentenced to death. She was summarily executed the following day despite a hasty appeal from the American Minister in Brussels.

The Allied and neutral nations were outraged by this act, believing that she should have been pardoned because of her sex. She had followed the laws of God and had to accept the consequences on earth; and according to German law the sentence was correct. Edith Cavell's body now lies in Norwich Cathedral. A statue of her stands in St Martins Place, London.

See also H. Judson, *Edith Cavell*, 1941; A. E. C. Kennedy, *Edith Cavell: Pioneer and Patriot*, 1965.   J.G.S.

Cavendish, Georgiana, Duchess of Devonshire (1757–1806), political hostess, the eldest daughter of John, first Earl Spencer. On her seventeenth birthday she married William Cavendish, fifth Duke of Devonshire. She became an indefatigable Whig hostess and a close friend of Fox, Sheridan, and the Prince of Wales; and in the election of April 1784 she personally canvassed for Fox in his Westminster constituency. Although she had three children between 1783 and 1790, her marriage was unhappy, for her ardent nature was unsatisfied by the cool and unresponsive Duke. She acquiesced in the Duke's relationship with Lady Elizabeth Foster, who became her closest friend despite the fact that she bore the Duke two children. In 1791 the Duchess became pregnant by Charles Grey, and this, combined with her reckless accumulation of gambling debts, produced a temporary separation from the Duke. She travelled on the Continent for almost two years, giving birth to Grey's daughter, Eliza Courtenay, at Aix-en-Provence in February 1792. After her return to England in 1793 her health deteriorated. She died at Devonshire House, Piccadilly, and was buried in St Stephen's Church, Derby.

Georgiana, Duchess of Devonshire, wrote a successful semi-autobiographical novel, *The Sylph* (1779), and a poem, *The Passage of the Mountain of St Gothard* (1802). In her political testament, written in 1802, she lamented the destruction of the Whig Rockingham connection and denounced the Tory-inspired extensions of executive power that had occurred over the previous decade.

See also B. Masters, *Georgiana, Duchess of Devonshire*, 1981. M.J.S.

Cavendish, Lucy, Lady Frederick (1841–1926), social reformer. Born Lady Lucy Caroline Lyttelton, she was a daughter of the fourth Lord Lyttelton. At Hagley, the family house in Worcester, she had an affectionate upbringing in a highly cultivated and intellectual society where particular emphasis was placed on the religious aspects of life. In her early twenties she became a Maid of Honour to Queen Victoria, and in less than a year she married Lord Frederick Cavendish, second son of the Duke of Devonshire. There followed eighteen years of happy marriage in the world of Liberal politics and high society.

As Gladstone's niece, Lady Cavendish knew many influential politicians on both sides of the House and was able to campaign effectively on behalf of the causes in which she was interested. But it was only after the death of her husband in the Phoenix Park murders of 1882 that she was able to devote herself to these causes, notably religious education, the union of peoples in South Africa, and peace in Ireland. Her hatred of oppression and her religious zeal prompted her concern for the plight of Christians in Turkey, and until her death she was president of the Friends of Armenia society. Her other main interest was education, especially that of young women, and as her brother-in-law was Minister of Education for some time, she was not without influence. Her knowledge of the subject was recognized by her appointment in 1894 as a member of the Royal Commission on Secondary Education. In 1904 she was awarded an honorary degree from the University of Leeds, and in 1965 the Lucy Cavendish Hall for women graduate students at Cambridge University was established as an acknowledgement of her work in this sphere.

Throughout her life Lady Cavendish was a most devoted and convinced supporter of the Church. As an admirable public speaker she campaigned on behalf of various religious or charitable causes, and few women were more consulted by the Church hierarchy. On a more practical level she undertook numerous services for the poor and sick. Lady Frederick Cavendish, who could have enjoyed at leisure the advantages of aristocratic birth, instead set an example of public service to other privileged women.

See also J. Bailey (ed.), *The Diary of Lady Frederick Cavendish*, 1927. J.G.S.

Cavendish, Margaret, Duchess of Newcastle (1623–73), writer, the youngest child of Thomas Lucas, an Essex gentleman who died when she was two. Despite her crippling shyness, Margaret Lucas succeeded in becoming Maid of Honour to Henrietta Maria, whom she accompanied on her flight to France in 1644, a terrifying experience and a recurring theme in Margaret's later writings. As a Royalist exile in Paris, she met William Cavendish, fifty-two-year-old Marquis of Newcastle, in 1645 and, 'Though I did dread marriage', Margaret fell completely in love with the romantic Marquis and became his wife in the same year despite the difference in their ages and social status. They spent most of their years of exile until 1660 in Antwerp.

Newcastle, a man of wide cultural and scientific interests and himself an author, encouraged Margaret to develop and publish her ideas. Although Newcastle had children by his first marriage, Margaret Cavendish proved barren. Her childlessness caused her little regret; as she pointed out, a woman loses her name on marriage and so has no 'line' to maintain, yet 'she hazards her life by bringing them into the world, and hath the greatest share of trouble in bringing them up'. Indeed, Margaret had absolutely no interest in conventional domesticity. For her, writing was an all-consuming passion. She had written compulsively since childhood, filling sixteen scrappy 'baby-books', but it was on a visit to England, in an unsuccessful attempt to redeem Newcastle's confiscated estates, that she decided to write consciously for publication. *Poems and Fancies* was published in March 1653, *Philosophicall Fancies* two months later; and for the next fifteen years Margaret showered her works on the public. She used most possible forms: essays, letters, orations, plays and verse, writing fantasies, fictions, and non-fiction on an extraordinary variety of topics. Her best-known work, the 1667 *Life* of her husband, is a splendid portrayal of his character and exile, but (having been written for public consumption) is less frank and therefore less valuable on Newcastle's public career than Lucy HUTCHINSON's comparable work. Margaret Cavendish wrote the *Life* after the Restoration (1660), when Newcastle was given scant reward for his Civil War sacrifices apart from being made a Duke. The couple lived in retirement at Welbeck, where Margaret Cavendish died before her elderly husband.

Margaret Cavendish's works were ridiculed by contemporaries; Dorothy OSBORNE, on reading her first book, claimed there were 'many soberer people in Bedlam'. They have perhaps also been undervalued by later critics. A woman who deliberately sought a public role ('All I desire is fame', she wrote) was an obvious target. Perhaps the best assessment of her is Virginia WOOLF's: 'though her philosophies are futile, and her plays intolerable, and her verses mainly dull, the vast bulk of the Duchess is leavened by a vein of authentic fire ... There is something noble and high-spirited as well as crack-brained and bird-witted.' She had vivid descriptive powers, a lively talent for fantasy, and her frank autobiographical passages and the fictions in which she gives her active, strong-minded heroines the public role and influence denied to herself and her contemporaries, remain of great charm and interest.

Margaret Cavendish's views on the relations between the sexes have not lost their relevance. Although she firmly believed men and women had different natures, she blamed women's restricted lives largely on men. Men undervalued women, so that they came to have a low opinion of themselves: 'our counsels are despised and laughed at, the best of our actions are trodden down with scorn by the overweening conceit men have of themselves'. Women were 'kept like birds in cages' and writing provided the only escape, 'all heroic actions, public employments, powerful governments and eloquent pleadings being denied' them. Her witty and committed analysis of what it meant to be a woman and a writer give the Duchess of Newcastle an important place in the history of feminism.

See also D. Grant, *Margaret the First*, 1957; M. R. Mahl and H. Koon (eds), *The Female Spectator*, 1977; V. Woolf, *Women and Writing*, 1979.   A.H.

Cecil, Mildred (?1526–1589), scholar and wife of Queen Elizabeth's chief minister. She was the eldest daughter of Sir Anthony Cooke of Gidea Park, Essex, and reputedly one of the most learned women of her time. The five Cooke sisters received a thorough humanist education from their erudite father, and were praised by the scholar-teacher Roger Ascham as eclipsing even the daughters of Sir Thomas More. Unlike her sister Ann BACON, Mildred Cecil published no works or translations of her own. However, her accomplishments can be gauged by her correspondence, and by Sir Richard Morison's letters to her husband, which contain many comments on her knowledge of Greek. In December 1545 she married William Cecil, later Lord Burghley, who skilfully survived the reigns of Edward VI and Queen Mary, and was immediately appointed chief secretary of state on Elizabeth's accession in November 1558. From this time Mildred Cecil came a little more into the public eye; she was described by different Spanish ambassadors as a tiresome bluestocking, and as a furious heretic with great influence over her husband. However, she was more concerned with domestic matters than with court life, though the Cecils frequently entertained Queen Elizabeth at their various houses. She was extravagantly mourned by Cecil, but it is impossible to say whether she exercised any real influence over him. Her importance lies in her remarkable erudition and her interest in learning, shown by charitable benefactions which she kept secret even from her husband. She provided an exhibition for two scholars and four quarterly sermons at St John's College, Cambridge, Cecil's old college, and gave books (some of them in Greek and Hebrew) to St John's, Cambridge, Christ Church, Oxford, and Westminster College.

See also J. A. Giles (ed.), *The Whole Works of Roger Ascham*, 1865; C. Read, *Mr Secretary Cecil and Queen Elizabeth*, 1955, and *Lord Burghley and Queen Elizabeth*, 1960.

M.D.

Cellier, Elizabeth (*fl.* 1679–88), political intriguer and midwife. Elizabeth Cellier came from a Buckinghamshire family. She became a Catholic and married a French merchant living in the parish of St Clement Dane's, London, where she practised as a midwife, acquiring a notable reputation and links with the Catholic community. She played an important role during the Popish Plot crisis of the late 1670s (when many Catholics were being arrested for supposedly participating in a widespread 'Popish' conspiracy), giving aid to Catholic prisoners and lodging witnesses who were to appear at their trials. Through these activities she met Thomas Dangerfield, a disreputable conspirator, and with him fabricated a conspiracy intended to make the Dissenters (Protestant nonconformists) seem guilty of concocting the Popish Plot. Their scheme was discovered in October 1679, becoming known as the 'meal-tub' plot, after the place in Cellier's house where forged documents were found. Elizabeth Cellier was imprisoned for high treason, but at her trial in June 1680 she secured an acquittal by her own spirited defence, proving that Dangerfield, who had turned King's Evidence and accused her of planning to assassinate Charles II, was a convicted robber and thus not a credible witness. Unfortunately she was not content with this triumph but produced a defence of herself in *Malice Defeated* (1680), which cast doubts (correctly) on the existence of any 'Popish Plot'. She was again tried, this time for libel, and was found guilty in September 1680, sentenced to be pilloried three times, fined £1000, and imprisoned. 'The Popish Midwife' became a bogey figure to English Protestants, who regarded the existence of an active female conspirator as conclusive evidence of the evils of Popery, and *Malice Defeated* attracted several vitriolic replies.

Elizabeth Cellier is also notable as one of several seventeenth-century midwives (for example Jane SHARP and Hester SHAW) who tried to raise the status of their calling. In a published address to James II of 1687 (reprinted in *The Harleian Miscellany*) she lamented the death of many women and their babies through the ministrations of unskilled midwives, and the murder of many illegitimate children by their 'wicked and cruel' or desperate mothers who had no way of providing for them. She proposed a neat solution to both problems: London midwives were to become a corporation, in which they would be closely supervised and carefully trained, while the fees paid for entry to the corporation were to be used to finance a hospital for the care and education of foundling children. Senior female midwives, under the overall supervision of a 'man-midwife' or physician, were

to be responsible for the midwives, while the children were to receive training in useful trades appropriate to their sex. Her plans came to nothing, however, as the overthrow of the Catholic James II in 1688 ended her influence in high places.

See also J. Donnison, *Midwives and Medical Men*, 1977.   A.H.

Centlivre, Susanna (1670?–1723), dramatist and poet. Little is known of her early life. She was probably educated by a Huguenot exile in Lincolnshire and after the death of her parents may have married a nephew of Sir Stephen Fox. This husband died, and in 1685 she married an army officer, Carroll, but was widowed again in 1687. Her first published work appeared in 1700, by which time she had settled in London. Before her first popular success she supplemented a scanty income by performing as a strolling player. Her marriage in 1707 to Joseph Centlivre, one of the royal cooks, did not curtail her dramatic output: she wrote numerous plays, including the most popular drama of the first half of the eighteenth century, *The Busy Body* (1709). Between 1712 and 1717 her poems and plays did political service in defence of the Protestant succession and the Hanoverian dynasty. This earned her the enmity of Alexander Pope, who attacked her in his pamphlet on Edmund Curll (1716), in the character of Phoebe Clinket in *Three Hours After Marriage*, and in *The Dunciad*. In the best of her plays, Susanna Centlivre's proficiency as a comic writer depended on her skill in adapting the Restoration techniques of Congreve to the sentimentalism popularised by such writers as Cibber and Steele. She is among the early dramatists who attempted to overcome the conventional hostility towards women writers by creating female characters of sense and integrity. Her works include *The Wonder* (1714) and *A Bold Stroke for a Wife* (1718).

See also J. W. Bowyer, *The Celebrated Mrs Centlivre*, 1952.   A.L.

Chadwick, Nora Kershaw (1891–1972), literary and historical scholar. The daughter of a Lancashire mill-owner, Nora Kershaw went to a private school in Southport before going up to Newnham College, Cambridge, where she distinguished herself in the Medieval and Modern Languages Tripos. After lecturing at St Andrews University (1914–19), she returned to Cambridge, where in 1922 she married her former teacher, H. M. Chadwick, who as Professor of Anglo-Saxon Literature had pioneered a broadly-based comparative approach to the study of philology and history. In the more than two decades of private work that followed, Nora Chadwick put together and published readers in Anglo-Saxon, Norse, early Irish and Russian literature; and she collaborated with her husband on their monumental *The Growth of Literature* (1932–40). She became a research fellow at Newnham College, Cambridge (1941–44), lecturer in the early history and culture of the British Isles at the University of Cambridge (1950–58), director of studies in Anglo-Saxon and Celtic subjects at Newnham (1950–59) and Girton College (1951–62), etc. Among her many publications were *Poetry and Letters in Early Christian Gaul*, 1955, *Celtic Britain*, 1963, *The Druids*, 1966, and *The Celts*, 1970.

N.H.

Chambers, Dorothea Katharine Lambert (1878–1960), tennis player, born at Ealing, the daughter of a clergyman. She won her first three Wimbledon ladies' singles under her maiden name, Miss D. K. Douglass, in 1903, 1904 and 1906. Then, after marrying Robert Lambert Chambers in 1907, she again won the singles in 1910, 1911, 1913 and 1914. She also won the Olympic ladies' gold medal in 1908. Twenty-three years after her first Wimbledon singles title, when she was already forty-seven years old, she played in the Wightman Cup team of 1925–6. She was probably the greatest woman player before 1918 and her match against the up-and-coming Suzanne Lenglen in the 1919 Wimbledon final made tennis history. Lenglen, twenty years younger than her rival, finally won after a total of 44 games over three gruelling sets. Asked to go to the Royal Box afterwards, both women had to refuse, as Mrs Lambert Chambers was exhausted and Mlle Lenglen's feet were bleeding. Such heroic encounters helped to transform women's tennis from a genteel pursuit into the modern game demanding great willpower and physical stamina.

See also M. Robertson, *Wimbledon 1877–1977*, 1977.

E.M.V.

Chapone, Hester (1727–1801), essayist. She was born Hester Mulso, of an old Northamptonshire family. Her precocity is evidenced by the composition at the age of nine of a romance, *Amoret and Melissa*. She was greatly admired by the novelist Samuel Richardson, and assumed a leading role in his coterie. It was at his house that she met her future husband and, after a long engagement during which she attempted to overcome her father's opposition to the match, the couple were married in 1760. Chapone died of a fever ten months later.

Hester Chapone's only piece of fiction, 'Fidelia', was printed in Dr Johnson's periodical *The Adventurer*, and she also contributed four letters to number 10 of his *Rambler* (1750). She corresponded with many literary figures in the Bluestocking group. A friendship with Elizabeth CARTER followed their meeting in 1749, and she became equally close to Elizabeth MONTAGU whom she met in 1762; she was also friendly with Fanny BURNEY. Her most distinguished work, for which she won royal recognition, was *Letters on the Improvement of the Mind*. It was written, shortly after her husband's death, for the edification of a favourite niece, and was dedicated to Elizabeth Montagu. The didacticism of this conduct book emerges in the treatment of such topics as 'Religion' and 'The Regulation of the Heart and Affections'.

See also G. B. Hill (ed.), *Boswell's Life of Johnson*, 1934.

A.L.

Charke, Charlotte (d. 1760?), actress and puppeteer, was the most eccentric member of a well-known theatrical family, the Cibbers.

She was brought up to the stage but was rarely an ornament to it. From childhood she preferred masculine pursuits and dress. She did, nonetheless, marry Richard Charke at an early age, but they separated within the year. She appeared on the stage between 1730 and 1737, chiefly in male parts. However, her behaviour and character were so unpredictable and irresponsible that she was unable to hold an engagement for any length of time.

Finally, Charlotte Charke fell out with her manager and wrote a play against him (*The Art of Management*, 1735). She was then employed at puppet-shows and booth theatres. Although she was regularly destitute, her father never forgave her for some offence she had committed against him, and never helped her. She was once bailed out by Covent Garden brothel-keepers. She was variously a sausage-seller, a tavern-keeper, and a gentleman's valet. A young woman proposed marriage to her, and at some point she gave birth to a daughter. On the death of her first husband she secretly re-married; her new spouse soon died, however, leaving her again destitute.

After 'a variegated scene of pitiable distresses' with strolling players in the provinces, Charlotte Charke returned to London, hoping to mend her fortunes by writing an autobiography. Although it was published in 1775, she died in abject poverty in Islington. 'Born in affluence, educated with care and tenderness, and who though possessing considerable talents terminated her miserable existence on a dunghill' (*Dramatic Table Talk*, 1825).

See also D. E. Baker, *Biographia Dramatica*, 1782; P. H. Highfill, K. A. Burnim, E. A. Langhans, *A Biographical Dictionary of Actors, Actresses, Musicians, Dancers, etc. in London, 1660-1800*, vol. 3, 1975. C.H.

Charlotte (1744–1818), George III's queen. She was born at Mirow on 19 May 1744, the youngest daughter of Charles, Duke of Mecklenburg-Strelitz, and Princess Elizabeth of Saxe-Hildburghausen. On 8 September 1761, she married George III at St James's Palace. Although it was an arranged match, the marriage proved to be successful, and between 1762 and 1783 she bore fifteen children, twelve of whom outlived her. The King never discussed affairs of state with her, and she was content to lead an entirely domestic life. She was a generous benefactor of charities, especially those devoted to the welfare of women and children, of which the Magdalen Hospital and Queen Charlotte's Maternity Hospital were the most notable. She also founded a Sunday School at Windsor, and encouraged the efforts of the Schools' originator, Robert Raikes. In addition, she is credited with playing a part in the passage of an Act in 1790 which abolished the penalty of burning at the stake for women convicted of certain offences. An enthusiastic amateur botanist, she patronized the Royal Gardens at Kew, and in 1773 a South African plant was named the *Strelitzia reginae* in her honour.

Her popularity received its first challenge during the Regency crisis of 1788–89, when the Whigs accused her of attempting to conceal the extent of the King's malady in order to prevent the Prince of Wales from assuming the Regency. Under the Regency Act of 1811, the care of the King's person and the man-

agement of his household were entrusted to the Queen. Her advice that nothing should be done that might impede the King's recovery was one factor in the Prince Regent's decision not to appoint a Whig administration. Her popularity diminished during her last years, since she took the side of the Prince Regent in his quarrel with his wife, Princess CAROLINE. Queen Charlotte died at Kew Palace and was buried in St George's Chapel, Windsor.

Queen Charlotte possessed neither the ability nor the desire to stamp her personality on public life. She presided over a decorous court, and the propriety of her private life was in marked contrast to the aristocratic morals and manners of the time.

See also P. Fitzgerald, *The Good Queen Charlotte*, 1899; O. Hedley, *Queen Charlotte*, 1975. M.J.S.

Chase, Marian Emma (1844–1905), painter. She was the second daughter of John Chase, a pupil of Constable, who published *A Practical Treatise on ... Water Colours* (1863). From her father she learnt water-colour painting and perspective, and she was given instruction on drawing by the Scottish artist Margaret Gillies. When she was young she practised as a miniaturist, painting interiors, landscapes, and gardens; but she is best known for her water-colour drawings of flowers and still life. She exhibited at the Royal Academy, the New Society of Painters in Watercolours, and the Dudley and Grosvenor galleries. She was elected an Associate of the New Society in 1875 and in 1888 was awarded the silver medal of the Royal Botanical Society in recognition of her flower painting. Examples of her work are in the Victoria and Albert Museum and a water-colour of roses is in the Aberdeen art gallery. Her sister Jessie was also a water-colourist.

See also E. C. Clayton, *English Female Artists*, 1876; W. S. Sparrow, *British Sporting Artists*, 1922. B.H.C.

Chatelain, (Henriette) Marie (1823–97), Catholic nun. She was born in Paris and baptized Henriette, but always used her confirmation name, Marie. Her parents died while she was young and the children were brought up in Geneva by an aunt and uncle. In 1844 her religious dedication led her to join the Sisters of Charity, and for twelve years her chief work was as secretary to the Mother

General, a position in which she displayed great practical ability despite tuberculosis. Her ability and dedication were again evident during her service as a nurse in the Crimea, the horrors of which she narrated in her letters. After a period as Superior in Constantinople, she was recalled to Paris in 1855 to take charge of a large new orphanage there, a difficult work for someone who was naturally reserved. As soon as the orphanage was established, she was sent to Sheffield to open a house and was confronted by hostility and poverty, a situation exacerbated by her poor English and ill health. Nevertheless, in a year she was able to report that the sisters were accepted and that their work was flourishing. They were invited to London by Catholic philanthropists, where Sister Chatelain started another house. Their first establishment was in an unsatisfactory situation, and it fell to Marie Chatelain to put the institution on its feet. This she did with great success, and within two years there were new recruits and a new house was built in Carlisle Place. There the sisters opened a school and a nursery and in the evenings taught men and boys who worked as street sweepers and hawkers during the day. The success of the work was largely due to the practical and spiritual leadership of Sister Chatelain. Always in the forefront of Catholic charitable work, she did much to break down prejudice in Britain against her faith.

See also A. Kerr, *Sister Chatelain*, 1900.

C.H.G.G.

Chatham, Hester, Lady. See PITT, HESTER, COUNTESS OF CHATHAM.

Cheesman, Evelyn Lucy (1881–1969), explorer and entomologist. The daughter of a prosperous shopkeeper in Ashford, Kent, she was educated at Ashford and Brighton and in 1904–05 spent two years abroad in France and Germany.

Unable to fulfil her ambition to become a veterinary surgeon, she worked as a canine nurse and then, during the First World War, as a temporary civil servant. She was introduced to Professor Maxwell Lefroy, Curator of the Insect House at Regents Park Zoo, and he asked her to become its Keeper in 1920. As she had received no formal scientific training she attended Professor Lefroy's general entomology course at Imperial College for two years.

In 1924 she was invited to join a scientific expedition travelling from the West Indies to the South Pacific. She remained on the Society Islands collecting insects, and on her return worked voluntarily at the British Museum classifying her specimens. Thereafter her life was divided between lone expeditions to the New Hebrides, Papua, Dutch New Guinea, and New Caledonia, writing and lecturing to subsidise her travels, and working as an unpaid honorary associate at the British Museum. She was awarded a Civil List Pension in 1953 and carried out her final expedition in 1954–55, when she was 74.

Her publications include *Everyday Doings of Insects*, 1924, *Hunting Insects in the South Seas*, 1932, *Land of the Red Bird*, 1938, and two volumes of reminiscences, *Things Worth While*, 1957, and *Time Well Spent*, 1960.

G.B.

Chenevix, Mrs (d. 1755), 'toy-woman'. Mrs Chenevix was the daughter of William Deards, toyman at the Star, Pall Mall, London. She married Paul Daniel Chenevix, also a toyman at the Golden Gate, opposite Suffolk Street, Charing Cross, and on his death in 1742 she carried on the business, earning for herself the reputation of the 'toy-woman à la mode'. Her sister Mrs Bertrand was 'the no less noted toy-woman at Bath'. In 1747 Horace Walpole purchased from Mrs Chenevix the lease of what became his famous residence, Strawberry Hill, Twickenham.

See also R. A. Austen-Leigh, 'The family of Chenevix', in *Proceedings of the Huguenot Society of London*, 1944–45; Mrs P. Toynbee (ed.), *The Letters of Horace Walpole*, 1903.

T.M.

Chester, Alice (d. 1485), Bristol businesswoman. After the death of her merchant husband in 1470 she developed an expanding trade with Spain and Flanders, exporting cloth and importing iron. She built an imposing house in the High Street with ground floor shop and three dwelling storeys above, and was also a great benefactress. For the city she funded the construction of a massive barrel crane, while her gifts to All Saints Church, High Street, included a rood screen, elaborate vestments, and a costly silver cross.

See also E. M. Carus-Wilson, *Medieval Merchant Venturers*, 1954. G.H.

Chesterton, Ada (Elizabeth) (1870–1962), journalist and philanthropist, born in London.

There was a strong journalistic tradition in her family, and she quickly established herself as a versatile feature writer, often under the pseudonym 'Sheridan Jones'. She became assistant editor to Cecil Chesterton (brother of G. K. Chesterton) on the *Eye Witness* (later the *New Witness*) and married him in 1917; he was drafted into the army shortly afterwards and died in 1918. Over the next few years Ada Chesterton travelled widely in Russia, Poland, and the East, recording her impressions in *My Russian Venture* (1931) and other books. However, she made her greatest impact on the public with *In Darkest London* (1926), based on her experiences among the destitute and homeless. Thereafter she worked devotedly to set up Cecil Houses, where homeless women could find decent food and accommodation for a small payment, and later Cecil Residential Clubs for the low-paid and aged. Among her many writings were novels (under the name John Keith Prothero) and a stage adaptation (in collaboration with Ralph Neal) of G. K. Chesterton's *The Man who was Thursday*, (1926). N.H.

Cheyne, Lady Jane (1621–69), active Royalist and writer, the daughter of William Cavendish, Duke of Newcastle, and step-daughter of Margaret CAVENDISH. In 1643, during the Civil War, she and her sister were put in charge of a small garrison at Welbeck, the family home; though temporarily successful, they were taken prisoner and roughly handled. Later, Lady Jane tried fruitlessly for a pardon for her exiled father, but interceded successfully for two of her brothers. When the family properties were despoiled she managed to secure some of the tapestries and Van Dycks. She supported her father abroad, selling her jewels and plate and sending him £1000 of her own money. Refusing to consider a match with anyone but a Royalist, she finally married Charles Cheyne of Cogenho, Northamptonshire, in 1654. Lady Jane Cheyne was buried in Chelsea Church, which she had re-roofed at her own cost, one of her various charitable acts.

Besides her active Royalism, she is interesting for her writings, notably religious poetry and a play, *The Concealed Fancies*, written with her sister Elizabeth. The manuscript of the play is in the Bodleian Library, Oxford; her works have never been published.

See also T. Faulkner, *Historical and Topographical Description of Chelsea*, 1829; A. Littleton, Funeral Sermon, 1669. M.D.

Chidley, Catherine (*fl.* 1590–1667), radical religious enthusiast. Catherine Chidley was the wife of Daniel, a Shropshire yeoman who became a tailor in Shrewsbury and burgess of the town in 1621. She had two sons, Samuel born in 1616 or 1617 and Daniel born in 1620.

During the 1620s, if not before, she belonged to an active group of religious separatists that incurred the wrath of Peter Studley, the rector of St Chad's, Shrewsbury, the Chidleys' parish. In 1628 the family was driven from Shrewsbury and settled in London, where Catherine's husband was employed as a haberdasher; her son Samuel followed the same trade.

Catherine Chidley was widowed in 1646. She and her son Samuel became well known in London sectarian circles and in 1646 she was described by the Presbyterian Thomas Edwards, an arch enemy of the sects, as 'an old Brownist' and a 'brazen-faced audacious old woman'. With the meeting of the Long Parliament she began to write and publish religious pamphlets, taking advantage of the breakdown of censorship. Her *Justification of the Independent Churches of Christ*, written with Samuel, appeared in 1641 with *A New-Yeares Gift for Mr Thomas Edwards* and *Good Counsel to the Petitioners for Presbyterian Government* following in 1645. All were appeals for toleration and attacks on Presbyterian authoritarianism; the first two were directed against Edwards in particular. Although her 1641 volume contained apologies for her lack of learning and appeals to her readers to accept it 'though it be from a woman', it does illustrate the liberating effect of religious radicalism on some women: 'I pray you tell me what authority the unbelieving husband hath over the conscience of the believing wife' she asked. Catherine Chidley did, though, acknowledge male authority in 'bodily and civil respects'.

In the summer of 1646, Catherine and Samuel 'convinced in conscience of the evil of the Church of England' and encouraged by the success of the New Model Army against the King, founded a gathered church in Bury St Edmunds. Soon afterwards Samuel became treasurer of the London radical group, the Levellers, while Catherine organised the Leveller women. She led the women's campaigns for the release of Leveller leader John Lilburne

Chidley, Catherine

93

from prison in 1649 and 1653, and is the probable author of Leveller petitions of April and May 1649. These were presented to Parliament by mass demonstrations of women who made the bold claim that 'we have an equal share and interest with men in the Commonwealth' and declared 'we are no whit satisfied with the answer you gave unto our Husbands'. In July 1653 she led a deputation of twelve women who brought the Barebones Parliament a petition signed by 6000 women, campaigning not only for the release of Lilburne but for Leveller causes in general.

Less is known of Catherine Chidley's personal life, although it is interesting to note that in 1651–52 she was making a good living from the sale of stockings to Parliament's Irish army. She lived in Bow Lane, perhaps until her death. Catherine Chidley is the most remarkable of all the women active in the political and religious radical movements of the 1640s and 1650s, and her life exemplifies the opportunities seized by women during the upheavals of the Civil War and republican period.

See also P. Higgins, 'The Reactions of Women' in B. Manning (ed.), *Politics, Religion and the English Civil War*, 1973.   P.M.H.

Chisholm, Caroline (1808–77), philanthropist, was born at Wootton, Northamptonshire, the daughter of a prosperous yeoman farmer. She was educated at home by her mother. She agreed to marry Archibald Chisholm, a captain in the East India Company's service, on condition that she could continue the philanthropic work that had occupied her youth. Her husband was a Roman Catholic and Caroline Chisholm was herself converted soon after her marriage.

In 1832 the Chisholms were posted to Madras. Shocked by the viciousness of barracks life, Caroline Chisholm founded a School of Industry for the daughters of soldiers, which continued to prosper after she left India for Australia in 1838. Arriving at Sydney, she was deeply moved by the helplessness of female immigrants, many of whom drifted into prostitution. Despite the indifference of the Governor, in 1841 Mrs Chisholm opened a home for the reception of immigrant girls. She also sought to provide them with work, and personally accompanied many into the bush in search of jobs on farms and ranches.

It was on her return to England that Caroline Chisholm began her most important work.

She became convinced that the best form of emigration was that of complete families, and assiduously sought government sponsorship for her ideas. She addressed a summary of her views to Lord Grey in her pamphlet *Emigration and Transportation relatively considered . . .* and enjoyed a limited success when the administration agreed to her request that the wives and children of liberated transportees be allowed to join them in the new homelands. For some time she had gathered and printed information on conditions prevailing in Australia, hoping to interest respectable families in emigration. In 1848 she founded the Family Colonization Loan Society, which prepared emigrants for the difficulties facing them, confided single women and children to the protection of married men, and also lent poorer families the price of their passage. This scheme proved popular with the colonial authorities, who were generally unenthusiastic about official emigration programmes.

Caroline Chisholm's writings included *The ABC of Colonization* (1850). She returned to Australia in 1854 and continued her work there for twelve years. She was granted a government pension of £100 a year in 1867, but nevertheless died in poverty.

Strongly motivated by an ideal of woman as a civilizing influence, Caroline Chisholm believed that virtuous wives encouraged the spread of moral goodness. The welfare of female emigrants was not therefore merely to be considered in terms of rescuing individuals; it also formed the only foundation upon which a properly ordered society could develop.

See also A. J. Hammerton, *Emigrant Gentlewomen*, 1979; E. Mackenzie, *Memoirs of Mrs Caroline Chisholm*, 1852.   J.V.L.

Chitenden, Agnes (*fl.* 1511), Lollard, of St George's parish in Canterbury, was interrogated by Archbishop Warham's commission of 1511 in Kent. She confessed to sharing the beliefs of such notorious heretics as Agnes GREBILL, and was compelled to witness several Lollard burnings.

See also D. Baker (ed.), *Medieval Women*, 1978.   K.R.D.

Cholmondeley, Mary (1859–1925), novelist, born in Hodnet, Shropshire. She was the daughter of a clergyman. Frail in health, she had a private education and until her late thirties lived in the country helping with parish work.

Her father retired in 1896 and she moved with him to a flat in London. She had already published four novels, including a detective novel, *The Danvers Jewels* (1887). Her best book, *Red Pottage* (1899), caused a minor scandal and made her a celebrity. Although it has a melodramatic, even implausible story, it is notable for its witty attack on clerical life and its compassionate understanding of poverty.

Mary Cholmondeley published five more novels and a book of memoirs, *Under One Roof* (1918). In later life she lived with her sister, moving between Suffolk and London, where she died.

See also P. Lubbock, *Mary Cholmondeley, A Portrait*, 1928.   P.L.

Christie, Dame Agatha (Mary Clarissa) (1891–1976), writer of detective fiction. She was born at Torquay, the daughter of an American who died when she was a child. Until she was sixteen she was educated at home by her mother, who encouraged her both to read and to write a great deal. In 1906 she went to Paris to study singing, and then moved to Cairo, where she began to write seriously.

When war broke out in 1914, Agatha Christie became a VAD in Torquay, and in the same year she married Colonel Archibald Christie. She divorced him in 1927 and three years later married Max Mallowan, an archaeologist. In subsequent years she accompanied him on many of his expeditions and has recorded her experiences in the book *Come Tell me How You Live* (1946).

Agatha Christie began to write her first detective novel towards the end of the First World War, having previously immersed herself in other novels of the genre. After many revisions *The Mysterious Affair at Styles* was published in 1920. She wrote a prodigious number of works, all of which have been best sellers, translated into almost every modern language, and many of which have been adapted successfully for the screen, television, and the stage. (The record-breaking *The Mousetrap* has been running in London's West End for 31 years.) Several of her works have become classics of the genre: *The Murder of Roger Ackroyd* (1926), for example, takes the 'least-likely-person' theme to its limit by

revealing at the end that the narrator is himself the criminal; and *The ABC Murders* (1936) is a brilliant play on the idea of the 'disguised motive'. Two of Agatha Christie's detectives have become household names: Hercule Poirot (*Murder on the Orient Express*, 1934, etc.) and Miss Marple (*The Body in the Library*, 1942, etc.). Under the pseudonym Mary Westmacott, Agatha Christie wrote two 'straight' novels, but neither had the same success as her detective fiction. She also published *An Autobiography* (1977).

See also H. R. F. Keating, *Agatha Christie, First Lady of Crime*, 1977; G. C. Ramsey, *Agatha Christie, Mistress of Mystery*, 1968; J. Symons, *Bloody Murder*, 1972.   J.M.

Christina of Markyate (1096?–1163?), founder of Markyate priory, took a vow of celibacy early in life. Forced into a marriage against her will, she steadfastly refused to countenance its consummation, and eventually escaped (about 1118) to become an anchoress at Markyate near St Albans under the guidance of Roger the Hermit. There she stayed for most of her life, devoting herself, after Roger's death, to his memory, secure in the patronage of Abbot Geoffrey of St Albans. She refused a request by Archbishop Thurstan of York to move north, preferring instead to live the life of a recluse. About 1131 she made some sort of monastic profession, and gradually became the focus for a community of sisters. In 1145 Abbot Geoffrey recognized the existence of a fully-fledged Benedictine nunnery at Markyate. Some ten years later Henry II ordered the payment of fifty shillings for Christina's support. The so-called St Albans' Psalter was almost certainly compiled for her use; and within a few years of her death an anonymous monk of St Albans, who clearly knew her well, composed an admiring *Life* (edited by C. H. Talbot, 1959), dwelling approvingly on Christina's successful struggle to maintain her chastity and making much of her frequent visions.

See also D. Baker (ed.), *Medieval Women*, 1978.   K.R.D.

Chudleigh, Elizabeth (1720–88), one of the supreme adventuresses of the 'Age of Scandal'. As a girl she lived penuriously in the country with her mother. However, Elizabeth Chudleigh was a great—and bold—beauty, and after she caught the eye of the future Earl of Bath she was soon brought to London and became Maid of Honour to the Princess of Wales. The nineteen-year-old Duke of Hamilton fell in love with her but was kept off; so she married Augustus John Hervey, a naval lieutenant who was the grandson of the Earl of Bristol. The wedding took place in secret, since both parties were poor; and Elizabeth Hervey was able to remain a Maid of Honour.

Over the next decade or so 'Miss Chudleigh' became notorious, even by the easy-going standards of George II's court; at a masquerade she appeared in a gauze dress that left nothing to the imagination except the small area concealed by a kind of floral g-string. She had long been parted from Hervey, and in 1769 swore on oath that they had never been married; she was thus able to wed the Duke of Kingston, whose mistress she had been for some years. But when the Duke died in 1773, his nephews had her indicted for bigamy, and she was tried and found guilty before the House of Lords; ironically, her first husband had succeeded as Earl of Bristol, so she was demoted only to the rank of countess. She left England in haste, lived for a time in Russia, and finally settled in France, where she was indiscreet, eccentric, and, apparently, fascinating to the end.　　　　　　　N.H.

Chudleigh, Lady Mary (1656–1710), author and feminist, was the daughter of Richard Lee of Winslade, Devonshire, and in about 1685 married Sir George Chudleigh of nearby Ashton. She had a daughter, whose death caused her immense sorrow, and two sons. Her marriage was an unhappy one, which heightened her awareness of the subject status of women, and she took refuge from her loneliness in reading and writing. She declared that in her poetry, which she described as 'the innocent Amusement of a solitary life', her readers would find 'a Picture of my Mind, my Sentiments all laid open to their view'. Two of her poems, which clearly provided an emotional outlet, followed the deaths respectively of her mother and daughter, and it seems reasonable to regard her poem addressed 'To the Ladies', which begins 'Wife and Servant are the same', as a revelation of her personal unhappiness and resentment. In her first publication, the poetic dialogue *The Ladies Defence*, printed anonymously at the instigation of friends in 1701, she argued vehemently against the tenets put forth by John Sprint, a Nonconformist minister, in *The Bride-Woman's Counsellor*,

a forty-four page commentary on wifely duties which took for its text the injunction that 'she that is Married careth for the things of the World, how she may please her Husband.' The first volume of poems to appear under Lady Chudleigh's name was published in 1703 and dedicated to Queen Anne, and in 1710 she published a volume of essays dedicated to the Electress Sophia. In all her writings she showed concern for the welfare and education of women. She wrote her own poems and essays for women in particular to read, and expressed her hope that they might be persuaded 'to cultivate their Minds, to brighten and refine their Reason, and to render their Passions subservient to its dictates', thereby improving their situations.

See also G. Ballard, *Memoirs of several Ladies of Great Britain . . .*, 1752; D. M. Stenton, *The English Woman in History*, 1957.

T.J.M.

Churchill, Arabella (1648–1730), mistress of James, Duke of York (the eventual King James II whose Catholic ardour cost him the throne). She was the sister of John Churchill, later a famous general and Duke of Marlborough. Hers was a typical Restoration career. In about 1665 she was appointed Maid of Honour to the Duchess of York, and she became James's mistress two or three years later; it is said that she was not particularly handsome, but that a fall from her horse revealed hidden charms that inflamed the Duke's ardour. She bore him two sons (dukes of Berwick and Albemarle) and two daughters before being pensioned off and marrying a civil servant.　　　N.H.

Churchill, Lady Clementine (Ogilvy Spencer-) (1885–1977), public figure as the wife of Sir Winston Churchill. The daughter of Sir Henry and Lady Blanche Hozier, she was educated at Berkhamsted Girls' School and at the Sorbonne in Paris. She married Winston Churchill in 1908, and thereafter devoted herself entirely to him and to their children; the marriage was a happy one despite the strains imposed by financial anxieties and the sometimes wayward manifestations of Churchill's genius. Apart from her activities during the World Wars (notably on behalf of the YMCA and YWCA), Clementine Churchill's public life was very much linked with her husband's: she evidently approached electioneering, speechmaking, etc. as duties rather than personal pleasures. She was created a baroness in 1965.

See also M. Soames, *Clementine Churchill*, 1979.   N.H.

Churchill, Lady Jennie Randolph (Spencer) (1851–1921), American-born public figure, wife of Lord Randolph and mother of Sir Winston Churchill. One of the three daughters of a financier, Jeanette Jerome was born in Brooklyn and brought up in New York and Paris. During a visit to Cowes Regatta on the Isle of Wight, she met Lord Randolph Churchill, the Duke of Marlborough's younger son; they fell in love virtually on the spot and overcame parental opposition to marry in April 1874; Winston arrived, six weeks early, on 30 November, and a second son, Jack, was born in 1880. As the wife of one of the country's most prominent men—an aristocrat who was briefly the prodigy of politics and leader of the 'fourth party'—Lady Jennie became one of the stars of English society. After Lord Randolph's death in 1895 she kept her position but widened the scope of her activities, starting a magazine (*The Anglo-Saxon Review*, 1899–1900) and spending four months on a hospital ship in South Africa during the Boer War. As well as charm and vigour (like many women in her position, she threw herself into electioneering on behalf of her menfolk), she possessed an undoubted sexual magnetism, twice marrying men over twenty years younger than she was. Her writings include *The Reminiscences of Lady Randolph Churchill* (1908).

See also P. Worsthorne and J. Mitchell, *Jennie*, 1974.   N.H.

Churchill, Sarah, Duchess of Marlborough (1660–1744), court favourite and adviser to Queen ANNE, wife of the great military leader John Churchill, Duke of Marlborough. She was born Sarah Jennings, at Sandridge near St Albans. In 1673 she was appointed an attendant to Princess Anne, who became devoted to her. In 1678 Sarah secretly married John Churchill. In 1683, on Anne's marriage to Prince George of Denmark, Sarah became her Lady of the Bedchamber, and during this time the two women began an intimate correspondence in which rank was put aside, Anne writing as 'Mrs Morley' and Sarah Churchill as 'Mrs Freeman'. During the Glorious Revolution, the Churchills' fortunes were advanced by their prompt desertion of James II for William and Mary; Sarah's influence was of some importance in persuading Anne to recognize the new régime. In 1689 Anne settled a £1000 a year pension on her friend. At the turn of the century two of the Churchills' daughters made marriages which helped cement a political alliance of great importance: one to the son of Lord Godolphin, the other to the son of Lord Sunderland.

On Anne's accession to the throne in 1702, the rewards of friendship increased proportionately: Sarah became Mistress of the Robes, Keeper of the Privy Purse, and Groom of the Stole. John Churchill became Commander-in-Chief of the British and Dutch armies, and won brilliant victories, while Godolphin and Sunderland controlled Parliament. In 1702 Anne decided to raise John Churchill to a dukedom, and he received a £5,000 a year grant for her lifetime. The Marlboroughs' ascendancy was complete, although their satisfaction was marred by the death of their only son Charles, first Marquis of Blandford, in 1703.

Good fortune did not improve Sarah Churchill's mercurial temper, and her relations with the Queen gradually deteriorated. Matters were not improved by Sarah's active promotion of Whig ministers, which ran counter to Anne's High Church Tory sentiments. By 1707 Sarah had been supplanted in the Queen's favour by Abigail MASHAM, acting in conjunction with the Tory politician Robert Harley. Sarah only made her already difficult position worse by engaging in violent outbursts against the Queen. Writers hostile to Sarah's politics seized the opportunity to defame the late favourite. Mary de la Rivière MANLEY cast her as Queen Zarah in the scandal-chronicle of the same name published in 1705, as the lubricious Marchioness of Caria in the *New Atalantis* (1709), and as the Empress Irene in *Memoirs of Europe* (1710). In *The Examiner* (1710) Swift accused her of appropriating £22,000 a year out of the Privy Purse, a charge she disproved by sending in her accounts. But by 1711 the offence taken by the Queen was so deep that the Marlboroughs were forced to resign their offices and retired abroad.

After George I's accession in 1714 they returned, and settled near Woodstock in Oxfordshire to build the magnificent Blenheim Palace. On Marlborough's death in 1722 Sarah controlled a jointure of £15,000 from the Duke and the right to spend £10,000 for five years to complete Blenheim. She divided her time between completing Blenheim and feuding bitterly with her children, her architect, Vanbrugh, and Sir Robert Harley. She also compiled memoirs of her own and her husband's life. She was evidently a woman of great personal force, and her marriage was perhaps the most remarkable political partnership in British history; it was all the more remarkable in that, despite Sarah Churchill's difficult temperament, she and her husband sustained a lifelong mutual devotion.

See also D. Green, *Sarah, Duchess of Marlborough*, 1967.　　　　　　　　　　A.L.

Cibber, Susannah (1714–66), actress and singer. She was the daughter of a prosperous Covent Garden upholsterer and younger sister of the composer Thomas Arne. Both she and her brother were fairly well educated and encouraged to take an interest in music. Her career as a singer began at the age of eighteen, when she appeared in Lumpé's opera *Amelia*. Later, in recognition of her superb voice, Handel chose her to sing Galatea in *Acis and Galatea*, and wrote contralto parts for her in *The Messiah* and the role of Micah in *Samson*. Two years after her marriage to Colly Cibber's son Theophilus she decided to pursue an acting career, making her début as Zarah in Aaron Hill's adaptation of Voltaire's *Zaïre* (1736). The marriage with Theophilus soon foundered: in 1738, and again the following year, he brought actions against William Sloper for 'criminal conversation' with his wife, being awarded substantial damages. Susannah Cibber subsequently left her husband and lived with Sloper. She was employed for the 1742–43 season by Rich, worked for Garrick in 1743, and then in 1753 joined Garrick on a permanent basis at Drury Lane, where she remained until her death.

See also L. Melville, *Stage Favourites of the Eighteenth Century* (undated).　　　　A.L.

Clairmont, Claire, properly Clara Mary Jane (1798–1879), mistress of the poet Byron. Her mother became the second wife of the philosopher William Godwin, and when her stepsister Mary Godwin (see Mary Wollstonecraft SHELLEY) eloped to the Continent with Shelley in 1814, Claire accompanied them. On their return to London she gained an introduction to Byron, whom she pursued with determi-

nation; as a result of the liaison their child Allegra was born in 1817. The child lived with Byron for almost three years, but in 1821, against Claire's wishes, she was taken to a convent near Ravenna, where she died in 1822. Claire Clairmont spent her remaining years in Russia, Paris and Italy, dying in Florence.

B.H.C.

Clare, Elizabeth de (1291?–1360), Lady of Clare and foundress of Clare College, Cambridge, was the third daughter of Earl Gilbert de Clare by Princess Joan, daughter of Edward I. In 1314, when her brother Gilbert was killed at Bannockburn, the extensive family lands were divided between Elizabeth and her two sisters, and she was henceforth known as *Domina Clarae*, 'Lady of Clare'. Her first husband, John de Burgh, by whom she had one son, William, died in 1313. In 1315 she married Lord Theobald Verdon, and, following his death in 1316, took as her third husband Lord Roger Damory, who fathered two daughters before his own demise in 1321.

Elizabeth de Clare seems to have been rather more than conventionally pious, and may well have had a genuine enthusiasm for learning. At all events, she so generously endowed University Hall, Cambridge, that by 1346 it had begun to be known as Clare College, and in 1359 she provided it with a body of governing statutes. When she died in November 1360, she left further money, plate, and books to her beloved college, as well as making a series of specifically religious bequests.　　　　　　　　　　K.R.D.

Clare, Mary (1894–1970), actress, born in London. Mary Clare's acting career spanned over fifty years, beginning in 1910 when she borrowed £50 to leave her office job and train in repertory. Her West End début was in *Turandot* (1913), after which she was almost constantly in the West End. Among her successes were *The Skin Game* and *The Ghost Train*, and in particular *The Likes of Her* (1923), in which she played opposite the sixteen-year-old Hermione Baddeley. In 1931 she appeared in Noël Coward's *Cavalcade*, apparently written especially for her.

In the 1920s Mary Clare was in some silent films. Her first 'talkie' was *Hindle Wakes* (1931). She took the title role in *Mrs Pym of Scotland Yard* (1940) and made many other films, usually appearing as formidable matrons.　　　　　　　　　　A.D.

Clarke, Elizabeth (d. 1645), witch. Elizabeth Clarke, an elderly, poor and disabled woman from Manningtree, Essex, was the first victim of Matthew Hopkins, the notorious witch-finder who conducted a fierce crusade against witches in East Anglia and the east Midlands in 1645–47. When Hopkins, an inhabitant of Manningtree, learnt of the suspicions against Clarke, he and some companions watched her for several days and nights, not allowing her to sleep, until they are said to have seen her summoning up her imps, or spirits sent by Satan. These were in the form of animals, like 'Vinegar Tom', a greyhound, and 'Jarmora', a fat white dog. Elizabeth said her imps came frequently in the night 'and told her they would do her no hurt, but would help her to a husband who should maintain her ever after.' Through her, a group of seven Manningtree witches was discovered which met at her house to conjure up devils. Their chief victim was Richard Edwards, one of the leading local landowners, and it was for bewitching his son to death that Clarke and one Anne Leech were condemned and hanged after a trial at Chelmsford. Elizabeth Clarke's experience is not typical of English witchcraft: mass trials, exotic practices, and witchfinders were rare, the usual witch being a solitary and more mundane figure. The onslaught in Essex, which came after a period of decline in witchcraft prosecutions, involved accusations against thirty-six women, nineteen of whom were executed while nine died in prison. Only one was acquitted while another was released after giving evidence against the others. Over ninety per cent of suspected witches in sixteenth- and seventeenth-century Essex were women, usually elderly and comparatively poor: witchcraft is an important element in female experience at this time.

See also A. Macfarlane, *Witchcraft in Tudor and Stuart England*, 1970; C. L. Ewens, *Witchcraft and Demonianism*, 1933.

A.H.

Clarke, Mary Anne (1776–1852), adventuress. In 1794 she eloped with Joseph Clarke, a stonemason, and had three children by him. From 1803 to 1806 she was the mistress of the Duke of York, third son of George III and Commander-in-Chief of the Army. It later transpired that because of her vast debts she had taken bribes to obtain army promotions from the Duke. She was examined by the Commons in 1809 and tried for libel in 1809 and 1813, when she was imprisoned. She withdrew to France about 1816 and died there alone and in poverty.

See also W. Clarke, *The Authentic and Impartial Life of Mrs Mary Anne Clarke*, 1809; P. Berry, *By Royal Appointment*, 1970.

J.R.

Clement, Margaret (1508–70), scholar and religious exile, born Margaret Gigs, the daughter of a Norfolk gentleman and adopted daughter of Thomas More, who brought her up with his own children. She was a gifted humanist scholar (her learning is mentioned in More's family letters and in John Coke's *The Debate* of 1550), and her speciality was probably algebra; More returned her algorism stone with his last letter from the Tower. About 1530 she married the humanist and royal physician John Clement, and in 1535 witnessed More's execution and helped his daughter Margaret ROPER bury him. In 1537 Margaret Clement personally relieved the sufferings of Carthusians condemned to starve to death in Newgate; perhaps for this reason she was mentioned in the interrogations of Geoffrey Pole, accused of treason in 1538.

As Catholics, the Clements fled to the Netherlands on the accession of Edward VI, returning under Mary in March 1554 and going back into exile on Elizabeth's accession. Margaret Clement died at Mechlin in 1570. She is remembered now for her scholarship and her association with Thomas More.

See also early *Lives* of Thomas More by W. Roper and others; and E. E. Reynolds, *Margaret Roper*, 1960.

M.D.

Clerke, Agnes Mary (1842–1907), scientific writer. She was born in County Cork, Ireland, the daughter of a bank manager who was also a classical scholar and astronomer, and the sister of Ellen Mary Clerke, a novelist and poet. She lived in Dublin and Queenstown, and was educated at home. From 1870 to 1877 she travelled in Italy, where she published tales and sketches in Italian periodicals. It was from Italy that she first began contributing to *The Edinburgh Review*. She returned to London, where she continued writing, although it was not until 1885 that her first book, the *Popular History of Astronomy during the Nineteenth Century*, was published. It was soon to become a standard work.

In 1888 Agnes Clerke went to the Cape of Good Hope, where she visited an observatory. The following year she travelled to Copenhagen, Stockholm, and St. Petersburg in the yacht *Palatine*. As well as writing for *The Edinburgh Review* she contributed articles on astronomy and astronomers to *The Encyclopaedia Britannica* and *The Dictionary of National Biography*. She won a prize from the Royal Institute in 1892, and in 1903 she was made an honorary member of the Royal Astronomical Society. Her interests were not entirely restricted to astronomy: she published *Familiar Studies in Homer* in 1892. Her other works include *The System of the Stars*, 1890, *Problems in Astrophysics*, 1903, and *Modern Cosmogonies*, 1905.

See also Lady M. L. Huggins, *An Appreciation of Agnes Mary and Ellen Mary Clerke*, 1907.

A.P.

Cleveland, Duchess of. See VILLIERS, BARBARA, COUNTESS OF CASTLEMAINE AND DUCHESS OF CLEVELAND.

Clifford, Lady Anne (1590–1676), great landowner and public figure, the daughter of George Clifford, third Earl of Cumberland, and Margaret Russell. Her mother was 'one of the most virtuous and religious ladies that lived in her time' and employed the poet and historian Samuel Daniel as her daughter's tutor. She also had a governess but her education concentrated on the 'female arts' of music, dancing, and cooking, and she was not allowed to learn foreign languages. Despite this, the poet John Donne could say of her, 'she knew well how to discourse of all things from predestination to slea-silk'.

In 1609 Lady Anne married Richard Sackville, third Earl of Dorset; she was widowed in 1624 and did not remarry until 1630, when she took as her second husband Philip Herbert, Earl of Pembroke and Montgomery. Her father had died deeply in debt in 1605, leaving all his estates to his brother Francis, the fourth Earl. Lady Anne and her mother hotly disputed the will, and for the next forty years she was obsessed with the recovery of what she regarded as her rightful property. She involved both her husbands in the dispute, and indeed she married them largely to use their power and influence in the cause. This soured her marriages, although she was also badly treated by both her husbands, Dorset at one stage bringing his mistress to live in the family

home. Attempts by both James I and the Archbishop of Canterbury to settle the family feud foundered on Lady Anne's determination. She separated from both her husbands and had her child taken from her, but she would not relinquish her rights.

In 1643 she came into her own when the death of her cousin, the fifth Earl of Cumberland, ended the male line of the Cliffords. She had abandoned her husband before his death in 1650 but had used his protection for her estates during the Civil War. In 1649 she took possession of her northern lands and became the greatest landowner and political influence in Craven and Westmorland until her death in 1676. She restored houses and churches, held court personally, and moved around in great style in a horse litter. In her will she styled herself 'High sheriffess by inheritance of the county of Westmoreland'. As Bishop Edward Rainbowe said, she was 'absolute mistress of herself, her resolutions, actions and time . . . she turned and steered the whole course of her affairs': an outstanding example of an independent and powerful aristocratic woman.

See also M. Holmes, *Proud Northern Lady*, 1977; R. T. Spence, 'Lady Anne Clifford . . . a Re-appraisal', in *Northern History*, 1979.

P.M.H.

Clifford, Rosamund (?–1176?), mistress of Henry II, was the daughter of Walter de Clifford. Her liaison with Henry, which probably pre-dated his imprisonment of Queen ELEANOR OF AQUITAINE in 1173, lasted until her death. Undoubtedly the woman he most deeply loved, she was buried in some style in the nunnery at Godstow. Many legends about 'Fair Rosamund' have come down to us, all of dubious authenticity, including the fanciful tale that a passionately jealous Queen Eleanor had her bled to death in a hot bath at Woodstock.

See also W. L. Warren, *Henry II*, 1973.

K.R.D.

Clinton, Elizabeth, Countess of Lincoln (1574–1630?), writer. The daughter of Sir Henry Knyvet, Elizabeth was married at the age of ten to Thomas Clinton, who became Earl of Lincoln in 1616. She bore eighteen children, several of whom died young, and was widowed in 1619.

Elizabeth Clinton has an interesting place

in women's history as the author of *The Countess of Lincoln's Nurserie* (1622), a short treatise encouraging upper-class women to breastfeed their own children. She wrote in part out of guilt at not doing so herself, 'partly I was over-ruled by another's authority, and partly deceived by some ill counsel, and partly I had not so well considered of my duty in this motherly office as since I did when it was too late'. Instead her children were entrusted to wet-nurses, many of whom proved 'wilful', 'froward', and 'slothful'; the deaths of one or two of her children were attributed to their neglect. She dismissed various objections to breastfeeding, such as that 'it is troublesome ... noisome to one's clothes ... makes one look old ...'; and lamented the bad example set by the 'better sort' who consigned their children to wet-nurses, poor women who often had to sacrifice their own babies 'for the entertaining of a richer woman's'. Breastfeeding, she argued, was enjoined by God's laws, and by the example of Biblical women from Eve to the Virgin Mary: 'we have followed Eve in transgression, let us follow her in obedience'. All truly religious and affectionate mothers should breastfeed, for, wrote the Puritan Countess, their baby might be 'one of God's very elect ... to whom to be a nursing mother is a Queen's honour'.

See also M. R. Mahl and H. Koon (eds), *The Female Spectator*, 1977.   A.H.

Clisby, Harriet (Jemima Winifred) (1830–1931), physician, journalist, and feminist. Harriet Clisby was born in London but emigrated to Australia with her family when she was eight years old. She spent her girlhood at Adelaide and on a farm in the Inman valley, then learned shorthand and took up journalism. From 1856 she worked in Melbourne, where she edited the *Southern Phonographic Harmonia*, a magazine in shorthand; and in 1861 she was involved in producing *The Interpreter*, the first magazine published by women in Australia.

Inspired by the life and writings of Elizabeth BLACKWELL, Harriet Clisby made up her mind to become a doctor. She experienced some financial hardship in the process, and worked for a time as a private nurse at Guy's Hospital in London before finding a more congenial atmosphere in the United States. Having qualified at the Medical College and Hospital for Women in New York, she practised in Boston from the early 1870s. There she founded a female equivalent to the YMCA, the Women's Educational and Industrial Union, of which she remained a leading spirit throughout the 1880s. Later she settled at Geneva, where she set up a Union des Femmes and enjoyed a long and active retirement. She died in London nine months after her hundredth birthday.   N.H.

Clitherow, Margaret (?–1586), Catholic martyr. The daughter of Thomas Middleton, citizen and wax-chandler of York, she married John Clitherow, butcher, in July 1571. She was converted to Catholicism about 1574, and was thereafter frequently prosecuted and imprisoned.

On 10 March 1586 Margaret Clitherow was arraigned at York, charged with sheltering Jesuits and seminary priests, the Queen's enemies, and hearing Mass. She did not deny harbouring priests, but, not considering them traitors, refused to answer to the charge. Several Protestants, including the Puritan minister Wigginton, went to argue with her in prison, but she was obdurate. Since she refused to plead, she was condemned to be pressed to death. Sentence was carried out at the Tollbooth near the prison on 25 March. Before dying, Margaret Clitherow sent her hat to her husband as a sign of her duty to him as her head, and her shoes and hose to her daughter Anne, to indicate that she should follow in her footsteps.

Margaret Clitherow is interesting as a post-Reformation convert to Catholicism, and as an example of female lay resistance to the Elizabethan settlement. One of the arguments put to her in prison, allegedly the opinion of a priest named Hart, was that it was lawful for unlearned women to conform and attend Anglican services. Margaret denied that this was Hart's opinion, and added that if he had said such a thing she would not have believed him. She is canonized by the Catholic Church among the Forty Martyrs of England and Wales.

See also the *Life* by Margaret Clitherow's confessor, John Mush, in J. Morris (ed.), *Troubles of Our Catholic Forefathers* 1877.   M.D.

Clive, Kitty (1711–85), actress. The daughter of an Irishman, William Raftor (by which surname she was known in her early career),

Clough, Anne Jemima

Catherine Raftor was said to have been 'discovered' singing while scrubbing the steps of a house in Drury Lane. A more plausible version is that she had rooms in the same house as Theophilus Cibber, who, impressed by her singing, recommended her to his father, Colley Cibber, then manager of Drury Lane.

After a successful début in 1728 she was given substantial comedy parts, making her name in an otherwise lamentable ballad-opera, *Damon and Phillida.* She went on to play Polly in *The Beggar's Opera,* and eventually most of the great English comedy roles. She played opposite Quin, Macklin, and Garrick, her main rival being Mrs WOFFINGTON, with whom she had a celebrated skirmish. Indeed her abrasive tongue and volatile temperament pained many managers, notably Garrick; but her fine voice and lively humour ensured her enduring popularity.

Uncharacteristically for her profession and period, she was famous for her chastity, holding predatory admirers and managers at arm's length. In 1733 she married a barrister, George Clive (second cousin of Clive of India); they separated in 1735 but never divorced, remaining on amiable terms.

Kitty Clive was a close friend of Horace Walpole, on whose estate she lived during her last thirty years. She retired in 1769, having suffered bouts of ill health. She spent her final fifteen years in domesticity at Twickenham, gaining the affectionate respect not only of Walpole but of Garrick and Dr Johnson, who said of her 'she was a better romp than any I ever saw in nature'. There are many portraits of her, notably by Cosway and Jeremiah Davison.

See also P. H. Highfill, K. A. Burnim, E. A. Langhans, *A Biographical Dictionary of Actors, Actresses, Musicians, Dancers, Managers and other Stage Personnel in London, 1660–1800,* vol. 3, 1975.   C.H.

Clough, Anne Jemima (1820–92), educationist, born in Liverpool; she was the sister of the poet Arthur Hugh Clough. Her father, a cotton merchant, took the family to South Carolina in the winter of 1822–23, but they returned to Liverpool in 1836. His death in 1846 drew Anne Jemima Clough closer to her brother, who had encouraged her first efforts at teaching; but she gave up her little school for poor children in the neighbourhood to concentrate on Sunday School teaching, being by now a devout High Anglican. Her own studies continued and she gained teaching experience at Borough Road, Southwark, and at the Home and Colonial School, both charitable establishments.

In 1852 she and her mother moved to Ambleside in Cumbria, where she opened a school for the children of friends: Mary Arnold (Mrs Humphrey WARD) was one of her first pupils. She showed a deep interest in each child, writing out individual timetables. However, family bereavements and physical exhaustion forced her to give up the school. But shortly afterwards she met Barbara BODICHON, one of the first to put forward a scheme for a women's college, and her interest in education was reawakened. In 1866 and 1867 she travelled to Liverpool and Manchester, becoming a leading figure on the North of England Council for Promoting the Higher Education of Women, of which she was Secretary from 1867 to 1870 and President from 1873 to 1874.

In 1871, Millicent FAWCETT and Henry Sidgwick persuaded her to take charge of a residence at Cambridge for women coming to attend the lectures, though it was to be quite distinct from their own organization, the aim of which was to enable women to attend lectures without chaperones. By 1875 a new residence, Newnham Hall, had been built, and by 1879 Newnham College, with Anne Jemima Clough as Principal, was fully established with resident lecturers. This led eventually to the opening up of all degree courses in Cambridge to women.

Anne Jemima Clough's whole-hearted devotion to the College led her to be too strict with the students at first. She did, however, encourage them to show that they were capable of achievement in spheres hitherto reserved for men. In 1885 she was among the first to be associated with the Cambridge Training College for Women, and in 1887 with the foundation by Henrietta BARNETT and Alice Grüner of the Women's University Settlement in Southwark. Her own students were encouraged to give weekly classes in non-academic subjects, and to go and teach in other parts of the Empire.

Enterprising and imaginative, Anne Jemima Clough was a widely respected authority on all educational matters, from the visiting of working-class primary schools to the higher education of the middle classes. As a moral reformer she believed that female education was something to be pursued as a good in itself, not simply as a means to preferment.

See also B. A. Clough, *Memoir of Anne Jemima Clough*, 1903; M. A. Hamilton, *Newnham, an Informal Biography*, 1936.

C.H.G.G.

Cobbe, Frances Power (1822–1904), writer and philanthropist. She was born in Ireland, the only daughter of Charles Cobbe, a landowner and magistrate. Brought up in a strict Evangelical home, she was educated by successive governesses. She then attended an expensive boarding school in Brighton (1836–38), but its emphasis on deportment and female accomplishments only served to alienate her from her studies. Back in Ireland she read widely and took classes in Greek and geometry from a local clergyman. Her religious and philosophical studies led in 1855 to the publication of what she later described as her *magnum opus*, *The Theory of Intuitive Morals*, which was stimulated by the philosophy of Kant. Left with £200 a year on the death of her father, she travelled to the Continent and the Holy Land in 1857. Italy was particularly dear to her, and she returned there many times in later life. In Italy she met Theodore Parker, a well-known Unitarian clergyman and writer, whose works she edited (1863–71).

Frances Power Cobbe's philanthropic career began in earnest in 1858, when she took part in Mary CARPENTER's work with pauper children at the Red Lodge Reformatory in Bristol. But her health was unsuited to the harsh conditions there, and she turned her attention to workhouse visiting, of which she was a pioneer. Her connections were extensive and she counted among her friends and correspondents Lord Shaftesbury, Cardinal Manning, and many of the most noted women of her day. Her interests were likewise broad. She wrote and lectured on a great variety of subjects, including poor relief, vivisection, immortality, and the law. Much of her work was concerned with the issue of women's rights and duties. In the 1860s she called for the admission of women to university degrees, the right of married women to hold property, and votes for women. In *Why Women Desire the Franchise* (1869) and *The Duties of Women* (1881) she argued that political emancipation was a means by which women could extend their

quality of compassion and thereby realize their social obligations.

The last thirty years of Frances Power Cobbe's life were largely devoted to the anti-vivisection crusade. In 1875 she was a founder of the Society for the Protection of Animals liable to Vivisection (the Victoria Street Society), and she acted as its joint secretary until 1884, when she moved from London to Barmouth in North Wales. Eventually she broke with this organization over a matter of principle and formed the British Union for the Abolition of Vivisection. Her last years were not altogether happy though she continued to speak out on behalf of various causes and entertained her many friends. She was a person of simple and uncompromising views, expressed with charm and humour, a strongminded but 'clubbable' woman. Her other works include *Essays on the Pursuits of Women*, 1863, *Italics*, 1864, *Darwinism in Morals and other Essays*, 1872 and *Life of Frances Power Cobbe by Herself*, 1894.

See also J. Chappell, *Women of Worth*, 1908.

F.K.P.

Cobham, Eleanor, Duchess of Gloucester (*c*.1405–1457), the daughter of Reginald Cobham of Sterborough, Kent., Eleanor served as lady-in-waiting to Jacqueline of Hainault, wife of Humphrey, Duke of Gloucester, youngest brother of Henry V. She became Humphrey's mistress and bore him two children. In 1428 Humphrey's marriage was declared invalid and he married Eleanor Cobham. The only one of her husband's intellectual interests the Duchess shared was astronomy. Contemporaries viewed her as beautiful and courageous but proud and ambitious, and they feared her domination of Humphrey and her influence on Henry VI, to whom her husband was heir-presumptive. In 1441 she was accused of practising witchraft to secure Henry's death. The trial was a great scandal and provided Humphrey's enemies with the opportunity to destroy him politically. The Duchess admitted some of the charges and was sentenced to do three days' public penance in London and to be imprisoned for life. She was divorced and deprived of dower, but her confinement at Chester, Kenilworth, the Isle of Man and Beaumaris, though strict, was not comfortless. She was the first peeress to be tried for treason and felony, in her case by a lay commission. As a result it was resolved in the Commons that in future peeresses, like peers, should be tried by the judges and peers of the realm.

See also R. A. Griffiths, *The Reign of King Henry VI*, 1981; K. H. Vickers, *Humphrey, Duke of Gloucester*, 1907.　　　　　　A.C.

Cohen, Harriet (1895–1967), concert pianist, the daughter of a businessman-cum-composer. She studied music at the Royal Academy from 1912 to 1917 before moving to the Matthay School, where, with Dame Myra HESS, she became one of the leading exponents of the 'new' relaxed and expressive method. She pioneered English appreciation of the sixteenth-century masters Byrd and Gibbons, and from the 1920s to the 1940s toured Europe and America playing modern English works (for example by Bax, Vaughan Williams, Ireland, and Walton) as well as the music of Bach. In 1932 these English composers, and others such as Bliss, Goossens, and Whittaker, presented her with a set of transcriptions of music by Bach in appreciation of her sympathetic interpretation of their works.

In spite of her unusually small hands, which made many of the virtuoso concertos impossible for her, Harriet Cohen gave many memorable performances, including Bax's epic Second Sonata, which he dedicated to her. In 1938 she was awarded the CBE for services to music. Her elegance and wit took her beyond the world of music into friendships with such people as Bernard Shaw, Arnold Bennett, and Ramsay MacDonald. Peter Racine Fricker wrote a piano concerto for her, and after she injured her right hand, Arnold Bax wrote for her a 'Concertante for Orchestra with Piano (Left Hand)'. It was Bax too who became founder and first President of the Harriet Cohen International Music Awards. She was a Freeman of the City of London and in the year of her retirement, 1960, she received an honorary doctorate from the National University of Ireland.

Harriet Cohen's memoirs were posthumously published as *A Bundle of Time* in 1969.　　　　　　E.M.V.

Cole, Margaret (1893–1980), writer and political activist. Margaret Cole was the daughter of John Percival Postgate, later Professor of Latin at the University of Liverpool. She was educated at a private school which catered mainly for the children of university teachers; at Roedean, which she hated; and at Girton College, Cambridge, where she took First Class Honours in Classics. At Cambridge she left behind the orthodox Anglicanism and basic conservatism of her childhood, becoming an atheist, a socialist, and a non-militant feminist. In 1916 she supported her brother's conscientious objections to military service, and was drawn into the world of politics, undertaking voluntary work at the Fabian Research Department, where she met G.D.H. Cole, whom she married in 1918. In 1925 she and her husband moved to Oxford, where she taught evening classes and worked part-time for the Labour Research Department. However, she disliked Oxford and the secondary status of a don's wife, and left it in 1929. In 1932 she visited the Soviet Union and was impressed by the people's enthusiasm and the state's welfare provisions, though she was later disillusioned with many aspects of Stalinism. The crushing of the Austrian socialists in 1934 caused her to turn away from pacifism, and she supported Britain's role in the Second World War while disliking some of its aspects. Throughout her adult life she worked for the Fabian Society and the Labour Party, and as a Labour member of the London County Council was involved in implementing the 1944 Education Act. She was awarded the OBE in 1965 and the DBE in 1970. Her writings include *Growing Up Into Revolution*, 1949, *The Story of Fabian Socialism*, 1961, and biographies of G. D. H. Cole, 1971, and Beatrice Webb, 1945, whose diaries she also edited (1952).　　　　　　J.E.

Coleridge, Mary (Elizabeth) (1861–1907), novelist and poet, born in London. Mary Coleridge was the granddaughter of the poet Samuel Coleridge's elder brother. She was educated at home, mainly by the poet and educationist W. J. Cory. She began writing poetry as a child, and by the age of twenty was a regular contributor of essays and reviews to a number of periodicals. Her first novel, *The Seven Sleepers of Ephesus*, was published in 1893, but was not a great success, though it was praised by Robert Louis Stevenson. In 1896, under the pseudonym 'Anados', she published a volume of poetry, *Fancy's Following*.

As a result of reading Tolstoy, Mary Coleridge was drawn towards philanthropic work. She began by teaching working women at her home, and then, in 1895, became a teacher at the Working Women's College. She was to continue teaching at the college until her death. Though she later claimed that she would rather have been a painter than a writer, she produced several further novels. *The King with two Faces*, 1897, a historical romance, was followed by *The Fiery Dawn*, 1901, *The Shadow on the Wall*, 1904, and *The Lady on the Drawing Room Floor*, 1906. A further volume of verse appeared in 1907 under the title *Poems Old And New*, and her biography of the Pre-Raphaelite painter Holman Hunt was completed shortly before her death and published posthumously in 1908.

See also W. de la Mare, *M. E. Coleridge: An Appreciation*, 1907.   J.H.S.

Coleridge, Sara (1802–52), translator, children's writer, and editor. The only daughter of the poet Samuel Coleridge, Sara was born at Keswick in Cumberland. As a result of her father's long absences from home and her parents' estrangement from each other, her education was left largely to the poet Southey, who allowed her the full use of his library. At an early age she was said to be well acquainted with the Greek and Latin authors, as well as being proficient in French, German, Italian and Spanish. Her linguistic abilities are indicated by the first works which she was to publish, a three-volume translation from the Latin of Dohbritzhoffer's *Account of the Abipones* (1821) and a two-volume translation from French, *The History of the Feasts, Guests and Prowess of the Chevalier Bayard* (1825).

In 1829 Sara Coleridge married her cousin Hartley Nelson Coleridge, a barrister, whom she had met at Highgate some seven years before. The couple had five children, only two of whom survived infancy. It was for these children, a boy and a girl, that Sara Coleridge wrote *Pretty Lessons in Verse for Good Children*, which she was persuaded to publish in 1834. The work was a considerable success, and it was followed in 1837 by *Phantasmion*, a fairy story set in the Lake District.

In 1843 Hartley Coleridge died. He had been appointed the literary executor of Samuel Coleridge, and Sara Coleridge undertook to continue his work. In 1844 she published a one-volume edition of Coleridge's poetry, and she went on to provide numerous annotations and introductions to her father's works.

See also E. Coleridge (ed.), *Memoirs and Letters of Sarah Coleridge*, 1873; E. L. Griggs,

Coleridge Fille: a Biography of Sara Coleridge, 1940.   J.H.S.

Collet, Clara (Elizabeth) (1860–1947), sociologist. Her father was the editor of *The Diplomatic Review*. Clara Collet showed early academic promise at the North London Collegiate School, where she was a pupil from 1873 to 1878. In October 1880 she took a BA at University College, London, and went on to take the Teacher's Diploma and an MA in Mental and Moral Science, winning the Joseph Hume Scholarship in Political Economy in 1886. For seven years she taught in the highest form of Wyggeston High School, Leicester.

Clara Collet left teaching to become Assistant Commissioner to the Royal Commission on Labour. Collaborating with Charles Booth on the classic *Life and Labour of the People in London* (1889), she contributed studies of women's work in East London and secondary education for girls. In 1893, having published studies, reports, and surveys on the position and status of working women in learned journals, she was appointed Labour Correspondent to the Board of Trade. She reported to the Royal Commission on Secondary Education in 1894 and presented a Report on the Money Wages of Indoor Domestic Servants to Parliament in 1899. In 1903 she became Senior Investigator for the Board of Trade and from 1917 to 1920 worked at the Ministry of Labour. Elected a Fellow of the Royal Statistical Society in 1893, she became a Fellow of University College, London, in 1896 and later a Governor of Bedford College and a member of the councils of the Royal Statistical and Royal Economic Societies.

As a feminist sociologist Clara Collet provided the first statistical analyses of the position of women at work, and addressed herself to a wide range of issues concerning the status of women. In *The Economic Position of Educated Working Women* (1890) she dismissed the question of difference between men and women as 'wholly irrelevant' and declared that 'the economic independence of women is as necessary to men's happiness as to women's'.

In 1924 she lectured in India on Joseph Collet, a former Governor of Madras, and an interest in genealogy led her to compile *The History of the Collet Family* (1935, with H. H. Collet). Her other works include: *Educated Working Women*, 1902 and *Women in Industry*, 1911.

See also North London Collegiate School for Girls, *Jubilee Calendar*, 1900; *North London Collegiate School for Girls Magazine* 1937, 1947.   C.B.

Collier, Constance (1878–1955), actress, born at Windsor. She made her first stage appearance at the age of four. In 1893 she became one of the famous Gaiety Girls before taking up serious parts. Her stage presence was so overwhelming that it limited her range, since she was not only beautiful but so tall that she usually towered over the rest of the cast. However, in 1902 the actor-manager Beerbohm Tree, himself very tall, engaged her, and she remained with him at His Majesty's Theatre for twelve years. One of her greatest parts was as Cleopatra, described by critics as 'superb and terrible', and she was also outstanding as Nancy in Comyns Carr's dramatization of *Oliver Twist*. Later she became a brilliant exponent of pointed comedy.

Her first American tour was in 1908; she returned frequently in Shakespearian and other parts. She also produced such plays as *Camille*, *Peter Ibbetson*, and *Hay Fever*. Her film career began in 1915, and after dividing her time between London and America she settled in Hollywood in 1933. She collaborated with Ivor Novello in writing two plays, and published her reminiscences, *Harlequinade: the Story of My Life*, in 1929.   A.D.

Collins, Anne (*fl.* 1653), poet, is unknown except as the author of *Divine Songs and Meditations*, published in 1653. The only biographical information which can be gleaned from her work is that she had suffered from some chronic illness since childhood, and lived a very retired life. Her book consists of some twenty-one poems, one of which runs to almost a hundred stanzas. Nearly all deal with religious topics. She justified her writing as a means of praising God, and hopes that her readers, by looking upon 'the image of her mind', will observe the grace of God to even his most lowly servant.   W.R.O.

Collins, Lottie (1866–1910), music hall artist. She gained lasting fame through one song and routine, 'Ta-Ra-Ra-Boom-De-Ay', which she introduced into the pantomime *Dick Whittington* at the Grand Theatre, Islington, in 1891. The song had been written originally by Harry Sayers, manager of an American minstrel troupe, and was first sung in a minstrel show called *Tuxedo*. Not until Lottie Collins performed it, however, did it achieve success. The version she used was an English adaptation written by B. M. Batchelor, and proved such a hit at the Grand that she was engaged to perform it at the Gaiety Theatre also, in a burlesque with the title *Cinder-Ellen-Up-Too-Late*. This ran concurrently with the pantomime, requiring Lottie Collins to rush from one theatre to the other in time to perform. The song itself was followed by an energetic dance of whirling skirts and high kicks. She took the song-and-dance all over England and America, making it her career and performing it for many years. Her daughter José was also an actress, best known for her playing in *Maid of the Mountains* (1917), which was also the title of her reminiscences (1932).   B.H.C.

Collyer, Mary (d. 1763), novelist and translator. She married the elder Joseph Collyer, a compiler and translator. Her learning was praised by such intellectual women as Elizabeth MONTAGU and Elizabeth CARTER, largely on the basis of her translation of Gessner's *Death of Abel*. Her *Letters from Felicia to Charlotte* (1750) had been called the first Romantic novel in English because of the extensive natural descriptions it contains. Mary Collyer also began a translation of Klopstock's *Messiah* which was completed by her husband after her death.

See also H. S. Hughes, 'An Early Romantic Novel' in *The Journal of English and Germanic Philology*, 1916.   A.L.

Colson, Phyllis (Constance) (1904–72), founder of the Central Council of Physical Education. She was educated at Huyton College and Bedford College of Physical Education. Between 1926 and 1930 she taught physical education. She was organizer of Physical Education for the National Association of Girls' Clubs (1930–33). In 1935 she founded the Central Council of Physical Recreation and was its General Secretary until 1963, being made Honorary Life Vice-President in 1966. Outside her busy working life, most of her time was devoted to the care of handicapped children.

Phyllis Colson was a remarkable woman whose great administrative ability, boundless energy, and sense of purpose enabled her to secure the co-operation of a wide variety of people. She became an Honorary Life Member of the Physical Education Association of Great Britain and Northern Ireland, and was awarded the Titre Honorifique de la Fédération Internationale d'Education Physique (1945), the King Gustavus Gold Medal (1945), and the William Hyde Award (1953). She received the CBE in 1964.   A.D.

Coltman, Constance Mary (1889–1969), the first woman in England to be ordained a minister. The daughter of George Todd, a Presbyterian, she read history at Somerville College, Oxford, and then obtained the consent of Mansfield College to read theology. Oxford did not in those days award theology degrees, so she did her BD at London and was ordained in the Congregational Church in 1917. She married Claude Martial Coltman, and together they were ministers at King's Weigh Church (1917–20), Cowley Road Church, Oxford (1924–32), Wolverton, Buckinghamshire (1932–40), and Haverhill, Suffolk (1940–53). Constance Mary Coltman retired in 1949 and died at Bexhill. As a person she was gracious and full of pastoral concern; she also did much to help other women who became ministers. Her passionate concern for peace led her to join the Fellowship of Reconciliation.

See also *The Congregational Yearbook*, 1969–70.   M.A.

Colville, Elizabeth, Lady Colville of Culross (*fl.* 1598–1630), poet. The daughter of Sir James Melville of Halhill, she married John Colville of Wester-Cumbrae who later inherited, though he did not assume, the title Lord of Culross. Their eldest son, Alexander, was born in 1620. The first mention of Lady Colville's poetic interests occurs in Alexander Hume's *Hymns and Sacred Songs* (1599) which he dedicated to her. He speaks of having seen her poetic compositions and declares that she 'excells any of your sex in that art'. Her only published work was *Ane Godlie Dreame, Compylit in Scottish Meter*, a poem of sixty eight-line stanzas, published in Edinburgh in 1603 and reprinted at least ten times up to 1737. It narrates a dream vision in which the author, after bewailing her sins and the trials of the saints in this 'wretched world', falls asleep and is visited by Christ in the form of an angel. He leads and supports her on a long, dangerous, and wearisome journey. She is granted a vision of the holy city, but has to

pass through hell where 'Puir damnit saullis. . . In flaming fire, war frying wonder fast'. Her terror is such that she awakes, and the final twenty stanzas are given over to pious exhortations.

Her only other surviving work is a manuscript sonnet addressed to a Presbyterian minister who was imprisoned on a charge of high treason around 1606. Contemporary accounts stress her exemplary piety and this, together with the subject matter of her poem, may have contributed to its wide popularity in the period.

See also D. Laing (ed.), *Early Popular Poetry of Scotland*, rev. ed. W. C. Hazlitt, 2 vols, 1895.   W.R.O.

Colvin, Brenda (1898–1981), pioneer landscape architect, born at Simla in India. She studied under Madeline Agar at Swanley Horticultural College, then started a large private practice in gardens in Britain and abroad. Both Gertrude JEKYLL and William Robinson greatly influenced her.

Brenda Colvin was one of the founders both of the Institute of Landscape Architects in 1929 (she was later its President, 1951–53) and of the International Federation of Landscape Architects. She was both idealistic and practical, aiming to achieve a satisfactory relationship between man and his surroundings, rather than merely to practise a decorative art. Her lectures influenced many post-war planners to 'create' landscapes, even to the extent of sculpting mountains, as in the ash disposal scheme for the Central Electricity Generating Board.

In 1969 Brenda Colvin went into partnership with Hal Moggeridge, one of their projects being the New Military Town of Aldershot; they introduced many schemes for the restoration of wasteland. She was awarded the CBE in 1973.   A.D.

Compton, Fay (Virginia Lillian Emmeline) (1894–1978), actress, born in London. She was the daughter of actor-manager Edward Compton and the sister of the novelist Sir Compton Mackenzie; Compton was the family's traditional stage-name. The name 'Fay' derived from a small sister's inability to pronounce 'Virginia', which evolved into 'Fay Ginger'.

Fay Compton was educated at Leatherhead Court, Surrey, and went on to the stage straight from school in 1911. So immediate was her success that she became known as 'the actress who is never out of work'. She appeared in the 'Follies' of her husband, H. G. Pélissier, whom she married in 1912. A year later he died leaving her a widow at eighteen with a son; she subsequently remarried three times.

Fay Compton could play any role with utter sincerity, whether in Shakespeare (Calpurnia, Ophelia, Titania), music hall, or contemporary drama. She was noted for the incredible range of her voice: she could be a tender, pathetic Ophelia or a shrieking harridan to equally convincing effect. She had the name part in *Mary Rose* (1920 and 1926), played Fanny Grey in *Autumn Crocus* (1931) and Gina Ekdal in Ibsen's *The Wild Duck* (1948), and gave many other notable performances. She was with the Old Vic for several seasons, and in the 1960s went to the Chichester Festival Theatre and the Yvonne Arnaud Memorial Theatre in Guildford. She also visited America in 1959, playing the lead in *God and Kate Murphy*.

Her film career began in 1917, and she made occasional appearances on the screen over the next sixty years; she played Emilia in Orson Welles's *Othello* (1952). She was also seen on radio and television, notably in the large-scale adaptation of Galsworthy's *The Forsyte Saga* (1967).   A.D.

Compton-Burnett, Ivy (1884–1969), novelist, a doctor's daughter, born in Middlesex. She spent her early life in Hove, Sussex, growing up with her own six brothers and sisters as well as the five older children of her father's first marriage. Until the age of fourteen she was educated at home in this enclosed Edwardian household ('One came between brothers and shared their tutor'), then at day- and boarding-schools. In 1902 she went to Royal Holloway College, where she read classics. After taking her degree in 1907, she returned to live at home to teach her younger sisters, and began work on her first novel. After her mother's death in 1907, she ran the household until the family circle broke up four years later. In 1919 she set up home in London with Margaret Jourdain, an expert on English furniture and decoration; they lived together until Margaret Jourdain's death in 1951.

Ivy Compton-Burnett's first novel, *Dolores* (1911), was acclaimed by critics as a highly original work, showing great promise. The author herself came to regard it as immature,

sentimental juvenilia; she disowned and tried to suppress it, expressing her detestation of the heroine's self-sacrifice, which she had applauded in 1911. She wrote nothing more until 1925, when the first work of her maturity appeared. *Pastors and Masters* is a short, extremely accomplished novel, set in a boys' private school. Ivy Compton-Burnett had by then achieved her distinctive style: a bare, stylized, highly dramatic dialogue, stripped of all wordiness and virtually all description, portraying, with a superb formalism of structure, a world utterly realistic within its own highly artificial confines. One critic likened the effect of her writing to that of the Cubist movement in painting.

Brothers and Sisters (1929) is the first of a long series of novels concerning family tensions that generate emotional tyranny, violence, and even crime. Her own family life provided a large part of the basic material. She lost her father when she was 17; both her two most dearly loved brothers died young; and two younger sisters committed suicide in 1916. Both homosexuality and incest are recurrent, if often muted, themes throughout her work. She described the first thirty-five years of her life as 'miserable'.

Ivy Compton-Burnett's novels, in which the doom-laden action of Greek tragedy is fused with a comedy of manners entirely English, have caused her to be likened both to Henry James and Jane Austen. The novels are characterized by precision of phrasing, scintillating aphorisms, an acute observation of eccentricity, and a ruthless exposure of hypocrisy and moral deceit. Despite discerning reviews, her readership at first was limited, and she was regarded by many as the object of a modish cult. Both her style and her essential subject-matter were perfected in the early 1920s; despite twenty novels (the last published posthumously in 1971), they never changed. But her compassionate wisdom and inimitable style have now given her an assured place in the canon of twentieth-century English writing, while dramatizations of her novels have made them accessible to a wider public. She won the James Tait Black Memorial Prize for *Mother and Son* (1955), received an Hon. D.Litt. from Leeds University in 1960 and was made a DBE in 1967.

See also C. Burkhart, *The Art of Ivy Compton-Burnett*, 1972; I. Compton-Burnett and M. Jourdain, *A Conversation*, 1945; E.

Sprigge, *The Life of Ivy Compton-Burnett*, 1973; H. Spurling, *Ivy When Young: the Early Life of I. Compton-Burnett 1884–1919*, 1974.
                                    J.E.E.H.

Cons, Emma (1838–1912), founder of the Old Vic theatre. Her childhood in central London ended abruptly when her father, a piano maker, became an invalid and could no longer work. With a talent for art and a determination to avoid the respectable but constricting career of governess, Emma Cons earned a living as an illuminator of manuscripts for John Ruskin, whom she met at one of his lectures. In the 1850s she and several friends set up a shop in Clerkenwell as watch engravers but the venture was sabotaged by male engravers who objected to women in their trade. Undaunted, she turned to designing stained-glass windows until an old school friend, Octavia HILL, introduced her to the slum housing projects which she had established in St Marylebone in 1864. A teetotaller and moral reformer, Emma Cons persuaded wealthy acquaintances to campaign for working-class coffee taverns as alternatives to public houses. On her own doorstep in Lambeth she seized the opportunity of re-opening the Old Vic music hall in 1880. This former temple of working-class temptation was turned by Emma Cons and her friends into the 'South London People's Palace', mixing ballad concerts with scientific lectures—and coffee. As well as running clinics and crèches, she became vice-president of the London Society for Women's Suffrage, and executive member of the Women's Liberal Foundation, and, in 1889, one of three women members of the first London County Council. Out of the Old Vic lectures grew the Morley College for working men and women, while the theatre itself became a national institution under Lilian BAYLIS.
See also L. Baylis and C. Hamilton, *The Old Vic*, 1926.   K.S.

Conti, Italia (1874–1946), actress and founder of a well-known stage school. She was the daughter of a naturalized singer, Luigi Conti, and was educated at Warden Court, Haywards Heath, and Kensington Academy.
Italia Conti appeared at the Lyceum in 1891, toured England and Australia, and played several successful London seasons before Charles Hawtrey asked her to train the children in *Where the Rainbow Ends*. She devoted the rest of her life to her stage school, imbuing even those who did not take up acting with a lasting social grace. Among her famous pupils were Gertrude LAWRENCE, Anton Dolin, and Noël Coward. She was called 'the governess of the English stage', claiming that she did not start her school; it 'came' to her. In 1918 the Board of Education asked her advice concerning the regulations for licensing stage children; today's laws are the direct result. She also founded the Rainbow League to help youth organizations and British hospitals.   A.D.

Conway, Anne, Viscountess Conway (before 1631–1679), author and philosopher, was the daughter of Sir Henry Finch, Recorder of London and Speaker of the House of Commons. Educated in Latin, Greek, philosophy and mathematics, she eagerly perused the ancient philosophers in their original languages, and developed a profound interest in metaphysics and mysticism. She formed an enduring friendship with Dr Henry More, the leading Cambridge philosopher of his day, who greatly respected her intellectual capacity, and was described by Richard Ward, More's biographer, as 'Heroine pupil' of 'incomparable Parts and Endowments'. In 1651 she married Edward Conway, Viscount and later Earl of Conway, and at Ragley Castle in Warwickshire she continued her studies. More visited regularly and corresponded with her for nearly thirty years.
Notwithstanding severe and persistent headaches, 'her Understanding continued quick and sound', and according to Ward she 'had the greatest facility imaginable for any, either Physical, Metaphysical, or Mathematical Speculations'. It was Lady Conway's 'Desire or Instigation' that prompted More to compose some of his most learned treatises, several of them while he was visiting Ragley. (However, despite More's disapproval Lady Conway ultimately joined the Society of Friends.) More wrote the preface to a proposed edition of her 'remains' and although the projected work never materialized, in 1690 a collection of philosophical treatises in Latin was printed at Amsterdam, including translation of work by 'a certain English countess'; it was ascribed by Leibnitz, on the information of her physician, to Lady Conway. In 1692 it was published in English as *The Principles of the most Ancient*

109

and Modern Philosophy, concerning God, Christ, and the Creatures.

See also M. H. Nicolson (ed.), *Conway letters: the Correspondence of Anne, Viscountess Conway, Henry More, and their friends, 1642–1684,* 1930; D. M. Stenton, *The English Woman in History,* 1957; R. Ward, *The Life of the Learned and Pious Dr Henry More,* 1710.   T.J.M.

Cook, Eliza (1818–89), poet. Eliza Cook was born in Southwark, the daughter of a brazier, and was entirely self-educated. She wrote poetry from the age of fourteen and published her first volume, *Lays of a Wild Harp,* in 1835. For many years she contributed poems to the *Weekly Despatch* and became very popular, mostly with people of little education whose feelings she could express in an acceptably sentimental form. Most of her subjects came from domestic life.

In 1849 she launched her own periodical *Eliza Cook's Journal,* a miscellany of verse and essays on current topics, but this survived only five years. Modern readers would find her writings tedious, but her books went into many editions, were popular in America, and were translated into German. Occasionally she influenced public events, as in her poem *Poor Hood,* which led to the erection of a monument to Thomas Hood in Kensal Green cemetery. Her *Collected Poems* appeared in 1870. She also published two prose books, *Jottings from My Journal* (1860), and *Diamond Dust* (1865), a collection of aphorisms.

See also S. J. Kunitz and H. Haycraft (eds), *British Authors of the Nineteenth Century,* 1936; R. Myers, *Dictionary of Literature in the English Language,* 1970.   P.L.

Cooper, Charlotte Reinagle (1871–1966), tennis player. Born at Ealing, 'Chattie' Cooper learnt to play tennis at the Ealing Lawn Tennis Club and won her first open singles title at Ilkley in 1893. By 1895 *The Sportfolio* considered her to be 'in the forefront of lady players' and in that year she became Irish champion and won her first Wimbledon ladies' singles championship. Praising her attack, *The Sportfolio* warned 'she has yet something to learn in regard of steadiness being apt to become wild at times in her hitting', but she came to be known for 'supreme steadiness' and great tactical ability. From 1894 to 1901 she led the field of women's tennis with

Blanche Hillyard, winning both singles and doubles titles all over the country. She won the Wimbledon title in 1895, 1896 and 1898 as Miss Cooper, and in 1901 and 1908 as Mrs Alfred Sterry. At the Paris games in 1900 she became the first woman to win an Olympic gold medal, defeating Hélène Prévost, the French champion, in the lawn tennis tournament, 6–1, 6–4, and winning the mixed doubles with R. F. Doherty from Hélène Prévost and H. S. Mahony. She became treble Wimbledon champion in 1908, defeating the great Mrs Lambert CHAMBERS in the singles and winning the mixed doubles with S. E. Casdagli and the ladies' doubles with Miss Garfit. In 1913, eighteen years after her first Wimbledon victory, she reached the final of the ladies' doubles. She was long remembered for her good temper, great sportsmanship, and 'irrepressible joie de vivre'.

See also M. Robertson, *Wimbledon 1877–1977,* 1977.   C.B.

Cooper, Gladys (Constance) (1888–1971), actress. Born in Lewisham, the daughter of a journalist, this woman of exceptional good looks began her long career at the age of six as a photographic model. In her teens and twenties she was a picture-postcard beauty, the 'pin-up girl' of the First World War.

Without any drama school training but with total self-confidence, Gladys Cooper auditioned in 1905 and gained her first job touring with Seymour Hicks in *Bluebell in Fairyland.* Equal success with her first London audition in 1907 won her a three-year contract as one of the famous Gaiety girls.

In 1911 she progressed to 'straight' acting as Cecily in Oscar Wilde's *The Importance of Being Earnest.* She took the lead as Dora in Sardou's *Diplomacy* (1913). She became joint manager with Frank Curzon of the Playhouse Theatre (1917), a responsibility she fulfilled for sixteen years, proving herself to be a capable business woman. Her fine performance in Pinero's *The Second Mrs Tanqueray* (1922) revealed that not only was she the most beautiful actress of her day but also one of the most gifted. She was totally professional: to her, acting was always hard and serious work, the way in which she earned a living.

Gladys Cooper made her American début in Keith Winter's *The Shining Hour* (1934). At the age of fifty-two she began a career in films, appearing in *Rebecca.* She played Mrs

Higgins in the film version of *My Fair Lady* (1964) and celebrated her eightieth birthday on stage in Ira Wallach's *Out of the Question*. Her last role was in Enid Bagnold's *The Chalk Garden* (1971) a few months before her death.

The critic Sir Harold Hobson praised Gladys Cooper's 'incomparable technique' and pronounced her to be one of the four best actresses he had ever seen. She was created DBE in 1967.

See also S. Morley, *Gladys Cooper, a Biography*, 1979.   P.L.

Cooper, Selina (Jane) (1864–1946), suffragist and socialist. Born in Cornwall, Selina was the sixth child of a navvy, later a sub-contractor, who worked under Brunel in the construction of the Great Western Railway. In 1876 he died of typhoid, and his penniless widow, with Selina aged eleven and a son aged eight, was taken in by Northern relatives. Selina went to work as a half-timer in a cotton mill (half the day at school, half at work). Aged about seventeen she left work to nurse her bedridden mother, taking in washing to earn money until her mother died in 1889. Then she returned to mill-work for a decade.

Meanwhile, she joined the Social Democratic Federation, addressing the Nelson SDF branch in 1896. A member of the Independent Labour Party (ILP), she campaigned in 1896 for Brierfield's first Labour councillor. In 1896 she married Robert Cooper, a socialist weaver. In 1898 she helped form Brierfield's Women's Co-operative Guild, becoming its first president.

By 1900, appreciating women's political powerlessness, Selina Cooper collected women mill-workers' signatures for a giant suffrage petition, which she accompanied to Westminster in 1901. She campaigned for Labour's support of women's suffrage, seconding the motion at the 1905 and 1907 Party Conferences. She had been elected an SDF-ILP Guardian (administrators of poor relief) to the Burnley Board 1901–07, and in 1907 she left the Guardians and became an organizer for Mrs FAWCETT's National Union of Women's Suffrage Societies (NUWSS). This took her campaigning throughout Britain, especially during 1912–14, when Labour agreed to support women's suffrage and NUWSS organizers backed Labour's by-election candidates.

During the First World War she was a pacifist, working for maternity and child welfare centres. Preferring to operate locally once women got the vote, she stood unsuccessfully in her Nelson Ward; but she became a magistrate in 1924. In 1928 she led a protest demonstration against the Burnley Guardians' harshness towards locked-out weavers, and in 1930 again became a Guardian. In 1933 she spoke at a Westminster mass meeting for married women's right to work. In 1934 she was widowed; she served on a delegation organized by Women Against War and Fascism to investigate Nazi treatment of women. In 1940–41 she joined the pro-Communist People's Convention, and was expelled from the Labour Party. The Cooper papers are in the Lancashire Record Office.

See also J. Liddington and J. Norris, *One Hand Tied Behind Us*, 1978.   J.R.L.

Corbett Ashby, Dame Margery. See ASHBY, DAME MARGERY CORBETT.

Corelli, Marie (1855–1924), novelist, was originally plain Mary Mackay, although she claimed to have been born in 1864 and to be the adopted daughter of Charles Mackay, a Scottish song writer. (She was in fact his daughter—originally illegitimate—by the woman who became his second wife.) Although she went to a convent for a short time, Mary Mackay was mainly educated by governesses. She was a talented pianist and intended to have a musical career, for which she chose her pseudonym, Marie Corelli; but in 1885 she had a psychic experience which turned her towards writing.

Marie Corelli's first novel, *A Romance of Two Worlds*, was published in 1886, and others followed; but it was not until the publication of *Barabbas* in 1893 that her great vogue began. Two years later *The Sorrows of Satan* (1895) had an initial sale greater than that of any previous English novel, making her the most popular novelist of her time.

Rooted in Christocentric Supernaturalism, Marie Corelli's novels are sensational, propagandist, and fantastic, being filled with trances, swoons, psychic experiences, religious conversions and ecstatic visions. Oscar Wilde once said to her, 'You certainly tell of marvellous things in a marvellous way', which was overkind; but in the 1890s her admirers ranged from Mark Twain to the Prince of Wales. Her popularity waned after 1900, and she enjoyed an extravagant, litigious, and eccentric decline.

Her other novels include *Thelma*, 1887,

Ardath, 1889, *The Soul of Lilith*, 1892, *The Mighty Atom*, 1896, *'Temporal Power'*, 1902, *The Life Everlasting*, 1911 and *The Young Diana*, 1917.

See also E. Bigland, *Marie Corelli: the Woman and the Legend*, 1953.   A.P.

Cork and Orrery, Countess of.
See MONCKTON, MARY, COUNTESS OF CORK AND ORRERY.

Cornford, Frances (1886–1960), poet. Frances Cornford was born into one of the most intellectually distinguished of 19th-century families. She was the only child of Francis Darwin, third son of Charles Darwin, and his second wife, Ellen Wordsworth, great-niece of the poet. She was educated at home. She met her husband, Francis Macdonald Cornford, Professor of Ancient Philosophy, in 1908, and they married in 1909.

The Cornfords' home in Cambridge became a meeting-place for writers and artists. Frances Cornford was a close friend of Rupert Brooke, and her writing owed much to the encouragement of Christopher Hassall. Her verse was essentially 'Georgian', and although she continued to write into the second half of the century, her work was little influenced by such figures as Eliot and Pound. Her first poems were published in 1910 and her *Collected Poems* in 1954. She also translated verse (*Poems from the Russian*, 1943). Her cousin Gwen RAVERAT illustrated several of her books.

See also G. Raverat, *Period Piece*, 1960.
                                      C.H.

Costello, Louisa Stuart (1799–1870), artist and writer. She was born in England, the daughter of an Irish army captain. Barely sixteen when he died, she began painting to support her mother and brother. She lived in Paris by painting miniatures, moving to London about 1820, where she exhibited at the Royal Academy. In 1835 she established a literary reputation with *Specimens of the Early Poetry of France*. Her brother Dudley assisted with this work and with the *Rose Garden of Persia* (1845), which was also illustrated by them. Although she wrote historical novels, it was her lively descriptions of travels in the Auvergne, the Pyrenees, Wales, and the Tyrol that were most popular.   B.H.C.

Cosway, Maria (Cecila Louisa) (*fl.* 1760–1833), miniaturist and engraver, born Maria Hadfield of an English hotel-keeper resident in Leghorn. Her life began in bizarre circumstances, and was to continue in similar vein. A mad nurse was discovered to have murdered her four older siblings in succession, and was about to despatch Maria when detected.

Maria Hadfield was educated in a convent and then sent to Rome, where she studied painting under Battoni, Mengs, and Fuseli. Her desire to become a nun on her father's death was forestalled by a visit to England, where she met the painters Angelica KAUFFMANN and Richard Cosway. In London she took up miniature painting, chiefly of mythological subjects, and first exhibited at the Royal Academy in 1781, the year in which she married Richard Cosway. As a painter she was an immediate success; her husband kept her secluded during her first year of marriage, supposedly because of her foreign speech and manners, but perhaps also through professional jealousy.

Maria Cosway's reputation as an artist was established by a portrait of the Duchess of Devonshire, while socially she enjoyed a great success among the minor aristocracy. Relations with her husband became strained, and she left for the Continent with an Italian tenor. Later she returned to London's social life, only to go back to the Continent once more in 1804, remaining there for three years. During this period her daughter died and her grief seems to have prompted her to execute several large religious pictures for churches. She lived in England and then in Paris, and while in France she attempted to found a College for Ladies; in fact she finally carried out this scheme at Lodi in Italy. It was at this period that she executed her master-work, the complete engravings of works in the Louvre.

The Cosways appear to have become reconciled at some time between 1815 and Richard Cosway's death in 1821. In 1826 Maria Cosway was arranging the engraving of her husband's drawings, and Cunningham (see below) writes of her in 1833 as still living. The date of her death is not known.

See also E. C. Clayton, *English Female Artists*, 1876; A. Cunningham, *The Lives of the most Eminent British Painters, Sculptors, and Architects*, 1829–33; J. T. Smith, *Nollekens and his Times . . .*, 1828.   C.H.

Coucy, Isabella de, Countess of Bedford (1332–79). She was the eldest daughter of Edward III and PHILIPPA OF HAINAULT. Several foreign marriages proposed for Isabella in her teens came to nothing and in 1351 she was betrothed to the son of the Sire d'Albret, her father's chief lieutenant in Gascony. She was given a generous dowry and sailed for Bordeaux. At the last minute, Isabella turned round and sailed home again. Forgiven by her indulgent father, allowed to retain her own dowry, and showered with other lands and gifts, she remained single and independent until 1365, when she decided to marry Enguerrand de Coucy, eight years her junior. He was a wealthy French peer being held as a hostage in England. Edward III created him Earl of Bedford and gave him a very large dowry with Isabella. There were two daughters of the marriage. Eventually Enguerrand had to choose between loyalty to either England or France. He chose France. Isabella accompanied him to France but soon left him to return to the more congenial atmosphere of her father's court. She remained settled in England until her death. Isabella seems to have been vain, selfish and spoiled, but her determination to lead her own life as she chose was virtually unprecedented among English princesses.

See also B. Tuchman, *A Distant Mirror*, 1978. A.C.

Courtauld, Louisa (1729–1807), silversmith. The daughter of Peter Ogier, of Spitalfields, a Huguenot refugee from Poitou, Louisa married the goldsmith Samuel Courtauld (1720–65) in 1749. She ran the business at the Crown, Cornhill, after her husband's death, taking his apprentice George Cowles into partnership and registering her mark at Goldsmith's Hall. Her work, executed in the Neoclassical style, can be seen in the Victoria and Albert Museum and the Museum of London. Her portrait, executed in about 1770, was at one time attributed to Zoffany.

See also S. L. Courtauld, *The Huguenot Family of Courtauld*, 1957; J. Hayward, *The Courtauld Silver*, 1975. T.M.

Courtenay, Gertrude (?–1558), political figure. She was the daughter of William Blount, Lord Mountjoy (Erasmus' patron and KATHERINE OF ARAGON's Chamberlain), by his first wife; her stepmother was Inez de Venegas, one of Queen Katherine's Spanish ladies. In October 1519 Gertrude Blount married Henry Courtenay, Earl of Devon, in the King's presence. Courtenay, a grandson of Edward IV, became Marquess of Exeter in 1525, and the couple had a son, Edward, in about 1526.

When Henry VIII set in motion his divorce from Katherine of Aragon, Lady Courtenay was an active partisan of Katherine, corresponding with her, giving information to her brother-in-law the Emperor's ambassador, and supporting Elizabeth BARTON, the Nun of Kent; in 1533 she was forced to send the King a fulsome apology (edited by Thomas Cromwell) for having visited the Nun. She returned to court after Anne BOLEYN's fall, but in November 1538 was arrested with her husband and son, Lord Montague, and other members of the Pole family, accused of plotting insurrection. She was a companion in the Tower of Margaret POLE. Exeter was executed on 9 December, and Lady Courtenay and her son were attainted in July 1539. She had been released by April 1540, though Edward remained in prison.

Lady Courtenay was a close friend of Queen Katherine's daughter, Princess Mary, and when Mary became Queen in 1553 her attainder was reversed and she became a lady-in-waiting. Her son Edward was restored to the earldom of Devon, and was encouraged by Bishop Gardiner to hope that he might marry the Queen. When Mary chose Philip of Spain instead, he became disaffected, and was implicated in Wyatt's rebellion of 1554. He was imprisoned, but was released and exiled at Easter 1555.

See also J. S. Brewer, *Letters and Papers, Foreign and Domestic, of the Reign of Henry VIII . . .*, 1920; J. E. Paul, *Catherine of Aragon and Her Friends*, 1966. M.D.

Courtneidge, (Esmeralda) Cicely (1893–1980), actress. She was born at Sydney, Australia, the daughter of Robert Courtneidge, an actor-manager. She made her first stage appearances in Sydney and Manchester in 1901.

Cicely Courtneidge married Jack Hulbert in 1916, two years after he had played opposite her in what was to be a life-long partnership. While he was in the army during the First World War she appeared in variety in the provinces. She made her London début in a revue with her husband, but despite their success they were unable to work together for much of the time. The British cinema boom in the 1930s helped them greatly, and they were together in many films, including *The Ghost Train* and *Jack's the Boy*. Cicely Courtneidge had a huge success in variety and revue, and made several films without Jack Hulbert before they came together on the stage in *Under Your Hat* (1938).

During the Second World War they acted together several times. Cicely Courtneidge also toured the Mediterranean for ENSA and formed the Ack-Ack Comforts Fund. Despite her success in serious plays such as *Dear Octopus*, she remained 'Cis' to the public. She was created CBE in 1951 and DBE in 1973. She and Jack Hulbert played together for the last time in *Breath of Spring* (1974). She wrote an autobiography, *Cicely* (1953).   A.D.

Courtney, Dame Kathleen (D'Olier) (1878–1974), worker for international peace. Kathleen Courtney was the daughter of Major D. C. Courtney of Milltown, County Dublin. She was educated at private schools and at Lady Margaret Hall, Oxford, where she read modern languages. She entered public life via the suffragette movement, her concern for the advancement of women leading on to a wider concern for humanity in a war-torn world. It was at the outbreak of the First World War that she abandoned her active campaigning for votes for women ('We had no knowledge of the causes of the war', she was to say) and devoted her life to studying international politics and building bridges towards international co-operation. She did not marry.

Until 1914 Kathleen Courtney was Honorary Secretary of the National Union of Women's Suffrage Societies, and spent some years helping organize the non-militant campaign. She was one of the founders of the Women's International League for Peace, serving for ten years as Chairman of the British section; when she left the League she did so partly because she found its brand of pacifism unrealistic. She took part in the famous International Women's Congress at The Hague in 1915, when delegates from fifteen countries, both neutral and belligerent, asked themselves on what foundations peace could be based and how women could help to realize it. Later in the war she did relief work among Serbian refugees and, after it, further relief work with

the Society of Friends in Austria, Poland, and Greece.

During her frequent visits to Geneva, Kathleen Courtney studied the activities of the League of Nations. In 1928 she was appointed a member of the Executive Committee of the British League of Nations Union; in 1939 she was elected its Vice-chairman. With her combination of sternness, clear vision, and graciousness, she proved to be an admirable Chairman. She was also a lively speaker, and during the Second World War twice toured America to lecture on behalf of the Ministry of Information.

Kathleen Courtney was at San Francisco in 1945 when the United Nations Charter was drawn up. Out of the defunct League of Nations Union she helped to build the United Nations Association, being appointed Vice-chairman of the British branch's executive. In 1949 she became Chairman, and in the same year joint President; she relinquished the chairmanship in 1951. She was awarded the CBE in 1946 and the DBE in 1952.   J.L.

Coutts, Angela Burdett-, Baroness. See BURDETT-COUTTS, ANGELA, BARONESS.

Cowley, Hannah (1743–1809), dramatist and poet, daughter of a Devon bookseller and cousin of John Gay. She married Captain Cowley of the East India Company. Hearing her express her contempt for a play, he challenged her to do better. She wrote *The Runaway*, which was produced by David Garrick at Drury Lane in 1776 with great éclat. Many plays followed, notably *The Belle's Stratagem* (1782). Her works were published, with an account of her life, in 1813. *The Belle's Stratagem* survived into the nineteenth century in performance.

Hannah Cowley declared herself indifferent to the success of her plays on the stage, but she nevertheless conducted newspaper battles with Hannah More over plagiarism. In 1795 she expressed her disgust for the debased taste of the times and ceased to write for the stage.

Her dramatic work has some originality and wit, though she herself plagiarized. She also published poetry, and under the name 'Anna Matilda' conducted a sentimental correspondence with Robert Merry in *The World*. These letters were collected in two volumes with portraits of the authors. Her verse lacks the fun and freshness of her comedies, and was mocked by William Gifford in *The Baviad* and *Maeviad*.

See also D. E. Baker, *Biographia Dramatica*, 1782.   C.H.

Craig, Ailsa. See CRAIG, EDITH.

Craig, Edith (Ailsa Geraldine) (1869–1947), actress. She was the daughter of Ellen TERRY and the architect E. W. Godwin, and the sister of the theatrical designer-director Gordon Craig.

Edith Craig's first stage appearance was at the Court Theatre; later she played with her mother and Henry Irving. In New York (1888), as Ailsa Craig, she played the name part in *Barbara*. In 1907 she acted as her mother's stage-manager on a tour of the United States. She later studied music at the Royal Academy of Music and in Berlin, but in 1911 she returned to the theatre to produce over 150 plays for the Pioneer Players. She had a genius for design; her costumes and scenery were exquisite. In 1929 she converted an Elizabethan barn at Small Hythe into a theatre for annual anniversary performances commemorating her mother's death. Many illustrious actors performed there.

Edith Craig was not submerged by her mother's personality. She was too firm, even peremptory, but her charm had people willingly obeying the orders given from the chaise-longue on which, because of illness, she spent her last years.

See also E. Adlard, *Edy*, 1949.   A.D.

Craig, Isa (1831–1903), poet, was born in Edinburgh, the daughter of a hosier and glover. Her parents died while she was young, and she was brought up by her grandmother. Her schooling was brief, but she educated herself and began writing poetry. Her poems were published in *The Scotsman*, and in 1853 she joined its staff. Three years later she moved to London, where she worked as secretary of the National Association for the Promotion of Social Science until 1866, when she married her cousin John Knox, an iron merchant.

Isa Craig continued to contribute to magazines, wrote a book for children, *The Little Folk's History of England* (1872), and was for a time editor of *The Argosy*. The popularity of her work declined after her death. Her other works include *Poems by Isa*, 1856, *Duchess Agnes*, 1864, *Esther West: a story*, 1870,

Songs of Consolation, 1874, and *Tales on the Parables*, 1872.   A.P.

Craighton, Elizabeth (*fl.* 1728–76), bookseller and publisher at Ipswich. Her first productions appeared in 1728. She held an interest in the *Ipswich Journal* produced by her brother William. The *Journal* appears to have got into difficulties under William's management and in 1765 she became joint printer with her nephew. She established herself as a partner in the enterprise upon William's bankruptcy in 1771.

See also H. R. Plomer, G. H. Bushnell, E. R. McC. Dix, *A Dictionary of the Printers and Booksellers who were at work in England, Scotland, and Ireland from 1726 to 1775*, 1932.   T.H.

Craigie, Pearl (Mary Teresa) (1867–1906), novelist and dramatist who used the pen-name 'John Oliver Hobbes'. She was born at Chelsea, near Boston, Massachusetts, the eldest child of a New York merchant who moved to London following Pearl's birth to run a manufacturing chemist's business. His family joined him in London and Pearl was educated at private day schools in London, a boarding school in Berkshire, and in Paris. She read widely and by the age of nine she was publishing stories in *The Fountain*, a newspaper owned by a family friend.

At the age of nineteen she married Reginald Walpole Craigie after a visit to America. The marriage was a failure: she left her husband following the birth of her son in 1890 and was granted custody of the child after a public trial. Pearl Craigie's first novel, *Some Emotions and a Moral*, was published in 1891, and the following year she became a Roman Catholic, taking the additional names 'Mary' and 'Teresa'.

Having established her reputation with her first novel, 'John Oliver Hobbes' went on to write *The Gods, Some Mortals, and Lord Wickenham*, 1895, *The School for Saints*, 1897, and its sequel *Robert Orange*, 1900, which had Disraeli as one of the characters, and *The Dream and the Business*, 1907. She also wrote plays, including *The Ambassador*, 1898, and *The Bishop's Move*, 1902, and journalism. Her work was noted for its wit and command of the epigram.

Pearl Craigie was involved in London's literary life, entertaining at her father's house.

115

She was president of the Society of Women Journalists in 1895 but was also a member of the Anti-Suffrage League: seeing herself as the exception to the rule, she said 'I have no confidence in the honour of the average woman or her brains'.

In 1903 she went to India, but a planned lecture tour of America two years later was prevented by her ill health. She was only thirty-nine when she died.

See also *The Life of John Oliver Hobbes Told in Her Correspondence with Numerous Friends*, 1911; J. Richards, *The Life of John Oliver Hobbes*, 1911. A.P.

Craik, Mrs. See MULOCK, DINAH (MARIA).

Crawford, Anne. See BARRY, ANNE.

Crompton, Richmal, pseudonym of Richmal Crompton Lamburn (1890–1969), author of the 'William' books for boys. The daughter of a clergyman, she was educated at St Elphin's School, Darley Dale, and Royal Holloway College, London. She taught classics at St Elphin's and then at Bromley High School for Girls, but retired in her thirties after an attack of polio. By this time she had already written 'William' stories for magazines, and in 1922 some of these were collected and published in book form as *Just William*. This and its many successors proved enduringly popular, and for forty years their hero, William Brown, remained the same scruffy, muddy, eleven-year-old savage, embarking on one wildly unrealistic scheme after another, almost always with disastrous and disruptive results. The William books have sold in millions, and have inevitably overshadowed Richmal Crompton's many other writings, mostly quiet tales of village and family life. N.H.

Crowdy, Dame Rachel (1884–1964), Commandant of VAD's and worker for the League of Nations. Born in London, she trained as a nurse at Guy's Hospital. She joined the Red Cross Volunteers in 1911 and there met Katherine FURSE. On the outbreak of the First World War they investigated the provision made for the wounded in France, and were instrumental in the establishment of rest stations. In 1914 Rachel Crowdy was appointed Principal Commandant of VADs in France and Belgium, and at the end of the war she was created DBE for her work.

This proved to be only the beginning of her public service, for, as the only woman to head an administrative section of the League of Nations, she did sterling work on Social Questions and the Opium Traffic. When, in 1931, her work for the League came to an end, she maintained her formidable record as a committee woman, sitting for example on the Royal Commission on the Private Manufacture of Armaments (1935) and the Royal Commission on the West Indies (1938–39), and going with the Parliamentary Commission to the Spanish Civil War in 1937. During the Second World War she was Regions Adviser to the Ministry of Information. E.M.V.

Crowe, Catherine Stevens (1800–76), novelist, was born at Borough Green, Kent, and educated at home. Her maiden name was Stevens; she married a Lieutenant-Colonel Crowe and settled with him in Edinburgh. She was thirty-eight when her first work, *Aristodemus*, a drama, was published anonymously. Her most successful novel, *Susan Hopley*, was published three years later.

Like Marie Corelli, Catherine Crowe was interested in phrenology, physiology, and spiritualism. Her novels and stories abound with ghosts and other supernatural happenings for which she attempts to find scientific explanations, most notably in her novel *The Night Side of Nature* (1848). She published many other works, but shortly after writing *Spiritualism and the Age we live in* (1859) she became temporarily insane. After her recovery she wrote little. Her other works include *Men and Women*, 1843, *Story of Lilly Dawson* 1847, *Pippie's Warning*, 1848, *Light and Darkness*, 1850, *Adventures of a Beauty*, 1852, *Linny Lockwood*, 1854, *Ghosts and Family Legends*, 1859, *Story of Arthur Hunter*, 1861, and *Adventures of a Monkey*, 1862. A.P.

Cullis, Winifred (Clara) (1875–1956), Professor Emeritus of Physiology at the University of London. She was born in Gloucester and educated at King Edward VI's High School for Girls, Birmingham, and Newnham College, Cambridge, where she read for the Natural Sciences Tripos. In 1901 she became demonstrator in physiology at the London (Royal Free Hospital) School of Medicine; in 1903 she was appointed a lecturer, and in 1912 Professor of Physiology.

Winifred Cullis was a brilliant teacher and lecturer; she broadcast widely for schools, and gave courses at the London School of Economics and the National Health Society and extension lectures for the University of London. She travelled widely, lecturing in the USA and in Canada, and being sent in 1919 by the Colonial Office to Gibraltar and Malta to lecture to the troops. For this work she was awarded first an OBE and then, in 1929, a CBE. In the Second World War, she again made extensive lecture tours of the Far East, China, Australia and New Zealand, as well as of Canada and the United States.

Winifred Cullis was deeply committed to the achievement of equality of status between professional women and their male counterparts, and to this end was one of the founders of the British Federation of University Women and of the International Federation. She is commemorated in the Winifred Cullis Lecture Fellowship of the British-American Association. E.M.V.

Cunard, Nancy (Clara) (1896–1965), public figure and writer, the only child of Sir Bache and Lady Emerald Cunard, a society hostess. Nancy Cunard's marriage to Sidney Fairbairn, an Australian Guards officer, lasted only twenty months. However, her fundamental seriousness was for a time concealed by her association with intellectual café society. In 1928 she founded the Hours Press to support contemporary writers such as George Moore, Louis Aragon, Robert Graves, Ezra Pound, and Samuel Beckett, using a printing press she had bought from an American newspaper man.

Nancy Cunard's cohabitation in London with a Negro jazz pianist, Henry Crowder, caused a major scandal. They escaped to Austria, where Nancy wrote a vitriolic pamphlet, *Black Man and White Ladyship, An Anniversary*, condemning the life-style and attitudes of her mother. With Henry Crowder she prepared an anthology called *Negro*, covering every aspect of Negro art. She celebrated its publication in 1934 by joining the Great North Road Hunger Marches. When eight Negro youths were condemned to death in Alabama for allegedly assaulting two white prostitutes (1932), she organized an inter-racial dance to raise funds for an appeal against this sentence. This anti-racism (or at any rate its practical expression) was extremely radical for its time.

At the outbreak of the Spanish Civil War, Nancy Cunard joined the International Brigade and went to Spain as a reporter for the *Manchester Guardian* and The Associated Negro Press, publishing anti-Fascist articles on the fighting. She continued to espouse various causes, such as Spanish War refugees, Franco's prisoners, and the gondoliers in Venice, but deteriorating physical and mental health hampered her activities in later years, and she died in France in 1965.

Her colourful personality and her continued presence in literary circles won her a place as a character in the literature of the 1920s and 1930s.

See also A. Chisholm, *Nancy Cunard*, 1979; D. Fielding, *Emerald and Nancy*, 1968.

M.G.B.

Cunningham, Lady Anne, Marchioness of Hamilton (d. 1647), political figure. Lady Anne Cunningham was the daughter of the Earl of Glencairn and came from a family noted for its early and zealous commitment to the Protestant cause in Scotland. In 1603 she married James, later second Marquis of Hamilton, a close associate of James VI and I, and was widowed in 1625 having borne two sons and three daughters.

Her importance is as a protector of the Presbyterian Church in Scotland against Charles I's attempts to impose what we should now call Anglicanism on his northern kingdom, and especially as an active adherent of the National Covenant movement of resistance to Charles's policies. Her son, the third Marquis, sided with Charles, and when he attempted in May 1639 to land an army on the Scottish coast she organized the defences and 'came forth armed with a pistol which she vowed to discharge upon her son if he offered to come ashore'. The Marquis's failure to land was popularly attributed to fear of his mother's wrath, although valid military explanations can also be found. She raised a troop of horse for the Covenanters and commanded them in person; their banner, a hand repelling a book (the hated prayer book), and their motto 'For God, the King, Religion, and the Covenant', reflected her views.

Commentators noted 'how the Ladies and gentlewomen, by her example do all practise their arms, in which new kind of housewifery they are very expert'. They were said to curse their sons and husbands 'wishing their . . . flesh to be converted into that of dogs, and their souls annihilated' if they did not oppose the English bishops. She was designated 'a notable

117

virago', a predictable comment on a determined, aggressive woman, who ignored contemporary opinions of a woman's proper role.

A.H.

Currie, Mary (Montgomerie Lamb), Lady (1843–1905), novelist, poet and essayist. Mary Currie was born at Beauport in Sussex, was educated privately, and began writing at an early age despite the disapproval of her family, publishing under the pseudonym 'Violet Fane', taken from Disraeli's *Vivian Grey*.

Mary Currie married twice. Her first husband, Henry Sydenham Singleton, was an Irish landowner. They lived in London, where she was celebrated for her beauty, charm and wit. In March 1893 Henry Sydenham Singleton died, and a year later she married Sir Philip Henry Wodehouse Currie, British Ambassador to Constantinople, where the couple lived until Currie was appointed Ambassador to Rome. Currie was made a peer in 1899. The Curries remained in Rome until his retirement in 1903, when they returned to England.

Mary Currie wrote a good deal in several literary forms. Her verse includes *From Dawn to Noon*, 1872, *Autumn Songs*, 1889, and *In Winter*, 1904. She published novels and stories such as *Laura Dibalzo*, 1880, *Sophy*, 1881, *Through Love and War*, 1886, and *The Story of Helen Davenant*, 1889. She also wrote a drama, *Antony Babington*, 1876, translated *The Memoirs of Marguerite de Valois*, and contributed articles and essays to magazines.

A.P.

Curtis, Dame Myra (1886–1971), civil servant. She was educated at Winchester High School and Newnham College, Cambridge (classical tripos, 1907). After coming down she worked as an editor of the *Victoria County History*. She began her Civil Service career in 1915, when she joined the temporary staff of the War Trade Intelligence Department. In 1918 she transferred to the Ministry of Food, specializing in personnel work. From 1920 to 1922 she was Deputy Assistant Secretary in the Establishment Branch.

After more than six years of temporary work which proved her to be one of the most promising of wartime recruits, Myra Curtis entered the permanent Civil Service in the junior administrative grade in 1923 via the first competitive examination for super-clerical grade women, in which she came first. After a short stint in the Ministry of Pensions, she went to the Post Office in 1924, first as superintendent of female staff of the Savings Bank Department and in 1934 as Principal in the Secretary's Office.

In 1937, from a field of the most distinguished women civil servants, she was selected for the post of Assistant Secretary and Director of Women's Establishments in the Treasury, in effect the premier women's post in the Civil Service. She retired in 1942 and was awarded the CBE and the DBE in 1949.

The focus of her activities in later life was education. She returned to Newnham as principal (1942–54), taking an active part in the campaign to secure for women full membership of the university.

Dame Myra Curtis inspired respect and liking rather than love. She was by temperament an administrator, and her work both in the Civil Service and at Newnham reflected this predilection. She had a marked flair for long-term planning as well as day-to-day management. 'The most competent woman civil servant' of her day, she sought equality of recruitment, conditions of service, and pay between men and women, and an end to segregation of the sexes. She pursued her feminist aims to effect in positions of considerable power. In collaboration with Hugh Townshend she published *Modern Money* (1937).

M.Z.

Curwen, Dame (Anne) May (1889–1973), administrator. Dame May Curwen was born at Birkenhead; she was educated at Birkenhead High School and Harrogate College, eventually going on to Newnham College, Cambridge, where she took a First in History. After a brief spell in teaching, she became organizing secretary of the Scottish Women's Hospitals in 1916, visiting Serbia late in 1918 to assess the post-war situation. In 1919 she joined the finance department of the Young Women's Christian Association, with which she remained for thirty years as Education Secretary (1920–30) and National General Secretary (1930–49). During the Second World War she travelled over much of the Continent setting up rest centres for servicewomen and nurses. Her appetite for fruitful activity persisted after her retirement in 1949, and she sat on numerous committees concerned with public welfare. However, the deepest commitment of her later years was to the world's refugees, in whose cause she travelled and worked with undiminished energy. She was the British delegate to the United Nations Refugee Fund from 1954 to 1958 and President of the British Council for Aid to Refugees from 1962 until her death.   N.H.

Cutpurse, Moll. See FRITH, MARY.

Cwoenthryth (*fl.* early ninth century), Mercian princess and abbess. Cwoenthryth was the daughter of King Coenwulf of Mercia and inherited substantial property from him; she may have been his only surviving child. By 811, before her father's death, she was an abbess, probably of the family monastery at Winchcombe. Her paternal inheritance also brought her the nunnery of Minster in Kent, and in her capacity as abbess there she was involved in a bitter dispute over land with Archbishop Wulfred. Her combination of the roles of heiress and abbess provided a dual power base. Later legends accused her of complicity in the murder of her half-brother Cynehelm because of her own desire to rule, with appropriate retribution when her eyes were torn out miraculously as she sang Psalm 108 backwards. Ninth-century Mercian history is too obscure for any aspect of the story to be verified, though rule by a woman in her own right would have been most unusual at that time.

See also W. Levison, *England and the Continent in the Eighth Century*, 1946.

                    P.A.S.

Cynethryth (*fl.* 772–98), Queen of Mercia. King Offa made his wife Cynethryth a queen, which in the eighth century probably meant that he had his marriage blessed by the Church. Such a step was not inevitable in Mercia at this date and the decision was related to Offa's wish to ensure his son Ecgfrith's succession to the throne: there were to be no doubts about Ecgfrith's legitimacy or the status of his mother, and Cynethryth received the title soon after her son's birth. The formal position Cynethryth thus acquired at court is attested in royal charters, in many of which the Queen's name appears with Offa's. Her name has also been linked with that of Offa in the murder of King Æthelberht of East Anglia while he was wooing their daughter; the possible motive and the truth of the accusation are totally obscure. Coins were struck in Cynethryth's name, an honour shared by no other Anglo-Saxon queen. Their issue may have coincided with the visit of the papal legates to Offa's court in 786, when they anointed Ecgfrith and pronounced injunctions requiring legitimate birth for all heirs to the throne; to honour Ecgfrith's mother with an issue of coin struck after the Byzantine example would have been a logical corollary.

Offa provided for Cynethryth's future by granting her monasteries and other properties, and she became abbess of Cookham in Berkshire after his death. She defended her abbey's lands with determination, and in 798 ended a long dispute with the Archbishop of Canterbury over possession of the nunnery by an exchange of lands.

See also P. A. Stafford, 'Charles the Bald, Judith, and Æthelwulf', in J. Nelson and M. Gibson (eds), *Charles the Bald*, British Archaeological Reports, 1981.   P.A.S.

D

Damer, Anne (Seymour) (1748/9–1828), sculptor. The daughter of Field Marshal Henry Seymour Conway, Anne Damer was born with powerful connections. She became a pet of Horace Walpole, showed precocious literary and artistic talent, and studied sculpture under Giuseppe Ceracchi and John Bacon.

In 1767 she married John Damer, son of the Earl of Dorchester. But in 1776, having exhausted his fortune and contracted huge debts, Damer shot himself after a last spree in Covent Garden. Left with a reasonable jointure, Anne Damer then devoted herself professionally to sculpture. She wintered on the Continent for her health; in Florence, she was introduced to Horace Mann by Walpole, who declared that 'she models like Bernini, and has excelled moderns in the similitudes of her busts'. She indeed executed busts of many distinguished people (including George III, Nelson, and Mrs SIDDONS), but her best-known works are the stone heads representing Thames and Isis on Henley Bridge (1785).

Anne Damer was also involved in Whig politics, canvassing for Charles James Fox in 1780. She knew Napoleon's wife, Josephine Beauharnais, and was invited to Paris to meet the First Consul during the Peace of Amiens. Napoleon presented her with a diamond snuff-box which is now in the British Museum.

Horace Walpole bequeathed Strawberry Hill to her for life. She lived there until 1811, when she passed it on to Lord Waldegrave. She was also friendly with two other friends of Walpole, the Misses BERRY, and produced a comedy by them at Drury Lane to universal condemnation.

Before dying, she directed that all her papers should be burnt, and that her working tools, her apron, and the ashes of her dog should be buried with her.   C.H.

Dancer, Ann. See BARRY, ANNE.

Dane, Clemence, pseudonym of Winifred Ashton (1888–1965), novelist and playwright. She was born at Greenwich and educated in England and abroad. She studied painting in Dresden and then spent three years at the Slade School of Art in London.

After a period as a teacher, Winifred Ashton decided to go on the stage. The First World War and her own poor health frustrated this ambition, however, and she turned to writing. Her first novel, *Regiment of Women* (1917), revealed the emergence of a distinctive new talent: she took her *nom de plume* from St Clement Dane, the church in the Strand near her home in Covent Garden.

Clemence Dane's first play, *A Bill of Divorcement* (1921), was a commercial and artistic triumph, but none of her subsequent plays were quite as successful. Her *Collected Plays* were published in 1961. Her novels were widely read, and *Broome Stages* (1931), the story of several generations of a theatrical family, was particularly popular. She also wrote radio plays, taking many of her plots from history, as in *Elizabeth I and Essex*. Her other works include *London Has a Garden* (1964).

See also S. J. Kunitz and H. Haycraft, *Twentieth Century Authors*, 1942.   P.L.

Daniell, Louisa (?–1871) and **Georgiana** (1835–94), Army mission workers. The early life of Louisa Daniell, born Louisa Drake, is obscure. Orphaned when very young, she was a lonely child whose only solace was religion. She later married Frederick Daniell, a captain in the East India Company and devout Christian whose intensity of belief complemented her own. After their marriage the couple left for India, where their daughter Georgiana was born, and where Mrs Daniell held prayer meetings and distributed religious tracts. Captain Daniell's death in 1837 later led the family to return to England, where Georgiana was sent to school in Brighton.

By 1857 the Daniells were living in Warwickshire, where Mrs Daniell had become concerned with the spiritual welfare of a local village. She instituted cottage Bible readings, held Scripture classes, and set up a Savings Bank. In 1860, having received substantial donations, she was able to build a Mission Hall. Impressed by her work, an associate at the County Town Mission Society suggested that she should embark upon similar evangelizing activities at the great army camp at Aldershot. Mrs Daniell conferred with her daughter, who approved of the proposal, and in 1862 they left for Hampshire.

Louisa Daniell believed that soldiers needed a place of relaxation that would be free from possible temptations. To this end, she set up the first Soldiers' Home and Institute, opened in 1863. It contained a library, a dining room, and a lecture hall; only non-alcoholic refreshments were served. A Total Abstinence Society was formed, and soldiers were encouraged to take the Pledge. The Daniells also sought to combat prostitution, and established refuge homes for friendless girls in Aldershot.

Organizations designed to assist soldiers' families were also established. The Soldier's Wife Aid Society provided a Savings Bank and sewing circle to augment slender incomes. In 1866 a Band of Hope was formed for camp children, and this developed into a school where basic tuition was provided by the soldiers themselves.

Louisa Daniell died in 1871, after a long illness, but her work was energetically continued by her daughter, a shrewd businesswoman who raised £30,000 to found new Soldiers' Homes. Georgiana Daniell also wrote *Aldershot: a Record of Mrs Daniell's Work amongst Soldiers, and its Sequel* (1879). Both mother and daughter form an excellent example of the formidable organizational and administrative abilities developed by nineteenth-century women committed to Christian philanthropy.

See also (anon.) *A Soldier's Daughter: a Short Memorial of Miss Daniell of Aldershot*, 1894.   J.V.L.

Darbishire, Helen (1881–1961), literary scholar, notable for her work on Milton and Wordsworth. She was born at Oxford, where her father was physician to the Radcliffe Infirmary, and spent most of her working life in the city. She was educated at Oxford High School and Somerville College, where she took a First in English Language and Literature. In 1904 she was appointed Visiting Lecturer at Royal Holloway College in London, but in 1908 she returned to Somerville as Fellow and Tutor in English; later (1926) she became a university lecturer in English Literature. Apart from a year (1925–26) as Visiting Professor at Wellesley College, Massachusetts, she remained at Somerville, of which she served as Principal from 1931 until her retirement in 1945.

Helen Darbishire's early publications included editions of Wordsworth's 1807 poems and De Quincey's criticism. Her 1931 edition of Milton's *Paradise Lost*, book I, was of particular scholarly interest in demonstrating the

coherence and utility of Milton's punctuation. *The Early Lives of Milton* followed in 1932, but thereafter she was largely occupied with her duties as Principal of Somerville during a period of rapid change and adjustment. In the 1940s she helped her early teacher and lifelong friend Ernest de Selincourt with his great edition of Wordsworth's poems, completing the last three volumes after his death. Her own edition of Milton's English poems (1952–55) was too conjectural for some tastes, but must still be consulted.

After her retirement, Helen Darbishire eventually left Oxford and settled at Grasmere, a village in the Lake District famous for Dove Cottage, the home of Wordsworth and his sister Dorothy. Helen Darbishire was a trustee, and from 1943 chairman, of Dove Cottage, which she did much to turn into a study centre. Even in old age, thanks to her knowledge of not only the Lake Poets but also the Lake District, she continued to be sought after for advice and information. Her last book was an edition of Dorothy Wordsworth's *Journal* (1958).   N.H.

D'Arblay, Madame. See BURNEY, FANNY.

Darling, Grace (1815–42), heroine. She was born at Bamburgh, Northumberland, the seventh child of William Darling, lighthouse keeper in the Farne Islands. Simple and submissive, she received an education that was narrowly religious and domestic. It is possible that she attended Spittal Boarding School, though evidence suggests that this may have been in the capacity of a servant. On 7 September 1838 her life took a dramatic turn, for the steamboat 'Forfarshire' was wrecked in a gale off Big Harker in the Farne Islands and she and her father, showing considerable skill and courage, rescued the survivors from the rocks in a small fishing boat. She soon became a celebrity, and a flood of journalists, poets, and portrait painters touched up her character and appearance; the details of the deed itself were lost in a hyperbolic mist. Patronized by the Duke of Northumberland, she received a gold medal from the Royal Humane Society. Subscriptions, gewgaws, day trippers, and begging letters poured in and made increasing demands on her. A private and sensitive girl, who before the incident would have expected to lead a life of unsung drudgery in the service of her overbearing father, she reluctantly saw herself translated into a legend. Her early death at the age of twenty-seven enhanced it, as did the obfuscations of her family and early biographers. She was buried in Bamburgh, the site of the Grace Darling Museum.

See also R. Armstrong, *Grace Darling: Maid and Myth*, 1965; C. Smedley, *Grace Darling and her Times*, 1932.   F.K.P.

Darusmont, Frances. See WRIGHT, FRANCES.

Dashwood, Edmée Elizabeth Monica. See DELAFIELD, E. M.

Davies, Lady Eleanor. See DOUGLAS, LADY ELEANOR.

Davies, (Sarah) Emily (1830–1921), pioneer of women's education. Born in Southampton, she was the fourth child of the Reverend John Davies, Rector of Gateshead. She was indifferently educated, but as an Evangelical clergyman's daughter developed a strong social conscience, turning her hand to district visiting and Sunday School teaching.

From an early age she was interested in the issue of women's rights and duties, and in her twenties became friendly with several leading women reformers, including Elizabeth Garrett ANDERSON and Barbara BODICHON. On a trip to London in 1859 she met various women associated with 19 Langham Place, which was the home of the Society for the Employment of Women and the influential *Englishwoman's Journal*. On returning to Gateshead she set up a Northumberland and Durham branch of the Society for the Employment of Women, with herself as Treasurer. She moved to London in 1862, after the death of her father, and campaigned with Elizabeth Garrett and others for the admission of women to degrees at London University and the right of women to enter the medical profession. Conscious of her own educational disabilities, she was concerned about the quality and appropriateness of girls' education generally. She therefore pressed, successfully, for the inclusion of female education in the Schools Enquiry Commission and gave telling evidence before that body in 1865. The Commission's recommendations were to lead to the reshaping of the secondary education of girls. In 1866 Emily Davies formed the London Schoolmistresses' Association, acting as its Secretary for twenty-two years. She also helped to organize the first female suffrage petition presented to Parliament in 1866 and was Assistant Secretary of the first Women's Suffrage Committee. From 1870 to 1873 she was an elected London School Board official.

Like many female reformers of her day she believed that specializing in one aspect of the women's movement was the best way forward, and so she withdrew from the suffrage campaign in 1867 to concentrate her energies on education. She was the practical genius behind the establishment in 1869 of a college for women at Hitchin, which opened with five students and moved to Cambridge, renamed Girton College, in 1873. She was the Honorary Secretary of Girton from 1873 to 1904, briefly treasurer, and Mistress from 1873 to 1875. Determined to prove that women were as capable as men of benefiting from higher education, she sought to prepare students for Cambridge degree examinations and opposed all plans to treat women separately. She did not, however, live to see the college fully incorporated into the University.

Once Girton was on a sound footing, she returned in earnest to the cause of women's suffrage, and in 1890 joined the Executive Committee of the London Society for Women's Suffrage. A constitutionalist and eminently respectable, she was shocked by the militant tactics of the suffragettes. In old age her life in London was simple and unpretentious, though frequently enlivened by trips to the Continent with female friends. She lived to vote in the general election of 1918, aged eighty-eight. Girton College may be seen as her monument.

Her writings include *The Higher Education of Women* (1866), and *Thoughts on some Questions relating to Women* (1910).

See also M. C. Bradbrook, '*That Infidel Place*': *A Short History of Girton College, 1869–1969*, 1969; B. Stephen, *Emily Davies and Girton College*, 1927.   F.K.P.

Davies-Colley, Eleanor (1874–1934), first woman Fellow of the Royal College of Surgeons. Eleanor, the second daughter of J. N. C. Davies-Colley, Honorary Consultant Surgeon to Guy's Hospital, was born at Petworth into a family with more than two hundred years of medical and surgical tradition. She attended Baker Street High School and Queen's College, Harley Street. She was a brilliant pupil, shy, high-minded and reserved. For some years after school she lived on a pittance in the East End of London, working for children's charities. She then decided to enter the medical profession and was eventually accepted at the London (Royal Free Hospital) School of Medicine for Women. She graduated MB, BS in 1907, took an MD in 1910, and in 1911 became the first woman Fellow of the Royal College of Surgeons of England.

Eleanor Davies-Colley's junior appointments included spells as Houseman at the New Hospital for Women and Children (Elizabeth Garrett Anderson Hospital from 1917 onwards) and Demonstrator in Anatomy and Surgical Registrar to the Royal Free Hospital. For many years she was Senior Obstetrician of the Elizabeth Garrett Anderson Hospital. Having helped Dr Maud Chadburn to found the South London Hospital for Women, she was an original member of its staff, serving for twenty-two years as an Honorary Consultant. She joined the surgical staff of the Marie Curie Hospital and was a member of its Cancer Research Committee, which made notable advances in the treatment of cancer of the uterus and breast by radium.

Eleanor Davies-Colley was beautiful, austere, and outspokenly honest. Modest and self-effacing, she never held office in any committee and her influence was exercised through her untiring work for private and hospital patients and for the hospitals themselves. She earned trust and affection and many young doctors profited by her clinical judgement, skill, and meticulous training in all aspects of their profession and professional conduct.

See also *Lives of Fellows of the Royal College of Surgeons of England*, vol. III, 1953.

R.B.

Daviot, Gordon. See TEY, JOSEPHINE.

Davis, Mary (c. 1650–after 1698), actress and royal mistress, was said to be the illegitimate daughter of Colonel Thomas Howard, later Earl of Berkshire. While still a child, she became one of the four principal actresses of the Duke's Company under the management of Sir William Davenant, in whose house she boarded. Her first recorded performance was in February 1662 in Davenant's *The Law against Lovers* as the 'very young' Viola, a role which appears to have been specially created to introduce the young actress and display her talents as a singer and dancer.

In 1667, as Celania in Davenant's *The Rivals*, she sang 'My Lodging It Is on the Cold Ground' so charmingly, it was said, that 'Not long after, it Rais'd her from her Bed on the Cold Ground to a Bed Royal'. In January 1668 Pepys heard that Moll Davis had become mistress to Charles II, who had given her a ring worth £600 and was furnishing a house for her in Suffolk Street. By the end of May she had left the stage permanently, returning only once more to sing in a performance at court in February 1675. Her daughter by Charles II, Lady Mary Tudor, was born in 1673 and married in 1687 to Edward, Viscount Radcliffe, later Earl of Derwentwater. In December 1686 she herself married the French flautist and composer James Paisible, who had come to England about 1674. The marriage of the former royal mistress and the well-known musician attracted considerable notice in court circles, and although it was initially satirized in prose and verse by wits and libellers, there is no evidence to indicate that it was unsuccessful. 'Moll' Davis was one of a bevy of obscure young women who took advantage of the new opportunities open to women as actresses on the Restoration stage (before the Civil War, all female parts had been played by boys), and whose beauty and talent brought them rewards off as well as on stage.

See also J. H. Wilson, *All the King's Ladies: Actresses of the Restoration*, 1958.

T.J.M.

Davison, Emily (Wilding) (1872–1913), suffragette. Born in Blackheath, she was educated at London University and in 1906 joined the Women's Social and Political Union, becoming one of its most prominent militants. In 1909 after a disturbance at Limehouse, she received a two-month prison sentence, although she was released early after a hunger strike. Stone-throwing in Manchester the same year earned her a similar sentence, while another such incident brought imprisonment with hard labour and forced feeding. In 1910 she broke a window in the House of Commons, was sentenced to a month's imprisonment, but was released after a hunger strike, and in 1911 she received a six months' sentence for setting fire to pillar boxes in Westminster. In 1912 she assaulted a Baptist minister whom she mistook for Lloyd George. The incident for which Emily Davison is remembered, however, occurred during the 1913 Derby, when she ran on to the course from Tattenham Corner and tried to grasp the reins of the king's horse, Anmer, dying a few days later from the injuries received.

B.H.C.

Davys, Mary (1674–1732), novelist and play-wright. She was born in Dublin, where she married the Reverend Peter Davys, master of the free school of St Patrick's Cathedral. After Davys's death in 1698 his widow left Ireland and was in London for a short period around 1700. She then retired to York, where she lived for fifteen years. During this time she petitioned her late husband's friend, Jonathan Swift, for money, which was sporadically granted before his departure for Ireland in 1714. Like the similarly impecunious Mary De La Rivière MANLEY, Mary Davys devoted most of her early literary career to writing plays. The first of these, *The Northern Heiress*, was presented in London in 1716. After failing to get a second play, *The Self Rival*, staged, she moved to Cambridge and opened a coffee-house. Mary Davys's early novel *The Fugitive* (1705), reprinted later as *The Merry Wanderer*, features a picaresque narrative with a heroine of engagingly earthy character. By the time *The Works of Mrs Davys* were printed in 1725, however, the author's didacticism had become more pronounced in conformity with the prevailing fashion for pious narratives. Included in this collection are a number of her plays and novellas including *The Reform'd Coquet* and *The Modern Poet*.

See also W. H. McBurney, 'Mrs Mary Davys: Forerunner of Fielding' in *Publications of the Modern Languages Association of America*, 1959.   A.L.

Dawson, Margaret (Mary) Damer (1875–1920), founder of the Women Police Volunteers. She was born in Sussex and educated privately, becoming a gold medallist of the London Academy of Music. In 1906 she became organizing secretary of the Congress of International Animal Protection (1906); her work for animal welfare was awarded silver medals by Finland and Denmark.

Shortly after the outbreak of war in August 1914, Margaret Damer Dawson found herself in charge of the transport of Belgian refugees to British homes, and was appalled to see obvious white-slavers waiting for them at railway stations. After a meeting with the Chief Commissioner of Police, Sir Edward Henry, she therefore formed a group of Women Police Volunteers to work in the metropolitan area. She trained hundreds of women for preventive work in munitions factories and organized rescue work during air-raids. The Home Office gave official recognition to a number of Volunteer patrols. Although not sworn-in and without the power of arrest, the members were recognized as part of the Metropolitan Police by Macready, Henry's successor.

Margaret Damer Dawson was awarded the OBE for services to the country in 1918, only to be sued by the Metropolitan Police in 1920 on the grounds that she and other volunteers had been 'impersonating police officers'. They were convicted, and had to pay a token fine. She died soon afterwards, but her work was continued by the co-founder of the Volunteers, Mary ALLEN.

See also J. Lock, *The British Police-woman—her story*, 1979.   A.D.

De la Hay, Nicola. See HAY, NICOLA DE LA.

Delafield, E. M., pseudonym of Edmée Elizabeth Monica Dashwood (1890–1943), née de la Pasture, (whence, presumably, 'de la Field'), popular novelist, born in Monmouthshire. Her mother, Mrs Henry de la Pasture, was a well-known novelist in the 1890s and 1900s, and E. M. Delafield was already writing copiously at the age of eight. Her first book was *Zelda Sees Herself* (1917); the next, *The War-Workers* (1918), was largely based on her experiences as a VAD in Exeter between 1914 and 1917. Thereafter she was notably prolific, writing at least one work a year until her death.

Her greatest success was *The Diary of a Provincial Lady* (1930), which originated as a serial for the magazine *Time and Tide*. In this novel, a succession of small crises enlivens but does not seriously threaten the essential security and comfort of family life—a story formula of the sort later exploited by several radio and television serials; not surprisingly, there were three more 'Provincial Lady' books. E. M. Delafield also wrote *A Messalina of the Suburbs* (1924), suggested by the Thompson-Bywaters murder case, and a number of plays.   N.H.

Delaney, Mary (1700–88), author of memoirs and collage artist. Born into an aristocratic family, Mary Granville was married against her will to an elderly disagreeable gentleman of substance. Fortunately for her, he died after a few years, leaving her with only her jointure. Through her influential relatives she was able to move in London and Dublin literary circles. In Dublin she met Swift and Dr Patrick Delaney, who followed her to London in 1743 and made her his wife.

The match was not favoured by her family, but the couple lived happily until his death in 1768. Much of Mary Delaney's time thereafter was spent with the Duchess of Portland, a tireless botanist, who introduced her to the Royal Family, with whom she became a great favourite. The King later gave Mary Delaney a house in Windsor and a pension. It was she who introduced Fanny BURNEY to the Royal Family.

The floral mosaics for which Mary Delaney is chiefly remembered were the result of a chance playing with pieces of coloured paper. Between 1774 and 1784 she completed nearly a thousand collages on floral themes, cut out by eye and pasted on paper. They were praised by Erasmus Darwin in *Loves of the Plants*.

Mary Delaney's six volumes of autobiography and letters were edited by Lady LLAN-OVER and published in 1861–62. They are remarkable chiefly for their amiable anecdotes of literary and social figures.

See also S. Dewes, *Mrs Delaney*, 1949; R. Hayden, *Mrs Delaney, her Life and Flowers*, 1980. C.H.

Dell, Ethel (Mary or May) (1881–1939), popular novelist. The daughter of an insurance agent, Ethel M. Dell, as she was generally known to her readers, was born in Streatham and educated at a private school there. She spent her early life at Knockholt, near Sevenoaks, later settling in Guildford, where she lived away from the glare of the publicity that her books had created.

Ethel M. Dell began writing when still a child. *The Way of an Eagle* (1912) was her first big success and is probably also her best-known book, although she had considerable difficulty in finding a publisher for it (the manuscript was rejected eight times). Further best-sellers followed by the year: *The Knave of Diamonds*, 1913, *The Rocks of Valpré*, 1914, *The Keeper of the Door*, 1915, *The Bars of Iron*, 1916, *The Hundredth Chance*, 1917, and *Great Heart*, 1918; her popularity during the First World War was immense. Her total output of thirty-four books also included *The Lamp in the Desert*, 1919, *Charles Rex*, 1922, *The Black Knight*, 1926, *Storm Drift*, 1930, and *The Serpent in the Garden*, 1938.

Ethel M. Dell's books are adventure stories for adults, with strongly delineated characters

(bold heroes, base villains) and a marked romantic element. Her writing is more substantial than that of her contemporary and fellow best-seller Ruby M. AYRES, but like her she has suffered an almost total eclipse. J.L.

Denman, Lady Gertrude Mary (1884–1954), administrator remembered above all for her development of the Women's Institute movement. She was the daughter of Viscount Cowdray and in 1903 married Lord Denman, whom she accompanied to Australia during his term as Governor-General (1911–14).

Lady Denman had been a member of the Women's National Liberal Federation Executive Committee while still in her twenties. In 1915, when the need for greater wartime food production had focused attention on the situation of rural Britain, she was appointed chairman of a Ministry of Agriculture sub-committee from which the policy of promoting Women's Institutes emerged. She remained Chairman of the National Federation of Women's Institutes until 1946, during which time the WIs functioned in a multitude of ways to improve not only the material conditions but also the quality of rural life. The WI headquarters and centre for residential courses, Denman College at Marcham Park in Berkshire, is Lady Denman's chief memorial. However, her devotion to the welfare of the countryside and its inhabitants went further. She worked on the Executive Committee of the Land Settlement Association from 1934 to 1939, when she became Director of the Women's Land Army; her home, Balcombe Place in Sussex, became its headquarters. It was typical of her protective attitude towards her charges that, as Chairman of the WLA Benevolent Fund, she became incensed at the government's decision not to offer 'land girls' the gratuities paid to other servicewomen, and resigned her offices. N.H.

Desmond, Astra, stage name of Gwendolin Mary Thomson (1893–1973), singer. She was born in Torquay and educated at Westfield College, London, taking a BA in 1914. She trained as a singer under Blanche Marchesi, and in Berlin under von Bos.

Astra Desmond's rich flexible contralto suited her broad musical sympathies. She was especially associated with Elgar, frequently singing under his direction. In 1928 she performed in the first broadcast of Stravinsky's

Oedipus Rex. She sang with the Carl Rosa Opera and as a guest artist at Sadler's Wells and Covent Garden. She also toured Europe for the British Council. A perfectionist, she worked to improve her understanding and execution by learning languages, including Norwegian for her 1937 Grieg recital.

Astra Desmond taught singing at the Royal Academy of Music from 1947 to 1963. She was President of the Incorporated Society of Musicians (1957–60), and of the Society of Women Musicians (1952–56), and served on the Arts Council Music Panel from 1953 to 1959. She was created CBE in 1949.   A.D.

Despard, Charlotte (1844–1939), suffragette and social reformer. She was the daughter of Captain John French, a wealthy Irishman. After her father's sudden death and her mother's resulting mental instability, Charlotte French was sent away to be cared for by relatives. Their strictness first brought out her rebelliousness. In 1870 she met and married Colonel Maximilian Despard; the marriage was happy, although childless. She began writing novels, the first of which, *Chaste as Ice, Pure as Snow*, was published in 1874.

On the death of her husband in 1890, Charlotte Despard went to live among the poor in Nine Elms, Vauxhall, where she became involved in Poor Law administration, the abuses of which she was fiercely critical. There she learnt about the particularly wretched lives of poor women. Her growing belief in socialist solutions led her to join Henry Hyndman's Social Democratic Federation. In 1902, however, she switched to the Independent Labour Party, which was more in tune with her views on women's suffrage. By now she had also been converted to Catholicism.

Already a feminist, she joined the Women's Social and Political Union in 1906, but soon came to consider it a tool of the Pankhursts; at the same time she felt that women's suffrage was not a broad enough issue. In the following year, therefore, the Women's Freedom League was born, and Charlotte Despard described its aims: 'Our cause is not only votes for women, but the binding together of all womanhood for human rights.' The League protested by constitutional boycotts and in 1909 adopted Gandhi's policy of non-violent resistance. Disappointment with the Liberals' Manhood Suffrage Bill of 1911 only confirmed the League in its pursuit of wider aims; and at the coming

of war in 1914 it was concentrating on the issues of women's employment and alcoholism. Meanwhile Charlotte Despard had created a miniature welfare state in Nine Elms; from her own money, she provided subsidized meals, free school dinners, and clinics, especially for young mothers.

In the post-war years her attention focused on international socialism and Ireland. A strong supporter of Home Rule, she settled in Dublin in 1921, becoming a friend of Maud GONNE and a supporter of Sinn Fein, despite the fact that her brother was Chief Secretary. However, Irish Catholic opinion was quick to condemn her visit to Russia in 1930 and the Workers' College she founded in Dublin, and she was forced to move to Belfast. She died there bankrupted by the cost of the many causes she had made her own.

See also A. Linklater, *An Unhusbanded Life*, 1980.   C.H.G.G.

Devlin, Margaret. See ASHFORD, DAISY.

Devonshire, Duchess of. See CAVENDISH, GEORGIANA, DUCHESS OF DEVONSHIRE.

Dilke, Emilia Frances, Lady (1840–1904), trade unionist, writer, and art historian. The daughter of an Indian army officer, she was educated privately at Oxford, where she early displayed an intellectual capacity and a taste for art. She studied art at South Kensington between 1859 and 1861, when she developed a mystical approach to religion which was later to appear in her writings. She married twice, but remained childless. Her first husband was the Reverend Mark Pattison, Rector of Lincoln College, Oxford. After their marriage in 1861 she soon became known as one of the most brilliant intellectual hostesses in Oxford, numbering George ELIOT among her friends. After Pattison's death, she became engaged to Sir Charles Dilke, an old friend, and married him in 1885. She supported him loyally during the Crawford divorce scandal, which, despite his eventual exoneration, effectively ended his political career, and for the rest of her life devoted herself primarily to his interests.

During her first marriage Lady Dilke became interested in the domestic and industrial conditions of working women. She joined the Women's Provident and Protective League, later the Women's Trades Union League, in 1876, and quickly became its dominant figure, guiding its course until her death. Under her leadership it became an effective organization, and part of the trades union movement as a whole instead of a separate feminine clique. A popular speaker at meetings, she attended Trades Union Congresses as the Women's League representative between 1889 and 1904, using the occasion to bring the conditions of labouring women to the fore and to try and promote co-operation between the sexes in the labour movement. Her interests led her to support votes for women, though she was not a prominent figure in that battle, reserving her energies for women's trade unionism.

Lady Dilke also had an interest in French art history. She published her first book on the subject, *The Renaissance of Art in France*, in 1879. Subsequent research provided the material for a series of volumes (1888–1902) on all aspects of eighteenth-century French art and artists. Her interest in the mystic also found an outlet in a number of stories based on mystical ideas; a posthumous collection, *The Book of the Spiritual Life*, was published in 1905.

See also N. Soldon, *Women in British Trade Unions*, 1978.   J.R.

Disraeli, Mary Anne, Viscountess Beaconsfield (1792–1872). Public figure as the wife of Benjamin Disraeli. She married Colonel Wyndham Lewis in 1815. It was a happy, though childless, marriage. In 1832 his political career brought her into contact with Disraeli, who became her protégé. Wyndham Lewis died in 1838, leaving Mary Anne his fortune, and after a year's courtship she married Disraeli in August 1839, disregarding the fact that she was twelve years older than him. A pretty and apparently feather-headed woman, she became Disraeli's greatest support. In his preface to *Sybil* he described her as 'the perfect wife'. Her maternal tenderness for him and unfailing belief in his capacity gave him great personal happiness, while her money ended his financial difficulties. She later remarked that he married her for her money but, given the chance, would remarry her for love. She enjoyed acting as his political hostess but her greatest reward came when Disraeli declined a peerage on his own account but asked for one for his wife, by way of tribute to her: in 1868 she was created Viscountess Beaconsfield. Her death left him heartbroken, and despite his friendships with other women he never remarried.

See also E. Lee, *Wives of the Prime Ministers*, 1968.   J.R.

Dixie, Lady Florence Caroline, (1857–1905), writer, traveller, and first woman war correspondent. The younger daughter of the Marquis of Queensberry, Lady Florence came of an eccentric aristocratic family. One of her brothers was killed in scaling the Matterhorn and the other, as the ninth Marquis, laid down the rules of boxing and was instrumental in ruining Oscar Wilde. In 1875 Lady Florence married Sir Beaumont Dixie, and although they had two sons, this did not deter her from seeking adventure on her travels in unknown Patagonia and big game hunting in Africa. She was the *Morning Post*'s correspondent in the Boer War of 1880–81, and although at first the idea of a woman acting in such a capacity was ridiculed, it soon became clear that she was quite up to the demands of the situation: 'With a glass of whisky in her hand', so it was said, 'she could hold her own in any mess tent.' On her return to England she was instrumental in obtaining the release and repatriation of King Cetewayo of Zululand. She continued to write about travel (in *Across Patagonia*) and politics (in *A Defence of Zululand and its King*), and to produce poetry and novels. A brilliant horsewoman and a crack shot, she later renounced all her sporting activities except riding and wrote forcibly against blood sports. Actively advocating the rights of women, she showed in her own life an aristocratic disregard for the conventions.

See also R. J. Wilkinson-Latham, *From our own Correspondent*, 1979.   E.M.V.

Dod, Lottie (1871–1960), sportswoman. Charlotte 'Lottie' Dod began playing tennis with her sister and two brothers; by the age of twelve she was known as 'the little wonder'. The first tennis prodigy, she won the women's singles title at Wimbledon in 1887 at the age of fifteen years and ten months, losing only two games to 'the indefatigable Blanche Bingley'. Her remarkable anticipation and powerful smash and volley brought speed to the game of women's tennis. She won the ladies' title at Wimbledon again in 1888, 1891, 1892 and 1893 (not competing in 1889 and 1890), and won the mixed doubles in 1889 and 1892 and the ladies' doubles (with Miss Langrishe) in 1886, 1887 and 1888; she also won the Irish championships in 1887. She never lost at Wimbledon, and in her entire tennis career was beaten only four times. After 1893 she gave up tennis for golf and as captain of the Moreton Club in 1904 won the British women's golf championship, defeating Miss Hezlet by one hole in a tense game. One of the best women archers in the country, Lottie Dod was also a champion skater and hockey international. The first woman all-rounder, she has been described as an early superstar of sport.

See also *Sporting and Athletic Register*, 1908; M. Robertson, *Wimbledon 1877–1977*, 1977.   C.B.

Dodd, Anne (*fl.* 1730), book- and pamphlet-seller in London. The evidence of the imprints on Anne Dodd's books indicates three consecutive business residences: Without Temple Bar; Peacock, near Temple Bar, in 1728; and near Essex Street in the Strand. In the eighteenth century the vendor as well as the writer and publisher of books and pamphlets was held responsible for their contents, and was thus liable to prosecution, especially where attacks on public figures were involved. Anne Dodd was a frequent victim of this law and was repeatedly subject to fines and imprisonments. In one of the petitions defending her actions she submitted that, as a widow with a large family, she was forced to sell pamphlets as a means of support.

See also H. R. Plomer, G. H. Bushnell, E. R. McC. Dix, *A Dictionary of the Printers and Booksellers who were at Work in England, Scotland, and Ireland from 1726 to 1775*, 1932.   A.L.

Dodgson, (Frances) Catharine (1883–1954), artist. She was born at Oxford, where her father was Warden of New College, and trained at Ruskin School, Oxford, the Royal Academy Schools, and the Slade. In 1913 she married Campbell Dodgson, Keeper of Prints and Drawings at the British Museum, and until his retirement in 1932 devoted herself mainly to home life. The only time she exhibited at the Royal Academy was in 1923, when she was represented by an oil portrait of Dean Inge, her cousin by marriage.

In the mid-1930s Catharine Dodgson again began to work, drawing in red chalk and/or bistre; she exhibited at Colnaghi's in 1936 and 1939. She had a flair for portrait-drawing, and also made some remarkably flamboyant sketches of the Rococo sculpture at Würzburg and Veitshöchheim.

Catharine Dodgson's extreme modesty and lack of confidence in her considerable talent prevented her work from being widely known during her lifetime.   A.D.

Domina Clarae. See CLARE, ELIZABETH DE.

Dormer, Jane (1538–1612), Duchess of Feria. The daughter of Sir William Dormer and Mary Sidney, she was a close friend in her childhood of the then Princess Mary, whose household she joined. As Queen Mary's Maid of Honour she met Don Gomez Suarez de Figueroa de Cordoba, envoy of Mary's husband, King Philip of Spain, and they were married in December 1558, after the Queen's death. (Jane Dormer had tended the dying Mary and had been entrusted with the jewels which were to be handed on to Queen Elizabeth.) In July 1559 she left England to follow her husband, and although he was hostile to the Protestant Elizabeth, she remained on good terms with the English court. In September 1559 she gave birth to a son, Don Lorenzo, in Brussels, and in 1560 the family moved to Spain. Throughout the 1560s she corresponded with English Catholics and her husband aided Elizabeth's rival, Mary Queen of Scots, financially. Nonetheless Jane Dormer maintained Elizabeth's good will and her patrimony in England was expressly exempted from the penalties against English Catholic exiles.

In 1571 Don Gomez, one of Philip's closest advisers and prospective Governor of the Netherlands, died leaving an estate deeply in debt. His duchess laboured to free the family from debt and raise her son, who was destined for high office in the service of Philip. She was also heavily involved in aiding English Catholic exiles, distributing material aid, supporting those who sought Spanish pensions, and helping the English colleges in Spain. Among those she aided were Sir Francis Englefield, Thomas Fitzherbert, and the English Jesuits Robert Persons and Joseph Creswell. Her position and influence was such that intrigues among the exiles often involved the unjustified use of her name; in the 1590s it was even rumoured that she was going to move to the Low Countries to assume a leading position among the Catholic exiles there or even become Regent, and that her son was to take charge of the Spanish army. Plans for her to succeed Cardinal Allen as chief of the exiles were adamantly opposed by her son.

Yet, unlike many exiles, Jane Dormer was never seen as a political dissident. On the accession of King James I it was even suggested that she return to England to become one of Queen Anne's ladies-in-waiting, and she herself wrote to the King expressing her loyalty. In the end she was never to leave Spain, and died there without ever playing the leadership role that others wished to thrust upon her.

See also A. J. Loomie, *The Spanish Elizabethans*, 1968; J. Stevenson (ed.), *The Life of Jane Dormer*, 1887.   G.Q.B.

Douglas, Lady Eleanor (1590–1652), prophetess, was the youngest daughter of George Touchet, Lord Audley and Earl of Castlehaven. She was well educated, and in 1609 married the poet and politician Sir John Davies, then Attorney-General for Ireland. They had at least one son, who died young, and a daughter, Lucy, who married Lord Hastings. According to her own account, the 'spirit of prophecy' fell upon Lady Eleanor in 1625. The discovery that her name, Eleanor Audeley, was an anagram of 'Reveale O Daniel' convinced her of her calling. Her first prophecies, however, were burned in manuscript by her husband. She thereupon prophesied his death within three years, and put on widow's weeds in anticipation: he died suddenly in 1626. After three months she married Sir Archibald Douglas, who likewise burned her writings. Although he lived until 1644, he 'escaped not scotfree', being unaccountably 'strooken bereft of his sences'.

Lady Eleanor Douglas was highly regarded by others as a prophet, and was even consulted by Queen Henrietta Maria. Her most notable achievement was her prediction in 1628 that the Duke of Buckingham 'should never see a day in September'. The Duke was indeed assassinated in August, but the success of this prophecy earned her the disapproval of the King. Undeterred, Lady Eleanor went to Amsterdam in 1633 to have her works printed. Her publications included verses referring to Charles I as Belshazzar, foretelling his destruction, and announcing that the Judgement Day would occur in January 1645.

Returning to England, she was brought before the Court of High Commission, charged with having taken 'upon her (which much unbeseemed her Sex) not only to interpret the Scriptures . . . but also to be a Prophetess', and with publishing 'scandalous matters . . . against Ecclesiastical persons and Judges of eminent place'. She was fined £3000 (though this seems never to have been paid), her books were burned, and she remained in prison for nearly two years.

Late in 1636 Lady Eleanor symbolically indicated her opposition to Laudian episcopacy by mounting the bishop's throne in Lichfield Cathedral, proclaiming herself Primate and Metropolitan, and sprinkling tar on the altar hangings. As a result she was sent first to Bedlam, where she continued to prophesy, and thence to the Tower, where she remained until September 1640. Between 1641 and her death she issued over thirty works, all written in an obscure, rhapsodical, fragmentary style, and relating Biblical texts to contemporary events.

She was imprisoned again briefly in 1646, and then reached the height of her fame in 1649, when a London printer reissued her prophecies of 1633, claiming that they had been fulfilled by the execution of the King. Cromwell, though apparently sceptical of her gifts, received her kindly, and in 1651 she addressed a laudatory 'Benediction' to him. She died the following year, and was buried beside her first husband under a flattering Latin epitaph. Her high birth, self-confidence, and persistence made her the most notorious of the prophets who abounded in seventeenth-century England.

See also *The Restitution of Prophecy . . . By the Lady Eleanor* (facsimile reproduction), 1978; C. J. Hindle, 'A Bibliography of the Printed Pamphlets . . . of Lady Eleanor Douglas . . .' in *The Edinburgh Bibliographical Society Transactions*, 1938; K. Thomas, *Religion and the Decline of Magic*, 1971.

W.R.O.

Douglas, Margaret, Countess of Lennox (1515–78), political figure. The daughter of Margaret Tudor, Queen of Scotland, by her second husband Archibald, Earl of Angus, Margaret was born at Harbottle. Her early years were mainly spent in Scotland, but she settled in England in 1528, when Angus fell from power. Her uncle Henry VIII sent her to Princess (later Queen) MARY, with whom she formed a friendship that remained warm even when she won the favour of Anne BOLEYN, who had supplanted Mary's mother as queen.

The extraordinary ups and downs of Margaret Douglas's subsequent career can largely be accounted for by the tangled matrimonial politics of Henry VIII's reign and her own closeness to the English throne. The second Act of Succession of 1536 bastardized Henry's two daughters and made Margaret first lady of the realm; consequently she was imprisoned on 8 June for her unauthorized betrothal to Thomas Howard, the Duke of Norfolk's brother. She was released on 29 October 1537, two days after Howard's death. Then the birth of a male heir, Prince Edward, made Henry anxious to reduce Margaret's status, so he had her declared illegitimate. She later returned to favour, but lost it in 1541 through her betrothal to Charles, brother of Katherine HOWARD. She was imprisoned again, but released when Henry needed her father's services in negotiations with Scotland.

On 6 July 1544 Margaret married Matthew Stewart, Earl of Lennox, who had a claim to the Scots throne. She quarrelled with Henry VIII over her conservative Catholic views, and was excluded from the succession.

Under the Protestant régime during Edward VI's reign, Margaret stayed in Yorkshire, but on Mary's accession she was recognized as the Queen's honoured friend; the authorities tried to implicate the Protestant Princess ELIZABETH in Wyatt's conspiracy so that Margaret could become Mary's heir. On Elizabeth's accession she retired to Templenewsam, thenceforward a centre of Catholic intrigue. Elizabeth cast doubts upon her legitimacy, and excluded her from the succession.

Margaret Douglas's machinations to marry her son Henry, Lord Darnley, to MARY Queen of Scots landed her in the Tower in 1562; she was not released until after Darnley's murder in March 1567. The Lennoxes demanded vengeance on Mary and her new husband, Bothwell, from Elizabeth, but soon after Lennox's death in September 1571 Margaret was reconciled with Mary.

In 1574 Margaret was again in the Tower, on this occasion for betrothing her son Charles to Elizabeth, daughter of the Earl of Shrewsbury. She was pardoned before spring 1577.

Margaret was highly important in dynastic terms because of her relationship to the Tudors and Stuarts. Though her four sons and four daughters predeceased her, her relationship to the English ruling house determined the careers of two grandchildren, King James I and VI and Arabella STEWART.

See also *Calendar of State Papers;* A. Strickland, *Lives of the Queens of Scotland,* 1850–59. M.D.

Douglass, Dorothea Katharine. See CHAMBERS, DOROTHEA KATHARINE LAMBERT.

Dove, Dame (Jane) Frances (1847–1942), pioneer of women's education, born at Bordeaux. Frances Dove, the daugher of a Lincolnshire curate, was the eldest of his ten children. She had a patchy education at home, at Queen's College in London's Harley Street, and at an inferior boarding school —experiences which seem to have provided the negative inspiration for her life's work. She was one of the first 'graduates' of Girton College, then newly established (but not of course recognized) at Cambridge. After working as an assistant mistress at Cheltenham Ladies' College, in 1877 she joined what was later to become St Leonard's School at St Andrews. She was Head Mistress from 1882 to 1896, when she left in order to found an English public school for girls that should be of equivalent distinction to St Leonard's. This was Wycombe Abbey School, which had become a flourishing institution by the time Frances Dove retired in 1910.

See also W. Peck, *A Little Learning,* 1952. N.H.

Dowriche, Anne (*fl.* 1589–96), poet, was born into the Edgcumbe family in Devonshire. She married Hugh Dowriche, rector of Honiton in Devon from 1587 until his death in 1598, and later Richard Trefusis of Trefusis, Cornwall. In 1589 she published a long poem, *The French Historie. That is, a lamentable Discourse of three of the chiefe, and most famous bloodie broiles that have happened in France for the Gospell of Jesus Christ.* This is composed in the lumbering poulter's measure (alternating Alexandrines and fourteeners), and is a melodramatic account of the persecution of French Protestants, supposedly related to the author by a godly French exile. It is dedicated to her brother Pearse (Piers) Edgcumbe. In 1596 Anne Downriche contributed commendatory verses to a sermon published by Hugh Dowriche, *The Jaylors Conversion.* Her work is notable as an expression of the anti-Catholic feeling generated in England by events on the Continent, especially in the wake of the threatened invasion by the Spanish Armada.

See also T. Corser, *Collectanea Anglo-Poetica*, Chetham Society, 1873.   W.R.O.

Drake, Judith (*fl*. 1696–1707), feminist writer. She was the daughter of a Cambridge solicitor, Robert Drake, and is now generally credited with the authorship of an important feminist tract, *An Essay in the Defence of the Female Sex*, published anonymously in 1696 and previously attributed to Mary ASTELL. An exceptionally entertaining, readable, and popular feminist book, already in its third edition by 1697, the *Essay* was clearly the work of a lively, intelligent, and worldly woman with a rare sense of humour and a pungent wit, who mocked the foibles of the opposite sex while illuminating the virtues of her own. Its purpose was to demonstrate the equal spiritual and intellectual capacities of the sexes; to show that women were qualified for the companionship of ingenious men; and to prove that men could improve and divert their minds generally in the company of women. The author differed strikingly from Mary Astell, both in her light-hearted tone and in her views on female education. She denied that 'learning' meant only the study of classical works, and recommended instead a liberal reading list of English prose, plays and poetry, including many authors of whom more sober contemporary feminists like Astell would surely have disapproved. It was mere idleness, the author held, not lack of ability or of higher education, that prevented women from acquiring greater knowledge.

The *Essay* was seen through its publication and promoted by James Drake, who wrote an essay and a lengthy poem commending the author, now assumed to be his sister Judith. Judith, like James, was probably born and bred in Cambridge, and joined her brother when in 1693 he came to London, where he made an immediate impression as a doctor, author, and Tory propagandist. In 1707 Judith published her brother's *Anthropologia Nova*, a highly acclaimed anatomical treatise completed shortly before his death. If Judith Drake was the author of *An Essay in the Defence of the Female Sex*, she was a talented writer, stylistically perhaps the most brilliant female author of her day, and a woman whose independent judgements and vigorous prose effectively defended and enhanced the reputation of her sex.

See also M. Reynolds, *The Learned Lady in England*, 1920; F. Smith, *Mary Astell*, 1916; D. M. Stenton, *The English Woman in History*, 1957.   T.J.M.

Dresdel, Sonia, stage-name of Lois Obee (1909–76), actress. She was born at Hornsea, Yorkshire, but her family moved to Scotland and she was educated at the High School and the University in Aberdeen. She then trained at the Royal Academy of Dramatic Art in London.

Her first part was Rosalie Quilter in *Almost a Honeymoon* (1931). After several years in repertory she joined the Old Vic Company in 1939 and toured as Portia, Viola, and Trilby. Her London début as Lady Faulconbridge in Shakespeare's *King John* (1941) was well reviewed; critics noticed her 'dark velvet' voice and her strong stage presence. In the title role of Ibsen's *Hedda Gabler* (1942) she brilliantly fulfilled the expectations of her admirers. She never had quite such a triumph again, although she starred in a near-melodrama, *This Was a Woman* (1945), which ran for over a year.

Sonia Dresdel frequently toured both in Britain and abroad. She had a year as director of productions at Harrogate and a season at the Mermaid Theatre (1961–63). She appeared in several films, including *The Fallen Idol* and *The Trials of Oscar Wilde*, and was well known on television, notably in *The Pallisers*, *Thérèse Raquin* and *The Onedin Line*.   P.L.

Drummond, Annabella (1350?–1401), Queen of Scotland as the wife of Robert III. She was the daughter of Sir John Drummond of Stobhall and niece of David II's queen, Margaret Logie. In 1367 she married John Stewart of Kyle, eldest son of Robert Stewart (grandson of Robert Bruce), who succeeded as Robert II in 1370. John, created Earl of Carrick, was lamed by a kick from a horse and became a semi-invalid. After years of childlessness, Annabella gave birth in 1378 to a son, David; her younger son, later James I, was born in 1394. In 1390 John succeeded his father, taking the title Robert III. He was an even less capable king than his father, resigning the government into the hands of his brother Walter, Earl of Fife, later Duke of Albany. Annabella, a woman of some determination, did her best to maintain the position of the Crown and her son. She seems to have been held in high esteem by the English kings, corresponding

131

with Richard II about a possible marriage alliance between their houses; and when Henry IV mounted an expedition to Edinburgh in 1400 he was reputed to have spared the countryside out of respect for Queen Annabella.

In 1398 David, now Duke of Rothesay, was appointed Governor of the realm in view of his father's continuing ill health. The Queen was one of the chief persons behind this move to curtail Albany's power, which proved largely unsuccessful. She died at Scone and was buried at Dunfermline, shortly before David's death in the custody of Albany. Annabella was celebrated for her beauty, graciousness, and generosity, and was a well-loved queen.

See also R. Nicholson, *Scotland: The Later Middle Ages*, 1974.　　　　　A.C.

Dudley, Lady Amy (1532?–1560), central figure of an Elizabethan political mystery. The only legitimate child of Sir John Robsart of Siderston, Norfolk, Amy was about eighteen when she married Robert Dudley, later Earl of Leicester, on 4 June 1550. Her next few years were spent in Norfolk, but when Dudley was in the Tower in 1553–54 for his part in the Jane GREY conspiracy, she was allowed to visit him. He was pardoned and released on 18 October 1554.

Amy became significant after the accession of ELIZABETH I, who plainly favoured Dudley; rumour said she meant to marry him, despite the existence of his wife. In early 1560, while Dudley remained at court, Amy moved to Cumnor Place near Abingdon, which was rented by her husband's friend Sir Anthony Forster. On 8 September 1560 she allegedly sent the whole household to Abingdon Fair; when the servants returned they found her dead at the foot of the stairs. The convenience of her death to Dudley and Elizabeth encouraged rumours of murder or suicide. The truth cannot be known, and in the event Amy's death did not facilitate Dudley's marriage with Elizabeth.

See also A. Harris, *Romance and Reality of Amy Robsart*, 1924; J. E. Jackson in *Wiltshire Archaeological and Natural History Magazine* XVII, 1877.　　　　　M.D.

Dudley, Lady Jane. See GREY, LADY JANE.

Dudley, Lettice, Countess of Leicester (1541?–1634), political figure. The daughter of Sir Francis Knollys, she had a famous and somewhat scandalous matrimonial career. She first married Walter Devereux, Earl of Essex. They had four surviving children, including Robert, later second Earl and favourite of Queen Elizabeth, and Penelope RICH.

Lettice Devereux, was on familiar terms with Robert Dudley, Earl of Leicester, staying with him at Kenilworth when he entertained Queen Elizabeth there in 1575. When Devereux died at Dublin in September 1576, gossip said that Leicester had poisoned him for love of Lettice. Leicester did indeed marry Lettice Devereux, but only in September 1578, when his hopes of winning the Queen's hand seemed to have disappeared. The news, carefully kept from Elizabeth, was broken to her in August 1579; she was furious, and the Leicesters were in disgrace for some time.

Leicester died in September 1588. This time it was rumoured that Lettice had poisoned him in order to marry his young gentleman of the horse, Christopher Blount. She did marry Blount in about 1589, but there is no evidence that Leicester was murdered. Blount was later involved in the rebellion of his step-son, the second Earl of Essex, and it was his two confessions of February 1601 which secured the Earl's conviction. Blount himself was executed in March; his wife survived him by over thirty years.

See also E. Jenkins, *Elizabeth and Leicester*, 1972.　　　　　M.D.

Duff-Gordon, Lady Lucie, or **Lucy** (1821–69), writer. She was educated at home, apart from visits to Germany, and among her childhood friends was John Stuart Mill. After marriage in 1840 to Sir Alexander Cornewall Duff-Gordon she gathered around her a brilliant circle of friends, including Dickens, Tennyson, and Thackeray. She also knew the German poet Heine well. She translated works from German and French, and in 1850 established a library for working men in Weybridge. It was not until 1840 that she did any original writing, the result of a visit to the Cape of Good Hope for her health; the letters written to her mother from abroad were later published. From 1862 she made her home in Egypt, where she was known as 'Sitt el Kebeer', the great lady. She is chiefly remembered for her *Letters from the Cape*, 1862–63, *Letters from Egypt*, 1863, and *Last Letters from Egypt*, 1875.

See also the revised edn. of *Letters from*

Egypt, 1924, with a memoir by her daughter, Janet Ross. B.H.C.

Dunbar, Agnes, Countess of Dunbar (*c.* 1300–*c.* 1369), Scottish heroine, known as 'Black Agnes'. She was the elder daughter of Thomas Randolph, Earl of Moray, who was a nephew of Robert Bruce. In 1320 she became the second wife of Patrick, Earl of March and Dunbar. Dunbar favoured the English, changing sides more than once, but in 1334 he joined the nationalist cause and remained loyal to it. In 1338 English forces held most of southern Scotland, and under the Earls of Salisbury and Arundel besieged Dunbar castle, which remained in Scots hands. Dunbar was campaigning elsewhere and so Agnes undertook the defence. She held out for nineteen weeks, although the castle nearly fell twice. A number of stories were told about Agnes's flamboyant stand, the chief being that in an effort to make her yield, the English brought up her brother John, Earl of Moray, threatening to kill their prisoner. Agnes mockingly replied that they might do so, since she was his heir. The English were finally forced to retire and grant the Scots a truce. In 1346 John of Moray was killed, whereupon Agnes inherited his earldom and several baronies, which passed later to her younger son. In 1368 Dunbar resigned his earldom to their eldest son and about the same time their daughter Agnes became the mistress of David II. Patrick and Agnes died at much the same time in 1369.

See also R. Nicholson, *Scotland: The Later Middle Ages*, 1974. A.C.

Dunbar, Evelyn (1906–60), painter. She studied at the Rochester and Chelsea Schools of Art before going to the Royal College of Art (1929–33). As a member of a team working under Cyril Mahoney (a member of the teaching staff of the RCA) she executed one of the decorations based on Aesop's Fables in the hall of Brockley County School in south-east London; her panel *The Country Girl and the Pitcher of Milk* first brought her to notice. With Cyril Mahoney she wrote and illustrated *Gardeners' Choice* in 1937, and with Michael Greenhill *A Book of Farmcraft* in 1942. During the Second World War she was commissioned as a War Artist to record scenes of women's war work, mostly painting landgirls and similar subjects. She was a visiting teacher at the Ruskin School of Art from 1950, and in

1952 she moved to Kent. There she led a very retired life, concerned with country pursuits and the painting of portraits. She was an infrequent exhibitor of pictures which have considerable atmospheric depth and charm of colour. The Tate has three of her works. L.M.M.

Durham, (Frances) Hermia (1873–1948), civil servant. Hermia Durham was the daughter of a noted surgeon. She was educated at Notting Hill High School and Girton College, Cambridge, where she studied history. In 1899 she was awarded the Alexander Medal by the Royal Historical Society. From 1900 to 1907 she served as honorary secretary of the Registry and Apprenticeship Committee of the Women's University Settlement in Southwark. From 1907 to 1915 she worked as organizer and inspector of technical classes for women under the London County Council. An efficient and imaginative administrator, she developed the trade schools for girls to a high technical standard and took a large part in the successful reconstruction of evening institutes.

In view of her expertise in job placement and technical training, Hermia Durham was approached by the Board of Trade in 1915 to spearhead its wartime programme of substitution of women's for men's labour. As chief woman inspector of the Employment Department of the Board of Trade, which was transferred in 1917 to the Ministry of Labour, she was concerned with the recruitment of women for a broad range of activities, including the women's branches of the armed services, munitions work, clerical work in government departments, and agricultural labour. She was awarded the CBE in 1918.

Hermia Durham was a firm believer in women's capacities and expended much time and energy in attempts to secure for women a larger place in the work force in general and the Civil Service in particular. At the end of the war she was put in charge of the Women's Training Department of the Ministry of Labour, but the activities of this department were restricted to preparing women to resume their pre-war jobs, chiefly in domestic service, and it was dissolved amid controversy. In 1923 she was promoted to the post of assistant secretary, the first woman in the Civil Service to rise so high, and she was put in charge of the Juvenile Employment Section. She established close contacts with business and industry and

Durham, Hermia

was thus able to promote practical schemes for fostering the employment of young persons. She retired from the Civil Service in 1933 and devoted her time to gardening and needlework as well as sitting as a co-opted member of the Education Committee of the Devon County Council.

See also *University Women's News*, July 1949.

M.Z.

E

Eadburh (*fl.* 789–802), West Saxon queen. Eadburh was the daughter of King Offa of Mercia, and her marriage in 789 to Beorhtric, King of Wessex, betokened an alliance between the two kings, if not Beorhtric's subjection to the powerful ruler of Mercia. Her fame is due to Asser's highly-coloured account of her tyranny at court, her murder of Beorhtric's courtiers and accidental poisoning of the King himself, her flight to the Carolingian court, and her eventual death in poverty in Pavia. The story has an anti-Mercian bias and smacks of propaganda put out by Egbert, Beorhtric's supplanter in Wessex and an enemy of Mercia. It was later elaborated to justify the West Saxon dislike of queens. However, Eadburh did play a large part at Beorhtric's court; her succour at Charlemagne's court is consistent with continental evidence; and her death at Pavia, if true, was an end shared by other Anglo-Saxon exiles on the pilgrimage route to Rome.

See also W. Stevenson (ed.), *Asser's Life of Alfred*, 1904.   P.A.S.

Eadgifu (before 905–*c.* 966), Anglo-Saxon queen. Eadgifu was the daughter of Ealdorman Sighelm of Kent, who died at the battle of the Holme (905) fighting on behalf of Edward the Elder, the West Saxon King of England. Eadgifu married Edward no later than 919 and bore him four children: two sons, Edmund and Eadred, and two daughters, Eadburh and Eadgifu.

Nothing is known of Eadgifu's career during the lifetime of her husband. At his death in 924 the throne passed to Edward's sons by earlier marriages: briefly to Ælfweard, then to Athelstan. The role of Eadgifu and her young sons during Athelstan's reign is obscure. She was certainly at court at some stage and perhaps now struck up her friendship with Dunstan, future Bishop of London and Archbishop of Canterbury and a leading figure in tenth-century politics. Athelstan was succeeded in 939 by Eadgifu's eldest son, Edmund, and Eadgifu may have played a part in securing the crown for him.

The accession of her nineteen-year-old son, followed at his death in 946 by the succession of her second son, Eadred, brought Eadgifu to the centre of politics. Between 939 and the death of Eadred in 955, the Queen-Mother was one of the most important and constantly consulted royal counsellors. Her position was unrivalled by that of any earlier West Saxon queen from at least the eighth century, and was scarcely equalled by any who came after her. She totally eclipsed the two wives of Edmund, neither of whom played any political role, while Eadred apparently never married. In the circumstances of tenth-century England, Eadgifu's power can be explained only in terms of her utility to her sons and the imponderable factor of personality. As her father's heir she had inherited substantial land in Kent, and this, together with her clients, must have been a source of strength; so too were the influential friends which a long career at court had brought. She used her influence with her sons to further the careers of two of these, Dunstan and Æthelwold, future leaders of the monastic revival. At her instigation Eadred persuaded Æthelwold to stay in England and made him Abbot of Abingdon.

Eadred had succeeded to the throne in 946 over the heads of his brother's young children. When he died in 955, his mother's dominant position at court was threatened. Eadwig, the eldest of her two grandsons, came to the throne, backed by a noble faction which had been alienated by Eadgifu's sons. When Eadwig took a wife and queen from this faction to strengthen his hand, his grandmother's influence at court was doubly endangered. At this stage, if not earlier, Eadgifu and her allies, most notably Dunstan, began to champion the claims of Eadwig's younger brother Edgar, then thirteen years old, a move which resulted in Dunstan's exile and the confiscation of Eadgifu's lands. When Edgar became King of all England in 959, he restored his grandmother's possessions, but she never regained her pre-eminence at court; Edgar had other allies. Eadgifu now retired, probably into a religious house, making only rare appearances at court, as in 966, when she celebrated with Edgar's third wife, ÆLFTHRYTH, the birth of a great-grandson.

See also P. A. Stafford, 'Sons and Mothers, family politics in the early Middle Ages', in D. Baker (ed.), *Medieval Women*, 1978.

P.A.S.

Eadgifu

Eadgifu (fl. 919–51), Queen of West Frankia. The daughter of King Edward the Elder, Eadgifu became the second wife of the beleaguered Carolingian King of West Frankia, Charles the Simple. In September 920 or 921 she gave birth to Louis, the future Louis IV, called 'd'Outremer' on account of his period of exile at the English court. The capture of Charles the Simple by his noble enemies in 923 forced Eadgifu and her son to flee to the refuge of the English court of Eadgifu's half-brother, Athelstan. The restoration of Charles the Simple in 927 was quickly followed by his death in 929 and Eadgifu and her son remained in England during the ensuing reign of King Ralph. In 936 they returned to France and the support of Eadgifu's English relatives proved crucial to her son's establishment as king. When Louis married in 939, Eadgifu retired from court to the nunnery of St Mary Laon. From there she fled in 951 to marry the lord of Vermandois, the son of her first husband's captor. Louis angrily confiscated his mother's lands, but Eadgifu was well provided for by her new family, receiving among other lands the Abbey of Soissons where she was buried.

See also P. Lauer, *Le Règne de Louis IV d'Outremer*, 1900.   P.A.S.

Eadgyth (before 918–946), Queen of Eastern Frankia. When the founder of the Ottonian dynasty, Henry the Fowler, sought a fitting bride for his heir, Otto, he turned to the English royal family. In 929, after negotiations through intermediaries, the English King Athelstan sent two of his sisters for Otto's consideration. Eadgyth, daughter of Edward the Elder and Athelstan's half-sister, married Otto early in 930 and bore him a son, Liudolf, within the year; a daughter, Liutgard, followed. The marriage and the introduction of a young queen at court apparently cooled relations between Otto and his mother Mathilda, who rarely appeared at court during Eadgyth's lifetime. Such resentment between mother-in-law and daughter-in-law was a common complicating factor in dynastic politics. Eadgyth's son did not live to be king, but the links that had been established by her marriage between England and the Ottonian Empire remained strong until the end of the century.

See also K. Schmid, 'Die Thronfolge Ottos des Grossen', in E. Hlawitschka (ed.), *Königswahl und Thronfolge in Ottonisch-frühdeutscher Zeit*, 1971.   P.A.S.

Ealdgyth (fl. 1057–1066), last Anglo-Saxon queen. This daughter of Earl Ælfgar of Mercia twice cemented the political alliances of her family through marriage. After 1057 her father gave her to his ally Gruffydd, King of North Wales. Gruffydd was murdered in 1063 but Ealdgyth proved an eligible widow. In 1065 Harold Godwinsson was searching for support for his designs on the English throne; he sought the friendship of Ealdgyth's brothers, the Earls Edwin of Mercia and Morcar of Northumbria, and therefore put aside his concubine and took Ealdgyth as his lawful wife. Nothing is known of her history after his death at Hastings in 1066.

See also F. Barlow, *Edward the Confessor*, 1970.   P.A.S.

Ealhswith (before 856–905), wife of King Alfred. In 868, at the age of twenty, Alfred married Ealhswith, daughter of Ealdorman Æthelred and of Eadburh, a woman of Mercian royal birth. The marriage was one of a series which cemented the alliance between ninth-century Wessex and Mercia against Viking attack. Ealhswith bore Alfred at least five children: the future king Edward the Elder, ÆTHELFLAED, who went on to become the famous Lady of the Mercians, Ælfthryth, Æthelgifu and Æthelweard. By contrast with her daughter's history, Ealhswith's career is totally obscure. Ninth-century West Saxon kings did not allow their wives a prominent political role, refusing even to give them the status of queens; they may have feared female intrigues over the succession to the throne at a time when young sons of kings were being passed over in favour of adult brothers in the interests of strong kingship. Alfred presented Ealhswith with dower lands, including Wantage, which she enjoyed during her six years of widowhood. She retired to Winchester, where she founded a religious house.

See also W. Stevenson (ed.), *Asser's Life of Alfred*, 1904.   P.A.S.

Eanflaed (626–?), Northumbrian queen. The eldest of King Edwin of Northumbria's four children by his second wife, Æthelburh, Eanflaed was born on Easter Sunday 626 and, seven weeks later, became one of the first Northumbrians to receive baptism. In 633

Edwin was killed and his family fled to Kent, where Eanflaed remained until she returned to Northumbria as the second wife of King Oswiu sometime between 641 and 645. The match, which provided Oswiu with at least four of his seven children, was important in two respects. It was primarily a political alliance between Edwin's only surviving offspring and a member of the dynasty that had succeeded him. However, Oswiu's desire to unify Northumbria also had religious ramifications, for at the synod of Whitby in 664 he ruled that the Irish Christianity that he had embraced should be abandoned for the Roman version practised by his wife. The Pope gratefully sent a cross with a golden key to Eanflaed along with his letter of congratulation to Oswiu, and praised her pious works and religious zeal. Eanflaed certainly seems to have taken an interest in ecclesiastical affairs, for she acted as Bishop Wilfrid of York's patron at the start of his career, and was responsible for getting her husband to found a monastery at Gilling, possibly in 658. Sometime between then and 685, probably after Oswiu's death in 670, she entered a monastery at Whitby, where she became joint abbess with her daughter, ÆLFFLAED. Due to their influence the body of Edwin (and possibly also that of Oswiu) was brought to Whitby, and on her death Eanflaed was buried beside him.

See also B. Colgrave and R. A. B. Mynors (eds), *Bede's Ecclesiastical History of the English People*, 1969; Eddius, *Vita Wilfridi*, ed. and trans. B. Colgrave, 1927.   J.C.

Eardley, Joan (1921–63), painter. She trained at the Glasgow School of Art (1940–43) but because of the war she then worked as a joiner's labourer for three years, painting and drawing in her free time. After the war she spent six months at Hospitalfield near Arbroath, working under James Cowie, Warden of the Allan-Fraser Trust. He influenced her by introducing her to the simple subjects which became her speciality: harbour scenes, men at work, and the like. In 1948, by means of a scholarship, she went to Italy, though this did little to affect the markedly social trend of her work. At this time she concentrated on drawing, and on her return to Glasgow she taught in the evening classes at the School of Art so as to be able to devote her days to drawings and paintings of scenes in the Glasgow tenements among which she lived. Her preferred

working area was the district round Hume Street, Tarbert Street, Cathedral Place and Balmano Brae, most of it now demolished in a slum clearance scheme, and in the port of Glasgow. She also worked at Catterline, a fishing village south of Aberdeen. She became a Royal Scottish Academician in 1963.

In Joan Eardley's work the social element is predominant. The subjects of her drawings and paintings are the Glasgow slums, graffiti, decayed buildings and portraits of the women and above all the children of the slums, as well as scenes of the fisher port and interiors of simple cottages like the one she herself lived in. In style she owes a lot to Sickert and his followers: her colour tends to be dark, and there is nothing in her work of the exuberant colour of Anne REDPATH, although they are alike in their technical ability. There are works by Joan Eardley in many of the major British galleries that exhibit modern artists.

See also W. Buchanan, *Joan Eardley*, 1976.   L.M.M.

Edgeworth, Maria (1767–1849), novelist, educationist and writer for children. She was born in Oxfordshire, the daughter of the educationist and agricultural reformer Richard Lovell Edgeworth. Her mother died when she was six, and Maria Edgeworth was educated in Derby between 1775 and 1780, and then in London. In 1782 the family settled on their estate, Edgeworthstown, in County Longford, Ireland. There Edgeworth began implementing a series of reforms to increase productivity on the estate and improve the condition of the resident farmers. He and his daughter were very close, and in later novels she would use him as a model to the Anglo-Irish gentry of an enlightened landlord and magistrate. Her first work, *Letters for Literary Ladies*, was published in 1795. In 1796 and 1801 she published the two volumes of *The Parent's Assistant*, which, with the later *Moral Tales*, were among the first original stories to be written specifically for children. In *Early Lessons* (1801) the aim is more decidedly educational: the characters grow older from one part to the next, and ideally the reader's maturity increases correspondingly. A textbook for teaching children, *Practical Education* (1798), was written by Maria with Richard Lovell Edgeworth and other members of her family; it was widely praised and made the Edgeworths well known.

137

Edith

In 1797 Maria Edgeworth accompanied her father and his fourth wife on their wedding trip to England, returning to Edgeworthstown in 1799. Her first novel, *Castle Rackrent*, was published in 1800. It is the book by which she is now remembered, a racy and far from complimentary account of Irish life; her drinking, fighting, litigious landlords and tenants, though entertainingly described, are very much realistic portraits as drawn by the daughter of an improving landlord. *Castle Rackrent* was followed in short order by her second novel, *Belinda* (1801). Then in 1802 the family travelled to France, where Maria frequented the Parisian *salons*. There she met the Swedish inventor and diplomat Abraham Niclas Clewberg-Edelcrantz, whose offer of marriage she refused, although she rightly suspected that her lack of physical attractions would make any other offers unlikely.

In March 1803 the Edgeworths returned to Ireland via England. *Popular Tales* (1804) and the novel *Leonora* (1806) were succeeded by more novels and *Professional Education*, a study of vocational education for boys, begun in 1807 and published nearly three years later with only her father's name on the title-page. The Irish novel, *Ennui*, published as one of the *Tales of Fashionable Life* (1809), and *Patronage* reflect the experience and knowledge gained in the process of researching *Professional Education*.

In 1817 the death of Richard Lovell Edgeworth, though long anticipated, proved a shattering blow to his daughter, though one which eventually led to considerable personal growth. In 1820 *Memoirs of Richard Lovell Edgeworth*, an autobiography begun by Edgeworth and completed by Maria, was published. Three years later, she first met and then stayed with Sir Walter Scott at Abbotsford. Her reputation was such that collected editions of her works appeared during her lifetime. Her last novel, *Helen*, was published in 1834.

See also M. Butler, *Maria Edgeworth: a Literary Biography*, 1972; C. Colvin (ed.), *Maria Edgeworth in France and Switzerland*, 1979. A.L.

Edith (*c*. 1020–1075), Edward the Confessor's queen. She was the eldest daughter of Earl Godwin of Wessex and his Danish wife Gytha, and had been well educated in the royally-connected nunnery of Wilton, which as queen she was later to rebuild. Edward's choice of Edith was determined by his desire for Godwin's support during the early years of his reign, and the queen's fate remained inseparable from that of her family.

The marriage took place in January 1045. Edith was consecrated as queen and took over her mother-in-law's place at court, but apparently played little role in politics during the 1040s. By 1050 it was clear that the marriage was barren and in 1051 Edward moved to divorce Edith, sending her into the keeping of his sister, the Abbess of Wherwell. The divorce had the backing of Robert, Archbishop of Canterbury. Edward was nearing fifty and an heir to the throne was essential, but the divorce was also inextricably entwined with high politics. In 1051 Edward acted against Edith's father and brothers, with the active support of Godwin's enemy, Archbishop Robert; he provoked their rebellion and banishment. The proposed divorce may have been a precipitating factor in a situation of growing mutual suspicion between Edward and Godwin, a situation which itself would have made Edith's presence at court increasingly unwelcome. If so, Edward miscalculated. In 1052 Godwin returned in triumph and Edith was restored to the royal bed, thus depriving Edward of the chance of an heir and initiating the sequence of events leading to the Norman Conquest.

Edith's period of greatest influence now began, waxing with that of her brothers, Earl Harold of Wessex and Tostig of Northumbria. She allegedly stood foremost in royal counsels. During the late 1050s she exercised power in ecclesiastical preferments, intervening in a Peterborough election in 1057 and securing the appointment of her close friend Herman to the bishopric of Sherborne in 1058 and of her chaplain Walter to Hereford in 1060. Queens regularly sought alliance with court ecclesiastics which were always open to misrepresentation by their enemies: Edith had been accused of adultery with the Bishop of Winchester during the divorce proceedings in 1051.

By the 1060s the main preoccupation of English politics was the succession. By 1065, if not before, Edith and her brothers were concerned to influence it, to act as king-makers if not to gain the throne themselves. At about this date Edith commissioned the so-called *Life of Edward*, a work originally planned as an encomium on the house of Godwin and on Edith in particular. Edith's precise hopes for the future are unclear, though it has been suggested that she favoured the claims of her younger brother Tostig. She has been accused of engineering on Tostig's behalf the murder of the Northern noble Gospatric at the Christmas court celebrations in 1064; motive and opportunity must have existed, but the general anti-feminist bias of the sources makes such accusations suspect. Whatever her plans, they were upset first by the dissensions between her brothers in 1065, then by William's conquest of England in 1066. The Norman King found Edith in possession of Winchester, part of the Anglo-Saxon queens' dower, which she was forced to yield. She died in 1075, having played little part in the politics of early Norman England. She swore her innocence of the charge of adultery on her deathbed and was buried beside Edward in Westminster Abbey.

See also F. Barlow, *Edward the Confessor*, 1970.   P.A.S.

Edith of Wilton, St (962?–984), abbess, daughter of King Edgar of England. When Edgar divorced his second wife, Wulfthryth, she was sent to the nunnery of Wilton, taking with her Edith, her infant daughter, a child no older than four. Edith was raised at Wilton by her mother the Abbess, and received the veil there from Bishop Æthelwold of Winchester. She later became abbess herself and built an oratory there dedicated to St Dionysius. Edith retained her noble life-style in the convent; Æthelwold had occasion to rebuke her for her costly apparel, eliciting her sharp retort that pride could lurk among rags. When her half-brothers fought for the throne between 975 and 978 Edith may have played some role; she was certainly present in 983 when the body of the murdered Edward was exhumed. Archbishop Dunstan attended her deathbed and thirteen years later had her tomb opened to discover her uncorrupted body.

See also A. Wilmart, 'La légende de Ste Edith en prose et vers par le moine Goscelin', in *Analecta Bollandiana*, 1938.   P.A.S.

Edwards, Amelia (Ann) Blandford (1831–92), novelist and Egyptologist, born in London, where her father worked for the London and Westminster Bank. She was chiefly educated at home. Amelia Blandford Edwards was seven when her first poem was published in a penny weekly. Later, she was torn between writing and music, which she studied under Mrs Mounsey Bartholomew between 1846 and 1853. She chose writing after receiving a cheque for a story published in *Chambers's Journal*. She continued contributing stories and art and drama criticism to a variety of periodicals, and she was on the staff of *The Saturday Review* and *The Morning Post*. Her first novel, *My Brother's Wife*, appeared in 1855, and the following year she published *A Summary of English History*.

As well as novels, historical works and poetry, Amelia Blandford Edwards wrote travel books. In the winter of 1873 she went to Egypt, a journey which was to change her life. It was there that she began her study of ancient Egypt and in 1877 she published her long-popular book *A Thousand Miles Up the Nile*. She became one of the founders of the Egypt Exploration Fund (1882), and lectured and contributed articles on Egyptology to *The Times* and *The Academy*. She received a number of honorary degrees and in 1889 made a lecture tour of the United States. While there, she broke an arm, an accident from which she never entirely recovered. Amelia Blandford Edwards died at Westbury-Super-Mare and her Egyptological collection and library were left to University College, London, together with a fund to establish the first chair in Egyptology in Britain. Her books include *The Ladder of Life*, 1857, *Hand and Glove*, 1859, *Lord Brackenbury*, 1880, *Untrodden Peaks and Unfrequented Valleys*, 1873, and *Pharaohs, Fellahs and Explorers*, 1891.

See also K. Macquoid, *Amelia Blandford Edwards*, 1897.   A.P.

Egerton, George. See BRIGHT, MARY (CHAVELITA).

Eleanor of Aquitaine (1122–1204), Duchess of Aquitaine and Queen of England. She was the eldest surviving child of William X, Duke of Aquitaine and Count of Poitou. On her father's death in 1137 she inherited his lands under the guardianship of Louis VI of France, who quickly married her to his own son. In the early years of their marriage, Louis VII seems to have been completely dominated by his wife, with unfortunate consequences for France. In 1147 Eleanor accompanied him on the Second Crusade. She was very active in the military preparations, but her huge baggage train considerably hindered the army and her Aquitaine contingent lacked discipline. Her relationship with her young uncle, Raymond of Antioch, was taken amiss by

Eleanor of Castile

Louis, who sent her home. The unsuitability of their marriage in personal terms had long been apparent, and it was a dynastic failure too, since Eleanor only bore Louis two daughters. Yet it seems clear that the annulment of their marriage was sought by Eleanor and not Louis.

In 1152 Eleanor returned to Poitiers and immediately married Henry, Count of Anjou, who inherited the throne of England two years later. In Henry II Eleanor met her match both physically and intellectually. For the next decade, despite bearing eight children (only one of whom failed to survive), the Queen travelled ceaselessly throughout England and the Angevin possessions in France. She seems to have shared in Henry's administration, acting as regent in England when Henry was in France, and vice versa. In 1168, at Henry's wish, Eleanor assumed the active government of Aquitaine on behalf of their second son, Richard. Henry's betrayal of his ageing wife with Rosamund CLIFFORD was probably one of the factors that turned her into an enemy who used even their children against him. In 1173, when Henry's heir, young Henry, rebelled against him, Eleanor supported her son but was captured. Henry II was too wise to divorce her and lose Aquitaine, but imprisoned her in England.

On Henry's death in 1189, Eleanor was immediately freed and poured her pent-up energies into securing the English throne for her eldest surviving and favourite son, Richard the Lionheart. Until his arrival in England she was chiefly responsible for the government of the kingdom, and such was her prestige that, even after years of imprisonment, nobody questioned her actions. Her pivotal role in England continued throughout most of Richard's subsequent absence on the Third Crusade, and without her frenzied efforts his enormous ransom would probably never have been raised. On his return she retired to Fontevrault Abbey in Anjou, but when he died in 1199 she came back to help ensure the accession of her last son, John. At the age of nearly eighty she crossed the Pyrenees to select one of her Castilian granddaughters as a bride for the future Louis VIII of France. She died at Fontevrault.

By any standards Eleanor was one of the outstanding women of the Middle Ages. To the end she remained fascinated by the exercise of power. Her extraordinary energy and force of character enabled her to act as regent in England for her husband and as virtual ruler for much of Richard's reign, and to retain the loyalty of her volatile vassals in Aquitaine for nearly seventy years. Her energies were not always directed towards worthwhile ends, but she played an important cultural role in patronage at the Courts of both her husbands. Like most of her comtemporaries she saw politics largely in personal terms, but she earned the continuing admiration of chroniclers. Roger of Devizes wrote of her at seventy-five as 'even now unwearied by any task and provoking wonder at her stamina'. He thought her 'an incomparable woman; beautiful yet gracious, strong-willed yet kind, unassuming yet sagacious'.

See also E. Brown, 'Eleanor as Parent, Queen and Duchess', in W. W. Kibler (ed.), *Eleanor of Aquitaine: Patron and Politician*, 1976; R. Pernoud (trans. P. Wiles), *Eleanor of Aquitaine*, 1967.　　　　　　　　　A.C.

Eleanor of Castile (*c*.1240–1290), Edward I's queen. She was the daughter of Ferdinand III, King of Castile and León. The negotiations for a match with Prince Edward, son of King Henry III, were carried out by her half-brother, Alphonso X, and the couple were married in 1254. In 1279, on the death of her mother, Eleanor inherited the county of Ponthieu. Between 1255 and 1284 she had fifteen or sixteen children (the exact number is in dispute) but only her youngest son, Edward, and five daughters survived to adulthood. During the civil wars in Henry III's reign, she stayed quietly at Windsor. In 1270 she accompanied Edward on crusade and while they were away he succeeded to the throne. This Eastern trip gave Eleanor a taste for the exotic and added brilliance and refinement to her court. Her accounts show her to have been fond of music, hunting and books. In 1290 she was corresponding with an Oxford scholar about one of her books and it seems likely that, unusually for her time, she could read and write.

Eleanor's marriage was a very happy one; her vital and energetic character made her highly suited to Edward. She was personally kind, devoted to the Church (patronizing in particular the Dominican Friars), and generous to the poor. But recent research into her business affairs has shown her in a less attractive light. She was hard-headed, and like

Edward she was eager to acquire land. Her business methods were highly unpopular, particularly her buying-up of debts owed to the Jews before their expulsion from England in 1290. On her estates her officials illegally extended her rights and arbitrarily raised customary dues in a way that suggested the Queen's authorization. Unfortunately no letter or document survives to illustrate her own thoughts or feelings. She died of a fever at Harby, Nottinghamshire, and as her body was borne to London the grieving Edward ordered a cross to be erected at each of the twelve stopping places. She was buried in Westminster Abbey.

See also J. C. Parsons (ed.), *The Court and Household of Eleanor of Castile in 1290*, 1977. A.C.

Eleanor of Provence (*c.* 1220–1293), Henry III's queen. The daughter of Raymond, Count of Provence, Eleanor was brought up at his highly cultured court, where both her parents were poets. In 1236 she was married to Henry III of England, over whom she soon developed a strong influence. They were a devoted couple and the family life of the future Edward I and their four other surviving children was very happy. In the country at large, however, Eleanor soon made herself highly unpopular by promoting the interests of her Provençal relatives and friends, who enriched themselves at the expense of the Crown. For this reason Eleanor was badly treated by the Londoners during the civil war of 1263–65. She also vainly attempted to raise a mercenary army for Henry in France, but when her funds were exhausted the troops melted away.

Eleanor was extremely devout, and on her widowhood retired in 1272 to Amesbury, a cell of Fontevrault Abbey, where she took the veil in 1286. She modified her vow of poverty by retaining her dower under special Papal dispensation, probably to pay off her large debts. In 1275 she had expelled all Jews from her estates and it was perhaps her influence that led her son, Edward I, to expel them from the kingdom in 1290. However, although she was rather a narrow, commonplace woman, her surviving correspondence, which is surprisingly informal in tone, shows Eleanor as pleasant and kindly within the limits of her sympathies.

See also M. Prestwich, *The Three Edwards*, 1980. A.C.

Eliot, George, pseudonym of Marian Evans (1819–80), novelist. One of five children, George Eliot was born at South Farm on the Arbury Hall estate near Coventry, where her father was the estate agent. After attending a number of private schools in the Midlands, she took charge of her father's household following the death of her mother in 1836. She continued her education at home, reading Latin and Greek with the help of a local schoolmaster and learning Italian and German.

During the early part of her life she was strongly influenced by the Evangelical movement, to which she had been introduced through her friendship with Maria Lewis, the principal governess at a school she had attended in Nuneaton. Her first publication was a religious poem which appeared, under her own initials, in *The Christian Observer* in 1840. However, Christianity began to lose its hold over her after she and her father moved to Coventry, where she became acquainted with Charles and Caroline Bray, who were both free-thinkers. It was through the Brays that she met Charles Hennell, a free-thinking writer whose wife had begun a translation of Strauss's rationalistic *Life of Jesus*. In 1844 she took over the work of translation from Mrs Hennell, and the book was published in 1846. Her father died in 1849 and, free to live her own life, she spent some time on the Continent and then settled in London.

From 1851 to 1853 Marian Evans was assistant editor of *The Westminster Review*. Her second translation was of another controversial work, Feuerbach's *Essence of Christianity*. It was published in 1854, the year in which she began living with George Henry Lewes, whom she had met three years previously; he was already married, so it was impossible to legalize their union. Because of her relationship with Lewes, a period of social ostracism ensued during which she began writing novels. It was Lewes who sent the first story of what was to become *Scenes of Clerical Life* to *Blackwood's Magazine* in January 1857; the three stories making up the *Scenes* had an immediate success, establishing 'George Eliot' as one of the leading writers of the day. In October 1857 she began work on *Adam Bede*, developing a story which had been told to her by her Methodist aunt many years before. The novel was published in 1859, and achieved tremendous popularity. Two further novels, *The Mill On The Floss* (1860) and

Elizabeth I, Queen

Silas Marner (1861), were published before she and Lewes left on their second Italian trip together in 1861. All these early books owe something to the scenes of George Eliot's own childhood or an even earlier rural England; her preoccupation with moral problems is apparent, but the flow of human sympathy and rustic humour keeps the didactic element in check. Her later novels, more consciously created, are more uneven. Out of the Italian visit came an historical novel, *Romola* (1863), which was followed by George Eliot's political novel, *Felix Holt the Radical* (1866). *Middlemarch*, published in 1871–72, was her greatest success, selling 20,000 copies within two years of publication; modern critics have come round to the Victorian opinion that this large-scale study of provincial life is George Eliot's masterpiece, giving an adult but unsensational account of human relations that is unique in nineteenth-century English fiction. Her last novel, *Daniel Deronda*, appeared in 1876, by which time she and Lewes had moved to Surrey, where Lewes died in November 1878. In May 1880 George Eliot married J. W. Cross, whom she had met in Rome over ten years before. She died seven months later.

One of the greatest of nineteenth-century novelists, George Eliot also published verse, notably *The Spanish Gypsy* (1868), and a large number of reviews.

See also G. S. Haight (ed.), *The George Eliot Letters*, 1954–55; G. S. Haight, *George Eliot, A Biography*, 1968; B. Hardy, *The Novels of George Eliot: a Study In Form*, 1959.

J.H.S.

Elizabeth I, Queen (1533–1603), one of England's greatest rulers. The daughter of Henry VIII and Anne BOLEYN, Elizabeth was heir to the throne at her birth, but when her mother was executed in 1536 she was declared illegitimate. Nevertheless her education was not neglected, her tutors including the humanists Roger Ascham and John Cheke; she became and remained an excellent scholar, fluent in Greek and Latin. After Henry's death she lived in the household of his last wife, Katherine PARR, and may have become emotionally involved with Katherine's husband, Thomas Seymour, who hoped to marry her and may have meditated the treason for which he was executed in 1549. Elizabeth herself came under suspicion and was interrogated. The years that followed were difficult ones. In 1553

the dying act of her brother Edward VI was to try to bar Elizabeth and her older half-sister MARY from the royal succession, as laid down by Henry's will, in favour of Lady Jane GREY. The attempt failed and Elizabeth and Queen Mary rode together triumphantly into London; but Elizabeth's Protestant sympathies and nearness to the throne endangered her life during the reign of her Catholic half-sister; after Wyatt's Rebellion she was committed to the Tower in March 1554, but no evidence against her was found. Released in May, she was held at Woodstock until briefly summoned to court for the last days of Mary's supposed (actually hysterical) pregnancy. She spent the rest of the reign conforming outwardly in religion and resisting plans to marry her off.

On Mary's death in November 1558, Elizabeth succeeded to the throne amid general rejoicing and set about consolidating her power, ably assisted by William Cecil. After sending ambiguous communications to a potentially hostile Catholic Europe, she established a moderate Protestant course that seemed best designed to unite the country and support her own claim to the throne (she was still a bastard in Catholic eyes, and MARY QUEEN OF SCOTS, supported by France, soon began to advance her own claims). Despite numerous offers of marriage from European princes and pleas from her Parliament to marry (especially after a near-fatal attack of smallpox in 1562), Elizabeth remained single, choosing to use the prospect of marriage as a political tool (a game which she continued until she was into her fifties) and to enjoy the vicarious pleasures of the romantic chase. The reasons for her celibacy may have been political: to marry an Englishman might have aroused dangerous factionalism, while to wed a foreigner might have entailed a sacrifice of English interests. But they may also have been emotional: Henry's judicial murder of her mother and Katherine Howard, and her experiences with Thomas Seymour, may have left permanent scars. Certainly throughout her life Elizabeth demonstrated an unpleasant hostility to the marriage of others, especially her ladies, clergy and courtiers. After a stable first decade of rule, Elizabeth faced two related threats: her rival, Mary, Queen of Scots, whose presence in England encouraged Catholic plots, and the hostility of Catholic Spain, spurred on by a papal bull of 1570 excommunicating and deposing Elizabeth. She spent the 1570s and 1580s coping with the plots, infiltration of priests, and dangers of invasion which these threats entailed. Her execution of Mary in 1587 and the defeat of the Armada in 1588 brought England through the crisis. The 1590s were marked by her churchmen's largely successful campaign against a Puritan tendency which Elizabeth had always disliked, and the struggle for influence over the ageing Queen waged by Robert Cecil and Robert Devereux, Earl of Essex. The contest ended in 1601 when Essex attempted a wild and incompetent coup and was executed. In her last years Elizabeth tacitly allowed Cecil to negotiate the succession of James VI of Scotland, saw important social legislation through Parliament, and strove to subdue Ireland. She was the last of the Tudors.

Elizabeth has had her critics. They point to her harsh treatment of English Catholics, her dangerous vacillations (particularly over Mary and the succession), her high-handed treatment of the Church, her vanity and her meanness. But there is much for which Elizabeth can take credit. England's maritime adventures and cultural achievements owed much to her inspiration. The good order and stability of the realm can be attributed to her ability to inspire devotion, minimalize factionalism, deal effectively with Parliament, and choose first-rate advisers. Most important, her intelligence and strength of personality maintained England's religious and national independence at a time when the powers arrayed against her seemed overwhelming.

See also F. Chamberlin (ed.), *The Sayings of Queen Elizabeth*, 1923; J. Hurstfield, *Elizabeth I and the Unity of England*, 1960; P. Johnson, *Elizabeth I*, 1974; J. Neale, *Queen Elizabeth*, 1934.   G.Q.B.

Elizabeth of Bohemia (1596–1662), daughter of James I and ANNE OF DENMARK. In 1613 she married the Elector Frederick V of the Palatinate, a leading German Calvinist, and moved to his court at Heidelberg. Her first son was born in 1614 and she had eleven more children before her husband's death in 1632. Her third child was Prince Rupert, the Royalist cavalry leader in the English Civil War.

From 1619 Elizabeth's fortunes became bound up with those of the Protestant side in the Thirty Years War, for her husband accepted the throne of Bohemia, traditionally occupied by the Catholic Habsburg Emperor.

Elizabeth's ambition has been blamed for Frederick's rash act, but the evidence shows only that she fully supported her husband. Frederick ruled Bohemia for barely a year: in October 1620 he, Elizabeth, and their family were forced to flee from Prague after a crushing defeat by the Emperor's forces. The Palatinate itself was lost by 1622, and thereafter Elizabeth lived in exile, chiefly in the Netherlands. She remained there on her husband's death despite an offer of hospitality in England from her brother Charles I. She was granted a pension by Charles, but after his execution she was dependent on the little money spared her by her son Charles Louis, who was restored to the Palatinate at the end of the Thirty Years War. She returned to England in 1661 after Charles II had paid her debts, and died the following year.

Although an exile for most of her adult life, Elizabeth has a significant place in English history. Before the Civil War she was for many English people the symbol of the Protestant cause, eulogized as the 'Queen of Hearts'. The failure of James I and Charles I to intervene effectively on behalf of European Protestants was one of the causes of their unpopularity. Elizabeth's personality, her cheerfulness in the face of a prolonged and impoverished exile, and her determined mobilization of international support for the Palatinate all added to the effectiveness of her role.

See also C. Oman, *Elizabeth of Bohemia*, revised edn, 1964.   P.M.H.

Elizabeth of York (1465–1503), Henry VII's queen, the eldest daughter of Edward IV and Elizabeth WOODVILLE. Elizabeth was betrothed in 1475 to the Dauphin of France, but his father, Louis XI, broke off the proposed match in 1482, shortly before Edward IV's death. After the presumed deaths of her brothers in the Tower during the reign of Richard III, Elizabeth became the heiress of the house of York. Her mother arranged that she should marry the exiled Henry Tudor, the Lancastrian candidate, provided his planned invasion proved successful. Henry VII did not marry Elizabeth, then nineteen, immediately after he had defeated Richard and gained the throne, largely because he did not wish to appear to owe the crown to his wife's superior claim; nor did he have her crowned for more than two years. The marriage itself seems to have been a happy one. Elizabeth, who was gentle and pious, made no attempt to interfere in politics, and she was a popular queen. Her popularity was a considerable help in persuading the English people to accept her husband. Her habits were simple and economical, but she made annual allowances to her three sisters, all married without dowry to peers loyal to Henry.

In 1502 the death of their eldest son, Arthur, soon after his marriage to Katherine of Aragon, was a great blow to Henry and Elizabeth. It left them with one surviving son, the future Henry VIII, and two daughters. Ten months later the Queen died in childbirth at the age of thirty-seven.

See also S. B. Chrimes, *Henry VII*, 1972.
                                                            A.C.

Ellis, Sarah (1810–72), writer and philanthropist. The daughter of a Quaker farmer, Sarah Stickney was born near Hull. Details of her early life are obscure, apart from her conversion to Congregationalism. A woman of considerable culture, she achieved literary acclaim in the 1830s with the publication of *The Poetry of Life* (1835) and the novel *Pictures of Private Life* (serialized 1833–37). In 1837 she married the missionary William Ellis, whose religious convictions she shared and to whom she was devoted. There were no children of the marriage, which was subject to lengthy separations, and she spent much of her time writing and doing philanthropic work in the vicinity of Hoddesdon, Hertfordshire, to which she and her husband moved in 1841.

Sarah Ellis's interests ranged from temperance and missionary work to female education, in which field she organized and directed a school for girls at Rawdon House in Hoddesdon. There she gave practical effect to the views on moral training and the development of character expressed in her many treatises. Four of the most important were *The Women of England*, 1838, *The Daughters of England*, 1842, *The Mothers of England*, 1843, and *The Wives of England*, 1843. One of the more prolific of early Victorian women authors, she wrote attractively on a variety of subjects, but her greatest influence lay in these widely read didactic essays on female behaviour, written for the middle classes.

As an exponent of the doctrine of separate spheres, Sarah Ellis regarded men as a race apart; they retained their best energies and intelligence for their careers and public work. Women, on the other hand, were softer, more domestic and moral, with a boundless capacity for love that was best expressed in marriage. She believed that wives must accommodate themselves to their husbands; this she achieved in her own marriage, for she rarely challenged her husband's decisions or authority. The essential aim of her writings, which sought to amuse as well as to instruct, was the moral improvement of her sex, which would lead to the greater glory of her country.

Though much of Sarah Ellis's writing is typical of the female literature of the time, there is some sharply observed social criticism and an underlying tension between her claims on behalf of women and her notions of Christian self-sacrifice, which makes her work an interesting example of Victorian stirrings toward female emancipation.

Sarah Ellis's other works include *Pique*, 1850, *Mothers of Great Men*, 1859, *Northern Roses*, 1868, and *Education of the Heart: Woman's Best Work*, 1869.

See also J. E. Ellis, *Life of William Ellis*, 1873; *The Home Life and Letters of Mrs Ellis*, compiled by her nieces, 1893.   M.N.

Elsie, Lily (1886–1962), musical comedy star, born at Wortley, Leeds. A woman of great beauty and grace, Lily Elsie became the most glamorous star of the Edwardian Theatre. She first appeared at Manchester in *Little Red Riding Hood* when she was ten, then performed as a child-mimic, 'Little Elsie'. Her first West End part was in *A Chinese Honeymoon*. At the Prince of Wales in *The Little Cherub*, she high-spiritedly kicked a football into the stalls during a 'sporting' number and was instantly fired. She later met the famous impresario George Edwardes when she was jobless, and he invited her to sing in *The Little Michus*, which was followed by *See-See* and a tour of *The New Aladdin*. Edwardes sent her to Vienna to see a new musical, *The Merry Widow*, and although she protested that it was too difficult he forced her to take the name part. Her performance at Daly's in 1907 was electrifying and has never been matched; overnight she became the rage of London.

Then came such successes as *The Dollar Princess* and *A Waltz Dream*. After marrying she retired temporarily, then returned with Beerbohm Tree in *Mavourneen* (1915). Her last appearance as leading lady was in Novello's *The Truth Game* at Daly's (1929), after which she retired.   A.D.

Elstob, Elizabeth (1683–1756), Anglo-Saxon scholar, was born in Newcastle-upon-Tyne, the daughter of a merchant. Both her parents were dead by the time she was eight years old. She seems to have become fascinated by the structure of language at an early age, and was for a time prevented by her guardian from following her studies, which he considered unseemly and unnecessary in a female child. However, upon taking up residence with her clergyman brother William at Oxford she began to learn Latin and seven other languages. Anglo-Saxon became her chief interest, and in 1709 she published the text and translation of the *English-Saxon Homily on the Nativity of St George*. Her edition of the homilies of Ælfric exists only in a printed fragment in the British Library and was never formally published in spite of some financial help from Queen Anne. The publication of her *Rudiments of Grammar for the English-Saxon Tongue* in 1715 necessitated the cutting of a special fount of new types. Her erudition brought her little practical advantage: she set up a school in Evesham, was dependent on small annuities and subscriptions from friends, and for the last two decades of her life was governess and dependant in the household of the Duchess of Portland.

See also M. Murphy, 'The Elstobs: Scholars of Old English and Anglican Apologists', in *Durham University Journal*, 1966.   T.H.

Emma (before 990–1052), queen of England as the wife of Æthelred and later Cnut (Canute). Emma was the daughter of Duke Richard of Normandy, and her marriage to the English King Æthelred II in 1002 sealed an anti-Viking alliance between king and duke. Emma replaced her mother-in-law ÆLFTHRYTH at court in the formal position of Queen, a title not enjoyed by Æthelred's earlier spouse (or possibly spouses). This, and her regular appearances in charter witness lists, indicates her importance during Æthelred's reign. In England she adopted the Anglo-Saxon name Ælfgifu.

As Æthelred's second or third wife Emma faced a brace of adult stepsons; as mother of two sons herself she worked hard for their accession. It was later claimed that her eldest, the future Edward the Confessor, was designated heir to the throne before his birth. The growing tensions within Æthelred's family which bedevilled the end of the reign were partly the result of these difficult step-relationships.

By 1013 Æthelred's England was on the brink of Viking conquest and Emma fled with her sons and youngest stepsons to Normandy. From there she returned in 1017 to marry Cnut, the victorious Danish king and son of her first husband's conqueror. Cnut hoped that by marrying his predecessor's widow he could buy off Norman support for her English sons; Emma's attitude to the marriage cannot be known, though she threw her support behind the new dynasty and behind Harthacnut, her son by Cnut. Emma was again a second wife with older stepsons; again she worked on behalf of her own son, this time to ensure Harthacnut's accession not only to Denmark, which he received before his father's death, but also to England.

Emma's power waxed under Cnut: she could offer the foreign king expertise in English politics and possibly acted as regent during his frequent absences in Scandinavia. She and Earl Godwin of Wessex, whose own career blossomed under Cnut, dominated the court, perhaps in alliance. Emma was associated in Cnut's ecclesiastical patronage and may have had personal control of the abbey of Evesham.

Cnut's death in 1035 threatened her power. The English throne was contested between her stepson Harold Harefoot and her son Harthacnut, who lingered in Denmark. Emma acted decisively, taking control of the treasury at Winchester and allying with Godwin. In 1036 her older sons by Æthelred, Edward and Alfred, arrived to claim the throne, perhaps at Emma's instigation, since Harthacnut was still absent, but more likely on their own initiative. These English princes received little support, and their arrival may have prompted the defection of Emma's ally Godwin to Harold. By 1037 Harold had triumphed and Emma was exiled, fleeing to Bruges in Flanders. Harold's untimely death in 1040 allowed Harthacnut's accession, Emma's return, and her acquisition of the coveted, influential status of queen-mother. She commissioned a Flemish monk to produce a justification of her actions in the *Encomium Emmae*. Emma looked to her future, and, perhaps anticipating Harthacnut's early death in 1042, invited her son Edward back to England in 1041. But if she hoped to win his gratitude she was sadly mistaken; Edward felt little love for the mother who had deserted him and married his father's enemy. After becoming king in 1042 one of his earliest actions was to dispossess Emma of her treasures. When Edward married Edith in 1045 Emma retired from court to Winchester, where she died.

Emma trod a tortuous path through the politics of eleventh-century England with a determination which has earned her unjustified attack. Her part in shaping events was of considerable importance.

See also A. Campbell (ed.), *Encomium Emmae Reginae*, in Royal Historical Society Camden 3rd Series, 1949; M. W. Campbell, 'Queen Emma and Ælfgifu of Northampton, Canute the Great's women', in *Medieval Scandinavia* (Odense University), vol. 4.   P.A.S.

Emmet, Evelyn Violet Elizabeth, Baroness Emmet of Amberley (1899–1980), politician, one of the pillars of the Conservative Party. Evelyn Emery, daughter of Lord Rennell of Rodd, was born at Cairo and educated at St Margaret's School, Bushey, Lady Margaret Hall, Oxford, and the London School of Economics. She also studied on the Continent and became fluent in several languages before returning to England, where she spent a year at the Toynbee Hall Settlement in London's East End. During the First World War she acted as secretary to her father, who was then British Ambassador in Rome. In 1923 she married T. E. Emmet of Amberley Castle, Sussex, and began her political career soon afterwards.

She was a member of the London County Council, chairing a number of committees, from 1925 to 1934; she lost her seat in the big swing to Labour that then occurred. During the Second World War she worked as Sussex county organizer for the Women's Voluntary Service. She returned to local politics as a member of the West Sussex County Council (1946–67), and was also elected an Alderman (1952–66). She was British delegate to the United Nations in 1952 and 1953.

Baroness Emmet held a number of important posts within the Conservative Party (member of the National Union Executive, Chairman of the Conservative Women's National Advisory Committee, Chairman of the National Union of Conservatives) and entered national politics in 1955 as Conservative MP for East Grinstead. She was created a Life Peer in 1964, and during her time in the Lords served as a Deputy Chairman of Committees (1968–77), a member of the Select Committee on the EEC (1974–77), and Chairman of the Legal Aid Advisory Committee (1966–72).   N.H.

Engelbach, Florence (1872–1951), painter. Her maiden name, under which she first exhibited, was Neumegen. Born in Spain of British parents, she always declared that Spain was her spiritual home. She studied at the Westminster School of Art and the Slade from around 1894, and also in Paris. Her early works, mainly portraits, showed an aptitude for careful drawing and painting in a low key that was fashionable at the time. In 1902 she married the president of the Institute of Automobile Engineers, and they had one son; she gave up painting for years, but around 1930 she started to work again in a totally changed style, with colour in a much lighter key, more fluid and freer drawing, and effects of light. She exhibited occasionally at the Royal Academy between 1934 and 1940, and at the Paris Salon. There are works by her in the Tate Gallery, London, and in the galleries of other large British cities, mostly the flowerpieces in which she came to specialize.   L.M.M.

Esdaile, Katherine (Ada) (1881–1950), art historian. Her father was secretary to the Girls' Public Day School Trust, and her mother the first Head Mistress of Norwich, Oxford and Bedford High Schools. She herself read classics at Oxford, where she acquired her interest in antique sculpture. After studying at the British School at Rome in 1907, she married A. S. R. Esdaile, later Secretary of the British Museum.

She did not begin her life's work on English post-medieval sculpture until 1919, after the birth of her children. Her researches took her principally to parish churches and the notebooks of George Vertue in the British Museum, which she prepared for publication by the Walpole Society. Her important *English Monumental Sculpture since the Renaissance* (1927) was followed by her *magnum opus*, *The Life and Works of Louis François Roubiliac* (1928), and from then until 1946 she produced a steady flow of books and articles on monumental sculpture. In 1928 she received the Royal Society of Arts Medal for her work.   C.H.

Essex, Countess of. See STEPHENS, CATHERINE.

Euphemia of Wherwell (?–1257), celebrated abbess, spent some forty years as a nun in the Benedictine house of Wherwell in Hampshire. A fourteenth-century cartulary includes a brief but vivid eulogy of her virtues and good deeds as abbess. According to this panegyric, Euphemia increased the number of nuns from forty to eighty and gave them an excellent example by her pious exhortations, regular discipline, holy conversation, charity and hospitality. She 'administered the necessaries of life with piety, prudence, care, and honesty'; and she 'so conducted herself with regard to exterior affairs that she seemed to have the spirit of a man rather than of a woman'. She died, amid the blessings of her sisters, in April 1257.

See also E. Power, *Medieval English Nunneries*, 1922.   K.R.D.

Eva. See KELLY, MARY ANNE.

Evans, Dame Edith (Mary) (1888–1976), actress, one of the leading stage performers of her generation. She was born in south London, the only daughter of a civil servant in the Post Office, and on leaving school at the age of fourteen was apprenticed to a milliner. She began acting as an amateur and in 1912 attracted the attention of William Poel, under whose direction she appeared with the English Stage Company at Cambridge in August 1912. Later that year she began her stage career proper in London with a performance of the title role in *Troilus and Cressida*, under Poel's direction.

For the next decade or so, Edith Evans gained experience in a variety of roles. A new phase of her career opened in 1924, when her talent for comedy found expression in a famous performance as Millamant in Congreve's *The Way of the World*. In the same year she brought to London the roles of the Serpent and the She-Ancient in Shaw's *Back to Methuselah*, which she had earlier created in Birmingham.

Over the ensuing twenty years she consolidated her reputation. Major Shakespearean roles with the Old Vic Company in their 1925 season included two of her most notable characterizations, Rosalind in *As You Like It* and the Nurse in *Romeo and Juliet*; in Restoration comedy (one of her favourite genres) she appeared as Mrs Fidget in *The Country Wife* and in the 1927 and 1930 revivals of *The Beaux' Stratagem*; while her association with Shaw was continued in her portrayals of Lady Utterword in *Heartbreak House* and Orinthia in *The Apple Cart*. In 1933 she appeared in the long-running popular success, *The Late Christopher Bean*, and in 1936 made her début in Chekhov as Irina Arkadina in *The Seagull*. The decade culminated with the 1939 revival of Wilde's *The Importance of Being Earnest*, in which she played a definitive Lady Bracknell. She was later to say that the role hung like a millstone round her neck for the rest of her life, but the celebrated octave swoop of 'A hand-bag?' still epitomizes convention mortally affronted, as well as being a potent reminder of a flawless high-comedy acting technique.

Firmly established after 1945 as one of the *grandes dames* of the English theatre, Edith Evans appeared in classical roles, including Mrs Malaprop (1946), Lady Wishfort, and Mme Ranevsky, and gave distinguished performances in modern plays such as James Bridie's *Daphne Laureola* (1949), N. C. Hunter's *Waters of the Moon* (1951), Christopher Fry's *The Dark is Light Enough* (1954, written specially for her) and Enid Bagnold's *The Chalk Garden* (1956). One of her most notable appearances was as Judith Bliss in the 1964 revival of Coward's *Hay Fever*. During this period she also reached a wider audience in films such as *The Queen of Spades*, *The Importance of Being Earnest*, *Look Back in Anger* and *Tom Jones*.

Wit, intelligence, vitality, all encompassed by the high professionalism of her technique, contributed to her long-lasting success as an actress. Her services to the English theatre were acknowledged by the award of the DBE in 1946, and by honorary degrees from London, Oxford and Cambridge.

See also B. Forbes, *Ned's Girl*, 1977; J. C. Trewin, *Edith Evans*, 1954.   K.W.

Evans, Dame Joan (1893–1977), author and antiquarian. Although born into a comfortable, educated background, Joan Evans had a somewhat lonely childhood. The only child of John Evans, paper manufacturer and amateur antiquary, and his third wife, one of Oxford's first women graduates, she was born when her father was seventy. Mrs Evans did not trouble to conceal her distaste for motherhood, so Joan Evans's childhood, and indeed much of her adult life, was spent with a much-loved nanny.

After a haphazard education she went up

147

to Oxford in 1914, having already completed a book on English jewellery, a subject which was to be a life-long interest. She remained in Oxford as a don until 1922, when she left to devote more time to her writing. She also spent much of her time in France, on whose art and history she wrote extensively. Her long career not only produced what was virtually a book a year but also an impressive list of offices and honours, among which were the Légion d'Honneur and the DBE.

Among her books are *Pattern: a Study of Ornament in Western Europe from 1100 to 1900*, 1931; *English Medieval Lapidaries*, 1933; *English Art, 1307–1461*, 1949; and *The Lamp of Beauty*, 1959. She also wrote on her family: *Time and Chance*, 1943, about her half-brother, the archaeologist, Arthur Evans; and *The Endless Web*, 1955, on her father's family, the paper-manufacturing Dickinsons. Her autobiography, *Prelude and Fugue*, published in 1964, is an enchantingly diffident account of a remarkable life.   C.H.

Evans, Marian. See ELIOT, GEORGE.

Ewing, Juliana (Horatia) (1841–85), children's author, born at Ecclesfield, Yorkshire. Her father was a clergyman and her mother, Mrs Gatty, a children's author. From an early age she entertained her eight siblings with stories. She published her first writings in Charlotte YONGE's *The Monthly Packet* and in Mrs Gatty's periodical *Aunt Judy's Magazine*. In 1867 she married Major Alexander Ewing, a noted hymn-writer, and accompanied him on his postings abroad whenever her health allowed. Although often gravely ill she was invariably cheerful, writing easily and with great enjoyment. *Mrs Overtheway's Remembrances*, 1869, *A Flat Iron for a Farthing*, 1872, and *Jan of the Windmill*, 1876, were followed by many others. Two of them, *Jackanapes*, 1884, and *The Story of a Short Life*, 1885, possibly appealed more to adults than to children.

Juliana Ewing had a deep love for the countryside; most of her characters are robust country children, high-spirited but with occasional lapses into naughtiness. Her tales usually have a moral but she always weaves this cunningly into the plot and leavens it with humour.

See also Gillian Avery, *Nineteenth Century Children*, 1965.

    P.L.

F

'Fair Maid of Kent'. See JOAN OF KENT.

Fairbrother, Sydney (1872–1941), actress. She was educated at Blackpool and Bonn. Her first appearance was a 'walking-on' part at the Haymarket in 1889. She was with the Kendals in America for two years and her subsequent varied career included a music-hall sketch, 'A Sister to Assist Her', with the elder Fred Emney (1912–14), Mahbubah in *Chu-Chin-Chow* (1916–20), Shakespearean roles such as Maria in *Twelfth Night*, and appearances in *Candida* and *The Ghost Train*. She was a fine character actress in later years; among her best parts was Mrs Badger in *The Young Person in Pink*. In 1915 she began a career in films.

B.H.C.

Fairfield, Cicily Isabel. See WEST, REBECCA.

Faithfull, Emily (1835–95), printer, editor and promoter of women's employment. The daughter of a clergyman, Emily Faithfull was born at Headley Rectory, Surrey. Her childhood was spent in the country but after attending a school in Kensington she became 'a thorough Londoner at heart'. Involvement with the 'Ladies of Langham Place' led her to join the founding committee of the Society for Promoting the Employment of Women in 1859. Having tried compositing herself, and encouraged by Bessie Rayner PARKES, she opened the Victoria Press at 9 Great Coram Street in March 1860 in order to give employment to women. She reported to the National Association for the Promotion of Social Science (NAPSS) in 1860 that nineteen female compositors were employed by the press, which was printing a weekly newspaper, the *Transactions* of the NAPSS, *The Law Magazine*, and *The Englishwoman's Journal*. The following year she published *The Victoria Regia* as 'a choice specimen of the skill attained by my compositors' and in June 1862 she was appointed 'Printer and Publisher in Ordinary to Her Majesty'. In 1863 she founded *The Victoria Magazine* (which she edited until 1880) and in 1865 *Women and Work*, a penny weekly. She also ran the Victoria Discussion Society, which gave women opportunities to speak for themselves. Withdrawing from the press in 1867 but keeping the imprint, she set up editorial offices in Princes Street, later moving to Praed Street. A moving force in founding the Women's Printing Society with Emma PATERSON, she was also manager of the Industrial and Educational Bureau for Women. She founded the Church and Stage Guild with Genevieve Ward and Mrs KENDAL in 1879, and in 1881 the International Musical, Dramatic and Literary Association. A lecture tour of North America in 1872–73 was followed by two more in 1877 and 1882–83, recounted in *Three Visits to America* (1884), where she draws comparisons between the movements for women's work in America and England. She was not one of the leaders of the women's movement as such; but her response was practical and lifelong to the need to create opportunities for women. Recognition of her work was shown by a gift of £100 from the Royal Bounty in 1886 and a Civil List Pension of £50 from 1889.

Her other writings include *On Some of the Drawbacks Connected with the Present Employment of Women* (1862), and *Change upon Change: A love story* (1868).

See also W. E. Fredeman, *Emily Faithfull and the Victoria Press*, 1973.

C.B.

Falconer, Lanoe. See HAWKER, MARY ELIZABETH.

Falkland, Viscountess. See CARY, ELIZABETH, VISCOUNTESS FALKLAND.

Fane, Violet. See CURRIE, MARY (MONTGOMERIE LAMB), LADY.

Fanshawe, Lady Ann (1625–80), author of memoirs, was the fourth child and elder daughter of Sir John Harrison of Balls, Hertfordshire. She described herself in her youth as what 'graver people call a hoyting girl', but changed completely at the age of fifteen, when her mother died and, at her father's request, she undertook the management of the house and family.

In 1643, in the middle of the Civil War, she accompanied her Royalist father (who had been deprived of his property by the Parliamentarians), to join the King at Oxford. There she met her equally impoverished second cousin, Sir Richard Fanshawe, a thirty-five-year-old diplomat, scholar, and poet, whom she married in May 1644, shortly before his appointment as Secretary for War to the Prince

149

of Wales. Throughout the twenty-three years of their married life, during which she bore fourteen children (only five survived their mother), she remained passionately devoted to her husband. During the Civil War and Interregnum she willingly suffered deprivation and discomfort in order to accompany him on the travels he undertook in the service of the Stuarts, criss-crossing the Channel frequently, often under perilous conditions, to join him or to raise money in England and carry it abroad. She had frequent opportunities to demonstrate her spirit and devotion; for example, in 1651, when her husband was imprisoned in Whitehall, she stood beneath his window daily in order to speak to him, and eventually procured his release on medical grounds. After the Restoration, Sir Richard continued to serve Charles II as a diplomat, and his wife dutifully accompanied him to Portugal and Spain. Heartbroken by his death in 1666, Lady Fanshawe thereafter devoted herself to the welfare of her children, but never fully recovered from her loss.

In 1676 she wrote her memoirs for her surviving son, Richard, aged eleven, to instruct the boy in the achievements of his forebears and particularly of his father. *The Memoirs of Ann, Lady Fanshawe* are the factually recorded and largely unemotional account of an eventful family career and a remarkably devoted wife and mother. The most recent edition is contained in *The Memoirs of Anne, Lady Halkett, and Ann, Lady Fanshawe* (1979), edited by John Loftis.   T.J.M.

Fawaz, Florence. See AUSTRAL, FLORENCE.

Fawcett, Millicent Garrett (1847–1929), leader of the women's suffrage movement. She was the seventh of the ten children of an East Anglian merchant and shipowner, and was educated at a school in Blackheath run by Miss Louisa Browning, an aunt of the poet. Hers was a closely-knit family, and she was much influenced by her older sister Elizabeth (later Mrs Garrett ANDERSON) and her sister's friend Emily DAVIES. In 1865 she met Henry Fawcett (1833–84), a blind Cambridge professor and Liberal MP for Brighton, and married him in 1867. It was a successful match: he gave her the benefit of his political experience; she acted for a time as his secretary and mixed easily with his political and academic friends, including John Stuart Mill, whose ideas she much admired. Their daughter Philippa, born in

1868, after being placed 'above senior wrangler' in the Cambridge Mathematics Tripos in 1890, went on to become an eminent educationist.

In 1867 Mrs Fawcett joined the first women's suffrage committee and the following year made her first political speech. Encouraged by her husband, she contributed articles to *Macmillan's*, wrote *Political Economy for Beginners* (1870), a lucid exposition of the philosophical individualism of Mill, and published a novel-cum-temperance-tract, *Janet Doncaster* (1875). She was active in university reform and called for married women's property rights. But it was her work for the suffrage movement that made the greatest claim on her time and talents. During a long and often discouraging campaign she brought to the struggle a determined optimism, political acuteness, and administrative skill which were invaluable.

An admirer of Josephine BUTLER, she also joined the moral reform movement after the publication of W. T. Stead's *The Maiden Tribute of Modern Babylon* in 1885 and worked actively for the National Vigilance Association. Moral reform and the suffrage cause were closely associated, and Millicent Fawcett, like many others, hoped that votes for women would work to eliminate venal and immoral relations between the sexes. In her pamphlet *Home and Politics* (1898) she advocated the extension of the franchise in the hope that it would lead to the 'womanly and domestic side of things' counting for more in public life.

In most matters, Millicent Fawcett was conservative and ultra-patriotic. She joined the Liberal Unionists in 1887 and spoke out against Gladstone's Home Rule policy (some small revenge, perhaps, for his having frustrated her hopes for women's suffrage). In 1901 she was sent to South Africa as the head of a commission of women looking into conditions in the concentration camps.

Back in England, she continued her work for female suffrage as president of the National Union of Women's Suffrage Societies (1897–1918). While not unsympathetic towards the suffragettes in their early days, she was temperamentally unsuited to militancy and thought the Pankhursts too autocratic. During the First World War she suspended her suffrage activities and supported the war effort. After the Act of 1918, which enfranchised women over thirty, she continued to take a prominent part in the campaign to secure a full equal franchise. In the 1920s she travelled widely, visiting Palestine four times. She was made DBE in 1925. She lived to see the passing of the Representation of the People Act of 1928, which conceded the vote to women on the same terms as men.

Millicent Fawcett's writings include *Essays and Lectures*, with Henry Fawcett, 1872; *The Women's Victory—and after: Personal Reminiscences, 1911–1918*, 1920; and *What I Remember*, 1924.

See also R. Strachey, *Millicent Garrett Fawcett*, 1931; C. Rover, *Women's Suffrage and Party Politics in Britain, 1866–1914*, 1967.

F.K.P.

Farjeon, Eleanor (1881–1965), writer, the daughter of a novelist. She had no formal schooling but grew up among theatrical and literary people and read ceaselessly in her father's huge library. At the age of seven she typed her first stories.

Impoverished by her father's death in 1903, Eleanor Farjeon began to write professionally, contributing a daily topical verse to *The Daily Herald* for thirteen years and a weekly poem for *Time and Tide*. She also published some novels. Her friendship with the poet Edward Thomas guided and strengthened her; the pain she suffered when he died may be said to have matured her.

She is now remembered for her children's books, though she insisted that she never wrote a book specifically for children. Her first best-seller, *Martin Pippin in the Apple Orchard* (1921), a perennial favourite with children, was in fact written to divert a soldier friend in the trenches.

All her work is joyous and full of fun and wonder. Among her most enduring books are *A Nursery in the Nineties*, 1935, *Silver Sand and Snow*, 1951, *The Children's Bells*, 1957, and *The Little Bookroom*, 1955, which won the Carnegie medal. Other honours were the Hans Andersen medal and the American Regina medal. With her brother Herbert she wrote operettas and plays, including *The Glass Slipper* (1944) and *The Silver Curlew* (1949). She also published her *Memoirs*, 1958.

See also D. Blakelock, *Eleanor*, 1966.　P.L.

Farren, Elizabeth (1759?–1829), actress. She began her career as a child with provincial strolling players. She mader her London début at the Haymarket in 1777, and in 1778 appeared at Drury Lane.

Playing between these two theatres, Elizabeth Farren became one of the leading exponents of refined comedy parts, taking over from Mrs ABINGTON on the latter's retirement. She played Angelica, Hermione, Olivia, Lydia Languish, Millament and many other parts. Her final appearance was in 1797 as Lady Teazle.

Her private reputation had always been excellent, and on her retirement from the stage she married Edward, Lord Derby, whose wife had recently died. Hazlitt commended her 'fine-lady airs and graces'. It was said that on her retirement comedy degenerated into farce. She was painted by Lawrence, Zoffany, Wheatley and Cosway, and sculpted by Anne DAMER.

See also Petronius Arbiter, *Memoirs of the Present Countess of Derby*, 1797.　C.H.

Farren, Nellie (1848–1904), actress. Born at Liverpool, Ellen Farren was the daughter of an actor and first appeared in 1853 at Exeter as the child Duke of York in *Richard III*. At nine she was at the Old Victoria Theatre in London, singing 'I'm ninety-five'. She excelled in comedy, as Lydia Languish in Sheridan's *The Rivals* and Maria in *Twelfth Night*, and with Edward Terry, Kate VAUGHAN, and Edward Royce formed a famous burlesque quartet. In 1868 she appeared in *On the Cards* for the opening of the Gaiety Theatre, where she remained a favourite until her last regular appearance in 1891. She became the leading 'principal boy' of her time, specializing in such parts as Sam Weller and Smike. In 1867 she married Robert Soutar, an actor and stage manager at the Gaiety. Having lost her savings in a management venture, she was provided for by a benefit performance in 1899.

B.H.C.

Faucit, Helen, stage-name of Helena Saville (1820–98), actress. She was the daughter of an actress. Her first appearance was at Covent Garden in 1836, after which she played in Shakespeare with Macready, as Desdemona, Cordelia, Portia, Lady Macbeth and Rosalind. She was at the Haymarket (1840) and Drury Lane (1842), and in 1851 married Theodore Martin, poet, essayist and translator, who, fascinated by her acting, adapted *King René's Daughter* for her from the Danish (1849).

Fell, Margaret

Martin's life of the Prince Consort (1875–80), written at Queen Victoria's request, brought the couple the Queen's friendship and Martin a knighthood. Lady Martin retired in 1865, but made brief appearances for charity. Of great beauty and charm, she did her best work, apart from Shakespeare, in new verse drama, some of which was specially written for her. She appeared in Browning's *Strafford* (1837) and *A Blot in the 'Scutcheon* (1843) and in plays by Bulwer Lytton. She wrote *On Some of the Female Characters of Shakespeare* (1885).   B.H.C.

Fell, Margaret (1614–1702), Quaker organizer, wife of George Fox. She was the daughter of John Askew, gentleman, of Marsh Grange, Dalton-in-Furness, Lancashire. She married Thomas Fell of Swarthmore Hall near Ulverston in 1632 and bore him nine children. Under her influence Swarthmore Hall became known as a centre of piety in the locality, and it was this which drew the young George Fox there in 1652. Fox, the founder of the Society of Friends (Quakers), convinced her of his teachings, but not her husband; nonetheless, from 1652 Swarthmore Hall became the centre of early Quaker missionary activity. During the 1650s Margaret Fell maintained a steady personal correspondence with Quaker missionaries and, along with Thomas Willan and George Taylor, organized the vital 'Kendal Fund' between 1654 and 1657. This fund helped provide for the expenses of the early movement, including the cost of travel, books, and the relief of prisoners. She also campaigned for the release of Quaker prisoners by writing personally to Oliver Cromwell, the Lord Protector.

In 1658 Thomas Fell died, and in 1660 Margaret Fell travelled to London, where she obtained an audience with Charles II to plead for the release of George Fox. The King ordered that Fox be tried in London, where she stayed until he was released. In 1663 she was summoned before the magistrates at Ulverston for allowing illegal Quaker meetings at her home, and in the following year was imprisoned. She remained in prison for twenty months and was formally released only in 1668. In 1669 she married George Fox at Bristol, and the following year was re-arrested and imprisoned until April 1671. From the mid-1670s until 1689 she spent most of her time at Swarthmore, and was occasionally

fined for allowing Quaker meetings to be held there. In 1697 she addressed a letter to William III, thanking him for the protection he had given the Quakers. Towards the end of her life she criticized the tendency of younger Quakers to make the wearing of formal 'Quaker' dress a mark of orthodoxy.

Margaret Fell's importance to the Quaker movement rested primarily on her organizational skill, especially in the first twenty years of the Society's history. She is often regarded as the 'mother' of the movement, and it would seem that her 'maternal' qualities were held in high regard by the early Quakers. She did much to spread Quaker influence both by deed and word; she wrote upwards of twenty-eight published works between 1655 and 1694, some of which were translated into Dutch and Hebrew. In her *Women's Speaking Justified, Proved and Allowed by the Scriptures* (1666) she defended women's right to preach publicly, and to take a prominent role in religious affairs in general; and indeed her entire career embodies the wide scope allowed women within the Quaker movement.

See also *A Brief Collection of Remarkable Passages and Occurrences relating to ... Margaret Fell ... together with Sundry of Her Epistles, Books, and Christian testimonies to Friends and Others*, 1710; M. Ross, *Margaret Fell, Mother of Quakerism*, 1949.
                                    T.O'M.

Fell, Sheila Mary (1931–79), painter, born at Aspatria, Cumbria, the only child of a miner. She was educated at Thomlinson Grammar School, Wigton, Carlisle School of Art, and St Martin's School of Art, London.

At her first London one-woman exhibition in 1955, the painter L. S. Lowry immediately recognized her gifts and bought twenty paintings. She exhibited annually in many British towns and sold her wild landscapes to galleries throughout the world. She received the Boise travelling scholarship (1958) and visited France, Italy and Greece. She was one of the relatively few women to be elected a Royal Academician (1974) and was classed among the best of contemporary British artists.

Most of her paintings represent aspects of her native Cumbria: the different activities that take place on the land, and the effect of changing light in relation to the earth. She said that she did not think of herself as a woman artist: 'Artists are either good or bad. Though I suppose it may be more difficult for a woman, having to do the cleaning and cooking as well as working.'

Her work hangs in the Tate and in many provincial galleries.

See also C. Parry-Crooke (ed.), *Contemporary British Artists*, 1979.   P.L.

Fenner, Mary (*fl.* 1734–57), printer and publisher. After William Fenner, who pioneered the stereotyping process in Britain, died in 1734, his widow began a determined effort to carry on the business. After four years in Cambridge during which she is only known to have published one work, she abandoned the lease of her premises after a dispute with the landlord. She then set up business at the Turk's Head in Gracechurch Street. Her last work was published in 1757.

See also H. R. Plomer, G. H. Bushnell, E. R. McC. Dix, *A Dictionary of the Booksellers and Printers who were at work in England, Scotland and Ireland from 1726 to 1775*, 1932.
                                          T.H.

Fenton, Lavinia (1708–60), actress and ballad-opera singer. Being illegitimate, Lavinia Fenton took the name of her step-father, a coffee-house keeper in Charing Cross. She early demonstrated her pretty voice and musical ear. Her début was at the Haymarket in 1726, where she had an instant success. As a result she was engaged by John Rich to perform at Lincoln's Inn Fields Theatre. It was there, in 1728, that she played the part with which she is always associated, Polly Peachum, in the first production of *The Beggar's Opera*.

Lavinia Fenton became the fashion of the day and the play had an unprecedented run. She had many admirers, but it was the Duke of Bolton who ran off with her after the last performance of the season. She abandoned the stage to become full-time mistress and later wife of the Duke. After her retirement she led a discreet life and was admired for her accomplishments, sense and good taste. Hogarth painted many versions of *The Beggar's Opera*. and made her the subject of one of his finest portraits.

See also P. H. Highfill, K. A. Burnim, E. A. Langhans, *A Biographical Dictionary of Actors, Actresses, Musicians, Dancers, Managers and Other Stage Personnel in London, 1660–1800*, vol. 5, 1978.   C.H.

Fenwick, Ethel Gordon (1857–1947), nursing reformer. The younger daughter of a farmer, she was born in Morayshire and educated privately. She trained as a nurse at the Children's Hospital, Nottingham (1878), and the Royal Infirmary, Manchester (1879), before going as a sister to the London Hospital (1879–81). She advanced rapidly to become matron and superintendent of nursing at St Bartholomew's Hospital, London, at the age of twenty-four, resigning in 1887 to marry a doctor, Bedford Fenwick, by whom she had one son.

From this time onwards Ethel Fenwick devoted her life to advancing the status of British nursing. The British Nurses' Association, which she founded in 1887, became in 1893 the first women's professional body to receive a royal charter. She also formed the Matron's Council of Great Britain and the National Council of Nurses.

For a quarter of a century much of her energy was devoted to the struggle to establish the state registration of nurses, a campaign which, despite powerful opposition (including that of Florence Nightingale), was eventually successful in 1919. She became a member of the first General Nursing Council. Her influence was also felt outside Britain through her formation of the International Council of Nursing. As editor of the *Nursing Mirror* she remained a force in the profession almost until her death.

Gifted with high intelligence, she was a formidable leader to whose efforts nursing owes much of its present status.   K.W.

Ferrier, Kathleen (1912–53), perhaps the best-loved British singer of the twentieth century. She was the daughter of a schoolmaster. As a schoolgirl she learned the piano, passing examinations and winning Festival prizes, but in the school choir she was told to sing softly. In 1928, when she was sixteen, she entered a *Daily Express* National Piano Competition. She won the prize in her local section but was not among the six winners, who included Cyril Smith and Phyllis Sellick. She continued piano lessons, gaining LRAM and ARCM diplomas, and in 1930 won the piano Gold Medal at the Liverpool Festival. She even broadcast as a pianist, and she was in demand as an accompanist at celebrity concerts. When she was taking part in the Carlisle Festival, her husband bet her a shilling that she dared not enter a singing contest. She won both a piano competition and the Silver Rose Bowl for the best

Field, Mary

singer of the festival. Maurice Jacobson, adjudicating, said her voice was one of the finest he had heard, and advised her to make singing her career. She was already twenty-five, but at least had a background of musical training. Realizing that she still had much to learn, in 1943 she started lessons with Roy Henderson. A few months later she sang *Messiah* and began her long association with the Bach Choir; she is the solo contralto on their recordings of *The St Matthew Passion* and *The Ascension Cantata*. From this time on her career developed at an astonishing speed. From Bach and Handel she turned to Elgar, making *The Dream of Gerontius* almost her own property. Among a number of works written specially for her was Arthur Bliss's *The Enchantress*. The BBC somehow managed to reject her at an audition for the 1944 Proms, but by 1945 her reputation stood so high that she had to be included, and she had a tremendous success. After the war she toured the USA and Europe, but in 1951 she had to undergo the first operation for the cancer that was eventually to kill her. In February 1953 Kathleen Ferrier, newly announced a CBE, was singing in *Orfeo* at Covent Garden; during the second performance her leg gave way and she sang to the end in great pain. This was her last professional appearance.

Kathleen Ferrier's career was a meteoric one: she died after a mere ten years as a famous artist. Yet over twenty-five years after her death one could still hear a professional musician remark that 'Nobody has ever moved me as Ferrier did.' Not only was the quality of her voice remarkable but she was strikingly good-looking, and her personality was a rare one; as an international celebrity she remained an unspoilt, down-to-earth Lancashire girl. Nevertheless this fabulous career was built on a solid foundation of training as a pianist and an all-round musician, and her rare gifts were complemented by a great capacity for hard work.

See also W. Ferrier, *Kathleen Ferrier: Her Life*, 1955.   R.G.

Field, (Agnes) Mary (1896–1968), maker of children's films and authority on film education. A solicitor's daughter, she was educated at Surbiton, at Bedford College, and at the Institute for Historical Research, London University.

After a spell in teaching, Mary Field joined British Instructional Films, eventually directing educational and documentary features. She moved to British Independent Producers in 1933, then (1934) joined G. B. Instructional Ltd. In 1944 she inaugurated the Children's Entertainment Films Division for the J. Arthur Rank Organization.

With Percy Smith, Mary Field made the award-winning *Secrets of Nature* series and *The Secrets of Life*. She joined the British Board of Film Censors in 1955, was made a Fellow of the Royal Photographic Society (1955) and a Fellow of the British Film Academy (1957), and became Chairman of the International Centre of Films for Children, Brussels. She also became children's programme consultant for ATV and ABC Television in 1955. She retired in 1963 as a recognized world authority on film education.
                                    A.D.

Fielding, Sarah (1710–68), novelist, born at East Stour, Dorset. She was the third sister of the classic novelist Henry Fielding. After the remarriage of her father in 1719 she was sent to boarding school in Salisbury and placed under the care of her maternal grandmother, Lady Sarah Gould. Although details of her education are lacking, she was clearly an excellent student, capable of reading French criticism, knowledgeable about classical poetry, and possessed of enough Greek to translate Xenophon's *Memorabilia* and *Apology*. By the 1740s Sarah Fielding was living in London, where she corresponded with the novelist Samuel Richardson and soon joined his circle at his country house at North End, Hammersmith. Despite Henry Fielding's characterization of her in the Preface to her first novel, *David Simple*, as 'unacquainted with the World', she knew and was respected by many London literary figures including Jospeh Warton, Edward Young and Warburton. She began to publish *The Adventures of David Simple in Search of a Faithful Friend* in 1744; Henry Fielding not only supplied a preface but also aided her in extensive revisions and wrote Letters XL-XLVI of this epistolary novel. The final volume appeared in 1753. After her brother's death in 1754 she settled near Bath under the patronage of the Ralph Allen so enthusiastically praised in *Tom Jones*. Like her brother, Sarah Fielding spent her life with the threat of indigence hanging over her, and it was probably that which initially drove her to write.

Sarah Fielding's works develop along the general lines indicated by innovations in the novel form between 1740 and 1760. Both *David Simple* and her most popular novel, *The Governess* (1749), typify 'Augustan' fiction in their overt didacticism and emphasis on hierarchical order. The theme at the heart of these novels, however—that sympathetic emotion rather than intellectual detachment is the proper basis for the ideal benevolent community—anticipates the dominance of the sentimental narrative from 1760 to 1780. Sarah Fielding's final novel, *Ophelia* (1760), conforms more completely to this genre than any of the others. Reworking themes and situations familiar from early eighteenth-century writers like Elizabeth Rowe and Penelope Aubin, she creates in the character of Ophelia a new kind of heroine. Active intelligence and imagination are here accorded a positive value unusual in an age which typically linked female self-determination with the sexually promiscuous woman or the virago.

Although Sarah Fielding did not write with the skill, vigour, and breadth of her brother, his greater reputation has tended to obscure her considerable achievement. Her carefully structured novels, with their acute moral analyses, have a secure place in the minor literature of her time. Her other works include *The Lives of Cleopatra and Octavia* (1757), and *The History of the Countess of Dellwyn* (1759).

See also W. J. Cross, *The History of Henry Fielding*, 1918; A. L. Barbauld (ed.), *The Correspondence of Samuel Richardson*, 1804.

A.L.

Fields, Gracie, stage-name of Grace Stansfield (1898–1979), stage and film entertainer, and one of the last great stars in the English music-hall tradition. She was the daughter of an engineer in Rochdale, Lancashire, where for a time she worked in a cotton mill and as a draper's assistant. Encouraged by her mother, she appeared in amateur shows from the age of eight and by the time she was fifteen was being paid 1s. a week for a solo turn with a juvenile company. Turning professional, she joined a touring revue, where she met her first husband, Archie Pitt, who wrote a successful revue, *It's a Bargain*, for her. Her talent for mimicry and high-spirited clowning, allied with a fine singing voice, steadily gained her a reputation, although it was not until 1923, when, after five years touring, the revue

Mr Tower of London came to the Alhambra, that she was seen in the West End. She became an overnight star.

The film *Sally* (1931) opened the most successful decade of her career. During the Depression and its aftermath, her unaffected warmth, comic gifts, and ability to strike a serious, often sentimental note made 'Our Gracie' something of a national heroine. She was given the freedom of Rochdale in 1937 and created CBE in 1938. At the outbreak of the Second World War, she gave troop concerts in France.

In 1940, however, public opinion swung against her when, after divorcing Pitt, she left for the United States with her second husband, Monty Banks, a film director of Italian descent who, in June 1940 with Italy's entry into the war, had been declared an undesirable alien. She was coolly received on wartime appearances from 1941 and, despite raising some £1,500,000 for the war effort in the USA, remained out of public favour for a number of years. On Banks's death in 1950, she retired to Capri, making the island her home from then on and in 1952 marrying her third husband.

As the resentments of the war years were forgotten, Gracie Fields returned to England for occasional concerts and was warmly greeted at the Royal Command Performances of 1957, 1964 and 1978; the last, her tenth appearance, came exactly fifty years after her first. She wrote an autobiography, *Sing as We Go* (1960), and in 1979 was created DBE.

K.W.

Fiennes, Celia (1662–1741), travel writer, was the daughter of Colonel Nathaniel Fiennes, and the granddaughter of the Parliamentarian leader Viscount Saye and Seale. Celia Fiennes' own Nonconformist, strong Whiggish views, and enthusiasm for William III all receive expression in the extraordinary journal of her travels. It also reflects her Puritan sobriety and utilitarian values, which helped to make her such a meticulous and down-to-earth observer of contemporary England.

Celia Fiennes' early journeys were made from the family manor house near Salisbury, where she lived until her mother's death in 1691; she probably then went to live in London near her sister Mary, who had married a businessman. In 1697 Celia Fiennes made her first great 'Northern Journey', in which she covered more than six hundred miles in six weeks,

155

followed by an even more remarkable 'Journey to Newcastle and to Cornwall' in 1698. Most of her journal was apparently written in 1701, and in her recorded journeys alone, which extended beyond the year 1703, she visited every county in England and crossed over briefly into Scotland and Wales.

Celia Fiennes was an enthusiastic and indefatigable traveller in an age when it was still almost unknown for anyone to go far without some practical end in view. Her lengthy and difficult journeys seem all the more remarkable for having been made by a woman. She was also an extraordinarily keen and impartial observer, so that her journal, first published in 1888, provides the first comprehensive survey of England since Elizabeth's reign. Very much in tune with the society in which she lived, with its rapidly expanding commerce and industry, she displayed a very 'masculine' interest in the national economy, making scrupulous notes on urban life, industry and communications. But the journal also gains much from having been written by a woman, for Celia Fiennes was more interested than most men would have been in such things as the manufacture of cheese and soap and the preparation of Cornish apple pie with custard and clotted cream.

A pioneer female traveller and author, Celia Fiennes probably knew more and certainly wrote more about what she had seen at first-hand in her travels throughout England in the late seventeenth and early eighteenth centuries than any other man or woman of her time, and her journals have proved to be not only a remarkable record of a woman's achievements but a source of inestimable value to historians. The most recent edition of her work is Christopher Morris's *The Journals of Celia Fiennes*, 1947.

See also M. Reynolds, *The Learned Lady in England, 1650-1760*, 1920.   T.J.M.

Finch, Anne, Countess of Winchilsea (1660-1720), poet, daughter of Sir William Kingsmill and wife of Heneage Finch, Earl of Winchilsea. She numbered Pope and Rowe among her literary friends. Her long poem *The Spleen* was published in 1701 and was highly regarded by contemporaries. A collected edition of her poems appeared in 1713. She was neglected for some time, and was rediscovered by Wordsworth, who pointed out her use of new images of 'external nature'.

Wordsworth considered that apart from her *Nocturnal Reverie* and a few lines of Pope, no poetry between Milton and Thomson's *Seasons* contained any true representations of the real world.   T.H.

Fisher, Mary (1623–98), Quaker missionary. She came from Yorkshire and was converted by George Fox in 1652. In the same year she was imprisoned in York for disturbing a congregation, and served sixteen months. While in prison she was the joint author of *False Prophets and False Teachers described* (1652). In 1654, after her release, she travelled with another Quaker, Elizabeth Williams, to Cambridge, where they preached in public; they were stoned by the scholars of Sidney Sussex College and whipped by the authorities. Soon afterwards Mary Fisher spent nine more months in York Castle for preaching at Pontefract, and she was imprisoned again in Buckinghamshire in 1655 for a similar offence.

Later in 1655 she travelled with Anne Austin to the West Indies and New England; they were among the first Quakers to do so. At Boston they had one hundred books confiscated and were arrested and examined as suspected witches. In 1660 Mary Fisher set out on a still more remarkable journey, determined to carry the Quaker message to the Ottoman Sultan, Muhammad IV; travelling mainly on foot, she finally obtained an interview with him at Adrianople. Returning to England, she married another Quaker, William Bayly, a mariner, in 1662. He died in 1675, and Mary published a *Testimony* to him in his collected *Works* (1676). She married John Cross in 1678, lived in London for a period, and eventually went to America. She appears to have been widowed again and was living in Charleston, Carolina, in 1697. She was a determined woman who endured much physical hardship while helping to establish the Quaker movement in England and America through her dangerous and adventurous missions.

See also M. R. Brailsford, *Quaker Women 1650–1690*, 1915.   T.O'M.

Fitton, Mary (1578–?), maid of honour to Queen Elizabeth from 1595 and perhaps the 'Dark Lady' of Shakespeare's sonnets. She became the mistress of William Herbert, Earl of Pembroke, who has often been suggested as the 'Mr W. H.' to whom the sonnets are dedicated. In 1601 Mary Fitton bore Herbert a son; there was a scandal during which Herbert declared his disinclination to marry and, after a brief imprisonment, discreetly set out on European travels. Mary Fitton's subsequent history is obscure, but she certainly had one or more husbands. The theory that she was the Dark Lady in a love triangle with Herbert and Shakespeare, seemingly described in the sonnets, received a check when a presumed portrait of her indicated that she was—fair.

N.H.

Fitzhenry, Elizabeth (d. 1790), actress. Born Elizabeth Flanagan in Dublin, the daughter of a tavern-keeper, she was married early to a sea captain, John Gregory. On the deaths of both her husband and her father, she turned to the stage for a living.

After some success in Dublin she appeared at Covent Garden in 1754 as Hermione in *The Distrest Mother*, to great applause. Arthur Murphy praised her in *The Gray's Inn Journal* (1754): 'Her Person being tall and graceful; her Features well-disposed . . . and her Voice clear, full and harmonious'. She was not, however, re-engaged, possibly because of her Irish accent, and so returned to Smock Alley, Dublin, for two seasons during 1754–56, playing Hermione, Zara and Volumnia. She appeared at Covent Garden in early 1757 and, later in the year, having married a lawyer, Edward Fitzhenry, in the summer, returned to Smock Alley where she was billed as Mrs Fitzhenry. During the 1760s she played both in London and Dublin, limiting herself to strong, matronly roles. Garrick employed her as a curb to the vexatious Mrs YATES, but she was increasingly criticized for her harshness of voice and violence of action. She finally returned to Ireland in 1767, appearing there until her retirement in 1774 on a legacy from her husband, who had died in 1772.

See also P. H. Highfill, K. A. Burnim and E. A. Langhans, *A Biographical Dictionary of Actors, Actresses, Musicians, Dancers, Managers and Other Stage Personnel in London, 1660–1800*, vol. 5, 1978; B. Victor, *History of the Theatres of London and Dublin*, 1761.

C.H.

Fitzherbert, Maria Anne (1756–1837), wife of George, Prince of Wales, later King George IV. She was born at Tong Castle, Shropshire, the elder daughter of Walter Smythe of Brambridge, Hampshire, a member of an old Catholic family. She was educated at an Ursuline convent in Paris, and in 1775 she married Edward Weld of Lulworth Castle, Dorset, who died later that year. Three years later she married Thomas Fitzherbert of Swynnerton Hall, Staffordshire, who died in 1781. In 1784 she met the Prince of Wales, who immediately fell in love with her; to escape his insistent addresses, having refused to become his mistress, she fled to the Continent. However, on 15 December 1785 they were married secretly in London. Under the Royal Marriage Act the ceremony was invalid, the Prince being under twenty-five and not possessing the King's consent; under the Act of Settlement, the Prince could have forfeited his right to the throne because she was a Catholic. Throughout her life, therefore, the marriage remained a closely guarded secret, known only to a handful of people, and Mrs Fitzherbert always maintained her own separate residences, both in London and Brighton.

In June 1794 the Prince, having come under the spell of Lady Jersey, broke off their relationship; the following April he married Princess CAROLINE of Brunswick. Although he soon sought a reconciliation, it was only after receiving the approval of Pope Pius VII that Mrs Fitzherbert agreed to return to him in June 1800. From 1807 the Prince was increasingly attached to Lady Hertford, and in June 1811 he and Mrs Fitzherbert separated for the last time. Thereafter she lived in retirement, dying at Brighton.

Mrs Fitzherbert was perhaps the only woman to whom the Prince was sincerely attached; he died and was buried with her miniature round his neck. Her discretion and dignity won her the respect and affection of the entire royal family; in 1830 she declined William IV's proposal to make her a duchess. Whether she had any children by the Prince of Wales will never be known.

The definitive works on Mrs Fitzherbert are two books by Sir Shane Leslie, *Mrs Fitzherbert: a Life*, 1939, and *The Letters of Mrs Fitzherbert*, 1940.

See also A. Leslie, *Mrs Fitzherbert*, 1960.

M.J.S.

Fitzroy, Mary (?–1557), daughter of Thomas Howard, third Duke of Norfolk, by Elizabeth Stafford, daughter of the Duke of Buckingham. In 1533 Mary married Henry Fitzroy, Duke of Richmond, Henry VIII's sole bastard son; the lack of a legitimate male heir made him a serious candidate for the succession. Because they were very young the couple lived apart, and when Fitzroy died in 1536 Mary had difficulty in claiming her jointure from the King since the marriage had not been consummated. In 1546 Norfolk offered her in marriage to Sir Thomas Seymour, one of several proposed alliances which never came about between the two great families which vied with each other during the reigns of Henry VIII and Edward VI.

Mary was of some political importance in 1546 when she gave damning evidence against her brother Henry, Earl of Surrey, who was accused of treason; apparently she resented his suggestion that she should become the King's mistress. However, she defended her father against accusations of treason, and later laboured for his release from prison.

After Surrey's execution she was given charge of his children, receiving an annuity from the crown of £100 towards their upbringing in 1552 and employing the martyrologist John Foxe as their tutor.

See also J. S. Brewer, *Letters and Papers, Foreign and Domestic of Henry VIII . . .*, 1920; G. Brenan and E. P. Statham, *The House of Howard*, 1907.   M.D.

Fletcher, Margaret (1862–1944), founder of the Catholic Women's League. An Anglican clergyman's daughter, Margaret Fletcher was educated by governesses, at Oxford High School for Girls, and at art schools in London and Paris. She believed that women, while essentially home-makers, should have a career; hers was pursued from home, as she cared for her father and four youngest siblings after her mother's death. She taught art in Oxford for nearly twenty years and exhibited her own work at the Royal Academy. In 1897 she joined the Roman Catholic Church, and thereafter was very active on its behalf. In 1906 she founded the Catholic Women's League, of which she was President from 1906 to 1919 and from 1923 to 1926. Previously she had founded *Crucible*, which became its journal; she was its editor for many years. She took part in many national and international conferences. Her autobiography, *O, Call Back Yesterday*, was published in 1939.   J.E.

Flower, Constance, Baroness Battersea (1843–1931), social reformer. Constance de Rothschild had all the advantages of being born into one of the richest and most important families in Europe. She was brought up with her younger sister Annie at the family home, Aston Clinton in Buckinghamshire, where she received an excellent education from her tutors. From her mother she acquired a profound interest in their Jewish faith as well as an interest in philanthropy. At an early age the two sisters taught at their local craft school, and later Constance also taught occasionally at the Jewish Free School in London. There she realized the inadequacy of the existing Jewish literature in English, and with her sister published *The History and Literature of the Israelites* (1870).

In 1877 Constance de Rothschild married Cyril Flower, a prominent Liberal, and threw herself into political affairs, speaking in several election campaigns. At the same time she became involved with the ubiquitous social purity movement of the late nineteenth century. As well as campaigning for temperance and higher moral standards, she was founder-member and Honorary Secretary of the Society for Preventive and Rescue Work. This body established rescue and training homes for Jewish prostitutes, and put Yiddish-speaking agents to work meeting immigrant Jews at London's docks.

In 1888 the Flowers moved to Overstrand in Norfolk and four years later her husband received a peerage. In 1894, after a request from Asquith, the now Lady Battersea undertook prison visiting at Aylesbury. In 1901 she was elected President of the National Union of Women Workers, an organization chiefly concerned with improving the social, moral, and religious position of women. After the death of her husband six years later she devoted herself to philanthropic work, as well as attempting to promote greater understanding between the Christian and Jewish faiths. In the last years of her life the building of the New Cromer Hospital was her chief interest. Her *Reminiscences* (1922) show her to have been a woman of influence and moral quality, a model of public service to other privileged women.

See also L. Cohen, *Lady de Rothschild and Her Daughters*, 1935.   J.G.S.

Flower, Eliza (1803–46), composer. She was born at Harlow, the elder daughter of a radical journalist. Her mother was astonished at the facility with which she learned a new tune when only four years old, and her music teacher, the organist of the village church at

Harlow, was impressed with the music which she composed in her early years. Her first musical publication was *Fourteen Musical Illustrations of the Waverley Novels* (1831), which set to music several of the songs in Sir Walter Scott's romances. This was followed by *Songs of the Seasons*, published in the *Monthly Repository* in 1834, and several other pieces. Among her few political compositions was 'The Gathering of the Unions', sung at a meeting of the Birmingham Political Union in May 1832. Her major work was the arrangement of a hymnbook for the congregation of the South Place Unitarian Chapel, Finsbury, compiled by its minister, W. J. Fox. Of the 150 hymns in the book, published by Fox in *Hymns and Anthems* (1841), she composed music for sixty-three, and arranged and adapted music for several more. Among the hymns which she set to music was the celebrated 'Nearer, My God, to Thee', written by her sister, Sarah Flower ADAMS. She and her sister both sang in the choir at the South Place Chapel.

The young Robert Browning had a boyish love for Eliza Flower, and became a lifelong friend; she inspired his poem 'Pauline'. For the last eleven years of her life she lived with Fox, and although their relationship was platonic, the connection brought a degree of social ostracism upon her.

See also R. Garnett, *The Life of W. J. Fox*, 1910; H. W. Stephenson, *Unitarian Hymn-Writers*, 1931, and *The Author of Nearer, My God, to Thee*, 1922.　　　　　M.J.S.

Fogerty, Elsie (1865–1945), founder and principal of the Central School of Speech Training and Dramatic Art. She was born in Sydenham to Irish parents, her father being an architect and engineer. During her childhood Elsie Fogerty travelled extensively with her parents, absorbing languages easily (she had an extremely retentive memory) and reading avidly, especially history. She was educated privately. She studied drama under Coquelin *aîné* and Delauney at the Paris Conservatoire, then with Hermann Vezin in London.

In 1889 Elsie Fogerty became a lecturer in English and Speech at Crystal Palace School of Art and Literature. For many years she taught in various schools in London and on the south coast, including Roedean (1908–37). She was also tutor in diction at Sir Frank Benson's London School of Acting.

In 1908 she worked out a three-year training course for speech and drama teachers. She thought the natural speaking of verse very important and fought against the artificialities of 'elocution' as it was then taught. At the Oxford Poetry Reading Competitions her students distinguished themselves. Pupils came to her from the United States and the Commonwealth as well as Britain. In 1923 she succeeded in establishing a diploma in dramatic art at London University.

Although short, Elsie Fogerty had a commanding presence and a dynamic personality. She also had great understanding of character and went to enormous trouble to fit her students for their various careers. Her great aim was to improve the standard of speech in all social classes. In 1912 she opened a speech clinic at St Thomas's Hospital and so became one of the first speech therapists. She gave university extension lectures for many years at the Royal Albert Hall and took evening classes for London County Council teachers. From its foundation she served on the British Drama League. In 1934 she was created CBE.

She published several acting editions of Greek plays and Shakespeare as well as books on stammering and speech defects, and translated Coquelin's *Art of the Actor*.　　A.D.

Forbes, Katherine. See WATSON-WATT, DAME KATHERINE (JANE TREFUSIS).

Forbes, Rosita (1890–1967), traveller and author, born at Swinderley, Lincolnshire; her father was a landowner and MP.

After a journey round the world, described in her first book, *Unconducted Wanderers* (1919), she became fascinated by the Islamic world. Disguised as a Muslim, she crossed the Libyan desert to the unexplored oasis of Kufura; *The Secret of the Sahara* (1921) described this expedition. *From Red Sea to Blue Nile* (1925) recounts a trek from Ankara to Afghanistan, and *Forbidden Road* (1937) a journey from Kabul to Samarkand. She also spent much time in India and visited South America, where she made a solo flight of 14,000 miles.

Slight of stature and very pretty, Rosita Forbes proved an intrepid traveller. The Dutch and French Geographical Societies awarded her a medal, as did the Royal Society of Arts. Her other books include (as editor) *Women of All Lands* (1938) and an autobiography, *Appointment in the Sun* (1949).　　P.L.

Forbes-Robertson, Jean (1905–62), actress. Born in London she was the daughter of Sir Johnston Forbes-Robertson, probably the greatest actor of his time, and the American actress Gertrude Elliott. She made her acting début in 1921, appearing with her mother's touring company in Durban. After another Commonwealth tour (1922–24) she appeared in London in *Dancing Mothers* (1925). The following year she was outstanding as Sonya in Chekhov's *Uncle Vanya,* and as Juliet in *Romeo and Juliet.* Slight and boyish, she played Peter Pan between 1927 and 1934, and also Puck and Jim Hawkins (1945). Her curious temperament made her a convincing 'boy who wouldn't grow up'; perhaps because of the difficulty in finding female parts that suited her, she was attracted to *travesti.*

During the Second World War, Jean Forbes-Robertson and her then husband André van Gyseghem toured with their own companies and with the Old Vic. Although successful both in acting and management she brought her career to an abrupt and premature end in 1962. A.D.

Ford, Isabella (Ormiston) (*c.* 1860–1924), social reformer. Isabella Ford was born of prosperous middle-class Quaker stock, the youngest daughter of Robert Lawson Ford, who ran one of the first night-schools in England, for local mill-girls. Meeting the girls gave Isabella and her sisters an insight into social injustice, and at the age of twelve she and a friend, Ellen Crofts (later Mrs Francis Darwin), took an oath 'to improve the state of the world'.

Her first efforts were in the field of female employment. When the tailoresses began to agitate for better conditions in the 1880s, she defied public obloquy by helping them form themselves into a trade union. Then in 1890 she associated herself with mill-girls on strike at Manningham, Bradford, and accompanied them on a march in a snowstorm. She taught herself to endure such physical hardship just as she was later to overcome her platform shyness and become a respected public speaker. The trade union movement acknowledged her efforts by electing her a life member of the Leeds Trades and Labour Council, and she was president of the Tailoresses' Union until it disappeared in an amalgamation.

Isabella Ford was in the forefront of both the Labour movement and the women's suffrage campaign. In 1903 she was elected to the executive of the Independent Labour Union, being an Independent Labour Party (ILP) delegate in that and succeeding years to the annual conference of the Labour Representation Committee (or Labour Party, as it became). In 1903 she was the first woman to speak at such a conference. However, at the 1918 general election she declined an offer to stand as a Labour Party candidate.

After the First World War she visited Germany, and was on the Society of Friends' Relief Committee formed to combat post-war German suffering. She was also, in 1922, a delegate to the International Peace Conference at The Hague.

Born to a life of cultured ease, Isabella Ford refused to take advantage of her position, dedicating herself to social work and the alleviation of distress. She was also an accomplished pianist and, assisted by her sister Bessie, who played the violin, arranged and took part in a series of free concerts in Leeds to bring good music to working people. She was a parish councillor and a member, until her death, of Leeds Juvenile Advisory Committee. Her wide circle of friends included the Labour politician Philip Snowden, the writer Edward Carpenter, and the American poet Walt Whitman. She published three novels: *Miss Blake of Monkshalton,* 1890, *On the Threshold,* 1895, and *Mr Elliott,* 1901, 'a story of factory life'.

See also J. Liddington and J. Norris, *One Hand Tied Behind Us,* 1978. J.L.

Forz, Isabella (1237–93), Dowager Countess of Aumâle, Countess of Devon, and Lady of the Isle of Wight, was the daughter of Baldwin de Redvers, Earl of Devon. She was an able, adventurous and ambitious woman whose great wealth, excessive litigiousness, and masterful personality earned her a formidable reputation. In 1249 she married William Forz, Count of Aumâle and Lord of Holderness, Skipton, and Cockermouth, who died in 1260 leaving her with a family of young children and effective control of his estates. Then, on the death of her brother, Earl Baldwin, in 1262 she became heir to the earldom of Devon and the Isle of Wight.

In the early 1260s the younger Simon de Montfort did his best to secure this young widow and her extensive estates, but she strenuously resisted his advances. Indeed she afterwards asserted that he pursued her so vigorously with horses and arms that she was forced to flee to Wales for a time. In 1267, when Isabella gave refuge to a dangerous pirate on the Isle of Wight, the island was temporarily possessed by the Crown. A few years later, following the death of Isabella's last surviving daughter in 1274, Edward I determined to secure permanent royal possession of this strategically vital island. Initially he met with no success, despite a notably generous offer, but eventually, when Isabella was on her deathbed in 1293, negotiations for the island's sale to the Crown did bear fruit.

See also F. M. Powicke, *King Henry III and the Lord Edward*, 1947.   K.R.D.

Fox, Elizabeth, Baroness Holland (1771–1845), political hostess. She was born in London, the only child of Richard Vassall, a wealthy Jamaican planter. In June 1786 she married Sir Godfrey Webster of Battle Abbey, Sussex, an irascible man more than twice her age. She made her début in Whig society under the guidance of the Duchess of Devonshire, but much of her first marriage was spent travelling in Europe. In January 1794 in Florence she met Henry Fox, third Baron Holland, and it was on the grounds of her adultery with him that her marriage was dissolved by Act of Parliament on 4 July 1797. Two days later, she and Holland were married at Rickmansworth.

Lady Holland ruled with imperious sway over the dining and drawing rooms of their home, Holland House in Kensington, which was not only the social centre of the Whig party, but became the salon of a luminous circle of wits, writers and statesmen. In the words of the diarist Charles Greville, it was 'a house of all Europe'. She was ambitious for her husband, who served as Lord Privy Seal in 1806–07 and was Chancellor of the Duchy of Lancaster almost continuously from 1830 until his death in 1840; but it was apparently because she was suspected of reading his correspondence that Holland was not invited to serve in Lord Goderich's administration in 1827. Her influence reached its height during the 1830s, when she was successful in securing patronage for various friends and associates; but as a divorcee she was never received at court, an exclusion she felt keenly.

She had three children by her first husband and five by Holland, including one born before their marriage. Her writings have been published (edited by the Earl of Ilchester) as *The Journal of Elizabeth, Lady Holland*, 1908, *The Spanish Journal of Elizabeth, Lady Holland*, 1910, and *Elizabeth, Lady Holland, to her Son, 1821–1845*.

See also J. Fyvie, *Notable Dames and Notable Men of the Georgian Era*, 1910; S. Keppel, *The Sovereign Lady*, 1974, and L. Mitchell, *Holland House*, 1980.   M.J.S.

Fox, Dame Evelyn (Emily Marion) (1874–1955), pioneer of the modern provision for the mentally handicapped. Her early education took place at home, which was Fox Hall in County Longford, Ireland; she was a descendant of the famous Whig leader Charles James Fox. Then she attended a high school at Morges in Switzerland before going on to Somerville College, Oxford; like other women of her generation, she became involved in philanthropic activity through the Women's University Settlement.

However, Dame Evelyn Fox's great contribution came with the passing of the Mental Deficiency Act in 1913 and the setting up of the Central Association for Mental Welfare in the same year. She became Honorary Secretary of this voluntary association, and made it a crucially effective agent of improvement in the decades before the organization of the National Health Service in 1946. Under her leadership, the Central Association mobilized public opinion through local associations and battled with local authorities and civil servants to improve facilities for the mentally handicapped and secure proper training for the teachers, medical officers, and social workers involved with them. Evelyn Fox was also the first Secretary of the Child Guidance Council, which ultimately merged with the Central Association for Mental Welfare and the National Council for Mental Hygiene to form the present National Association for Mental Health.   N.H.

Franklin, Lady Jane (1792–1875), social reformer and traveller. A minor heiress, she received a spasmodic education since she accompanied her father on his travels. In 1828 she became the second wife of the explorer Sir John Franklin; they had no children but the marriage was a happy one, and Lady Franklin went with her husband on his postings to the Mediterranean and Australasia. When

Sir John's 1845 expedition was lost, she was the prime mover of several expeditions to discover his fate. The last, fitted out largely at her expense in 1857, brought back proof of her husband's death in 1847, but also proved that his party had discovered the North-West Passage. In 1860 the Royal Geographical Society conferred their Founder's Medal on her in recognition of her efforts in the search, efforts which were also commemorated in songs and poems of the time. Lady Franklin's early travels had given her an interest in social reform which found full scope in her married life. During her husband's Lieutenant-Governorship of Tasmania she seconded his efforts to liberalize conditions there, using her fortune generously, in particular to improve the lot of female convicts.   J.R.

Franklin, (Stella Maria) Miles (1879-1954), Australian novelist. Miles Franklin was born at Talbingo Station, near Tumut in New South Wales, and grew up on a farm, the setting for her ironically titled *My Brilliant Career* (1901). Hailed as 'the very first Australian novel to be published', it described a young girl's rebellion against her narrow environment. *My Career Goes Bung*, from the same period, was such strong meat for its time that it was not published until 1946.

From 1905 Miles Franklin lived in the United States and Britain, working for the women's suffrage and labour movement, as a journalist, and, during the First World War, as a hospital assistant in Macedonia. In 1933 she returned to Australia and wrote *All That Swagger* (1936), a saga novel of the country's pioneer past, more romantic and nostalgic than her earlier work. She was also almost certainly the author of a series of novels in a similar vein by 'Brent of Bin Bin', starting with *Up the Country* (1928). Miles Franklin's other books include the novel *Old Blastus of Bandicoot*, 1931; the reflective and critical *Laughter, Not for a Cage*, 1956; and the autobiographical *Childhood at Brindabella*, 1963.

See also M. Barnard, *Miles Franklin*, 1967; V. Coleman, *Miles Franklin in America: Her Unknown (Brilliant) Career*, 1981.   N.H.

Franklin, Rosalind (1921–58), X-ray analyst in biophysics. Rosalind Franklin worked for some years in Paris, carrying out X-ray analysis of three dimension forms in carbon. She had wished to turn her attention to biology; and

in 1951 was invited to build up an X-Ray diffraction unit at Randall's biophysics unit at King's College, London. There she built a high resolution X-Ray camera to analyse the structure of DNA. At the time Francis Crick and James Watson of Cambridge were working on a model of the form of DNA, an approach with which Franklin disagreed. In 1952 Rosalind Franklin's fellow King's researcher, Maurice Wilkins, showed Watson her best X-Ray diffraction picture of the B form of DNA, which demonstrated that the structure was helical, a vital piece of information. Unknown to her, Crick and Watson were also shown a copy of one of her papers. They formulated a new model, which Rosalind Franklin accepted, and in 1953 *Nature* published three papers on the discovery: by Watson and Crick, Wilkins and Stokes, and Franklin and Gosling.

Disliking the atmosphere at King's, Rosalind Franklin moved to Birkbeck College, London. She worked on the tobacco mosaic virus, and had begun work on the polio virus shortly before her death from cancer at the age of thirty-seven.

In 1962 Watson, Crick and Wilkins were awarded the Nobel Prize for their work on the structure of DNA; the story of the discovery is told in Watson's *The Double Helix* (1968). The text contains a number of slighting and revealingly sexist references to Rosalind Franklin, although the Epilogue makes some amends recognizing the importance of her work and the problems faced by an intelligent woman within the scientific community.

See also R. Hubbard, 'Reflections on the Story of the Double Helix', in *Women's Studies International Quarterly*, 1979; A. Sayre, *Rosalind Franklin and DNA*, 1975.   J.E.

Freeman, Mrs. See CHURCHILL, SARAH, DUCHESS OF MARLBOROUGH.

Freeman, Ann (1797–1826), preacher, born at Horathorne, Devonshire, the fourth child of William Mason, a farmer. At fifteen she was apprenticed to a dressmaker, but developed consumption and was unable to complete her training. Raised as an Anglican, she was preoccupied with religious matters from childhood, but her illness intensified her spiritual restlessness. In 1815 she and her sister joined a local Methodist connection, which led to her temporary banishment from the family home. On her return she succeeded in converting her mother and brothers.

In 1816 Ann Mason believed she had finally achieved eternal salvation. Despite opposition from friends, she subsequently joined the Arminian Bible Christians, or Bryanites, and became a class-leader. Convinced that her vocation lay in communicating the grace she enjoyed to others, she began to preach publicly, enduring the hostility this provoked. She undertook a lengthy preaching tour of south-west England, although her health began to decline very rapidly. In 1823 she visited London, where she met Henry Freeman, a fellow-Bryanite, whom she married the following year. Together they left for Ireland, where they preached in the streets of Dublin. Their denial of the value of the Sacraments led to frequent stonings and abuse, which destroyed the remnants of Ann Freeman's health; she returned to England and died at her father's house.

Confident of the divine nature of her calling, Mrs Freeman disregarded the criticisms levelled at her, and expressed bitter regret that other, weaker women were prevented by prejudice from exercising their vocations. *A Memoir of the Life and Ministry of Ann Freeman . . . written by Herself . . .* (1826) provides a vivid insight into the absolute nature of convictions which enabled her to set aside social conventions; it also conveys the emotional fervour and intensity of belief which characterized enthusiastic religion in the early nineteenth century.   J.V.L.

Frere, Mary (Eliza Isabella) (1845–1911), writer. She was born in Gloucestershire, the daughter of the colonial administrator Sir Henry Bartle Frere, and was educated privately in London. At the age of eighteen she went out to Bombay, where her father was governor. During the absence of her mother in 1864 she acted as hostess for her father at Government House. She also went with him on his tours round the country and became deeply interested in the peoples of India, listening with fascination to the tales recounted by her ayah (maid), which the ayah had originally heard from an aged grandmother. Mary Frere published twenty-four of these stories in 1868 as *Old Deccan Days*, with illustrations by her sister Catherine. The book was of some historical significance in giving added impetus to the study of folklore.   B.H.C.

Frith, Mary (1584?–1659), criminal and folk heroine. The daughter of a shoemaker of the Barbican, Mary was well educated but refused to submit to discipline. As a young girl she was sent into domestic service, but since she loathed housework and looking after children she soon adopted male dress and devoted herself to a life of crime, becoming infamous as a forger, pickpocket, fortune-teller, and receiver. Her usual sobriquet was 'Moll Cutpurse', and she numbered among her friends the highwaymen Richard Hannam and Captain Hind. Once, in a fit of drunken sentimentality, she did penance at Paul's Cross. Her criminal activities were evidently profitable; she was sent to Newgate for robbing General Fairfax on Hounslow Heath (incidentally wounding him in the arm and shooting two of his servants' horses), but was set free when she paid him £2,000. She died at an advanced age.

Mary Frith is of some interest as a folk-heroine. There are numerous allusions to her in contemporary writings, and she is the subject of a comedy by Middleton and Dekker, *The Roaring Girl* (1611), which presents her in a very attractive light.

See also *The Life and Death of Mrs Mary Frith*, anonymous, 1662; Alexander Dyce (ed.), *The Works of Thomas Middleton*, 1840.
                M.D

Fry, Elizabeth (1780–1845), prison reformer. Born at Norwich, she was the third daughter of John Gurney, a member of a prominent Quaker banking family. She enjoyed a stimulating childhood, studying a varied curriculum under her mother's supervision and moving in a lively circle of friends and relatives. But an unhappy love affair when she was sixteen left her melancholic and introspective. She became increasingly discontented with her spiritual life and in 1798 was deeply impressed by the preaching of the American Quaker William Savery. Shortly afterwards, to her family's dismay, she adopted the distinctive Quaker dress and speech. She studied the Scriptures with a new intensity, and opened a Sunday School for local children. In 1800 she married a fellow Quaker, Joseph Fry, who was to support her unfailingly throughout her career. Childbearing absorbed her energies until 1809, when she became a Quaker minister.

Elizabeth Fry's first contact with prisons occurred in 1813 when, on a friend's recommendation, she visited Newgate. However, it was not until 1816 that she became committed to improving conditions there. Appalled by the situation of the women convicts, she established an Association for the Improvement of Female Prisoners in Newgate, run by a committee of Quaker ladies. Plans for reform were drawn up and immediately approved by the prisoners themselves. The women were provided with paid employment, supervised by a matron and monitors. A school was set up for their children, and immoral behaviour was discouraged by lady visitors and regular Scripture readings. The scheme proved successful, and received much publicity. In 1818 Mrs Fry undertook an investigative tour of the North and Scotland, founding Ladies' Visiting Associations wherever possible. The British Society for Promoting the Reformation of Female Prisoners was established in 1821 to encourage and integrate the activities of these voluntary groups.

Elizabeth Fry's rehabilitative principles were outlined in her *Observations . . . on Female Prisoners*, published in 1827. However, public opinion at that time was already moving towards a harsher prison policy based on deterrence. Her husband's bankruptcy in 1828 curtailed Elizabeth Fry's activities just when her proposals were meeting increasing hostility from prison authorities and government. After 1836, when an Inspector's report strongly criticized conditions in Newgate, Elizabeth Fry concentrated her attention on Europe, undertaking several tours to foster continental prison reform.

She also engaged in many other philanthropic activities. She urged the government to improve conditions for women prisoners sentenced to transportation, encouraging the Ladies' Committees to visit prison hulks. A stay in Brighton in 1824 resulted in her establishment of a model district visiting society, and in the founding of libraries for isolated Sussex coastguards. In Germany she assisted the growth of an institution for training nurses, and she later set up a similar body in London.

Often accused of neglecting her nine children, Elizabeth Fry was very conscious of the competing claims of home and her wider social mission, but justified her actions in terms of her religious vocation. She was typical of her generation in her preoccupation with the material and moral condition of women; improving their political status did not concern her.

She was an assiduous diarist, and her journals present the most intimate and illuminating record of her life. Forty-four volumes of these can be found in the Library of the Society of Friends; two others exist in the Norfolk Record Office.

See also K. and R. Fry, *Memoirs of the Life of Elizabeth Fry*, 1847; J. Rose, *Elizabeth Fry: a Biography*, 1980.   J.V.L.

Fry, (Sara) Margery (1874–1958), penal reformer. Of Quaker ancestry, Margery Fry was the daughter of a distinguished judge and the sister of the painter and critic Roger Fry; her sisters Agnes and Isabel also had distinguished careers. Margery Fry was educated at Miss Lawrence's School, Brighton (later Roedean), and Somerville College, Oxford. In 1899 she became Somerville's Librarian, and in 1904 Warden of a new residence for women students at Birmingham. Made independent by a legacy, she worked from 1915 to 1917 for the Quakers' War Victims' Relief Mission in France. In 1919 she became Secretary of the Penal Reform League, and was instrumental in securing its merger with the Howard Association in 1921. In that year, too, she was made one of the first women magistrates; and in 1922 she became the first official education adviser to Holloway prison. By 1923 she had become convinced that capital punishment was wrong, and gave evidence on the matter, on behalf of the Howard League, to the Select Committee of 1929. In 1926 she resigned as the League's Secretary, and became, until 1931, Principal of Somerville. During the 1930s she toured China and the United States, predicting in 1941 that before the end of the century China would play a major part in world affairs. In 1946 she represented Britain at the International Penal and Penitentiary Congress; and in 1947, by invitation, she submitted a memorandum on human rights to UNESCO. She presented a League memorandum to the 1949 Royal Commission on the death penalty, and worked for the cause behind the scenes. She was the author of various pamphlets on penal reform; her book *Arms of the Law* was published in 1951. From 1937 to 1939 she was a Governor of the BBC, and for many years she sat on the University Grants Committee. She did not marry.

See also E. Huws Jones, *Margery Fry*, 1966.   J.E.

Fullerton, Lady Georgiana (Charlotte) (1812—85), novelist and philanthropist, was born at Tixall Hall, Staffordshire, the youngest daughter of Lord Granville Leveson-Gower and Lady Harriet Elizabeth Cavendish. She was educated at home; her father was Ambassador in Paris and Lady Georgiana learned French while living there. She married Alexander George Fullerton, an officer in the Irish Guards, when she was twenty-one. Her first two novels were *Ellen Middleton* (1844) and *Grantley Manor* (1845). *Ellen Middleton* was a melodramatic murder story, and when published it created a furore, although Gladstone praised its 'tremendous moral'. She wrote over thirty books but after the tragic death of her son in 1854 she decided to devote her life to charity. Having been a Roman Catholic since 1846, she joined the Order of St Francis, wrote a biography of the Saint in 1855, and translated his *Fioretti* into English for the first time.

Lady Georgiana Fullerton was a successful novelist in her day; her books were praised for their moral tone and she was admired by Cardinal Newman. Her other work includes *Too Strange Not to be True*, 1864; *Constance Sherwood*, 1865; *A Stormy Life*, 1867; and *A Will and a Way*, 1881.

See also P. Craven, *Lady Georgiana Fullerton*, 1888.   A.P.

Furse, Dame Katharine (1875–1952), first Director of the Women's Royal Naval Service (WRNS or 'Wrens'). She was the daughter of the historian John Addington Symonds. In early life she lived abroad, mainly in Switzerland and Italy. In 1900 she married Charles Wellington Furse, a distinguished painter, who died four years later. Katharine Furse was the model for one of his best-known pictures, *Diana of the Uplands* (Tate Gallery, London).

When her two sons were old enough, Katharine Furse travelled constantly, and was evidently searching for an outlet for her enormous energy. In 1912 she joined the Red Cross. By 1914 she was a Commandant, impatient at unreadiness for war and the official attitude towards women volunteers. Matters came to a head over VAD accommodation in 1917; she resigned in protest, being immediately invited to set up 'a Naval organisation of women'.

Some of those who had resigned with her helped to devise a structure for the WRNS which served not only for 1917–19 but for the 1939–45 War and the subsequent Permanent Service. Katharine Furse was appointed Director in November 1917, and by 11 November 1918 there were over 5,000 ratings and nearly 450 officers. The service was disbanded in 1919, but in 1920 Katharine Furse formed the Association of Wrens, of which she was president until 1952.

In the inter-war years she worked for Sir Arnold Lunn running mountain holidays, served on numerous ex-service committees, and represented the World Association of Girl Guides and Boy Scouts at the League of Nations. To her disappointment, she was not called on or consulted by the WRNS in the Second War. She wrote an autobiography, *Hearts and Pomegranates* (1940).

See also U. Stuart Mason, *The Wrens 1917–1977*, 1977.   U.S.M.

G

Gardiner, Marguerite, Countess of Blessington (1789–1849), famous beauty, society woman, and writer, 'Georgeous Lady Blessington'. Born Marguerite Powell at Knockbrit near Clonmel in Ireland, she was virtually sold by her parents to a brutal officer whom she married and left before she was fifteen. Her subsequent adventures culminated in her becoming the mistress of Lord Blessington, who is said to have bought off her previous protector for £10,000. In 1818, following the death of her first husband, she became Blessington's wife, and her beauty, intelligence, and wit made her house one of the most fashionable centres of London society. In 1822 the Blessingtons began a continental tour, forming an apparently amiable *ménage à trois* with the celebrated dandy Count Alfred D'Orsay. 'The Blessington Circus' travelled in Italy, spending two months at Genoa with the poet Lord Byron, and in France, where Blessington died (1829). Lady Blessington returned to England in 1831 and resumed her sway as a society hostess—an expensive sway which she financed by a quite extraordinary activity as author of three-volume novels, editor of periodical publications, and freelance journalist; for years her annual income from writing is reckoned to have been about £2–3,000, a huge sum for that time. Nevertheless she went bankrupt in April 1849; first D'Orsay and then Lady Blessington fled to Paris, where she died a few weeks later. Only her *Conversations with Lord Byron* (1834) now finds readers.

N.H.

Garnett, Constance (Clara) (1861–1946), translator of Russian classics. She was the intensely shy sixth child of the Brighton coroner, David Black. At seventeen she won a scholarship from Brighton High School to Newnham College, Cambridge, where she read classics and was bracketed top in the final examinations.

Influenced by socialist ideas, she became librarian at the People's Palace in London's East End. In 1889 she married the well-known man of letters Edward Garnett. After resigning her job, and while expecting her only child, David (the later novelist, born 1892), she learnt Russian, encouraged by her Russian revolutionary friends Felix Volkhovsky, Prince Kropotkin, and Sergey Stepniak. In the winter of 1892–3 she visited Russia, taking money for famine relief and papers for her socialist friends. On this trip she met Tolstoy at his home, Yasnaya Polyana. In 1904 she made another journey to Russia, accompanied by her son.

Her first translations were published in 1894. Thereafter she continued translating with prodigious rapidity and concentration; in later years her failing eyesight required her to dictate her English version after hearing the Russian read aloud. The seventy volumes of her translations include all the novels of Dostoyevsky, seventeen volumes of Turgenev, thirteen volumes of Chekhov's stories and two of his plays, Herzen's memoirs, six volumes of Gogol, and Tolstoy's *War and Peace* and *Anna Karenina*.

When Constance Garnett began her work, Russian literature was enjoying a certain vogue in Britain but was patchily known, often in poor translations made from French versions rather than the originals. Idiomatic, readable, and with very few inaccuracies, her translations introduced millions of readers in Britain and America to a strange and fascinating new literature which was to profoundly influence Western sensibilities.

See also D. Garnett, *The Golden Echo*, 1954; C. G. Heilbrun, *The Garnett Family*, 1961.

A.V.C.

Garrod, Dorothy (Annie Elizabeth) (1892–1968), archaeologist, daughter of the Regius Professor of Medicine at Oxford. Dorothy Garrod was educated privately, and at Newnham College, Cambridge, and Oxford University. In 1925 and 1926 she excavated in Gibraltar; then in 1928 she directed an expedition to South Kurdistan. She was Research Fellow of Newnham from 1929 to 1932. In 1932, at Mount Carmel in Palestine, she uncovered human skeletons thirty thousand years old, the oldest ever found. In 1934 she was a Leverhulme Research Fellow, and in 1936 President of Section H of the British Association. From 1939 to 1952 she was Disney Professor of Archaeology at Cambridge, the first woman to hold an 'Oxbridge' chair. From 1942 to 1945 she served as section officer in the Women's Auxiliary Air Force. In 1949, near Poitiers, she discovered sculptures dating back to around 50,000 BC; in the same year, she became head of Cambridge's Department of Archaeology and Anthropology. In 1957 she delivered the British Academy Reckitt Lecture, and in 1962 gave the Huxley Memorial Lecture to the Royal Anthropological Society. She was awarded the Huxley Medal, and was the first woman to receive the Gold Medal of the Society of Antiquaries. In 1965 she was created CBE. Her works include *The Upper Palaeolithic Age in Britain*, 1926; *The Palaeology of South Kurdistan*, with M. A. Bate, 1930; and *The Stone Age of Mount Carmel*, 1937.   J.E.

Gaskell, Elizabeth (Cleghorn) (1810–65), novelist, usually called 'Mrs Gaskell'. She was born in Chelsea, the daughter of William Stevenson, Keeper of the Treasury Records. After the early death of her mother, she was brought up by an aunt, Mrs Lumb, at Knutsford in Cheshire. She attended a boarding school at Burford and later one at Stratford-on-Avon, where she received an unusually good education.

In 1832 she married the Reverend William Gaskell, minister of Cross Street Unitarian Chapel in Manchester, where mural inscriptions commemorating the Gaskells can be seen. Mrs Gaskell lived in Manchester for the rest of her life and often helped her husband in his work, teaching and organizing relief. Her marriage was happy albeit unusual for the time: William's work kept him in Manchester while Elizabeth frequently travelled alone. Attractive and intelligent, she made many friends whom she visited, and she also travelled to do the research for her writing. She bore six children, of whom four daughters survived; her letters reveal her close relationship with them.

Mrs Gaskell's first publication was in 1840. Following the death of her son in 1844 she wrote her first novel, *Mary Barton: a tale of Manchester life*, published in 1848. It was one of the earliest novels to deal with the condition of the working class, and was an instant success. Among those who welcomed her to the literary world was Dickens, and several of her works were serialized in his periodical *Household Words*. Throughout her career she wrote frequently for periodicals, and collections of her shorter tales were published.

Her next major work, *Cranford* (1853), describes the daily life of a small Cheshire village in the 1830s (it was based on Knuts-

ford). Although sentimental, the novel is a delicate and humorous portrayal of a small female world, and is an established minor classic. The less important *Ruth* (1853) advocated more lenient treatment of unmarried mothers, and created a furore. By this time Mrs Gaskell was friendly with Charlotte Brontë, whom she met in 1850, and Charlotte agreed to delay the publication of her own novel *Villette* for a few months, hoping to avoid the inevitable comparisons between female novelists from the male critics of the day.

North and South (1855) is generally regarded as the third and last of Mrs Gaskell's major novels. The regional contrast and the preoccupation with problems of industrial unrest give it distinction, along with its unusually passionate and forceful heroine. Her next work was *The Life of Charlotte Brontë* (1857), written at the request of Charlotte's father. It was criticized at the time for detailing the family troubles of the Brontës, but its honesty and integrity have long been recognized. Mrs Gaskell's last three novels were all set in the past: *Sylvia's Lovers* (1863) centres on the activities of a press gang in eighteenth-century Yorkshire; *Cousin Phyllis* (1865) takes place in a rural area facing the coming of the railway; *Wives and Daughters* (1866) examines the conflict between town and country attitudes.

Mrs Gaskell was one of the first authors of 'condition of England' novels and a major provincial writer. Her work constitutes an important record of nineteenth-century life, particularly the life of women, and her career provides an interesting example of a woman writer successfully coping with male critics and editors. Her other works include *Lizzie Leigh and Other Tales*, 1854; *Round the Sofa*, 1859; and *Lois the Witch and Other Tales*, 1861.

See also J. A. V. Chapple and A. Pollard (eds.), *Letters of Mrs Gaskell*, 1966; W. Gérin, *Elizabeth Gaskell*, 1980; A. Pollard, *Mrs Gaskell: Novelist and Biographer*, 1965.   J.H.

Gaunt, Elizabeth (d. 1685), political martyr, was the wife of a yeoman, William Gaunt of St Mary's, Whitechapel, in London, where she herself kept a tallow chandler's shop and became known as a good and charitable woman. Despite her poverty she gave freely to the poor of all denominations, to dissenting

Genée, Dame Adeline

ministers, and to political and religious exiles. She herself was an Anabaptist. Among those she helped was a man called Burton, who later took refuge in her house after taking part in Monmouth's rebellion of 1685 against the Catholic King James II. He was discovered, and sought mercy by incriminating Elizabeth Gaunt. In a show trial at the Old Bailey on 19 October 1685, she was found guilty of high treason and sentenced to be burned at the stake four days later. At her execution at Tyburn she rejoiced in her martyrdom for the cause, and died with such cheerfulness that onlookers were moved to tears. Elizabeth Gaunt was the last woman to be executed in England for a political offence.

See also T. B. Howell, *A Complete Collection of State Trials*, vol. II, 1811; *Mrs E. Gaunt's Last Speech . . .*, 1865; *A True Account of . . . Eliz. Gaunt*, 1685.   T.J.M.

Genée(-Isitt), Dame Adeline (1878–1970), dancer, born Anita Jensen in Hinnerup, Denmark. Her uncle Alexander Genée was a professional dancer who encouraged her love of dancing. He also made himself responsible for her education and, when she took his surname, chose for her the forename Adeline. She studied classical ballet in a particularly pure and disciplined form, revealed in her later performance which was very refined but which some found 'a little hard and cool'.

Adeline Genée travelled widely in Europe, first in the corps de ballet of her uncle's company and then in leading roles, making *Coppelia* particularly her own. In 1897 she first appeared in London and during the next ten years there became famous both in classical roles and in the solos where she showed her gift of characterization. Before her day, dancers had tended not to be received in society, but the rectitude of her life was such that in 1905 she was received at Chatsworth and performed for Edward VII and Queen Alexandra. She toured the United States in 1907, and on her return to London produced a number of ballets while continuing her dancing career. Her marriage in 1910 to the businessman Frank Isitt was long and happy. He died in 1939. In 1914 she announced her retirement, but in fact danced on until 1917, and in 1920 became President of the newly-formed Association of Teachers of Operatic Dancing, which sought to raise the standard of teaching. She persuaded Queen Mary to grant her patronage

in 1928, and in 1936 the Association was granted its charter as the Royal Academy of Dancing.

Adeline Genée worked all her long life in the cause of the dance, particularly for its development and recognition in her adopted country. Not only was she one of the best-loved dancers of her time, but also one of the founders of British ballet as it exists today. She was created DBE in 1950 for her services to ballet, having been granted an honorary doctorate in music by London University in 1946. She continued as President of the Royal Academy of Dancing until 1954, when she was succeeded by Dame Margot Fonteyn.

See also I. Guest, *Adeline Genée*, 1958.
E.M.V.

Gibson, Margaret Dunlop (1843–1920), traveller and joint discoverer of the Sinai Palimpsest. She was the younger twin daughter of John Smith, a solicitor, and the sister of Agnes LEWIS. She was educated with her sister in Scotland and London. In 1883 she married James Young Gibson, a Spanish translator, who died in 1886. After her sister's husband also died, the two women lived together. They were very close, and alike in many respects. Margaret was the lesser scholar, but she was fluent in conversational Greek, and in 1892, on their trip to St Catherine's Monastery in the Sinai, to examine Syriac manuscripts, greatly eased their task by her personal charm. She was responsible for photographing many of the manuscripts (including the Sinai Palimpsest), a number of which were exhibited at the International Congress of Orientalists in the same year. She later wrote *How the Codex was Found* (1898), based on her sister's journals.
J.R.

Gilbert, Elizabeth (1824–85), pioneer of employment for the blind. She was the third child of the Principal of Brasenose College, Oxford, who was later Bishop of Chichester. An attack of scarlet fever at the age of three left her blind, but her parents resolved to educate her as if she were normal and to develop her musical ability. Using books with the newly invented raised letters, she was able to tackle many subjects, and later learned to use Foucault's writing frame. On a visit to the St John's Wood blind school in Avenue Road, London, she was taught an early form of typewriting by a blind teacher, William Levy. This visit made her aware of the difficulties faced by blind people without family assistance or other means of support, and, prompted by her father, she decided to use her inheritance to help them.

In 1854, with the help of Levy and his wife, Elizabeth Gilbert began to employ seven men to make household goods in their own homes: materials were purchased for them at cost price, and the goods sold at a small profit. Later a workroom was rented with Levy as manager. Though it was successful in many respects, blindness made bookkeeping difficult, and money was not used to best advantage. A visit to the Blind School in Edinburgh in 1856 gave her new ideas which resulted in the opening of new premises financed by donations from an appeal. At the same time the Association for the General Welfare of the Blind was formed and a report sent to Queen Victoria, who donated £50. By now blind women had joined the men in the workrooms, and Elizabeth Gilbert and Levy had written *Blindness and the Blind*, which was not however published until 1872.

Despite physical and financial difficulties, a shop in Oxford Street was opened, later to be the Institution for the Welfare of Blind People, and in 1869 the Prince of Wales became Vice-Patron on his own request. Meanwhile Elizabeth Gilbert had introduced the idea of peripatetic instructors for rural areas, and attempted to have provisions for the blind inserted in the 1870 Education Act. She was now advocating long-term aid from the State for the blind, but her failing health forced her to leave this campaign to others. Perhaps her greatest achievement was to make others more aware of the social problems associated with blindness and to create projects which helped the blind help themselves.

See also Frances Martin, *Elizabeth Gilbert and her work for the Blind*, 1891.

C.H.G.G.

Gilmore, Dame Mary (Jean) (1865–1962), Australian poet, progressive and journalist. Born Mary Cameron, at Goulburn, New South Wales, she became a teacher at the age of sixteen. In Sydney she fell under the influence of the socialist journalist William Lane, and went out to New Australia, a utopian colony he had set up in Paraguay; there she met W. A. Gilmore, who became her husband in 1897. After the collapse of the colony she worked in Patagonia and Buenos Aires as a teacher and journalist, only returning to Australia in 1920.

She then became well known as a Labour activist and as an editor and columnist for the Sydney *Worker*. She also established herself as Australia's leading woman poet, publishing several collections of verse beginning with *Marri'd* (1910). Her work reflects her socialist and feminist preoccupations, often with an unexpected imaginative slant (which is also apparent in her use of the life and culture of the Aborigines as poetic material); but her achievement was limited by her failure to break with the stilted diction and conventions of Victorian verse. She wrote two autobiographical books, *Old Days, Old Ways*, 1934 and *More Recollections*, 1935. N.H.

Ginner, Ruby (1886–1978), dancer-teacher, a revivalist of the Greek dance whose career in many respects resembled that of her American contemporary Isadora Duncan. Ruby Ginner, a doctor's daughter, was born at Cannes and went to school at Brighton before running away to become a dancer. She made her first stage appearance in *The Comedy of Errors* (1903). At the height of her performing career she was principal dancer with the Beecham Opera Company (1910–12), then organized her own company and toured with it. After the First World War she founded a school of dance and drama in partnership with the mime Irene Mawer, and for years she and her pupils were celebrated for the open-air performances they gave by the Serpentine in Hyde Park and at Stratford-upon-Avon. In 1923 she founded the Greek Dance Association to promote her ideas.

Ruby Ginner created a number of ballets and wrote two books, *The Revived Greek Dance* (1933); and *Gateway to the Dance* (1960). N.H.

Ginner, Sarah. See JINNER, SARAH.

Girling, Mary Anne (1827–86), religious enthusiast, leader of the People of God sect. The daughter of a Suffolk farmer, she married a seaman named Girling, later a general dealer at Ipswich, and they had several children. They parted after she began to have religious revelations. She was largely self-educated, and her reading seems to have been the trigger for her belief, from about 1864, that she was a fresh incarnation of God. She produced the stigmata and evidently liked describing in detail the emotions she experienced at the moment of revelation. From 1864 she proclaimed the New Coming. She gathered a group around her, mostly working-class, calling themselves the People or Children of God. Under the force of Mrs Girling's undoubted personality and will, the community lived an industrious, celibate existence, enduring hardship in the belief that they would live for ever with their 'mother'. She died of cancer, despite a belief that she was not mortal, and the community collapsed. She published one tract, *The Close of the Dispensation*, signed Jesus First and Last.   J.R.

Gladstone, Catherine (1812–1900), philanthropist, wife of the great Liberal leader. She was born the elder daughter of Sir Stephen Glynne, who died when she was three, and the Honourable Mary Neville, through whose family she was related to four prime ministers. Educated by successive governesses at Hawarden, the family home, she was an ebullient girl, quick but tenacious. Her beauty and social position made her a desirable catch, and she rejected several suitors. In 1839, after a courtship in Italy, she married William Ewart Gladstone, whose character and political promise aroused her sense of drama and expectation. Although they were temperamentally unalike, the marriage was a long and happy one, despite minor problems caused by Gladstone's addiction to work and her unmethodical habits. Catherine Gladstone shared her husband's political secrets and, given her impetuous temperament, showed remarkable discretion.

In a life given over to the support of her husband and the care of a large family, she still found time to pursue an active philanthropic career. She organized relief during the Lancashire cotton famine. She worked for a number of metropolitan charitable institutions including the House of Charity in Soho, from which she developed the Newport Market Refuge and Industrial School in the 1860s. A frequent hospital visitor, she was in daily attendance at the London Hospital during the cholera epidemic of 1866, and established a Home at Woodford, Essex, for some of the survivors. At Hawarden she founded an orphanage and an asylum for aged women. In 1882 she became president of St Mary's Training Home for the Protection and Care of Young Girls. Given her social position, she was constantly called upon to raise money for various causes and institutions, which she did

with marked success, though she alienated some of her guests at Hawarden by passing the plate round with the breakfast dishes.

In 1887, in an attempt to help her husband politically, Catherine Gladstone reluctantly agreed to become President of the Women's Liberal Federation. This organization promoted Liberal principles among women, though it did not support women's suffrage; on the issue of votes for women Mrs Gladstone accepted her husband's view that women were best suited to making their presence felt through other channels. Her presidency of the Federation (1887–93) was something of a trial for her, for she did not like public speaking or large political meetings; but membership increased rapidly under her leadership, from 9,000 in 1887 to 43,000 three years later. In her eighties she continued her charitable work with remarkable vigour and managed to wheedle Gladstone out of his Temple of Peace at Hawarden whenever she needed him to promote a cause. Perhaps appropriately for the wife of the Grand Old Man, she came to be known as G.D. or 'Grande Dame' to her friends.

See also G. Battiscombe, *Mrs Gladstone: The Portrait of a Marriage*, 1956; M. Drew, *Catherine Gladstone*, 1919; J. Marlow, *Mr and Mrs Gladstone: An Intimate Biography*, 1977.   F.K.P.

Glasse, Hannah (1707/8–1770), writer of cookery books. The eldest child of probably wealthy Northumbrian parents, she married John Glasse and after his early death seems to have supported her family through trade; a reference to Hannah Glasse 'Habit Maker to Her Royal Highness, the Princess of Wales' appears in the third edition of *The Art of Cookery, made Plain and Easy*, published in 1748, while she may also be the 'Hannah Glass of St Paul's, Co. Garden, Warehouse-keeper' declared bankrupt in *The Gentleman's Magazine* of May 1754.

Hannah Glasse's most famous book, *The Art of Cookery* won widespread popularity, running into thirty-four editions between 1747 and 1842 and being published in London, Dublin, Edinburgh and America. Although rivals such as Ann Cook cited weak points (lack of originality, organization, economy, simplicity), later writers of cookery books copied items and recipes and followed the book's format, which, together with its persuasive and impressive preface, may account for its instant success.

Hannah Glasse published *The Servant's Directory or Housekeeper's Companion* in 1760 and, probably about 1770, *The Compleat Confectioner or the Whole Art of Confectionery made Plain and Easy*. Little is known of her except her books and, supposedly, authorship of the proverb 'First catch your hare', although its nearest written expression is 'Take your hare when it is cased' in *The Art of Cookery*.

See also M. H. Dodds, 'The rival cooks: Hannah Glasse and Ann Cook', in *Archaeologica Aeliana*, 1938; A. Whittaker, *English Cookery Books to the Year 1850*, 1913.

A.M.N.

Gleichen, Lady Feodora Georgina Maud (1861–1922), sculptress. She was born in London, the daughter of Admiral Prince Victor of Hohenlohe-Langenburg, who was also a sculptor. She studied at the Slade School and in Rome and, beginning about 1890, exhibited at the Royal Academy, the Grosvenor Gallery, and the New Gallery. In 1900 she received the medal for sculpture in Paris. Among her best-known pieces are a life-size group of Queen Victoria surrounded by children for the children's hospital, Montreal, the Edward VII memorial at Derby, and external decorations for the foundling hospital in Cairo. She produced the Diana fountain for Rotten Row in Hyde Park, and made various busts of the famous; many of her works were royal commissions. She was made a posthumous member of the Royal Society of British Sculptors, the first woman to receive the honour. C.B.

Gloucester, Eleanor Cobham, Duchess of. See COBHAM, ELEANOR, DUCHESS OF GLOUCESTER.

Glover, Julia (1779–1850), actress. She was born in Newry, Ireland, the daughter of an actor named Betterton or Butterton, who claimed descent from the famous actor Thomas Betterton. She began touring with her father about 1789, taking such parts as the Duke of York in *Richard III* and Tom Thumb. She made her first appearance at Bath in 1795. She played in tragedy as Desdemona and Lady Macbeth, but it was in comedy, notably as Lydia Languish, that she excelled. Her father treated her badly, took her salary, and sold her for a thousand pounds (never paid) to Samuel Glover, the supposed heir to a large fortune, whom she married in 1800. She played at Drury Lane in 1802 and at Covent Garden, becoming one of the leading actresses on the London Stage. In 1810 she made her first appearance at the Lyceum with the Drury Lane company, whose own theatre had burned down. She played with Kean, Macready, and Thomas Dibdin, and in 1813 was the original Alhadra in Coleridge's *Remorse*.

Julia Glover was fair and plump, growing very stout with age. Her Mrs Malaprop was a character in which her rich comic gift and hearty humour could be given free reign, and it was as Mrs Malaprop that she appeared in her farewell benefit at Drury Lane in 1850, so ill that she could hardly speak. (She died four days later.) Her own life was unhappy. Her father preyed on her until his death at the age of eighty, and so for a time did her husband.

The foremost comedy actress during the middle years of her career, Julia Glover had a phenomenal memory and was called by Macready a 'rare thinking actress'. One of her sons became a musician, another an actor-manager, and on one occasion her daughter acted as Juliet to Kean's Romeo while her mother played the Nurse. B.H.C.

Glyn, Elinor (1864–1943), novelist, born in Jersey. Her father, a civil engineer, died within months of her birth; her maternal grandmother, a fearsome person of aristocratic French origins, delivered homilies on *noblesse oblige* that the young Elinor enthusiastically absorbed. She was educated by governesses and through her avid reading in the library of her stepfather's house in Jersey. An exotic beauty with flame-red hair and a pale complexion, she married Clayton Glyn, a wealthy but spendthrift English landowner, in 1892, and had two daughters. However, the romantic love for which she craved always escaped her (among the objects of her unrequited affection were Lord Milner and Lord Curzon); and it was in her novels that this love found its sublimated expression. Significantly, her autobiography is called *Romantic Adventure* (1936).

Elinor Glyn's highly successful first novel, *The Visits of Elizabeth* (1900), was a light-hearted concoction about country-house life, based on her own diaries. With *Three Weeks* (1907) she achieved fame and notoriety; this story about an affair between a handsome, athletic, but rather vacuous young English aristocrat and a seductive older woman who turns out to be a Balkan Queen, includes passages of passionate purple prose that caused the book to be banned at Eton, though by modern standards it is innocuous. Elinor Glyn's best-known novels, including *His Hour*, 1910, *The Reason Why*, 1911, and *The Man and the Moment*, 1915, represent the epitome of a style of popular romantic fiction that—because of its class-conscious snobbery, its hot-house emotions, and the artificially contrived situations that keep its two 'soul-mates' apart until the final pages—now seems hilariously dated.

With her novella *It* (1926) she coined a new word for sex-appeal, given wide currency by the Clara Bow film (1927) in which Elinor Glyn herself makes an appearance. Her popularity as novelist led to a spin-off career as counsellor on love and marriage in books like *The Philosophy of Love* (1923), published in America. She spent much of the 1920s in Hollywood, writing film-scripts and taking a hand in the direction of films.

Elinor Glyn (1955) is a sympathetic biography by her grandson, Anthony Glyn.   J.L.

Godgifu or **Godiva** (*fl.* 1041–after 1066), noblewoman, the legendary 'Lady Godiva'. Godgifu was the wife of Leofric, Earl of Mercia, and probably the mother of his son and successor Ælfgar. Leofric controlled Midland England through the critical years of the mid-eleventh century, but is also remembered as a monastic patron, an activity shared by his wife. In 1043 they founded the Abbey of Coventry, the family monastery where both were buried, and Godgifu was the benefactress of the monasteries of Leominster, Chester, Wenlock, Stow St Mary, Worcester, Evesham, and Spalding. In an age when abbeys controlled great lands and wielded political influence, church benefactions had both religious and political significance, and the couple's piety confirmed their status and power in the Midlands. Leofric's lands, including the leasehold property he held from the Church at Worcester, seem largely to have passed to his wife; the Domesday Survey of 1086 gives some impression of the extent of her property. Godgifu is chiefly remembered for her legendary ride naked through the streets of Coventry, supposedly undertaken to persuade her husband to relieve the burden of taxation on the

city. The truth of the story, which occurs only in later sources and was often elaborated in the interests of the borough, cannot be ascertained, but it is another indication of Godgifu's importance; nonentities do not attract such legends. Godgifu outlived her husband (he died in 1057), survived the Norman Conquest in 1066, and died at some date before 1086.

P.A.S.

Gonne, Maud (1865?–1953), Irish nationalist. The daughter of a colonel in the British Army and of a member of a wealthy business family, Maud Gonne was born near Aldershot. Motherless from the age of five, she and her sister were brought up in Ireland, London, and France. She was never sent to school, but was taught by a republican French governess. In Dublin in 1882 she played hostess to high-ranking army officers but, horrified by the plight of evicted tenants, vowed to work for Irish independence. Her father died in 1886 and Maud Gonne, rebelling against London relatives, sought independence as an actress. Prevented from succeeding by ill health, she recuperated in France, where she met the Boulangiste deputy Lucien Millevoye, with whom she formed an alliance against the British Empire and had a secret affair, bearing two children, one surviving as her 'niece' Iseult Gonne.

Travelling between France and Ireland, she became an independent crusader, since no Irish nationalist organization then admitted women. She campaigned on behalf of evicted tenants, the Treason Felony Prisoners, and famine victims in Mayo; and she organized counter-demonstrations at Queen Victoria's Jubilee and centenary celebrations for the 1798 rising. She established a journal in France, *L'Irlande Libre*, and toured France and the United States lecturing and fund-raising. During the Boer War she stepped up her activities in the hope of exploiting British difficulties. Queen Victoria's visit to Ireland to encourage recruiting prompted her famous attack *The Famine Queen*. In 1900 she formed The Daughters of Erin, which became a focus for women's political activity.

In 1903 she married John MacBride, who was to be executed after the Easter Rising of 1916. A son, Sean (later important in Irish politics), was born in 1904, but within a year Maud Gonne was suing for divorce. 'If a woman has something worthwhile doing in the world . . . marriage is a deplorable step.' After nursing in France during the War she returned to Ireland but was disillusioned by the Free State and the partition agreement. As secretary of the Women's Prisoners' Defence League she worked for imprisoned IRA members still fighting for unity and independence. Until her death she campaigned for prison reform and fair treatment of political prisoners.

Maud Gonne's patriotic fervour on behalf of her country of adoption was often expressed by involvement in small, specific issues, and she does not figure prominently in Irish political histories. But her striking physical appearance and her powers of oratory made her a legend. Working from a sense of duty, extraordinarily vibrant and committed, she had an indignant and passionately sympathetic heart. She is now remembered for the poet Yeats's long courtship of her, though neither he nor the mystic world she sometimes shared with him were central to her life. She wrote A Servant of The Queen, 1938, and illustrated two books by Ella Young, Celtic Wonder Tales, 1910, and The Rose of Heaven, 1920.

See also S. Levenson, Maud Gonne, 1976.

C.B.

Gordon, Jane, Duchess of Gordon (1748–1812), political hostess. She was born in Edinburgh, the second daughter of Sir William Maxwell of Monreith. In October 1767 she married Alexander Gordon, fourth Duke of Gordon, by whom she had two sons and five daughters. Energetic and ambitious, she became a leader of society in London and Edinburgh, and her house in Pall Mall was the social centre of the Tory Party from the late 1780s to 1801. She pursued a systematic course of family aggrandizement, and was a consummate matchmaker, three of her daughters marrying dukes and a fourth marrying a marquis. Her eldest daughter, Lady Charlotte, was apparently destined for the Prime Minister, William Pitt, whom the Duchess later described as 'the immortal and ever to be regretted Pitt'.

Subsequently the Duchess became estranged from her husband, and for the rest of her life led a nomadic existence. She died at the Pulteney Hotel, Piccadilly, and was buried at Kinrara, Inverness-shire.

See also A. Fergusson, The Honourable Henry Erskine, Lord Advocate for Scotland, 1882; J. Wyllie Guild, An Autobiographical Chapter in the Life of Jane, Duchess of Gordon, 1864.

M.J.S.

Gordon, Dame Maria (May) (1864–1939), geologist. Maria Ogilvie was the eldest daughter of the Revd D. A. Ogilvie, a distinguished educationalist. She was educated at the Ladies' College, Edinburgh; the Royal Academy of Music in London; Heriot-Watt College, Edinburgh, where her brother was Principal; and University College, London. In 1893 she was awarded the D.Sc. of London University. From 1891 to 1895 she studied geology and palaeontology at the University of Munich; in 1900 she gained its Ph.D., with the highest honours, one of the first women doctorates awarded at Munich. In 1895 she married Dr J. Gordon of Aberdeen; she had three children.

Maria Gordon conducted important research on the stratigraphy, palaeontology, and tectonics of the South Tyrol; and several of her many books concerned that area. In 1927 she produced two volumes on aspects of the geology of the Dolomites; a supplementary volume followed in 1929. Of her nearly thirty original scientific works, rather more than half were written in German. Among her fellowships and honorary fellowships were those of the Linnean Society, the Geological Society, and the Geological Society of Vienna. In 1932 she was awarded the Lyell Medal, and a grant from the Lyell Geological Fund. She held honorary doctorates of the universities of Edinburgh, Sydney, and Innsbruck.

She was also a major worker for the rights of women and children, and for this was created DBE in 1935. She was Honorary Secretary (1904–09), and then (1909–38) first Vice-President of the International Council of Women. From 1916 to 1920 she was President of the National Council of Women, and she also served as Honorary President of the National Women's Citizens' Association and the Association of Women's Friendly Societies. One of the first women JPs, she was also the first woman chairman of a London Borough Court.

J.E.

Gore-Booth, Eva (Selina) (1870–1926), a leading figure among the Northern radical suffragists whose industrial and Labour orientation set them somewhat apart from other groups. She was born and brought up in idyllic surroundings at Lissadell in County Sligo, Ireland, where her father was a wealthy land-owner. She and her sister, later the famous Countess MARKIEWICZ, founded a suffrage society in Sligo, but the decisive event in her life took place in 1896 on an Italian holiday, when she met Esther ROPER, then the secretary of the North of England Society for Women's Suffrage (NESWS). In the belief that she was dying of tuberculosis, Eva Gore-Booth settled in Manchester with Esther Roper, determined to give her remaining time to helping working women. Over the next few years she sat on the executive committee of the NESWS, became joint secretary of the Manchester and Salford Women's Trade Union Council, served on the city's Education Committee, and edited *The Women's Labour News*. She exerted a strong initial influence over the young Christabel PANKHURST. In partnership with Esther Roper she promoted the industrial organization of women, particularly the thousands of female textile workers. The two friends also played leading roles in the 1906 Wigan election and in the foundation of the Manchester Barmaids' Association (to defend barmaids' jobs against a new Licensing Act). In 1913 they moved to London for the sake of Eva Gore-Booth's health, and during the First World War worked ardently for pacifist causes. Eva Gore-Booth published several volumes of poetry, mainly on Irish themes. The *Collected Poems of Eva Gore-Booth* appeared in 1929, edited by Esther Roper.

See also J. Liddington and J. Norris, *One Hand Tied Behind Us*, 1978.   N.H.

Gosse, (Laura) Sylvia (1881–1968), painter and etcher. She came from a family distinguished for its scientific, literary, and artistic interests. Her grandfather was Philip Henry Gosse, naturalist and marine biologist, and her father Sir Edmund Gosse, author of the classic *Father and Son* (1907). Sylvia Gosse's mother Nellie was herself a pupil of Ford Madox Brown.

Sylvia Gosse was a painfully shy and retiring woman, but of the kind that copes in a crisis. Her private income enabled her to be independent of painting for a livelihood, and also to be of considerable help to the painter Walter Sickert and his successive wives. This was the most important involvement of her life. From 1910 to 1914 she was the co-principal of Sickert's Rowlandson School of Painting and Etching, at 140 Hampstead Road, and only her

dedication enabled it to survive for as long as it did. She and the Sickerts had villas first at Neuville, near Dieppe, and later further inland at Envermeu, and she nursed Christine, Sickert's second wife, until her death in 1920, after which she managed his household for him. She was also, with Thérèse LESSORE, one of the assistants whom he used in the boring chores of his work—stretching canvases or squaring up his drawings for transfer to canvas. Often, and as unobtrusively as possible, she helped him by buying pictures or arranging for their purchase by friends, and she was one of the organizers of the Sickert Fund, raised in 1934 to enable him to work without financial anxiety.

Like Sickert, and almost certainly because of his influence, Sylvia Gosse used photographs as a starting point for her pictures, and her style is in general very dependent on his. While it may be (and has been) argued that his employment of her as a domestic and artistic maid-of-all-work impeded her own development as an artist, it remains true that without his influence and stimulus she would probably not have created anything worth noticing. Among the few works in public collections, the Tate Gallery has a portrait of Sickert based on a photograph taken in 1923, the National Portrait Gallery has portraits of George Lansbury and Henry Austin Dobson, and there are etchings in the Victoria and Albert Museum, the Fitzwilliam Museum, Cambridge, and elsewhere. Sylvia Gosse was a member of the Royal Society of British Artists, and was admitted to the Camden Town Group in 1914. In later years she moved from London to Ore, near Hastings, where she died, afflicted by cataract.   L.M.M.

Gould, Eliza (1770–1810), philanthropist and founder of Sunday Schools. She was born at Bampton, Devonshire, the eldest daughter of John Gould of Dodbroke. She worked as a governess for several families, and she established a Sunday School in the village near Bedford where one such family resided; it soon had over 100 pupils. She then founded a boarding school at South Molton, Devonshire, but was obliged to abandon it around 1794 on account of the hostility she incurred through her patronage of a radical newspaper, *The Cambridge Intelligencer*, edited by Benjamin Flower. On 20 June 1795 a letter of hers in the paper condemned the confinement of women to 'those trifling employments which men have assigned us', and argued for the better education of women; she declared herself 'a disciple of the justly admired Wollstonecraft [sic]'. In 1799 she visited Flower, whose acquaintance she had already made, during his imprisonment in Newgate for libelling the Bishop of Llandaff; the following year, they were married. At Cambridge she established a Benevolent Society for the Relief of the Sick and Aged Poor, and was its secretary and visitor. In 1803 she gave birth to Eliza FLOWER, and two years later to Sarah Flower ADAMS. She suffered constantly from ill health, and died as a result of premature childbirth; at the time of her death she was helping to establish a Sunday School in Cambridge.

See also her obituary in *The Monthly Repository*, 1810.   M.J.S.

Goward, Mary Ann. See KEELEY, MARY ANN.

Grand, Sarah, pseudonym of Francis Elizabeth McFall (1854–1943), writer and feminist. She was born Frances Elizabeth Bellenden Clarke at Donaghadee in Ireland, of English parents. At the age of sixteen she married David C. McFall, an army surgeon. She spent five years with him in the East, and at thirty-four had her first success with *Ideala* (1888). It was five more years before she made her name with a long novel, *The Heavenly Twins* (1893), that made a great stir through its 'indelicate' view of marriage and especially its discussion of venereal infections. Its complicated plot was narrated in a highly coloured style and it became a best-seller. Having left her husband three years earlier, she had adopted the pseudonym 'Sarah Grand', by which she was thereafter universally known.

Sarah Grand had been interested in the women's movement since the publication of *Ideala* and became a well-known lecturer on the subject. There were distinct limits to her feminism, however; she was a believer in marriage, though outraged by the 'profligacy' of men, whom she wished to see as 'clean' as respectable women were supposed to be. Her other novels included the strongly autobiographical *The Beth Book*, 1897, *Babs the Impossible*, 1901, *Adnam's Orchard*, 1912, and *The Winged Victory*, 1916. Among other achievements Sarah Grand was six times mayoress of Bath, in 1923 and from 1925 to 1929.

See also G. Kersley, *Darling Madame: Sarah Grand and Devoted Friend*, 1983.   B.H.C.

Granuaile. See O'MALLEY, GRANIA.

Gray, Eileen (1878–1976), interior decorator, furniture designer, and architect. She began learning lacquer work in the repair workshop of D. Charles, in Dean Street, London, in 1898. She went to Paris in 1902, and France remained her real home until her death. By 1907, after studying drawings at the Académies Colarossi and Julien, she began to work on lacquer with the Japanese artist Sugawara, and exhibited with the Société des Artistes Décorateurs in 1913, selling furniture to the collector Paul Doucet, for whom she made in 1914 her only signed and dated work (a screen). She passed the war years 1914–18 in London, returning to Paris in 1919 to resume her career from her gallery in the rue de Faubourg-St-Honoré called 'Jean Désert'.

Eileen Gray worked for many years with Evelyn Wyld in the designing of carpets and rugs—with great success, since they were less expensive than her lacquered furniture, which entailed a lengthy process of manufacture. The partnership ended in 1927, by which time she had become more interested in architecture. She shut her shop in 1930, ultimately because what had been her 'novelty' in style and finish had become popular and had been down-graded in quality. Her final statement as a decorator was a 'Room Boudoir for Monte Carlo' at the Salon des Artistes Décorateurs in 1923, but her meticulously orchestrated swan-song was greeted with abuse and virulent criticism. However, it earned her the unstinted praise of J. P. P. Oud, the leading Dutch architect of the De Stijl group, and a successful exhibition of her work followed in Amsterdam. From 1925 onwards she worked with the Romanian architect Jean Badovici, building villas on the Riviera which were much admired by Le Corbusier. In 1932–34 she built a villa at Tempe a Pailla, near Menton, which was looted and wrecked by succeeding waves of invaders during the Second World War. She restored it, but in 1956 increasingly bad eyesight forced her to return to Paris, and she sold the house to Graham Sutherland.

Eileen Gray was an original in that she was always in the forefront of modern furniture design throughout her career, an achievement equalled only by such contemporaries as Marcel Breuer, Le Corbusier, and Mies van der Rohe. She designed chrome and leather chairs, chaises-longues that followed the line of the body, and rectangular tables and cabinets of austere simplicity of line that were finished in a gleamingly hard lacquer, either in black and white or in deep, glowing colour.

See also S. Johnson, *Eileen Gray*, 1979.

L.M.M.

Gray, Maria Emma (1787–1876), conchologist and algologist. She was born at Greenwich Hospital, where her father, Lieutenant Henry Smith, RN, was living. In 1812 she married Francis Edward Gray, who died two years later, leaving her with two daughters. In 1826 she married John Edward Gray, a cousin of her first husband and thirteen years her junior, who was employed as an assistant in the Natural History Department at the British Museum. Mrs Gray was an educated woman, fond of music and acquainted with a wide circle of scientific and literary men. She had money of her own, which gave her husband the means to travel and visit European naturalists and their collections, a factor which influenced his appointment as Keeper of the Zoological Department in 1840.

Mrs Gray's own interests were in molluscous animals and algae. She arranged and mounted the greater part of the Cuming collection of shells at the British Museum and etched thousands of plates of marine animals, privately published in five volumes as *Figures of Molluscous Animals* (1857–74). In 1842 the Grays spent a holiday in Ilfracombe collecting algae. In the 1850s Mrs Gray was helped with her collection by Dr George Johnston of Berwick and in 1859 she visited Professor W. H. Harvey in Dublin. Her knowledge of seaweeds, both in the living state and in the herbarium, was so highly regarded that Sir William Hooker entrusted to her the arrangement of the British algae at Kew, and J. J. Bennett, Keeper of Botany at the British Museum, invited her to order the general collection of algae. In order to promote the study of the subject she arranged collections which she presented to schools, and her own collection, together with her husband's, was bequeathed to the Museum of the University of Cambridge. As a tribute to her work her husband coined the name *Grayemma* for a newly discovered genus of algae from the Gulf of Mexico.

See also A. E. Gunther, *A Century of Zoology at the British Museum*, 1975. S.G.

Grebill, Agnes (1451?–1511), Lollard, of Tenterden in Kent, was converted by John Ive towards the end of Edward IV's reign. By 1511, when Archbishop Warham of Canterbury launched a full-scale campaign against Lollardy in Kent (rife there since the early fifteenth century), Agnes had achieved a considerable reputation. She was duly indicted as a heretic (along with her husband and two sons), found guilty, and burned at the stake in company with four other women Lollards.

See also J. A. F. Thomson, *The Later Lollards 1414–1520*, 1965. K.R.D.

Green, Alice Sophia Amelia (1847–1929), historian and Irish radical, known as Mrs Stopford Green. Born at Kells, County Meath, the daughter of the Revd E. A. Stopford, archdeacon of Meath, she taught herself Greek to help her father, but at seventeen became partly blind. Her reading time was severely restricted until an operation restored her sight in 1871. When her father died in 1874 the family moved to England, where in 1877 she married the historian John Richard Green. After his death in 1883, she completed his *Conquest of England*, and began to write her own historical studies, including *Henry II* (1888) and *Town Life in the Fifteenth Century* (1894). Her friends included such notable people as Florence NIGHTINGALE, Mary KINGSLEY, and Winston Churchill. She grew increasingly radical and became a zealous supporter of Home Rule for Ireland, studying early Irish history to refute the prevalent view that Ireland had no native civilization before the Tudor conquest. As a result she published *The Making of Ireland and Its Undoing, 1200–1600* (1908). Increasingly anti-English and anti-Imperialist, she was a close friend of Sir Roger Casement. In 1917 she returned to Ireland, where her name appeared on the first list of Irish senators nominated in 1922. B.H.C.

Green, Mary Anne Everett (1818–95), historian. She was born at Sheffield, the daughter of a Methodist minister, and her childhood was spent in Lancashire and Yorkshire. She was educated at home and in 1841 went to London, where she pursued her own course of study in the British Museum reading room. She published *Letters of Royal Ladies of Great Britain* under her maiden name of Wood. She began to write *Lives of the Princesses of Great Britain* in 1843, but delayed publication until 1849 owing to the appearance of Agnes STRICKLAND's *Lives of the Queens of England*

(1840–48). In 1846 she married a painter, George Pycock Green, travelling with him to Paris and Antwerp and returning two years later to London. In 1853 she was appointed to prepare Calendars of state papers, which required scholarly research at the Public Record Office. She edited forty-one volumes altogether over a period of forty years. When her husband became disabled in an accident, she learned perspective in order to help with his work, and, having taken a close interest in her own children's studies, wrote a book on education.   B.H.C.

Green, Mrs Stopford. See GREEN, ALICE SOPHIA AMELIA.

Greenaway, Kate (1846–1901), children's book illustrator. Born at Hoxton, Catherine Greenaway was the daughter of a wood-engraver. In her childhood she acquired a love of nature and began to draw from her father's collection of magazines and from copies of Cruikshank's engravings. As a hard-working art student at the Royal College she won the Bronze medal in 1861 (for her decorative art), the National Medal in 1864, and the Silver in 1869; she then went to Heatherley's and the Slade School at University College for life classes. In 1868 she began to exhibit, and her first commercial illustrating was done for *The People's Magazine* and *The Illustrated London News*. Throughout the 1870s she drew for children's novels and designed Christmas, birthday and Valentine cards.

In 1878 Kate Greenaway began to work with Edmund Evans, the pioneer colour engraver: his new process, giving greater variety of tone, was used in *Under the Window* (1879), the first work that she both wrote and illustrated. It was an immediate success in Britain and abroad. Her drawings for a yearly almanack and her *Kate Greenaway's Birthday Book for Children* (1880) were among the many works she illustrated in the following decade, making her a household name.

Her distinguished admirers included such people as John Ruskin, the literary editor Locker-Lampson, and the novelist George Eliot. She worked in the Pre-Raphaelite tradition, and expressed her dislike for the style of contemporaries such as Beardsley and Whistler. In the 1890s she realized that her style was going out of fashion and turned to sculpture and oil painting, but without success. Just

before her death she started illustrations for William Blake's *Songs of Innocence*.

A strong religious instinct was evident in Kate Greenaway's search for beauty and goodness in her art, though she was not an orthodox Christian. A diligent and strong character, she rejected the women's movement, remarking that she had always been fairly treated by men. Besides being an innovative artist she was one of the few women to have made a commercial success of her profession.

See also R. K. Engen, *Kate Greenaway*, 1976; B. Holme, *The Kate Greenaway Book*, 1977; M. H. Spielmann and G. S. Layard, *Kate Greenaway*, 1905.   C.H.G.G.

Gregory, Mrs. See FITZHENRY, ELIZABETH.

Gregory, Lady (Isabella) Augusta (1852–1932), playwright and patron, a major figure in the Irish Literary Renaissance. Born at Roxborough, County Galway, née Persse, she was the daughter of a wealthy landowner. She was educated privately and grew up in the Protestant tradition, but learned much about Irish peasant life from the stories of her Catholic nurse. In 1880 she married Sir William Gregory of Coole Park, former Governor of Ceylon; they had one son who was killed in the First World War. After her husband's death in 1892 she filled her life with literature and with intense devotion to Ireland.

In 1896 Augusta Gregory met the poet W. B. Yeats and felt certain he was the man for whom Ireland was waiting. Coole Park became his second home and he repaid her care by directing her energies into channels that would help their country. She learned Gaelic, collected the folklore of Galway and translated many of the old Irish sagas in, for example, *Cuchulain of Muirthemne* (1902) and *Gods and Fighting Men* (1904).

After the opening of the Abbey Theatre in 1904, all Lady Gregory's abilities were concentrated on this venture. She became known as the godmother of the theatre; Bernard Shaw went further and called her its charwoman. Because of the Abbey she became a playwright. Though she tried her hand at tragedy (for instance in *Grania*), she was at her best with comedy, one of the most successful being *Spreading the News* (1904). She wrote nearly thirty plays, mostly based on her observation of rural life, and also translated Molière into the idiom of Western Ireland.

Lady Gregory travelled with the Abbey

players and was with them in America during the riots over Synge's *Playboy of the Western World* in 1911 and 1912. She continued to work for the theatre and for Ireland until old age, dying at Coole. Her other works include *A Book of Saints and Wonders* (1907) and *Seven Short Plays* (1907). *Lady Gregory's Journals 1916–30*, edited by L. Robinson, appeared in 1958.

See also E. Coxhead, *Lady Gregory, a Literary Portrait*, 1961; H. Howarth, *The Irish Writers*, 1958.   P.L.

Grenfell, Joyce (Irene) (1910–79), actress. The daughter of an architect, she began her career as a journalist, contributing radio criticism to the *Observer*. However, she soon turned to writing and broadcasting satirical character monologues and in 1939 transferred these to the stage in the *Little Review*. Thereafter she appeared regularly in a succession of revues that included *Diversions, Light and Shade, Sigh No More, Tuppence Coloured*, and *Penny Plain*.

Joyce Grenfell developed a one-woman show consisting of monologues and songs (written by her in collaboration with the composer Richard Addinsell), which she presented in the West End and on tour, scoring a great success on her first visit to the United States in 1955. A series of films during the 1950s brought the gawkily enthusiastic but hapless characters in whom she specialized to a wider audience. They included *The Happiest Days of Your Life, Genevieve* and the St Trinian's series. She was a regular performer on radio and television, both in her own material and in shows such as Stephen Potter's *How to . . .* series and the TV quiz programme *Face the Music*. After retiring from the stage in 1973, she took up writing again, producing *Joyce Grenfell Requests the Pleasure* (1976) and *In Pleasant Places* (1979), both autobiographical, and a quantity of verse. She was President of the Society of Women Broadcasters and Writers and served on the Pilkington Committee on Broadcasting (1960–62).

A conscientious and disciplined artist, Joyce Grenfell achieved success through accurate observation and the essential kindliness with which she treated her subjects. She was awarded the OBE in 1946.   K.W.

Greville, Frances Evelyn, Countess of Warwick (1861–1938), social reformer. Born in London, the elder daughter of a wealthy landowner, she inherited extensive family estates in 1865 following the deaths of her father and grandfather, the third Viscount Maynard. In 1881 she married Lord Brooke, heir to the Earl of Warwick, by whom she had three sons and two daughters. As a member of the Prince of Wales's Marlborough House set, she led an extravagant social life, taking numerous lovers, and eventually, in 1889, attracting the attention of the Prince himself, becoming his mistress for the next nine years.

Attacks on her way of life by W. T. Stead and Robert Blatchford in the radical press activated her social conscience and, without abandoning her position in society, she worked for progressive causes, eventually joining H. M. Hyndman's Social Democratic Federation. She promoted a number of schemes of her own, including Bigods, a school to encourage rural occupations at Dunmow in Essex, and Studley Castle, to train women in horticulture and agriculture. Many of her projects foundered on her improvidence, which on occasions brought her close to bankruptcy. A proposal to convert her family home, Easton Lodge, Essex, into a Labour university came to nothing, and in 1923 she was defeated as Labour candidate for Warwick and Leamington by Anthony Eden, a relative. She contributed to the authorship of a number of books, although in fact these were largely the work of the writer R. L. Bensusan.

Despite her failings, the Countess was a woman of immense vitality and genuine philanthropy whose commitment to socialism, often inconsistent and highly emotional, helped to keep it in the public eye.

See also M. Blunden, *The Countess of Warwick*, 1967; T. Lang, *My Darling Daisy*, 1966.   K.W.

Grey, Elizabeth, Countess of Kent (1581–1651), author, the second daughter of the Earl of Shrewsbury. She married Henry Grey, a nephew of the sixth Earl of Kent in 1601, and when her husband succeeded as eighth Earl in 1623 they made their home at Wrest Park, Bedfordshire. Elizabeth Grey thus became responsible for the running of a large aristocratic household and for the well-being of its inhabitants. Her husband died in 1639 and she went to live in London until her own death in 1651. She had no children.

Elizabeth Grey was acquainted with several

well-known writers; the lawyer and antiquary John Selden served as steward to her family for many years; and poets such as Samuel Butler (Selden's secretary) and Thomas Carew received hospitality at her houses. The main interest of her life, however, lies in her *A Choice Manuall or Rare and Select Secrets in Physick and Chyrurgery: Collected and practised by the Right Honourable Countess of Kent... whereto are added ... most Exquisite waies of Preserving, Conserving, Candying, etc*, posthumously published in 1653 from the Countess's manuscript collection of favourite recipes and trusted cures for common ailments. This work illustrates some of the responsibilities of the mistress of a great household and is also an example of a very popular published cookery book, running to at least twelve editions by 1708. The Countess was thus unwittingly a pioneer in the domestic literary genre in which many women have been successful.

See also L. R. Conisbee, 'Elizabeth, Countess of Kent', in *The Bedfordshire Magazine*, 1969.

P.M.H.

Grey, Lady Jane (1537–54), the 'nine days' Queen' of England. The daughter of Henry Grey, Marquess of Dorset, and Frances Brandon, she was the granddaughter (on her mother's side) of Henry VIII's sister MARY, QUEEN OF FRANCE and Duchess of Suffolk. As a possible claimant to the throne (Henry's will named Mary's issue directly after his own children) she was destined to be a pawn in Tudor dynastic and religious politics. She entered Katherine PARR's household at the age of nine, and after Katherine's death in 1548, Katherine's husband, Thomas Seymour, bought Jane's wardship from Dorset, promising to marry her to the boy King Edward VI, son of Henry VIII. On Seymour's execution for treason in 1549 Lady Jane returned to her parents, continuing her studies under John Aylmer, later Bishop of London. She was a considerable humanist scholar, corresponding with Bullinger at Zurich and being praised by Roger Ascham.

Lady Jane Grey was increasingly caught up in the dangerous politics of Edward VI's reign. The Protector, Somerset, planned to marry her to his son, the Earl of Hertford. Then on Somerset's fall, Jane's father, created Duke of Suffolk in 1551, allied with the Duke of Northumberland, who had established a dominat-

ing influence over Edward VI. On 21 May 1553 Jane married Guildford Dudley, Northumberland's fourth son; she protested against the match, but was forced to submit by her father. Influenced by Northumberland and by his own wish to ensure a Protestant régime, Edward VI altered the succession so that Lady Jane Grey would inherit instead of his sisters Mary and Elizabeth.

King Edward died on 6 July 1553, and on 9 July Northumberland presented Lady Jane to the Council, while Ridley preached in her favour at Paul's Cross. On 10 July she was brought to the Tower, and a proclamation announced her accession. But on 9 July Princess Mary wrote to the Council claiming the throne; popular support for her ensured her victory over Northumberland's forces, and on 19 July she was proclaimed Queen throughout the country. Mary pardoned the Suffolks, and refused to have Jane executed.

However, on 14 November Jane was arraigned for treason at the Guildhall with her husband, his brothers, and Thomas Cranmer, Archbishop of Canterbury. She pleaded guilty and was condemned to death, though sentence was suspended. Her father's involvement in Wyatt's rebellion sealed her fate, and she and Dudley were beheaded on 12 February 1554.

Lady Jane Grey was no more than a political figurehead, but her accession might have changed the religious and political history of England. She was a reluctant pawn, swooning when told she was Queen, refusing to allow Dudley to call himself King without Parliament's consent, and gladly resigning her title. She was also a sincere Protestant, and ably defended her views against theologians who visited her in prison.

See also H. Chapman, *Lady Jane Grey*, 1962.

M.D.

Grey, Katherine, Countess of Hertford (1538?–68), second daughter of Henry Grey, Duke of Suffolk, by Frances Brandon, and sister of Lady Jane GREY. Katherine Grey married Henry Herbert, later Earl of Pembroke, in May 1553. The marriage was one of political expediency and was apparently never consummated; after Lady Jane Grey's fall, Herbert had it dissolved.

From 1558 Katherine Grey was of dynastic importance, since various deaths left her as Queen ELIZABETH's heir by the terms of Henry VIII's will. In 1560 Philip II planned to kidnap and marry her in order to press her claim against Elizabeth's. But in November or December 1560 Katherine Grey secretly married Edward Seymour, Earl of Hertford, despite the statute of 1536 which forbade marriage with a person of royal blood without the monarch's approval. By summer 1561 she was obviously pregnant, and was sent to the Tower for questioning. In September Hertford joined her in prison, where she gave birth to a son. Elizabeth was outraged, and appointed a commission to investigate the marriage. Since the priest who had performed the ceremony could not be produced, the commission declared that there had been no marriage. John Hales challenged this decision in a pamphlet which came to official attention in April 1564, giving rise to a public furore, the 'tempestas Halesiana'.

Katherine Grey and her husband met illicitly in the Tower, and in February 1563 she gave birth to another son. In August 1563 she was put in the custody of her uncle, Lord John Grey, and spent the rest of her life in various places of confinement. Despite frequent appeals she was never allowed to rejoin her husband, and died at Cockfield Hall.

See also H. Chapman, *Two Tudor Portraits*, 1960.   M.D.

Grey, Maria (Georgina) (1816–1906), campaigner for women's education. Maria Grey was the daughter of Admiral Shirreff and younger sister of Emily SHIRREFF. She spent much of her childhood abroad, and was educated privately. Her family returned to England in 1834, and in 1841 she married her first cousin, William Grey, a wine merchant. She had a very close relationship with her sister and they continued to live together for much of the time after the marriage. They published two books together, a novel, *Passion and Principle* (1841) and *Thoughts on Self-Culture addressed to Women* (1850).

Maria Grey's public involvement in the campaign to improve women's secondary education began a few years after the death of her husband in 1864. She founded the National Union for the Improvement of the Education of Women of All Classes, later the Women's Education Union (WEU). She set up two of the WEU's most influential offshoots, the Girls' Public Day School Company (later Trust), incorporated in 1872, and the Teacher Training and Registration Society, established

in 1877. By 1879 the GPDSC had seventeen schools providing relatively cheap secondary education for girls; the TTRS sought to provide adequate training for the teachers such schools required, and thereby to open up teaching as a profession for middle-class women. Maria Grey lectured throughout the country on women's education, and addressed the British Association and the Social Science Association on several occasions, as well as publishing many letters and articles. Her other works include *Love's Sacrifice* (a novel, 1868) and *Last Words to Girls on Life in School and After School* (1889).

Maria Grey was also a life-long member of the Central Society for Women's Suffrage and published several pamphlets on the suffrage question. Her political sympathies became increasingly radical, and in the 1880s she showed an interest in socialism and the co-operative movement. However from 1877 onwards ill-health increasingly forced her to withdraw from public life.

See also E. W. Ellsworth, *Liberators of the Female Mind*, 1979.   K.C.

Grierson, Constantia (1706–33), poet and classical scholar, born in comparatively humble circumstances at Kilkenny, Ireland, but clearly a 'natural' scholar from an early age. Her verse, an example of which appeared in *Poems on Several Occasions* (1734), edited by Mary BARBER, is not remarkable, but her careful editions of several of the classics was admired at the time and for years afterwards. At the age of eighteen she produced a Virgil, and subsequently editions of Terence (1727) and Tacitus (1730). These were well printed in pocket editions for scholars by her husband's press in Dublin. As was customary, her husband's name appears on the title page, and the role of the female editor is nowhere publicly acknowledged.

See also G. Ballard, *Memoirs of several Ladies of Great Britain, who have been celebrated for their writings or skill in the learned Languages, Arts, and Sciences*, 1752. T.H.

Griffiths, Ann (1776–1805), writer of Welsh hymns. Ann Thomas was the eldest daughter of a farmer in Montgomeryshire. Legend has it that she was a frivolous girl until deeply affected by a sermon which caused her to join the Independents and later (1797) the Methodists. In 1804 she married Thomas Griffiths of

Meifod; she died the following year after giving birth to a child. She wrote down few of her compositions, and her works were preserved only because she had habitually recited them to a servant, Ruth Evans, who was still able to recall them after Ann Griffiths' death; Ruth Evans and her husband, the Methodist minister John Hughes, were thus responsible for preserving some of the best-known hymns in the Welsh language. They were published posthumously, in 1805, 1806, and 1808, and definitively in 1905 in O. M. Edwards, *Gwaith Ann Griffiths*. N.H.

Grote, Harriet (1792–1878), biographer, born Harriet Lewin at The Ridgeway near Southampton. Tall, spirited, and athletic, she was brought up at Bexley, where in 1815 she met and became engaged to George Grote, the son of a banker. Family differences kept them apart until they married in secret in March 1820. Seriously ill after the birth and death of a child, Harriet Grote suffered from neuralgia ever afterwards.

In 1832 George Grote was elected to Parliament as a reformer, and the couple lived at the centre of Radical politics. Unconventional, outspoken and clever, Harriet Grote made an impression on London intellectual circles. Cobden and Place asserted that she might have led the Radicals if she had been a man. In 1839, with the Radical Party reduced to 'Grote and his wife', she became disillusioned with politics and turned to the arts. Maintaining two households and helping her husband through the writing of his monumental *History of Greece* she also entertained frequently and often travelled to France. She befriended Mendelssohn, helped Anna JAMESON with research, and was instrumental in bringing Jenny LIND to London in 1847. From 1842 to 1852 she contributed to the *Spectator* and during the 1850s promoted the Society of Female Artists. Her first book, *Memoir of the Life of Ary Scheffer* (1860), was the biography of a painter. In 1861 she contributed to *The Victoria Regia*, supporting the Society for the Promotion of Employment for Women. Her *Collected Papers* (1862) reflect a variety of interests from political comment and biography to art appreciation. A real Radical-individualist, she condemned the Crimean War as springing from 'timorous panic and delusion', attacked welfare policies which encouraged the poor to depend on the rich or the state, deprecated the French policy of centralization, and urged reforms in the Law of Marriage to give women equal rights over property. George Grote died in 1871, and two years later she published *The Personal Life of George Grote*. A friend of artists, intellectuals, and politicians in France and England, Harriet Grote was famed for her witty, intelligent conversation and notable eccentricities. Her other works include *The Philosophical Radicals of 1832* (1866) and *A Brief Retrospect of the Political Events of 1831–1832* (1878).

See also M. L. Clarke, *George Grote*, 1962; Lady Eastlake, *Mrs Grote*, 1880; J. Fournet, *Madame Henriette Grote*, 1879. C.B.

Grymeston, Elizabeth (before 1563–*c.* 1603), author, was the daughter of Martin Bernye and Margaret Flynte, of Gunton Hall in Norfolk. Her writings show her to have been well educated in classical literature, the Bible, and the Church Fathers, and proficient in Latin, Greek, and Italian. She also had some musical training. In 1584 she married Christopher Grymeston, then a student at Caius College, Cambridge, and later Bursar until his dismissal in 1592; he entered Gray's Inn in 1593 and was admitted to the Bar in 1599. Both the Bernye and Grymeston families were accused at various times of recusancy, and her husband's Roman Catholic sympathies, which she fully shared, may have brought upon him what she refers to as 'eight severall sinister assaults' against his life. They had nine children, eight of whom died prematurely.

As a legacy for her remaining son, Bernye, so that he might know 'the true portrait of thy mother's mind', Elizabeth Grymeston wrote a little volume entitled *Miscelanea. Meditations. Memoratives*, published after her death in 1604 and in a further three enlarged editions. After a dedicatory letter to her son, the work comprises a series of short meditations on religious themes. Her prose is full of paraphrases of the Fathers, and she frequently quotes pieces of poetry by the Catholic poets Robert Southwell and Richard Verstegan, along with others drawn from a popular anthology of 1600, *England's Parnassus*. These quotations are usually skilfully adapted to fit in with her own ideas. The book ends with a series of elegantly turned moral maxims.

See also R. Hughey and P. Hereford, 'Elizabeth Grymeston and her *Miscellanea*', in *The Library*, 1934–35. W.R.O.

Guest, Lady Charlotte (Elizabeth) (1812–95), scholar, businesswoman, collector and diarist, born at Uffington House, Lincolnshire, the daughter of Albemarle Bertie, ninth Earl of Lindsey. She had an unhappy childhood due to differences with her clergyman stepfather, the Revd P. W. Pegus, and sought solace in reading. At twenty-one, against her family's wishes, she married John (later Sir John) Guest, a Welsh ironmaster. The marriage was happy and they had ten children. Three years after his death in 1852 she married Charles Schreiber, her eldest son's tutor, who died in 1884. She had gone blind by 1893, but remained vigorous to the end.

A woman of forceful personality, proficient in French, German, Italian, Welsh, Greek, Latin and Hebrew, Lady Charlotte Guest put her learning and abilities to use in a number of ways. During her first marriage she was her husband's private secretary. She spent eight years preparing the text and making a fine translation of fourteenth-century Welsh tales, published as *The Mabinogion* (1849). After Sir John's death she took over the management of the Dowlais steelworks, near Merthyr Tydfil, improved profits, and embarked on welfare schemes for her workers and tenants. She gave up business after her second marriage and began collecting. She was the first private person to collect English china, eventually donating a superb collection to the Victoria and Albert Museum in Schreiber's memory. Subsequently she began collecting fans and playing cards, building up another unique collection, donated to the British Museum. With the onset of blindness she undertook the publication of reproductions of these collections in five volumes (1888–93). Her last years were spent knitting comforters for London cabmen and keeping up her diary, written from the age of ten. Edited by the Earl of Bessborough, it has been published as *The Diaries of Lady Charlotte Guest* and *The Diaries of Lady Charlotte Schreiber* (1952).

J.R.

Gunning, Susannah (1740?–1800), novelist. Born Susannah Minifie, she collaborated with her sister Margaret in writing a number of novels. The title page of such mutual efforts as *The History of Lady Frances S – – and Lady Caroline S – –* (1763) declares the author to be the Miss Minifies of Fairwater, Somersetshire. After her marriage to John Gunning in about 1765 she continued writing in the popular sentimental style. In *The Cottage* (1769) the excessive emotional refinement of the sentimental novel is handled with a degree of self-consciousness that approaches decadence. Its themes and structures are typical of her other works, which include *Barford Abbey*, 1768, *Anecdotes of the Delborough Family*, 1792, *Memoirs of Mary*, 1793, *Delves: A Welch Tale*, 1796, *Love at First Sight*, 1797, and *Fashionable Involvements*, 1800.

When Susannah Gunning's daughter Elizabeth was turned out of the house by her father during a quarrel, her mother also left; John Gunning subsequently retired with his mistress to Naples, where he died in 1797. Susannah Gunning's last novel, *The Heir Apparent*, was revised and augmented by her daughter and published posthumously in 1802.

A.L.

Gurney, Anna (1795–1857), scholar. The youngest child of Richard Gurney of Keswick, she contracted polio at ten months and never walked. Despite her incapacity she lived a busy, active life, and was renowned for her cheerful personality. She never married. After her mother's death in 1825 she lived with a cousin, Miss Sarah Buxton, at Northrepps Cottage, in Norfolk. After Sarah's death in 1839, Anna Gurney lived alone. Her determination enabled her to make a trip to Rome and Greece, and she was planning a journey to the Baltic when she died.

Anna Gurney's strong will gave her a full life in other ways also. She studied both modern and classical languages, as well as Anglo-Saxon, and published (anonymously, in a limited edition) *A Literal Translation of the Saxon Chronicle* (1819), a work much praised by contemporary scholars. Her knowledge of and interest in the Anglo-Saxon era led her to become the first lady member of the British Archaeological Association in 1845. She was a deeply religious woman with a sense of social responsibility. She was interested in missionary work and in educating the local children. At her own expense she installed a device at Cromer for helping rescue shipwrecked seamen, and often had herself carried down to the beach to direct difficult rescues.

See also E. Hoare, *The Coming Night* (funeral sermon), 1857; Viscount Templewood, *The Unbroken Thread*, 1949.

J.R.

Gwyn, Nell (1650–87), actress and royal mistress. Ellen Gwyn was probably born in or near the Covent Garden district of London where she grew up. Her father seems to have died in a debtors' prison, and she was raised by her mother, a disreputable woman who drank excessively and was not averse to her daughter being 'brought up in a bawdyhouse to fill strong waters to the guests'. This and other employments such as raking cinders and selling apples and herrings provided a rough school for Nell Gwyn, who at thirteen became an orange girl at the Theatre Royal through the influence of her sister, Rose, a courtesan.

Bright, attractive, and ambitious, she at some time learned to read and write, took lessons in acting, singing, and dancing from the actors of the King's Company, and made her début on stage in November 1664. She developed rapidly into a popular and accomplished comedian, playing opposite her lover, Charles Hart, and giving her most memorable performance in Dryden's *Secret Love* in March 1667 as Florimel, a role especially created for her.

A brief liaison with Lord Buckhurst, an intimate of the King, led to a lifelong friendship with the Lord and his court circle. Towards the end of 1667 Nell Gwyn became one of the mistresses of Charles II, whom, alluding to her previous liaisons with Buckhurst and Hart, she impudently dubbed her 'Charles III'. Although temporarily eclipsed by Moll DAVIS, she persevered in her new career as part-time royal mistress and full-time actress for nearly two years, returning to the stage even after the birth of her son Charles in 1670, until the King firmly acknowledged her as his mistress and purchased a magnificent house for her in Pall Mall. Sustained by her frank sensuality, bawdy wit, and the advice of her courtier friends, she maintained against formidable competition a permanent place in the King's ménage, supplying him with an evidently irreplaceable brand of entertainment and relaxation.

Nell Gwyn was strongly identified with the Protestant interest at Court, although her political ties seem to have been based mainly on personal friendships, notably with Buckingham and Monmouth. A fond, indulgent, and ambitious mother, she strove successfully to have her sons Charles and James duly acknowledged and provided for (they eventually became respectively Duke of St Albans and Lord Beauclerc). She also acquired during the King's lifetime an annual pension of £5,000 besides additional grants. On his deathbed Charles is said to have issued the memorable injunction to his brother James, 'Let not poor Nelly starve.'

See also B. Bevan, *Nell Gwyn*, 1969; J. H. Wilson, *Nell Gwyn, Royal Mistress*, 1952.

T.J.M.

Gwynne-Vaughan, Dame Helen (1879–1967), botanist and organiser of the Women's Army, born Helen Fraser. She was educated at Cheltenham Ladies' College and King's College, London, obtaining her B.Sc. in Botany in 1904 and her D.Sc. at the age of twenty-eight. She carried out research in mycology, and especially in the cytology of the sex cycle in fungi; she was given her own research school of fungal cytology at Birkbeck College, London, where she became head of the Botany Department in 1909. In 1911 she married the palaeobotanist Professor T. G. Gwynne-Vaughan, who died in 1915.

From 1914 to 1918 Helen Gwynne-Vaughan was called upon to organize a women's army, becoming Chief Comptroller of the Women's Army Auxiliary Forces with the British Army in France. Until 1919 she was Commodore of the Women's Royal Air Force; in that year she was awarded the DBE for her wartime service and resumed her scientific career. In 1920 she gained the Trail Medal of the Linnean Society. In 1928 she became President of the British Mycological Society and of Section K of the British Association. She was an influential member of the university Board of Studies in Botany and served on the Senate from 1929 to 1934. In 1929 she was awarded the GBE. Between 1930 and 1937 she wrote a series of substantial papers on the cytology of fungi, putting forward a stimulating but now discredited theory. Called back to the Women's services in 1939, she served with the Auxiliary Territorial Service with a rank equivalent to major-general. In 1941 she returned to Birkbeck until her retirement in 1944. Later she carried out welfare work for ex-servicemen and became Head of the County Office in London of the Soldiers', Sailors' and Airmen's Families Association, carrying on her work vigorously into old age.

Her publications include *Fungi: Ascomycetes, Ustilaginales, Uredinales* (1922) and a standard textbook on fungi, with B. Barnes (1926 and 1930).

J.E.

H

Hadow, Grace (Eleanor) (1875–1940), educationist, the daughter of a clergyman. Her
mother and brother (the later scholar Sir William H. Hadow) were the strongest influences
on her, both in childhood and later. She went
to Somerville in 1900 to read for the Honours
School of English Language, became English
tutor there in 1905, and moved to Lady Margaret Hall in 1906. After her mother's death
in 1917 she became director of a subsection of
the Ministry for Munitions, in charge of
women workers' welfare, an experience that
fired her interest in the social services. In 1920
she became Secretary of Barnett House,
Oxford, with the aim of furthering the social
services, becoming recognized as an authority
on adult education. In 1929 she became Principal of the Society of Oxford Home Students
(St Anne's) and succeeded in raising the status
of the Society considerably. The Women's
Institute movement also owed much to her:
she recognized its educational and social value
for women and was Vice-Chairman of its
National Federation (1916–40). She collaborated with her brother on *The Oxford Treasury
of English Literature* (1906–08). Her work in
adult and women's education was of major
significance, and her dedication and tolerance
made her popular.

See also H. Deneke, *Grace Hadow*, 1946.

J.R.

Haldane, Elizabeth Sanderson (1862–1937),
social reformer. Born in Edinburgh, she was
the only daughter in a large and distinguished
family. She received tuition alongside her
brothers Richard, John and William (later outstanding as, respectively, politician, scientist
and lawyer), but was denied the university
education and career opportunities that came
to them as a matter of course. She did attend
a private school in Edinburgh, but from 1877
spent much of her time caring for her widowed
mother both at Cloan, the family home in
Auchterarder, and in London.

As a young woman she took an increasing
interest in social reform; after working briefly
with Octavia HILL she set up a housing project
in Edinburgh and in 1890 was a founder
member of the Scottish Women's Benefit
Society. Education and health were to be her
principal areas of activity. Her early work

included workhouse visiting, duties on the
local School Board, the establishment of a
library in Auchterarder, and the formation of
the Westminster Health society. She was
instrumental in the formation of the Territorial
Forces Nursing Service in 1908. She was also
in later years a governor of Birkbeck College
and a member of the Scottish Universities
Committee, the General Nursing Council, and
the Board of Management of Edinburgh Royal
Infirmary. During the First World War she
played an important role in the extension of
nursing services and in 1918 was appointed
CH in recognition of this work.

At Cloan, Elizabeth Haldane met with
numerous people of influence; her friendship
with Andrew Carnegie resulted in her appointment in 1914 as the first woman trustee of the
Carnegie UK Trust, a post which she held
until her death. She also served on a number
of government bodies, notably the Inter-
Departmental Committee on Outdoor Staff,
appointed under the National Insurance Act
of 1911, and the 1912 Royal Commission on
the Civil Service. She gave evidence before
both the 1904 Departmental Committee on
Poor Law Medical Relief and the 1909 Royal
Commission on the Poor Laws, when she was
in favour of the Webb Minority Report.

An author and critic of some distinction, she
published twelve books including *The Wisdom and Religion of a German Philosopher*,
1897, *Descartes: His Life and Times*, 1905,
and *From One Century to Another: the Reminiscences of E. S. Haldane*, 1937. She was the
first woman to receive an Honorary LL D.
from St Andrews University and was also the
first female JP in Scotland. She was a leading
thinker on welfare reform, believing that the
plight of the poor should not be left to the
vagaries of charity. She was also a staunch but
non-militant supporter of women's rights,
employing her talents to promote greater freedom of opportunity throughout society. J.G.S.

Hale, Cicely (1884–1981), suffragette and
social worker. She became an active member
of the Women's Social and Political Union in
1908, remaining a member until the outbreak
of the First World War ended its activities.
She then trained as a social worker and worked
among Jewish and Polish women in White-

184

chapel. At the end of the war she moved to Marylebone, continuing her social work there for sixteen years, and then to Littlehampton, where she was a health visitor. For nine years she conducted the baby circle of the magazine *Woman's Own*, encouraging a large correspondence. In retirement she continued working with young people in the Girl Guide movement, and was also in demand in schools as a popular speaker on the suffragette movement. She published a lively and moving account of these experiences in her book *A Good Long Time* (1973), written at the age of eighty-nine.   B.H.C.

Halkett, Lady Anne (1623–99), author of *Memoirs*, the daughter of Thomas Murray, Provost of Eton College and a tutor to Charles I. Her father died shortly after her birth and the formative influence on her life was her mother, Jane Drummond Murray, who provided her with a deeply religious upbringing and a conventional education. Information about Anne's life comes mainly from her *Memoirs*, composed in 1677–78 and covering her life up to her marriage in 1656 to Sir James Halkett. Although Lady Halkett was by this time a sober and respectable widow (her husband had died in 1670), her *Memoirs* are of immense interest as one of the first female autobiographies to concentrate on their author's romantic life; by contrast her twenty or so works of piety, some published from her manuscripts in the eighteenth century, are now forgotten.

Lady Anne recounts, in fluent prose, her relationship with two men she loved but could not marry; her struggles to reconcile her own impulses with her wish to obey her mother's commands; and her adventures as a resourceful and intelligent young woman, freed from the usual constraints on women's lives by the upheavals of civil war. Her first attachment was to Thomas Howard, heir to Lord Howard of Esrick, whom she was forbidden to see because of her poor dowry. She refused to marry against her parents' wishes but continued to meet Thomas in secret, but with her eyes blindfolded so she could not actually see him. She vowed to remain faithful to Howard but the relationship ended with his marriage to the daughter of a peer in 1646.

Shortly afterwards she met the great romance of her life, Colonel Joseph Bampfield, a Royalist secret agent, with whom she remained

in intermittent contact until 1653, despite persistent rumours that the Colonel, who posed as a widower, in fact had a living wife. In April 1648 Anne helped the Colonel effect the escape of James, younger son of Charles I, from St James's Palace by dressing him in women's clothes, and in the early 1650s she spent two years in Scotland treating wounded Royalist soldiers and caring for the poor. The Colonel promised her marriage, but doubts about his wife caused her much emotional distress and periods of physical collapse. Her brother-in-law was badly wounded in a duel with Bampfield after he had taxed the Colonel with deceiving her, and in 1653 she obtained definitive proof that his wife was still alive. At this point Anne decided to settle for a quiet life with marriage to the sober and reliable Halkett, a middle-aged widower with four children who had courted her for some years. She bore him four children, none of whom survived.

At the Restoration Lady Halkett failed to recover the property lost on account of loyalty to the Crown, and after her husband's death she had to supplement her reduced income by teaching. Her circumstances improved in 1685, when James II (the Prince she had rescued in 1648) awarded her an annuity. Her later life was uneventful. *The Memoirs of Anne, Lady Halkett* were edited by J. Loftis and published in 1979.

See also 'S. C', *The Life of Lady Halkett*, 1701; L. Stone, *Family, Sex and Marriage in England*, 1977.   P.H.

Hall, Marie (1884–1956), violinist. She was born at Newcastle-on-Tyne, the daughter of a harpist. At the age of nine she was heard playing the violin by Emile Sauret, who recommended that she should attend the Royal Academy of Music (RAM) in London. However she continued with her own teacher, receiving occasional lessons from eminent musicians such as Elgar, Wilhelmj, and Max Mossel. She won a scholarship to the RAM but was unable to take it up and was tutored by Johann Kruse.

In 1901 Marie Hall was heard by Jan Kubelik. On his advice she went to Prague to complete her studies under Ševčik (1903). Her public performances there led to engagements in London and Vienna. After a long illness she returned in 1905 to tour Britain, America, and the Commonwealth.

Hall, Radclyffe

She was considered one of the greatest violinists of her day. Vaughan Williams composed *The Lark Ascending* (first performed 1921 under Boult) for her. She also broadcast with her daughter Pauline Baring, the pianist.

A.D.

Hall, (Marguerite) Radclyffe (1880–1943), poet and novelist. Born in Hampshire, she grew up in London with her mother, step-father, and maternal grandmother, her parents having been divorced soon after her birth. She was educated at home and studied for a year at King's College, London. At twenty-one she inherited her grandfather's money and was able to live the life of a wealthy and independent woman, maintaining homes in London and the country, and travelling extensively in Europe and the United States.

A number of poems in Radclyffe Hall's first volume of verse, *'Twixt Earth and Stars* (1907), were set to music, and their popularity led to her meeting Mabel Batten ('Ladye'), a society beauty of fifty who was a talented amateur soprano. Radclyffe Hall was Ladye's lover until the latter's death. She published four more volumes of poetry. 'The Blind Ploughman', in *Songs of Three Counties* (1913), became especially popular in 1918 in a musical setting by Coningsby Clarke.

After Ladye's death in 1916, Radclyffe Hall became deeply occupied with work for the Society for Psychical Research and with a tumultuous personal life. She embarked on a life-long relationship with Una, wife of Admiral, later Sir Ernest Troubridge. In 1920, she was involved in a widely-reported slander trial, following a charge of immorality made against her by a member of the Council of the Society for Psychical Research. She won the case, and in 1921 became a member of the Council.

The Unlit Lamp (1924), her first novel, was well received, and 1926 saw the appearance of her major work, *Adam's Breed*, the story of an illiterate Soho waiter and his search for God. Reprinted seven times in the first year, it was awarded two prestigious literary prizes. Encouraged by her literary and social success, Radclyffe Hall then wrote a novel dealing openly with the subject of lesbianism in a serious attempt to engage public sympathy for, and understanding of, the plight of the 'congenitally invert'. More of a tract than a novel, *The Well of Loneliness* was prefaced with a Note by Havelock Ellis, the pioneer investigator of sexual abnormality. Its appearance in 1928 occasioned a famous trial for obscenity; evidence as to its literary merit having been disallowed, the novel was ruled an 'obscene libel' and suppressed. This once-notorious book has undoubtedly had a profound influence on the law and on social attitudes, if not on the course of the English novel.

Radclyffe Hall's other works include *A Sheaf of Verses*, 1908; *Poems of the Past and Present*, 1910; *The Forgotten Island*, 1915; *The Forge*, 1924; *A Saturday Life*, 1925; *Master of the House*, 1932; *Miss Ogilvy Finds Herself*, 1934; *The Sixth Beatitude*, 1936.

See also V. Brittain, *Radclyffe Hall: A Case of Obscenity?* 1968; L. Dickson, *Radclyffe Hall at the Well of Loneliness*, 1975; Una, Lady Troubridge, *The Life and Death of Radclyffe Hall*, 1961.

J.E.E.H.

Hallé, Lady. See NORMAN-NERUDA, MADAME.

Hamill, Cicely Mary. See HAMILTON, CICELY MARY.

Hamilton, Lady Anne, Duchess of Hamilton (1630–1716), influential Scottish noblewoman. Anne Hamilton was the daughter of James, third Marquis and first Duke of Hamilton (and hence grand-daughter of Anne CUNNING-HAM). In 1651 she became the heiress to the Hamilton title and estates, but did not gain her inheritance until the Restoration of 1660, when her husband, William Douglas, took the title of Duke of Hamilton in right of his wife. The couple married in 1656 and had seven sons and three daughters; the Duke died in 1694. The Duchess is not as flamboyant a figure as her grandmother, but her eminence, piety and integrity gave her a significant influence in late seventeenth-century Scotland. She and her husband were Royalists, but also Presbyterian sympathizers, and, more consistently than Douglas, Anne attempted to moderate the periodic religious persecutions that occurred before 1689. She protected ejected ministers and tried, unsuccessfully, to bring about an accommodation between the Presbyterians and the established order. Her charity including religious endowments and bequests to Glasgow University, earned her the title 'Good Duchess Anne'. In her old age she was a determined opponent of the 1707 union of Scotland and England, fearing for the independence of the Presbyterian Church;

and she is also important as the friend and patron of the historian Gilbert Burnet.

See also J. Anderson, *The Ladies of the Covenant*, 1886.   A.H.

Hamilton, Marchioness of. See CUN-NINGHAM, LADY ANNE, MARCHIONESS OF HAMILTON.

Hamilton, Cicely Mary (1872–1952), actress and writer. The daughter of an impoverished army officer, she always earned her own living, first in teaching (which she detested), and then as an actress in provincial repertory and in London (where she changed her name from Hamill to Hamilton). She is best remembered as a playwright, novelist, and travel journalist, making her name in 1908 with the play *Diana of Dobson's* (for which she had precipitately sold the rights for £100). She wrote some twenty plays in all, including two suffrage dramas.

She was an uncompromising representative of the brand of Edwardian feminism which viewed the economic subordination of women as the central issue, and which believed that women should expect to compete with men on men's terms. Most of her writing reflects her strong views; *Marriage as a Trade* was the most biting example of her feminist polemic, stripping away the romance surrounding marriage. During the inter-war years she was an active member of the Open Door Council, which strove to improve the legal and economic position of women.

After the First World War she became preoccupied with finding an explanation for the growth of 'the aggressive instinct' and came to link the militant suffrage activity of the pre-war years to the 'combative impulse' she deplored. As a thorough-going individualist, she distrusted all aspects of organized life and feared the growth of what she termed 'irresponsible democracy'.

Her other works include *Life Errant*, 1935, her autobiography, *Just to Get Married*, 1911; *William an Englishman*, 1921; a history of the Old Vic with Lilian BAYLISS, 1926; and *Lament for Democracy*, 1940.   J.E.L.

Hamilton, Lady Emma (1765–1815), mistress of Lord Nelson and second wife of Sir William Hamilton, British Ambassador at Naples. Born Amy Lyon, a Cheshire blacksmith's daughter, she entered service and came to London at the age of fourteen. Calling herself Emma Hart, she was briefly the mistress of Sir Harry Fetherstonhaugh of Up Park, then from 1781 the mistress of Charles Greville, who taught her to sing, dance, and act. In 1786 Greville ceded her to his uncle Sir William Hamilton, who at the same time paid his nephew's debts. In love with Greville, Emma Hart at first resented the arrangement. In 1791, however, she married Sir William and as ambassador's wife became the confidante of Maria Carolina, Queen of Naples. Her subsequent political role was far from negligible: she informed Sir William of Spain's intention to ally with France, and later helped the King and Queen of Naples to escape to Sicily.

In 1793 Lady Hamilton met Horatio Nelson for the first time. In 1798 she used her influence to enable his ships to obtain stores in neutral Sicily and pursue the French fleet, which they destroyed at the Battle of the Nile. When Nelson returned to Naples he fell in love with her, and by the time they returned to England with Sir William she was pregnant with his child, Horatia, born in January 1801. Nelson and the Hamiltons formed a devoted threesome; whether Sir William, now over seventy, realized the exact state of affairs is unclear. He died in 1803 and Nelson in 1805. Both provided generously for Lady Hamilton in their wills, but she gambled and was extravagant; she died at Calais, destitute and hounded by creditors.

In her time Lady Hamilton was widely admired: as a young woman she was evidently beautiful, vivacious and fascinating. Many Italian and English artists painted her (Romney in particular was obsessed by her); later, when she was fat and famous the cartoonist Gillray satirized her cruelly.

See also N. Lofts, *Emma Hamilton*, 1978; H. Tours, *The Life and Letters of Emma Hamilton*, 1963.   A.M.N.

Hamilton, Mary Agnes (1884–1962), Labour MP, writer, and public servant. She was the eldest daughter of Robert Adamson, Professor of Logic at Glasgow University. Educated at Glasgow Girls' High School, she went up to Newnham College, Cambridge, in 1902 to study economics. She took First Class Honours. But her real interest, even at university, was politics, and she joined the Independent Labour Party. She married early and unhappily, but retained her married name. She had been writing for some time when, in 1916, her

Hammond, Barbara

novel *Dead Yesterday* caused something of a sensation with its account of the dilemma of the British intellectual in August 1914 and after. She was by this time a well-known journalist and spoke often for the Labour Party.

Throughout her life, Mary Agnes Hamilton was in demand as a committee member. She sat on the Balfour Committee on Trade and Industry (1924–29) and the Royal Commission on the Civil Service (1929–31). She stood twice unsuccessfully for Parliament before being elected in 1929 as Labour Member for Blackburn, and she quickly became Parliamentary Private Secretary to the Postmaster General, Clement Attlee. She enjoyed parliamentary life and looked set for a distinguished career. However, in spite of her success in the House, and at the Assembly of the League of Nations, which she attended in 1929, political events were to overtake her: she lost her seat in the débâcle of 1931.

She never returned to Parliament, but she continued her public service, becoming a Governor of the BBC (1933–37) and a London Alderman (1937–40). In 1940 she entered the Civil Service and became head of the United States section of the Ministry of Information. She was created CBE in 1949. Apart from her political work, she is perhaps best remembered for her writing, particularly the biographical sketches she did of Mary Macarthur and Margaret Bondfield, and her biography of Arthur Henderson (1938), probably the best of her many books. She wrote memoirs, *Remembering my Good Friends* (1944) and *Uphill all the way* (1953).   E.M.V.

Hammond, (Lucy) Barbara (1873–1961), social historian who, with her husband, wrote classic accounts of the sufferings inflicted by the Industrial Revolution and the popular movements in protest against them. Barbara Bradby was the daughter of a clergyman and former headmaster of Haileybury College. She went to St Leonard's School at St Andrews, and was a brilliant classics student at Lady Margaret Hall, Oxford. In 1901 she married John Lawrence Hammond, and the bulk of their work thereafter was done in collaboration. Their great trilogy, *The Village Labourer*, 1911, *The Town Labourer*, 1917, and *The Skilled Labourer*, 1919, described the conditions of work and workers between 1760 and 1832, the transitional period between the

old and the new ways of life; *The Age of the Chartists*, 1930 and *The Bleak Age*, 1934, give an account of the 1830s and 1840s from a similar standpoint. The Hammonds were Liberals, not socialists, but their emphasis on social misery represents the traditional 'left wing' view, and has intermittently come under attack from historians of the other persuasion, who have argued that living standards actually improved under early industrial capitalism. The issue continues to be hotly debated; what is not in doubt is the value of the Hammonds' contribution to the debate. Their other joint works included a life of the social reformer Lord Shaftesbury (1923) and *The Rise of Modern Industry* (1925). In 1933, with a proper sense of the appropriate, the University of Oxford awarded both husband and wife an honorary D.Litt. on the same day.   N.H.

Hammond, Kay, stage name of Katharine Standing (1909–80), actress. She was born in London, the daughter of the actor Sir Guy Standing, and was educated at The Lodge, Banstead, and the Royal Academy of Dramatic Art. Her first London appearance was in *Tilly of Bloomsbury* (June 1927), after which she was never out of work. Excellent in comedy, she could be both seductive and charmingly ridiculous, as in Rattigan's *French Without Tears*. From 1931 she acted in several films, including *Blithe Spirit* (1945).

During the Second World War she was in Coward's *Blithe Spirit* and *Private Lives* (with John Clements, who became her second husband). Under Clements' direction she played in Dryden's *Marriage à la Mode* and, in 1949, in Farquhar's *The Beaux' Stratagem*, which ran longer than any previous classical play in the history of the English theatre. Kay Hammond and John Clements broadcast weekly in *We Beg to Differ*, achieving great popularity.   A.D.

Hancock, Dame Florence (1893–1974), trade-union official. She was born at Chippenham, the daughter of textile workers, and one of a large family of fourteen. Her first job, on leaving school at the age of twelve, was in a café kitchen where she worked a twelve-hour day for a wage of 3s. a week. At fourteen she began work in a local condensed-milk factory where in 1913 she joined a newly formed branch of the Workers' Union. Increasing commitment to unionism led to her appointment in 1917 as district officer for Wiltshire and, in 1918, for Gloucestershire.

Florence Hancock remained in the West of England until 1942, serving from 1929 as Women's Officer in Bristol for the Transport and General Workers' Union (TGWU). In 1942 she moved to London to become Chief Women's Officer for the TGWU, a post she held until her retirement in 1958. Her own early years of poverty made her a staunch campaigner for the 200,000 women members of the union, most of whom were unskilled, and she pressed hard for equal pay, the provision of day nurseries, and improvement in the conditions of domestic workers.

By the outbreak of war she had already made her name in the trade-union movement, being elected to the TUC General Council in 1935 and representing it at the International Labour Organization. From 1941 to 1945 she served on the committee that advised the government on women's war work, and was the TUC's appointee in the South-West to help maintain production in the event of an invasion.

Her career in trade-unionism culminated in her election in 1947 as the third woman chairman of the TUC. Created DBE in 1951, she retired from the General Council in 1958. Outside the trade union movement she served on many official bodies, including the Royal Commission on Capital Punishment (1949), the Piercy Committee on the disabled (1953), and the Franks Committee on administrative tribunals (1955). She was a governor of the BBC from 1956 to 1962.

Held in high esteem by her contemporaries (she and other leading women trade-unionists such as Anne LOUGHLIN were viewed with awe by Walter Citrine), she was a woman of cheerful common sense and a leading figure in the postwar trade-union movement.

See also S. Lewenhak, *Women and Trade Unions*, 1977.   K.W.

Harding, Sarah (*fl.* 1725–28), printer in Dublin. After the death of her husband John Harding, his widow Sarah continued the business for a few years from two addresses, 'opposite the Hand and Pen in the Blind Key', and then 'next door to the Crown in Copper Alley'. She printed *The Intelligencer* and some pamphlets for Jonathan Swift. Imprisonment in 1728 for printing a satirical poem may have persuaded her to abandon printing. Her husband had

been prosecuted in 1724 for printing Swift's *Drapier's Letters*.

See also H. R. Plomer, G. H. Bushnell, E. R. McC. Dix, *A Dictionary of the Booksellers and Printers who were at work in England, Scotland, and Ireland from 1726 to 1775*, 1932.   T.H.

Harley, Lady Brilliana (1598?–1643), Civil War heroine and letter-writer. She was the daughter of Sir Edward, later Viscount, Conway, a Warwickshire gentleman, and was born in Brill (hence her name) in the United Provinces, where her father was a commander. She had a deeply religious upbringing. The Conways lived in England from 1606 and in 1623 Brilliana became the third wife of Sir Robert Harley of Brampton Bryan, Herefordshire. She and her husband were thorough-going Puritans and Sir Robert, a member of the Long Parliament, was one of very few Herefordshire gentry to side with Parliament in the Civil War. Edward, the eldest of their seven children, served in the Parliamentary army.

Lady Harley's part in the Civil War, her views on current political and religious affairs, and much about her family life, are found in the hundreds of her surviving letters. From these emerges a picture of a deeply religious, literate woman, fluent in French: she wrote in 1638, 'I had rather read anything in that tongue than in English.' She closely supervised the education of her children, with a particular concern for their religious beliefs, was an able manager of the family estates during her husband's frequent absences on parliamentary business, and was a patron of many local ministers. She had decided views on the developments of the early 1640s, writing in February 1641, 'I have always believed that the Lord would purge his church from all these things and persons that have been such a hindrance to the free passage of his glorious gospel; and I trust, now is the time.' She welcomed the downfall of the bishops and the execution of the Earl of Strafford, Charles I's chief adviser.

Lady Harley became increasingly fearful for the safety of her home and younger children once the Civil War began, isolated as she was in a Royalist county. She begged her husband for permission to join him in London but he refused, preferring to leave her in charge of Brampton Bryan, presumably as a focus for the Parliamentarian cause in Herefordshire. Estate management became increasingly difficult as her tenants refused to pay rent and her cattle were driven away by the Royalists. She was forced to let her servants go because she could not pay them. Nevertheless she managed to supply the house with food, muskets and shot, ready for an attack. From February 1643 she was virtually confined to her own home after she refused to allow the Royalists to garrison Brampton. In July 1643 a full siege began, led by Sir William Vavasour. Lady Harley refused all demands for her surrender, arguing that she was simply obeying the laws of the land in protecting what was hers. After seven weeks Vavasour was forced to retreat on hearing that the Parliamentarians under the Earl of Essex were approaching Gloucester. Despite Lady Harley's protestations to the king that she had only 'some few muskets ... to keep me from the plundering of the soldiers' she seems to have been in charge of about a hundred people during the siege including fifty musketeers. An eyewitness described her as 'this noble lady who commanded in chief, I may truly say with such a masculine bravery both for religion, resolution, wisdom and warlike policy, that her equal I never yet saw.' Her health had always been poor and she did not long survive the siege, dying in October 1643. Her letters are printed in *The Historical Manuscripts Commission*, Bath MSS vol. 1 and Portland MSS vol. 3; and (edited by T. T. Lewis) in *Camden Society*, 1854.   P.M.H.

Harraden, Beatrice (1864–1936), novelist and suffragette. The daughter of an importer of musical instruments, she was born at Hampstead in London and went to school at Dresden and Cheltenham before going on to Queen's and Bedford Colleges; her London University BA in classics and mathematics was still an unusual achievement for a woman in the 1880s. Despite her early success as an author, Beatrice Harraden was extremely shy; nevertheless she became one of the leaders of the Women's Social and Political Union and the Women Writers' League. She campaigned vigorously for the vote, speaking, writing, and selling newspapers on behalf of the suffragette movement; her descriptions of events are prime sources. Her books, written in a now dated 'poetic' vein, had a considerable vogue in their day; *Ships That Pass in the Night*, 1893, was a best-seller, and *In Varying Moods*

1894 (short stories), *Katharine Frensham*, 1903, and *Out of the Wreck I Rise*, 1907, found readers down to the 1920s.   N.H.

Harrison, Jane Ellen (1850–1928), classical scholar. The daughter of a timber merchant, Jane Ellen Harrison was educated by governesses, one of whom was to become her stepmother; then at Cheltenham Ladies' College, which left her with an abiding dislike of schools; and at Newnham College, Cambridge, to which she won a scholarship in 1874. She gained the highest place in the Second Class in Classics, the best result for a woman until then. She moved to London to study archaeology at the British Museum, lecturing on Greek art in the Museum's galleries and at boys' schools. In 1898 she returned to Newnham as lecturer in classical archaeology; and from 1900 to 1903 she was the College's first Research Fellow.

With Gilbert Murray and Frances Cornford, Jane Ellen Harrison furthered a new movement in classical studies, turning from textual criticism to studies informed by anthropology, archaeology, and philosophy. In 1882 she published *Myths of the Odyssey in Art and Literature*, and in 1885 *Introductory Studies in Greek Art*. Turning her attention to religion she produced *Mythology and Monuments of Ancient Athens* (1890) and the widely admired *Prolegomena to the Study of Greek Religion* (1903). *Themis* (1912) was written with Cornford and Murray. *Epilegomena to the Study of Greek Religion* (1921) was influenced by Freud and Jung, and by a conviction of the biological value of religion. With her friend and student Hope Mirrlees she also translated from the Russian, notably the early prose classic *The Life of the Archpriest Avvakum*. In 1925 she published *Reminiscences of a Student's Life*. She was Vice-President of the Hellenic Society from 1889 to 1896. One of the first women magistrates in Cambridge, she disliked politics, but emphatically supported female suffrage. She viewed family life as confining, and never married.

See also J. Stewart, *Jane Ellen Harrison*, 1959.   J.E.

Harrison, Mary (1788–1875), flower painter, was born in Liverpool, the daughter of a prosperous hat manufacturer. In 1814 she married William Harrison; they went to live in France but returned to Liverpool after the birth of their first child in 1815.

Later, when her husband lost his money in disastrous commercial enterprises, Mary Harrison rose to the occasion and became the sole support of the family of twelve children. A talented amateur artist, she now turned professional and devoted herself to painting flowers. In 1829 she moved to London and became one of the founder-members of the New Society of Painters in Watercolours, later called the Royal Institute of Painters in Watercolours. She exhibited her fruit and flower compositions annually at the Society's gallery in Pall Mall. After a period of obedience to the fashion for painting cut specimens of plants, she struck out in a new direction with pictures of growing flowers and fruit. She loved wild flowers, and went on long country walks to find them.

To the French, who greatly admired her, Mary Harrison was 'the Rose and Primrose painter'. Her most famous work was *The History of a Primrose*, done in three panels: Infancy, Second Maturity, and Decay. In her lifetime she exhibited more than 300 pictures. Examples of her work can be seen in the Victoria and Albert Museum, London.

See also C. Wood, *Dictionary of Victorian Painters*, 1971.   P.L.

Harrison, Mary St Leger. See MALET, LUCAS.

Hartley, Elizabeth (1751–1824), actress and famous beauty. Born at Berrow, Somerset, she first appeared on stage at the Haymarket Theatre (1769) and then toured the provinces for several years. In 1772, as Jane Shore at Covent Garden, she had an enthusiastic reception and stayed at the theatre for the remaining eight years of her career. She was Elfrida in Mason's tragedy, Rosamund in Hull's *Henry II*, and the original Lady Touchstone in Mrs Cowley's *The Belle's Stratagem* (1780); and she played Desdemona and Lady Macbeth. Most critics thought her weak in tragedy and advised her to attempt no emotion stronger than pathos.

But no one faulted her beauty. Auburn-haired, fine-featured, and with a lovely figure, she posed for many artists and was the favourite model of Sir Joshua Reynolds. She is quoted as deriding his compliments: 'Nay, my face may be well enough for shape, but sure 'tis freckled as a toad's belly.' She retired from the stage in 1780 and died at Woolwich.   P.L.

Harvie Anderson, Betty (1914–79), Conservative MP and first woman Deputy Speaker.

Born in Stirlingshire, she went to school at St Leonard's School, St Andrews. She began her political career in local government and became a district councillor in Stirlingshire in 1938. She served during the war on anti-aircraft sites and saw action when the Germans raided the Forth in 1941–42. In 1943 she was made commander of the mixed Heavy Anti-Aircraft Brigade, with which she stayed until 1946.

She maintained her political interests during this period and was elected to Stirlingshire County Council in 1945, becoming leader of the 'Moderate' group in 1953. She was awarded the OBE in 1955 for services to politics and education. She stood three times in Parliamentary elections before she was selected for the safe Conservative seat of Renfrewshire (East), which she won in 1959 and held for the next twenty years; she continued to be known by her maiden name, although she was married by this time to Dr John Skrimshire, a hospital consultant.

In the House, Betty Harvie Anderson's reputation was that of a tireless and diligent committee woman rather than a charismatic speaker. She was a member of the executive of the powerful Conservative backbenchers' 1922 Committee from 1962 to 1970 and again from 1974 to 1979. She sat on the Wheatley Commission on Local Government in Scotland and on the Historic Buildings Council for Scotland. She was made a Privy Councillor in 1974. The high point of her political career, however, was probably her service as Deputy Chairman of Ways and Means, in which capacity, as Deputy Speaker, she became the first (and so far the only) woman to sit in the Speaker's Chair. She did the job competently and with characteristic lack of fuss. When she retired in 1973, it was because she wanted to be free to oppose Scottish devolution. She did not stand in the General Election of 1979 and was created a Life Peeress as Baroness Skrimshire; but she died only a few days after taking her seat.

See also E. Vallance, *Women in the House: A Study of Women Members of Parliament*, 1979.   E.M.V.

Haslett, Dame Caroline (Harriet) (1895–1957), engineer. Caroline Haslett was born in Sussex, the eldest daughter of a railway signal fitter and pioneer of the co-operative movement. She attended Haywards Heath

High School and began work as a secretary with an engineering firm. She asked to be transferred to the works and during the First World War got the experience which allowed her to qualify first in general and then in electrical engineering.

In 1919 she founded the Women's Engineering Society, of which she was for many years secretary. She was a pioneer in breaking down employers' prejudices against female labour, and in persuading the professional engineering institutions to allow women to qualify. She edited *The Electrical Handbook for Women* and *Household Electricity*, and in 1924 founded the Electrical Association for Women, which grew into a nation-wide organization with over ninety branches and ten thousand members.

In 1930 Caroline Haslett was the sole woman at a power conference in Berlin, and she thereafter took up many public appointments, including a governorship of the London School of Economics and the Presidency of the Federation of Business and Professional Women. In 1947 she was appointed part-time member of the British Electrical Authority and promoted to DBE (having been created CBE in 1931). A most able organizer and committee woman, she did much by her efforts and her own example to open up to women the hitherto male world of engineering.   E.M.V.

Hastings, Selina, Countess of Huntingdon (1707–91), promoter of Methodism. The daughter and co-heiress of Washington Shirley, second Earl Ferrers, she married Theophilus Hastings, Earl of Huntingdon, in 1728. They retired to Donington Park, Leicestershire, where the Countess soon became well known for her charities. At Donington she was converted to Methodism by her sister-in-law, Lady Margaret Hastings, and although her husband disapproved of her adherence to the movement he made no effort to curtail her growing involvement. After the death of two of her sons from small-pox in 1743 and of her husband in 1746, she left Donington Park and took a house at Ashby with her children and sisters-in-law. The death of her husband left her in control of considerable funds, which enabled her to set up chapels and support their ministers. By 1749 she had settled in London, opening her house in Chelsea to the evangelist George Whitefield in order that his preaching might reach a wider audience. Much of her life was devoted to attracting the aristocracy to Methodist doctrines, for which purpose she extended her evangelical activity to the fashionable circles of Bath, Tunbridge Wells, and London. With the proceeds from the sale of her jewels in 1761, she sponsored the first regular chapel at Brighton. In 1768 she opened Trevecca House in North Wales as a seminary for ministers, and subsequently devoted much time and energy to furthering the college. Her interest in missionary work overseas (which ultimately cost her £10,000) began in 1770, when Whitefield bequeathed his foundations in America to her.

The Countess of Huntingdon's efforts to advance the Methodist cause met with several checks. At a time when Methodists still thought of themselves as reforming members of the Church of England, the Countess operated on the principle that a peeress could constitute an unlimited number of priests as her chaplains and appoint them to livings in chapels which she had built; but in 1779 the Consistory Court of London overrode her freedom of appointment and forced her to register her chapels as dissenting meeting houses. The Countess also became involved in the dissensions that culminated in a break between Wesley and George Whitefield, whose Calvinistic Methodism she supported. Finally, in 1790, she founded her own 'Countess of Huntingdon's Connexion'. Dubbed by Horace Walpole 'Queen of the Methodists', the Countess of Huntingdon was pre-deceased by all her four sons and left her large fortune to be used for religious purposes.

See also, H. Keddie, *The Countess of Huntingdon and Her Circle*, 1907; A. Valentine, *The British Establishment 1760–1784*, 1970.
                                                      A.L.

Hathaway, Anne (1555/6–1623), wife of William Shakespeare. She was probably the daughter of Richard Hathaway, a prosperous yeoman of Shottery, a village just outside Stratford-upon-Avon. Anne Hathaway and Shakespeare were married in haste, by special licence, in November 1582, when he was eighteen; she was sixty-seven at her death and must therefore have been eight years older than her husband. Their first child, Susanna, was born six months after the wedding, in May 1583, and the twins Hamnet and Judith followed in January or February 1585. Apart from mentions in two wills, nothing else is known about

Anne Hathaway—not even how often the poet visited her in Stratford after he had made a career for himself in London; at his death he left her 'my second best bed with furniture'.

N.H.

Havergal, Frances Ridley (1836–79), poet. She was born at Astley Rectory, Nuneaton, Warwickshire, daughter of William Henry Havergal, who published sermons and composed sacred music. Her brother, Henry East Havergal, was also a talented musician and composer. Her verse was mainly religious and included many hymns and devotional poems. Much of her material was reprinted for many years. Her hymns included 'True-Hearted, Whole-Hearted', 'O Saviour, Precious Saviour', and 'Tell it out Among the Heathen'. Some were set to music by famous composers, including Gounod. *Poetical Works* appeared in 1884 and *Ministry of Song* in 1870. Among her chief works were *Loyal Responses*, 1878, *Life Chords*, 1880, and *Life Echoes*, 1883. For children she wrote *Bruey: A Little Worker for Christ*, 1872, *Little Pillows: or Good Night Thoughts*, 1874, and *Morning Bells: or Waking Thoughts*, 1874.

See also *Memorials of Frances Ridley Havergal*, 1880, by her sister, M. V. H. Havergal.   B.H.C.

Hawker, Mary Elizabeth (1848–1908), short story writer who used the pseudonym 'Lanoe Falconer'. She was born at Inverary, Aberdeenshire, the daughter of a soldier. Although she had no formal education, she read a good deal and during time spent abroad learned German and French. It was not until the age of forty-two that she achieved success with her *Mademoiselle Ixe*, a short story which was among the best of its time and which included Mr Gladstone among its admirers. Although popular abroad, the work was banned in Russia because the heroine, an English governess, becomes involved with Russian Nihilists. Her other works include *Cecilia de Noël*, 1891, *Hotel d'Angleterre and Other Stories*, 1891, *Old Hampshire Vignettes*, 1907, *Shoulder to Shoulder*, 1891, and *The Wrong Prescription*, 1893. Although she continued writing, ill-health blighted her later career.   B.H.C.

Hay, Lucy, Countess of Carlisle (1599–1660), political intriguer. She was the second daughter of Henry Percy, ninth Earl of Northumberland, who spent fifteen years in the Tower for his alleged involvement in Catholic plots. In 1617 she became the second wife of James Hay, a Scots favourite of James I, greatly angering her proud father, who 'could not endure that his daughter should dance any Scotch jigs'. Hay, created Earl of Carlisle in 1622, was a good-natured spendthrift, almost twenty years Lucy's senior, and theirs seems to have been a comfortable, unexacting marriage, entirely suited to the Countess who apparently enjoyed harmless flattery and flirtation rather than closer personal commitments. She was, wrote Edmund Waller, one of her many eulogists, 'Born for no-one, but to delight the race of men'; or, as her sister, the Countess of Leicester, more critically described her, 'Her great fortune, the observations of powerful men, and the flatteries of some mean ones, doth make her less sufferable than ever she was.' Lucy Hay had no children and did not remarry after Carlisle's death in 1636.

Her historical role was that of an inveterate political intriguer, an accomplished practitioner of the informal manipulation through which women have often influenced public affairs. Her beauty, intelligence, and wit ensured her a prominent place at Charles I's court, and she was one of the oldest and closest friends of HENRIETTA MARIA. She was part of the Protestant group which included the Earls of Northumberland, Leicester, and Holland (her brother, brother-in-law, and intimate friend), and which found common ground with the Catholic Queen in hostility to Spain. With apparent inconsistency she was also close to Thomas Wentworth, Lord Deputy of Ireland and later Earl of Strafford, a great rival of the 'Puritan' courtiers. All these men relied heavily on her influence with the Queen at Court during the 1630s.

In 1641, after Strafford's execution, Lady Carlisle became a covert ally of the parliamentary opposition, reporting on the secret, ineffectual plotting going on round Henrietta Maria. This has been interpreted as a treacherous revenge on the court which had acquiesced in Parliament's demand for Strafford's death; but a more coherent policy may have been behind it, that of working for a strongly Protestant monarchy, limited by aristocratic influence. On this view it is Lady Carlisle's association with Strafford that is an aberration, prompted by personal attraction. Her later actions can certainly be interpreted according to this theory. She remained with Parliament on the outbreak of Civil War, but her contacts with the Court were used in 1646–47 by the Parliamentarians who were seeking a compromise peace with the King, and during the second civil war she conspired with the Scots, London Presbyterians, and her old ally Holland to raise men and money for Charles I. For this last intrigue she spent eighteen months in the Tower and a further period under house arrest, but she was again active in the Presbyterian interest in 1659–60.

A.H.

Hay, Nicola de la (c. 1160–after 1218). The eldest daughter and heir of Richard, Lord de la Hay, she was married to Gerard de Camville, a notable sheriff of Lincolnshire. Gerard was deprived of his office during the reign of Richard I for being a follower of Richard's younger brother, John. In the troubles of John's own reign, Nicola de la Hay, by then a widow, remained one of his most loyal supporters. She was the hereditary castellan of Lincoln castle and in 1216 John appointed her joint sheriff of Lincolnshire with Philip Mark, already sheriff of Nottingham. In the next year she successfully defended Lincoln when it was besieged by the forces of the rebel Earl of Lincoln. After John's death Nicola's tenure of the sheriff's office, rarely held by women, was confirmed by Henry III. The date of her death is unknown.

See also J. C. Holt, *The Northerners*, 1961.

A.C.

Hayes, Catherine (1825–61), singer. She was born at Limerick, where the Bishop helped to raise funds for her to study singing in Dublin. Her first concert appearance was in 1839 at the city's Rotunda, but after hearing *Norma* in 1841 she decided on an operatic career, studied in Paris and Italy, and appeared at the Italian Opera House in Marseilles, where she was enthusiastically received. An engagement at La Scala, Milan, followed. She sang in Vienna and at Covent Garden, and visited the United States, South America, Australia, and India. In 1857 she married William Bushnell, who died the following year. Her voice was sweet and tuneful over the whole range, including the lower tones, which were accounted very beautiful for a real soprano. Tall and graceful, she was also an effective actress.

B.H.C.

Hays, Mary (1760–1843), radical and feminist novelist, the child of a Dissenting family in Southwark. Her political education was influenced by the radical Dissenter and free-thinker Robert Robinson, who advised on her reading and introduced her to a circle of well-known radicals, including William Frend. Later, after the publication of her pamphlet *Cursory Remarks on an Enquiry into the Expediency and Propriety of Public or Social Worship*, which defended the public worship of Dissenters, she came to know Godwin, Blake, Tom Paine, and Mary WOLLSTONECRAFT. Her *Letters and Essays, Moral and Miscellaneous* (1793) are strongly influenced by Wollstonecraft's *Vindication*, but despite her emphatic plea for equality and respect in male-female relationships, her critics were chiefly impressed by her religious opinions. Her next work, *Memoirs of Emma Courtney* (1796), was one of the earliest feminist novels, and attracted much more adverse criticism by its frank declaration of female feelings in a love-affair. It was clearly a *roman à clef* in which both William Frend, who did not return her love, and Godwin, as her friendly mentor, make appearances.

As society turned against the radicals under the impact of the the French Revolution, Mary Hays came increasingly under attack, mostly through ridicule in the press; the hunt was led by *The Anti-Jacobin*, an establishment newspaper started by Canning. Mary Hays struck back with her remarkable *Appeal to the Men of Great Britain on Behalf of Women*. In 1799 she published her second novel, *The Victim of Prejudice*, and in 1802 her *Female Biography* in six volumes. The tone of this latter work is less aggressive, and in the ensuing years she appeared less in print, preferring to conduct a private correspondence with friends. Her later friendship with Hannah More encouraged her to further efforts, however, and in 1815 Hannah More's publishing company printed Mary Hays' novel, *The Brother or Consequences. A Story of what happens every Day* in 1815, and in 1817 *Family Annals, or the Sisters;* both books were intended as popular educators. Her last work was *Memoirs of Queens, Illustrious and Celebrated* (1821).

After 1800 Mary Hays' views seem to have lost something of the militant acerbity apparent in her earlier writings, either by mellowing with time or, as some suggest, from aversion to continued public conflict. Her feminism, unlike Mary Wollstonecraft's, always retained a strong religious element.

See also J. P. Baylen and N. J. Grossman, *Biographical Dictionary of Modern British Radicals*, vol. 1, 1979; K. N. Cameron (ed.), *Shelley and his Circle*, 1961; G. Kelly, *The English Jacobin Novel 1780–1805*, 1976. T.H.

Haywood, Eliza (1693?–1757), novelist, journalist, and playwright. Born Eliza Fowler, the daughter of a London tradesman, she appeared on the Dublin stage in 1715 and soon afterwards moved to London. Even her contemporaries disagreed about the details of her early life. Friends contested her critics' view that her two children were illegitimate, asserting that her husband had abandoned her and that she had turned to writing as a means of support. The alternative view is typified by Lord Egmont's summary of her career on hearing a premature report of her death: 'a whore in her youth, a bawd in her elder years, and a writer of lewd novels, wherein she succeeded tolerably well.'

In fact, Eliza Haywood's success was more than 'tolerable': the early novel *Love in Excess* (1719) was, with *Gulliver's Travels* and *Robinson Crusoe*, one of the three most popular fictional works before the publication of Samuel Richardson's *Pamela* in 1740. Its subject-matter explains much of the hostility directed toward its author throughout her life. Plot and characterization are here distinctly secondary; the chief aim is to provoke vicarious erotic pleasure in the reader. Eliza Haywood also incurred the hostility of Pope (who attacked her in *The Dunciad*), Swift, and Walpole in her role as Mary de la Rivière MANLEY's successor in the writing of scandal chronicles. Like Mary Manley's *New Atalantis*, Eliza Haywood's *Memoirs of a Certain Island Adjacent to the Kingdom of Utopia* (1725) uses thinly veiled characters to depict public figures in a variety of unflattering, and often libellous, situations.

In this first phase of her career, which lasted until 1728, her narratives are consistently erotic. Between 1721 and 1733 she also wrote a number of plays, none very successful. A limited output in the early 1730s was suceeded by a period lasting from 1736 to 1742 in which she published no new works. When her writing career resumed, she adapted her talents to the prevailing taste for didactic literature. She was the first woman to produce periodicals for

women: *The Female Spectator* (1744–46) and *The Parrot* (1746). Her novel *Life's Progress Through the Passions* (1748) typifies the worst aspects of the new style of writing in the numbing inevitability of its moral line. But *The History of Miss Betsy Thoughtless* (1753) is considerably more successful. Carefully constructed with attention to psychological plausibility, this novel traces the adventures of an impetuous heroine who learns through long experience to control her vanity.

See also B. MacCarthy, *Women Writers, Their Contribution to the English Novel 1621–1744*, 1946. A.L.

Hazzard, Dorothy (d. 1674), religious radical. Her first husband was Anthony Kelly, a Bristol grocer who died in about 1631. The widowed Dorothy continued to run the shop. As a woman of convinced Puritan views she regarded Christmas day and similar festivals as superstitious relics of popery; so she defied the established church by keeping her shop open, and sat 'sewing in her shop in the midst of the city . . . like a Deborah . . . with a strength of holy resolution in her soul from god'.

Before 1639 she married a local cleric, Matthew Hazzard, who had lost a parochial living through his Puritan views and was then working as a preacher in Bristol. Dorothy Hazzard was much more opposed to the established church than was her husband, and she frequently caused him embarrassment in the years before the Civil War. She refused to attend the parish church because of its 'popish' ceremonies and images, and when Matthew obtained a parish of his own she refused to attend his services because he still used the Book of Common Prayer. Instead, with a group of allies, she would sweep into the church late in the service to listen only to the sermon. Her house was a refuge for religious dissidents on their way to New England and she was an active opponent of the ceremony of churching women after childbirth. This last was obviously a particularly female, even feminist, concern, for the ceremony implied that women were unclean. Dorothy enabled women from all the Bristol parishes to evade the ritual by allowing them to give birth in her own house, since Matthew Hazzard did not impose the ceremony in his parish.

In the early 1640s Dorothy and her allies in her husband's parish gradually organized a completely separate congregation. They met in her home for prayer and, under the influence of Mr Canne, a Baptist preacher, constituted the first Baptist church in Bristol with some 160 members. In 1643 Bristol was besieged by the King and despite the efforts of Dorothy Hazzard and other staunch Parliamentarians, who tried to block up the gates with woolsacks and earth, the Royalists took the city. The congregation was then dispersed, but reformed in 1645, when Parliament took Bristol again. Dorothy Hazzard played an active part in its affairs until her death; although her religious views conflicted with her husband's, they lived together, apparently happily, until Matthew's death around 1670.

Many facets of women's experience in the seventeenth century meet in the life of Dorothy Hazzard: the economic and personal autonomy of many widows; the opportunity for unusual activity afforded by the Civil War; and especially the comparative freedom offered by religious radicalism. Like several other women Dorothy Hazzard played an important part in founding and maintaining a separatist congregation, and, again like other women, she found in her religious beliefs a sanction for independent activities, even for open defiance of her husband.

See also Claire Cross, 'He-Goats Before the Flocks' in *Studies in Church History* (The Ecclesiastical History Society), volume 8.

P.M.H.

Heelis, Mrs Beatrix. See POTTER, (HELEN) BEATRIX.

Hemans, Felicia (Dorothea) (1793–1835), poet. She was born Felicia Browne in Liverpool, and was a precocious child whose early interest in poetry was encouraged. She published her first volume of verse in 1808 at the age of fifteen. It was followed by *The Domestic Affections* in 1812, the year in which she married Captain Alfred Hemans, an Irish officer. Five sons were born, but in 1818 the couple separated, Captain Hemans living in Italy and his wife in Wales, Lancashire, and Dublin. Her verse is pleasant and, at its best, graceful. Some of her more sentimental poems became very popular and ran into numerous editions which had an avid readership among young ladies. They include *The Forest Sanctuary*, 1825, *Records of Woman*, 1828, and *Songs of the Affections*, 1830. 'Mrs Hemans' is probably best remembered today for the

famous and often parodied lines beginning 'The boy stood on the burning deck'.

B.H.C.

Henrietta Maria (1609–69), Charles I's queen. Henrietta Maria, the youngest daughter of King Henri IV of France and his second wife, Marie des Médicis, married Charles I in 1625. Initially the marriage of the vivacious sixteen-year-old to the reserved English king was not a success, but after assassination removed Charles's favourite, Buckingham, in 1628, the birth of a still-born child in 1629 brought Charles and Henrietta Maria together, and they became a devoted couple. Henrietta Maria's first living child, the future Charles II, was born in 1630, and seven more children followed by 1644, of whom two died very young.

Lively and frivolous, the Queen wholeheartedly enjoyed the cultural life of the court, particularly the extravagant and elaborate masques, which aroused much criticism among Puritans. Her leading role in Walter Montagu's *The Shepheard's Paradise* in 1633 probably provoked the publication of William Prynne's *Histrio-Mastix*, in which the Puritan lawyer castigated women actors as 'notorious whores'. For his audacity Prynne had his ears cropped, and was sentenced to life imprisonment. Henrietta Maria's Catholicism was another source of disapproval, and also of fears that it might prove infectious: in the 1630s there were several Catholic conversions among fashionable courtiers and in 1636 her chapel at Somerset House was opened for public celebration of the mass.

However, it has recently been argued that Henrietta Maria's influence with Charles was not used simply in a pro-Catholic direction but that she had a group of 'Puritan' followers including the Earls of Holland and Northumberland and her close friend Lucy HAY, Countess of Carlisle. Their alliance was based on common hostility to Spain and on opposition to the King's chief (and pro-Spanish) advisers, Wentworth (Strafford), Laud, and Weston. Henrietta Maria's opportunistic political stance meant that she kept in touch with potentially threatening nobles until she switched her support to Laud and Wentworth in 1639, cutting the Court off from a group that might have reached agreement with the parliamentary leadership and prevented civil war.

In 1641, as the crisis deepened, Henrietta Maria became involved with extremist hotheads such as her close friend Henry Jermyn, who tried to organize military coups against the Long Parliament. Fears for her safety were an important influence on Charles's actions in 1641–42: he agreed to Wentworth's execution in May 1641 during popular demonstrations in London which attacked the 'popish Queen'; and his abortive attempt on the 'Five Members' and the precipitate flight of the royal family from London in January 1642 occurred amid rumours that Parliament would accuse Henrietta Maria of complicity in the Irish rebellion of the previous October.

Early in the Civil War, Henrietta Maria spent a year in Holland raising support for the Royalist cause. She was reunited with Charles and the Court at Oxford in July 1643. Her influence was directed against any compromise peace and she was much involved in the destructive faction fights among the Royalists. She left Charles for the last time in April 1644 and fled to France shortly after giving birth to her youngest child, HENRIETTE ANNE, in June. She continued to offer advice from a distance to her husband, alternately recommending a hard line and opportunistic concessions while hoping for foreign aid. After the shattering blow of Charles's execution, her influence with her son, the young Charles II, was resisted by his more sober advisers. Although Charles II was restored in 1660, she remained in France until 1662, spending only three years in England before returning finally to her native land.

Henrietta Maria has usually been seen as a malign influence on Charles I, but her importance has probably been overrated: ultimately the King followed his own fatal counsels. However, her frivolity, her taste for intrigue, her religion, and the contemporary conviction that she dominated her obviously devoted husband, must have harmed the Royalist cause.

See also Q. Bone, *Henrietta Maria*, 1972; R. M. Smuts, 'The Puritan Followers of Henrietta Maria in the 1630s', in *The English Historical Review*, 1978.   P.M.H.

Henriette Anne, Duchess of Orléans (1644–70), sister of Charles II and intermediary between him and Louis XIV. The seventh and youngest child of Charles I and HENRIETTA MARIA, Henriette was born in Exeter during the Civil War and conveyed safely to France in 1646. Brought up strictly in the Catholic faith and better educated than most royal children, she led a relatively secluded life in which occasional court festivities and the visits of her brother Charles were welcome interludes.

After a family reunion in England after Charles II's restoration in 1660, Henriette returned to France to marry Louis XIV's younger brother, Philippe, Duke of Orléans, known as 'Monsieur' (hence she is generally called 'Madame'). Although a suitable political alliance, which produced two surviving daughters, Henriette's marriage to the homosexual Duke was a personal disaster. Monsieur was jealous not merely of Madame's person but of her popularity and her credit with his brother, who had a high opinion of her intelligence and ability to influence the King of England. According to Charles II's own testimony, his beloved sister 'Minette' was the only woman he ever entirely trusted, and it was she in whom he confided his true political intentions and chose to mediate with Louis XIV in his covert negotiations for an alliance, which culminated in the secret Treaty of Dover in 1670, often called the Traité de Madame. Only a month after their brief and emotional reunion at Dover, which her husband had strenuously opposed, Charles II and his court were shattered by the news of his sister's death, subsequently shown to be from natural causes and not, as was first suspected, of poison. The Treaty of Dover, which she did so much to bring about, remains susceptible to various interpretations, as indeed does the question of where Madame's ultimate loyalties lay.

See also J. Cartwright, *Madame: a Life of Henrietta, Daughter of Charles I and Duchess of Orléans*, 1894; C. H. Hartmann, *The King My Brother*, 1954.   T.J.M.

Hepworth, Barbara (1903–75), sculptor. She was born at Wakefield, studied for one year (1919) at the Leeds School of Art, and then from 1920 to 1924 at the Royal College of Art, London. In 1924 a travelling scholarship enabled her to go to Florence and Rome for two years; she married the sculptor John Skeaping in 1925 in Florence, and they had one son. Between 1928 and 1939 she had a studio in Hampstead, and her circle of friends included Henry Moore, Arp, Brancusi (who influenced her a good deal), Mondrian, and Picasso. In 1931 she separated from John

Skeaping and began her long association with Ben Nicholson, whom she divorced in 1951. In 1939 she and Ben Nicholson moved with their triplets to St Ives in Cornwall, where the financial difficulties caused by lack of commissions for sculpture during the war were overcome by camouflage painting and running a market garden. She maintained a working studio in St Ives to the end of her life, and bequeathed it to the nation as a museum of her works. She was created DBE in 1956.

Barbara Hepworth's early sculptures are in marble, English stone, and wood, and are figurative in a highly simplified way. By 1931, partly though not entirely through the influence of Ben Nicholson, her work had become far more abstract, and she began to use pierced forms. By 1940 she was combining such forms, often in varied colours, with precisely placed stringing in wire or string, creating the effect of a musical instrument and giving movement and contrasts of light to the large masses, which in general are smoothly rounded, with great sensitivity in the carving (always done direct on to the stone). From about 1955 she worked a great deal in bronze, often cast from forms partly carved in plaster rather than entirely modelled. There are works in almost every large collection of modern art all over the world, and some of her large metal forms may be seen in London (State House, Holborn: *Meridian*, 1959; the John Lewis store, Oxford Street: *Winged Figure*, 1963; Dulwich Park: *Divided Circle*, 1969) and in New York, where she created the Hammarskjöld Memorial outside the United Nations building, 1963. Other open-air forms are on a hillside in Cornwall (a large group), and at Harlow New Town, Essex; Hatfield, Hertfordshire; and the Royal Festival Hall, London. She made a *Madonna* for the church at St Ives as a memorial to her son, who was killed in action in the RAF during the Malayan Emergency in 1953. She published *Drawings for a Sculptor's Landscape* (1967).

See also A. Bowness, *Barbara Hepworth, 1960–69*, 1971; B. H. Hodin, *Barbara Hepworth*, 1961.   L.M.M.

Herschel, Caroline (Lucretia) (1750-1848), astronomer, sister and assistant to the famous astronomer Sir William Herschel. Born in Hanover, Germany, she was the daughter of a musician in the Hanoverian Guard. She was taught the violin by her father, but received little formal education since her mother required her help with the housework. In 1772 she joined her brother William, who was studying music and astronomy in Bath, as his housekeeper and assistant. There she studied English and arithmetic, took singing lessons, and received coaching for stage appearances. Her promising career as an oratorio singer was curtailed because William increasingly required her assistance with his astronomical work.

Beginning in 1782, Caroline Herschel herself observed the skies with a small Newtonian reflector, and the following year discovered three new nebulae. In addition to making her own observations, she noted down those made by her brother and carried out the necessary calculations. She reorganized Flamsteed's *British Catalogue* (a listing of nearly 3,000 stars) into zones of one degree each to enable William to search the skies more systematically, prepared his catalogues and papers for publication, and ground and polished mirrors for telescopes. In 1787 she was officially recognized as William's assistant and given a salary of £50. After her brother's marriage in 1788 she lived in lodgings but collaborated with him as before. Between 1786 and 1797 she discovered eight comets, establishing her reputation as an astronomer in her own right. In 1798 the Royal Society published her *Index to Flamsteed's Observations of the Fixed Stars* together with her *Collection of Errata* to those observations. After William's death in 1822 she returned to Hanover where she spent the rest of her life. In 1828 she received the Gold Medal of the Royal Astronomical Society for her *Reduction and Arrangement in the form of a Catalogue in Zones of All the Star Clusters and Nebulae Observed by Sir William Herschel*. Although never published, this work was indispensable to her nephew John Herschel's review of northern nebulae.

In her old age Caroline Herschel received many honours, including election as honorary member of the Royal Astronomical Society in 1835 and of the Royal Irish Academy in 1838. She was entirely without personal ambition and always disclaimed any credit for herself for fear it might detract from that due to her brother. She lived to see the publication of John Herschel's *Results of Astronomical Observations at the Cape of Good Hope* (1847), which completed the comprehensive survey of the heavens to which she had contributed.

See also M. C. Herschel, *Memoir and Correspondence of Caroline Herschel*, 1876; C. A. Lubbock, *The Herschel Chronicle*, 1933.

S.G.

Hertford, Countess of. See GREY, KATHERINE, COUNTESS OF HERTFORD.

Hervey, Lady Mary (1700–68), letter-writer, beauty, and wit. Her father was a brigadier-general in Marlborough's army, and was able to procure advancement at court for his daughter, so that as a young woman she was a maid of honour as well as holding a commission in the army, an anomaly uncommon even during this period. She became part of the literary circle of Pope (who hung her portrait in 'the best Room fronting the Thames' of his villa at Twickenham), Gay, and Chesterfield, but her role seems mainly to have been the passive one of receiving admiration and dedicatory verses for her beauty. Her wit was also praised, however, and her letters, not published until 1821, are not without interest. Her married life involved ignoring a good deal of neglect and infidelity on the part of her husband (the author of the well-known *Memoirs*), and she seems to have been modest about her learning: Chesterfield thought she had more learning than was proper for a woman, no doubt with his own famous definition of the sex (as 'children of a larger growth') in mind, and praised the way in which she concealed her own knowledge of Latin. He recommended his son to visit her in Paris in 1750, saying she has '*le ton de la parfaitement bonne compagnie, les manières engageantes, et le je ne sçais quoi qui plait*'.

See also D. M. Stuart, *Molly Lepell, Lady Hervey*, 1936.

T.H.

Hess, Myra (1890–1965), pianist. Myra Hess started her musical education at the Guildhall School of Music and Drama, but at the age of twelve won a scholarship to the Royal Academy of Music, where she worked with Tobias Matthay for five years and developed the beautiful piano tone for which she was later to become famous. In November 1907 she played Beethoven's Fourth Piano Concerto with Beecham and his orchestra at Queen's Hall, and in time her interpretation of this piece, at a slow tempo but with an unusual warmth of tone and depth of feeling, became

so beloved of musicians and audiences that many younger pianists became nervous of performing it. She subsequently toured in Holland, Germany, and France, and from 1922 onwards in America and Canada. She was created CBE in 1936.

During the Second World War Myra Hess established the famous midday chamber concerts, given daily at the National Gallery in London and attended by many workers during their lunch-hour; the eating of sandwich lunches was allowed during the performances, and this was always done with exemplary quietness. The concerts, given by artists of considerable stature (including Myra Hess herself), were made financially possible by a standard soloist's fee of five guineas. It was for her service in organizing this splendid series that she was created DBE in 1941; but musicians had long regarded her as being worthy of such an honour for her performances alone, and she was soon known throughout the profession simply as The Dame. Having small hands, she was better suited to classical works than to 'war-horses'. Despite her many performances of Mozart, Beethoven, and Schumann, the work most connected with her and best loved by the public was her own arrangement of Bach's chorale prelude 'Jesu, Joy of Man's Desiring'.

R.G.

Hewley, Lady Sarah (1627–1710), philanthropist and Nonconformist. The only daughter and heir of Robert Wolrych, bencher of Gray's Inn, she married John Hewley of Wistow, Yorkshire, Recorder of Doncaster and MP for Pontefract and York. They had two sons, who both died in infancy. The Hewleys were devout Presbyterians, John founding a chapel at York in 1692. After his death in 1697 Sarah Hewley showed her own importance as a local philanthropist and patron of Nonconformity. In 1700 she established an almshouse at York for ten poor Presbyterian women, and in 1705 she donated £200 to charity schools in the city and conveyed to trustees a landed estate whose income was to be used after her death for charitable purposes, including the support of poor preachers.

M.D.

Hickman, Rose (1526–1613), Protestant autobiographical writer. She was the daughter of Sir William Locke, a wealthy merchant of Cheapside; her brother, Henry, was the husband of Anne LOCKE. As a child she was taught from the Scriptures by her mother. In 1543 she married Anthony Hickman, a merchant adventurer in partnership with her brother Thomas. During the reign of Edward VI the Hickmans gave financial support and encouragement to Protestant ministers like John Knox and John Foxe, and continued this practice after the accession of the Catholic Queen MARY I. This led to the imprisonment of Anthony Hickman in the Fleet in 1554. He was eventually released, partly through influence and partly through judicious bribery, and immediately left England for Antwerp. Rose Hickman went to Oxfordshire to await the birth of their child, and there corresponded with the imprisoned bishops, Latimer, Ridley, and Cranmer, on the validity of Catholic baptism. She later joined her husband in Antwerp, where she had another child. They remained there until the accession of the Protestant Queen ELIZABETH I. After their return to England Rose Hickman maintained her contacts with Protestant ministers. Her husband died in 1573, and Rose married Simon Throckmorton of Brampton, Huntingdonshire.

In her old age Rose Hickman compiled an autobiographical narrative, a nice blend of practical and spiritual concerns, which includes reminiscences of her family, particularly her father's role as an importer of Biblical translations for Queen Anne BOLEYN. She also recounted her own experiences in the reigns of Edward VI and Mary, and thus provides uniquely valuable evidence of how the political and religious changes of the age affected the lives of Protestant merchants.

See also M. Dowling and J. Shakespeare, 'Religion and Politics in Mid Tudor England through the eyes of an English Protestant Woman', in *The Bulletin of the Institute of Historical Research*, May 1982.   J.S.

Higgs, Mary (1854–1937), social reformer most noted for her work on vagrancy. Born in Devizes, Wiltshire, she was the daughter of a Congregationalist minister who moved with his family to Bradford when Mary was eight. She was devoted to the Church from an early age, and retained a lifelong deep religious conviction. In 1871 she won a scholarship to the first women's college at Hitchin (later Girton College, Cambridge) from which she graduated in natural sciences. After five years of teaching she married the Reverend Thomas Higgs and in 1891 settled with him in Oldham.

Surrounded by the poverty of the industrial North, Mary Higgs sought to find the causes and the remedies for the social ills she saw. Becoming increasingly aware of the plight of the destitute, she founded a lodging home for workhouse women. Then, in the summer of 1903, she took up the life of a tramp for five days, an act that proved to be the start of her travels to experience at first hand the hardships of life on the road. Her work aroused much interest and concern, and in Oldham alone three houses for the destitute were subsequently established. After the death of her husband in 1907 she was able to devote herself wholly to social reform, addressing herself to national issues such as unemployment and infant welfare. She also campaigned for international friendship and co-operation, and in 1916 joined the Society of Friends to work for peace. The homeless, however, remained her primary concern, and after the war she campaigned by word and deed to ameliorate the worsening vagrancy problem. In all she gave evidence before three departmental committees enquiring into vagrancy (1906), casual ward reform (1924), and relief of the casual poor (1929–30).

In 1936 she was awarded the OBE for her services to Oldham; but through her determination to bring about more humane treatment and better provision for those on the road, Mary Higgs succeeded in extending her influence throughout the country. Her writings include *Three Nights in Women's Lodging Houses*, 1905, *Down and Out: Studies in the problem of Vagrancy*, 1924, and *Casuals and Their Casual Treatment*, 1928.

See also M. K. Higgs, *Mary Higgs of Oldham*, 1954.   J.G.S.

Hild (614–80), Northumbrian abbess. Northumbrian politics were bedevilled by dynastic quarrels, and Hild spent her early childhood in exile with her parents, Hereric and Breguswith, at the court of King Cerdic of Elmet. Not long after her birth her father was slain by his uncle Edwin's dynastic rival, King Æthelfrith. In 617, however, Æthelfrith was killed and Edwin seized the throne. Hild and her family were therefore able to return to Northumbria, and were certainly there by April 627, when she was baptized at York.

Nothing more is known of her life until 647, when she went to East Anglia, where her nephew Ealdwulf was king; she hoped to join his mother, her sister Hereswith, at the Frankish monastery of Chelles. After spending a year with Ealdwulf, however, she was persuaded by Bishop Aidan of Lindisfarne to return to Northumbria, where she was given land on the north side of the River Wear on which to live the religious life. She remained there, with a small band of companions, until 649, when she was made Abbess of Hartlepool. There her first priority was to establish a Rule for the community; and, although she had been baptized by a Roman missionary, she based her Rule on the teachings of the Celtic Church, drawing on the advice and example of Irish ecclesiastics such as Aidan who dominated religious life in Northumbria. At Hartlepool Hild quickly established a reputation for wisdom and piety which won the admiration of her fellow-churchmen and also of the court, for in 655 King Oswiu entrusted his infant daughter Ælfflaed to Hild to train as a nun.

In 657 Hild transferred the community to a new monastery at Whitby, where she continued to make a powerful impact on the religious life of Northumbria. One of her monks, Caedmon, became famous for his religious songs; six others went on to become bishops. The advice of Hild herself was much sought after, and Whitby was selected to be the site of the synod which in 664 decided the Roman–Celtic schism in favour of Rome. Although Hild was often ill for the last five or six years of her life, she continued to play an active role in ecclesiastical affairs, sending a representative to the Pope in 679 to argue against giving back Bishop Wilfrid his see, part of which had gone to her former pupil Boso; and in the year of her death she built a daughter-house at Hackness, thirteen miles from Whitby.

See also B. Colgrave and R. A. B. Mynors (eds) *Bede's Ecclesiastical History of the English People*.   J.C.

Hill, Octavia (1838–1912), philanthropist and housing reformer. The daughter and granddaughter of social reformers, Octavia Hill was born at Wisbech, Cambridgeshire, the third child of her father's third marriage to Caroline Smith, a writer on educational theory. Her childhood was unsettled; in 1840 her father's corn-dealing business failed and he suffered a mental breakdown. The family split up and the children went to live with relatives. In 1851 Octavia Hill went with her mother to London. Mrs Hill was to act as manager of the Ladies' Co-operative Guild, a Christian Socialist project which sought to provide work for the genteel poor and to train needy children. Here Octavia Hill met F. D. Maurice, who impressed her deeply by his desire to link religious commitment with social responsibility, and encouraged the development of her Christian principles.

The various philanthropic and administrative tasks which she undertook for the Guild familiarized Octavia Hill with the appalling housing conditions endured by the poor. She became convinced that existing landlords would never countenance improvement on the scale required, and persuaded her friend John Ruskin to purchase three Marylebone houses for her to manage personally. She sought to secure her tenants' trust, repairing buildings and establishing clubs, classes, and savings banks for their benefit. In return, regular rent payments were demanded: in her view, sound finances were essential if independence and self-reliance were to be encouraged among the poor.

In 1869 Octavia Hill helped to found the Charity Organization Society, designed to combat indiscriminate and demoralizing alms-giving. Under the Society's auspices, she took charge of the Walmer Street district of Marylebone and put her principles into practice. All undirected charity was abolished, while volunteer visitors were employed to seek out and assist the truly deserving.

Meanwhile, Octavia Hill's model housing schemes proliferated and her reputation as an expert on property management grew. Her recommendations greatly influenced the Artisans' Dwelling Bill of 1875. She gave evidence to the Royal Commission on Housing of 1884, and in the same year accepted the Ecclesiastical Commissioners' invitation to manage their extensive South London property. She was particularly active on the Commissioners' behalf in Southwark, where she established a large body of enthusiastic volunteer workers who improved buildings and helped clear waste ground to provide play areas. In 1889 she joined the Committee of the Southwark Women's University Settlement, a scheme in which educated women lived and worked in poor districts in an attempt to foster mutual sympathy between the classes. At the Southwark settlement a thorough training in social work was offered to women, intended to qualify them for a professional career or voluntary service.

Octavia Hill's concern for the quality of urban life inspired her alarm at the disappearance of public open spaces. She fought unsuccessfully to preserve Swiss Cottage Fields, and in 1875 founded the Kyrle Society to provide cities with trees and gardens. She helped raise £70,000 to purchase the threatened Parliament Hill Fields, acquired in 1889, thus extending and securing Hampstead Heath for public use. Other triumphs followed, and Octavia Hill assisted in the creation of the National Trust to administer the property thus conserved.

Although she never married (she terminated a brief engagement in 1873), Octavia Hill thought highly of traditional family life. She believed that the domestic impulse was universal, surmounting class barriers. Women, with their maternal sympathies, were natural philanthropic workers, possessing an inherent understanding of the problems of their poorer counterparts. She disliked the idea of female suffrage, fearing that it would undermine feminine commitment to practical service in favour of nebulous political activity. Her writings include *Homes of the London Poor* (1875) and *Our Common Land* (1877).

See also E. Moberley Bell, *Octavia Hill*, 1942; C. E. Maurice (ed.), *Life of Octavia Hill*, 1913; D. Owen, *English Philanthropy 1660–1960*, 1964.   J.V.L.

Hill, Rosamond Davenport (1825–1902), school and prison reformer. Born in Chelsea, she was the eldest daughter of Matthew Davenport Hill, Recorder of Birmingham and prison reformer. She attended boarding school at Clapton for six years before studying at home with a governess until she was twenty-one.

In 1851 the family moved to Bristol, where she became a firm friend of Mary CARPENTER, assisting her in the running of a Ragged School. She also set up an Industrial School for Girls and devoted much time to it. Her father influenced her greatly and their mutual interest in prison reform resulted in many travels abroad inspecting criminal institutions. On returning from Dublin in 1856, she wrote a paper 'A Lady's Visit to the Irish Convict Prisons', and in the same year founded a society to study reformatory legislation, which developed into

a society to promote the social sciences in general. She strongly believed in the reformatory rather than punitive aims of detention and put similar ideas into practice in the educational sphere.

In 1872 Matthew Hill died, and Rosamond, accompanied by her sister Florence, who was active in helping juvenile paupers, undertook a long trip to Australia. There they inspected various schools and prisons, also giving evidence on the English system of boarding out paupers before a Public Charities Commission in New South Wales. They published their impressions of the country in a book, *What We Saw in Australia* (1875).

The sisters settled in London in 1879, and Rosamond Davenport Hill was elected to the City Division of the London School Board, carrying out its work for the next eighteen years. She was particularly influential as Chairman of the Cookery and later Domestic Sciences Committee and a valued member of the Industrial Schools Committee. In this capacity she fought hard to have the practical and moral aspects of life included in the school curriculum. A major personal triumph was the reorganization of Brentwood Industrial School, which she put on a sound business footing. In 1896 the school was renamed the Davenport-Hill Home for Boys.

In 1895 she was appointed a life governor of University College, London, and in the following year gave evidence before the Departmental Committee on Reformatory and Industrial Schools. In 1897 she moved to Oxford, where she died after a long illness. Her other writings include *Lessons in Cookery* (1885), and with Florence Davenport Hill, *The Recorder of Birmingham: a Memoir of Matthew Davenport Hill* (1878).

See also E. E. Metcalfe, *Memoir of Rosamond Davenport Hill*, 1904.   J.G.S.

Hilton, Marie (1821–96), pioneer of crèche provision. Orphaned in infancy, she was brought up at Richmond, Surrey, by her maternal grandmother. She developed a passion for reading and religion and became a Sunday school teacher at Westminster Congregational Church before moving to Brighton in 1843 as a governess. Here she was drawn to the Society of Friends, and to a particular member, John Hilton, whom she married in 1853.

Eight years later and now the mother of

five children, she moved with her husband to Bromley-by-Bow, in the heart of London's dockland. Appalled by the poverty, she joined the Quaker mission in Ratcliff and introduced a crèche. Derided by pessimists as an invitation to hard-pressed parents to abandon their children, and initially dismissed by locals as a foreign import, the 'crouch', as the East Enders called it, became a model institution which was soon copied in the major cities of Britain, the United States, and the colonies. In its first week in 1871 the crèche admitted ten infants and fifteen young children. 'We never take a child whose mother is capable of looking after it', said Marie Hilton; but by 1893 she and her nursing staff had a hundred children on their books at 16 Stepney Causeway. Fed on a diet of Irish stew and rice pudding the children of coalheavers, dockers, shirtmakers, and charwomen glimpsed an alternative life of toys, singing, and hygiene, though Marie Hilton admitted that some families in the grip of alcohol were beyond help. After twenty-five years the crèche had been visited by 30,000 people and had developed its own welfare network, which included an infirmary, a temporary home for incapacitated mothers, accommodation for nurses, and a country retreat at Feltham in Middlesex. Marie Hilton's own account of her work is *The Crèche at Ratcliff* (1872).

See also J. D. Hilton, *Marie Hilton: Her Life and Work*, 1897.   K.S.

Hoare, Lady Nora (Mary) (?–1973), public figure remembered for her activities on behalf of thalidomide victims. Lady Hoare was the wife of Sir Frederick Hoare, who was elected Lord Mayor of London for 1961–62. She was associated with good causes from an early age, working for refugees, invalid children, the Red Cross, the deaf, and the Royal National Lifeboat Institution. As Lady Mayoress she launched an appeal to help the victims of thalidomide, a sedative drug that was found to produce serious deformities of the limbs in new-born children whose mothers had taken it during the early stages of pregnancy. The limited public response, and the realization that compensation would not be rapidly forthcoming, led to the setting up of the Lady Hoare Trust for thalidomide and other physically handicapped children. Under her guidance, the Trust organized a team of home visitors and set up a centre for research into

artificial limbs; the intention, executed with remarkable success, was that all but the most severely handicapped should be enabled to live at home and attend ordinary schools. At the time of Lady Hoare's death, the Trust cared for some nine hundred children.

N.H.

Hobbes, John Oliver. See CRAIGIE, PEARL (MARY TERESA).

Hoby, Elizabeth (1528–1609), humanist. She was the third daughter of Sir Anthony Cooke, and received an excellent education under his guidance; her correspondence throughout her life demonstrates her knowledge of Latin and Greek. While living in the household of her sister, Mildred CECIL, and her husband William, Elizabeth met Sir Thomas Hoby, whom she married in June 1558. They had two surviving sons, one (Thomas Posthumous) born after the death of his father. Elizabeth Hoby commemorated the deaths of her two infant daughters by composing a Latin inscription for their tomb.

Thomas Hoby died on an embassy visit to France in 1566. In 1574 Elizabeth Hoby married John, Lord Russell, by whom she had two daughters. After his death in 1584, Elizabeth was involved in various law suits, notably against the Earl of Nottingham in the Star Chamber (1606), regarding the occupation of the castle and lands of Donington. During the hearings she was very outspoken, and even went so far as to attack her opponent physically.

Elizabeth Hoby was a strong Protestant and helped to support Puritan preachers, notably Thomas Cartwright, who wrote to her from the Fleet prison in August 1591, thanking her for her offer to intercede on his behalf with her brother-in-law, William Cecil, now Lord Burghley and Queen Elizabeth's chief minister. She passed Cartwright's letter on to Burghley and it is to be found among his papers, endorsed by her, 'God my Lord rede this thorow and do what good yow can to the pore man.' In 1605 she published her translation from the French of *A Way of Reconciliation touching the true Nature and Substance of the Body and Blood of Christ in the Sacrament*, dedicating it to her daughter Anne, then Lady Herbert.

Elizabeth Hoby's connections with some of the most influential families in England, including the Cecils and Bacons, as well as her friendship with Queen Elizabeth, ensured her a high place at court. She derived great benefit from the humanist education she received, and this, coupled with a forceful and intelligent mind, made her one of the most interesting women of her age.

See also D. M. Meads (ed.), *The Diary of Lady Margaret Hoby*, 1930.   J.S.

Hoby, Lady Margaret (1571–1633), diarist. She was the daughter and heiress of Arthur Dakins, a landed gentleman of Linton, East Riding, and received a general education in the household of the Countess of Huntingdon. She was married three times. In May 1589 she became the wife of Walter Devereux, the younger brother of the Earl of Essex, Queen Elizabeth's favourite. He died at the siege of Rouen in 1591, and in the same year she married Thomas Sidney, brother of the poet Sir Philip Sidney. On his death in 1595 she married Sir Thomas Posthumous Hoby, the son of Sir Thomas and Elizabeth HOBY, in August 1596. They lived at Hackness, Yorkshire. They had no children.

Margaret Hoby is noteworthy as one of the earliest female diarists. *The Diary of Lady Margaret Hoby* (edited by Dorothy M. Meads, 1930) gives a clear picture of the life of a country gentlewoman of this period. Her main concerns were religious; much of the diary, which is written in a laconic but informative style, concerns daily religious exercises, including both public and private prayers, and attendance at sermons. Her chaplain, Richard Rhodes, was much in her company. The diary also reveals that Margaret Hoby spent a considerable amount of time in running her household and kept careful accounts. She visited the sick of the neighbourhood and seems to have been an excellent nurse. During the years covered by the diary she made several trips to York and London, notably during Essex's rebellion, but she makes very few references to public events of any kind. The diary ends abruptly, and it is possible that part of it has been lost.   J.S.

Hodgkins, Frances (1869–1947), painter. She was born at Dunedin, New Zealand, but from 1901 travelled in Europe and North Africa until 1904. She returned to New Zealand until 1906, but left because she could not adjust to the life there, and also because her first attempts to exhibit seriously met with no suc-

cess. She came to London, visited Venice in 1906, and in 1907 settled in Paris, where she earned her living teaching water-colour painting at the Académie Colarossi and later at her own school. She gained wide recognition as a water-colour artist working in a *plein-air* style. In 1912–13 she returned to exhibit in New Zealand and Australia, this time with great success. At the outbreak of the First World War she moved from Paris to Cornwall, where she first began to work in oils, finding it as expressive a medium as water-colour. She went back to Paris in 1920, when there was a considerable change in her style. From 1925 to 1927 she lived in Manchester, teaching, and making a short-lived attempt to become a textile designer. In 1939 she moved to Dorchester, remaining there for the rest of her life.

Frances Hodgkins' early works are sub-Impressionist, with overtones of Bonnard and Vuillard and a very free handling with which she strove to express a feeling of light. Her later works, particularly after 1930, show a number of influences—some passing, some lasting—not only from Gauguin, Matisse, and Chagall, but also from lesser but attractive figures on the Parisian scene such as Dufy and Marie Laurencin. Her subject matter is quietly domestic: figures, the occasional portrait, flower-pieces, still life, and landscapes with a strongly lyrical use of colour. Although she spent virtually all her working life in Fance and England, she is claimed as one of New Zealand's major artists. There are works by her in the Tate Gallery, London, at Bristol and Temple Newsam, and in New Zealand (Auckland, Dunedin, and elsewhere).

See also M. Day and others, 'Frances Hodgkins', in a commemorative issue of the periodical *Ascent*, December 1969; M. Evans, *Frances Hodgkins*, 1948; E. H. McCormick, *The Works of Frances Hodgkins in New Zealand*, 1954.   L.M.M.

Hodson, Henrietta (1841–1910), actress. The daughter of an Irish singer-comedian who kept an inn, she was born in Westminster but learnt her acting in Glasgow, appearing first at the Theatre Royal in 1858. At Greenock she acted with the young Henry Irving and went with him to the Theatre Royal, Manchester. At Bath and Bristol she was popular as a soubrette and burlesque actress. Having retired on her marriage to a solicitor, she returned to the stage following his early death and played at the Queen's, London. One of the theatre's proprietors was Henry Labouchère, then MP for Windsor, whom she married in 1868. In 1870 she took over management of the Royalty, where she had several disputes with the dictatorial W. S. Gilbert when staging his plays. She retired from the stage in 1878. Her best parts were those suggesting an underlying mischief; pathos and deep sentiment were not her forte. She was also instrumental in introducing Lillie LANGTRY to the stage.

B.H.C.

Hoey, Frances Sarah (1830–1908), writer and journalist. She was born near Dublin, one of eight children, and was educated at home, chiefly by her own efforts. On her sixteenth birthday in 1846 she married Adam Murray Stewart, who died in 1855. She then went to London, where she met and married John Cashel Hoey. In 1853 she had begun to contribute reviews and articles on art to Dublin papers and journals, and she continued writing from then onwards, with novels, translations from French and Italian, and journalism. In 1865 she began a long association with *Chambers's Journal* with her story 'Buried in the Deep'. For it she wrote two serial novels, *A Golden Sorrow* (1892) and *The Blossoming of an Aloe* (1894). In all she wrote eleven novels, mostly concerning fashionable society. She often visited Paris, and returned from there at Easter 1871 with the 'scoop' news of the Paris Commune, on which she wrote an article, 'Red Paris', for *The Spectator*.

B.H.C.

Holland, Lady. See FOX, ELIZABETH, BARONESS HOLLAND.

Holme, Constance (1880–1955), novelist. Born at Milnthorpe, Westmorland, she was the daughter of a land-agent and JP. In 1916 she married Frederick Burt Punchard, a land-agent.

All her books are set in the north-west corner of England, where she lived all her life. Her stories are about the land, families, property, and the threat of hostile natural forces. Her characterization is often humorous (though her heroines are splendidly spirited and independent) but her view of life tends towards the tragic. Her first novels, *Crump Folk Going Home* (1913) and *The Lonely Plough* (1914), cover a fairly long span of time. In later work the period is shorter, the psychological insight is deeper, and there is an effective unity of

setting and action. *The Splendid Fairing* (1919) won the Femina Vie Heureuse prize. Constance Holme received a rare accolade with the inclusion during her lifetime of her work in the Oxford University Press 'World's Classics' series.

See also M. Crosland, *Beyond the Lighthouse: English Women Novelists in the Twentieth Century*, 1981.

P.L.

Holtby, Winifred (1898–1935), writer, journalist, and social reformer. She was born at Rudston, Yorkshire, the younger daughter of a farmer, and educated at Queen Margaret's School, Scarborough, and Somerville College, Oxford. During the First World War she served in the Women's Army Auxiliary Corps in France (1918–19) as hostel forewoman. In 1926 she lectured in South Africa, and until her death the political and social conditions there were a major preoccupation, absorbing much of her time, energy and money. She was also a leading figure in the feminist movement, publishing *Women and a Changing Civilisation* (1934), and prevailing injustices and inequalities led to her becoming a prominent supporter of Viscountess RHONDDA's Six Point Group. A brilliant journalist, she became a director of *Time and Tide* in 1926 and contributed to numerous newspapers and periodicals. For the last five years of her life she suffered with fortitude from a progressive kidney disease.

Winifred Holtby's 'magnificent epitaph' is the posthumously published classic regional novel *South Riding* (1936), awarded the James Tait Black Memorial Prize (1936), filmed (1938), and more recently serialized on television (1974). She was an exceptionally versatile writer, but her Yorkshire heritage was a lasting influence on her work. She published *Anderby Wood*, 1923, *The Crowded Street*, 1924, *The Land of Green Ginger*, 1927, *Poor Caroline*, 1931, and *Mandoa! Mandoa!*, 1933. Her evocative letters and short stories are also of outstanding merit: *Letters to a Friend*, 1937, *The Selected Letters of Winifred Holtby and Vera Brittain 1920–1935*, 1960; *Truth is Not Sober*, 1934; *Pavements at Anderby*, 1937. She also published a play and the first critical study of Virginia Woolf.

See also V. Brittain, *Testament of Friendship*, 1940; M. Waley, *Winifred Holtby: a Short Life* (printed privately), 1976; E. White, *Winifred Holtby as I Knew Her*, 1938.

P.B.

Holy Maid of Kent. See BARTON, ELIZABETH.

Hone, Evie (1894–1955), stained-glass artist. She was born in Dublin, and was descended from Joseph Hone, the brother of the 18th-century painter Nathaniel Hone, and from Galyon Hone, a 16th-century glazier who made a large number of stained-glass windows for King's College Chapel, Cambridge. She was crippled by infantile paralysis when eleven years old, and for many years depended on nursing attendants. She was briefly a pupil of Sickert's at the Westminster School of Art, and after various other unsatisfactory art-school experiences finally went to Paris with her life-long friend Mainie Jellett. There she worked first under André Lhote and then from 1921 intermittently until 1931 under Albert Gleizes.

About 1924 Evie Hone began to be interested in stained glass, probably encouraged by seeing work by Georges Rouault. She found it difficult to obtain any instruction in the art, but from about 1933 she began to work with Michael Healy at the An Túr Gloine (the Tower of Glass), in the communal studios and workshops. Michael Healy was some twenty years her senior, but he encouraged her and taught her. She travelled in Italy, notably to Ravenna for the mosaics and surviving stained glass.

Evie Hone became a Roman Catholic in 1937, and she worked extensively for churches and hospital chapels in Ireland. Her principal works outside Ireland are the windows she made for Eton College Chapel (1949–51); the Jesuit church in Farm Street, London (1953); Washington Cathedral; Lanercost Priory, Bournemouth; All Hallows, Wellingborough; and St Michael's, Highgate, London. Drawings for some of her designs are in the Tate Gallery, London.

In style her windows are figurative, not abstract, and are never either bitten with acid, nor undercut — both common practices in modern stained glass work.

See also Stella Frost (ed.), *Evie Hone*, 1958.

L.M.M.

Hooton, Elizabeth (*fl.* 1600–1672), Quaker activist and missionary. She was the wife of Oliver Hooton of Skegby (d. 1657), by whom she had a son. She was probably the first person to be convinced by the founder of the Society of Friends, George Fox, whom she met in Nottinghamshire. In 1650 she became a travelling Quaker activist. At Derby in 1651 she was imprisoned for challenging a clergyman. In the following year she was held in York Castle for disturbing a congregation, and in 1654 she served five months at Lincoln for a similar offence. She went on a missionary journey to America with Joan Brocksopp of Derbyshire in 1661 and arrived at Boston, Massachusetts, in 1662. In Boston she was subject to the harsh anti-Quaker laws then in force and, for visiting imprisoned Quakers, was jailed and then ejected from the settlement. She returned to England and obtained a licence from Charles II to settle in any American colony, but on revisiting New England was nevertheless imprisoned and whipped.

Elizabeth Hooton returned to England and continued her work, receiving another period of imprisonment at Lincoln in 1665 for interrupting a church service. In 1670 she and another Quaker, Thomas Taylor, published *To the King and Both Houses of Parliament*. In the same year, with Hannah Salter, she lobbied Parliament on behalf of the Quakers and delivered over two hundred books to MPs. She returned to America, this time with George Fox, and died in February 1672 at Port Royal in Jamaica.

An important contributor to the early Quaker movement, Elizabeth Hooton again illustrates how courageous women found in Quakerism the opportunity for remarkably adventurous and emancipated activities.

See also E. Manners, *Elizabeth Hooton*, 1914; and the unpublished *Dictionary of Quaker Biography* in Friends House Library, London.

T.O'M.

Hope, Laurence, pseudonym of Adela Florence Nicolson (1865–1904). Poet. Born at Stoke Bishop, Gloucestershire, she was the daughter of a colonel in the Indian Army. She went out to join her parents in India and married Colonel Malcolm Hassels Nicolson, who was aide-de-camp to Queen Victoria (1891–94). Experience of the East prompted her to write passionate poems with oriental settings, such as *The Garden of Karma* (1901), in which the influence of Swinburne is also apparent. Some became very popular as songs, notably 'Pale Hands I Loved Beside the Shalimar'. General Nicolson died in Madras in 1904 and, acutely depressed, his widow poisoned herself two months later. Two more volumes of verse were published, *Stars of the Desert* (1903) and *Indian Love Lyrics* (1905). Some of these last poems are best known in their musical settings by Amy Woodford Finden.   B.H.C.

Hopkins, (Jane) Ellice (1836–1904), moral and legal reformer. Born at Cambridge, she was the younger daughter of the mathematician William Hopkins. As a girl she was given a broad scientific education by her father, whose influence on her was marked and whose memory she revered. In the mid-1850s she began her charitable career among the navvies in Barnwell, a suburb of Cambridge; she recorded her experiences in *An Englishwoman's Work among Working Men* (1875), which, like much of her best writing, combined a lively sense of humour with clarity of expression. After her father's death in 1866, she moved to Brighton, where she came into contact with the work being done among prostitutes by Fanny Vicars and Sarah ROBINSON. Fearless, she began to visit the pubs and brothels of Brighton and soon became an acknowledged leader in the field of rescue work.

She believed, however, that prevention was better than cure: 'We are not going to quench this pit of hell in our midst by emptying scent bottles upon it.' And so Ellice Hopkins organized a crusade to reform the law concerning women and children. In this campaign she was given considerable moral support by her friend the philosopher James Hinton. (Her *Life of James Hinton*, 1878, is a work of literary distinction.) In 1880 she originated what came to be called the Ellice Hopkins' Act, which gave magistrates increased powers over children found in the company of prostitutes. Two years later she gave testimony before the Select Committee of the House of Lords on the Law relating to the Protection of Young Girls. In 1883, with the help of the Bishop of Durham, she founded the White Cross Army, which recruited only men, who pledged themselves to extend the 'law' of social purity equally to men and women and to forgo indecent behaviour. On behalf of this society she wrote numerous pamphlets and addressed meetings of up to two thousand working men. Though unprepossessing in appearance she impressed her audiences by her beautiful voice and a religious conviction untouched by bigotry.

Ellice Hopkins was prominent in the women's campaign to secure the passage of the Criminal Law Amendment Act of 1885, and she was active in the National Vigilance Association, which sought to monitor the Act and to promote further legal reform. She also supported female suffrage, believing that if women had political power, men might be made to rise to the standard which women set for them.

Her health, for many years precarious, deteriorated in later life, and she spent much of her time at home writing on behalf of moral reform. These works, and several of her earlier books, including a novel and some poetry, suggest that if she had chosen writing as her career she might have become a noted author. Her other works include *English Idylls and other Poems*, 1865; *Notes on Penitentiary Work*, 1879; and *The Power of Womanhood*, 1899.

See also R. M. Barrett, *Ellice Hopkins: a Memoir*, 1907; E. Bristow, *Vice and Vigilance*, 1978; F. K. Prochaska, *Women and Philanthropy in Nineteenth-Century England*, 1980.   F.K.P.

Hopton, Susanna (1627–1709), devotional author, was born in Staffordshire. She was largely self-educated, and was particularly well read in theological controversy. During the Civil Wars she was an ardent Royalist, and was converted to Roman Catholicism by a Father Turberville. Some time before the Restoration she married Richard Hopton, an ex-Parliamentarian soldier who had turned Royalist. After the Restoration she returned to the Church of England, and her husband was appointed to a chief justiceship on the Welsh circuit. They lived at Kington in Herefordshire, and became one of the leading families there.

At Kington, Susanna Hopton's house became the centre of a religious society, or 'family', which probably included the mystic and poet Thomas Traherne, then rector at neighbouring Credenhill. He was certainly a close friend of Susanna Hopton's, and it is now believed that he wrote his *Centuries* for her. In 1699 she arranged for the posthumous publication of his *Thanksgivings*. Her own publications were issued anonymously by her friend Dr George Hickes. They comprised a devotional manual, *Daily Devotions* (1673), and an adaptation of a Catholic devotional manual, *Devotions in the Ancient Way of Offices Reformed by a Person of Quality* (second edition 1701), which ran to many editions.

207

Horan, Alice

After her death another clerical friend, Nathaniel Spinckes, issued *A Collection of Meditations and Devotions* (1717), ascribing two of the works in it to her. One of these, *Meditations on the Six Days of the Creation*, has been shown to be by Traherne; the other, *Meditations on the Life of Christ*, may be her own. In *A Second Collection of Controversial Letters* (1716) Hickes printed a long letter which she had written to Father Turberville, explaining her re-conversion to the Anglican Church. This letter, and contemporary accounts of her, suggest that she was a woman of very considerable abilities.

See also G. I. Wade, *Thomas Traherne*, 1946.   W.R.O.

Horan, Alice (1895–1971), trade-union organizer, one of the notable generation of women trade unionists that included Florence HANCOCK and Anne LOUGHLIN. Alice Horan was the daughter of a London tailor, the eldest child of a family of nine. She began work at the age of fourteen as a packer in a stationery factory, then worked for a court dressmaker for 1s. 6d. a day. She was drawn into trade unionism by a strike over piecework by the two thousand girls at a factory making service equipment where she was employed during the First World War. She became a shop steward and then, with advice and encouragement from Mary MACARTHUR, Secretary of the National Federation of Women Workers. She also went on to further education, winning a scholarship to Ruskin College for two years and gaining a diploma in political science.

In 1926 Alice Horan became a full-time union official; the recently formed National Union of General and Municipal Workers appointed her its Women's District Organizer for Lancashire. Over the twenty years during which she held the position, membership expanded dramatically (it multiplied seven times), and in 1946 she was appointed National Women's Officer by the Union. She had already been involved with union affairs at a national level during the Second World War, when she had helped work out a code regulating women's earnings in war factories (the Extended Employment of Women Agreement of May 1940). She was, for a number of years until 1958, a member of the Labour Party National Executive.

Sturdy and humorous, Alice Horan was modest about her achievements, claiming merely to have helped to consolidate the work of such pioneers as Susan LAWRENCE and Margaret BONDFIELD.

See also S. Lewenhak, *Women and Trade Unions*, 1977.   K.W.

Horniman, Annie (Elizabeth Fredericka) (1860–1937), theatre manager, pioneer of modern drama and repertory. She was born at Forest Hill, London, the daughter of Frederick John Horniman, the tea merchant and Liberal MP who founded the Horniman Museum. She was educated privately and studied art at the Slade School under Professor Legros. Thanks to the family money, she travelled widely, studying astrology and other occult subjects, Wagnerian opera, art, and architecture. Seeking some direction, she became involved with the magical Order of the Golden Dawn, where she met W. B. Yeats, then became interested in the theatre, despite the intense disapproval of her family. Her first venture, undertaken secretly, was in 1894 at the Avenue Theatre, London: she financed *Arms and the Man*, the first play by Bernard Shaw to be seen by the general public. It proved an expensive experiment, but Annie Horniman regarded it as 'a fruitful failure'.

In 1904 she took over the old theatre of the Mechanics' Institute in Abbey Street, Dublin, and lent it, rent free, to the Irish National Theatre Society. This became the famous Abbey Theatre, the dramatic vehicle of the Irish literary renaissance initiated by Yeats, J. M. Synge, and Lady GREGORY. Annie Horniman acted as unpaid secretary to Yeats at the Abbey Theatre for some time, although she ultimately severed her connection with it.

She returned to Manchester in 1907 and won such public acclaim with a series of modern plays that in 1908 she bought, and practically rebuilt, the Gaiety, which she ran as a repertory theatre—the first in Britain. Her policy was to sell seats at prices everybody could afford, to handpick her actors and actresses (Sybil THORNDIKE was one), and to put on plays by a wide variety of authors from Euripides and Shakespeare to Maeterlinck, Shaw, and St John Ervine. Hundreds of plays were produced at the Gaiety, of which over a hundred were new. The enterprise finally collapsed in 1921. In 1933 Annie Horniman was made a CH.

See also R. Pogson, *Miss Horniman and the Gaiety Theatre*, 1952   A.D.

Horsburgh, Florence, Baroness Horsburgh (1889–1969), the first woman Conservative Cabinet Minister. She was born in Scotland and educated at Lansdowne House in Edinburgh and St Hilda's, Folkestone. She never married but gave twenty-three years service to the House of Commons before going to the Lords. She entered politics in 1931, as Conservative member for Dundee, a seat she was to hold continuously until 1945. In 1936 she was the first woman to move the address in reply to the King's Speech. In 1939 her Private Member's Bill, which had emerged from her membership of the Committee on Adoption Societies and Agencies, was passed into law as the Adoption of Children (Regulation) Act. This was to be a major step towards the reorganization of the law affecting deprived children which was introduced after the war.

In 1939 Florence Horsburgh was appointed Parliamentary Secretary to the Ministry of Health. During the war years she was responsible for arranging for the evacuation of children from London and other cities, and was herself on one occasion injured by bomb blast during an air raid on London. In the period immediately after the war she was Parliamentary Secretary to the Ministry of Food, but she lost her seat in the Labour landslide of 1945. In 1950 she stood again, for Midlothian and Peebles, and was defeated. However, when the Conservative candidate for Moss Side (Manchester) died before polling day, the election there had to be postponed and Florence Horsburgh was persuaded to stand. She was duly elected with a majority of over 8,500, some two weeks after the rest of the country had voted.

In 1951, when the Conservatives came back into power, Florence Horsburgh was made Minister of Education in Churchill's Government. This was not at first a Cabinet post, but in 1953 it became so, making her the first Conservative woman member of a Cabinet. She resigned in 1954, when she was made a Dame Grand Cross of the Order of the British Empire. In 1959 she was made a Life Peeress.

See also E. Vallance, *Women in the House: a Study of Women Members of Parliament*, 1979.   E.M.V.

Houston, Dame (Fanny) Lucy (1857–1936), philanthropist. The fourth daughter of a warehouseman, she was born in Kennington, South London, and after a sketchy education suc-

ceeded by the age of eighteen in establishing herself on the stage, playing small parts. She became a well-known café society beauty, attracting many wealthy admirers, and in 1883 married her first husband, Theodore Brinckman, who inherited a baronetcy. The marriage was dissolved in 1895, but she rose further in society with her second marriage, in 1901, to the ninth Lord Byron. Energetic, wilful, and with a cockney irreverence, she was a keen supporter of women's rights, an interest that found practical expression in the foundation and financing of the first rest home for nurses. For this she was created one of the first five DBEs in 1917, the year her second husband died.

In 1924 she married the shipowner Sir Robert Houston, nicknamed the 'Robber Baron', and at his death two years later came into an immense fortune of some five and a half million pounds, a sum that allowed full rein to her flamboyant personality. From this time until her death she was rarely out of the news. Successfully resisting the Exchequer's claim for estate duties (Houston had established domicile in the Channel Islands), she then presented the Chancellor (Winston Churchill) in person with a £1,500,000 cheque as an *ex gratia* payment. A romantic, if strident patriot, in 1931 she made a gift of £100,000 that enabled the British team to win the Schneider Trophy in an aircraft that became the prototype of the Battle of Britain Spitfire. In 1933 she financed the first flight over Mount Everest, and the same year bought the long-established *Saturday Review* which, as editor, she turned into a vehicle for her idiosyncratic right-wing views (she was obsessed with the 'Red Menace' and the 'treachery' of Ramsay MacDonald). Her extravagant generosity found innumerable outlets, including gifts of £30,000 to the Miners' Relief Fund and of £100,000 to St Thomas's Hospital.

Pugnacious, quirky, shrewd, 'implacable in her hatreds', she was insatiable in her kindnesses', a larger-than-life character who might have stepped from an Evelyn Waugh novel. She died childless and intestate, her well-managed fortune barely diminished.

See also W. Allen, *Lucy Houston, DBE*, 1947.   K.W.

Howard, Elizabeth, Duchess of Norfolk (1494–1558), public figure. The daughter of Edward Stafford, Duke of Buckingham (executed in 1521), Elizabeth was betrothed to Ralph Neville, later Earl of Westmorland. However, she married Thomas Howard, later Duke of Norfolk, about Easter 1513. They had three children: Henry, Earl of Surrey, the poet; Thomas, Viscount Bindon; and Mary, Duchess of Richmond. Elizabeth accused Howard of atrocious ill-treatment after Mary's birth in 1519; he was a violent man, and the marriage was notoriously unhappy.

Elizabeth Howard became significant in politics during the royal divorce crisis of Henry VIII's reign, when she sided with KATHERINE OF ARAGON; by contrast, Howard was a prominent member of his niece Anne BOLEYN's party. In November 1530 Elizabeth Howard sent the Queen a useful letter from one of Henry VIII's agents in Rome, hidden in a hollow orange. In May 1531 she was banished from court because of her outspoken hostility to Anne Boleyn.

In 1533 the Howards separated, Elizabeth living at Redbourne, Hertfordshire, on a meagre allowance and complaining frequently to the chief minister, Thomas Cromwell. Refusing Norfolk a divorce, she enjoyed some measure of revenge in 1546, when, like his mistress, she testified against him when he was accused of treason.

See also J. E. Paul, *Catherine of Aragon and her Friends*, 1966. M.D.

Howard, Frances, Countess of Essex and Somerset

Howard, Frances, Countess of Essex and Somerset (c. 1593–1632), scandalous public figure and, perhaps, · murderess. Frances, daughter of Thomas Howard, Earl of Suffolk, was married to Robert Devereux, third Earl of Essex, in 1606. Immediately after the wedding the young bridegroom left for the Continent, leaving Frances to enjoy a frivolous existence at court, where she probably became the lover of Robert Carr, James I's Scots favourite, aided by potions obtained from the famous astrologer Simon Forman. On Essex's return in 1610, Frances lived with him on her father's insistence, detesting life on his Staffordshire estates after the pleasures of the court. Forman was now consulted for ways to keep Essex impotent. With Frances' family keenly aware of the political advantages of a Carr marriage, influential pressures resulted in the establishment of a nullity commission in May 1613, which the following September voted by seven to five that the marriage should be annulled on the grounds of non-consummation, concluding that Essex was impotent and, more improbably, that his Countess remained a virgin.

Sir Thomas Overbury, a courtier and literary figure closely associated with Carr, remained a barrier to a new marriage. Overbury was committed to the Protestant wing at court, and although he had no objections to his friend having a Howard mistress, he opposed a marriage which would ally Carr politically with the pro-Catholic Howards. Furthermore, as Carr's intimate he could discredit the picture of a virginal Countess presented to the nullity commissioners. Consequently Overbury was confined to the Tower on a pretext in April 1613, and died there in mysterious circumstances in September. Frances Howard may or may not have murdered him, but it seems clear that she attempted to do so. Howard influence ensured a pliable Lieutenant of the Tower and keeper for Overbury, while Frances' lady-in-waiting, Anne Turner, found an apothecary to provide poison. All this remained undetected, and Frances, still only twenty, was married to Carr, created Earl of Somerset for the occasion, in December 1613. But less than two years later rumours about Overbury's death began to circulate, strengthened by Carr's evident panic. A commission of inquiry, established in October 1615, resulted in the execution of lesser conspirators, including Turner. The Countess's trial was delayed by the birth of her only daughter in December 1615 but early in the new year she was indicted, immediately confessed, and was confined to the Tower. At the trial in May 1616 she pleaded guilty and Carr not guilty, but both were convicted and condemned to death. Luckier than her subordinates, the countess was immediately pardoned; Carr, who may well have been innocent, was spared, but was not pardoned until 1624. The couple remained in prison until 1622 and were thereafter obliged to live in retirement. Frances Carr seems to have died of cancer of the womb, to the delight of hostile commentators who saw this fate as entirely appropriate. Her self-destructive egotism had launched a scandal astounding even by the standards of James's reign, and significantly influenced contemporary views of the court and political alignments within it.

See also B. White, *Cast of Ravens*, 1965.

A.H.

Howard, Henrietta, Countess of Suffolk (1681–1767), mistress of George II, was married apparently at an early age to Charles Howard. As one of the ladies-in-waiting of Caroline, Princess of Wales, in 1714 she was noticed by the Prince and soon became his mistress. When he became king in 1727 some courtiers and politicians imagined that Henrietta Howard was influential enough to be worth the trouble of pleasing. Robert Walpole was better informed, or more observant: the King was ruled by his wife, Queen CAROLINE. Henrietta Howard remains an example of a non-intriguing royal mistress, pleasing, well-mannered, and content with a passive role in public life. Her sense of propriety was such that some observers thought that her connection with the King was merely platonic. Although not celebrated for her intellect, she was not without some wit, and enjoyed the society of Pope, Swift, and Gay. She became Lady Suffolk in 1731 and Groom of the Stole to the Queen, patiently enduring the embarrassments that inevitably accompanied Hanoverian family life. She retired from Court in 1734. Her portrait in the National Gallery (attributed to Charles Jervas) is a fine Rococo statement of pulchritude and amiability.

See also J. W. Croker (ed.), *Letters to and from Henrietta Countess of Suffolk and her Second Husband, The Hon. George Berkeley, from 1712–1767*, 1824; C. C. Trench, *George II*, 1974.   T.H.

Howard, Katherine (1521?–1542), fifth queen of Henry VIII. The daughter of Edmund Howard, an impoverished younger son of Thomas, second Duke of Norfolk, Katherine Howard was brought up by her step-grandmother, the Dowager Duchess Agnes. She became Lady in Waiting to Anne of Cleves early in 1540, and the King's attraction to her gave the Catholics at court the chance to undermine the new Lutheran Queen. Bishop Gardiner entertained Henry and Katherine at his house, and it was thought that she would become Henry's mistress. Instead, he divorced Anne on 9 July, and on 28 July Henry and Katherine were married.

Katherine's ruin was engineered by the Protestant party. John Lassells heard from his sister Mary (who had lived with Katherine) that about 1536 she had been scandalously familiar with her music teacher, Henry Mannocks, and later was secretly betrothed to Francis Dereham, a kinsman of hers in the Dowager

Duchess's service. More recently, she had entertained her cousin Thomas Culpepper late at night while on progress with the King.

On 1 November 1541 Henry ordered his confessor to give thanks with him for the good life he was leading with the Queen, but next day at mass Cranmer handed him Lassells' accusations. He refused to believe the evidence, but Dereham and Mannocks were arrested and Katherine was interrogated. Being almost deranged with terror, she admitted promiscuity before marriage, but persistently denied adultery with Culpepper and the precontract with Dereham, which would in fact have invalidated her marriage, and so saved her.

Culpepper and Dereham were condemned on 1 December, and several Howards were attainted of treason or misprision of treason. Henry promised Katherine mercy, but on 11 February 1542 he assented to her attainder. When informed on 12 February that she would die next day, she asked for the block so she could rehearse her own execution. She died with dignity. Though of little personal political influence, Katherine Howard is important as a pawn in the faction-fights of Henry VIII's last years.

See also L. Baldwin Smith, *A Tudor Tragedy*, 1961.   M.D.

Howard, Rosalind Frances, Countess of Carlisle (1845–1921), political and temperance reformer, the daughter of Lord Stanley of Alderley. In 1864 she married George Howard, later Earl of Carlisle, by whom she had eleven children. She was brought up with an interest in politics and a strong sense of social duty. When her husband took up a political career, she became a prominent Liberal hostess. Husband and wife disagreed over Home Rule (which she favoured), so she gave up London politics to concentrate on running the family estates with energy and efficiency. Her main interest remained women's enfranchisement and she was widely acknowledged as one of the best women speakers of the day. Her talent for debate made her an important asset to the moderate branch of the women's movement. From 1891 to 1901 and from 1906 to 1914 she was President of the Women's Liberal Federation. Her other major interest, shared with her husband, was teetotalism, a theme she pursued tirelessly, closing public houses on the Carlisle estates. In 1903 she became President of the National British Women's Temperance Association.   J.R.

Howitt, Mary (1799–1888), writer. She was born into a Quaker family at Coleford, Gloucestershire, and was brought up in Uttoxeter. Her upbringing was strict but she was close to her 'nanny', a great story-teller to whom she later attributed her own 'flights of fancy'. In 1821 she married William Howitt and went to live in Hanley. They had seven children, but only two of them survived her. They kept a chemist's shop but were chiefly interested in writing, and their first joint publication, *The Forest Minstrel, and other Poems*, appeared in 1823.

A move to Nottingham brought the Howitts into a wider social and literary circle, and they became interested in radical politics. Another volume of poems followed a walking tour of the Lake District in 1827 and they gave up the shop to write for a living. Visits to the countryside resulted in *The Book of the Seasons* (1830) and *Sketches of Natural History* (1834). Mary Howitt met and corresponded with other women writers of her day, including Felicia HEMANS and Joanna BAILLIE. As a result of a stay in Edinburgh the Howitts started to contribute regularly to *Tait's* and *Chambers's* magazines.

After they had settled at Esher in 1837, Mary Howitt began to produce her long and successful series of tales for children. She also translated the tales of Hans Christian Andersen and the novels of Frederika Bremer. The failure in 1846 of *The People's Journal*, which her husband had helped to finance, led the following year to the foundation of *Howitt's Journal* 'to urge the labouring classes to self-education'; but it lasted for only a year. In 1848 the Howitts became increasingly interested in radical demands for compulsory national education, extension of the suffrage, and women's rights. In 1854 Mary Howitt shocked the young Anne Thackeray by calling for women MPs, and in 1856 she was a signatory of the petition calling for married women's property rights.

The Howitts collaborated on many works of popular non-fiction, notably *Biographical Sketches of the Queens of England*. Their eventual break with the Quakers led them to Spiritualism and Unitarianism. They settled in Italy, and although, on the death of her husband in 1879, Mary Howitt was awarded a

Civil List pension of £100, she stayed on in Rome. She was received into the Catholic Church shortly before her death.

Mary Howitt's name can be found on well over a hundred works, mostly forgotten. Her autobiography, however (edited by Margaret Howitt, 1889), is a very useful source for many important nineteenth-century figures.

See also A. Lee, *Laurels and Rosemary: the Life of William and Mary Howitt*, 1955; C. R. Woodring, *Victorian Samplers: William and Mary Howitt*, 1952.   C.H.G.G.

How-Martyn, Edith (*c.* 1875–1954), suffragette. Edith How was born at Cheltenham and educated at Bath, the North London Collegiate School, and University College, Aberystwyth. An associate of the Royal College of Science, she gave up a lectureship at Westfield College to devote herself to the suffrage campaign, and in 1899 married a science lecturer, Herbert Martyn. She was secretary of the first London group of the Women's Social and Political Union and was among the first women sent to prison (1906). In 1907 she broke from the WSPU and became secretary of the Women's Freedom League. She stood as a candidate in the first parliamentary election after women had gained the vote (1918) and in 1919 became the first woman member of the Middlesex Council. As Director of the Birth Control International Information Centre, she travelled the world, wrote *The Birth Control Movement in England* (1930), and formed the first Play Centre in Hampstead Garden Suburb. In 1939 she went with her husband to Australia, where she died. Founder of the Suffragette Fellowship, she was its president until her death.   B.H.C.

Hubbard, Louisa (Maria) (1836–1906), editor who worked to advance employment opportunities for women. Born in St Petersburg, she was the eldest of a family of seven. Her father was a merchant in Russia but in 1843 the family returned to England, settling at Leonardslee near Horsham, where Louisa Hubbard was privately educated.

Louisa Hubbard was particularly drawn to the plight of women of her own class left alone or without means. In the Victorian era the unmarried woman tended to be considered a burden on society, and Louisa Hubbard set herself to promote a new self-respect and self-reliance in her. As a first venture she actively encouraged the 'deaconess movement', publishing *Anglican Deaconesses: or, Is there no Place for Women in the Parochial System?* From 1867 to 1878 she annually compiled a *Guide to all Institutions for the Benefit of Women.* From 1875 to 1893 she edited *The Handbook of Women's Work,* later *The Englishwoman's Yearbook.* To supplement this the monthly magazine *Woman's Gazette* was produced at her own expense as another means of convincing gentlewomen of the respectability of work and to give practical advice on obtaining employment. Renamed *Work and Leisure* in 1880, in an attempt to make it self-supporting, it was a pioneer in the field of women's papers. It did much to remove the stigma attached to existing professions such as nursing and teaching, as well as publicizing new areas of woman's work such as typing, gardening, and massage.

Around these influential publications numerous schemes and societies grew up, instigated both directly by Louisa Hubbard and also through correspondence in her journals. They included the Working Ladies' Guild, the British Women's Emigration Society, the Matrons' Aid Society, and the Church of England Women's Help Society. She was also particularly interested in promoting the provision of suitable accommodation for working women, and was instrumental in establishing the National Union of Women Workers.

This exceedingly active career ended in 1893, when her health gave way; and five years later she suffered a stroke while in the Tyrol. Although Louisa Hubbard had concentrated her efforts upon a particular class of woman, her struggle to remove the prejudices against the single working woman, and to give practical help to those in employment, made an important contribution to the changing position of women in Victorian society. Her other writings include *Work for Ladies in Elementary Schools* (1872) and *The Beautiful House and Enchanted Garden* (1885).

See also E. A. Pratt, *A Woman's Work for Women,* 1898.   J.G.S.

Hughes, Margaret (d. 1719), actress and royal mistress. Peg Hughes appears for the first time in theatrical records in 1668. She was almost certainly the 'pretty woman newly come, called Pegg, that was Sir Charles Sidley's mistress', whom Samuel Pepys kissed at the King's

Theatre on 7 May. She performed a number of important roles, including Desdemona in *Othello,* before leaving the theatre to become the mistress of Prince Rupert, whose daughter, Ruperta, she bore in 1673. In 1676 she returned to the stage, giving her final performance in May 1677. The Prince, a devoted and generous lover, is said to have bought her a palatial house, worth about £25,000, and at his death in 1682 divided estates worth about £12,000 equally between his mistress and daughter. It was said that she gambled away her bequest, and she may have spent her old age dependent upon her daughter.

See also J. H. Wilson, *All the King's Ladies,* 1958, and 'Pepys and Peg Hughes', in *Notes and Queries,* October 1956.   T.J.M.

Hunt, Dame Agnes (Gwendoline) (1866-1948), pioneer in the care of the physically handicapped. The daughter of a Shropshire landowner, she grew up as one of a large Victorian family, but at the age of ten was left permanently crippled by osteomyelitis. A severe but loving family régime developed her independence and self-reliance. After the death of her father, she spent some years in Australia with her mother and other members of her family, returning to begin a determined and eventually successful struggle to qualify as a nurse, completing her training at the Salop Infirmary in 1896.

Agnes Hunt spent some years as a district nurse and then in 1900, with the backing of her mother and the assistance of a close friend, Emily Goodford, started a little convalescent home in her native village of Baschurch that developed into a hospital for twenty-five crippled children. Convinced that physical handicaps could be overcome through self-reliance, she improvised open-sided accommodation in rough sheds taken from her family home. Somewhat alarmed by her own temerity, she managed to enlist the aid as consultant of a well-known Liverpool orthopaedic surgeon, Robert (later Sir Robert) Jones.

During the First World War the hospital was enlarged to accommodate disabled servicemen, and in 1921 it was moved to a former military hospital near Oswestry. After-care clinics, backed up by voluntary social workers, reinforced the work of the hospital in neighbouring counties. With government backing, similar hospitals and clinics were established in other parts of the country, and in 1927

Agnes Hunt was persuaded to extend her pioneer work by founding the Derwen Cripples' Training College to provide instruction in a variety of trades.

Unconventional and adventurous, Agnes Hunt overcame constant physical pain to inspire her co-workers by her vision and devoted professionalism. Her work helped bring about radical changes in the social and medical treatment of physical disability. She published an autobiography, *This is My Life*, 1938.   K.W.

Hunt, Arabella (d. 1705), musician, a vocalist and lutenist who was teacher to the court of Queen MARY. All we know of Arabella Hunt's background is that she was unhappily married and probably attended one of the many girls' boarding schools which sprang up in and around London in the early 17th century.

Arabella Hunt excelled as a singer, lutenist, and teacher (Princess Anne was among her pupils); she was also a noted beauty, which undoubtedly assisted her rise to fame. Both Blow and Purcell were her friends and composed songs for her. Sir John Hawkins records that her voice was described as 'the pipe of a bull-finch' and that not only was she 'celebrated for her beauty, but more for a fine voice and an exquisite hand on the lute'. After her death Congreve wrote an ode, 'On Mrs Arabella Hunt Singing', which is quoted in part beneath the painting of her by Kneller. Hawkins also records Arabella Hunt's popularity with Queen Mary, 'who would frequently be entertained in private with her performance, even of common songs'. We glimpse an amusing sidelight on life at court in one such performance. Growing tired of Purcell's songs, the Queen asked Arabella Hunt to sing the Scots ballad 'Cold and Raw', which she did, accompanying herself on the lute, and evidently to good effect. Purcell swallowed his pride, and in his next Birthday Song, for the year 1692, included the tune 'Cold and Raw' as the bass line to the air.

A notable exception to the rule that English court musicians have invariably been men, Arabella Hunt was a very gifted as well as socially acceptable court musician, equally at ease in both folk and art songs, and commanding the respect of no less a composer than Purcell.

See also J. D. Brown and S. S. Stratton, *British Musical Biography*, 1897; Sir J. Hawkins, *A General History of the Science and Practice of Music*, 1776.   D.H.

Huntingdon, Countess of. See HASTINGS, SELINA, COUNTESS OF HUNTINGDON.

Hutchinson, Lucy (b. 1620), author of the indispensable *Memoirs*, was born in the Tower of London, the daughter of Sir Allen Apsley, Lieutenant of the Tower. According to her own account, she was a studious girl: 'play amongst other children I despised'; she preferred sermons and books to the conventional female accomplishments of dancing and music. Her parents encouraged her intellectual development, and she excelled her brothers in learning Latin.

In 1638 Lucy married a Nottinghamshire gentleman, John Hutchinson of Owthorpe. In her life of her husband she refers to their courtship as 'not worthy mention amongst the greater transactions' but in fact tells it as a highly romantic story. John Hutchinson fell in love with her simply through hearing of her accomplishments. The couple felt an immediate attraction on meeting and married despite the disapproval of Lucy's mother and friends at her refusing 'many offers which they thought advantageous', and despite the ravages to her beauty from a recent attack of small-pox.

Lucy Hutchinson's devotion to her husband led her to compose after his death in 1664 the *Memoirs of the Life of Colonel Hutchinson* (most recent edition by James Sutherland, 1975), based in part on her diaries of the 1640s and 1650s. The *Memoirs* were not intended for general consumption and were not published until 1806. Their purposes were to console her in her loss; to provide a picture of their noble father for her eight surviving children; and to justify John Hutchinson's political career, particularly his partial recantation at the Restoration, when he expressed 'penitent sorrow' for his part in Charles I's execution. The *Memoirs* and Lucy's fragmentary surviving autobiography reveal above all the Hutchinsons' profound commitment to radical Puritan religion. John Hutchinson was Governor of Parliament's garrison at Nottingham throughout the Civil War, and Lucy also lived there, frequently tending wounded soldiers. She believed completely in the subjection of women: she criticized Charles I for allowing HENRIETTA MARIA to dominate him, and claimed that she disobeyed her husband only once, when she wrote his letter apologizing for regicide in 1660. Unwittingly, however, she presents herself as an active and independent woman, in many ways a stronger personality than her husband. It was on her initiative that the couple took the radical step of rejecting infant baptism, after Lucy had studied the question during her pregnancy in 1646. It was she who lobbied and campaigned to save Hutchinson's life in 1660, while he lapsed into a melancholic lassitude; and she did all she could to alleviate the hardships of his imprisonment from 1663 until his death the following year at the age of forty-eight.

Lucy Hutchinson also translated Virgil and Lucretius, and composed two religious treatises, *On Theology* and *On the Principles of the Christian Religion*, for one of her daughters. But it is as the author of the *Memoirs* that she is principally important. Although in part an apologia, the *Memoirs* are still a valuable source for English social, political, and religious developments, quite apart from their obvious importance as a record of her husband's career. Her vivid descriptions of the rivalries among Nottingham Parliamentarians, and her memorable pronouncements on the characters of her narrative, have put historians in her debt.   P.M.H.

Hyde, Anne (1637–71), Duchess of York, was the eldest daughter of Sir Edward Hyde, later Earl of Clarendon, Lord Chancellor to Charles II. Like many other Royalists after the Civil War, she lived in exile, spending the early years of the Interregnum with her family in Antwerp and Breda. In 1654 she became Maid of Honour to the Princess of Orange, the elder sister of Charles II and his brother James, Duke of York.

During a visit to Paris in 1656 she met James, who fell passionately in love with her and, when she refused to yield to his advances, entered into a secret contract of marriage with her in 1659. After she became pregnant James put pressure on Charles to allow the wedding, and they were finally married secretly on 3 September 1660, a month before the birth of their son. This inappropriate match between the daughter of a commoner and the heir presumptive to the throne (to which Charles had been restored in May 1660) was violently opposed by the bride's father and the Queen Mother, and James himself had second thoughts. But the King insisted that the situation was beyond remedy and James publicly acknowledged the marriage in December.

A dutiful royal wife, Anne produced eight children in eleven years, but she was an indifferent mother, devoting her considerable energy and skills to organizing the ducal household, administering her husband's finances, participating in court entertainments, and consolidating her position. Although she offended many courtiers by her haughtiness, foreign visitors found her court, with its many talented inhabitants, more interesting than the Queen's. James's passion for his wife quickly subsided and she had to tolerate a succession of mistresses. Over-eating, illness, and repeated pregnancies made her increasingly obese and unattractive, but she continued to dominate her husband in financial and political matters. 'The Duke', as Pepys put it, 'in all things but his cod-piece is led by the nose by his wife.' A highly literate woman, who wrote 'very correctly', she helped her husband to transform his journal into memoirs, and having become a Catholic, wrote a persuasive paper explaining the reasons for her conversion (published by James in 1686). She exerted considerable pressure on him to acknowledge publicly his own subsequent conversion—an act whose remote consequence, ironically, was to make Anne Hyde's Protestant daughters, Mary and Anne, Queens of England.

See also J. S. Clarke (ed.) *Life of James II . . . collected out of memoirs writ of his own hand*, 1816; A. Fea, *James II and His Wives*, 1908; E. Hyde, Earl of Clarendon, *The life of Edward, Earl of Clarendon*, 1857; J. Miller, *James II, a Study in Kingship*, 1978.
                                      T.J.M.

I

Inchbald, Elizabeth (1753–1821), actress, dramatist and novelist. Born at Standingfield near Bury St Edmunds, the second youngest child of a large Catholic family, Elizabeth Inchbald educated herself at home. Leaving secretly in 1772 to pursue a theatrical career, she made her début in Bristol, playing Cordelia to the Lear of Joseph Inchbald, her husband. Later in the same year the couple joined West Digges's Company in Scotland but were forced to leave after Joseph Inchbald's 'great dispute' with an Edinburgh audience. In 1776 they travelled to Paris intending that she should study French and he painting, but returned penniless to England after only a month. The couple subsequently joined Younger's Company in Liverpool, where Elizabeth met the actress Sarah SIDDONS.

In 1777 she began an outline of her first novel, *A Simple Story*, which was completed soon after Joseph Inchbald's death in 1779. When it was declined by the publisher, Elizabeth resumed her acting career in London and Dublin, and began to write plays. Her farce *The Mogul Tale* was first performed to great acclaim in 1784 and published in 1786. By 1789 the success of this and subsequent comedies allowed her to give up acting and support herself solely by writing. Aided by Thomas Holcroft and William Godwin, she extensively revised *A Simple Story*, for which the publisher Robinson paid £200 in 1791. Her early critics recognized the key significance of dramatic technique in this novel, especially in the effective use of dialogue. The central characters of the first half, Miss Milner and Dorriforth, are based on Elizabeth Inchbald herself and John Philip Kemble, the brother of Sarah Siddons, whom the author had first met in 1777 when he joined Younger's Company. Through its emphasis on personal psychology, *A Simple Story* establishes Elizabeth Inchbald as one of the founders, with Robert Bage, of the Jacobin novel.

In her second novel *Nature and Art*, published in 1796, the protagonists are again characterized in terms of their relationship to society and thus the book can be said to have set the pattern for the later regional novels of Maria EDGEWORTH and the historical ones of Sir Walter Scott. Her adaptation of August von Kotzebue's *Das Kind der Liebe (Child of Love)* as *Lovers' Vows* (1798) encouraged the reading of the German dramatist in England and is remembered for its appearance in Jane Austen's *Mansfield Park*. Two further plays were completed before 1806–09, when she wrote the prefaces for the twenty-five volume work *British Theatre*. After retiring to Kensington House in 1819 she burned her *Memoirs* on the advice of her confessor, and at her death two years later left an estate of between £5,000 and £6,000.

See also J. Boaden, *Memoirs of Mrs Inchbald*, 1833; S. R. Littlewood, *Mrs Inchbald and her Circle*, 1921. A.L.

Ingelow, Jean (1820–97), poet and novelist. Born at Boston, Lincolnshire, the eldest child of a banker, she was educated at home by governesses and tutors, moving with her family to Ipswich when she was about fourteen. In 1850 *A Rhyming Chronicle of Incidents and Feelings* was published, after which Tennyson commented 'I declare, you do the trick better than I do', but it was her first series of *Poems*, published in 1863, that established her reputation as a lyric poet. That year she moved to London, where she was to spend most of her life.

Jean Ingelow wrote three books of poetry. Her most popular poem was 'Divided', while 'The High Tide on the Coast of Lincolnshire' is regarded as among the finest of modern ballads. Many other pieces were set to music. She also wrote novels, the best known being *Off the Skelligs* (1872), and stories for children, including *Mopsa the Fairy* (1869) which has been compared to *Alice in Wonderland* and is still read today.

A shy and nervous woman, she never married and once said 'If I had married, I should *not* have written books'.

See also E. Stedman, *An Appreciation*, 1935. A.P.

Inglis, Elsie Maud (1864–1917), doctor. The seventh of nine children, Elsie Inglis lived in north India until 1875 and then in Hobart, Tasmania. In 1878 her parents settled in Edinburgh. The Edinburgh School of Medicine for Women opened in 1886 and Elsie studied there until 1889 when the founder, Sophia

JEX-BLAKE, high-handedly dismissed two students for a trivial offence. Outraged, Elsie, her father, and influential friends were instrumental in opening the Edinburgh Medical College for Women. Her clinical training was completed at the Glasgow Royal Infirmary and its district. Appointed Resident Medical Officer at the New Hospital for Women (now the Elizabeth Garrett Anderson), she assisted the director and surgeon Mary SCHARLIEB and Mrs Garrett ANDERSON. On graduating MB, CM (Edin.) from the Faculty of Medicine, which was opened to women in 1899, she was appointed lecturer in gynaecology at the Medical College for Women, and opened a small and successful hospital where for the first time obstetric anaesthesia in childbirth was available to the poor. Meanwhile, as honorary secretary, she lectured indefatigably for the Federation of Scottish Suffrage Societies.

When in 1914 the Royal Army Medical Corps rejected her services, Elsie Inglis appealed for funds and founded the Scottish Women's Hospitals. This eventually approached the size of the Red Cross and St John Ambulance Association, and raised £450,000 by the end of the war. Fourteen self-sufficient units served in France, Serbia, Corsica, Salonika, Romania, Russia and briefly in Malta. Dr Inglis herself led a unit to Serbia in 1915, was interned at Krushevatz, arrested as a spy, and suffered great privation. She returned to help the Serbians but by the end of 1917 was dying of cancer.

Welfare measures now commonplace were pioneered by Elsie Inglis; her logical approach and epic war record also played a notable part in gaining women's suffrage. She received the Serbian Order of the White Eagle and was posthumously decorated with the highest awards by Russia and Serbia, the Gold St George Medal and White Eagle with Swords, never previously awarded to a woman. No British honour was given, although Arthur Balfour, Secretary of State for Foreign Affairs, paid this tribute: 'A wonderful compound of enthusiasm, strength of purpose and kindliness. In the history of this World War, alike by what she did and by heroism, driving power and the simplicity with which she did it, Elsie Inglis has earned an everlasting place of honour'.

See also M. Lawrence, *Shadow of Swords, A Biography of Elsie Inglis*, 1971; E. Shaw McLaren, *Elsie Inglis*, 1919.   R.B.

Inglis, Esther (1571–1624), calligrapher and miniaturist. The daughter of Nicholas Langlois (Inglis is an anglicized version) and Marie Prisott, she was probably born in Dieppe. Her Protestant family fled from France after the St Bartholomew Massacre in 1572 and by 1578 were settled in Edinburgh, where her father was master of a French school. About 1596 she married Bartholomew Kello of Leith, a minister who moved to a living in Essex in 1607. She bore him a son and two daughters.

Esther Inglis was probably instructed in calligraphy by her mother, and while penmanship and drawing were conventional pastimes for ladies, her work is of exquisite quality. Over forty of her manuscript books survive, some still in the original velvet bindings which she embroidered herself. About half the volumes consist of illustrations from the Bible and many have dedications, to Elizabeth I, James I, and Prince Maurice of Nassau, amongst others. These dedications suggest that she received payment for her work. The latest known volume was finished in the year of her death and was dedicated to the future Charles I. She wrote that she needed the spirit of an 'Amazon lady' to offer him this product of two years' labour which contained her adaptations of fifty-one emblem woodcuts with French and Latin verses written calligraphically attached to each. Several English and Scottish scholars praised Esther Inglis's skill and learning in verse, and her work shows the degree to which women's traditional accomplishments could be made the basis for a highly regarded artistic career.

See also P. Hogrefe, *Tudor Women*, 1975.
                                        P.M.H.

Iron, Ralph. See SCHREINER, OLIVE EMILIE ALBERTINA.

Irwin, Margaret (Emma Faith) (?–1967), popular historical novelist. Margaret Irwin was born in London, but both her parents died when she was a child and she was brought up by an uncle, a master at Clifton, where she went to school. She read English at Oxford and published her first book, *Still She Wished for Company*, a ghost story, in 1924. In 1929 she married the author-illustrator J. R. Monsell. She found her métier with *None So Pretty* (1930), which won first prize in a competition for historical novels. The books that followed are still widely read. She chose 17th-century settings for *Royal Flush*, 1932 (the story of

Isaacs, Adelaide Mary

Charles II's sister Minette—see HENRIETTE ANNE), *The Proud Servant*, 1934 (about Montrose, Charles I's commander in Scotland), and *The Stranger Prince*, 1937 (about Rupert of the Rhine, leader of the Royalist cavalry in the Civil War). Then she turned to the previous century for *The Gay Galliard*, 1941 (about Mary Queen of Scots and Bothwell), and her trilogy on Queen Elizabeth, *Young Bess*, 1944, *Elizabeth, Captive Princess*, 1948, and *Elizabeth and the Prince of Spain*, 1953. Among her other works was a biography of Sir Walter Raleigh, *That Great Lucifer*, 1960.   N.H.

Isaacs, Adelaide Mary. See REEVE, ADA.

Isaacs, Stella, Marchioness of Reading (1894–1971), founder of the Women's Royal Voluntary Service. She was born in Constantinople where her father, Charles Charnaud (of Huguenot descent), was director of the state tobacco monopoly of the Ottoman Empire. The family returned to England shortly before the First World War. In 1931 she married Rufus Isaacs, first Marquess of Reading, as his second wife, and a short, ideally happy marriage followed. He died in 1935. Meanwhile she had taken up social work, notably as Chairman of the Personal Service League (1932–38). In 1938, when war seemed imminent, the Home Secretary invited her to form a women's organization to assist the local authorities with air raid precautions. This was the start of Women's Voluntary Service for Civil Defence. The last three words were dropped after the war, and the accolade 'Royal' bestowed in 1966. To this organization, the Marchioness of Reading devoted the rest of her life.

Thousands of volunteers were enrolled, and on the outbreak of war in 1939 the new organization was ready to help in the evacuation of women and children from the cities, in setting up rest centres and information points during air raids, and in providing canteens and welfare service for the troops, at first at home and then overseas. A second great achievement was to adapt the organization to peacetime. WVS continued as an 'emergency service', ready to help the civil authorities at a moment's notice with disasters large and small. Simultaneously it found various ways to serve the community, at a time when many people thought there was no longer any need for voluntary services because the state would provide all. 'Home helps' and 'meals-on-wheels' were pioneered

by WVS, which also provided clubs for the elderly, canteens and shops in hospitals and mental institutions, housing for retired people, welfare services for prisoners and their families, 'Good Companions', and family support generally.

Lady Reading gave practical expression to the ideal of voluntary service by putting it on an organized basis, so facilitating the integration of statutory and voluntary services. In 1958 she was made a Life Peer as Baroness Swanborough and was one of the first four women to take her seat in the House of Lords.

See also *Stella Reading: Some Recollections by Her Friends*, WRVS publication, 1979.

A.P.

Isaacs, Susan (Sutherland) (1885–1948), child psychologist. She was born in Lancashire where her father, William Fairhurst, was a journalist and Methodist lay-preacher. When she professed agnosticism, her father took her away from school before she was fifteen, claiming that 'If education makes women Godless, they are better without it'. Deciding that she wanted to be a teacher and having gained some practical experience, she realized that training was necessary and began a non-graduate course in infant teaching at Manchester University. Her teachers were so impressed that they asked her to take a degree course, for which she gained the necessary language qualifications in Greek and German in three months. She read philosophy and was remembered later by a former fellow student Ellen WILKINSON, by then a Cabinet minister, as 'our star student'. Having taken a first-class degree, she went on to work at Cambridge. Thereafter, already fascinated by child development, she lectured in education at Darlington. In 1916 she married William Brierly. The marriage was dissolved in 1921 and in 1922 she married Nathan Isaacs, who proved a potent influence on her thinking and intellectual development.

In the spring of 1924, having given up plans to read medicine, Susan Isaacs answered an advertisement which led her to begin the research at an experimental school—The Malting House—for which she became well-known through her books. The school was 'liberal' in its organization and attempted to encourage children to think for themselves. In 1933, she became Head of the newly formed Department of Child Development at the University of London Institute of Education. At first very small and poorly serviced, this department was built by her efforts into a centre of international renown. A few months before her death in 1948 she was awarded the CBE in recognition of work which had contributed immeasurably to an increased understanding of children, their upbringing and education.

See also D. E. M. Gardner, *Susan Isaacs*, 1969. E.M.V.

Isabella of Angoulême (1188–1246), Queen of England. The daughter of Aymer, Count of Angoulême, Isabella was betrothed as a child to Hugh, Lord of Lusignan. In 1200 the English King John, her father's feudal overlord, visited Angoulême and immediately married Isabella himself. Although there were strong political reasons for his action, it seems likely that having seen her, John was determined to have Isabella regardless of the consequences. Contemporaries firmly believed that the affront to the Lusignans led ultimately to the loss of the English-held Angevin lands in France. In the early years of their marriage John was regarded as bewitched by Isabella to the neglect of his duties, but their later relationship seems to have been closer to hatred. They had two sons and three daughters, but on John's death in 1216 the Queen, notoriously guilty of adultery, was allowed no say in advising her young son Henry III. Her unpopularity in England led her to retire to Poitou, where she immediately married the son of her former Lusignan betrothed, bearing him nine children. Problems with his mother and step-father troubled Henry III for years; he was always generous to them, but they never hesitated to desert him in a crisis or transfer their loyalty to Louis IX of France. It is difficult to authenticate the many crimes and misdeeds attributed to Isabella, but clearly public opinion was very much against her and her letters to Henry III show her to have been greedy, selfish and arrogant.

See also W. L. Warren, *King John*, 1961. A.C.

Isabella of France (1296–1358), Queen of England, nicknamed 'the She-Wolf'. The daughter of Philip IV of France, Isabella was betrothed to the future Edward II in 1299 when his father, Edward I, married her aunt, MARGARET OF FRANCE. Edward and Isabella were married in 1308 and by 1321 had two sons and two daughters, but there is no doubt that they were temperamentally unsuited. Isabella found the Queen's role of confidante already usurped by her husband's friend, Piers Gaveston; she disliked Edward's unkingly pursuits and found herself slighted and ignored. Gaveston's successors, the Despensers, regarded her as an enemy and by 1321 she was virtually a prisoner, her estates having been seized. Baronial opposition to Edward provided a weapon for the Queen and when in 1325 Edward was forced to send her to France to negotiate over Gascony with her brother Charles IV, Isabella seized her chance. She persuaded her husband to send their eldest son, Edward, to France to do homage for the province of Gascony and then ignored his demands that they return. The Queen became the centre of a group of English exiles and the mistress of one of them, Roger Mortimer of Wigmore. The French promoted Prince Edward's marriage to PHILIPPA OF HAINAULT and in return Isabella renounced her claim to the French throne, leaving her cousin, Philip of Valois, to succeed on the death of her last brother.

Isabella, Prince Edward and Mortimer landed in Suffolk in 1326 with their Hainault-backed force. Edward and the Despensers were so loathed that they met little opposition; the King was deposed in favour of his son and eventually murdered. It is an open question as to who ruled England for the next three years, but Isabella certainly appears to have had equal rule and responsibility with Mortimer. In 1330 Edward III rejected their rule and took power himself. Mortimer was executed and for a time Isabella was disgraced. Her position gradually improved, although she ceased to have any political influence, and from 1337 she led the affluent, retired life of a queen-dowager, hawking, reading and collecting relics. In old age she took the habit of the Poor Clares and in 1358 was buried with her husband's heart in her coffin as a sign of remorse for his murder.

Isabella's actions were governed by personal rather than political motives, but, having seized power, she was not afraid to use it. Her adultery and the King's murder, to which she was almost certainly not a party, made her extremely unpopular in her own time and blackened her reputation for posterity.

See also N. Fryde, *The Tyranny and Fall of Edward II, 1321–1326*, 1979. A.C.

219

Isabella of Valois

Isabella of Valois (1387–1410), Queen of England. The eldest daughter of Charles VI of France, Isabella was married at the age of eight to Richard II, to prevent him from making a Spanish match. Richard's first wife, ANNE OF BOHEMIA, had died in 1394. Isabella adored her husband and after his deposition and death in 1399 refused to countenance a marriage with the future Henry V, son of her husband's usurper. She returned to France and in 1406 married her cousin, Charles, Duke of Orléans. She died in childbirth in 1410.

See also A. Steel, *Richard II*, 1941.

A.C.

Iurminburg (*fl.* 678–685), Queen of Northumbria. The daughter of unknown parents, Iurminburg became the second wife of King Ecgfrith of Northumbria some time between 672 and 678. Her influence over her husband seems to have been considerable, and she therefore played an important part in Northumbrian history. Her hostility to Bishop Wilfrid of York, possibly because he had been so close to her predecessor ÆTHELTHRYTH, caused her to persuade Ecgfrith to expel Wilfrid from his see in 678, and then, after Wilfrid returned from Rome in 681 with a papal judgement in his favour, to imprison him. Shortly after this Iurminburg fell ill, and was cured only after the King was advised by the Abbess ÆBBE of Coldingham, at whose foundation the royal couple were staying, to release Wilfrid and return the reliquary that Iurminburg had taken from him. Despite this warning, the Queen continued to harry Wilfrid, using her influence to prevent him from finding refuge either in Mercia or Wessex. Yet Iurminburg was not hostile to all ecclesiastics. In 685, for instance, St Cuthbert warned her of his vision that her husband had been killed while fighting the Picts. Cuthbert advised her to leave her sister's monastery, where she was staying to await the outcome of the battle, and take refuge in nearby Carlisle. When the prophecy proved true, Iurminburg decided to take the veil. Cuthbert consecrated her, and she entered a monastery at Carlisle, presumably her sister's house, where she spent the remainder of her life, first as a nun, and then as the monastery's well-respected abbess.

See also B. Colgrave (ed. and trans.), *Vita Cuthberti*, 1940, and Eddius, *Vita Wilfridi*, 1927.

J.C.

J

Jackson of Lodsworth, Baroness. See WARD, BARBARA (MARY).

James, Eleanor (*fl.* 1688–1715), printer and pamphleteer, 'that she-state-politician'. Little is known of her except that she was the wife of Thomas James, a London printer; was committed to Newgate prison in 1689 for 'dispersing scandalous and reflective papers'; and carried on the printing business after her husband's death in 1711. Her own single-sheet pamphlets indicate that she secured interviews with Charles II and James II; her main concern was to defend the rights and privileges of the Church of England, although she strongly opposed the ejection of the Catholic King James II. Her writings are self-important and exhortatory ('Mrs James' Advice to the Citizens of London') in the style of the time.

N.H.

Jameson, Anna Brownell (1794–1860), writer. Anna Murphy, the eldest daughter of an Irish miniature painter and his English wife, was born in Dublin but lived in London from 1806. Educated by a governess, she was talented at languages and sketching, and at sixteen became a governess herself to help family finances. After fifteen years' intermittent work as such, she married Robert Jameson, a lawyer, in 1825. Their marriage was not a success and they lived together only briefly, Anna visiting him for the last time in 1836 when he was Vice Chancellor of Upper Canada. She had begun writing while still a governess and published *A Mother's First Dictionary* in 1825. *The Diary of an Ennuyée* (1826) was the fruit of a trip to the Continent in 1821. Led by necessity to write for the popular market, her next works were sentimental biographies, *Memoirs of the Loves of the Poets* (1829) and *Memoirs of Celebrated Female Sovereigns* (1831). A study of Shakespeare's heroines, *Characteristics of Women* (1832), dedicated to Fanny Kemble, was her first critical success, and it entered the canon of Shakespeare criticism. She also published three collections of 'fugitive pieces', notable for their discussions of German thought and the position of women in society. In 1840, commissioned to write guidebooks to public and private galleries in London, she also contributed articles on art to *The Athenaeum*. Her greatest undertaking, the series known as *Sacred and Legendary Art*, extended to six volumes and was completed after her death by Lady Eastlake. In this comprehensive survey of Christian iconography she guided her readers towards a moralistic view of the world's great art, a school of criticism which was soon to be outmoded by the mid-century reaction in taste. Her work continued to be reprinted for many years and her contribution to the dissemination of art history earned her the appellation 'mother of art criticism'. Other works published include *Winter Studies and Summer Rambles in Canada* (1838) and *Memoirs and Essays on Art, Literature and Social Morals* (1846).

Throughout her life Anna Jameson formed strong friendships with other women, in particular Ottilie von Goethe and Lady Byron, and her writing is imbued with a nascent feminist sympathy. Her first discussion of women's rights had appeared anonymously in *The Athenaeum* in 1843, and in the 1850s she returned to the question in two lectures: *Sisters of Charity* (1855) and *The Communion of Labour* (1856). In her last years, still struggling to support her sisters and her adopted niece Gerardine, she became an inspiration for a younger generation of women. At her suggestion *The Englishwoman's Journal* and the Society for the Promotion of Employment for Women, of which she was a founder member, were established. A courageous, hard-working, independent woman, she both catered to, and influenced, the popular culture of her time. Although not of the intellectual standing of her idol, Madame de Staël, she earned affection and respect for her work.

See also C. Thomas, *Love and Work Enough, The Life of Anna Jameson*, 1967.

C.B.

Jeans, Ursula (1906–73), actress. Born in Simla, India, the daughter of Major Charles McMinn, she was educated at the Sacred Heart Convent in Cavendish Square, London, and later trained at RADA. Her first stage appearance was at Nottingham's Theatre Royal in *Cobra* (1925). She acted in small but conspicuous parts very successfully before playing opposite Noël Coward in S. N. Behrman's *The Second Man*. Her first London appearance was in *The Firebrand* (1926). In *The First*

Jebb, Eglantyne

Mrs Frazer (1929) she played with Marie Tempest and underwent a nerve-racking time as the star gave her a 'lesson in stage-manners'. However, Ursula had courage and put this experience to good use. Her next performance, in *Grand Hotel*, was widely acclaimed and Tyrone Guthrie invited her to join the company for his Old Vic season (1933), with such stars as Charles Laughton, Flora Robson, Marius Goring and Roger Livesey (whom she married after the death of her first husband, the actor Robert Irvine).

In 1939, still with Guthrie, she played Kate Hardcastle in *She Stoops to Conquer* and in *The Taming of the Shrew*. During the Second World War she toured extensively in the Middle and Far East with ENSA, appearing in such plays as *Dear Brutus* and *Watch on the Rhine*. After playing in J. B. Priestley's *Ever Since Paradise* the author described her as 'astonishingly versatile and brilliant'. She returned to the Old Vic for *Captain Brassbound's Conversion* and *The Merry Wives of Windsor*, and then with her husband toured Australia and New Zealand in *The Reluctant Debutante;* they were together again in Wilde's *An Ideal Husband*, her last London appearance.

Ursula Jeans's film career began in 1931 with *The Gypsy Cavalier*. She also appeared in *Cavalcade* (1933), *Dark Journey* (1937), and *The Dam Busters* (1955). She served the English theatre with distinction for forty years and achieved what Ellen Terry described as her own ambition — to be 'a useful actress'.

A.D.

Jebb, Eglantyne (1876–1928), founder of the Save the Children Fund. The daughter of a Shropshire landowner, she read history at Oxford and, after training in London, became an elementary-school teacher in Marlborough. Forced by ill-health to abandon her career, she returned home to care for her widowed mother. In 1913, at the request of her sister Dorothy, wife of the politician Charles Buxton, she travelled to Macedonia to administer a relief fund for the victims of the Second Balkan War.

Following the 1918 Armistice, reports from Europe that 4·5 million children were starving as a result of the continued Allied blockade moved Eglantyne and Dorothy to set up an emergency relief fund, the Save the Children Fund, in 1919. Within two years the Fund had collected almost £1,000,000. The move-ment quickly spread to other countries, and in 1920 Eglantyne Jebb set up the Save the Children International Union, which, from its headquarters in Geneva, administered a huge relief programme that included the daily feeding of hundreds of thousands of children throughout Europe, as well as the provision of health and educational facilities.

As the post-war emergency was contained, Eglantyne Jebb and her supporters acted to establish the movement on a permanent basis. In 1923 she drafted a 'Children's Charter' which was adopted the following year by the League of Nations as the 'Declaration of Geneva'. She became a member of the League's advisory council for the protection of children and, working mainly from Geneva, inspired and co-ordinated the International Union's long-term programmes in the creation of infant welfare centres, children's hospitals and model villages.

Tireless and dedicated, within the short space of nine years she had created a great relief organization and, in the words of UN Secretary-General Dr Kurt Waldheim, made 'a profound impact upon the values and attitudes of a whole generation'.

See also F. M. Wilson, *Rebel Daughter of a Country House*, 1967.

K.W.

Jekyll, Gertrude (1843–1932), landscape gardener and writer. Born in London, she was the daughter of a former captain in the Grenadier Guards. Her mother was a pupil of Mendelssohn. The family moved in intellectual circles and, after studying art at the Kensington School, Gertrude shone in this milieu. She had been widely travelled from girlhood, and had learnt innumerable arts and crafts, as well as gaining an encyclopedic knowledge of the countryside during her childhood in Surrey.

At the age of 48, acute myopia forced her to abandon the arts of embroidery and painting for gardening. She created over 200 gardens, many with Sir Edward Lutyens, frequently devising complex planting arrangements from plans of the terrain alone. Few of these gardens survive as she envisaged them, but Great Dixter in East Sussex, a Lutyens project of 1910 in which she did not directly participate, is a good extant example of her style.

Gertrude Jekyll held the Victorian medal of honour and the Veitchian gold medal, both from the Royal Horticultural Society, and the G. R. White gold medal of the Massachusetts

Horticultural Society. She contributed to *Garden* and *Country Life* and was briefly editor of the latter, working ceaselessly under painful handicaps. Her books include *Gardens for Small Country Houses* (written with Lawrence Weaver, 1912), and *A Gardener's Testament* (1937). These and other books, articles, and copious correspondence, conducted with the great and unknown alike, gained her an international reputation. She surpassed other great gardeners in botanical knowledge through her instinct for colour, light and shade. An advocate of the natural garden, champion of the hardy annual and the herbaceous border, and drawing on inspiration found in cottage gardens, she exercised a lasting influence that is still apparent in the beauty of English gardens today.

See also B. Massingham, *Gertrude Jekyll*, 1964.   A.D.

Jephcott, (Agnes) Pearl (1900–80), sociologist, mainly concerned with the welfare of young people. After graduating from the University College of Wales, Aberystwyth, Pearl Jephcott spent some years as organizing secretary of girls' clubs in Birmingham and County Durham; she later wrote a handbook for club leaders. Her first sociological work was *Girls Growing Up* (1942), a study of working girls' lives based on periodic interviews and on records kept by the girls themselves, followed by *Rising Twenty: notes on some ordinary girls* (1948). As a member of the Department of Social Science at Nottingham University, Pearl Jephcott undertook a study of adolescent boys and girls in three widely different areas, afterwards published as *Some Young People* (1954). Then, as research fellow at the London School of Economics, she worked under Professor Richard Titmuss to produce the report *Married Women Working* (1962; with N. Seear and J. H. Smith); as part of her investigation she took a job at the Peek Frean biscuit factory in Bermondsey. *A Troubled Area* (1964) examined the racial tensions of Notting Hill; it was followed, after a move to Glasgow University, by *Time of One's Own: leisure and young people* (1967).

Pearl Jephcott remained active and socially aware into old age. She persuaded Birmingham Housing Committee to let her occupy one of their tower-block flats for two years; the outcome was a list of practical suggestions for Birmingham and *Homes in High Flats: some of the human problems involved in multi-storey housing* (1971), identifying drawbacks of high-rise living which have since become widely appreciated.   N.H.

Jersey, Countess of. See VILLIERS, MARGARET (ELIZABETH CHILD-), COUNTESS OF JERSEY.

Jesse, F(ryniwyd) Tennyson (1889–1958), novelist and expert on crime, born at Chislehurst in Kent; her clergyman father was a nephew of the poet Tennyson. In her teens she started to train in Cornwall as a painter, exhibiting some pictures and illustrating a book before turning to journalism in 1911. She wrote for the *Daily Mail*, *The Times*, and other newspapers, worked for the Ministry of Information during the First World War, and spent some time as a freelance reporter at the front. In 1919 she published *The Sword of Deborah: first-hand impressions of the British Women's Army in France*. After her marriage in 1918 to the playwright H. M. Harwood, they collaborated on a number of successful light comedies such as *Billeted* (1919), *The Pelican* (1924), and *How To Be Healthy Though Married* (1930).

However, F. Tennyson Jesse is now remembered as a novelist, notably for *The Lacquer Lady* (1929), an historical novel set in Burma, and for *A Pin to See the Peepshow* (1934), suggested by the Thompson-Bywaters case of 1922, in which a woman's young lover murdered her husband and as a result brought both to the gallows. *A Pin to See the Peepshow* examines the woman's life from the inside: Julia Almond is shown to be the victim of her poor circumstances, her constricted life as a woman, and her consequent capacity for living in a romantic fantasy world. F. Tennyson Jesse's interest in crime was sustained and serious: she edited and provided substantial introductions for a number of volumes in the 'Notable British Trials' series, and her *Murder and its Motives* (1924) put forward the then startling theory that there are 'born victims' as well as perpetrators of crimes.   N.H.

Jewsbury, Geraldine (Endsor) (1812–80), novelist. She was born at Measham, Derbyshire, the fourth of six children of a merchant from Manchester. Her older sister, Maria Jane Jewsbury (afterwards Mrs Fletcher) was herself a successful writer, the author of *Phantasmagoria* (1824) and *The Three Histories* (1830). After the death of their mother, Maria brought up and educated her brothers and sisters until her marriage in 1832 when Geraldine took over the household responsibilities. She cared for her father until his death in 1840 and her brother until his marriage in 1853. In 1841 she met Thomas Carlyle and his wife becoming their intimate friend and, thirteen years later, moving to London in order to be near Jane Carlyle. By this time she had already published several novels, including: *Zoe: The History of Two Lives*, 1845, *The Half Sisters*, 1848, and *Marian Withers*, 1851. She was prevented by ill-health from fulfilling her desire to be a journalist, although she occasionally contributed to magazines and was a publisher's reader for Bentley's, exercising considerable influence over the choice of books for Mudie's circulating library. She required novels to have a moral tone with nothing 'unpleasant', and subscribed to belief in the 'eternal importance of love in the financial and popular success of a novel'. Her own books concerned working-class life in northern England, or were historical, with titles including *The Sorrows of Gentility*, 1856, *Right or Wrong*, 1859, and *Constance Herbert*, 1855. But it is as the correspondent and intimate friend of Jane CARLYLE that she is now chiefly remembered.

See also *Letters to Jane Carlyle*, 1892; S. Howe, *Geraldine Jewsbury*, 1935.　　A.P.

Jex-Blake, Sophia (1840–1912), physician. Born in Hastings, the youngest daughter of well-connected parents, she was an audacious child whose 'wildness' shocked her stern Evangelical father. He sent her to various boarding schools, one of which expelled her—an event marking the first in a round of struggles between the unladylike Miss Jex-Blake and educational authority. After a successful period at Queen's College, London, where she went on to teach mathematics, she became a keen educational reformer, taking posts in Germany and America. In Boston she met Dr Lucy Sewall, who stimulated her interest in medicine, and in 1869 returned to England to try for a medical degree. She applied to Edinburgh University, urging the demand of women for doctors of their own sex. Rejected but undaunted, she and four women friends eventually won the right to sit the matriculation examination, which they passed. The vital, final MD examination, however, still eluded them. Harassed by male undergraduates and

hounded by the medical faculty, Miss Jex-Blake and her friends became the centre of national controversy. Their campaign was strengthened by the fact that women who had qualified abroad were already practising in England.

In 1874 Miss Jex-Blake opened the London School of Medicine for Women, but the problems remained of obtaining clinical education in a hospital, and of sitting an MD examination. Two years later Parliament passed an Enabling Bill which gave universities permission to examine women for medical degrees. In 1877 at Queen's University, Dublin, Miss Jex-Blake and Elizabeth Pechey passed their MD and their names were added to the Register of the General Medical Council. In the same year the Royal Free Hospital of London agreed to take women for clinical training; the next year London University admitted women to all degrees.

The battle won, Miss Jex-Blake returned to Edinburgh, where she started a school of medicine and opened the Edinburgh Hospital and Dispensary for Women and Children in 1885. The campaign for women doctors had found in Miss Jex-Blake an indomitable personality which resisted all compromise and which supplied the cutting edge to the patient diplomacy of fellow campaigner Elizabeth Garrett ANDERSON. Her publications included *Medical Women* (1886) and *The Care of Infants* (1884).

See also E. Bell, *Storming the Citadel*, 1953; M. G. Todd, *The Life of Sophia Jex-Blake*, 1918.　　K.S.

Jinner (or Ginner), Sarah (*fl.* 1658–64), writer of almanacs. Sarah Jinner is known only through her published almanacs: *An Almanac or Prognostication* for the years 1658, 1659 and 1660; *An Almanac* for 1664, and *The Woman's Almanac or a Prognostication for Ever* (1659). The almanacs for 1658 and 1659 include portraits, and the publications describe her as a 'Student in Astrology'.

Almanacs, which were the most popular literature of seventeenth-century England, combined the practical handbook with escapist sensationalism. They offered an annual astrological and astronomical calendar, with useful practical advice on legal affairs, health, farming, the weather, and much besides. In addition they included sexual, social, and political comment. The genre was almost unrelievedly misogynist, portraying the contemporary stereotypes of women as garrulous, promiscuous, extravagant and exceedingly dangerous to men. Only three women writers of almanacs have been identified. Of these Jinner was the earliest, the most prolific, and the only one to write general almanacs as well as ones specifically directed to women.

In her almanacs Sarah Jinner supported women's right to a public voice: 'it is as lawful for us to be judges and plead our own causes in our own gowns as lawyers to plead for others'; and pointed out that 'it is the policy of men to keep us from education and schooling wherein we might give testimony of our parts by improvement'. Much space was given to matters of particular concern to women, such as cures for disorders of menstruation and childbirth, and methods for detecting the sex of unborn children. But in general she accepted women's subordinate position, protesting that she had no wish to usurp men's breeches, and she largely endorsed contemporary views of women as wantons and scolds. Her vivid and bawdy style was also similar to that of many male writers: 'When men come sober home and go to bed by daylight our sex are in election to be merry at candlelight'. However, her burlesque is written decidedly from a woman's point of view. Her consciousness of the dangers of promiscuity for women is not often found in almanacs by male authors, for example. In 1659 she wrote that 'more maids than do' would engage in sexual activity 'were it not for the fear of the rising of the apron which usually detects such actions', and in 1664 she recommended an anti-aphrodisiac to women, 'this may be a good medicine for the preventing of young girls throwing themselves away upon madcap fellows'.

Jinner also included radical political and social comment in her almanacs, arguing that people were not bound to obey a bad government, and bemoaning the lack of 'one grain or two of honesty' among money-grubbing lawyers. She was no democrat, however, and was extremely hostile to the radical religious movements of the later 1650s. Her significance as a rare woman contributor to an important aspect of popular literature is complemented by the example of a woman's intervention partially transforming an overwhelmingly misogynist literary genre.

See also B. Capp, *Astrology and the Popular Press*, 1979.   A.H.

Joan (?–1237), Princess of North Wales. The daughter of King John by his mistress Clementia, Joan was legitimized by Pope Honorius III in 1226. In 1204 she married the Prince of North Wales, Llywelyn ap Iorwerth, and soon became prominent as a peacemaker between Wales and England. In 1211, when John led an army into North Wales, Joan persuaded him to accept her husband's submission. She was instrumental in preventing a further English invasion in 1213, secured the release of Welsh hostages in 1215, and continued to act as mediator following the accession of Henry III in 1216. In 1230 Joan was imprisoned for adultery, and her lover, William de Braose, executed; but on her death she was buried in Anglesey 'with sore lamentations', and Llywelyn founded a Franciscan house in her honour.   K.R.D.

Joan of Kent (c. 1328–85), the 'Fair Maid of Kent', Princess of Wales. The daughter of Edmund, Earl of Kent, younger son of Edward I, Joan was married at the age of twelve to William Montagu, Earl of Salisbury. Five years later the marriage was annulled on the grounds of her previous secret marriage to Sir Thomas Holand. The Holand marriage being confirmed by the Pope, the couple subsequently had several children before his death in 1360. Joan then immediately married her cousin Edward, the Black Prince, and they made their home in the Prince's province of Aquitaine. Joan was deservedly popular and her death in 1385 removed a good, strong influence from her young son, Richard II.

See also J. Harvey, *The Black Prince and his Age*, 1976.   A.C.

Joan of Kent. See BOCHER, JOAN.

Joan of Navarre (c. 1373–1437), Queen of England. The daughter of Charles II, King of Navarre, Joan became the third wife of Duke John IV of Brittany in 1386. On his death in 1399 she became regent for her young son, John V, but in 1402 relinquished this position to marry Henry IV of England. Their own marriage was childless, but Joan enjoyed a friendly relationship with the future Henry V and her other step-children. When the King died in 1413, Joan continued to preside at the court of the bachelor Henry V. However, in 1419 she was arrested and accused of using witchcraft aimed at procuring the King's death. She was never tried, but her possessions were sequestrated. After an initial period of imprisonment she lived in style and comfort at her own castle of Leeds. The charges were probably not believed, and certainly Joan had nothing to gain from Henry's death, but for three years the war-impoverished crown secured substantial additional income from her lands. Conscience-stricken on his death-bed, Henry restored her freedom in 1422 and she was treated with affection and generosity by Henry VI until her own death in 1437.

See also J. L. Kirby, *Henry IV of England*, 1970.   A.C.

Joan, Queen of Scotland. See BEAUFORT, JOAN.

Joanna (1165–99), Queen of Sicily. The youngest daughter of Henry II and ELEANOR OF AQUITAINE, Joanna was married at the age of eleven to William II, King of Sicily. There were no children. On his death in 1190 Joanna was held hostage by the usurper Tancred of Lecce and was rescued by her brother, Richard I, on his way to the Third Crusade. After further adventures in Cyprus she accompanied Richard and BERENGARIA to the Holy Land. There it was suggested that she marry Saladin's brother and rule the kingdom of Jerusalem jointly with him. On returning to England, however, Richard married her to Raymond, Count of Toulouse, who was succeeded by the son Joanna bore him. While attempting to put down a rebellion against her husband, Joanna, who was pregnant, was forced to flee for aid to her brother, but learned of Richard's death on the way and went instead to her mother's abbey of Fontevrault. Here she insisted on taking vows, shortly before her death in childbirth. Despite her two marriages, Joanna's first loyalty seems always to have been to her mother and brother.

See also R. Pernoud, *Eleanor of Aquitaine*, trans. P. Wiles, 1967.   A.C.

Jocelin, Elizabeth (1596–1622), author. Elizabeth's parents were Sir Richard Brooke of Norton, Cheshire, and Joan Chadderton, daughter of the Bishop of Lincoln, but after their separation she was educated by her maternal grandmother, 'in languages, history and some arts' but mainly in 'studies of piety'. Her extraordinary memory is said to have permitted her to write out whole sermons word for word. In 1616 she married Tourell Jocelin of Cambridgeshire and gave birth to a daugh-

ter, Theodora, in October 1622, but died within a fortnight. Having experienced a foreboding that she would not survive, she had, while pregnant, composed *The Mother's Legacie to her Unborne Child*. This work of piety, exhorting her child to live a godly life, is prefaced with a letter to her husband giving him advice on child-rearing. Despite her own relatively advanced upbringing, she advised confining a daughter's education to basic literacy, housewifery, and religion; 'other learning a woman need not'. The *Legacy* was published in 1624 with a third edition by 1625. Its composition reveals one seventeenth-century woman's fears of the dangers of childbirth, while its publication shows the increasing emphasis of the period on the importance of family life.   P.M.H.

John, Gwen (1876–1939), painter. She was the daughter of a solicitor and elder sister of the artist Augustus John. The family had no previous connection with the arts, and their father could not understand how it had produced two such artists. Gwen John studied at the Slade from 1895, and in Paris from 1899, where she worked in Whistler's Academy and shared a room with Ida Nettleship, who later married Augustus. She was probably the model for Rodin's abandoned first project for the Whistler monument (the maquette is now in the Library of Congress, Washington). Her disappointing association with Rodin ended in 1906. Between 1906 and 1908 she was friendly with the poet Rilke, and in 1913 became a Roman Catholic. While she certainly knew the influential Catholic philosopher Jacques Maritain, his influence on her art has been much exaggerated; her long and intimate friendship with Maritain's sister-in-law, Véra Oumançoff, was of greater importance in the demands it made on her time and energy.

Gwen John lived all her life in poverty and retirement, not to say squalor, and was shy and timid, but obstinate in her search for solitude and independence. Her work had in common with Post-Impressionists only a similar concern for simplified contours and flattened surfaces. Unlike them she worked in a consistently muted colour range. Her gifts as a draughtswoman were encouraged by Tonks at the Slade; her concern for meticulous technique came from Whistler's rigorous discipline. Her subjects are usually domestic; clothed or nude models are normally seated in simple, straightforward poses; there is also the occasional landscape or still-life. Gwen John had only one major exhibition of her work, in 1926, although she exhibited irregularly with the New English Art Club (1900–11), shared an exhibition with her brother in 1903, and showed irregularly at the Salon des Tuileries from 1923. Augustus said that one day he would be remembered as Gwen John's brother.

Her life ended in the loneliness she always insisted upon. One day in 1939 she felt she would like a change of air, took the train to Dieppe, collapsed on arrival, and died in the local hospital. Characteristically, she had no luggage with her, but in her will had made adequate provision for her cats.

There are works in London (the National Portrait Gallery and the Tate Gallery); the Fitzwilliam Museum, Cambridge; Leeds; Manchester; the Museum of Modern Art, New York; Norwich; Sheffield; and elsewhere.

See also S. Chitty, *Gwen John*, 1982; J. Rothenstein, *Modern English Painters: Sickert to Smith*, 1952; introduction by Taubman to the catalogue of the Arts Council exhibition, 1968.   L.M.M.

Johnson, Amy (1904–41), aviator. Born in Hull, she took a degree in economics at Sheffield University and began flying in 1928, gaining her pilot's licence. Only two years later she made the solo flight halfway round the world which caused newspapers to hail her as 'Queen of the Air'. Whereas other women pilots had been wealthy, Amy Johnson had no such financial backing to help her to success. However, she achieved not only her pilot's licence, but also a ground engineer's licence and took courses in meteorology, direction-finding and signalling. Her aim was to fly solo to Australia in an attempt to equal the record of Hinkler, an Australian test pilot, who had flown from London to Darwin in fifteen and a half days. Setting off from Croydon on 5 May 1930 in her biplane *Jason*, she reached Vienna on the first lap. From there she flew to Istanbul, across Asia Minor and south to Aleppo. After some mishaps, she reached the Indian sub-continent on 11 May, beating Hinkler's time by forty-eight hours. She then encountered weather problems and was forced to land near Rangoon, damaging the propeller and undercarriage. Her aircraft repaired, she continued to Bangkok and Sin-

gapore and thence, again in bad weather, to Darwin, where her welcome on 24 May was rapturous.

Amy Johnson perhaps never quite came to terms with her fame, for both her personal and professional life from then onwards were flawed. Her marriage failed and her later flying exploits were often less than successful. In January 1941 she was delivering an aeroplane to Kidlington when she crashed and was killed. Nonetheless, her 1930 triumph had in the words of the *Manchester Guardian*'s report, given 'heartening proof of a courageous spirit and a supreme command of air skill'.

See also C. Babington Smith, *Amy Johnson* 1967.   E.M.V.

Johnson, Dame Celia (1908-82), actress. Born in Richmond, the daughter of a doctor, she was educated at St Paul's Girls' School and RADA. In 1935 she married the author and explorer Peter Fleming.

Her career began in *A Hundred Years Old* at the Lyric (1929). Mediocre plays followed but she was always singled out by the critics; her delicate touch, expressive eyes and perfect timing made her an elegant comedienne. Her best early part was in *Cynara* with Gerald du Maurier. She often played 'bright young things' but was Ophelia (New York, 1931) to Raymond Massey's Hamlet, while her Elizabeth Bennet in *Pride and Prejudice* (1936) showed a sure sense of period. After her marriage she devoted herself to her family, often leaving a play before the end of the run to be with them. She played only two important roles between 1937 and 1944: Mrs de Winter in *Rebecca* (1940) and Jennifer in *The Doctor's Dilemma* (1944). She was, however making a name in films, including *In Which We Serve* (1942), *This Happy Breed* (1943), *Brief Encounter* (1945), and *The Astonished Heart* (1950). In 1944 her *Saint Joan* at the Old Vic divided the critics, but her exquisite playing of Olga in Chekhov's *Three Sisters* (1951) won universal acclaim. Between these two appearances she left the stage, returning to tour Italy as Viola, the part she played in *Twelfth Night* at the Old Vic in 1950, and after Olga again had a 'rest' period. She returned to the theatre in *The Reluctant Debutante* (1955) and, in 1957, *Flowering Cherry*.

Celia Johnson could be tragic or pathetic without sentimentality, as in *The Dame of Sark* (1974), and in her later career became the finest television actress of her generation, for, despite her performance of restrained passion opposite Trevor Howard in the film *Brief Encounter* (1945), by which she has been immortalized, Celia Johnson actually reached the peak of her career in middle and old age. Her Gertrude to Alan Bates's Hamlet in 1971, for example, portrayed a distraught mother and overwhelmed the audience.   A.D.

Johnson, Esther (1689–1728), friend of Jonathan Swift. She was reputedly the natural daughter of Sir William Temple, but this, as so much of her history, is obscure. In literary history she is known as 'Stella', the pseudonym bestowed upon her by Swift. Her existence was retired, even cloistered, and was spent almost entirely in Ireland. Here she lived mainly in Dublin, remote from the world almost as a troubadour's lady, the passive, often sorrowing companion of Swift's Irish exile, the object of his tenderness and his bullying. The possibility of a secret marriage between them about the year 1716 has been a question much discussed. It is by virtue of her association with Swift and its enigmatic nature, not by any positive achievement of her own that her place in literary history is assured.

See also S. de Brocquy, *Swift's Most Valuable Friend* (1968); H. Williams, ed., *Jonathan Swift. Journal to Stella*, 2 vols (1948).   T.H.

Johnson, Pamela Hansford (1912–81), novelist, critic and broadcaster. Born in south London and educated at Clapham County Secondary School, she began writing at a very early age and while employed in her first job as a secretary won the *Sunday Referee* competition for poetry. In 1934 she published a volume of verse, *Symphony for Full Orchestra*. The favourable critical reception of her first novel, *This Bed Thy Centre* (1935), made her decide to make writing her career. *Too Dear for my Possessing* (1940) established her as a serious professional novelist. Her first popular book, *Catherine Carter* (1952), concerned Victorian theatre and was based on intimate knowledge of the subject, her mother having been an actress and her grandfather manager to Sir Henry Irving. She wrote critical essays on Dickens, Trollope, Ivy Compton-Burnett, and Thomas Wolfe, and through radio broadcasts, later published in book form, gained a reputation as an authority on Proust. As one of the reporters at the trial of the Moors

murderers, she wrote a commentary, *On Iniquity* (1967).

Pamela Hansford Johnson developed in the tradition of broad realism exemplified by George ELIOT. Her concern was with morality and duty and she had total empathy with her characters. These were often comic, as in *The Unspeakable Skipton* (1959), based on the career of the notorious Baron Corvo. Her view of life was not specifically feminine and she could write convincingly in the first person as a man. Twice married, to Gordon Stewart (1936) and the novelist C. P. Snow (1950), she had three children.

See also I. Quigley, *Pamela Hansford Johnson*, 1968.   P.L.

Jones, Agnes Elizabeth (1832–68), pioneer of workhouse nursing, born of Irish parents in Cambridge. Her father was a lieutenant-colonel in the army, and when she was five his regiment moved to Mauritius, where she spent six happy years and where her passionate altruism was first aroused by refugee Madagascar Christians. A reserved and religious child, she was educated at home and later by a governess, but though diligent she was not a distinguished pupil. At sixteen she attended Stratford on Avon School, leaving on the death of her father two years later. Much of her time in the following years was taken up by teaching in ragged schools and visiting the poor. A trip to the Continent in 1853 took her to Kaiserswerth, on the Rhine, where Pastor Fliedner had established a Protestant sisterhood for the training of nurses. She was anxious to join the eight-month course, but domestic considerations prevented her from doing so until 1860.

After training at Kaiserswerth she intended to prepare herself at a London hospital for a post which Florence Nightingale had arranged as head of the new nurses' home and training school at the Liverpool Infirmary. But her mother, who did not think nursing a respectable career for her daughter, objected to this plan and it had to be postponed. In 1861, with her mother's blessing, she worked in London for the Bible and Female Domestic Mission established by Ellen RANYARD, where she gained valuable experience as an overseer of slum visitors. She entered St Thomas's Hospital in 1863 as a probationer, Miss Nightingale's 'best and dearest pupil', and after her year's work joined the staff of the Great Northern Hospital. In 1865 she was offered the post as matron at the Liverpool Infirmary. Under a scheme supported by the Liverpool philanthropist William Rathbone, she took charge of a staff of over 50 nurses, 150 pauper scourers and about 1,300 patients. Although there were disagreements with the Infirmary authorities, her talents as a teaching nurse and an administrator soon reduced the chaos and squalor of the wards, improved the health of the inmates, and, not least, cut costs. Selfless and indefatigable, though without Miss Nightingale's tact, she convinced the Liverpool Vestry of the economy and humanity of using trained nurses. In so doing she had raised infirmary nursing to a profession. Her promising career was short-lived, however, for in 1868, aged thirty-five, she died of typhus contracted in the workhouse.

See also J. Jones, *Memorials of Agnes Elizabeth Jones*, 1871; C. Woodham Smith, *Florence Nightingale*, 1950.　　　F.K.P.

Jones, Katherine, Viscountess Ranelagh (1615–91), intellectual. Katherine was the seventh child of Richard Boyle, first Earl of Cork, the leading Anglo-Irish magnate. In 1630 she married Arthur Jones, later second Viscount Ranelagh and another prominent Anglo-Irishman. Contemporary comment suggests that Jones was a drunken boor, a totally unsuitable husband for the learned and pious Katherine. The marriage produced three daughters and a son, the last born in 1641, and it is probable that thenceforth the couple lived apart for most of the time until Jones's death in 1670. After the rising of 1641, Katherine was besieged by Irish rebels in Athlone Castle for two years, then obtained a safe conduct for England where she lived until her death. However, she was active on behalf of her husband and family, successfully petitioning the English authorities to compensate for her considerable losses during the uprising.

In the 1640s Katherine's London home became a focus for the Irish Protestants in exile and for many leading intellectuals and scientific figures. Among these were Benjamin Worsley, Samuel Hartlib, John Dury, whose wife was her kinswoman, and Henry Oldenburg. Oldenburg was a German emigré, Secretary of the Royal Society, who, with the poet John Milton, helped to tutor her son. Katherine took great interest in contemporary scientific, religious and philosophical debates, but, like many women, was patron and facilitator rather

than a direct participant. During the 1650s she encouraged schemes for reform of the legal and medical professions, and took an especial interest in educational improvement, which she saw as the vital foundation of a truly learned and religious commonwealth. She was particularly concerned for the education of girls. More significant, perhaps, was the encouragement she gave to her younger brother Robert Boyle, the eminent scientist. Through Lady Ranelagh he gained access to a stimulating scientific circle, and from 1668 he lived in her Pall Mall house, where a laboratory was built for him.

While holding pronounced religious and political views, Katherine used her influence generously and without bias. She had sided with Parliament in the 1640s, but interceded on behalf of defeated Royalist friends and at the Restoration attempted to moderate the new government's policies towards religious non-conformists. Described as a Presbyterian but an 'honest sectary', Lady Ranelagh was reputedly sympathetic to Quakers but seems generally to have conformed to the Church of England after 1660. Her beloved brother Robert died a week after her death, declaring that his heart was broken, and his eulogy included a tribute to Katherine which spoke of her as 'the greatest figure in all the revolutions of these kingdoms for above fifty years, of any woman in that age'.

See also R. E. W. Maddison, *The Life of the Honourable Robert Boyle*, 1969; C. Webster, *The Great Instauration*, 1975.　　A.H.

Jones, Sheridan. See CHESTERTON, ADA (ELIZABETH).

Jordan, Dorothy (1761/2–1816), actress, also known as Dorothea. One of the best-loved actresses of her time, she made early stage appearances in Dublin, Waterford, and Cork as Dorothea Bland. It was after an affair with the nefarious Daly, manager at Cork, that she fled to Yorkshire, heavily pregnant, under the name 'Mrs Jordan'. From 1782 to 1785 she played the York circuit with the provincial company of Tate Wilkinson, and first appeared in London at Drury Lane in *The Country Girl*. Until 1809 she played there and at the Haymarket a range of 'breeches' and hoyden parts, such as Viola, Rosalind, Miss Tomboy, Sir Harry Wildair and Miss Prue. She also wrote a farce, *The Spoiled Child*. Between 1811 and 1814 she appeared at Covent Garden, her final role being that of Lady Teazle. Dorothea Jordan was seen as the Comic Muse, counterpart to the Tragic Muse of Mrs Siddons. She did not shine in tragic parts and her creation of the role of Cora in Sheridan's *Pizarro* was a notable failure.

Although she acted almost continuously for thirty years, she not only had five children by Daly and Sir Richard Ford, but also ten by the Duke of Clarence. The eldest of these was created Earl of Munster. In 1811, under pressure from the royal family, he shamefully abandoned her. She left for France in 1815, and died there in poverty. Anecdotes are told of her philanthropy during these last years, while throughout her life she supported her mother, brothers and sisters, and numerous children, even as adults. Hazlitt wrote of her, 'She was all gaiety, openness and good nature; she rioted in her fine animal spirits, and gave more pleasure than any other actress, because she had the greatest spirit of enjoyment herself'. She was painted by Hoppner, Romney, De Wilde, Reynolds, and Gainsborough. The Duke of Clarence, as William IV, commissioned a statue of her by Chantrey.

See also A. Aspinall (ed.), *Mrs Jordan and her family*, 1951; A. G. Fothergill, *Mrs Jordan, portrait of an actress*, 1965.　　　　C.H.

Jordan-Lloyd, Dorothy (1889–1946), biochemist. One of four children of a professor of medicine, Dorothy Jordan-Lloyd was educated at King Edward's High School, Birmingham, and Newnham College, Cambridge. She gained first class honours in both parts of the Natural Sciences Tripos, and was Bathurst Student. From 1914 to 1921 she was a Fellow of Newnham; and from 1914 to 1918 conducted research for the Medical Research Committee (later Council) on substitute culture media for bacteriology, and the causes and prevention of ropiness in bread. She later joined the staff of the British Leather Manufacturers' Federation, becoming its director in 1927. She was Vice-President of the Royal Institute of Chemists, and in 1939 was awarded the Fraser Moffatt Muir Medal of the Tanners Council of America. She also held a D Sc from London University. Her works include *The Chemistry of the Proteins* (1926). An accomplished mountain climber, in 1928 Dorothy Jordan-Lloyd carried out the first ascent and descent in one day of the Eiger by the Mittelegi route. She was also a fine rider, competing at

the Richmond Royal and International Horse Shows.　　　　J.E.

Judith (844–after 870), Frankish princess and Queen of Wessex. Judith was the eldest daughter of the Carolingian King Charles the Bald and his first wife Ermintrud. In 856, at the age of twelve, she married the fifty-year-old West Saxon King Æthelwulf, who was visiting Charles on the way from Rome. The Carolingian marriage was a prestigious match for Æthelwulf, while Charles struck a bond with a warrior king fresh from victory against the Vikings who controlled the northern shores of the English Channel. But Charles was concerned for his daughter's future in a remote country, for her potential difficulties with stepsons older than herself, and for the fertility of her ageing husband. To safeguard her position he hedged the marriage with a unique event, her anointing as queen. The occasion marked the first known anointing of a queen in England or Frankia. When Æthelwulf returned to Wessex, he found his eldest son Æthelbald in rebellion. Æthelbald objected to a stepmother whose anointing as queen might enhance the prospect of accession to the throne by any sons she might bear, thus threatening his hopes of succession. The king's wife in Wessex was normally excluded from all power in order to avoid the fomenting of family dissension. Æthelwulf was forced to divide the kingdom with his son, but died in 858 before Judith bore a child.

Æthelbald succeeded to all of Wessex and promptly married his stepmother, hoping to gain from the match the same advantages as his father; but this second marriage was again short-lived. By 861 Æthelbald was dead and Judith, still apparently childless, was selling her English lands to return to Frankia. Twice widowed before the age of eighteen, she remained unbowed and soon eloped with Baldwin of Flanders. As Countess of Flanders she produced a son, Baldwin, who married Ælfthryth, a granddaughter of Judith's first husband.

See also P. A. Stafford, 'Charles the Bald, Judith and Æthelwulf', in *Charles the Bald*, British Archaeological Reports, 1981.

　　　　P.A.S.

Juliana of Norwich (1343?–1443?), mystical writer and recluse who spent most of her life as an anchoress in the churchyard of St Julian of Norwich. Her *Revelations of Divine Love* (edited by H. Collins in 1877) is an entirely mystical work, derived from powerful religious experiences which she underwent while seriously ill in 1373. By the early fifteenth century, this remarkably long-lived visionary had come to enjoy a great reputation for piety, compassion, spiritual calm, and a deep, unflinching love of God. Her writings, described by a contemporary as containing 'very many cheering and deeply moving words for all those who want to be Christ's lovers', have won her a reputation as the 'first English woman of letters'. K.R.D.

K

Katherine of Aragon (1485–1536),first Queen of Henry VIII. The youngest daughter of Ferdinand of Aragon and Isabella of Castile, Katherine was destined from infancy to marry Arthur, son of Henry VII. This accorded with Aragonese foreign policy, which aimed to forge dynastic alliances between the royal houses of Aragon and other countries surrounding France. As a child she witnessed her mother's final crusade against the Moors, culminating in the fall of Granada in 1492. She also received a thorough humanist education.

Katherine arrived in England during October 1501, marrying Arthur in London on 14 November. The couple proceeded to the Welsh Marches, but on 2 April 1502 Arthur died of the sweating sickness at Ludlow. Since both Henry VII and Ferdinand wished to continue the alliance, Katherine was shortly afterwards betrothed to Arthur's brother Henry, a papal dispensation being procured because of their near relationship. But both kings were reluctant to conclude the marriage while they could use their children as dynastic bargaining counters, and so Katherine lingered in England, an impoverished widow, until Henry VII's death. Henry VIII married her on 11 June 1509, and she was crowned with him on 24 June.

In the early years of the reign Katherine was politically important because of the alliance between England and Aragon against France. When Henry VIII invaded France in 1513, Katherine was appointed Regent in his absence; the battle of Flodden against the Scots was won under her authority and direction. The Anglo-Aragonese rapport ended in 1514 when Ferdinand made a separate peace with France without Henry's knowledge, and the latter in retaliation married his sister Mary to Louis XII. However, Katherine's political influence can also be discerned after 1519, when her nephew Charles became Holy Roman Emperor. Henry and Charles combined against France in an alliance which was to last almost until the royal divorce and during the course of which Katherine's daughter was betrothed to Charles.

Katherine also played an important part as patron in cultural and religious matters, assisting such scholars as Erasmus and commissioning polemical works against Luther and Melanchthon in the 1520s. But her most important—and political—achievement was the preparation of Princess Mary for the throne. A long succession of miscarriages and stillbirths had left Katherine and Henry with only one child, a daughter. Despite the fact that there was no encouraging precedent for female rule in England, Katherine commissioned the Spanish humanist Juan Luis Vives to produce a comprehensive and uniquely innovatory scheme of education which would equip Mary for rule as well as for private life. She herself marked her daughter's exercises and sent reading-matter to her.

Steps towards the royal divorce began in 1527 when Henry, worried by his lack of a male heir and attracted by Anne Boleyn, claimed concern that the dispensation for his marriage was insufficient and that the union was consequently null. Katherine opposed this vigorously, asserting that her marriage to Arthur was void because unconsummated, refusing to admit the competence of a papal court opened in London to try the case, and recruiting scholars to defend her. In 1531 Henry separated from her, and in January 1533 he secretly married the pregnant Anne Boleyn. Katherine's marriage was annulled by Archbishop Cranmer in May, Anne was crowned in June, and her daughter Princess Elizabeth was born in September. The 1534 Act of Succession disinherited Mary.

Katherine, ailing in health but still defiant, lived in a succession of unhealthy prison-houses, and finally died at Kimbolton on 7 January 1536. She had exerted considerable political influence at different times, had broken new ground in the field of women's education, and had affected political and ecclesiastical history by her intransigence over the divorce.

See also J. S. Brewer, *Letters & Papers, Foreign and Domestic, of the Reign of Henry VIII . . .*, 1920; *Calendar of State Papers, Spanish;* G. Mattingly, *Catherine of Aragon,* 1944.   M.D.

Kauffmann, Angelica (1741–1807), historical and portrait painter. She was born in Switzerland, the daughter of a minor painter. With her father she travelled widely through Switzerland, Austria, and northern Italy in search of commissions, and from a very early age

232

won recognition as a child prodigy. She was introduced to the Neo-classical style in Naples, 1762, through its main exponents, Benjamin West, Johann Friedrich Reiffenstein, and later Abbé Winckelmann. During this period her linguistic skills enabled her to pursue international contacts, and in 1766 she travelled to London under the patronage of Lady Wentworth, the wife of an English diplomat. Her success there is shown by her inclusion as a founding member of the Royal Academy (1768). The paintings she exhibited at the Academy, which include *Interview of Hector and Andromache* and *Venus Showing Æneas and Achates the Way to Carthage*, gain historical significance through the choice of genre. Angelica Kauffmann was the first woman to prove successful in history-painting, a style previously the exclusive domain of men. In addition to her major paintings she also worked in the decorative arts, designing for Wedgwood and painting interior panels in collaboration with the architect Robert Adam.

In 1767 she married a Swedish adventurer, the 'Count de Horn', but it soon emerged that he was a commoner named Brandt and was already married. Although they soon separated, Angelica's devout Catholicism caused her to wait until he died in 1780 before marrying the painter Antonio Zucchi the following year. The couple returned to the Continent shortly afterwards, and settled in Rome. There she enjoyed the patronage of a large portion of European nobility, including Grand Duke Paul of Russia. After her husband's death in 1795, Angelica's output declined, but her wealth and reputation made her home in Rome a centre for artists and visitors. Her total *oeuvre* of over 500 paintings contributed significantly to the development of Neo-classicism in eighteenth-century Europe.

See also A. S. Harris and L. Nochlin, *Women Artists 1550–1950*, 1976. A.L.

Kavanagh, Julia (1824–77), novelist. Although born at Thurles in County Tipperary, she spent much of her childhood and early adulthood in France. She was the only child of a writer and linguist who later claimed that he was the author of her publications and that his own worst work had been written by her. She was educated at home, remaining single and looking after her invalid mother.

In 1844 Julia Kavanagh moved to London where she began writing magazine stories and children's books. Her first novel, *The Montyon Prizes*, was published in 1846 and proved very popular, as did her other books, most of which were set in France. She also wrote three biographical and historical works: *Women in France in the Eighteenth Century*, 1850, *French Women of Letters*, 1861, and *English Women of Letters*, 1862. On the death of her mother, Julia Kavanagh moved to Nice where she lived until her death at the age of fifty-three. Her other works include *Natalie*, 1851, *Madeleine*, 1848, *Daisy Burns*, 1853, *Adele*, 1858, *Grace Lee*, 1855, *Queen Mab*, 1863, and *Bessie*, 1872. A.P.

Kaye-Smith, Sheila (1887–1956), writer. She was the daughter of a physician at Hastings, where she mainly lived until her marriage in 1929 to an Anglo-Catholic priest, Theodore Penrose Fry; the couple later converted to Roman Catholicism. Sheila Kaye-Smith's first published novel was *The Tramping Methodist* (1908), after which she produced at least one book a year. Her works generally had a rural Sussex background which sometimes suggested comparisons with Thomas Hardy's use of 'Wessex' settings. *Sussex Gorse: The Story of a Fight* (1916) is typical in its narrative of Reuben Blackfield's ruthless struggle to gain and master the moorland he believed to be rightfully his. The 'earthy', 'passionate' novel would seem difficult to consider seriously since Stella Gibbons's merciless parody of Mary Webb's *Precious Bane* in *Cold Comfort Farm*, yet *Sussex Gorse*, along with *Green Apple Harvest* (1920), *Joanna Godden* (1921), and others, still commands a readership.

See also S. Kaye-Smith, *Three Ways Home*, 1937. N.H.

Keeley, Mary Ann (1806–99), actress. She was born Mary Ann Goward at Ipswich, Suffolk, and trained as a singer, first appearing in 1825 at the Royal Opera House, later the Lyceum, in London. She then began a career as an actress and had already achieved considerable individual success when in 1829 she married the actor and comedian Robert Keeley and thereafter appeared with him.

Her small, neat physique contributed to the success she had in pathetic roles and in boys' parts, such as Smike in *Nicholas Nickleby*, although it was as the notorious criminal Jack Sheppard that she created her most notable character. The couple were at the Haymarket

with Kean, and also played for five years at
the Adelphi. In 1833 they went to America
and in 1838 joined Madame VESTRIS at the
Olympic, remaining until 1841 when they
were with Macready at Drury Lane. From
1844 to 1847 they were involved together in
management of the Lyceum, where they produced adaptations from Dickens's novels and
burlesques. After Robert Keeley's death in
1869, his widow retired from the stage,
although she survived for another thirty years.
Her daughters were both actresses, one,
Louise, playing with Irving.   B.H.C.

Keene, Mary (Frances Lucas) (?–1977), anatomist. She was educated at Eversley, Folkestone, and at what was then the London School
of Medicine for Women (now the Royal Free
Hospital School of Medicine); its development
into one of the leading London teaching hospitals owes a good deal to Mary Keene. Her
entire working life was bound up with the
School, where she was successively Lecturer
in Embryology and Senior Demonstrator in
Anatomy, head of department, and ultimately
President. On retirement she became Professor
Emeritus in Anatomy at the University of
London. She played an important part in the
Medical Women's Federation and the Anatomical Society of Great Britain, becoming
president of both bodies. She was also a vice-
president of the Medical Protection Association.   N.H.

Kello, Esther. See INGLIS, ESTHER.

Kelly, Frances Maria (1790–1882), actress
and singer. Born in Brighton, she first appeared
at Drury Lane at the age of seven, playing in
her uncle Michael Kelly's opera *Bluebeard*.
She remained a favourite at Drury Lane for
thirty-six years, acting many of the parts formerly associated with Mrs JORDAN. Considered
pre-eminent in melodrama, she also covered
all the leading comedy characters, while her
appearances as Ophelia to Kean's Hamlet in
1812 helped to restore the theatre's fortunes
after its destruction by fire. She was twice shot
at on stage by lunatics, first in 1816, when
some of the shot landed in the lap of Mary
LAMB. She was in the audience with her
brother Charles, who wanted to marry Fanny
Kelly. On retirement in 1835, she opened a
dramatic school for actresses, beginning at the
New Strand Theatre. She later built the Royalty in Soho, but fell into debt, after which

she gave private tuition and Shakespearean
readings.   B.H.C.

Kelly, Mary Anne (1826-1910), poet and Irish
patriot, known as 'Eva'. She was born at Head-
ford in Galway, Ireland, the daughter of a
gentleman farmer, and contributed patriotic
verse to *The Nation*, organ of the Young
Ireland movement. She was engaged to the
patriot Kevin Izod O'Doherty, who leaned to
revolutionary views, was arrested for treason
and transported to Australia. He visited Ireland
secretly in 1855 and they married. In 1856 he
was granted an unconditional pardon, qualified as a doctor and entered Australian politics.
He was also elected an Irish nationalist MP.
She died in Brisbane, having been supported
in later years by a fund raised by the Irish
people.   B.H.C.

Kemble, Adelaide (1814?–79), singer and
writer. She was born in London, the younger
daughter of Charles Kemble, manager of Covent Garden, and niece of Sarah SIDDONS.
Adelaide Kemble first sang professionally in
1835 and performed in Germany, Prague,
Paris and Italy, while continuing her studies.
Her first operatic performance was in *Norma*.
She travelled abroad with her sister, accompanied for a time by Liszt, and in 1842 left
the stage, marrying Edward John Sartoris the
following year. She then began to write. *A
Week in a French Country House* was published in *The Cornhill* magazine and, in 1867,
as a book. Other publications were *Medusa
and Other Tales* (1868) and *Past Hours* (1880).
Hers was a brilliant, brief, singing career. She
performed lieder by Schumann and Mendelssohn, excelled in Rossini and Bellini, but was
distinguished most by her intellectual gifts.
Her career was of rare value in proving to the
cynical that an Englishwoman could reach the
forefront of art.   B.H.C.

Kemble, Elizabeth (1763–1841), actress. Born
in London, the daughter of an instrument-
maker named Satchell, she joined the famous
theatrical family of Kemble when she married
the actor-manager Stephen Kemble in 1783.
Her first recorded stage appearance was at
Covent Garden as Polly in *The Beggar's Opera*
(1780). She played Margaret in *A New Way
to Pay Old Debts* (1781), followed by appearances as Juliet, Ophelia, and Celia in *As You
Like It*. Her first role opposite Stephen Kemble

was as Desdemona to his Othello. Afterwards they often acted together and it was said that she greatly contributed to his fortune and often outshone him on stage. Contemporary critics praised her fulsomely, declaring that she was the best Ophelia, had genius rather than talent, and though in stature a little woman she was a mighty actress. They also applauded her delightful singing voice. Among other performers she was notorious for her violent temper, and sometimes bit her fellow actors. Elizabeth Kemble died in retirement at Durham and was buried in the cathedral by her husband's side.   P.L.

Kemble, Frances Anne (1809–93), actress and author. Fanny Kemble was the daughter of Charles Kemble, actor and part-owner of Covent Garden, and the actress-playwright Maria Theresa de Camp. A 'troublesome and unmanageable' child, she was sent to school in France where she developed a passion for reading and an ambition to be a writer. At seventeen she wrote her first play, *Francis I*, published and performed in 1832. Financial difficulties led her parents to launch her as an actress and she made a triumphant, though reluctant, début at Covent Garden on 5 October 1829, as Juliet. For three years she combined work as a leading lady, hailed as successor to her aunt, Mrs SIDDONS, with society life. This was followed in 1832 by a two-year tour of America with her father.

Welcomed by American society, she was critical of the New World and her outspoken *Journals*, published in 1835, offended many and caused the first rift with her husband Pierce Butler, a rich Philadelphian she had married in 1834. Once married, she discovered him to be a slave-owner with plantations in Georgia, and when she visited these in 1838 her attempts to improve conditions for the slaves increased the tension in her marriage. Butler banned publication of her *Journal of a Residence on a Georgian Plantation* (published finally in 1863), while she resented the limitations imposed on her by being housewife, mother to two daughters, and subordinate to her husband after independence as an actress. Separations and attempted reconciliations between the two continued until a divorce settlement was agreed in 1850. In 1847 Fanny established her independence by returning to the English stage for one tour and a season with Macready, and from 1848 she spent

twenty years in giving public readings of Shakespeare on both sides of the Atlantic. From 1877 until her death she remained in England, publishing three volumes of *Records*, 1878, 1882, 1890, based on her journals and letters, and, aged eighty, her only novel, *Far Away and Long Ago*, 1889. Other works included *Poems*, 1844, 1865, 1883, and *Plays*, 1863, as well as *Notes Upon some of Shakespeare's Plays*, 1882.

Fanny Kemble was surprised at her own success as an actress; uninterested in theatrical life, she was happier in her readings where she held the stage alone. As a writer, she was prolific and talented but undisciplined. Her journals and records, considered by Henry James to form 'one of the most animated autobiographies in the language' bear witness to an exuberant personality, an indomitable but sensitive woman unusually aware of the social inconsistencies of her time.

See also D. Marshall, *Fanny Kemble*, 1977; E. Ransome, *The Terrific Kemble*, 1978. C.B.

Kempe, Margery (1373?–?), celebrated mystic and pilgrim, the daughter of John Burnham, burgess and sometime member of parliament of Lynn in Norfolk. About 1393 she married a Lynn freeman, John Kempe, bore him many children, and for some fifteen years lived a notably worldly life. By about 1410, however, this forceful and determined woman had become firmly committed to celibacy, prayer, fasting, and wearing a hair shirt. She experienced visions, which won her some fame, and developed a tendency to indulge in frequent bouts of noisy, uncontrolled weeping. These were no doubt instrumental in finally persuading her husband to forgo his conjugal rights.

For several years she journeyed around the country, impressing some with her devotion and humility, but irritating others by her spiritual arrogance, hysteria and manifold eccentricities. In 1413 she visited Thomas Arundel, Archbishop of Canterbury, at Lambeth; and towards the end of the year embarked on a pilgrimage to the Holy Land, during the course of which she managed to alienate most of her fellow pilgrims. Further pilgrimages followed, to St James of Compostella in Spain, and to Eastern Europe in 1433. From about 1418, however, she mainly lived at Lynn.

Not surprisingly, Margery's orthodoxy was questioned more than once. In the late summer of 1417, for instance, she was arrested at Leicester and closely questioned about her beliefs before being allowed to go free. At York soon afterwards she was again examined about her faith, but seemingly proved more than a match for Archbishop Bowet. On her way south she was arrested once more, amid considerable popular hostility, with women apparently clamouring for 'this fals heretyk' to be burnt. In fact Margery Kempe was not a Lollard (follower of the Protestant forerunner John Wyclif), but these dramatic experiences may have prompted her return to Lynn. Many burgesses of the town clearly sympathized with her husband, and may even have regarded her as 'an antisocial virus in the body politic'. But she did have powerful supporters, both lay and clerical, who ensured her immunity from the impact of local hostility.

About 1436, towards the end of her life, Margery persuaded one or more clerics to record her life-story and mystical experiences in the so-called Book of Margery Kempe (edited by S. B. Meech and H. E. Allen, 1940). Not unreasonably described as 'our first biography in English', this remarkably lucid and deeply personal work throws much light not only on popular religious beliefs and attitudes, but also on the dilemmas facing a determinedly pious laywoman in the early fifteenth century.

See also D. Baker (ed.), Medieval Women, 1978; H. S. Bennett, Six Medieval Men and Women, 1955.   K.R.D.

Kemp-Welch, Lucy (1869–1958), animal painter. She studied at the school of art in Bushey, Hertfordshire, run by Sir Hubert von Herkomer, RA, which specialized in animal painting. From 1895 onwards Lucy exhibited at the Royal Academy and enjoyed phenomenal success, having works bought by the Chantrey Bequest from 1897. She took over the running of the Herkomer School in 1904, and after its closure in 1911 had one of the large studios re-erected in the garden of her own house in Bushey, where she ran the Lucy Kemp-Welch School of Art. One of her more remarkable works was Forward the Guns!, painted in 1917. For this work the Commanding Officer of Bulford Camp on Salisbury Plain ordered eight batteries of horse artillery to gallop past her so that she might catch accurately the movement and effect of the charge. In 1924 she completed a large panel commem-

orating women's work during the First World War for the Royal Exchange.

After closing her art school in 1926 she turned to subjects drawn from gypsy and circus life, and these works show some appreciation of the changes in art which had taken place during the previous thirty years. Her colour became brighter, the handling looser, and there was even some hint of the consequences of Impressionism. Despite her undoubted ability, however, the great reputation she enjoyed in her heyday has not lasted. Her art is essentially narrative and illustrative; indeed she did the illustrations for Sparrow's In the Open Country (1905) and for the 1915 edition of Anna Sewell's classic Black Beauty. Besides two works in the Tate Gallery, there are several by Lucy Kemp-Welch in the Chantrey Bequest, and others in Bournemouth, Sheffield, Bristol, the Imperial War Museum, London, and elsewhere. After her death, her remaining works were assembled into a collection at Church House, Bushey.

See also D. Messum, The Life and Work of Lucy Kemp-Welch, 1976.   L.M.M.

Kendal, Dame Madge (1848–1935), actress. The youngest of twenty-two children in the fifth generation of a theatrical family, Margaret Robertson started acting when she was five. By the age of twenty-one she was an experienced actress, having played leading roles in several major companies. In 1869 she married William Hunter Kendal, an actor five years her junior, and, vowing to her father that they would never act apart, the Kendals began a highly successful partnership which lasted until the end of their careers. They joined John Hare in management at the Court and the St James's theatres in London, and took their own companies on tours of England, and, after 1889, the United States. Rigid disciplinarians, they were concerned not only to raise standards of acting and improve conditions for actors, but also with enhancing the moral standing of the profession. They were almost fanatical about respectability, and, careful in their choice of repertoire, refused to meet actors who appeared in plays of dubious morality.

Madge Kendal was an actress of great verve and technical prowess. Notably a comedienne, she played a range of parts, not cast to type. Henry James praised her above all others in 1880 as a 'thoroughly accomplished, business-like actress' and James Agate considered her one of the six best actresses he ever saw. In 1902 she appeared, without her husband for once, as Mistress Ford in Beerbohm Tree's production of *The Merry Wives of Windsor* with Ellen TERRY. The Kendals retired together in 1908, making their last appearance in *The House of Clay* at the Coronet, Notting Hill Gate. The partnership was apparently happy, although as parents they were alienated from their five children, never speaking to one daughter after she divorced.

Widowed in 1917, Madge Kendal continued as a public speaker, given to outbursts against trends of which she disapproved. Her memoirs, published in 1933, catalogue her own virtues pitted against the world's iniquities and are full of sanctimonious self-righteousness. 'The Matron of the Drama' was created DBE in 1926, as a great actress and benefactor of the theatrical profession. She died at her home in Hertfordshire, aged eighty-seven.

See also R. Findlater, *The Player Queens*, 1976; E. Johns, *Dames of the Theatre*, 1974.
C.B.

Kendall, Marie (1875–1964), music-hall comedienne. Born in East London, she first appeared at the age of five as 'Baby Chester', after which she played pathetic melodramatic roles for ten years. When fifteen she toured as principal boy in *Aladdin* and was a noteworthy Dandini in *Cinderella* at Mile End. Her first variety success came during sixteen consecutive weeks at Camden Town, singing 'I'm One of the Girls'. She made the song the rage of London and was booked for the Britannia theatre in Hoxton. As principal boy she had earned 30s 0d. weekly; at the Britannia she was paid £15. Appearing at seven London music-halls nightly for several weeks, in two years she had raised her salary to £100 a week.

An original star of the Vintage Variety Company (1931), Marie Kendall appeared at the Royal Variety Performance of 1932, and after playing in non-stop variety shows during her sixties without any sign of strain, retired in 1939. Shortly before her death she appeared on television, where, reminiscing about the disappearing music-hall, she displayed charm, dignity and wistfulness. She was the grandmother of another well-remembered actress, Kay Kendall.
A.D.

Kennedy, Margaret (1896–1967), popular novelist and playwright who wrote under her maiden name. She was the daughter of a barrister, and in 1925 married David (later Sir David) Davies QC. Educated at Cheltenham Ladies' College, she took a history degree at Somerville College, Oxford, and first published a history textbook, *A Century of Revolution* (1922). She wrote a novel, *The Ladies of Lyndon* (1923), and followed it with *The Constant Nymph* (1924), which achieved an astonishing popular—and international—success; a tale of illicit passion, caused and romanticized by the 'artistic temperament' (in this case musical), it exactly met the 1920s' taste for daring, high-toned but fundamentally sentimental fiction. The dramatization of *The Constant Nymph*, written in collaboration with Basil Dean in 1926, proved an effective vehicle for the actress Elisabeth Bergner, for whom Margaret Kennedy later wrote the play *Escape Me Never* (1933); both works became popular films. *The Fool of the Family* (1930) was a sequel to *The Constant Nymph*, but Margaret Kennedy never repeated her early, overwhelming triumph, although *Lucy Carmichael* (1951), *Troy Chimneys* (1953), and others were well received. She also published *The Outlaws on Parnassus* (1958), a less than enthusiastic examination of twentieth-century fiction.

See also V. Powell, *The Constant Novelist*, 1983.
N.H.

Kennet, (Edith Agnes) Kathleen, Lady (1878–1947), sculptor. Born Kathleen Bruce, she married Captain Robert Falcon Scott in 1908. In 1922 she became the wife of Sir Edward Hilton-Young, later Lord Kennet, following the death of her first husband in the Antarctic Expedition of 1912.

Kathleen Bruce studied at the Slade, and between 1901 and 1906 in Paris at the Atelier Colarossi and under Rodin. She exhibited at the Royal Academy from 1913 to 1947, while enjoying great sucess as a sculptor of portrait busts, mostly in bronze. She also made semi-allegorical figures. Her style conforms to the conventional academic sculpture of the period, untouched by any of the new ideas then current. Her best-known work is the bronze statue of her first husband which stands in Waterloo Place in London. Executed in 1915, it depicts him in heavy Antarctic clothing. There is also a bust of the Earl of Oxford and Asquith in the Tate Gallery (1912). A book of photographs, *Homage, a book of Sculpture by Kath-*

leen Scott, with commentary by Stephen Gwynn, was published in 1938. *Self-portrait of an Artist* was published posthumously in 1949.   L.M.M.

Kenney, Annie (1879–1953), suffragette. She was born at Leeds near Oldham, her parents' fifth child. Starting work in the Woodend Mill cardroom in 1889, where she soon lost a finger while minding the frames, her thirst for education inspired the launching of a library campaign among the millhands. When the mill closed she was unemployed for fifteen months before finding work for herself and several workmates. She then successfully organized the women into obtaining a small increase in pay, subsequently representing women on the Trade Union Council. The 15s 3d. which she earned fortnightly for this work was spent on a correspondence course at Ruskin College, Oxford, although she was forced to give this up because of political commitments.

Annie Kenney moved to London where she lived with the Pankhursts. She was the only working-class woman to be involved in the decision-making leadership of the suffrage movement, and was useful in justifying the claim of the Women's Social and Political Union that it wanted the vote for all women and not just the educated middle class. At meetings she appeared in her clogs and shawl.

On Friday 13 October 1905, Annie and Christabel Pankhurst gained publicity for the movement by interrupting a meeting at the Free Trade Hall, Manchester, which was being addressed by Sir Edward Grey and Winston Churchill. Annie spent three days, and Christabel a week, in Strangeways Prison. Most of Annie's work was done in the West of England, where she organized women's suffrage during 1908–09. She also helped suffragettes to win the right of trial by jury. During Christabel Pankhurst's exile in Paris, Annie crossed the Channel weekly, despite violent sea-sickness, to receive instructions. She called herself 'Christabel's blotting paper'. She was also prominent in the fight to allow women to work in munitions factories during the First World War and, in 1914, went to America to seek support for the movement. In Australia she formed a friendship with the Prime Minister, W. M. Hughes.

Once women won the vote, Annie felt 'exhausted to death'. She joined the newly-formed Theosophical Society and never again

returned to Lancashire. In 1924 she published her memoirs *Memories of a Millhand*.

Called 'a Joan of Arc of the mill', Annie lived by her mother's teaching: 'One thing above all others my mother impressed upon us—always to fight for the weak'.

See also J. Liddington and J. Norris, *One Hand Tied Behind Us: the Rise of the Women's Suffrage Movement*, 1978. A.D.

Kenny, Elizabeth (1886–1952), nurse who devised a controversial treatment to relieve paralytic conditions, particularly those caused by poliomyelitis, or infantile paralysis. Sister Kenny was born at Warialda in New South Wales, Australia; she was brought up there and at Nobby in Queensland. The extent of her formal training for nursing is unclear. She began to develop her distinctive methods while working in the Queensland outback, and later with the Australian Army Nursing Service during the First World War. After some years of private nursing, she set up a clinic for paralytics at Townsville, Queensland, with the aid of voluntary subscriptions. Her results were so startling, and the ensuing publicity so favourable, that the Australian government was persuaded to take over the clinic. However, the medical profession remained hostile to the 'Kenny treatment', and in 1935 it was condemned by a Royal Commission. The essential difference between the Kenny and the professional techniques derived from a conflict of opinions as to how soon after injury movement of the limbs and manipulation of the muscles should begin. The orthodox view was that limbs should be splinted for several weeks, whereas the 'Kenny Treatment' involved movement from a very early stage, which critics wrongly expected to damage the muscles. Despite continuing opposition, Sister Kenny was able to open clinics in England and other countries. Her greatest triumph was the establishment of the Kenny Institute in Minneapolis for the treatment of paralysis and the training of nurses in her methods. Among her publications were *The Kenny Concept in Infantile Paralysis and its Treatment* (1942), and an autobiography, *And They Shall Walk* (with Martha Ostenso, 1943). N.H.

Kent, Countess of. See GREY, ELIZABETH, COUNTESS OF KENT.

Kenyon, Dame Kathleen (Mary) (1906–78), archaeologist whose excavations at Jericho were of decisive importance in revealing the antiquity and significance of cities in the development of civilization. She was educated at St Paul's School for Girls and Somerville College, Oxford, and then began her long career of excavation as assistant at three important sites: Great Zimbabwe, in what was then Southern Rhodesia (1929); Verulamium near St Albans (1930–35) when, under the aegis of Mortimer Wheeler, the famous Roman theatre was discovered; and at Samaria during the winters of 1931–34, which gave her a grounding in Palestinian fieldwork. She then became director of several British digs—in Leicestershire and Shropshire, at Southwark in London, and at Sutton Walls in Herefordshire. As acting Director she steered the University of London Institute of Archaeology through the war years; and between 1944 and 1949 she played an equally valuable part as Secretary of the Council for British Archaeology.

But Kathleen Kenyon's greatest achievements lay in the post-war period. After directing an excavation at the Roman town of Sabratha in North Africa (1948–49, 1951), she became Director of the British School of Archaeology in Jerusalem and began work on the mound of Jericho. The excavations at this, the oldest known urban settlement in the world, were carried out between 1952 and 1958. The huge mass of evidence from Jericho was still being evaluated when urban redevelopment made it imperative to conduct new and difficult digs in Jerusalem. These Kathleen Kenyon directed (1961–67) in spite of a new and heavy commitment: she was Principal of St Hugh's College, Oxford, from 1962 to 1973, a period of material expansion and testing social change.

Kathleen Kenyon's many publications include *Verulamium Theatre Excavations*, 1935, and records of subsequent excavations; *Beginning in Archaeology*, 1952, *Digging Up Jericho*, 1957, *Archaeology in the Holy Land*, 1960, and *Digging Up Jerusalem*, 1974.

N.H.

Kéroualle, Louise de, Duchess of Portsmouth (1649–1734), mistress of Charles II. Born into an impoverished noble Breton family, she was nineteen when influential friends gained her an appointment as maid of honour to HENRIETTE ANNE, wife of Louis XIV's younger brother and the devoted sister of Charles II.

She quickly became a favourite of her mistress and in 1670 accompanied her on a visit to Charles II, who immediately became infatuated with Louise. A few months later, Charles requested her appointment as maid of honour to his wife, and she returned to England with the blessing of Louis XIV who hoped to make use of her influence with Charles.

Louise became the King's mistress in October 1671 when a mock wedding ceremony was held at the home of the Earl of Arlington. Approximately nine months later she gave birth to her only child, Charles Lennox, subsequently created Duke of Richmond. A devoted and ambitious mother, she obtained the lucrative post of Master of the Horse for her son in 1681. She herself was created Duchess of Portsmouth in 1673, and through her pleading and scheming, as well as Charles's generosity and pressure on Louis XIV, she amassed enormous wealth in England and France, where in 1684 she finally acquired the coveted possession of a French duchy. The ascendancy of Barbara VILLIERS, Duchess of Cleveland, was nearly ended by 1671, and Louise's chief rival Nell GWYN, whom she could never displace, presented no serious challenge to her position as *maîtresse en titre*. This Louise maintained until Charles's death in 1685, despite serious opposition provoked by her nationality, religion, arrogance, and greed. Besides her physical charms, the King was attracted by her intelligence and artistic tastes. He became increasingly dependent on her during his last years, when their relationship became comfortably domestic.

A consummate political intriguer and opportunist, Louise de Kéroualle played an important role at Charles's court, where she was feared, respected, and cultivated by politicians and diplomats. Although she was with some justice regarded as a French agent, her support of French interests was inconsistent, especially when they conflicted with her own ambitions or the welfare of her lover. She nevertheless remained a valuable intermediary between the French and English kings.

See also B. Bevan, *Charles the Second's French Mistress*, 1972. T.J.M

Keynes, Lady. See LOPOKOVA, LYDIA VASILIEVNA, LADY KEYNES.

Kilham, Hannah (1774–1832), linguist and missionary. Born at Sheffield, the seventh child of small tradespeople, she was expected from an early age to perform household duties to counteract a delicate constitution. She attended a local day-school until her mother's death in 1786, when she took upon herself the care of her father and brothers. Orphaned in 1788, she was then sent to a boarding-school in Chesterfield, where she displayed such aptitude for the study of grammar that she displeased her schoolmaster with her unfeminine enthusiasm.

In 1796 she joined the Wesleyan Methodists, although objecting to some aspects of church government. Such views drew her to Alexander Kilham, founder of the separatist New Connexion, whom she married in April 1798. Following his death only eight months later, she opened a day-school. When her daughter also died, Hannah Kilham joined the Society of Friends, and devoted several years to philanthropic work in Sheffield. A Society for Bettering the Condition of the Poor was established there, due principally to her efforts; she also promoted Bible societies and temperance associations. Always aware of the claims of home and family, she carefully sought to balance domestic duties with other commitments.

Preoccupied for some years by the problems of Africa, she became convinced of the desirability of using African languages transcribed into print to encourage the spread of Christianity. Acquiring a knowledge of Mandingo and Jaloof from two African sailors living in England, in 1818 she produced an elementary grammar for the missionary school in Sierra Leone. She decided to visit Africa herself, and in 1823, under the auspices of the Friends' Committee for Promoting African Instruction, she set sail for the Gambia. Ignoring the ridicule of British settlers, she established schools there and in Sierra Leone for the teaching of English. In 1827 she returned to Sierra Leone, this time visiting hundreds of villages and transcribing the basic elements of twenty-five native dialects. She made her third and final trip to Africa in 1830, when she took charge of children rescued from slave-ships, and organized a large school to train them as missionaries and teachers. A similar scheme took her to Liberia, where she arranged for children of influential Africans to be educated in England. Returning to Sierra Leone, her ship was struck by lightning. She never recovered from the shock and died at sea.

Mrs Kilham was one of the first Europeans to regard African languages as a fit and necessary subject of study. Although her fundamental aim was to make Christian converts, she also helped to extend intellectual opportunities for Africans by making increased communication possible. Her sympathy with the lowly situation of African women caused her to publicize, and thus possibly to alleviate, some of the cruelties and oppressions to which they were subject. Among her publications were *Lessons on Language* (1818), and *The Claims of Africa to Christian Instruction* (1830).

See also *Memoir of Mrs Kilham*, by her step-daughter Mrs Biller, 1837.   J.V.L.

Killigrew, Anne (1660–85), painter and poet, born into a noted theatrical family in London. Her father, Dr Henry Killigrew, was a theologian and sometime dramatist who became master of the Savoy Hospital and chaplain to the Duke of York, later James II. Two uncles and two cousins were also associated with the theatre. Anne became Maid of Honour to Mary of Modena, Duchess of York; one of her companions in the household was the poet Anne FINCH, Countess of Winchilsea. In 1685 Anne Killigrew fell victim to the smallpox, and died on 16 June.

After her death Anne's father collected and published her poems, together with the famous prefatory 'Ode To Mrs Anne Killigrew' by Dryden. The slim volume contained twenty-six completed poems together with a few fragments. They have a rather austere moral tone, her themes including stern criticism of unrestrained ambition and greed for money. Dryden's 'Ode' indicates that he had read her poems in manuscript; that he had seen her paintings is certain because he describes them in some detail. She seems to have painted portraits, landscapes, and Biblical subjects. To these last she refers in her poems, according to which the subjects included John the Baptist in the Wilderness, and Herodias's daughter presenting John's head to her mother on a charger. Only three of her paintings are known to have survived. Her portrait of James, Duke of York, hangs at Windsor; two others, a portrait of Mary, Duchess of York, and her *Venus and Adonis* are in private collections. An engraving of her self-portrait is prefixed to her poems. These works reveal considerable technical ability in so young a painter. Her varied talents and exemplary character do much to justify the tributes paid by friends at her untimely death.

See also *Poems by Mrs Anne Killigrew*, facs. rep., 1967; G. Greer, *The Obstacle Race*, 1979.

W.R.O.

Killigrew, Catherine (?1530–83), Protestant patron and humanist, the fourth daughter of Sir Anthony Cooke of Gidea Hall, Essex, who had once been tutor to Edward VI. She was, like her sisters, educated in accordance with her father's precept that 'sexes as well as souls are equal in capacity', and was proficient in Latin, Greek, and Hebrew. On 4 November 1565 she married Sir Henry Killigrew, who in 1554 had been involved in the West Country rebellion against Mary I, helping the ringleaders to escape abroad. Subsequently he, too, went into exile, but unlike his brothers did not play an active part in later rebellions against Mary, and returned to England in 1558 to a successful diplomatic career. Catherine does not seem to have rejoiced in his absences abroad, since she sought her sister Mildred's influence with her husband Sir William Cecil to excuse Henry from an embassy to France. As befitted a daughter of Sir Anthony Cooke, she expressed this wish in Latin verse. It can be seen in Thomas Fuller's *The Worthies of England* (1662). Catherine had four daughters, Anne, Elizabeth, Mary, and Dorothy, and died after giving birth to a stillborn child in 1583. Her tomb, since destroyed, bore an inscription by Andrew Melville.

Catherine and her sisters were great supporters of the Protestant cause, and befriended Puritan prelates such as Edward Dering who, although forbidden to preach, corresponded with Catherine until his death in 1576, giving spiritual advice, and thanking her for medicines and other gifts. Catherine and her sisters were principally important because of the humanist education which they received, demonstrating that women as well as men could become skilled linguists. The fact that she was related by marriage to the influential families of Cecil, Bacon, and Hoby meant that she could offer more than just financial support to the Puritan divines she befriended.

See also P. Collinson, *A Mirror of Elizabethan Puritanism: The Life and Letters of 'Godly Master Dering'*, 1964; C. H. Garrett, *The Marian Exiles*, 1938.

J.S.

Kimmins, Dame Grace (1871–1954), pioneer of work with crippled children. Grace Thyrza Hannan was the daughter of James and Thyrza Hannan. Her family, which was comfortably middle-class, gave her a firm belief in the importance of work for others and she was early impressed by the suffering of the physically handicapped. In 1894 she began the meetings which were to lead to the foundation of the Guild of the Brave Poor Things, which aimed to bring together physically handicapped people, regardless of age or creed. Then, as later, she attracted an impressive number of celebrated supporters to the venture, originally including the Duchess of Bedford and Emmeline PETHICK-LAWRENCE, and later, Queen Mary, and Queen Elizabeth, the Queen Mother.

The Guild was originally housed in the West London Mission, and branches were established in many parts of the country. But all the time Grace, who had married the educationist Dr Charles Kimmins in 1897, was dreaming of starting a school for crippled children. This became a reality in 1903, at Chailey, where the first such residential school was established. From an original seven boys housed in primitive conditions, it grew to cater for more than 500 children, in the most modern buildings, but with the same basic aim of training the physically handicapped to become independent, self-supporting citizens.

In 1927, she was made a CBE and became DBE 1950. Until well into her seventies, she provided the energy and driving force behind this unique venture. Even after it had become part of the Health Service, she maintained strong connections with her beloved schools and hospitals.

E.M.V.

King, Augusta Ada, Countess of Lovelace (1815–52), mathematician. Ada was the only child of Lord Byron's marriage to Lady Noel Byron, and was brought up by her mother after her parents separated when she was a few months old. Her intellectual talents were recognized from childhood and were encouraged by her mother, who engaged William Frend, the Cambridge mathematician, and later Augustus de Morgan, Professor of Mathematics at London University, to teach her. From the mid-1820s she became a close friend of Mary SOMERVILLE, whose achievements she longed to emulate. In 1835 she married Lord King (elevated to the earldom of Lovelace in 1838), by whom she had three children.

In spite of domestic and social obligations

241

and poor health, Ada continued to study mathematics after her marriage. She hoped to be of assistance to Charles Babbage in his work on the 'Analytical Engine', his prototype computer, designed to be capable of any mathematical operation. In 1843 she translated from French a description by the Italian military engineer L. F. Menebrea which explained the machine and the principles on which it would operate. To this she added annotations three times the length of the original article and examples, for which she herself worked out the algebra, to demonstrate the machine's powers. The translation, annotations, and examples, published in *Taylor's Scientific Memoirs*, vol. 3 (1843), constitute the best available contemporary account of the machine and show Lady Lovelace to have thoroughly understood the principles of a programmed computer. From 1845 onwards she and Babbage directed their mathematical abilities towards the development of a system for predicting the outcome of horse races. As a result Lady Lovelace died heavily in debt and at the mercy of blackmailers.

See also D. L. Moore, *Ada Countess of Lovelace: Byron's Legitimate Daughter*, 1977.

S.G.

King, Jessie M(arion) (1876–1949), book-illustrator. She was born at Bearsden, Glasgow, the daughter of Dr James King of New Kirkcudbright Church. Art was not considered a fit occupation for a daughter of the manse, and Jessie hid her drawings to prevent her mother destroying them. Nevertheless, her father let Jessie attend Glasgow School of Art, where Francis Newbury allowed her to develop her individual linear expression, and from which she won a travelling scholarship to Italy and Germany. Influenced by Botticelli, Burne-Jones and Rossetti, her work, mostly on parchment, has elaborate borders with stylized foliage and birds; an example is *The High History of the Holy Graal*. A book of plants, *Budding Life*, is drawn with minute exactitude.

In 1909 she married the artist and furniture designer E. A. Taylor, and moved to Paris in 1911 to run the Shealing Atelier until the outbreak of the First World War. During this time she also contributed to *The Studio*. Small, robust, with long golden hair, she was intensely practical, designing masque and pageant costumes and later producing Batik dresses and jewellery commercially. A member of the Lady Artists' Club; the Royal Scottish Academy, Edinburgh; and the Fine Art Institute, Glasgow, she finally settled with her husband in Kirkcudbright.

A.D.

Kingsford, Anna (1846–88), writer and doctor, whose maiden name was Bonus. She was born at Stratford, Essex, and in 1867 married a Shropshire vicar, Algernon Godfrey Kingsford. In 1870 she was converted to Roman Catholicism. Her early writing was for *The Penny Post*, to which she contributed stories, (1868–72). She then bought *The Lady's Own Paper* (1872) editing it for a year and in it supporting the movement against vivisection.

In 1874 she began studying medicine in Paris and, on receiving her degree in 1880, practised in London. She had by this time become a vegetarian. An extended translation of her thesis was published in 1881 as *The Perfect Way in Diet*. Particularly successful with women patients, she was also a pioneer in the cause of higher education for women, but spent much time in investigating mystical subjects. She became president of the Theosophical Society in 1883, and in 1884, together with Edward Maitland, a Californian 'forty-niner' who had settled in London, founded the Hermetic Society. Her aim as a religious teacher was to reconcile Christianity with her own mystical theories and to emphasize its connection with Eastern faiths. Also with Edward Maitland, she collaborated on *Keys of the Creeds* (1875), and *The Perfect Way; or the Finding of Christ* (1882). While on a visit to Pasteur's laboratory in 1887, she caught a cold, from which she never fully recovered, and died the following year.

Among Anna Kingsford's other publications were *Beatrice, a Tale of the early Christians*, 1863, written while very young, *River Reeds*, 1866, a book of verse, *Astrology Theorised*, 1886, and *Health, Beauty and the Toilet*, 1886, a reprint of letters which appeared in *The Lady's Pictorial* and which attracted adverse criticism for supposedly sanctioning artificial aids to beauty. Posthumously published, and edited by Edward Maitland, were *Dreams and Dream Stories*, 1888, and *Clothed with the Sun* (1889), an idiosyncratic collection of 'illuminations'.

B.H.C.

Kingsley, Mary (1862–1900), traveller and writer. She was born in Islington, the eldest child of Dr George Kingsley, the traveller, and niece of the novelist Charles Kingsley. Soon after her birth her parents moved to Highgate, where she spent most of her youth. Her childhood was an isolated one, for her mother was often ill and her father, whom she idolized, frequently away from home. She received no formal education but read omnivorously in her father's scientific library, subscribed to *The English Mechanic*, and learned German by joining her brother's lessons. When her parents became invalids Mary Kingsley took charge of the household and helped to prepare for publication her father's notes on sacrificial rites in West Africa. Her parents' deaths and the departure of her brother for China left her free to plan her own travels to West Africa, where she hoped to finish her father's work and to collect zoological specimens for the British Museum.

In 1893 Mary Kingsley set out on the first of her two remarkable journeys, which were to take her to areas hitherto unexplored by Europeans. She lived among, and as, the Africans, paying her way by trading in oil and rubber, while retaining conventional European dress. On returning to Britain from the second journey of 1895, she wrote a narrative of both trips, *Travels in West Africa* (1897), which was based on her detailed diaries. In 1899 *West African Studies* appeared, reflecting the variety of her interests and containing some of her most mature work. Her knowledge of West African culture was extensive. She wrote and lectured widely on the subject, and her advice was occasionally sought by colonial administrators, including Joseph Chamberlain, but she did not hesitate to criticize colonial policy and missionary activity where they failed to respect African culture. Essentially an enlightened imperialist, she sought to improve relations between the races as a condition of judicious British rule. Practical and compassionate, she gave much of her time to charitable schemes. Though not opposed to female emancipation, she did not support votes for women, for she believed that women needed to be better informed and more active in local government before they entered the wider political arena. She died of typhoid fever while on duty as a camp nurse in the Boer War.

See also S. Glynn, *Life of Mary Kingsley*, 2nd ed., 1935; C. Howard, *Mary Kingsley*, 1957.   C.H.G.G.

Klein, Melanie (1882–1960), psychoanalyst, famous for her radical and controversial theories of child development. Melanie Klein was born in Vienna, where her father practised as a physician. She herself studied medicine until 1903, when she married her second cousin Stephan Klein, a chemical engineer; they had three children, but the marriage was unhappy and the couple were divorced in 1923.

Melanie Klein's involvement with psychoanalysis began just before the First World War in Budapest, where she read Freud's book on the interpretation of dreams. She was analysed by Freud's Hungarian follower Sandor Ferenczi, who encouraged her to work in his children's clinic and to write her earliest papers. In 1921, under the influence of another leading analyst, Karl Abraham, she settled in Berlin. Her work there had already become controversial when she met Freud's future biographer, Ernest Jones, who in 1925 invited her to give a series of lectures in London. In the following year she settled permanently in England, becoming naturalized in 1934.

Melanie Klein's methods of working with children quickly attracted disciples, but they also aroused hostility on the part of those who considered them unscientific and un-Freudian. For many years the British Psycho-Analytical Society was split between Kleinians and followers of Freud's daughter Anna. By using what would now be termed 'play therapy—providing children with drawing materials and other toys—Melanie Klein claimed to have created a situation equivalent to that of orthodox analysis: instead of verbal 'free association', the child revealed psychic patterns and associations through free play. Such a method was open to the objection that it relied on intuition rather that verifiable facts; and Klein's interpretations, which emphasized the aggressive impulses of young children and traced neuroses back to the earliest phase of life, were inevitably controversial. Her findings are set out in *The Psycho-Analysis of Children*, 1932, *Contributions to Psycho-Analysis*, 1948, *Envy and Gratitude*, 1957, and *Narrative of a Child Analysis*, 1961.

See also H. Segal, *Introduction to the Work of Melanie Klein*, 1964; forthcoming biography by P. Grosskurth.   N.H.

Knel, Joan. See BOCHER, JOAN.

Knight, Dame Laura (1877–1970), painter. Her early years were spent in Nottingham, where her mother taught in the School of Art at which Laura later became a pupil and where she met Harold Knight, whom she married in 1903. The couple lived in Staithes, on the Yorkshire coast, before moving to Newlyn in Cornwall. Here they were in touch with the artists who formed the so-called Newlyn School: Stanhope Forbes, Lamorna Birch, and the Proctors. Another visitor was Sir Alfred Munnings, whom Harold Knight detested, although Laura found him attractive for his boisterous good humour.

She began painting stage and ballet subjects about 1914, but her interests were deflected by an appointment as a Canadian War Artist in 1916 and she did not return to ballet subjects again until 1919, when both the Diaghilev Ballet and Pavlova provided her with opportunity and subject matter. She became an Associate of the Royal Academy in 1927, the first women since Annie SWYNNERTON, and later Royal Academician, as well as DBE in 1929. She visited the United States in 1922 and 1926, and after her work as an official war artist was at Nuremberg to paint a large group picture of the war trials. Her interest in circus subjects, which began in 1929, led to her fascination with gipsies and their encampments.

In style, her art is derived from nineteenth-century realism, treated with a certain freedom of manner which she was angered to find described as 'sketchy'. Colourful, factual, picturesque, technically competent, sound in drawing, popular in imagery, she was totally untouched by any of the modern movements in art, and found modern French painting utterly distasteful. There are works in London (at the Tate Gallery, the Royal Academy, the Imperial War Museum), Ottawa, and elsewhere.

Her autobiography of 1936, *Oil Paint and Grease Paint*, was extended by a further volume in 1965, *The Magic of a Line*, and a volume of circus reminiscences, *A Proper Circus Omie*, 1962.

See also J. Dunbar, *Laura Knight*, 1975.

L.M.M.

Knox, Marjory. See BOWES, ELIZABETH.

Kyteler, Alice (*fl.* 1320s), alleged witch. Alice Kyteler was related through her fourth husband, John le Poer, to the Seneschal of Kilkenny. In 1324 she was accused, together with two accomplices, of heresy and witchcraft by Richard, Bishop of Ossory. Alice was additionally charged with poisoning her three previous husbands. Condemned to the stake, one of the accused accomplices denounced Alice's son, William Outlaw. Though imprisoned, he bribed the Seneschal to release him and to arrest the Bishop. Alice was summoned to appear at Dublin, but first used her influence to have the Bishop arraigned before a disciplinary hearing. She was then smuggled to England by the local gentry.

G.H.

L

L. E. L. See LANDON, LETITIA ELIZABETH.

Ladies of Llangollen. See BUTLER, LADY ELEANOR.

Lake, Claude. See BLIND, MATHILDE.

Lamb, Lady Caroline (Ponsonby) (1785–1828), novelist. The only daughter of the third Earl of Bessborough and Lady Henrietta Frances Spencer, Lady Caroline lived in Italy between the ages of three and nine, after which she was sent back to England to be looked after by her grandmother and educated with her cousins. When only sixteen she married the Hon. William Lamb, afterwards second Viscount Melbourne, but was soon to suffer a passionate infatuation for the poet Byron. It was she who wrote of him that he was 'mad, bad, and dangerous to know'. Byron discarded her in 1813 to the accompaniment of endless public and private scenes, and Lady Caroline's always unstable mind was so affected that her husband decided on a separation. They were reconciled, however, on the day that legal separation was due to take place. Her first novel, *Glenarvon*, published anonymously in 1816, contained a caricature of Byron. In a letter the poet wrote, 'If the authoress had written the truth . . . the romance would not only have been more romantic, but more entertaining. As for the likeness, the picture can't be good; I did not sit long enough'. The novel was translated into Italian in 1817 and republished in 1865 as *The Fatal Passion*.

In 1819 Lady Caroline Lamb canvassed in Westminster for her brother-in-law, George Lamb. The same year she published *A New Canto*. Her second novel, *Graham Hamilton*, was published in 1822, followed the next year by *Ada Reis, A Tale*. Further writing was brought to an abrupt end, however, when by accident she saw Byron's funeral procession on its way to Newstead in 1824. The shock so deranged her that her husband, having suffered her hysterical, drug-induced behaviour, coupled with numerous infidelities, could take no more and they separated.

Lady Caroline Lamb lived for the rest of her life chiefly at Brocket Hall, Hertfordshire, with her father-in-law and her imbecile son George Augustus Frederick Lamb, who died in 1836 at the age of twenty-nine. She herself died at Melbourne House, Whitehall, on 26 January 1828 at the age of forty-two. Some of her poems were collected in Isaac Nathan's *Fugitive Pieces and Reminiscences of Lord Byron . . . also some original Poetry, Letters and Recollections of Lady Caroline Lamb*, 1892.

See also David Cecil, *The Young Melbourne*, 1954, E. Jenkins, *Lady Caroline Lamb*, 1974.   A.P.

Lamb, Elizabeth, Viscountess Melbourne (d. 1818), Whig hostess and improving landowner. Lady Melbourne was a capable organizer and administrator of the family fortune and properties, in marked contrast to her husband, the first Viscount Melbourne, who was notable only for his extravagance and improvidence. Byron thought her 'the cleverest of women'. She made her own garden at Brocket Hall a paying concern, and then turned to the improvement of the estate. Towards the end of the eighteenth century she began carrying out drill husbandry on her land, 'after the principle of Mr Ducket', in a county (Hertfordshire) then backward in that respect. The seed drill invented by Jethro Tull had been in use for a large part of the century, but was employed unevenly throughout the country. For a full effect it required larger estates. Lady Melbourne was a member of that enthusiastic band of female agricultural innovators selected for special praise in the writings of Arthur Young. She also invested in one of Salmon's Woburn chaffcutters, which Young records was capable of cutting up to twenty bushels of chaff in an hour.

See also David Cecil, *The Young Melbourne*, 1954; Arthur Young, *A General View of the Agriculture of Hertfordshire*, 1804.

                                                                T.H.

Lamb, Mary (Ann) (1764–1847), author. Born in London, eleven years older than her famous brother Charles, she was the 'Bridget' of his essays, his 'poor, dear, dearest'. Her education was slight, but she read widely in English literature.

After Mary had killed their mother in a fit of madness, Charles, then only twenty-one, assumed total responsibility for her. They lived together harmoniously except when she

245

Lamburn, Richmal Crompton

required treatment in a private asylum for recurrences of her illness. Charles wrote, 'we house together, old bachelor and maid, in a sort of double singleness'. She entertained liberally, despite their straitened means, helped to educate their adopted daughter, and acted as Charles's critic and occasional collaborator. She survived her brother by thirteen years.

Mary Lamb wrote the preface to *Tales From Shakespeare*, 1807, and three-quarters of this enduring children's classic was her work. She contributed a similar share to the stories in *Mrs Leicester's School*, 1809, and the verses in *Poetry For Children*, 1808.

See also E. V. Lucas, *The Life of Charles Lamb*, 1921.   P.L.

Lamburn, Richmal Crompton. See CROMPTON, RICHMAL.

Landon, Letitia Elizabeth (1802–38), poet and novelist. She was born in Hans Place, Chelsea, where she went to school.

In 1815 her family moved to Old Brompton, where she met William Jerdan, an editor who had been shown some of her verse. Her first poem, 'Rome', appeared under the initial 'L' in *The Literary Gazette* during March 1820. She subsequently took over the paper's music reviews and wrote more verse: *The Fate of Adelaide*, 1821, *The Improvisatrice*, 1824, *The Golden Violet*, 1827, and *The Venetian Bracelet*, 1829. Her first novel, *Romance and Reality*, was published in 1831 but her best work of fiction, *Ethel Churchill*, appeared six years later in 1837.

Letitia Landon helped to support her mother with her writing while living at various houses in Hans Place. But after experiencing a broken engagement she was precipitated into hasty marriage with George Maclean, who was governor of Cape Coast Castle and considerably older than herself. She returned to Africa with him, but soon after her arrival was found dead from an overdose of poison, thought to be prussic acid, which she took to relieve spasms. Although it seems most likely that her death was accidental, there was some conjecture that had she committed suicide or was murdered by her husband.

Letitia Landon was a conventional, somewhat sentimental, poet and novelist whose popularity waned after her death. Most of her writings appeared under the initials 'L.E.L.', among them: *The Troubadour*, 1825, *The Vow*

of the Peacock, 1835, *Flowers of Loveliness*, 1838, and *The Zenana*, 1839.

See also D. E. Enfield, *L.E.L. A Mystery of the Thirties*, 1928.   A.P.

Lane, Jane (d. 1689), Royalist heroine. Jane's father was Thomas Lane of Bentley, Staffordshire, a staunch Royalist, while her mother Anne Bagot also came from a leading Staffordshire Royalist family. Her fame derives from the part she played in the escape of Charles II after his defeat at the battle of Worcester on 3 September 1651. Bentley Hall was one of Charles's Midland refuges and it was from there that he left on September 10, dressed as a servant and posing as Jane's chaperone. After a dangerous week's journey to the south-west, evading Parliamentarian search-parties, Jane and her companions guided the King safely to the home of Francis Wyndham near Sherborne, from where he escaped to France. Jane then returned home, but when stories of the King's escape were printed she and her brother thought it prudent to leave England although they had not been named. Disguised as peasants, they fled to Yarmouth and thence to France where they joined Charles's exiled court. Jane's later life was uneventful. At the Restoration a grateful king granted her an annual pension of £1,000, and she married a Warwickshire baronet, Sir Clement Fisher. She had no children.

See W. Matthews (ed.), *Charles II's Escape from Worcester*, 1967.   P.M.H.

Langtry, Lillie (1853–1929), actress. Emilie Charlotte Le Breton was the daughter of the Dean of Jersey. Intelligent and highly attractive, she benefited from the lessons given to her brother and soon found society in Jersey too restricting. Largely to escape from this she married Edward Langtry, a wealthy yachtsman, but the marriage proved a disaster; she did not share his passion for sport, and he was not interested in society. On their first visit to London she determined to make her own mark. Subsequently, Oscar Wilde fell in love with her; Millais painted her portrait *The Jersey Lily;* and Leopold of the Belgians made himself foolish by demanding her attentions. Despite the disapproval of Queen Victoria, the Prince of Wales invited her to join his Marlborough House set; she befriended his wife while becoming his first publicly-acknowledged mistress.

The friendship of Sarah Bernhardt, a previous mistress of the Prince, coupled with her own ambition, enabled Lillie to start a career as an actress and to succeed despite initial setbacks. Great acclaim was first given to her talent in the United States, where a town was named in her honour. This and her friendship with the playboy Freddie Gebhard led her to become an American citizen, but when the affair ended she returned to England and to an abortive attempt at theatre management. Another liaison, this time with the millionaire George Bird, gave her at his sudden death the ownership of several racehorses. When her colt 'Merman' won the Cesarewitch she became the first woman member of the Jockey Club, by order of the Prince of Wales. The Prince had previously persuaded her to end a relationship with Prince Louis of Battenberg, despite her strong feelings and not before the birth of a daughter, Jeanne Marie. Her daughter forgave neither this, nor Lillie's refusal to see her husband before his death of alcoholism in an asylum. Her second marriage was to Hugo de Bathe, twenty-one years her junior, who took her to Monte Carlo where his famous villa and gardens became her final home.

As Lillie de Bathe she wrote *All at Sea* (1909) and in 1929 her autobiography, *The Days I Knew*. Her chequered career had proved that women could be independent, but she had little sympathy with the ideals of the suffragette movement, as was evident when she played the leading role in *Helping the Cause*, a satire on it staged in 1912. It was her combination of beauty, intelligence, and ruthlessness that enabled her to succeed in society and to become a setter of tastes and fashions.

See also E. Dudley, *The Gilded Lily*, 1958.
C.H.G.G.

Lanier, Emilia (c. 1570–1645), poet. Her parents, Baptist Bassano, one of the court musicians, and Margaret Johnson, were unmarried. Her father died in 1576, her mother in 1587, and Emilia was taken up as the mistress of Henry Carey, Lord Hunsdon, who was the Lord Chamberlain. Upon becoming pregnant, she was married in 1592 to Alphonso Lanier, who was a musician in the King's Music from 1594 until his death in 1613 and also served abroad for some years as a soldier. Emilia's son by the Lord Chamberlain was named Henry after him, and she had a daughter, Odilla, who died in infancy. Her marriage seems not to have been happy, and

between 1597 and 1600 while her husband was away, she was visiting an astrologer, Simon Forman, with whom she had sexual relations. The references to her in Forman's notebooks have led one scholar to argue that she was the 'Dark Lady' of Shakespeare's sonnets, although this opinion is not generally shared.

In 1611 Emilia Lanier published a long religious poem, *Salve Deus Rex Judaeorum*, which reveals her as a well-educated and fairly sophisticated poet. The book opens with a series of nine flattering dedicatory poems to aristocratic ladies, together with a prose address to Margaret, Countess Dowager of Cumberland, for whom the work was written. The poem itself is composed in *ottava rima* and is a sternly moral work describing the passion of Christ. Her preface to the reader indicates a committed feminist point of view and this is apparent elsewhere in the poem where she defends Eve and blames Adam for the Fall. Since men are at fault, she demands equality for women: 'Then let us have our Libertie againe, / And challendge to yourselves no Sov'raigntie ... Your fault being greater, why should you disdaine, / Our beeing your equals, free from tyranny?' The book ends with a poem in rhyming couplets in praise of Cookham, where she had spent happy times with her patron, the Dowager Countess of Cumberland, and her daughter Anne, later Countess of Dorset.

After her husband's death, Emilia apparently set up a school in a fashionable part of London, but was sued by the landlord for non-payment of rent and arrested for debt when she left the house in 1619. In the 1630s she was involved in legal disputes with her brothers-in-law over her husband's estate. She died in 1645 and was buried at Clerkenwell. As a poet she must rank high among other women writers of her time, while her work speaks with an individual, strongly feminist voice.

See also A. L. Rowse (ed.), *The Poems of Shakespeare's Dark Lady*, 1978.   W.R.O.

Lauderdale, Duchess of. See MURRAY, ELIZABETH, DUCHESS OF LAUDERDALE.

Lawrence, (Arabella) Susan (1871–1947), Labour MP. The daughter of Nathaniel Tertius Lawrence, she was born in London into a family well-established in the legal profession, prosperous and politically Conservative. She was educated at Newnham College, Cambridge, where she read mathematics. In 1900 she became a member of the London School Board and so began her career in politics. An arresting figure, she was tall and rather severely dressed, sporting a monocle.

In 1910 she was elected to the London County Council as a Conservative, but her political views were changed by the experience of trying to organize factory girls in the East End of London and by the revelation of the position of charwomen employed by the LCC. She became a socialist. The initial reaction of cockney audiences to this tall, gaunt, upper-middle-class radical was, according to Margaret Bondfield, that they treated her 'as a comic turn and roared with laughter' at her refined voice. However, her patent sincerity soon won their confidence and even affection. From 1919 to 1921 she was assistant to Mary Macarthur in organizing the National Federation of Women Workers. Also in 1919 she was elected to the Poplar Borough Council, having already been the first woman Labour representative on the LCC. In 1920 she stood for the first time as a parliamentary candidate, in Camberwell, but was unsuccessful, and in 1921 went to prison with other Poplar Guardians, including George Lansbury, for refusing to collect the poor rate. She treated her imprisonment with the contempt she thought it deserved — 'a lark', she called it—and spent the time writing a pamphlet on taxation.

In 1923 she was elected as Labour member for East Ham North, where 'our Susan' was extremely popular with her constituents. In the House of Commons she was a sharp critic of social and industrial conditions. Her formidable appearance gave her a reputation for severity which was scarcely deserved, for besides great clarity and precision of thought and presentation, she also had a biting wit. She became Parliamentary Secretary to the Ministry of Health in 1929, and in 1930 was appointed Chairman of the Labour Party. Defeated in 1931, she never returned to Parliament. If she had, there can be little doubt that she would have achieved high office. Rather, she is remembered, as her *Times* obituary maintained, as 'the most transparently honest and unegotistical of politically-minded women'.

See also E. Wilkinson, *Peeps at Politicians*, 1931.   E.M.V.

Lawrence, Elizabeth. See BURY, ELIZABETH.

Lawrence, Frieda (1879–1956), wife of D. H. Lawrence: a major influence on his career and writings, and a personality of considerable interest in her own right. Emma Maria Frieda Johanna von Richthofen was born into an aristocratic family at Metz, then a German city; she had the rank of baroness and as a girl led the privileged existence of her class. In 1899 she married Ernest Weekley, newly appointed professor of French at the University College, Nottingham, where she lived a comfortable but evidently stultifying life with a husband fourteen years her senior and three children. Lawrence, six years younger than she, was not Frieda Weekley's first lover, but his intensity and directness changed her outlook almost at once: a former student of Weekley's, he called on her in March 1912, and at the beginning of May the couple eloped to Metz. They were eventually married in 1914, and after the First World War (when Frieda's nationality led to highly unpleasant experiences in England) shared an impecunious wandering life that took them to various places in Europe, Australia and New Mexico. The importance of their relationship is clear from Lawrence's writings—as is its tempestuous nature: Frieda refused to submit to him as he wished, and was not sexually faithful. After Lawrence's death she returned to their house at Taos, New Mexico, where she married again. She wrote an account of Lawrence, 'Not I But The Wind' (1935), that at times achieves an idiosyncratic force, and for years worked at memoirs, posthumously edited by E. W. Tedlock as *Frieda Lawrence: the Memoirs and Correspondence* (1961).

See also R. Lucas (English translation by Geoffrey Skelton), *Frieda Lawrence*, 1972.
                                                    N.H.

Lawrence, Gertrude (1898–1952), musical comedy actress. Gertrude Lawrence was born in London into a theatrical family. Her father, Arthur Lawrence Klasen, was Danish and was divorced from his English actress mother while Gertrude was still a baby. She spent most of her formative years on tour with her mother and made her stage début at the age of nine, as a dancer at the Brixton Theatre. She studied dancing, elocution, and acting under Italia Conti, and in 1911 appeared in Charles B. Cochran's spectacular Christmas show *The Miracle*. For the next few years she toured the provinces and in 1916 had her first real success as principal dancer at London's

Vaudeville Theatre. Although not classically beautiful, she became the ideal musical comedy star. She was glamorous, had a true clear voice, and danced 'with magical lightness'. Her friendship with Noël Coward began when they were teenagers and continued for the rest of their lives. It was for her that Coward wrote *Private Lives* (1930), and it is for her performances in his plays, tailored to her gaiety and chic, that she will largely be remembered, although she was also a talented serious actress. She was twice married, the first marriage ended in divorce, but the second, to the theatrical producer Richard Aldrich, lasted until her death. When she died, lights were dimmed both along Broadway and in London's West End.

See also S. Morley, *Gertrude Lawrence*, 1981.   E.M.V.

Lawrence, Maude (1864–1933), civil servant. Maude Lawrence was the fifth and youngest daughter of the first Lord Lawrence of the Punjab, Viceroy of India. She was educated at home and at Bedford College. In 1900 she was co-opted as a member of the London School Board and the following year was elected for Westminster. Upon the abolition of the School Board and the transfer of its powers to the Education Committee of the London County Council in 1904, she was asked to remain as one of the special non-elected members.

In 1905, as part of the reorganization of the Board of Education in the wake of the 1902 Education Act, she was invited by Sir Robert Morant to take the newly-created post of Chief Woman Inspector. Morant was concerned about national physical deterioration and hoped to improve 'the physique and moral nurture of the rising generation', in part by giving a sound domestic education to girls within the elementary and secondary systems. A dedicated band of women inspectors was vital to the scheme, and Morant appointed Maude Lawrence because as 'a well-known name' with important social connections she would give it prestige and be able to subdue the warring factions within the women's inspectorate. Without professional qualifications or teaching experience and armed only with a commanding personality, Maude Lawrence proved successful in seizing control of her department and overseeing the expansion of its functions, particularly on the teacher-training side.

In 1920 she was again asked to undertake a pioneer post, as Director of Women's Establishments at the Treasury. This was, in effect, the premier women's post in the Civil Service and had been instituted in response to an overwhelming demand by women civil servants for some form of representation at the Treasury. Although Maude Lawrence sat on all committees dealing with the problems of women civil servants, her advocacy of the women's cause was, to say the least, lukewarm. To the Royal Commission on the Civil Service in 1930 she advocated retention of the marriage bar, requiring women to leave work on marriage, and unequal pay, in direct opposition to the wishes of organized women civil servants. Her chief interest was the Civil Service Sports Council, where she was particularly assiduous in promoting golf and hockey. She was awarded the DBE in 1926.   M.Z.

Lawson, Dorothy (1580–1632), Roman Catholic activist. Both Dorothy's parents, Margaret Dormer and Sir Henry Constable of Burton Constable, Yorkshire, were members of leading Roman Catholic families and brought up their daughter in the same faith. In 1597 Dorothy married Roger Lawson, heir of a prominent Newcastle mercantile and landed family. Although the family had Catholic connections, the Lawsons were conforming Protestants until the arrival of this determined young bride. It was just a week before Dorothy introduced the first Catholic priest into the house, and she quickly converted most of her husband's family, although Roger himself remained a Protestant until a deathbed conversion in 1613, stimulated by his wife who had hastened to London to be with him.

The most important period of Dorothy's Catholic proselytizing came after 1605 when she settled at Heaton near Newcastle. Her barrister husband's frequent absences in London gave her the opportunity gradually to employ Catholic servants. She held elaborate daily religious exercises in her home, had the major responsibility for the estates, and was active in charitable and healing works in the neighbourhood. She comforted local women in childbirth before baptizing their infants as Catholics, and was a tireless catechizer. The neighbourhood, which had lacked a single Catholic family in 1605, held some 100 converted families by 1632.

Dorothy's importance to Catholicism was

national, or even international, for she built before 1623 a house at St Anthony's near Newcastle, designed especially as a centre for Jesuit missionaries. She herself kept a Jesuit chaplain and annual exercises of the Society were held at St Anthony's. In addition, she bore fifteen children between 1597 and 1613. All were Catholics and two daughters became nuns. Most of them adopted a Catholic celibacy. The leading role that women played in supervising feasts and fast days; the female exemplars of the Virgin and the Saints; and women's relative immunity from legal prosecution all made Catholicism attractive to many women. Dorothy Lawson, like other determined Catholic matriarchs, played a vital role in maintaining and spreading the outlawed faith.

See also J. D. Hanlon, 'These be but Women', in *From the Renaissance to the Counter Reformation*, ed. C. H. Carter, 1966.

A.H.

Lead, Jane (1624–1704), religious author and mystic. Jane Ward was born into a family of Norfolk gentry. At the age of fifteen she suffered a spiritual crisis and a period of severe depression which lifted following an ecstatic vision experienced when she was eighteen. She was sent for six months to her brother in London, where she frequented the sectarian gatherings that had appeared after the outbreak of the Civil War. On returning to Norfolk, having disagreed with her family about prospective husbands, she married a distant relative, William Lead. They had four daughters.

Around 1663 Jane Lead joined a small religious group led by John Pordage, an Anglican cleric who was a follower of the German mystic, Jacob Boehme. After her husband's death in 1670 she moved into Pordage's household and recorded her experiences there in a spiritual journal, later published in four volumes as *A Fountain of Gardens* (1697–1701). In 1681 she published her first book, a theological treatise entitled *The Heavenly Cloud Now Breaking*. She wrote voluminously in both prose and verse, and published at least fifteen more books and pamphlets. Some were translated into German and Dutch and gained a wide readership.

Following Pordage's death in 1681 she struggled to lead his congregation, but support dwindled and by 1692 she was living alone in Stepney. Around 1694 she was joined by a

young scholar and physician, Francis Lee, who acted as her secretary and editor after she became blind in 1695. They reorganized her congregation as the Philadelphian Society, basing their beliefs on her interpretation of Boehme's theosophical doctrines. The Society flourished for a time, but declined after Jane Lead's death in 1704. Her writings remain valuable as vividly subjective chronicles of female experience, using visionary, poetic language to communicate her mystical ideas.

See also C. F. Smith, 'Jane Lead: Mysticism and the Woman Cloathed with the Sun', in *Shakespeare's Sisters*, ed. S. M. Gilbert and S. Gubar, 1979.

W.R.O.

Leadbeater, Mary (1758–1826), poet and chronicler of Irish life. Born into an Irish Quaker family, she was allowed a good education. She wrote poetry, most of which has not survived, but her claim to notice rests on her publications in the genre of 'improving literature'. Her *Extracts and Original Anecdotes for the Improvement of Youth* (1794) represents an advance on the usual type of juvenile literature then available. The writing makes a more ambitious claim on the understanding of the young, and the subject-matter includes more radical theories than those commonly found in such works, such as the brotherhood of man, irrespective of colour or creed. *Cottage Dialogues of the Irish Peasantry* (1811–13) calls attention to the misery of Irish rural life, while the *Annals of Ballitore from 1768–1824* (not published until 1862) contains much original and interesting observation of contemporary life. It includes her eye-witness account of the sacking of Ballitore during the French invasion of 1798.

T.H.

Leavis, Q(ueenie) D(orothy) (1906–81), literary critic, closely associated with her more famous husband, F. R. Leavis, whose highminded and abrasive outlook she shared. As Q. D. Roth she was educated at Latymer School and Girton College, Cambridge, where she took a first class degree and became a research fellow. In the same year, 1929, she married. Together she and her husband founded the influential magazine *Scrutiny* in 1932, and over the next twenty years Q. D. Leavis was a frequent contributor. In their writing and teaching the two insisted on the central importance of literary culture, emphasized the role of a small creative minority in forming standards, and restricted the 'great tradition' in modern literature to a handful of writers. Q. D. Leavis's most substantial achievement was *Fiction and the Reading Public* (1932), a pioneering study in the sociology of literature which examined changes in reading habits and the development of separate high-, middle-, and low-brow markets for novels. Despite the Leavises' impact on several generations of students, Q. D. Leavis never received any university appointment —in part, at least, a measure of the hostility she and F. R. Leavis provoked. After her husband's retirement from Cambridge she went with him to Harvard; their joint *Lectures in America*, 1969, contains her 'A Fresh Approach to *Wuthering Heights*'. Her most notable collaboration with F. R. Leavis is *Dickens the Novelist* 1970.   N.H.

Ledingham, Una (Christina) (1900–65), physician, one of the first generation of women to make distinguished careers in medicine. Una Ledingham was the daughter of the journalist J. L. Garvin, who became editor of *The Observer*. She went to South Hampstead High School and had a distinguished student career at the Royal Free Hospital School of Medicine (then called the London School of Medicine for Women). The greater part of her life's work was accomplished at the Royal Free Hospital, where she was house physician (1924), medical registrar (1925–28) and first assistant to the children's department (1929–31) before her election in 1932 to the consultant staff. She ultimately became senior consultant physician. She was also an able teacher and examiner for the University of London. Her special field was diabetes; she was physician-in-charge of the diabetic clinic at the Royal Free Hospital and Hampstead General Hospital, and made a number of contributions to the literature of the subject.
                N.H.

Lee, Ann (1736–84) founder of the Shaker sect. She was born in Manchester, the daughter of a blacksmith, and had no formal education. Her marriage in 1762 to another blacksmith, Abraham Stanley, was unhappy and was probably responsible for inducing in her that invincible disgust with physical love which became so important a doctrine in the Shaker sect. In 1758 she joined a small group led by two Quaker apostates, James and Jane Wardley. This group confidently expected the Second Coming of Christ and their meetings were punctuated by prophecies and violent physical seizures. After the death of Ann Lee's fourth child she intervened decisively in the movement, believing herself to be ordained by God to reveal the manifold, and above all the sexual, corruptions of the age. As her mission was not notably successful in Britain, she moved to America in 1774. After an initial period of poverty and failure, by the late 1770s she began to establish her sect. Conversions and persecution followed. She died in 1784, by which time the American Shakers numbered about a thousand. The sect continued to flourish long after her death, its doctrines firmly based on the holiness of celibacy and the duality of God expressed in a male form as Christ and in a female as Ann Lee.

See also J. F. C. Harrison, *The Second Coming. Popular Millenarianism 1780–1850*, 1979; J. M. Whitworth, *God's Blueprints: A Sociological Study of Three Utopian Sects*, 1975.   T.H.

Lee, Sarah (1791–1856), writer and artist. Born in Colchester, Essex, she married the naturalist Thomas Edward Bowdich at the age of twenty-two. Sharing her husband's interest in natural history, she visited Africa with him in 1815. In 1818 they visited the famous French naturalist Baron Cuvier and spent about four years in studying his collections. They set off once more for Africa in 1823, where the following year, near the Gambia River, Thomas Bowdich died. Five years later she married Robert Lee and spent much of her time in popularizing natural science, illustrating some of her own books. *The Freshwater Fishes of Great Britain* (1828) was perhaps her most valuable work, its faithful colouring achieved because the fish, specially caught for Mrs Lee, were painted as they lay on the river bank, before their colours had dulled.
                B.H.C.

Lee, Vernon. See PAGET, VIOLET.

Lehmann, Liza, properly Elizabeth Nina Mary Frederica (1862–1918), singer and composer, born in London of German-Scottish parents. Her father was the painter Rudolf Lehmann and her mother a singer. There was an artistic atmosphere at home, which was variously in Germany, France, and Italy, where Liszt was a guest. She studied in London and Germany, making her first appearance in

Leigh, Dorothy

London in 1885. In 1894 she married the painter and composer Herbert Bedford and retired from the stage, taking seriously to composition. Liza Lehmann became the first English woman composer to enjoy widespread success in Britain and America, known primarily for her song cycles, especially *In a Persian Garden* (1896). This piece for four voices with piano accompaniment employs words from FitzGerald's *Rubaiyat of Omar Khayyam*; the music is conventional but with effective vocal parts. In 1910 she toured America, giving concerts of her songs and accompanying herself at the piano. Her memoirs, *The Life of Liza Lehmann, by Herself*, appeared in 1919.   B.H.C.

Leigh, Dorothy (*fl.* 1616), author. Dorothy Leigh, 'gentlewomen', was the author of *The Mother's Blessing* which, first published in 1616, was reputedly in its fourteenth edition by 1629. Its success shows the increasing emphasis which contemporaries placed on a religious family life. To some extent *The Mother's Blessing* is a conventional example of pious exhortation, referring to no literature besides the Bible, and representing the fulfilment of Dorothy's promise to her dead husband to provide their four sons with the means to 'grow in godliness' and find the 'right and ready way to heaven'. But it does include trenchant remarks on the dangers of worldliness in clergymen and many vivid passages on the dangers of sin, and in some ways escapes from the conventionality of its genre. It is significant that as a woman, Dorothy Leigh felt bound to include a long passage justifying her decision to show 'to the view of the world' her private advice to her sons. There are also interesting signs that she was frustrated by the limitations of her life and sought to fulfil her own desires through her children, 'Methinks if I were a man, and preacher of God's word, as I hope some of you shall be . . .'.   A.H.

Leigh, Vivien (1913–67), actress. She was born Vivien Mary Hartley in Darjeeling, India, educated in English and French convents, and later accompanied her parents on a five-year tour of Europe. Acting was her vocation from childhood. In 1931 she enrolled at the Royal Academy of Dramatic Art but gave this up a year later on her marriage to Herbert Leigh Holman. Shortly after the birth of her daughter in 1933 she returned to acting, and after

a few small film parts was cast as the heroine in Carl Sternheim's *The Mask of Virtue* (1935), a role that required a woman of exceptional beauty. She was outstandingly successful and Alexander Korda, the film producer, then offered her a contract.

In *Fire Over England* (1937) she starred with Laurence Olivier. The partnership marked the beginning of a life-long devotion to the great actor who became her second husband in 1940 and whose inspiration helped her to realize her childhood declaration: 'I am going to be a great actress'. In the same year she played Ophelia to his Hamlet at Elsinore. Film and stage triumphs proliferated. She received an Oscar (1939) for her unforgettable Scarlett O'Hara in *Gone With The Wind*, she was Emma in *Lady Hamilton*, Cleopatra in *Caesar and Cleopatra*, Anna in *Anna Karenina*, and won a second Oscar as Blanche Dubois in *A Streetcar Named Desire*. She acted on stages throughout the world in plays which included Shaw's *The Doctor's Dilemma* (1942), Thornton Wilder's *The Skin of Our Teeth* (1946), and *Duel of Angels* by Giraudoux (1958), as well as much of Shakespeare. She sang and danced in the musical *Tovarich* on Broadway (1957), receiving the Antoinette Perry Award.

Her life of incessant travel, work, and excitement exacted a high price; she had a manic-depressive illness that recurred with increasing severity, eventually alienating Olivier who divorced her in 1960. The new theatre of 'angry young men' did not appeal to her although she continued to tour the world with previous successes and won another award, the French Etoile Crystal, for her part in the film *Ship of Fools* (1965). She died at her home near Guildford.

See also A. Dent, *Vivien Leigh — A Bouquet*, 1969; A. Edwards, *Vivien Leigh*, 1977.
                                                    P.L.

Leighton, Margaret (1922–76), actress. She was born in Worcester and educated at Birmingham, where at the age of sixteen she joined the repertory company to scrub floors. She toured with ENSA in 1940, rejoining the company at Birmingham a year later. She then played at the Old Vic in London for three years (1944–47), before appearing in *The Cocktail Party* (1950), which established her in the West End. She was the leading lady at Stratford in 1952, played Orinthia opposite

252

Coward's Magnus in *The Apple Cart* (1953), and appeared in *Separate Tables* (1954).

In 1959 in New York she played a brilliant Beatrice to John Gielgud's Benedick, and remained in the city for several years following a return visit in 1961. For *The Night of the Iguana* she won the 1961–62 Antoinette Perry Award, and also played in *The Chinese Prime Minister* (1964). Her many films included *The Go-Between*, for which she won the Best Supporting Actress Award of 1971.

Margaret Leighton married Max Reinhardt (1947), Laurence Harvey (1957), and Michael Wilding (1964). Despite her tough repertory experience, she was always nervous and amazed at her success. Everyone described her in terms of light: 'silver', 'gleaming', 'moonlight'. She was appointed CBE in 1974

A.D.

Leitch, Cecil, properly Charlotte Cicelia Pitcairn (1891–1977), golfer. Born in Silloth, Cumberland, Cecil Leitch was acknowledged by 1914 as the leading woman player in the country. She was British lady champion in 1914, 1920, 1921 and 1926, and English champion in 1914 and 1919. She won the French Open five times and the Canadian Open in 1921, beating her rival Miss M'Bride by the remarkable margin of 17 up, 15 to play. Later, her matches with Joyce Wethered (Lady Heathcote-Amory) became almost legendary and focused attention on the new style and calibre of woman's golf. When they first met in the final of the English Championships at Sheringham in 1920, Miss Wethered surprisingly won. But the next year Miss Leitch had her revenge by defeating her rival in both the British Open at Turnberry and the French at Fontainebleau. She brought to the women's game a vigour it had never known before. She used a wide stance and played the ball well away from herself, unperturbed that this might be thought unfeminine. Before her time, women golfers had played like ladies. Cecil Leitch showed that power, strength, and determination were not the prerogatives of men.
See also C. Price, *The World of Golf*, 1963; Steel and Ryde (eds.), *Shell International Encyclopaedia of Golf*, 1975.   E.M.V.

Lejeune, C(aroline) A(nne) (1897–1973), film critic. Born in Manchester, the youngest child of a Frankfurt cotton-merchant, she was educated at Withington Girls' School and Man-

chester University. In 1925 she married Edward Roffe Thomas. C. P. Scott helped her to begin writing for the *Manchester Guardian*.

Although fond of opera, Caroline loved the new and still not acceptable medium of the cinema. Seeing the possibilities of an unusual career, in 1922 she persuaded the *Guardian* to let her write a weekly column: 'The Week on the Screen'. In 1928 she moved to *The Observer* where she stayed for the rest of her career, while also writing for other publications. After the war she reviewed television plays, and adapted the Sherlock Holmes stories, among others, as television serials. She lost interest in films through distaste for postwar sexual explicitness and after leaving *The Observer* in 1960 never again visited the cinema. Her passions were her home, family, dogs, and roses. Caroline Lejeune criticized without malice, but with wit, percipience and kindness. Her work is part of film history. She wrote an autobiography, *Thank You for Having Me*, 1964; *Cinema*, 1931; *Chestnuts in her lap* (collection of reviews), 1947; and *Three Score Years and Ten* (her completion of Angela THIRKELL's unfinished novel), 1961.

A.D.

Lemmens-Sherrington, Helen (1834–1906), singer. She was born at Preston, Lancashire, the daughter of a mill manager, but following the family's financial ruin in a bank failure, in 1838 moved to Rotterdam when her father took a post there. She was taught music by her mother, who before retiring on marriage had been a promising singer. The daughter, too, proved to have a rich, pure soprano voice, and in 1852 she began studying at the Brussels Conservatoire. During this time she became engaged to Nicolas Jacques Lemmens, who encouraged her to travel with him to England in 1856. As a stranger in her native country she found it difficult at first to gain engagements, but her early performances were very impressive and as a result she appeared with the famous tenor Sims Reeves. She studied oratorio and took part in Mendelssohn's *Elijah*.

In 1857 she married Lemmens and settled down in London, where she took her place among the leading English sopranos of the day. Indeed, after the retirement of Clara NOVELLO in 1860, she had hardly any rivals. Although she sang in opera, her career was mainly devoted to the concert platform, where from 1870 she completed a quartet of great vocalists, with Janet PATEY, Sims Reeves and Charles Santley. She was particularly successful in Haydn's *Creation*. Although her husband was a professional pianist, it was mostly left to her to make provision for their family of seven children, and consequently she worked too hard. In 1881 she accepted the post of singing teacher at the Brussels Conservatoire, although her husband died just before she was due to take it up. She remained at this post in Brussels until 1891 and then taught for a time in London and Manchester. She died in Brussels.   B.H.C.

Lennox, Charlotte (1730?–1804), novelist. In a petition for support to the Royal Literary Fund in 1792, Charlotte Lennox described herself as daughter of Colonel James Ramsay, born in 1720 at New York where her father served as Lieutenant-Governor. This biographical untruth designed to upgrade her family connections, survives in numerous critical works. In fact, she was probably born in Gibraltar and arrived in America only in 1739, settling near Albany where her father had been appointed captain of an independent company of foot. She emigrated to England after the death of her father (1742) and from 1743 to 1746 was patronized by Lady Finch and the Countess of Rockingham.

In 1747 Charlotte Lennox's *Poems on Several Occasions* were published and in 1749 her first novel, *The Life of Harriot Stuart*. *The Female Quixote* (1752) firmly established her reputation and she was subsequently lionized by Samuel Johnson who proclaimed her superiority to all other women. In 1753 a novel, *Henrietta*, was published, while a number of translations and a dramatic pastoral were also completed (1756–57). She was supported during her illness in the years 1759 to 1761 by the Duchess of Newcastle, but also managed to write a magazine, *The Lady's Museum*, and a novel, *Sophia* (1761). While *The Female Quixote* was the most successful, both financially and artistically, of Charlotte's novels, her literary significance is secured by the subject-matter of her first novel *Harriet Stuart* and her last, *Euphemia* (1790). Although she was not a native of the United States, the fictional realization in these works of the author's experiences there between 1739 and 1742 have earned her the title of the first American novelist.

See also P. Séjourné, *The Mystery of Charlotte Lennox* 1967; M. R. Small, *Charlotte Ramsay Lennox*, 1935.   A.L.

Leofgyth or Leoba (*fl. c.* 724–771), abbess. The only child of Dynne and Æbbe, members of the West Saxon aristocracy, Thrutgeba, better known as Leofgyth or Leoba was born no later than 724. When she was old enough, her parents decided to dedicate their daughter to God in thanksgiving for her long-awaited birth, and placed her in a monastery at Wimborne. There she gained a reputation for piety and holiness which led Boniface, a relation of Æbbe and correspondent of Leofgyth, to ask whether she could travel to Germany and help him in his missionary work. Permission was granted and Leofgyth became abbess of Bischofsheim, founding many daughter-houses and taking part in the great Anglo-Saxon missionary activity in eighth-century Germany. Boniface had a high regard for her and expressed the wish that they should be buried together. After his death in 754 Leofgyth remained in Germany, a respected figure in both ecclesiastical and court circles, and particularly dear to Charlemagne's wife Hildegard. Leofgyth eventually retired to a convent at Scoranesheim, near Mainz, where she died on 28 September, some time between 771 and 783. Her body was taken to Fulda where she was buried, not with Boniface as he had requested but near the high altar. Her bones were translated twice; once in 819, and again in 837.

See also Rudolf's *Vita Leobae*, in C. H. Talbot, *The Anglo-Saxon Missionaries in Germany*, 1954.   J.C.

Lepell, Molly. See HERVEY, LADY MARY.

Lessore, Thérèse (1884–1945), painter. She was the daughter of a French painter and etcher, Jules Lessore, who settled in England in 1871; her grandfather had also been a painter and well-known china decorator. Thérèse studied at the Slade, 1904–09, and then married Bernard Adeney, later president of the London Group. After the marriage ended she entered the entourage of the painter Walter Sickert, and in 1926 she married him. Thérèse, like Sylvia GOSSE did much of the donkey-work for Sickert in his later career by squaring-up drawings for transfer to canvas, laying-in the early stages (and sometimes substantial parts of the later ones), taking the snapshots on which many of his late works were based, and similar chores. These did not entirely prevent her from working on her own account, although her work was inevitably influenced by his outlook and technique. There are works by Thérèse Lessore in Birmingham, Bristol, and a few other galleries. L.M.M.

Lewis, Agnes (1843–1926), scholar and discoverer of the Sinai Palimpsest. Agnes was the elder twin daughter of a solicitor, John Smith, and the sister of Margaret GIBSON. She was educated in Scotland and London and in 1887 married Samuel Savage Lewis, an antiquary and librarian. After her husband's unexpected death in 1891, she lived with her sister.

Agnes's early interest in the Mediterranean civilization had been fostered by her marriage and the interests of her husband. She had a liking for history and a talent for languages, particularly the ancient ones. Both sisters also spoke fluent modern Greek. In 1892 they went to the recently rediscovered monastery of St Catherine's, Mount Sinai, and there discovered a number of early Syriac manuscripts. On examining one eighth-century script, Agnes noticed traces of an earlier text written underneath, which she identified as coming from the Gospels. The importance of the discovery was confirmed when photographs of the text were examined by experts in England. A return visit was made in 1893, a transcript of the Gospel made, and the result published in 1894. Although two further trips were made and resulted in further publications of texts, none were of equal merit to the first discovery. Agnes received several awards for her work, including the gold medal of the Royal Asiatic Society (1915) and several honorary degrees.

See also M. D. Gibson, *How the Codex was Found*, 1898. J.R.

Lewis, Rosa (1867–1952), hotelier. She was born in Leyton, east London, the daughter of a watch repairer and undertaker named Ovenden. At the age of twelve she became maid-of-all-work to a middle-class Victorian couple, earning 1s. 0d. a week, and rose to become the greatest cook in Europe by 'picking others' brains'. By way of the exiled Comte de Paris, Lady Randolph Churchill, the Asquiths, and others, she became 'housekeeper' in a house in Eaton Terrace kept for Edward VII's private pleasures. A marriage to Excelsior Lewis, a footman, was arranged by Lord Savile to give Rosa respectability, but she eventually parted

from her unhappy alcoholic husband in 1903. By the age of thirty, Rosa was the most sought-after cook in the land, preparing meals at Sandringham and for the Kaiser when he was in England.

A year after Edward VII's succession, Rosa bought the Cavendish Hotel in Jermyn Street and soon made it into the most fashionable and racy establishment in London. Edward could not frequent the hotel, although he always relied absolutely on Rosa's discretion. She herself never recovered from the King's death in 1910. The television series *The Duchess of Duke Street* was inspired by her story.

See also A. Masters, *Rosa Lewis*, 1977. A.D.

Leyel, Hilda Winifred (1880–1957), herbalist. She was the daughter of Edward Brenton Wauton of Uppingham School and was educated at Halliwick Manor. After joining F. R. Benson's company she was given a few acting parts, and then met and married Carl Leyel (1900). Charming and practical, she soon turned to organizing elaborate fancy-dress balls which became part of London's society life before the First War. She initiated The Golden Ballot, raising £350,000 for ex-servicemen and hospitals, and was prosecuted under both the Betting and the Lottery Acts. She won both cases, thereby legalizing the holding of ballots for charity. She then took up herbalism, founding the Society of Herbalists and the Culpeper shops. Her books show a lack of scientific training, although as a small child Edward Thring had taught her botany. They include *Herbal Delight*, 1937; *Diet and Commonsense* 1936; and *The Gentle Art of Cookery*, 1925. She was a Life Governor of St Mary's, the West London and the Royal Orthopaedic hospitals, and the French Government awarded her the *Palme Académique* (1924). A.D.

Lind, Jenny, properly Johanna Maria (1820–87), Swedish soprano. Born in Stockholm, the daughter of Niclas Jonas Lind and Anna Maria Fellborg, Jenny Lind spent her early childhood in care. She enrolled as 'actress-pupil' at the Royal Opera House School in September 1830, making her stage début in November. Tutored by Isak Berg, she appeared in minor roles at the Opera House before her formal début as Agathe in *Der Freischütz* on 7 March 1838. Small and unprepossessing, she was outstanding in performance and in 1840 was appointed Court Singer. Her voice became overstrained and was saved only by ten months' tuition in Paris from Manuel Garcia, from which she returned, with renewed force, on 10 October 1842 as Norma.

She sang in Finland and Denmark in 1843 and was invited to Berlin to sing in *Ein Feldlager in Schlesien*, composed for her by Meyerbeer. Touring Germany in 1845 she sang at Leipzig, under Mendelssohn's direction, and in 1846 made her début in Vienna. She first sang oratorio at Aachen. Reluctant to relearn her roles for England, she finally appeared at Her Majesty's Opera House on 4 May 1847 as Alice in *Robert le diable*. 'Jenny Lind fever' gripped London, but she shrank from the adulation and resolved to leave the stage. A tour of England, a second season in London, and another tour were to constitute her farewell to opera, but, persuaded to give six final performances at Her Majesty's, her last operatic appearance was on 10 May 1849 in *Robert le diable*.

In 1850 the second stage of her career, as a concert singer, began with a tour of North America managed by the entrepreneur Phineas T. Barnum. Her tour of ninety-three concerts, accompanied by Julius Benedict and Giovanni Bellatti, was a tremendous popular and financial success. She stayed to give another forty concerts accompanied by Otto Goldschmidt, whom she married on 5 February 1852. Returning to Europe, Madame Lind-Goldschmidt continued to give concerts in Germany, Austria, Holland, and England, where she settled after 1858. Her voice was now past its best and after 1867 she would perform only on special occasions, above all for charity. In 1883 she made her last public appearance in Malvern and was appointed first Professor of Singing at the Royal College of Music. She died at Wynds Point, Herefordshire, on 2 November 1887 and a plaque in Poet's Corner, Westminster Abbey, was unveiled in 1894.

Although her operatic career was over before the age of twenty-nine, Jenny Lind was the most celebrated singer of her time. Her combination of musicianship and acting ability was unequalled; her voice was remarkable in its range of two octaves and a sixth, and her breathing control was such that her sustained notes, her pianissimo, and her shake became legendary.

256

See also J. Bulman, *Jenny Lind*, 1956; H. S. Holland and W. S. Rockstro, *Jenny Lind the Artist*, 1891.   C.B.

Lindsay, Lady Anne (1750–1825), poet. She was the daughter of James Lindsay, Earl of Balcarres, and spent the early part of her life in her native Fifeshire. She and her widowed sister Margaret moved to London sometime before 1793, the date when she married Andrew Barnard, son of the Bishop of Limerick. They settled in the Cape of Good Hope, where Barnard was Colonial Secretary. Here she wrote her *Journals and Notes* of life at the Cape (published in *Lives of the Lindsays*, below). In 1807 her husband died and she returned to London, once more taking up residence with her sister. Although her sister re-married, Lady Anne remained with her, and their home became a literary salon; Burke, Sheridan, and the Prince of Wales were among the habitués.

The ballad upon which Lady Anne Lindsay's fame rests, 'Auld Robin Gray', was actually published when she was only twenty, but her authorship remained concealed until 1823, others claiming authorship in the meantime. She in fact confided her secret to Sir Walter Scott, telling him that it was based on an old melody to which there were improper words, and to which he had wished to attach 'some little history of virtuous distress in humble life'. She indeed loaded her lachrymose heroine with disasters. The sequels to the poem were less successful.

See also A. W. C. Lindsay, *Lives of the Lindsays*, 1849.   C.H.

Linton, Eliza Lynn (1822–98), novelist and essayist who was born at Keswick, the daughter of a clergyman. The youngest of twelve children, she was just five months old when her mother died. Eliza Lynn educated herself, learning French, German, and Italian, and then at the age of twenty-three went to London to become a journalist. With the help of an allowance from her father she was also an independent woman. Between 1849 and 1851 she was on the staff of *The Morning Chronicle*, where she earned a guinea a week, and worked for *All the Year Round*. Her first novel, *Azeth, the Egyptian*, was published in 1847, but this book and its successors, *Amymone* (1848) and *Realities* (1851), were unsuccessful. She therefore went to Paris and stayed there until 1854, working as a correspondent for London newspapers.

In 1858 Eliza Lynn married W. J. Linton, a wood engraver and poet. Their marriage did not last, but they separated amicably, remaining friends for the rest of their lives. Eliza Lynn Linton continued novel-writing, achieving particular success with *The True History of Joshua Davidson* (1872), *Patricia Kemball* (1874), and *Christopher Kirkland* (1885). The novels produced after her marriage lost the cloying sentimentality of those written before: they were both better written and more realistic.

From 1866 Eliza Lynn Linton worked on the staff of *The Saturday Review*. She was a hard-working, dedicated journalist but despite the fact that she was economically, professionally, and personally independent she was extremely critical of the generation that succeeded her and violently anti-feminist. Among her other works were *Witch Stories*, 1861, *Grasp Your Nettle*, 1865, *Under Which Lord?*, 1865, *The Girl of the Period and Other Essays*, 1883, and *My Literary Life*, 1899.

See also G. S. Layard (ed.), *Mrs Eliza Lynn Linton. Her Life, Letters, and Opinions*, 1901.   A.P.

Lisle, Viscountess. See PLANTAGENET, HONOUR, VISCOUNTESS LISLE.

Lisle, Alice (1614?–85), political martyr who was executed after the Duke of Monmouth's rebellion. She was the daughter of Sir White Beckenshaw of Moyles Court, Ellingham, Hampshire, and in 1630 became the second wife of John Lisle, whose political career as a regicide and Cromwellian undoubtedly contributed to her own fate. Her husband took refuge in Switzerland at the Restoration, only to be assassinated in 1664, but she chose instead to retire to Ellingham, where she became known for her piety, charity, and sympathy with Nonconformist ministers. Shortly after Monmouth's defeat at Sedgemoor, two rebels, John Hicks, a fiery Nonconformist preacher of her acquaintance, and Richard Nelthorpe, took refuge at Alice Lisle's house. They were betrayed before their arrival and captured by Colonel Thomas Penruddocke, whose father had been condemned to death by John Lisle, and who had laid a trap to ensnare their hostess with them. The trial of this partially deaf, seventy-year-old gentlewoman at Winchester

on 27 August 1685 was carefully calculated by Chief Justice Jeffreys as a terrible warning to Westcountrymen of the dangers of harbouring traitors. A reluctant jury found Alice guilty and she was executed at Winchester on 2 September. A brave and sympathetic woman, Alice Lisle was largely a victim of circumstances, who achieved fame and martyrdom as the first and best-known casualty of the Bloody Assizes.

See also G. W. Keeton, *Trial for Treason*, 1959; J. G. Muddiman (ed.), *The Bloody Assizes*, 1929.   T.J.M.

Livingstone, Janet (*fl.* 1674), Presbyterian activist. Janet Livingstone was the widow of an eminent Presbyterian minister and played a prominent role in organizing a protest against religious persecution in Scotland. A deputation of women, mainly the wives or widows of ministers, petitioned the Scottish Privy Couicl against the ending of religious toleration in June 1674. They organized as women in the belief that they would be less likely than the ministers themselves to face legal recriminations. But the protest, which attracted a large crowd, so alarmed the Councillors that some of the women were imprisoned and others, including Mrs Livingstone, banished briefly from Edinburgh.

See also J. Anderson, *The Ladies of the Covenant*, 1866.   A.H.

Llanover, Augusta, Lady (1802–96), promoter of Welsh culture. She was the younger daughter of Benjamin Waddington of Llanover and married Sir Benjamin Hall, later Baron Llanover, in 1823. Her childhood in Wales had given her a deep interest in Celtic culture, history, and language, which was fostered by her marriage to a man similarly interested in Welsh traditions. She herself spoke little Welsh, but she organized her house on traditional Welsh lines. Her domestic and Welsh interests came together in *Good Cookery and Recipes Communicated by the Hermit of the Cell of Gower* (1867). Another major influence was Thomas Price (Carnhuanawc), the Welsh historian and activist. Encouraged by him she became an early member of Cymreigyddion y Fenni (The Welsh Society of Abergavenny), and helped the Welsh Manuscript Society as well as the Welsh Collegiate Institution, Llandovery. She also edited the *Autobiography* *and Correspondence of Mary Granville, Mrs Delaney* (1861), who was an ancestress.

Altogether, Lady Augusta made a significant contribution to the preservation and encouragement of Welsh culture in all its aspects.   J.R.

Llewelyn Davies, Margaret (1861–1943), General Secretary of the Women's Co-operative Guild. She was the daughter of J. Llewelyn Davies, a minister and member of the Christian Socialist group, and niece of Emily Davies, founder of Girton College, Cambridge, which Margaret later attended. She died at the age of eighty-two having spent thirty-two years as General Secretary of the Women's Co-operative Guild (formed in 1883). She never accepted a salary and for years ran the Guild's affairs from her father's vicarage at Kirkby Lonsdale in Westmorland.

Under her leadership the Women's Co-operative Guild became a remarkable campaigning body, developing social attitudes which were often far ahead of the co-operative movement as a whole. As early as 1895 the Guild set up an inquiry into the working conditions of 2,000 women employed in co-operative stores. In 1907 its Central Committee asked guilds to co-operate with local trade union branches in pressing for a minimum wage for all women employees, and continued this campaign until, by 1912, 200 retail societies and the Co-operative Wholesale Society itself had complied.

From 1909, Margaret Llewelyn Davies gave evidence to a Royal Commission on divorce law reform, the WCG began to advocate divorce on the same terms for women as for men, and in 1912 it passed a resolution urging that divorce by mutual consent after two years' separation should be legalized. This aroused strong opposition and the Central Board of the Co-operative Union decided to withhold its annual grant of £400 unless the divorce campaign was dropped. Margaret Llewelyn Davies was adamant that in no circumstances could the WCG forfeit its independence and for four years branches raised sufficient funds to carry on unpaid.

The Guild supported the suffrage cause from 1904, and Margaret Llewelyn Davies walked with Margaret BONDFIELD (who became the first woman Cabinet Minister) in a peaceful sandwich-board picket of Parliament in 1912. Other campaigns she initiated were for maternity benefit to be paid to the mother, and for

greatly improved ante-natal, natal, and post-natal care in order to bring down the high infant mortality rate (1913–14). Her greatest achievement, however, was to give under-educated, homebound, working-class women the confidence to take part not only in the affairs of the co-operative movement but in public life, and to have the courage of the convictions that grew out of their hard experience. Many of these convictions are expressed eloquently in *Maternity* (which was published in 1915 with an introduction by Sir Herbert Samuel) and *Life as We Have Known It* (with an introduction in 1931 by Virginia Woolf, a close friend of Margaret Llewelyn Davies).

                                                  M.S.

Lloyd, Elizabeth. See BURY, ELIZABETH.

Lloyd, Marie (1870–1922), music-hall artist. Born Matilda Alice Victoria Wood in Hoxton, London, she was the eldest of a large family. Her father made artificial flowers and worked as a part-time waiter at The Grecian Music Hall, where on Saturday 9 May 1885 'Bella Delmere' made her first appearance on stage. By 22 June she was appearing as 'Marie Lloyd' (taking the name from a popular newspaper) and on 17 August she was already fourth on the bill at Bermondsey. The following year she appeared in the West End, working several halls in one evening; in 1891 she had a year's engagement at the Oxford; and for the next three Christmases she appeared in pantomime at Drury Lane with Dan Leno, Little Tich, and Herbert Campbell.

From the start of her career, this cockney girl singing songs such as 'The Boy I Love is up in the Gallery' was loved for her youthful energy. Not until she was in her thirties did her act mature. Saucy, witty, and coquettish, famous for her wink and once questioned by the local council for being too risqué, she sang 'Oh Mr Porter' and 'Everything in the Garden is Lovely' while increasingly adding character studies to her repertoire. She married the first of her three husbands in 1887 and had a daughter. Separated after 1893, she then lived with Alec Hurley, 'the Coster King', whom she married in 1906. In 1910 she fell in love with a young Irish jockey who won the Derby, but although she stayed with him until she died, the relationship was not happy. She was exuberant, fun-loving, and compulsively generous, both to individuals and to charity, paying for 150 beds in a hostel for the destitute and providing shoes for East End children. In 1906 she joined the music-hall strike, picketing the halls, and in 1909 appeared in *How The Vote Was Won* in support of women's suffrage. At the height of her career in 1912 she was not among those invited to appear in the first Royal Command Performance. So she hired the London Palladium for the same evening, billing her show 'By Public Demand' and played to a packed house. During the First World War she visited hospitals and gave concerts for soldiers. She retired to run a public house, but after two years returned to the halls, popular as ever, though forced by illness, drink, and private troubles to shorten her act.

Famous for her impeccable timing and stage sense, the alluring but down-to-earth Marie Lloyd is today the best remembered of the music-hall stars. Admired by Max Beerbohm, Sarah Bernhardt, and T. S. Eliot, she was the most popular performer of her time, not only in London, but also in Paris, Berlin, New York, Australia, and South Africa. Her last performance was at the Edmonton Empire, where during the song 'One of the ruins that Cromwell knocked about a bit. . .' she collapsed, in character, so that the audience remained unaware that she was ill. She died a few days later at her home in Golders Green.

See also D. Farson, *Marie Lloyd and Music Hall*, 1972; N. Jacob, *Our Marie*, 1936; C. Macinnes, *Sweet Saturday Night*, 1967.

C.B.

Lloyd George, Lady Megan (1902–66), Liberal, later Labour MP. Born at Criccieth, Wales, she was the younger daughter of David and Dame Margaret Lloyd George. From the ages of eight to twenty-two she lived in Downing Street, where her father was successively Chancellor of the Exchequer, Minister of Munitions, Secretary of State for War, and Prime Minister. A very clever child, she was often said to be most like her father, both in appearance and temperament, of all his children. From him she inherited a passionate love of politics, a formidable intelligence, and an uncompromising radicalism. She went with Lloyd George to the Peace Conference in Paris after the First World War and at the age of seventeen, often acting as her father's hostess, met and talked with the most eminent statesmen, soldiers, and diplomats of the time. It was a remarkable, and perhaps unique, political education.

Lady Megan never married, but contrived to prepare herself for a political life to which she seemed destined. She went to India for a year in 1924 and was closely associated from 1925 onwards with all her father's political activities. In 1929 she was elected as Liberal member for Anglesey, conducting her campaign (as she did subsequent ones) largely in Welsh. Her brother Gwilym was also an MP and the three members of the family sat in the House together. In 1949 Lady Megan became Deputy Leader of the Parliamentary Liberal Party, but became increasingly disenchanted with what she saw as the Party's drift to the right. In 1951 she was defeated in Anglesey by the Labour candidate, Cledwyn Hughes, a great blow after she had represented the constituency for twenty-two years. Between 1952 and 1955 she turned her radicalism to Welsh affairs and became President of the 'Parliament for Wales' campaign, but in 1955 she joined the Labour Party and in 1957 was back in the Commons, this time as Labour member for Carmarthen.

She was never given office, but this was probably as she preferred it. First and foremost she was a radical and fighter for the underdog, and these roles could be fulfilled most adequately from the backbenches. The women MPs of all parties presented her with a book to mark her twenty years in Parliament, the preface of which described her most aptly as 'a true daughter of the Welsh Wizard: she bewitches friend and foe alike'.

E.M.V.

Locke, Anne (*fl.* 1530–90), Protestant exile. Anne Locke was brought up in an evangelical household and by 1552 had married Henry Locke, a London mercer and merchant adventurer, the brother of Rose HICKMAN. From the same period dates her longstanding friendship with John Knox, the Scottish reformer, which was of considerable importance to both. Knox sent Anne his writings and advised her on religious matters, and it was to her, in a letter of December 1556, that he issued his famous invitation to leave Marian England for 'that maist perfyt schoole of Chryste', Geneva. Anne accepted this invitation, arriving in Geneva with her two small children, but without her husband, on 8 May 1557. Her daughter, Anne, died within a few days. There she made a translation of *Some Sermons of John Calvin upon the song that Ezechias made*, which was published in London in 1560 and dedicated to

Lodge, Eleanor

Catherine BERTIE, Dowager Duchess of Suffolk. By mid-June 1559 Anne had returned to England, now ruled by the Protestant Queen Elizabeth. Her relationship with her husband appears to have remained close, despite her absence, for when Henry Locke died in 1571 he left her all his property and made her sole executrix of his will. Their son was the minor Elizabethan poet, Henry Locke.

By 1573 Anne had married Edward Dering, a prominent Puritan divine some ten years her junior, and following his death in 1576 she married (before 1583) her last husband, Richard Prowse, an eminent draper of Exeter and three times mayor of that city. In 1590 she published *Of the markes of the children of God, and of their comfort in affliction*, a translation from the French work by Jean Taffin, which she dedicated to Ann, Countess of Warwick.

Anne Locke is an excellent example of the devout, intelligent women who were so important to the early Protestant Church through their support of its ministers. In particular, the independence shown by her stay in Geneva provides an insight into the relative freedom of women of her class in this period.

See also P. Collinson, 'The role of Women in the English Reformation, illustrated by the life and friendships of Anne Locke' in *Studies in Church History II*, 1965.   J.S.

Lodge, Eleanor (Constance) (1869–1936), historian. The daughter of a businessman, Eleanor Lodge spent a largely unremarkable middle-class childhood in the county of Stafford. She was educated first at home, subsequently in small private schools, and in 1890 went to Lady Margaret Hall, recently founded at Oxford, where she began to cultivate her enthusiasm for history. After graduating she spent a year in Paris studying at the Ecole des Chartes and the Ecole des Hautes Etudes. Returning to Oxford in 1895, she joined the staff of her old college as Librarian. She later became official history tutor and in 1906 was appointed Vice-Principal. During the First World War, before the complete recognition of female membership was finally granted at Oxford, she became the first woman to lecture for the university. In 1921 she left to become Principal of Westfield College, Hampstead, in the University of London, a post she retained until her retirement a decade later.

Eleanor Lodge's year in Paris concentrated her interest on the history of France, especially that of Gascony, and much of her subsequent research was in this field. Her work on villeinage in Gascony appeared in the *English Historical Review* and she wrote in the *Cambridge Medieval History* on the communal movement in France. In her own estimation her best work was that on the *Estates of Saint André of Bordeaux* (1912). Among other publications were a school-book, *The End of the Middle Ages 1273–1453*, 1909, *Gascony under English Rule*, 1926, and *Sully, Colbert and Turgot*, 1931.

Throughout her career Eleanor Lodge was tirelessly active in various administrative capacities and served on a host of committees. At Oxford she sat on the Council of Lady Margaret Hall, was a member of the Delegacy for Women Students, and was later involved in the campaign for degrees for women. In London she sat on the Hampstead Borough Council, became President of the Association of University Women Teachers, and was a Fellow and Vice-President of the Royal Historical Society. She also took a strong interest in elementary education. In 1928 she became the first woman to be admitted by Oxford University to the degree of D Litt, and in 1932 she was made CBE. Eleanor Lodge began her academic life at a time when the doors of universities were still largely closed to women. A reformer rather than a radical, she was nevertheless a firm believer in the benefits of higher education for women, and her career both reflected and assisted the improving position of women in academia.

See also her reminiscences *Terms and Vacations*, ed. J. Spens, 1938; O. Lodge, *Past Years*, 1931.   H.O.

Londonderry, Marchioness of. See VANE-TEMPEST, EDITH HELEN, MARCHIONESS OF LONDONDERRY.

Long, Margaret Gabrielle. See BOWEN, MARJORIE.

Longsword, Ela, Countess of Salisbury (1187–1261), Abbess of Lacock, the only daughter and heiress of William, Earl of Salisbury. At the Earl's death in 1196, Richard I gave Ela and her earldom to his bastard half-brother, William Longsword. The couple had four sons and three daughters. In 1220 they laid the third and fourth stones at the founding of Salisbury Cathedral. On William's death in 1226, Ela did homage for her inheritance, but was required to surrender Salisbury castle, for neither this nor the sheriffdom was regarded as belonging to the family inheritance. The county of Wiltshire was committed to her during the King's pleasure and she held it until 1228 and again from 1231 to 1236.

Although Ela was a great admirer of the Cistercians, Lacock Abbey, which she founded in 1229, adopted the Augustinian rule because of the Cistercian suspicion of nunneries. She secured a grant of confraternity with the Cistercians, however, and dedicated her house jointly to the Virgin and St Bernard. Ela took the veil at Lacock in 1238 and became abbess in 1240, but surrendered her position in 1257 owing to ill-health.

See also D. Baker (ed.) *Medieval Women*, 1978.   K.R.D.

Lonsdale, Dame Kathleen (1903–71), crystallographer. Kathleen Yardley was born in Newbridge, southern Ireland, the youngest in a family of ten. She inherited a passion for information from her father, a self-educated post-office worker, and high moral principles and pacifism from her Scottish mother. She was educated at Newbridge Village School and Downshall Elementary School, London (1908–14), winning a scholarship to the County High School for Girls, Ilford (1914–19). Her physics, chemistry, and higher mathematics were studied at the boys' school in Ilford. At sixteen she won a County Major Scholarship to Bedford College and headed the list for graduating in physics three years later. Among the examiners was W. H. Bragg, who invited her to University College, London (1922) and the Royal Institution (1923) to work with his brilliant young team on X-ray crystallography.

In 1927 she married a fellow scientist, Thomas Jackson Lonsdale, and the couple spent two scientifically valuable years in Leeds before returning to London. In 1935 both joined the Society of Friends, for which Kathleen worked indefatigably and travelled widely. In 1943 she spent a month in Holloway Prison as a conscientious objector and engaged in agitation for penal reform for the rest of her life.

For sixteen years her work at the Royal Institution was supported by grants. In 1946 she was appointed Reader in Crystallography, and Professor of Chemistry and Head of the Department of Crystallography at University College, London, in 1949. A brilliant mathematician and elegant experimenter, she made notable contributions to crystallography. In 1945 she was the first woman elected a Fellow of the Royal Society in Section A (Physical Sciences); she was created DBE in 1956; and received honorary doctorates from many universities. The Royal Society awarded her the Davy Medal (1957) and elected her a Member of the Council and Vice-President (1960–61). She was Vice-President of the International Union of Crystallography (1960–66) and President in 1966. From 1959 to 1964 she was General Secretary of the British Association, President of the Section of Physics in 1967, and its first woman President in 1968. The theme of her presidential address was 'Science and the Good Life', for she was preoccupied with the need for the wise and humane application of science and knowledge.

See also D. M. C. Hodgkin, 'Kathleen Lonsdale' in *Biographical Memoirs of Fellows of the Royal Society*.   R.B.

Lopokova, Lydia Vasilievna, Lady Keynes (1892–1981), ballerina, born at St Petersburg in Russia. Her father was a commissionaire at the Marinsky Theatre, her mother of Scots descent. She studied at the Imperial School of Ballet until the age of sixteen. Lopokova was not the typical classical dancer. She was short and stocky, without the flowing limbs associated with ballerinas, and paid scant attention to her make-up or appearance. Her magic lay in an infectious *joie de vivre*; an ability to make her audience feel happy. Her histrionic talents were nearly as good as her dancing and she later took up acting, although hampered by a strong Russian accent.

Diaghilev invited her to dance the exacting part of *The Firebird* at the Paris Opera in 1910, and she also performed in *Scheherezade* and *Le Festin*. After this triumph she spent some years in America playing in musical comedy and in *The Young Idea* (1914), her first acting role, before rejoining Diaghilev in 1915. A year later she appeared as a puppet for the first performance of *Petrushka*. In 1918 she was at last seen in London, dancing Princess Aurora in *The Sleeping Princess* at the Alhambra (1921). Although this classical part did not suit her, she triumphed nevertheless because of her bewitching personality. In 1919 she was sensational as the can-can dancer in

Loraine, Violet

La Boutique Fantasque, her gaiety and exuberance exactly fitting the role. She was in *Façade* for the Camargo Society (London, 1931).

After the end of her first marriage to Diaghilev's manager, Randolfo Barocchi, she married the economist John Maynard Keynes and thereafter danced only occasionally. She supported her husband when he founded the Arts Theatre in Cambridge in the 1930s, and she acted there in Ibsen's *A Doll's House* and *The Master Builder*. Her remaining performances included a season at the Old Vic (*A Doll's House*) and at the Criterion (*The Master Builder*), but she soon abandoned the stage to devote herself to her ailing husband, accompanying him on all his economic missions abroad until his death in 1946. As a member of the Arts Council, she took up the ballets fostered by them but soon retired altogether from public life.

See also Milo Keynes, *Lydia Lopokova*, 1983.   A.D.

Loraine, Violet (Mary) (1886–1956), musical comedy actress and singer. Violet Loraine, the daughter of a clerk, was born in Kentish Town, London, and educated at Trevelyan House in Brighton. At sixteen she joined the chorus of *Mother Goose* at Drury Lane, and over the next few years played in musical comedy and pantomime, as well as appearing solo on the halls. Already well known, she achieved enormous popularity playing opposite George Robey at the Alhambra in *The Bing Boys Are Here* (1916), 'a picture of London in seven panels' which appealed to wartime audiences. Violet Loraine's numbers, especially 'If you were the only girl in the world' and 'Let the great big world keep turning' became favourites with the armies in France. She appeared in two sequels, *The Bing Girls Are There* (1917) and *The Bing Boys on Broadway* (1918), but married and retired in 1921, still at the height of her fame. She made occasional reappearances, the last in 1945 for an RAF pageant at the Albert Hall.   N.H.

Loudon, Jane (1807–58), writer on horticulture. Born at Ritwell House near Birmingham, Jane Webb began to earn her own living when her father died in 1824. Her first published book, which appeared anonymously, was a novel, *The Mummy, a Tale of the Twenty-Second Century* (1827), and it so impressed the writer and landscape gardener John Loudon that he asked to meet the author. His astonishment on discovering the novelist to be a woman changed to love, and seven months after their meeting they married (1830). It was the popularity of his wife's horticultural writings that rescued John Loudon when he fell into debt over the enormous printing costs of his own *Arboretum*. *Instructions in Gardening for Ladies*, 1840, was succeeded by *The Ladies' Companion to the Flower Garden*, 1841, which achieved nine editions. Other equally useful books followed, including *The Lady's Country Companion or How to Enjoy a Country Life Rationally*, 1845.

In a modest way Jane Loudon was a pioneer of women's emancipation, for through the example of her writings and her own life, thousands of women found freedom and creative joy in gardening. Widowed in 1843, she then received a Civil List pension of £100.

See also M. Hadfield, *Gardening in Britain*, 1960.   P.L.

Loughlin, Dame Anne (1894–1979), trade-union official. She was born in Leeds, one of five children of a footwear operative. Both her parents died by the time she was sixteen and she went to work in a clothing factory to help support the family. She was soon involved in union affairs and became a full-time organizer when she was twenty-one, guiding the famous 1916 strike of clothing workers at Hebden Bridge. Appointed as national women's officer in 1920 at a time of rising unemployment, falling wages, and declining union membership, she fought to rebuild union strength and to combat the notorious 'sweatshop' conditions in the industry. A series of amalgamations in the inter-war years, in which she played a prominent part, resulted in the formation of the National Union of Tailors and Garment Workers, of which she was appointed General Secretary in 1948.

By this time she had been for many years a respected figure in the trade-union movement. Elected to the TUC General Council in 1929, during the 1930s she served on many joint industrial bodies and government committees, as well as on the Royal Commission on Equal Pay. During the Second World War she advised the government on the industrial welfare of women workers and on the wartime organization of the clothing industry. She was created DBE in 1943—the first trade unionist to receive the honour—and in the same year, following her election as Chairman of the TUC in 1942, became the first woman President of the Trades Union Congress.

An energetic speaker and compelling personality, she was one of the leading women trade unionists of her generation. Ill-health forced her early retirement in 1953.

See also S. Lewenhak, *Women and Trade Unions*, 1977.   K.W.

Louise (Caroline Alberta), Princess (1848–1939), the sixth child of Queen Victoria. Princess Louise was born in Buckingham Palace. In 1871 she married the Marquess of Lorne, future Duke of Argyll, and accompanied him to Canada during his governor-generalship; Lake Louise is named after her. By the standards of her milieu, Princess Louise was unusually intellectual and artistic in her tastes, writing magazine articles as 'Myra Fontenoy', entertaining the leading artists of the day, and herself practising as a sculptor. The statue of Queen Victoria at Kensington Palace was carved by her. She patronized a number of deserving causes, most notably the National Union for the Higher Education of Women, of which she was co-founder (1872) and first president.   N.H.

Lovelace, Countess of. See KING, AUGUSTA ADA, COUNTESS OF LOVELACE.

Lowe, Eveline Mary (1869–1956), public figure in London local government. She was born in Rotherhithe, where her father was a Congregational minister, and went to school at Milton Mount College, training as a teacher at Homerton College which at that time was in London. She became a lecturer and then vice-principal of the college, but resigned in 1903 on her marriage to G. C. Lowe, a Bermondsey medical man and active socialist.

Retirement merely meant the beginning of a long career in local government for Eveline Lowe, and she evidently found it completely satisfying, since she never attempted to enter national politics. She was elected to the Bermondsey Board of Guardians, and served the borough faithfully for many years. In 1919 she was co-opted as a member of the LCC's education committee and in 1922 was elected to the LCC as Labour member for West Bermondsey, which she represented until her retirement in 1946. She specialized in educational policy, becoming leader of the opposi-

tion on the education committee and then, when Labour won a majority on the LCC (1934), committee chairman. In 1929 she was elected Deputy Chairman of the LCC itself, and in 1939 became its first ever woman Chairman. Even after her retirement she was co-opted on to the education committee for a further three years. During her career she also sat on a dozen other committees and represented the LCC on the Burnham Committee and various other bodies.   N.H.

Lowndes, Mrs M(arie Adelaide) Belloc (1868–1947), novelist and autobiographer. She was born in London of an English mother (the feminist editor Bessie Rayner PARKES) and a French father who died when she was only four. The writer Hilaire Belloc was her brother, and she herself published as M. A. Belloc before her marriage to the journalist F. S. Lowndes. After a childhood divided between England and France, she became a prolific writer of historical studies and, above all, novels. Many were inspired by criminal mysteries (she also wrote a study of the Lizzie Borden case, 1934), and during her lifetime her best-known book was *The Lodger* (1913), a novel inspired by the Jack the Ripper murders; another novel, *Letty Linton* (1931), has been reprinted (1976). In old age she wrote three charming volumes of family history and autobiography which are perhaps the most likely of her works to survive: *I, Too, Have Lived in Arcadia*, 1941, *Where Love and Friendship Dwelt*, 1943, and *Merry Wives of Westminster*, 1946.   N.H.

Lutyens, (Agnes) Elisabeth (1906–83), composer, daughter of the architect Sir Edwin Lutyens. She was born in London and studied at the Ecole Normale de Musique in Paris and the Royal College of Music, London.

Elisabeth Lutyens made a relatively conventional start as a composer, and she later repudiated many works dating from before about 1940, when she became increasingly devoted to serialism. Though strongly influenced by Webern, she was increasingly successful in evolving a personal idiom; its wide cultural reference—from ancient Egypt to modern philosophy as represented by Wittgenstein—is one of its notable features. At the time, serialism was not popular or even critically respectable in Britain, and a new work by Lutyens often remained unperformed for a decade or more. Recognition came only in the 1960s, culminating in her appointment as CBE in 1969.

Elisabeth Lutyens composed film and radio scores, much instrumental and choral music, and a number of operas including *The Pit*, 1972, *Time Off?—Not a Ghost of a Chance!*, 1968, and *Isis and Osiris*, 1970. She published an autobiography, *A Goldfish Bowl*, 1972.

N.H.

Lyall, Edna. See BAYLY, ELLEN ADA.

Lytton, Lady Constance (1869–1923), suffragette. Daughter of the first Earl of Lytton, she was born in Vienna and spent most of her childhood and youth abroad, being educated privately. In 1908, aged thirty-nine, she joined the campaign for women's suffrage. The first of four arrests occurred in 1909, and she was sent to Holloway. In October that year she was arrested in Newcastle, and sentenced to four weeks' imprisonment. Having undergone a fifty-six-hour hunger strike, she was released without being forcibly fed because of a heart condition discovered by the prison doctor. The Home Secretary (Herbert Gladstone)

announced in the Commons that she had a 'serious heart disease' and that no preferential treatment had been accorded because of her rank. To prove the hypocrisy of this statement, Lady Constance cut short her hair, donned glasses, and posed as a working-class woman, Jane Warton. She was arrested while protesting outside Walton Jail in Liverpool and sentenced to fourteen days' hard labour. After four days on hunger strike she was forcibly fed; she had not been medically examined. She was released after eight days because of weakness and loss of weight, but not because of her heart condition. Lady Constance was now seriously ill. Her brother Lord Lytton took up her cause and wrote to *The Times* on 30 March 1910, pointing out the difference between the treatment of Lady Constance the aristocrat, and that of Jane Warton the working woman. He demanded a public enquiry which the Home Office refused.

Lady Constance wrote a pamphlet, *No Votes for Women* (1909), and a book, *Prisons and Prisoners, some Personal Experiences by Constance Lytton and Jane Warton* (1914).

A.D.

M

Macarthur, Mary (1880–1921), trade unionist. The daughter of a Glasgow draper, she was educated at the Girls' High School, Glasgow. In 1896 she went to Germany for a year, from which she returned with a good working knowledge of French and German, but with the problem of her career unresolved. While helping in her father's shop, she went to a meeting of shop assistants in a local school and heard John Turner, the organizer of the shop assistants' union. This was her introduction to trade unionism and, although the 'boss's daughter', she later joined the union and became secretary of the Ayr branch. In 1902 she was made president of the Scottish council of the union, and at the Scottish annual conference met Margaret BONDFIELD. Through the union she also met Will Anderson, who became her husband. Her increasing interest in trade unionism led to disagreements with her father, and in 1903 she left Ayr for London, where from Margaret Bondfield's flat in Gower Street she started her life's work as Secretary of the Women's Trade Union League.

Throughout those early years, she saw not only the extent of sweated labour among women working in factories and shops, but the even more desperate conditions among women out-workers and their children, labouring long hours at home. She was instrumental in forming the Anti-Sweating League, and in demanding that trade boards be set up, with power to fix minimum wages. In 1910 the Wages Board Act dealt with the shocking conditions that Mary had uncovered, for instance, among women chain-makers at Cradley Heath and women lace-workers at Nottingham. Probably her hardest campaign, however, was for the thousands of women who worked in munitions factories during the First World War. In this fight she came into contact with ministers, departments, trade unions, government leaders, and with Queen Mary. The size of the problem she faced is shown by the fact that in 1914 there were 350,000 women members of trade unions, but by 1918 the number had risen to 1,960,000. By the time the war ended, Mary Macarthur's name was not only known throughout Britain but also in allied nations, especially the United States. Both she and her husband were defeated in the 1918 general election. Will Anderson died in the influenza epidemic of 1919, two years before her own death.

See also M. A. Hamilton, *Mary Macarthur, A Biographical Sketch*, L. Middleton (ed.), *Women in the Labour Movement*, 1977.

L.M.

Macaulay, Catherine (1731–91), historian and polemicist, the second child of Elizabeth, a London banker's daughter, and John Sawbridge of Olantigh, Wye, Kent. Catherine received a private education and from her lessons in Roman history became inspired by libertarian and republican ideals. In 1763, she published the first of her eight-volume *History of England from the Reign of James I to that of the Brunswick Line*, in which she championed the republican cause and praised the Long Parliament as the greatest monument of human virtue. Completed by 1783, Catherine's *History* was important for helping to sustain the tradition of radical Whiggism, which, dating from Cromwell's Commonwealth, had been severely undermined by David Hume's elegantly and persuasively written defence of Charles I in the 1750s. Although Hume's *History of England* remained unchallenged for literary genius, Catherine's volumes sold well and were translated into French between 1791 and 1792, probably at Mirabeau's instigation.

Catherine also wrote many pamphlets, including *Loose Remarks on certain Positions to be found in Mr Hobbes' Philosophical Rudiments of Government and Society* (1767), a *Reply to Burke's Pamphlet entitled 'Thoughts on the Causes of the Present Discontents'* (1770), and a *Modest Plea for the Property of Copyright* (1774). A keen supporter of the notion of liberty, Catherine delighted in the American and French Revolutions. In 1775 she wrote an *Address to the People of England, Scotland and Ireland on the present, important Crisis of Affairs*, in which she attacked the British government for its Quebec Act and taxation of America. In 1790 she published *Observations on the Reflections of the Rt Hon Edmund Burke on the Revolution in France in a letter to the Earl of Stanhope*. She also wrote *Letters on Education with Observations on Religious and Metaphysical Subjects* (1790) in which she advocated the same sports and studies for boys and girls, believing that women's privation lay in a lack of education and the inability to make themselves more than simply pleasing in appearance to men. She had nothing against dress, however. Her own was striking and bold and provoked critical comments from John Wilkes and Samuel Johnson.

In 1760 Catherine married George Macaulay, a Scots physician of Brownlow Street Lying-in Hospital, London, who died in 1766. In 1774 she moved to Bath, where she was especially admired by Dr Thomas Wilson, the non-resident rector of St Stephen's Walbrook. In 1778, however, she lost many friends when she married William Graham, brother of a quack doctor and twenty-six years her junior. She left Bath to visit France, where her admirers included Benjamin Franklin, Turgot and Madame Roland. In 1784 she visited North America and was the guest of George Washington for ten days at Mount Vernon in 1785. She died at Binfield, Berkshire, in 1791, something of an international figure, admired by Madame Roland and Mary WOLLSTONECRAFT for her judgement, energy, and abilities, and by Horace Walpole for her *History of England*.

See also D. L. Hobman, 'Mrs Macaulay. Historian and Controversialist' in *Fortnightly*, Vol. 171, 1952. A.M.N.

Macaulay, Rose (Dame Emilie Rose) (1881–1958), novelist and travel-writer. The daughter of a lecturer in English literature at Cambridge, she lived for a time in Italy as a child but went to school and university in Oxford (Somerville College.) Here she began to write, and her first novel, *Abbots Verney*, was published in 1906. She never married and devoted the rest of her life to writing and travelling. A great admirer of Virginia WOOLF, Rose Macaulay's novels are distinguished by their elegance of style and their detached, caustic wit. Some critics have seen her work as superficial, and at times she herself denied any serious intentions as a writer, but there is a strong satirical vein in her work, particularly in *Potterism* (1920), a fierce attack on the Victorian nuclear family. Other critics have labelled her work as feminist, but while her novels may be regarded as sharing with those of other women writers certain modes of awareness and preoccupations, they are not radically critical. Indeed, *The Towers of Trebizond* (1956), through the stylistically innovatory device of abandoning masculine and feminine pronouns, attempts to deny the existence of any significant difference between the situations of its hero and heroine. Her other works include *Told by an Idiot*, 1923; *Staying with Relations*, 1930; and *The World my Wilderness*, 1950.

See also C. Babington Smith, *Rose Macaulay*, 1972; A. R. Benson, *Rose Macaulay*, 1969; W. C. Frierson, *The English Novel in Transition*, 1965. J.M.

McCarthy, Dame Emma Maud (1859–1949), army nurse. Born in Sydney, the daughter of William McCarthy, a solicitor, she grew up and was educated in Australia. She travelled to England and in 1891, after a three-year visit, decided to stay and take up nursing, training at the London Hospital. Nursing was a logical choice for a girl imbued with a strong sense of philanthropy and a medical family tradition. By 1899 she had achieved sufficient standing to be among the six volunteers chosen to form the Princess of Wales's own nursing sisters' service in South Africa. Her experiences during the Boer War were a major factor in her subsequent career, for she never returned to civilian nursing. Instead, on her return to England in 1902 she was instrumental in forming the Queen Alexandra's Imperial Military Nursing Service (Queen Alexandra's Royal Army Nursing Corps), her service as matron revealing her exceptional administrative talents, as well as her nursing ability.

In 1910 Emma McCarthy became Principal Matron at the War Office. On the outbreak of war in 1914 she went immediately to France, and in 1915 was made Matron-in-Chief of the British forces there. She retained this post to the end of the war, coping ably with the vast increase in numbers of nurses and hospitals. After the war, in 1920, she became Matron-in-Chief of the Territorial Army Service, retiring from active nursing in 1925, although maintaining her interest in the profession's progress. She had played a major role in establishing a permanent military nursing service, and in advancing nursing generally. Among the many awards she received were the GBE (1918) and the Florence Nightingale medal (1919).

See also G. W. Macpherson, *History of the Great War: Medical Services, General History*, vol. vii, 1923. J.R.

McCarthy, Lillah (1875–1960), actress. Born at Cheltenham, her first amateur stage appearance was in 1895 with A. E. Drinkwater's company as Lady Macbeth. Her performance was reviewed encouragingly by George Bernard Shaw in *The Saturday Review*, and as a result Lillah McCarthy visited the playwright. They became great friends and he advised her to gain professional experience. Having studied elocution with Herman Vezin and voice production with Emil Behnke, she then joined Ben Greet, touring with his company and then with Wilson Barrett until 1904. In 1905 she took over the part of Nora for Shaw in a revival of *John Bull's Other Island* at the Court Theatre, where she went on to make her reputation by creating the part of Ann Whitefield in Shaw's *Man and Superman*. A year later she married the Court's director, Granville-Barker. She made a great contribution to the English theatre, her striking appearance helping to create many Shavian heroines, including Ann Whitefield (in the first performance of *Man and Superman*), Mrs Dubedat, and Lavinia. She also played Hermione, Helena and Viola in her husband's Shakespearian productions. Overseas tours included America, New Zealand, Australia, and South Africa.

In 1911 she took over management of the Little Theatre, producing *The Master Builder* and playing Hilda Wangel. She became manager of the Kingsway in 1912, and later of the Savoy, playing Jocasta in *Oedipus Rex* and the title role in *Iphigenia of Taurus*. In 1914–15 she went to New York. Divorced from Granville-Barker in 1918, Lillah continued to work. She again took the Kingsway, producing Arnold Bennett's *Judith* and Eden Phillpotts' *St George and the Dragon*. She played in *The Wandering Jew* and *Blood and Sand* with Matheson Lang and, in 1932, toured South America to speak English verse. After her marriage to Sir Frederick Keeble she lived in Oxford in semi-retirement. In December 1932 she made a final London appearance in *Iphigenia* and in 1935 appeared at the Oxford Playhouse in *Boadicea*. Among her publications were an autobiography, *My Life* (1930), and memoirs, *Myself and My Friends* (1933).

A.D.

MacDonald, Flora (1722–90), heroine of the Jacobite rebellion of 1745. Born and brought up in the Hebrides, she was the daughter of Ranald MacDonald, a gentleman farmer of South Uist, and his second wife Marion. During Prince Charles Edward Stuart's flight after his defeat at Culloden in 1746, his companion, Colonel O'Neill, asked Flora for help. Although apprehensive, she agreed to row the Prince, disguised as a spinning maid, from Long Island to Skye. Her deed was discovered and she was imprisoned in the Tower of London until released under a general amnesty in 1747.

In 1750 Flora married Alan MacDonald of Kingsburgh and later they migrated to North Carolina, as did many Highlanders. During the American War of Independence, Flora and her husband supported the Crown, for which he fought while she rallied the support of her countrymen. In 1779 she returned to Scotland and died in Kingsburgh in 1790. Although acclaimed a heroine by Jacobites, her part in their cause was overrated; her main contribution was to help save their defeated leader, which she did more from personal sympathy than from political disposition. Ultimately, she came to see that Scotland's best interests lay in peace with the Hanoverians.

See also E. G. Vining, *Flora MacDonald. Her Life in the Highlands and America*, 1967.

A.M.N.

MacDonald, Margaret (Ethel) (1870–1911), pioneer in the Labour movement. She was the daughter of John Hall Gladstone, FRS, and his second wife, Margaret, who died three weeks after the baby was born. The sense of Christian service which inspired the home, mingled with her father's devotion to science, fostered in Margaret a desire to serve those around her, as well as a love of accuracy and interest in statistics. She was educated mostly privately and at Doreck College, afterwards attending classes on a wide variety of subjects at the Women's Department of King's College, London.

As a young woman, she tried to use her energy, ability, and income to help those in need, all the while learning what was needed to bring about the ideal society she believed to be implicit in a true understanding of the Christian faith. Politically, she started as a Liberal and an ardent supporter of Mr Gladstone, but the experience of her social work, work on school boards, her reading, and the views she discussed with her friends, together with the poverty and suffering which she saw around her, led her to become a member of the Independent Labour Party. In 1895 she met her future husband, James Ramsay Mac-Donald, having sent him a subscription to his election fight that year in Southampton. They married a year later. At their home in Lincoln's Inn Fields six children were born, but Margaret, despite family responsibilities, found time for the kind of social work she had undertaken when single. Additionally she toured abroad with her husband, and shared his interests and his campaigns while continuing to concentrate her work on the welfare of women and children.

In 1900 the Labour Representation Committee, later the Labour Party, was founded, and Ramsay MacDonald was its first Secretary. All its early secretarial work and many of its committees and social gatherings took place at 3 Lincoln's Inn Fields. In 1905, a letter was sent to the Party from the Railway Women's Guild, pleading for a chance for working women to understand Labour politics. Mr MacDonald and his assistant, J. S. Middleton, decided to ask their wives for help. As a result, the Women's Labour League was formed in 1906, with Margaret MacDonald as its Chairman and Mary Middleton as Secretary. Together they brought into being a political organization of women which has never been surpassed in Britain. In 1911 first Mary Middleton and then Margaret MacDonald died. A clinic for children in Kensington became a memorial to them both.

See also L. Herbert, *Mrs Ramsay MacDonald*, 1924; I. M. Holmes, *The Girlhood of Margaret Ethel MacDonald*, 1938; J. R. MacDonald, *Margaret Ethel MacDonald*, 1912; L. Middleton (ed.), *Women in the Labour Movement*, 1977.　　　　L.M.

MacDuff, Isabel, Countess of Buchan (c. 1285–after 1313), supporter of Robert Bruce. Isabel was the daughter of Duncan, Earl of Fife, and married John Comyn, Earl of Buchan. A near kinsman of her husband's was another John Comyn, one of Robert Bruce's rivals for the throne of Scotland. The hereditary right to crown the Scottish kings belonged to the earls of Fife. In 1306 the Earl of Fife, who was Isabel's brother, was a prisoner of the English. Desire to exercise the family right overcame marital loyalty and Isabel stole her husband's horses to ride to Scone and place the circlet of gold on Bruce's head. A few months

later when Edward I's army overran southern Scotland, his vengeance on Bruce's family and adherents did not spare women. Isabel was captured and held in a cage in one of the towers of Berwick castle where she could be gazed on by passers-by. Bruce's sister Mary suffered a like fate at Roxburgh. Isabel was treated like a beast in a menagerie for four years until in June 1310 she was removed to Berwick's Carmelite convent. In 1313 she was released into the custody of Sir Henry Beaumont. Her husband meanwhile had been defeated by Bruce and had retired to England, his estates forfeit. There were no children of the marriage and it is not known when Isabel died.

See also G. W. S. Barrow, *Robert Bruce*, 1976.　　　　A.C.

McFall, Frances Elizabeth. See GRAND, SARAH.

Mackay, Mary. See CORELLI, MARIE.

Mackintosh, Elizabeth. See TEY, JOSEPHINE.

Macklin, Maria (1732–81), actress. The illegitimate daughter of the actor Charles Macklin, Maria was educated for the stage. Her father ensured her accomplishment in music and languages, but his autocratic behaviour finally alienated her from him. Although no beauty, she had an elegant figure and musical talents which were suited to 'breeches' parts. Her most famous role was as Portia to her father's Shylock, but her self-consciousness and coldness on stage limited her popularity. She led a piously austere and celibate life, dying before her father and still estranged from him.

See also W. Appleton, *Charles Macklin*, 1961.　　　　C.H.

M'Lehose, Agnes (1759–1841), sometime muse of the poet Robert Burns. She was the daughter of a Glasgow surgeon, and at seventeen married a law agent, James M'Lehose, who eventually separated from her and left for the West Indies. After the death of her father, she and her four children lived in Edinburgh on a small annuity.

In December 1787 Mrs M'Lehose met Burns and invited him to tea; but he injured his knee and was confined to his room, so the couple began a correspondence. Even after meeting they continued to write to each other with some ardour, he as 'Sylvander', she as 'Clarinda'; her religious scruples and situation as an abandoned wife almost certainly prevented the relationship from developing beyond the epistolary. Burns left Edinburgh in February 1788, and 'Clarinda' was alienated by the discovery of his more down-to-earth love affairs and common-law marriage. However, there was a reconciliation and final meeting in December 1791, shortly before Mrs M'Lehose sailed for Jamaica in an unsuccessful attempt to mend her marriage. Burns commemorated the event with the touching 'Ae fond kiss, and then we sever'.   N.H.

Macmillan, Chrystal (1882–1937), barrister. Born in Edinburgh, she was educated at St Leonard's School, St Andrews, Edinburgh University, and Berlin. One of Edinburgh's first women graduates, she was called to the Bar in 1924, having begun legal work some years earlier. She was the first woman to plead before the House of Lords when in 1908 she advocated the Scottish women graduates' claim to the vote, and she appeared before numerous committees of enquiry on matters of concern to women, including those on street offences and unemployment insurance. Her life was devoted to feminist causes, for which she worked nationally and internationally, especially for those of women's suffrage, women's wages and status in industry, and women's equality of citizenship. On the last issue she was involved in trying to alter the law which forced a woman to lose her citizenship if she married a foreigner. Chrystal Macmillan was secretary of the International Women Suffrage Alliance (1913–20); joint initiator and secretary of the Hague International Women's Congress, and delegated by it to the Paris Peace Conference in 1919; and a founder member of the Open Door Council, aiming to remove legal restrictions applying only to women and to bring about the economic emancipation of the woman worker. In 1914, on the day after the fall of Antwerp, she organized the dispatch of the first food sent from Britain to Belgian refugees in Holland, and in 1935 she stood unsuccessfully for North Edinburgh as a Liberal in the parliamentary election.   B.H.C.

McMillan, Margaret (1860–1931), educationist. Born in New York of Scottish parents, she went to Scotland at the age of five with her mother and sister Rachel McMILLAN after the death of her father. She was educated in Inverness and travelled in Europe before going to London in 1883 as a governess and lady's companion. In 1893 a deputation from Bradford, impressed by her work in the London socialist movement, invited her to participate in the newly-founded Independent Labour Party. She accepted this offer, and the following year also became a member of Bradford School Board.

One of her main aims at this time was to force the government to admit its responsibility for the health of schoolchildren, and in Bradford she took part in the first medical inspection of schoolchildren under government auspices.

In 1902 she returned to London and six years later, after successfully campaigning for government expenditure on child health care, opened the first school clinic in London at Bow. Financial support for the venture came jointly from Joseph Fels, a wealthy American businessman, and a local authority grant. In 1910 a larger, more successful, health centre was founded at Deptford, followed by a camp school for needy girls and then boys. An elementary day school was later opened, without local authority support, and in 1913, when joined by her sister Rachel on a full-time basis, a larger garden nursery for slum children was built. From 1919 to 1922 she was a Labour member of the London County Council, and in the following year was elected President of The Nursery Schools Association. In 1917 she was appointed CBE, the award of CH being bestowed thirteen years later. The culmination of her many achievements was the opening in 1930 of the Rachel McMillan Training College for nurses and teachers, in memory of the sister who had been her spiritual guide and constant source of inspiration.

Margaret McMillan was able successfully to harness her idealism to the practicalities of running nurseries, schools, and clinics for the children of the poor. By her continued emphasis on the duty of the state to the schoolchild she was instrumental in bringing about compulsory medical inspection and treatment of schoolchildren. She was a woman of remarkable vision who, despite her support of the suffragette movement and lifelong devotion to the Labour Party, ultimately dedicated her life to the children of Deptford and in so doing influenced education throughout the country. Among her written works were *Education through the Imagination* (1904) and *The Life of Rachel McMillan* (1927).

See also P. B. Ballard, *Margaret McMillan. An appreciation*, 1937; A. Mansbridge, *Margaret McMillan, Prophet and Pioneer*, 1932.

J.G.S.

McMillan, Rachel (1859–1917), educationist. Born in New York, Rachel McMillan was brought up at Inverness in Scotland and, after attending Inverness High School and a Midlands boarding school, spent eleven years there nursing her grandmother. Towards the end of this period she was deeply influenced by the writing of W. T. Stead, as well as by contemporary socialist thinkers in Edinburgh, and determined to devote her life to the alleviation of human suffering. She thus joined her sister Margaret McMILLAN in London, taking employment in a working girls' hostel in Bloomsbury and quickly becoming part of the London socialist movement. After a brief spell in Bradford, she trained as a sanitary inspectress and took a post in Kent as a travelling teacher of hygiene. In the following years she saw much of the poverty of south-east London but, until joined in 1902 by Margaret, her schemes for helping the children of the slums remained untried.

Before 1913, when she resigned her teaching post, she had helped with her sister's work in education but had become increasingly convinced that more should be done for children of pre-school age. She envisaged a nursery where such children could be given facilities lacking at home, and planned a large, bright garden with shelters instead of rooms, and hot water for bathing. This notion was contrary to the accepted ideas on pre-school education, but in 1913 the Rachel McMillan Open Air Nursery School was established. According to one government inspector, the devotion of its founder caused it subsequently to become 'the largest and most important in England'. As a memorial to Rachel's vision and determination, Margaret, who had always regarded her sister as the true originator of all their ideas, established the Rachel McMillan Training College in 1930.

Rachel McMillan had been a strong supporter of socialism and votes for women from girlhood, although seldom actively participating. Instead she saw as her goal the need to help the neglected children of the slums. In so doing, she introduced important new ideas

into pre-school education, founding a modern nursery school five years before such institutions were officially recognized in the 1919 Fisher Act.

See also P. B. Ballard, *Margaret McMillan. An appreciation*, 1937; M. McMillan, *The Life of Rachel McMillan*, 1927.

J.G.S.

Macpherson, Annie (1824?–1904), philanthropist who pioneered child emigration to Canada. Born in Campsie by Milton, Stirlingshire, she was the oldest of three sisters. On completing her education in Glasgow, she decided to follow her father into the teaching profession but at the age of nineteen experienced 'a divine revelation' after which the love of God became the ruling force of her life. Following a brief spell in Cambridgeshire, where she undertook evangelical work, she moved to London with her mother. Appalled by the misery and deprivation she found, she immediately began mission work in the East End. She was particularly moved by the child slavery of the matchbox industry and resolved to devote her life to these children. With donations collected chiefly through *The Revival* paper, in 1870 she procured a large workshop which she turned into the 'Home of Industry', where such children could work while receiving education and nourishment. Annie Macpherson was firmly convinced, however, that the real solution for these children lay in emigration to a country of opportunity. An emigration fund was duly started and in the first year, 500 children, trained in the London homes, were dispatched to Canada. This was the start of a massive operation which sought to find homes and careers for 14,000 of Britain's needy children. Annie Macpherson herself made the voyage across the Atlantic over 120 times. Initially one distribution centre was opened in Ontario but this was soon followed by other regional centres. An important section of the operation was founded in Liverpool by Annie's sister, Louisa Birt, and a number of other philanthropic societies, which recognized the benefits of emigration, made use of this network. The scheme received wide acclaim and was much copied abroad.

As well as her work on emigration, Annie Macpherson sought to help the poor in many other ways, and a number of missions, for example a Bible Flower Mission and a Prison Mission, had their origins in the Home of Industry. She was a far-sighted woman whose unwavering faith enabled her to realize an idea which she believed would give opportunities to those born with none. In so doing she inspired others to follow where she had led; a philanthropist with wide-ranging interests, she is above all renowned as the 'Children's Home Finder'. Her works included *Canadian Homes for London Wanderers* (1870) and *The Little Matchbox Makers* (1870).

See also L. M. Birt, *The Children's Home Finder*, 1913.   J.G.S.

Macpherson Mackay, Helen Marion (1891–1965), physician. Her father was in the Indian civil service and her mother the daughter of an army officer. After an early childhood spent in Burma, she was educated at Cheltenham Ladies' College and the London School of Medicine for Women (later the Royal Free Hospital). She held appointments in London and then from 1919 to 1922 worked in Vienna as a Beit Memorial Fellow, studying nutritional deficiencies produced as a result of the Allied blockade. This gave her a lifelong interest in the dietetic problems of children, the treatment of which was transformed by her research.

She became a member of the Medical Research Council and part-time consultant paediatrician to the London County Council, but although she attended the necessary committees, her interests were not in medical politics. Her interventions were not always pleasing to administrators and politicians, but were based on facts and practicability. This, combined with her obviously sincere and unselfish concern for patients' welfare, often converted opponents.

She was awarded an Ernest Hart Memorial Scholarship (1925–27) and was the first woman elected to a Fellowship of the Royal College of Physicians of London (1934). Elected President of the Section of Paediatrics of the Royal Society of Medicine in 1944, in the following year she became the first woman member of the British Paediatric Association. She demanded and received the highest possible standard of work, as well as the affection and awe of her assistants.

See also R. R. Trail (ed.) *Lives of the Fellows of the Royal College of Physicians of London*.   R.B.

Maitland, Agnes Catherine (1850–1906), writer and educationist, born near Hyde Park in London. Her father settled in Liverpool as a merchant when she was five and she was educated there, at home. From 1880 to 1885 she studied cookery at the Domestic Science Training School in Liverpool and became a recognized authority on domestic economy. She wrote several cookery books, such as *The Afternoon Tea Book* (1887), *What Shall we Have for Breakfast?* (1889) and *The Rudiments of Cookery: a Manual for use in Schools and Homes*. She also wrote novels for young girls, all of an educationally informative nature.

Having taken a keen interest in the higher education of women, in 1889 she became principal of Somerville Hall, Oxford, where she proved a talented administrator, developing the tutorial system with a view to making Somerville a genuine college and not just a hall of residence. To that end she urged students to take the full degree courses. Although autocratic, she took a strongly liberal view in politics and, despite her early Presbyterian background, preserved the college's undenominational atmosphere. Somerville was incorporated as a college in 1881. To her it owes the college library, which received the collection of John Stuart Mill.   B.H.C.

Makin, Bathsua (fl. 1641–73), feminist and educationist. She was the daughter of John Pell, rector of Southwick, Sussex, whose death in 1616 was followed by that of his wife a year later, leaving three remarkable children: Thomas, a Gentleman of the Bedchamber to Charles I; John, an eminent linguist and mathematician; and Bathsua, who was proficient in science and mathematics, as well as ancient and modern languages, and acquired an early reputation for her learning. About 1641 she was appointed tutor to Charles I's children and was apparently at liberty to follow her own ideas concerning the education of women with her star pupil, the Princess Elizabeth, who, by the time she was nine, was proficient in Greek, Latin, Hebrew, French, Italian, Spanish, and mathematics. Bathsua had a number of other distinguished female pupils, and even before the death of the Princess in 1650 may have been in charge of a school for gentlewomen in Putney.

Her remarkable *Essay to Revive the Antient Education of Gentlewomen* was issued in 1673 with a prospectus for the new school she had recently established at Tottenham High Cross. Half of her pupils' time was devoted to the subjects ordinarily taught in other schools for girls: religion, dancing, music, writing, and accountancy. The other half of the curriculum consisted of rudimentary Latin and French and a general study of such topics as natural history, astronomy, geography, history, and arithmetic. Domestic science was rather oddly bound up with a course in art, and optional subjects included Greek, Hebrew, Italian, Spanish, and experimental philosophy. The elective principle was paramount, and students were allowed to take 'more or few' courses as they wished. The basic tuition was £20 per annum with additional fees for advanced instruction in languages and other optional courses. That Bathsua anticipated opposition to this novel scheme for educating girls in the arts and sciences is shown by the famous *Essay* which accompanied the prospectus. In it she first produced a long list of famous women who had been pre-eminent for their academic attainments, so demonstrating that women were capable of becoming successful scholars. She further argued that those women who possessed the necessary ability, wealth, and leisure to undertake such studies ought to be given the opportunity to pursue them. Finally, after meeting the standard objections to a serious education for women, she indicated the advantages that such an education would bring to them and their families and the pleasure they would derive from improving their minds.

Bathsua was one of the earliest and most significant feminists and educationists of the seventeenth century, outstanding in her combination of theory and practice. Her own reputation for prodigious scholastic achievement, the prestige she had acquired at court, her courage, and originality made her an authoritative figure in the field of women's education. Her school at Tottenham introduced a new conception of the learning which women could achieve. Her proposals for a liberal education for women form the earliest known attempt to organize a systematic scheme of serious study for girls, and were based on the important and novel assumption of the value of an education in the arts and sciences for women as well as men.

No records have yet emerged concerning Mrs Makin's marriage, but a letter from 1668 indicates that she had a son. She also wrote

The Malady and . . . Remedy of Vexations and Unjust Arrests and Action (1646).

See also M. R. Mahl and H. Koon (eds), *The Female Spectator, English Women Writers before 1800*, 1977; M. Reynolds, *The Learned Lady in England, 1650–1760*, 1920.

T.J.M.

Malet, Lucas, pseudonym of Mary St Leger Harrison (1852–1931), novelist. Mary Harrison was the youngest daughter of the novelist Charles Kingsley, and was born at his rectory at Eversley in Hampshire. She studied at the Slade School, but gave up any idea of an artistic career on her marriage to the Rev. William Harrison, from whom she was eventually separated. All her novels were written under the pen-name 'Lucas Malet', who first came to notice with *Colonel Enderby's Wife* (1885), *The Wages of Sin* (1891). and *The History of Sir Richard Calmedy* (1901). These novels, rhapsodic and unreal to modern eyes, were considered quite daring, and indeed Mary Harrison revised some parts of them after converting to Roman Catholicism in 1902.

N.H.

Manley, Mary de la Rivière (?1667/1672–1724), journalist, playwright, and author of scandal chronicles. She was the daughter of the Royalist Sir Roger Manley, who was Lieutenant-General of Jersey at the time of her birth. The family settled after 1680 at Landguard Fort in Suffolk. Roger Manley died shortly after the 1688 revolution, leaving two of his daughters in the care of their cousin John Manley, who entered into a bigamous marriage with Mary which produced a son. She then became a companion to the Duchess of Cleveland (1693–94) and after a two-year residence in the country returned to London to see two of her plays produced. She was mistress to John Tilley, Warden of the Fleet Prison, from 1696 to 1702, when she left for Bristol, returning again to London in 1704. In 1706 her best tragedy, *Almyna*, opened at the Haymarket.

The first of her great *romans à clef*, *The Secret History of Queen Zarah and the Zarazians*, had been published in 1705. In *The New Atalantis* (1709), *Memoirs of Europe* (1710), and the autobiographical *Adventures of Rivella* (1714), she refined the genre (novels about real people under disguised names), merging political scandal and erotic fantasy in disjointed narratives critical of the Whigs. The ascendancy of the Tory Harley ministry (1710–14), provided a welcome measure of protection after her arrest for the libellous *New Atalantis*. Like Swift she was engaged during this period in writing Tory propaganda both in novels and as editor of the journal *The Examiner*. The defeat of the Tories ended her political writing and she turned to less polemical forms, writing a tragedy, *Lucius* (1717), and *The Power of Love* (1720).

Mary Manley's popularization of the *chronique scandaleuse*, established as a distinct genre in seventeenth-century France, set the pattern for her successor in the tradition, Eliza HAYWOOD. Underlying the two characterizations of women in her works—the sexually voracious virago and the passive victim—is the recognition that such roles are a function of the male hegemony. Despite this model's crudeness, Mary Manley's insight into the female psyche proved valuable to future generations of authors.

See also P. B. Anderson, 'Mistress De La Rivière Manley's Biography' in *Modern Philology* 33, 1936; and *The Novels of Mary De La Rivière Manley*, facsimile edition, 1971.

A.L.

Mann, Cathleen Sabine (1896–1959), painter. She was born in Newcastle upon Tyne, daughter of the Scottish portraitist Harrington Mann, and was taught by her father and Dame Ethel Walker. She also studied at the Slade School and in Paris. During the First World War she served with an ambulance unit, and during the Second was an official war artist, working chiefly on portraits. She married the eleventh Marquess of Queensberry in 1926 and in 1946, following her divorce, J. R. Follett. His death in 1953 caused a nervous breakdown, although the same period also saw a revival of her painting. Indeed, some of her best work, including child studies and landscapes, was produced in her last ten years, when she also tried abstract painting and sculpture. A study of some boys by the Serpentine, completed within days of her death, is among her best work. She had limitless energy, but also suffered bouts of nervous exhaustion and during one of these she committed suicide. Much of her work is in private ownership. B.H.C.

Manning, Olivia (1915?–1980), novelist. The daughter of a commander in the Royal Navy,

she was born in Portsmouth but spent much of her early life in Ireland. Just before the Second World War she married R. D. Smith, then a British Council lecturer, and they lived for a while in Bucharest where he was teaching. Her experiences and observations of this period form the basis of her later work *The Balkan Trilogy*.

In 1942 they were both evacuated to Cairo, where she was Press Officer to the United States embassy, and then to Jerusalem where they spent the rest of the war, she as information officer of the British Council and he as the head of the Palestine broadcasting station; these events provided the background for *The Levant Trilogy*. They returned to London in 1946 where she worked as a freelance journalist and book reviewer.

Although her first novel, *The Wind Changes* (1938), was published just before the war it was *The Balkan Trilogy* (*The Great Fortune*, 1960, *The Spoilt City*, 1962, and *Friends and Heroes*, 1965) which brought her widespread critical recognition. The range and accuracy of her characterization and the 'objectivity, restraint, and proportion' of her observations received particular praise. She was described by Anthony Burgess as 'the most considerable of our women novelists'. By contrast, a later novel, *The Play Room* (1969), is a macabre study of the growing awareness of sex and violence in the lives of two adolescent girls. Before her death she completed work on *The Levant Trilogy*, which continues the story of the earlier trilogy; it consists of *The Danger Tree* (1977), *The Battle Won and Lost* (1979), and *The Sum of Things* (1980). Olivia Manning was awarded the CBE in 1976. J.M.

Mansfield, Katherine (1888–1923), writer of short stories. Kathleen Mansfield Beauchamp was born in Wellington, New Zealand, one of five children of a successful businessman and banker. From 1893 to 1898 the family lived in Karori, some way outside Wellington, but they returned to the city where Kathleen went to a day school until 1903. In this year the whole family sailed to London, and for the next four years, Kathleen and her two sisters attended Queen's College in London, the first institution to have been formed for the higher education of women. Here she wrote her first stories under the name 'Katherine Mansfield' and met Ida Baker, who was to be her lifelong friend and companion. The years 1907 to 1908 were spent at her old school in Wellington; then Katherine Mansfield returned to London alone, determined to become a writer. For the next three years she led a tumultuous life. She had a number of love affairs; married a singing teacher in 1909 but left him after only one day; became pregnant by another man but lost the baby. Her miscarriage occurred in Bavaria, where she wrote a series of sketches published over two years in the periodical *The New Age*. These stories were collected in 1911 under the title *In a German Pension*, which was a considerable success.

At the end of 1911 she met John Middleton Murry, an undergraduate editing a literary magazine called *Rhythm*. In 1912 he left Oxford to live with her in London, and she became joint editor of the magazine, which changed its name to *The Blue Review* in 1913. In the years that followed they often lived apart, partly because of her deteriorating health, which obliged her to spend long periods in France, Italy, and Switzerland. In 1917 it was confirmed that she had tuberculosis. In 1918 she obtained a divorce, and married Murry. Her second collection of stories, *Bliss*, was published in 1920 and contained 'Prelude', a vivid observation of a New Zealand childhood. Planned as the prelude to a novel, the story is considered her best. From 1919 to 1920, she was also regularly reviewing new books for *The Athenaeum*, of which Murry was editor. Her collected reviews, all except one, were published after her death under the title *Novels and Novelists* (1930). *The Garden Party* appeared in 1922 and was an immediate success.

Katherine Mansfield died at the age of thirty-four at Fontainebleau, just outside Paris. Murry devoted himself to making her work known, and his overzealous attempts to form a 'cult of Katherine' brought severe criticism for, it was said, trying to take advantage of the value of his dead wife's talent. In the resulting opprobrium, her reputation also declined. Murry's editions of her letters and journal idealized her character by excising the more acidic and the most sensual passages. Recent biographies present a fuller picture of her short and largely unhappy life, setting into relief an appreciation of the delicate precision of her writing—writing which was, as one critic has put it, 'a function of her dying'. She revolutionized the English short story, and her

place as a major influence in twentieth-century writing is now assured.

See also A. Alpers, *The Life of Katherine Mansfield*, 1980; J. Mayers, *Katherine Mansfield: A Biography*, 1978; J. M. Murry (ed.), *Katherine Mansfield's Letters to John Middleton Murry, 1913–1922*, 1951; *The Journal of Katherine Mansfield*, rev. ed. 1954; *Letters of Katherine Mansfield*, 1928.   J.E.E.H.

Mapp, Sarah (d. 1737), bonesetter. Born in Hindon, Wiltshire, she learned the art of bonesetting from her father. After a quarrel with him, she travelled from town to town, calling herself 'Crazy Sally'. Her success as a bonesetter was so impressive that in 1736 the inhabitants of Epsom raised a subscription of 100 guineas to induce her to settle there for a year. She married Hill Mapp, a footman, who disappeared with her money a week later. Undaunted, she continued to practise in Epsom, driving weekly in a coach-and-four to London, where she operated at the Grecian Coffee House. She cured the niece of Sir Hans Sloane, President of the Royal Society, whose shoulder had been dislocated for nine years. A popular figure, she inspired a 'Mrs Mapp' Plate' at Epsom Races, and a play called *The Husband's Relief*, in which her achievements were invoked to mock the pretensions of physicians. Hogarth depicted her in his satirical print *Consultation of Physicians*, placing her above the physicians, between two famous 'quacks'. The reasons for her sudden decline are unknown, but she died a penniless alcoholic. Celebrated in the press, Mrs Mapp's undeniable abilities demonstrated to her contemporaries that successful healing was not the monopoly of 'regularly' educated physicians.

See also J. Caulfield, *Portraits, Memoirs and Characters*, 1820; C. J. S. Thompson, *The Quacks of Old London*, 1928.   C.C.

Marcet, Jane (1769–1858), didactic writer. The only daughter of a Swiss businessman, Jane Haldimand was born in Geneva but brought up in London. Her early life is obscure; little is known of her circumstances before 1799 when she married Alexander Marcet, a prosperous physician by whom she had two children. In 1806 she published her first work, *Conversations on Chemistry intended more especially for the Female Sex*, in which she sought to familiarize women with the basic principles of the science by use of an informative dialogue. It was among the earliest attempts to convey scientific knowledge to lay readers in a simple, comprehensible form. Her book was well received both in Britain and America, where it sold over 160,000 copies. Encouraged, Mrs Marcet embarked on her most famous piece, the *Conversations on Political Economy*, which appeared in 1816 and again adopted the form of a dialogue to discuss the fundamental elements of economic science. Jane Marcet was most insistent that women should understand such concepts, for while accepting that their overt political role was restricted, she thought their indirect influence vitally important. An ill-informed mother would transmit erroneous ideas to her children, thus assisting in the propagation of ignorance. Her work was highly regarded by her contemporaries; the economist Jean-Baptiste Say described her as 'the only woman who had written on political economy and showed herself equal even to men'. Harriet MARTINEAU, later a close friend of Mrs Marcet's, attributed her own interest in the subject to a youthful reading of *Conversations on Political Economy*. Mrs Marcet produced a number of other 'conversations', tackling *Natural Philosophy* (1819), *Vegetable Physiology* (1829), and *Different Kinds of Government* (1836). She also wrote a series of books designed to assist in the education of children, including several elementary works on history and grammar.

See also *Allibone's Dictionary of English Literature*, 1870. J.V.L.

Margaret, Queen of Scots (1240–75), consort of King Alexander III. She was the eldest daughter of Henry III of England and was born at Windsor, where she grew up with her brother Edward, the later 'Hammer of the Scots'. In 1251, when she was just eleven years old, she married the scarcely older King Alexander, who had succeeded to the throne in 1249. The king's guardians, suspicious of possible English influence, treated her badly and kept her in isolation. In 1255 an English physician, sent to examine her, expressed his indignation freely and died shortly afterwards in suspicious circumstances, perhaps by poison. Matters subsequently improved, although the couple remained under certain constraints until Alexander reached manhood. Margaret had three children, Margaret, Alexander, and David. N.H.

Margaret of Anjou (1429–82), Queen of England. She was the daughter of René, Duke of Anjou, titular King of Sicily, Naples, and Hungary, and was educated in Italy. At the time of her marriage in 1445 to Henry VI of England, Margaret was regarded as both beautiful and learned. The marriage brought a truce in the war between England and France, but Margaret was dowerless and her extravagance was a strain on the war-impoverished crown. For eight years she was childless until the birth in 1453 of Edward, Prince of Wales. The character of Henry VI enabled the strong-minded Margaret to exercise a powerful influence over him, particularly in regard to the war with France. In English politics she was often unwise, failing to appreciate that the English crown was expected to be above faction. When Henry fell ill in 1453 she bitterly opposed York's regency, and this led ultimately to civil war between York's supporters and the Queen's Lancastrian forces. After Edward IV seized the throne in 1461, Margaret escaped to Scotland, offering to cede Berwick to the Scots in return for aid. From there she returned to France and set up a Lancastrian court in exile. With the help of Louis XI she organized expeditions against Edward in the north of England, where most of her support lay.

Margaret's opportunity came in 1470 when the defection from Edward of Warwick the Kingmaker brought her an unexpected ally. Political necessity dictated the marriage of her son to Warwick's daughter, Anne NEVILLE, and the alliance led to the temporary restoration of Henry VI. In 1471 Edward IV defeated Warwick at the battle of Barnet and Margaret's forces at Tewkesbury, where Prince Edward was killed. Immediately afterwards Henry VI was murdered in the Tower. Margaret was captured and imprisoned, mainly at Wallingford, until in 1476 Louis XI ransomed her. She was forced to renounce all her rights in England and returned to Anjou. On the death of Duke René in 1480, Louis obliged her to resign all reversionary rights in her paternal inheritance in return for a small pension. She lived in retirement until her death two years later.

Margaret was both vindictive and aggressive, and her lack of political judgement had much to do with the downfall of the House of Lancaster. But she fought bravely and long to regain the throne for her husband, and in her personal life paid a bitter price for her mistakes.

See also J. J. Bagley, *Margaret of Anjou*, 1948; R. A. Griffiths, *The Reign of Henry VI*, 1981.   A.C.

Margaret of France (*c*. 1277–1318), Queen of England. The daughter of Philip III of France, Margaret became the wife of the widower Edward I in 1299. She was regarded as gentle, beautiful, and devout, and quickly won the affection of her step-children. She bore Edward two sons and a daughter, and despite her youth when widowed in 1307 did not choose to marry again. She began the building of the church of the Grey Friars in London and was buried there in 1318.

See also L. F. Salzman, *Edward I*, 1968.
                                                    A.C.

Margaret of Scotland, Saint (*c*.1038–93), Queen of Scotland. Margaret was the daughter of an exiled Anglo-Saxon prince, Edward, and his Hungarian wife Agatha. In 1057 she returned with the rest of her family to the English court of her uncle Edward the Confessor, where they spent the next nine years. There her brother Edgar was groomed as heir to the childless Edward. The Norman Conquest dashed all their expectations, however, and in 1067 she fled with her mother, brother, and sister to Scotland. There King Malcolm III Canmore received them and made Margaret his wife. Between 1071 and 1082 she produced six sons, Edward, Edmund, Æthelred, Edgar, Alexander, and David, and two daughters, Mary and Mathilda/Edith. Their names recall Margaret's identification with England, as do her attempts at religious reform in Scotland, but to consider her in anti-Celtic terms is anachronistic. The King and Queen were patrons of the native ascetic Culdee movement, but Margaret also tried to widen the contacts of the Scottish Church. She called on Lanfranc, the Archbishop of Canterbury, to send monks for her Benedictine foundation at Dunfermline, and her links with Durham are demonstrated by Thurgot, who became her close spiritual adviser and later her biographer.

Margaret's religious reforms belong with those of the Scottish royal family as a whole; as matriarch of that family her canonization was later sought for dynastic reasons. Her Anglo-Saxon links were always apparent. In 1075 her brother Edgar was twice received at

court, and his attempts to gain an English inheritance were supported by Malcolm and Margaret. Her sister Christina became abbess of the Anglo-Saxon royal nunneries of Romsey and Wilton, and both Margaret's daughters were sent to their aunt for upbringing. One of these girls, Edith, became Henry I's wife and later commissioned a biography of her mother. Allegations that Margaret brought foreign ways, with habits of splendour and luxury to the Scottish court provoked a Scottish reaction at her death, but such accusations were often levelled against foreign queens. She was buried at Dunfermline.

See also 'A Nursery of Saints, St Margaret of Scotland Reconsidered', in *Medieval Women*, ed. D. Baker, 1978.   P.A.S.

Margaret of York (1446–1503), Duchess of Burgundy. She was the youngest daughter of Richard, Duke of York, and Cecily NEVILLE. Her brother Edward IV strengthened the close ties between England and the Low Countries by marrying Margaret to Charles the Bold, Duke of Burgundy, in 1468. Charles was uninterested in women and spent very little time with his new wife. There were no children. When Edward was exiled in 1470, Charles and Margaret gave him shelter and aid. At this time Burgundy was the cultural centre of western Europe and Charles had many intellectual interests, but Margaret's primary love was books. She patronized the printer William Caxton in Bruges, and later recommended him to her brother.

Margaret's political role in Burgundy increased with the years. She proved energetic and effective, retaining her influence even after Charles's death in 1476 and the accession of her step-daughter, Mary. In 1480 she visited Edward IV and was the chief intermediary in England's alliance with Burgundy against France. Margaret was fiercely hostile to Henry VII, who supplanted her family on the English throne in 1485. She remained involved in English affairs, by supporting the pretenders Lambert Simnel and Perkin Warbeck, and sheltering exiled Yorkists, as long as she lived.

See also R. Vaughan, *Charles the Bold*, 1973.
                                                    A.C.

Margaret Tudor. See TUDOR, MARGARET.

Marie de Guise (1515–60), Queen of Scotland. The daughter of Claud de Guise, one of the most powerful nobles in France, in 1534 she married Louis, Duc de Longueville, the Grand Chamberlain. A son, Francis, was born in 1535, followed by Louis in 1537, two months after his father's death. Marie was then courted by both Henry VIII of England, who wished to thwart a French-Scottish alliance, and James V of Scotland. Having married James by proxy in 1538 she moved to Scotland, where she soon gave birth to two sons. Both boys died in 1541, but a daughter, Mary, was born in 1542, a week before the death of James who had been sickened by the disastrous defeat of his army by the English at Solway Moss.

Marie's life after this was given to preserving the power of her daughter, MARY, QUEEN OF SCOTS and maintaining French influence in Scotland. To do this she had to struggle against both the Regent, James Hamilton, Earl of Arran, and Henry VIII, who wished to absorb Scotland through the marriage of his son Edward to the young Queen Mary. In 1543 she succeeded in reverting Scotland to the French alliance and in the following year, while failing to unseat Arran as Regent, Marie forced him to be guided by a council in which she played a prominent role. In 1548 Mary, Queen of Scots was sent out of reach of the English to France, where Marie visited her in 1550.

Returning to Scotland the next year, she resumed her struggle for power and in 1554 finally assumed the Regency on the resignation of Arran, now the Duc de Châtelherault. She proceeded to strengthen French influence in Scotland, naming Frenchmen to Scottish offices, and to deal with the rising Protestant party. Her earlier attempts at reconciliation with the Protestants gave way to armed confrontation. By July 1559 they had forced her to concede a certain freedom of worship and in October they declared her regency suspended, with the powers to be assumed by a council led by Châtelherault. In 1560, close to total defeat, Marie died. In her last moments she revealed the double loyalties that had governed her life, affirming that she always favoured 'the welfare of the realm of Scotland as much as France'. Despite John Knox's opinion that it was as fitting for Marie to rule as to put a saddle on the back of an unruly cow, she was an able, intelligent woman. In playing a difficult political game, she achieved more success and dignity than either her mother-in-law Margaret TUDOR in similar circumstances, or, in later years, her daughter Mary.

See also E. M. McKerlie, *Mary of Guise - Lorraine*, 1931; R. Marshall, *Mary of Guise*, 1977.

G.Q.B.

Markham, Violet (1872–1959), public administrator. She was the daughter of a wealthy colliery owner of Chesterfield in Derbyshire, and was educated at home and at West Heath, Ham Common. For some years she was involved locally in efforts to improve the miners' conditions of life and as a Liberal activist. She often spoke on anti-suffrage platforms, but nonetheless stood for parliament (unsuccessfully) at the first opportunity, in 1918. She became a town councillor and ultimately mayor of her native Chesterfield.

The First World War brought Violet Markham splendid new opportunities for achievement. With the help of an influential civil servant, Sir Robert Morant, she was appointed to the executive committee of the National Relief Fund. Then, in 1917, she became deputy director of the women's section of the newly established National Service Department. After the war she sat on a multitude of committees, councils, and courts, concerned with such interests as women's training, women JPs, trade, and industry. The culmination of her career was her appointment as deputy chairman of the Assistance Board (1937–46), which has been described as the most important administrative post held by a woman up to that time. In addition, during the Second World War she ran a canteen, sat on an appeal tribunal concerned with internments under the Defence of the Realm Act, and even chaired a committee set up to investigate the morals of servicewomen (the results of which were interpreted as reassuring).

Violet Markham wrote several books about South Africa. *A Woman's Watch on the Rhine* (1921), was based on observations made when her husband, Lieutenant-General Carruthers, was posted to Cologne, and *Paxton and the Bachelor Duke* (1935), concerned her maternal grandfather Joseph Paxton, gardener and architect of the Crystal Palace.

See also her reminiscences, *Return Passage*, 1953, and *Friendship's Harvest*, 1956.

N.H.

Markievicz, Countess Constance (1868–1926), Irish nationalist and first woman elected to the House of Commons. Born in London, she was the eldest child of Sir Henry Gore-

Marsh, Catherine

Booth of Lissadell, Ireland. She grew up in Ireland with perhaps more freedom than most girls of her class and became an outstanding horsewoman and competent sailor. The country at the time was dominated by the Land Question and Home Rule controversy, and even such relatively enlightened landlords as the Gore-Booths were constantly attacked by the Land League. In spite of a fairly conventional Victorian upbringing, which included being presented at court in 1889, Constance developed a passion for politics, initially supporting women's suffrage which her sister, Eva GORE-BOOTH advocated and fought for all her life. In 1893 she went to study at the Slade and from 1898 to 1900 settled mostly in Paris to paint. There, in 1899, she met the Polish Count Casimir Dunin-Markievicz, also an artist. They married in 1900 and had one daughter.

In 1903 the couple settled in Dublin, where the Countess became involved in nationalist politics and joined Sinn Fein. She came under the influence of James Connolly, the Labour leader, and was involved in raising and training the Citizen Army. Having fought in the Easter Rising, she was condemned to death with the other leaders, but her sentence was commuted to life imprisonment. She served over a year in prison in England before being released in 1917 and returning to Ireland. In 1918 she was again imprisoned, in Holloway, following a round-up of Sinn Fein leaders. In the general election of that year her name was put forward for the St Patrick's Division of Dublin, which she duly won, thus becoming the first woman elected to the House of Commons. She did not, however, take her seat, refusing with the other Sinn Feiners to take the oath of allegiance. For the rest of her life she worked for a free united Ireland, travelling widely in Britain and America, and going to prison several times. She died of peritonitis, deeply mourned. At her funeral people lined the streets in their thousands and sent eight lorry-loads of flowers for her grave.

See also A. Marreco, *The Rebel Countess*, 1967; E. Roper (ed.), *Prison Letters of Countess Markievicz*, 1934.   E.M.V.

Marsh, Catherine (1818–1912), philanthropist and writer. Born at Colchester, the youngest daughter of a vicar, Catherine Marsh was raised in a family distinguished for its ener-getic Christian commitment. The children were actively engaged in parochial work from an early age; Catherine Marsh held Sunday School classes at the age of eleven, and regularly spent her pocket money on the poor.

In 1839 her father moved to Leamington, where Catherine Marsh made her first contact with the navvies building the railway there. She distributed Bibles and tracts among them, and was encouraged by their response. However it was not until 1853 that her work began in earnest. Living then at Beckenham, near the site of the Crystal Palace, she was struck by the spiritual ignorance of the 3000 navvies involved in its construction. In her own words, Catherine Marsh 'sought them out', holding Bible classes in their cottages and circulating testaments among their gangs. Her *English Hearts and English Hands*, published in 1858, was an account of her mission to labourers. In it, she emphasized the 'fine character' of working people and stressed their desire for Christian knowledge, their immense capacity for moral improvement, and urged the rich to cultivate closer relationships with their poorer neighbours. Immediately popular, *English Hearts* was a vastly influential book which inspired many other Christians to involve themselves in philanthropic work among the poor. She herself preached anywhere; she addressed meetings in schools and workhouses, and on board ships.

Following the outbreak of a severe cholera epidemic in 1866, Catherine Marsh regularly attended the London Hospital in Whitechapel to comfort and pray with the dying. She undertook the care of many children orphaned by the disease and established a home at Beckenham for their reception. Together with fellow-hospital workers Catherine Tait and Catherine GLADSTONE she founded a convalescent home in Brighton which became a permanent institution, having treated 19,000 patients by the turn of the century. Catherine Marsh continued well into old age to propagate the gospel among working people. In 1899 she was appointed Honorary Life Governor of the British and Foreign Bible Society. She was also a most prolific writer and published over fifty works, including *Memorials of Captain Hedley Vicars* and *A Light on the Line*.

See also: F. K. Prochaska, *Women and Philanthropy in Nineteenth-Century England*, 1980; L. E. O'Rorke, *The Life and Friendships of Catherine Marsh*, 1917.   J.V.L.

Martin, Sarah (1791–1843), prison visitor. Born in Caister near Great Yarmouth, she was the only child of a small tradesman and his wife. She was orphaned at an early age, and her grandmother, a glovemaker, put her to the dressmaking trade when she was fourteen. It was during a Sunday outing in 1810 that she attended a sermon in Great Yarmouth which resulted in her conversion to evangelical Christianity. She began Sunday School teaching about this time and first entered the Yarmouth Workhouse to read the Scriptures to the inmates. After much difficulty, in 1819 she received permission to visit Yarmouth Gaol, which was notorious for its unruliness. Here, in addition to her religious mission, she suggested and oversaw employments for the prisoners, including book-binding for the men and needlework for the women. She meticulously entered details of prison life in accounts and 'every day books', and by various means raised money to extend her philanthropic schemes. From 1836 Elizabeth Fry's British Ladies' Society contributed annual donations, and in 1841 the Yarmouth Town Council, in recognition of her services to the community, gave her an annual grant of £12.

Sarah Martin also led the prison congregation in Sunday services, and the Prison Inspector, William John Williams, who attended one of her services in 1835, was impressed by her stylish delivery and moral authority. Celebrated in women's magazines, penny tracts, and *The Edinburgh Review*, Miss Martin is perhaps the best nineteenth-century example of a humble philanthropist taken up by the religious establishment. She represents Church and King, deference and conservative reform, and stands for the views of a wide section of working-class opinion. After Mrs FRY, with whom she was often compared, she is perhaps the most widely known female prison visitor of the nineteenth century. She is commemorated in a window of St Nicholas's church in Yarmouth.

See also *A Brief Sketch of the Life of the Late Miss Sarah Martin*, 1845; F. K. Prochaska, *Women and Philanthropy in Nineteenth-Century England*, 1980; D. Stippings, *Miss Sarah Martin*, 1969.   F.K.P.

Martin, Violet Florence (1862–1915), author. Born at Ross House, County Galway, the youngest of eleven children, she was educated at Alexandra College, Dublin. Despite poor eyesight she was a fearless horsewoman, but after a bad fall while hunting she sustained injuries from which she never completely recovered. She lived mostly at Ross and at Drishane, the home of her cousin Edith SOMERVILLE. The two women first met in 1886; Violet Martin, a very pretty woman, often posed as model for her cousin's drawings. They were devoted friends and seldom apart. The famous literary collaboration of 'Somerville and Ross' began in 1898 when she took the pseudonym 'Martin Ross'. In addition to their joint books she published two autobiographies, *Some Irish Yesterdays* (1906) and *Strayaways* (1920). These showed a delightful sense of fun and deep understanding of people, especially Irish characters. An ardent feminist, she was vice-president of the Munster Women's Franchise League.

See also M. Collis, *Somerville and Ross*, 1968.   P.L.

Martindale, Hilda (1875–1952), civil servant. Hilda Martindale, whose father, a City merchant, died before her birth, was first educated by governesses in Germany and Switzerland and then at Brighton High School for Girls. In order to prepare for a career in social work she took courses at the Royal Holloway College, the Royal Sanitary Institute, and Bedford College. She then acquired practical experience by inspecting workhouses in Paddington for the Charity Organization Society and working at Dr Barnardo's Baby Home at Hawkhurst, Kent. In 1900–01 she travelled around the world, studying the treatment of children in the various countries she visited.

Upon her return home, her command of the subject so impressed Adelaide Anderson, head of the Women's Branch of the Factory Department, that she was invited to take a temporary appointment as a lady factory inspector under the Home Office. This was made permanent in 1902. Initially she divided her time between Ireland and the Potteries but in 1905 was assigned full-time to Ireland. She remained there until 1912, as senior lady inspector after 1908. She covered the whole of Ireland and, though stationed at Belfast, travelled over 16,000 kilometres (10,000 miles) a year. In 1912 she moved to the Midland Division and in 1918, having been awarded the OBE, to the South-Eastern Division. When the Factory Department was reorganized in 1921 she became superintending inspector of the Southern Division, with responsibility for both men and women (one of only two women with such assignments). In 1925 she was appointed a deputy chief inspector (one of three and the only woman) and in this post presided over a large increase in the women staff and the further integration of male and female staff.

In 1933 she was appointed director of women's establishments at the Treasury, in effect the premier women's post in the Civil Service. She found that her official duties (mostly sitting on selection boards of the Civil Service Commission and on various committees, including the Official Side of the National Whitley Council, the Committee on Women's Questions, and the Committee on the Admission of Women to the Consular and Diplomatic Services) were insufficient to occupy her fully, and therefore embarked on a series of inspections of the various government departments and of outside firms. Armed with this comprehensive knowledge she was an able advocate for women civil servants in their struggle to achieve equality. She retired in 1937.

Hilda Martindale then returned to her first interest, child welfare, and became in 1938 the first woman member of the Council of Dr Barnardo's Homes. She was also a governor of Bedford College. She wrote a history of the employment of women in the Civil Service, *Women Servants of the State: A History of Women in the Civil Service, 1870–1938* (1938) and two books of memoirs, *From One Generation to Another, 1839–1944: A Book of Memoirs* (1944) and *Some Victorian Portraits and Others* (1948).

See also *University Women's Review*, 1953.

M.Z.

Martineau, Harriet (1802–76), didactic writer. The sixth of eight children of Thomas Martineau, a cloth manufacturer, Harriet was born in Norwich. Her family were prominent Unitarians and led a lively social and intellectual life, although Harriet Martineau took little part in this; a nervous and sickly child, she was already beset by the deafness which was to become almost total in later life. She nevertheless received an excellent education, attending schools in Norwich and Bristol. In 1826 she was 'virtually engaged' to a Unitarian minister, but terminated the relationship when he became insane. Henceforth she remained single, believing herself unsuited to marriage. The collapse of the family business in 1829

left Harriet Martineau without an income, and for some years she survived by sewing and writing. Her first article, 'Female Writers on Practical Divinity', written at her brother's suggestion, had been printed in *The Monthly Repository* in 1821, and she now produced a wide variety of articles and tales. Impressed by the work of Mrs MARCET, she began to consider writing a series of stories designed to explain aspects of political economy. She had long been an advocate of the principles of Smith, Malthus, and Ricardo, and now sought to convey them to a wider audience. Between 1832 and 1834 she produced a story each month as *Illustrations of Political Economy*. A resounding success, *Illustrations* ushered Miss Martineau into literary and political life which she embraced with great enthusiasm. In 1834 she visited America and was horrified to witness slavery. Her life-long support for the Abolitionist cause is reflected in her *Society in America*, published in 1836.

During the early 1840s she was much troubled by a painful illness. Persuaded to attempt a cure by Mesmerism, she recovered rapidly and became a zealous devotee, publishing a series of 'Letters on Mesmerism' in *The Athenaeum* in 1844. In Mesmerist circles she met Henry Atkinson, with whom she conducted a lengthy correspondence published in 1851 as *Letters on the Laws of Man's Social Nature and Development*. Its severe criticism of the clergy and organized religion, combined with its foggy mysticism, guaranteed it a hostile reception. As Harriet Martineau lost confidence in orthodox religion, she looked elsewhere for a new faith, and was much attracted by Positivism. In 1853, with the approval of Auguste Comte, she translated and condensed his *Positive Philosophy*.

In later life she devoted herself to journalism. She wrote leading articles for the liberal *Daily News* for fourteen years, and contributed extensively to numerous periodicals, including Dickens's *Household Words* and *The Westminster Review*. One of her most important pieces, 'On Female Industry', appeared in *The Edinburgh Review* of 1859. Here Harriet Martineau drew attention to the situation of 'redundant women' who were reliant upon their own efforts for their livelihood, and argued that changes must be made in the political and social organization of the state to reflect the independence and aspirations of these women. Immediately influential, the article inspired Jessie BOUCHERETT to found the Society for Promoting the Employment of Women. However, Harriet Martineau remained equivocal on the value of legislative action in this respect, believing it to be of primary importance that women should first acquire sound education and experience of self-determination, as she herself had done. A brilliant didactic writer at a time when the desire for instruction was at its height, Harriet Martineau was perhaps the foremost disseminator of liberal opinion of her time.

Her other works include *Life in the Sickroom*, 1843; *History of England during the Thirty Years' Peace*, 1849; and *Autobiography*, 1877.

See also V. K. Pichanick, *Harriet Martineau, the Woman and her Work*, 1980; R. K. Webb, *Harriet Martineau, a Radical Victorian*, 1960.　　　　　　　　　　J.V.L.

Marx, (Jenny Julia) Eleanor (1855–98), socialist. The youngest daughter of Karl Marx, Eleanor was born at 28 Dean Street in Soho, London. Her childhood in the crowded, impoverished household, the centre of revolutionary exiles in London, left her well versed in international politics and literature, as well as fluent in German and French. At seventeen she began to earn her living by teaching private pupils and devilling at the British Museum, work which was later supplemented by freelance typing. An ambition to be an actress was not fulfilled, but she performed at playreadings and 'entertainments' and her championing of Ibsen was an important contribution to the theatre. She arranged the first reading of *A Doll's House* in 1885 and translated *An Enemy of Society* (1888) and *The Lady from the Sea* (1890). Other literary translations were the first in English of *Madame Bovary* (1886) and a German translation of Amy Levy's *Reuben Sachs* (1889).

Despite her literary and theatrical interests, Eleanor Marx's main sphere of activity was political. On her father's death in 1883 she wrote two articles for *Progress* in which her clear exposition of the theory of surplus value showed a rare combination of theoretical understanding and human sympathy. As Marx's daughter and Engels's protégée she carried their theories into action, involved in the battles within the movement for an International Socialism. In her own right she became a distinguished member of the move-

ment and a forceful, much sought-after public speaker. Throughout her life she also contributed to socialist journals, *To-Day*, *Commonweal*, *Time* and *Justice*, depending on their affiliations, and in 1895, after translating Plekhanov's *Anarchism and Socialism*, she wrote analyses of British affairs for *Russkoye Bogatstvo*. She played a major part in organizing the Second International in Paris in 1889 and at later congresses in Halle, Brussels, Zürich, and London worked as organizer, speaker and interpreter.

Her battles were not limited to intellectual affairs, however. A demonstrator on 'Bloody Sunday' in 1887, she identified with the problems of the poor, and the strikes of 1889 found in her an indefatigable supporter. She formed the Women's Branch of the National Union of Gasworkers, on whose executive she served until 1895, and dedicated herself to the twelve-week strike at Silver's. Recognizing her Jewish ancestry, she sympathized with the Jews in East London, working to bring them into the movement.

After Engels's death, she took charge of Marx's papers, working on the fourth volume of *Capital* with Kautsky and editing *The Eastern Question* (1896), *Value, Price and Profit* (1898), and Engels's *Revolution and Counter-Revolution* (1896). From 1884 she lived openly with Edward Aveling as his common-law wife, appending his name to hers. They worked together, writing and lecturing, but his constant borrowings and infidelities strained the relationship. With him she produced *The Woman Question* (1886), and she also wrote *Der Böse Maitag* (in *Die Neue Zeit* 1893–94). Eleanor Marx killed herself by taking prussic acid on 31 March 1898.

See also Y. Kapp, *Eleanor Marx*, 2 vols, 1972, 1975.　　　　　　　　　　C.B.

Mary I, Queen (1516–58), Queen of England. The only surviving child of Henry VIII and KATHERINE OF ARAGON, Mary was the subject of the usual dynastic marriage bargaining, promised at various times to the Dauphin, the French King, and to the Emperor. To train her for eventual rule she was named Princess of Wales and moved, with her own household, to Ludlow. However, Henry's desire for a divorce from Katherine soon caused difficulties for Mary, who remained loyal to her mother. She was forbidden to see Katherine in 1531, was declared illegitimate and stripped

281

of her titles in 1533, and pressured formally to accept her bastardy and the altered succession. Even after the death of her stepmother Anne BOLEYN, the pressure for Mary's submission continued until, under threat of treason charges and her will broken, she acknowledged her illegitimacy, the unlawfulness of her parents' marriage, and the Henrician Supremacy. She was then forgiven and accepted at court.

Until her father's death in 1547 Mary remained in the political background but was still too dangerous as a potential claimant to the throne, despite her bastardy, for Henry to allow her to be married abroad. His will and the Succession Act of 1544 placed Mary after her brother Edward in line to the throne. During Edward's reign Mary was occupied by resisting plans to marry her to a foreign Protestant and by trying to maintain her own Catholicism in the face of pressure to conform. When pressed to cease attending Mass, she successfully appealed to the Emperor Charles V, who had previously supported her and whose ill-will the English were unwilling to provoke. Throughout Edward's reign Mary therefore remained the symbol of the conservative opposition. In 1553 Edward was dying, and under the influence of the Duke of Northumberland tried to divert the succession to Jane GREY. Mary asserted her own claim, eluded the Duke, proclaimed herself Queen, and witnessed the failure of Northumberland's coup. On August 3, Mary entered London in Triumph. She was crowned on October 1, the first queen regnant in English history.

Now wishing to marry, she rejected all English candidates and turned to the Imperial-Spanish connection, choosing Philip of Spain. This news prompted Wyatt's unsuccessful rebellion in January 1554, but the wedding was nevertheless celebrated in July. Despite Mary's deep emotional commitment, the marriage was unsuccessful. Her countrymen hated the Spaniards who in turn resented their ill-treatment and the failure of the English to crown Philip. After an embarrassing hysterical pregnancy in 1555, Mary was deserted by her husband who returned only in 1557 when he needed to win English participation in the war against France.

The other matter dearest to Mary's heart, her religious policy, was also a failure. Although she restored England to Catholicism, the revival of the heresy laws and the cam-

paign of burning Protestants, begun in 1555, only served to blacken her reputation. The disastrous war with France which resulted in the loss of Calais caused further unpopularity. Another hysterical pregnancy and the final departure of Philip in 1558 left Mary a broken woman. She died in November, aware of the failure of her marriage, her foreign policy, and, with the succession of her Protestant sister ELIZABETH, her religious policy. Although greatly responsible for the religious persecution which earned her the title of 'Bloody Mary', she was also responsible for putting England on a sound financial footing, restoring the English navy, enhancing the wealth of the Church, and helping to ensure the survival of Catholicism in England. Pious, brave, and merciful to her secular opponents, Mary deserves a better reputation than history has granted her.

See also D. Loades, *The Reign of Mary Tudor*, 1979; H. Prescott, *Spanish Tudor*, 1953.   G.Q.B.

Mary II, Queen (1662–94), Queen of England. Mary was the eldest surviving child of James, Duke of York, later James II, and his first Duchess, Anne HYDE. As the prettiest, cleverest, and most responsive of their children, she was her father's favourite. Both parents were Catholic converts, and when her mother died in 1671 Mary and her sister Anne were made wards of the state. To ensure their Protestant upbringing they were placed in the charge of their governess, Lady Frances Villiers. They grew up with the Villiers daughters and other suitable companions, who shared their lessons in French, singing, dancing, and drawing. Mary was an apt pupil, but her education was superficial and proved inadequate for her future role. After her marriage she felt the need to supplement her learning by extensive reading. Her religious training, supervised by Henry Compton, Bishop of London, laid the foundation for the staunch Protestantism that was to guide and sustain her.

The death of her two brothers in 1671 placed Mary second in line to the throne, and in 1677 a political marriage was arranged by her uncle, Charles II, to her staunchly Protestant first cousin Prince William III of Orange. The prospects of marriage and leaving England caused Mary great distress, hardly lessened by the unprepossessing appearance and manners of her future husband. The warm reception she met in Holland; the ardour, sincerity, and sympathy which underlay William's taciturn exterior; and the stories she heard of his extraordinary courage and piety, which appealed to her romantic temperament, rapidly changed aversion to a love akin to hero-worship. William's guidance and example served to expand her horizons, inspiring in her a wish to help him achieve his political and religious ambitions. She was willing and eager to subordinate herself to her husband in all matters, domestic and political. She endured his liaison with Elizabeth VILLIERS, his frequent neglect, and his extended absences, maintaining an unwavering loyalty to him.

It was this wifely devotion and her staunch Protestantism that led Mary to support the Revolution of 1688 which deposed her father, James II. She endorsed her husband's wish that they be crowned joint sovereigns, passing over her own stronger claims. As Queen, she continued to defer to William in all political matters; was reluctant to accept responsibility for administering the kingdom in his absence; and was diffident about taking decisions without him. William had always been able to delegate to Mary the ceremonial and social aspects of monarchy, which he disliked and in which she excelled, but to everyone's surprise she also proved a capable administrator. Her faithful adherence to William's instructions, refusal to follow an independent policy, and increasing ability to deal with administrative details made the joint arrangement tenable. It enabled William, during his extended campaigns on the Continent, to be effectively in two places at once. Mary's premature death of smallpox in 1694 left her husband inconsolably grief-stricken.

A charming, dignified, and intelligent Queen, Mary, by her personal popularity and loyalty to William, helped to ensure the success of the revolutionary settlement and the Protestant succession, despite the fact that she had no children of her own.

See also H. W. Chapman, *Mary II, Queen of England*, 1953; E. Hamilton, *William's Mary*, 1972; *Memoirs of Mary, Queen of England, 1689–1693*, ed. R. Doebner, 1886.

T.J.M.

Mary, Queen of France (?1496–1533), daughter of Henry VII of England. She was contracted to Charles of Castile from 1507 to 1514, when the match was broken off after Imperial and Spanish doubledealing in the combined war with England against France. By a separate English peace with France, Mary married Louis XII, an elderly invalid, on 9 September; he died on 1 January 1515. Her brother Henry VIII had promised that she could choose her next husband herself, but fearing this would not be honoured she secretly married Charles Brandon, Duke of Suffolk, in Paris. Henry was outraged, but eventually mollified by the Suffolks' promise to pay him her dowry. In May they were married publicly at Greenwich in Henry's presence, although the union was generally unpopular. Mary was a friend of KATHERINE OF ARAGON, and an implacable enemy of Anne BOLEYN. In 1532 a brawl allegedly arose because she used 'opprobrious language . . . against Madame Anne'. She died on 24 June 1533.

Mary's importance was dynastic. Her children were Henry, Earl of Lincoln; Eleanor; and Frances, mother of Jane GREY. In 1514 Henry VIII promised the Hapsburgs to make her his heir if he died childless, and he bequeathed the succession to her issue after his own. It was therefore through her that Jane Grey's claim to the throne was advanced.

See also J. S. Brewer, *Letters & Papers of Henry VIII*; J. Paul, *Catherine of Aragon and Her Friends*, 1966.

M.D.

Mary, Queen of Scots (1542–87). The daughter of James V of Scotland and MARIE DE GUISE, she was born a week before her father's death, and as the infant Queen of Scotland was sought by Henry VIII as bride for his son Prince Edward. Although promised to Edward and due to be sent to England, Mary went in 1548 to be educated at the French court. There she developed into a refined and attractive French princess. In 1558 she married the Dauphin, signing a secret treaty which would give to the French crown her claims to the thrones of Scotland and England should she die childless. On the advice of her father-in-law, Henri II, she quartered her arms with those of England, openly asserting her claim. With Henri's death in 1559, her husband became Francis II and Mary was Queen of France. But, by the following year Francis was dead and Mary a widow.

Returning to Scotland in 1561, Mary faced a powerful Protestant party and a country torn by religious strife. Though wishing to restore

Catholicism, Mary first attempted conciliation. She attempted no alteration of religion, reasoned with the unreasonable John Knox, and created her half-brother James Stewart the Earl of Moray. Choosing to marry, she rejected European candidates and her cousin ELIZABETH I's nominee, Robert Dudley, settling on Henry, Lord Darnley. The marriage in July 1565 strengthened Mary's claim to the English throne, as Darnley was the grandson of Margaret TUDOR but it also outraged Elizabeth, already suspicious of Mary's intentions, and Moray. Darnley's jealousy, ambition, and resentment at being denied the crown matrimonial led him to participate in the brutal murder of Mary's unpopular aide David Riccio in March 1566, before the eyes of the pregnant Queen. In June 1566 she gave birth to the future James VI, and turned her thoughts to being rid of Darnley, who was murdered the following February in spectacular fashion. Whether Mary actively plotted his death is uncertain, but her subsequent relations with the man who planned Darnley's end, James Hepburn, Earl of Bothwell, brought her universal condemnation. She shielded Bothwell from prosecution, allowed him to abduct her, and married him in May 1567. Seized by her nobles, she was forced in July to abdicate in favour of her son.

An attempt in May 1568 to revoke her abdication and resume power failed, so Mary fled to England, calling on Elizabeth to restore her to the Scottish throne. Elizabeth replied by keeping her in captivity, an unwelcome guest too dangerous to release but almost as dangerous as a prisoner. Over the next eighteen years Mary became the focus of attempts by Catholics in England and Europe to place her on Elizabeth's throne, and was herself a party to conspiracies against the life of her captor. After the failure of the Babington plot to assassinate Elizabeth, the English Queen was at last convinced that Mary must die. Playing the role of a Catholic martyr whose faith had sustained her in her years of imprisonment, Mary was beheaded in February 1587.

Few politicians have crammed so many mistakes into so short a term in power as Mary. Her marriage to Darnley, the clumsy handling of his murder, her relationship with Bothwell, and the crowning folly of her flight to England were all cardinal errors which her rival Elizabeth, a much less appealing figure personally, would never have made. The romance and tragedy of her life have often obscured Mary's failings as a ruler.

See also *Letters of Mary Stuart*, ed. W. B. D. D. Turnbull 1845; A. Fraser, *Mary, Queen of Scots*, 1969.   G.Q.B.

Mary of Guelders (*c.* 1433–63), Queen of James II of Scotland. She was the daughter of Arnold, Duke of Guelders, and niece of Philip, Duke of Burgundy. Her marriage to James II in 1449 strengthened both Scottish commercial ties with the Low Countries and political ties with France. It also brought to an end James's minority. Mary was beautiful, devout, and a patron of the arts. She fulfilled her dynastic duty by bearing three sons and two daughters; she also founded the Collegiate Church of the Holy Trinity, Edinburgh, with its hospital, and built Ravenscraig castle in Fife.

On James's unexpected death in 1460 at the siege of Roxburgh, Mary showed both vigour and political intelligence. She assumed the headship of state, ruling with the aid of a regency council on behalf of her nine-year-old son James III, and continued the war with England, bringing the siege of Roxburgh to a successful conclusion. Late in 1460 she received and aided with troops the Lancastrian Queen MARGARET OF ANJOU and her son Prince Edward. The next year, following the accession of the Yorkist Edward IV, she demanded and received the surrender of Berwick in return for further aid to the Lancastrians. But this did not stop her from negotiating with Edward as well, since she was wise enough to see that Scotland's best interests lay in making peace with the English King. Her policy was supported by many of the younger lords, but opposed by their seniors.

Mary did not make another marriage although her name was linked with the exiled Duke of Somerset and Adam Hepburn of Hailes. Possibly as a result of this, but possibly also because of ill-health, her political influence waned and she died in 1463, aged thirty.

See also C. Bingham, *The Stewart Kingdom of Scotland, 1371–1603*, 1974.   A.C.

Mary of Modena (1658–1718), Queen of James II. She was the only daughter of Alfonso IV, Duke of Modena, who died when she was four. Her mother, Laura Martinozzi, then became regent. She was a formidable woman from a well connected Roman family, and strictly supervised the education and religious upbringing of her son and daughter. Mary was an accomplished young woman, fluent in Italian, French, Latin, and subsequently in English. She was musical and enjoyed reading and riding, but her dearest childhood ambition was to become a nun. Thus she was violently opposed to the marriage arranged for her at the age of fourteen with the English Duke of York, a forty-year-old widower. It took the Pope to persuade her that marriage to the Catholic heir-presumptive to the English throne was a more worthy sacrifice than taking the veil. The marriage in 1673 of the Duke to an Italian Catholic was received with great hostility by the English parliament and the majority of the English people. The Duke himself was immediately captivated by the beauty and charm of his young bride and was to remain, despite his extra-marital affairs, a devoted and affectionate husband. She came in time to love her husband so passionately that his continued infidelities caused her the greatest anguish and his fondness for his illegitimate children intensified her grief at her incapacity to produce a healthy heir.

During her twelve years as Duchess of York, Mary took little active part in affairs of state. Her principal duty, she believed, was to provide a Catholic heir, and she endured numerous pregnancies resulting in miscarriages or the birth of children who died young. After the accession of James in 1685, however, her political role as Queen was more active and crucial. She became an ardent supporter of her husband's Catholicizing policies and exerted considerable influence on the King and those around him. At the centre of an inner group of ultra-Catholic and Francophile ministers, she became after the birth of the Prince of Wales in June 1688 a key figure at court as potential regent for her son. Ironically, it was the birth of a Catholic heir that served as a catalyst for the events leading to her husband's deposition and her dramatic flight with her son to France, where she was subsequently joined by her husband.

In exile she played an active role in Jacobite conspiracies, seeking military and financial support for her husband's endeavours to regain his throne. James, who had always found her a source of comfort and strength, became increasingly dependent upon her in old age. She exerted a similar influence over their son, James, the Old Pretender, after her husband's death in 1701.

A devoted wife, Mary was a conscientious mother to her children, James and Louise. Bound to her husband by mutual ties of love and affection and by common religious and political goals, she proved an extremely able and influential consort, who significantly affected the history of her time.

See also C. Oman, *Mary of Modena*, 1962.

T.J.M.

Mary of Teck, properly Victoria Mary Augusta Louise Olga Pauline Claudine Agnes (1867–1953), Queen of Great Britain as the wife of George V. Princess Victoria Mary of Teck was the granddaughter of the Duke of Württemberg, who had married a Hungarian countess and so disqualified his children from succeeding. Mary's father settled in England and married a cousin of Queen Victoria. Although extremely shy and not an outstanding beauty, she was thought a suitable bride for Albert, elder son of the Prince of Wales, and they became engaged in 1891. A few months later Albert died, apparently of influenza, and Mary was quickly engaged to his younger brother, George. It seems likely that she had more in common with the younger son, who was solid and dependable where his brother had been more charming but less stable, and the marriage, which took place in 1893, was long and successful.

The couple had five children. The eldest, Edward (known in the family as David), succeeded his father in 1936, but abdicated the following year. Mary and George were rather stiff and unapproachable parents, but they inculcated values of duty and moral uprightness which they believed were the necessary underpinnings of a popular and successful monarchy. These ideals were largely rejected by their eldest son, but remained very much the basic beliefs of their second, Bertie, who was to become George VI. It is perhaps inevitable that Mary should be associated in most people's minds with the abdication — 'the dreadful goodbye' as she called it — and her traditionalism is often blamed for Edward's stubborn desire to assert himself. Yet it should not be forgotten that the King and Queen were enormously popular during the First World War, when their devotion to duty and their frugal personal living standards raised the monarchy as high in public esteem as it had ever been in the modern period. She suffered with great dignity personal tragedies, including the losses of her husband and two sons, George VI and the Duke of Kent, who was killed in an air crash in 1942, as well as the trial of the abdication. Yet she lived to see with satisfaction her granddaughter, Elizabeth, in whose upbringing she had perhaps taken a more personal interest than that of her own children, become Queen.

See also U. Bloom, *The Great Queen Consort*, 1976; James Pope-Hennessy, *Queen Mary*, 1959. E.M.V.

Masham, Abigail (1670–1734), royal favourite. Abigail Hill was the daughter of a Levant merchant who died insolvent. She was taken from a menial serving post into the household of her cousin Sarah CHURCHILL, who introduced her in 1697 into the service of Princess (later Queen) Anne. From 1705, Sarah was often absent from court on family business, and in deputizing for her, Abigail drew closer to the Queen. In 1707, when she married Samuel Masham, a wealthy gentleman, she had begun to oust her cousin from royal favour. Queen Anne attended the wedding and provided 'a round sum' for her dowry. At about the same time Robert Harley, leader of the Tory opposition to the Churchills and a relative of Abigail's, began to use her friendship with the Queen to discredit the Churchills and the Whig government. In 1711 she replaced Sarah Churchill as Keeper of the Privy Purse and took over her lodgings in St James's Palace. At the same time her husband was appointed Comptroller of the Household, in place of Francis Godolphin, the Churchills' ally. Harley and the Tory government made political use of her proximity to the Queen, but the real successor to Sarah Churchill was the Duchess of Somerset; Mrs Masham was never more than a servant.

She was a quiet, placid woman. Swift described her as 'a person of plain, sound understanding . . . firm in her friendship for the Queen, her mistress'. She provided Anne with relief from Sarah Churchill's domination, but beyond a few letters and an unproven portrait, left very little trace of herself. After Anne's death she faded into obscurity.

See also I. Butler, *The Rule of Three*, 1967; E. Gregg, *Queen Anne*, 1980. C.H.G.G.

Masham, Damaris, Lady (1659–1708), philosopher and author. The daughter of Dr Ralph Cudworth, the philosopher and theologian, she

was brought up in Cambridge, where her father was Regius Professor of Hebrew. At an early age she showed exceptional promise, and her father, from whom she acquired a strong taste for philosophical studies and extensive knowledge, took great pride in providing her with a scholarly education. In 1682 she met the philosopher John Locke. Under his influence the Platonic philosophy she had inherited from her father was much modified, but she was never converted entirely to Locke's more empirical way of thinking, and remained her father's daughter as well as Locke's disciple. But it was more than intellectual companionship that bound the pair together. Soon after their meeting they formed a romantic attachment, exchanging love letters and verses which reveal the full nature of their relationship. Whether they contemplated marriage is not known, but in 1683 Locke fled for political reasons to Holland, where he remained until after the Revolution of 1688. In 1685 Damaris married Sir Francis Masham, an unremarkable widower with nine children, and in 1686 gave birth to their only child.

The extensive household over which Lady Masham presided included Locke after 1691. He had been a regular visitor since his return from Holland, and after a serious illness became a permanent paying guest of Sir Francis and Lady Masham until his death in 1704. The arrangement worked remarkably well. A conscientious wife and mother, Lady Masham still found time to contribute to contemporary intellectual discussions. In the 1690s she and Mary ASTELL were ranged on opposite sides in a theological disputation between Locke and John Norris, a clergyman with whom she had communicated earlier on the subject of Platonic love and who had dedicated a treatise to her in 1689. Lady Masham's contributions consisted of her *Discourse concerning the Love of God*, published anonymously in 1696 and generally attributed to Locke,' and her *Occasional Thoughts in Reference to a virtuous Christian Life*, published in 1700. She also wrote a brief account of Locke for the *Great Historical Dictionary*. Her lengthy letter to Jean Le Clerc, Locke's friend and earliest biographer, has been a major source for later biographers.

An advocate of better educational opportunities for women, whom she felt were the victims of male ignorance and insecurity, she expressed her views strongly in *Occasional*

Thoughts. According to Locke, Lady Masham was so well versed in theology and philosophy and was of such an original mind that very few men could equal her in knowledge or in the ability to use it. He praised her excellent judgement, clarity of thought, and extraordinary capacity to solve problems beyond the range of most men. The great respect inspired by her ability to combine intellectual pursuits with motherhood and other more 'feminine' virtues helped to discredit the assumption that women were born with lesser intellects and to dispel the prejudice against their education.

See also M. W. Cranston, *John Locke: a biography*, 1957; P. Laslett, 'The Rise and Fall of an English Family, Masham of Otes', in *History Today*, 1953. T.J.M.

Mason, Charlotte (Maria Shaw) (1842–1923), educationist. The only child of a Liverpool merchant and his wife who taught her themselves, she was orphaned at sixteen and left without relatives or means. After one year's teacher training at the Home and Colonial Training College, she left, only qualifying later when already teaching at the Davison School in Worthing. While there, and as Vice-Principal of the Bishop Otter College in Chichester, her own educational philosophy began to take shape. This was based on faith in the response of all children to living ideas presented in a literary form. Concentration was taught by the single reading of a passage, to be narrated immediately afterwards without interruption. Once the child's mind had acted directly upon the book, its content would be known and revision would be unnecessary. Foremost, children must enjoy their lessons. The desire to know should be the only motivation, rewards or competition being discouraged. Charlotte Mason also appreciated the importance of parental involvement to the child's confidence and progress.

Living in Bradford from 1880 to 1891, she began lecturing on education and formed the Parents' National Educational Union. Following lecture tours of England, she gained support from many prominent people in both education and the Church. At the same time she remained independent of the contemporary movement in girls' and women's higher education. From 1890 onwards she edited *The Parents' Review*, and, moving to Ambleside in 1891, started a correspondence school.

Termly programmes of work, chosen by specialists, were sent out to all children enrolled in the Parents' Union School. By 1923, 117 secondary schools, 175 elementary schools, and countless home school-rooms in England and abroad were working in the PUS. The demand for governesses to implement her methods caused her to train young women and to raise their status by insisting on adequate salaries and conditions of work. These students were trained in her Ambleside home, now the Charlotte Mason College. Much of the best practice in modern primary schools can be traced to her influence. Her works included *An Essay towards a Philosophy of Education* (1923).

See also E. Cholmondeley, *The Story of Charlotte Mason*, 1960. S.B.

Mason, (Marianne) Harriet (1845–1932), civil servant. Harriet Mason was born at Moreton Hall in Nottinghamshire, the daughter of a country squire. She was educated at home. Until the age of forty her pursuits were those of leisured countrywomen, with one significant exception. Her 'high ideals and great energy' gave her a deep interest in social problems, particularly as they affected the young. She became voluntary supervisor of the boarding out of children for the poor law unions in Nottinghamshire, and guided the poor law activities of the Girls' and Young Men's Friendly Societies. She was also a member of the Charity Organization Society, the Association for Befriending Boys, and the National Association for the Care of the Feeble-Minded.

As an expert in the care of the young in the poor law system, she was invited by the Local Government Board to become its inspector of boarded-out children in 1885. This controversial post had lapsed after the retirement of its first holder in 1874, and in reviving it the Board signalled its renewed interest in finding a system of care for children, humane as well as efficient, which involved fostering rather than institutionalization. At the time of her appointment Harriet Mason was the only woman inspector in the Civil Service, and she thus became the doyenne of the women inspectors who were appointed from the 1890s onwards. Her interest in her young charges was personal as well as professional, for she acted as friend and adviser to many long after they were adults. She pushed hard for the extension of the boarding-out system and for the increased employment of women as inspectors. With the hiring of additional women inspectors in 1889 she became head of her department. She retired in 1910.

Harriet Mason then embarked on a series of travels in Africa, exercising her talents as botanist and water-colourist. She also published a collection of nursery rhymes. Her last years were spent in South Africa and she died at Rondebosch.

See also H. Martindale, *Women Servants of the State, 1870-1938: A History of Women in the Civil Service*, 1938.   M.Z.

Mathews, Dame Vera Laughton (1888–1959), Director of the Women's Royal Naval Service. She was the daughter of the naval historian Sir John Laughton and his second wife, who was Spanish. Educated at convents in London and Belgium, and then at King's College, London, she showed great all-round ability as athlete, painter and musician. Her early career in journalism was interrupted by the First World War, and when the Women's Royal Naval Service (WRNS) was formed in 1917, she immediately joined the 'Wrens' and was quickly put in charge at the Crystal Palace naval depot. After the war, she was awarded the OBE. In 1924 she travelled to Japan to marry Gordon Dewer Mathews and there the first of their three children was born. Returning to England in 1927, she gave much time to the Girl Guide movement, becoming a District Commissioner in 1928 and, in 1930, a Division Commissioner. Always a strong supporter of the women's suffrage movement, in 1928 she joined the Executive Committee of St Joan's Social and Political Alliance.

With this background of public service, in 1939 she was appointed Director of the WRNS with responsibility 'for the recruitment, efficiency, welfare and discipline of the WRNS, and ... all matters concerning the entry, promotion, accommodation, medical attendance, pay, allowances, travelling expenses, leave of absence and retirement and discharge of members of the service'. These duties she carried out with great efficiency and personal charm, the greatest monument to her achievement undoubtedly being the decision to establish the WRNS as a permanent feature of the Royal Navy. Retiring from the WRNS in 1946, Dame Vera became Chairman of the Domestic Coal Consumers' Council and served on the South Eastern Gas Board.

See also V. Laughton Mathews, *Blue Tapestry*, 1948.   E.M.V.

Matilda (?–1083), Queen of William the Conqueror. She was the daughter of Count Baldwin V of Flanders; her mother was Adela, daughter of Robert and sister of Henry I, Capetian kings of France. In 1049 Duke William of Normandy was struggling to counteract the disadvantages of his illegitimacy and to assert his authority over a notably turbulent province. He determined to secure a firm alliance with his powerful Flemish neighbour by marrying Matilda. The match did not gain the approval of the reforming Pope Leo IX, however, and was prohibited by the Council of Rheims in October 1049. William and Matilda were perhaps too nearly related, but the decision was more probably a result of political pressures. The marriage was nevertheless concluded, probably in 1051, and eventually received Papal recognition from Nicholas II in 1059. It appears to have been a happy union and a productive one. Matilda bore four sons: Robert, who succeeded his father as Duke of Normandy; Richard, who met with a hunting accident in the New Forest; and William Rufus and Henry, both later Kings of England. There were also at least five daughters.

When William mounted his invasion of England in 1066, Matilda both provided a splendid ship for his personal use and undertook to serve as Regent in Normandy during his absence. Not until William was firmly established on the English throne did Matilda herself cross the Channel, in the spring of 1068, attended by a great retinue of lords and ladies. The journey culminated in her solemn crowning as Queen at Westminster on Whit Sunday, by Archbishop Aldred of York. Her main role continued to be in Normandy, however, superintending the affairs of the duchy, often in association with her eldest son Robert. Robert was the cause of her only known quarrel with her husband when, in 1079, she was discovered to be secretly sustaining him in exile with all manner of valuables.

Matilda died in Normandy after a lengthy illness and was buried in the church of Holy Trinity at Caen. Here she founded a nunnery to atone for her years of illicit union in the 1050s. The Conqueror, who is said by the early twelfth-century chronicler William of Malmesbury to have wept for days at her passing and mourned for the rest of his life, erected a magnificent tomb to her memory.

See also D. C. Douglas, *William the Conqueror*, 1964.   K.R.D.

Matilda (1080–1118), first Queen of Henry I of England. She was the daughter of Malcolm III of Scotland and MARGARET, sister of Edgar Aetheling. Matilda became Henry's wife on 11 November 1100, and bore two children who survived infancy: William, drowned in 1120, and MATILDA, Henry's designated successor. John of Salisbury later dubbed the King's marriage an 'incestuous union', since Matilda was 'a nun whom Henry had dragged away from Romsey Abbey and deprived of the veil'. But significantly, St Anselm failed to find any impediment to the match. It was Stephen, the rival claim of Henry's daughter Matilda for the English throne, who deliberately revived doubts about her parents' union.

Matilda, a pious, virtuous, and intelligent woman, was at best a reluctant Regent for her husband during his frequent absences on the Continent. She reputedly wore a hair shirt, washed the feet of lepers, and built a hospital for them. Literate herself, she was an ardent patron of scholars, poets, and musicians. 'The goodness that she did in England', declared an enthusiastic contemporary, 'cannot all here be written, nor by any man understood.' She was buried at Westminster in May 1118.

K.R.D.

Matilda (1102–67), Holy Roman Empress, the daughter of Henry I of England and his first wife, MATILDA. In 1110 she was despatched to Germany to marry the Emperor Henry V and after years of rigorous training for the role of Empress finally became his wife in 1114. Ironically, in view of the almost universal condemnation she later received from English chroniclers, the Empress won much admiration on the Continent as the 'good Matilda', and her father's insistence that she return to England following her husband's death in 1125 was genuinely regretted. It appears that Matilda herself felt little enthusiasm for a country she had left at the age of eight. But consolation was forthcoming when the Anglo-Norman baronage, albeit reluctantly, recognized her in 1127 as Henry I's rightful heir following the death of her only brother. In 1128 she acquired her second husband, Geoffrey Plantagenet, the young heir to the

county of Anjou. Initially their relationship was tumultuous, until both realized the political advantages of the match. Then Matilda gave birth, in rapid succession, to Henry (1133), Geoffrey (1134), and William (1136).

On her father's death in 1135 the lack of enthusiasm felt by Anglo-Norman barons for a female ruler, especially the haughty, domineering, and German-speaking Matilda; the unpopularity of Geoffrey of Anjou; and the uncharacteristic efficiency of his own manoeuvring enabled her cousin Stephen of Blois to seize the throne. The Empress had no intention of accepting what she regarded as the illegal overthrow of her claim by men who had sworn to uphold it. In 1139 she landed in the West Country and became firmly established, largely thanks to Stephen's typically misplaced generosity in not taking her when he had the chance. Matilda showed no such weakness when Stephen was captured in 1141: on the contrary, he was incarcerated in Bristol Castle. But Matilda's behaviour thereafter ensured a short-lived triumph. She treated her chief supporters, Earl Robert of Gloucester and Bishop Henry of Winchester, in a foolishly high-handed manner; failed to conciliate many men who might have been won over; and, if we are to believe the contemporary *Gesta Stephani*, the new 'Lady of England and Normandy . . . had no pity on her people and demanded of them what was intolerable'. As a result she was driven from London, forced to release Stephen, and barely managed to escape with her life from Oxford in December 1142. Her shattered fortunes never recovered, and she retired to Normandy in 1148.

In later years the Empress mellowed and her influence on her son Henry II of England was generally constructive. By the time she died, optimistically clothed in nun's habit, this formidable veteran—graphically described by Arnulf of Lisieux as 'a woman who had nothing of the woman in her'—had even gained a reputation for piety and good works.

See also H. A. Cronne, *The Reign of Stephen*, 1970; R. H. C. Davies, *King Stephen*, 1967.   K.R.D.

Matilda of Boulogne (1103?–52), wife of King Stephen of England. The only child of Count Eustace III of Boulogne and Mary, daughter of Malcolm III of Scotland, she inherited both the strategically significant county of Boulogne and substantial estates in England. Her marriage to Stephen in 1125 notably strengthened his position as a potential successor to Henry I. Equally crucial was her support, political, military, and psychological, for her ineffectual husband once he had secured the English throne in 1135. She reconciled Stephen with her uncle, David I of Scotland, in 1139 and in 1140 negotiated a marriage for her son Eustace with Constance, sister of Louis VII of France. In 1141, when Stephen was imprisoned by the Empress MATILDA, she raised an army in Kent, secured London, relieved Winchester, captured Robert of Gloucester, and exchanged him for her husband before the year was out. Without the support of this courageous, energetic, and forceful woman, Stephen's failure might well have been more abject than it was. Certainly, her death deprived the ageing king of a faithful wife, sagacious counsellor, and loyal champion.

See also R. H. C. Davis, *King Stephen*, 1967.
K.R.D.

Matthews, Jessie (Mary) (1907–81), actress. Born in Soho, London, she was educated at Pulteney Street School. She studied classical ballet with Madame Elise Clerc and Miss Freedman of Terry's Juveniles, appearing first as a child-dancer in *Bluebell in Fairyland* in the Edgware Road (1919).

She worked for C. B. Cochrane in *The Music Box Revue* at the Palace Theatre (1923) and, the same year, was in the chorus of *London Calling*. In 1924 she was in New York, at the Times Square Theatre in André Charlot's Revue, which reopened at the Selwyn Theatre. When the show moved to Toronto the following year she took over the lead from Gertrude LAWRENCE and again played the lead in the Charlot Show of 1926 in London. In 1927 C. B. Cochrane put her under contract, and *One Dam Thing After Another* (1927); *Jordan* (1928); *This Year of Grace* (1928); and *Wake Up and Dream* (1929) all followed, with Jessie Matthews in leading roles. She was in the sixth Royal Command Variety Performance (1935). One of her greatest successes was in *Ever Green* at the Adelphi (1930) opposite Sonnie Hale, who became her second husband. Later she acted in the film version. After six years in films, which included *Beloved Vagabond* (silent version, 1926), *Head Over Heels*, and *Gangway*, she returned to the stage in *I Can Take It* (1939). Many other engagements followed, including overseas tours, before she

worked for ENSA in Normandy (1944). She returned to revue and straight plays, touring Australia, South Africa, and America (1950–1960). Her numerous radio broadcasts included six years in the serial *The Dales*. At the height of her fame Jessie Matthews found time to read and send hand-written replies to all her fan-letters. *A Tribute to Jessie Mathews* was given at the Huntington Hartford Museum (New York, 1965).

See also her autobiography, *Over My Shoulder*, 1974.
A.D.

Maud Charlotte Mary Victoria, Princess Maud of Wales, Queen of Norway (1869–1938). The fifth child of Edward VII and Queen Alexandra, she married Prince Christian, second son of the Crown Prince of Denmark, when he was a lieutenant in the Danish Navy. They had one child, Alexander, later Crown Prince Olav, born in 1903. In 1905 her husband was elected to the throne of Norway and accepted reluctantly, becoming Haakon VII. Maud was also reluctant but convinced of her duty. Although shy, she made a great and successful effort to learn the ways of her new country. The Norwegian court soon acquired a reputation for simplicity and informality which the Norwegians themselves appreciated. In private, Maud was vivacious and fond of practical jokes. She remained essentially English, loving country life, horses, dogs, and children. She never lost her love for England, making annual visits there. She died in London and was buried in Norway. Maud's contribution to establishing the Norwegian throne on a secure base cannot be underestimated.

See also T. Aaronson, *Grandmother of Europe*, 1976.
J.R.

Maxwell, Mrs. See BRADDON, MARY (ELIZABETH).

Melba, Dame Nellie (1861–1931), opera singer. Born at Richmond, near Melbourne, she was the daughter of a pioneer Scottish building contractor called Mitchell. She sang in public when only six, but her father refused to let her make singing her career even though her voice was obviously outstanding. She managed to take lessons from a famous teacher, Pietro Cecchi, but these were cut short when in 1882 she married Captain Charles Armstrong and went to live in Queensland. She left him a year later, taking custody of their baby son.

She travelled to Paris in 1886 to study under Mathilde Marchesi, who interrupted the audition to call out to her husband, 'Enfin, j'ai trouvé une étoile!'. The following year she made her début as Gilda in *Rigoletto* at the Théâtre de la Monnaie, Brussels, taking her professional name from her native city. The performance was greeted rapturously. Critics said her voice was a revelation, unique in quality, with a remarkable trill. Her first appearance at Covent Garden in the title role of *Lucia di Lammermoor* (1888) was received more coolly. Despite the silvery tone of her soprano voice it was thought she still had a long way to go.

Nellie Melba kept on going with increasing brilliance. People raved about her Ophelia in Ambroise Thomas's work at the Paris Opera (1889); Gounod himself gave her personal instruction for Marguerite in *Faust*; Verdi went through the part of Desdemona with her. For years she appeared every season at Covent Garden; these were known as 'Melba Nights' and people paid inordinate sums to hear her. Listening to her sing for the first time was described as an emotional experience beyond everyday living. She toured Europe, sang to royalty in their palaces, and was adored in America. She was created DBE (1918) and GBE (1927). Her only serious failure was attempting the role of Brunnhilde in *Siegfried*, after which she had to rest her voice for three months.

Having become immensely wealthy, she was famous for her generosity, giving many concerts in aid of charity and always ready to help talented young singers. Her official farewell to England took place at Covent Garden in 1926. She took her final leave of the operatic stage in Sydney (1928) and retired to Coldstream, Victoria. Her autobiography, *Melodies and Memories*, was published in 1925. She died in Sydney.

See also J. Hetherington, *Melba*, 1967; B. and F. Mackenzie, *Singers of Australia*, 1968.

P.L.

Melbourne, Lady. See LAMB, ELIZABETH, VISCOUNTESS MELBOURNE.

Mellon, Sarah Jane (1824–1909), actress. She was born at Gosport, Hampshire, the daughter of a tailor who had taken to the stage and who, though not completely successful himself,

nevertheless trained her well and guided her career. She first performed in London in 1843 at the Adelphi, being known as 'Bella' Woolgar from her appearance as Bella Wilfer in an adaptation of Dickens's *Our Mutual Friend*. The most successful phase of her career was after the re-opening of the Adelphi in 1844. After marriage to a musician, she became Mrs Alfred Mellon. She was at the Lyceum for a time (1856–58), and in 1867 became supervising manager of the Adelphi. She retired in 1883, owing to ill-health. An accomplished actress, she was praised as Anne Chute in the first London production of *The Colleen Bawn*, played Black-Eyed Susan in Douglas Jerrold's drama, and was a notable Mrs Cratchit. Towards the end of her career, her style appeared stilted compared with the contemporary trend towards 'natural' acting.

B.H.C.

Melville, Elizabeth. See COLVILLE, ELIZABETH, LADY COLVILLE OF CULROSS.

Menuhin, Hephzibah (1920–81), pianist. The daughter of Ukrainian Jews, Hephzibah was born in San Francisco, California. She was educated at home in a very sheltered environment, as was her elder brother, the violinist Yehudi Menuhin. She immediately showed promise on the piano and in 1927 her playing so impressed Marcel Ciampi that he agreed to give her lessons. Her first solo recital on 25 October 1928 at San Francisco's Scottish Rite Hall caused a sensation, as did her débuts in New York in 1932 and Paris in 1934. Also in 1934, at the instigation of Enesco, she made her début with Yehudi in the Queen's Hall, London, so beginning their life-long partnership of sonata recitals. Their duet-playing was instinctive, and on one occasion both simultaneously started the third movement of a sonata, omitting the second. Together they made not only recordings of such classical composers as Mozart, Beethoven, Brahms, and Schumann, but also of Enesco, Bartok, and Elgar. Hephzibah would only play these sonatas because they contained a true dialogue between piano and violin. As a soloist, her interpretations of Mozart's concertos were particularly famous. She was, however, a modest performer, preferring chamber recitals to solo appearances. Many of her solo performances took place in Australia. Here she made her home with her first husband, Lindsay Nicholas,

Meredith, Susanna

the brother of Yehudi's first wife, Nola. They married in 1938 and had two sons.

Hephzibah combined a musical career with an active interest in social problems, especially after her marriage to the sociologist Richard Hauser in 1956. Together they ran a settlement house in the East End of London for reformed alcoholics, drug-addicts, and recently-released mental patients. She was also involved in the women's movement and was President of the Women's League for Peace and Freedom.

See also L. M. Rolfe, *Menuhins: A Family Odyssey*, 1979; Y. Menuhin, *Unfinished Journey*, 1978.   M.G.B.

Meredith, Susanna (1823–1901), pioneer of rehabilitation for women criminals. Born in the south of Ireland, Susanna Lloyd was the eldest daughter of the governor of Cork County Gaol. She was a lively, strong-willed child with a great love of music and study. At the age of seventeen she married a successful young physician who shared her firm religious beliefs, but he died after only seven years of marriage. The shock of this early widowhood prompted her to help with various philanthropic schemes, including an industrial school to provide employment for girls in lacemaking.

After the death of her father in 1860, Susanna moved with her mother to London and there became involved in advancing the limited sphere of female employment, editing a magazine, *The Alexandra*, which advocated greater opportunities for women. A desire to give service, coupled with a suggestion that she might aid friendless women in prison, resulted in her obtaining permission from the Home Secretary to visit Brixton Prison. The misery and degradation she encountered there convinced her that she should provide spiritual and practical help for the female criminal. Home Office regulations forced her to begin by concentrating on discharged prisoners, and she started a small mission house opposite Tothill Fields Prison to provide breakfast for women newly released. There they were urged to start afresh, and some initial employment in the form of sewing was provided.

The public was at first unsympathetic to the work of the prison mission and there were initial financial difficulties. In time funds grew, enabling the purchase of a larger house and laundry in south London to provide much-needed employment for the women. Deter-

mined that the children of criminals should not follow the same path, Susanna Meredith planned village homes for these youngsters, each headed by a 'mother', along with a school, hospital, and church. In 1871 the first home at Addlestone, Surrey, was opened by Princess Mary. To protect her scheme, Susanna successfully petitioned to amend the laws concerning guardianship of children of convicted criminals. She also gave evidence before the Gladstone Committee on prisons which reported in 1895.

Her last years were spent at Addlestone, where she died in December 1901. She had done much to improve the spiritual and physical welfare of prisoners, and was perhaps the most widely recognized female prison visitor in the generation which followed Elizabeth FRY. She published *A Book about Criminals* (1881) and *Saved Rahab! An Autobiography* (1881).

See also M. A. Lloyd, *Susanna Meredith; A Record of a Vigorous Life*, 1903.   J.G.S.

Mew, Charlotte (Mary) (1869–1928), poet. Born in London and educated privately, she lived briefly in Paris and then in London with her youngest sister. Her life was a losing battle aginst poverty, illness, despair. She wrote prose before poetry, publishing her first stories in *The Yellow Book* (1894), and then contributing essays and stories to leading journals. Her first volume of poems, *The Farmer's Bride* (1916), won her the friendship of Thomas Hardy, who considered she was undoubtedly the best woman poet of the time. Other writers praised her sincerity and poignancy. She often used a narrative form of a strange and disturbing power. Extremely self-critical and secretive, she destroyed much of her work. In 1923, to mitigate her dire poverty, friends procured a Civil List pension of £75. She became seriously ill in 1927 and the death of her sister proved too great a loss to bear; she committed suicide. Her second volume of poems, *The Rambling Sailor*, was published posthumously.

See also *Collected Poems*, preface by A. Monro, 1953; L. Untermeyer, *Lives of the Poets*, 1960.   P.L.

Meynell, Alice Christiana Gertrude (1847–1922), poet, essayist, and critic. She was born at Barnes in London, but lived as a child in Italy, France, and Switzerland. Her father, T. J. Thompson, a friend of Charles Dickens, educated her thoroughly. In 1872 she followed her mother's conversion to Roman Catholicism, as subsequently did her father and sister.

In 1875 her first first volume of verse, *Preludes*, was produced by Tennyson's publisher. Two years later she married the journalist and literary critic Wilfred Meynell, who greatly encouraged her literary activities. The couple were both busy with journalistic work. Alice contributed to *The Pall Mall Gazette*, *The National Observer*, *The Spectator*, and *The Saturday Review*. She also helped with her husband's Catholic periodicals, *The Weekly Register* and *Merry England*.

The Meynells lived in London for most of their married life. Their family comprised four girls and four boys, one of whom died in infancy, and they also cared for the poet Francis Thompson. Their home was comparatively poor, yet they were a hospitable couple, frequently entertaining such important literary figures of the time as Ruskin, Rossetti, Tennyson, Browning, George Eliot, and Meredith.

Alice Meynell wrote numerous essays published as books. They included *The Rhythm of Life*, 1893, *The Colour of Life*, 1896, *London Impressions*, 1898, *Ceres' Runaway*, 1909, and *The Second Person Singular*, 1921. But it is for her poetry that she will be remembered: *Poems*, 1893, *Other Poems*, 1896, *Later Poems* 1902, *A Father of Women*, 1917, and *Last Poems*, published posthumously in 1923.

See also V. Meynell, *Alice Meynell: A Memoir*, 1929.   A.P.

Middleton, Mary (1870–1911), political activist. The daughter of Walter Muir, an overman in the mining industry, Mary was born at Carnworth, Scotland, and grew up in various mining villages in the area. She wanted to be a teacher, but the low wages made this an impossible ambition for a girl from a large family, so she went into domestic service in the Workington area.

During this time she became acquainted with J. S. Middleton, who was then working as a printer/reporter on his father's paper, *The Workington Star*. After the young couple married they decided to seek employment in London. It was while working on a north London newspaper that Jim and Mary Middleton came to know James Ramsay MacDonald, then Secretary of the recently formed Labour Representation Committee, afterwards the Labour Party. He offered Middleton a part-time post as his assistant, and so began a fruitful association for both. The secretarial work of the embryo Labour Party was at that time being done at the MacDonald flat in Lincoln's Inn Fields. In 1905 a letter arrived from the Railway Women's Guild asking that women should be given the opportunity for political education in the Labour Party and helping in its work. When a similar request came from Mrs Cawthorne, a docker's wife in Hull, the two men decided to ask their wives to help. The result was the formation of the Women's Labour League in 1906, with Margaret MAC-DONALD as chairman and Mary Middleton as Secretary.

Both women worked unsparingly over the next five years to lay the foundations for what was to become perhaps the finest political organization of women in Britain, or even the English-speaking world. Mary Middleton was not to see the full results of their work, for she died in the spring of 1911. Having started a scheme for the establishment of a baby clinic in her memory, Margaret MacDonald died the same year. The clinic became a memorial to them both.   L.M,

Mildmay, Lady Grace (c. 1552–1620), diarist. Grace was the second daughter of Sir Henry Sherrington, a Wiltshire landowner, and was given a strict religious upbringing as well as a grounding in the medical skills she later practised. In 1570 she entered another sober Puritan household when, after some hesitation on the groom's part, she married Anthony, son of Sir Walter Mildmay, a leading Elizabethan politician. Her early married life was lonely as her husband was 'much away' at court but Grace resisted the temptation to follow suit. 'God had placed me in the world in this house and if I found no comfort here, I would never seek it out of this house.' The marriage led to the birth of one daughter. It was perhaps not entirely happy, but Grace was a dutiful wife. She recorded on her husband's death in 1617, 'I carried always that reverend respect towards him . . . that I could not find it in my heart to challenge him for the worst word or deed which ever he offered me . . . but in silence passed over all such matters between us'. Grace's journal covers 1570 to 1617 and gives a clear insight into the full life of a sixteenth-century 'godly gentlewoman'. That life was based on the home, but on a home that was a vital part of the wider neighbourhood. Grace supervised the strict religious observances within the household, and was fully occupied with medical and charitable works on her estate. Her philanthropic interests were revealed in her will, which left funds to provide work for the poor, to finance the projects of young tradesmen, and to educate poor scholars at Emmanuel College, Cambridge, her father-in-law's Puritan foundation.

See also R. Weigall, 'An Elizabethan Gentlewoman', in *Quarterly Review* 428, 1911.

A.H.

Millar, Gertie (1879–1952), actress. This most famous and beautiful of the Gaiety Girls was born in Bradford, the daughter of a millworker. She made her first stage appearance at thirteen in the pantomime *Babes in the Wood* at Manchester. Then followed other provincial musicals before her London appearance in *Cinderella* (December 1899). In June 1901 she was in *The Toreador* at the Gaiety Theatre, where she stayed for seven years except for a short time in *A Waltz Dream* at the Hicks Theatre (1908). In 1902 she married the composer, Lionel Monckton. She made her New York début in *The Girls of Gottenberg*. In January 1909 she returned to the Gaiety in *Our Miss Gibbs*. An exquisite dancer with a small, sweet voice and an enchanting smile, Gertie Millar played in many musicals, including *The Quaker Girl* (1910) and *The Critic* at the Gala Performance of June 1911. Her first variety performance was in a repertory of songs. After *Flora* (1918) she retired from the stage. Following Monckton's death in 1924 she married the second Earl of Dudley (1931).

A.D.

Milner, Violet Georgina, Lady (1872–1958), periodical editor. Her parents were incompatible, and her childhood was divided between them; at its end she spent two years in Paris with her father, Admiral Maxse, during which she studied art. In 1894 she married into one of England's great political families; her husband, Lord Edward Cecil, was the son of Lord Salisbury and made a distinguished career in the army and the Egyptian civil service. He died in 1918, and in 1921 Lady Cecil married the imperialist administrator Lord Milner, who died in 1925.

Lady Milner's own public career began when she ran *The National Review* during the illness of her brother Leo Maxse. After his death she took it over permanently. Under her editorship (1932–48) *The National Review* was right-wing, albeit often eccentric— fiercely conservative, imperialist, anti-internationalist, pro-French and anti-German.

See also Lady Milner's reminiscences, *My Picture Gallery 1886–1901*, 1951.

N.H.

Mitchell, Hannah Maria (1871–1956), suffragette and socialist. She was born in Alport Dale, Derbyshire, the daughter of a farmer and a domestic servant. Educated at home, she spent a year apprenticed to a dressmaker, and later worked as a dressmaker or maid. In 1895 she married Gibbon Mitchell, a tailor's cutter, by whom she had one son. She deliberately curtailed her family, aware of the restrictions imposed on women's public ambitions by marriage and motherhood. She had moved before her marriage to Bolton, where she was converted to socialism through the various influences of Robert Blatchford, *The Clarion*, visiting speakers, and her husband. With her husband she joined the Labour Church, the Clarion Van movement, and the Independent Labour Party. In 1904 and 1906 she was elected ILP member to Ashton-under-Lyne Board of Guardians.

Hannah Mitchell's feminism germinated early, as she perceived the disadvantages women experienced. It was fostered through membership of the Women's Co-operative Guild and through contact with Emmeline and Christabel PANKHURST in the ILP Manchester branch. She joined the Women's Social and Political Union in 1903, was imprisoned briefly for militancy in 1906, and became a speaker and part-time organizer in the North. Recovering from a nervous breakdown in 1907, she joined the Women's Freedom League and was their organizer in East Fife, Scotland, in the summer of 1908. She continued suffragette activities until the First World War when, as a pacifist, she supported the No Conscription Fellowship and the Women's International League for Peace and Freedom.

In 1918 she resumed her activities to extend women's suffrage and her work for the ILP. She was elected Labour member (as ILP nominee) of Manchester City Council in 1924, 1926, 1929, and ILP member in 1932. From 1926 to 1946 she was City Magistrate for Manchester. After the war she also began writing, producing dialect sketches for *The North-*

ern Voice and articles for *Manchester City News*. She recorded her life story in *The Hard Way Up* (1968). L.W.

Mitford, Mary Russell (1787–1855), author. She was the only child of George Mitford, who was disliked by most of his acquaintances and who succeeded in gambling away most of the family fortune. At the age of ten, Mary chose for him a lottery ticket which won £20,000, thus retrieving the family finances, at least for a time. Most of her adult life, however, was spent in efforts to maintain her parents by writing. In spite of severe strains and difficulties, she remained touchingly and indeed perversely loyal to her father until his death in 1842.

Miss Mitford is chiefly remembered for her accurate and affectionate portrait of life in an English village. First published as occasional sketches in *The Lady's Magazine* from 1822, it was so popular that it increased sales of the magazine considerably, and it was later published several times in collected form as *Our Village*. The author would probably have been surprised and perhaps vexed at the opinion of posterity, for she thought more highly of her dramatic works. Her first play, *Julian*, was produced at Covent Garden in 1823, although it lasted for only eight nights. Macready played the principal part, noting somewhat coolly in his diary: '*Julian* ... had but a moderate success ... the performance made but little impression, and was soon forgotten'. Another drama, *Foscari*, followed in 1826, and a third, *Rienzi*, in 1828. The last, with its rather elaborate moral purpose, was probably her best dramatic production. It ran much longer on the stage than its predecessors and sold several thousand copies. Mary also wrote some poetry which Coleridge found interesting, and other dramatic pieces as well as fiction.

If her reputation rested on these productions alone Mary Russell Mitford would no doubt be forgotten. *Our Village* remains her major achievement. It has points of resemblance to Lamb, Mrs Gaskell, and Jane Austen. The style is straightforward, familiar, and unmannered. Its purpose was to give a picture of the environment and inhabitants of a quiet south-country parish. The first page is a prospectus, announcing her theme as the 'little world of our own, close-packed and insulated like ants in an ant-hill'. The detailed descriptions that follow show an amused tolerance for mankind and

a great love for natural things. Elizabeth Barrett praised the 'Dutch minuteness and high finishing' of the sketches. Many of the scenes are set outdoors and involve walks to collect the flowers and fruits of the countryside. The weather is a constant matter for comment. In many ways *Our Village* is a pioneer of the 'Countryside Column' of modern journalism, which attempts to satisfy the yearning of an increasingly urbanized society for news from the world outside the town. The effect upon the real setting of the sketches, a village called Three Mile Cross near Reading, was to make it into an early tourist attraction.

In her last years Mary moved to nearby Swallowfield, still receiving the visits of admirers and maintaining a correspondence with, among others, W. S. Landor and Ruskin. Her final years were more tranquil, especially as her father's debts had finally been paid off. She died in 1855, having never married, leaving her property to her two servants, save for her well-stocked library, which was distributed among her circle of friends.

See also I. Jack, *English Literature 1815–1832*, 1963. T.H.

Mitford, Nancy (Freeman) (1904–73), novelist and biographer. The Hon. Nancy Mitford was the eldest of the second Baron Redesdale's six daughters. Born in London, she grew up there and in the Cotswolds, learning to ride and to speak French but receiving no other formal education. She remained a francophile for life; after the Second World War she settled in France, first in Paris and later at Versailles. From 1933 until their divorce in 1958 she was married to the Hon. Peter Rodd; they had no children.

It was after 'coming out' in London society and associating with its literary figures —including Evelyn Waugh, a friend whose sense of comedy she shared—that she began to write. Her first novel was *Highland Fling* (1931). Seven others were to follow. *The Pursuit of Love* (1945) and its sequel *Love in a Cold Climate* (1949) were immensely popular. *The Blessing* (1951) was filmed in 1959 as *Count Your Blessings*. Her novels were written in a simple and unpretentious style, painting a witty, irreverent portrait of upper-class manners. While critics debated whether or not she was a 'serious' writer, her books were reprinted continuously and have recently acquired a

Molesworth, Mary Louisa

period flavour in their depiction of a vanished era. Many of their characters were drawn from life, including the portrayal of her father as the eccentric Uncle Matthew.

Three biographical studies of eighteenth-century France were scholarly and founded on careful research, but also popular with the general reader, especially *Madame de Pompadour* (1954) and *The Sun King, Louis XIV at Versailles* (1966). A fourth biography, of Frederick the Great (1970), was researched and written when she was already suffering from cancer. Among her other works are an English translation of Mme de la Fayette's *The Princess of Cleves* (1950); an adaptation and translation of André Roussin's play *The Little Hut* (1951); and a book of essays *The Water Beetle* (1962). She edited and contributed to *Noblesse Oblige* (1956), in which she included Professor Alan Ross's paper on 'U' (upper class) and 'non-U' (non-upper class) usage, written two years earlier; it was he, not she, who coined the terms.   J.L.

Molesworth, Mary Louisa (1839–1921), children's author. She was born in Rotterdam, where her father was a merchant. The family moved to Manchester in 1841 and she described her childhood there in *The Carved Lions* (1895). Educated mostly at home, she was taught by her mother.

In 1861 she married Major Richard Molesworth, and narrated her first stories to her own children, of whom there were seven. She then wrote for them and about them, giving a child's-eye view of life. She excelled in portraying very young children, who usually inhabited a strict but loving world in which Nurse often had more reality than parents. The poet Swinburne hailed her as a perfect portrayer of children.

After legal separation in 1878 from her husband, whose personality had been deranged by a head wound received in the Crimea, she wrote continually, in order to support her family. Among her best-loved books were *Tell Me A Story*, 1875; *Carrots*, 1876; *The Tapestry Room*, 1879; and *Nurse Heatherdale's Story*, 1891. Children today still read her tales. She died in 1921, having published more than a hundred books.

See also G. Avery, *Nineteenth Century Children*, 1965; R. Lancelyn Green, *Tellers of Tales*, 1969.   P.L.

Monckton, Mary, Countess of Cork and Orrery (1746–1845), conversationalist, bluestocking, and hostess, the daughter of Viscount Galway. As a young woman she held well-attended *conversazioni* at her mother's house in Berkeley Square, and she entertained on an even grander scale after her marriage in 1786 to the Earl of Cork. The diarist Fanny Burney, while admitting that Mary Monckton was 'handsome', made pertinent observations about her shortness, fatness, fantastic mode of dress, and over-use of rouge. As a hostess, however, she had the advantages of liveliness of manner and a flow of witty and agreeable talk that evidently made for social ease. She was a favourite with Dr Johnson—his 'dearest dunce', and according to Boswell 'her vivacity enchanted the sage'. Thanks to her unflagging ardour and longevity, she played hostess to several generations of celebrities, from Johnson and Burke to Byron and Scott. Her company continued to be sought even in extreme old age and despite mild fits of kleptomania.   N.H.

Montagu, Elizabeth (1720–1800), bluestocking. Born Elizabeth Robinson, she showed early signs of intellectual tastes. Her marriage in 1742 to the fifty-one-year-old Edward Montagu made her cousin-in-law of Lady Mary Wortley MONTAGU and Laurence Sterne. She contributed anonymously to Lyttleton's *Dialogues of the Dead* (1760) and wrote *Essay on the Writings and Genius of Shakespeare* (1769). Samuel Johnson dubbed Elizabeth Montagu 'Queen of the Blues', in reference to her membership of the 'bluestocking' circle of learned women which included Mrs DELANY, Mrs Boscawen, Mrs CHAPONE, Mrs CARTER, and Hannah MORE.

After her husband's death in 1776 Elizabeth Montagu consolidated the control she had gained over his business interests in his old age. Some of the considerable wealth she amassed was invested in a magnificent house in Portman Square. In the construction and embellishment of her properties, which included the estates Sandleford, Allerthorpe, and Denton, Elizabeth Montagu employed the greatest designers of her age. 'Athenian' Stuart, Robert Adam, Cipriani, Capability Brown, and Angelica Kauffman were all set to work. In the salons of these houses Elizabeth Montagu gathered round her such eminent figures of literary London as Gilbert West, Edward Young, Lord Lyttleton, and James Beattie.

See also A. A. Hufstader, *Sisters of the Quill*, 1978.   A.L.

Montagu, Lady Mary Wortley (1689–1762), essayist, poet, and letter writer. Born Mary Pierrepont, daughter of the future Marquess of Dorchester, she spent her childhood isolated from others of her age but enriched by acquaintance with her father's friends Addison, Steele, Congreve, and Garth. Following an erratic courtship conducted secretly because of her father's disapproval, she eloped in 1712 with Edward Wortley Montagu. The accession of George I in 1714 ensured Montagu's political career, and in 1715 Lady Mary emerged from retirement in Yorkshire to aid her husband in London. Her first published work, an anonymous essay in *The Spectator* (1714), was succeeded by collaboration with Pope and Gay in the writing of satiric eclogues. These were circulated privately until Curll pirated them in a pamphlet entitled *Court Poems* (1716).

In 1716 she followed her husband to Turkey, where he had been appointed ambassador to the Porte. Here her observation of the practice of inoculation for smallpox, from which she had suffered in 1715, led her to campaign for immunization after her husband's recall to England in 1717. The *Embassy Letters* written during her years in Turkey were published posthumously to great acclaim in 1763. Pope's love for her was repulsed on her return, and his growing enmity ultimately found expression in *The Dunciad* (1728). At the same time Wortley Montagu's engrossment in business and political affairs contributed to the breakdown of their marriage. In 1736 Lady Mary met the Italian Francesco Algarotti, and letters written soon after the event reveal her deep infatuation. For the next two years she was involved in political journalism in support of the government.

She left England for the Continent in 1739, ostensibly to improve her health, but in fact to pursue Algarotti, whom she met only briefly in Venice. The wandering life of the expatriate which lasted until 1762 led her through Italy to settlement in Avignon (1742–46) and Brescia (1746–56). The voluminous correspondence of these years reveals troubled relations with her son, but great love for her daughter Lady Bute. In 1756 she moved to Venice and then Padua, where she stayed until her husband's death prompted her return to England. In later life she considered that her extensive knowledge and famed wit had been negative gifts because of their isolating effects. Letters to her granddaughters cautioned them to conceal their learning at the expense of inviting envy.

See also R. Halsband, *The Life of Lady Mary Wortley Montagu*, 1956.   A.L.

Montez, Lola (1818–61), dancer and adventuress who was born Marie Dolores Eliza Rosanna Gilbert, in Limerick. The family went with her soldier father to India, where he died of cholera in 1825. Upon her mother's remarriage, she was sent back to her stepfather's family in Scotland in 1826. In order to avoid an unwanted marriage she eloped to Ireland with Captain Thomas James, whom she married in 1837 and accompanied to India, but on their return in 1842 he applied for divorce on the grounds of her adultery on the voyage home. She then studied drama, but showed more promise as a dancer and first appeared at Her Majesty's in London as 'Lola Montez, Spanish dancer', without great success.

More enthusiasm was stimulated in Dresden, Berlin, Warsaw, and St Petersburg, where she was received by the Emperor Nicholas and showered with presents. In Paris, she was party to a sensational duel and trial, at which the novelist Alexandre Dumas appeared as a witness. In 1847 she was in Munich, where her dancing completely captivated the old King Ludwig of Bavaria, who granted her naturalization, titles, a pension, and a mansion. Thereupon she more or less ruled Bavaria, showing unexpected ability and liberal views. However, opposition quickly developed, and after a period of disorder, she was banished, and the King forced to abdicate.

In 1849 she went to England where her marriage to George T. Heald, who was just of age, resulted in a summons for bigamy. The couple fled to Spain, and in 1853 he was reported drowned at Lisbon. She then appeared in America, on Broadway, and in 1853 was briefly married to P. P. Hull. She visited Australia and France, gave lectures on beautiful and heroic women, and published *The Art of Beauty* (1858). But her health was shattered. As a result of meeting an old schoolfriend in 1859 she had a complete change of heart and devoted herself to helping 'fallen

297

women' at the Magdalen Asylum near New York. While engaged in this work, she was stricken with paralysis and died, penitent, after much suffering.

See also *Autobiography and Letters of Lola Montez*, 1858; A. Darling, *Lola Montez*, 1972.

B.H.C.

Montfort, Eleanor (1252–82), Princess of Wales. The only daughter of Earl Simon de Montfort, she was betrothed to Prince Lly-welyn ap Gruffydd of Wales during her father's short-lived ascendancy in England in the 1260s. The project was revived but in 1275, while on her way to her marriage in Wales, she was captured and brought instead to Edward I at Windsor. There she remained until 1278 when, following Llywelyn's sub-mission to the King, the marriage was at last celebrated. Eleanor died, giving birth to a daughter, in June 1282.

See also F. M. Powicke, *King Henry III and the Lord Edward*, 1947.

K.R.D.

Moore, Mary (1861–1931), actress and theatre manager. Her father was Charles Moore of Dublin, a prosperous parliamentary agent in London until his ruin in 1873. At the age of sixteen Mary therefore left Warwick Hall, Maida Vale, to follow her sister on the stage and to help with the family finances. She made a good start at the Gaiety Theatre in pantom-ime and light opera, having a sweet singing voice and a pretty face. In the same year (1878) she married the brilliant but erratic forty-year-old dramatist James Albery, and left the stage. She returned in 1885 to support her now invalid husband and three sons. Given a touring engagement as understudy by Charles Wyndham, manager of the Criterion Theatre, she soon became Wyndham's leading lady in a revival of John O'Keefe's *Wild Oats* in May 1886. Her name was made overnight.

Famous for portraying helpless little women, 'she knew to a shade how to make them foolish without making them tiresome, and helpless without being intolerably silly'. In real life she was an excellent business-woman, managing her own affairs wisely after her husband's death in 1889.

Her partnership with Wyndham, first in acting and then after 1896 in business, was one of the most famous in theatrical history. The Wyndham Theatre opened in 1899 and the New Theatre in 1903. As actors they were famous in the United States, Russia, and Ger-many until 1913, when failing memory forced Wyndham's retirement at the age of seventy-six, despite his still youthful appear-ance and manner. Mary did little acting after that, and married her partner in 1916 to care for him in his widowhood. After Wyndham's death in 1919, apart from charity perform-ances she made one successful appearance as Lady Bagley in *Our Mr Hepplewhite* and then devoted herself to theatrical management, founding Wyndham Theatres Limited in 1924, helped by her stepson Howard Wynd-ham, and her son Bronson Albery.

A.D.

Moore, Monica. See WILSON, MONA.

More, Hannah (1745–1833), writer and moral reformer. Born at Stapleton, Gloucestershire, she was the fourth of five daughters of a schoolmaster who encouraged her early enthusiasm for learning. She later attended her sisters' boarding-school, and became fluent in French, Spanish, Italian, and Latin. In 1767 she accepted a proposal of marriage from a Mr Turner, but the marriage date was repeat-edly postponed by him and the engagement eventually broken. Subsequently, Hannah More resolved never to marry, although she continued to receive offers.

In 1774 she visited London, where she met the actor David Garrick who introduced her to literary circles. She became friendly with Mrs MONTAGU and other 'bluestockings', who provided her with material for her poem *Bas Bleu*, written in 1786. She also met Burke, Reynolds, and Dr Johnson, who was fond of her. In 1777 her tragedy *Percy* was successfully performed at Covent Garden. But after Gar-rick's death in 1779 she gradually drew away from her literary friends and became increas-ingly hostile to the stage. In 1787 she was much impressed by the preaching of the Evan-gelical John Newton, and later in the same year met William Wilberforce, beginning a life-long friendship. These new sober influ-ences are very apparent in her next works, *Thoughts on the Importance of the Manners of the Great to General Society*, published in 1788, and *An Estimate of the Religion of the Fashionable World* (1790). Both sought to demonstrate the vital distinction between real and superficial religious convictions and are classic expositions of nascent Evangelical opinion.

In 1789 Hannah More and her sister Martha visited Cheddar with Wilberforce, who was astonished at the degradation and ignorance of its poor inhabitants. At his suggestion, the More sisters set up a Sunday School there, later establishing others in neighbouring parishes. The schools were to provide a Christian education suitable for the pupils' social position. Children were taught to read the Bible and the Catechism, but there was no instruction in writing. In 1800, Hannah More was accused by the curate of Blagdon of allowing Methodist doctrine to be propagated in her schools. An acrimonious struggle ensued, during which the schools were repeatedly closed and re-opened. In 1803 she secured the support of the new Bishop of Bath and Wells, and the controversy gradually died away.

Apprehension caused by the spread of democratic ideas after 1789 led the Bishop of London to urge Miss More to produce a popular pamphlet discouraging sedition. In 1792 she published *Village Politics*, which was rapturously received by the loyal establishment. Encouraged, she composed many similar works over the next few years, known collectivly as the *Cheap Repository Tracts*. By 1799, two million copies were said to have been sold. With the return of unrest after 1815, she produced a further series of anti-radical pieces, culminating in the *Moral Sketches* of 1819. She wrote little after this, and her health began to fail.

Perhaps the most influential woman of her day, Hannah More was a crucial figure in the development towards high moral and religious seriousness which was to characterize Victorian Britain. An acute intelligence enabled her to criticize the pretensions of the society in which she had herself moved, while her enthusiasm for practical benevolence illustrates the increased sense of responsibility for the spiritual welfare of the poor which preoccupied committed Christians from the late eighteenth century onwards. Her other works include *Coelebs in Search of a Wife* (1809) and *Practical Piety* (1811).

See also M. G. Jones, *Hannah More*, 1952; H. Thompson, *Life of Hannah More*, 1838.

J.B.L.

Morley, Mrs. See ANNE, Queen of Great Britain and Ireland.

Morrell, Lady Ottoline (Anne Violet) (1873–1938), literary hostess. Born in London,

she was the daughter of Lieutenant-Colonel Arthur Bentinck, heir to the fifth Duke of Portland. Bentinck's early death made his son by his first wife heir to the dukedom, but Disraeli, who was grateful for the Bentincks' political support, induced Queen Victoria to bestow titles on all the children.

Ottoline was six feet tall, gauche, intellectual, and solitary. However, her fascinating conversation, unorthodox views, and exotic clothes often gave an impression of beauty. Educated at home, Ottoline spent a short time at Somerville College, Oxford, studying politics and Roman history. Her love of literature gained her the friendship of H. H. Asquith from 1898. In February 1902 she married Philip Morrell, a solicitor who became MP for South Oxfordshire in 1906, the year in which Ottoline gave birth to twins; only the daughter lived. Ottoline began her 'At Homes' at 44 Bedford Square, London, in 1908. She entertained all the great political and literary figures of the day, including W. B. Yeats to whom she remarked 'It's wonderful how the Irish have got so much more sensible now—none of that Celtic twilight stuff anymore'. Their friendship nevertheless survived.

Ottoline was notorious as the mistress of many famous men, among them Axel Munthe, Augustus John, Henry Lamb, and Bertrand Russell, who wrote her over 2000 letters. But she also campaigned vigorously for her husband helping him to win Burnley in 1911 for the Liberals. She was often the first to recognize a special talent, and also gave practical help to struggling artists, among them T. S. Eliot, who was probably her truest friend. But among the famous who accepted her hospitality, including many members of the 'Bloomsbury set', some frequently derided her. Lytton Strachey, a lifelong friend wrote of her 'hobbling through the buttercups wearing cheap shoes', while D. H. Lawrence and Aldous Huxley both caricatured her mercilessly in their novels, causing her sadness and bewilderment.

In 1927 an operation for necrosis of the jaw left her badly scarred. Eleven years later she entered Dr Cameron's Tunbridge Wells Clinic to be treated with injections of the powerful antibiotic Prontosil. She made a return visit to the clinic, despite the doctor's suicide after threats of official investigation because of Prontosil's results on other patients. She died while a nurse was injecting the drug, the official cause of death being given as 'heart failure'.

Morris, Margaret

Margot Asquith in her *Times* obituary wrote: 'I never heard her utter an unkind word—of how many clever women can we say the same?'.

See also S. J. Darrough, *'Ottoline', the life of Lady Ottoline Morrell*, 1976.　　A.D.

Morris, Margaret (1891–1980), dancer. Born in London, Margaret Morris lived with her parents in France until the age of five when she returned to England. Her mother was determined that her daughter should go on the stage. She had no formal academic education, but went to dancing classes where she soon rebelled against classical ballet and began to compose exercises of her own. In 1909 she met Raymond Duncan, who taught her the six classical Greek dance positions. She adapted and used these as the basis of her own system of movement, and in 1910 choreographed the dances for Gluck's *Orpheus and Eurydice*. At this time she met John Galsworthy, who encouraged her to open her first school in London. By 1913 she was again in France, where in Paris she met J. D. Fergusson, a Scottish painter who later became her husband and who was an important influence on her work. He introduced her to the Paris art world and with her in 1915 started the Margaret Morris Club, which became a centre for discussion and the presentation of creative ideas. It was patronized by Augustus John, Katherine MANSFIELD, and Ezra Pound, among others.

Becoming convinced of the remedial possibilities of the movement system she had developed, Margaret Morris took a massage and medical gymnastic training which she passed with distinction in 1930. She had great faith in the value of her system to the handicapped, believing that 'the more normal you make people feel the more normal they would become'. She extended her exercises into sports training, writing a book with the tennis star Suzanne Lenglen, and tried to have her methods accepted in schools by the education authorities. Although she achieved only limited acceptance in this area, her influence was immense on the modern practice of physical education, on remedial work, and in choreographic innovation.

See also M. Morris, *My Life in Movement*, 1971.　　E.M.V.

Moser, Mary (1744–1819), flower painter. Her father was a Swiss gold-chaser and enameller who was appointed first Keeper of the Royal Academy in London. Mary Moser herself exhibited flower paintings at the Academy when she was still a child, and was a founder member at the age of twenty. With Angelica Kauffmann she was included in Zoffany's depiction of Academy members, *Life School of the Royal Academy*, as portraits hanging on the wall. She continued to exhibit there regularly between 1768 and 1790, and although she did attempt occasional history paintings, it is as the first significant British flower painter that she is best known. She was patronized by Queen Charlotte, who paid her £900 to decorate the ceiling and walls of a room at Frogmore, Windsor. After her marriage in 1797 to Captain Hugh Lloyd she ceased to work professionally.

See also G. Greer, *The Obstacle Race. The Fortunes of Women Painters and Their Work*, 1979; A. S. Harris and L. Nochlin, *Women Artists: 1550–1950*, 1976.　　A.L.

Mosley, Lady Cynthia (1899–1933), Labour MP. The daughter of Lord Curzon of Kedleston, she became one of the wealthiest women in the country when she inherited a fortune from her maternal grandfather, a Chicago millionaire. She met Oswald (later Sir Oswald) Mosley when both were campaigning for Lady ASTOR in Plymouth. Sir Oswald was Conservative MP for Harrow and the two seemed set for a glamorous political life when they married in great style, with the King and Queen among their wedding guests. They had three children.

Lady Cynthia was not content to be a passive political wife, however, and when Mosley crossed the floor of the House to join the Independent Labour Party she joined with him. He became Labour MP for Smethwick and in 1929 she won Stoke-on-Trent. They thus became, after the Runcimans and the Daltons, the third married couple to sit in the House together and were seen as 'a pair of magnificent cuckoos in the Labour Party nest'. She was never a strong speaker but was much liked in the Commons, and when her husband began his New Party (later to become the British Union of Fascists) many believed that it was loyalty rather than political conviction which led her to support him and resign from the Labour Party. She died young of peritonitis and was commemorated by the building of the Cynthia Mosley Day Nursery at Kennington.

See also P. Brooks, *Women at Westminster*, 1967.   E.M.V.

Mountbatten, Lady Edwina (Cynthia Annette), Countess Mountbatten of Burma (1901–60), public figure, born in London. Edwina Ashley was descended on her father's side from the nineteenth-century social reformer Lord Shaftesbury, and on her mother's from the great financier Sir Ernest Cassell. On Cassell's death in 1921 she became a rich woman, having inherited the interest on part of his immense fortune. In 1922 she married Lord Louis Mountbatten, then a lieutenant in the Royal Navy, and was thereafter the partner in his long and distinguished career, culminating in his appointment in 1946 as last Viceroy of India, responsible for the transition of the sub-continent to independence.

However, Lady Mountbatten also succeeded in making a career of her own as a patron and organizer of voluntary work, and especially of hospitals and nursing. During the Second World War she began her long commitment to the St John Ambulance Association, travelling tirelessly as its superintendent-in-chief. When Lord Mountbatten was appointed Chief of Combined Operations in 1942, and later Supreme Allied Commander in South-East Asia (1943–46), his wife took over the arduous job of organizing the welfare side of these commands, which became increasingly important with the need to care for large numbers of prisoners of war and displaced civilians. Later, during the outbreaks of mass violence and vast population transfers that accompanied partition in India, she was chiefly responsible for forming the United Council for Relief which co-ordinated the efforts of the various voluntary organizations. In the 1950s she continued to work for the Red Cross, the WVS, the Royal College of Nursing, and many other organizations. But the St John's Ambulance Brigade remained her overriding concern, and it was in North Borneo, on one of her long, exhausting tours of inspection, that she died.   N.H.

Mountfort, Susanna (*c.* 1667–1703), actress. The daughter of Thomas Percival, a minor actor in the Duke's Company, she made her début in 1681 with the King's Company, which offered greater opportunities for young actresses. A natural mimic and an attractive woman, particularly admired in male attire, Susanna had no inhibitions about donning grotesque clothing or make-up and developed rapidly into an outstanding comedienne, equally accomplished in broad comedy or subtle satire. In 1686 she married a rising young actor, William Mountfort, and the couple, growing in professional stature, often performed together on stage. Their first child, Susanna, also became a comic actress and was probably born in 1688. A second daughter was born in 1692, but died when eight days old. Her mother, who apparently found motherhood compatible with her career and took little time off from acting, returned to work several months later. Two further tragedies shattered her life soon afterwards. Her husband was killed in a duel by Captain Richard Hill, who suspected him to be a rival for the affections of Anne BRACEGIRDLE. Susanna was left alone to bear another daughter, Mary, in 1693. In October of that year her father was condemned to death for clipping coins. Susanna's intercession with Queen Mary led to the sentence being commuted to transportation, but Thomas Percival died on the way to his ship.

Persevering in her career, she married another successful young actor, John Verbruggen, in January 1694. Too ill to accompany her fellow actors to Bath in the summer of 1703, Susanna died several months later in childbed. The 'mistress of more variety of humour' than Colley Cibber had ever known in a single actress, Susanna Mountfort was a dedicated performer, unrivalled as a comic actress.

See also A. S. Borgman, *The Life and Death of William Mountfort*, 1935; J. H. Wilson, *All the King's Ladies*, 1958.   T.J.M.

Mulock, Dinah (Maria) (1826–87), novelist. She was born at Stoke-on-Trent, Staffordshire, where her father was a Nonconformist clergyman, and educated at Brampton House Academy in Newcastle under Lyme. At thirteen she taught elementary Latin in a small school where her mother was a teacher.

In 1846 the family moved to London, where Dinah continued her studies, but three years later she took her mother back to Staffordshire in order to get away from her unstable father; her mother died the following year. In 1847 the elder of her two brothers died in an accident and Dinah and her remaining brother, Benjamin, had to live on their mother's diminished estate.

Her first novel, *The Ogilvies*, was published in 1849, followed by *Olive* (1850) and *The Head of the Family* (1851). The copyright in each book was sold to Chapman and Hall for £150. In 1856 her most famous work, *John Halifax, Gentleman*, was published. The novel's hero is an orphan boy, poor and humbly born, yet possessing all the true qualities of a gentleman, who, largely by his own efforts, rises in the world and finally marries the heroine.

By now she was well known in literary society and a friend of Alexander Macmillan, Charles Mudie and Margaret OLIPHANT. She moved to Hampstead with her brother in 1859, but he died four years later and she sold the house in 1864. The next year Dinah married George Lillie Craik, a partner and editor in the publishing house of Macmillan. They built a house in Bromley where they lived until her death. She remained childless but adopted a girl, Dorothy, in 1872. A generous woman who used her pension (granted in 1864) to help needy authors, Dinah Mulock Craik was also a good business woman. At the end of her life she could command £2000 for the copyright of a story. As well as novels, plays, and poetry, she wrote biography, travel books, didactic essays, and a children's story, *The Little Lame Prince*, 1874. Her other novels include *A Life for a Life*, 1859, *Christian's Mistake*, 1865, and *Young Mrs Jardine*, 1879.   A.P.

Munnings, Hilda. See SOKOLOVA, LYDIA.

Murray, Hon. Mrs. See AUST, SARAH.

Murray, Alma (1854–1946), actress. Born in London, the daughter of an actor, she was educated privately and first performed as a child. As an adult she played at the Olympic Theatre in 1870, in *The Princess*. From 1875 to 1877 she toured in the provinces and in 1876 married Alfred Forman, the translator of Wagner's *Ring of the Nibelung, Tristan and Isolde, Parsifal*, and *Tannhäuser*. In 1879 she was at the Lyceum with Irving, and at the Prince's Hall in 1884 made her first appearance in poetic drama, in Browning's *In A Balcony*. The following year she played Colombe in *Colombe's Birthday*. Browning

described her as a 'poetic actress without a rival and a woman of genius'.

Alma Murray was indeed outstanding in poetic drama and tragedy, and secured a great personal triumph as Beatrice in the one performance of Shelley's banned *The Cenci* put on at the Grand, Islington, in 1886. Another triumph was the role of Mildred Tresham in Browning's *A Blot in the 'Scutcheon* in the 1888 revival. Other parts were Rosalind in *As You Like It* (1897), Mrs Maylie in *Oliver Twist* (1905), the part in which she also made her final appearance, and Jane in Jerome K. Jerome's *Fanny and the Servant Problem* (1908). She played the original Raina in *Arms and the Man* (1894), which was the first play by Shaw to appear in a commercial theatre and which he produced himself. She also played Mrs Eynsford-Hill in *Pygmalion* (1914) at His Majesty's Theatre. Retiring from the stage in 1915, she lived to be ninety.   B.H.C.

Murray, Elizabeth, Duchess of Lauderdale (*c.* 1627–97), political figure. She was the eldest daughter of William Murray, first Earl of Dysart, whose title and property she inherited in 1650. A woman of great beauty, she had studied theology, philosophy, history, and mathematics, and possessed 'a wonderful quickness of apprehension and an amazing vivacity in conversation'. She was also excessively ambitious, extravagant, avaricious, and would stop at nothing to 'compass her ends'. Among the many admirers of this brilliant woman was Oliver Cromwell, and she was apparently employed by Charles II to exert her influence on the Protector. It was rumoured that she had been Cromwell's mistress, a dubious claim which she herself later encouraged. In 1647 she married Sir Lionel Tollemache, a Suffolk baronet, and had eleven children, of whom three sons and two daughters survived.

During the late 1660s she formed a liaison with John Maitland, Earl of Lauderdale, who allegedly owed his life to her intervention with Cromwell and whom she married in February 1672, a few years after the death of her husband and less than two months after the death of Lauderdale's wife. In learning, knowledge of affairs, and financial acumen she was a fit wife for the powerful Secretary of State and Lord High Commissioner for Scotland. The Earl, created Duke shortly after their marriage, was completely captivated by his wife, whose influence over him had been observed while she was still his mistress. He had ignored the objections of his friends, who feared the political effects of the marriage and urged him to marry a younger woman who could bear him children. To her evil influence contemporaries ascribed his misgovernment and excessive taxation of Scotland, as well as the marked deterioration in his character and reputation from about 1670 onwards. Charges of bribery, corruption, nepotism, and lavish expenditure levelled against the Duchess were well founded. She personally controlled a vast amount of political, judicial, and religious patronage and entered into partnership with Lauderdale's brother and deputy, Halton, to engage in a number of dubious enterprises. The extent of her patronage and the corruption in which these two were involved in various Scottish government departments were exposed by the Duke of York when he reorganized Scottish administration in the early 1680s. After her husband's death in 1682 she became involved in extensive litigation with her brother-in-law, the new Earl, and was later suspected of furnishing funds to the Duke of Argyll for the Monmouth rebellion.

A woman of extraordinary intellect and few scruples, Elizabeth Murray chose to exercise her ability in the spheres of politics and finance. One of the most powerful and fascinating women at the Restoration court, she wielded considerable influence over the King's chief minister in Scotland, exercised extensive patronage, and substantially increased their income by her corrupt practices.

See also W. C. Mackenzie, *The Life and Times of John Maitland, Duke of Lauderdale, 1616–1682*, 1923.   T.J.M.

Murray, Margaret (1863–1963), Egyptologist. The daughter of a British businessman and a former missionary, Margaret Murray was born in Calcutta and spent much of her childhood and adolescence in India. In 1893 she was urged by her sister to enrol for a course of study under Flinders Petrie at University College, London. At the time there was no training in Egyptology except at Oxford, where the language only was taught. In 1895, aided by Petrie, she published her first article; and in 1898, having never passed an examination in her life, she was given charge of his elementary hieroglyphics class. In 1899 she became junior lecturer in Egyptology at University College, and in 1902 joined Petrie's excavation group in Egypt. Thereafter she took part in numerous excavations. She was made a Fellow of University College in 1922, and in 1924 Assistant Professor; she also served as Secretary of the Board of Studies in Anthropology, and as member of the Professorial Board. During the First World War college duties made work in Egypt impractical, and her attention turned to Western Europe. The result of her researches, published in 1921 as *The Witch Cult in Western Europe*, made her known to a wider public. Its thesis—that witches were neither innocent victims nor devil-worshippers, but adherents of a pre-Christian 'old religion'—was, and remains, controversial.

Having retired from her post, Margaret Murray worked during the Second World War for an organization that sent lecturers to army outposts in the UK. She also conducted research on Cambridge at the time of the Tudors and Stuarts. Her works include *Egyptian Sculpture*, 1930; *Egyptian Temples*, 1931; *The God of the Witches*, 1933; *The Splendour that Was Egypt*, 1949; and *The Divine King in England*, 1954. She was a supporter of the suffragettes, worked quietly for the good of women students, and greatly admired Marie STOPES.

See also her autobiography, *My First Hundred Years*, 1963, an extraordinary feat for a centenarian.   J.E.

N

Nairne, Carolina, Baroness Nairne (1766–1845), Scottish ballad writer, born Carolina Oliphant, whose strongly Jacobite background coloured much of her literary work. Another early influence was Burns. Her first song appeared anonymously in 1792, and thereafter the long list of her well-known Scottish ballads includes 'Charlie is my Darling' and 'Will ye no' come back again'. Although one of the foremost contributors to the revival of Scottish poetry and song in the late eighteenth and early nineteenth centuries, she seems to have accepted the customary notion of women as modest and retiring, and preferred her work to remain anonymous. Therefore even her husband, Major William Murray Nairne, whom she married in 1806, was unaware of her achievement. Most' of her energies were absorbed by caring for the comfort and education of her only son.   T.H.

Neilson, (Lilian) Adelaide (1846–80), actress whose real name was Elizabeth Ann Brown. She was born in Leeds, the daughter of a strolling player, and lived in Skipton during her unhappy childhood. She then worked as a mill-hand in Guiseley, where she had been a pupil at the parish school. Calling herself Lizzie Ann Bland, she later made her way secretly to London, where she took work as a barmaid near the Haymarket and gained quite a reputation for declaiming Shakespeare. She had as a child recited passages from her mother's playbooks. Subsequently changing her name to Lilian Adelaide Lessont and then to Neilson, she appeared as Juliet in 1865 at Margate and made her first London appearance in the same part at the Royalty Theatre in 1865. Although the audience was small, it contained several critics who were greatly impressed.

For several years she appeared in Shakespeare both in London and the provinces, and also in dramatizations from Sir Walter Scott, achieving great success as Amy Robsart in *Kenilworth* (1870–71). Her marriage to Philip Lee, son of a rector, was unhappy and they divorced in 1877.

In 1872 Adelaide Neilson paid her first visit to America, where she went on tour. This proved so great a success that further visits were made, in 1874, 1876, and 1879. She returned from her last tour in 1880 and soon afterwards left for Paris, complaining of illness. She died after drinking iced milk in the Bois de Boulogne. Her best original parts were in *Kenilworth* and as Rebecca in *Ivanhoe* (1871), while in Shakespeare she excelled as Rosalind, Beatrice, and Imogen. She was popular with her fellow actors, as well as the public.   B.H.C.

Neilson, Julia (Emilie) (1868–1957), actress. Born in London, she studied music at Wiesbaden and at the Royal Academy of Music, London, where she won prizes for singing. She was prompted to take to the stage by W. S. Gilbert, appearing in his *Pygmalion and Galatea* in 1888. Later she toured with Beerbohm Tree and was engaged as his leading lady at the Haymarket, where her successes included Drusilla Ives in *The Dancing Girl* and Hester Worsley in Wilde's *A Woman of No Importance*. It was at this time that she met Fred Terry, youngest brother of ELLEN. She later married this handsome romantic actor and regularly acted with him, either on tour or with their own company in London. Between 1896 and 1898 she played Rosalind in *As You Like It* during the longest run then recorded for a London theatre.

From 1900 she managed the Haymarket with her husband, and the Strand from 1915. At the Haymarket they achieved great popularity with costume melodramas such as *Sweet Nell of Old Drury* and *The Scarlet Pimpernel*. After her husband's death she appeared with Seymour Hicks in *Vintage Wine* (1934). Her stage jubilee was celebrated in 1938 and following some years in retirement she returned for a final performance in 1944 as Lady Ruthven in *The Widow of Forty*.

See also her memoirs, *This for Remembrance*, 1940.   B.H.C.

Nesbit, Edith (1858–1924), children's novelist. She was born in London, where her father was principal of an agricultural college. The large family of which she was the youngest daughter was to become the model for the Bastable family and the 'five children' who figure in her best known stories. She was educated in France and Germany, and in 1880 married the journalist Hubert Bland. Three years after his death in 1914 she married Terry Tucker, an engineer. She had four children.

Initially it was financial pressure experienced in her first marriage that made 'E. Nesbit' take up writing as a profession. To begin with she simply published hack-work — light romances and occasional verse — but became established as a children's novelist when the *Pall Mall Gazette* and *Windsor Magazine* began to publish instalments of *The Treasure Seekers*. Subsequent stories were then serialized in *The Strand Magazine*, and her growing literary fame brought her into contact with writers such as Shaw and Wells. Although her adult novels and poetry are of little interest now, the children's stories have become classics, transcending their Edwardian context by the idiosyncratic humour and fantasy with which E. Nesbit describes the adventures of her characters. Indeed, the importance of fantasy for those who, perhaps like the author herself, are denied the chance to live life as 'beautifully' as they might wish, is stressed in her study of child psychology *Wings and the Child* (1913). Her best known works include *The Story of the Treasure Seekers*, 1899; *The Five Children and It*, 1902; and *The Railway Children*, 1906. *Long Ago When I Was Young*, 1896, contains reminiscences of her childhood.

See also D. L. Moore, *E. Nesbit: A Biography*, 1967; A. R. Ruck, *A Story-teller Tells the Truth*, 1935.   J.M.

Neumagen, Florence. See ENGELBACH, FLORENCE.

Neville, Anne (1456–85), Queen of England. The younger daughter of Richard, Earl of Warwick, 'the Kingmaker', Anne was married in 1470 to Henry VI's only son, Edward. The purpose of the union was to cement an alliance between her father and Queen MARGARET OF ANJOU, aimed at restoring Henry VI to the throne. Edward was killed at Tewkesbury in 1471 and Anne then married her cousin, Richard, Duke of Gloucester, Edward IV's brother. When she and Richard III were crowned in 1483 they had one son, Edward, Prince of Wales, who died a year later. Anne died early in 1485, possibly of tuberculosis. Suspicions that she was poisoned by her husband are unfounded.

See also C. Ross, *Richard III*, 1981.
                                        A.C.

Neville, Cecily (1415–95), Duchess of York, mother of Edward IV and Richard III. She was the daughter of Ralph Neville, first Earl of Westmorland, by his second wife Joan Beaufort. As wife of Richard Plantagenet, Duke of York, she bore many children, including Edward (who seized the English crown as Edward IV in 1461), George (created Duke of Clarence, and 'drowned in a butt of malmsey' in 1478), and Richard (who usurped his nephew's throne in 1483, and ruled as Richard III until his own violent end on the battlefield at Bosworth in 1485).

Cecily's life was involved with politics and war. She accompanied Richard of York to France and Ireland in the 1440s and in 1459 was captured by the Lancastrians at Ludlow. Her husband's condemnation by the Coventry Parliament followed, although Cecily herself was granted an annual sum of 1000 marks by Henry VI 'for the relief and sustention of her and her young children that have not offended against us'. She rapidly joined Richard of York on his return from exile in 1460, and after his death, helped her son Edward to establish himself on the throne in 1461. Indeed, it was reported on the Continent that 'the Duchess of York . . . can rule the King as she pleases'. She was apparently furious at Edward's marriage to Elizabeth WOODVILLE in 1464, and may even have cast doubts on his legitimacy. In 1469 she probably tried to prevent her son George from joining Warwick the Kingmaker in rebellion, and certainly helped to reconcile him with Edward IV in 1471.

In her later years Cecily retired from public life, becoming virtually a recluse in Berkhamsted Castle, where she followed a strict daily routine of religious observance along Benedictine lines. Surviving household ordinances from about 1485 show a deeply pious old lady, profoundly influenced by the writings of great mystics such as St Catherine of Siena and St Bridget of Sweden, whose life was entirely devoted to God.

See also P. M. Kendall, *The Yorkist Age*, 1962.   K.R.D.

Newcastle, Duchess of. See CAVENDISH, MARGARET, DUCHESS OF NEWCASTLE.

Nicholls, Agnes (1876–1959), singer. Agnes Nicholls won a scholarship to the Royal College of Music in 1894, and studied singing for six years under Visetti. She also learned the violin, and in later years took pride in having been one of the first solo singers to be an all-round musician. Her début was in 1895 as Dido in Purcell's *Dido and Aeneas,* an occasion of considerable historic importance as it marked a renaissance of interest in English music. Her voice was of a rare purity (almost like a boy's voice on the few records that remain) and must have been ideal for the part. Rather unexpectedly, in view of her generous figure, she made her Covent Garden début in 1901 as the Dew Fairy in *Hansel and Gretel,* and when Richter conducted the first production of *The Ring* in English at Covent Garden in 1908, she sang Sieglinde in *Die Walküre.* According to herself, at a performance of *Götterdämmerung* on tour, she had a real white horse for the final scene which she led into the flames 'because I was too fat actually to ride it'!

It was, however, as an oratorio singer that Agnes Nicholls was mainly famous. She appeared in many important festivals, at the Crystal Palace, in Manchester, in Birmingham, and in Cincinnati. Parry wrote a number of parts for her, but her most memorable appearance was perhaps as the Blessed Virgin in the first performance of Elgar's *The Kingdom.* In 1904 she married the pianist, conductor, and composer Hamilton Harty, who had often accompanied her in recitals.

Agnes Nicholls was one of the last of the old-style prima donnas. She was also an innovator, however. She claimed that by insisting on appearing under her own name of Nicholls, rather than Nicolini, she was the first British singer to reach Covent Garden principal level without pretence of foreign birth. She was made a CBE, and is commemorated by the Agnes Nicholls trophy awarded to the outstanding singer of the year at the Royal College of Music.   R.G.

Nicolson, Adela Florence. See HOPE, LAURENCE.

Nightingale, Florence (1820–1910), reformer of nursing and public health. Florence Nightingale was born in Florence. Her parents belonged to the new wealthy middle class and with her elder sister she enjoyed all the advantages of a privileged childhood. From her father she received an unusually broad classical education, becoming fluent in French, Italian, and German. When she was seventeen the family toured Europe and on their return she was presented at court; however, she began

to find fashionable life deeply unsatisfying. She had already at sixteen experienced a 'call from God', and in 1845 Samuel and Julia Ward Howe urged Florence to follow her vocation for nursing. Her parents were appalled, as nursing was at that time not considered a fit occupation for women of good family, and the next six years were spent miserably striving to reconcile her inner aspirations with her duty to them.

In 1851 Miss Nightingale spent three months nursing with the Protestant Deaconesses at Kaiserswerth on the Rhine, and by 1853 her father was finally convinced that she must follow her inspiration. With the help of her friend Henry (later Cardinal) Manning she entered a Paris convent to observe nursing practice, and while there was offered the post of Superintendent in the Hospital for Gentlewomen in London. This was the turning point in her career. A year's practical experience made her the most eligible choice to take charge of the band of nurses who were sent out to care for the victims of the Crimean War. She arrived on the eve of the Battle of Inkerman, and with a mixture of consummate tact and ruthless efficiency set about organizing the nursing care and reforming the hospital administration of the British Army. In 1856 she returned to Britain a legend and was summoned to Balmoral to receive the thanks of the Queen. She used her influence to force reluctant Ministers to set up the Royal Commission on the Sanitary State of the Army and for the next year laboured unceasingly to produce its Report, visiting hospitals and barracks by day, and writing up the evidence by night.

In August 1857 she collapsed and was so ill that it was thought she would die. She recovered, but never again appeared in public. From her bed she supervised the publication of the Report of the Royal Commission and undertook the work of carrying out its recommendations. She next turned her attention to the Indian Army, and was instrumental in setting up the Royal Commission on the Sanitary State of the Army in India. This led to a deep interest in all aspects of Indian life and she published many articles on India during the ensuing forty years.

Meanwhile the Nightingale School of Nurses opened at St Thomas's Hospital in 1860, and before the end of the decade trained staffs were sent out to Liverpool Workhouse Infirmary, to Netley military hospital, and to Australia. Within twenty years most of the large voluntary and workhouse hospitals throughout the country had trained nursing staffs and many had their own nursing schools.

Florence Nightingale claimed to have had 'more political power than if I had been a borough returning two MPs'. Nevertheless, while sympathizing with the women's suffrage movement, she felt that their lack of the vote was the least of the evils under which women laboured. Her achievement in establishing nursing as a well-paid profession for women of all classes had the most profound influence on the position of women in society. Her published works include *Notes on Nursing* (1860) and *Notes on Hospitals* (1863).

See also W. J. Bishop and S. Goldie, *A Bibliography of Florence Nightingale*, 1962; Sir E. Cook, *The Life of Florence Nightingale*, 1913; S. Goldie, *A Calendar of the Letters of Florence Nightingale*, 1981; C. Woodham-Smith, *Florence Nightingale*, 1950.　　S.G.

Nihell, Elizabeth (1723–?), midwife. Born in London, she had the unusual privilege of studying midwifery at the Hôtel-Dieu in Paris (1747–49). She then married a surgeon-apothecary and practised in the Haymarket. Mrs Nihell deplored the growing fashion for man-midwives and opposed their use of metal instruments. In her view the popular devaluation of female midwives was eroding an important field of employment for women. Her *Treatise on the Art of Midwifery* (1760) contained a spirited invective against the eminent 'great-horse-godmother of a he-midwife', William Smellie. His male pupils, she charged, were inadequately trained and lacked patience, delicacy, and skill. Mrs Nihell's arguments and bombastic language were ridiculed at length by Tobias Smollett in *The Critical Review* (1760). Her treatise was translated into French in 1771, and she was still in practice in the Haymarket in 1772. Mrs Nihell's defence of her profession contributed to public awareness of an important contemporary issue. Other works include *An Answer to the Author of The Critical Review*.

See also J. Donnison, *Midwives and Medical Men*, 1977.　　C.C.

Norfolk, Duchess of. See HOWARD, ELIZABETH, DUCHESS OF NORFOLK.

Norgate, Kate (1853–1935), historian. The only child of Frederick Norgate, a bookseller, she was brought into contact with a group of writers active in Norwich by her grandfather, Thomas Starling Norgate, a writer and journalist. In particular she was influenced by the historians J. R. Green and his wife, Alice STOPFORD GREEN, whose protégée she became. Her first book, *England under the Angevin Kings* (1887), was the result of fifteen years work and was soon acclaimed as authoritative, being an advance on the work of Agnes STRICKLAND

Encouraged, Kate Norgate produced a number of other histories, notably *John Lackland*, 1902; *The Minority of Henry III*, 1912; and *Richard the Lion Heart*, 1924. All were well-received by the public, although increasingly less so by scholars, who detected a neglect of primary sources. Green died before his protégée achieved success, but she showed her gratitude by working with his widow to edit much of his work. She outlived her contemporaries and her popularity, dying largely forgotten. Only Somerville College gave her belated recognition, electing her an honorary Fellow in 1929. She had proved, however, that a woman could write valuable works of history.　　J.R.

Norman-Neruda, Madame, stage-name of Lady Hallé (1839–1911), violinist, born Vilemina Marie Franziška Nerudová at Brno. She was the daughter of Joseph Neruda, a violinist, and was trained by Leopold Jansa in Vienna. She was a child prodigy. Hanslick heard her in 1846, and in 1847 she performed in Prague. After a German tour with her musical family, she appeared in London in 1849. Later, after a Scandinavian tour, she was appointed Court Chamber Virtuoso (1863). In 1864 she married the Swedish composer Ludwig Norman, from whom she separated five years later. Three years after his death in 1885 she married Sir Charles Hallé. As Madame Norman-Neruda she appeared frequently in Hallé's recitals from 1877 onwards, and was in demand as a violinist all over Europe. She was so popular in England that the nobility presented her with a magnificent Stradivarius. Hallé died in 1895, and in 1898 she left London and settled in Berlin at the Stern Conservatory.　　A.D.

North, Marianne (1830–90), artist and naturalist. She was the daughter of Frederick North, Liberal MP for Hastings, and grew up there and on the family estate in Norfolk. She was taught singing and the piano but had little formal education, apart from a few unhappy months at school in Norwich. She showed an early aptitude for painting, in which she was self-taught, and enjoyed studying plant life in the hot-houses of the Hastings Botanic Gardens and at Kew. She travelled widely in Europe with her parents and after her mother's death in 1855 travelled with her father to Turkey, Syria, and Egypt, filling many sketch-books with pictures of what she saw. After the death of her father in 1869 she resolved to devote her life to painting plant life in its natural surroundings.

In 1871 she travelled alone to Jamaica, where she rented a deserted house on the hillside outside Kingston. Each morning she went out at daylight to paint, returned to the house for the afternoon, and explored the surrounding countryside in the evening. In 1873 she returned to England and took lessons in etching on copper. Two years later she set out for Quebec, crossed North America by train, and visited California and the Yosemite Valley. She continued her journey to Japan, Singapore, and Sarawak where, on a mountain excursion, she discovered the largest of all pitcher plants, *Nepenthes northiana*. In 1877 she began a tour of India, visiting Madura where 'starvation, floods, and fever were all around' and making an excursion to the Himalayas where she was carried up the foothills in a litter on the heads of bearers. Subsequent journeys took her to Australia, South Africa, and the Seychelles, where she discovered the previously unclassified capucin tree *Northia seychellana*. Her last journey, begun in 1884, was to Chile, where she painted the great tree *Araucaria imbricans* (monkey puzzle) in the mountains above Santiago.

On her return to England in 1879 she had responded to the interest shown in her paintings by offering to present them to Kew. The North Gallery, built at her own expense, opened in July 1882. Within a month 2000 copies of the catalogue were sold, and she received a letter of thanks from the Queen, regretting that no honour equivalent to a knighthood was available for women. Her autobiographies *Recollections of a Happy Life* (1892), and *Further Recollections of a Happy Life* (1893), contain vivid accounts of her travels, enhanced by her acute powers of observation and sense of humour.

See also *A Vision of Eden: The Life and Work of Marianne North*, 1980.   S.G.

Northampton, Marchioness of. See PARR, HELENA, MARCHIONESS OF NORTHAMPTON.

Norton, Caroline (Elizabeth Sarah) (1808–77), poet and campaigner for the rights of divorced women. Caroline Sheridan was the third of seven children, the granddaughter of the famous playwright Richard Brinsley Sheridan. Strikingly attractive, intelligent but wayward, she was sent at sixteen to a Surrey boarding school in an attempt to discipline her high spirits. There she met George Norton, son of a local landowner, whom she married in 1827. It was an unsuccessful marriage. Norton was a dull and morose man, embittered by the failure of his career as a barrister. He resented his wife's literary success, which began with the publication of her poem *The Sorrows of Rosalie* in 1829. It sold well and paid for Mrs Norton's first confinement. She was to live by her pen for the rest of her life, producing numerous poems, plays, and novels. Perhaps her most famous and characteristic work is *The Lady of La Garaye*, a sentimental poem much admired when published in 1861.

Mrs Norton's literary talent was not of the highest order, and her pieces were too much the product of contemporary taste to appeal to the modern reader. Of more lasting significance was the campaign she waged after the breakdown of her marriage to secure for divorced women a right to the custody of their children and control of their property. In 1835 Norton instigated divorce proceedings, naming Lord Melbourne as co-respondent. He lost his case but, following the couple's legal separation, was granted custody of their children in the customary manner. Mrs Norton was denied access to them and responded by publishing in 1836 *The Natural Claim of a Mother to the Custody of her Children*. She argued that custody should be granted by the Court of Chancery on consideration of individual circumstances. The Infant Custody Act of 1839 incorporated many of her suggestions, and was supported at all its stages by her efforts.

Mrs Norton's relations with her husband continued to decline. He refused to pay her an allowance, or to return to her vital publishing contracts essential to her work. Finding herself without legal redress, Mrs Norton produced her most bitter and influential work, *English Laws for Women in the Nineteenth*

Century. Published in 1854, it demonstrated what little protection the law afforded married women and their property. The passage of the Divorce Bill during 1855–56 enabled Mrs Norton to keep the issue of married women's rights before the public and she worked tirelessly in its favour. The final provisions of the Divorce Act of 1857 owed much to her influence, particularly the clauses securing to the divorced or separated woman sole rights to her subsequent earnings.

Although she tried hard to improve the legal status of married women, Mrs Norton personally rejected the idea of sexual equality, believing in the natural inferiority of women. For this reason she thought that their situation demanded the greatest possible protection from the law, to compensate for their inherent deficiencies. She always regarded a good husband as a better protector than the best laws, however, and married again herself after Norton's death in 1875.

See also A. Acland, *Caroline Norton*, 1848; J. G. Perkins, *The Life of Mrs Norton*, 1909.
J.V.L.

Novello, Clara (Anastasia) (1818–1908), singer. She was born in London, the daughter of Vincent Novello, music publisher and founder of the firm Novello & Co., and at the age of fourteen achieved the remarkable feat of singing the soprano solo in Beethoven's *Missa Solemnis*. She studied piano and singing in London and started at the Paris Conservatoire in 1829, returning home the following year because of the revolution.

After performing at Windsor in 1832, she was engaged for the Philharmonic Society and the major music festivals. In 1837 Mendelssohn chose her for the Gewandhaus concerts. She sang in Berlin, Vienna and St Petersburg, and while visiting Rossini at Bologna was advised to study opera for a year. Having taken lessons in Milan, she made her first operatic appearance at Padua in 1841, in Rossini's *Semiramide*. The same composer later sent for her to take the soprano part in his recently-completed *Stabat Mater*. In 1843 she returned to England, performing in English opera at Drury Lane and appearing in Handel's *Acis and Galatea*. The same year saw her marriage to Count Gigliucci, after which she retired for some years, but in 1848 their property was confiscated and the Countess decided to resume her professional career, reappearing to sing in concert and opera, mainly in England and Italy. She made her farewell performance at a benefit concert in 1860, her voice in the same good form as it had been six years earlier at the re-opening of the Crystal Palace at Sydenham. Perhaps her greatest singing took place at the 1859 Handel Festival, however, for Handel's music was particularly suited to her style. She was greatly admired by Schumann, who called some of his pieces 'Novelettes' in affectionate deference to her, and after the retirement of Catherine STEPHENS, she had no serious rival. She retired to Rome and died in her ninetieth year.

See also A. Mackenzie-Grieve, *Clara Novello*, 1955.
B.H.C.

Nun of Kent. See BARTON, ELIZABETH.

Nutt, Elizabeth (*fl.* 1720), printer and bookseller. She was one of a number of eighteenth-century women who continued commercial ventures after the death of a husband. Apart from the fact that she probably succeeded her husband John in the business, little is known of Elizabeth Nutt. She is known to have printed in the Savoy from 1720 to 1731 and to have produced T. Cox's *Magna Britannia* in six volumes. She also kept a pamphlet shop at the Royal Exchange.

See also H. R. Plomer, *A Dictionary of the Printers and Booksellers who were at work in England, Scotland and Ireland from 1668 to 1725*, 1922.
T.H.

O

Obee, Lois. See DRESDEL SONIA.

Oberon, Merle (1911–79), film actress. Estelle Merle O'Brien Thompson was born in Tasmania. The family moved to India when she was seven, and she was educated at La Martinière College, Calcutta. In 1928 she went to England, taking work as a dance-hostess at the Café de Paris, London, and as a film extra. The film producer Alexander Korda noticed her dark beauty and offered her a seven-year contract. After her success as Anne Boleyn in *The Private Life of Henry VIII* (1933) she received offers of work from Hollywood and thenceforth made her home in America. Hollywood transformed her from an exotic but rather uninspired actress into an international star. Films such as *The Dark Angel* with Fredric March and *Wuthering Heights* with Laurence Olivier won her a huge following.

After the British film *The Lion Has Wings* (1939) came many years of mediocre parts. Not until 1952 did interest in her revive with *Twenty-four Hours of a Woman's Life*. *The Oscar* (1965) and *Hotel* (1966) were other successes.

Merle Oberon ranked among the most highly-paid film stars. She married four times, Alexander Korda (1939), Lucien Ballard (1945), Bruno Pagliari (1957), and Robert Wolders (1975).

See also D. Shipman, *The Great Movie Stars*, 1979. P.L.

O'Brien, Charlotte Grace (1845–1909), Irish author and social reformer. She was the daughter of William Smith O'Brien, an Irish nationalist politician transported for treason in 1849, and spent most of her life in Ireland. After her parents' death she looked after her brother's motherless children from 1864 until his remarriage in 1880. Thereafter she lived alone, increasingly afflicted by deafness. Talented and courageous, much influenced by her father, she was taught to be proud of her Irish descent. Irish patriotism guided many of her actions and writings and she was a supporter of Parnell and Home Rule. Her novel *Light and Shade* (1878) was based on the Fenian Rising of 1869. Charlotte O'Brien's published poetry and her letters to *The Pall Mall Gazette* also reflected her nationalism, but she was not a good or very successful writer (although later

works on the flora of the Shannon were of value). She was more successful in her social reforms. The conditions of Irish emigrants to America having caught her attention, she set about trying to remedy them, particularly for women. In 1881 she established boarding houses for girls about to embark for America from Queenstown, following this with homes to give them temporary shelter on reaching New York. Her efforts, including the exposure of existing conditions, did much to improve matters.

See also C. O'Brien, *Selections from Her Writings*, 1909. J.R.

Old Demdike. See SOUTHERN, ELIZABETH.

Oldfield, Anne (1683–1730), actress, commonly known as 'Nance' Oldfield. She was the successor to Mrs BRACEGIRDLE and the leading actress of the pre-Garrick era. It was the playwright George Farquhar who introduced her to the stage, following the first of many liaisons, but it was Colley Cibber who, substituting her at the last moment for his leading lady in *The Careless Husband* (1703), placed her in the public eye. He himself acknowledged his debt to her: 'Whatever favourable reception this comedy has met from the public, it would be unjust in me not to place a large share of it to the account of Mrs Oldfield'. From then on she enjoyed a triumphant career, creating the parts of Maria in Addison's *Cato* (1714), Jane Shore in Rowe's play of that name (1714), Mrs Sullen and Sylvia in Farquhar's *Beaux' Stratagem* (1707) and *The Recruiting Officer* (1706) respectively, and Lady Townley in Cibber's *The Provok'd Husband* (1727). She excelled in comedy, particularly in coquette roles, although she was also successful in tragedy. She seems to have earned an unusual respect from her colleagues, for Cibber and Wilkes considered taking her into partnership in the management of Drury Lane in 1708, and in 1709 she was chosen to represent her fellow actors' interests before the Lord Chamberlain in their campaign against the theatrical producer John Rich. Of her final and perhaps most successful part as Lady Townley, Cibber wrote: 'The qualities she had acquired were the genteel and the elegant. The one in her air and the other in her dress, never had her equal on the stage'.

Mrs Oldfield was buried in Westminster Abbey, although she was not allowed a monument on account of her somewhat irregular domestic arrangements. She had sons by both General Churchill and Arthur Mainwaring. However, 'notwithstanding that the amorous connections of this highly distinguished actress were publicly known, she was invited to the houses of women of fashion, as conspicuous for unblemished character as for elevated rank'. She was also a favourite with the Royal Family.

See also *Authentick Memoirs of Mrs Oldfield*, 1730; R. H. Barker, *Mr Cibber of Drury Lane*, 1939; C. Cibber, *Apology for the Life of Colley Cibber*, 1739.　　　　C.H.

Oliphant, Carolina. See NAIRNE, CAROLINA, BARONESS NAIRNE.

Oliphant, Margaret (1828–97), novelist. She was born at Wallyford, near Musselburgh in Midlothian, the daughter of a customs official at Lasswade, near Edinburgh. Her first novel, *Mrs Margaret Maitland* (1849), was published when she was twenty-one. In 1857 she married her cousin Francis Wilson Oliphant, a painter and stained glass designer, and they moved to London, where Mrs Oliphant gave birth to a son and a daughter. Because they also had to support her brother's family, Mrs Oliphant began her never-ending battle against bankruptcy. In 1859 they went to Rome in an attempt to improve Francis Oliphant's failing health but he died the same year, leaving numerous debts and a pregnant wife. Margaret gave birth to another son and continued writing at great speed. In 1864 her daughter died and two years later she moved near Eton in order to send her sons to school there, on the proceeds of her writing.

Mrs Oliphant's best known work is *The Chronicles of Carlingford*, published anonymously between 1863 and 1876, after its serialization in *Blackwood's Magazine*. Included in this series are *Salem Chapel* and *The Rector and the Doctor's Family* (1863), *The Perpetual Curate* (1864), and *Miss Marjoribanks* (1866), and *Phoebe Junior,* (1876). Her novels were mainly concerned with Scottish life, for example *The Minister's Wife* (1869), *Effie Ogilvie* (1886), and *Kirsteen* (1890), but some, such as *A Beleaguered City* (1880) and *A Little Pilgrim of the Unseen* (1882), were strongly supernatural. She also wrote history, translations, travel books, criticism, and biography, including the lives of St Francis of Assisi, Edward Irving, and Principal Tulloch. Virginia WOOLF felt that Mrs Oliphant's enormous finacial burdens were responsible for the poor quality of her art: 'Mrs Oliphant sold her brain, her very admirable brain, prostituted her culture and enslaved her intellectual liberty in order that she might earn her living and educate her children'.

She died the year her *Annals of a Publishing House: William Blackwood and his sons* was published. Her autobiography was published posthumously in 1899. Other works include *The Ladies Lindores*, 1883; *Makers of Florence*, 1888; and *Makers of Venice*, 1889.

See also V. and R. Colby, *The Equivocal Virtue: Mrs Oliphant and the Victorian Literary Marketplace*, 1966.　　　　A.P.

O'Malley, Grania or Grace (*c*. 1530–*c*. 1600), clan leader who played a prominent role in Irish struggles against the enforcement of English authority. Grace was the daughter of Dubhdara O'Malley, whose family dominated the western coast of Connacht. The O'Malleys were noted seafarers, feared as privateers and raiders. Her first husband, by whom she had two sons, was the chief of the O'Flaherty, a west Connacht clan. By her second marriage, to Sir Richard Burke (d. 1583), leader of the Mayo Burkes, she had one son. Supported by the O'Malleys and their powerful galleys, Grace exerted a political influence on her own account besides that gained through her marriages. When questioned by the English in 1593 she explained that married Irish women maintained strong links with their families. Their dowries were delivered up only for as long as the marriage lasted. This was partly because Irish chiefs usually died in debt and were not able to provide adequately for their widows, but also because 'the husband now and then without any lawful or due proceeding do put his wife from him and so bringeth in another so as the wife is to have sureties for her dowry for fear of the worse'.

In 1576 the Lord Deputy, Sir Henry Sidney, described her as 'a most famous feminine sea captain', but his belief in her loyalty proved ill-founded. After risings in 1580 she surrendered when many of her followers were put to the sword, and Burke was starved into submission on the O'Malley stronghold of Achill Island. In 1586 her eldest son Owen O'Flaherty was killed in a rising against the

O'Neill, Eliza

English, and Grace herself only escaped the gallows through the last-minute intervention of a Burke stepson. She later claimed to have lived a poor 'farmer's life' in Connacht after 1586, but her leadership of O'Malley raiding parties troubled the authorities until the end of the century, although her sons were mainly loyal to the increasingly dominant English. In 1593 the governor of Connacht branded her 'a notable traitress and nurse to all rebellions in this province for forty years'. A.H.

O'Neill, Eliza (1791–1872), actress, later Lady Becher. She was born in Ireland, the daughter of an actor who was stage manager at the Drogheda theatre. It was in Drogheda that she had her brief education, in one of its small schools, and made her early appearances, while still a child, at her father's theatre. After spending two years in Belfast, she went to Dublin, where she appeared as Juliet and Jane Shore. From there she moved on to London, and at Covent Garden in 1814 scored a notable success as Juliet to Conway's Romeo. She was hailed with enthusiasm as 'a younger and better Mrs SIDDONS', enjoying such favour for about five years and acting in both tragedy and comedy. Although excellent in parts such as Lady Teazle, it was in tragedy that she achieved her most memorable successes, as Juliet, Belvidera in Otway's *Venice Preserv'd*, Mrs Haller in *The Stranger*, and Mrs Beverley. Extravagant and no doubt exaggerated stories were told of the effects of her acting on those who experienced it; it seems that after witnessing one of her tragic performances, some gentlemen in the audience were so moved that they fainted and had to be carried away.

Eliza O'Neill's last appearance was as Mrs Haller in 1819, the year in which she married William Becher, an Irish MP who was created a baronet at William IV's coronation in 1831. She had a deep mellow voice and possessed classic beauty, although her carriage was affected by a slight stoop. Hazlitt and Macready held her in high esteem, though others accused her of excessive vehemence. She maintained a good name throughout her theatrical career, apart from a reputed tendency towards meanness. B.H.C.

O'Neill, Maire (1887–1952), actress. Born in Dublin, she was the younger sister of Sara ALLGOOD, also a famous Irish actress. Her first stage appearance was as a member of the Irish National Theatre Society at the Abbey Theatre. She remained until 1913 at the Abbey, where she created the part of Pegeen Mike in *The Playboy of the Western World*, and subsequently appeared at the Liverpool Repertory Theatre. She also acted in Beerbohm Tree's 1913 Shakespeare Festival. A long and distinguished career in London and New York followed. Her first husband was G. H. Mair, and after his death she married Arthur Sinclair, with whom she often acted in Irish plays. She also appeared with her sister. Later performances included parts in *The Shadow of a Gunman* and *Juno and the Paycock*. Her theatrical career continued until the early 1950s, while she also appeared in numerous films, the first, *Sing as we go*, in 1934. B.H.C.

Opie, Amelia (1769–1853), novelist and poet, born in Norwich. Her education consisted chiefly of French, music, and dancing. Her father was a doctor and on her mother's death in 1784 she ran the home and entered enthusiastically into Norwich society, where she was popular for the ballads which she composed and sang. After 1794 she made many trips to London, where she met the painter John Opie, becoming his second wife in 1798.

Her literary reputation was founded with *Father and Daughter* (1801), the story of a seduction and its effect on the heroine's father, which was influential in the development of the popular novel during the nineteenth century. *Adeline Mowbray* (1804) was based on the life of Mary WOLLSTONECRAFT. Other writings include *Valentine's Eve* (1816) and *Madeline* (1822). Her novels display vivid descriptive powers, but tend to the overly pathetic. She knew many famous people of her day, including Sydney Smith, Sheridan, Madame de Staël, the Kembles, and Mrs Siddons. In 1825 she became a Quaker. She helped Elizabeth FRY in philanthropic work and was active in the anti-slavery movement. Novels were given up, at some cost to this lover of sparkling society, for moral tracts and articles.

See also A. G. K. L'Estrange, *The Friendships of Mary Russell Mitford*, 1822. B.H.C.

Orczy, Emmuska, Baroness (1865–1947), romantic novelist and dramatist. She was born in Tarna-Eörs in Hungary, the only child of the composer and conductor Baron Felix Orczy and his wife Emma. Her upbringing was both cosmopolitan and cultured. Wagner, Liszt, Gounod, and Massenet were all frequent visitors to the family house, and she was educated in Brussels, Paris, and finally London, at the Heatherly School of Art. Here she met and married Montagu Barstow, an artist. They had one son.

She had some early success as an illustrator, with paintings exhibited at the Royal Academy, but in the late 1890s she began writing short stories for popular magazines. Her first real success in this sphere came in 1905 when the play *The Scarlet Pimpernel*, which she wrote in collaboration with her husband, became a great public, if not critical, success and the novel of the same title also appeared. These two works initiated a long series of 'Pimpernel' fictions, all featuring Sir Percy Blakeney as the deceptively foppish hero who secretly performs feats of daring and courage. Her novel *The Old Man in the Corner* (1909) has also been seen among historians of detective fiction as one of the earliest examples of the 'intuitive' or armchair school later exemplified in G. K. Chesterton's Father Brown stories.

In later life Baroness Orczy moved to Monte Carlo, where she continued writing, although she never repeated the success of her early novels.

See also E. Orczy, *The Scarlet Pimpernel Looks at the World*, 1934.   J.M.

Orléans, Duchess of. See HENRIETTE ANNE.

Ormerod, Eleanor Anne (1828–1901), economic entomologist. Born at Sedbury Park in Gloucestershire, she was educated in basic subjects by her mother and taught herself Latin and modern languages. With her sister Georgiana she studied painting under William Hunt, and both became competent artists. Eleanor showed an interest in natural history from childhood, observing the animal, bird, and plant life on her father's estate, and, beginning in 1852, she studied entomology systematically. In 1868 she helped the Royal Horticultural Society to form a collection of 'insects beneficial or injurious to Man', for which she was awarded the Society's Silver Flora medal. In 1872 she prepared models of insects injurious to plants, as well as electrotypes of plants, fruits, and leaves, for the International Polytechnic Exhibition in Moscow. After the death of her father in 1873 she and her sister lived first in Torquay and then moved to Isleworth in order to be near Kew Gardens. At Isleworth she undertook a series

of meteorological observations, for which she was elected Fellow of the Meteorological Society in 1878.

Miss Ormerod generously gave advice to her many correspondents, particularly on the eradication of agricultural pests, and hospitably entertained visitors from abroad. In 1877 she began her *Annual Reports of Observations of Injurious Insects* (1877–1900) with the object of finding means to prevent agricultural damage by insects. These reports, fully illustrated and compiled with the assistance of observers throughout the country and abroad, were printed at her own expense and sent free to all who requested them. She was Honorary Consulting Entomologist to the Royal Agricultural Society (1882–86), and sat on the Committee of Economic Entomology appointed by the Department of Education (1882–92), giving advice on the improvement of the collections in the South Kensington and Bethnal Green museums. In addition to her advisory work, she published a number of important books and papers, and was highly regarded as a lecturer, holding the post of special lecturer on economic entomology at the Royal Agricultural College (1881–84). Ten lectures delivered at the South Kensington Museum were published as a *Guide to the Methods of Insect Life* (1884).

She received many honours from agricultural societies throughout the world and in 1900 was the first woman to be awarded an honorary LLD by Edinburgh University. Other works include *A Manual of Injurious Insects*, 1881; *A Text-Book of Agricultural Entomology*, 1892; and *Handbook of Insects Injurious to Orchard and Bush Fruits*, 1898.

See also her *Autobiography and Correspondence*, ed. R. Wallace, 1904.   S.G.

Osborne, Dorothy (1627–95), letter writer. She was the youngest daughter of Sir Peter Osborne of Chicksands, Bedfordshire, an ardent Royalist during the Civil War. An intelligent, beautiful, and accomplished young woman, Dorothy was an avid reader, proficient in Latin, French, and Italian. In 1648 she was on her way to join her father in exile, when she met William Temple, the twenty-year-old heir of Sir John Temple, a noted Cromwellian, and himself a future diplomat, statesman, and author. The couple fell immediately in love but parental objections caused their courtship to last for seven years.

In 1649 Dorothy's father was allowed to live on his sequestered estates, and, on the death of her mother in 1650, Dorothy became mistress of the household, nursing her father during a prolonged illness. Her correspondence and occasional meetings with Temple sustained her during these years, for she was determined to marry him, rejecting all other suitors. In 1654 Dorothy's father died, and despite continuing opposition from her brothers, she married William on Christmas Day 1654.

The couple lived for extended periods in Brussels and the Hague during Sir William's embassies, but on his retirement in 1681 they moved to a country seat near Farnham. Two of their nine children survived infancy, a daughter who died at fourteen, and a son who committed suicide in 1689. Their household after 1689 included Temple's secretary, Jonathan Swift, who decribed Lady Temple as 'mild Dorothea, peaceful, wise, and great'. Dorothy proved valuable to her husband in many capacities, most notably in his conduct of the negotiations for the marriage of Princess Mary and William of Orange, in which she played an active role. She became a close friend and correspondent of Queen Mary, and her grief at the Queen's death was said to have hastened her own. Contemporaries praised her as a wife, ambassadress, patron, and correspondent, who was 'greatly admired', wrote her sister-in-law, 'for her fine style and delicate turn of wit and good sense in writing letters'. It was this epistolary talent that has earned her a place in literature. 'All letters', wrote Dorothy, 'should be free and easy as one's discourse', and her application of this principle provides the chief explanation for the continued charm of the letters written during her courtship. Their chief social and historical interest lies in the indications they provide of changing attitudes towards marriage, which ought, so the Temples believed, to be based on love and 'perfect friendship'.

See also *The Letters of Dorothy Osborne to William Temple*, ed. G. C. Moore Smith, 1947; *The Life and Correspondence of Martha, Lady Giffard*, ed. J. G. Longe, 1911.
                                                                T.J.M.

Osburh (*fl.* mid-9th century), wife of Æthelwulf of Wessex. Osburh was the daughter of Oslac, a great noble at the court of King Æthelwulf of Wessex and a descendant of Stuf and Wihtgar, the legendary first rulers of south Wessex. Her birth determined her choice as wife. She was mother of the future King Alfred and probably of his four brothers and one sister. It is said to have been Osburh who fostered Alfred's early love of learning by encouraging him to learn vernacular poetry. Æthelwulf never made her his queen and gave her no prominence at his court, and our knowledge of her derives solely from her son's biography.

See also W. Stevenson (ed.), *Asser's Life of King Alfred*.   P.A.S.

Osthryth (?–697), Queen of Mercia, the daughter of King Oswiu of Northumbria and his second wife, EANFLAED. Osthryth married Ethelred, the son of King Penda of Mercia, some time before 679. It was one of three matches between offspring of Oswiu and Penda that formed part of the long and often violent struggle for supremacy between Northumbria and Mercia in the seventh century. Ethelred became King of Mercia in 675. As his queen, Osthryth enjoyed a position of some importance. Not only did she have responsibilities of her own, such as the welfare of the monastery she held at Fladbury, Worcestershire, but she was also privy to affairs of state, as her subscription as a witness to one of Ethelred's charters shows. She seems to have used her influence with Ethelred primarily to further the interests of Northumbria. In 681, for instance, she gained Ethelred's help for her brother, King Ecgfrith, in his vendetta against Bishop Wilfrid of York by forbidding Ethelred's nephew to shelter the exiled priest. But her greatest coup was to encourage Northumbrian allegiances in Lindsey, a kingdom lying between Northumbria and Mercia which had recently come under Mercian suzerainty. This she did by translating the saintly bones of her uncle, the Northumbrian King Oswald, to Bardney Abbey, a Lindsey foundation that professed anti-Northumbrian sentiments. However, in this she may have over reached herself. In 697 she was killed by a group of Southumbrian nobles, Mercians who may have disliked her pro-Northumbrian policies. She was survived by Ethelred and one son, Ceolred.

See also B. Colgrave and R. Mynors, (eds.), *Bede's Ecclesiastical History of the English People*, 1969.   J.C.

Otté, Elise (1818–1903), linguist, scholar, and historian, born in Copenhagen of a Danish father and English mother. Her stepfather was

Benjamin Thorpe, Anglo-Saxon scholar and philologist, who was the major influence in her life. As part of a comprehensive education, Thorpe taught her Anglo-Saxon and Icelandic; she also spoke Danish, Swedish, and French fluently and was considered one of the most learned women of her day. Her life was wholly absorbed by a desire to increase her own knowledge and to pass it on through her publications. As a girl she assisted Thorpe in his work. At twenty-two she went to America to escape his tyrannizing, interesting herself in science and studying physiology at Harvard. She rejoined Thorpe and helped him with his edition of the *Edda of Saemund* (eventually published in 1866), but again his behaviour drove her away. In 1849 she went to St Andrews to work on scientific translations for Dr Day. After his death in 1872 she pursued an active literary career in London, publishing a *History of Scandinavia* (1874), translations of standard Scandinavian works, Scandinavian grammars, and contributions to scientific periodicals. Despite her learning, however, she was not a good writer of English.   J.R.

Ouida. See RAMÉE, LOUISE DE LA.

Owen, Alice (d. 1613), philanthropist. The daughter of Thomas Wilkes, an Islington landowner, Alice was married three times: to Henry Robinson, a brewer, by whom she had six sons and five daughters; to William Elkin, a London Alderman, by whom she had a daughter; and finally to Thomas Owen, a judge, who died in 1598. As a widow, Alice had the independence to undertake the philanthropic work that attracted many pious wealthy women. Most of her benefactions were to Islington, and legend suggests that this was in gratitude for a providential deliverance as a child when a stray arrow pierced her hat while she was playing in Islington fields. She endowed a chapel, almshouses, a hospital for ten poor widows, and a school. She herself drew up the rules for the school, which still survives, although it moved from Islington to Potters Bar in the 1970s. At her death Alice Owen left generous donations to Oxford and Cambridge universities and to Christ's Hospital.   P.M.H.

P

Paget, Dame Mary Rosalind (1855–1948), nurse. The daughter of John Paget, Whig author and police magistrate, and his wife Elizabeth Rathbone, Mary was descended from a long line of social reformers. Her cousin Eleanor RATHBONE also worked in this field. Mary's parents inspired in her an early desire to devote herself to public service. Following the example of such women as Florence Nightingale, she turned to nursing as the medium to relieve suffering, and trained at the Westminster Hospital. Later experience at the British Lying-In Hospital showed her the need for better midwifery training. In 1881 she was among the founders of the Midwives Institute (later the Royal College of Midwives), and worked for the Midwives Act of 1902 which provided for their registration. Her interests also extended to district nursing and to the founding of the Chartered Society of Physiotherapy. A major force in gaining improved nursing training, particularly for midwives, she worked devotedly and was created DBE in 1935 in recognition of her services.

J.R.

Paget, Lady Muriel (Evelyn Vernon) (1876–1938), philanthropist. Daughter of the twelfth Earl of Winchilsea, she married Richard Paget in 1897. They had five children, one of whom died in infancy. Rarely in good health, she suffered greatly during the last years of her life, despite which she continued with her relief work. Brought up with the idea that position carried responsibility, her adult interest in philanthropy was a natural development. She involved herself in a number of British organizations, such as the Invalid Kitchens of London, but the First World War gave her wider scope. She organized and later administered the Anglo-Russian Hospital at Petrograd, together with its frontline field hospitals. In 1924 she returned to Russia to organize relief for stranded Britons, and thereafter maintained her Russian interest. She also worked for Romania from 1917, headed the Paget Mission to Czechoslovakia in 1919, worked for the Red Cross, and continued her interest in various London organizations. She received the OBE (1918), CBE (1938), and various Russian, Romanian, and Czechoslovakian decorations.

See also W. J. W. Blunt, *Lady Muriel Paget and Her Work*, 1962. J.R.

Paget, Violet (1856–1935), author. She was born in France, the daughter of Henry Ferguson Paget and Matilda Lee-Hamilton. She was educated in France and Italy, where she spent most of her life, and became an able linguist and scholar. Her mother and half-brother, Eugene Lee Hamilton, were the strongest influences on her life, particularly on her intellectual development; her pseudonym, Vernon Lee, was adopted with reference to her half-brother, although the two grew apart after their mother's death.

Material collected over the years formed the basis of her first book, *Studies of the Eighteenth Century in Italy* (1880), which created a wider interest in Italian culture of the period. Over the next half-century she published some thirty assorted works, those on the Italian Renaissance (*Euphorion*, 1884, and *Renaissance Fancies and Studies*, 1895) winning her particular acclaim. Her novels were readable, if not great, but her later excursions into philosophy tended to be obscure and turgid. Always a controversial figure, particularly in London society, her notoriety increased after 1903 with her advocacy of sociological ideas and pacifism. She had a vivid personality, was a witty and dominating debater, and mixed with the leading intellectual figures of the day. Yet she remained a private person, requesting that there be no biography of her. For many, she epitomized the cosmopolitan culture of her age; she promoted the study of Italian art, and her influence on others is undoubted.

See also P. Gunn, *Vernon Lee*, 1964. J.R.

Pankhurst, Dame Christabel (Harriette) (1880–1958), suffragette and co-founder of the Women's Social and Political Union. She was the eldest daughter of Richard and Emmeline PANKHURST, both active feminists. Her father was a barrister, a friend of John Stuart Mill, while her mother's father had been in 1865 a founder member of the original Women's Suffrage Committee. When her father died in 1898, she helped her mother to bring up the family and they became very close. She shared and encouraged her mother's sympathies for the Independent Labour Party and for the

Society for Women's Suffrage, joining the latter's Executive Committee in 1901. In 1903, mother and daughter jointly established the Women's Social and Political Union.

Meanwhile, Christabel had studied law at the Victoria University, Manchester, and applied for admission to Lincoln's Inn but was refused. It is often said that this refusal made her a revolutionary and militant, but it was her arrest with Annie KENNEY in 1905 which brought her this reputation. She promptly became the movement's first martyr. The effect was immediate: the question of female suffrage, which had been talked about and around in largely the same terms for over forty years, was suddenly something which could no longer be ignored. Christabel Pankhurst had shown that if they refused to accept the politicians' rules, women could win, and she continued breaking those rules, enduring imprisonment twice more for the cause.

For many, she had a gift for inspiring loyalty, and the genteelly brought up middle-class girls who followed her were able to leave the confines of their backgrounds for militancy only because of her example. Yet others saw her as a megalomaniac, egotistical and arrogant. When she escaped to Paris in 1912, wanted by the police again, it was claimed that her insistence on running the campaign from there proved that she was really only interested in personal power. This judgement was made by her sister, Sylvia PANKHURST, who disagreed in many respects with the campaign as masterminded by Christabel. Sylvia wanted more working-class women in the movement and a greater involvement with radical social reform in general. Here the elder sister's political intuition was perhaps more sensitive. She pointed out that working-class women did not have the time or the newsworthiness of their middle and upper-class sisters, and that to dilute the issue of suffrage with other claims, however worthy, would be wrong-headed.

With the outbreak of war, the WSPU declared an immediate truce, and the members set themselves to do war-work. In 1918, when women over thirty received the vote, Christabel stood for parliament for the Women's Party, but failed to be elected then or in subsequent attempts. She was created DBE in 1936 and spent much of her later life in America, a committed Christian, convinced of the imminence of the Second Coming.

See also D. Mitchell, *Queen Christabel*, 1977; C. Pankhurst, *Unshackled*, 1959.

E.M.V.

Pankhurst, Emmeline (1858–1928), suffragette and political reformer. Born in Manchester, the daughter of a manufacturer, she was educated at a dame school and in France. In 1879 she married Dr Richard Marsden Pankhurst, a legal scholar and radical reformer, and had three daughters and two sons.

In Manchester she supported her husband's political ambitions, while working for women's suffrage and for married women's property reform. Living in London from the mid-1880s, she helped Annie BESANT in the Match Girls' strike, joined the Women's Liberal Federation, and convened the inaugural meeting of the Women's Franchise League. Following the death of a son and the failure of her retail shop, the family returned to Manchester where she and Dr Pankhurst allied themselves with the embryonic Independent Labour Party (ILP). She was adopted (though not elected) as their candidate for the Manchester School Board in 1894 and during her work for the unemployed in the hard winter of 1894–95 was elected to the Chorlton Board of Guardians. The death of Dr Pankhurst in 1898 placed financial constraints on his widow, who resigned from the Chorlton Board and became their salaried Registrar of Births, Marriages, and Deaths. Gradually she resumed political work. She was elected to the Manchester School Board in 1900, to the Executive Committee of the ILP Manchester Central Branch in 1902, and to the ILP National Administrative Council in 1904.

An active member of the North of England Society for Women's Suffrage, after 1900 Emmeline Pankhurst tried to nurture the cause within the Labour movement, but found some of its members (advocates of manhood or adult suffrage) antagonistic to her aims. With her daughters she founded in Manchester in 1903 the Women's Social and Political Union (WSPU), using militant tactics to gain women's suffrage on the same terms as those enjoyed by men. She moved to London in 1907 to further what had become a national movement helped by paid organizers and devoted volunteers. Charismatic and eloquent, with unflinching resolve, she endured hunger strikes while imprisoned under the notorious 'Cat and

Mouse' Act, and made the WSPU a political force which roused the country and embarrassed the Liberal government. She was greatly influenced by her eldest daughter Christabel PANKHURST, whose increasingly autocratic methods caused secessions from their ranks. The movement's withdrawal from the ILP in 1907 and the escalation of militancy from 1911 alienated many members.

Mrs Pankhurst suspended WSPU activities at the outbreak of the First World War, and then directed its energies into conscription propaganda. In 1916 she toured America, lecturing on the war effort and social hygiene, and in 1917 visited Russia under the auspices of the British government in an attempt to persuade the Bolsheviks back into the war. The same year she founded with Christabel the Women's Party, which collapsed after Christabel's failure as a candidate in the general election of 1918. She then sailed to North America, settling in Toronto in 1920 with the illegitimate children she had fostered during the war, and supporting herself as a lecturer. After a brief stay in France, she returned to London in 1925 where her involvement with the campaign to extend women's suffrage was minimal. In 1926, having joined the Conservative Party, she became their candidate in the constituency of Whitechapel and St George, but the strain of renewed public work hastened illness and her death.

See also her autobiography *My Own Story* 1914; S. Pankhurst, *The Suffragette Movement*, 1931; S. Pankhurst, *The Life of Emmeline Pankhurst*, 1935; A. Rosen, *Rise Up, Women!* 1974.   L.W.

Pankhurst, (Estelle) Sylvia (1882–1960), suffragette and socialist. Daughter of the political reformers Emmeline and Richard PANKHURST, she was born in Manchester and educated at Manchester High School for Girls and the Royal College of Art in South Kensington. Growing up in an active political family, she attended Independent Labour Party (ILP) meetings from an early age. In 1904 she joined the Fulham branch while studying in London and, much influenced by her friendship with Keir Hardie, remained a staunch socialist all her life. She was also involved in the Women's Social and Political Union (WSPU) founded in 1903 by her mother and elder sister, Christabel PANKHURST. Based in London and supporting herself initially as a freelance artist, she worked

for the WSPU as organizer and speaker, visiting the USA in 1911. She was also a writer (*The Suffragette*, 1910) and designer (the cover of *Votes for Women*), and from 1906 an early militant. In the same year she helped to found the London Committee of the WSPU.

As the organization became controlled by the increasingly autocratic Christabel, from 1912 Sylvia directed her energies into building a democratic mass movement in London's East End. Initially called the East London Federation of the WSPU, from 1914 it was known as the East London Federation of the Suffragettes. She edited its journal, *The Workers' Dreadnought*, was imprisoned many times under the infamous 'Cat and Mouse' Act, and journeyed abroad lecturing on suffragette militancy, to Scandinavia in 1913 and central Europe in 1914.

The years 1914–18 saw Sylvia preoccupied with war relief work, always with the East London Federation. They established maternity welfare clinics, a toy and garment factory for unemployed women workers, cost-price restaurants, a day nursery, a Montessori school, and organized the League of Rights for Soldiers' and Sailors' Wives and Relatives to fight for better pensions and allowances. She pursued her pacifism through the Women's International League for Peace and Freedom, and continued agitation for women's suffrage through the Labour Council for Adult Suffrage. She travelled to Moscow to meet Lenin, attended the second congress of the Third International, and started a People's Russian Information Bureau. The later part of her life was spent in fighting against fascism and for Ethiopian independence. She helped to establish the Abyssinian Association, published *Ethiopia, A Cultural History* in 1955, and moved the following year to Addis Ababa where she eventually died. Her writings include *Writ on Cold Slate*, 1922, a collection of poems; *India and the Earthly Paradise*, 1926; *The Suffragette Movement*, 1931; and *The Life of Emmeline Pankhurst*, 1936.
                                              L.W.

Pardoe, Julia (1806–62), writer, born in Beverley, Yorkshire. Her father was an army officer who fought at Waterloo. She began writing while very young and one volume of poetry, published when she was fourteen, reached a second edition. For a time she lived in Portugal, about which she wrote a book of travel. In 1835 she went with her father to

Constantinople, acquiring a knowledge of Turkey unrivalled by any Englishwoman since Lady Mary Wortley MONTAGU and revealed in her book *The City of the Sultan and Domestic Manners of the Turks* (1837). She had by this time written her first novel, and thereafter produced popular historical novels and works on French history. Among them are *Louis XIV and the Court of France in the Seventeenth Century*, 1847; *The Jealous Wife*, 1847; *The Court and Reign of Francis the First, King of France*, 1849; *Flies in Amber*, 1850; and *The Life and Memoirs of Marie de Médicis, Queen and Regent of France*, 1852.

See also the memoir in *The Court and Reign of Francis the First*, vol. 1, 1887 ed.

B.H.C.

Parkes, Bessie Rayner (1829–1925), editor. Born into a family with pronounced liberal sympathies, Bessie Parkes was a descendant of Joseph Priestley and only daughter of the radical lawyer Joseph Parkes. She taught herself to read and had completed all Scott's novels by the age of seven. Later she was sent to school in Warwickshire. From early childhood she was a close friend of Barbara BODICHON and in 1850 they visited the Continent together, travelling unchaperoned. Both believed in rational dress, refusing to wear corsets. Convinced of the need for a speedy improvement in the political status of women, the couple were prominent members of the committee which drew up a petition calling for a Married Woman's Property Bill. Although the committee produced a mass of information and secured over 24,000 signatures in favour of the measure, the Bill failed at its second reading.

Bessie Parkes was increasingly persuaded that the women's movement needed a means of expression to communicate new ideas to a wider audience. In 1858 she purchased *The Englishwoman's Journal* with Barbara Bodichon and from the outset envisaged the periodical as being run by and for women. Particularly concerned to expand the horizons of its readers, it ran numerous articles on women's career prospects, seeking to encourage feminine ambition by detailing the achievements of prominent professional women. As editor, Miss Parkes adopted a cautious tone. Her desire not to cause offence can perhaps be attributed to the derision and outrage which greeted her own essay *Remarks on the Education of Girls*, published anonymously in 1854, in which she inveighed against the narrowness of female instruction. Notwithstanding, *The Englishwoman's Journal* played a crucial role in stimulating interest in women's issues, reaching an eager, receptive audience. Jessie BOUCHERETT arrived from Lincoln to help in its production; Maria Rye and Emily FAITHFULL were also involved from its earliest days.

In 1867 Bessie Parkes married Louis Belloc and lived mostly in France until his death in 1872. The couple had two children, both of whom became writers (Hilaire Belloc and Mrs Belloc LOWNDES. Mme Belloc had been received into the Roman Catholic church in 1864 and became increasingly devout as she grew older. She spent the rest of her life in Sussex, where she wrote poems, children's stories, and a reflective work, *A Passing World*, published in 1897.

See also: H. Burton, *Barbara Bodichon*, 1949; M. Belloc Lowndes, *I, Too, Have Lived in Arcadia*, 1941.

J.V.L.

Parr, Helena, Marchioness of Northampton (1549–1635), courtier. Helena Snakenborg, the daughter of a Swedish knight, travelled to England in 1565 as the attendant of a visiting Swedish princess. William Parr, the fifty-two-year-old Marquis of Northampton and brother of Katherine PARR, became infatuated with her, but the couple could not marry because his first wife, from whom he had a divorce of dubious legality, was still alive. Helena had also attracted the attention of Queen Elizabeth, and instead of returning home became one of her courtiers. At the Queen's insistence she married Parr in 1571, but the Marquis died six months later; Helena remained Elizabeth's companion, receiving a substantial landed income. The Queen was angered by her later marriage to a prominent courtier, Sir Thomas Gorges, but the relationship was repaired and Helena was chief mourner at Elizabeth's funeral. She had four sons and three daughters by Gorges, and is buried with him in Salisbury Cathedral.

See also G. Sjogren, 'Helena, Marchioness of Northampton' in *History Today*, September, 1978.

A.H.

Parr, Katherine (1512–48), sixth Queen of Henry VIII. Although she was daughter of Sir Thomas Parr of Kendal, Master of the Wards and Controller of the Household to Henry

VIII, Katherine's early life is shrouded in obscurity. About 1523 she married one Edward Borough, who was dead by 1529, and then John Neville, Lord Latimer, of Snape Hall, Yorkshire. Latimer died in late 1542 or early 1543, whereupon Katherine was courted by Thomas Seymour, brother of Jane SEYMOUR. But when the King showed interest in her she interpreted it as a call from God to work for reformed religion at court, and married Henry on 12 July 1543. From July to October 1544 she was Regent during Henry's absence at the siege of Boulogne, and an Act was passed allowing him to settle the succession on her future children.

Katherine's radical religious views led to a conservative attack on her led by Bishop Gardiner and the Chancellor, Wriothesley. The Queen liked to argue theology with her didactic husband, and Henry's irritation at her views made him listen to imputations of heresy against her. Fortunately, alerted by the reform faction within the King's Privy Chamber, she made a timely submission to the King, and the plot rebounded on its instigators.

Soon after Henry VIII's death in 1547 Katherine married Thomas Seymour, later gaining the approval of Edward VI. Princess Elizabeth resided with them, but scandalous talk of Seymour's relations with the girl made Katherine send her away. Katherine also quarrelled over court precedence with the Protector's wife, Anne, Duchess of Somerset, and the Seymours moved to Sudeley in Gloucestershire. There Katherine gave birth to a daughter, Mary, on 30 August 1548, but she succumbed to puerperal fever and died on 7 September.

Katherine's importance has been exaggerated by recent commentators. However, she is interesting as a cultured and pious court lady, who sponsored the translation of Erasmus's *Paraphrases* into English. Katherine herself composed two devotional treatises: the *Prayers or Meditations*, printed in 1545; and *The Lamentation of a Sinner*, published posthumously.

See also J. S. Brewer, *Letters and Papers Foreign and Domestic, of the Reign of Henry VIII*, 1920; *The Acts and Monuments of John Foxe*, ed. S. R. Cattley, 1837; J. K. McConica, *English Humanists and Reformation Politics*, 1968.   M.D.

Parry, Blanche (*c*. 1508–90), courtier. Blanche Parry was born into a leading Herefordshire family related to several other important border families such as the Stradlings and the Herberts. She was brought to court by a Herbert kinswoman in 1536 and became a gentlewoman to the young Princess Elizabeth. A distant cousin and close friend was William Cecil, later Lord Burghley, who was probably influential in her rise to the position of Queen Elizabeth's chief gentlewoman of the Privy Chamber in 1565. She never married and it has been conjectured that she modelled herself on her mistress, the Virgin Queen.

Blanche Parry's close personal relationship with the Queen made her a significant influence at court, and leading administrators often used her as an intermediary with Elizabeth, to whom she could present their activities in a favourable light. She was particularly important as a channel of communication for the gentry of Wales and the border, to whom she frequently transmitted royal orders and for whom she interceded at court. She is also important as a patron of Welsh culture, encouraging the work of David Powel, whose *Historie of Cambria, now called Wales* was published in 1584. Powel praised her as a 'singular well wisher and furtherer of the weale publike' of Wales. The extensive property she was granted by the Queen during her long service at court was used for charitable bequests in London and Herefordshire, and for the advancement of her relatives. Her tomb in St Margaret's, Westminster, thus commemorates her as 'beneficial to her kinsfolk and countrymen, charitable to the poor. . . . She died a maid'. Blanche Parry illustrates the way in which women have frequently wielded informal political power despite their exclusion from formal political structures.

See also *The Dictionary of Welsh Biography Down to 1940*, 1959.   A.H.

Passfield, Baroness. See WEBB, (MARTHA) BEATRICE.

Paston, Margaret (d. 1482), household manager and principal correspondent in the famous Paston family letters. The heiress of John Mautby, she was born at Reedham, Norfolk, and married John Paston I about 1440. The letters give invaluable information on fifteenth-century life and manners and on conditions during the Wars of the Roses. John was often away on business and, for a time, in prison, where Margaret visited him. She had to run the family home and sometimes organize its defence against military attack by the men of Sir John Fastolf, Lord Moleyns, and other powerful neighbours. In her letters to John in London, she informs him of the military situation, complains of difficulties in disciplining her soldiers, and asks him to buy spices, dress materials, and crossbow quarrels. Margaret dealt with the tenants, used agents to monitor proceedings in the county court, and bought the bulk supplies. After her husband's death in 1466 she lived mostly in the town of Norwich, moving to her own family's home of Mautby about 1474.

See also N. Davis (editor), *Paston Letters. . .,* Part I, 1971.   G.H.

Paterson, Emma (Ann) (1848–86), organizer of women's trade unions. She was born in London, the only child of a headmaster of a National Society school in Hanover Square. Educated by her father, she was for a time apprenticed to a bookbinder. She showed an early interest in the political and industrial status of women, and worked as assistant secretary to the Working Men's Club and Institute Union from 1867 to 1872. From 1872 until her marriage the following year to Thomas Paterson, a cabinet-maker, she acted as secretary to a women's suffrage association. During her year's honeymoon in America she observed women's trade unions, in particular the Female Umbrella Makers' Union of New York.

On her return to London she established the Women's Provident and Protective League in 1874, with the assistance of trade unionists and middle-class philanthropists. The League formed unions along craft lines, starting first in London among women dressmakers, milliners, upholsterers, bookbinders, and shirt and collar makers. Apart from the Society of Women Employed in Bookbinding, the unions were short-lived, for low wages, unskilled status, and the tendency of workers to move from one occupation to another made permanent organization difficult. In its early years the League opposed both protective legislation and strikes. It received little sympathy from male trade unionists, who, anxious to protect their living standards, did not wish to compete with low-paid women.

In an attempt to strengthen the movement, Emma Paterson worked alongside men's unions and gained admission to the Trades Union Congress in Glasgow in 1875, representing the Bookbinders. She and Edith Simcox were the first women delegates to be admitted. Thereafter she attended Congress every year until the end of her life, except in 1882 when her husband was dying. Nominated several times for a seat on the Parliamentary Committee, she was particularly interested in the establishment of women factory inspectors; and in 1878 she succeeded in carrying a resolution in the TUC calling for their appointment. Parliament did not concede this issue until 1892. She lectured widely and from 1876 edited *The Women's Union Journal*, a record of the League's proceedings. In that year she also founded the Women's Printing Society in Westminster and mastered the printer's craft. Tactful but determined, she held the fundamental belief that working women must organize on their own behalf, albeit in harmony with men, if they were to improve their economic position. In their *History of Trade Unionism*, Sidney and Beatrice WEBB called her 'the real pioneer of modern women's trade unions'.

See also H. Goldman, *Emma Paterson*, 1974; S. Lewenhak, *Women and Trade Unions*, 1977; R. Strachey, *The Cause*, 1928.   L.W.

Patey, Janet Monach (1842–94), singer. She was born in Holborn, London, the daughter of a Scottish businessman called Whytock. Having first been taught singing by John Wass, she made her initial appearance in public at Birmingham in 1860, where she sang under the name of Ellen Andrews. The performance was successful, but made her so nervous that she lost her voice for six months afterwards. Continuing to make steady progress from this time onwards, her promise was such that she was given further musical instruction by Ciro Pinsuti and Mrs Sims Reeves.

She made her first concert tour in 1865, travelling in the provinces with a group that included the famous soprano Helen LEMMENS-SHERRINGTON. In 1866 she married the operatic and oratorio singer John Patey. She sang as principal contralto at the various English festivals, including Worcester (1866), Birmingham (1867), and Norwich (1869), and after the retirement of Charlotte Sainton-Dolby was left without a rival as the principal English contralto. An American tour took place in 1871, and on her return she appeared at all the major festivals and concerts with increasing success. In Paris, which she had visited in

1875 to take part in four performances of *Messiah* in French, she was compared favourably to the distinguished Madame Marietta Alboni, and to the Italians she became known as 'the English Alboni'. In 1890 she toured Australia, New Zealand, China, and Japan, and began a farewell tour of the English provinces in 1893. After an appearance and an enthusiastic reception at Sheffield, she suffered an apoplectic fit and died in the concert-room. Her pure, rich, sonorous contralto, heard in innumerable oratorios and ballad performances, was unrivalled in England for a quarter of a century.   B.H.C.

Paton, Mary Ann (1802–64), singer. She was born in Edinburgh, the daughter of a writing master and amateur violinist. Her grandmother had played the violin before the Duke of Cumberland on his way to Culloden. The family settled in London in 1811. She had sung in concerts as a child and in 1820 appeared in Bath, in 1821 at Huntingdon, and in 1822 she joined the Haymarket company, singing her first operatic part, Susanna in *The Marriage of Figaro*. Subsequently she sang at Covent Garden, before she was twenty-one and was enthusiastically received, although some critics noted a tendency to exaggerated ornamentation. Forced by her father to end an engagement to a medical practitioner named Blood, she married Lord William Pitt Lennox in 1824, was divorced in 1831, and in that year married the tenor Joseph Wood.

At the premiere of Weber's *Oberon* in London in 1826, she sang the part of Rezia. Weber conducted the sixteen rehearsals and the performance itself, just two months before his death. His verdict was that 'she was created for the part... she sang exquisitely even at the first rehearsal'. After a visit to America in 1840 she retired for a year to a convent, reappearing to sing at concerts with her husband. Her very fine soprano voice could manage lyric and coloratura parts equally brilliantly.   B.H.C.

Patti, Adelina (1843–1919), singer. Adelina Patti was born in Madrid, into an Italian family of singers. She made her world début in New York at the age of sixteen as Lucia in Donizetti's *Lucia di Lammermoor*. Her London début (1861) in Bellini's *La Sonnambula* was an immense success and the beginning of her twenty-five-year reign at Covent Garden. The British came to regard her as one of themselves,

especially when she made the song 'Home Sweet Home' an indispensable item in her lieder recitals. With her third husband, Baron Rolf Cederström, who became a naturalized British subject, she settled in a Welsh castle.

Patti's voice was considered extraordinary for its purity, still apparent in recordings made in her sixties, while her remarkable range made her one of the great nineteenth-century coloratura singers. Verdi and Rossini were her favourite composers. Her official farewell concert took place at the Albert Hall in 1906, but she appeared once more in a Red Cross benefit concert (1914) and sang 'Home Sweet Home' for the very last time.

See also H. Klein, *The Reign of Patti*, 1926; S. Sadie (ed.), *The New Grove Dictionary of Music and Musicians*, 1981.   P.L.

Pattison, Dorothy (1832–78), nurse. Born in Hauxwell, Yorkshire, she was the tenth child of a clergyman. Her childhood was sombre, owing to a joyless evangelical upbringing and her father's mental instability. Her elder brother Mark's interest in the Oxford Movement, which Dorothy shared, caused further family tensions. She tried to escape from her oppressive home environment through marriage, encouraging the attentions of two suitors simultaneously, but finally chose not to marry for convention alone. Eventually, in 1861 she took a post as village schoolmistress near Newport Pagnell in Buckinghamshire.

In September 1864, having recovered her faith after a period of agnosticism, Dorothy entered the Christ Church Sisterhood, one of the first Anglican religious orders, taking the name of Sister Dora. During her training she worked in the Coatham convalescent home, where she did her first nursing. In 1865, she went as a nurse to the new Cottage Hospital in Walsall, a grim Black Country town in which there were very many industrial accidents. It was here that she did her major work. In the same year her father died, and in 1866 she broke her engagement to a doctor when she realized that marriage would mean the end of her career as a nurse.

In 1867 the Sisterhood was reconstituted into a proper religious order and Dora was given the opportunity of taking vows. She elected instead to remain at the Walsall hospital as an associate of the Community, and eventually became Sister-in-charge. Her work gave her complete personal fulfilment and she wrote in 1870 that 'Eternity has become real'. In 1875 she had to cope with the summer smallpox epidemic and Walsall's worst-ever industrial accident, the explosion at a blast furnace. One result of this accident was a decision to build a new hospital better fitted for such emergencies; but Dora died before this was finished. Although she never became a full member of her community, religion was the mainstay of Sister Dora's life. She was also a profoundly passionate and feminine woman, constantly torn between love and duty. She stands in the great tradition of Victorian philanthropy and her skill set a standard for the new nursing profession.

See also M. Lonsdale, *Sister Dora*, 1880; J. Manton, *Sister Dora, the Life of Dorothy Pattison*, 1971. M.A.

Pembroke, Countesses of. See ST POL, MAIRIE DE, COUNTESS OF PEMBROKE; SIDNEY, MARY, COUNTESS OF PEMBROKE.

Penrose, Dame Emily (1858–1942), educationist. The eldest daughter of Francis C. Penrose, archaeologist and architect, she was educated at a private school in Wimbledon, later studying languages and archaeology in Europe. She lived in Athens with her father, developing a great love for Greece. Religion was a mainstay and, although reserved, she was unfailingly generous to those in trouble. She went to Somerville in 1889, concentrating on ancient languages, and three years later was the first woman to achieve a first-class degree in the school of *literae humaniores*.

Emily Penrose then turned to the academic world rather than practical archaeology, displaying great aptitude for administration and finance. In 1893 she became Principal of Bedford College. She was Professor of Ancient History (1894), and from 1898 Principal of Royal Holloway College. In 1907 she returned to Somerville as Principal, leaving in 1926. She sat on many commissions and committees, including the Royal Commission on University Education in Wales (1916). An important figure in the advance of women's university education during this period, she had a decisive effect on all the institutions with which she was connected. She was awarded the OBE (1918), created DBE (1927), and died in retirement at Bournemouth. J.R.

Penson, Dame Lillian (1896–1963), historian and educationist. Lillian Penson was educated privately and at Birkbeck and University Colleges, London. She obtained a degree in history in 1917 and a PhD in 1921. From 1917 to 1919 she worked for the government and helped to edit the Peace Handbooks used at the Paris Conference. She became part-time lecturer at Birkbeck in 1921, and from 1923 to 1925 at East London College (now Queen Mary College). After obtaining a full-time post at Birkbeck in 1925, in 1930 she gained the Chair of Modern History. Although her early interests lay with the colonies, her main field was diplomatic history, which she established in the university at both undergraduate and postgraduate level. Her writings include *Documents on the Origins of the First World War (1898–1914)* with G. P. Gooch and Harold Temperley (1928–1938); *A Century of British Blue Books*, with Temperley (1938); *Foundations of British Foreign Policy* (1938); and a revision and continuation of Grant and Temperley's *Europe in the Nineteenth and Twentieth Centuries* (1952).

Lillian Penson was also active in university affairs. She joined the Senate in 1940, became Chairman of the Academic Council in 1945, and a member of the University Court in 1946. In 1948 she was unanimously elected Vice-Chancellor of the University, the first woman to hold such a post within the Commonwealth. She was instrumental in establishing the Institute of Commonwealth Studies; and helped to develop the Courtauld and Warburg Institutes, the School of Slavonic and East European Studies, and the School of Oriental and African Studies. From 1949 to 1956 she was a member of the US Educational Commission in the UK. She took a great interest in the growth of higher education in the Commonwealth, and served on the Asquith Commission on Higher Education in the Colonies. In 1951 she was created DBE. J.E.

Pentreath, Dorothy, called Dolly (1685–1777), Cornish fish-seller whose churchyard monument states that she was 'the last person who conversed in ancient Cornish, the peculiar language of this county from earliest records till it expired in the eighteenth century in this parish of St Paul'. She was born nearby, at Mousehole, and is said to have spoken no English before the age of twenty. Dolly Pentreath was not in fact the last Cornish speaker, but was described as such to the Society of Antiquaries, probably thanks to her forceful

323

presence: she charged sixpence to say anything in Cornish, and abused in good fishwife English anyone who refused to pay.   N.H.

Perham, Dame Margery (Freda) (1895–1982), expert on African affairs, a major influence on both the academic study and the actual policy of colonial administration. She was educated at St Stephen's College, Windsor, St Anne's School, Abbots Bromley, and St Hugh's College, Oxford, from which she emerged with a first-class degree in modern history. In 1922, as an assistant lecturer at Sheffield University, she was forced to take a year's sick leave which she spent in British Somaliland. The experience fixed the direction of her future interests. She subsequently became Tutor and Fellow of St Hugh's; then a series of travelling fellowships enabled her to study problems of government, and particularly African colonial government, at first hand.

The publication in 1937 of *Native Administration in Nigeria*, with its penetrating analysis of indirect rule (that is, the system of controlling a populous colony through native rulers), at once established Margery Perham as an authority. Over the next few years she was increasingly consulted by colonial officials, maintaining her grasp of affairs by frequent visits to the colonies. Meanwhile she became reader in colonial administration at Oxford, and in 1939 found a congenial academic base at Nuffield College, then newly endowed, of which she became the first fellow. The Institute of Colonial (now Commonwealth) Affairs at Oxford owed much to her, and its outstanding library was in the first instance largely her creation. Her many publications included *Africans and British Rule*, 1941; a two-volume life of Lord Lugard, 1956, 1960; *The Colonial Reckoning*, 1963, based on her Reith lectures of 1961; two volumes of 'chronological commentary upon British colonial policy', *The Colonial Sequence, 1930 to 1949*, 1967, and *The Colonial Sequence, 1949 to 1969*, 1970; and such autobiographical accounts as *African Apprenticeship*, 1929.
   N.H.

Perrers, Alice (?–1400), mistress of Edward III, a woman of obscure origins, possibly (as her enemies alleged) of low birth. By October 1366 she entered the service of Queen PHILIPPA OF HAINAULT, and had become the King's mistress before Philippa's death in 1369.

She certainly bore the king a son, openly acknowledged at court as John Sotherey, and, following her marriage to William de Windsor about 1376, gave birth to the two legitimate daughters who were her heirs.

Alice Perrers has an unenviable reputation as an ambitious, grasping, and evil influence on an increasingly senile king and in an ever more corrupt court. This at least partly results from the hostile tone of a St Albans' chronicler, influenced by his own abbot's failure to defeat the royal mistress in a manorial dispute. She had 'such power and influence in those days', he asserted, 'that no one dared prosecute a claim against her'. It is also no doubt a result of the massive attack on Alice Perrers made in the Good Parliament of 1376: 'it would be a great profit to the kingdom', declared the Commons' Speaker Peter de la Mare, 'to remove that lady from the king's company so that the king's treasure could be applied to the war, and wardships in the king's gift not so lightly granted away'. Yet there seems little reason to reject such judgements. By 1376 she had become a substantial landowner and had received many gifts (especially jewellery) from the King. The Good Parliament had no hesitation in pronouncing a sentence of banishment and forfeiture, but she was soon back in royal favour, and, at Edward III's death in 1377, this rapacious woman is said to have stolen the very rings from his fingers.

See also G. Holmes, *The Good Parliament*, 1975.   K.R.D.

Pethwick-Lawrence, Lady Emmeline (1867–1954), suffragette and social reformer. Born in Bristol, the eldest child of Henry Pethwick JP, she was educated at private schools in England, France, and Germany. She then devoted herself to social work as a 'Sister' at the West London Mission. With a colleague, Mary Neal, she founded the Esperance Working Girls' Club near St Pancras, and set up holiday hostels for club members and their children. She also opened a co-operative dressmaking establishment, Maison Esperance, with such innovations for its staff as an eight-hour working day, minimum weekly wage (15s. 0d.), and annual holiday.

In 1901 she married Frederick William Lawrence, editor of the London evening newspaper *The Echo*, and four years her junior. He was also involved in work among London's poor, and later recalled how her 'liberated' ways had attracted him: she smoked, went out walking without gloves, and could jump off a moving omnibus. Their hyphenated married name was a gesture to the principle of sex equality. Emmeline was already a member of the Suffragette Society. In 1906 she joined the more militant Women's Social and Political Union founded by Mrs Emmeline PANKHURST and her daughter Christabel PANKHURST, becoming its honorary treasurer. Her husband wholeheartedly supported the suffragist cause, in which the Pethwick-Lawrences, together with the Pankhursts, were now the driving force.

From 1907 to 1914 Emmeline and Frederick edited the weekly paper *Votes for Women*. In 1906 and on four subsequent occasions she was imprisoned for her suffragette activities; in 1908 she led a band of colleagues who chained themselves to the railings of 10 Downing Street. Her husband was imprisoned—and went on hunger-strike —with her in 1912. In the same year the Pankhursts decided on a policy that involved widespread attacks on property, including the burning of pillar-boxes. With this extreme militancy the Pethwick-Lawrences disagreed, and they were expelled from the WSPU. Two years later they joined the newly-formed United Suffragists. When. in 1914, Emmeline was invited to America to promote the Women's International League for Peace, she also helped to inaugurate the campaign that led to the enfranchisement of American women. She attended the 1915 International Women's Congress at The Hague, and became honorary treasurer of the Women's International League in Britain.

At women's first opportunity to stand for parliament, in 1918, she was Labour candidate at Rusholme, Manchester, but was not elected. Subsequently she supported her husband's political campaigns: he was a Labour MP (1923–31 and 1935–45), and in 1945 was appointed Secretary of State for India and Burma, having been created Baron Pethwick-Lawrence of Peasdale. In later years Emmeline campaigned actively for the causes of women's welfare and international peace, to which she brought qualities of humanity, tolerance, eloquence, and efficiency. For many years she was president of the Women's Freedom League, and in 1953 was elected its President of Honour, but the suffragette victory to which she had so largely contributed

remained her proudest achievement. In her autobiography *My Part in a Changing World* (1938) she described it as 'the greatest bloodless revolution since history began'.

See also Roger Fulford, *Votes for Women*, 1957; J. Kamm, *Rapiers and Battleaxes, the Women's Movement and its Aftermath*, 1966; S. Pankhurst, *The Suffragette Movement*, 1931. J.L.

Peto, Dorothy (Olivia Georgiana) (1886–1974), Superintendent of the Metropolitan Women's Police. Educated at home, during the First World War she became deputy director and later director of the Bristol Training School for Women Patrols and Police, which was established to train women in policing duties. After the war she became detective inquiry officer in the Birmingham City Police, leaving in 1925 to set up the British Social Hygiene Council.

Women police were not officially recognized at this time, however. In 1914 Dame Mary ALLEN had, with Mrs Damer DAWSON, set up a voluntary organization of women who wore uniform and exercised some police functions. This had been tolerated, but hardly welcomed, by the official force, especially Scotland Yard. After the war the unofficial force was allowed to co-operate with the police, albeit within strictly defined limits The women's organization, with the recruiting drive of Mary Allen behind it, became so large and important that it could be ignored no longer by the authorities, who were gradually convinced of the need to add women to the official police force.

In 1930 the Metropolitan Police appointed Dorothy Peto to the rank of Superintendent with the object of building up the new force. She thus became the first woman in Britain to command and train an official force of policewomen. She retired in 1946, having been awarded the King's Police Medal in 1945.

See also J. Lock, *The British Policewoman: her story*, 1979. E.M.V.

Philippa of Hainault (*c.* 1315–69), Queen of England, the daughter of William II, Count of Hainault, Holland, and Zeeland. Philippa's marriage (1328) to the future Edward III was arranged when she was a child and expedited by his mother, Queen ISABELLA, in return for Hainault's support of her invasion of England. Philippa bore Edward a large family, and it is much to her credit that all remained on

Philips, Katherine

affectionate terms, particularly with their father. A highly active woman, she accompanied Edward on his campaigns in France and kept close ties with her own home. She was shrewd, likeable, aware of the responsibilities of kingship, and won the universal praise of chroniclers. She acted as an appeaser and conciliator, and there is no reason to disbelieve the famous story of her intervention on behalf of the Burghers of Calais. Edward held her in deep affection and relied on her judgement, although he was not always faithful to her, particularly during the last years of her life.

Philippa introduced foreign poets and writers, including Froissart, to England, and encouraged native ones such as Chaucer, who married one of her ladies. Although hopelessly extravagant, she did much to promote trade with the Low Countries, establishing Flemish weavers at Norwich. She also encouraged coal-mining on her estates near Newcastle. She died after a long dropsical illness.

See also P. Johnson, *The Life and Times of Edward III*, 1973.   A.C.

Philips, Katherine (1632–64), poet and translator. She was the daughter of John Fowler, a wealthy London merchant, and Katherine Oxenbridge, who came from a noted Puritan family. After her father's death in 1642, her mother married Sir Richard Phillipps and then, when he died within two years, the Parliamentary Major-General, Philip Skippon, who died in 1660. Katherine's education was begun at home by a cousin, but from the age of eight she attended Mrs Salmon's school for girls at Hackney, where she may have learned some French and Italian. At fifteen she went to live with her mother in Wales. In 1648 she married James Philips, a leading Parliamentarian who was related to Sir Richard Phillipps and who had been married to one of his daughters. He was aged fifty-four; she was not yet seventeen. A son was born in 1655, but died within two months. Their daughter was born the following year.

Katherine began to be known as a poet in the 1650s, her earliest published verses appearing prefixed to the works of William Cartwright in 1651. Her poems circulated in manuscript among what she called her 'Society of Friendship', a circle of correspondents who were assigned classical names. The closest of these friends were Mrs Mary Aubrey

('Rosania') and Mrs Anne Owen ('Lucasia'), to whom she was known as 'Orinda'. One of the most important themes in her poems is that of love between women friends.

Although Katherine's family and her husband's associates were all Parliamentarians, her own friends were Royalists. With the Restoration of Charles II in 1660 she was able to express her sympathies openly in panegyrics to the returning royal family. She became a close friend of Sir Charles Cotterell, Charles's Master of Ceremonies, whom she named 'Poliarchus', and her *Letters from Orinda to Poliarchus* (1705, 1729) provide some insight into her personality and activities. In 1662 she accompanied 'Lucasia' to Ireland, remaining there for nearly a year to look after property claims for her husband. She completed a translation of Corneille's heroic tragedy *Pompey*, which was produced to great applause in Dublin in 1663, and immediately published. This is notable as the first work by an Englishwoman to have been performed on the stage. On her return to Wales she began translating Corneille's *Horace*, which was completed after her death by Sir John Denham and staged in 1688 and 1689. To her apparent consternation, an unauthorized collection of her poems was published in 1664. She returned to London that year, but contracted smallpox and died within three months. Her death called forth extravagant tributes by Abraham Cowley and others which were printed with her collected poems and translations in 1667 (reprinted 1669, 1678, 1710). She remains significant as the first woman to be publicly recognized and accepted as a poet in England, and the fact that she was frequently held as an example by later women writers suggests that her success did much to open the way to literary activity for women.

See also P. Elmen, 'Some Manuscript Poems by the Matchless Orinda', in *Philological Quarterly*, XXX, 1951; W. Roberts, 'The Dating of Orinda's French Translations', in *Philological Quarterly*, XLIX, 1970; G. Saintsbury (ed.), *Minor Poets of the Caroline Period*, 1905, rep. 1968; P. W. Souers, *The Matchless Orinda*, 1931.   W.R.O.

Phillips, Marion (1881–1932), political activist and Labour MP. Born in Melbourne, Australia, she was educated at Melbourne University and the London School of Economics (1905–06). She impressed Beatrice

WEBB, who found her work as an investigator under the Royal Commission on the Poor Law, 1907–08. In 1907 she joined the Fabian Society, becoming a member of the Executive and a leader of the Fabian Reform Committee. An active suffragist and member of the National Union of Women's Suffrage Societies, she supported herself by lecturing on the Poor Law and by journalism. During the First World War she was appointed to the Central Committee for Women's Employment, the Reconstruction Committee, and the Consumers' Council of the Ministry of Food. Afterwards she served as a JP and sat on the Advisory Committee of Magistrates for the County of London.

Her powerful intellect and forceful personality caused Marion Phillips to emerge as a leading figure in the Labour movement. At first she concentrated her efforts on local government, serving on the London Labour Electoral Committee. She was adopted as Labour candidate for Bow and Bromley in the LCC elections, and in 1912 served on the Borough Council of Kensington. Her major contribution to Labour politics, however, was through her work in organizing women. She had served an apprenticeship under Mary MACARTHUR during the Bermondsey strikes in the summer of 1911, had joined the Fabian Women's Group in 1908, and was secretary to the Industrial Women's Insurance Advisory Board. Her great triumph came in 1913 when she wrested the general secretaryship of the Women's Labour League from Margaret BONDFIELD. This paved the way to her appointment as Chief Woman Officer of the Labour Party in 1918, a position from which she could mould an effective network of politically educated and trained women who strengthened the Labour Party and began to realize some of the potential of working women. As Secretary of the Standing Joint Committee of Industrial Women's Organizations (SJC) formed in 1915, she was able to influence the National Conferences of Labour Women to which the SJC reported and gave guidance on policy. She also played a major part in Women's International Labour Conferences, edited *Labour Woman*, organized the Relief Committee for Miners' Wives and Children in 1926, and was Labour MP for Sunderland (1929–31). She commanded respect for her immense energies and gained enemies in the pursuit of the power needed to enforce her views.

Marion Phillips edited *Women and the Labour Party* (1918), and wrote *Women and the Miners' Lock-Out* (1927) and *The Working Woman's House* (1920, with A. D. S. Furniss).

See also L. Middleton (ed.), *Women in the Labour Movement*, 1977.   L.W.

Phillpotts, Dame Bertha (Surtees) (1877–1932), literary scholar specializing in Scandinavian studies. She was born at Bedford, where her father was headmaster of the grammar school. She was taught by the masters there, and then went up to Girton College, Cambridge, where in 1901 she took a first-class degree in the medieval and modern languages tripos. In the pre-war years she devoted herself to Scandinavian studies, and in 1913 was elected a Fellow of Somerville College, Oxford. After war-work at the British Legation in Stockholm, she became Principal of Westfield College, London (1919–21), and Mistress of Girton (1922–25). A temporary retirement to look after her father was followed by a university lectureship at Cambridge, where she also became director of Scandinavian Studies. In 1929 she married H. F. Newall, Cambridge Professor of Astrophysics. Her publications included *Kindred and Clan in the Middle Ages and After* (1913) and *Edda and Saga* (1931).   N.H.

Pilkington, Laetitia (1712–50), writer. Born in Dublin, she was the daughter of a Dutch obstetrician. In 1730 she married the Rev. Matthew Pilkington, later the author of the *Dictionary of Painters* (1770). They were both friends of Swift, who found a post for Matthew in London. When he returned to Dublin he divorced Laetitia in a highly publicized case in 1737. Swift thought him a rogue and her 'the most profligate whore in either Kingdom'. Laetitia then moved to London, where she set up house in St James's. She was taken up by Colley Cibber and others, writing poetry and a burlesque which was performed though not published. In 1742 she was imprisoned for debt in the Marshalsea. Cibber helped her to gain her freedom, and for a while she ran a shop for prints, pamphlets, and copying. After this failed she returned to Dublin, ending her days with the consolations of low company and alcohol. Her lively *Memoirs* (1748–54), in which she protests her innocence a little unconvincingly, enjoyed considerable success and set off a minor pamphlet war. She forms the subject of a charming biographical sketch by Virginia Woolf in *The Common Reader* (1925).

See also I. Barry (ed.), *Memoirs of Mrs Letitia Pilkington,* 1928; *Poems by Eminent Ladies* vol. II, 1755; *Mrs Pilkington's Jests; or, the cabinet of wit and humour,* 1751

G.E.H.H.

Pinsent, Dame Ellen (Frances) (1866–1949), pioneer of mental health care. She was born in Claxby, Lincolnshire, the eighth and youngest child of a Church of England clergyman. In 1888 she married a solicitor, H. C. Pinsent, by whom she had three children.

Ellen Pinsent became involved in Birmingham local government and particularly with the problems of the mentally handicapped, serving as chairman of the Birmingham special schools sub-committee from 1901 to 1913. The only woman member on the Royal Commission on the Feeble-Minded, after the passing of the Mental Deficiency Act in 1913 she was appointed an honorary commissioner of the Board of Control. Meanwhile in 1911 she had been elected the first woman member of Birmingham City Council, retiring two years later when she left the city with her husband. Following his death in 1920, she became a permanent commissioner of the Board of Control and in 1931, the year before her retirement, a senior commissioner. Right up to her death Ellen Pinsent continued to take an active interest in mental health, notably from 1936 to 1939 as a member of the Feversham Committee on the Voluntary Mental Health Services. She was created DBE in 1937.

A woman of great warmth, vitality, and intelligence, she devoted much of her life to advancing the interests of the mentally handicapped, both as an administrator and in helping to promote legislation. In addition, she was the author of four novels: *Jenny's Case, Children of this World, No Place for Repentance,* and *Job Hildred.* Her daughter, Hester Adrian, continued her mother's interest in mental health into prison reform, becoming president of the Howard League.   K.W.

Piozzi, Hester. See THRALE, HESTER LYNCH.

Pitt, Hester, Countess of Chatham (1721–1803), political wife. There must be many sensible women of strong character of

her type who have left no memorial. Her claim to a place in history largely depends on her supportive role in the career of a brilliant but erratic statesman, possibly mentally ill for much of his later life, and undeniably in his fits of depression dependent upon the constant ministering of a helpmate. Brought up at Stowe surrounded by the members of the ambitious Grenville connection, Hester seems to have acquired a liking for William Pitt at a tender age, perhaps fourteen. Their marriage did not take place until 1754, when she was 33 and he 46. For the next two years her love and companionship were invaluable. Pitt, impatient in the subordinate office of Paymaster-General which he had occupied for years, was fretting over a career that seemed at a standstill, if not at an end. But in 1757 he re-emerged with full powers as Secretary of State to direct the course of the war with France (until 1761). Hester's position was as important in success as in adversity. She took care to shield him from difficulties, nurse his depressions and mitigate the consequences of his financial extravagances, always a serious matter in a man who was obsessed with interior decorating and the embellishment of country properties. Her absences always had an unsteady effect on him. In 1766, now Earl of Chatham, he formed his own administration. A total breakdown in his faculties shortly followed, and Hester again assumed the task of nurse and protector, communicating his wishes to his cabinet colleagues and taking power of attorney to manage his tortuous affairs.

Her later years were saddened by the wreck of her husband's career. The strain of protecting him from reality, even to the extent of consuming her own fortune, so that he might know nothing of the family financial crises, began to tell. After Chatham's death in 1778 she achieved a measure of calm and happiness in her last years in the contemplation of the career of her son William Pitt the younger, whom she lived to see Prime Minister.

See also K. McLeod, *The Wives of Downing Street,* 1976.   T.H.

Pix, Mary (1666–*c.* 1720), dramatist. She was the daughter of Roger Griffith, an Oxfordshire clergyman, and although she claimed an inclination to poetry from childhood, her literary style indicates little formal training. Though fluent in French and well acquainted with English and French dramatic literature, she was no scholar; contemporaries asserted that she possessed little learning of any sort. In 1684 she married George Pix, a merchant tailor of London whose family was associated with Hawkhurst in Kent, where the couple's only child was buried in 1690.

In 1696 her first play, *Ibrahim, the Thirteenth Emperour of the Turks*, a heroic tragedy, was produced at Dorset Garden and subsequently printed. In the same year she published a novel, *The Inhuman Cardinal*, and a comedy, *The Spanish Wives*, which had enjoyed considerable success on stage. Over the next ten years she wrote assiduously for the theatre, producing and publishing under her own name and as an anonymous female author. Modern critics find only her comedies of intrigue are interesting, and then chiefly as relics of a style being rapidly submerged by its debased farcical form. The action of Mrs Pix's plays never lags, and this has been suggested as the chief reason for their acceptance year after year by the Drury Lane and Lincoln's Inn Fields theatres, where they enjoyed reasonable runs.

By 1698 Mary Pix and Catherine Trotter, another novice playwright, were under the protection of the great dramatist, William Congreve. The strong prejudice which women playwrights faced is illustrated by the highly popular production of *The Female Wits*, by 'W.M.', in 1697. In this play Mrs Pix, who was notorious for her corpulence and love of good food and wine, was unmistakably characterized as Mrs Wellfed, 'a fat Female Author', and mercilessly satirized together with Miss Trotter and Mrs MANLEY.

The quality of Mrs Pix's plays cannot be compared with those of Aphra BEHN or Susanna CENTLIVRE. Her importance lies rather in the quantity of her output, her dedication to her self-appointed role as a professional female dramatist, and the success which she enjoyed as a result. Her career must be seen within the context of a period of exceptional activity by female playwrights, beginning, in 1696, seven years after the death of the pioneering Mrs Behn, and ending with the demise of Mrs Centlivre in 1723. Mary Pix's other works include *Adventures in Madrid* (1706).

See also A. Nicoll, *A History of English Drama, 1660-1900*, vols 1 and 2, 1952; M. Reynolds, *The Learned Lady in England, 1650-1760*, 1920.   T.J.M.

Plantagenet, Honor, Viscountess Lisle (*fl.* 1528–63), political figure and letter-writer. The daughter of Sir Thomas Grenville, Honor first married Sir John Basset, who died in January 1528 leaving her with a large family. In February 1531 she married Arthur Plantagenet, Viscount Lisle, a bastard son of Edward IV. Two years later he was appointed Deputy of Calais, but his government was hindered by debt, religious controversies in the town, and quarrels among the garrison. He was recalled in April 1540 and sent to the Tower in May, suspected of complicity in a plot to deliver Calais to the Pope and Cardinal Pole. Honor 'immediately upon his apprehension, fell distraught of mind, and so continued many years after', and was imprisoned at Calais with two of her daughters. Lisle died in March 1542, apparently of excitement at the news of his restoration to royal favour. His widow survived him by over twenty years.

Honor is chiefly important for her voluminous correspondence, which throws light on domestic life and court etiquette, besides sometimes touching on greater events. Her efforts to place her daughters in the service of successive queens-consort, and her attempts to curry favour with leading courtiers, are particularly interesting.

See also J. S. Brewer, *Letters and Papers, Foreign and Domestic, of the Reign of Henry VIII*, 1920; D. Mathew, *Lady Jane Grey*, 1972.
M.D.

Pole, Margaret (1473–1541), political figure. Her father was George, Duke of Clarence; her mother Isabel Neville, daughter of Warwick the Kingmaker. Edward, Earl of Warwick, executed for treason in 1499, was her brother. About 1492 Margaret was married beneath her station to Sir Richard Pole, chief gentleman to Arthur, Prince of Wales. The couple accompanied Arthur and KATHERINE of Aragon to Ludlow after their marriage. Richard Pole died in 1505, leaving five children; Henry, later Lord Montague, Arthur, Reginald, Geoffrey, and Ursula.

Margaret's fortunes improved under Henry VIII, who called her the most saintly woman in England. She received an annuity of £100 in August 1509, and was created Countess of Salisbury in 1513. By 1520 she was governess to Princess Mary, and although the Poles were under a cloud in 1521 she retained the post until late 1533, when Mary's household was dissolved. Since Margaret had the confidence of the repudiated Queen Katherine, she was forbidden to serve her daughter Mary, although she offered to do so at her own expense.

After Anne Boleyn's fall, Margaret returned to court. Her son Reginald became a Cardinal in 1536 and published an attack on Henry VIII, *Of the Unity of the Church*. Margaret admonished him in strong terms, denouncing him to her servants as a traitor. Nonetheless, suspicion of the family's loyalty led to the arrest of Montague and Geoffrey Pole in 1538. Margaret was interrogated, and a search of her house produced letters, papal bulls, and a treasonable coat armour. She was put in the Tower and attainted in May 1539. In April 1541 a Catholic uprising in Yorkshire under Sir John Neville gave Henry VIII the pretext to execute her, and in May she was brutally butchered by a novice executioner. Margaret, last of the Plantagenets, is significant as an innocent victim of politics, who suffered for Reginald Pole's defection to Rome.

See also J. S. Brewer, *Letters and Papers, Foreign and Domestic, of the Reign of Henry VIII*, 1920; J. E. Paul, *Catherine of Aragon and Her Friends*, 1966.   M.D.

Pollock, Mary. See BLYTON, ENID (MARY).

Polwhele, Elizabeth (*c.* 1651–1691), dramatist who cannot be identified with any certainty, except as the author of two plays unpublished in her lifetime, *The Faithfull Virgins* and *The Frolicks*. She may have been the daughter of a nonconformist clergyman, Theophilus Polwhele of Tiverton, the first of whose three marriages took place in 1650 and whose eldest daughter was named Elizabeth. She married Stephen Lobb, also a nonconformist minister, who became prominent in ecclesiastical and political affairs in the 1680s. The first of their five children was born in 1678. There is nothing to connect this Elizabeth Polwhele with the author of the two plays in question, but although she seems an unlikely person to have been a playwright, no alternative candidate has yet been discovered.

The Faithfull Virgins is a high-flown melodramatic rhymed tragedy which includes a dumb-show and an elaborate allegorical masque. It was almost certainly given a professional performance by the Duke's Company, probably in 1670. Polwhele's second play, *The Frolicks, or The Lawyer Cheated*, written in 1671, is very different in style and content. This is a lively sex-intrigue comedy constructed around two plots, an imaginary cuckolding and a complicated elopement. Many of the characters were to become stock figures in Restoration comedy: foolish elderly husband, young wife, and handsome young gallant. Perhaps the most impressive character is Clarabell, the witty, independent daughter of a wealthy lawyer who frustrates her father's attempts to marry her off to rich fools, and marries a rakish young bankrupt instead. The play is both typical and forward-looking in its concerns. Whoever 'E. Polwhele' was, she deserves to be remembered as author of the first comedy written by a woman for the professional stage in England.

See also E. Polwhele, *The Frolicks*, ed. J. Milhous and R. D. Hume, 1977.   W.R.O.

Ponsonby, Sarah. See BUTLER, LADY ELEANOR.

Poole, Elizabeth (*fl.* 1640–53), prophetess. Described variously as from Hertfordshire and Berkshire, Poole belonged to a London Baptist congregation, but by 1648 had parted from them acrimoniously and set up as a prophetess. In December of that year she was given a lengthy hearing at the Whitehall Debates, where the General Council of the Army was discussing the fate of Charles I and the future constitution of England. The occasion provides a remarkable instance of the serious consideration given to prophets in this period. She was closely questioned about a vision she had experienced illuminating 'the disease and cure of the kingdom' and dealing specifically with the army's role. At a later meeting she warned the officers against the King's execution, arguing that kingly government was ordained by God. More scepticism about the divine origins of her visions was expressed here, but her views were still thought worth discussion. Having failed to convince the army, she accordingly denounced both it and Parliament in a pamphlet of May 1649, attacking the murder of the King and warning, 'I have seen *your* carcasses slain upon the ground'. She was still active in 1653, uttering 'many strange expressions, to the great grief of the people' in London. By this time she was the object of some ridicule, but her brief political interventions in 1648–49 indicate how a woman claiming to represent God's word could demand an

330

official hearing which women speaking on their own account usually could not.

See also A. S. P. Woodhouse, *Puritanism and Liberty*, 1974 ed.   P.M.H.

Pope, Elizabeth (?1744–97), actress, also known as Miss Younge. A milliner's apprentice, Elizabeth Pope secured an introduction to David Garrick, who gave her a successful Drury Lane début in 1768, as Imogen. The death of Hannah PRITCHARD in the same year provided her with further opportunity, and the following season she was assigned a variety of comic and tragic parts. She maintained this wide range throughout her career. In spite of disagreements, she remained one of Garrick's leading ladies until his retirement in 1776, playing parts such as Desdemona, Cleopatra, Lady Macbeth, Portia, and Lydia Languish. Her own acting style was said to approach most nearly that of Garrick. Although surpassed by others in tragedy and in comedy, no other actress succeeded so well in both genres.

She joined Covent Garden for the final years of her career, and in 1785 married a younger actor, Alexander Pope. It was not a happy marriage, although her reputation remained irreproachable. She was painted as Viola by Wheatley.   C.H.

Pope-Hennessy, Dame Una (Constance) (1876–1949), biographer. She was the daughter of Sir Arthur Birch and in 1910 married Major-General Ladislaus Pope-Hennessy. In 1920 she was awarded a DBE for voluntary work during the First World War. Una Pope-Hennessy's early writings included books on jades and historical studies on such topics as secret societies, but her vocation as a biographer became apparent with her lives of the seventeenth-century artist and scholar Anna van Schurman and the French Revolutionary figure Madame Roland. Among her best known works were *Three English Women in America* (1929), describing the American experiences of three very dissimilar characters (Frances Trollope, Fanny Kemble, Harriet Martineau), and studies of Edgar Allan Poe (1934), the royal biographer Agnes Strickland (1940), and Charles Dickens (1945). *The Closed City* (1938) is an interesting account of a visit to Leningrad during the Stalin period. Una Pope-Hennessy's last books were a translation, *A Czarina's Story* (1948), and *Canon*

Charles Kingsley (1948). The art historian Sir John Pope-Hennessy and the biographer James Pope-Hennessy were her sons.   N.H.

Porter, Jane (1776–1850), writer. She was born in Durham, the daughter of an army surgeon, but after her father died in 1779 the family moved to Edinburgh, where she was educated. Among her schoolfriends was Sir Walter Scott. She enjoyed studying literature and legends and listening to the old Scottish tales told to her by a neighbour. This background is apparent in her novels, two of which were highly successful. The first was *Thaddeus of Warsaw* (1803), an early example of the historical novel, and the second *The Scottish Chiefs* (1810), the story of William Wallace. This was translated into German and Russian with enormous success, although the novels lack historical accuracy and the characterization is somewhat artificial. Later works were *The Pastor's Fireside* (1815), a story of Stuart times, and *Tales Round a Winter's Hearth* (1824), produced with her sister Anna Maria, who also wrote novels.   B.H.C.

Potter, (Helen) Beatrix (1866–1943), author and artist. She was born in Kensington to affluent middle-class parents, both of whom had inherited wealth from the cotton mills of Lancashire. Her brother was six years younger, and, a lonely child, she lived in her own world of fantasy and pets. While very young she exercised her talent for drawing, training the powers of observation which led to her interest in natural science. The Potters rented houses for long summer holidays in Scotland and the Lake District, where Beatrix had the opportunity to study nature and to paint. One special interest was in fungi, and her research, continued with the aid of the newly-built museums in Kensington, led to a paper which was read to the Linnaean Society in 1895.

Between 1881 and 1896 she wrote a diary in code, revealing the extent of her loneliness and social isolation, as well as her parents' apparent indifference. She was fortunate in her governesses, however, and her first published book, *The Tale of Peter Rabbit* (1900), grew from a picture-letter written to the child of one of these former teachers. *The Tailor of Gloucester* followed two years later. Beatrix Potter had an urge to write, but lacked experience and so kept strictly to the world about her, saying 'it is dangerous to fly in the face of nature'. She was most particular to attribute to her animals only recognizable characteristics, and, a child at heart, wrote as much to please herself as others. Believing that long words held no problems for children, she often insisted on retaining these, against professional advice.

Her publishers, the Warne family, gave her great encouragement, particularly Norman Warne, to whom she became engaged, against her parents' wishes because he was 'in trade'. Tragically, he died suddenly. The Warne family remained life-long friends and still hold the copyright of her books, which are now classics of children's literature, translated into many languages. The success of her books enabled her to buy her own home; and in 1905 she settled at Hill Top Farm, Sawrey in the Lake District. This was the prelude to her most productive years. *The Tale of Jeremy Fisher* (1906), *The Tale of Tom Kitten* (1907), and *The Tale of Jemima Puddleduck* (1908) were among the works closely associated with her life in the Lake District.

At the age of forty-seven, and again in face of her parents' opposition, she married William Heelis, the solicitor who had helped her to buy the farm. She wrote only four more books after her marriage, as her sight was now too poor for her to be able to draw the detailed pictures they required. In her last years she happily devoted her energy to breeding Herdwick sheep and to saving areas of the Lakes for the National Trust.

See also M. Lane, *The Magic Years of Beatrix Potter*, 1978; *The Journal of Beatrix Potter*, transcribed by L. Linder, 1966; L. Linder, *A History of the Writings of Beatrix Potter*, 1971.   S.B.

Power, Eileen (Edna le Poer) (1889–1940), economic historian. The eldest of three daughters of a stockbroker, Eileen Power was educated at Oxford High School for Girls, Girton College, Cambridge, the Sorbonne, and the London School of Economics. At Cambridge in 1909 and 1910 she gained first-class honours in both parts of the history tripos, and was Gilchrist Research Fellow; in 1910–11 she studied at the University of Paris and the Ecole des Chartes; and from 1911 to 1913, she was Shaw Research Student at the LSE. She was Director of Studies in History at Girton (1913–21), and Pfeiffer Fellow (1915–18). From 1920 to 1921 she was the first woman

Albert Kahn Travelling Fellow, and visited China. She became Lecturer in Political Science at the LSE in 1921; in 1924 Reader of the University of London; and in 1931, Professor of Economic History. In 1938–39 she became the first woman to give the Ford Lectures at Oxford. A year earlier she had married Michael Postan, who had left the LSE for Cambridge in 1935, and gained the Cambridge Chair of Economic History in 1938.

Eileen Power's special interests were the economic position of women in the thirteenth and fourteenth centuries, the life of the medieval peasant, and the wool trade. Her writings include *The Paycockes of Coggeshall*, 1919; *Medieval English Nunneries*, 1922; *Medieval People*, 1924; *The Goodman of Paris*, 1928; *Tudor Economic Documents*, edited with R. H. Tawney, 1924; and *Studies in the History of English Trade in the Fifteenth Century*, with Michael Postan, 1932. A gifted researcher, who illuminated new fields, she was also a distinguished teacher.   J.E.

Powles, Matilda Alice. See TILLEY, VESTA.

Pratt, Anne (1806–93), botanist and writer. Born in Strood, Kent, the daughter of a wholesale grocer, she was educated at Eastgate House School, Rochester. Frail health caused her to lead a sedentary and studious life, but when a friend suggested botany as a subject of interest she espoused the idea with zest, devoting her life to the study of plants. Her eldest sister gathered specimens for her, enabling Anne to form a large herbarium, and the sketches she made from her collection provided the basis for her book illustrations. In 1849 she went to Dover, where she wrote her monumental five-volume work *The Flowering Plants and Ferns of Great Britain* (1855).

In 1866 Anne Pratt married John Peerless, lived for a time in East Grinstead, Sussex, and then moved to Redhill, Surrey where she died. She published sixteen books, many of which went into several editions. Among her titles are *The Poisonous, Noxious and Suspected Plants of Our Fields and Woods* (1857) and *The Ferns of Great Britain and Their Allies* (1871). Her popular style of writing enabled a wide readership to share her knowledge and enjoyment.   P.L.

Preedy, George. See BOWEN, MARJORIE.

Price, (Lillian) Nancy Bache (1880–1970), actress and theatre manager. Born at Kinver,

Worcester, she was educated at Malvern Wells and auditioned in Shakespeare while at school, joining F. R. Benson's company at the end of term in September 1899. In 1900 she appeared at the Lyceum. She triumphed as Calypso in Tree's production of *Ulysees* (1901), sharing her success with Constance Collier. In Pinero's *Letty* (1903) she earned her first special curtain-call on the opening night, imitating the aristocratic drawl of West End dressmakers' customers. Max Beerbohm declared 'every sentence rings dramatically true'. She had a dry, deflatory humour and outstanding physical grace, for which she was chosen to play an elegant Parisienne in Bataille's *Dame Nature* (1910). In 1907 she married the actor Charles Maude, grandson of Jenny Lind.

Although in the 1920s she appeared in many plays, including Pirandello's *Naked* (in which the main part was created for her), the younger generation discovered her only in the 1930s. From this time dates the work for which she is best remembered, as the inspiration of the People's National Theatre (1930) in London. In a few years she produced over fifty plays, ranging from Euripides to Pirandello. Her last stage appearance was in 1950, the year she was appointed CBE.

She worked hard for the blind, toured for the troops during the First World War, and wrote many books about the countryside, as well as *Shadows on the Hill* (1935), her reminiscences. A.D.

Pringle, Dr Mia (Lilly) Kellmer (1920–1983), educational psychologist and child welfare expert, first director of the National Children's Bureau. She was born and educated in Vienna, came to Britain in 1938, and taught in primary schools (1940–44) while studying psychology at Birkbeck College, London. She took a Dip. Ed. (1945) and a PhD. (1950), meanwhile working as an educational and clinical psychologist for the Hertfordshire Child Guidance Service (1945–50). In 1950 she joined the staff of Birmingham University as a lecturer in educational psychology, becoming senior lecturer (1960–63) and deputy head of the Department of Child Study (1954–63).

The climax of Mia Kellmer Pringle's career was her appointment as director of the newly-founded National Children's Bureau, which she ran until her retirement in 1981. In her hands the Bureau became a repository of carefully collated information and an initiator of new research, notably the National Child Development Study. The influence of the bureau was strengthened still more by Mia Kellmer Pringle's activities on a variety of public committees. Her many publications included *The Emotional and Social Adjustment of Physically Handicapped Children*, 1964; *The Challenge of Thalidomide*, 1970; *Growing Up Adopted*, 1972; *The Needs of Children*, 1974; and *Psychological Approaches to Child Abuse*, 1980. She was appointed CBE in 1975. N.H.

Pritchard, Hannah (1711–68), actress. Under her maiden name of Vaughan, Mrs Pritchard first made her reputation at the London fairground theatres. She married an actor and after a short engagement at the Haymarket in 1773, went to Drury Lane, playing mainly in comedy before David Garrick's arrival in 1741. She was Garrick's favourite leading lady, being not only sympathetic to his acting style but also blessedly equable in temperament. Her style was best suited to rage and horror; she played the great tragic heroines, and with Mrs SIDDONS was probably the finest Lady Macbeth of the century. She was not beautiful, and increasing stoutness made her unsuitable for light comedy parts, but the dignity and propriety of her manner, and her fine clear voice ensured her popularity beyond the fading of her looks.

As the only exponent of the title role in Dr Johnson's *Irene*, she earned his lasting rancour. The audience could not stomach the strangling scene, and drove her and the play from the stage. Johnson attributed this to her stupidity, damning her to posterity as 'a vulgar idiot' and marvelling at 'how little mind she had'. It was said that she had never read to the end of *Macbeth*, while Garrick also remarked on her tendency 'to blubber her sorrows'. Her final performance as Lady Macbeth was painted by Zoffany in 1768. She was also painted by Hayman and R. E. Pine. Her private life was one of conspicuous rectitude.

See also A. Vaughan, *Born to Please*, 1980. C.H.

Procter, Adelaide Anne (1825–64), poet. Adelaide Procter was the eldest child of the writer and lawyer Bryan Waller Procter (also known as Barry Cornwall) and his wife Anne Skepper. Her first verses were transcribed by her mother before she could write. In this literary environment she learnt French, Italian, and German and showed 'true taste and sentiment' in her drawing and piano playing. Her first published poems appeared in *The Book of Beauty* in 1843 and others subsequently in the *Cornhill Magazine* and *Good Words*. Her association with *Household Words* began in 1853 when she submitted a poem to the editor, Charles Dickens, under the pseudonym of 'Miss Mary Berwick'. As Dickens was a family friend she wanted to compete 'fairly with the unknown volunteers' and it was two years before her identity was revealed. About one-sixth of all the poems published in *Household Words* were hers and a collection, *Legends and Lyrics*, was published in 1858, a second series in 1861, and a collected edition, with an introduction by Dickens, in 1866.

Adelaide Procter's conversion to the Roman Catholic faith with her sisters in 1851 informed both her writing and her devotion to charitable works. She joined the founding committee of the Society for the Promotion of Employment for Women, and in 1861 edited *The Victoria Regia*, a literary miscellany with contributions from Matthew Arnold, Harriet MARTINEAU, Tennyson and Thackeray, published by Emily FAITHFULL at the Victoria Press. She contributed verse and prose to *The Englishwoman's Journal* and published *A Chaplet of Verses* (1862) in aid of the Providence Row Night Refuge for Homeless Women and Children.

'Graceful and delightful', Adelaide Procter's poetry appealed to the sentiment of the time. She was Queen Victoria's favourite poet, and in 1877 her work was second in demand only to Tennyson's. Published also in America and translated into German, she is best known for 'The Lost Chord', 'The Message' and some poems which became hymns. A sufferer from tuberculosis, she tried the cure at Malvern in 1862, but died in February 1864 and was buried at Kensal Green Cemetery.

See also *The Complete Works of Adelaide A. Procter*, introduction by Charles Dickens, 1905; B. R. Belloc, *In a Walled Garden*, 1895; F. Janku, *A. A. Procter, ihr Leben und ihre Werke*, 1912; A. Lohrli, *Household Words*, 1973.   C.B.

Prothero, John Keith. See CHESTERTON, ADA (ELIZABETH).

Puddicombe, Anne Adalisa (1836–1908), novelist who wrote under the pseudonym of Allen Raine, a name suggested to her in a dream. Born in Carmarthenshire, the daughter of a solicitor, she was educated at Cheltenham and at Southfields, where she saw many literary people, including Dickens and George Eliot. From 1856 she spent sixteen years in Wales, her colloquial grasp of Welsh gaining her the friendship of local people. In 1872 she married Beynon Puddicombe, foreign correspondent of a London bank. She suffered almost continual ill-health herself, and then in 1900 her husband became mentally ill. They moved to Wales, where he died in 1906 and she two years later, of cancer.

Anne Puddicombe began writing fiction seriously in 1894, and that year shared the prize in the National Eisteddfod at Carnarvon for a serial story describing Welsh life. Her first novel was *A Welsh Singer* (1897), a simple love story of peasant and sea-faring peoples, setting the pattern for most of its successors. *Hearts of Wales* (1905) was an historical romance set at the time of Glendower's rebellion, and *Queen of the Rushes* (1906) embodied incidents of the 1904–05 Welsh revival. *All in a Month* (1908) dealt with her husband's illness and *Under the Thatch* (1910) with her own.

B.H.C.

Pym, Barbara (1913–80), novelist. She was born Mary Crampton at Oswestry and educated at Huyton College, Liverpool, and St Hilda's College, Oxford. In the 1950s, with five novels including *Some Tame Gazelles* (1950), *Excellent Women* (1952), and *A Glass of Blessings* (1958), she acquired a significant, if relatively restricted, following. But her subjects were increasingly unfashionable areas of experience—being 'on the shelf', loneliness, old age and retirement, backbiting and petty intrigue at the office—and during the 1960s, after *No Fond Return of Love* (1961), she found it impossible to get her work published.

For a decade and a half Barbara Pym concentrated on her work as editorial secretary of the International African Institute and assistant editor of the anthropological journal *Africa*. In 1973 she retired to live in Oxfordshire. Renewed interest was shown in her writing from 1977, when *The Times Literary Supplement* published articles by Lord David Cecil and Philip Larkin which named her as one of the century's underrated novelists. As a result her books were reissued, she began to publish new works (*Quartet in Autumn*, 1977; *The Sweet Dove Died*, 1978), and she enjoyed a considerable reputation until her death. A last novel, *A Few Green Leaves*, appeared posthumously in 1980, and her seventh novel, *An Unsuitable Attachment*, which had been rejected by publishers in 1963, was issued in slightly edited form in 1982.   N.H.

R

Rackham, Clara Dorothea (1875–1965), socialist and factory inspector. The daughter of an Essex farmer, she was educated at Newnham College, Cambridge, where she studied classics. During student days she was a well-known hockey player, captaining Newnham College Club and Cambridge Ladies Club, while her interest in politics was also evident. In 1901 she married Harris Rackham, a Fellow and Tutor of Christ's College. Her early public activities were both social and political, including membership of the Cambridge Board of Guardians and appointments as Secretary of the Cambridge Charity Organization and Founder-President of the Cambridge Women's Co-operative Guild. She was an active member of the Cambridge Women's Suffrage Society. In 1915 the Home Office appointed her as one of the first women factory inspectors working in Lancashire. As the need for more women inspectors grew with the rapidly increasing number of women employed on munitions work, she was transferred to the London area. In 1918 she was appointed Director of Social Studies at Bedford College, but did not take up the post because of the crucial need at that time for women factory inspectors. In 1919 she was elected to Cambridge Borough Council, and later to the City Council. Twice she stood as a Labour parliamentary candidate, in Chelmsford in November 1922, and in 1935 at Saffron Walden. A great worker for the causes that she served, she was also a superb hostess, welcoming both academic and political visitors to her Cambridge home.

See also L. Middleton (ed.), *Women in the Labour Movement*, 1977.   L.M.

Radcliffe, Ann (1764–1823), novelist. She was born in London, the only daughter of a tradesman, and at the age of twenty-three married William Radcliffe, editor and proprietor of *The English Chronicle*. Ann Radcliffe's first novel, *The Castles of Athlin and Dunbayne*, was published anonymously in 1789, followed in 1790 by *A Sicilian Romance*, which Scott thought the first modern English example of the poetical novel. She became famous for a novel published the next year, *The Romance of the Forest* (1791), which achieved a fourth edition by 1795, was translated into French

and Italian, and dramatized in 1794. But her best-known novel is *The Mysteries of Udolpho* (1794), which revealed her mastery of suspense and horror writing; it was widely regarded as the supreme example of the 'Gothick' novel, and was satirized as such by Jane AUSTEN in *Northanger Abbey*. While it was in the course of publication, Ann Radcliffe went travelling with her husband and as a result published *A Journey Made in the Summer of 1794 Through Holland and The Western Frontier of Germany, With a Return Down the Rhine* (1795).

The Italian (1796) was the last novel to be published in Mrs Radcliffe's lifetime. It was dramatized as *The Italian Monk* and produced at the Haymarket on 15 August 1797. She then went into retirement, living as a recluse near Leicester, suffering from asthma and dying from an attack on 7 February 1823. Her husband's memoir appeared with *Gaston de Blondeville*, a work published posthumously in 1826. Mrs Radcliffe's other writings include *Poems, 1815–1816*.

See also *I*. Grant, *Ann Radcliffe: A Biography*, 1951; C. MacIntyre, *Ann Radcliffe in Relation to Her Time*, 1920; A. Wieten, *Mrs Radcliffe: Her Relation to Romanticism*, 1926.   A.P.

Raftor, Catherine. See CLIVE, KITTY.

Raine, Allen. See PUDDICOMBE, ANNE ADALISA.

Rambert, Dame Marie (1888–1982), founder of the Ballet Rambert; the family's name was originally Rambam. She was born in Warsaw and educated at Warsaw Gymnasium, becoming fluent in French, German, and Russian. She studied dancing under Slowacki of the Warsaw Opera. Having arrived in Paris (1910) to study medicine, she met Emile Jacques-Dalcroze and instead studied his theory of eurythmics, emulating Isadora Duncan. When Diaghilev, director of the Ballets Russes, asked Jacques-Dalcroze's help for Nijinsky to decode the complex rhythms of *Le Sacre de Printemps*, he sent Rambert, who remained with the Russians in the *Corps de ballet*, assisting with the choreography (1913).

War broke out in 1914 on her return to Paris. She travelled to London where she began teaching, continuing even after she had made a name as a dancer (1917). That year she met the playwright Ashley Dukes and in 1918 married him. He was a 'ballet hater' who nevertheless dedicated his life to her company. Rambert studied classical ballet with Astafieva and then Cecchetti. With Dukes she opened a studio in Kensington in 1920, encouraging the students to create new ballets themselves. This tiny woman had a tremendous driving force so that, although not herself creative, she drew out the latent creativity in others. Among her pupils was Frederick Ashton, a dancer who became a great choreographer.

The company prospered during the 1930s, Karsavina joining them after their public performance at the Lyric. In 1931 the Dukes opened The Ballet Club at the Mercury, with Markova and Harold Turner dancing, to be joined later by Fonteyn, Helpmann, and others. Antony Tudor and Walter Gore were among the choreographers. By 1939 the Ballet Rambert was established. Throughout the London blitz they gave lunchtime performances in factories, bringing the dance to thousands of people who had never seen it.

In 1946 a projected six-week tour of Australia lasted eighteen months, and virtually destroyed the company, as many dancers chose to remain behind and the costs were enormous. At home, many classics were revived in order to restore the company financially, and eventually Rambert was able to assemble a small group of soloists and choreographers whose aim was to create new ballets, exploring all the possibilities of dance under Norman Morrice. Ill health and the death of her husband had taken the heart out of 'Mim', but she retained her interest in the company, intervening in rehearsals and reducing ballerinas to tears with her acid tongue. Nevertheless, she was adored for her generosity, whether with her time, knowledge, or possessions. Among the honours she was awarded were the Royal Academy of Dancing's Queen Elizabeth II Coronation Award (1956); the Légion d'Honneur (1957); DBE (1962); D Litt, University of Sussex (1964); and Order of Merit of the Polish People's Republic (1979). A.D.

Ramée, Marie Louise de la (1839–1908), novelist who used the name 'Ouida', which came from a mispronunciation of 'Louise'. She was born at Bury St Edmunds with an English mother and a French father, Louis Ramé, who was a teacher. She was educated at local schools until her family moved to Paris, where her father disappeared at the time of the Paris Commune of 1871, perhaps killed in street fighting. Louise and her mother then returned to England, and after meeting the popular author William Harrison Ainsworth, Louise began contributing to *Bentley's Miscellany*.

Her first novel, *Held in Bondage*, was published when she was twenty-four. She went on to write another forty-two novels, of which *Under Two Flags* (1867) was the most successful. These books were largely about high society, although Ruskin praised *A Village Commune* (1881) as a faithful picture of peasant life. The German publisher Tauchnitz took up her work, and from 1860 she lived mainly in Italy, renting a large villa in Florence. Here she lived an expensive and affected life, surrounded by dogs—she was known as *La Signora dei Cani* in Italy—and frequently falling prey to hopeless passions for English and Italian aristocrats. In 1894 she moved to Lucca, where her style increased in grandeur despite the fact that her popularity was waning. Ouida was so sure of her genius that she could write: 'English literature is very sorry stuff nowadays. You must make much of me, for now George Eliot is gone there is no one else who can write English'.

Although Ouida's novels were much ridiculed, particularly for their ludicrously incorrect rendition of men, she was very popular and, as G. K. Chesterton wrote, 'It is impossible not to laugh at Ouida; and equally impossible not to read her'. However, her books did stop selling, and Ouida lived in poverty for some years, reliant on a civil list pension. She died at Viareggio, having lost the sight of one eye, and was buried at Lucca.

Her other works include: *Strathmore*, 1865; *Chandos*, 1866; *Tricotrier*, 1869; *Puck*, 1870; *Folle Farine*, 1871; *Two Little Wooden Shoes*, 1874; *Moths*, 1880; *In Maremma*, 1882; and *Bimbi*, 1882.

See also E. Bigland, *Ouida*, 1950; Y. Ffrench, *Ouida, a Study in Ostentation*, 1938; M. Stirling, *The Fine and the Wicked*, 1957. A.P.

Rande, Mary. See CARY, MARY.

Randolph, Agnes. See DUNBAR, COUNTESS OF.

Ranelagh, Viscountess. See JONES, KATHERINE, VISCOUNTESS RANELAGH.

Ranyard, Ellen Henrietta (1810–79), founder of the Bible and Female Domestic Mission.

Rathbone, Eleanor

She was born in Nine Elms, London, the eldest daughter of a cement manufacturer, John Bazley White and raised in a Nonconformist home. Her gift for painting and reciting poetry in the family reading circle was evident at an early age. At sixteen she began to visit the poor in her neighbourhood with a friend, who contracted typhus as a result of one outing and died. Deeply moved by this tragedy, Ellen White joined the Ladies' Bible Committee at Kennington, so beginning a lifelong connection with the Bible Society. Her family moved to Swanscombe, Kent, and there she married Benjamin Ranyard in 1839. She worked for the Bible Society in Kent and had four children, one of whom, Arthur Cowper Ranyard, became a noted astronomer. In 1852 she wrote *The Book and its Story*, which sought to interest young people in the Bible. An enormous success, it illustrated her talent for presenting the work of scholars in a popular form.

In 1857 she moved to London with her family, and in that year while walking through St Giles, 'the misery of our sisters there. . . brought forth the idea of the Bible-woman'. This Bible-woman was to be a paid, native agent in the slums, a seller of Bibles and an adviser on domestic matters. Within ten years Mrs Ranyard had recruited 234 working-class women to serve in London's poorest districts and had raised £133,000. The idea of the Bible-woman spread to other parts of Britain and to other countries. The work of the Bible and Female Domestic Mission, as it was then called, is described in *The Book and its Mission* (1856–64) and *The Missing Link Magazine* (1865–79). Mrs Ranyard had not only inaugurated a 'women's mission to women', but also the first paid corps of social workers in Britain.

Always interested in the problems of sick visiting, in 1868 she gathered together a staff of poor women to work as itinerant nurses. Trained in the lying-in wards of Guy's Hospital, they eventually complemented her corps of Bible-women. The programme was one of the earliest examples of district nursing in London, and has been hailed as a pioneering achievement. As with her earlier schemes, the Bible-nurses showed her to be a most imaginative, unsectarian reformer, whose work was widely admired and imitated. She died of bronchitis in London and is buried in Norwood cemetery. Her other works include *Life Work; or the Link and the Rivet*, 1861; *The True Institution of Sisterhood: or a Message and its Messengers*, 1862; *London, and Ten Years Work in it*, 1868.

See also Ranyard Papers in the Greater London Record Office; F. K. Prochaska, *Women and Philanthropy in Nineteenth-Century England*, 1980; R. E. Selfe, *Light Amid London Shadows*, 1906.   F.K.P.

Rathbone, Eleanor (Florence) (1872–1946),

Independent member of parliament. She was born in London while her father, William Rathbone VI, was Liberal MP for Liverpool. Her family was steeped in the traditions of politics and public service; its members had, through six generations, enormous influence on the civic and intellectual life of Liverpool, as councillors, founder members of the university, and finally MPs. The Rathbone family fortune, based on ships and trading, was used in ways which reflected the thrifty and public-spirited attitudes of their Quaker origins. Eleanor herself reflected these attitudes in a public life of remarkable devotion to duty, diligence, and self-sacrifice. She went to Somerville College, Oxford, in 1893, and was considered an outstanding student, especially in philosophy. Academic life did not attract her, however, and all her interest was directed towards the reorganization of society along lines which were more compassionate and coherent. Her philosophical training was put to use in marshalling conclusive arguments for women's suffrage, child allowances, and widows' pensions. She did much organized social work in Liverpool, from which derived some impressively documented empirical studies (*How the Casual Labourer Lives*, 1909; *The Conditions of Widows under the Poor Law in Liverpool*, 1913).

During the course of these studies, Eleanor Rathbone became convinced that the condition of women was particularly unfair. They worked hard in the home for no wages, outside the home for much less than men, they had no financial help with children, no claims as widows, wives, or mothers, and no vote. She tackled the last problem first, becoming in 1897 Parliamentary Secretary to the Liverpool Women's Suffrage Society, the non-militant wing of the suffrage movement under Mrs FAWCETT. When women's suffrage was granted, she turned her attention to the wider position of women in Britain and abroad. In the late 1920s she was impressed and horrified

Read, Mary

by Katherine Mayo's book *Whither India*, which depicted the sufferings and indignities experienced by Indian women, and in 1929 was elected as Independent MP for the Combined English Universities, the only woman ever to stand successfully without the backing of a political party. In Parliament throughout the 1930s she continued her fight for family allowances (she had written *The Disinherited Family* in 1924), and supported an aggressive opposition to Hitler (*War can be Averted*, 1937.) She was not always popular in the House, but inspired enormous admiration and some trepidation. As Harold Nicolson said, 'the persistence and zeal with which she identified herself with her own causes... taught the House of Commons that such identification, while intense, could be completely selfless. She added objective ardour to subjective sympathy'. It was characteristic of her to refuse all political honours and to accept only the honorary degrees conferred on her by the universities of Durham (1930), Liverpool (1931), and Oxford (1938).

See also M. Stocks, *Eleanor Rathbone*, 1949.
E.M.V.

Raverat, Gwen(dolen Mary) (1885–1957), wood-engraver. Born in Cambridge, née Darwin, she was the daughter of the Plumian Professor of Astronomy and Experimental Philosophy and granddaughter of Charles Darwin. She was educated at home and at boarding school. From 1908 to 1911 she studied art at the Slade School in London and learned the rudiments of wood-carving from her sister-in-law, Mrs Elinor Darwin. She married Jacques Raverat in 1911 and had two daughters.

Gwen Raverat was one of the first members of the Society of Wood-Engravers, founded in 1920, and also a member of the Royal Society of Painters-Etchers-Engravers. It was said of her work that one looked 'through' the engraving, as if through clear glass, to the meaning as felt by her imaginative, sympathetic mind. In her style of work and choice of subject she was without self-consciousness and, although intensely imaginative, never fanciful. Both with the knife and graver she was a superb craftswoman. One of her admirers, Eric Gill, wrote that she was quite, or nearly quite, the best of all contemporary engravers.

She illustrated several books, including *The Cambridge Book of Poetry for Children* (1932), and in 1952 published *Period Piece*,

a delightful account of her childhood and youth with her own illustrations. She also designed the scenes for Vaughan Williams's ballet *Job* (1931), which remained in use for twenty years. For the last six years of her life she was handicapped by paralysis of her left side. She had just finished a new translation of Perrault's *Fairy Tales*, to be illustrated by her friend Joan Hassall, when she died in Cambridge.

See also A. R. Stone, *The Wood-Engravings of Gwen Raverat*, 1957.
P.L.

Read, Catherine (*d*. 1778), portrait painter and miniaturist. The daughter of a Scottish laird, Catherine Read studied in Paris and Rome. On her return to England she became immensely fashionable, exhibiting almost annually from 1760 at the Society of Artists, the Free Society, and the Royal Academy, and attracting commissions away from such artists as Hudson and Reynolds. She specialized in painting aristocratic ladies and their children, work which culminated in portraits of Queen Charlotte and the Prince of Wales. Her work was widely engraved but her popularity was short-lived, and after a visit to India in 1771 she lost favour. It is uncertain whether she died in India or in London.

Fanny Burney wrote of her, 'Miss Reid (sic) is shrewd and clever when she has an opportunity given her to make it known, but she is so very deaf that it is a fatigue to attempt conversation with her. She is most exceedingly ugly and of a very melancholy, or rather discontented humour' (1774).

See also Lady V. Manners, 'Catherine Read, The English Rosalba', in *The Connoisseur*, LXXXVII, 1932.
C.H.

Read, Mary (?1692–1721), pirate. According to *A General History . . . of the Most Notorious Pyrates* (1724), by Captain Charles Johnson (Daniel Defoe?), she was born near Plymouth in 1692, the illegitimate daughter of unknown parents. Mary was raised as a boy and put into service at the age of thirteen as a foot-boy to a 'French lady.' But 'growing bold and strong, and having also a roving Mind, she entered herself on Board a Man of War'.

After her time at sea, Mary spent some years in romantic and military adventures as a soldier with forces in Flanders. She eventually took ship for the West Indies but on the way

339

was taken by English pirates, whom she joined. As a pirate Mary became known for her bravery and swordsmanship, even fighting a duel to save a mate she had taken a fancy to. But her new career was cut short in October 1721 by the intervention of a Jamaican warship, and she was brought to trial.

The record of the trial is deficient of the bravado and wit that later writers have attributed to her. According to the witnesses called against her, she took no active role in the fighting but was content to shout and swear while passing ammunition to the men. She offered no defence and spoke only to enter a plea of pregnancy when her sentence was read. Her execution was never carried out, and she is said to have died in prison on 4 December 1721, but as with so many events of her life this is difficult to verify. It can be demonstrated that she spent some seven weeks involved in minor, but nonetheless remarkable, piracies, but as to the other more colourful incidents of her life, the reader 'may be tempted to think the whole Story no better than a Novel or a Romance'. 					D.D.H.

Reading, Marchioness of. See ISAACS, STELLA, MARCHIONESS OF READING.

Redpath, Anne (1895–1965), Scottish painter. She was the daughter of a tweed designer in Galashiels, and studied at the Edinburgh School of Art (1913–18), where her teachers included Adam Bruce Thomson and D. M. Sutherland, who influenced her strongly. A travelling scholarship (1919) enabled her to visit Belgium, Paris, and Italy, where she was deeply affected by Sienese Trecento painting, notably through the works of Ambrogio Lorenzetti, whose *Buon Governo* in the Palazzo Pubblico, Siena, remained a continuing inspiration and influence on her vision of colour and perspective. In 1920 she married James Beattie Michie, an architect employed by the War Graves Commission, and went to live in France, first near Boulogne and later at Cap Ferrat on the Riviera. She did little work during these years, which were occupied by running a household and bringing up three sons, her chief outlet being the decoration of homely objects of everyday use. In 1934 she returned to Hawick, moving to Edinburgh in 1949. Various journeys abroad inspired her: to Spain (1951), Corsica (1954) Canary Islands (1959), Portugal (1961), Amsterdam (1962), and Venice (1963). She was elected Associate

of the Royal Scottish Academy (1947), becoming a full RSA in 1952; to the Royal West of England Academy (1959), an ARA (1960), and was awarded an OBE in 1955. She made a number of broadcasts reviewing exhibitions and, more valuable, setting out the basis of her attitudes to her subjects and the world around her.

From the beginning of her career colour was the vital aspect of Anne Redpath's art, and the *matière*—the very substance of the paint—which she used in strong impasto, was an important expressive factor. Her work exploits contrasts: black and white modulated through greys, strong colours in opposing harmony. Her perspective is dictated by her expressive response to her subject, and has nothing to do with conventional angles of vision. The subject matter ranges over still-life, landscape, town- (or rather village-) scapes, interiors, and flowers, but only rarely do the figures in her pictures possess an identity of their own; they are subordinate to the needs of the composition. There are works in museums in Aberdeen, Adelaide, Edinburgh (Royal Scottish Academy, National Gallery of Modern Art), Glasgow, London (Royal Academy, Tate), Manchester (City, Whitworth), Sydney, Vancouver, Wellington, and elsewhere.

See also G. Bruce, *Anne Redpath*, 1974. 					L.M.M.

Rees Williams, Ellen Gwendolen. See RHYS, JEAN.

Reeve, Ada (1874–1966), music-hall performer whose real name was Adelaide Mary Isaacs. Born in Mile End, London, she was the daughter of Franco-Dutch theatrical parents. Her first stage appearance was in 1882 at Dewsbury, in *East Lynne*. East End pantomimes followed, before her débuts first in music-hall, at Hackney (1886), and then in the West End (1888) at the Hungerford Hall. After playing in New York, she made her first appearance at the Gaiety in *The Shop Girl* (1894). She topped the bill in a two-year tour of Australia in *The Gay Parisienne*, before returning to London. For the next ten years, she was a leading soubrette in musical comedy, notably *Florodora* (1899–1900). After other tours of the Empire she spent the First World War years entertaining the troops, before settling in Australia (1917–35), where she enjoyed great popularity and founded her own stage school. She also sang and acted on Australian radio. She returned to England in 1936 to appear in C. B. Cochrane's revues. Other successes followed, including eight films. In 1947 she played Queen Victoria in *Mr Gladstone* on television. She was twice married. A.D.

Reeve, Clara (1729–1807), novelist, born at Ipswich, the daughter of a clergyman. After her father's death in 1755 her mother moved with Clara and two of her sisters to Colchester. Clara's career as a writer began in 1769 with *Original Poems on Several Occasions*, and three years later, a translation of Barclay's *Argenis* entitled *The Phoenix*. In 1777 she published anonymously *The Champion of Virtue*, which was re-named *The Old English Baron* in 1778 when her name appeared on the title-page. By the end of the nineteenth century this enormously popular work had gone through at least nineteen editions, had been translated into French and German, and had been dramatized as *Edmond, Orphan of the Castle*. The novel established a countertradition within the Gothic novel: on the one hand, Walpole's sensational *Castle of Otranto*, which is thematically linked to such later works as Lewis's *The Monk*; on the other, Clara Reeve's somewhat more subdued and credible *Old English Baron*, which set the pattern for the Gothic classics of Ann RADCLIFFE.

The Two Mentors (1783) and *The School for Widows* (1791) were written in the prevailing sentimental style. In 1785 Clara Reeve published her critique of the eighteenth-century novel in dialogue form, *The Progress of Romance*. A survey of both major and minor fiction, the work's significance lies in the author's refusal to apologise for her subject. Unlike most of her contemporaries, she discusses the novel as a serious literary form, while retaining the conventional view that a narrative should be judged by its didactic value. Her last historical narrative was *Memoirs of Sir Roger de Clarendon* (1793). She died unmarried in her native Ipswich.

See also E. Birkhead, *The Tale of Terror*, 1921; J. M. S. Tompkins, *The Popular Novel in England, 1770–1899*, 1932. A.L.

Rhondda, Viscountess. See THOMAS, MARGARET HAIG, LADY RHONDDA.

Rhys, Jean (?1890–1979), novelist whose real name was Ellen Gwendolen Rees Williams.

She was born in Dominica in the West Indies, where her father was a doctor, and attended a convent school until at sixteen she went to England. After spending a term at the Perse School in Cambridge, she studied for a year at RADA, and then took a job as a chorus-girl. While working intermittently in the theatre she had her first love affair, the aftermath of which is described in *After Leaving Mr Mackenzie* (1931). In 1919 she met and married Jean Lenglet and they moved to Paris. They had one son, who died at three weeks, and a daughter. She divorced Lenglet in 1932 and married Leslie Tidden Smith. Two years after his death in 1945 she married her third husband, Max Hamer.

She began writing soon after she moved to Paris, translating Lenglet's articles for newspapers and writing a few of her own. Some of her short stories were shown to Ford Madox Ford, who encouraged her to publish them, and her first book, *The Left Bank and other Stories*, appeared in 1927. During the next twelve years she wrote several novels, receiving limited critical recognition. Her work of this period is in many ways autobiographical and 'therapeutic', portraying the lives of passive and self-destructive women, but exploring with considerable frankness such subjects as prostitution, lesbianism, and abortion.

After 1939 she virtually stopped writing, except for a few short stories, but in the late 1950s began work on *Wide Sargasso Sea*, which was published in 1966. The novel retells the Jane Eyre story from the point of view of the mad wife, Bertha Mason, portraying her as an oppressed and betrayed figure and emphasizing her Creole background. This at last brought Jean Rhys widespread fame. She was given the RSL award and the W. H. Smith Annual Literary Award in 1966, and received an Arts Council Bursary in the following year. She then published two volumes of short stories, *Tigers are Better Looking* (1968) and *Sleep it off Lady* (1976) and, posthumously, an unfinished autobiography *Smile Please* (1979), edited by D. Athill.

See also W. L. G. James, *Jean Rhys*, 1978; T. F. Staley, *Jean Rhys*, 1979. J.M.

Rhys Williams, Lady Juliet (Evangeline) (1898–1964), public figure, active in the United Europe Movement and other causes. She was the daughter of the novelist Elinor GLYN, and went to school at Eastbourne, leaving to do war-work in 1914. In 1918–19 she was a civil servant at the Admiralty and with the War Cabinet Demobilization Committee, after which she worked as private secretary to Rhys Williams, Parliamentary Secretary to the Minister of Transport; they were married in 1921.

Lady Rhys Williams's varied later life included a spell in Hollywood sorting out her mother's affairs, during which she wrote the continuity for a film based on an Elinor Glyn novel. She also made contributions to welfare on both the practical and the theoretical level. She was a founder-member of the National Birthday Trust Fund and its chairman from 1957 to 1964, organizing several important research projects. Despite their persuasiveness, her writings on welfare arrangements, and the radical schemes set out in *Taxation and Incentive* (1952) and *An Economic Policy for Britain* (1963), had less visible impact. Her deepest post-war commitment was to the United Europe Movement, of which she was secretary (1947–50) and ultimately chairman (1958–64).

N.H.

Rich, Mary, Countess of Warwick (1625–78), autobiographer. Mary was the seventh daughter of Richard Boyle, first Earl of Cork, by his second wife Catherine Fenton, and the younger sister of Katherine JONES, Viscountess Ranelagh. She is important as a diarist and for her autobiography. This was written in the 1670s, like Anne HALKETT's as a justification for her youthful actions, and provides valuable insights into the childhood and married life of an upper-class woman. She describes her initial 'aversion to marriage, living so much at my ease that I was unwilling to change my condition'; and her defiance of her beloved father by refusing, at the age of thirteen, a wealthy suitor he had found for her. Her father was further displeased when she fell in love with Charles Rich, who was only a second son, albeit of the Earl of Warwick. Fortunately Cork was persuaded to agree to the match and the couple were married in 1641. Thereafter Mary lived chiefly at the Warwick seat of Lees Priory, Essex, where she became mistress in 1659 on her husband's succession to the earldom following the deaths of his father and brother. In 1642 Mary bore a daughter, who died a year later, and in 1643 a son. When he died in 1664, Mary, aged thirty-eight, hoped for more children, but in vain; a judgement,

she believed, for her earlier 'proud conceit' of fearing she would lose her looks by bearing children so soon after marriage.

It is probable that interesting aspects of the psychology of many seventeenth-century women are revealed in Mary's description of her development from a frivolous girl, occupied 'in reading romances, in seeing and reading plays .., in curious dressing and playing cards' to a Puritan matron, determined 'to glorify God . . . and to do what good I could to all my neighbours'. This transformation was influenced both by her distress at the death of her baby daughter and by the pious atmosphere at Lees, where there was constant preaching from a resident chaplain and visiting divines. As a godly noblewoman, Mary found fulfilment in middle age, voraciously reading religious works and writing 'occasional meditations' of a devotional nature, diaries, and her autobiography. Her piety also enabled her to cope patiently with a difficult husband who suffered twenty years of wretched health before his death in 1673.

See also the 'Autobiography', *Percy Society* vol. 22, 1848; C. Fell Smith, *Mary Rich*, 1901; Diaries and 'Meditations', British Library Additional MSS 27, 351–58.

P.M.H.

Rich, Lady Penelope (?1562–1607), political and literary figure. Penelope Rich was the daughter of Walter Devereux, Earl of Essex, by Lettice KNOLLYS, and sister of Robert Devereux, Queen Elizabeth's favourite. When aged about fourteen, Penelope won the admiration of Philip Sidney; however, in 1581 her guardian the Earl of Huntingdon requested the Queen's consent for her marriage with Robert, Lord Rich. The marriage was intensely unhappy, and according to a later statement Penelope protested before and during the wedding. The couple had seven children. Penelope's attachment to Sidney continued until his death in 1586 and she is immortalized as the heroine of the poet's *Astrophel and Stella*. Before 1595 she became the mistress of Charles, Lord Mountjoy, and her subsequent five children were later acknowledged by him. In 1599 she interceded unsuccessfully with Elizabeth for her disgraced brother Essex. She was often with him during the rebellion of 1601, and was present when royal troops surrounded Essex House. Rich abandoned her after Essex's execution and she then lived openly with Mountjoy.

James I showed Penelope Rich marked favour and she was prominent at his court, being among the ladies who escorted Anne of Denmark to London in May 1603, and playing in Ben Jonson's *Masque of Blackness* on Twelfth Night 1605. She and Rich were divorced by mutual consent, but when she married Mountjoy (now Earl of Devon) on 20 December 1605, the King's anger was extreme, and he banished the couple from court. Penelope died within a year of her husband, in 1607.

An unconventional and self-willed woman, Penelope Rich was important as a literary patron and inspiration, receiving the dedications of Richard Barnfield's *Affectionate Shepherd* (1594) and Bartholomew Yonge's *Diana of George of Montemayor* (1598), as well as the tributes of Sir Philip Sidney.

See also Kingsley Hart (ed.), *Astrophel and Stella*, 1959; Duke of Manchester, *Court and Society from Elizabeth to Anne*, 1864; M. S. Rawson, *Penelope Rich and her Circle*, 1911.
M.D.

Richardson, Dorothy (Miller) (1873–1957), novelist. Born in Berkshire, the daughter of a tradesman, she was educated at a private school in England and then in Germany. She carried the burden of many responsibilities in a family where the father was unreliable and the mother depressed and semi-invalid. It was only in 1895, when her mother committed suicide, that she was free to move to London. Here she began work as a teacher, but later took to translating and journalism. For several years she moved in various intellectual circles and societies, and after a series of unsuccessful love affairs, in 1917 married the artist and illustrator Alan Odle. They had no children.

Dorothy Richardson was nearly forty when she began work on her first novel, *Pointed Roofs* (1915). This began the twelve-volume work *Pilgrimage*, a semi-autobiographical study of the life of Miriam Henderson, which has frequently been linked to the work of Proust and Joyce in its treatment of the heroine as emerging artist. Her work has also been linked to that of Joyce because of its innovatory use of the 'stream of consciousness' technique, although she rejected this term as a 'perfect imbecility', preferring the more traditional 'dramatic monologue'. She herself regarded her technique as one seeking to create a female form and a female language which would be able to accommodate multiple perspectives, impressions, and associations. It would thus reflect the qualities of receptivity and empathy which she regarded as the distinguishing characteristics of the female consciousness.

She worked on *Pilgrimage* for the rest of her life, and in many ways it became an extension of herself to be completed only by her death, for although the initial twelve volumes had been completed by 1938, the manuscript for a final section was found among her papers and published posthumously as *March Moonlight* (1967). Other titles in the series include *The Tunnel*, 1919; *Revolving Lights*, 1923; and *Dimple Hill*, 1938.

See also H. Gregory, *Dorothy Richardson: An Adventure in Self Discovery*, 1967; J. Rosenberg, *Dorothy Richardson: The Genius they Forgot*, 1973.
J.M.

Richardson, Ethel Florence Lindesey. See RICHARDSON, HENRY HANDEL.

Richardson, Henry Handel, pseudonym of Ethel Florence Lindesey Richardson (1870–1946), novelist. She was born in Melbourne and educated there at the Presbyterian Ladies' College. In 1887 her mother took her to Europe, where she studied the piano at Leipzig Conservatorium and met her future husband, J. G. Robertson. They were married in 1895 and lived in Strasbourg and London, where Robertson occupied university chairs until his death in 1933. His widow's last years were spent in Sussex.

Henry Handel Richardson turned to writing after realizing that she was temperamentally unsuited to the career of a concert pianist. Significantly, her novels are reticent. 'Objective' and factual in presentation, they carefully conceal the author's feelings and opinions despite their origin in personal or family history. *Maurice Guest* (1908), for example, draws on her experience of German musical life, while *The Getting of Wisdom* (1910) is based on her schooldays. Her best-known work is the trilogy *The Fortunes of Richard Mahony* (*Australia Felix*, 1917; *The Way Home*, 1925; *Ultima Thule*, 1929), which was inspired by the erratic, tragic career of her father, an Irish doctor, in the Ballarat gold rush and afterwards. Henry Handel Richardson also wrote *The Young Cosima* (1939) and a memoir, *Myself When Young* (1948).

See also studies by N. Palmer, 1950, and L. Kramer, 1967.
N.H.

Richardson, Mary Raleigh (1889–1961), suffragette. Brought up in Canada, the granddaughter of a bank manager, at the age of twenty Mary Richardson started her campaign for women's suffrage by trying to speak at lunchtime in a Holborn restaurant, where wealthy gentlemen pelted her with bread. Becoming one of the most militant suffragettes, she was arrested nine times in 1913–14 and was one of the first two women to be forcibly fed under the 'Cat and Mouse'. Act. She once presented a petition to George V by leaping on to the running board of his carriage, but gained true notoriety in 1914 for slashing the 'Rokeby Venus' in the National Gallery with a chopper (for which she was given the nickname 'Slasher Mary'). The marks on the painting can still be seen. *Laugh a Defiance* told of her suffragette experiences. She also wrote poems and novels.   B.H.C.

Riddick, Kathleen (1907–73), conductor. Kathleen Riddick studied at the Guildhall School of Music and Drama, where she held scholarships for 'cello and composition. Although at this time it was considered impossible for a woman to become a conductor, R. J. Forbes, Principal of the Royal Manchester College of Music, encouraged her to make conducting her career. On his recommendation she went to Salzburg to study at the Mozarteum with Bruno Walter and Nicolai Malko. Returning to England, she formed the professional chamber ensemble known as the Riddick Orchestra. This was well known in London before the Second World War, and Kathleen Riddick's professional status as a conductor was taken for granted by younger musicians, a turning-point for British women musicians, since even Ethel SMYTH was known as a conductor only for her own compositions. In 1934 Kathleen married George Bixley, and ten years later their daughter Susan was born.

During the Second World War, she benefited from the temporary inability of the BBC to import a large number of its conductors from abroad. She mainly broadcast with her own orchestra, but also with the BBC Symphony Orchestra, BBC Scottish Orchestra, and BBC Northern Orchestra. Once the war was over, however, she (and some of her male colleagues) suffered as the BBC gradually returned to employing foreign conductors for guest appearances. Kathleen Riddick also conducted the London Symphony Orchestra, and

was the first woman to conduct a public concert in the Royal Festival Hall, shortly after its opening in 1951. In 1961 she was awarded the OBE for her services to music. She continued with her symphonic work and in addition from 1964 to 1967 conducted the London Opera Group. Her colleagues and players regarded her as a thoroughly professional musical director, and she is remembered not so much as Britain's first successful woman conductor, but simply as a good conductor.
                                         R.G.

Ritchie, Lady Anne (Isabella) (1837–1919), writer. The eldest daughter of William Makepeace Thackeray, she was born in London and educated privately in London and Paris. She was always her father's close companion and through him knew all the literary figures of her time. In 1877 she married after a long courtship a second cousin, Richmond Thackeray Ritchie, who was later knighted. They had one son and one daughter.

It is for her biographical writings that Anne Ritchie is most valued. She contributed articles to *The Dictionary of National Biography*, including one on Elizabeth Barrett Browning, and her memoirs include *Records of Tennyson, Ruskin, and Browning*, 1892; *Lord Tennyson and his Friends*, 1893; and *Chapters from Some Memoirs*, 1894. In 1908 she edited her father's work. Her best known novels are *The Village on the Cliff* (1867) and *Old Kensington* (1873). Anne Ritchie's niece was Virginia Woolf, who wrote of her, 'she will be the unacknowledged source of much that remains in men's minds about the Victorian age. . . . Above all and for ever she will be the companion and interpreter of her father'. Her other works include *The Story of Elizabeth* (1863) and *Mrs Dymond* (1885).

See also W. Gérin, *Anne Thackeray Ritchie*, 1983; H. Ritchie, *Letters of Anne Thackeray Ritchie*, 1924.   A.P.

Ritchie, Margaret Willard (1903–69), singer. Born in Grimsby, she was educated in Italy and at the Royal College of Music. She later studied with Henry Wood. In a student performance at the College she attracted attention as Pamina in *Die Zauberflöte* and soon, at first as Mabel Ritchie, became leading soprano of Frederick Woodhouse's Intimate Opera Company. In 1944 at Sadler's Wells she was a distinguished Dorabella in *Così fan tutte*, and

in 1946 sang Lucia in the first performance of Britten's *Rape of Lucretia*. As Miss Wordsworth in the same composer's *Albert Herring* she played the prim schoolmistress with a charming sense of comedy. She joined the English Opera Group in 1947. Although her voice was small, her pure clear soprano and florid technique made her equally at ease in madrigals, Monteverdi, Britten, and even the songs of Liszt. Later in her career she taught, opening a summer school for singers in Oxford (1960), and giving master classes in London.
A.D.

Robinson, Mary (1758–1800), actress, novelist, and poet. The daughter of an American sea-captain named Darby, Mary Robinson began her education at a school in Bristol run by Hannah MORE's sisters. She attended two further establishments in Chelsea before the age of thirteen, when she temporarily assisted her mother in running a school. Her father then sent her to a finishing academy in Marylebone. Through the dancing master there she met David Garrick, who offered her the role of Cordelia to his Lear, but her marriage at the age of sixteen to an articled clerk named Thomas Robinson deferred her début. After two years of lavish spending, Mary accompanied her husband to a debtor's prison. There she wrote a volume of poems published with the aid of the Duchess of Devonshire (author of *The Sylph*) in 1775.

From 1776 to 1780 she pursued with great success an acting career at Drury Lane. Her performance as Perdita in Shakespeare's *A Winter's Tale* attracted the attention of the Prince of Wales, the future George IV, and she became his mistress. Numerous pamphlets, including *Letters from Perdita to a Certain Israelite* (1781), mounted vehement attacks on her relationship with the Prince and her interest in politics. The affair lasted two years and although the Prince defaulted on a promised bond, she did receive £8,000 in jewels and an annuity of £500. She travelled on the Continent between 1783 and 1788 and returned to begin an affair with an army officer, Colonel Banastre Tarleton. It was while making a journey on his behalf that she contracted an illness which led to her partial paralysis.

Mary Robinson's later career was directed to the writing of novels. In a series of works comprising *Vaucenza*, 1792, *The Widow*, 1794, and *Walsingham*, 1798, she established

a position on the fringe of the revolutionary circle of writers. Her liberal viewpoint typifies this group, which includes Elizabeth INCHBALD and Charlotte SMITH, but she achieves distinction in her perception of the close relationship between sexual, social, and economic forms of tyranny. In each of her novels sexual mastery is linked with reactionary social views, self-aggrandizement with corruption, and egotism with political injustice. The ideal state is imagined as a benevolent community in which women could play a fuller role. Mary Robinson died at Englefield Cottage, Surrey.

See also B. MacCarthy, *The Later Women Novelists 1714–1818*, 1948.
A.L.

Robinson, Sarah (1834–?), reformer, particularly concerned with the welfare of soldiers. Born in Blackheath, the fourth of six children, she moved while still young to Sussex, when her father bought an estate near Lewes. She was a shy girl of delicate health, brought up in a stern Calvinist tradition. At the age of ten she was sent to boarding school, but after the death of her mother and with her own health deteriorating, she returned home. She had little interest in religion as a child but in her late teens went through a conversion experience and, as for so many women of her generation, faith resulted in good works. Initially she engaged in house-to-house visiting and Sunday School teaching.

In 1858 the family settled in Guildford, where Sarah Robinson first came into contact with the army. She began corresponding with a regiment in Burma and helped with mission work among the soldiers of Aldershot, undertaking midnight meetings, brothel-visiting, and forming a total abstinence society. Her aim was to improve the health, manners, and morals of British soldiers by removing them from their unseemly haunts and by putting them in touch with Christian influences. For eight years from 1865 onwards she visited soldiers in their barracks, calling on over 190 different camps. This courageous and unprecedented work, which sometimes aroused violent opposition, attracted much attention from army authorities and Miss Robinson was given permission to use regimental facilities; her name appeared as a lecturer in the 1870 Parliamentary Blue Book on military education.

Her visits to brothels and barracks convinced Sarah Robinson that lasting good required the establishment of a permanent base with Christian workers. Portsmouth was chosen as an ideal site and in 1874 she opened the 'Soldiers' Institute', which provided accommodation, refreshments, reading, and work-rooms for soldiers, sailors, and their families. Several other such institutions followed, and eventually she extended her labours to include the poor of Portsmouth, forming a temperance society and opening a coffee house, public laundry, and various night schools. Ill health caused her gradually to withdraw from active work, after which she concentrated her energies on fund raising. In 1899 she retired to Burley.

Fearless and determined, Sarah Robinson was the most widely known female reformer in the field of rescue work among soldiers, and her work can be compared to that of Agnes WESTON. It should be seen in the context of the wider moral reform movement of the late nineteenth century, which was dominated by women advocating a single standard of chaste behaviour for both sexes. Her works include *The Soldiers' Friend. A pioneer's record* (1913) and *My Book: A personal narrative* (1914).

See also J. C. Hopkins, *Active Service; or [Miss S. Robinson's] Work among our Soldiers*, 1872; E. M. Tomkinson, *Sarah Robinson. Agnes Weston. Mrs Meredith*, 1887.

J.G.S.

Robsart, Amy. See DUDLEY, LADY AMY.

Rogers, Annie Mary Anne Henley (1856–1937), educationist. The daughter of the political economist Thorold Rogers, she was born in Oxford and privately educated there. She headed the list of successful candidates in the Oxford senior local examinations of 1873. Although she was interested in all aspects of women's advancement, women's education was her major concern. In 1879 she joined the Committee of the Association of the Higher Education of Women in Oxford, a private organization formed to improve facilities for the teaching and examining of women to university standards. She was secretary from 1894 until its dissolution in 1920. The Committee's efforts led to partial recognition of women students by the University in 1910 and to full membership in 1920, developments in which she played a major role. Her administrative abilities were also employed for the Society of Oxford Home Students (St Anne's) and for St Hugh's, both of which owed much to her.

Degrees by Degrees, a narrative of her work for women's education, was published posthumously in 1938.

J.R.

Roper, Esther (*c*. 1870–1938), suffragette. She was educated at Victoria University, Manchester, and thereafter devoted most of her time and energies to the causes of peace and international friendship. She was secretary of the Lancashire and Cheshire Women's Suffrage Society, and organizer of the Barmaids' Political Defence League when their employment was threatened by crusading moralists. She campaigned in Wigan with her friend Eva GORE-BOOTH for the first woman's suffrage candidate to stand at a general election, and helped various minority groups, including conscientious objectors during the First World War. In later years she worked to secure equal treatment for men and women in industry and the professions, and for the abolition of capital punishment.

B.H.C.

Roper, Margaret (1505–44), scholar. Eldest and favourite child of Sir Thomas More, Margaret married William Roper in 1521. The couple lived in More's household, as did his other children and their spouses. On Wolsey's fall in 1529 More became Lord Chancellor of England but resigned the post in 1532, alleging reasons of health although in fact his tacit opposition to Henry VIII's proposed divorce made it impossible for him to remain in office. In 1534 he was arrested and committed to the Tower for refusal to take the oath of supremacy. Margaret corresponded with him and was allowed to visit him in prison because she was prepared to persuade him to take the oath. After his execution in July 1535 she buried her father, bribing the executioner to fetch his head from London Bridge; consequently she was imprisoned for keeping the head as a sacred relic, and for trying to have More's works printed. After her release she lived quietly, and died at Christmas 1544. Her husband composed the first biography of Thomas More.

Besides her filial piety, Margaret is important as an outstanding humanist scholar. More's household was a pioneering centre of feminine education, where his daughters Margaret, Elizabeth, and Cecily were educated to the same degree as his son John. The More sisters' learning was praised in many works, including Vives's *Instruction of a Christian Woman* and

Erasmus's colloquy *The Priest and the Learned Woman*. About 1525 they held a philosophical disputation in the King's presence. Margaret, the most notable student among More's daughters, corresponded with Erasmus and translated his *Devout Treatise on the Pater Noster* (published anonymously in 1524), while he dedicated a commentary on Prudentius to her. Margaret also restored a corrupt passage in the Greek text of St Cyprian, and composed at her father's request a treatise on the 'Four Last Things' which has not survived. In later life she attempted unsuccessfully to secure Roger Ascham as tutor to her own children. Her daughter Mary Bassett, praised by Ascham for her learning, later translated More's *History of the Passion* from Latin into English.

See also early *Lives* of More by Roper, Harpsfield, Stapleton, and Cresacre More; E. E.Reynolds, *Margaret Roper*, 1960.   M.D.

Rose of Burford (*fl.* 1300–30), London businesswoman. Born into the London merchant family of Romaine, Rose married John of Burford, alderman and sheriff of London, and during his lifetime built up a trade in wool and cloth. Queen ISABELLA purchased a cope from her as a present for the Pope. Before he died in 1318, John made a loan to the Crown, and Rose was allowed to secure its repayment out of customs due on her own wool shipped out of London. In 1323 the mayor and corporation exerted influence on her behalf in a dispute over one of her cargoes with the Dover authorities.

See also E. Power, *Medieval Women*, 1975.   G.H.

Ross, Martin. See MARTIN, VIOLET FLORENCE.

Rossetti, Christina (Georgina) (1830–94), poet. Born in London, Christina was the daughter of Gabriele and Frances Polidori Rossetti. Her Italian father, a political exile, taught Italian and became a professor at King's College, London in 1831. His passion for Dante's works was a major influence on his family. Christina was the youngest of four children and with her sister was educated by their mother, who intended that they should become governesses. Ill-health, however, meant that Christina could never work regularly and she spent most of her life at home with her mother, making only two trips abroad. After her father's retirement she helped the family finances by teaching with her mother in a day school in Camden, and afterwards at Frome from 1851 to 1853.

Christina was extremely religious, a strict Anglican as was her mother, but attracted by the devotional appeal of Catholicism. Her sister Maria became an Anglican nun. In 1850 Christina's engagement to James Collinson, the Pre-Raphaelite painter, was cancelled because he was a Roman Catholic. This sorrowful renunciation is the subject of her sonnet sequence *Monna Innominata* and other poems. In 1866 she also rejected Charles Bagot Cayley, a close family friend, who was a free-thinker. It has also been suggested that many poems of the 1850s and early 1860s were inspired by love for William Bell Scott, a married man.

Christina's first recorded verses were written for her mother's birthday in 1842 and privately printed by her grandfather, as was a small volume of her verse in 1847. In 1848 her brother Dante Gabriel and his friends formed the Pre-Raphaelite Brotherhood, and Christina was closely associated with this group, although not a formal member. She contributed to their journal *The Germ*, using the pseudonym 'Ellen Alleyne'. Her first publication was *Goblin Market and Other Poems* (1862), the fantastic and sinister story of the sisters whom the goblins tempt with their luscious fruits being perhaps her most famous work. In 1866 she published *The Prince's Progress* and in 1870 a collection of stories, *Commonplace*. Her next works were collections of nursery rhymes (*Sing-Song*, 1872) and of tales for children (*Speaking Likenesses*, 1874).

Much of Christina's writing, particularly her later work, was religious, including devotional manuals and works of religious edification. These had a wide circulation, popularizing her name, and included a book of prayers, *Annus Domini*, 1874; *See and Find*, 1879; and *Letter and Spirit*, 1883. For ten years she undertook voluntary work at a Home for Fallen Women in Highgate and several of her narrative poems use this theme. After spending many years as an invalid, she died of cancer in December 1894 and is buried in Highgate cemetery.

Christina's literary reputation declined after her death but she is today recognized as a major poet. *Goblin Market* places her within the new movement in poetry, away from

Rowe, Elizabeth Singer

Tennysonian conventions. Her love lyrics are particularly fine, while the clarity and smoothness of her sonnets reveal considerable skill in poetic construction. In 1904 her brother William edited her *Poetical Works*, adding a memoir and notes. Her other works include *A Pageant* (1881).

See also G. Battiscombe, *Christina Rossetti*, 1981; R. W. Crump, *Christina Rossetti: A Reference Guide*, 1976; W. M. Rossetti, *The Family Letters of Christina Georgina Rossetti*, 1908.   J.H.

Rowe, Elizabeth Singer (1674–1737), novelist and poet. She was the daughter of Walter Singer, a nonconforming minister of Ilchester, who hired a master to instruct her in music and painting. The publication of *Poems on Several Occasions* (1696) gained her the patronage of Lord Weymouth of Longleat, whose son Henry Thynne subsequently tutored Elizabeth in French and Italian. At the age of thirty-six she married a much younger man, Thomas Rowe, who died in 1715 at the age of twenty-eight. After his death she left London and settled on an estate at Frome, from which she corresponded with her friend Elizabeth CARTER.

Elizabeth Rowe's works were published to great acclaim in the eighteenth century. *Friendship in Death* (1728) went through at least eighteen editions by 1800; *Letters Moral and Entertaining* (1729) through three. According to Samuel Johnson, the appeal of these epistolary novels lay in their 'attempt to employ the ornaments of romance in the decoration of religion'. Influenced by theological and neo-Platonic thought, Elizabeth Rowe stressed the wide-ranging power of God and the beneficence of the divine order. *Friendship in Death* comprises twenty letters from the dead to the living in which the immortal bliss of heaven is held out as a reward to those who live without sin on earth. Within the necessarily narrow limits of her chosen theme, she crafts an extraordinarily well-written and compelling narrative. Again, Johnson best defines the special quality of her work in his analysis of the 'copiousness and luxuriance' of her language and 'her brightness of imagery, her purity of sentiments'. Although the genre in which she excelled did not continue to exert a great influence on eighteenth-century literature, Elizabeth Rowe was among the first female authors to exploit the potential of language to great effect in popular narrative.

See also Boswell's *Life of Johnson*, vol. I, ed. G. B. Hill, 1934; H. F. Stecher, *Elizabeth Singer Rowe, the Poetess of Frome*, 1973.   A.L.

Royden, (Agnes) Maude (1876–1956), preacher and feminist. The youngest daughter of Sir Thomas Royden, a former mayor of Liverpool, she was educated at Cheltenham Ladies' College and Lady Margaret Hall, Oxford. Returning to Liverpool, she worked for the Victoria Women's settlement and then went to South Luffenham to help the vicar, the Rev. Hudson Shaw. The two became indispensable to each other, and Maude Royden later wrote the remarkable book *A Threefold Chord* (1947), describing their love, shared by Shaw's first wife, which maintained a strict regard for the Christian view of marriage.

In 1908 she joined the National Union of Suffrage Societies, becoming a member of the executive, editor of *Common Cause*, and a frequent and effective speaker. She also lectured in English literature. Although increasingly drawn to spiritual concerns, she could not, as a woman, preach within the Anglican Church. In 1917 she was asked to preach at the City Temple, London, and then at other non-Anglican meetings.

In 1920 Maude Royden founded with Dr Percy Dearmer the interdenominational 'Fellowship Services' in Kensington Town Hall and a year later Eccleston Square Church was acquired for the Fellowship Guild, opening as the Guildhouse, Eccleston Square. Throughout the 1920s and 1930s she travelled widely, often the centre of vigorous controversy and attracting great praise as a preacher. During the 1930s she became more and more devoted to the cause of peace, and was one of the organizers of the 'Peace Army'. She resigned from the Guildhouse ministry in 1936 to travel and lecture further on peace. In 1930 she was created a Companion of Honour and in 1931 was made DD by Glasgow University. She finally married Hudson Shaw, now over eighty, in 1944, but he died soon afterwards.

E.M.V.

Russell, Lucy, Countess of Bedford (d. 1627), literary patron. Daughter of John, first Lord Harington of Exton, Lucy married Edward

Russell, third Earl of Bedford, in 1594. She died childless. Lucy had wide cultural interests and probably wrote poetry, although none is known to have survived. As with so many women, her major role was as a patron and inspiration of poets rather than as a writer. John Davies of Hereford, Michael Drayton, and Samuel Daniel were among the poets who addressed verses and dedications to her. Ben Jonson described her as 'Life of the Muses' day, their morning star', and she acted in several of his masques, especially after 1603 when she had a prominent place at court. Above all she is remembered for her close association with John Donne, particularly in the years 1608–15. Their relationship cooled in later years after Lucy's financial difficulties made it impossible for her to fulfil a promise to pay his debts. Several of Donne's poems were addressed directly to the Countess, while the famous 'Twicknam Garden' commemorates her London home.

See also P. Hogrefe, *Tudor Women: Commoners and Queens*, 1975.   P.M.H.

Russell, Mary, Duchess of Bedford (1865–1937), aviator. Born Mary de Caurroy Tribe, she was the daughter of a clergyman who later became Anglican Archbishop of Lahore, and was educated at Cheltenham Ladies' College, then under the headship of the celebrated Miss BEALE. Returning to India she met, and in 1888 married, Lord Herbrand Russell, who succeeded his elder brother as Duke of Bedford in 1893. They had one son. The Duchess was a keen sportswoman, enjoying walking, climbing, and shooting. She also had a passion for bird-watching and built cottages on the islands of Barra and Fair Isle where she appreciated the solitude which she was to seek later in flying. Her dislike of official and court life was probably increased by her deafness, a legacy of typhoid fever which she had contracted as a girl in India. However, she was not a recluse and devoted herself for over thirty years to hospital work. She built and managed a cottage hospital at Woburn, where she assisted as theatre sister in operations and ran the radiology department. During the First World War the hospital became a military one.

Until she was sixty-one the Duchess had never been in an aeroplane, but she was advised that the constant buzzing in her ears, a feature of her deafness, would be helped by

flying. She therefore decided to try it, flying with a pilot to India and back, and to the Cape. In March 1937, aged 72, the Duchess took off from Woburn to complete her two hundred hours of solo flying. She was never seen again, although parts of her aeroplane were later washed ashore. Although not a pioneer in the manner of Amy JOHNSON, she brought long-distance flying to the notice of the public at a crucial stage in its development.

See also John, Duke of Bedford, *The Flying Duchess*, 1968.   E.M.V.

Russell, Lady Rachel (1636–1723), political figure and letter writer. She was the second daughter of Thomas Wriothesley, Earl of Southampton, Lord Treasurer of Charles II, and in 1653 married Francis, Lord Vaughan, who died in 1667. Two years later she became the wife of William Russell, second son of the Earl of Bedford. Their marriage was one of exceptional affection and devotion, and produced two daughters and a son. In 1678, on the death of his elder brother, William became heir to the earldom. He was already a prominent politician, a leader of the Country party (or Whigs), a staunch opponent of Popery and arbitrary government, and a prime mover of the bill to exclude the Duke of York from the throne. In 1683 he was accused of complicity in the Rye House Plot, a conspiracy by Whig extremists against the lives of Charles II and the Duke of York. During his trial for high treason, Russell was sustained by his wife, whose courage evoked admiration even from her husband's enemies. She played an active part in the preparations for his defence, and assisted as a recorder at the trial, where she took notes and made observations on his behalf. Even after he was sentenced to execution, she made strenuous if futile efforts to obtain his pardon, bravely encouraging him while he awaited death and helping him to prepare his apologia. Heartbroken by his execution, she struggled to attain a Christian resignation and devoted herself mainly to the education and welfare of her children.

Lady Russell was highly regarded for her good judgement and piety, and was consulted by many men and women in prominent positions. It was largely her influence that determined Princess Anne's adherence to the post-1688 regime, Tillotson's acceptance of his Archbishopric, and the future Lord Chancellor Cowper's early appointment as king's counsel.

She was instrumental in the reversal of her husband's attainder, thus securing for her son the family title and estates, many of which she managed on his behalf. Lady Russell was a discriminating reader and a voluminous letter writer. Her letters, some of which were first published in 1773 and went through numerous and enlarged editions, are of great social, political, and religious interest. They have won her a place in history as much as her wifely and spiritual devotion.

See also *Letters of Rachel, Lady Russell*, ed. Lord John Russell, 1853; M. Guizot, *The Married Life of Rachel, Lady Russell*, trans. J. Martin, 1855; Gladys Scott Thomson, *The Russells in Bloomsbury*, 1940.   T.J.M.

Rutherford, Dame Margaret (Taylor) (1892–1972), actress. Born in London, she was brought up by an aunt following the death of her mother when she was three. She was educated at Wimbledon High School and Raven's Croft, Seaford. After gaining her ARCM she taught the piano for five years, and later elocution, but, always keen to act, she used a small inheritance to join the Old Vic Company as a student in 1925. She was forced to return to teaching at the end of nine months, but two years later persuaded Nigel Playfair to engage her, and then went on to play in weekly repertory in London, Epsom, and Oxford. She made her first West End appearance in melodrama and proceeded to build a reputation as a leading comedy player, notably as Miss Prism in the 1939 revival of *The Importance of Being Earnest*.

During the 1940s and 1950s she created a series of memorable stage roles: the eccentric medium Madame Arcati in *Blithe Spirit*, Madame Desmortes in *Ring Round the Moon*, and the Duchesse de Pont-au-Bronc in another Anouilh play, *Time Remembered*. In 1950 and 1956 she played Lady Wishfort in *The Way of the World* and followed this in the 1960s with two further classic eighteenth-century comic roles as Mrs Candour in *The School for Scandal* and Mrs Malaprop in *The Rivals*.

Eccentricity tempered with shrewdness; authority vitiated by indecisiveness—these were the distinguishing features of her comic creations. They were transferred to the screen with resounding success, notably in *Passport to Pimlico* (1949) and *The Happiest Days of Your Life* (a film version of her 1948 stage success). She also appeared with her husband Stringer Davis, whom she married in 1945, in a series of films based upon Agatha Christie's detective, Miss Marple. Her performance in *The VIPs* (1963) won her an Academy Award as best supporting actress. She was appointed DBE in 1967.

See also: E. Keown, *Margaret Rutherford*, 1956.   K.W.

Rye, Maria (1829–1903), promoter of female emigration. The eldest of nine children of a London solicitor, Miss Rye was considered a delicate girl. Her education was interrupted by illness and mostly conducted at home. Convinced at an early age of the virtues of emigration, at sixteen she personally arranged for a family servant to leave for Australia. She later contributed articles to *The Englishwoman's Journal*, proposing female emigration as a solution to the lack of suitable work for middle-class women in Britain. In 1859 she undertook the management of a law-copying office, supported by the Society for Promoting the Employment of Women. At the Social Science Congress of 1861 she read a paper entitled 'The Emigration of Educated Women', urging that assistance be given to unemployed women needed in the colonies as teachers and governesses. As a result, the Female Middle-Class Emigration Society was founded in the following year, with Miss Rye as secretary. A public subscription was raised, enabling loans to be extended to emigrant women.

Miss Rye's own interests were increasingly concerned with working-class emigration. Of the 400 women she personally helped emigrate in 1862, only forty were governesses. Lengthy visits to New Zealand and Australia confirmed her belief that the colonies needed women prepared to perform hard manual labour, and after her return to England in 1866 she concentrated exclusively on encouraging poorer women to emigrate. Like Caroline CHISHOLM, Miss Rye hoped that female emigration would elevate the moral tone of the colonies, but difficulty in finding adults of the requisite personal standards led her to consider the emigration of children. In 1869 she set up a home for waifs and strays in Canada, to which orphan girls were sent and trained in preparation for domestic service. A similar institution was established in London, where girls were received until vacancies arose in Canada. By 1897, over 4000 children had passed through these homes.

Miss Rye was granted a small government pension in 1871, but not until her father's death did she become financially secure. He had always refused her a regular allowance, maintaining that as her domestic comforts were provided by him, she could have no further use for money. It was an ironic situation for a woman whose life had been devoted to helping other women earn their livelihood and achieve independence. In 1895 Miss Rye retired from public work to care for an invalid sister.

See also: A. J. Hammerton, *Emigrant Gentlewomen*, 1979; E. A. Pratt, *Pioneer Women in Victoria's Reign*, 1897.   J.V.L.

S

Sackville-West, Victoria (1892–1962), poet, novelist, critic, and biographer. She was born and grew up at Knole, Kent, the ancestral home of the Sackvilles, Earls of Dorset. She was the only child of the third Baron Sackville. Her parents were cousins: her mother was an illegitimate daughter of the second Baron Sackville by a Spanish gypsy dancer; her father was the second Baron's nephew and heir. Vita's character was greatly influenced by her unusual heritage, part Spanish peasant, part English aristocrat, and by her deep love of Knole, which, since she was an only daughter, she could not inherit. In 1913 she married the diplomat Harold Nicolson and had two sons. The marriage was seriously threatened by, but survived, her intense love affair with Violet Trefusis, a childhood friend. In 1930 the Nicolsons bought the derelict Sissinghurst Castle, where during the next ten years they restored the Elizabethan buildings and created one of the most beautiful gardens in England.

Her knowledge and intense love of the rhythms of traditional English rural life, under increasing threat from industrial and agricultural progress, were distilled in her poem 'The Land' (1926). which won the Hawthornden Prize. Often anthologized, her poetry perfectly captures the atmosphere of a rural England that vanished with the Second World War. Her last long poem, 'The Garden', won the Heinemann Prize. *Heritage* (1919), her first novel, was likewise highly acclaimed. *The Edwardians* (1930) centred on the lives of the 'smart set' around 1905 and was a best-seller, while *All Passion Spent* (1931), perhaps her best novel, is a study of extreme old age.

Vita Sackville-West was also an accomplished historian and biographer. Her histories included *Knole and the Sackvilles* (1922) about her home and family; among her biographies were *Aphra Behn* (1927), *Andrew Marvell* (1929), and the story of her Spanish grandmother, *Pepita* (1937). Her literary criticism was extensive, and two travel books were produced after visits to Persia. She also wrote about gardening and flowers. Virginia Woolf's *Orlando* (1928) is a fantastical biography of her, which her son has described as 'the longest and most charming love-letter in literature'. In 1947 she was made a Companion of Honour for services to literature. Her works also include *Collected Poems* (1933) and *Challenge* (1924).

See also V. Glendinning, *Vita*, 1983; N. Nicolson (ed.), *Harold Nicolson: Diaries and Letters 1930–1962*, 3 vols, 1966–68; N. Nicolson, *Portrait of a Marriage*, 1973; M. Stevens, *V. Sackville-West: A Critical Biography*, 1973.
J.E.E.H.

St Pol, Marie de, Countess of Pembroke (*c.* 1304–77), benefactress. She was the daughter of Guy de Chatillon, Count of St Pol, and in 1321 married Aymer de Valence, Earl of Pembroke. Marie was his second wife and they had no children. On the Earl's death in 1324 she began a long and independent career of her own. Although she faced severe financial difficulties in connection with Pembroke's will and her own dowry, her keen business sense eventually triumphed. She made her home in England, and though on good terms with Edward III and his family, was rarely seen at court.

Religion played an immense part in her life. Despite the brevity of their marriage, she never ceased to associate Pembroke's name with all her religious works. She re-founded and re-endowed Denny Abbey, Cambridgeshire, but her most important foundation was that of Pembroke College, Cambridge. The college charter is dated 1348, and over a lengthy period Marie endowed her foundation with lands, in the management of which she took a keen interest. She reserved the right to eject any Fellow of the college and made special provision for French scholars. On her death in 1377 her considerable wealth was divided between her household, religious foundations, and the poor.

See also H. Jenkinson, 'Marie de Sancti Pauli, Foundress of Pembroke College, Cambridge', in *Archaeologia*, XVI, 1915.
A.C.

Salinas, Maria de (*fl.* 1514–47), Castilian attendant of KATHERINE of Aragon. She does not occur in records of Katherine's original retinue, and probably arrived in England during her widowhood. In 1514 the Spanish ambassador named Maria as one of the 'bad influences', urging Queen Katherine to forget Spain and devote herself to England. In 1516 Maria was naturalized, and married Baron

Willoughby d'Eresby. They received a grant of lands from the King, who named one of his ships the *Mary Willoughby*. Maria had two sons, one of whom died in infancy; a daughter, Katherine, was born in 1519. She continued to serve the Queen and was present at the Field of Cloth of Gold in 1520. She was widowed in 1527 and in 1528 Charles, Duke of Suffolk bought her daughter Katherine's wardship, and although she was contracted to his son, Henry, Earl of Lincoln, married her himself in 1533.

Maria's firm support, particularly during the royal divorce, was appreciated by Katherine, who reported, 'She has faithfully served me, and in the hours of trial has comforted me'. From 1531 she was forbidden to serve the Queen, doubtless because of the affection between them, but from 1533 her influence won Suffolk's sympathy for Katherine, as Maria herself informed Charles V's ambassador, Chapuys. Her requests to attend the sick Queen were refused, despite an ingenious petition which avoided both Katherine's disputed titles by referring to her simply as 'my mistress'. In January 1536, when the Queen was plainly dying, Maria gained access to her by pretending to have a royal licence. Katherine died in her arms. Maria was still living in 1547, and on her death was buried quietly in Queen Katherine's tomb at Peterborough.

See also J. S. Brewer, *Letters and Papers, Foreign and Domestic, of the Reign of Henry VIII*, 1920; *Calendar of State Papers, Spanish*; F. Claremont, *Catherine of Aragon*, 1939.

M.D.

Salisbury, Countesses of. See LONGSWORD, ELA, COUNTESS OF SALISBURY; POLE, MARGARET, COUNTESS OF SALISBURY.

Salt, Dame Barbara (1904–75), diplomat and first woman to be appointed as a British ambassador. The granddaughter of Sir Thomas Salt, Chairman of Lloyds Bank and MP for Stafford, she received her education at Downs School, Seaford, and the universities of Munich and Cologne. During the Second World War she was Vice-Consul in Tangier, and in 1946 joined the United Nations Department of the Foreign Office. She became a permanent member of the Foreign Service (as it was then called) and in 1950 was sent to Moscow as First Secretary. Illness, which was to plague her professional life, forced her to return to London in the same year.

In 1951 she went to Washington as First Secretary, and in 1957 was appointed Counsellor and Consul-General at Tel Aviv. She was appointed CBE in 1959. In 1960 she became Deputy Head of the United Kingdom Disarmament Delegation to the United Nations in Geneva, and, the following year went to New York on the Economic and Social Council of the UN. She returned to the United Kingdom in 1962 on her appointment as Ambassador to Israel, the first woman to be so appointed. However, illness again struck and she was unable to take up the post. being confined thereafter to a wheelchair. In spite of this bitter disappointment, which she bore with great courage, she continued to work in the Foreign Office until her retirement in 1972.

E.M.V.

Sanders, Mary Dolling. See BRIDGE, ANN.

Sandes, Flora (1876–1956), soldier in the Serbian army. She was the youngest daughter of a former Rector of Whitchurch, County Cork, and was born in England after the family moved there. She displayed an early love for adventure, enjoying riding and shooting, and learning to drive in the days when motoring was distinctly experimental. In 1914 she went to Serbia with a small nursing unit of the St John Ambulance Association. There she joined the Serbian Red Cross, and found herself a dresser in the ambulance of the Second Infantry Regiment of the Serbian army. As the Serbians were slowly driven back through the Albanian mountains, she became increasingly involved in fighting rather than nursing. It was not unusual for peasant girls to fight with the army, and Flora Sandes finally removed her Red Cross Badge to join the Second Regiment as a private. For the next seven years she was regarded by the regiment as a considerable asset. She was seen as a representative of England and idolized for her great courage and outstanding cheerfulness and sympathy. She fought with her regiment in every battle until in 1916 she was badly wounded by a grenade and taken to a British military hospital, where she was decorated with the Order of the Kara-George for bravery in the field.

On sick leave in England she raised funds, and in 1917 returned to her regiment. She was commissioned in 1919 and promoted to lieutenant in 1922 when demobilization came. In 1926 she received the rank of captain. In 1927 she married Yurie Ydenitch, a White Russian who had escaped during the Russian Revolution and joined the Serbian army. They lived in France and then in Belgrade, where they were interned by the Germans during the Second World War. Her husband died in 1941 and after the war she returned to England to settle in Suffolk, where she lived until her death.   E.M.V.

Saville, Helena. See FAUCIT, HELEN.

Sayers, Dorothy L(eigh) (1893–1957), poet, novelist, and playwright. She grew up in the Fen country, where her father was a clergyman, and was educated at home and at the Godolphin School, Salisbury. In 1912 she went as a Scholar to Somerville College, Oxford, graduating in 1915 with first-class honours in French. In 1921 she joined Benson's Advertising Agency as a copy-writer, and stayed for eleven years. An illegitimate son, born secretly in 1924, was given to a cousin to be brought up. In 1926 she married a journalist, Atherton Fleming.

After two small volumes of poetry she published her first detective novel, *Whose Body?* (1923). It was the first of a series featuring the aristocratic sleuth Lord Peter Wimsey; the best of these is *The Nine Tailors* (1934), a highly atmospheric novel set in the Fen country. By 1928 she was established as a successful writer of detective fiction; in 1949 she became President of the Detection Club, an office she held until her death. In middle age she returned to an interest in religion, which had been a theme of her early poetry. Her first religious play, *The Zeal of thy House*, was performed at Canterbury Cathedral in 1937. In 1941 her series of plays on the life of Christ, *The Man Born to be King*, was broadcast by the BBC, causing great controversy. It was regarded by critics as a breakthrough in religious broadcasting.

The last decade of her life was absorbed by work on her translation of Dante, which she did not live to complete. Her translations, into which she put great care and research, have never received scholarly acclaim: she herself considered that her success as a writer of detective stories eclipsed her credentials as a scholar. She was President of the Modern Language Association from 1939 to 1945, and received an Hon. D Litt from Durham University in 1950. Her works include *Op 1*, 1916; *The Man Born to be King*, 1943; *The Song of Roland*, 1957; *Dante's Hell*, 1949; *Purga-*

tory, 1955; and *Paradise*, with Barbara Reynolds, 1962.

See also J. Brabazon, *Dorothy L. Sayers: The Life of a Courageous Woman*, 1981; J. Hitchman, *Such a Strange Lady*, 1975.

J.E.E.H.

Scharlieb, Dame Mary Ann Dacomb (1844–1930), doctor. Born in London, Mary was the eldest child of William Chandler Bird, a merchant. Her mother died ten days after her birth, and her happy childhood and good education were owed to her maternal aunt, her stepmother, and sympathetic father. In 1865 she married William Scharlieb, a barrister, by whom she had two sons and a daughter, and sailed for Madras. She helped her husband to publish two monthly law journals and reviewed Freyer's *Medical Jurisprudence*. This work, and reports of women in purdah, convinced her of the need for medically qualified women. Having approached Surgeon General Balfour, she entered Madras Medical College with three other women in 1875. All qualified three years later.

Returning to England, she entered the London School of Medicine for Women in 1878, and in 1882 she and Edith Shove were the first women medical graduates of London. Mary won honours in all subjects, the Gold Medal, and the Scholarship in Obstetrics. On her return to Madras in 1883 her practice flourished, and a small hospital for Hindu and Moslem women was founded.

Ill-health forced her to leave in 1887. In England she was appointed to the staff of the New Hospital (now the Elizabeth Garrett Anderson), where she proved a gifted teacher and surgeon. She was the first woman to gain the MD of London University, in 1888; the first appointed consultant to a general teaching hospital (the Royal Free); and one of the first six women magistrates (1920). She led deputations to successive secretaries of state which finally resulted in the establishment of the Indian Medical Service for Women in 1916.

Mary Scharlieb acknowledged that her achievements as clinician, teacher, and reformer would not have been possible without the support of family, colleagues, and a profound religious faith. She published *Reminiscences* in 1924 and was created DBE in 1926.

See also I. Thorne, *Sketch of the Foundation and Development of the London School of Medicine for Women*, 1905.   R.B.

354

Schreiber, Lady Charlotte. See GUEST, LADY CHARLOTTE ELIZABETH.

Schreiner, Olive (Emilie Albertina) (1855–1920), novelist, born at Wittebergen Mission Station, Basutoland. Her father was a Methodist missionary of German descent and her mother was English. She was the sixth of twelve children. Olive Schreiner was self-educated and at the age of fifteen became governess to a Boer family. She was still in her teens when she began *The Story of an African Farm* (1883) which was published under the pseudonym of 'Ralph Iron' by Chapman and Hall, whose chief reader, George Meredith, helped to revise it. The sensation caused by its religious heteredoxy and feminist viewpoint has long been forgotten, but *The Story of an African Farm* survives as a superb evocation of a way of life. Olive Schreiner had moved to England two years previously, in search of a publisher, and in 1884 met Havelock Ellis, with whom she was to have a very close friendship. Ten years later, however, she returned to South Africa and married Samuel Cronwright, a politician who gave up his work as farmer and lawyer to become her literary assistant and later her literary executor. He accompanied his wife on frequent trips to England and around Africa.

The bulk of Olive Schreiner's work was written after her return to South Africa: *Trooper Peter Halket of Mashonaland*, 1897; *From Man to Man*, 1926; *Undine*, 1928; and collections of short stories including *Dreams*, 1891; *Dream Life and Real Life*, 1893; and *Stories, Dreams and Allegories*, 1920. Her classic work, in the opinion of some critics, is *Woman and Labour* (1911). Her *Letters* were published in 1924.

See also D. L. Adler, *Olive Schreiner: her friends and times*, 1955; J. Berkman, *Olive Schreiner: Feminism on the Frontier*, 1979; R. First and A. Scott, *Olive Schreiner*, 1980; V. B. Gould, *Not without Honour. The Life and writings of Olive Schreiner*, 1948; S. C. C. Schreiner, *The Life of Olive Schreiner*, 1924.   A.P.

Schulenburg, (Ehrengard) Melusine von der, Duchess of Kendal (1667–1743), mistress of George I of England. Born in Emden, Saxony, the daughter of a noble official in the household of the Elector of Brandenburg, in 1690 she became a maid of honour to Sophia, the Elec-

tress of Hanover. She soon attracted the notice of Sophia's son, Georg Ludwig, who was already seeking solace from the tantrums of his wife Sophia Dorothea. During 1691 Melusine became Georg Ludwig's mistress, and the first of their children was born a year later. In 1694 occurred the dramatic and tragic exposure of the love-affair between Sophia Dorothea and Count Konigsmarck, followed by his murder and her subsequent divorce and sequestration in a fortress. Although this no doubt strengthened Melusine's position, she was probably not entirely secure until Georg Ludwig went to England as George I in 1714. Even so, her three children by him, although privately cherished, were never acknowledged as such by their father. His granddaughter later spoke of a morganatic marriage, but this remains unproved.

Melusine's influence after 1714 was considerable, although oblique and subtle. Lord Stanhope found her assistance useful in 1719 when he procured the disgrace of Bernstorff and the signing of the Prussian treaty. Robert Walpole called her 'as much Queen of England as ever was' and took care to cultivate good relations with her, even though he often used his colleague Townshend, whom Melusine preferred, as an intermediary. No one could make George I do something against his will. But politicians realized that the amiable mistress was the ideal intermediary for broaching a matter likely to be ill-received.

In general her conduct was surprisingly unambitious. Her gains during the South Sea Bubble were unspectacular, and the only serious criticism of her financial dealings arose over the monopoly she sold to Wood to make copper coins for Ireland. It is evident from the recently-discovered will of George I, in which he left her £23,000, that he was worried about her financial prospects in the case of his death. The notion of the rapacious German mistress, held in some circles at the time, seems to have been a fallacy.

See also J. M. Beattie, *The English Court in the Reign of George I*, 1967; R. Hatton, *George I*, 1978.   T.H.

Scott, Elisabeth Whitworth (1898–1972), architect. Born in Bournemouth, the daughter of a doctor, she nevertheless had architectural connections. Her grandfather was a brother of Sir Gilbert Scott, the great Victorian architect, and her grandmother was sister to George

Frederick Bodley. Sir Giles Gilbert Scott, the architect of Liverpool Cathedral, was a cousin. Elisabeth was educated at Redmoor School, Bournemouth, and at the School of the Architectural Association where she gained her diploma in 1924. She was assistant successively to Louis de Soissons, Oliver Hill, and Maurice Chesterton, with whom she went into partnership for the construction of the new Shakespeare Memorial Theatre at Stratford-upon-Avon. The old theatre had been destroyed by fire, and her design for its replacement was one of seventy-two originally submitted from all over the world. In 1928 the assessors unanimously selected Miss Scott's design, of which George Bernard Shaw said it was the only one which showed any theatre sense. She later worked on the extension of Newnham College, Cambridge, the first part of which was opened by Queen Mary in 1938.   E.M.V.

Scott, Kathleen. See KENNET, (EDITH AGNES) KATHLEEN, LADY.

Sellon, Priscilla Lydia (1821–76), founder of Anglican sisterhoods. Born in Hampstead, she was the daughter of a naval commander. Her mother died in 1823 and she was brought up by her father and a Scottish governess, who developed in her a strong will. In 1848 she met Edward Pusey, leader of the High Church Movement, and visited his convent in Regent's Park. She abandoned a visit to Italy for her health in order to respond to a call from Bishop Phillpotts of Exeter for help among the poor of Devonport, Plymouth, and Stonehouse. At considerable personal expense she eventually set up a community of women to work in the three towns, establishing an orphanage and a school for training female printers. The support given by Pusey soon attracted hostility from Low Church groups which led to a public enquiry into her activities. Her exoneration by Bishop Phillpotts did not prevent a rash of pamphlets against her 'Romish practices', which she and her father answered.

The adoption of a Rule and the formal establishment of three sisterhoods saw the beginnings of female Anglican monasticism. A number of these sisters were sent to nurse in the Crimean War, and convents were opened in London, Bristol, and Berkshire. Miss Sellon's forceful personality created divisions within the communities, however, and her enforcement of strict rules of poverty and obedience led, in 1852, to Bishop Phillpotts'

resignation as Visitor to them. Attacks against her were renewed in 1862 with the publication of *Experiences of a Sister of Mercy* by an ex-nun; and even some High Church clergy abhorred the 'pseudo-asceticism of Mother Lydia'. But the sisters earned admiration for their work in Spitalfields during the cholera epidemic of 1886 and opened a fever hospital there despite the opposition of the Bishop of London. By that time, at Pusey's prompting, Miss Sellon had sent sisters to work in Honolulu, with considerable success. She visited them herself in 1867.

Always given to poor health, from 1872 she suffered increasingly from paralysis, and eventually a stroke led to her death. Pusey had called her 'the restorer', after three centuries, of Anglican monasticism, and *The Times* spoke in admiration of her as 'the founder of Anglican Sisterhoods'. Her works include *A Few Words to some women of the Church of England* (1850).

See also A. M. Allchin, *The Silent Rebellion: Anglican religious communities, 1845–1900*, 1958; T. J. Williams, *Priscilla Lydia Sellon*, 1965.   C.H.G.G.

Senior, Jeannie, properly Jane Elizabeth Hughes (1828–77), philanthropist and civil servant. Jeannie Hughes was one of ten children of a country squire. Her elder brother was Thomas Hughes, Christian Socialist and author of *Tom Brown's School Days*. She was educated at home and in 1848 married Nassau John Senior, son of the political economist. She belonged to a brilliant political and intellectual circle to which she contributed her beauty and musical talents and counted among her friends G. F. Watts, who painted her portrait, Octavia HILL, Florence NIGHTINGALE, Jenny LIND, and the Thackeray family. In the late 1850s her health began to fail, but this did not prevent Jeannie Senior from undertaking substantial charitable work. As a lady visitor, she undertook a thorough study of the poor law system and the measures needed to ameliorate its harshness to the poor, particularly children. She became an advocate of the boarding-out system, whereby children were removed from workhouses and placed in foster care or in small family-like homes.

In 1873 the Local Government Board decided that it needed 'feminine insight' into the poor law system, and on the recommendation of Octavia Hill, Jeannie Senior was asked to take an experimental post as inspector of workhouses and workhouse and district pauper schools. She thus became the first woman inspector in the Civil Service and one of very few married women to serve until after the Second World War. She immediately set out to discover at first hand the conditions then prevailing in pauper schools and the effect of pauper education on young persons' later careers. In her report of January 1874 she condemned the stultifying nature of pauper education and pleaded for boarding-out and the end of institutionalization. She criticized the shortcomings of the system in the placing of girls in work and advocated a support network of voluntary befriending to supplement the state's efforts. She also stressed the need for inspection of workhouses by women. In February 1874 her appointment was made permanent, but illness forced her to resign later that year. From her sick-room she tried to put into effect her scheme for the after-care of workhouse girls, and with the support of Octavia Hill and Lord Shaftesbury founded the Metropolitan Association for Befriending Young Servants in 1875.

See also F. D. How, *Noble Women of Our Time*, 1901; E. A. Pratt, *Pioneer Women in Victoria's Reign*, 1897. M.Z.

Sergeant, (Emily Frances) Adeline (1851–1904), novelist, born in Derbyshire. Her father was a Methodist missionary and her mother wrote devout stories and verses. Educated at a Nonconformist school at Clapham and Queen's College, London, she joined the Church of England in 1870. During the 1880s she was a Fabian and agnostic, a phase reflected in her best novel, *No Saint* (1886). In 1893 she inclined towards High Church opinions and in 1899 became a Roman Catholic. For ten years a governess, she visited Egypt and there wrote *Jacobi's Wife*, a novel which received a prize from *The People's Friend* of Dundee, a journal to which she then regularly contributed. She was interested in reform and relief work, spending generously what she earned from writing. She produced over ninety novels, writing six a year and sometimes eight. Although without literary value, they are sometimes of interest as pictures of the domestic life of middle-class provincial Nonconformist families. *Esther Denison*

(1889) is partly autobiographical; other works include *The Story of a Penitent Soul* (1892) and *The Idol Maker* (1897). B.H.C.

Seward, Anna (1749–1809), writer, the 'Swan of Litchfield'. Born in Eyam, Derbyshire, the daughter of a clergyman, she moved to Lichfield in 1754 when her father became canon and tenant of the Bishop's Palace. She lived in the Palace for the rest of her life. Anna could recite the first three books of *Paradise Lost* at the age of nine, and started to write poetry early. Erasmus Darwin advised her family against poetry, suggesting that it might unduly tax her mind. He later encouraged her talents, however, and used some of her verses in his *Botanic Garden*. He may also have written sections of her *Elegy on Captain Cook* (1780). This elegy and Anna's *Monody on Major André* (1781) were considerable successes, and Darwin said she had invented their form, the epic elegy. Her *Memoir of the Life of Dr Darwin* (1804) remains a valuable source on Darwin, despite inaccuracies.

Anna said she was 'dead to the world' at Lichfield, but numbered among her acquaintances Dr Johnson, Mrs THRALE, Scott, Southey, Hannah MORE, and Helen Maria WILLIAMS. She knew the famous ladies of Llangollen, wrote a poem on 'Llangollen Vale' (1796), and left the ladies a bequest in her will (see BUTLER, LADY ELEANOR). She was a copious letter writer and her lively and malicious *Letters* (six volumes, 1810) have finally brought her more admirers than her poetry. Although passionately fond of a series of men and women, she never married. In later years she caused some scandal by her devotion to John Saville, a cathedral singer who lived apart from his wife.

Her literary remains were bequeathed to Scott, who published her poetry and extracts from the letters (1810), although he thought most of the poems 'absolutely execrable'. Romantic in her enthusiasms, she was an early admirer of Coleridge, Scott, and Southey, but it is unlikely that she really understood the new poetry. She thought Wordsworth 'must be mad'.

See also M. Ashmun, *The Singing Swan*, 1913; E. V. Lucas, *A Swan and her friends*, 1907; S. H. Monk in *Wordsworth and Coleridge. Studies in honour of George McLean Hayter*, ed. E. L. Griggs, 1962. G.E.H.H.

Sewell, Anna (1820–78), author of *Black Beauty*. She was born in Yarmouth, the daughter of Mary Sewell, poet and author of children's books. In 1835 the Sewells moved to Brighton, where Anna's father became a bank manager. They were not a wealthy family and Mary Sewell wrote in order to educate her children. It was also a strict Quaker household and Anna devoted her life to work for the poor and underprivileged.

As the result of a fall in early childhood Anna became lame. The family moved to Lancing in 1845, visited Germany the following year, and later lived in various parts of England. In 1856 Anna and her mother again went to Germany, for a year, so that Anne could receive treatment. When they returned, Anna could walk again, and the following year they went to Spain to visit Anna's brother, Philip. On her return she moved to Old Catton, near Norwich, but her health declined and the last seven years of her life were spent indoors, being cared for by her mother.

Inspired by Horace Bushnell's *Essay on Animals*, Anna wrote *Black Beauty* (1877) in an attempt to improve the treatment of horses. It was an immediate success, becoming a children's classic.

See also M. J. Baker, *Anna Sewell and Black Beauty*, 1956.　　　　　　　　　　A.P.

Sewell, Elizabeth (Missing) (1815–1906), writer and educationist. She was born at Newport, Isle of Wight, the daughter of a solicitor. Educated at Newport and Bath, she returned home at sixteen to teach her younger sisters. Her father died in 1842, leaving debts which Elizabeth helped to pay off with her literary earnings. Most of her works were tales for young people, strongly Anglican in outlook. She published *Amy Herbert* (1844), a popular girls' story, *Laneton Parsonage* (1846), indicating the practical use of the Catechism, and *Margaret Perceval* (1847), defending the Church of England. *The Experience of Life* (1852) and *Ursula* (1858) were other popular novels.

To supplement her income Elizabeth Sewell decided, with her sister Ellen, to take pupils. She had pronounced views on education, eschewed examinations, and made her pupils read widely and take an interest in current affairs. Convinced of the need for better education among middle-class girls, she founded the St Boniface School at Ventnor in 1886. Her autobiography appeared posthumously in 1907, edited by Eleanor Sewell.

B.H.C.

Sexburga (*fl.* 640–95), Queen of Kent and abbess. Eldest of King Anna of East Anglia's four daughters, Sexburga married King Eorcenberht of Kent in 640. She bore him two sons, Egbert and Lothar, both of whom became kings of Kent. Of her two daughters, Eorcengota became a nun at the Frankish monastery of Faremoutiers, and Ermenhild married King Wulfhere of Mercia, becoming the mother of St WEREBURGA.

Eorcenberht died in 664, whereupon tradition has it that Sexburga acted as regent for her son Egbert until he came of age. She then appears to have founded a monastery at Sheppey which she ruled as abbess, having received the veil from Archbishop Theodore some time after 668. Some time after 675 she made her daughter Ermenhild her successor at Sheppey in order to go and receive instruction at the monastery recently founded at Ely by her sister Æthelthryth. In 679 Sexburga succeeded Æthelthryth as abbess there, and sixteen years later was responsible for translating her sister's bones from the wooden coffin in which she was buried to a new stone sarcophagus. The ceremony was marked by a number of miracles. When Sexburga died, at an unknown date, she was buried near Æthelthryth and was succeeded as abbess at Ely by her daughter Ermenhild. Sexburga's feast day is 6 July.

See also B. Colgrave and R. Mynors (eds.), *Bede's Ecclesiastical History of the English People*, 1969; E. O. Blake (ed.), *Liber Eliensis*, Camden Ser. 3, vol. 92, 1962.　　J.C.

Seymour, Anne (1497–1587), political figure. Daughter of Sir Edward Stanhope of Sudbury, Suffolk, Anne married Edward Seymour before 1536. A statute of 1540 settled his estates on her children, four sons and six daughters, instead of those of his divorced first wife. In March 1536 she was installed at Greenwich Palace with Seymour and his sister Jane, and the couple benefited from Jane's marriage to Henry VIII in May. In October 1537, shortly after the birth of his nephew, Prince Edward, Seymour was created Earl of Hertford; and on Edward's accession in 1547 he became Lord Protector and Duke of Somerset.

Though formerly a religious associate of Queen Katherine PARR, Anne now quarrelled with her over precedence at court, a symptom of the political rivalry between their husbands, the Seymour brothers. When Somerset was arrested on treason charges in October 1551, Anne followed him to the Tower. He was beheaded on 22 January 1552, and she subsequently married his steward, Francis Newdigate. Anne's political influence was minor, but during Edward's VI's reign she was an important patron of Protestant learning, receiving the dedications to several treatises, including those *Paraphrases* of Erasmus translated by her protégé John Olde.

See also J. K. McConica, *English Humanists and Reformation Politics*, 1968; State Papers of Henry VIII and Edward VI. M.D.

Seymour, Jane (?1509–37), third Queen of Henry VIII. Daughter of Sir John Seymour of Wolf Hall, Wiltshire, she became lady-in-waiting successively to the King's first two wives, KATHERINE OF ARAGON and Anne BOLEYN. Princess Mary later alluded to Jane's kindness to her before her marriage with Henry, so possibly she was one of the unnamed women who attracted him in 1534–35. In March 1536 she was installed with her brother Edward and his wife Anne SEYMOUR in apartments at Greenwich to which Henry had private access. She refused to become his mistress, but was the mouthpiece of the faction which plotted to remove Anne Boleyn. On the day of Anne's execution (19 May) Henry visited Jane, and Archbishop Cranmer gave a dispensation for the marriage without the publication of banns. They were married on 30 May. In July parliament settled the succession on her issue.

Little is known of Jane's opinions, although Cardinal Pole heard 'good things' about her and Luther heard that she was an enemy to the gospel. Cardinal Du Bellay was told that she begged the King on her knees to restore the dissolved abbeys, but was told not to meddle in affairs unless she wished to share her predecessor's fate. Her sole contribution to politics was to give birth to the long-desired male heir, Edward, on 12 October 1537. She died twelve days later.

Henry was deeply moved by her death, but told Francis I that his grief was outweighed by his joy in his son. The attitude was widely shared, and numerous epitaphs depicted Jane as the phoenix dying in order to give birth. Her significance was felt indirectly in the next reign, when their relationship to Edward VI

enabled her brothers Edward, Duke of Somerset, and Thomas, the Lord Admiral, to play important (and fatal) political roles.

See also J. S. Brewer, *Letters & Papers, Foreign and Domestic, of the Reign of Henry VIII*, 1920; M. A. S. Hume, *The Wives of Henry VIII*, 1929. M.D.

Sharp, Jane (*fl.* 1671), midwife. She was author of the first textbook on midwifery written by an Englishwoman, *The Midwives Book or the whole Art of Midwifry Discovered*, which was published in 1671 and achieved four editions by 1725. Nothing is known of her private life although the 1671 volume describes her as a 'practitioner in the art of midwifry above thirty years', and reveals her as a widely read, pious, and accomplished woman. Her distress at 'the many miseries women endure in the hands of unskilful midwives' who practised only 'for lucre's sake' prompted her work, which was based on her own wide experience and on study of midwifery treatises in several languages. *The Midwives Book* was conventional enough and inferior to contemporary Continental works, but by English standards was a comprehensive and down-to-earth account which emphasized the midwife's need for both theoretical knowledge and practical experience. It dealt fully with the male and female reproductive systems; conception, pregnancy, and childbirth, and their associated complications; and ended with comments on diseases in childbearing women and young children. Her recommendations frequently involved good diet, exercise, and common herbal remedies. Treatment advised for teething troubles, for example, was to rub the child's gums with honey and fresh butter.

In the seventeenth century 'men-midwives' were becoming increasingly common, and Sharp's work is important for its staunch defence of women's predominant role in pregnancy care and childbirth. Although men alone could study anatomy at the universities, women could learn from each other and from 'long and diligent practice'. 'Men-midwives' were not mentioned in the Bible, while 'poor country people' who had 'none but women to assist' fared at least as well in childbirth as 'the greatest ladies in the land' who called on men for help. Midwifery was thus 'the natural propriety of women', and Sharp's pride in this threatened female preserve is evident: 'The

Shaw, Hester

Art of Midwifery is doubtless one of the most useful and necessary of all arts for the. . . well being of mankind'.

See also A. Clarke, *Working Life of Women in the Seventeenth Century*, 1968; J. Donnison, *Midwives and Medical Men*, 1977.

A.H.

Shaw, Hester (1613–60), midwife. Hester Shaw was practising as a midwife in London before 1613. In 1634 Peter Chamberlen, the 'man-midwife' from the family which invented, and kept secret, the midwifery forceps, proposed that midwives be incorporated into a society under his supervision. He was opposed by the sixty midwives led by Mrs Shaw and Mrs Whipp, who argued that it was in Chamberlen's interest to keep midwives unskilled so that he could take over difficult cases. They petitioned the King and briefed counsel who sucessfully defended their position at an enquiry under the Archbishop of Canterbury. However, the women's attempt to improve standards by tightening up the traditional episcopal licensing of midwives, failed.

Hester's husband was John Shaw, citizen and turner. As churchwarden of All-Hallows-by-the-Tower in 1629 he recorded his wife's gift of a damask cloth for the communion table. By 1643, when Thomas Clendon became minister, she was a widow. Although her husband's family had paid their tithes for sixty years, Hester made the minister an additional annual payment of £8, but ceased the gift when Clendon tried to publicize her charity to encourage other parishioners. This caused animosity between them. In January 1650, Mrs Shaw's house in Tower Street was one of five blown up by an explosion. Sixty-seven people were killed, including her son-in-law Daniel Dun or Donne, and three of her grandchildren, Thomas, Hester, and Elizabeth. She claimed to have lost £3000 without recompense. In addition, £953 6s 8d. which she had in bags inside the house was blown out and subsequently, she alleged, taken to the minister's house for safe-keeping. Clendon refused to return it. In 1653 Clendon complained of her allegations against him in his pamphlet, *Justification Justified*, and she responded with *A Plain Relation of my Sufferings* and *Mrs Shaw's Innocency Restored*. Affidavits were taken before Lord Mayor Thomas Viner, who had befriended her in 1650.

360

In 1650 Hester Shaw was described as a midwife of 'good esteem and quality'. She had a wide circle of contacts, and Clendon was stung to self-defence by her accusations 'at all the meetings she came to, in the way of her calling'. Although it is unclear to what extent her considerable wealth came from her own labours, she spoke of losing 'above forty years toilsome gleaning in way of my laborious calling' by the explosion. Clearly Clendon found her formidable, and admitted that she was 'by many reputed Religious, having by her good education, and volubility of tongue, and natural boldness, and confidence, attained some ability in prayer, and in speaking of matters of Religion'. In her will, proved in November 1660, she mentions her daughter, Dame Elizabeth Bludden, her son-in-law George Farrington, and her grandson John Donne.

See also J. Donnison, *Midwives and Medical Men*, 1977; *Death's Masterpiece: or a true relation of that great and sudden Fire in Tower-Street*, January 1650.

P.C.

Shearing, Joseph. See BOWEN, MARJORIE.

Shelley, Mary Wollstonecraft (1797–1851), author. Mary was born in London, the daughter of the radical philosopher William Godwin and Mary WOLLSTONECRAFT, the feminist writer. Her mother died soon after Mary's birth and Godwin remarried in 1801. It was a large household, with five children, including Wollstonecraft's elder daughter, and Godwin found it hard to make ends meet. Mary's step-mother was an unsympathetic woman, so that the girl spent much time with her father, imbibing ideas from his discussions with intellectual friends. Throughout her life she read voraciously, and she mastered four languages.

Mary first met the poet Percy Bysshe Shelley in 1812 but it was in 1814, after Mary's return from visiting friends in Dundee, that they fell in love. In July they eloped to France, accompanied by Claire CLAIRMONT, Mary's foster sister. The suicide of Shelley's first wife in 1816 enabled the couple to marry. Their relationship was intense but troubled. Frequent moves, scandal, debt, and the births and deaths of children all brought strain and distress. Godwin's initial hostility to the couple was replaced by numerous requests for loans.

Mary Shelley's first work was *Frankenstein: or, The Modern Prometheus*, inspired by a dream and finished in 1817. It was published the following year. While her husband encouraged Mary in her work, it was definitely her own creation. After Shelley's death in 1822 Mary stayed in Italy with friends, returning to London the following summer. Of her four children only one, Percy, had survived, and through him she received a small and uncertain allowance from Shelley's father, who remained antagonistic towards her. When Percy became heir to the baronetcy in 1826 Mary's financial position improved, but the money from her writing was needed to pay for her son's education. She produced several historical romances and novels, of which the most interesting are *The Last Man* (1826), with characters based on Shelley and Byron, and *Lodore* (1835), which is markedly autobiographical. Much of her work consisted of stories which appeared in annuals such as *The Keepsake*.

In 1840 Percy received a settlement and Mary was able to rest from her work. Between 1840 and 1843 she visited Europe with him, describing these travels in *Rambles in Germany and Italy* (1844). By the time Percy became a baronet in 1844, hard work had affected Mary's health. She had edited Shelley's poetry and prose in 1839–40 but now found the task of writing his biography too much for her. In 1851 she died in London, and was buried at Bournemouth. Mary is chiefly remembered for *Frankenstein*. Although overshadowed by Shelley's reputation, she is an important figure in literary history as the creator of a work that has fascinated the Western imagination. Her other works include *Mathilda* (1819); and *Valperga* (1823).

See also F. L. Jones (ed.), *Mary Shelley's Journal*, 1947 and *The Letters of Mary W. Shelley*, 2 vols, 1944; W. H. Lyles, *Mary Shelley: An Annotated Bibliography*, 1975; E. Nitchie, *Mary Shelley*, 1973.   J.H.

Sheridan, Clare Consuelo (1885–1970), sculptor and writer, the only daughter of a Sussex family called Frewen. Her mother was Lady Randolph Churchill's sister. Her friends included Princess Margaret of Connaught, Henry James, and Axel Munthe, whom she met while in Stockholm with the Princess after her marriage to Prince Gustaf of Sweden. In 1910 she married Wilfred Sheridan, a descendant of the playwright, who was killed in 1915, leaving her with two children. Another child had died earlier, and while modelling an angel for the grave, she discovered her talent for

sculpture. Soon she was holding exhibitions, and such famous figures as Asquith and Winston Churchill ordered busts, as did the first Soviet delegates to London in 1920. She was invited to return to Russia with them, to sculpt portraits of Lenin and Trotsky, which she did, despite the civil war. After two months in the Kremlin she returned home to mixed eulogy and abuse. Excerpts from her diary appeared in *The Times* and she found herself a journalist.

She covered the Irish Civil War, and the Turco-Greek war, and interviewed Mussolini and Ataturk. *Nuda Veritas* (1927) records such occasions. With her brother she travelled across south Russia on a motorbike, detailing the journey in *Across Europe with Satanella* (1925). Later came *A Turkish Kaleidoscope* (1926) and *Arab Interlude* (1936), describing life on the edge of the Sahara. In 1938 *Redskin Interlude* chronicled six months spent on a reservation carving portraits from tree stumps. In England she carved trees into church statuary and in 1942 became a Roman Catholic. *To the Four Winds* (1957) brought her autobiography up to date.   B.H.C.

Sheridan, Elizabeth (1754–92), singer. Richard Brinsley Sheridan was eighteen and staying with his father in Bath when he met and fell in love with Elizabeth Linley, then aged sixteen and already famous for her beauty and musical talents. Her father, the composer Thomas Linley, had arranged a marriage for her to an elderly gentleman of large fortune, but Miss Linley was much besieged by other suitors, notably Major Mathews, a married man with dishonourable intentions. The elderly gentleman of fortune, on being taken into her confidence, benevolently broke off the match and even settled £3000 on Miss Linley. Major Mathews, however, pursued his intentions with threats of suicide and blackmail. Harrassed, and afraid of her father, Miss Linley confided in Sheridan, who urged flight to France under his protection. Inevitably they married (1772) and after paternal wrath and a duel with Mathews, all parties were reconciled.

After her marriage Elizabeth sang only at private gatherings. Sheridan, with the help of her £3000, sought his independence in London as manager of Drury Lane and as a playwright, drawing amusingly on his courtship of Miss Linley in *The Rivals* (1774). Elizabeth assisted

361

her husband in the management of the theatre and in his political career, canvassing for him and for Charles James Fox in 1780. She was painted by both Gainsborough and Reynolds, and retained her extraordinary beauty until her death of consumption at the age of 38.

See also C. Black, *The Linleys of Bath*, new ed. 1971; M. Bor and L. Clelland, *Still the Lark: a Biography of Elizabeth Linley*, 1962.

C.H.

Sheridan, Frances (1724–66), novelist and playwright. Born Frances Chamberlaine in Ireland, the daughter of a clergyman, she wrote her first novel, *Eugenia and Adelaide*, at the age of fifteen. In 1747 she married Thomas Sheridan, manager of the Theatre Royal, Dublin, but financial difficulties forced their departure to London where Frances Sheridan's friends included Young, Dr Johnson, Richardson, Elizabeth MONTAGU, Sarah Scott, and Sarah FIELDING. Her novel *Sidney Biddulph* (1761) was published after her husband's unsuccessful attempt to re-establish himself in the Dublin theatre. Her first play, *The Discovery*, accepted by Garrick and successfully produced in 1763, was followed by a failure, *The Dupe*. In 1764 financial pressures forced the family to flee the country and they settled in France near Blois, where Frances Sheridan wrote a last novel, *Nourjahad*, before her death there in 1766. Among her seven children was the playwright Richard Brinsley Sheridan.

See also J. Boswell, *Life of Johnson*, ed. G. B. Hill, 1934.

A.L.

Sherwood, Mary Martha (1775–1851), writer. Mary Butt was born at Stanford, Worcestershire, the daughter of George III's chaplain. Educated strictly at home, she went in 1790 to a French school at Reading where among her contemporaries were Mary Russell MITFORD and Letitia Elizabeth LANDON, also writers. She married a cousin, Captain Henry Sherwood, in 1803 and lived in India from 1805 to 1816. There she wrote *The Infant's Progress* (1814), *Little Henry and his Bearer* (1815), and began *The History of the Fairchild Family: or, The Child's Manual* (1818–47), a three-part work which became a children's classic. *Little Henry and his Bearer* went through 100 editions up to 1884 and was translated into a dozen languages, while middle-class Victorian children were brought up on *The History of the Fairchild Family*. Despite some insight into the working of children's minds, her books are pious, didactic, and chillingly Calvinistic. Mrs Sherwood founded the first orphan asylum in India and adopted three orphans in addition to her own family of five.

B.H.C.

Shirreff, Emily (Anne Eliza) (1814–97), educationist, promoter of women's education and of the kindergarten system. The second daughter of Admiral Shirreff, Emily Shirreff was educated by a governess at home and briefly at a boarding school in Paris. The family followed their father to various postings in Europe, returning to England permanently in 1834. Miss Shirreff's formal education came to an end in her early teens and thereafter she was largely self-educated, following a regular daily plan of study. She published two books with her sister Maria GREY, *Passion and Principle* (1841), a novel, and *Thoughts on Self-Culture* (1850). Her views on women's secondary education are expounded in *Intellectual Education* (1858), which she wrote alone.

Miss Shirreff became actively involved in the campaign to improve women's education only in her fifties. In 1870 she was for a short time the principal of Emily Davies' college for women at Hitchin, the future Girton College, and after her resignation remained on its council. She was honorary secretary of the Women's Education Union, set up by her sister in 1871, and with G. C. T. Bartley, edited its periodical, *The Journal of the Women's Education Union*. She sat on the council of the Girls' Public Day School Company (later Trust) from 1872 to 1896 and was its Vice-President in 1896–97. She was also involved in the Teachers' Training and Registration Society. The main focus of Miss Shirreff's work, however, was the Froebel Society. She was present at its inauguration in 1874, and a year later became President, a position she held until her death. A training college for kindergarten teachers was started by the society in 1878, which later merged with the Maria Grey Training College. She wrote numerous articles and several books on the kindergarten system and presented several papers on education at the Social Science Association.

Other works include *The Kindergarten. Principles of Froebel's System and their Bearing on the Education of Women*, 1876; *The*

Kindergarten at Home, 1884; *Moral Training; Froebel and Herbert Spencer*,1892.

See also E. W. Ellsworth, *Liberators of the Female Mind*, 1979; M. Grey, *Memorials of Emily A. E. Shirreff, with a Sketch of her Life*, 1897.   K.C.

Shore, Jane (c. 1450–1526/7), mistress of King Edward IV. She was born Elizabeth Lambert, daughter of a London mercer, and was married young to another mercer, William Shore. In 1476, when Jane was already a royal favourite, a papal commission heard her suit for the annulment of her marriage on the grounds of William's impotence. Edward called Jane the merriest of his concubines. Sensual, witty, and well read, she was also generous in using her influence. One tradition holds that she persuaded Edward not to disendow Eton College, founded by the deposed Henry VI. On Edward's death in April 1483 Jane was protected by Lord Hastings, but in June he was executed for treason by Richard III. Jane was accused of sorcery and forced to do public penance as a harlot. Her next protector, the Marquess of Dorset, was also arraigned for treason and Jane was imprisoned. By 1487 she was married to Thomas Lynom, but she died in poverty and alone

See also N. Barker, 'the Real Jane Shore', in *Etoniana*, no. 125, 1972.   G.H.

Shrewsbury, Countess of. See TALBOT, ELIZABETH, COUNTESS OF SHREWSBURY.

Shuard, Amy (1924–75), singer. She was born in London and studied at Trinity College of Music before starting her career in South Africa. Returning to England in 1942, she was engaged by the Sadler's Wells opera, where she first appeared as Marguerite in *Faust*, and remained until 1955 when she joined the Covent Garden company to begin a brilliantly successful career there.

At Sadler's Wells she sang most of the leading lyric soprano parts, while at Covent Garden she made her reputation as a singer of international promise. Her Turandot in 1958 was the first by a British singer since the performance of her teacher Dame Eva Turner. Then came Wagnerian roles, as well as Lady Macbeth and Aïda. In 1964 she became the first English-born singer to perform the complete Brunnhilde cycle at Covent Garden. She appeared in Buenos Aires, San Francisco, Milan, as Brunnhilde in *Die Walküre* at the

Vienna State Opera, and in 1965 sang at Bayreuth. Her final appearance at Covent Garden was in 1974, in Janáček's *Jenufa*. Among the leading post-war British lyric and dramatic sopranos, she was one of the few outstanding interpreters of Turandot and Brunnhilde, while her dramatic ability and intense singing were also ideal for Janáček, many of whose parts she created in Britain.   B.H.C.

Siddons, Sarah (1755–1831), actress. Born in an inn at Brecon, Wales, she was the daughter of Roger Kemble and thus a member of a famous theatrical family. From the age of three, when she first appeared on stage, she belonged to her father's Company of Comedians touring the West Country, and attended school only when a long-running play held the family for some time in one town. After a two-year interlude in the service of the Greatheed family house, Guy's Cliffe near Warwick (1771–73), she returned to the stage. Against her family's wishes she married in 1773 a former player in her father's company, William Siddons, who then rejoined the Comedians. Together they joined the Chamberlain and Crump Company in 1774 and the Younger Company in 1775.

After a failed season at Garrick's Drury Lane theatre, Mrs Siddons returned to the provinces and from 1778 to 1782 was employed by the Theatre Royal, Bath, where she consolidated her reputation as a great tragic actress. When her fame reached London she was recalled for a second season at Drury Lane (1782) which was massively successful. Sarah Siddons was subsequently lionized as the most eminent actress of the age, befriended by Dr Johnson and Walpole and painted by Lawrence, Gainsborough, and most memorably by Reynolds in the pose of the Tragic Muse. Her definitive performances included Isabella in *The Fatal Marriage*, Belvidera in *Venice Preserv'd*, Constance in *King John*, Zara in *The Mourning Bride*, Desdemona in *Othello*, and, her most lauded role, Lady Macbeth. Her career after 1782 was pursued not only at Drury Lane but in tours of Ireland and appearances in Edinburgh. A farewell performance as Lady Macbeth in 1812 was followed by a return in 1819 as Lady Randolph in *Douglas*, in a benefit performance for her brother Charles. Her dramatic technique was considered by this point, however, to be regressively uniform and unenlivened. In fact, her

Sidgwick, Eleanor Mildred

1782 opening at Drury Lane marked the high point of her acting ability and the years following witnessed a steady decline in her power to move the audience.

Mrs Siddons had seven children, three of whom survived infancy. She died in 1831 of erysipelas.

See also K. Mackenzie, *The Great Sarah, The Life of Mrs Siddons*, 1968; B. Marinacci, *Leading Ladies, A Gallery of Famous Actresses*, 1961.   A.L.

Sidgwick, Eleanor Mildred (1845–1936). Principal of Newnham College, Cambridge. Born in East Lothian, she was eldest of the nine children of James and Blanche Balfour. Her family moved in political circles, associating with the Gladstones and the Cecils, and her younger brother Arthur later became prime minister. The children were raised by their mother who took considerable care with their education, considering it essential that both girls and boys should be properly informed. Her mother's teaching aroused that fascination with mathematics which was to last throughout Eleanor Balfour's life. She coached her brothers for their Cambridge entrance examination, and through them met Henry Sidgwick, then a lecturer at Trinity, later Professor of Moral Philosophy. They were married in 1876.

Dr Sidgwick was closely involved in attempts to establish a hall of residence for women students at Cambridge, and soon infected his wife with his enthusiasm for the cause of female education. When the woman's hall was built at Newnham, Mrs Sidgwick immediately committed herself to its administration. In 1876 she became treasurer, a post which she held until 1919, while accepting the office of Vice-Principal in 1880 and that of Principal itself in 1892. The flourishing state of Newnham at the time of her retirement owed much to her unobtrusive and untiring hard work. She also donated over £30,000 to college funds. Although a woman of considerable intellect, Mrs Sidgwick never took her degree, deciding it would interfere with her marital responsibilities. She continued to study, however, and during 1881–82 worked with her brother-in-law Lord Rayleigh in researching electrical standards of measurement.

Also interested in psychical phenomena, she was a founder member of the Society for Psychical Research, which was set up by her husband in 1882 to examine evidence of the supernatural by scientific means. She contributed frequently to the Society's *Proceedings* and *Journal*, and wrote an entry on spiritualism for the *Encyclopaedia Britannica*. She exposed numerous frauds, including Mme Blavatsky, the theosophist. Highly regarded as an expert on educational issues, Mrs Sidgwick sat on the Royal Commission on Secondary Education of 1903, one of the first women to be so appointed. A life-long believer in equality of educational opportunity for both sexes, she fought hard to persuade the Cambridge authorities to admit women students on the same basis as men. She strongly favoured the principle of female suffrage but considered militant suffragettes as misguided and dangerous, maintaining that their tactics made women appear violent and irresponsible, thus undermining the solid achievement of their more moderate sisters.

See also E. Sidgwick, *Mrs Henry Sidgwick*, 1938.   J.V.L.

Sidney, Mary, Countess of Pembroke (1561–1621), poet, translator, and patron of letters. She was the fifth child of Sir Henry Sidney and Lady Mary Dudley and was evidently well educated, proficient in French, Italian, and Latin, and able to play the lute. In her youth the family lived at Penshurst Manor and Ludlow Castle. Her father was Lord Deputy of Ireland from 1565, and the family spent a year there in 1570. From 1575 until her marriage two years later, Mary lived at court as a lady in waiting to Queen Elizabeth. Her husband, Henry Herbert, second Earl of Pembroke, was twenty-five years her senior and had been married twice before. His seat was Wilton House in Wiltshire, where their four children were born.

At Wilton began her active patronage of literature, attested by the numerous dedications of works to her. From 1580, when he was out of favour at court, her brother Sir Philip Sidney, poet, soldier, courtier, and one of the most famous men of his age, spent long periods at Wilton. At her urging he wrote *The Countess of Pembroke's Arcadia*, and his *Apology For Poetry* may also have been written there. His death in 1586 followed those of Sir Henry and Lady Mary Sidney earlier the same year.

In the following years, the countess engaged in a number of literary projects. Her translations of Philip du Plessis-Mornay's *A Discourse* of *Life and Death* and Robert Garnier's *The Tragedie of Antonie* were published together in 1592. The former was an important expression of the Calvinist Protestant ideology to which the Sidney circle adhered. The latter introduced into English drama a pseudo-classical Senecan tragedy which had been highly successful in France. Her translation provided an influential model for dramatists such as Kyd, Daniel, and perhaps Shakespeare. Following the appearance of an incomplete, pirated edition of her brother's *Arcadia*, in 1593 the countess edited and supervised publication of a new edition fulfilling Sidney's intentions. In 1598 she edited for publication his sonnet sequence *Astrophel and Stella*, and between 1586 and 1599 translated Petrarch's *The Triumph of Death*. From 1593 until about 1600 she was working on what she seems to have regarded, with justice, as her most important literary achievement. This was a translation of the Psalms which had been begun together with her brother, who completed the first forty-three. The Countess translated Psalms 44–150, the major part of the series both in length and quality. Her renderings display an extraordinary range of stanza forms, metres, and rhyme schemes in her attempt to unite theme and form.

After her husband's death in 1601, she spent some time with her brother Robert's family, and travelled abroad, apparently for her health. Much of her time was employed in managing the estates left to her by her husband, and dealing with problems created by her wayward sons. In 1615 she built a fine house, Houghton Lodge, near Ampthill, Bedfordshire. She died of smallpox in 1621 at her London home and was buried with her husband in Salisbury Cathedral.

Although remembered as a great patron of letters, Mary Sidney's own literary achievements have been overshadowed by her brother's work. Her contribution to literature and her wide-ranging intellectual activities make her the foremost representative of the learned Elizabethan ladies.

See also *The Psalms of Sir Philip Sidney and the Countess of Pembroke*, ed. J. A. C. Rathmell, 1963; F. B. Young, *Mary Sidney, Countess of Pembroke*, 1912.　　　W.R.O.

Simmonds, Martha (1624–65/7), Quaker. Martha was born in Somerset, the sister of a

radical publisher Giles Calvert. She later married the printer Thomas Simmonds of London and in 1654 became a Quaker. Her husband was also a convinced believer, publishing many early Quaker books. Martha Simmonds testified to her new beliefs by walking through the streets of London in sackcloth and ashes. In December 1655 she was imprisoned for speaking to a priest, and she suffered further imprisonment in 1657. By early 1656 her strong belief in the importance of following the promptings of the 'inner light' was coupled with a growing attachment to the Quaker leader James Nayler. With some other women she began to insist that Nayler, and not George Fox, was the most important Quaker leader. In July 1656 London Quakers sent Nayler to Bristol to escape from what they saw as Martha's damaging influence. Soon afterwards he was arrested and imprisoned at Exeter, and while there had a bitter and divisive meeting with Fox, who had come to visit him. By this time one of his followers had styled Nayler the 'only begotten Son of God', and Martha is supposed to have encouraged Nayler to accept this belief.

Nayler was released from Exeter jail on 20 October 1656 and four days later, along with eight other Quakers including Martha, reached Bristol. They entered the city in a fashion which mimicked Christ's entry into Jerusalem on Palm Sunday and the affair caused a national scandal. Nayler was found guilty of blasphemy by an incensed parliament, while the incident weakened Cromwell's policy of religious toleration. The Quakers were also severely damaged by the affair, and the subsequent divisions within the movement were still apparent twenty years later.

Martha Simmonds is seen as the prime mover in this episode, and as such had a profound influence on both the public reception of the early Quakers and the internal history of the movement. Her career also shows how religious beliefs could provide a sanction for unconventional female behaviour. There is evidence to suggest she was reconciled to the movement by 1659, and she is reported to have died in 1665 or 1667. Among her writings were *When the Lord Jesus came to Jerusalem* (1655) and *A Lamentation for the Lost Sheep of the House of Israel* (1655).

See also K. Carroll, 'Martha Simmonds, a Quaker enigma', in *Journal of the Friends Historical Society*, 53, 1972.　　　T.O.'M.

Simpson, Dame Florence (Edith Victoria)
(1874–1956), senior women's army officer. The
daughter of a lieutenant-colonel, she married
Captain Burleigh Leach, later Brigadier General Burleigh Leach CMG. The marriage was
dissolved after twenty-five years, and in 1922
Dame Florence married Edward Percy Simpson, a widower with two daughters. Her distinguished career began in 1915 when, without
any experience, she volunteered her services
as a cook with the Women's Legion. This
organization had been recently formed by the
Marchioness of Londonderry to provide 'a
capable and efficient body of women whose
services could be offered to the state, to take
the place of men needed in the firing line or
in other capacities'. She first worked at Sum-
merdown Convalescent Camp at Eastbourne,
but soon became Commandant of the Military
Cookery Section of the Legion, taking on more
and more catering for the army.

In February 1917 she was appointed Controller of Cooks, and in September brought all
7000 Women's Legion cooks and waitresses
into the Women's Army Auxiliary Corps which
had been formed earlier in the year. Later she
was appointed Controller of Recruiting to the
WAAC, and was awarded the CBE in the 1918
New Year Honours. In February 1918 she
became Chief Controller WAAC at the War
Office and in July was promoted Controller-
in-Chief (Major General), becoming the senior
officer of 57,000 women serving at home and
overseas. Meanwhile she had been received by
Queen Mary, who agreed to be their
Commandant-in-Chief, and in future the
Corps was known as Queen Mary's Army
Auxiliary Corps.

In the New Year Honours of 1919 Florence
Simpson was appointed DBE, the first Dame
Commander in the Military Division. When
the Queen Mary's Army Auxiliary Corps Old
Comrades Association was formed in 1919
Dame Florence was elected president. She
retired from QMAAC in 1920 and lived for
many years with her step-daughters in South
Africa. She died in a clinic in Switzerland.

D.R.M.P.

Sinclair, May (1870–1946), writer. She was
born in Cheshire and educated at Cheltenham
Ladies' College. Beginning her writing with
poetry and philosophical criticism, she published verse in 1887 and 1890. Her first novel,
Audrey Craven (1896), brought her recogni-

366

tion as a leading novelist and pioneer of the
'stream of consciousness' technique. With
Divine Fire (1904) she founded a reputation
for realism, being compared by some to Giss-
ing, while *The Creators* (1910) led to her
consideration as one of the leading writers of
the time.

An active feminist and suffragette, she
served during the First World War with a
field ambulance, an experience which produced *Journal of Impressions in Belgium*
(1915). She was an invalid for some years and
in later life grew interested in psychic phenomena. Herself a spiritualist, she wrote stories
with supernatural themes. In *The Three Sisters* (1914), *Divine Fire*, and *Anne Severn and
The Fieldings* (1922) she analyses character
with perception, and in *Mary Olivier; A Life*
(1919) explores the subconscious. *The Dark
Night* (1924) is a novel in verse while *Uncanny
Stories* (1923) and *The Intercessor* (1931) are
short stories. She also wrote metaphysical
essays and works on philosophical Idealism.

B.H.C.

Sitwell, Dame Edith (Louisa) (1887–1964),
poet and critic. The daughter of Sir George
and Lady Ida Sitwell of Renishaw, Derbyshire,
Edith was born in Scarborough and privately
educated. Her brothers Osbert and Sacheverell
were also writers. She held honorary doctorates
in Literature from Leeds, Durham, Oxford,
Sheffield, and Hull universities, and when
created DBE in 1954 was the first poet to be
thus honoured. In 1955 she became a Roman
Catholic.

Edith Sitwell has been described as the 'high
priestess of twentieth-century poetry'. The
description certainly accords with the nature
of her later verse, with its vatic if sometimes
confused and over-elaborate symbolism, and
with her physical appearance: she was nearly
six feet tall, with striking elongated features,
and fingers heavily-laden with rings. She spoke
of her affinity with Queen ELIZABETH I, and
affected a somewhat Tudor style of dress. Her
prose works include *Fanfare for Elizabeth*
(1946) and *The Queens and the Hive* (1962),
a study of Elizabeth and MARY QUEEN OF
SCOTS. Another book was *The English Eccen-
trics* (1933). Although she denied being an
eccentric herself, she was certainly a baroque
personality.

From 1916 to 1921 she edited *Wheels*, an

anthology of avant-garde poetry repudiating the gentle charms of Georgian verse. In 1923 her experimental poem-sequence *Façade* was given its first public performance at the Aeolian Hall in London, being intoned through a megaphone, from behind a curtain, to music by William Walton. The performance was greeted with uproar and derision. Noël Coward expressed the reaction in a mischievous revue-sketch parodying the original performance, and in a slim volume of eccentric verse, *Chelsea Buns*, by 'Hernia Whittlebot'; Edith and her brothers were deeply offended. Later poems of the decade included *Bucolic Comedies* (1923), *Elegy on Dead Fashion* (1926), and an attack on the evils in society, *Gold Coast Customs* (1929). The 1930s were devoted largely to works of criticism, including a study of *Alexander Pope* (1930), and a novel that took Swift as its subject, *I Live under a Black Sun* (1937). From the 1940s Dame Edith's poetry became more sombre and hieratic; *Three Poems for the Atomic Age* was inspired by news of the destruction of Hiroshima. Her autobiography *Taken Care Of* was published posthumously in 1965.

'Abstract patterns in sound' and 'experiments in texture' were two of her descriptions of *Façade*. She was to elaborate at length on the technical developments in her poetry, for example in the introduction to her *Collected Poems* (1957), but without always providing further illumination. It was certainly one of her achievements to gain acceptance for the synthesis of senses, and of sense, illustrated in such phrases as 'the creaking empty light', 'the rain squawks down', and 'decoy-duck dust'—phrases that were shocking innovations but are now part of generally accepted poetic idiom. She admired, and exercised an influence on, the work of Dylan Thomas.

See also *Selected Letters 1919–1964*, ed. J. Lehmann and D. Parker, 1970; J. Lehmann, *Edith Sitwell*, 1952; R. L. Megroz, *The Three Sitwells*, 1927; E. Salter, *The Last Years of a Rebel: a memoir of Edith Sitwell*, 1967; V. Glendinning, *Edith Sitwell: Unicorn Among Lions*, 1981.   J.L.

'Slasher Mary'. See RICHARDSON, MARY RALEIGH.

Slessor, Mary (Mitchell) (1848–1915), missionary. Born in Aberdeen, Mary Slessor was the second of seven children. Her father Robert Slessor was a shoemaker and her mother

Mary a weaver. Educated at Sunday School, when the family moved to Dundee in 1859 she became a 'half-timer' in a linen factory, alternating work with lessons. Family responsibilities and full-time work did not impair her commitment to the Church, however, and she began home missionary work in Dundee. In 1875 she volunteered for service in West Africa, and after three months' training started teaching in Duke Town, Calabar. Eager and active, she was frustrated by the conventions of the mission; she befriended natives and quickly became fluent in Efik.

On return from home leave in 1879, she was in sole charge at Old Town and her success brought praise from mission officials, who made an exception in allowing her to stay alone, setting the pattern for her later pioneering work. Her ambition to work among 'the untouched multitudes' inland was delayed by sick leave, the deaths of her mother and sisters, and mission deliberations. Finally in 1888 she moved to Ekenge to work with the Okoyong, and began fifteen years of fighting ritual human sacrifice, running schools and dispensaries, and adopting abandoned children. She became engaged in 1890 to a teacher eighteen years her junior, but his ill-health and her work prevented marriage. Appointed Vice-Consul in 1892, the 'White Ma' dispensed a commonsense justice with a sympathy for native traditions which deeply impressed Mary KINGSLEY on a visit in 1895. By 1897 the Okoyong had migrated and Miss Slessor transferred her mission to Akpap, but concern for peoples further inland made her move again, and in 1902 she began pioneering work with the Ibibios, spending the rest of her life travelling and setting up new stations in Enyong and Ibibio.

A fearless, independent missionary, Mary Slessor combined a strong faith and conviction in 'God's purpose' with an unconventional, down-to-earth approach. Her success, often in the face of danger to herself, made her a missionary heroine. In 1913 she was honoured by the Order of St John of Jerusalem, and a hospital and home for girls in Arochuku are named after her.

See also C. Christian and G. Plummer, *God and One Redhead: Mary Slessor of Calabar*, 1970; W. P. Livingstone, *Mary Slessor of Calabar, Pioneer Missionary*, 1915; United Free Church of Scotland, *Women's Missionary Magazine*, March 1915.   C.B.

Slingsby, Lady Mary (d. 1694), actress. She joined the Duke's Company under her maiden name of Aldridge in 1670, but almost immediately became Mrs Lee, probably through marriage to an insignificant actor, John Lee. Following his death, probably about 1677, she married in 1680 her second husband, who may have been Sir Charles Slingsby, a baronet of Bifrons in Patrixbourne, Kent. She continued to perform as Lady Slingsby, with a long list of impressive performances to her credit, until her retirement from the theatre in 1685. From all descriptions she was an exceedingly attractive and talented actress, who excelled in romantic and tragic roles. Lady Slingsby's career was all the more remarkable because she persevered in it even after acquiring a position and wealth.

See also J. H. Wilson, *All the King's Ladies*, 1958.   T.J.M.

Smith, Charlotte (1749–1806), novelist. She was the daughter of Nicholas Turner and Anna Towers. Her mother died in 1752, and in 1764 her father decided, prior to his second marriage, that a husband must be found for Charlotte. She subsequently married in 1765 Benjamin Smith, son of an East India Company director with whom they initially lived. Benjamin Smith's unstable and spendthrift character involved the couple in considerable difficulties. Part of the year in which Charlotte published her first work *Elegiac Sonnets and Other Essays* (1784) was spent in prison with her husband, who had been arrested for debt. In 1787, after the birth of twelve children, the couple finally separated. In the years following, her prodigious output, averaging four volumes a year, was largely determined by financial need. Many of the painful experiences of her private life found expression in these novels: her husband appeared as the villain Stafford in *Emmeline* (1788) and the rapacious lawyers who were involved in litigation over her father-in-law's will have their fictional counterparts in *The Old Manor House* (1793).

Charlotte's novels, like those of Eliza HAY-WOOD, serve as a summary index of the themes explored by her contemporaries. Her early works, *Emmeline*, *Ethelinde* (1789), and *Celestina* (1791), mark the emergence of a new type of heroine, secure enough in her own intelligence to remain unthreatened by exclusion from society. The heroines of these novels are further distinguished by their sensitivity to landscape, an emotion which Charlotte identified as characteristic of her own happy childhood at Bignor Park near the Arun river. Her probable influence on Wordsworth's early poetry stems from a similar attraction to wild, untamed scenery, and a shared belief that landscape stimulates the imagination. In *Desmond* (1792) she expressed the liberal viewpoint common to writers sympathetic with revolutionary activities in France. But as public sentiment turned against the French after 1793, her novels absorbed the predominant Burkean conservatism. *The Banished Man* (1794) thus reviles the new régime as tyrannical and salutes the British parliamentary system as guarantor of liberty. Her last novel, *The Young Philosopher*, was published in 1796, after which she confined her writing to didactic tales for children. Charlotte's poetry, especially the volume *Beachy Head*, published posthumously in 1807, is in the Romantic mode of Wordsworth and Coleridge, both of whom she met.

See also A. H. Ehrenpreis, 'Introduction' to *The Old Manor House*, 1969; A. K. Elwood, *Memoirs of the Literary Ladies of England*, vol. I, 1843.   A.L.

Smith, Elizabeth (1776–1806), poet and scholar. The daughter of a country gentleman, she was educated at home, largely by being let loose in her father's library at Burn Hall, near Durham. She began to learn French and Italian in 1786, and Arabic, Persian, and Latin in 1794. Hebrew followed in 1796. Her verse was undistinguished, and her moral judgements, on the upbringing of children, the bad effects of the French Revolution on behaviour, and upon the convergence of reason and revelation in human knowledge, are fairly conventional, although she makes some interesting points about Locke on the perceptions. She believed that learning in women was no bad thing, only the vanity that went with it. The philological productions of her short life are impressive, however. Extracted posthumously from her papers, these include translations from the Old Testament, including a highly-regarded version of the Book of Job (1810) and a Hebrew, Arabic, and Persian vocabulary, possibly the first production of its kind.   T.H.

Smith, Florence Margaret, known as Stevie (1902–71), poet and novelist. She was born in

Hull, but when she was three the family moved to her aunt's house in Palmers Green, London, where she lived for the rest of her life. Since her father was almost entirely absent from the family, and her mother, who suffered frequently from ill health, died when she was a child, the 'Lion' aunt became a figure of considerable importance in her life and appears frequently in her writing.

As a child she spent some time in hospital but was later educated at the North London Collegiate School for Girls. When she left, she went to work for Newnes-Pearson, the magazine publishers, where she became a private secretary until her retirement in the late 1950s. Her first attempt to have her poems published was in 1935, when she was told to 'go away and write a novel'. This she did, and *Novel On Yellow Paper* was published the following year. Her first volume of poems, *A Good Time was had by All*, was published in 1937 and established her reputation as a considerable poetic talent. She wrote only two more novels, *Over the Frontier* (1938), an extraordinary adventure story which also studies the psychology of war, and *The Holiday* (1949). Eight more collections of poems appeared, however, many of them illustrated by her own drawings. She was also a very popular reciter. Several recordings and broadcasts were made of her reading and singing her poetry to her own music, which was largely based on Gregorian chant and hymn tunes.

Both Stevie Smith's poetry and her novels are extremely personal and idiosyncratic in style, and she never regarded herself as part of any contemporary tradition. Although she admitted that her work was frequently written from 'struggle and melancholy', it is also distinguished by a very particular blend of wit and fantasy. She won the Cholmondeley Award for Poetry and, in 1969, the Queen's Gold Medal for Poetry. *Stevie* (1977), a stage play by Hugh Whitemore based on her life and writings, was later adapted into a successful film.

The Collected Poems of Stevie Smith, appeared in 1975, and subsequent reissues of her novels, and publication of uncollected writings (*Me Again*, 1981), indicate the quality and continuing relevance of her work.

J.M.

Smith, Lucy Toulmin (1838–1911), scholar. Born in Boston, Lucy was the daughter of Joshua Toulmin Smith, lawyer and reformer, who returned to England in 1842. She was educated at home, largely by her father, becoming his amanuensis at an early age. Between 1857 and 1865 she worked with him on his periodical *The Parliamentary Remembrancer*, and after his death concentrated on scholarship, where her early training proved invaluable. From 1870 she worked on the early English period, with a particular interest in editorship, and between 1906 and 1910 edited Leland's *Itinerary*. Among other important works were editions of the York Mystery Plays, and a number of texts for the Early English Text Society and the Camden and New Shakespeare Societies. In 1894 she became Librarian of Manchester College, Oxford, the first woman to head such a library. She held the post until her death, and her house in Oxford became a centre for scholarly meetings. Throughout her life she also maintained the importance of the traditional female accomplishments, believing that women's progress depended on a combination of the traditional and the new. She was skilled in the domestic arts and a keen gardener, for instance. Her ability as a scholar and editor left its mark both on the College and on those whom she helped.

J.R.

Smith, Maria Constance (?1853–1930), civil servant. Maria Constance Smith was one of the youngest of the ten children of Philip Smith, Professor of Classics and Ecclesiastical History at New College, Oxford. Educated at home, she later assisted her father with his researches. She joined the Savings Bank Department of the Post Office as a clerk in 1875, and, her exceptional abilities having been noted, she was appointed lady superintendent in 1876 at the age of twenty-three. The whole of her official career of thirty-seven years was passed in this department, over which she reigned supreme, and during the course of which the staff under her control grew from forty to 2000. M. C. Smith viewed her staff, the first women assigned to clerical duties in the Civil Service, as the nucleus from which other departments would in time draw their staffs. She therefore concentrated her energies on preparing for the expansion of the employment of women in clerical work. She emphasized strict attention to regulations and a high level of efficiency, in order to demonstrate that women were as capable as men.

Smith, Mary Harris

Eventually other government departments took for their budding clerical staffs women hand-picked by her.

These ambitions for women did not, however, rest on a belief in the absolute equality of men and women. M. C. Smith, who abstained from participation in the feminist movement, believed that in their work women should be segregated by class and occupation. She fought hard to retain the clerical grades as the exclusive preserve of middle-class women (and against penetration by the working- and lower-middle-class women already in sorting and telegraphist grades). She also strove to keep women in self-contained sections in order to avoid contact with male civil servants and the public. In her dealings with male colleagues at the most senior level she maintained the utmost reserve. While insisting on her powers and independence, she nevertheless refrained from claiming for herself the public attributes of her position. A more discreet role was in her opinion more satisfying. She was, however, awarded the Imperial Service Medal in 1902, one of the first women to be so honoured. She retired in 1913 and went to live at Folkestone.

See also H. Martindale, *Women Servants of the State, 1870-1938: A History of Women in the Civil Service,* 1938.   M.Z.

Smith, Mary Harris (1847–1934), first woman chartered accountant. The daughter of a banker who recognized and encouraged her talents, Mary Harris Smith was sent at the age of sixteen to King's College, London, to study mathematics. There she proved a brilliant student and went on to work as an accountant in commerce while building up a practice of her own, a thing unheard of for a woman at the time. In 1888 she applied for membership of the Institute of Chartered Accountants and was refused on the legalistic grounds that the words 'he' and 'his' in the Charter did not encompass 'she' or 'her'. When the question of her membership was raised again in 1895, the President, Charles Fitch Kemp, claimed that to manage a staff composed partly of women would be so embarrassing that he would rather retire from the profession than contemplate it.

It was the other professional body, the Society of Chartered Accountants, which in 1918 finally changed its rules to allow women to join. This, however, was not immediately to Miss Harris Smith's advantage, for the reorganization involved the Society in giving up its powers, long fallen into disuse, of electing members, directly without examination, in special cases. Her first application officially to join her profession having been turned down by the Institute thirty-one years before, it now looked as if Miss Harris Smith would be unsuccessful with the Society. In fact, they made her an Honorary Fellow and it was another two years before any woman was admitted by examination. The Sex Disqualification (Removal) Act of 1919 forced the Institute to follow the Society and open its doors to women. Mary Harris Smith renewed her application of 1888 and was made a Fellow, to become, in 1919, the first woman chartered accountant in the world.

See also A. A. Garrett, *History of the Society of Incorporated Accountants, 1885-1957,* 1961.   E.M.V.

Smith, Sarah (1832–1911), author who wrote under the name of Hesba Stretton. She was born in Shropshire. Her father Benjamin Smith was a bookseller and publisher, and his wife Anne held strong evangelical views. Sarah Smith thus took over from her parents the two preoccupations that dominated her life: writing and religion. She was educated at a girls' day school, but also read her father's stock avidly. She never married, maintaining a somewhat austere way of life.

Sarah began writing young, without thought of publication. Her sister Elizabeth, who was Sarah's lifelong companion and admirer, then sent *The Lucky Leg* to Dickens in 1859. After its appearance in *Household Words,* Sarah embarked on her career as one of the most prolific and popular Victorian girls' authors. She adopted the name Hesba Stretton for greater distinction, using it in private and public life thereafter. Although sentimental and extremely pious, her works also revealed a personal knowledge of slum conditions. She was a friend of Baroness BURDETT-COUTTS and helped in various charitable works, taking a prominent part in founding the London Society for the Prevention of Cruelty to Children (1884). Her first love remained writing, however, and through it she supported herself and her sister. *Jessica's First Prayer* (1866) brought her greatest fame: constantly in print long after her death, and translated into many languages.   J.R.

Smith, Stevie. See SMITH, FLORENCE MAR-
GARET known as STEVIE.

Smithson, Harriet (Constance) (1800–54),
actress. Little is known of the early life of this
Irish actress of startling beauty and promise
who accompanied Kemble to Paris (1827) after
playing opposite Kean in London. At the Salle
Favart she was acclaimed for her Shakespearean heroines; critics said that she had 'revealed
Shakespeare to France'. The composer Hector
Berlioz saw her and fell instantly in love with
'his Ophelia'. She toured France before playing opposite Macready in *Macbeth* (1828),
when she had another unprecedented success.

Knowing little French, she was restricted to
dumb roles in French productions, and the
Opéra-Comique engaged her as the dumb
Cécilia in *L'Auberge d'Auray*, but the directors absconded without paying her. Replying
to her pathetic appeal, the Minister of the
Interior answered that 'the Ministry has no
money for this purpose'. Then Berlioz, volatile
and jealous, hearing 'horrible truths' (later
disproved), became engaged to another,
although he was jilted within months. Harriet,
having renounced him in return, met him
again and they married at the British Embassy
on 3 October 1833. They had one son. Berlioz
made Harriet renounce the stage, but her
frustration, allied to her jealousy of his philan-
dering with his professional colleagues, eventually caused them to part in 1844. Poor and
with her looks gone, Harriet sought oblivion
in alcohol. She died in Paris.   A.D.

Smyth, Dame Ethel (1858–1944), composer
and suffragette. A colourful character in the
history of British music, Ethel Smyth was the
daughter of General J. H. Smyth. For a short
time in 1877 she studied music at Leipzig
Conservatory, and two of her works, a string
quintet and a violin-and-piano sonata, were
performed in Leipzig with success in 1884 and
1887 respectively. Ethel Smyth, the feminist,
well expressed the average male attitude to
women musicians in the 'myth' used as an
introduction to her book *Female Pipings in
Eden*. According to this, 'The legend relates
that one afternoon while Adam was asleep,
Eve, anticipating the great god Pan, bored
some holes in a hollow reed and began to do
what is called "pick out a tune". Thereupon
Adam awoke: "Stop that horrible noise", he
roared, adding, after a pause, "Besides which,

if anyone's going to make it, it's not you but
me".'

Her musical career was a remarkably successful one. The *Serenade in D* was performed
at the Crystal Palace in 1890, and an overture,
Antony and Cleopatra, appeared the same
year. The following year her *Mass in D* was
performed in the Albert Hall and she was
established as the most important woman composer of her time, perhaps of any time up to
that date. Surprise was expressed by male
critics at the lack of 'femininity' in her music,
which, thoroughly professional in construction
and orchestration, was accorded the unexpected adjective 'virile'. In spite of its success,
the Mass was not performed again until 1924,
but by this time Ethel Smyth had made her
name—largely as an ardent suffragette—and
had been awarded an Honorary DMus, and in
1922 made a DBE. She was also established as
an important figure in the world of opera,
although it is salutary to remember that her
most important work in this medium, *The
Wreckers*, reached England in 1909 having
been produced in Leipzig (as *Standrecht*) and
in Prague, with considerable success, three
years previously. During the earlier part of
her career she lived largely on the Continent,
but with the success of *The Wreckers* her
name was made in her own country, and she
returned home.

For some time this name was connected
with suffragette notoriety rather than musical
fame, perhaps stimulated by stories of her in
prison, conducting fellow suffragettes in her
'March of the Women' from her cell window
with a toothbrush. (The theme of this march
came from the overture to her other well-
known opera, *The Boatswain's Mate*, produced by Beecham at the Shaftesbury Theatre
in 1916.)

See also S. Sadie, (ed.), *The New Grove
Dictionary of Music and Musicians*, 1981.
                                            R.G.

Sokolova, Lydia (1896–1974), ballerina. Born
Hilda Munnings in Wanstead, she was a niece
of Sir Alfred Munnings, President of the Royal
Academy. She trained with Pavlova and began
her career in 1911 with Mikhail Mordkin's
company, touring America. She then danced
with Feodor Kosloff at the Coliseum.

In 1913 she became the first English girl to
join Diaghilev's Ballets Russes, the company
completely accepting her as one of themselves.

Diaghilev himself showed special affection for, and trust in, her. She remained with him except for short periods until his death in 1929, when her own career virtually ended. Sokolova was closely connected with Massine's ballets; the choreographer created for her the role of Kikimora in *Contes Russes* and the tarantella in *La Boutique Fantasque*, and cast her as 'the chosen maiden' in *The Rite of Spring*. She was tremendously successful in this last arduous part, showing great dramatic force. She also danced frequently for Fokine. In 1935 she emerged from retirement to join Leon Woizokovski's company, and did so again (1962) for Massine's revival of *The Good Humoured Ladies*. Her memoirs, *Dancing for Diaghilev*, (1960) demonstrate her humour and relate many stories about the company. Sokolova's success showed that it was possible for an English dancer to be the equal of the hitherto supreme Russians.　　　　A.D.

Somerset, Lady Isabella (1851–1921), temperance campaigner. Isabella Somers-Cocks was the eldest daughter of Earl and Countess Somers. She was educated by a succession of governesses, learning French, Italian, German, and other fashionable accomplishments. As a girl she read widely, particularly enjoying the works of Macaulay and J. S. Mill. Courted by a number of suitors, she accepted Lord Henry Somerset whom she married in 1872. A son was born in 1874 but shortly afterwards Lady Somerset was separated from her husband on account of his promiscuous homosexuality. 'Cut' by polite society, she returned to her parents' house where she led an increasingly intense spiritual life. Attracted by Methodism, she was also interested in temperance, and in 1887 took the Pledge along with the rest of her household.

Although she initially disliked public speaking, Lady Somerset disciplined herself to address local meetings on abstinence, and soon developed an easy, persuasive manner. She undertook a series of lecture tours, usually in working-class districts, living among her audiences as a guest in their homes. She would preach anywhere, on one occasion addressing miners at the coal-face. In 1890 she was appointed President of the British Women's Temperance Association. She visited America the following year, addressing large and enthusiastic crowds, and on her return to Britain gave impressive evidence to the Royal Com-

mission on the Liquor Licensing Laws. She also worked hard for the Liberal election campaign, with which the temperance cause was closely associated. Her most famous work began in 1895, when she established a Home for Female Inebriates at Duxhurst in Surrey. Women spent up to a year at the establishment, where they were cured of their addiction and encouraged to regain their self-respect.

Although she was elected President of the World Women's Christian Temperance Union in 1898, Lady Somerset's public career thereafter suffered some reverses. Her rejection of prohibition made her unpopular among some temperance workers while her open discussion of the Social Purity issue in 1897 outraged the sensibilities of many more. Lady Somerset resigned as President of the BWTA in 1903 and declined to stand for re-election to the WWCTU in 1906. The author of numerous articles on temperance, she also edited *The Women's Herald*, organ of the WWCTU, and established *The Women's Signal* to promote the general cause of women's work.

See also K. Fitzpatrick, *Lady Henry Somerset*, 1923.　　　　J.V.L.

Somerville, Edith Anna Œnone (1858–1949), novelist. Born in Corfu where her father, a soldier, was stationed, she returned in 1859 with her family to their home at Drishane, County Cork. She was educated at Alexandra College, Dublin, and studied painting in London, Paris, and Düsseldorf. Until she met her cousin Violet MARTIN her chief interests were horses and painting. She had one-woman exhibitions in London and New York and was the first female Master of Foxhounds.

The meeting with her cousin in 1886 was described by Edith Somerville as 'the hinge of my life, the place where my fate and hers turned over'. Their first book signed 'Somerville and Ross' was *An Irish Cousin* (1889). When 'Ross' died (1915) they had published fourteen titles, including the very popular *Experiences of an Irish R.M.* (1899). Edith Somerville believed that her cousin's death caused no break in the partnership and that she still received help and inspiration from her.

A woman of tremendous energy, Edith Somerville shared in the management of a farm, was organist at the parish church for seventy-five years, founded and directed the Castlehaven Nursing Association, and chaired the Munster Women's Franchise League. She received an Hon. DLitt from Dublin University and the Gregory gold medal from the Irish Academy of Letters (1941). She died at Drishane. Other works include *The Real Charlotte* (1894) and *The Big House at Inver* (1925).

See also G. Cummins, *Dr. E.O. Somerville*, 1952; M. Collis, *Somerville and Ross*, 1968.

P.L.

Somerville, Mary (1780–1872), writer on science. Born in Jedburgh, Scotland, she was the fifth of the seven children of Vice-Admiral Sir William Fairfax. Her only formal education was received at a fashionable boarding school in Musselburgh, which she attended for one year. This was supplemented by private study and first-hand observation of nature. In 1804 she married her cousin, Samuel Greig, captain in the Russian navy, who had little sympathy with her scientific interests. His early death in 1807 gave her the independence and means she needed to educate herself. Ignoring the ridicule of relatives and acquaintances, she found time from domestic and social obligations to read Newton's *Principia* and study higher mathematics and physical astronomy. She received advice and encouragement from Edinburgh intellectuals, including William Wallace, later Professor of Mathematics at Edinburgh University. In 1812 she married another cousin, William Somerville, an army doctor, who supported his wife's intellectual aspirations and took pride in her achievements. He encouraged her to systematize her studies and take up Greek, botany, geology, and mineralogy.

In 1816 the family moved to London, where they associated with the foremost scientific and literary figures. Mrs Somerville's first published work described experiments she had designed and carried out on the magnetizing effect of sunlight. It appeared in *Philosophical Transactions of the Royal Society*, vol 116 (1826). This paper was widely praised and, although its conclusions were later disproved, gave impetus to further investigation of the alleged phenomenon. Her first book, *The Mechanism of the Heavens* (1831), an English version of Laplace's *Mécanique Céleste*, received excellent reviews, sold well, and was used at Cambridge for advanced courses. Even higher acclaim was accorded *On the Connexion of the Physical Sciences* (1834), a consideration of the mutual dependence of the physical sciences, and *Physical Geography* (1848). Honours bestowed upon her in recognition of these publications included a civil pension, election to scientific societies in Britain and abroad, and the award of the Victoria Gold Medal of the Royal Geographical Society. Her final work, *On Molecular and Microscopic Science* (1869), was already outdated on publication but was nevertheless received with deferential interest by the public.

Through her writings Mrs Somerville brought before a wider public the newest and most authoritative scientific ideas of the time. She was always an advocate of higher education for women and of women's suffrage, causes which were advanced by her example. Somerville College, Oxford, founded in 1879, is named after her.

See also *Personal Recollections from Early Life to Old Age of Mary Somerville*, ed. M. Somerville, 1873; E. C. Patterson, *Mary Somerville 1780–1872*, 1979.

S.G.

Somerville, Mary (1897–1963), radio producer. Born in New Zealand, the daughter of a clergyman, she was educated at the Abbey School, Melrose, and Selkirk High School. She went up to Somerville College, Oxford, where she took her degree in English in 1925. In the same year she joined the BBC, where she worked for thirty years, eventually becoming Controller of Talks.

Mary Somerville is probably best remembered for her contribution to school broadcasting, which was established largely as a result of her zeal. She saw the enormous potential of radio for educational purposes and fought hard to convince sceptics and win allies in her cause. Convinced that education must be a reciprocal process, she realized that the BBC had to know the reactions of the listening children, and in 1926 a project financed by the Carnegie Trust provided the data which set the pattern for schools broadcasting as a partnership between the BBC, the then Board of Education and local Education Authorities, and school teachers.

In 1928 she married Ralph Penton Brown and had one son. The marriage was dissolved in 1945 and in 1962 she married E. Rowan Davies. She received an OBE in 1935 and an Honorary MA from Manchester University in 1943. A superb producer, she had a wide-ranging influence over radio production all her working life and even into her retirement, when the BBC asked her to make regular appraisals of their programmes.　　E.M.V.

Southcott, Joanna (1750–1814), prophetess. Born at Tarford, Devonshire, the fourth daughter of an unsuccessful farmer, Joanna Southcott worked as a domestic servant and later as an upholsteress. As a young woman she rejected numerous proposals of marriage and determined to remain single. She was brought up as an Anglican, but became spiritually restless after her mother's death, and briefly attended Methodist services at Exeter. In 1792 she began to hear divine voices which supplied her with her first prophecies. Although she had no formal education, she resolved to write these down and seal them up for later reference. Between 1792 and 1814 she produced some sixty-five pamphlets and a quantity of unpublished material, much of which was autobiographical. Her first published work, *The Strange Effects of Faith*, appeared in 1801, financed from her own meagre savings. This attracted her first believers, a small circle with established millennarian sympathies, including two Anglican clergymen and the engraver William Sharp. Encouraged by her followers, she visited London in 1802, and from 1804 until her death lived there in the house of the wealthy Jane Townley, who acted as her patron and secretary.

In 1802 she received instructions to begin 'sealing' true believers. Converts signed a petition calling for the establishment of Christ's kingdom on earth, and were presented with a seal as a token of their faith. In 1803 tours in the North and West were undertaken, and Southcottian congregations established there. About 14,000 seals had been issued by 1807, but the practice declined after 1809, when the witch and murderess Mary Bateman was alleged to have been associated with a Yorkshire congregation.

Southcottian theology appealed strongly to women, who formed the majority of Miss Southcott's following. She stressed the importance of woman's role in the Bible and argued that just as woman had been responsible for the Fall, she would also be the instrument by which mankind would be saved. It was not until 1814 that her own role in the expected Second Coming became clear to Miss Southcott. In March she announced that she was to give birth to Shiloh, the anticipated Messiah. She developed all the symptoms of pregnancy,

and although she was then sixty-four years old, six of the nine doctors who examined her thought her pregnant. She grew steadily weaker throughout the winter, and died on 27 December. An autopsy was performed, but no evidence of a pregnancy found.

Miss Southcott was perhaps the most influential of many prophets and visionaries who fascinated the popular imagination during the unsettled first decades of the early nineteenth century. By providing a divine answer to apparently insoluble worldly problems, she offered her followers both solace and hope. A Southcottian society still exists today, and occasionally advertises Miss Southcott's writings. Among her works was *Divine and Spiritual Communications* (1803).

See also J. Fairburn, *Life of Joanna Southcott*, 1814; J. F. C. Harrison, *The Second Coming*, 1979.　　J.V.L.

Southern, Elizabeth (d. 1612), witch. Elizabeth Southern, known as 'Old Demdike', headed a whole family of witches active in the remote forest region of Pendle, Lancashire. By 1612 she was reputedly eighty years old, and blind. She had been a witch for half a century and besides initiating her daughter and grandchildren as witches, had instructed a neighbour, Anne Whittle, who then ungratefully set up with her family as rival practitioners. In April 1612 local complaints led Roger Nowell, a Puritan Justice of the Peace, to commit the two old women to prison in Lancaster, along with a granddaughter of each. Several of Old Demdike's relatives then held a meeting with other witches in Pendle Forest, allegedly to plot the blowing up of Lancaster Gaol. They, too, soon arrived at the same prison, chiefly on the evidence of Janet Device, Southern's nine-year-old granddaughter. Most of the Southern family confessed to witchcraft and eagerly incriminated one another. Elizabeth Southern died in prison before the trial in August 1612, but some ten witches were executed. They included her rival Whittle and Whittle's daughter, and Elizabeth's own daughter, granddaughter, and grandson.

This sort of mass activity is not usual in English witchcraft, (compare the case of Elizabeth CLARKE), but accusations against Elizabeth Southern reveal a common pattern in witchcraft persecution. One allegation was that she had caused the death of a daughter of Richard Baldwin, a local mill-owner. Baldwin had turned Elizabeth and her daughter off his land, calling them 'witches' and 'whores' when they had gone to demand payment for work done at the mill. Guilt at unkindly acts against marginal members of local society, and fear of their revenge, often prompted witchcraft accusations.

See also E. Peel and P. Southern, *The Trials of the Lancashire Witches*, 1969.   A.H.

Speght, Rachel (*fl.* 1617), feminist controversialist. Very little is known about the personal life of Rachel Speght; a fellow author described her as a minister's daughter, and her father was possibly one Thomas Speght. She was probably under twenty in 1617. She is important as a participant in the controversy occasioned by Joseph Swetnam's *The Arraignment of Lewd, Froward and Unconstant Women* (1615), an hysterical outburst of misogyny which characterized all women as 'ungrateful, perjured, full of fraud, flouting and deceit, unconstant, waspish, toyish, light, sullen, proud, discourteous and cruel'. This immensely popular work (with ten editions by 1634) stimulated four direct replies besides a play, *Swetnam the Woman-hater, arraigned by Women*, published in 1620. One reply was by a man, Daniel Tuvil, and two others presumably by women, using pseudonyms. The last was Rachel Speght's *A Mouzell for Melastomus, the Cynicall Bayter of and Foule Mouthed Barker against Evah's Sex: or an Apologetical Answere to the Irreligious and Illiterate Pamphlet made by Jo. Sw.* (1617). This work contains some grand attacks on arguments quoting the Bible to support the theory of women's inferiority, but on the whole Speght's argument is directed against the intemperance and comprehensiveness of Swetnam's attack on women. She accepted that 'man is the woman's head' and that man should protect woman as 'the weaker vessel'. Indeed it was dissatisfaction with the mildness of Speght's rebuke to Swetnam that prompted a pseudonymous woman author, Esther Sowernam, to join the fray with her more robust *Esther hath hang'd Haman* (1617). However, it is difficult to imagine how a thorough-going defence of women's equality could have been constructed within the ideological framework of the early seventeenth century, and Speght, with her two unknown sisters, was among the earliest public female defenders of women from misogynist attacks. Moreover, the whole Swetnam controversy suggests that literate women at least were more assertive and threatening than their formal inferiority would suggest.

See also C. Camden, *The Elizabethan Woman*, 1952; C. Crandall, *Swetnam the Woman-Hater*, 1969.   A.H.

Spence, Catherine Helen (1825–1910), reformer and author. She was born in Scotland, the daughter of a lawyer and banker who emigrated to South Australia in 1839 as a result of financial difficulties. Her ambition was to be a great writer, and she published a number of novels including *Clara Morison* (1854), the first novel about Australia written by a woman. These works were only moderately received, largely because of the socialist political ideas that increasingly appeared in them. However, she won respect as a literary critic and social commentator in both Australian and British journals. She became keenly interested in the political future of South Australia, and in the political destiny of its women. As a result she began to campaign and to write pamphlets in favour of proportional representation, soon being acknowledged as an accomplished speaker.

From 1891 she campaigned more specifically for women's suffrage, becoming a vice-president of the Women's Suffrage League of South Australia, and when women there were enfranchised in 1894, she carried on the fight elsewhere. In 1895 she founded the Effective Voting League of South Australia, and in 1897 was Australia's first female political candidate. Although never elected, she was an important influence on the political system, providing an inspiration for later Australian women. Religion was also an important factor in her life: in later years she preached as a Unitarian. Interested in social conditions, particularly those of children, in 1872 she helped to form the Boarding-Out Society to place orphaned and destitute children in families. She herself raised three families of orphans.

See also her *Autobiography*, ed. J. F. Young, 1910; L. S. Morice, *Life and Work of Catherine Helen Spence*, 1978.   J.R.

Spiers, Dorothy Beatrice (1897–1977), first woman actuary. She was the second of three daughters of a headmaster of the Jewish Free School, and was educated at Wilton Road School and the City of London Girls' School.

From there she went to Newnham College, Cambridge, where she read mathematics, receiving her degree in 1918. She then worked in the Guardian Insurance Company, studying in her spare time for the actuarial examinations and qualifying as a Fellow of the Institute of Actuaries in 1923, the first woman ever to do so. She made a positive contribution to the meetings of the Institute of Actuaries, where it is customary to invite newly-qualified actuaries to open the discussion. This she did in March 1926. In 1931 she married Henry Michael Spiers, and from then onwards devoted herself primarily to her home, husband, and two sons. She did not, however, lose touch with the profession and worked part-time with the Guardian until the war, when she worked for the Eagle Star, returning to the Guardian in 1946 until 1954.

Dorothy Spiers had wide-ranging interests outside the actuarial profession, and devoted much time and energy after 1955 to the League of Jewish Women, where she was a member of the Council and National Treasurer. In her work for the League, her helpful commonsense was noted, as well as her mathematical ability. She clearly also brought these attributes to her professional life where she was such an eminently successful pioneer for women in the actuarial sphere.   E.M.V.

Spry, Constance (1886–1960), author, cook, and flower-arranger. Born in Derby, she was educated in Ireland, where she spent her youth. During the First World War she worked for the Ministry of Aircraft Production and did welfare work in the East End. It was towards the late 1920s that she began to work with flowers. She opened a little shop at Victoria (1929), and then a larger one in Burlington Gardens, followed by one in South Audley Street. By now she was also chairman of the Constance Spry Flower School. Her passion was for plants, and she was greatly aware of them as 'living things', her own garden being filled with rare and beautiful specimens. Constance Spry also loved organizing grand occasions, from gala performances at Covent Garden to state occasions including Queen Elizabeth II's wedding and coronation, when she was adviser to the Ministry of Works on flower decoration in the Westminster Abbey annexe and on the processional route. For this work she was awarded the OBE (1953).

Her work in cookery led her to become joint-principal of the Cordon Bleu Cookery School, and to her most ambitious venture, at Winkfield Place, Berkshire, where girls were trained in the arts of entertaining, cooking (English and French), choosing wines, and creating beautiful homes. Her one criterion was beauty, and she expressed this in all the versatile aspects of her work, from flower-arrangements to cookery. Among her publications were *A Garden Notebook* (1940) and *The Constance Spry Cookery Book* (1956, with Rosemary Hume).

See also E. Coxhead, *Constance Spry*, 1975.
A.D.

Standing, Dorothy Katharine. See HAMMOND, KAY.

Stanhope, Lady Hester (Lucy) (1776–1839), traveller. She was born at Chevening, Kent, the eldest daughter of Charles, third Earl Stanhope, and his wife, Hester Pitt. From 1803 to 1806 she acted as housekeeper and confidante to her uncle, William Pitt the Younger, and during the invasion scare of 1803 was made honorary Colonel of the Berkshire Militia and the 15th Light Dragoons. In 1809 she suffered the deaths at Corunna of Sir John Moore, her favourite suitor, and her half-brother, Charles. To restore her health she left England the following year and travelled through the Levant, becoming in 1813 the first European woman to visit Palmyra.

In 1814 Lady Stanhope settled at Mar Elias, a convent on the foothills of Mount Lebanon, moving soon after to Dar Djoun, a hilltop monastery nearby. She increasingly adopted Eastern customs and, dressed in the attire of a Turkish male, held court over her retinue of servants. Her growing interest in astrology led the credulous to ascribe prophetic powers to her, while her fearless horsemanship excited the admiration of the Arabs. In political affairs, her influence was exerted to uphold the authority of the Turkish Sultan against the usurpations of his rebellious vassals, the Emir Bechir, Prince of the Druses, and Mehemet Ali, Pasha of Egypt. She gave sanctuary to the Europeans who sought her protection following the battle of Navarino in 1827, and to some 200 refugees from the siege of Acre in 1832.

Her final years, which were spent in seclusion, were clouded by impoverishment produced by her charitable munificence and financial mismanagement; in 1838 the British government appropriated her crown pension to satisfy the demands of a creditor, a blow from which she never recovered. Lady Stanhope died 23 June 1839 at Dar Djoun, where she was buried. She had little of the explorer or the antiquarian in her, and her travels were mostly undertaken in the search for health and the acquisition of a romantic celebrity among the orientals.

See also I. Bruce, *The Nun of Lebanon*, 1951; Duchess of Cleveland, *The Life and Letters of Lady Hester Stanhope*, 1897; J. Haslip, *Lady Hester Stanhope*, 1934; C. L. Meryon, *Memoirs of the Lady Hester Stanhope*, 3 vols, 1845, and *Travels of Lady Hester Stanhope*, 3 vols, 1846; J. Watney, *Travels in Araby of Lady Hester Stanhope*, 1975.

M.J.S.

Stannard, Henrietta (Eliza Vaughan) (1856–1911), writer under the pseudonym of John Strange Winter. She was born in York, daughter of a rector called Palmer who had been a Royal Artillery officer and whose family had produced generations of soldiers. She was educated at Bootham House School, York, and in 1874 began writing under the pseudonym of Violet Whyte, for *The Family Herald*. Over ten years she wrote forty-two short stories and many long serials for this journal, mainly on the theme of military life. *Cavalry Life* (1881) and *Regimental Legends* (1883) were published under the name of John Strange Winter, a character from *Cavalry Life*, and it was generally assumed that these were the work of a cavalry officer. She wrote *Houp-la* (1885) and *Bootle's Baby: a story of the Scarlet Lancers* (1888), which sold two million copies in its first ten years. She was first president of the Writers' Club (1892) and president of the Society of Women Journalists (1901–03). Ruskin, an admirer of her work, declared that to her 'we owe the most finished and faithful rendering ever yet given of the character of the British soldier'. She died, as a result of an accident, aged 55.

B.H.C.

Stansfield, Grace. See FIELDS, (DAME) GRACIE.

Stansfield, Margaret (1860–1951), pioneer of physical training for women. Born in London, the daughter of a baker, she became a student teacher after attending Bloomsbury dayschool. She trained under Madame Osterberg in Hampstead, and her first teaching post was at Bedford High School, which lacked gymnastic equipment and had only a gravel playground. With vision and enthusiasm, as well as a powerful vocabulary, she set about campaigning to build a permanent gymnasium and managed also to acquire a splendid playing-field.

Margaret Stansfield founded the Bedford Physical Training College in 1902, sending her students all over the world. She left the High School in 1918, but remained interested in physical education all her life, displaying an outstanding grasp of its practice and theory. She insisted always on the very best, believing that health education should be part of the general curriculum. At the age of eighty-nine she returned to guide her old college on the sudden death of its principal, showing her usual generosity and courage.

A.D.

Stark, Helen (?–1543), Protestant martyr. One of the earliest Scottish Protestant martyrs, Helen Stark, or Stirke, was executed by drowning in Perth. She was among a number of heretics condemned there at the visitation of Cardinal David Beaton, Archbishop of St Andrews, in January 1543. She was charged with having refused to call upon the Virgin Mary in childbirth, and with having claimed that the Virgin had no special qualities which made her superior to other women. Helen's husband, James Ranoldsone, or Rannelt, was condemned with her. They seem to have been a devoted couple, for Helen appealed, unsuccessfully, to be allowed to share her husband's bonds and his death by hanging. The townspeople sought to save the accused, but to no avail, since the local priests refused to intercede for any found guilty of such crimes. Helen left several children, including her baby, to the care of the townspeople.

Helen's religious beliefs, though perhaps not definitively Protestant, were strong enough to cause her death, and thus give her a prominent place in Scottish martyrologies.

See also J. Foxe, *Acts and Monuments*, 1653; A. R. Macewen, *A History of the Church in Scotland*, 1913–18.

J.S.

Starkie, Enid Mary (1897–1970), scholar. Daughter of W. J. M. Starkie, the distinguished classicist and Resident Commissioner of National Education for Ireland, Enid Starkie was educated at Alexandra College, Dublin, and Somerville College, Oxford. In 1920 she gained a first-class degree in French, with

377

distinction in the colloquial use of the language. From 1921, as Gilchrist Student, she studied at the Sorbonne; the hardship of her life at this time was itself reflected in later life in her habits of rigorous personal economy. In 1927 a thesis on Émile Verhaeren gained her the Doctorate of the University of Paris with the highest distinction, as well as a prize from the French Academy. From 1925 to 1928 she taught at University College, Exeter, and in 1928 returned to Somerville as the first Sarah Smithson Lecturer in French Literature. In 1933 she gained a university lectureship, and in 1934 was elected Fellow and Tutor of her College. In 1939 she was awarded the first Doctorate of Letters conferred in her faculty, and from 1946 to 1965 was University Reader in French Literature. The post of Professor, however, was to elude her.

She was made Chevalier de la Légion d'Honneur in 1948, and in 1967 awarded the CBE. She was a Visitor at the universities of Berkeley, Columbia, and Seattle; and at Hollins College, Virginia. Herself a rebel, and interested as much in the creators of literature as in their works, she was drawn to the socially rebellious among French authors. She published books on Baudelaire (1933), Rimbaud (1938), and Gide (1954), but her most ambitious efforts were *Flaubert: the Making of a Master* (1967) and *Flaubert the Master* (1971). *A Lady's Child* (1941) evokes her early life. Also deeply committed to teaching and to university politics, she was widely known for her involvement in successive elections to the Oxford Chair of Poetry, proceedings which her activity greatly publicized.

See also J. Richardson, *Enid Starkie*, 1973.

J.E.

Stead, Christina (Ellen) (1920–83), novelist whose considerable stature was recognized only late in life. She was born in Sydney, Australia, where she graduated at the University Teachers' College in 1922. She later studied business practice and worked in London (1928–29 and Paris (1930–35) before settling in the United States, where she was for a time senior writer for MGM and an instructor at New York University. After the Second World War she returned to England, married her companion of many years William J. Blake, and set up house in Surbiton. In 1969, after Blake's death, she went back to Australia, holding a Fellowship in Creative Arts at the

Australian National University until her retirement in 1980.

Christina Stead's work was remarkably cosmopolitan in setting. Apart from Australian novels such as *Seven Poor Men of Sydney* (1934), she portrayed modern America convincingly in *The Man Who Loved Children* (1940) and *A Little Tea, A Little Chat* (1948), and post-imperial Britain in *Cotter's England* (1966). Most of her writing is in a forceful naturalistic vein; the corruption and injustices of society loom large (above all in *House of All Nations*, 1938) but individual obsessions and sexual conflicts also preoccupied her. *The Man Who Loved Children*, often considered her masterpiece, is an epic of marital agony; its American reissue in 1965 began the overdue reappraisal of Christina Stead's achievement. Her other works include *For Love Alone* (1944), *Letty Fox, Her Luck* (1946), and many short stories.

N.H.

Stebbing, (Lizzie) Susan (1885–1943), philosopher. A barrister's daughter, Susan Stebbing was educated privately, at Girton College, Cambridge, and at the University of London. She gained a degree in History and Part I of the Moral Sciences Tripos; and in 1912 was awarded the London MA with Distinction. From 1911 to 1924 she was visiting lecturer and then Director of Studies in Moral Science Studies at the colleges of Girton and Newnham. She was lecturer in Philosophy at King's College, London, from 1913 to 1915; and then at Bedford College, from 1915 part-time and full-time from 1920. In 1927 she became Reader, and in 1933 was appointed Professor, the first woman to hold a Chair of Philosophy in Great Britain. From 1933 to 1934 she was President of the Aristotelian Society; and in 1935, President of Mind. She delivered the annual philosophical lecture to the British Academy in 1934; and in 1943 was Hobhouse Memorial Lecturer.

Susan Stebbing's writings include *Pragmatism and French Voluntarism* (1914); *A Modern Introduction to Logic* (1930); *Logic and Practice* (1933); *Philosophy and the Physicists* (1937); *Thinking to Some Purpose*, (1939); and *Ideals and Illusions* (1941). To the regret of many, the interest in the philosophy of science shown in her book of 1937 was never fully developed. Susan Stebbing believed that ethics had no superhuman foundation, but came from reason alone; and that clear thinking would lead to political and social good. She was interested in the logical positivism of the Vienna Circle, and befriended those of its members exiled after 1933.   J.E.

'Stella'. See JOHNSON, ESTHER.

Stephens, Catherine, Countess of Essex (1794–1882), singer and actress. Born in London, the daughter of a carver and gilder, she first studied with Gesualdo Lanza and from 1812 with Thomas Welsh. After she appeared at Covent Garden in 1813, responsibility for her success was disputed by the two teachers. She played Ophelia and Hermia and, in 1819, Susanna in the theatre's first production of *The Marriage of Figaro*. The fifth Earl of Essex became her husband in 1838 but died, in his eighties, the following year. Her simple, unaffected soprano was thought the sweetest of its time, ideally suited to the ballad-singing at which she was unequalled, while Hazlitt spoke of her and Kean as his only theatrical favourites.   B.H.C.

Stephens, Joanna (?–1774), medical practitioner. Born in Berkshire, she developed a medicine for dissolving bladder stones, curing such eminent sufferers as David Hartley, Sir Robert Walpole, and the Bishop of Bath. Her remedy offered an attractive alternative to surgery. Hartley published *Ten Cases of Persons Who Have Taken Mrs Stephens's Medicines for the Stone* (1738), in which he announced that she would make her recipe public for £5000. A subscription raised £1400, but Joanna would not lower her price and so her supporters petitioned parliament for public funds. After a parliamentary commission found the evidence for her cures 'unexceptionable', in March 1739 she was awarded her £5000 and the recipe was published. Analyses of the remedy, made by Fellows of the Royal Society, the College of Physicians, and the Académie Royale des Sciences, found that two of the ingredients (soap and calcined shells) contained a high proportion of lime, which could dissolve certain kinds of stone. Joanna faded into obscurity with her fortune, and died in Hammersmith at an advanced age.

See also C. J. S. Thompson, *The Quacks of Old London*, 1928; A. J. Viseltar, 'Joanna Stephens', in *Bulletin of the History of Medicine* 42, 1968.   C.C.

Stephenson, Marjory (1885–1948), physician. The youngest of four children, Marjory Rogers was born at Burwell. Both parents came of well-educated Fenland land-owning farmers. As Chairman of the County Council, her father supported the founding of the Cambridge University School of Agriculture, and awakened his daughter's interest in applied science. She received a sound general education at Berkhamsted High School for Girls, but scientific training was poor. In 1903–06 at Newnham College, Cambridge, she read chemistry, zoology, and physiology. Lack of funds prevented her from reading Medicine, therefore she trained and taught at Gloucester County Training College for Domestic Science and King's College of Household Science, London. In 1911 she embarked on research and advanced teaching at University College, London, but gave up the Beit Memorial Fellowship for Medical Research, awarded in 1914, to undertake war service with the British Red Cross in France and Salonika. She was mentioned in dispatches in 1917 and appointed Associate of the Royal Red Cross and MBE. In 1919 the scholarship was resumed on joining Professor (later Sir) Gowland Hopkins in the Biochemistry Laboratory, Cambridge, where she remained until her death. Hopkins's influence was profound.

She became ScD (Cantab.) in 1936 and Reader in Chemical Microbiology in 1947. In 1945 she was the first woman elected Fellow of the Royal Society in the Biological Division (B). Enthusiastic, impetuous, and 'inclined to include dynamite among her reforming measures', she possessed an intellectual honesty which made her an outstanding developer rather than director of young research workers. She was largely responsible for establishing bacterial chemistry as a separate discipline in Britain and was President of the Society of Chemical Microbiology when she died.

See also M. Robertson, 'Marjory Stephenson', in *Obituary Notices of Fellows of the Royal Society*, vol. VI, 1949.   R.B.

Stern, G(ladys) B(ronwyn) (1890–1973), popular novelist. Gladys Bertha (later changed by herself to Bronwyn) Stern was born in London and went to Notting Hill High School until she was sixteen. She travelled in Germany and Switzerland with her parents, spent two years at the Academy of Dramatic Art, but then became a professional author; she had composed plays and poems since childhood, and her first novel was written when she was only twenty. All her work was lively and entertaining, and she was extraordinarily prolific. Although early predictions of greatness were not fulfilled, she achieved wide popularity and still has her readers. Her most substantial achievement is the series of novels, ranging over several generations and countries, about a matriarch-dominated Jewish family: *Tents of Israel*, 1924; *A Deputy was King*, 1926; *Mosaic*, 1930; *Shining and Free*, 1935; and *Young Matriarch*, 1942. Her own cosmopolitan existence and idiosyncracies are described in *Monogram* (1936), *Another Part of the Forest* (1941), and similar volumes.   N.H.

Sterry, Mrs Alfred. See COOPER, CHARLOTTE REINAGLE.

Stevenson, Flora (Clift) (1839–1905), educational administrator. One of eleven children, including her sister Louisa STEVENSON, she moved to Edinburgh with her family in 1854 when her father retired from his prosperous chemical business. Educated privately herself, she developed an early interest in the provision of popular instruction, and when still a young girl, organized evening classes for illiterate women. Elected to Edinburgh's first School Board in 1873, she sat on every successive Board until her death, becoming Chairman in 1900. As an educational expert, she served on many commissions of enquiry, and gave important evidence to the Endowed Schools Commission of 1883.

Flora Stevenson was particularly concerned with the education of the poor. Her public career had begun as a member of the Association for Improving the Condition of the Poor, where she won the recognition which led directly to her appointment to the School Board. Her attention was always concentrated on schools in depressed urban areas, where she tried hard to root out parental connivance at children's irregular attendance. Her familiarity with the condition of Edinburgh's poor resulted in her accepting many administrative and advisory posts, including the directorship of the Blind Asylum, and membership of Lord Balfour's Committee investigating the treatment of inebriates.

Miss Stevenson was a keen politician, Vice-President of the Women's Liberal Unionist Association, the Women's Free Trade Union, and the National Union of Women Workers; she was also a member of the National Society for Women's Suffrage.

Always aware of the importance of the public work performed by women like herself throughout the country, she regarded the honours granted her in later life (including an honorary doctorate and the Freedom of the City of Edinburgh) as recognition of the wider principle of such women's utility.

See also L. Stevenson, *Recollections of the Public Work and Home Life of Louisa and Flora Stevenson*, 1914.   J.V.L.

Stevenson, Louisa (1853–1908), educational reformer. Like her sister Flora STEVENSON she spent most of her life in Edinburgh. Her involvement in educational reform began with her appointment as secretary to the Edinburgh Association for the University Education of Women. Initially, the Association confined itself to providing supervised instruction for women outside the university, but under Miss Stevenson's influence it began to press for their full admission to recognized degree courses. She gave important evidence to the Commission of Enquiry into Higher Education, and the eventual achievement of female entrance in 1894 owed much to her perseverance.

Miss Stevenson was one of the first women elected to membership of the Parochial Board. With a longstanding interest in medical matters, she paid particular attention to the nursing arrangements in the Poor House. Success in this sphere led to her managing the Scottish branch of the Jubilee Nurses Institution, the Colonial Nurses Scheme, and her active participation in a campaign for the registration of nurses. Her greatest successes, however, were those in which she made use of her administrative abilities. She sat on the Board of Managers of the Edinburgh Royal Infirmary, and, disarming initial opposition to women's presence there, was re-elected six times.

Although Miss Stevenson had always taken a keen interest in women's suffrage, the main thrust of her life's work was directed towards achieving more specific goals. Her career illustrates the way in which a forceful and intelligent woman could do much to undermine local antipathy to female participation in public life. This was not achieved without personal sacrifice; neither of the Stevenson sisters married, and their private lives were necessarily subordinated to the demands of their work.

See also Louisa's *Recollections of the Public*

Work and Home Life of Louisa and Flora Stevenson, 1914.   J.V.L.

Stewart-Murray, Katharine Marjory. See ATHOLL, DUCHESS OF.

Stirling, Fanny (1815–95), actress, born Mary Anne Kehl. She was born in Mayfair, London, the daughter of a military secretary at the War Office, and first appeared at the East London theatre in 1829, where she met the actor Edward Stirling, who became her husband. She was brilliantly pretty, a successful soubrette and good in comedy, as one of the last exponents of the grand style. Peg Woffington in *Masks and Faces*, Mrs Malaprop and Juliet's Nurse were her most successful parts. After retiring in 1870 she gave elocution lessons and recitals. She had long been separated from her husband, and following his death in 1894 she married Sir Charles Hutton Gregory.
B.H.C.

Stocks, Mary (Danvers), Baroness (1891–1975), economist and broadcaster. As Mary Brinton she went to St Paul's School for Girls and the London School of Economics, and later took some part in the suffragette movement. Then in 1913 she married an Oxford Fellow, John Stocks. She became an economics lecturer during the First World War, after which she followed her husband to Manchester, working for the university as an extension lecturer and extra-mural tutor (1924–37). Soon after John Stocks's death she became Principal of Westfield College, London (1939–51).

By this time Mary Stocks was nationally known as a broadcaster; her incisive opinions made her a popular panellist on *The Brains Trust* and *Any Questions?* She also sat on various government committees and published several books, including histories of the Workers' Educational Association and of district nursing, and the biographies of two social reformers, Eleanor RATHBONE (1949) and Ernest Simon (1963). She was made a baroness in 1966.

See also her autobiographies, *My Commonplace Book*, 1970, and *Still More Commonplace*, 1973.   N.H.

Stokes, Margaret M'Nair (1832–1900), archaeologist. The daughter of William Stokes, physician to the Queen in Ireland, she was privately educated, showing an early love for history and an aptitude for art. A dutiful daughter, she was occupied with domestic responsibilities until her parents' deaths, when, in middle age, she was able to indulge her taste for research into Celtic art and archaeology. Her girlhood had brought her into contact with many antiquaries, including George Petrie and Earl Dunraven, who had fostered her sense of history and provided her with the training she later needed.

Her first important work was not intended for publication. It comprised a set of illustrations for Sir Samuel Ferguson's poem 'The Cromlech'; a new edition of the poem with these illustrations subsequently appeared to wide acclaim in 1861. She contributed much to the study of Irish archaeology, although her *magnum opus*, *The High Crosses of Ireland*, partly published in 1898, was left unfinished at her death. She became an Honorary Member of the Royal Irish Academy and the Royal Society of Antiquaries of Ireland, in recognition of her valuable contribution to the knowledge of Celtic art.   J.R.

Stone, Sarah (*fl.* 1701–37), midwife. Daughter of a well-known midwife, she studied six years with her mother and some months in London under the patronage of the Duchess of York. She began to practise in Bridgwater, Somerset, in 1701, but soon moved to Taunton, where there was no man-midwife as competition. In addition to her own extensive practice there, she was routinely called to difficult deliveries by less skilled midwives, often at a great distance. The hardships of country work led her to settle in Bristol in 1721. In 1736 she retired to Piccadilly, where she wrote her textbook *A Complete Practice of Midwifery* (1737). A defender of female practitioners, she nevertheless deplored their lack of training. She argued that it was not improper for women to see dissections and read anatomy, as she herself had done. She also recommended an apprenticeship of at least three years to an experienced midwife. Her daughter practised midwifery from 1727, and to her Sarah Stone passed on her secret method of stopping haemorrhage by 'touch'.

See also J. H. Aveling, *English Midwives: their History and Prospects*, 1872, repr.1967.
C.C.

Stopes, Marie (Carmichael) (1881–1958), Pioneer of birth-control. Born in Edinburgh, the eldest daughter of an archaeologist and anthropologist, Marie Stopes was thus brought up in an academic family and her interest in science was encouraged from the first. She was educated at St George's in Edinburgh and the North London Collegiate, and went from there to University College, London, with a chemistry scholarship. She took her BSc, gaining gold medals in botany, and went on to take her PhD at Munich. In 1904 she started teaching at Manchester University and in 1907 visited Japan to do research, particularly into fossils. On her return she lectured in fossil botany at Manchester and in palaeo-botany at University College, and published widely in those areas.

Her first, brief, marriage having been annulled, in 1918 she married Humphrey Verdon-Roe, the aircraft pioneer and builder. They had two sons. In 1918 she also published what were to be her best-known books, *Married Love* and *Wise Parenthood*, and so began her notorious second career as an advocate of sexual fulfilment and contraception. It was not only the content of her books which shocked genteel 1920s society, but the form in which they were presented. In spite of her scientific background and training in objectivity, she wrote in a totally tendentious and committed way, in language more rhapsodic than precise, of the joys of married love between equal partners where parenthood was chosen rather than the almost automatic result of sexual activity. This approach was indicative of her appeal, which was not to men of science, or even to the educated women of her own class, so much as to ordinary men and women for whom she transformed this whole area of social and personal life from one of mystery and taboo into one openly discussed.

She was opposed at every stage. Her writing was condemned as brazen, immodest, and shocking, even as irreligious, and her early birth control clinics in London, Aberdeen, and Leeds were opened amid heated controversy. Through all this she showed the single-mindedness and determination which later were to manifest themselves as arrogance and dogmatism when she found it impossible to work with others or to co-operate in the, by then respectable, Family Planning Association. Yet she had established the necessity for intelligent and humane discussion of sexual problems, thereby changing the attitudes and aspirations of more than her own generation.

See also R. Hall, *Marie Stopes*, 1977.

E.M.V.

Storace, Ann Selina (1765–1817), singer, also known as Nancy or Anna. She was the daughter of an Italian double bass player who settled in Dublin, and her brother was Stephen Storace, the composer. Her parents were ambitious for her success as a singer, and launched her public career in Florence when she was only fifteen. In 1783 she went to Vienna, where she was patronized by the Emperor Joseph II. Having sung in a number of operas, she proved more suitable to comic roles. She was Susanna in the first performance of *Le Nozze di Figaro*, and Mozart wrote a concert aria for her. On her return to England she and Michael Kelly did much to raise the standards of singing in playhouses. Although much admired by discerning judges such as Dr Burney, she seems to have been less appreciated by the public in London than abroad. Her private life was punctuated by storms: her disastrous first marriage failed, and quarrels with her lover, the tenor John Braham, saddened the closing years of her life.

See also *The New Grove Dictionary of Music and Musicians*, 1981. T.H.

Strachey, Philippa (1872–1968), feminist pioneer. She was born in London and grew up in a famous family as one of ten children, including Lytton Strachey, at the heart of the 'Bloomsbury set' in Gordon Square. With such a background she could not fail to be open to the ideas and philosophies of the day. During the early years of the movement for women's suffrage she was secretary of the London Society for Women's Suffrage, forerunner of the Fawcett Society, of which she was honorary secretary. Working closely with Dame Millicent FAWCETT, she proved a born administrator 'behind the scenes'. It was she who organized the society's first open-air rally, the 'Mud March' of 1907, when 3000 women marched to the Strand from Hyde Park, setting the pattern for future demonstrations of the sort. She inspired loyalty, had a phenomenal memory and, dying at the age of ninety-six, had the satisfaction of seeing the results achieved by the movement she served with such dedication. B.H.C.

Strachey, Ray (Rachel Conn) (1887–1940), writer and feminist. Born Costelloe, she came of American stock and was brought up by her grandmother Hannah Whitall Smith, a well-known religious preacher and writer. Educated at Kensington High School, she read mathematics at Newnham College, Cambridge (1905–08) where she was caught up in the suffrage movement. She became a close friend and principal lieutenant of Millicent FAWCETT, leader of the law-abiding suffragists. After a year at Bryn Mawr College, Philadelphia, she studied electrical engineering and then married Oliver Strachey, brother of Lytton, himself a convinced feminist, and had two children. During the First World War she fought to open all fields of war work to women, negotiating pay and status with government, employers, and unions. She stood for parliament in 1918 as an Independent and again in 1922 and 1923.

Rachel Strachey wrote novels and biographies, and her history of the women's movement, *The Cause* (1928) is a classic. She founded the Women's Employment Federation to obtain more responsible and better paid work for women, edited the feminist newspaper *The Common Cause*, worked for the League of Nations and the Anti-Slavery Society, and was an extremely skilful lobbyist for women's rights. She was also an indefatigable chairwoman, raiser of funds, writer of innumerable articles, and frequent broadcaster on current affairs as well as women's problems. Her books included *Frances Willard, her life and work*, 1912; *Shaken by the Wind*, 1927; *Millicent Garrett Fawcett*, 1931; *Careers and Openings for Women*, 1937.

See also B. Strachey, *Remarkable Relations*, 1980.   B.H.

Stretton, Hesba. See SMITH, SARAH.

Strickland, Agnes (1796–1874), historian. Agnes Strickland was born in London, the second in a family of six sisters, five of whom became published writers. Her father was a businessman employed by a firm of shipowners, and it was he who attended to his daughters' education, providing them with a useful intellectual grounding. Agnes began to write early in life, and encouraged by the success of her sister Elizabeth and spurred on by financial need after the death of her father, she took to authorship for a living.

She began by publishing verse. *Monody upon the Death of the Princess Charlotte of Wales* appeared in 1817; *Worcester Field; or, the Cavalier* (1827) and *The Seven Ages of Woman* (1827) came later but secured little success. In addition to poetry she produced

many books for children, among them *Historical Tales of Illustrious British Children* (1833), written in collaboration with Elizabeth. Agnes's best known work, *Lives of the Queens of England*, was also a joint venture with her sister, who consistently declined publicity. First published in twelve volumes between 1840 and 1848, the *Queens* proved highly popular, reaching a fourth edition by 1854. Unfavourable business arrangements, however, limited the authors' financial return. After the *Queens*, Agnes concentrated for the most part on historical biography. She edited and published *The Letters of Mary Queen of Scots*, 1842, and produced *The Lives of the Queens of Scotland*, 1850–59, and *The Lives of the Bachelor Kings of England*, 1861. Her final work, on the lives of the last four Stuart princesses, appeared in 1872.

Agnes Strickland won considerable fame for her biographies; her presentation at the court of Queen Victoria in 1840 provides some indication of her social success. Although her scholarship was not of a high standard, the books were enjoyed for their close attention to domestic detail. Her work was based on original research at a time when a woman's access to public documents was severely limited: it required the intervention of someone as influential as Lord Normanby before Agnes and her sister were permitted to use the State Paper Office. The sisters also visited many of the historic houses of Britain, while Agnes made trips to France and Holland to study directly from the sources. The Stricklands have been admired by a contemporary historical biographer, Lady Antonia Fraser, for having founded 'a whole new school of vivid readable history aimed at the general reader, inadequately served in the 1840s either by the pedantic scholar or the over-imaginative historical novelist'. Other works include *How Will it End?* (1865) and *Lives of the Tudor Princesses* (1868).

See also U. C. Birch, *Agnes Strickland, Biographer of the Queens of England*, 1940.
                                                       H.O.

Stuart, Arabella (1575–1615), political figure. Arabella was the daughter of Charles, Earl of Lennox, and Elizabeth Cavendish, a daughter of Elizabeth TALBOT, known as 'Bess of Hardwick'. Her father was the younger brother of Lord Darnley, husband to Mary Queen of Scots, and Arabella was therefore a direct descendant of Henry VIII's sister MARGARET. She was thus a serious claimant to the English throne after Elizabeth I's death. During Elizabeth's reign she was occasionally allowed at court and encouraged to hope for some great marriage, but this was merely a stratagem employed by the Queen to keep James VI of Scotland, the only realistic choice as her successor, in suspense. Most of Arabella's time was spent as a virtual prisoner at Hardwick.

In 1602 Arabella conceived a hare-brained plan to escape from this restraint, by offering marriage to Edward Seymour, the last man she would have been allowed to marry as he too had a claim to the throne through his grandmother Catherine Grey. Her scheme was discovered and she was subjected to a closer imprisonment that prompted mental and physical collapse. On James I's accession, however, she was brought to court and treated with greater kindness. In February 1610, at the age of thirty-five, she became engaged to William Seymour, the twenty-two-year-old younger brother of Edward. The marriage was forbidden by the Privy Council, but solemnized secretly in June. Barely two weeks later her secret was discovered. Arabella was placed under house arrest and William confined to the Tower. In June 1611 the couple arranged a co-ordinated escape; Arabella, dressed as a man, reached a ship in the Thames, but was recaptured in the Channel. William, with greater luck, reached France safely. Thereafter Arabella was imprisoned in the Tower. She lost all will to live, refusing food and medical attention before her death in September 1615.

Arabella's tragedy is not a romantic story: she had never met Edward Seymour in 1602, and barely knew his brother in 1610, although her stubborn and unwise refusal to renounce her marriage suggests that some loyalty and affection had developed between the couple. Her personality remains baffling; her significance is as the unlucky victim of dynastic politics.

See also D. N. Durant, *Arabella Stuart*, 1978. A.H.

Suffolk, Countess of. See HOWARD, HENRIETTA, COUNTESS OF SUFFOLK.

Summerskill, Edith, Baroness (1901–79), Labour MP, the youngest of three children of a doctor. Her father was probably the most important formative influence of her life, with his opinions about preventive medicine, radical political ideas, and strong feminist bias. With him she visited poor families, seeing how squalid and unhealthy were the conditions in which they lived, and the results of chronic malnutrition. In 1918 she went to King's College, London, to study sciences and then to read medicine. She qualified in 1924 and in 1925 married another doctor, Jeffrey Samuel. They had two children, a son and a daughter, Shirley, who later followed her mother into both medicine and politics.

In 1933 Edith Summerskill was co-opted on to the Maternity and Child Welfare Committee of her Urban District Council and her political career was formally under way. In 1934 she was elected to the Middlesex County Council and also stood in the General Election of that year. She contested Putney, a Conservative stronghold, for Labour, reducing the majority by 18,000 votes. In 1935 she stood in Bury, where she encountered for the first time strong antagonism to her radical social and feminist stand. Her advocacy of birth control infuriated the local Catholic Church and when she refused to recant, the priests instructed their congregations to vote for the Conservative candidate. Her third attempt to gain a parliamentary seat was successful, however, and in 1938 she was returned for Fulham West, which she represented until 1955. From then until 1960 she represented Warrington.

In parliament her major interests were in preventive medicine, extending into National Insurance and the Health Service, and feminism, with demands for equal pay and analgesia in childbirth (she wrote *Babies without Tears*, 1941, on this subject). She was an unremitting champion of women in every sphere, as consumers, mothers, wives, and single women. Edith Summerskill was an original supporter of the National Council for the Single Woman and Her Dependants. During the Second World War she insisted that women had an active part to play in Home Defence, even to the extent of learning to shoot, and was a member of the 1942 government enquiry into the women's services. In 1945 she became Parliamentary Secretary to the Ministry of Food, a difficult and frustrating job in the years of shortages and rationing immediately after the war. One of her more difficult tasks was to persuade the housewives of Britain to buy snoek, a South African fish which provided a source of much-needed protein. To

Edith Summerskill, its nutritional value was the significant consideration and she was surprised and irritated when snoek was rejected, apparently because of its unfamiliar name and appearance. In many ways, this incident typifies her approach—sensible, rational, and utilitarian—and perhaps her limitation. In her work as Minister of National Insurance (1950–51) she displayed this same practicality, the keynote of her politics being her down-to-earth stance, with a strong moral tone. Yet her own rather severe manner often belied a great compassion, which she saw best expressed in deeds rather than words. She was created a Life Peeress in 1961 and a Companion of Honour in 1966.

Her other writings include *A Woman's World* (1967), *Letters to my Daughter* (1957).

E.M.V.

Sutherland, Dame Lucy (1903–80), historian. Lucy Sutherland's father was a civil engineer of Scottish extraction. She was born in Australia but soon afterwards the family moved to South Africa, where she spent her school days and early university career, gaining a first-class honours degree in 1924 at the University of Witwatersrand. In 1927, having moved to Oxford to read Modern History, she achieved another first and went on to a tutorship and fellowship in Economic History and Politics at Somerville College. She had a particular interest in the eighteenth century, and among her best-known works were *The East India Company in Eighteenth-Century Politics* (1952) and the second volume of *The Correspondence of Edmund Burke*, which she meticulously edited.

Her academic career was interrupted by the Second World War when she joined the Board of Trade, becoming an Assistant Secretary. Here her administrative abilities became apparent, and after leaving the Civil Service she was in demand on commissions and committees for the rest of her life, serving on, among others, the Committee of Inquiry into the Distribution and Exhibition of Films, the Royal Commission on Taxation of Profits and Incomes, and the Committee on Grants to Students. In 1947 she was appointed CBE. From 1945 to 1971 she was Principal of Lady Margaret Hall, and was enormously successful in facilitating its development to full collegiate status. Her own standards of academic excellence and of tutorial responsibility were brought to her role of Principal and, in 1960,

to that of first woman Pro-Vice-Chancellor. In 1969, in recognition of her contribution to Oxford academic life and women's education, she was created DBE.

E.M.V.

'Swan of Lichfield'. See SEWARD, ANNA.

Swanborough, Baroness. See ISAACS, STELLA, MARCHIONESS OF READING.

Swanwick, Anna (1813–99), scholar and author. She was educated at home, where she showed an early aptitude for, and love of, learning, and to further her education was sent to Berne, where she studied languages, particularly German and Greek. Returning to England in 1843 she began a series of translations, first from German and later from Greek. *Faust* appeared in two parts (1850 and 1870), being much praised for its accuracy and vigour. Her translation of the dramas of Aeschylus (1873) was similarly well-received. Anna Swanwick was also interested in furthering women's education, and sat on the councils of Queen's and Bedford Colleges, London. She was Principal of the former, and helped to found both Somerville and Girton colleges. Her work in this field resulted in her helping to carry out the will of Mrs Emily Pfeiffer (d. 1890), who left money to promote women's higher education. Linked with this interest was her support for women's suffrage; she was a signatory to J. S. Mill's Petition in 1865. Although she had no desire to become famous herself, her work brought her many famous friends, including Tennyson and Gladstone.

See also M. Bruce, *Anna Swanwick*, 1965.

J.R.

Swynford, Catherine (1350?–1403), mistress and third wife of John of Gaunt, Duke of Lancaster. She was the daughter of Sir Payne Roelt, a Hainault knight who came to England in the entourage of Edward III's queen, PHILIPPA. In 1367 she married Sir Hugh Swynford, a household retainer of the immensely powerful and wealthy John of Gaunt, but he was killed while fighting on the Continent in 1372. Catherine, meanwhile, had become governess to Gaunt's two daughters by his first wife, Blanche, and on the Duchess's death in 1369 may even have assumed charge of his household. In 1371 the Duke took as his second wife Constance of Castile. By then, in all probability, Catherine Swynford had accepted the duties and privileges of ducal mistress.

According to the St Albans' chronicler,

Gaunt's openly sinful liaison with Catherine resulted in a good deal of unsavoury rumour in the later 1370s, so much so that in 1381 he repented of his conduct and withdrew from her company. By then four children had been born, all of whom took the surname Beaufort: John, who eventually became Earl of Somerset; Henry, the future Bishop of Winchester and cardinal; Thomas, later Duke of Exeter; and Joan, who ultimately became the second wife of Ralph Neville, Earl of Westmorland.

The situation changed dramatically following Constance of Castile's death in March 1394, leaving John of Gaunt free to marry once more. Remarkably enough, for such a move hardly accorded with medieval conventions, he decided to make Catherine his third wife. Richard II was anxious to please his uncle and readily sanctioned the marriage, which was duly celebrated in January 1396. There remained, of course, the problem of the couple's bastard issue, but in September 1396 Pope Boniface IX pronounced the children legitimate, and in February 1397 the King in turn issued letters patent of legitimation which were subsequently confirmed by parliament. Initially there were no reservations regarding the Beauforts, but when Henry IV (Gaunt's son by his first wife) confirmed their legitimate status in 1407, the words 'excepta dignitate regali' were interpolated. By then both John of Gaunt himself and his third wife had been dead for some years.

See also S. B. Chrimes, Lancastrians, Yorkists and Henry VII, 1964.   K.R.D.

Swynnerton, Annie Louisa (1844–1933), painter. Annie Robinson received her early training at Manchester School of Art, and with her sister painted small watercolours for a living. She then studied in Paris and Rome, and exhibited at the Royal Academy from 1879 until 1886, after which there was a gap of sixteen years. In 1883 she married Joseph Swynnerton, a Manx sculptor, and they lived mainly in Rome until his death in 1910.

When she came to London her first sponsors were Burne-Jones and G. F. Watts. Her work was also much admired by Sargent, who bought several of her pictures, including The Oreads which he presented to the nation. She was much influenced by Watts, and many of her subjects were of the allegorical or symbolic type which was his forte. Her drawing was solid, and she had a sculptural grasp of form allied to fresh, broken colour displaying affinities with Impressionism. She was particularly successful at painting children, with or without ponies. The Academy appears to have taken umbrage at her early success and the support she received from Sargent, so that it was not until 1922, by which time she was nearly blind, that her merit was finally acknowledged with an ARA. She thus became the first woman to be made an Associate since Angelica KAUFMANN and Mary MOSER were made full members at its foundation in 1768.

There are works in Melbourne, Paris (Mater Triumphalis, given by Rodin to the then Musée du Luxembourg), and New York (Metropolitan Museum), and several works in the Chantrey Collection, and a Diploma Work at the RA. The Tate Gallery has six works, and the City Art Gallery, Manchester, has a representative group which is augmented whenever the opportunity arises.   L.M.M.

T

Talbot, Elizabeth, Countess of Shrewsbury (1518–1608), political figure. Daughter of John Hardwick of Hardwick, Derbyshire, Elizabeth is familiarly known as 'Bess of Hardwick' and is famous for becoming increasingly wealthy through a series of marriages. At the age of fourteen she married Robert Barlow of Barlow, near Dronfield; he died soon afterwards, on 2 February 1533, having settled his estate on Bess and her heirs. Next, on 20 August 1549 she married Sir William Cavendish; of their children (Bess's only issue) three sons and three daughters survived infancy. Cavendish died in 1557, and Bess's third husband was Sir William St Loe, Queen Elizabeth's captain of the guard; he was so completely under his wife's influence that he bequeathed her his whole estate, to the exclusion of his own children. Finally, in 1568 Bess married George Talbot, sixth Earl of Shrewsbury, having first married her daughter Mary to his son Gilbert and her son Henry to his daughter Grace.

In December 1568 Elizabeth I gave Shrewsbury the custody of Mary Queen of Scots, who arrived at Tutbury on 2 February 1569. Bess and the Queen were friendly at first, working many elaborate embroideries together, but relations later soured. The Countess hinted to Elizabeth that Shrewsbury was amorously involved with Mary, and assiduously stirred up trouble between the Earl and his sovereign; Bess herself intrigued with both queens. Mary was taken from Shrewsbury's custody in 1584, and the Earl died in 1590, estranged from his wife and dominated by Eleanor Britton, a servant.

Before this, Bess had become involved in an intrigue of dynastic importance. In October 1574 Margaret, Countess of Lennox, and her son Charles Stuart stayed with Bess at Rufford on their way to Scotland. A marriage was speedily concluded between Charles and Bess's daughter Elizabeth; the Queen was furious, and committed both countesses to the Tower. Shrewsbury laid all the blame on his wife in a letter to Burghley; however, she was released after three months. The Stuarts' daughter Arabella STUART, born in 1575 and a potential heir to the throne, was a favourite with Bess until the old lady's domineering ways alienated the girl. Before March 1603 Arabella was taken from Hardwick Hall to the care of the Earl of Kent, and Bess disinherited her by a codicil to her will.

Besides her matrimonial career and talent for intrigue, Bess is famous as a builder. Her second husband, Cavendish, bought Chatsworth from her relatives and began a new manor house which she completed after his death. She also built the family seats of Worksop, Bolsover, and Oldcotes, besides a new Hardwick Hall, finished in 1597. An interesting, though improbable, family tradition tells of a prediction that she would not die while she was building, and claims that when she died on 13 February 1608 there was a severe frost which made building work impossible.

See also E. Carleton Williams, *Bess of Hardwick*, 1959; British Library: Lansdowne Manuscript 34, containing some of her letters.

M.D.

Tate. See ÆTHELBURH.

Taylor, Elizabeth (1912–75), novelist and short story writer. Born in Reading, she was educated there at the Abbey School, and began writing in secret when very young. Later she worked as a governess and librarian, married John Taylor in 1936, and had two children. Her first novel, *At Mrs Lippincote's*, was published in 1946 and four years later came her best-selling *A Wreath of Roses*. She was a painstaking craftswoman who said that a sentence would sometimes take a whole page of scratching out before she was satisfied. She was perhaps at her best with short stories. Angus Wilson said of her that she had 'a warm heart, sharp claws, and exceptional powers of formal balance'. She lived in Penn, Buckinghamshire, loved village life, and was happy to believe that her books were truly English. Other works include *Mrs Palfrey at the Claremont* (1972).

See also S. J. Kunitz and H. Haycraft, *Twentieth Century Authors*, 1st supplement, 1955.

P.L.

Taylor, Eva (Germaine Rimington) (1879–1966), geographer. Born at Highgate in London, she was the daughter of a solicitor, and was educated at Camden School for Girls, the North Collegiate School for Girls, and Royal Holloway College, taking a London University degree in chemistry. Working as a schoolteacher, she became interested in geography at Oxford, where she managed to combine work with study at the university. Having qualified, she stayed on at Oxford (1908–10) as private assistant to the Head of the School of Geography. Then she spent six years in London writing school textbooks with J. F. Unstead; 'Unstead and Taylor' were very widely used in their day. After lecturing at colleges in Clapham and East London, she found a congenial home at Birkbeck College, London, where she was Lecturer (1921–30), Professor of Geography (1930–44), and subsequently Emeritus Professor and Fellow.

During the 1940s Eva Taylor became involved as an adviser on post-war planning, but her main interests remained scholarly. Work on her preferred period of history culminated in the publication of *Tudor Geography* (1930) and *Late Tudor and Early Stuart Geography* (1934). Retirement merely meant more time to write, and some of Eva Taylor's best work was done in her seventies and eighties. She was a great expert on all aspects of navigation; the most popular of her books on the subject was *The Haven-Finding Art: a history of navigation from Odysseus to Captain Cook* (1956). *The Mathematical Practitioners of Tudor and Stuart England* had already appeared in 1954, and it was eventually followed by *The Mathematical Practitioners of Hanoverian England* in 1966, the year of her death at the age of eighty-seven.   N.H.

Taylor, Harriet (1807–58), advocate of women's rights. Born Harriet Hardy, the daughter of a surgeon, she was one of seven children. An unhappy home possibly drove her into early marriage with John Taylor, a Unitarian druggist, in 1826. They had three children, and although there is evidence for their happiness in the first years, her intellectual and artistic leanings were frustrated. Through William Fox, the Unitarian minister at South Place Chapel and editor of *The Monthly Repository*, she met John Stuart Mill at a dinner party in 1830. Their mutual attraction and intellectual rapport led them into a deep and loving friendship. In 1833 the Taylors agreed to a trial separation, but she decided to remain Taylor's wife without relinquishing Mill, whom for the next seventeen years she continued to meet regularly. Mill

worshipped her and his eulogies of her excellence possibly exacerbated their colleagues into less than generous estimates of her character, offending Mill and making their relationship more exclusive. As an intellectual companion, Harriet Taylor helped Mill to revise his manuscripts and discussed his work with him. It has been difficult to determine how much is attributable to her, as nothing apart from poems and reviews in *The Monthly Repository* was published under her name.

In 1832 they corresponded in the form of essays on the position of women where it is evident that she was more radical than Mill, impulsive, and far less intellectually disciplined; but her position brought home to him 'the vast practical bearings of women's disabilities' which later made him an ardent campaigner for women's rights. The article 'On the Enfranchisement of Women' in *The Westminster Review* (1851) was attributed to her later when Mill declared his share to have been 'little more than that of an editor and amanuensis'. A cogent plea for equality, it declares that 'high mental powers in women will be but an exceptional accident, until every career is open to them and until they, as well as men, are educated for themselves and for the world, not one sex for the other'. There is a note of personal bitterness in the recognition that young girls are expected to marry, the only qualification being that of not understanding the terms of the contract. Apart from his work on women, Mill also attributed a chapter in *Principles of Political Economy* (1848) on the future condition of the working class as 'wholly an exposition of her thoughts', and *On Liberty* (1859) as 'more directly and literally our joint production than anything else'.

In 1851, two years after the death of John Taylor, they married at Melcombe Regis, Weymouth. Mill recorded a formal protest against the existing laws of marriage, repudiating all rights over her. They settled in Blackheath and led a secluded life. Both were ill and often separated by convalescent holidays on the Continent, although after Mill's retirement from India House in 1858 they went together to the South of France. Harriet became seriously ill and died at Avignon on 3 November 1858.

See also F. A. Hayek, *John Stuart Mill and Harriet Taylor*, 1951; J. Kamm, *John Stuart Mill in Love*, 1977; A. S. Rossi (ed.); *John*

Stuart Mill and Harriet Taylor, Essays on Sex Equality, 1970.   C.B.

Taylor, Helen (1831–1907), advocate of women's rights, The youngest child of John and Harriet TAYLOR, Helen Taylor was born in London, at the beginning of her mother's relationship with J. S. Mill. Educated by her mother, she was her constant companion, and only after her mother's marriage to Mill in 1851 did she assert her independence. She took acting lessons with Fanny STIRLING who found her a position in Newcastle in 1856. Under the name of 'Miss Trevor' she took a few leading roles and might have become successful had she not abandoned the stage on her mother's death in 1858 to look after Mill. She became his housekeeper and secretary, filling her mother's role of intellectual companion. Having edited the *Miscellaneous and Posthumous Works of H.T. Buckle* (1865) and worked with Mill on *The Subjection of Women* (1869), she became his literary executor when he died, editing his *Autobiography* (1873) and essays.

Outspoken, independent, and domineering, she had strong feminist principles and radical sympathies. Her political work began in 1865 when, as a member of the Kensington Society with Emily DAVIES, she campaigned for Mill's election to parliament and for women's suffrage. On her initiative the London National Women's Suffrage Society was formed, although intransigence on some issues led to her later exclusion. In 1876 she was returned for Southwark as a radical member of the London School Board, and for eight years she campaigned for universal free education, smaller classes, the abolition of corporal punishment, and the restitution of charitable endowments. At her own expense she provided meals and clothing for the poor children of the borough and fought malpractices in Industrial Schools.

Moving towards socialism, she presided over meetings of the Irish Ladies' Land League and worked for land nationalization as a leading member of the Land Reform Union and the League for Taxing Land Values. In 1881, involved in setting up the Democratic Federation, she served on its first executive committee and in 1885 became the first woman to attempt to stand for parliament. Accepted as a radical candidate for North Camberwell on a platform of universal suffrage, women's rights, prevention of war, and Home Rule for Ireland, she held only one public meeting which was disrupted by the Liberals and her nomination was refused by the returning officer.

She retired from public life, living in Avignon until 1904, when her niece brought this now senile, passionate eccentric back to England. She died in Torquay.

See also J. Kamm, *John Stuart Mill in Love*, 1977; B. Simon, *Education and the Labour Movement 1870–1920*, 1965; F. W. Soutter, *Recollections of a Labour Pioneer*, 1923.

C.B.

Teerlinck, Lavinia (*fl.* 1545–62), painter and miniaturist. Lavinia Teerlinck, or Terling, was a Flemish woman who presumably received her training as an artist from her father, named Bennick, himself a painter and miniaturist. She served as an artist at the courts of Henry VIII, Edward VI, Mary and Elizabeth, receiving the considerable annual sum of £40. She owed her initial appointment to the patronage of Lady Herbert, sister of Queen Katherine Parr. Unfortunately, none of her works are known to have survived, but her long court service suggests that she was a highly regarded and successful artist.

See also P. Hogrefe, *Tudor Women: Commoners and Queens*, 1975.   A.H.

Tempest, Dame Marie (1864–1942), actress. In her heyday the leading comedienne of the English stage, Marie Tempest was born Mary Susan Etherington, the daughter of a London stationer. She was educated in Sussex, Belgium, and Paris, and, after training at the Royal Academy of Music, began her career as a singer in operetta, making her début in 1885 in Suppé's *Boccaccio*. Over the next fifteen years she played leading roles in a number of successful musical comedies, including *The Geisha*.

In 1901 she gave up the musical theatre and developed her talent for comedy with great success in a long series of plays by authors such as Henry Arthur Jones, Arnold Bennett, Maugham, Barrie, and Coward. From October 1914, however, she was not seen in London for nine years. This period was spent in touring North America (she had already spent the years 1890–95 in New York), Australasia, and the Far East. On her return she re-established her position only with some difficulty.

A notably intelligent and hardworking

actress, she captivated audiences by her stylish and graceful performances. She was three times married; her second husband, C. G. Gordon-Lennox, a grandson of the fifth Duke of Richmond, wrote one of her most popular comedies, *The Marriage of Kitty*.

See also H. Bolitho, *Marie Tempest*, 1936.
K.W.

Temple, Lady. See OSBORNE, DOROTHY.

Tennant, May (1869–1946), civil servant. Margaret Mary Edith Abraham was born at Rathgar, County Dublin. She was educated at home, and when her father's death in 1887 left the family in financial straits, she went to London to seek her fortune. She was employed as secretary to Lady Dilke and later as treasurer of the Women's Trade Union League. Her contacts with Liberal and labour activists provided her with an informal but invaluable education. She supported the dock strike in 1889 and then helped to organize laundresses. In 1891 she was appointed one of four women assistant commissioners on the Royal Commission on Labour.

When the Home Secretary H. H. Asquith decided to appoint women factory inspectors in 1893, May Abraham was his first choice. By 1895 there were five women inspectors, and the Home Office established the Women's Branch of the Factory Department with May Abraham as superintendent. Her fine presence and sharp wit made her especially successful on the legal side of inspecting work. She wrote a summary of factory legislation, *The Law Relating to Factories and Workshops. Pt. I: A Practical Guide to the Law and Its Administration* (1896). In 1895 she was appointed to the Departmental Committee on Dangerous Trades, and in the course of her investigations into the dangers of white lead met H. J. Tennant, Asquith's parliamentary secretary and brother-in-law, who was committee chairman. They were married in 1896 and the next year May Tennant resigned to devote herself to family responsibilities.

Marriage and five children did not, however, altogether end her work. She remained a member of the Committee on Dangerous Trades, and in 1898 became chairman of the Industrial Law Indemnity Fund, which provided compensation to workers victimized by employers. In 1909 she served on the Royal Commission on Divorce. She was a founder member of the Central Committee for Women's Employment

and its treasurer from 1914 until 1939. During the First World War she worked as a welfare adviser at the War Office. In 1917 she was appointed director of the Women's Department of the National Service Department, but her tenure in that unhappy department was brief, and she subsequently went to the Ministry of Munitions. She was made a Companion of Honour in 1917.

After the war she gradually withdrew from political concerns, although her interest in maternal and child welfare remained strong and she served on several investigating bodies, including the Committee on Maternal Mortality (1928) and the Committee on Maternal Health (1937). She was a governor of Bedford College, London.

May Tennant was a great character and great adventurer. Shrewd, caring, hard-working, humorous (as a factory inspector she once fell into a barrel of lime while fixing a notice and came out laughing), she grasped the chances which life offered her.

See also V. Markham, *May Tennant: a Portrait*, 1949. M.Z.

Terry, Dame (Alice) Ellen (1847–1928), actress. Born in Coventry, where her parents Ben and Sarah Terry were on tour, Ellen was brought up with her eleven brothers and sisters in the theatre and had no formal education. She was trained by the Keans, making her début with their company as Mamilius in *The Winter's Tale*, aged nine. A successful child actress, she left the stage in 1864 to marry G. F. Watts, the painter, who was thirty years her senior. Separated within a year, she was acting at the Haymarket in 1867 when she ran away with the architect Edward Godwin, by whom she had two children, Edith CRAIG and Edward Gordon Craig. Penury led her back to the stage in 1872 and she established herself as a leading actress with the Bancrofts' and John Hare's companies. Divorced by Watts in 1877 and parted from Godwin, she married, briefly, an actor called Charles Kelly.

In 1878 the title role in *Olivia* confirmed her reputation and Henry Irving invited her to join him at the Lyceum as his leading lady. Their partnership dominated London theatre for the next twenty years. Irving, an autocratic actor-manager, planned the repertoire to suit himself, often leaving Ellen Terry with only minor roles. George Bernard Shaw, who corresponded with her for many years, thought this 'a heartless waste of an exquisite talent', but she was happy to be useful and she had financial security as the best paid actress in England. She advised on staging and design, managed company relations, and played hostess to writers and artists at the Lyceum. Best-loved as Portia, Beatrice, and Olivia, she was praised for her naturalness and sympathetic spontaneity. The equal and friend of Bernhardt and Duse, she may have lacked variety and technique, but her magnetic, graceful stage presence ensured her popularity.

Difficulties at the Lyceum ended the partnership with Irving. In her fifties she tried modern plays for the first time and turned to management herself, though unsuccessfully. She played Mistress Page and Hermione with Beerbohm Tree, and in 1906 celebrated her jubilee with a 'mammoth matinee' attended by many celebrities and twenty members of her own family. From 1910 she toured England, America, and Australia with her Shakespearean lecture-recitals ('the living, laughing, triumphant, scornful words of a great actress who is proud to be a woman'). A respected figure, she made guest appearances in parts of decreasing importance, including five films, giving her last performance in 1925. In the same year she was created DBE. Her third marriage in 1907 to James Carew, a young American actor, lasted only two years and she spent the rest of her life with her daughter and her friend Christopher St John. Her autobiography, *The Story of My Life*, appeared in 1908. Ellen Terry died in 1928 at her cottage in Smallhythe, Kent, which is now the Ellen Terry Museum.

See also R. Manvell, *Ellen Terry*, 1968; C. St. John (ed.) *Ellen Terry and Bernard Shaw: a Correspondence*, ed. C. St John, 1931.

C.B.

Tey, Josephine, pseudonym of Elizabeth Mackintosh (1896–1952), novelist and playwright. She was born at Inverness and educated at Inverness Academy. Having qualified as a physical training instructress at Anstey College in Birmingham, she taught the subject (see her *Miss Pym Disposes*, 1946) until called home in 1923 to take care of her parents. She published verse and short stories as 'Gordon Daviot' before turning to play-writing with *Richard of Bordeaux* (1932), a study of the 'generation gap' set in the fourteenth century,

which ran for a year in the West End of London. 'Gordon Daviot's' later plays made less of a mark.

Elizabeth Mackintosh regarded the crime novels she published under the name of 'Josephine Tey' as no more than a diversion, calling them 'my yearly knitting', but in the event they outlived her other works. Her historical interests gave her approach to matters criminal a distinctive quality in *The Franchise Affair* (1948), which transposes a famous eighteenth-century mystery into a modern setting, and *The Daughter of Time* (1951), in which a bedridden police inspector conducts an investigation into the character and alleged crimes of King Richard III.

See also J. Mann, *Deadlier Than the Male*, 1981.

N.H.

Teyte, Dame Maggie (1888–1976), singer. She was born in Wolverhampton and first studied singing in London, where her practising disturbed her famous neighbour, George Bernard Shaw. Her first public appearance was at a small church in Maiden Lane. Later she studied in Paris with Jean de Reszke. Reynaldo Hahn and Debussy were also numbered among her teachers. Her first operatic performance was in 1907 as Zerlina at Monte Carlo, and thereafter she gained popularity as an opera and concert singer in the United States and Europe. It was to gain the correct pronunciation of her surname in France that she changed the spelling from Tate to Teyte.

In 1908 Debussy, who once described a bird as singing 'almost as well as Miss Teyte', chose her to play Mélisande, the part for which she became most famous. She was supreme as an interpreter of French song, of Ravel as well as Debussy, excelling also in Mozart and as Butterfly, Mimi, Manon, and Marguerite. She was at the Opéra-Comique (1909–10) and with Sir Thomas Beecham's opera company in London (1910–11). In America she appeared with the opera company in Chicago and with the Boston Grand Opera Company from 1915 to 1917. During the Second World War she continued recitals of French music in London and also toured the provinces. At the age of fifty-seven she made a triumphant return to the United States, finally achieving, three years later, her ambition to sing Mélisande in New York. Her farewell appearance in 1957 was in *Dido and Aeneas*.

The most famous English singer of her generation, Maggie Teyte became an international celebrity, outstanding as an operatic soprano and in musical comedy. She was married and divorced twice, pioneered light opera on BBC radio, was decorated in France, and created a DBE in 1958. Her autobiography, *A Star on the Door*, appeared in the same year.

See also G. O'Connor, *The Pursuit of Perfection*, 1979.   B.H.C.

Thirkell, Angela (1890–1961), novelist, born Angela Mackail in Kensington. Her father was Oxford Professor of Poetry and one of her grandfathers was the Pre-Raphaelite painter Burne-Jones. She was educated at St Paul's Girls' School, where she was a brilliant all-rounder, and then at a finishing school in Paris. In 1911 she married James McInnes and had two sons, but the couple were divorced in 1917. A year later she married George Thirkell and went with him to Australia. She had another son but this marriage also proved disastrous. In 1930 she returned to England, where she lived in her parents' Kensington house and enjoyed a social life in which she was known for her 'magnetic if acid personality'. She also became a highly successful professional writer.

Her first book, *Three Houses* (1931), a picture of childhood, was followed by her first novel, *Ankle Deep* (1933), after which there was an entertaining new novel every year. Critics accused her of snobbery, while in fact she depicted precisely the life of the upper-classes on the verge of extinction. It was also said that her work lacked substance and depth. Nevertheless, she kept her thousands of readers satisfied and first editions of her novels are now collectors' pieces. She died at Bramley, Surrey, and was buried beside her Burne-Jones grandparents at Rottingdean, in Sussex. Other works include *Wild Strawberries* (1934) and *Pomfret Towers* (1938).

See also G. McInnes, *The Road to Gundagai*, 1965; M. Strickland, *Portrait of a Lady Novelist*, 1977.   P.L.

Thomas, Margaret Haig, Viscountess Rhondda (1883–1958), owner-editor of the magazine *Time and Tide*. She was the only child of D. A. Thomas, a mine owner and politician who became Viscount Rhondda in 1916. Although she succeeded to her father's title in 1918, her attempt to claim a seat in the House of Lords failed after involved legal proceedings.

Margaret Haig Thomas was born in London and educated at Notting Hill High School, St Leonard's School at St Andrews, and, briefly, Somerville College, Oxford. Shortly after her marriage in 1908, she came into contact with the suffragette movement and began a course of self-education and militant activity. She was eventually sent to prison for trying to destroy letters in a post-box with a chemical bomb, but was quickly released after she went on hunger-strike. By the First World War she had become an efficient businesswoman through participating in her father's dealings. Returning from a trip to the United States on the *Lusitania* in May 1915, she was fortunate enough to be rescued after the ship was torpedoed by a German submarine, a notorious incident in which over a thousand passengers lost their lives.

After her father's death, Lady Rhondda started the venture for which she is now remembered: the magazine *Time and Tide*, which she founded in 1920 and herself edited from 1926, when she took over from Helen ARCHDALE, until her death. *Time and Tide* was very much a personal vehicle, reflecting Lady Rhondda's strong convictions—emphatically, though not always orthodoxly, on the political right. However, she had an eye for good writing, and the magazine was notable for the distinction of its editorial staff and its contributors. Over the years, Lady Rhondda sank her entire fortune of some half a million pounds into *Time and Tide*, which was in dire straits by the time of her death in 1958. She wrote several books, including a memoir of her father and the autobiographical *This Was My World* (1933).   N.H.

Thompson, Flora (June) (1876–1947), author of *Lark Rise to Candleford*, which has already achieved classic status. Flora Timms was born at Juniper Hill, a hamlet in Oxfordshire near the border with Buckinghamshire, She was educated at a nearby school, which she left at fourteen to work in a local post office.

After her early marriage to a postmaster, Flora Thompson settled with her husband at Bournemouth. Apart from some poems, her literary efforts consisted for many years of pot-boiling fiction written to help support her growing family. Her first serious, substantial work was *Lark Rise*, a portrait of an Oxfordshire hamlet in the 1880s, published when she was 62; it was followed by *Over to Candleford* (1941) and *Candleford Green* (1943), the three volumes being published together in 1945 as *Lark Rise to Candleford*. The trilogy is essentially autobiographical: 'Lark Rise' is Juniper Hill, and the chief character, 'Laura', is Flora Thompson herself. Her keen observation, power of recall and quiet, limpid style created a literary classic that was also a pioneering account of a rural society pauperized and just beginning to abandon its old customs and values under the onslaught of modern industrial society. More recent attempts to record rural ways before they disappear owe a good deal, directly or indirectly, to Flora Thompson. *Still Glides the Stream* was published in 1948, and the selection *A Country Calendar and other writings* appeared in 1979.

See also M. Lane, *Flora Thompson*, 1976.
N.H.

Thorndike, Dame (Agnes) Sybil (1882–1976), actress. The daughter of a clergyman, she trained first at the Guildhall School of Music and then, overcoming family opposition, for the stage with Ben Greet, afterwards accompanying his Shakespeare company to the United States. Her marriage in 1908 to Lewis Casson, a fellow-member of the Horniman repertory company in Manchester, inaugurated a notable partnership that endured until his death in 1969. Inspired by Casson, an ardent socialist, she joined the Women's Social and Political Union, and remained for the rest of her life an unflagging supporter of progressive causes. She also worked to further the repertory movement, appearing in realist plays by Galsworthy, Granville Barker, and others.

From 1914 to 1919 she played major Shakespearean roles at the Old Vic, and in the post-war years in management with Casson and others, gave powerful performances in Greek tragedy. Her appearance as Beatrice Cenci in Shelley's drama stimulated George Bernard Shaw to write *Saint Joan* for her. Presented in London in 1924, the play provided Sybil Thorndike with her most famous role, and one that she continued to act for the next eight years in London and abroad.

During the Second World War she played leading roles in the Olivier-Richardson seasons with the Old Vic, and in the immediate post-war years scored notable successes in Priestley's *The Linden Tree* and in plays by N. C. Hunter. With Casson she made extended world tours, and in England acted with undiminished vitality in a wide range of productions from Chekhov to *Arsenic and Old Lace*. In 1969 she opened the theatre at Leatherhead, Surrey, named after her.

Sybil Thorndike brought to her life and work a moral intensity that, as she herself admitted, tended at times to overtax her acting technique. Despite this, she remained for more than fifty years one of the leading figures of the English stage. She was created DBE in 1931 and Companion of Honour in 1970.

See also E. Sprigge, *Sybil Thorndike Casson*, 1971.
K.W.

Thornton, Alice (1626/7–1707), autobiographer. Alice was the fifth child of Christopher Wandesford and Alice Osborne, both from prominent Yorkshire families. Her father rose to importance through his friend and cousin, Thomas Wentworth, Earl of Strafford, and was Lord Deputy of Ireland on his death in 1640. Alice was educated largely in Dublin with Wentworth's children, but her life changed drastically for the worse with her father's death and the Irish Rising of 1641. After several alarms, her mother brought the family safely, but much impoverished, to her Yorkshire home. In 1651 Alice married a minor north Yorkshire gentleman, William Thornton, whose own improvidence compounded his existing economic difficulties. Alice had been reluctant to marry, believing before 1641 that she had the financial security to remain single, a 'happy and free condition', and suffered a physical collapse on her wedding day, but seems to have become genuinely fond of her feckless husband by the time of his death in 1668.

It was perhaps the frustrating contrast between her privileged childhood and her straitened married life that prompted Alice to compose, throughout her life, some 900 pages of autobiography. The more overt motive was vindication of her role in a variety of property disputes with her own and her husband's families. The autobiography was left to one of her daughters and first published, in part, in the nineteenth century. This deeply religious work reveals Alice's moderate but convinced royalism and Anglicanism, but is important mainly for its fascinating insights into her family life. Alice bore nine children between 1652 and 1667, only three of whom survived to adult-

393

hood, and the autobiography is especially moving its recollection of her sorrows at the deaths of her children, and her fears of 'the pangs of childbearing, often remembering me of that sad estate I was to pass and dangerous perils my soul was to find'.

See also C. Jackson (ed.), *The Autobiography of Alice Thornton of East Newton*, Surtees Society, 1875.   A.H.

Thrale, Hester Lynch (1741–1821), diarist, poet, and friend of Samuel Johnson. Daughter of Hester Maria Cotton and John Salusbury, landowner of a heavily mortgaged Welsh estate, Hester received a broad education in French, Italian, Spanish, and Latin, as well as in literature. In 1763 she married Henry Thrale, a brewer, and MP for Streatham from 1765. Excluded by him from riding and from running the household, Hester devoted herself to writing and bringing up her children. Unlike her husband, she was a warm, sentimental, and artistic person. In 1764 she became acquainted with Samuel Johnson, who became a close friend and frequent visitor. It may have been he who inspired her to begin her *Children's Book*, a journal describing their education and physical growth. In 1772 her activities took her outside the home, helping to relieve her husband of debt and to manage the brewery until he died in 1781. In 1774 she visited Wales with Dr Johnson, following which she wrote her first travel journal, describing the people and places visited. She also engaged in philanthropic work, helping to manage 'The Ladies' Charity School for Training Girls and Servants', and seeking benefactors for the needy.

From 1776 Hester wrote continually. At Johnson's suggestion she began *Thraliana*, a repository for anecdotes of living people, and between 1779 and 1781 wrote the clever *Three Dialogues on the Death of Hester Lynch Thrale*, character sketches presented in conversation at familiar gatherings. In 1784, after the break with Johnson which occurred because of her marriage to the Italian musician, Gabriel Piozzi, she travelled to Italy. There she contributed to *The Florence Miscellany*, a collection by various writers, and also heard news of Johnson's death. Between 1785 and 1786 she wrote *Anecdotes of Dr Johnson*, desiring to explain why she deserted him after a friendship of sixteen years which was an inspiration to both parties. In 1788 she published *Letters to and from the Late Samuel Johnson*, which won her fame as well as much criticism. In 1794 she wrote *British Synonymy*, describing the origins, meanings, alterations in use, and variations of words.

Hester Piozzi died in 1821, estranged from her daughters, leaving everything to her nephew and adopted son, John Salusbury Piozzi. Among her friends, who included Joshua Reynolds, Edmund Burke, and Mrs MONTAGU in addition to Johnson, she was respected as a clever woman whose writing was widely read.

See also *Thraliana, The Diary of Mrs Hester Lynch Thrale*, ed. K. C. Balderston, 1942; J. L. Clifford, *Hester Lynch Piozzi (Mrs Thrale)*, 2nd ed. 1952.   A.M.N.

Thynne, Joan (1558–1612), mistress of Longleat, the daughter of Sir Rowland Hayward, alderman and Lord Mayor of London. After a 'virtuous' education, she was married at sixteen to John Thynne, heir to Longleat in Wiltshire. After spending four years as a hated interloper with her in-laws, she became mistress of the mansion and estate of Longleat, where forty was frequently the number at dinner. She was also concerned with the birth and care of her four children, while the running of the estates fell increasingly on her shoulders, because her husband was in London seeking advancement. Joan also visited the court, and advised her husband on tactics to pursue there.

She set up a household and became influential in Shropshire as well, involving herself in a long legal battle with Lord Stafford to gain possession of Caus Castle, Shropshire, the jointure which she had brought to the match with Thynne. Stafford had refused to release the castle after selling it to Joan's father in 1574, ignoring Privy Council commands to do so. The Thynnes took Caus by force in 1591, and Joan established herself there to occupy and defend it, sleeping with muskets in her bedroom. She selected jurymen for the legal actions, discussed matters with the sheriff and under-sheriffs, and established a group of supporters (and enemies) among the gentry, freeholders, and others. Both before and after Thynne's death in 1604 she ran the estate, dealing with leases and tenants; the buying and selling of crops and livestock; and the masons and plumbers repairing the castle. She also tried to become an industrial entrepreneur, 'digging for lead upon the Mendips', but was unsuccessful.

Joan Thynne was a patron of art and music; John Maynard dedicated to her a set for viol, lute, and voice, writing that they had their origin in her household 'when by nearer service I was obliged yours'. She was important as a strong-willed gentlewoman who undertook on her own a wide range of activities common to men.

See also B. Botfield, *Stemmata Botevilliana*, 1843, *Victoria County History*, Shropshire, viii; A. D. Wall (ed.), *Two Elizabethan Women: Correspondence of Joan and of Maria Thynne 1574–1612*, Wiltshire Record Society, vol 38.   A.W.

Thynne, Maria (*c.* 1575–1611), daughter of George, Lord Audley, by his wife Lucy (Marvin). Maria's education was probably similar to that of her sister Lady Eleanor DAVIES. She apparently knew Latin, which was unusual for women, and used very individual turns of phrase in writing and invective. She spent some time at Queen Elizabeth's court. Her family were the feuding arch-enemies of the Thynnes, and her youthful secret marriage in 1594 to their son and heir Thomas Thynne, immediately following the young couple's first meeting and in circumstances closely resembling those of the early part of *Romeo and Juliet*, probably prompted Shakespeare to write the play about a year later. Shakespeare's company was playing near by and his patron Lord Hunsdon, the Lord Chamberlain, knew both the Thynnes and their enemies. The secret marriage was later discovered and legally disputed, but was declared valid by Doctor Donne, Dean of the Court of Arches, in 1601. Thomas and Maria took up life as husband and wife, and in 1604, on the death of her father-in-law, Maria took charge of Longleat in Wiltshire from her mother-in-law Joan THYNNE, amid mutual hatred. Later, during her husband's absences at parliament and court, Maria saw to the running of the large and complex estates, dealing with stewards and tenants, collecting large sums of money, and other such tasks. She had three children, dying in childbed in 1611; the infant survived.

See also 'The Feud and Shakespeare's *Romeo and Juliet*: a Reconsideration', in *Sydney Studies in English* v, 1979–80; A. D. Wall (ed.), *Two Elizabethan Women: Correspon-* dence of Joan and of Maria Thynne 1574–1612, Wiltshire Record Society, vol. 38.   A.W.

Tilley, Vesta (1864–1952), male impersonator and entertainer. Born Matilda Alice Powles, she was the daughter of the manager of St George's Hall, Nottingham, where she made her first stage appearance aged three and half, billed as 'the Great Little Tilley'. Her first appearance in male costume was a year later in Birmingham, as 'The Pocket Sim Reeves' (after the famous tenor). Later her clothes were made in Savile Row and were impeccably elegant, although she lost none of her femininity and grace.

Vesta Tilley first performed in London at the Royal, Holborn, on 25 March 1876, and was soon playing three music halls a night, the Canterbury, Lusby's, Mile End, and Marylebone. After appearing in *Robinson Crusoe* in Portsmouth at the age of thirteen, she played many principal boy parts, notably Captain Tra-la-la in the Drury Lane pantomime *Sinbad* under Augustus Harris in 1880. She appeared in all the great music-halls in Britain, as well as in Chicago and New York, retaining her popularity throughout her career with such songs as 'Burlington Bertie', 'Jolly good luck to the girl who loves a sailor', and 'Fairly knocked the Yankees in Chicago'. She was known as 'The London Idol' and retired from the stage on 5 June 1920 with a final appearance at the Coliseum where she took seventeen curtain calls.

In 1934 she wrote *Recollections of Vesta*, in which she said that she had run through the whole gamut of female character songs, from baby tunes to old maids' ditties and 'I concluded that female costume was rather a drag. I felt I could express myself better if I were dressed as a boy'. Because of her patriotic songs she was called 'England's Greatest Recruiting Sergeant', and on her retirement was presented with a set of books containing signatures of two million admirers—*The People's Tribute to Vesta Tilley*. She was married to the MP Sir Walter de Frece, and died in Monaco.   A.D.

Tipping, Isabella (d. 1598), draper. The wife of Richard Tipping, a leading Manchester linen draper who died in 1592, Isabella continued the business during her widowhood, and at her own death in 1598 was among the wealthiest drapers in the town. She owned an eight-roomed mansion, substantial cloth in London and Manchester, £500 in cash, and a large library. She is representative of innumerable 'middle-class' women in Tudor and Stuart England who played a significant role in commercial life and whose experiences have only recently been investigated by historians.

See also T. S. Willan, *Elizabethan Manchester*, Chetham Society, 1980.   A.H.

Tofts, Katherine (?1680–?1758), singer. Of obscure origins, Katherine Tofts was said to be connected to the family of which Bishop Burnet was also a member. She was first heard in a series of subscription concerts during 1703–04, when she sang in both Italian and English. A much-publicized rivalry sprang up between her and the Italian singer Margherita de L'Epine, culminating in 1704 when Mrs Tofts' maid threw oranges at her rival. Mrs Tofts herself disowned the action. The two singers appeared at Drury Lane during the brief period of English opera, but L'Epine did not become prima donna until Tofts retired.

During this period, 1705–07, Mrs Tofts appeared in Clayton's *Arsinoe* and Haydon's *Camilla*, both of which enjoyed some success. The latter was a bi-lingual production with a prologue by Mrs OLDFIELD, the actress. The performance also afforded Mrs Tofts an affecting scene with a wild boar, demonstrating savagery being overcome by vocal and personal charm. She joined the Haymarket Company in 1707 under Owen MacSwiney, but her brilliant career came to an abrupt end in 1709 after a performance of *Lover's Triumph*, amid rumours of a mental breakdown.

Apparently recovered, and possessed of a considerable fortune, she left for Italy, where by 1711 she was successfully singing at assemblies. By 1716 she had married the wealthy British consul in Venice, Joseph Smith, but by 1740 her health had relapsed and she was some years under restraint before her death in 1757 or 1758.

Her voice was soprano, and although experts found fault with her singing style, Colley Cibber believed these to be superseded by her natural gifts, 'the exquisitely sweet silver tone of her voice, with that peculiar rapid swiftness of her throat, were perfections not to be imitated by art or labour'.

See also C. Cibber, *Apology for the Life of Colley Cibber*, 1739; C. Gildon, *Life of Tho-*

mas Betterton, 1710; S. Sadie (ed.), *The New Grove Dictionary of Music and Musicians*, 1981; M. Sands, *Mrs Tofts, 1685–1756*, Theatre Notebook, Vol X, 1966.   C.H.

Trapnel, Anna (*fl.* 1642–60), Fifth Monarchist prophetess. The daughter of a shipwright of Stepney, around 1642 she joined a Baptist congregation at Allhallows which was led by a Fifth Monarchist preacher, John Simpson. During the Civil War she supported Parliament, claiming to have sold her plate and rings to raise money.

Fifth Monarchists believed that Christ's return to reign on earth was imminent, and Trapnel achieved prominence when she began to have millenarian visions. Her claims to have foreknowledge of political events, however, occasioned 'threatning speeches' against her by the authorities. In 1654 she became widely known after experiencing an apparently cataleptic trance at Whitehall. While attending the examination of a leading Fifth Monarchist she was 'seized upon by the Lord', and remained in bed at a nearby house for about twelve days, fasting and uttering ecstatic prayers and spiritual songs. Her prophecies were recorded by an observer and published as *The Cry of a Stone* (1654).

Later she journeyed to Cornwall, and her account of her activities there in *Anna Trapnel's Report and Plea* (1654) provides a vivid glimpse of the impact made by the singing prophetess. Local clergy and magistrates, alleging that she was 'aspersing the Government', had her arrested. Because of the notoriety of the case, she was subsequently taken to London, and kept in the Bridewell prison for two months. Her friends published her spiritual autobiography which related earlier visions and prophecies. In 1655 she was back in Cornwall, visiting an imprisoned Fifth Monarchist leader. Her opposition to Cromwell's government grew bitter; when questioned by soldiers she and her companions retorted 'Thy Lord Protector we own not; thou art of the Army of the Beast'. A collection of prophetic poems appeared in 1658 in which she looked forward to the speedy return of King Jesus who would 'strike down' Cromwell and inaugurate the rule of the saints. Her brief career indicates how the possibilities for female self-expression were augmented by the radical sects which appeared during the seventeenth century.

See also B. S. Capp, *The Fifth Monarchy Men*, 1972.   W.R.O.

Travers, Rebecka (1609–88), Quaker. Rebecka was the widow of William Travers, a tobacconist at the Three Feathers in Watling Street, London, and had one daughter who was named after her mother. Originally a Baptist, she attended a public meeting at the Glasshouse in Broad Street where she heard James Nayler speak and was converted to Quakerism. She subsequently became a prominent writer and minister on behalf of the movement. In 1656 she helped to nurse Nayler after he had been whipped for blasphemy. She visited Quaker prisoners, and was imprisoned herself in the early 1660s. Rebecka Travers had a very good relationship with George Fox, who stayed regularly at her house on his visits to London. Her house was also used, along with those of Gerrard Roberts and James Claypole, for the important Second Day Morning Meeting. It is difficult to know whether she regularly helped this committee in its task of censoring Quaker publications, although one such case is recorded in 1677. She was a member of the London Women's Meeting and was one of the Friends appointed to supervise the right conduct of Quaker marriage ceremonies. She was also a member of the influential Six Weeks Meeting, which was formed to supervise the secular needs of London Quakers. Along with Dorothy WHITE and Margaret FELL she was the most prolific of Quaker women writers. She published *Testimonies* to fellow Quaker women, including Susanna Whitrow (1677), Alice Curwen (1680), and Anne Whitehead (1686).

Rebecka Travers provided the movement with a firm base in London from the early years and did much to build the organization which enabled the Quakers to survive in the difficult climate of late Stuart England. Her publications include *This is For All of Any Those (by what name or title soever they be distinguished) that resist the Spirit* (1664) and *A Testimony For God's Everlasting Truth, as it hath been learned of and in Jesus* (1669).

See also N. Penney (ed.), *The Short Journal and Itinerary Journals of George Fox*, ed. N. Penney, 1925; J. Smith, *A Descriptive Catalogue of Friends' Books*, 2 vols, 1867, supplement, 1893; the unpublished *Dictionary of Quaker Biography* in Friends House, London.   T.O'M.

Tredway, Lettice Mary (1593–1677), Roman Catholic educationist. Daughter of Sir Walter Tredway of Beckley, Buckinghamshire, Lettice was professed a nun of the Augustinian convent at Douai in 1615. In 1624 the nunnery moved to Sin-le-Noble, where Lettice met Thomas Carre and planned with him the establishment of an English convent school at Douai. However, George Leyburne, President of Douai College, persuaded her that Paris would be a better location. Until the school opened English girls could be educated at Sin; two arrived in 1632 from Dover, where they had been arrested.

Richard Smith, Bishop of Chalcedon, used his influence with Richelieu to obtain letters patent from the French King in 1633, and the school opened a year later with five pupils. Eminent English Catholics began sending their daughters to Lettice, although French girls were not admitted as pupils until 1655. There was financial difficulty during the Civil War because the nuns' dowries were invested in England, but help came from the artist Charles Le Brun, their neighbour, who asked Chancellor Séguier for financial aid.

Lettice was abbess until 1674, receiving the dedication of Carre's English version of Thomas à Kempis. She was an important Catholic educationist at a time when English Catholics were handicapped by penal laws.

See also F. C. Husenbeth (ed.), *Notices of English Colleges and Convents established on the Continent*, 1849.   M.D.

Tree, Lady (Helen) Maud (1863–1937), actress. Born in London, Helen Maud Holt was educated at Queen's College, London, where she read classics and performed in Greek drama. Her first stage success came as Hester Gould in *The Millionaire* at the Court Theatre in 1883, the year of her marriage to Sir Herbert Beerbohm Tree, the actor-manager. She excelled in comedy, in Shakespeare, Sheridan, Shaw, and Barrie, and during her distinguished career appeared in most of the lavish productions with which her husband came to be associated. In 1899 she gave three weeks' salary, £1700, for reciting Kipling's 'Absent-Minded Beggar', to the South African War Fund. From 1902 she directed Wyndham's Theatre for a while, and continued on the stage after her husband's death in 1917, playing Mistress Quickly at the age of seventy, before retiring in 1935. She also appeared in films. Her daughter Viola, also an actress, managed the Aldwych Theatre.   B.H.C.

Trefusis, Anne. See DOWRICHE, ANNE.

Trevelyan, Hilda, stage-name of Hilda Tucker (1877–1959), actress. Her first stage appearance was made while still at school, in *The Silver King* (1889), and at the age of fourteen she toured in *A Gaiety Girl.* Always closely associated with the playwright J. M. Barrie, she was the original Wendy in *Peter Pan* (1904) and thereafter played the part many times. Also in 1904 she toured with Sir John Hare in *Little Mary.* She appeared briefly in *Alice-Sit-by-the-Fire,* and then took the leading role in Tree's *Oliver Twist,* (1905), giving a superb performance as the terrified orphan. She acted in many famous plays, including *Quality Street, The Admirable Crichton* (1906), *Trelawny of the 'Wells';* and *Mary Rose* (1926), but Barrie gave her her greatest chance as Maggie Wylie in *What Every Woman Knows,* (1908). Author and actress combined with consummate skill to portray a girl completely lacking in self-confidence who evolves into the courageous wife of a politician. After an unsuccessful period of management with Edmund Gwenn she was again successful in *A Kiss for Cinderella* (1916). Barrie wrote parts especially for her and she played his Lady Babbie nearly 700 times. Critics described her as having 'a fragrant naturalness' in all her work. Her last stage appearance was in 1939. She was married to the actor-playwright Sydney Blow.   A.D.

Trimmer, Sarah (1741–1810), didactic writer. Born at Ipswich, Sarah Kirby was the only daughter of a prosperous landscape artist. She attended a local boarding-school, where she acquired fluent French, until the family moved to London in 1755. Here she met and married James Trimmer of Brentford, by whom she had twelve children. With her husband's encouragement, she educated her large family herself, and with such success that friends persuaded her to publish the lessons. In 1782 her *Early Introduction to the Knowledge of Nature* appeared. Some years later, much impressed by Madame de Genlis' *Adèle et Théodore,* she developed the idea of illustrating lessons with prints, to be hung with an explanatory text in school-rooms. Eventually bound and published as *New and Compre-*

hensive Lessons, this work proved extremely popular.

Always a devout Christian, Sarah Trimmer produced many books designed to introduce children to Christian principles. Between 1782 and 1784 her *Sacred History . . . adapted to the Comprehension of Young Persons* appeared in six volumes. She also published many shorter pieces explaining some of the central tenets and customs of Christianity, many of which were issued by the Society for the Propagation of Christian Knowledge. Her *Abridgements* of the Old and New Testaments sold 250,000 copies during the seventy years that they remained on the Society's lists.

Throughout her life Mrs Trimmer was preoccupied with the education of the poor, and wrote many pamphlets designed to better the content and organization of their instruction. From 1788 she edited *The Family Magazine,* which contained both sermons and informative articles, thus combining moral improvement and useful knowledge in a palatable form. From 1786 she was actively involved in running the first local Sunday Schools, opened largely due to her own exertions. Her success in this field attracted the attention of Queen CHARLOTTE, who sought her advice on founding Sunday Schools in Windsor, and encouraged her to set down her knowledge of their promotion and management. This resulted in the publication in 1786 of the highly influential *Economy of Charity,* a handbook of philanthropic advice.

Mrs Trimmer did much to improve the quality of basic education for children of all classes. She saw clearly the need to capture the attention of the young, and, at all levels, sought to present suitable knowledge in an interesting and manageable form. Her career illustrates the considerable influence that women could exert from within the traditional sphere if their work could be seen as an extension of domestic duties rather than in conflict with them.

See also Mrs A. K. Elwood, *Memoirs of the Literary Ladies of England,*1843.   J.V.L.

Trollope, Frances (1780–1863), author. Born at Stapleton in Somerset, Frances Milton was the daughter of a vicar. In 1809 she married Thomas Anthony Trollope and had six children, one of whom became the famous novelist Anthony Trollope. Her writing career did not begin until she was over fifty, when the endless financial disasters of her husband compelled her to become the breadwinner. Her first book, *Domestic Manners of the Americans* (1832), partly based on her experiences of trying to start a bazaar in Ohio, was a sensation, scathing in its comment on America and Americans. From then onwards she made enough money to keep her dependants in comfort, and continued writing until she was seventy-six, having then published 114 books.

Her working day began before dawn, for she combined authorship with household management and the care of her children, four of whom predeceased her. Her son Thomas wrote that she had many troubles, but 'of all people I have known she was the most joyous'. She published travel books and dozens of novels. The most esteemed were *The Vicar of Wrexhill* (1837), a portrait that mingled vice and religion, *The Widow Barnaby* (1838), with its coarse, humorous heroine, and *The Life and Adventures of a Clever Woman* (1854). Her special gift, oddly for a Victorian lady, was the depiction of rather bawdy characters. Her son Anthony agreed that she was remarkably creative but said 'she was neither clear-sighted nor accurate—and was unable to avoid the pitfalls of exaggeration'. In 1844 she moved to Florence, where she died.

See also J. Johnston, *The Life, Manners and Travels of Fanny Trollope*, 1979; T. A. Trollope, *What I Remember*, 1887.   P.L.

Tucker, Charlotte Maria (1821–93), writer and missionary. She was born in Barnet, the daughter of an authority on Indian finance. Her mother's family was related to James Boswell, biographer of Dr Johnson. Charlotte was educated at home, where she wrote verse and plays from childhood. Her father had disapproved of the idea that she should publish any of her work, but after his death in 1851 she wrote at least one book for children every year, giving all the proceeds to charity. Her work appeared under the pseudonym of 'ALOE' (A Lady Of England).

In 1869 Charlotte Tucker's mother died and, although almost fifty, she decided to become a missionary. She studied Hindustani and set off for India, going to Amritsar in 1875 and Lahore in 1876. Here she wrote numerous tracts and worked hard teaching her faith to Indian women. Although her books are mostly pious allegories and parables conveying obvious morals, she also wrote on natural history, and these works are more straightforward and entertaining. Her titles include *The Rambles of a Rat*, 1854; *Wings and Stings*, 1855; and *Old Friends with New Faces*, 1858.

See also A. Giberne, *A Lady of England: The Life and Letters of Charlotte Maria Tucker*, 1895.   B.H.C.

Tuckwell, Gertrude (Mary) (1861–1951), social reformer. A daughter of William Tuckwell, well known in his day as the 'radical parson' and the Master of New College School, Gertrude Tuckwell was born in Oxford, where she grew up in an atmosphere of progressive thought. Her aunt was Lady DILKE, a pioneer of women's trade unions. Gertrude worked as an elementary teacher under the London School Board from 1885 to 1892, teaching the children of the poor. She then became Lady Dilke's secretary, being appointed honorary secretary to the Women's Trade Union League until her aunt's death in 1904, when she succeeded her as the League's president. She remained president until the WTUL's work was taken over by the General Council of the Trades Union Congress in 1921.

With the help in parliament of the Liberal statesman Sir Charles Dilke, the League gained notable successes in, for instance, its campaign against white-lead poisoning in the china and earthenware industries, and against 'phossy jaw'—contamination by phosphorus suffered by match-makers. In these campaigns Gertrude Tuckwell played a leading part. Under Sir Charles's influence she had become convinced that philanthropy alone could never right women's wrongs: women must be helped to help themselves. As a result she supported trade unionism. She also fought for the setting up of wages boards. In 1906 she presided over an Exhibition of Sweated Goods that publicized the harshness of factory conditions for women. The 1909 Trades Board Act resulted from such efforts.

In later years Gertrude Tuckwell was to espouse the cause of the welfare of working women during pregnancy and in childbirth; with Mary MACARTHUR she led a national campaign against preventable maternal mortality. She was a member of the Royal Commission on National Health Insurance (1924–26); presided over the Women Public Health Officers' Association for much of the 1920s; and was a member of the Women's Central Committee on Women's Training and

Tudor, Margaret

Employment. In 1920 she was the first woman to be sworn a Justice of the Peace for the County of London. An active member of the Labour Party and a persuasive speaker, she frequently addressed annual TUC conferences.

Gertrude Tuckwell developed a lucid literary style, and with Stephen Gwynn wrote a two-volume life of Sir Charles Dilke (1917). Other works include *The State and its Children* (1894) and *The Worker's Handbook* (1908).

See also L. Middleton (ed.), *Women in the Labour Movement*, 1977.   J.L.

Tudor, Margaret (1489–1541), Queen of Scotland. The daughter of Henry VII and Elizabeth of York, she had been proposed by England as the bride of James IV of Scotland in 1495, in order to persuade the Scots against supporting the claim to the English throne of the impostor Perkin Warbeck. It was not until August 1503, however, after much negotiation, that Margaret entered Scotland to marry James IV. During the next nine years she bore him six children, only one of whom, the future James V, survived infancy.

If Henry VII had hoped to bind Scotland closer to England by marrying his daughter to James, the policy was, in the short term, a failure. By 1513 the two countries were at war, despite Margaret's attempts to prevent Scotland from engaging in hostilities. In September of that year James died at the battle of Flodden, leaving a seventeen-month-old heir and Margaret, pregnant again, as effective head of state. Her English background and marriage to the pro-English Archibald Douglas, Earl of Angus, lost her support among the Scottish nobility, who recalled the Duke of Albany from France to become Regent. Albany forcibly secured custody of the young King and his brother, and Margaret, after failing to recapture them, fled to the court of Henry VIII in 1515. In England she gave birth to a daughter, Margaret, who was to become the Countess of Lennox and grandmother of King James VI.

Angus, returning to Scotland without her, regained his estates and made peace with the Albany faction, so that when Margaret returned in 1517 to continue the struggle for power, she and her husband found themselves in opposition. Because Henry VIII refused to aid her in obtaining a divorce from Angus, his ally, Margaret sided with Albany, who had influential connections in Rome. Angus was then banished by Albany, but Margaret repaid his help by betraying his invasion plans to the English. When Albany left Scotland in 1524 to return to France, Margaret enjoyed a brief period of success, as she obtained custody of the King and with it the position of head of state. In late 1525, however, Angus seized control of the King and, despite several attempts by Margaret to rescue him, kept control until James escaped in 1528 and forced Angus into exile in England.

Margaret and her third husband, Henry Stewart, Lord Methuen, now became the young King's closest advisers, although her influence with James was to a large extent lost following his discovery that she had betrayed his secrets to Henry VIII. Nor were her relations with her third husband any better, for she often complained to her brother and son of Lord Methuen's treatment and sought a divorce. In her last years she had little influence. She lived to see her son married to MARIE DE GUISE, who seems to have won the approval of her querulous mother-in-law, and died at Methuen Castle.

Personally unsuited to the demands of ruling, and always inclined to favour England, her adopted country's greatest enemy, Margaret Tudor was not a successful Queen of Scotland. Her inability to sustain a relationship with her last two husbands and her two surviving children partly reflects her own personality, but also the demands made by the position of a marriageable princess in European dynastic politics.

See also 'Tudor Intrigues in Scotland', in *Scottish Review*, 1894; H. W. Chapman, *The Sisters of Henry VIII*, 1969; B. Seton, 'The distaff side', in *Scottish History Review*, 1919.
      G.Q.B.

Tussaud, Anne Marie (1760–1850), waxmodeller. Born in Strasbourg, she was the posthumous daughter of Johannes Gresholtz, a soldier. Her mother became housekeeper to Philippe Curtius the wax-modeller and founder of the Cabinet de Cire, who was the major influence on her life. Her education was undertaken by Curtius, whose apprentice she became after they moved to Paris in 1767, and she soon became a skilled sculptress in wax. In 1780–89 she was art tutor to Madame Elizabeth at Versailles, where she grew to know the court well, only leaving for fear of the Revolution. Although she survived the Revolution, it had a lasting impact on her, particularly as she was forced to model the death masks of many she had known, including her patron. She was later to use many of the grisly scenes of the Revolution in her subsequent exhibitions.

Curtius died in 1794, leaving Anne Marie as his heir, and thereafter she ran his exhibition. She married François Tussaud, a civil engineer eight years her junior in 1795 and her two surviving sons were born in 1798 and 1800. The Tussauds separated about 1800 and there was no reconciliation. Subsequent financial and domestic strains persuaded her to take the exhibition to London in 1802; it never returned to France. She signed the French property over to her husband, and with her eldest son, Joseph, spent nearly thirty years in touring with the exhibition before finding a settled home in Baker Street (1833), by which time the other son, François, had joined them. The exhibition proved a consistent success because of her determination, talent as an advertiser, skill in wax-modelling, and her realization of the importance of expanding the exhibition and keeping it up-to-date. She believed her show must be entertaining and instructive and, above all, accurate. As a result she created the outstanding waxwork exhibition of her age, and an abiding tradition. She died in England, leaving the exhibition there jointly to her sons.

See also L. Cottrell, *Madame Tussaud*, 1965.

J.R.

Twining, Louisa (1820–1912), poor law reformer. Born in London, she was the youngest child of the tea merchant and philanthropist Richard Twining. Intelligent and energetic, in early years she had interests that were largely artistic, and in 1852 she published *Symbols and Emblems of Early and Medieval Christian Art*, with her own drawings. In the late 1840s she began to visit the poor near her home in the Strand, and joined her father in helping to set up a Church of England nursing sisterhood. In 1853 she first entered the Strand Union Workhouse, eventually being allowed to hold afternoon services and give sermons.

To increase her knowledge of poor relief, Louisa Twining visited other workhouses around the country and gave papers at meetings of the National Association for the Promotion of Social Science, where she met many of the people prominent in poor law reform. When the NAPSS sanctioned the formation of the Workhouse Visiting Society in 1858, she became its secretary, and established a home for workhouse girls sent out to service in 1861. In the same year she gave evidence before a Select Committee on Poor Relief.

One of her main interests was the field of workhouse nursing, and in 1879 she became the secretary of the Association for Promoting Trained Nursing in Workhouse Infirmaries and Sick Asylums. A campaigner for women in local government, she was chairman of the Society for Promoting the Return of Women as Poor Law Guardians. From 1884 to 1890 she was herself a Poor Law Guardian for Kensington, and from 1893 to 1896 for Tunbridge Wells. In later years she was president of the Women's Local Government Society, but did not ignore women's political involvement at national level, as she believed that votes for women would lead to legislation for improving public morality and women's employment opportunities.

Throughout her long and active life she wrote extensively on poor relief and related issues and was a frequent contributor to *The Times*. No woman of her generation did more to raise the standard of poor law administration or to reduce the widespread prejudice against women in local government. Her other works include *Workhouses and Women's Work*, 1858; *Recollections of Workhouse Visiting and Management during Twenty-Five Years*, 1880; *Recollections of Life and Work*, 1895; and *Workhouses and Pauperism*, 1898.

F.K.P.

Tyler, Margaret (*fl.* 1578), translator, known only for her translation of the first part of a lengthy Spanish romance by Diego Ortuñez de Calahorra. Published about 1578 as *The Mirrour of Princely Deedes and Knighthood*, the work was very popular with Elizabethan readers and was certainly known to Shakespeare, who may have drawn on it for an episode in *The Tempest*.

Margaret Tyler's prefatory address to the reader is of some interest in the history of the struggle for women's literary emancipation. She begs indulgence for her translation 'for that it is a woman's woork, though in a story prophane, and a matter more manlike than becometh my sexe'. But she goes on to defend herself by pointing out that men have previously dedicated their writings to women, and therefore, if worthy to have works dedicated to them, 'then may we read such of their works as they dedicate unto us, and if we may read them, why not farther wade in them to the search of a truth . . . it is all one for a woman to pen a story, as for a man to address his story to a woman'. Her forthright declaration in favour of women's equality in reading and writing is a notable forerunner of the feminist controversies of the early seventeenth century.

See also H. Thomas, *Spanish and Portuguese Romances of Chivalry*, 1920; *Notes and Queries*, March 1946.   W.R.O.

Tynan, Katharine (1861–1931), poet and novelist. She was the daughter of a prosperous County Dublin farmer, and some of her best poems are based on her childhood memories of him at work, and on the round of life in the countryside. Her convent education at Drogheda was cut short by the appearance of ulcers on her eyes following a bout of measles, and her sight remained poor. In 1883 she married the barrister and novelist H. A. Hinkson and lived with him in England until 1916; after his death in 1919 she lived variously in England and Ireland and on the Continent.

Katharine Tynan's first book of poems was *Louise de la Vallière*, published in 1885. It was successful enough to bring her to the attention of W. B. Yeats, AE (George Russell) and other prominent figures in the 'Irish Renaissance'. Her association with them perhaps led to an overvaluation of her work, which is notable for its strong religious feeling. She also wrote *The Way of a Maid* (1895) and more than a hundred similarly sentimental novels that irritated critics but evidently provided a useful income.

See also her five autobiographical volumes, *Twenty-Five Years*, 1913; *The Middle Years*, 1916, etc.   N.H.

U

Underhill, Evelyn (1875–1941), poet and mystic. She was born in Wolverhampton, the only child of Sir Arthur Underhill, a barrister, and educated mainly at home. At King's College for Women, London, she read history and botany, becoming a Fellow in 1927. In 1907 she married Hubert Stuart Moore, a barrister and childhood friend, and the following year saw her final conversion to Christianity. Initially attracted to Rome, she did not become a Roman Catholic as she felt that this would compromise her intellectual integrity. In 1911 she published her first important work, *Mysticism*, and through it met Baron Friedrich von Hügel, who was to become an important influence and eventual spiritual director.

Her writings stress the complementary importance of the spiritual and the social—she would often say 'To give Our Lord a perfect service Martha and Mary must combine'—and her religious work was divided between contemplation and action. Mornings were spent in writing and afternoons in visiting the poor and directing their souls. She became a practising Anglican in 1921, and in 1924 began to conduct retreats, which formed the basis for several of her books. She wrote three novels, two books of verse, and many philosophical and religious works, including *Concerning the Inner Life* (1926) and *The Life of the Spirit and the Life of Today* (1922), from her 1921 Upton lectures on religion at Manchester College, Oxford.

During the First World War she worked for naval intelligence but became a Christian pacifist in 1939, joining the Anglican Pacifist Fellowship and writing an uncompromising pamphlet, *The Church and War* (1940). She had a lively sense of humour and a vivid personality. Although shy, her love for souls, her hatred of manipulating those under her spiritual direction, and her determination to let them grow in their own way won her the love and affection of all. A.D.

Ursula, St (*fl.* possibly *c.* 400), legendary saint and virgin martyr whose supposed life history constitutes an entertaining piece of medieval myth-making. She is said to have been a British princess who made a pilgrimage to Rome with 11,000 accompanying virgins. On their way back they were martyred *en masse* at Cologne after Ursula had refused to wed the Hunnish chieftain there. In the eleventh century the cult of St Ursula and the trade in relics received a fillip from the discovery at Cologne of great quantities of bones, actually of both sexes and various ages, which were taken to be the remains of the martyrs. St Ursula later inspired a cycle of paintings by the Renaissance artist Carpaccio, and gave her name to the Ursuline teaching order.

Historians have traced the story back to a Latin inscription of *c.* AD 400 in the Church of St Ursula at Cologne. It says nothing more than that somebody called Clematius restored a ruined church in honour of some local virgin martyrs. The most fantastic of the later elaborations, the virgin multitude, may well derive from a misreading of XI MV ('eleven virgin martyrs') as XIM V ('eleven thousand virgins'). Since 1969 the feast of St Ursula no longer appears in the universal calendar of the Roman Catholic Church, although certain local celebrations of it are still permitted.

N.H.

Uttley, Alison (1884–1976), writer. Born at Cromford, Derbyshire, Alison Taylor was the daughter of a farmer. She was educated at Bakewell Grammar School and Manchester University, where she graduated with an honours degree in physics, and then studied education at Cambridge for a year before becoming a teacher. In 1911 she married a scientist, James Uttley, who died in 1930, leaving her with a son.

Alison Uttley was a natural writer and turned to this as a livelihood that would enable her to be at home during her son's childhood. Her first book, *The Country Child* (1931), was illustrated by C. F. Tunnicliffe, as were so many of her writings for adults. It was the forerunner of many books about the countryside, through which she created a special place for herself in the field of rural *belles-lettres*. Although firmly rooted in her scientific training, she allowed her imagination to fly free without ever losing her readers' trust. Ghosts, dreams, and country superstitions were as real to her as light, rocks, or trees. Her children's books were also very popular and are perhaps her most widely known works today. Drawing on her own observation of animals, she created Little Grey Rabbit, Little Red Fox, Brock the badger, Sam the pig, and many other creatures. The greater part of her adult life was spent in Buckinghamshire, and she died there, in High Wycombe.

Other works by Alison Uttley include *The Stuff of Dreams*, 1953; *A Traveller in Time*, reissued 1963; and *A Ten O'Clock Scholar*, 1970. Most of her essays are autobiographical, and she also published an autobiography, *Ambush of Young Days*, 1951.   P.L.

V

Vanbrugh, Dame Irene (1872–1949), actress. She was born in Exeter, the daughter of a clergyman, and educated at Exeter High School and in Paris. Trained in Margate by Sarah Thorne, she first appeared there at the Theatre Royal in 1888, as Phoebe in *As You Like It*. In the same year she played the White Queen in *Alice in Wonderland* at the Old Globe in London. She appeared at the Haymarket with Beerbohm Tree, and then with George Alexander at the St James's. In 1898 she played Rose Trelawny in *Trelawny of the 'Wells'*, and at the Old Globe in 1899 came her first great success when she appeared in another Pinero comedy *The Gay Lord Quex*. Two years later she married Dion Boucicault, the actor-manager and son of the famous playwright.

Irene Vanbrugh gained a reputation for portraying the heroines of Sir Arthur Pinero and J. M. Barrie, in such works as *The Admirable Crichton* (1902) and as Agnes Ebbsmith in Pinero's *The Notorious Mrs Ebbsmith*. She toured New Zealand and Australia (1923–25 and 1927–29), while earlier in her career she had acted in America, appearing with her brother-in-law Arthur Bourchier. She also performed in South Africa. In 1941 she was created a DBE, having celebrated her stage golden jubilee in 1939 with a matinée at His Majesty's Theatre. With her sister Violet VANBRUGH she shared the family height, dark expressive eyes, a magnificent presence, and great charm. The Vanbrugh Theatre at the Royal Academy of Dramatic Art was named after Irene and Violet Vanbrugh by their brother, Sir Kenneth Barnes, who was principal from 1909 to 1955.

She wrote an autobiography, *To Tell My Story* (1948).   B.H.C.

Vanbrugh, Violet (Augusta Mary) (1867–1942), actress. She was born in Exeter, the older sister of Irene VANBRUGH, and educated at Exeter High School, in France, and in Germany. Her first London appearance was in 1886 at Toole's Theatre, in burlesque. Two years later she joined the company at Margate, where she had been trained by Sarah Thorne, playing Ophelia. She then went with the Kendals on their American tour, and on her return played Ann Boleyn in Irving's production of *Henry VIII*, also understudying Ellen Terry. She proved a great success.

After marrying the actor-manager Arthur Bourchier in 1894, she appeared as his leading lady at the Royalty, where much of her husband's success was due to her popularity. Roles with which she was particularly associated were in *The Ambassador, Hearts are Trumps,* and *The Wedding Guest*. She was also known for her Shakespearean performances, playing Portia at Windsor Castle in 1905 by command of Edward VII. Later she appeared in films, including *Pygmalion*, 1938.   B.H.C.

Vane-Tempest-Stewart, Edith Helen, Marchioness of Londonderry (1879–1959), public figure. Her father was the prominent Conservative Henry (later Viscount) Chaplin, and her mother a daughter of the Duke of Sutherland. She was brought up mainly at Dunrobin Castle and Lancaster House, London, and in November 1899, when not quite twenty, married Viscount Castlereagh. During the First World War she was founder and director-general of the Women's Legion, becoming the first woman to receive the military DBE; but for most of her life her destiny was intertwined with her husband's. By birth and inclination she was ideally suited to be the wife of a social and political magnate (Castlereagh was Conservative MP for Maidstone from 1906 to 1915, when he succeeded his father as Marquess of Londonderry), and she became a famous political hostess who knew—and perhaps unobtrusively influenced—the great figures of her time. Among her publications were *Henry Chaplin, A Memoir*, 1926, *The Magic Inkpot*, 1928, and two edited volumes of nineteenth-century letters.

See also her reminiscences, *Retrospect*, 1938.   N.H.

Varley, Julia (1871–1952), social reformer and trade unionist. Born in Bradford, Julia Varley was the daughter of a mill-worker and herself began work as a 'half-timer' in a textile mill when only ten. To later generations she was to describe that childhood routine: to the mill by 6 a.m., a half-hour breakfast break at 8.30 a.m., then further work until 12.30 p.m., when they left for dinner and school. 'It was a hard life yet we felt ourselves important, part of the scheme of things, because were we not breadwinners?' At sixteen she joined the Weavers' and Textile Workers' Union, becoming its Bradford branch secretary.

In 1904 Julia Varley was one of the Independent Labour Union's woman delegates to the Labour Party conference, the other being Isabella FORD. She took a leading part in the public campaign against women's sweated labour. With Mary MACARTHUR and others she helped to organize the historic strike of women chain-makers at Cradley Heath (near Halesowen) in 1910, at a time when the chain-makers' wages were only 1*d*. an hour. It was a successful strike, which represented a milestone in the organization of women workers.

In 1913 she was appointed an organizer for the Workers' Union, and when this was amalgamated with the Transport and General Workers' Union in the 1920s, she became its Chief Woman Organizer until her retirement in 1935. She was on the General Council of the Trades Union Congress from 1921 to 1935, with one year's break, and in the inter-war years frequently spoke on behalf of the TUC at International Labour Organisation conferences.

'I learned when young,' she once said, 'that there were three kinds of life for thousands of people: tramp-wards, lodging-houses and prison. I've known all three.' As a militant suffragette she twice went to prison in the years before the First World War. To experience tramp-wards at first hand she walked from Bradford to Liverpool, assuming the identity of a poverty-stricken wife looking for her husband; and in another deliberate experiment she spent weeks experiencing some of London's worst lodging-houses, against the filthy, verminous conditions of which she was later to campaign.

Denied any higher education herself, Julia Varley would tell how, as a mill-girl, she and four colleagues were once taken to Girton College, Cambridge, 'where I learnt the possibilities of life that education could bring'. Her passionate interest in the education of women remained with her.

See also L. Middleton (ed.), *Women in the Labour Movement*, 1977.   J.L.

Vaughan, Hannah. See PRITCHARD, HANNAH.

Vaughan, Kate (*c.* 1852–1903), dancer and actress. She was born Catherine Candelon in

406

London, the daughter of a theatre musician, and trained as a dancer, first appearing in music hall with her sister Susie. Ignoring the stage conventions of the time, she inaugurated a new school of skirt dancing. She also played in burlesque, and from 1876 to 1882 formed part of the quartet at the Gaiety which included Nellie FARREN, Edward Terry, and E. W. Royce.

When forced to give up dancing to safeguard her health, she concentrated on classic comedy, playing Lydia Languish, Peg Woffington, Miss Hardcastle, and Lady Teazle. With H. B. Conway she organized a touring company and then began management at the Opéra Comique. In 1884 she married the Hon. Frederick Wellesley, from whom she was divorced in 1897, afterwards travelling abroad for her health. She died in South Africa. In grace and magnetism she has been called the century's greatest English dancer, owing most to innate rhythm and little to training.

B.H.C.

Vaux, Anne (*fl.* 1605–35), Roman Catholic activist. The daughter of William, Lord Vaux of Harrowden, and a cousin of Francis Tresham, one of the Gunpowder Plotters, Anne was aide to the Jesuit Henry Garnett. With her sister, Eleanor Brooksby, she hired houses notably White Webbs near Enfield, for Jesuit meetings. Tresham and other conspirators often met there, although Anne and Garnett were probably ignorant of their plans. The tradition that she wrote the famous letter to Lord Monteagle warning him not to attend parliament on 5 November 1606 can be discounted.

After the Gunpowder Plot Anne was kept in custody for a time. She was with Garnett at Hindlip, near Worcester, where he was arrested on 25 January, and while he was in the Tower she sent him letters partly written in orange juice (invisible until exposed to heat) until his keeper denounced them. She was arrested in March and herself taken to the Tower, receiving rough treatment, but was released in September. Later she kept a Catholic school at Stanley Grange, near Derby, which was dissolved by warrant of the Privy Council in 1635.

Anne gave valuable service to the Catholic cause at a time of persecution, and as an independent single woman her commitment to Catholicism provided a fulfilling role.

See also *Calendar of State Papers, Domestic, 1603-10.* J. Morris, *Troubles of our Catholic Forefathers*, 1872.   M.D.

Vere, Lady Mary (1581-1670), religious gentlewoman. The basic account of her life is contained in a stereotyped 'godly life', or funeral sermon, reprinted by Samuel Clarke. While highly conventional, the account does reveal how a commitment to religion could broaden the horizons of pious gentlewomen and strengthen the control which they could exercise over their own lives and experience. After the death of her first husband, William Hoby, she married Sir Horace Vere in 1607. Vere was the leading English soldier for the Protestant cause on the Continent in the early seventeenth century, and Lady Mary was herself patron, friend, and confidant to many eminent Puritan divines. She therefore shared her religious commitment with her husband. In her relations with the Puritan ministry, the normal bond between patron and client was broadened into real friendship, and in correspondence with a number of ministers, Lady Vere can be seen acting as spiritual adviser and comforter to them, almost an exact reversal of the customary relationship between a single lady and her clerical protégés.

In her own household, over which she must have presided alone during Sir Horace Vere's periods abroad and after his death in 1637, the pursuit of 'godliness' served to turn the domestic establishment into a spiritual community, centred on Lady Vere as the focal point. More generally, her charitable works and concern for the 'saints' served to create a number of linked activities for her to undertake in the domestic and semi-public arenas. Her reputation as a stalwart of the Puritan cause stood so high that by 1645 parliament consigned to her the care of the King's children, Elizabeth and Henry, Duke of Gloucester. Lady Vere had five daughters by Sir Horace Vere, whom she outlived by over thirty years. The very model of the Puritan matriarch, Lady Mary Vere represents the epitome of the 'godly lady' of the early seventeenth century, her life spanning the history of English Puritanism.

See also British Library, Additional Mss 4275; S. Clarke, *The Lives of Sundry Eminent Persons of this Later Age*, 1683.   P.G.L.

Vestris, Lucia Elizabeth, or Elizabetta (1797-1856), actress, singer, and theatre manager. She was born in Soho, London, granddaughter of the engraver Bartolozzi, and was educated at Manor Hall, Fulham Road. At the age of sixteen she married Auguste-Armand Vestris, dancer and ballet-master at the King's Theatre. He was son of the French dancer Auguste Vestris, who had set a new style of ballet with his brilliant technique and leaps. Her husband, having some occasion to doubt her fidelity, left her four years later and she spent some time in Paris. She was an excellent singer, said to have a perfect, though not fully trained, contralto voice which could have been successful in grand opera. Instead she chose to appear in lighter entertainment, moving from early performances in Italian opera (1815) to gain fame in comedy and burlesque.

Her first success came in *Giovanni in London* (1817), a burlesque of Mozart's *Don Giovanni*. She appeared at Drury Lane in 1820, became famous in *The Haunted Tower*, and scored great success as Phoebe in *Paul Pry*. In 1830 she took over the lease of the Olympic Theatre, opening with *Olympic Revels*, the first in a series of spectacular extravaganzas supplied by James Robinson Planché. She was a theatrical innovator, particularly with regard to costume and scenery, and her sets were models of good taste. She insisted on good costumes, was among the first to have historically correct details, introduced real properties instead of fakes, and is credited with being the first (1832) to use a box set with walls and ceiling to replace wings and backcloth. An exceptional and firm manageress, she was known as 'Madame Vestris'. In 1838 Charles Mathews, an actor at the Olympic, became her second husband, and she helped him in managing Covent Garden (1839-47) and the Lyceum (1847-54).   B.H.C.

Vezin, Jane Elizabeth (1827-1902), actress. The daughter of a merchant, Jane Thomson was born during her actress mother's tour of England, and as a child went with her parents to Australia, where she gained a reputation as a child prodigy with her singing and dancing. In 1845 she played at the Victoria Theatre in Melbourne, and in Tasmania in 1847 married a comedian, Charles Frederick Young. She also appeared in Shakespeare.

Moving to London, in 1857 she played at Sadler's Wells and at Covent Garden, where, as Mrs Charles Young, she appeared with Samuel Phelps, playing Julia in *The Hunch-*

back and being enthusiastically received. From this time onward she was strikingly successful in Shakespeare and classic comedy and from 1858 to 1875 had few rivals in this field. She played at the Haymarket and the Lyceum, and at the opening of the Princess's Theatre, when Henry Irving made his début on the London stage. When Sadler's Wells re-opened under the sole managership of Phelps in 1860, she appeared as Rosalind, playing for the first time with the American actor Hermann Vezin as Orlando.

Vezin had made his way to England in 1850 and, apart from a tour of the United States from 1857 to 1858, thereafter acted exclusively in England. She divorced Charles Young and in 1863 married Vezin, accompanying him on a tour of the provinces. At Stratford in 1864 she played Rosalind at the tercentenary celebrations of Shakespeare's birth. Another particularly notable performance was as Peg Woffington in Charles Reade's *Masks and Faces* at the Princess's Theatre in 1867. Graceful and earnest, she could be successful in both comedy and tragedy. The death of her only daughter in 1901 unbalanced her and the following year she committed suicide. She is buried in Highgate cemetery.   B.H.C.

Victoria, Queen (1819–1901), Queen of Great Britain and Ireland and Empress of India. Alexandrina Victoria was born at Kensington Palace on 24 May 1819, the only child of Edward, Duke of Kent, fourth son of George III, and Princess Victoria of Saxe-Coburg-Saalfeld. She ascended the throne on the death of her uncle, William IV, on 20 June 1837, and was proclaimed Empress of India on 1 May 1876. On 10 February 1840 she married at St James's Palace Prince Albert of Saxe-Coburg-Gotha: she bore nine children, six of whom outlived her. After her husband's death from typhoid on 14 December 1861, she retired into a grief-stricken seclusion which prompted a rash of republican sentiment in the early 1870s; but the Golden Jubilee of 1887 marked her re-emergence into public life.

Although always desirous of maintaining Britain's prestige, her attitude to foreign policy was coloured by her concern for the security of the dynasties into which her children had married, especially the German royal families. This attitude led to conflict with her ministers on several occasions, one such example being the Schleswig-Holstein dispute of 1863–64,

while her Russophobia, first kindled during the Crimean War, seriously embarrassed Disraeli during the Eastern Crisis of 1877–78. In home affairs her political sympathies were initially Whig, but from the 1870s they acquired a virulently anti-Gladstonian hue, and she came to regard the Conservative Party as the sole repository of 'true Liberalism'. She was an indefatigable reader of state papers and a voluminous correspondent, but her political influence was largely confined to a choice of prime minister where there was no obvious candidate: Lords Aberdeen and Rosebery, for example, were her personal appointees. In addition, she helped to mediate between the two Houses of Parliament over the disestablishment of the Church of Ireland in 1869, and over the Reform Bill in 1884. A soldier's daughter, the Queen identified herself closely with the army, and she held no prerogative more tenaciously than that which gave her nominal control over the army through the appointment of the Commander-in-Chief. She also exerted considerable influence over preferment in the Church of England, favouring Broad Churchmen as bishops, and promoted the Public Worship Act of 1874, designed to check the growth of Anglo-Catholic ritualism.

Her refusal to open parliament personally on more than seven occasions after 1861, as well as her frequent foreign visits, weakened the public's perception of the Crown's central role in government, however. Her neglect of Ireland, as opposed to her love of Scotland, only assisted the advance of separatism; and she was remiss in depriving the admittedly indiscreet Prince of Wales of access to the whole range of state papers until 1892. Although she was no friend of 'this mad, wicked folly of "Woman's Rights", with all its attendant horrors', her other views were enlightened: she opposed class snobbery, racial prejudice, and religious intolerance, and she favoured the extension of the franchise in 1867 and 1884.

After the longest reign in English history, Victoria died at Osborne House, Isle of Wight, on 22 January 1901, and was buried in the Frogmore Mausoleum. She had transformed the standing of the monarchy and become the symbol of imperial unity and the matriarch of the royal families of Europe.

She published two works, *Leaves from the Journal of our Life in the Highlands, from 1848 to 1861* (1868), and *More Leaves from the Journal of our Life in the Highlands, from 1862 to 1882* (1884).

See also F. Hardie, *The Political Influence of Queen Victoria 1861–1901*, 1935; E. Longford, *Victoria R.I.*, 1964; Lytton Strachey, *Queen Victoria*, 1921. M.J.S.

Victoria Adelaide Mary Louise, Princess Royal, Empress of Germany (1840-1901). The eldest child of Queen Victoria and Prince Albert, in 1858 she married Prince Frederick Wilhelm of Prussia, later Crown Prince of Germany and, briefly, Emperor (1888). She had eight children, of whom two died young and the eldest became Kaiser Wilhelm II. Her husband died of cancer in 1888, after which she lived in retirement until her death, also of cancer, in August 1901.

Her early display of intellectual alertness delighted her parents, who lavished particular care on her upbringing. Her father had a lasting influence, instilling in her the liberal convictions which were to make her so unpopular in Germany. She was a talented artist and linguist, and showed an early interest in politics and philanthropy. Her marriage, although a love match, fulfilled the dearest wishes of her parents, and she went to Germany feeling that she had a mission to promote Anglo-German friendship and to liberalize the Prussian (later German) system. Her husband already had liberal tendencies and her influence on him was strong.

Victoria, never able to hide her love for England and things English, made little effort to adapt herself to the rigid Prussian environment. This, with her tendency to act impulsively and speak out unwisely, earned her the nickname 'die Engländerin'. Moreover, the success of Prussian militarism under Bismarck made her and her husband's ideas unpopular, divided them from the government, and created a rift between them and their eldest son.

Victoria encouraged the arts in Germany, and forty-two educational and philanthropic institutions were under her patronage. She also gave an important impetus to modernizing nursing and to improving women's education. In her last years she founded the Empress Frederick Institution. None of this dispelled her general unpopularity, however, and her hopes of liberalizing Germany were destroyed by her husband's death.

See also editions of letters to her mother; T. Aaronson, *Grandmother of Europe*, 1968. J.R.

Villiers, Barbara, Countess of Castlemaine and Duchess of Cleveland (1640–1709), mistress of Charles II. The only child of William Villiers, Viscount Grandison, a Royalist commander killed in 1643, Barbara was brought up in reduced circumstances in the country until her early teens, when she moved to London. Here her striking beauty and good connections gained her immediate entry into a fast set of young Royalists. In 1656 she began an affair with Philip, Earl of Chesterfield, which was still in progress in 1659 when she married Roger Palmer. A sober Royalist of modest fortune, Palmer had pressed his suit despite parental objections, only to discover that their apprehensions concerning Barbara's character had been fully justified.

It was in the spring of 1660, when she was sent as a messenger to the exiled court at Brussels, that she became the King's mistress, a position she consolidated immediately after the Restoration. Charles II's marriage to CATHERINE OF BRAGANZA did nothing to diminish his infatuation with Barbara, whom he finally succeeded in appointing a Lady of the Queen's Bedchamber in 1663. In 1661, in order to bolster her position, Charles created her husband Earl of Castlemaine. After claiming paternity of her first two children, subsequently acknowledged by Charles II, Castlemaine prudently left the scene. Barbara was an excellent hostess, and her house in King Street was a major meeting place for the King and aspiring young politicians. It soon became the focal point of opposition to the Lord Chancellor, Clarendon, whose downfall was procured in 1667.

In addition to her extraordinary physical attractions, Barbara was endowed with a shrewd intelligence, a highly developed knowledge of the workings of the court, and an outstanding business acumen. She was thus able to retain her hold on the King, extend her power, and reap colossal material benefits from her position through enormous gifts from Charles, as well as bribes from foreign diplomats and anyone else who sought to use her influence at court. For ten years she remained the King's mistress *en titre* and when forced to yield her place to others, retained a permanent hold on the King's affections and his purse, and a prominent place in the inner circles of power. In 1670 she was created Duchess of Cleveland, and, an ambitious mother, she worked hard to ensure the future of her children. Three sons and two daughters were acknowledged by the King and achieved titles, property, and lucrative marriages. Her youngest daughter, Barbara, was presumably the child of John Churchill, whose mistress she became in 1671.

As a Catholic convert, who had consistently supported religious toleration, the Duchess fared well at the court of James II. Her abstention from associating with the ultra-Catholic party and the support of her son, the Duke of Grafton, for the Protestant Revolution, ensured that she was tolerated at the court of William and Mary. But by the turn of the century her fortunes had declined drastically. In 1705 she became a widow and married an ageing roué, 'Beau' Fielding, who treated her badly and, as it emerged, had married another woman two weeks previously. The humiliation of her so-called marriage and Fielding's trial for bigamy seriously affected her health and hastened her death. She left behind a ducal dynasty and an extraordinary legend of the beauty, wit, and opportunism with which she had captivated Charles II and dominated his court for ten years.

See also E. Hamilton, *The Illustrious Lady, A Biography of Barbara Villiers*, 1980. T.J.M.

Villiers, Elizabeth (*c.* 1655–1733), royal mistress and political confidante. She was the eldest of eight children of Colonel Edward Villiers, a Cavalier and royal servant under Charles II. Her mother, Frances, was governess to the princesses Mary and Anne, with whom Elizabeth was brought up. With her own sister Anne, Elizabeth accompanied Mary to Holland as maid of honour in 1677, on the princess's marriage to William of Orange.

Having had a brief affair with a Scottish officer attached to the Dutch army, Elizabeth became the mistress of the Prince. Mary was aware of the relationship, always conducted with great discretion, from 1680, but matters were forced into the open in 1685 by trusted members of her entourage, acting as agents of her father James II. William dismissed his wife's servants as spies, but Mary sent Elizabeth back to England. Encouraged by her father, Elizabeth returned at once and, although Mary initially refused to receive her,

she soon resumed her relationship with William, which continued after he became King of England in 1689.

'Squinting Betty', as the Dutch called her, was unprepossessing in appearance but admired for her shrewdness. Her wit, ability, and common sense were appreciated by the overworked and anxious William, who obtained solace and wisdom in her conversation and companionship. Greatly in demand at social gatherings, Elizabeth served William as an intelligence agent, reporting on the conversations of unsuspecting diplomats and politicians and their wives. Her influence was used to persuade Shrewsbury to become Secretary of State, and although unsuccessful, she received this telling tribute: 'When you, madam, have attempted to persuade, and have failed, you may conclude the thing is impossible.'

After Mary's death in 1694, filled with remorse at his former behaviour, William terminated his relationship with Elizabeth, but settled upon her estates worth £30,000 a year and encouraged her marriage to Lord George Hamilton, whom he created Earl of Orkney. Elizabeth then acted as a great society hostess at Cliveden, where in the reign of Anne she entertained the Whig leaders, and she subsequently gave parties and did the honours for George I at Hampton Court. She remained a political personality, whose advice was sought by her husband and other politicians, including Walpole. Swift described her as the wisest woman he knew, yet her accomplishments were in subsequent centuries undervalued until she recently received her due as a remarkable woman, who for nearly fifteen years provided William with emotional and political support, while wielding considerable power and influence behind his throne.

See also H. Chapman, *Mary II*, 1953.

T.J.M.

Villiers, Margaret (Elizabeth Child-), Countess of Jersey (1848–1945), public figure. Born at Stoneleigh Abbey in Warwickshire, she was the daughter of Baron Leigh and sister of the Duke of Westminster. In 1872 she married the Earl of Jersey, and until her husband's death in 1915 was hostess to the powerful and famous at her great house at Osterley. She lived in New South Wales when her husband was Governor-General there (1891–93), and became a devout believer in the mission of the

Empire; she was one of the founders of the Victoria League, of which she was president for twenty-six years. She wrote plays for children, many articles about her extensive travels, and an autobiography, *Fifty-One Years of Victorian Life* (1922). N.H.

W

Waddell, Helen (1895–1965), scholar of the medieval period. Daughter of a clergyman, Helen Waddell was educated at Victoria College, Queen's College, Belfast, and Somerville College, Oxford. Her entry to Oxford was postponed for some years while she cared for her invalid mother; during this period, because of time lost, she abandoned plans to study Greek and decided to concentrate on Latin. In 1921 she was Cassell Lecturer at St Hilda's College, Oxford; from 1922 to 1923 lecturer at Bedford College, London; and from 1923 to 1925 Susette Taylor Fellow at Lady Margaret Hall, Oxford. In 1932 she became a member of the Irish Academy of Letters, and in 1937 a corresponding Fellow of the Medieval Academy of America. She held honorary degrees from the universities of Durham, Belfast, Columbia, and St Andrews. Her scholarly works include the pioneering *The Wandering Scholars*, 1927; *Medieval Latin Lyrics*, 1929; a translation of *Manon Lescaut*, 1931; and *The Desert Fathers*, 1936. Her novel *Peter Abelard* (1933) made her known to a wide audience.

See also M. Blackett, *The Mark of the Maker: A Portrait of Helen Waddell*, 1973.

J.E.

Wakefield, Priscilla (1751–1832), philanthropist and writer. Born of Quaker parents, she married Edward Wakefield, a London merchant, in 1771. Edward Gibbon Wakefield and Elizabeth FRY were among her relatives. Her considerable philanthropic achievements included the establishment of several early savings banks and a charity for lying-in women. She was also a tireless producer of books for the intellectual and moral improvement of young people. Such works were mainly of the type which explain the world of plants and animals in a way calculated to excite interest and demonstrate the proofs of natural religion. Several of these went through numerous editions; her *Family Tour through the British Empire* (1804) was reprinted fourteen times. Of more interest to feminists today is her *Reflections on the Present Condition of the Female Sex, with Suggestions for its Improvement* (1798). Priscilla Wakefield believed that the talents of women ought to be directed less into indolent and trifling amusements and more into useful, and indeed financially profitable, pursuits. Women engaging in trade ought not to be excluded from polite society, and if they preferred the same tasks as men, ought to receive the same reward. She pointed out that if the occupations of women were less trivial, they would gain in self-confidence.

See also P. Bloomfield, *Edward Gibbon Wakefield*, 1961.

T.H.

Walker, Dame Ethel (1861–1951), painter. Born in Edinburgh, she decided to become an artist after seeing an exhibition there of Chinese art, in which the landscapes particularly impressed her. She studied at Westminster School of Art and worked in the evening classes organized by Sickert. A visit to Madrid, where she copied works by Velazquez, enabled her on the return journey to visit Paris, where she saw the Manet memorial exhibition in 1884. She was at the Slade (1892–94) and continued periodically to work there until 1922, studying both drawing and sculpture. She exhibited at the Royal Academy from 1898, became an ARA in 1940, and was made a Dame in 1943. Most of her working life was spent in London, although she also worked at Robin Hood's Bay in Yorkshire.

Dame Ethel Walker's work consisted mainly of portraits, generally commissioned, among which those of women are the more appealing. She also executed some large-scale decorations, however, as well as flower pieces and seascapes. Her main decorations are the *Nausicaa* series, probably begun in 1919 but continued until the late 1930s, and the 'Zones', influenced by her enthusiasm for the doctrines of Swedenborg and Taoist philosophy. The *Zone of Hate* depicted the misery and suffering caused by the First World War, and the *Zone of Love*, finally completed in the 1930s, the joys of peace in an idyllic manner.

Her style was at first sober and restrained and her colour low in tone, as was natural for someone influenced by Sickert before the turn of the century, and by Velazquez and the early Manet. Later, however, she began to use a lighter palette and more lyrical and expressive colour, possibly through the influence of the New English Art Club, of which she was a member and which, at the turn of the century, was dedicated to the advancement of Impressionism. It may be argued that in her acceptance of Impressionism she remained closer to Whistler and Wilson Steer than to Manet, particularly in his later works.

There are ten works in the Tate Gallery, London, including the *Nausicaa* and the *Zones*. L.M.M.

Ward, Anne (*fl.* 1759–89), printer in York. After the death of her husband, Caesar Ward, Anne continued the publication of *The York Courant* for thirty years. In 1775 she produced the first edition of Mason's *Poems of Gray*, and she may have printed the first edition of Sterne's *Life and Opinions of Tristram Shandy* in 1759. Her son-in-law, George Peacock, carried on the business after her death in 1789.

See also H. R. Plomer, et al., *A Dictionary of the Printers and Booksellers who were at work in England, Scotland and Ireland from 1726 to 1775*, 1932. T.H.

Ward, Barbara (Mary) (1914–81), economist, known for her concern with the problems of world poverty, aid, and development. She was born in Yorkshire and brought up at Felixstowe, where she received a convent education; her religious beliefs played an important part in her policy recommendations. She studied in France and Germany, acquiring an excellent knowledge of the languages, before going up to Somerville College, Oxford, where she took a first in Modern Greats (now Politics, Philosophy, and Economics). Between 1936 and 1939 she worked as a university extension lecturer; she was already, and remained, a Labour Party activist.

In 1939 Barbara Ward joined the staff of *The Economist*, of which she eventually became foreign editor, and the magazine's subsequent position of authority and influence owed much to her, as well as to its editor, Geoffrey Crowther. She became nationally known as a broadcaster on *The Brains Trust*, while making a solid professional reputation with such works as *The West at Bay* (1948) and *Policy for the West* (1951). Her influence, already felt in the United States, was much increased by her spell as visiting scholar at Harvard between 1957 and 1968, while American grants made possible the research and writing of *India and the West*, 1961, *The Rich Nations and the Poor Nations*, 1962, and

Nationalism and Ideology, 1967. She became Schweitzer Professor of International Economic Development at Columbia University, and President (1973–80) and Chairman (1980-81) of the Institute for the Environment and Development. The best known of her later works was *Only One Earth: the care and maintenance of a small planet* (1972, in collaboration with René Dubos).

Barbara Ward's interests were cultural as well as economic; at various times she was a governor of the BBC, Sadler's Wells, and the Old Vic. She married Robert (later Sir Robert) Jackson in 1950, and in 1976 was created a Life Peer as Baroness Jackson of Lodsworth. N.H.

Ward, Mrs Humphrey. See WARD, MARY AUGUSTA.

Ward, Ida Caroline (1880–1949), linguist. She was born and went to school in Bradford, where her father was a wool merchant, and then studied at Darlington Training College and Durham University. After sixteen years as a schoolteacher she became a lecturer in phonetics at Univeristy College, London. She published *Speech Defects and their Cure* (1923) and *The Phonetics of English* (1930).

Having become interested in African languages, she joined the staff of the School of Oriental and African Studies in 1932, becoming successively lecturer, reader, and professor of West African languages. From 1937, as head of the School's new Department of African Languages and Cultures, she presided over a great expansion of African studies, an achievement probably even more significant than her scholarly contributions in analysing the phonetic and tonal structures of African languages. She published several books, including introductions to Ibo (1936) and Yoruba (1949). N.H.

Ward, Mary (1585–1645), Catholic educationist. Born Joan Ward, she came from a prominent Roman Catholic family living near Ripon. Like many other daughters of English Catholic families, she became a nun, joining the 'Poor Clares' at St Omer in 1606. Though happy and fulfilled in the enclosed life, she felt that the way of life of the existing orders was not for her and that God had destined her for some other work. Returning to England, she gathered together a small group of followers. To avoid detection and persecution they wore normal clothes rather than religious habits. By 1609 or 1610 she had returned to the Continent with her companions, but visited England frequently until 1618. In St Omer she founded a boarding school for English girls and a day school for the poor, a pattern afterwards followed in her other foundations. By 1621 she had foundations in Liège, Cologne and Trèves.

In that year she went to Rome to seek papal blessing for her new congregation, popularly known as 'the English Ladies', but despite a four-years stay in Italy failed to obtain it, although she founded several schools there for the poor. After 1625 she set up convents and schools in Germany, Austria, and Hungary, but in 1630 was arrested as a 'heretic and schismatic'. Her release was obtained after her sisters petitioned the Pope, but her Institute of two or three hundred members was dissolved. She was allowed to continue working for religious education in Rome, provided that she and her friends took merely private vows. In 1639 she returned to England, hoping to evangelize her native land, under the patronage of HENRIETTA MARIA. She planned to give girls an education equal to that of boys, but the outbreak of civil war dashed her hopes. Her health, always precarious, gave way, and she died at York in 1645.

Mary Ward advocated an active unenclosed religious life for women, setting aside the directives of the Roman Catholic Church for congregations of women and modelling her Institute on the Jesuits. She tried to educate girls and women towards greater independence, and to give them an intellectual and religious grounding comparable to that received by their brothers, in order to fit them for their responsibilities as wives and mothers, or for the religious life. These ideas were too radical for the seventeenth-century Catholic hierarchy, which suppressed the Institute.

See also M. C. E. Chambers. *The Life of Mary Ward*, 1885.   P.M.H.

Ward, Mary Augusta (1851–1920), novelist known as Mrs Humphry Ward. Born in Hobart, Tasmania, she was the granddaughter of Thomas Arnold of Rugby and niece of the poet Matthew Arnold. In 1865 the family moved to Oxford, where Mary grew up to know Mark Pattison, T. H. Green, Edmond Scherer, and Pater. In 1872 she married T. Humphry Ward who was a Fellow of Brasenose College. In 1881 she moved to London

when her husband was given a post on the staff of *The Times*. Three years later, her first novel, *Miss Bretherton*, was published. She researched early Spanish and Visigothic Christianity for an article in the *Dictionary of Christian Biography*, and this led her to question the value of certain aspects of contemporary Christianity. As a result came her most famous novel, *Robert Elsmere* (1888), which caused a furore by proposing that Christians should devote themselves to social endeavours rather than theology and similar concerns. *Robert Elsmere* was quoted in pulpits, denounced by Marie Corelli, discussed by Gladstone, and translated into dozens of languages. Her thirteen other novels (tiresomely didactic to modern tastes) were also concerned with religious, social, or political reform. They include *David Grieve*, 1892; *Marcella*, 1894; *The Story of Bessie Costrell*, 1895; *Helbeck of Bannisdale*, 1898; *The Marriage of William Ashe*, 1905; and *The Case of Richard Meynell*, 1911.

Although Mrs Humphry Ward worked tirelessly for social reform and women's higher education, she was a vehement opponent of women's suffrage and became the first president of the Anti-Suffrage League in 1908. She concerned herself with charitable agencies and settlement houses, doing much good work for London's poor. She also became one of the first women magistrates in England. She published her autobiography, *A Writer's Recollections*, in 1918. Her other works include *Eleanor*, 1900: *Lady Rose's Daughter*, 1903; *Fenwick's Career*, 1906; and *The Testing of Dinah Mallory*, 1908.

See also E. H. Jones, *Mrs Humphry Ward*, 1973; J. P. Trevelyan, *The Life of Mrs Humphry Ward*, 1923.   A.P./G.B.

Warner, Sylvia Townsend (1893–1978), novelist and short-story writer. She was born at Harrow-on-the-Hill, Middlesex, the daughter of a schoolmaster, and was educated privately. Music was one of her passions, and for the best part of a decade she was an editor of a ten-volume collection of Tudor Church Music. She published *The Espalier* (1925) and other volumes of verse, but made her reputation with the novel *Lolly Willowes* (1926), in which the tradition of spinster-becomes-witch is taken up and told, with great good humour, as a contemporary event. It was followed in 1927 by *Mr Fortune's Maggot*, a touching, heterodox tale of a missionary on a South Sea island. The success of these two novels owes much to the light touch with which they are written, and the even-handed matter-of-factness with which both fantasy and commonplace are treated, to the exclusion of archness and whimsy. They remain Sylvia Townsend Warner's best-known works, although her talent was stronger and more various than her reputation suggests: in novels such as *The True Heart*, 1929, *Summer Will Show*, 1936, *The Corner That Held Them*, 1948, and *The Flint Anchor*, 1954, she wrote of settings that ranged from a medieval convent to the revolutionary Paris of 1848.

Sylvia Townsend Warner's only public gesture was her work on behalf of the Spanish Republic against the Fascist threat. Her life was intensely private, although also extremely sociable, yet she became a transatlantic presence: *Lolly Willowes* was named as the first American 'book of the month'; its author went to New York for a time as guest critic of the *Herald Tribune*, and for over forty years her short stories appeared regularly in *The New Yorker*. The last of her many story collections was *Kingdoms of Elfin* (1977). N.H.

Warren, Elizabeth (*fl.* 1646–49), religious pamphleteer, known only by three pamphlets which she published in the late 1640s. She apparently lived in Woodbridge, Suffolk, and may have been the wife of the Rev. John Warren, headmaster of Woodbridge school from about 1632. Her first tract was a defence of the ordained clergy against lay preachers, *The Old and Good Way Vindicated* (1646, two editions), and in 1647 she issued a long work entitled *Spiritual Thrift*, comprising a series of meditations on religious themes. This reveals her to have been a well-educated woman who knew Latin and wrote well. Her third work, *A Warning—Peece from Heaven against the Sins of the Times* (1649), was a lament on the breakdown of authority in the home, church, and state.

Unlike many female pamphleteers of the 1640s, Elizabeth Warren seems to have accepted a subordinate role for women even in spiritual matters. She published only reluctantly, 'conscious to my mentall and sex-deficiencie', and believed that women were more susceptible to error than men: 'wee of the weaker sex, have hereditary evill from our Grandmother Eve' and so were 'created subordinate by divine institution'. She provides some insight into the difficulties faced by women who wanted to write: her own educational, social, and family commitments, together with poor health, she says, 'put mee continually upon such imployments, as straightens my leisure in affaires of this nature'.

See also K. Thomas, 'Women and the Civil War Sects', in *Past and Present*, 13, 1958; E. M. Williams, 'Women Preachers in the Civil War', in *Journal of Modern History*, I, 1929.
W.R.O.

Warriner, Doreen (1904–72), economic historian. Educated at Malvern Girls' College and St Hugh's College, Oxford, she was awarded a Ph D by the University of London in 1931. After research posts at the London School of Economics and Somerville College, Oxford, she became a lecturer at University College, London.

Having specialized in East European studies, Doreen Warriner travelled widely in the region before publishing *Economics of Peasant Farming* (1939). In 1938–39 she proved herself as much a woman of action as of thought. In the period between the Munich agreement and the final dismemberment of Czechoslovakia, she worked in that country on behalf of the British Council for Refugees, saving the lives of hundreds of Jews and Social Democrats. Her methods were unorthodox and sometimes risky. To obtain visas she bribed the Polish consul with postage stamps, and on occasion made use of the quietly purloined visiting card of a senior general. During the Second World War she worked for the Ministry of Economic Warfare and in the political intelligence department of the Foreign Office; then (1944–46) she took charge of United Nations food supplies to refugees in Yugoslavia.

From 1947 Doreen Warriner was successively lecturer, reader, and professor at the School of Slavonic Studies in London University. She travelled widely, extending her abiding interest in land reform and the problems of economic development until it encompassed virtually the entire world. Her publications included *Land and Poverty in the Middle East* (1948) and *Revolution in Eastern Europe* (1950,) N.H.

Warwick, Countesses of. See GREVILLE, FRANCES EVELYN, COUNTESS OF WARWICK; RICH, MARY, COUNTESS OF WARWICK.

415

Waste, Joan (1534?–56), Protestant martyr. Daughter of a Derby barber and rope-maker, Joan was blind from birth but learned how to knit hose and turn ropes. Becoming a Protestant in the reign of Edward VI, she bought a New Testament and asked either friends, or persons who would do so for a penny or two, to read it to her. In this way she came to learn the Scriptures by heart, and was renowned for her ability and willingness to use Scripture to attack sin and what she considered as religious abuses. Her forthrightness continued into the reign of Queen Mary and the Catholic restoration, causing her to be examined by the ecclesiastical authorities. Questioned about her sacramental beliefs, she termed herself a 'blind, poor, and unlearned woman', but refused to recant the Protestant doctrines she had imbibed. Condemned for heresy, she was burnt to death outside Derby in 1556.

The execution of a blind woman by the forces of Catholicism furnished John Foxe, the Elizabethan martyrologist, with a powerful argument in his attempt to link the Roman religion with tyranny and repression. The examples of Joan Waste and those other handicapped martyrs executed under Mary, such as John Appice, were used to remind Elizabethan Englishmen of what might lie in wait for them if their Queen were to die and Catholicism to be restored.

See also J. Foxe, *Acts and Monuments*, 1563.   G.Q.B.

Watson-Watt, Dame Katherine (Jane Trefusis) (1899–1971), first Director of the Women's Auxiliary Air Force (WAAF). She was born Katherine Forbes in Chile, the daughter of an engineer. During the First World War she served from 1916 to 1918 in the Women's Volunteer Reserve. She owned and ran a kennels from 1922 to 1938 and was also manager of a building estate from 1932 to 1939. In 1935, with Dame Helen Gwynn-Vaughan and Lady Trenchard, she founded the Emergency Service to undertake the training of officers for what was to become the Auxiliary Territorial Service (ATS). She became Chief Instructor to the ATS and was later seconded for duties with the RAF.

With the rank of Senior Controller, Katherine Forbes became the first Director of the WAAF in June 1939. In 1943 she was promoted to Air Chief Commandant and travelled in various service tasks to North America and

the Far East. In 1944 she became a DBE (having been created CBE in 1941), and retired from WAAF.

Joining the staff of the Control Commission in Germany, she became its Deputy Director and finally Director for Welfare. She was also active as Vice-President of the RAF Association and in many other service organizations. In 1966 she married Sir Robert Watson-Watt, a pioneer in the field of radar. Two years later St Andrews University made her an honorary Doctor of Law.

Throughout her life Dame Katherine Watson-Watt displayed great imagination, enthusiasm, and energy in the service of her country, as well as outstanding organizational ability.   F.F.

Watt, Margaret Rose (1868–1948), founder of the British Women's Institute movement. Born in Canada, the daughter of Henry Robinson, QC, she married Alfred Tennyson Watt, a medical officer of health in British Columbia. After her husband's death in 1913 she returned to England to educate her two sons.

Her interest in the Women's Institute Movement, an essentially rural organization at first, began in British Columbia. Wartime experience in England convinced her that the movement would be of value there, by encouraging countrywomen to make the best use of all available foods, for example. With the aid of the Agricultural Organization she started the first Institutes in 1915, after which the movement rapidly spread and became popular. She then planned world-wide links through associations of rural women, for the interchange of help and advice. In 1930 the Associated Country Women of the World was created, with Margaret Watt as president until 1947. Her work earned many awards, including the MBE (1919). By her efforts she transformed a rural Canadian movement into a major British institution with international links. She died in Montreal.   J.R.

Webb, (Martha) Beatrice (1858–1943), social reformer and historian. Born near Gloucester, the eighth daughter of the financier Richard Potter, Beatrice was educated privately and spent a solitary and often sickly childhood. Her father, whom she nursed in later life, was a strong influence on her: 'The only man I ever knew who genuinely believed that women were superior to men, and acted as if he did; the paradoxical result being that all his nine daughters started life as anti-feminists!'. Through her parents' friendship with the philosopher Herbert Spencer, and her own activities among Lancashire cotton workers and in the East End of London, she became interested in social problems, assisting Charles Booth in research for his massive survey *Life and Labour of the People in London*. Her first independent project was *The Co-operative Movement in Britain*, published in the year of her father's death (1891).

Her marriage the following year to the Fabian Sidney Webb strained her friendship with Spencer, who disapproved of Webb's politics and rescinded his decision to make Beatrice his literary executor; but it created a partnership that was curiously complementary. Webb was the researcher, linguist, and committee man; Beatrice's special gift was a skill at social intercourse and, at the beginning of her career at least, the advantage that as a woman, she was not taken seriously. She revelled 'in observing and recording the sayings and doings of men' and in the 'happy-go-lucky acquisition (by guile, not theft) of confidential documents'. Their works together included *The History of Trade Unionism* (1894) and its sequel *Industrial Democracy* (1897), as well as their monumental multi-volume work on English local government. Together they participated in establishing the London School of Economics (1895) and *The New Statesman* (1913).

As Fabians, the Webbs began as élitists, indifferent to party and confident that they could influence the ruling groups in the direction of social reform. They eventually changed their minds and backed the Labour Party; and it was Beatrice who wrote *A Constitution for the Socialist Commonwealth of Great Britain* (1920).

Like her husband, Beatrice Webb believed in investigating public questions by Commission, and served on many during her long life, beginning with that on the Poor Law and Unemployment (1905–09). The Webbs were mainly responsible for the minority report on this subject, which acted as a spur to socialist reform. Later she was a member of the War Cabinet Committee on Women in Industry (1918–19) and, as a JP in London from 1919 to 1927, on the Lord Chancellor's Advisory Committee for Women Justices (1919–20).

Mrs Webb became Lady Passfield in 1929, when her husband was created Baron, but she preferred to use the title only on formal occasions. Two years later the Passfields visited Russia, where they were much impressed by the workings of the socialist state. Their study of Soviet Communism was reprinted many times. Other publications include *Men and Women's Wages: Should they be Equal?* (1919). Beatrice Webb's ashes are buried in Westminster Abbey.

See also her *My Apprenticeship*, 1926, and *Our Partnership*, 1948; N. and J. MacKenzie, *The Diary of Beatrice Webb*, Vol. 1, 1982, continuing; *Lives* by M. A. Hamilton, 1933, and K. Muggeridge and R. Adam, 1967.

J.S.R.

Webb, Mary (1881–1927), author, born at Leighton, Shropshire. Her father was a school-master and she was educated mainly at home. Her very happy childhood fostered a deep love for the surrounding countryside, so that early in life she developed a pantheistic, mystical view of creation. At the age of twenty a serious illness with Graves' disease left her a legacy of frail health and slight disfigurements that aggravated her natural shyness. In 1909 the death of her father, with whom she had a great affinity, shattered her security. It was never entirely regained, although the early years of her marriage (1912) to a young school-master, Henry Webb, were happy.

Her literary career began with journalism in her twenties. The first novel was *The Golden Arrow* (1916), followed by *Gone to Earth* (1917) and *The House in Dormer Forest* (1920). With their brooding fatalism and immersion in the countryside, the books shared similarities with Hardy's novels, and she became to Shropshire what he had been to Dorset. The works received high critical praise but sales were minimal. Depressed by their failure and by her childlessness, she fell ill in 1920. A hopeful move to London, where she shyly entered literary circles, brought optimism. *Precious Bane* (1924) won the Femina prize (1926) and improved the Webbs' finances. She also published poems and essays. Her marriage deteriorated, however, and she also developed pernicious anaemia. Six months after her death in 1927, the prime minister Stanley Baldwin made a speech at a public dinner extolling her gifts. This brought her posthumous fame and great wealth to both her publishers and her estranged husband.

See also G. M. Coles, *The Flower of Light*, 1978.   P.L.

Webster, Clara Vestris (1821-44), dancer. She was born in Bath, where she was taught by her father, and first appeared in a *pas de deux* with her brother Arthur in 1830. In 1836 she went to London, appearing at the Haymarket, and subsequently to Dublin, Liverpool, and Manchester. She was one of the first English dancers to perform the Cachuchu, Cracovienne, and, with her brother, the Tyrolienne. During a Drury Lane performance of *The Revolt of the Harem*, she touched an oil burner which set her gauzy costume alight and caused burns from which she died three days later.

See also I. Guest, *Victorian Ballet Girl*, 1957.   B.H.C.

Webster, Margaret (1905–72), actress and director, known as Peggy. She was born in New York, the daughter of Ben Webster and May WHITTY, was educated in England, and began her career in London in 1924 with Sybil THORNDIKE in *The Trojan Women*. In 1935 she began to direct, producing *Richard II* in New York in 1937 and then *Hamlet*. Among further Shakespearean plays, she directed *Othello*, herself playing Emilia to Paul Robeson's Moor. She toured America and Canada with her own company, was the first woman to direct at the Metropolitan Opera House, and, in England, directed Donald Wolfit in *The Merchant of Venice* at Stratford, and *Measure for Measure* at the Old Vic. Her book *Shakespeare Today* (1956) gives some idea of the quality of her work. She was active in the campaign to start Equity in Britain, and was one of the few established women directors, indeed the only one to be truly successful at directing Shakespeare in America.

                                    B.H.C.

Webster, Mary Louise. See WHITTY, DAME MAY.

Wenham, Jane (d. 1730), the last woman condemned for witchcraft in England. Although the European witch-craze declined in the late seventeenth century, there remained a gulf between the educated world and that of the fearful superstitious folk of remoter country districts. The confrontation between these two worlds was strikingly demonstrated in the case of Jane Wenham, whose apparently equivocal behaviour caused her neighbours in Walkern, Hertfordshire, to accuse her of sorcery. The jury found her guilty but the judge secured a pardon from the Crown, and Jane Wenham lived until 1730 under the protection of charitable well-wishers. The laws against witchcraft were repealed in 1736, although cases of bullying of eccentric old women continued to occur in villages for some years.

See also K. Thomas, *Religion and the Decline of Magic*, 1971.   T.H.

Wenman, Lady Agnes (?–1617), Catholic activist. The daughter of Sir John Fermor of Easton-Neston, Northamptonshire, Agnes married Richard, first Viscount Wenman. Their two surviving sons both succeeded to the title, Thomas as second and Philip as third Viscount.

Agnes is important for her Catholic activities. John Gerard, the Jesuit missionary, once held a discussion at her house with George Abbot, later Archbishop of Canterbury, on the spiritual state of a predestinarian who committed suicide while firmly believing in his salvation. A friend of Elizabeth Vaux, sister-in-law of Anne VAUX, Agnes corresponded with her and consequently was suspected in connection with the Gunpowder Plot. In December 1605 she and her husband were questioned separately about the conspiracy, but were released after a brief term of imprisonment. Agnes is also interesting for her translation of Johannes Zonaras, from the French of Jan de Maumont; the manuscript is now in Cambridge University Library. She was buried at Twyford on 4 July 1617.

See also J. Morris, *Life of John Gerard*, 1881; Calendar of State Papers, Domestic, 1603–10.   M.D.

Wentworth, Anne (*fl.* 1677–79), prophetess, known only by two pamphlets, *A Vindication of Anne Wentworth* (1677) and *The Revelation of Jesus Christ* (1679). She apparently lived with her husband in White-Cross Street in London, where they were associated with nonconformist congregations led by Hanserd Knollys and Nehemiah Cocks. Around 1677 she claimed to have had nightly visitations from the Lord, who imparted to her revelations warning of judgements to befall England as punishment for spiritual apathy, and encouraging the persecuted saints. These revelations were written down by her the following morning 'just as he spake it in verses at several times, and sometimes in prose'.

Unfortunately, her husband and other religious friends did not accept her claims of divine inspiration, but called them 'delusions and disobeying of thy husband'. Following this the revelations became more specific; her husband and three other named individuals were warned to repent on pain of losing their souls. Eventually her husband commanded her to leave the house, and when she refused he removed all the furniture. In the middle of 1677 he sent three of her cousins to evict her by force.

The response to Anne Wentworth's claims to spiritual inspiration in the late 1670s was in marked contrast to the respect enjoyed by earlier prophetesses in the Civil War period. Her reception possibly indicates a significant tightening of restraint on female claims to spiritual equality, even among the nonconformist sects.

See also K. Thomas, 'Women and the Civil War Sects', in *Past and Present*, 13, 1958.

W.R.O.

Wereburga (*fl.* 675–700), abbess. According to the late hagiographical documents which are the only source for her life, Wereburga was the daughter of King Wulfhere of Mercia and a Kentish princess, Ermenhild. She received many offers of marriage in her youth, including proposals from an unknown West Saxon prince and from Werbod, chief steward of the palace, who engineered the deaths of two of her brothers when they opposed his request. She refused them all, however, and entered the monastery that her maternal great-aunt ÆTHELTHRYTH had founded at Ely some time between 673 and 679. Here she remained until after 697, when she took the place of her mother (who wished to go to Ely herself) as superior at her maternal grandmother's foundation at Sheppey in Kent. On her mother's death Wereburga returned to Ely, where she was made abbess. She left again before 704, when her uncle, King Ethelred of Mercia, asked her to be superintendent of some, or all, of the nunneries in his kingdom. Wereburga founded four new houses in Mercia (at Trickingham; Hanbury, in Staffordshire; Weedon, in Northamptonshire; and Repton, in Derbyshire) and quickly established a reputation for piety and healing. Shortly before her death, she visited all her foundations and requested that she should be buried at Hanbury. However, the community at Trickingham, where she died between 700 and 707, refused to honour this wish, and the Hanbury residents had to claim her corpse by force. Wereburga's body was translated twice; once by King Ceolred, nine years after her death, and then during the Viking invasions, when it was taken to Chester. Here it became a centre of pilgrimage, Wereburga's feast-days being 3 February and 21 June.

J.C.

West, Rebecca. Pseudonym of Cicily Isabel Fairfield (1892–1983), journalist, critic and novelist. She was born in London but spent much of her childhood in Edinburgh, where she attended George Watson's Ladies' College for a time. She arrived in London to study at the Royal Academy of Dramatic Art, but her stage career was brief; it did, however, provide her with her pseudonym 'Rebecca West', taken from the heroine of Ibsen's *Rosmersholm*. In 1911 she ventured into journalism as a reviewer for the feminist *Freewoman*, and when it closed she joined the staff of *The Clarion* as a political writer, ardent in the cause of female suffrage.

The authority—and the cutting edge—of Rebecca West's writing made an immediate impression on contemporaries, and not least on H. G. Wells. The subsequent ten-year liaison (1913–23) between Rebecca West and Wells, a famous and married man, was necessarily clandestine and fraught with difficulties, especially after the birth of their son Anthony in 1914. Nevertheless Rebecca West managed to publish a study of Henry James (1916) and two novels, *The Return of the Soldier* (1918) and *The Judge* (1922).

In 1923 she broke with Wells and made her first visit to the USA, forming an important connection with the *New York Herald Tribune*. Much of her career was in fact occupied with high-quality journalism, some of which supplied material for such critical books as *The Strange Necessity*, 1928, *Ending in Earnest*, 1931 and *The Court and the Castle*, 1957. Her special gift for combining observation, vivid on-the-spot description and historical reflection found its most ambitious expression in *Black Lamb and Grey Falcon* (1941), on the people and history of Yugoslavia, which is widely considered her masterpiece. Reporting the Nuremberg trials after the Second World War prompted *The Meaning of Treason* (1949), revised and expanded several times until the definitive *New Meaning of Treason* (1964). She was created CBE in 1949, DBE in 1959. Rebecca West's fiction displays her intellectual preoccupations and gifts but is not the work of a born novelist. *The Fountain Overflows* (1958), with evident autobiographical elements, is perhaps her best novel. Others are *Harriet Hume*, 1929, *The Thinking Reed*, 1936, and *The Birds Fall Down*, 1966.

During her last years Rebecca West's reputation increased dramatically, partly thanks to public interest in early feminism. A generous selection of her works, *Rebecca West: A Celebration* (1977), was published, *Black Lamb and Grey Falcon* was reissued, and some of her early writings (1911–17) were reproduced in *The Young Rebecca* (1982). She herself published the nostalgic *1900* (1982) and was said to be working on an autobiography at the time of her death.

See also M. F. Deakin, *Rebecca West*, 1980; G. N. Ray, *H. G. Wells and Rebecca West*, 1974.   N.H.

Westmacott, Mary. See CHRISTIE, DAME AGATHA (MARY CLARISSA).

Weston, Agnes (Elizabeth) (1840–1918), reformer concerned with the welfare of sailors. She was the eldest child of a barrister who took his family to live in Bath in 1845. There she attended school, receiving additional tuition in music from Dr S. S. Wesley, the organist at Gloucester Cathedral. Although not especially religious as a child, she gradually became converted and by her late twenties was actively engaged in various forms of Christian work. The Somerset Militia assembled each year in Bath, and Agnes started to help with reading- and coffee-rooms for the soldiers. She struck up a correspondence with many of the armed forces abroad, both soldiers and sailors, and eventually published a monthly letter to seamen which became known as *Ashore and Afloat*. After Agnes had been invited by Sophia Wintz to address a meeting of sailors' wives in Devonport, the two women began their life's work of fighting against 'godlessness and intemperance' among sailors.

The National Temperance League had just started work in the navy, but its members were often refused permission to speak on board ship. Agnes Weston was allowed to do so,

however, and in 1873 she first spoke aboard a man-of-war, thereafter forming numerous branches of the League. In order to promote this work further, a house in Devonport was procured and a 'Sailors' Rest' set up in 1879, where 'Coffee, Comfort, and Company' were the order of the day. The 'Sailors' Rest', which received the Royal Warrant in 1892, was also to become the centre of the Royal Naval Christian Union. In 1881 a similar institution opened in Portsmouth.

Agnes Weston was always concerned with the welfare of sailors' dependants, and in 1896 gave evidence before a Select Committee on the Royal Patriotic Fund regarding national assistance for widows and orphans of seamen. Prior to this she had appeared before the Farrar Commission to press for reform in the method of payment to sailors' wives. In 1901 she became the first woman to receive an honorary LLB from the University of Glasgow, and in 1918 both she and Miss Wintz were awarded the OBE in recognition of their services during the First World War. On her death in October 1918 she was afforded a naval burial, the first woman so honoured.

Her work, like that of Sarah ROBINSON, must be seen as part of the wider Social Purity movement of the late nineteenth century, in which Agnes Weston particularly sought to bring moral reform to the navy.

See also her *My Life Among the Bluejackets*, 1912; S. G. Wintz, *Our Bluejackets*, 1894.
                                                    J.G.S.

Wharton, Anne (1632?–85), poet. The daughter of Sir Henry Lee of Ditchley in Oxfordshire, and his wife Ann Danvers, in 1673 she was married to Thomas Wharton (later the Marquis of Wharton), whose chief interest in her appears to have been her large dowry. Little is known of her life except that she was unhappy in her marriage and considered leaving her husband, but was persuaded not to do so by Dr Gilbert Burnet, with whom she corresponded regularly and exchanged poems. Around 1680 she was in France for her health.

Anne Wharton's poems seem to have been passed round in manuscript, and she was admired by many of the leading literary figures. As well as poems, she left a manuscript play, *Love's Martyr, or Witt above Crowns*, a five-act tragedy in blank verse, in which Caesar tries to force his daughter Julia to marry Marcellus, while she secretly loves the poet Ovid. The work is dedicated to her friend Mrs Mary Howe. The only work to have been published in her lifetime was her poem 'The Despair', which Aphra BEHN included in a *Miscellany* edited in 1685. In 1688 some of her poems were published together with Edward Young's *The Idea of Christian Love*. An anthology of 1695, *The Temple of Death*, contained her paraphrase of 'The Lamentations of Jeremiah' and six other poems, including one to Mrs Behn. In the *Examen Miscellaneum* (1702) her elegy to her kinsman the Earl of Rochester was reprinted, together with glowing tributes to her work by Edmund Waller and others. Her translation of the 'Epistle of Penelope to Ulysses' was included in Jacob Tonson's collection, *Ovid's Epistles, Translated by Several Hands* (1712).

Although her work is not great either in quantity or quality, the praise it received from contemporaries and its inclusion in numerous anthologies indicates the extent to which the whole field of literature had been opened to women by the end of the seventeenth century.

See also J. P. Malcolm (ed.), *Letters between the Rev. James Granger . . . and many of the most Eminent Literary men of his time*, 1805.
W.R.O.

Wheeler, Anna Doyle (1785–1848), Irish radical and feminist, born in western Ireland, the daughter of an archdeacon. Her godfather was the Irish statesman Henry Grattan. Anna sought to acquaint herself with the new ideas of the age, absorbing them from political literature. Mary WOLLSTONECRAFT and the French *philosophes* proved crucial in her political development. After a dozen disastrous years of marriage to an alcoholic wastrel, she escaped from her husband in 1812 and took refuge with her uncle, Sir John Doyle, Governor of Guernsey. During this period she tactfully suspended her political activities, but recommenced them on arriving in London in 1816.

For a time she was a leading member of a St Simonian community at Caen in Normandy which practised equality of the sexes. In 1823 she met and came under the influence of William Thompson. Although it appeared under Thompson's name, the book *Appeal of One-Half of the Human Race, Women, against the Pretensions of the Other Half, Men, to retain them in Political and thence in Civil and Domestic Slavery* (1825) was

dedicated to Anna. Thompson also acknowledged her contribution to the work, derived from their exhaustive discussions on the question of female subjugation. In fact he described himself merely as 'scribe and interpreter' of her ideas. If this is so, then Anna Wheeler deserves to take her place with Mary WOLLSTONECRAFT and John Stuart Mill as one of the notable precursors of the modern feminist view. Curiously, the book was intended as a counterblast to Mill's father James, who wrote that women's interests resembled those of children, that is being entirely subsumed in those of their families. Apart from its description of the dependent and frequently wretched position of women, the book is notable for its view that sexual equality and mutual respect would be difficult to achieve unless the principle of competition were to be replaced by that of co-operation.

After this date Anna became an indefatigable lecturer, often in dissenting chapels, at a time when for a woman to speak in public at all was extremely uncommon. She continued to correspond with and visit the leading French socialists, insisting that the differences between St Simon, Fourier, and Owen were unimportant, and survived long enough to hear of the rising in Paris in 1848. Although a tireless worker, she never reduced her ideas to a permanent written form, existing for posterity only in the *Appeal* of Thompson.

See also R. K. Pankhurst, *William Thompson*, 1954, and 'Anna Wheeler: A Pioneer Socialist and Feminist', in *Political Quarterly* 25, 1954.
T.H.

White, Antonia (1899–1980), novelist. Antonia White's father was a writer of textbooks, and her own literary gift was precocious and fluent. By the age of sixteen she was writing tales for the twopenny papers, and later she became an advertising copywriter (1924–31) and a freelance journalist (1931–34). She returned to copywriting with the well-known firm of J. Walter Thompson (1934–35), and was appointed fashion editor of *The Daily Mirror* (1935–37). During the Second World War she worked for the BBC (1940–43) and in the political intelligence department of the Foreign Office (1943–45).

Antonia White's first novel, *Frost in May*, made an impression on its publication in 1933; like her later work, it is essentially autobiographical, in this instance reflecting with

White, Dorothy

intense bitterness the rigours of her schooling at the Convent of the Sacred Heart in Roehampton. Marital and mental difficulties delayed further publication, and form much of the subject-matter of the trilogy (in effect a tetralogy with *Frost in May* that at last appeared after the war: *The Lost Traveller* (1950), *The Sugar House* (1952), and *Beyond the Glass* (1954). Antonia White also published two books about her cats Minka and Curdy, a volume of correspondence about the problems of religious belief, and over thirty translations of Colette, Simenon, and other French Language authors.   N.H.

White, Dorothy (*fl.*1659–84), Quaker writer. Little is known of her apart from the fact that she lived in Weymouth, Dorset, from which she dates her pamphlet *A Diligent Search* (1659) and a letter of January 1661. She knew the Quaker leaders George Fox and Francis Howgill, and at the end of 1660 visited London where she tried to deliver a message to the 'King, Rulers, and Priests', but returned home unsuccessful. She may have been prosecuted for her beliefs, as in *A Call from God out of Egypt by His Son* (1662) she styles herself 'a Sufferer for the name of Jesus, and for the testimony of his Truth'. The same tract also contains two pages of poetry. Although a Dorothy White died in Cripplegate, London, on 6 January 1686, she may not have been the same person.

Dorothy published about nineteen separate items between 1659 and 1684, most of which appeared during the years 1659–64. The pamphlets of these years are filled with Biblical rhetoric and with warnings to the rulers of England that the wrath of God was about to be visited upon them for their sinfulness and ill treatment of the Quakers. Titles such as *This is to be delivered to the Councellors that are sitting in Counsel as a Warning from the Lord unto them* (1659) reflect the belief among some groups at the time that radical change was imminent, and illustrate how religious conviction could give women the confidence to pronounce on public affairs. Other writings reflect her concern to console and encourage Quakers during the years of heavy persecution which followed the Restoration of Charles II in 1660. Like many Quakers, Dorothy White was convinced that she was a channel through which God chose to deliver messages to the world, and her writings

helped promote the radical image of Quakers in the early 1660s.

See also J. Smith, *A Descriptive Catalogue of Friends' Books*, 2 vols, 1867, supplement 1893.   T.O'M.

Whitty, Dame May (1865–1948), actress. She was born Mary Louise Whitty in Liverpool, the daughter of a journalist and granddaughter of the founder-editor of the *Liverpool Daily Post* and chief constable of Liverpool. She began acting in 1881 and, after appearing at the Comedy Theatre in 1882, joined the company of Hare and the Kendals. In 1892 she married Ben Webster (the third of that name in a theatrical family) and with him joined Irving's company (1895–98), playing rather colourless characters completely the opposite of her own. During 1905–07 she was in America, where her daughter Margaret WEBSTER was born.

Having been concerned with the cause of women's suffrage from about 1900, May Whitty was chairman of the Actresses' Franchise League. She was also a pacifist until the outbreak of the First World War, but thereafter put her considerable energies and organizational skills into war work, forming a Women's Emergency Corps which pioneered women's land work, camp shows for the troops, and work rooms for unemployed actresses.She also chaired the British Women's Hospitals Committee, which created the Star and Garter Home for disabled servicemen at Richmond, and in 1918 was created DBE for such services.

After the war she returned to the theatre and at the age of seventy had the greatest success of her long and distinguished career in Emlyn Williams's *Night Must Fall*, repeating the part in New York in 1936 and on film in 1937. She also appeared in such films as *Mrs Miniver* and *The Lady Vanishes*, and made her home with her husband in Hollywood. Both were interested in actors' organizations, and British Actors' Equity was founded at their London home.   B.H.C.

Wilkinson, (Cecily) Ellen (1891–1947), journalist and Labour politician. Born in Manchester, Ellen, whose father was a cotton worker turned insurance clerk, often boasted of being 'born into the proletarian purple'. She was the third of four children in a happy Methodist home, and attributed to the traditions of the Methodism she always upheld her earliest speaking successes. After her education at Ardwick Higher Elementary School and a period of pupil teaching, which she abominated, Ellen won a scholarship to Manchester University, an exceptional feat for a girl of her background in 1910. A keen member of the Independent Labour Party, at university she was active in the Fabian and university socialist societies; became briefly engaged to Walton Newbold (Communist MP 1922–23), who shaped much of her early left-wing thinking; and took a second-class degree in history.

A period as suffrage organizer in Manchester followed, after which Ellen entered the trade union field, first as woman organizer to the Amalgamated Union of Co-operative Employees (AUCE, later NUDAW and now USDAW) in 1915. Energetic and eager, she proved a hard-working, astute negotiator, demanding economic equality for the burgeoning, largely female, wartime membership. She was a founder member of the British Communist Party, which she left in 1924; won a seat on Manchester City Council (1923–26), where she consistently advocated women's rights and help for the unemployed; and lost a parliamentary battle at Ashton under Lyne. She won Middlesbrough East for Labour in 1924, however, and entered parliament. Although she failed to keep her seat in 1931, she was successful at Jarrow in 1935. A year later she marched with 200 unemployed constituents on the Jarrow Crusade, petitioning the government to act on unemployment, as she described in *The Town that was Murdered* (1939).

During the Second World War she was part of the National Government, taking responsibility for air-raid shelter provision, which led to strain and ill-health, In 1945 she became a member of the Privy Council and Minister of Education in Attlee's government. During her brief tenure she widened opportunities for university entrants, reduced the number of direct grant schools, expanded the provision of free milk and school meals, and, above all, fought to avert postponement of the raising of the school leaving age. A feminist who triumphed in the male dominated worlds of trade unionism and parliament, she never married, but rose to Cabinet rank by sheer ability and determination. Her writings included *Peeps at Politicians* (1930); and with E. Conze *Why Fascism?* (1934).

See also B. Vernon, *Ellen Wilkinson*, 1982.

B.V.

Wilkinson, Jane (?–1557), Protestant exile. Her parents were probably of gentle birth, and her husband, John Wilkinson, was certainly wealthy. Jane was a silkwoman at the court of Queen Anne Boleyn, and was later greatly renowned for her financial support of those Protestants in prison or exile under Mary I. She was a friend and benefactress to John Bradford, Hugh Latimer, Nicholas Ridley, John Hooper, and Thomas Cranmer, among others, all of whom expressed their gratitude to her in letters still surviving.

In the autumn of 1553 Cranmer wrote to Jane, now a widow of Soper Lane, London, advising her to flee the country, but she did not go until 1556, when she arrived in Frankfurt with 6100 florins, the richest of the Marian exiles. She had left England without licence, and in the summer of 1556 John Brett was sent to deliver letters from the Queen summoning certain prominent exiles home. Of these, Jane Wilkinson was the first to be approached by Brett, on 8 July 1556. She claimed to be abroad only for the sake of her health, which she hoped would be improved by the Continental spa waters, and accepted the letters. By early 1557 she was dead, and in July the exile church at Frankfurt was squabbling over the execution of her will, which gave liberal relief to the poor among the exiles. She left one daughter in Frankfurt.

Jane Wilkinson was one of the wealthy and devout women who so greatly contributed to the Protestant cause. Her kindness to imprisoned preachers led her into danger and so into exile, but she is remembered as a 'sustainer' of those in trouble for their beliefs.

See also J. Foxe *Acts and Monuments*, 1563; C. H. Garrett, *The Marian Exiles*, 1938.

J.S.

Williams, Anna (1706–83), author and friend of Dr Johnson. She was the daughter of Zachariah Williams, the eccentric scientist, and was a lively, intelligent child who might have made a literary career but for the blindness which overcame her in her early twenties. Her translation from the French of the *Life of the Emperor Julian* (1740) has some merit, and she published some verse, but could achieve little on account of her handicap. She is therefore chiefly remembered for her friendship with Dr Johnson, with whom she lived on intimate terms for many years. The impression given in Boswell's life of Johnson is of an entertaining, but latterly rather peevish, companion.

See also W. Jackson Bate, *Samuel Johnson*, 1978; J. Boswell, *Life of Samuel Johnson*, 1791. T.H.

Williams, Ellen Gwendolen Rees. See RHYS, JEAN.

Williams, Grace (1906–77), composer, born in Wales; music was part of her life from the first, for her father was a music teacher and conductor of the well-known Romilly Boys' Choir. After graduating from Cardiff, she went to the Royal College of Music and then, for further training in composition, to Vienna.

Grace Williams was always aware of her Welsh heritage. In her dedication of the *Sea Sketches* (for string orchestra) she expressed thanks to her parents, who 'had the good sense to set up home on the coast of Glamorgan', and much of her music reflects the grandeur of that coastline. Besides music of specifically Welsh inspiration, such as the *Fantasia on Welsh Nursery Tunes* and *Castell Caernarfon*, written for the Investiture of the Prince of Wales, she also wrote *The Parlour*, an opera based on a story by de Maupassant. When commissioned by the BBC to write for the Cheltenham Festival, she set six of the poems of Gerard Manley Hopkins for contralto and strings.

For many years Grace Williams lived in London, but she eventually returned to Wales, where she was consistently active in musical life both as composer and as a regular supporter of other Welsh composers. R.G./M.G.-E.

Williams, Helen Maria (1762?–1827), novelist. After the death of her father in 1769, the family left London for Berwick-on-Tweed, where Helen was educated by her mother. Her career as an author began with the publication of the poem *Edwin and Eltruda* (1782), which drew her back to London and membership of a literary circle that included Elizabeth MONTAGU, Fanny BURNEY, Dr Johnson, Anna SEWARD, and Robert Burns.

By the close of the decade her friendships with Priestley, Godwin, and Price marked a growing political consciousness which culmi-

nated in her departure for revolutionary France in 1790. Frequent visits to France in the following three years consolidated her support for the Revolution and provoked increasingly bitter attacks from the English press. These reached their most vitriolic form in 1794 when she retired to Switzerland with John Hurford Stone, an act which was seized upon as evidence of the intrinsic relation between 'promiscuity' and revolutionary politics. In her writings she opposed the more extreme revolutionaries, the Jacobins, and later Napoleon as opponents of true republicanism.

In addition to her novels *Julia* (1790) and *Perourou* (1801), she translated both Bernardin de St. Pierre's *Paul and Virginia* (1795) and Xavier de Maistre's *The Leper of the City of Aosta* (1817). She died in Paris in 1827.

See also J. G. Alger, *Englishwomen in the French Revolution*, 1889; J. Baylen and N. Gossman, *Biographical Dictionary of Modern British Radicals*, vol. I, 1979. A.L.

Williams, Ivy (1877–1966), lawyer, first woman to be called to the English Bar. Born in Oxford, she was the only daughter of a solicitor and was educated at home. In 1896 she became a member of the Society of Oxford Home Students, now St Anne's College, and in 1900 took a second-class degree in jurisprudence. She passed the BCL examinations in 1902 and a year later received her LL D. Women were not at the time allowed full membership of the University in Oxford, although they were allowed to sit examinations. As soon as degrees were open to women, however, she received her BCL.

In 1920 women were admitted to the Inns of Court, and she was sponsored by Sir John Simon to join the Inner Temple. She was called to the Bar in May 1922, six months after Miss Frances Kyle was called to the Irish Bar, but with a Final Bar Examination Certificate of Honour (first class) which excused her two terms' dinners. She published *The Sources of Law in the Swiss Civil Code* (1923) and received her DCL. She never practised, but pursued her academic career as tutor and lecturer in law at Oxford from 1920 to 1945.

After the Second World War, when she realized that her eyesight was failing, she studied Braille and became an authority on work for the blind, publishing a Braille primer (1948), and teaching others to read and write Braille almost to the end of her life. She was elected an Honorary Fellow of St Anne's College in 1956. E.M.V.

Williams, Jane (1806–85), historian and writer who employed the pseudonym of 'Ysgafell'. She was born in Chelsea, London, the daughter of an official in the Navy Office, and was descended from Henry Williams of Montgomeryshire, a prominent Welsh nonconformist during the time of Cromwell. Ill-health led to her spending the early part of her life in Breconshire, where she first became interested in the Welsh language and its literature and, through a friendship with Lady LLANOVER, was introduced to others with similar interests. Her writings include *Miscellaneous Poems* (1824) and *Cambrian Tales*, a series of Welsh sketches for *Ainsworth's Magazine* (1849–50), but her best work is her *History of Wales derived from Authentic Sources* (1869). This was the result of much patient, if at times rather uncritical, research, and covered Welsh history up to the end of the Tudor dynasty. She lived in London from 1856. B.H.C.

Wilson, Florence. See AUSTRAL, FLORENCE.

Wilson, Margaret (1667–85?), radical Presbyterian. Margaret Wilson was the daughter of a yeoman farmer of Wigtownshire. Although her parents were Episcopalians, Margaret and her younger sister Agnes were fervent Presbyterians, adherents of the radical 'Cameronian' group which refused to give up arms after the defeat of the Scottish Presbyterian rising of 1679. In 1685 Margaret and Agnes, with Margaret MCLAUCHLAN, were seized by the authorities and charged with rebellion and attendance at conventicles. They refused to take an oath abjuring the Cameronian movement and were found guilty. All three women were sentenced to be tied to stakes in the waters of Bladenoch near Wigtown, in order to be drowned by the incoming tide. It is certain that Agnes, who was but thirteen, was reprieved through the efforts of her father, but it has not been definitely established whether the sentence on McLauchlan and Margaret Wilson was in fact carried out, and thus whether these two brave women paid the ultimate sacrifice of martyrdom for their radical religious and political cause.

See also J. Anderson, *The Ladies of the Covenant*, 1866; G. Donaldson, *Scotland James V–James VII*, 1965. A.H.

Wilson, Mona (1872–1954), civil servant and author. The eldest daughter of the Rev. James Wilson, headmaster of Clifton School and Canon of Worcester, Mona Wilson was educated at Clifton High School, Bristol; St Leonard's School, St Andrews; and Newnham College, Cambridge. After leaving university she became interested in social and industrial problems, and through the influence of Lady DILKE and Gertrude TUCKWELL joined the Women's Trade Union League. She later became its secretary and under its aegis undertook a series of first-hand investigations into social conditions, publishing her findings in *Our Industrial Laws: Working Women in Factories, Workshops, and Laundries and How to Help Them* (1903) and, with E. G. Howarth, *West Ham: A Study in Social and Industrial Problems* (1907). She also became a member of the trade boards for chain-making and paper-box-making and of the Home Office's Committee on Industrial Accidents.

In 1911, in recognition of her knowledge of labour conditions and social welfare, she was appointed to the post of National Health Insurance Commissioner for England, newly constituted under the National Insurance Act of 1911. Along with the three other women commissioners (one each for Scotland, Ireland, and Wales) she received, at Lloyd George's insistence, the same salary as the male commissioners and incidentally the highest salary paid to a woman civil servant. During the years 1917 to 1918 she was on loan to the National Service Department and the Ministry of Reconstruction, where she was a strong advocate of women's rights. Her seven-year term as commissioner having ended in 1919, she retired to her home at Oare near Marlborough, Wiltshire. She did, however, serve as a member of the Industrial Fatigue Research Board from 1919 to 1929 and as a local JP.

Mona Wilson had a lifelong devotion to literature and a wide circle of literary friends, including the poet Thomas Sturge Moore. Her only work of fiction was the sentimental novel *The Story of Rosalind Retold from her Diary*, written under the pseudonym of Monica Moore in 1910. After her retirement she wrote elegant and scholarly works of criticism, including *These Were Muses: Essay on English Women Writers*, 1924; *The Life of William Blake*, 1927; *Sir Philip Sidney*, 1931; and *Jane Austen and Some Contemporaries*, 1938.

She also wrote two biographies, *Queen Elizabeth* (1932) and *Queen Victoria* (1933).

See also Sterling Library, University of London, T. S. Moore Papers.   M.Z.

Winchilsea, Lady. See FINCH, ANNE, COUNTESS OF WINCHILSEA.

Winter, John Strange. See STANNARD, HENRIETTA (ELIZA VAUGHAN).

Woffington, Peg (1714–60), actress. Humbly born in Dublin, Margaret Woffington was engaged as a child to Madame Violante's juvenile company. Attracting the attention of theatre managers, she was booked to play at Smock Alley Theatre. Her first major success was as Sylvia in *The Recruiting Officer*, but it was her 'breeches' role as Sir Harry Wildair in *The Constant Couple* that took Dublin by storm in 1739. She was now supporting her entire family and, with better prospects offered in London, sailed for England.

Having secured an engagement with Rich at Covent Garden, she played Sylvia with instant success, and then Sir Harry Wildair, to unprecedented acclaim, for ten consecutive nights. In 1741 she was engaged by Drury Lane to play leading roles, notably Cordelia to the Lear of another newcomer, David Garrick. Between London and Dublin, Garrick and Mrs Woffington had a hugely successful run. It is claimed that they became lovers, and set up house together with Charles Macklin in an unlikely *ménage à trois*, but three such short tempers ensured that by 1743 whatever there had been was over. It is said that Mrs Woffington was more anxious for marriage than Garrick, and there is no evidence among Garrick's papers, beyond several poems in her honour, for a liaison. The evidence comes from secondary biographical sources.

Peg Woffington remained at Drury Lane for a few seasons, but had formidable rivals in Mrs PRITCHARD and Mrs CLIVE, both of whom detested her. With these ladies, and with Mrs BELLAMY and Mrs CIBBER, she had noisy and publicized battles. Between 1749 and 1751 she was at Covent Garden, playing more serious roles as well as her comedy parts, in rivalry with Mrs Bellamy. From 1753 to 1754 she was back in Dublin for her greatest successes, bringing prosperity to herself and the theatre, before returning to Covent Garden in 1754. In 1757 she collapsed on stage, but lingered on, in ill-health, until 1760.

Although her private life was somewhat scandalous, Peg Woffington retained public favour and was much sought after socially for her liveliness and wit. She was supreme in refined comedy roles such as Millamant, Lady Townly, and Angelica, rarely venturing into tragedy.

See also J. Dunbar, *Peg Woffington and her World*, 1968; J. C. Lucey, *Lovely Peggy*, 1952.   C.H.

Wollstonecraft, Mary (1759–97), feminist author. She was born in Epping Forest, the daughter of an unsuccessful farmer of tyrannical temper and the second of seven children. She moved a great deal as a child and adolescent, her only formal education being acquired at a day school in Yorkshire. Between 1778 and 1780 she worked as companion to a Miss Dawson in Bath, after which she lived with her childhood friend Fanny Blood. When her sister Eliza left her husband and child, the three women established a school at Newington Green. The practical experience gained there formed the basis for the exposition of Mary Wollstonecraft's educational theories in *Thoughts on the Education of Daughters* (1787). In 1785 she left for Portugal to assist the pregnant Fanny Blood, married earlier that year in Lisbon, but returned to England on the death of the mother and child. After the closure of her school in 1786 she accepted a job as governess to the Kingsborough family in Ireland. While at Bristol Hot-Wells (1787) she wrote the novel *Mary, A Fiction*, and on dismissal from her post determined to pursue a literary career.

She completed a number of translations and journalistic writings, including contributions to *The Analytical Review*, and published *Mary, A Fiction* and *Original Stories from Real Life*. Mary Wollstonecraft's *Vindication of the Rights of Men* (1790), one of the first of the numerous replies to Burke's *Reflections on the Revolution in France*, contrasts the 'demon of property' with man's 'natural rights'. Her radicalism, expressed in this work as opposition to the hereditary principle, acquired a more cogent and articulate form in *A Vindication of the Rights of Women*, the feminist tract published in 1792. Her exposure of sexual, political and economic double standards was later rendered fictionally in the incomplete novel *The Wrongs of Women, or Maria* (1798). The heroine's summation of her experience—'was not the world a vast prison, and women born slaves?' —encapsulates the author's view of the female condition.

As with many of her contemporaries, Mary Wollstonecraft's acceptance of revolutionary principles involved faith in the emergence of a new age of liberty. In 1792 she left for France, where she met the English supporters of the French Revolution, including Helen Maria WILLIAMS, Archibald Hamilton Rowant, and Tom Paine. In 1793, the same year which saw publication of her critical analysis *An Historical and Moral View of the French Revolution*, she met and began an affair with Gilbert Imlay, a former officer in the American Revolutionary Army. As the relationship foundered, she was abandoned for long periods to care alone for their child Fanny, born in 1794. She left France for England in 1795, attempted suicide on discovering Imlay's infidelity, travelled through Scandinavia, and then again attempted suicide by jumping off Putney Bridge when she returned to England and found Imlay living with another woman.

In 1796 she renewed her acquaintance with the philosopher William Godwin, whom she had originally met in 1791. *Letters from Sweden* was published and work began on *The Wrongs of Women* (1796). In December of that year she became pregnant, and in March 1797 married Godwin. A daughter, Mary GODWIN, the future wife of Shelley and author of *Frankenstein*, was born in August. Mary Wollstonecraft died of complications from the birth the following month.

The brevity and intensity of her life exercise a romantic appeal to which is owed much of her present high reputation. Neither the two incomplete novels nor her critical writings are of particularly high calibre, but as a polemicist she excelled in focusing attention on social and sexual inequities.

See also V. Gornick and B. K. Moran (eds.), *Women in Sexist Society, 1971;* E. W. Sunstein, *A Different Face. The Life of Mary Wollstonecraft,* 1975.   A.L.

Wood, Ellen (1814–87), novelist known as Mrs Henry Wood. She was born in Worcester, the eldest daughter of a glove manufacturer, and brought up by her grandmother. She was educated at home, suffering from curvature of the spine which made her a lifelong invalid. In 1836 she married Henry Wood, a banker, of whom her son said 'he had not a spark of imagination'. The family lived in France for most of the following twenty years, and from there she contributed immensely popular stories to *Bentley's Miscellany* and *The New Monthly Magazine*. Her first novel, *Danesbury House* (1860), was written in twenty-eight days and for it she won a prize of £100 from the Scottish Temperance League. Her greatest success, however, was *East Lynne* (1861). Having been rejected by two publishers, the story was serialized in *The New Monthly Magazine* and sold over half a million copies. It was translated into a number of languages and made into a popular stage melodrama in England, for which the book's author received not a penny.

Mrs Henry Wood had a large family; she wrote all her novels propped up on a sofa, producing them at an incredible rate. Her son said that 'she never knew what it was not to be in the humour for writing' although she always maintained that 'no home duty was ever neglected or put aside for literary labours'. Other popular, though less melodramatic, books were *Mrs Halliburton's Troubles* and *The Channings*, both published in 1862. In 1867 she became the proprietor and editor of the magazine *Argosy*. Her husband died in 1866 and her son, Charles, helped her to edit the paper. She was always conservative in her views, and an anti-labour novel, *A Life's Secret*, published anonymously in 1867 by the Religious Tract Society in *Leisure Hour*, caused a near-riot.

Other works by her include *The Shadow of Ashlydyat,* 1863; *Lord Oakburn's Daughters,* 1864, *Lady Adelaide's Oath,* 1867, *Roland Yorke,* 1869, *Dene Hollow,* 1871, *Within the Maze,* 1872, *Edina,* 1876, and *Pomeroy Abbey,* 1878. Mrs Henry Wood died in St John's Wood at the age of seventy-three. Her son Charles became her biographer.

See also C. W. Wood, *Memorials of Mrs Henry Wood,* 1894.   A.P.

Wood, Mrs Henry. See WOOD, ELLEN.

Woods, Margaret Louise (1856–1945), novelist and poet. Born at Rugby, she was the daughter of the Dean of Westminster, and married the Rev. H. G. Woods, who became president of Trinity College, Oxford. She wrote several novels, beginning with *A Village Tragedy* (1887), considered highly realistic in its day. Others included *Sons of the Sword,* 1901, *The Invader,* 1907, and *The Spanish Lady,* 1927. She also wrote poetic dramas and published verse, brought together in the *Collected Poems* of 1914.　　　　　　N.H.

Woodville, Elizabeth (*c.*1437–92), Queen of England, wife of Edward IV. She was the eldest daughter of Richard, Earl Rivers, and Jacquetta of Luxembourg, widow of John, Duke of Bedford. Elizabeth was a maid of honour to Queen MARGARET, and in 1452 married Sir John Grey, son and heir to Lord Ferrers. They had two sons before Grey was killed in 1461. When and where the young Edward IV met and courted the Lancastrian widow who refused to become his mistress is unknown, but in May 1464 Elizabeth became the first Englishwoman since the Conquest to marry her King. For Edward it was a major political error. It deprived him of an advantageous foreign match and encumbered him with the Queen's numerous and greedy family. Elizabeth managed her own financial affairs carefully, and although the Woodvilles received only modest gains from the Crown in cash and lands, she ensured that through other means, particularly by marriage, her family were well provided for, to the chagrin of many of their peers. Elizabeth bore Edward two sons and six daughters who survived, although the future Edward V was not born until 1471, during the period when his father temporarily lost his throne.

Although Edward's infidelities to his Queen were well-known, she continued to have considerable influence over him, most notably in the advancement of her family's interests, where she persuaded Edward into manoeuvres as dubious legally as they were morally. Both the Queen and her family were therefore deservedly unpopular. Elizabeth was designing and ambitious. Her attempt to secure complete Woodville control of the government on the accession in 1483 of her young son Edward V was almost directly responsible for the usurpation of Richard III and the consequent death of both her sons. Richard had her marriage declared invalid and her children bastards, but gave her a generous pension for herself and her daughters.

In concert with Margaret BEAUFORT, Elizabeth then set to work to promote a marriage between her eldest daughter, ELIZABETH OF YORK, and Margaret's exiled son, the future

Henry VII. Henry's invasion in 1485 was successful, and Elizabeth's position as Queen-dowager was restored, after his accession to the throne, although she did not regain all her dower lands. She remained on good terms with Henry VII and was suggested as a possible wife for the widowed James III of Scotland. In 1487 she retired to Bermondsey Abbey on the grounds of ill-health, surrendering her property to her daughter, the Queen, in return for a pension. She died there in 1492.

See also C. Ross, *Edward IV,* 1974.

　　　　　　A.C.

Woodward, Joan (1917–71), industrial sociologist. Joan Woodward was educated at the universities of Oxford and Durham. She gained first-class honours in politics, philosophy and economics in 1936, a Durham MA in medieval philosophy in 1938, and the Oxford Diploma in Social and Public Administration in 1939. During the war she worked in management, and became Senior Labour Manager of the Royal Ordnance Factory at Bridgwater, thereby gaining useful practical insight into industrial problems. She worked briefly in the Civil Service; and taught at the University of Liverpool, South-East Essex Technical College, and the Department of Social and Public Administration at Oxford. In 1951 she married Leslie Thompson Blakeman.

She became Senior Lecturer in Industrial Sociology in the Department of Mechanical Engineering at Imperial College, London, in 1962; and in 1969 became the second woman professor there, as well as head of the new Industrial Sociology Unit. There she set up a unique teaching programme. She acted as adviser to various government bodies, including the Post Office and the Department of Employment; and on the training of nurses and the administration of hospitals. She also served on two sub-committees of the Social Science Research Council, and the Mallabar Committee on government industrial establishments. From 1968 to 1970 she was a part-time member of the National Board on Prices and Incomes. Her writings include *The Dockworkers,* 1954, *The Saleswoman,* 1960, *Industrial Organization: Theory and Practice,* 1960, and *Industrial Organization: Behaviour and Control,* 1970.　　J.E.

Woolf, (Adeline) Virginia (1882–1941), novelist, essayist, and critic. Virginia Stephen was born in London, daughter of the writer Leslie Stephen, and of Julia Duckworth. For both parents it was a second marriage, and Virginia grew up with her own sister and two brothers and her older Duckworth step-siblings. She was educated at home, by her parents and by tutors in the classics. The family lived in London, but spent every summer in Cornwall; recollections of St Ives appear in much of her work.

She began writing at an early age. At the age of nine, she wrote the first issue of a weekly family 'newspaper', which continued for four years: its reception by her parents gave her a first experience of public criticism. An essentially happy childhood came to an end in 1895 with the death of her mother, and soon afterwards Virginia suffered her first breakdown. Her step-sister died two years later, aged 28. A few months after her father's death in 1904, she had a second, more serious mental breakdown, and made the first of many suicide attempts.

Her career in literary journalism was launched in 1904 with the publication of her first review in *The Manchester Guardian*. The four Stephen children set up house together in Gordon Square, where their entertainment of Thoby Stephen's literary and artistic friends from Cambridge marked the beginning of the cultural phenomenon that came to be known as 'Bloomsbury'. Virginia Stephen became a regular reviewer for the newly-founded *Times Literary Supplement*, and started to teach at Morley College, an evening institute for working people. Thoby Stephen died in 1906, aged 26, after contracting typhoid on a trip they made to Greece; the following year Vanessa Stephen married his friend Clive Bell, and Virginia became more closely drawn into their circle. In 1909 she agreed to marry Lytton Strachey, but both immediately changed their minds, and in 1912 she married Leonard Woolf. The following year she completed her first novel, became ill, and attempted suicide for the second time. *The Voyage Out* was published in 1915; by this time it was clear that her mental breakdowns would persist.

In 1917 the Woolfs founded the Hogarth Press in Richmond. Their first publication was Katherine Mansfield's *Prelude* in 1918; they also published the early work of Sigmund Freud and the poetry of T. S. Eliot. In 1919 they bought a house at Rodmell, near Lewes in Sussex, which was to remain their country home. Virginia Woolf's second novel, *Night and Day* (1919), received rather mixed reviews, but she was already making a name for herself as a literary critic. By the time her fifth novel was published, in 1927, she was assured of a major place among twentieth-century writers. *To the Lighthouse* was the most extensively reviewed of her novels to date and achieved the most successful sales. Its mastery of 'stream of consciousness' technique, experimental handling of time sequences, and its autobiographical interest cause it to remain the most widely admired of all her works. It was awarded the Prix Femina Vie Heureuse in 1928. *Orlando* (1928), begun 'as a joke' in 1927, is a highly fictionalized 'biography' of her lover Vita SACKVILLE-WEST.

Throughout her life, Virginia Woolf was deeply concerned to improve the quality of life for women, especially for intellectual women like herself—'the daughters of educated men'. In 1910 she undertook voluntary work for the Adult Suffrage movement, and in 1915 was actively involved with the Women's Co-operative Guild. *A Room of One's Own* (1929) and *Three Guineas* (1938) are impassioned pleas for women's education and women's financial independence. Her persistent refusal of the many academic honours offered to her (by Cambridge and Manchester Universities in 1933; by Liverpool University in 1939) was caused in part by her long-standing resentment at the patronizing way in which the universities continued to treat women. She herself always regretted not having been allowed to have a 'real' education.

Virginia Woolf's fiction was a major contribution to the break with the 'realism' of the nineteenth-century novel. She was also a brilliant essayist, diarist, and letter-writer, and an outstanding literary critic, who reviewed the work of numerous contemporary writers. In February 1941, sensing the onset of another mental breakdown, she committed suicide by drowning, in Sussex.

Her works include *Jacob's Room*, 1922, *Mrs Dalloway*, 1925, *The Waves*, 1931, *The Years*, 1937, *Roger Fry: A Biography*, 1940, *Between the Acts*, 1941 and the following posthumous publications: *A Writer's Diary*, 1953, *Collected Essays*, 4 vols., 1966–67, *Letters*, 6 vols., 1975–80, *Moments of Being: Unpublished Autobiographical Writings*, 1978, *Diary*, 4 vols., 1977–82, continuing.

See also Q. Bell, *Virginia Woolf: A Biogra-*

Woolley, Hannah

phy, 2 vols., 1972; J. Lehmann, *Virginia Woolf and her World*, 1975.   J.E.E.H.

Woolley, Hannah (*c*.1623–after 1677), author, feminist, and educationist. A well-educated and spirited young woman of obscure background, she was orphaned at fourteen and had become mistress of a small school before she was fifteen. Her musical ability and knowledge of Italian attracted the patronage of a noble-woman, who employed her as governess for her daughter. In this employment, and in a subsequent post in a noble household, Hannah acquired a thorough grounding in domestic skills, household management, deportment, French, and medicine, all of which were to be of great value later in her career.

When she was twenty-four, she married Mr Woolley, master of the free school at Newport, Essex, by whom she had four sons. Both at Newport and at Hackney, a fashionable London suburb for schools to which the couple moved seven years later, they had a number of boarders and as many as sixty pupils under their tuition. In 1661 she published her first cookery book, *The Ladies' Directory*, followed by *The Cook's Guide* in 1664. Mr Woolley died before 1666, the year in which Hannah married Francis Challoner of St Margaret's, Westminster, but she was again widowed. By 1674 she was living at the house in the Old Bailey of Richard Woolley, Master of Arts and Reader at St Martin's, Ludgate, probably her son. A pragmatic woman, always ready to support herself by hard work, she was now, in addition to writing for publication, selling remedies at 'reasonable Rates' and training gentlewomen who wished to enter service.

In 1670 she published one of her most famous books, *The Queen-like Closet*, which ran through many editions and in 1674 was translated into German. In 1673 she published another popular book, *The Gentlewoman's Companion*, a comprehensive 'Guide to the Female Sex' on the correct behaviour and conversation appropriate to various capacities and circumstances from childhood to old age. An authoritative writer on such subjects as female deportment, cookery, household management, medicine, and cosmetics, Hannah Woolley in no way felt that a woman's knowledge should be limited to such domestic accomplishments. In the introduction to her latest work, which also reached numerous editions, she lamented the almost universal neglect of the 'right education of the female sex'. She felt bitterly the lack of educational opportunities available to women and the limitations that this imposed on their lives. In vituperative language she condemned the popular consensus that a woman was 'learned enough if she can distinguish her Husband's bed from anothers'. Asserting the essential intellectual equality of the sexes, she insisted that women were capable of the same improvement as men, if given the same educational advantages. She advised girls to become serious scholars and recommended the study of Latin, which would help them to speak and write more eloquent English. She also believed that French and Italian were important acquisitions for young ladies, especially useful for travel.

The fact that women such as Hannah Woolley and Bathsua MAKIN were earning a living by writing and teaching indicates the growing concern with women's education. An authoritative and highly successful author of books on domestic science and manners, Hannah was also among the earliest and most vocal champions of women's education. Her other works include *The Ladys Delight* (1672) and *The Accomplish'd Ladys Delight in Preserving, Physick, Beautifying and Cookery* (1677).

See also D. M. Stenton, *The English Woman in History*, 1957.   T.J.M.

Wordsworth, Dorothy (1771–1855), diarist. The only sister of the poet William Wordsworth, Dorothy was born at Cockermouth in Cumberland, where her father was steward and agent of the Lowther family. On her mother's death in 1777, she was sent to live with her mother's cousin, the daughter of a Unitarian minister in Halifax. Dorothy lived in Halifax for the next ten years, attending day schools in the area, except for a period of six months spent at a boarding school. In 1787 she went to live with her maternal grandparents at Penrith, but the interlude was not happy. Dorothy's uncle, William Cookson, had secured a living in a curacy at Forncett in Norfolk, and in 1788 she joined him. She lived in Norfolk until 1794, when together with her brother William she took a house at Racedown in Dorset.

For the rest of her life, with the exception of brief visits elsewhere, Dorothy was to stay with her brother. Together with Wordsworth and Coleridge, in 1803 she made a six-week tour of Scotland, which became the subject of her posthumously published work. In 1820, in company with Wordsworth and his wife, and a cousin and his bride, she visited the Continent. On both these and subsequent trips, Dorothy kept a journal; there was some talk in 1822 of publishing her work, but nothing came of it. In April 1829 Dorothy became violently ill. She recovered, but her strength had vanished. She suffered a severe mental breakdown in 1835, and was never fully to recover, dying in January 1855.

Dorothy Wordsworth began writing her journals while she was living with her brother at Alfoxden in Somerset. Although she claimed that she wrote them only 'to give William pleasure', there is evidence to suggest that both he and Coleridge drew on her work extensively in the composition of a number of poems. Her works include *Recollections Of A Tour Made In Scotland AD 1803* (1874) and the *Journals*, most recently edited by Mary Moorman (1971).

See also A. M. Ellis, *Rebels And Conservatives, Dorothy and William Wordsworth and their Circle*, 1967; E. Gunn, *A Passion For The Particular*, 1981.   J.H.S.

Wordsworth, Dame Elizabeth (1840–1932), founding Principal of Lady Margaret Hall, Oxford. Oldest of seven children, Elizabeth Wordsworth was the daughter of Christopher Wordsworth, headmaster of Harrow and later Bishop of Lincoln, and sister of John, Bishop of Salisbury. Her father was nephew of the poet Wordsworth, and her family had wide and distinguished academic and literary connections. For a year she attended a Brighton boarding school, but was otherwise educated by her father and governesses.

In 1878 she became the first Principal of Lady Margaret Hall, which opened formally in 1879. She had to contend both with conservatives, among them many Anglicans, who opposed women's education, and with those who disliked the Hall's religious character. In 1883 she helped to found the University Women's Settlement for social work in London, and in 1897 was instrumental in founding the Lady Margaret Hall Settlement. She presided over the Hall until 1909, in 1886 founding St Hugh's Hall, later St Hugh's College. In 1893, during her tenure, all Oxford Honours Schools were opened to women, although degrees were awarded only from 1920. In 1921 she was granted an honorary Oxford MA, and in 1928, at the Hall's Jubilee, a DCL; in the same year she was also created DBE.

In 1876 and 1883 Elizabeth Wordsworth published novels under the name of Grant Lloyd; and in 1888, with J. H. Overton, *Christopher Wordsworth, Bishop of Lincoln*. Other publications included *Glimpses of the Past*, 1912, *Essays Old and New*, 1919, and *Poems and Plays*, 1931. Despite her furthering of university education for women, ideally she would have liked them to be taught as she had been; she realized that for most, however, this was impractical. She placed great emphasis on religion, believing it to be especially important in the lives of those women who had left traditional confines for a new role lacking customary supports.   J.E.

Wright, Frances (1795–1852), Utopian socialist, and elder daughter of a wealthy radical merchant, James Wright of Dundee, where she was born. Frances Wright was orphaned young and brought up with her sister Camilla by maternal relatives in London. In 1830 she married William Phiquepal D'Arusmont, a French physician and educationist, whom she later divorced.

Frances Wright was beautiful and intelligent, with a compelling personality, but she had no wish to follow the conventional path laid down for English ladies. A lonely child, she took refuge in study, reading widely among the sciences, literature, and the classics. From an early age this led her to believe that British society was unjust and that the United States of America was a better constituted and freer nation. She drew on the ideas of Jeremy Bentham and other radical thinkers to form a creed that included the abolition of slavery, women's emancipation, the necessity of birth control, and the relaxation of the marriage tie. In 1818 she and her sister sailed for the USA where she lived for two years. On her return she published an account of her experiences: *Views of Society and Manners in America*. Its pronounced liberal sympathies brought her to the notice of European reformers, resulting in friendships with Bentham, Lafayette and others. She so much admired Lafayette that she followed him back to the USA in 1824. During this trip she visited the South and became interested in the problem of slavery. Her investigations convinced her that it could be abolished without legislation and she decided to set up a community based on co-operative labour and complete equality between black and white where ex-slaves could be trained in independence and civic responsibility before receiving both their freedom and waste land to cultivate. Confident that her example would be widely imitated, she bought property at Nashoba, Tennessee, for the experiment but it was bedevilled by bad management and the settlement ended after one year. Frances Wright then left for New Harmony, the Utopian community run by Robert Owen, whose principles had greatly influenced her thinking. There she undertook the editorship of *The New Harmony Gazette and Free Enquirer*, discussing in its pages a variety of social and religious issues. Believing firmly in the importance of rationality in human behaviour, she distrusted religious enthusiasm in any form.

In 1828 Frances Wright visited Cincinnati, a centre of revivalism, to deliver a lecture attacking all institutions which retarded the progress of reason. From this grew the *Course of Popular Lectures* which she presented in New York and many other American cities between 1829 and 1836. She attacked the subordinate position of women, criticizing the narrowness of their education and their lack of legal status. She repudiated marriage and advocated birth control. Attempts were made to prevent her speeches, but their delivery also led to the formation of Fanny Wright Societies dedicated to the promotion of her principles.

In later years, preoccupied by the breakdown of her marriage, she gradually withdrew from public life. Frances Wright was sometimes lacking in judgement and her ideas were rarely her own, but her enthusiasm and zeal did much to popularize them and influenced Robert Dale Owen, a close friend, Mrs Frances TROLLOPE, and many others.

See also M. Lane, *Frances Wright and the Great Experiment*, 1972.   J.V.L./J.R.

Wroth, Lady Mary (*c*.1586–?1653), author. The eldest daughter of Sir Robert Sidney, Earl of Leicester, and his wife Barbara Gamage, she spent most of her childhood at Penshurst, but often travelled to the Low Countries where her father was Governor of Flushing. In 1604 she married Sir Robert Wroth of Loughton Hall, Essex. She took a prominent part in court life, and acted in a court production of Ben Jonson's *Masque of Blackness*. Her activities as a literary patron were celebrated in many dedications and complimentary verses, and in 1610 Jonson dedicated *The Alchemist* to her. In 1614 her husband died, leaving her deeply in debt. Her only son, born less than a month before his father's death, died in 1616. For the next few years she struggled to control her financial affairs, without success. Rumours of a possible marriage in 1619 were not fulfilled, but in 1623 the Crown granted her protection from creditors by an order which was renewed annually.

Lady Mary's only published work appeared in 1621, entitled *The Countesse of Montgomerie's Urania*. The title indicates a close association with her uncle Sir Philip Sidney's famous work *The Countess of Pembroke's Arcadia*, which is reinforced on the richly ornamented frontispiece where she is described as the daughter of Robert Sidney, and the niece of Sir Philip Sidney and Mary, Countess of Pembroke (see SIDNEY). The *Urania* is a long pastoral romance with an elaborate plot concerning the wanderings and adventures of characters such as Urania, a shepherdess who is really a princess. Parselius, with whom she falls in love, is searching for the long-lost daughter of the King of Naples; his son Amphilanthus and his love Pamphilia are also important characters. The prose narrative is punctuated by poems expressing the characters' distress and joy, and bound together with the romance, with separate pagination, is a sequence of songs and sonnets entitled *Pamphilia to Amphilanthus*.

On publication, the *Urania* met with an extremely hostile reception in the Jacobean court, where various nobles apparently saw in it satirical allusions to themselves. One, Lord Denny, claimed that he and his family had been libelled, and a reading of the relevant passages does suggest some justification for his complaint. He and Lady Mary exchanged angry letters and satirical poems about the matter, but pressure from the court was such that she was forced to withdraw the book from sale.

Although she published nothing more, Mary Wroth deserves attention as the first woman to attempt long prose fiction, and as one of the earliest secular women poets in English.

See also *Pamphilia to Amphilanthus*, ed. G. F. Waller, 1977; *Notes and Queries*, December 1977.   W.R.O.

Wyndham, Lady Mary. See MOORE, MARY.

Wynyard, Diana (1906–64), actress. Born Dorothy Isabel Cox, in London, she was educated at Woodford School, Croydon, and later studied voice-production with various teachers. She adopted her stage name by deed poll in 1936.

Her first stage appearance was in *The Grand Duchess* (1925), after which she toured for a year playing many roles and learning the essentials of her craft. A year with the Liverpool Repertory Company followed, and then came London fame in *Sorry You've Been Troubled* (1929), followed by another triumph in Congreve's *The Old Bachelor*. In 1933 she was Charlotte Brontë in Clemence Dane's *Wild Decembers*, subsequently taking on the management of the play. She thrilled New York in *The Devil Passes* (1932), a success that led to Hollywood where critics declared her early film work to be 'quite, quite stunning'. Her most memorable film was probably *Cavalcade* (1933).

Diana Wynyard represented British theatre at the Paris Exhibition (1937) and then had a period with the Old Vic. From 1943 to 1944 she toured for ENSA. She was with the Shakespeare Memorial Theatre at Stratford-upon-Avon (1948–49), giving consistently fine performances as Portia, Gertrude, Beatrice, Lady Macbeth, and Hermione. She toured Australia with the company in 1950.

She starred in several British films, including a memorable *Gaslight* (1940), and in 1953 was created CBE. She married first Carol Reed and later Tibor Csato. At the time of her death she was rehearsing a revival of *Hay Fever*.

See also D. Shipman, *The Great Movie Stars*, 1979.   P.L.

Y

Yates, Elizabeth (1799–1860), actress. Born in Norwich, Elizabeth Brunton first appeared in 1815 at her father's theatre at Lynn, playing Desdemona to Charles Kemble's Othello. Her father thought her better suited to comedy, however, and cast her as Letitia Hardy in *The Belle's Stratagem*, after which she was engaged to play in Birmingham, and elsewhere. In 1817 she was at Covent Garden, and after a three-year period with the company, spent some time in the country before joining her father in 1822 at the West London Theatre. This arrangement was not altogether successful and she again retired to the country, where she met, and at Bath in 1823 married, Frederick Yates. They played together at Cheltenham and at Drury Lane, and after his death in 1842 she tried management at the Adelphi but found it too taxing. She played the 1848–49 season at the Lyceum and then retired from the stage, dying after a long illness.

B.H.C.

Yates, Frances A(melia) (1899–1981), scholar of the Renaissance period. Her father was a naval architect and his work involved the family in frequent moves. Frances A. Yates's home environment and self-education were therefore more important to her than the teaching at Laurel Bank School in Glasgow, Birkenhead High School, and elsewhere. Despite her BA and MA in French at University College, London, she remained outside the academic system and was hardly affected by its outlook. Between the world wars she worked on her own, publishing a biography of John Florio, the Italian who lived in Elizabethan England and translated Montaigne into English, and a study of Shakespeare's *Love's Labour Lost*.

From the beginning of the Second World War she worked as an ambulance attendant; meanwhile, having joined the Warburg Institute in 1941 as a research assistant, she became a lecturer there and eventually (1956–67) Reader in the History of the Renaissance. *The French Academies of the Sixteenth Century* (1947) and *The Valois Tapestries* (1959) were followed by two books that made her widely known: *Giordano Bruno and the Hermetic Tradition* (1964), which traced the influence of 'Egyptian' magical-mystical writings on a central figure of the Renaissance; and *The Art of Memory* (1966), a fascinating examination of a technique once vital to the cultural tradition. These displayed her characteristic ability to throw new light on occult and other 'discredited' or outmoded ideas, the historical significance of which had been neglected. The mass of new information she uncovered, and the daring, often controversial speculations she based on it, made Frances A. Yates's books intellectual adventures in which the reader fully shared the author's sense of excited discovery. Her later works included *The Rosicrucian Enlightenment*, 1972, *Astraea: the imperial theme in the sixteenth century*, 1975, *Shakespeare's Last Plays*, 1975, and *The Occult Philosophy in the Elizabethan Age*, 1979.

N.H.

Yates, Mary Anne (1728–87), actress. The wife of the comedian Richard Yates, she was coached by him and by Garrick for the stage. Mrs CIBBER reigned at Drury Lane and Mrs Yates's début in 1754 was unremarked. On Mrs Cibber's death, however, she held the field in classical tragedy. Her rather stiff style and sing-song voice were suited neither to comedy nor sentiment. Mr and Mrs Yates fell out with Garrick over money and defected to Covent Garden. Her last appearance was in 1785.

See also J. Genest, *Some Account of the English Stage*, 1832.

C.H.

Yonge, Charlotte Mary (1823–1901), novelist and writer of children's books. She was born at Otterbourne, near Winchester, and came from a clerical background. Her father was a retired army officer who had fought at Waterloo. She led a secluded and uneventful life, and was educated at home by her parents, who gave her excellent instruction in modern languages, history, and literature. She began Sunday School teaching at the age of seven and continued it for seventy-one years. Her upbringing was, as she admitted, 'old fashioned even for the Victorian age'. As a child she was forced to take a diet of milk and dry crusts for breakfast and supper, and so conformist was she that she denounced a nursemaid who 'out of misplaced pity' brought her bread with butter on it.

Charlotte Yonge lived in the house where she was born until her father died and her brother married. Before publishing her first story her family held a council to discuss whether or not to allow publication. They agreed on the understanding that any money earned would be used for good works: it was considered unladylike to benefit from one's own writing. At first she had to read to her father everything she had written, and make changes as he indicated. Later, John Keble, her 'pope' and mentor who had prepared her for confirmation, censored her manuscripts. It was under his influence that she became a leading exponent of Oxford Movement principles in fiction.

Charlotte Yonge gained fame with the publication of *The Heir of Redclyffe* (1853), the nobly self-sacrificing hero of which, Sir Guy, became something of a cult figure. Her later books, including *The Little Duke*, 1854, *The Lances of Lynwood*, 1855, and *The Daisy Chain*, 1856, were written for children. She earned £2000 from *The Daisy Chain*, using the money to establish a missionary college in Auckland, New Zealand. The profits from *The Heir of Redclyffe* went to a missionary schooner for the South Seas. Between 1851 and 1890 she edited the children's magazine *The Monthly Packet*, and contributed to *The Magazine for the Young*.

Charlotte Yonge's two hundred books, sentimental and pious, are no longer read, though they retain some interest as chronicles of the Oxford Movement and Victorian family life.

See also G. Battiscombe, *Charlotte M. Yonge*, 1943; C. Coleridge, *Charlotte Mary Yonge: Her Life and Letters*, 1903; E. Romane, *Charlotte Mary Yonge: An Appreciation*, 1908. A.P.

York, Duchess of. See HYDE, ANNE, DUCHESS OF YORK; NEVILLE, CECILY, DUCHESS OF YORK.

Young, Mrs Charles. See VEZIN, JANE ELIZABETH.

Young, Elizabeth (*fl.* 1558), Marian exile. During the Catholic restoration of Mary I, hundreds of English Protestants fled the country. Among this number were many who became involved in the smuggling of books and pamphlets back into England for distribution among the faithful. Elizabeth Young,

a married woman of middle age with three small children, had experienced difficulties with the ecclesiastical authorities and joined the exile colonies at Frankfurt and Emden, centre of the illicit printing activities. Late in Mary's reign she was captured in London while attempting to smuggle and distribute copies of the Protestant tract *Antichrist* by the exile John Olde. She was then imprisoned, together with a colleague named Dixon.

Throughout her thirteen separate examinations, Elizabeth Young lied to her interrogators, refusing to answer truthfully those questions that would have endangered her exile friends. She claimed not to have sold any books, although at least one of her customers, an apprentice called Thomas Green, had already been captured and had confessed. She also claimed to have bought the books in Amsterdam, hoping to sell them at a profit, while the authorities knew them to have come from Emden. At first equally reluctant to give ground when questioned on her beliefs about the sacrament, Elizabeth eventually allowed herself to be saved from prosecution by agreeing to an ambiguous use of words in a declaration on the real presence, and was released.

Bishop Ponet, exiled at Strasbourg, had declared that three sorts of people were required for a successful pamphlet war against Queen Mary and her supporters: the learned to write tracts, the rich to pay for them, and the poor to distribute them. By far the most dangerous of these roles was the last. Without women such as Elizabeth Young, willing to risk imprisonment and death, the Protestant propaganda campaign could not have had the success it did.

See also J. Foxe, *Acts and Monuments*, 1563; C. Garrett, *The Marian Exiles*, 1938. G.Q.B.

Younge, Miss. See POPE, ELIZABETH.

Younghusband, Dame Eileen (Louise) (1902–81), pioneer of social work training. She was born in London but spent her childhood in Kashmir, where her father was British Resident. In 1924 she became involved in settlement work in Bermondsey and Stepney. She took a certificate in social studies and a diploma in sociology at the London School of Economics, where she taught from 1929 to 1957. During the Second World War she was principal officer for employment and training with the National Association of Girls' Clubs (1939–44) and director of the British Council for Social Welfare Courses (1942–44); she also conducted a survey of welfare facilities for the Assistance Board, trained youth leaders, and set up one of the first Citizens' Advice Bureaux. Later, she was seconded to work with the United Nations Relief and Rehabilitation Administration.

In the post-war period, Eileen Younghusband's reports on the employment and training of social workers (1947) and on social work in Britain (1951) emphasized the need for an integrated system of training in social work and a proper career structure. Much had been accomplished in this direction at the LSE by the time of her retirement, and the work of the 'Younghusband Committee' on local authority health and welfare services was similarly effective in a non-university context; the National Institute for Social Work Training was set up, with Eileen Younghusband as its principal adviser (1961–67). At the same time she was involved with the International Association of Schools of Social Work, of which she was president from 1961 to 1968. Even in the 1970s she continued to write articles and influential pamphlets, such as *Social Work with Families* and *New Developments in Casework* (both 1971), and in 1978 published her two-volume *Social Work in Britain 1950–75*.

N.H.

Ysgafell. See WILLIAMS, JANE.